BUCHANAN AND BRECKINRIDGE.

THE

DEMOCRATIC HAND-BOOK,

COMPILED BY

MICH. W. CLUSKEY,

OF

WASHINGTON CITY, D. C.

RECOMMENDED BY THE

DEMOCRATIC NATIONAL COMMITTEE.

The success of the Democracy essential for the preservation of the Union and the protection of the integrity of the Constitution.

WASHINGTON:
PRINTED BY R. A. WATERS.
1856.

PREFACE

TO THE

DEMOCRATIC ELFCTORAL HAND-BOOK.

The demand for authentic documents disproving the unprecedented charges against the Democratic candidate, and refuting the unblushing pretensions of the Black Republican Know-Nothing nominees for the Presidency, has rendered it important in the opinion of leading members of the Democratic party, that some compilation of argument and fact derived from indisputable authorities should be prepared and published.

In the execution of this work, selections have been made from the works of the Democratic leaders—Leaders who represent the uniform and united opinions of the Democracy, North and South, whilst the motives of those patriotic citizens who have forgotten the prejudices of party, to bestow their support upon the only National candidate, are illustrated in the speeches and letters of the old line Whigs, vindicating their course of action in that respect.

The Electoral Hand Book, will be found to contain, also, the most important enactments and reports bearing upon the great issues of the day, with a mass of other matter sufficient to furnish any enquirer with the means of making up an impartial opinion upon the questions involved in the canvass, and to furnish speakers and writers with the material for defence or assault.

The author can only add, that having access to the whole magazine of political missiles, proper for employment in the present campaign, and enabled by his position and pursuits, to furnish any specific information from the published political records of the country, it will afford him pleasure to communicate any answer to any inquiry which may be made of him, and which is not satisfactorily responded to in the "Hand-Book."

Appealing to the magnanimity of his fellow-democrats to attribute any omission, to the hurried manner in which he is necessitated to prepare his work, he submits it for their judgment and use.

THE MISSOURI COMPROMISE.

The excitement created by the repeal of a geographical line, the existence of which Mr. Jefferson said "would be recurring on every occasion, and renewing irritations, until it would enkindle such mutual and moral hatred as would render seperation preferable to eternal discord," has induced us to republish the unfortunate act of Congress which first gave existence to what was called the Missouri Compromise line.

Missouri having applied for admission into the Union as a State, the House of Representatives, on the 16th of February, 1819, passed a bill providing for her admission, and affixing as a condition thereof, the prohibition of slavery within her limits. On the 27th of February, 1819, the Senate struck out of the bill the clause prohibiting slavery, and thus amended, sent it back to the House. On the 2d of March, 1819, the House refused to concur in the amendment of the Senate. On the same day the Senate insisted upon its amendment, and the House adhered, so that bill was lost.

On the 6th of January, 1820, the Committee on the Judiciary of the Senate reported a bill from the House admitting Maine into the Union, which contained no prohibition whatever, with an amendment admitting Missouri without any clause concerning slavery. It was then that Mr. Thomas introduced as an amendment what is called the Missouri Compromise which was adopted, and the bill as amended, passed the Senate on the 18th of February, 1820. The bill came to the House. After numerous messages between the two Houses, informing each other of their disagreements, and after motions had passed both Houses te insist on their respective positions, a joint committee of conference was appointed. Whilst this committee was in session, an independent bill to admit Missouri was taken up in the House and passed, containing a clause prohibiting slavery in said State, which was sent to the Senate, amended by it, and returned. Upon its return, the managers of the conference reported, that the Senate recede from its amendment to the bill admitting Maine, and that the House bill, admitting Missouri, should be amended by striking out the clause prohibiting slavery, and inserting in lieu thereof, what is now known as the Missouri Compromise. The bill thus framed, was, after one disagreement on the part of the two Houses, passed, and is as follows:

An ACT to authorize the People of the Missouri Territory te form a Constitution and State Government, and for the admission of such State into the Union on an equal footing with the original States, and to prohibit Slavery in certain Territories.

SEC. 1. *Be it enacted by the Senate and House of Representatives of the United States of America in Congress assembled*, That the inhabitants of that portion of the Missouri Territory included within the boundaries hereinafter designated, be, and they are hereby authorized to form for themselves a Constitution and State Government; and to assume such name as they shall deem proper; and the said State, when formed, shall be admitted into the Union, upon an equal footing with the original States, in all respects whatsoever.

The 3d, 4th, 5th, 6th, and 7th sections of the law, embrace mere matters of detail, having no connection with the great question which is now agitating the country. The 8th section, which is what is generally known as the Missouri Compromise, is as follows:

SEC. 8. *And be it further enacted*, That in all that territory ceded by France to the United States, under the name of Louisiana, which lies north of thirty-six degrees and thirty minutes north latitude, not included within the limits of the State contemplated by this act, slavery and involuntary servitude, otherwise than in the punishment of crimes, whereof the parties shall have been duly convicted, shall be, and is hereby forever prohibited; *Provided always*, That any person escaping into the same, from whom labor or service is lawfully claimed, in any state or territory of the United States, such fugitive may be lawfully reclaimed and conveyed to the person claiming his or her labor or service as aforesaid. [*Approved* 6 *March*, 1820.]

The action of Congress after the passage of the foregoing act rejects the idea that it was a compact, or that the Missouri Cnmpromise embraced in the 8th section thereof was at all a condition to the subsequent admission of Missouri. After the enactment of that law, Missouri applied for admission as a state, and her application was rejected. Congresss disregarded the act establishing the geographical line and shut the door on Missouri. The following act was afterwards passed and she was admitted:

RESOLUTIONS.

[No. 1.] RESOLUTION providing for the Admission of the State of Missouri into the Union, on a certain Condition.

Resolved by the Senate and House of Representatives of the United States of America in Congress assembled, That Missouri shall be admitted into this Union on an equal footing with the original States, in all respects whatever, upon the fundamental condition, that the fourth clause of the 26th section of the third article of the constitution submitted on the part of said state to Congress, shall never be construed to authorize the passage of any law, and that no law shall be passed in conformity thereto, by which any citizen, of either of the states in this Union, shall be excluded from the enjoyment of any of the priviieges and immunities to which such citizen is entitled under the constitution of the United States: *Provided*, That the legislature of the said state, by a solemn public act, shall declare the assent of the said state to the said fundamental condition, and shall transmit to the President of the United States, on or before the fourth Monday in November next, an authentic copy of the said act; upon the receipt whereof, the President, by proclamation, shall announce the fact; whereupon, and without any further proceedings on the part of Congress, the admission of the said state into this Union shall be considered as complete. [*Approved.* 2 *March*, 1821.]

From this it will be seen that the only condition under which Missouri was admitted, is contained in the proviso of the last act, which Missouri in her acceptance of the terms of admission denied the right of the United States to make whilst she nevertheless yielded and became a part of the Union. The effect of this condition was to force Missouri to agree to admit within her limits to the same privileges which white citizens of other states might have, the negro where he is recognised as a citizen by any state.

Mr. Jefferson's opinion of the enactment of a geographical line in the country' referring to that instuted by the Missouri act of 1820.

THOMAS JEFFERSON to WM. SHORT.

MONTICELLO, *April* 13, 1820.

DEAR SIR: * * * * Although I had laid down as a law to myself, not to write, talk, or even think of politics, to know nothing of public affairs, and therefore had ceased to read newspapers, yet the Missouri question aroused and filled me with alarm. The old schism of Federal and Republican, threatened nothing, because it extended in every State, and united them together by the fraternalization of party. But the coincidence of a marked principle, moral and political, with a geographical line, once conceived, I feared would never more be obliterated from the mind; that it would be recurring on every occasion, and renewing irritations, until it would enkindle such mutual and moral hatred as would render separation preferable to eternal discord. I have been the most sanguine in believing that our Union would be of long duration. I now doubt it much, and see the event at no great distance, and the direct consequences of this question, not by the line which has been so confidently counted on—the laws of nature control this—but by the Potomac, Ohio and Missouri, or more probably the Mississippi, upwards to our northern boundary. My only *comfort and confidence is that I shall not live to see this;* and I envy not the present generation the glory of throwing away the fruits of their father's sacrifices of life and fortune *and of rendering desperate the experiment which was to decide ultimately, whether man is capable of self-government. This treason against human hope will signalize their epoch in future history as the counterpart of their predecessors.*

THOMAS JEFFERSON to JOHN HOLMES.

MONTECELLO, *April* 20, 1820.

I tnank you, dear sir, for the copy you have been so kind as to send me of the letter to your constituents, on the Missouri question. It is a perfet justification to them. I had for a long time ceased to read newspapers, or pay any attention to public affairs, confident they were in good hands, and content to be a passenger in our bark to the shore from which I am not far distant. But this momentuous question, like a fire-bell in the night, awakened and filled me with terror. I considered it at once as the *Knell* of the Union. It is hushed indeed for the moment, but this is a reprieve only, not a final sentence. A geographical line, coinciding with a marked principle, moral and political, once conceived and held up to the angry passions of men, will never be obliterated; and every new irritation will mark it deeper and deeper. An abstinence, too, from this act of power, would remove the jealousy excited by the undertaking of *Congress to regulate the condition of the different descriptions of men composing a State. This certainly is the exclusive right of every State, which nothing in the Constitution has taken from them and given to the General Government. Could Congress, for instance, say that the non-freemen of Connecticut should be freemen, or that they shall not emigrate into any other State.*

EXTENSION OF THE MISSOURI LINE TO THE PACIFIC.

On the 10th of August 1848, in the Senate of the United States, the Oregon bill being under consideration, the question was taken on the amendment extending the Missouri Compromise line to the Pacific, and it was decided in the affirmative as follows:

YEAS—Messrs. Atchison, Badger, Bell, Benton, Berrien, Borland, *Bright*, Butler, Calhoun, *Cameron*, Davis of Miss., *Dickinson*, *Douglas*, Downs, *Fitzgerald.* Foote, *Hannegan*, Houston, Hunter, Johnson of Maryland, Johnson of Louisiana, Johnson of Georgia, King, Lewis, Mangum, Mason, Metcalf, Pearce, Sebastian, Spruance, *Sturgeon*, Turney, and Underwood—33.

NAYS.—Messrs. *Allen*, *Atherton*, *Baldwin*, *Bradbury*, *Breese*, *Clarke*, *Corwin*, *Davis* of Mass., *Dayton*, *Dix*, *Dodge*, *Felch*, *Greene*, *Hale*, *Hamlin*, *Miller*, *Niles*, *Phelps*, *Uphham*, *Walker*, *Webster and* Wescott—22.

"The Bill with this amendment came before the House on the next day, and the amendment of the Senate extending the Missouri line to the Pacific was non-concurred in by the following vote:

YEAS—Messrs Adams, Atkinson, Barringer, Barrow. Bayly, Beale, Bedinger, *Birdsall*, Bocock, Botts, Bowdon, Bowlin, Boyd, Boydon, *Brodhead*, *Chas. Brown*, A. G. Brown, Buckner, Burt, Cabell, Chapman, Chase, Beverly L. Clarke, Clingman, Howell Cobb, Williamson R. W. Cobb, Cocke, Crozier, Daniel, Donnell, Garnett Duncan, Alexander Evans, Featherston, Flournoy, French, Fulton, Gayle, Goggin, Greene, Willard P. Hall, Haralson, Harmanson, Hairiss, Haskell, Hill, Hilliard, Isaac E. Holmes, Geo. S. Houston, *Chas. J. Ingersoll*, Iverson, Andrew Johnson, Robert W. Johnson, Geo. W. Jones, John W. Jones, Kaufman, Thomas Butler King, Ligon, Lumpkin, McDowell, McKay, McLane, Meade, Morehead, Outlaw, Pendleton, Phelps, Pillsbury, Preston, Rhett, Roman, Sheppard, Stanton, Stephens, Thomas, Jacob Thompson, J. B. Thompson, Robert A. Thompson, Tompkins, Toombs, Venable, Wallace and Woodward—82.

NAYS—*Messrs. Abbott*, *Ashmun*, *Bingham*, *Blanchard*, *Brady*, *Butler*, *Canby*, *Cathcart*, *F. Clark*, *Collamer*, *Collins*, *Conger*, *Cranston*, *Crowell*, *Cummins*, *Darling*, *Dickey*, *Dickinson*, *Dixon*, *Duer*, *Daniel Duncan*, *Dunn*, *Eckert*, *Edsall*, *Edwards*, *Embree*, *Nathan Evans*, *Faran*, *Farelly*, *Ficklin*, *Fisher*, *Freedly*, *Fries*, *Gott*, *Gregory*, *Grinnell*, *Hale*, *Nathan K. Hall*, *Hammons*, *Jas. G. Hampton*, *Moses Hampton*, *Henly*, *Henry*, *Elias B. Holmes*, John W. Houston, *Hubbard*, *Hudson*, *Hunt*, *Joseph R. Ingersoll*, *Irvin*, *Jenkins*, *Kellogg*, *Kennen*, *D. P. King*, *W. T. Lawrence*, *Sydney Lawrence*, *Lincoln*, *Lord*, *Lynde*, *Ma-*

clay, McClelland, McClernand, McIlvaine, Job Mann, Horace Mann, Marsh, Marvin, Miller, Morris, Mullen, Murphy, Nelson, Nes, Newell, Nicoll, Palfrey, Peaslee, Peck, Petrie, Pettitt, Pollock, Putnam, Reynolds, Richey, Robinson, Rockhill, Jno. A. Rockwell, Rose, Root, Rumsey, St. John, Sawyer, Schenck, Sherrill, Sylvester, Slingerland, Smart, Caleb B. Smith, Robert Smith, Truman Smith, Starkweather, Andrew Stewart, Chas. E. Stuart, Strohm, Strong, Tallmadge, Taylor, James Thompson, Richard W. Thompson, William Thompson, Thurston, Tuck, Turner, Van Dyke, Vinton Warren, Wentworth, White, Wick, *Williams and* Wilmot.—121.

The House having thus non-concurred with the Senate, the question was decided in the Senate, on the 12th of August, 1848, in favor of receding from its amendment, running the Missouri line to the Pacific, by yeas and nays, as follows:

YEAS.—*Messrs. Allen, Baldwin,* Benton, *Bradbury, Breese, Bright, Cameron, Clarke, Corwin, Davis, of Mass., Dayton, Dickinson, Dix, Dodge, Douglass, Felch, Fitzgerald, Greene, Hale, Hamlin, Hannegan,* Houston, *Miller, Miles, Phelps,* Spruance, *Upham, Walker and* Webster—29.

NAYS—Messrs. Atchison, Badger, Bell, Berrien, Borland, Butler, Calhoun, Davis of Miss., Downs, Foote, Hunter, Johnson of Maryland, Johnson of Louisiana, Johnson, of Georgia, Lewis, Mangum, Mason, Metcalfe, Pearce, Rusk, Sebastian, Turney, Underwood, Westcott and Yulee—25.

So the Senate receded, and the Compromise line was not extended.

By analyzing this vote it will be seen that upon its being first proposed in the Senate to extend the Missouri line to the Pacific, the entire North in that body with seven exceptions voted against it, whilst the entire South with one exception voted for it.

In the House the entire North with four exceptions voted against it, whilst the entire South with one exception voted for it.

Upon receding in the Senate the entire North voted to recede whilst the entire South with two exceptions voted against it.

NOTE—Those in Italics are from the North. Those not in Italics are from the South.

LEGISLATION OF 1850, SUPERSEDING THE MISSOURI COMPROMISE.

We do not deem it necessary to burden this book with a publication of the whole of the Territorial laws of the memorable year 1850. The extracts bearing directly on the subject are all that is necessary.

The Act approved September 9, 1850, for the organization of the Territory of New Mexico, being a part of the act fixing the boundaries of Texas, contains the following proviso in its second section.

"*Provided further*, That when admitted as a State, the said Territory or any portion of the same shall be received into the Union, with or without slavery as their constitution may prescribe at the time of their admission."

The Act apprved the same day for the organization of the Territory of Utah, contains an identical provision with that cited from the New Mexico Act.

A portion of New Mexico lies north of 36.30. The whole of Utah lies north of that line.

THE WHIG AND DEMOCRATIC PLATFORMS OF 1852 ENDORSE THE LEGISLATION OF 1850, SUPERSEDING THE MISSOURI COMPROMISE.

We here subjoin the Whig platform of 1852. It will be seen that it fully endorsed the legislation of 1850, and afforded the South ample guarantees for the protection of its institutions.

NATIONAL WHIG PLATFORM OF 1852.

The Whigs of the United States, in convention assembled, firmly adhering to the great conservative republican principles by which they are controlled and governed, and now, as ever, relying upon the intelligence of the American people, with an abiding confidence in their capacity for self-government, and their continued devotion to the Constitution and the Union, do proclaim the following as the political sentiments and determinations, for the establishment and maintainance of which their national organization as a party is effected.

1. The Government of the United States is of a limited character, and it is confined to the exercise of powers expressly granted by the Constitution, and such as may be necessary and proper for carrying the granted powers into full execution, and that all powers not thus granted or necessarily implied are expressly reserved to the States respectively and to the people.

The State Governments should be held secure in their reserved rights, and the General Goverement sustained in its constitutional powers, and the Union should be revered and watched over as "the palladium of our liberties."

3. That while struggling freedom, everywhere, enlists the warmest sympathy of the Whig party, we still adhere to the doctrines of the Father of his Country, as announced in his Farewell Address, of keeping ourselves free from all entangling alliances with foreign countries, and of never quitting our own to stand upon foreign ground. That our mission as a Republic is not to propagate our opinions, or impose on other countries our form of government, by artifice or force, but to teach by example, and show by our success, moderation, and justice, the blessings of self-government, and the advantages of free institutions.

4. That where the people make and control the Government, they should obey its Constitution, laws, and treaties, as they would retain their self-respect, and the respect which they claim, and will enforce, from foreign powers.

5. Government should be conducted upon principles of the strictest economy, and revenue sufficient for the expenses thereof, in time of peace, ought to be mainly derived from a duty on imports, and not from direct taxes; and in levying such duties, sound policy requires a just discrimination and protection from fraud by specific duties, when practicable, whereby suitable encouragement may be assured to American industry, equally to all classes and to all portions of the country.

6. The Constitution vests in Congress the power to open and repair harbors, and remove obstructions from navigable rivers; and it is expedient that Congress shall exercise that power *whenever such improvements are necessary for the common defence or for the protection and facility of commerce* with foreign nations or among the States; such improvements being, in every instance, national and general in their character.

7. The Federal and State Governments are parts of one system, alike necessary for the common prosperity, peace, and security, and ought to be regarded alike with a cordial, habitual, and immoveable attachment. Respect for the authority of each, and acquiescenee in the constitutional measures of each, are duties required by the plainest consideration of national, of State, and individual welfare.

8. The series of acts of the 31st Congress, commonly known as the Compromise or Adjustment, (the act for the recovery of fugitives from labor included,) are received and acquiesced in by the Whigs of the United States, as a final settlement, in principle and substance, of the subjects to which they relate, and so far as these acts are concerned, we will maintain them, and insist on their strict enforcement, until time and experience shall demonstrate the necessity of further legislation to guard against the evasion of the laws on the one hand, and the abuse of their powers on the other, not impairing their present efficiency to carry out the requirements of the Constitution, and we deprecate all further agitation of the question thus settled, as dangerous to our peace, and will discountenance all efforts to continue or renew such agitation, whenever, wherever,

or however made; and we will maintain this settlement as essential to the nationality of the Whig party and the ittegrity of the Union.

The Democratic platform of 1856 embraces the whole of the platform of the same party in 1852, with the exception of the two following sections. ☞ See platform ol 1856 in proceedings of National Convention, contained in this volume.

IX. "*Resolved*, That the war with Mexico, upon all the principles of patriotism and the laws of nations, was a just and necessary war on onr part, in which every American citizen should have shown himself on the side of his country, and neither morally nor physically, by word or deed, have given 'aid and comfort to the enemy.'

X. "*Resolved*, That we rejoice at the restoration of friendly relations with our sister republic of Mexioo, and earnestly desire for her all the blessings and prosperity which we enjoy under republican instituons : and we congratulate the American people upon the results of that war, which have so manifestly justified the policy and conduct of the Democratic party, and insured to the United States "indemnity for the past and security for the future.' "

Upon these platforms the two parties went into that contest—their candidates standing uneqvivocally upon their distinctive features. The candidate of no other party carried a single State. Every State in the Union endorsed one or the other of those platforms. Both platforms endorsed the Legislation of 1850. Therefore, every State endorsed the legislation of 1850.

THE NEBRASKA AND KANSAS ACT OF 1854.

This act contains the following section, repealing in direct terms the 8th section of the Act approved March 6th, 1820, commonly known as the Missouri Compromise.

"Sec. 14. * * * * * * That the Constitution and all the laws of the United States which are not locally inapplicable shall have the same force and effect within the said Territory of Nebraska (or Kansas, the language being the same in reference to both,) as elsewhere within the United States, except the 8th section of the act, preparatory to the admission of Missouri into the Union, approved March sixth, eighteen hundred and twenty, which, being inconsistent with the principles of non-intervention by Congress with slavery in the States and Territories, as recognised by the legislation of eighteen hundred and fifty, commonly called the compromise measures, is hereby declared inoperative and void; it being the true intent and meaning of thls act not to legislate slavery into any Territory or State, nor to exclude it therefrom, but to leave the people thereof perfectly free to form and regulate their domestic institutions in their own way, subject only to the Constitution of the United States. *Provided*, That nothing herein contained shall be construed to revive or put in force any law or regulation which may have existed prior to the act of 6th March, 1820, either protecting, establishing, prohibiting, or abolishing slavery."

This act passed the House by a vote of 113 to 100—44 northern men, all Democrats, and 69 southern men voted for it in the House.—91 northern men and 9 southern men voted against it.

The final vote on its passage in the Senate, was 35 to 13.

In that body, 11 Southern men and 14 Northern men—the latter all Democrats, voted for it.—11 Northern men and 2 Southern men voted against it.

READ THE PLATFORMS OF THE OPPONENTS OF THE DEMOCRACY.

KNOW-NOTHING PLATFORM OF 1855.

1. The acknowledgment of that Almighty Being who rules over the Universe—who presides over the Councils of Nations—who conducts the affairs of men, and who, in

every step by which we have advanced to the character of an independent nation, has distinguished us by some token of Providential agency.

2. The cultivation and develooment of a sentiment of profoundly intense American feeling; of passionate attachment to our country, its history and its institutions; of admiration for the purer days of our National existence; of veneration for the heroism that precipitated our Revolution, and of emulation of the virtue, wisdom and patriotism that framed our Constitution, and first successfully applied its provisions.

3. The maintainance of the union of these United States, as the paramount political good; or, to use the language of Washington, "the primary object of patriotic desire." And hence—

First. Opposition to all attempts to weaken or subvert it.

Second. Uncompromising antagonism to every principle of policy that endangers it.

Third. The advocacy of an equitable adjustment of all political differences which threaten its integrity or perpetuity.

Fourth. The suppression of all tendencies to political division, founded on "geographical discriminations, or on the belief that there is a real difference of interests and views" between the various sections of the Union.

Fifth. The full recognition of the rights of the several States, as expressed and reserved in the Constitution; and a careful avoidance, by the General Government, of all interference with their rights by legislative or executive action.

4. Obedience to the Constitution of these United States as the snpreme law of the land, sacredly obligatory upon all its parts and members; and steadfast resistance to the spirit of innovation upon its principles, however specious the pretexts. Avowing that in all doubtful or disputed points it may only be legally ascertained and expounded by the Judicial power of the United States.

First. A habit of reverential obedience to the laws, whether National, State, or Municipal, until they are repealed or declared unconstitutional by the proper authority.

Second. A tender and sacred regard for those acts of statesmanship, which are to be contra-distinguished from acts of ordinary legislation, by the fact of their being of the nature of compacts and agreements; and so, to be considered a fixed and settled national policy.

5. A radical revision and modification of the laws regulating immigration, and the settlement of immigrants—offering the honest immigrant, who, from love of liberty or hatred of oppression, seeks an asylum in ths United States, a friendly reception and protection, but unqualifiedly condemning the transmission to our shores of felons and paupers.

6. The essential modification of the Naturalization Laws.

The repeal by the Legislatures of the respective States, of all State laws allowing foreigners not naturalized to vote. The repeal, without retrospective operation, of all acts of Congress making grants of land to unnaturalized foreigners, and allowing them to vote in the Territories.

7. Hostility to the corrupt means by which the leaders of party have hitherto forced upon us our rulers and our political creeds.

Implacable enmity against the present demoralizing system of rewards for political subserviency, and of punishments for political independence.

Disgust for the wild hunt after office which characterizes the age.

These on the one hand. On the other—

Imitation of the practice of the purer days of the Republic; and admiration of the maxim that "office should seek the man, and not man the office," and of the rule that the just mode of ascertaining fitness for office is the capability, the faithfulness, and the honesty of the incumbent candidate.

8. Resistance to the aggressive policy and corrupting tendencies of the Roman Catholic Chnrch in our country by the advancement to all political stations—executive, legislative, judicial, or diplomatic—of those only who do not hold civil allegiance, directly or indirectly, to any foreign power, whether civil or ecclesiastical, and who are Americans by birth, education, and training—thus fulfilling the maxim, "AMERICANS ONLY SHALL GOVERN AMERICA."

The protection of all citizens in the legal and proper exercise of their civil and religions rights and privileges; the maintainance of the right of every man to the full, unrestrained, and peaceful enjoyment of his own religious opinions and worship, and a jealous resistance of all attempts by any sect, denomination, or church, to obtain an ascendency over any other in the State, by means of any special privilege or exemption, by any political combination of its members, or by a division of their civil allegiance with any foreign power, potentate, or ecclesiastic.

9. The reformation of the character ef our National Legislature, by elevating to that

dignified and responsible position men of higher qualifications, purer morals, and more unselfish patriotism.

10. The restriction of executive patronage—especially in the matter of appointments to office—so far as it may be permitted by the Constitution, and consistent with the public good.

11. The education of the youth of our country in schools provided by the State; which schools shall be common to all, without distinction of creed or party, and free from any influence or direction of a denominational or partisan character.

And, inasmuch as Christianity, by the Consttitutions of nearly all the States: by the decisions of the most eminent judicial authorities, and by the consent of the people of America, is considered an element of our political system, and as the Holy Bible is at once the source of Christianity, and the depository and fountain of all civil and religious freedom, we oppose every attempt to exclude it from the schools thus established in the States.

12. The American party, having arisen upon the ruins, and in spite of the opposition of the Whig and Democratic parties, cannot be held in any manner responsible for the obnoxious acts or violated pledges of either. And the systematic agitation of the Slavery question by those parties having elevated sectional hostility into a positive element of political power, and brought our institutions into peril, it has, therefore, become the imperative duty of the American party to interpose, for the purpose of giving peace to the country and perpetuity to the Union. And as experience has shown it impossible to reconcile opinions so extreme as those which separate the disputants, and as there can be no dishonor in submitting to the laws, the National Council has deemed it the best guarantee of common justice and of future peace, to abide by and maintain the existing laws upon the subject of Slavery, as a final and conclusive settlement of that subject, in fact and in substance.

And regarding it the highest duty to avow their opinions upon a subject so important in distinct and unequivocal terms, it is hereby declared as the sense of this National Council, that Congress possesses no power, under the Constitution, to legislate upon the subject of Slavery in the States, where it does or may exist, or to exclude any State from admission into the Union because its Constitution does or does not recognize the institution of Slavery as a part of its social system: and expressly pretermitting any expression of opinion upon the power of Congress to establish or prohibit Slavery in any Territory, it is the sense of the National Council that Congress ought not to legislate upon the subject of Slavery within the Territory of the United States, and that any interference by Congress with Slavery as it exists in the District of Columbia, would be a violation of the spirit and intention of the compact by which the State of Maryland ceded the District to the United States, and a breach of the National faith.

13. The policy of the Government of the United States, in its relations with foreign governments, is to exact justice from the strongest, and do justice to the weakest; restraining, by all the power of the government, all its citizens from interference with the internal concerns of nations with whom we are at peace.

14. This National Council declares that all the principles of the Order shall be henceforth everywhere openly avowed; and that each member shall be at liberty to make known the existence of the Order, and the fact that he himself is a member; and it recommends that there be no concealment of the places of meeting of subordinate councils.

E. B. BARTLETT, of Kentucky, President of National Council.
C. D. DESHLER, of New Jersey, Corresponding Secretary.
JAMES M. STEPHENS, of Maryland, Recording Secretary.

PLATFORM OF THE AMERICAN PARTY, ADOPTED AT THE SESSION OF THE NATIONAL COUNCIL, FEBRUARY 21st, 1856,

1st. An humble acknowledgment to the Supreme Being, for His protecting care vouchsafed to our fathers in their successful Revolutionary struggle, and hitherto manifested to us, their decendants in the preservation of the liberties, the independence, and the union of these States.

2d. The perpetuation of the Federal Union, as the palladium of our civil and religious liberties, and the only sure bulwark of American Independence.

3d. *Americans must rule America*, and to this end, *native*-born citizens should be selected for all State, Federal, and municipal offices, or government employment, in preference to all others: nevertheless.

4th. Persons born of American parents residing temporarily abroad, should be entitled to all the rights of native-born citizens; but

5th. No person should be selected for political station, (whether of native or foreign birth,) who recognises any allegiance or obligation of any description to any foreign prince, potentate or power, or who refuses to recognise the Federal and State constitutions (each within its sphere) as paramount to all other laws as issues of political action.

6th. The unqualified recognition and maintenance of the reserved rights of the several States, and the cultivation of harmony and fraternal good will, between the citizens of the several States, and to this end, non-interference by Congress with questions appertaining solely to the individual States, and non-intervention by each State with the affairs of any other State.

7th. The recognition of the right of the native-born and naturalized citizenss of the United States, permanently residing in any Territory thereof, to frame their constitution and laws, and to regulate their domestic and social affairs in their own mode, subject only to the provisions of the Federal Constitution. with the privilege of admission into the Union whenever they have the requisite population for one Representative in Congress. *Provided always*, that none but those who are citizens of the United States, under the constitution and laws thereof, and who have a fixed residence in any such Territory, ought to participate in the formation of the constitution, or in the enactment of laws for said Territory or States.

8th. An enforcement of the principle that no State or Territory ought to admit others than citizens of the United States to the right of suffrage, or of holding political office.

9th. A change in the laws of naturalization, making a continued residence of twenty-one years, of all not hereinbefore provided for, and indispensable requisite for citizenship hereafter, and excluding all paupers, and persons convicted of crime, from landing upon our shores; but no interference with the vested rights of foreigners.

10th. Opposition to any union between Church and State; no interference with religious faith, or worship, and and no test oaths for office.

11th. Free and thorough investigation into any and all alleged abuses of public functionaries, and a strict economy in public expenditures.

12. The maintenance and enforcement of all laws constitutionally enacted, until said laws shall be repealed, or shall be declared null and void by competent judicial authority.

13. Opposition to the reckless and unwise policy of the present administration in the general management of our national affairs, and more especially as shown in removing "Americans" by designation and conservatives in principie, from office, and placing foreigners and ultraists in their places; as shown in a truckling subserviency to the stronger, and an insolent and cowardly bravado towards the weaker powers; as shown in re-opening sectional agitation, by the repeal of the Missouri Compromise; as shown in granting to unnaturalized foreigners the right of suffrage in Kansas and Nebraska; as shown in its vacillating course on the Kansas and Nebraska question; as shown in the corruptions which pervade some of the departments of the government; as shown in disgracing meritorious naval officers through prejudice or caprice; and as shown in the blundering mismanagement of our foreign relations.

14th. Therefore to remedy existing evils, and prevent the disastrous consequences otherwise resulting therefrom, we would build up the "American party" upon the principles hereinbefore stated.

15th That each State Council shall have authority to amend their several constitutions, so as to abolish the several degrees, and institute a pledge of honor, instead of other obligations for fellowship and admission into the party.

16th. A free and open discussion of all political principles embraced in our platform.

REPUBLICAN PLATFORM.

(*Adopted March* 12, 1856.)

Resolved, That we regard the Republican movement and organization as having been forced upon the country by the unconstitutional and despotic measures and aggressions of the national administration, and the want of any other party occupying a position suitable for combining public sentiment, and rendering it effective for resisting such aggressions, for defending the rights of the people, and vindicating the principles of freedom.

Resolved, That the recent convention at Pittsburg, which first inaugurated the Republican movement as a national organization, was demanded by the circumstances of the country; that its proceedings were patriotic and judicious, and meet our hearty approval, believing that they have already exerted a powerful influence in inspiring confidence and awakoning exertions in the cause which the convention so ably represented.

Resolved, That this convention, representing a portion of the people of the State, and believing that a majority of our citizens approve our principles and sympathise in our objects, deem the present an auspicious occasion to inaugurate the Republican party in this State, with anticipations that it will form a new political era, productive of results highly beneficial to the interests and honor of the State, and in its relations to the Union, conducive to the peace, the welfare, and freedom of the country.

Resolved, That we regard it a leading object of the Republican movement to vindicate and defend the Constitution against the perversions, interpolations, excisions, and assaults of a sectional monoply interest; to restore the government to its original opinions, and to insure its administration, not in the interests of slavery, but in the interests of freedom, and in the same spirit in which it was founded, and its powers exercised by the fathers of the republic.

Resolved, That the aggressive acts originating in sectional monoply interests which have agitated and alarmed the country, having been consummated in disregard of the plainest provisions of the Constitution, admonish us of the necessity and wisdom of an adherence to those republican doctrines that prevailed in the early days of the republic, which regarded our political system, not as a national or centralized government, but as a compact between sovereign States, each containing all its sovereignty except so far as it had voluntarily surrendered a part of its powers to the confederacy, and which regarded the federal system as having originated from the States, and as possessing only special and limited powers which had been granted to it by the States, and that this grant was the extent and measure of its authority, which cannot be enlarged by construction or implication, or by the exercise of assumed or doubtful powers, without an invasion of the reserved rights and sovereignty of the States. And in accordance with these sound doctrines, there being no grant of power to the federal government in respect to slavery, it cannot uphold or defend it in the Territories, or anywhere else under the flag and authority of the Union, without the exercise of unconstitutional powers.

Resolved, That recent events and disclosures respecting the passage of the Kansas-Nebraska act, and the subsequent action of the administration on the subject, have stamped upon that measure a darker shade of corruption, fraud, injustice, despotism, and violation of public faith unparalleled in the records of modern legislation.

Resolved, That the conduct of the administration in relation to Kansas, both in what it has done and in what it has neglected to do, affords conclusive evidence that it has been its settled purpose to make Kansas a slave State, regardless of the wishas of the people, and in violation of the principles of "popular sovereignty," the establishment of which was alleged to be the object of the Kansas and Nebraska act.

Resolved, That as the federal government has exclusive jurisdiction over the Territories, it is the duty of the President to enforce the laws of Congress, and to protect the people of Kansas; and in the refusal of the President to do so, and in removing Gov. Reeder, who was upholding the authority of the law, the administration is justly responsible for the disorders, lawless acts, and crimes which have been perpetrated there, and all the calamities inflicted on the unoffending people of the Territory.

Resolved, That the recent proclamation of the President, and the instructions of the Secretary of War to the officer in command in Kansas, have placed the administration in the position of co-operating with the border ruffians to subjugate the people of Kansas, and to compel them, by military force, to submit to the usurpation and despotic laws which the Missourians have established over them. This illustrates his doctrine of popular sovereignty.

Resolved, That in view of the present distracted and alarming condition of the country, we see no safety, no way of deliverance, except in the success of the Republican movement; and that we earnestly appeal to the people to complete their organizations in every town in the States, and to sustain the Republican cause with an earnestness and zeal commensnrate with its importance, and with the momentous issues depending upon it.

Resolved' That we sympathise with the people of Kansas, exposed to the outrages of the border ruffians, on the one hand, and the unjust acts of the administration on the other; and should the President attempt to execute his threats of compelling, by military force, their submission to usurpation and despotism for the evident purpose of forcing slavery upon them against their will, and against the principle of the organic law of the Territory, we trust that the friends of justice and freedom in the West and North will not quietly witness such wrong to the free people of the Territory, and to their own interests, but will promptly afford them such succor as circumstances may demand, let the consequences be what they may.

THE OBJECTS OF THE ANTI-WAR DISUNIONISTS IN 1812, IDENTICAL WITH THOSE OF THE BLACK REPULBLICAN LEADERS NOW.

More than forty years ago the patriotic Mathew Carey, of Philadelphia, startled the American people by publishing and proving in his invaluable book "The Olive Branch," "That there existed a conspiracy in New England to effect a dissolution of the Union at every hazard, and to form a separate Confederacy."

The object of that warning was to abjure the American people to forget their party names of Democrat and Federalist which separated them, and come up to save the country from a secret and malevolent enemy.

His proof consisted in the demonstration that this conspiracy was governed but by one principle, and that was the creation of a sectional hostility by which they could overthrow this Union. Read his description of the Anti-War and Disunion party of that day."

"They are possessed of inordinate wealth—of considerable talents—great energy and overgrown influence. A Northern Confederacy has been their grand object for a number of years. They have repeatedly advocated in the public prints a separation of the States."

* * * * * * * * * * *

"To sow discord, jealousy and hostility between the different sections of the Union, was the first and grand step in their eareer, in order to accomplish their favorite object of a separation of the States."

"In fact, without this efficient instrument, all their efforts would have been utterly unavailing. It would have been impossible had the honest yeomanry of the Eastern States continued to regard their Southern fellow citizens as friends and brethren, having one common interest in the promotion of the general welfare to make them instruments in the hands of those who intended to employ them to operate the unholy work of destroying the noble, the august, the splendid fabric of our Union."

"For eighteen years therefore the most unceasing endeavors have been made to poison the minds of the people of the Eastern States towards and to alienate them from their fellow citizens of the Southern. The people of the later section have been portrayed as demons incarnate, and destitute of all the good qualities that dignify or adorn human nature."

One of their writers says:

"The Northern States can subsist as a Nation or Republic without any connection with the Southern. * * * I shall endeavor to prove the impossibility of a Union for any long period in future, both from the moral and political habits of the citizens of the Southern States."

"It thus happens, that a people proverbially orderly, quiet, sober, and rational, were actually so highly excited as to be ripe for rovolution, and ready to overturn the whole system of social order. A conspiracy was formed, which, as I have stated, and as cannot be too often repeated, promised fair to produce a convulsion—*a dissolution of the Union—and a civil war.*"

In order to embarrass the government of Mr. Madison these disunionists opposed the war of 1812. Belonging chiefly to the commercial interests, they opposed a war made to protect those interests. They sympathized with the slave in bondage, and were as ready at that day as this to sever the Union rather than sit in council with the masters, whilst at the same time they traitorously opposed a war as the means of releasing their own sea-faring fellow citizens from worse than servile bondage, their being "eight hundred and seventy-three persons sailing under the American flag which ought to have insured their protection, imprisoned with every circumstance of outrage, oppression, injury injustice.

The patriotic Carey goes on to depict the slavery to which the American seamen were reduced, from which the disunionists opposed the means of their release.

"We were ordered off the quarter deck, and the captain called for the master at arms, and ordered us to be put in irons. We were then kept in irons about twenty-four hours, when we wer taken out. brought to the gangway, ☞ STRIPPED OF OUR CLOTHES, TIED AND ☞ WHIPPED, EACH ONE DOZEN AND A HALF LASHES, AND PUT TO DUTY."—*Deposition of Richard Thompson, of New York, page* 211, *Olive Branch.*

He goes on to recite innumerable affidavits of the same character.

One Hiram Thayer, a native of Greenwich, Mass., was told by Captain Stackpole a British officer, that "if they fell in with an American man of war, he did not do his duty, ☞ HE SHOULD BE TIED TO THE MAST AND SHOT LIKE A DOG."

But they wanted to dissolve the Union, and they resisted the efforts of a Southern President to set their *own fellow citizens free* from bondage.

They did not hate slavery. They hated the Union. It is the same case now.

HOW THEY OPPOSED THE WAR.

Some of the clergy at that day, as at this, denounced the government for passing an act (The Declaration of War,) of which they did not approve. Let us compare them with their successors.

The Rev. Mr. Gardiner, Rector of Trinity Church, Boston, on the 23d July 1812, said:

"The alternative then is, that if you do not wish to become the slaves of those who own slaves, and who are themselves the slaves of French slaves, you must either in the language of the day, ☞ CUT THE CONNEXION, or so far altar the national compact, as to insure yourselves a due share in the government."

"THE UNION HAS BEEN LONG SINCE VIRTUALLY DISSOLVED; AND IT IS FULL TIME THAT THIS PART OF THE DISUNITED STATES SHOULD TAKE CARE OF ITSELF." Idem, page 19.

Rev. David Osgood pastor of the Church at Medford, said:

"If at the command of weak or wicked rulers, they undertake an unjust war, each man who volunteers his services in such a cause, or loans his money for ite support, or by his conversation, his writings, or any other mode of influence, encourage its prosecution that man is an accomplice in the wickedness, ☞ loads his conscience with the blackest crimes, ☞ brings the guilt of blood upon his soul, and ☞ IN THE SIGHT OF GOD AND HIS LAW IS A MURDERER." *Discourse delivered June* 27, 1812, page 9.

Rev. Elijah Parish, D. D., said:

"*Here we must trample on the mandates of despotism*!!! or here we must remain slaves forever." Idem, page 13.

"You may envy the privilege of Israel, and mourn that *no land of Canaan has been promised to your ancestors.* You cannot separate from that mass of corruption, which would poison the atmosphere of paradise. You must in obstinate despair bow down your necks to the yoke, and with your African brethren drag the chains of Virginia despotism, *unless you discover some other mode of escape.*" Idem, page 15.

"The legislators who yielded to this when assailed by the manifesto of their angry chief, *established iniquity and murder by law.*" Idem, page 9.

Compare the Disunion preached of that day with the Disunion preached at the present day. Look at the treasonable sentiments of the Beecher of 1855, contained in the pamphlet entitled "Fearful Issue, &c.," in this volume, and compare them with those of the Gardiners, Osgoods and Parishes of Mr. Madison's time. They assailed him and the Union then, as they assail the Kansas Act and the Union now.

But it happens that we can from the public records identify at least one individual who was the active advocate of dissolution then, and has avowed the same sentiments now. He was then indifferent to the far worse than plantation bondage in which we have shown his own fellow-citizens were held by the British *then*, yet he affects to make his horror of slavery *now*, his excuse for avowing the same doctrines:

"Mr. Quincey repeated and justified a remark he had made: which, to save all misapprehensions, he committed to writing in the following words:

"If this bill passes, it is my deliberate opinion, that it is virtually A DISSOLUTION OF THE UNION; that it will free the States from their moral obligation; and as it will be *the right of all*, so it will be the *duty of some*, TO PREPARE FOR A SEPARATION, *amicably if they can*—VIOLENTLY IF THEY MUST."

NOW HEAR THE SAME JOSIAH QUINCEY!

Josiah Quincey is the venerable head of a large class of men in Boston, who are constantly at work against the Union. During the late war with England he began his crusade against the Union, and surpassed its worst adverseries. He assailed Mr. Jefferson for his purchase of Louisiana, in 1803, because this was intended, in his opinion, to extend the area of Slavery. Though past eighty-five, he is still the enemy of the Democracy. ***He is now in the field for Fremont.*** What his views now are, may be seen from the following extract from his speech, at Boston, on the 18th of August, 1854.

"The Nebraska fraud is not that burden on which I intend now to speak. There is one nearer home, more immediately present and more insupportable. Of what that burden is, I shall speak plainly. The obligation iucumbent upon the free States to deliver up fugitive slaves is that burden—*and it must be obliterated from that Constitution, at every hazard.*"

"And such an obliteration can be demonstrated to be as much the interest of the South as it is of the North."

This man knows that we should have no Union or Constitution, but for this very provision!

Josiah Quincy is still in the land of the living; and though approaching his ninetieth year, is still as hostile to the Union as he was fifty-three years ago, while Jefferson was President, or at a later period, when Jackson was chief magistrate.—***Fearful Issue.***

For the sentiments in detail of the noted Black Republican disunionists of the present day, which afford the striking resemblance between them and those in Mr. Madison's time, we must refer our readers to the admirable document in this volume before referred to, from which the preceding pointed observations upon Mr. Quincey are taken.

PLANS OF THE DISUNIONISTS THEN—PLANS OF THE BLACK REPUBLICANS NOW.

They attempted to "stop the wheels of Government" by preventing the loan of money to carry on the war.

"Let no man who wishes to continue the war by active means, by vote or lending money, DARE TO PROSTRATE HIMSELF AT THE ALTAR ON THE FAST DAY; for they are actually as much partakers in the war, as the soldier who thrusts the bayonet; and THE JUDGMENT OF GOD WILL AWAIT THEM."

"By the magnanimous course pointed out by governor Strong, that is, by withholding all voluntary aid in prosecuting the war, and manfully expressing our opinion as to its injustice and ruinous tendency, we have arrested its progress; and driven back its authors to abandon their nefarious schemes, and to look anxiously for peace. What then if we now lend them money? They will not make peace; they will still hanker for Canada; they will still assemble forces, and shed blood on our western frontier. Mere pride, if nothing else, would make them do it. The motives which first brought on the war, will still continue it, if money can be had. But some say—will you let the country become bankrupt? no, the country will never become bankrupt. BUT PRAY DO NOT PREVENT THE ABUSERS OF THEIR TRUST BECOMING BANKRUPT."

"It is very grateful to find that the universal sentiment is, that ☞ ANY MAN WHO LENDS HIS MONEY TO THE GOVERNMENT, AT THE PRESENT TIME, WILL FORFEIT ALL CLAM TO COMMON HONESTY AND COMMON COURTESY AMONG ALL TRUE FRIENDS TO THE COUNTRY!!!!!!"

"☞ My brother farmers, if you have money to let, let it lay. ☞ If the war continues, you will purchase your stock at four years old, cheaper than you can raise it; so unjust is this offensive war, in which our rulers have plunged us, in the sober consideration of millions, that ☞ they cannot conscientiously approach the God of armies for his blessing upon it."—[Boston Centinel, 13th January, 1813.

The Disunionists attempted to exhaust the means of the Middle and Southern States which supported the war, by draining their banks of specie.

"It may not be uninstructive to the reader to explain this process a little more in detail. New York purchased goods largely in Boston, partly for bank notes and partly on credit. For the latter portion promissory notes were given, which were transmitted from Boston to the New York banks for collection. Very large purchases were likewise made in Boston by citizens of Philadelphia, Baltimore, Richmond, Petersburg, &c. Payments were made in bank notes, of the middle and southern States, and in promissory notes. Both were sent on to New York, the first for transmission to the banks whence they were issued—and the second for collection.

"This state of things suggested the stupendous idea, at which the reader will stand aghast, of wielding the financial advantages then enjoyed by Boston, to produce the effect which the press and the pulpit had failed to accomplish—that is, *to stop the wheels of government by draining the banks in the middle and southern States of their specie, and thus producing an utter disability to fill the loans!!!* This scheme was projected in the winter of 1813-14—and immediate arrangements were made to carry it into execution."

"A fearful alarm spread through the community. The issue was looked for with terror. Wagons were loading with specie at the doors of our banks almost every week. There have been three at one time loading in Philadelphia. The banks throughout the middle and southern States were obliged to curtail their discounts. Bankruptcies took place to a considerable extent."

The result was that the Banks in Massachusetts soon had $4,945,444 specie in their vaults to $2,000,601 circulation.

"To render the stroke at public credit more unerring—and to place the result wholly out of the reach of contingency, there was an arrangement made by some persons at present unknown, with agents of the Lower Canada, whereby an immense amount of British government bills, drawn in Quebec, were transmitted for sale to New York, Philadelphia, and Baltimore, and disposed of to monied men, on such advantageous terms as induced them to make large purchases. And thus was absorbed a very large portion of the capital of these three cities."

By such means they were determined then to repeal the declaration of war as their successors are now to repeal the Legislation of Kansas.

The further effect in the Middle and Southern States is shown by Mr. Carey.

"These drafts were carried to such a great extent, that on the 26th of August the banks in Baltimore—on the 29th those in Philadelphia—and on the 31st those in New York, were reduced to the painful neeessity of suspending the payment of specie."

THE DISUNIONISTS DICTATED THE HIGHER LAW AS THE MEANS OF DEFEATING THE GOVERNMENT.

"Administration hirelings may revile the Northern states, and the merchants generally, for ☞ *this monstrous depravation of morals,* ☞ *this execrable course of smuggling and fraud* But there is a just God who knows how to trace the causes of human events: and ☞ *he will assuredly visil upon the authors of this war, all the iniquties of which it has been the occasion.* ☞ *If the guilty deserve our scorn or our pity,* ☞ *the tempters and seducers deserve our execration.*"

Thus we have the Higher Law recommended by the Disunionists as justifying resistance to an "odious and unjust war," as it has been since in resisting what is called by them, an "unjust and odious" Fugitive Slave Law.

Can there be any further doubt that the objects and plans of these two parties are the same?

We have only to recapitulate, to bring to the eyes and mind of the reader the identity of the two.

Both resorted to Anti-Slavery agitation, to divide the two sections.

The Disunionists of 1812 said that the South governed the North by its slave representation.

The Disunionists of 1856 say that the South commits an act of aggression upon the North, by leaving to the people of Kansas to choose whether they will own slaves or not.

Both employed a minority to effect their purposes.

The Disunionists of 1812, having no department of the Government, employed the wealth and corporate combination of an outside minority.

The Disunionists of 1856 employ the Legislative majority of two or three in one branch of the National Congress to compel the passage of an act which they want, and which the other Branch and Executive Departments of the Government do not want, as a condition to their consent to the passage of an act alike indispensable to the interests of all.

Both attempted to embarrass the Government into compliance with their purposes, by stopping the supplies necessary to national defence. The Disunonists of 1812, by defeating the War loan. The Disunionists of 1856, by withholding the pay of the officers, soldiers and artificers, and thus disbanding the army.

The object of the one was the repeal of the act declaring war against Great Britain.

The object of the other was the repeal of the act authorizing the admission of Kansas with a free or slave constitution.

Are not their purposes identical, and should you not fellow citizens sacrifice your party differences now, as your fathers did then, to the peace of the country and the duration of the Union?

HYPOCRISY OF ABOLITION ORATORS.

House of Representatives,
August 11, 1856.

"Sir:—In compliance with your request, I forward to you a copy of the bill of sale from Dr. Joseph E. Snodgrass, the travelling Abolition orator, conveying to Daniel Burkhart two slaves. I cannot comply with your farther request to have it certified under the seal of the Clerk of the County Court. It has never been recorded, as it is not usual in Virginia to record such instruments, nor does the law require it where the sale of a slave, or other personal cheatel is accompanied by the transfer of possession rom grantor to grantee, as was the case in the transfer of the slaves by Dr. Snodgrass to Mr. Burkhart. The copy I send to you is in the handwriting of Mr. Burkhart, with which I am well acquainted, and who in person handed it to me. Mr. Burkhart is a gentleman of great intelligence and worth. He was for many years a magistrate of the county of Berkley, and is at this time the cashier of the Bank of Berkeley, Virginia. Dr. Snodgrass will not dare to deny the genuineness of this paper, nor will he dare to deny that he first made sale of all the slaves which he inherited from his father, and put the price of flesh and blood into his pocket, before he assumed the vocation of teaching his fellow men what an atrocious crime it is to hold a human being in bondage. Such hypocrites and impostors should be scouted from every stand from which they attempt to address the people.

Know all men by these presents, That I, Joseph E. Snodgrass, of the city of Baltimore, in the State of Maryland, for and in consideration of the sum of eight hundred dollars to me in hand, paid by Daniel Buckhart. the receipt whereof is hereby acknowledged, have bargained and sold, and by these presents do bargain and sell into the said D. Buckhart, a negro man, named Charles, of about the age thirty-six years; also, a negro woman, wife of the said Charles, named Emily, aged abont nineteen years, together with the natural increase of the said Emily. And I, the said Joseph E. Snodgrass, for myself and my heirs, executors, and administraters, do hereby warrant the said negroes and their increase to be slaves for life. In testimony whereof, I have hereunto set my hand and seal this 1st day of December, 1838.

(A copy,) JOSEPH E. SNODGRASS. [SEAL.]

A STUPENDOUS IMPOSTURE EXPOSED.

The Black Republicans are circulating for the purpose of poisoning the minds of our Irish fellow-citizens thousands of a fraudulent pamphlet purporting to be an address from their countrymen in Washington, imposing the acquittal of Mr. Herbert for killing Thomas Keating upon the Democratic party of the country. The following card from the alleged signers of the address exposes the fraud.

A CARD.

WASHINGTON CITY, *August* 28, 1856.

Finding our names appended to a printed document, published in this city for the benefit of the Republican party in the pre ent political canvass, headed "THE KIILLING OF THOMAS KEATING.—AN ADDRESS FROM IRISHMEN OF WASHINGTON CITY TO THE CITIZENS OF THE UNITED STATES," we desire to make known the fact that some of us have not signed it, and that all of us disapprove, disavow, and deny its political statements. Those of us who did sign it were induced so to do by misrepresentation of its purport and contents on the part of an individual who, in asking our signatures to it, assured us that it was only to be a history of the killing of Thomas Keating, and of the circumstances of the imprisonment, trials and final acquittal of Philemon T. Herbert, the perpetrator of that act, designed as a precursor of the publication of the speech of Mr. Preston delivered on the last trial of Herbert, printed in advance of the publication of that speech, so that the distant public might have a reliable key to his argument.

* * * * * * * * * *

We pronounce false the statement of the aforesaid document intimating that the Secretary of State—Mr. Marcy—sought to screen the accused, by lending his influence to prevent Mr. Dubois, the Netherlands Minister from testifying in the case; that gentleman's Government having expressly forbid him from testifying under circumstances wherein he would be compelled to submit himself to the usual cross-examination, the only system of giving testimony known to our laws, and Mr. Dubios having asked permission of his Government to testify in that way at the suggestion and solicitation of Secretary Marcy.

* * * * * * * * * * *

We are humble men, but we respect ourselves and our rights which have been outraged by those unknown to us, who have undertaken for political effect to use our names as we have explained above. We have to ask those conducting journals of all parties who respect the truth, to spread before their readers this brief card.

Patrick M. Keating,	Charles Quinn,
Rd. B. Gardiner,	James Quinn,
Daniel Shea,	Jere H. Riordan,
Peter Mansville,	John Green,
John Enright,	John Roach,
Wm. Roach,	John Keating.
Edmund Roach,	Edward Gorman,
Patrick Branagan,	David Roach,
Wm. Scherager.	

FREMONT THE DUELLIST.

The Black Republicans have been poisoning the northern mind with the idea that the Southern men are all bullies and fighting men, disposed rather to resort to the persuasion of the bludgeon than to the arguments of reason.

The case of the Hon. Preston S. Brooks, and other incidents resulting from an extraordinary existence of excitement, have been cited to sustain this assertion. We do not blame Col. Fremont for what he has done in that line, but we publish the following as antidotes to the poison which has been infected into the public mind by his friends.

These incidents show him to be the cool calculating, revenge-seeking duellist.

His first challenge was sent to Col. Mason, in 1847. It was as follows:

"Cuidad de los Angeles, April 14, 1847.

"Sir:—An apology having been declined, Major Reading will *arrange the preliminaries for a meeting requiring personal satisfaction.*

Very respectfully, your obodient servant,
"J. C. FREMONT,
"Lieut. Col. Mounted Riflemen.

"Col. R. B. Mason,
"First dragoons, Cuidad de los Angeles."

Col. Mason requested time to go to Monterey to arrange his *private* afiairs previous to their meeting. Col. Fremont thus replied:

"Cuidad de los Angeles, April 15, 1847.

"Sir:—I am in receipt of your letter of this date, and in reply have the honor to state that I will hold myself in readiness for a meeting at Monterey, at such time as you may designate.

"I am, very respectfully, your obedient servant,
"J. C. FREMONT,
"Lieut. Col. Mounted Riflemen.

"Col. R. B. Mason,
"First Dragoons, Cuidad de los Angeles."

Col. Fremont repaired to Monterey, and presented himself at Col. Mason's headquarters, to let Mason see he was in Monterey, but would not sit down. Gen. Kearney and Com. Biddle, hearing of the proposed meeting, wrote the parties, forbidding the meeting.

Col. Fremont thus replied to Col. Mason's letter.

"Monterey, May 22, 1847.

"Sir:—I have the honor to acknowledge the receipt, on yesterday, of your note of the 19th inst., accompanied by a copy of a letter from Com. Biddle to yourself.

"The object of your note appears to be to induce me to consent to a further, and indefinite postponement of a meeting. If such be your desire I am willing to comply with it, trusting that you will apprise me *of the earliest moment at which the meeting can take place consistently with your convenience and sense of propriety.*

"I am, most respectfully, your obedient servant,

"JOHN C. FREMONT.

"Col. R. B. Mason, Monterey."

THE FOOTE AND FREMONT DIFFICULTY.

The difficulty between Senators Foote and Fremont grew out of the circumstance that Foote charged Fremont, in the Senate, with seeking legislation in reference to the gold mines for the sake of his own private advantage, which Fremont pronounced false.

Afterwards they met in the ante-chamber, when Fremont struck Foote and brought blood. They were immediately separated by Senator Clarke. Subsequently, Fremont addressed a note to Foote, demanding a retraction of the language used by him in debate, to be signed in the presence of witnesses, and a challenge note was left if he refused.

Mr. Foote declined to sign the paper, but addressed a note in reply to Fremont, disclaiming any intention of giving any personal offence in the language used by him in debate.

The friends of both parties considered this satisfactory to Fremont. but, at his instance, the note of Mr. Foote was submitted to Col. Benton, who consented to an arrangement. The following card was the result:

Washington, September 28, 1850.

A. Card.—The unnersigned are authorized to state that the difficulty between the Hon. H. S. Foote and the Hon. J. C. Fremont, growing out of certain expressions used by the former in relation to the California bill in the Senate last evening, has been adjusted satisfactorily and honorably to both those gentlemen.

Signed, A. C. Dodge,
W. M. Gwin,
Henry W. Sibley,
Rodman M. Price.

CHARGE OF BARGAIN AND INTRIGUE.

Referring to the document entitled "Short Answers, &c.," embraced In this volume, relative to the connection of Mr. Buchanan with the charge of bargain and intrigue against Mr. Clay, we cite some additional facts bearing thereon. See what Gov. Letcher, in a recent speech at Mayslick, Kentucky, said, "that Mr. Buchanan was his personal friend—that he was a gentleman and a patriot, for whom he entertained a high regard—*and he could not say a word against his character as a man.* He did not like his political sentiments, and opposed him on that account."

Gov. Letcher, be it remembered, is the witness upon whom the opposition editors have relied to prove Mr. Buchanan the calumniator of Mr. Clay!

George E. Badger a prominent supporter of Mr. Fillmore in North Carolina connection with the charge. Mr. Badger is one of those old line Whigs who can't support Mr. Buchanan.

Mr. Badger, in his address to his constituents in 1828, said:

"Mr. Clay, of Kentucky, was one of the four candidates for President; but having the lowest number of electoral votes, was excluded from the House. The State from which he came had instructed her members, in the event which had then happened, to support General Jackson; but, under the influence of Mr. Clay, a man of intrigue, and of eloquence, of unbounded ambition, and of talents above mediocrity, these members, with those of other western States, voted for Mr. Adams, and his election was the result. Immediately after his elevation, Mr. Adams appointed Mr. Clay Secretary of State, in power and influence the second station of our government, and generally thought to be an introduction to the first.

"Between these two gentlemen there had been previously neither confidence nor affection; and Mr. Clay had public expressed, in language not to be misunderstood, a disbelief of Mr. Adams's politcal integrity and patriotism. How, then, are you to account for Mr. Clay's support of Mr. Adams, in opposition to the declared wishes of Kentucky.

* * * * * * * * * *

"Take the facts, and answer for yourselves whether it be harsh or uncharitable to conclude that he voted for Mr. Adams in the expectation of being Secretary of State, and that this expectation decided his vote. Let the friends of Mr. Clay protest against the conclusion with whatever of earnestness they can press into the service, and the common sense of mankind will still find in his conduct the grounds of serious suspicion. They may contend that there is not proof to convict him in a court of justice, and subject him to an ignominious punishment. If this were allowed, it will avail them nothing, for the inquiry is not about inflicting punishment on Messrs. Adams and Clay; it is about the propriety of continuing them in public stations of power and influence; and, with due submission, the difference is vastly important. We pity the miserablh wretch dragged to the bar, for whom the scaffold or whipping-post is in waiting; and the humanity of the law coincides with our own compassion in pronouncing that doubt shall be followed by acquittal; but to him who claims our confidence, probable suspicion is just ground for refusal; and many are the men dismissed by an acquittal from a court of justice, who, upon grounds which the law cannot notice, stand condemned before the tribunal of public opinion. Aaron Burr was acquitted—and rightfully acquitted, too—for want of evidence; but think you he is a fit object to attract confidence?—is he entitled to support?

Andrew Jackson Donelson, the Know-Nothing candidate for the Vice-Presidency, connection with the Bargain and Intrigue slander.

Now, A. J. Donelson, in August, 1844, as chairman of a Democratic Mass Meeting, in announcing the circumstances which prevented the arrival of Hon. Lynn Boyd, of Kentucky—

"Called the attention of the meeting to the fact that Mr. Boyd was the distinguished Kentuckian who had charged and proved upon Mr. Clay, in his place in Congress, the charge of 'Bargain, Intrigue and Corruption' in the Presidential election of 1825, and who had been sustained by his constituents in his course, he therefore proposed nine cheers for Lynn Boyd and the Democracy of his district."

There is consistency.

MR. BUCHANAN AND THE BANKRUPT BILL.

The enemies of Mr. Buchanan are charging him with having voted for the Bankrupt Bill. The Hon. David S. Reid, a Senator from North Carolina, has written a letter entirely disproving the charge. We extract from it the following record evidence:

"At the time this act was passed, Mr. Buchanan was in the United States Senate, and on July 24, 1841, he is recorded as voting against the passage of the bankrupt bill. See Senate Journal for that session, page 115. On the same day Mr. Buchanan made a speech against the bill. (See appendix to Congressional Globe for that session, p. 205.)

"On February 25, 1843, Mr. Buchanan is recorded as voting for the repeal of the bankrupt law. (See Senate Journal for that session, p. 229.)

"When the act passed Mr. Fillmore was a member of the House of Representatives, and on August 18, 1841, he is recorded as voting for the bankrupt bill. (See House Journal for that session, p. 879.) Mr. Fillmore made a speech in favor of the passage of the bill August 16, 1841. (See appendix to Congressional Globe for that session, p. 480.)

"On January 17, 1843, Millard Fillmore is recorded as voting against the repeal of the bankrupt act. (See House Journal for that session, page 215.)

"It will, therefore, be seen that Mr. Buchanan *did not* vote for the bankrupt law, but that Mr. Fillmore *did;* and moreover that Mr. Buchanan voted *for the repeal* of the law, while Mr. Fillmore voted *against the repeol.*"

MR. BUCHANAN VINDICATED FROM THE CHARGE OF HAVING VIOLATED THE SUB-TREASURY LAW BY DEPOSITING MONEY IN SIMON CAMERON'S BANK.

We wish to fix attention on the specific charge that "Mr. Buchanan, while Secretary of State, wrote to Mr. Polk recommending $50,000 to be deposited in Simon Cameron's bank," &c. This letter, the Post is informed, contains sufficient evidence to send Mr. Buchanan to the state prison for a violation of the sub-treasury law. If this charge is true, Mr. Buchanan ought not to be elected president; and if true, the proof ought to be obtained from the proper department to establish it. To show how basely false the charge is, we ask attention to the following facts, which appear by the official records:

"Mr. Buchanan entered upon his duties as secretary of State, under Mr. Polk, *on the 4th of March*, 1845. The sub-treasury law was passed *on the 6th of August*, 1846.

"On the 4th of November, 1844, the books of the treasury department show that the deposits of $50,000 was made in Mr. Cameron's bank at Middletown, Pennsylvania.

"The deposite, therefore, which the Post says was recommended by Mr. Buchanan's letter addressed to Mr. Polk, was made by Mr. Tyler, just four months before Mr. Buchanan was appointed secretary of State by Mr. Polk, and just twenty-one months before the sub-treasury law was passed."

TRIUMPHANT VINDICATION OF MR. BUCHANAN BY THE MECHANICS OF HARPER'S FERRY, VA.

MEETING OF THE MECHANICS OF HARPER'S FERRY, VIRGINIA.

A very large and enthusiastic meeting of the mechanics of Harper's Ferry was held in that place on the 12th of August, 1856, at which, on motion, JOHN PRICE, Esq., was called to the chair, and Thomas W. Shriver, Esq., appointed secretary.

On motion, a committee, consisting of Captain William H. More, T. S. Duke, and Michael E. Price, Esqs., was appointed to draught resolutions expressive of the sense of the meeting in regard to the base calumnies which have been circulated, charging Mr. Buchanan with being unfriendly to the interests of the working men of the country.

The committee, retiring for a short time, came into the meeting and made their

REPORT.

The mechanics of Harper's Ferry having seen, with much regret, the unprincipled effort of the enemies of the Hon. James Buchanan to revive and fasten upon him the charge of having advocated a reduction of the wages of mechanical labor to the rate of "ten cents a day," have deemed it a duty to one who has so long and so consistently represented the interests of the industrial classes, to examine and refute this infamous charge, as contrary to history and reason, and contradictory to the whole tenor of his private life and public record.

In proceeding with this refutation, we cannot suppress our honest indignation at the impudent imputation upon the intelligence of the American mechanics which the circulation of this calumny implies. Who are the mechanical classes of our country? Are they like the menial millions of Europe, oppressed by class combinations, kept in the most profound ignorance of everything except the manual skill necessary to execute some special article of social consumption, and living upon an allotted pittance of their own labor?

Are they so far debarred the privilege to read and reason as that they may be misled by the charge that one who has been through life their benefactor and advocate has deliberately tried to deprive them of a just compensation for their labor and the honest support of their families?

Is it supposed that they cannot discriminate between truth and falsehood? or distinguish an honest friend from a concealed enemy?

Enjoying, then, the same advantages of acquiring information with other citizens of the republic, accustomed to discuss and investigate for themselves public questions in which their rights are involved, they have appealed to the records of the country to testify upon the truth or falsity of the charge referred to.

Before, however, proceeding with the investigation of the subject, the mechanics of Harper's Ferry may be pardoned in taking a peculiar interest, when it is known that they stand under especial obligations to the statesman whose character they intend to vindicate.

It will be remembered that, in the year 1841, an effort was made to commit the direction of the mechanical labor employed in the manufacture of fire arms to officers of the army of the United States. The injustice of this measure accasioned an appeal to Congress, and amongst the most earnest and efficient advocates of continuing the mechanical construction of military weapons in the hands of a practical and mechanical civilian was the Hon. James Buchanan, as will be seen by reference to his whole congressional history, and the following letter addressed by him to a member of the committee sent from the Armory at this place to advocate the desired relief:

(Here the Mechanics publish Mr. Buchanan's letter of July 24, 1842, contained on page 25 of the document called Short Answers, in this volume.)

We proceed with a narrative of historical facts, necessary to the intelligent comprehension of this infamous charge.

During the currency war, which followed the delivery of the country from the monster monopoly of the United States Bank, Mr. Buchanan advocated the establishment of the independent treasury. One argument used by the enemies of this indpendent measure was that it was designed to prostrate the whole banking system, and introduce a metallic currency. Assuming that this was the purpose of its advocates, it was a natural inference that such a financial revolution must paralyze the monetary and industrial interests of the country. The wages of the mechanic and laborer must sympathize with this universal embarrassment, and great suffering would result to all who depended upon the sweat of their brows for an honest maintenance. Such were the consequences attributed by its enemies to the establishment of the independent treasnry. The consequences then were denied and controverted by its friends. They disavowed any intention to overthrow the institution of credit. They demonstrated that such an effect treasury would reduce the wages of labor.
would not follow the measure. They denied that the establishment of the independent

It was a bold step on the part of the panic-makers that they should have ascribed to Mr. Buchanan an admission of the very imputation which himself and others so vehemently denied. Yet it seems that a senator of that day, whose *soubriquet* of *honest* John Davis was not certainly conferred upon him for the merit of fairness towards his political antagonists, charged Mr. Buchanan with having advocated the independent treasury for the express purpose of bringing down the wages of labor. Having assumed that this consequence was intended and desired by Mr. Buchanan, this honest John Davis added in the appendix of his speech the rates of daily labor allowed as the rule of mechanical compensation under the despotisms of Europe, as that to be established by the independent treasury in this country; another and an inferior set of calumniators reduced this fallacy to a simpler formula of falsehood, and asserted that Mr. Buchanan had declared himself in favor of fixing the wages of American laborers and mechanics "at ten cents a day!" Thus did this calumny originate.

Time has vindicated the wisdom of Mr. Buchanan and of those who aided him in separating the federal government from the monetary concerns of the country. It has shown that the predictions of the panic-makers have been falsified by the whole fiscal history of the country. The Bank of the United States has been discontinued; yet the currency is uniform and readily convertible. Domestic exchanges rule below the average rate during the bank regime. Commerce is prosperous. Manufactures flourish, and the wages of labor are steady and liberal. If the object of those who introduced the independent treasury had been to reduce the wages of labor, they should long since have set about its repeal. The preposterous consequences predicted by the panic-makers have not followed its establishment. The friends of the independent-treasury system point to the prosperity which prevails as a vindication of the wisdom that designed it.

Mr. Buchanan was never the representative of corporate or associated wealth. The Bank of the United States, with its whole affiliated influence, located in the metropolis of his own State, appealed to him in vain. He steadily represented the great agricultural, mechanical, and mineral interests. He still represents their interests, and it would be ridiculous to say that he had deserted them, and that they have nevertheless continued their unabated confidence in him for more than twenty years.

If any specific evidence of the interest taken by Mr. Buchanan in the misfortunes of the mechanic was wanting, it will be found in the following letter to the Secretary of the Navy, imploring him to afford temporary employment to five hundred mechanics thrown suddenly out of work at the Philadelphia navy-yard in 1837:

(Here the mechanics publish Mr. Buchanan's letter of December 26, 1837, contained on page 26, of the document called Short Answers, in this volume.

It will be seen from this report that we have examined this charge against Mr. Buchanan historically, logically, and by the test of those motives which usually influence the relation between representative and constituent. From this investigation we are satisfied that the charge is absurd, groundless, and malicious, and that it ought to be withdrawn by every antagonist who makes the least pretension to fairness or to justice.

Resolved, therefore, that the mechanics of Harper's Ferry have seen with regret that the malignant spirit of party has endeavored to impair the confidence of the laboring men of the country in the integrity of Hon. James Buchanan, by charging him with a wish to reduce the rates of compensation for their labor to a degrading scale of wages, established by the class-combinations of Europe.

Resolved, That the whole public history of Mr. Buchanan proves him to have been the representative of the laborious and intelligent class of American citizens upon which the power and prosperity of the republic must depend, of which he is a native, to which he owes every representative position which he has ever held, and to which he has dedicated the patriotic labors of a long and virtuous life.

Resolved, That with an impartial determination to examine every charge brought against the candidate of their choice, the mechanics of Harper's Ferry are satisfied that the charge that the Hon. James Buchanan has ever advocated a low rate of wages for the laboring man is contrary to the whole tenor of his private acts, to the charity and justice of his nature, and to the democratic theory by which his whole public actions have been regulated, and we pronounce these charges false, absurd, and malicious.

On motion, the above preamble and resolutions were adopted unanimously.

The meeting then adjourned.

JOHN PRICE, Chairman,

THOMAS W. SHRIVER, Secretary.

OLD LINE WHIGS OF THE COUNTRY IN FAVOR OF MR. BUCHANAN.

OLD LINE WHIGS IN MARYLAND FOR BUCHANAN.

Hon. Thomas G. Pratt, Hon James Alfred Pearce, present United States Senators.

Hon. William D. Merrick, former United States Senator.

Capt. Richard T. Merrick, son of the above.

Hon. Thomas F. Bowie, of Prince Georges, now in Congress.

Hon. Revedy Johnson, former United States Senator and Attorney General under General Taylor.

William R. Gaither, President of the State Senate.

Hon. John B. Eccleston, of Kent, one of the Judges of the Court of Appeals.

Hon. Ezekiel F. Chambers, former United States Senator and Judge of this Judicial District.

Hon. Isaac D. Jones, of Somerset.

Hon. John W. Crisfield, of Somerset.

Samuel Hambleton, Esq., of Talbot, former State Senator.

Henry H. Goldsborough, Esq., lawyer of Talbot.

Daniel F. Henry, Esq., of Dorchester, former Whig candidate for Congress.

George W. P. Smith, Esq., editor of the Snow Hill Shield.

Hon. William T. Goldsborough, formor State Senator and Whig candidate for Governor.

R. W. Dirickson, of Worcester, former member of the Legislature.

Col. Joseph Wickes, of Charlestown, former Deputy Attorney General for Cecil and Kent.

Hon. Alexander Evans, of Cecil, former Representative in Congress.

George Earl, Esq., of Cecil.

John A. Croswell, of Cecil.

John C. Morgan, of St. Mary's.

John T. Dorsey, of Howard county, former member of the Legislature and member of the Reform Convention.

William H. Dorsey, of Baltimore, brother of the above.

S. Teakle Wallace, of Baltimore, a prominent lawyer and former Whig speaker.

Thomas Yoates Walsh, of Baltimore, former member of Congress.

William H. Gatchell, Esq., lawyer of Baltimore.

Robert M. Magraw, Esq., of Baltimore, President of Susquehannah Railroad.

Thomas Donaldson, Esq., of Howard county, former member of the Legislature and member of the Convention which formed the present constitution of the State.

John K. Longwell, of St. Mary's county, former member of the Legislature.
Benedict I. Heard, of St. Mary's county, a prominent Whig.

OLD LINE WHIG LAWYERS IN CINCINNATI FOR MR. BUCHANAN.

Judge James,
Judge M. R. Tilden,
Judge Saffin,
C. Anderson, Esq.,
Joshua Bates, Esq.,
N. Longworth, Esq.,
T. Nesmith, Esq.,
D. Worthington, Esq.,
J. Worthington, Esq.,
Judge T. M. Key,
Judge W. Johnson,
Hon. E. H. Spencer,
Alex. Johnson, Esq.,
A. S. Sullivan, Esq.,
L. Anderson, Esq.,
Patrick Mallon, Esq.,
T. Jones, Esq.,

We add the following:

Hon. George Evans, Maine,
Hon. E. W. Farley, Maine,
Hon. Rufus Choate, Mass.,
Hon. James C. Jones, Tenn.
Hon. A. G. Talbott, Ky.,
Hon. William Preston, Ky.,
Hon. J. P. Benjamin, La.,
Hon. Josiah Randall, Penn.,
Hon. William B. Reed, Penn.,
Hon. I. E. Hiester, Penn.,
Hon. T. J. Michie, Va.,
And a host of others,

TO THE OLD LINE WHIGS.

The following address taken from the National Intelligencer of the 27th of October' 1840, was issued by the State Whig Central Committee to the Whig Party in Maryland' and shows the doctrine of the Whig party, both as to the naturalization and the Catholic question.

Many sincere Whigs, who in the present contest are heart and hand with the Democratic party, will rejoice to know that the Whig doctrine, years ago, was that a discussion of religious creeds should not be brought into political contests. They stand *now* where they stood in 1840, and extend the hand of fellowship to all who fight the same great battle:

TO THE WHIGS OF MARYLAND.

The undersigned, as members of the Whig Central Committee of the State, have deemed it their duty to present this statement of their views. The Whigs of Maryland will, we have no doubt, sustain this proceeding, and acquiesce in its propriety.

Gen. Duff Green, as editor of the Pilot, has discussed in his paper subjects which, in the opinion of the undersigned, have no proper connection with the Presidential election. Within a few days this gentleman has published a prospectus for a newspaper, in which he expresses his determination to continue, after the election, discussions on questions with which the Whig party has not been, and will not be identified. As an individual, Gen. Green has an undoubted right to take such a course as his own judgment may approve. As an editor of a party paper, he has thought proper to persevere in conduct which he knew was disapproved of by the Whig party of Maryland. He has repeatedly been requested to avoid all discussions in reference to religious sects, but such requests have always been disregarded. He has ever assumed the position that he alone is responsible for what may appear in his editorial columns. This is undoubtedly true; and our object now is to make this manifest beyond all dispute to the people of Maryland. We now emphatically declare that the Whig party is not in any way, or to any extent, responsible for what has heretofore been published in the Pilot on the subject of Catholicism and naturalized voters, and will not be responsible for what Gen. Green may be pleased hereafter to do.

It is our decided conviction that the election contests in this country are already sufficiently exciting and absorbing in their character. If the differences of opinion between the religious denominations are to be appealed to, and to be used as incentives to party action, no man can forsee how terrible may be the result. Heretofore, after the elections have been settled by the ballot box, a calm has succeeded the political storm. With the close of the contest have subsided the excited and often angry feelings which prevailed during its continuance. Those who were alienated one from the other by political discussions have generally returned to their friendly relations after the settlement of the questions which divided them. But if, in addition to the causes of discussion which ordinarily exist, a religious controversy is to take place, who can allay the excitement which these combined causes may produce, and when will such a contest be finally settled.

In this country every man is permitted to worship his Maker in snch way as his conscience may approve. Our laws and constitutions were framed to secure to all this glorious privilege. The native and naturalized citizens are equally entitled to the blessings of our government. All are equal; and when a stranger takes up his abode here, and has remained among us durlng the time prescribed by the naturalization laws, he has a right to become a citizen, and will be entitled to the privileges of citizenship.

Such being the views of the Committee, and, as they believe, of their constituents, the great Whig party of the State of Maryland, they hereby declare their disavowal of any concurrence in the present or prospective editorial course of General Green, and devolve upon him alone the entire responsibility of his course.

N. F. Williams, Chairman.

Geo. R. Richardson,	William Chesnut,
Wm. H. Gatchell,	John P. Kennedy,
James Grieves,	Sam'l McLellan,
Samuel Harden,	A. G. Cole,
Geo. W. Krebs,	Hugh Birckhead,
Asa Needham,	Jas. L. Ridgely,
Chas. H. Pitts,	Gustav W. Lurman,
Neilson Poe,	Jas. Frazier,
Geo. M. Gill,	Wm. R. Jones,
James Harwood,	T. Yates Walsh.

THE NORTHERN SUPPORTERS OF MR. FILLMORE.

The first suggestion of the Revolutionary means of redressing what the Abolitionists call the wrongs of Kansas came from the Hon. George Grundy Dunn, of Indiana, a candidate for Elector on the Fillmore ticket in that State. In a speech in the House of Representatives on the 21st of July last he said:

"I would cut off the supplies and stop the wheels of government, rather than let it move an inch further in its present most ill-directed and perilous course. If those who control that course are refractory—if they will not heed the clear and distinct utterances of an overwhelming public sentiment, justly aroused to indignation against a great wrong—if the dangers that threaten us will not warn or check them, I would *cut off the sinews of power and thus compel submission* to an overwhelming public necessity. [Cries of 'Good!' 'That is it!' 'That is the doctrine!'"

He was speaking in favor of a restoration of the Missouri Compromise at the time. The public sentiment to which he alluded was that which he supposed to be in favor of such restoration. In the same speech he said:

"I shall most cheerfully give my vote to that candidate who both hails from, and lives in, New York, and not to him who hails from, and lives in Pennsylvania, or to him who, living in New York, for the purpose of this canvass, hails from California—or to any other, who is amphibious, either in his home or his principles." [Laughter.]

The following is from Mr. Bayard Clarke, a member of Congress from New-York, a prominent Know-Nothing and an ardent supporter of Mr. Fillmore:

"Some have wondered that a certain class of our naturalized citizens should be found sustaining the Cincinnati platform, and the Presidential candidate who has merged his individuality in that platform, while another class sustain the platform of freedom in opposition to the aggressions of slavery. But to me there is no mystery in all this. It only illustrates the natural affinity of Jesuitism with slavery. That part of our foreign born population who support Mr. Buchanan are, with rare exceptions, the subjects of the Roman hierachy, and consequently friendly to the despotic *principle*, of which slavery is a logical necessity. On the contrary, the foreign born voters who oppose the extension of slavery, with the platform and candidate of the Cincinnati convention, are generally a more intelligent class of citizens, owing no allegiance to Rome, and disdaining all alliance with the slave power, which degrades labor, and despises the laborer. The former are Catholics, the latter Protestants. Of course there are exceptions in both cases, but this classification will be found generally correct, and the explanation of the fact will also be found in the natural affinity of one despotic system with another. Said I not rightly that Protestantism is significant of all that contributes to the elevation, the progress, and freedom of our race? As a Protestant I can do no less, then, than oppose the aggressions of the slave-power; and when I find Jesuitism allying itself with that power, and striving to secure the success of its platform and its candidate, I cannot fail to remark, that consistency demands from all who love the Protestant principle, opposition to the usurpations of slavery, no less than relentless hostility to the aggressions of popery. They are TWIN DEMONS; and, God helping me, I am resolved, within the limits of constitutional action, to give no quarter to either."

The New Albany Tribune, the leading Fillmore paper in Indiana, has the following ticket at the head of its columns:

FOR PRESIDENT, MILLARD FILLMORE.
FOR VICE PRESIDENT, A. J. DONELSON.

Electors for the State at large.

George G. Dunn, of Lawrence county, Andrew L. Osborne, of Laporte.

District Electors.

1. James G. Jones, of Vanderburf.
2. David T. Laird, of Ferry.
3. John Baker, of Lawrence.
4. William E. White, of Dearborne.
5. Fred. Johnsonbough, of Wayne.
6. Henry H. Bradley, of Johnson.
7. William K. Edwards, of Vigo.
8. James Prather, of Montgomery.
9. Thomas S. Stanfield, of St. Joseph.
10. John B. Howe, of Langrange.
11. William R. Hale, of Wabash.

The same paper contains the following:

COALITION BETWEEN FILLMORE AND FREMONT.

The Fillmore State Convention of Indiana have just united with the Fremont or Black Republican party, by nominating the same Electoral ticket for the State. If any of our Democratic friends have been feeding themselves up with the hope of a division among the American and Republican parties, upon the State ticket, they would do well to give that hope up as utterly futile.

The fusion of the parties for the Presidency is now complete, which seals the fate of Buchanan Democracy in Indiana.

The friends of Mr. Fillmore should now go to work to secure a majority of the popular vote of the State of Indiana for him; if they succeed, of which we have no doubt, the Electoral vote will be cast for him. *Let there be no crashing between the friends of Fillmore and Fremont, because their cause is one cause.* Let the energies of the friends of each be directed against Buchanan, and we will have *no more slave soil to curse our government.*

The Huntington (Indiana) Gazette, a Fremont paper, has the same Electoral ticket in its columns, headed as follows:

FOR PRESIDENT, JOHN C. FREMONT, of New York.
FOR VICE PRESIDENT, W. L. DAYTON, of New Jersey.

MORE FUSION.

The Gazette published at Mauch Chunk, Pennsylvania, has the following ticket at its head:

WHIG, AMERICAN AND REPUBLICAN UNION TICKET.

FOR CANAL COMMISSIONER, THOMAS E. COCHRAN, of York County.
FOR AUDITOR GENERAL, DARWIN PHELPS, of Armstrong county.
FOR SURVEYOR GENERAL, BARTHOLOMEW LAPORTE, of Bradford county.

IS NOT THE FUSION COMPLETE?

The Eagle, a Fillmore paper published at Newark, New Jersey, has the following caption to the American platform adopted at Philadelphia, Februrary 21, 1856:

THE PLATFORM MR. FILLMORE ENDORSES AND STANDS ON!

AMERICA FOR AMERICANS, AND OPPOSITION TO THE REPEAL OF THE MISSOURI COMPROMISE.

AMERICANISM AT THE NORTH.

THE KNOW-NOTHING PLATFORM OF THE STATE OF MAINE.

BANGOR, *February* 1*st*, 1855.

"*Resolved*, That the Declaration of Independence, the tone and tenor of the constitution, the ordinance of 1787, the words and deeds of the founders of this republic, all indicate that our forefathers intended that slavery be sectional, not national—temporary, not permanent.

"*Resolved*, That *native-Americanism*, *anti-slavery*, and *temperance* are the foundation stones of our order, equally deserving our consideration; and that before giving our political support to any man, for any office, we will imperatively demand his entire committal in favor of these great and cardinal principles.

"*Resolved*, That we solemnly protest against the repeal of the Missouri Compromise, the passage of the Nebraska-Kansas bill, and the fugitive slave law, as violations of the rights of the free States, and tending to the destruction of the free institutions of our country."

KNOW-NOTHING PARTY OF NEW HAMPSHIRE ON SLAVERY.

"*Resolved*, That the Declaration of Independence, the tones and deeds of the founders of this republic, all indicate that our forefathers intended that slavery should be sectional, not national—temporary, not permanent.

"*Resolved*, That as a political party pledged to regard and watch over the best interests of the whole Union, and to labor for its integrity and perpetuity we solemnly protest against the repeal of the Missouri Compromise, the Kansas and Nebraska bill, and the fugitive slave law, as violating the spirit of the Constitution, and tending to the destruction of the free institutions of the country.

"*Resolved*, That we never will, under any circumstances, consent to the admission of slavery into any portion of the territory embraced in the compact of 1820, and from which it was then excluded by the mutual agreement of both the northern and southern States."

MR. FILLMORE IN FAVOR OF ALIEN SUFFRAGE.

Mr. Filmore signed the Washington Territorial bill in 1853. That bill gives aliens the right of suffrage.

WASHINGTON TERRITORY.

"Every white male inhabitant above the age of twenty-one years, who shall have been a resident of said Territory at the time of the passage af this act, and shall possess the qualifications hereinafter prescribed, shall be entitled to vote at the first election, and shall be eligible to any office within the said Territory; but the qualifications of voters, and of holding office at all subsequent elections, shall be such as shall be prescribed by the Legislative Assembly: *Provided*, That the right of suffrage, and of holding office, shall be exercised only by citizens of the United States above the age of twenty-one years, anb those above that age who shall have declared on oath their intention to become such, and shall have taken an oath to support the Constitution of the United States and the provisions of this act.

THE STATES, AND NOT CONGRESS, HAVE ALONE THE RIGHT TO REGULATE SUFFRAGE WITHIN THEIR RESPECTIVE LIMITS.

The Know-Nothing orators clamor about aliens voting in some of the states. They promised the people if they were elevated to power that they would stop it. Have any of them attempted to do it in Congress? No! Why? Because they know Congress has no power over the subject. Congress can make a man a citizen of the United States, but not a voter in the states, nor can it take from him the right of voting therein. The states have the controlling power in that respect. Thus Virginia years since prescribed in her constitution that a man without a property qualification could not vote. The man thus prescribed was a citizen of the United States. Such citizenship it will thus be seen did not give him the right to vote. Virginia controlled that matter and decided that he should not vote. This fact is merely cited as an illustration.

FOREIGN PAUPERS AND CONVICTS.

Alabama, California, Delaware, Georgia, Louisiana, Maine, Maryland, Massachusetts, New Hampshire, New Jersey, New York, Pennsylvania, Rhode Island, South Carolina, Texas, Vermont and Virginia, the only states, through the seaports of which foreign paupers and convicts can find access to our shores, have already on their statute books, ample law to prevent the immigration of convicts, and to reimburse those States the damages arising from the support of paupers.

PROTESTANT EPISCOPAL ENGLAND SATISFIED THAT NO TEMPORAL ALLEGIANCE IS DUE, BY CATHOLICS, TO THE POPE.

The odious Catholic disabilities which existed in Protestant Episcopal England for so many years, were, no doubt, established on account of the idea that Catholics owed a Temporal Allegiance to the Pope. Mr. Pitt, on the part of the British Government, instituted the following inquiries, and received the subjoined answers. The result was that nearly, if not all, of the disabilities were removed by England:

"1. Has the Pope, or cardinals, or any body of men, or any individual of the Church of Rome, any civil authority, power, jurisdiction, or pre-eminence whatsoever, within the realm of England?

"2. Can the Pope, or cardinals, or any body of men, or any individual of the Church of Rome, absolve or dispense with his Majesty's subjects, from their oath of allegiance, upon any pretext whatsoever?

"3. Is there any principle in the tenets of the Catholic faith by which Catholics are justified in not keeping faith with heretics, or other persons differing from them in religious opinions, in any transaction, either of a public or a private nature?"

These questions were sent for answer to the Catholic universities of Paris, of Douay, of Alcala, of Valladolid, and of Salamanca. These several universities are conducted by the most learned men of Europe, and they all responded with frankness and promptness to the questions. We have space only for the answer of one, though we have them all before us, and state that the answers of all are strictly the same. To show what they all answered, we select the response of the University of Paris, as follows:

Abstract from the answers of the Sacred Faculty of Divinity of Paris to the above queries.

After an introduction, according to the usual form of the university, they answer the first query by declaring—

Neither the Pope, nor the cardinals, nor any body of men, nor any other person of the Church of Rome, hath any civil authority, civil power, civil jurisdiction, or civil pre-eminence whatsoever, in *any* kingdom, and, consequently, none in the kingdom of England, by reason or virtue of any authority, power, jurisdiction, or pre-eminence by divine institution inherent in, or granted, or by any other means belonging to the Pope, or the Church of Rome. This doctrine the sacred faculty of divinity of Paris has always held, and upon every occasion maintained, and upon every occasion has rigidly proscribed the contrary doctrines from her schools.

Answer to second query. Neither the Pope, nor the cardinals, nor any body of men, or any person of the Church of Rome, can, by virtue of the keys, absolve or release the subjects of the King of England from their oath of allegiance.

This and the first query are so intimately connected, that the answer of the first immediately and naturally applies to the second, &c.

Answer to the third query. There is no tenet in the Catholic church by which Catholics are justified in not keeping faith with heretics, or those who differ from them in matters of religion. The tenet that it is lawful to break faith with heretics is so repugnant to common honesty and the opinions of Catholics, that there is nothing of which those who have defended the Catholic faith against Protestants have complained more heavily than the malice and calumny of their adversaries in imputing this tenet to them; &c., &c., &c.

Given at Paris, in the general assembly of the Sorborne, held on Thursday, the 11th day before the calends of March, 1789. [Signed in due form.]

IDENTIY OF PRINCIPLE BETWEEN HARTFORD CONVENTIONISM AND KNOW NOTHINGISM.

Every one recollects the odious Hartford Convention, held during the War of 1812—a Convention, representing constituencies in the New England States, who opposed their country in that war and hung blue lights out on the coast to enable the ships of the enemy to know the movements of our own gallant navy and conspire the more easily to defeat it. It had its secrecy, like the Know Nothings.

The first resolution read:

Resolved, That the most inviolate secrecy shall be observed by each member of this Convention, including the Secretary, as to all propositions, debate, and proceedings thereof, until this injunction shall be suspended or altered.

A part of its platform, like that of the Know Nothings, proscribed naturalized citizens.

ONE OF THE RESOLUTIONS OF THE HARTFORD CONVENTION.

Resolved, That no person who shall hereafter be naturalized shall be eligible as a member of the Senate or House of Representatives of the United States, nor capable of holding any civil office under authority of the United States.

THIRD ARTICLE OF THE KNOW NOTHING PLATFORM OF 1856.

3. *Americans must rule America;* and, to this end, *native*-born citizens should be selected for all State, Federal, and municipal offices, or government employment, in preference to naturalized citizens.

THE BIBLE VS. KNOW NOTHINGISM.

"If a *stranger* sojourn with thee in your land, *ye shall not vex him;* but the stranger that dwelleth with you shall be unto you *as one born among you,* and thou shalt love him as thyself, for ye were strangers in the land of Egypt. I am the Lord your God.—*Book of Leviticus,* 19*th chapter,* 33*d and* 34*th verses.*

GEORGE III, A KNOW-NOTHING.

Amongst the counts in that grand indictment framed by our Revolutionary fathers – the Declaration of Independence, is one charging his Royal highness with the infliction upon the American Colonies of one of the very abuses now sought to be engrafted upon the policy of the country by the Know-Nothing party. Read from that Declaration of Independence with what emphasis they rebuked the Know-Nothingism of that Royal tyrant.

"He has endeavored to prevent the population of these States; for that purpose obstructing the laws for the naturalization of foreigners, refusing to pass others to encourage their migration hither, and raising the conditions of new appropriations of land."

PRINCIPLE OF THE NATURALIZATION LAWS VINDICATED BY THE WAR OF 1812.

In a paragraph preceding this we show the identity of principle between Know-Nothingism and Hartford Conventionism. The Hartford Conventionists opposed the war of 1812. The war of 1812 was fought by this country for the reason that England denied the right of a man born under her flag to swear away his allegiance to her Government and become a citizen of the United States. Denying this right she attempted to search our vessels, take from them those in the service of the United States who were born under English dominion. War was the result. Victory for our arms ended the contest. The basis principle of the naturalization laws was vindicated. The Know-Nothings are endeavoring to destroy these laws, with the halo of the glory of the revolution and the war of 1812 thrown around them. Think of this and read the following paragraph:

FOREIGN INFLUENCE.

It was against this kind of foreign influence that Washington advised his countrymen when he said:

"Against the insidious wiles of foreign influence, (I conjure you to believe me fellow citizens,) the jealousy of a free people ought to be *constantly* awake."

Washington was not thinking of the poor emigrant, but of influence like the following, which appeared in the London Chronicle, one of Victoria's organs, in referemce to our Presidential contest:

"We should be sorry to see Mr. Buchanan elected, because he is in favor of preserving the obnoxious institutions, as they exist, AND THE UNITY OF THE STATES. There is no safety for European monarchial governments, if the progressive spirit of the Democracy of the United States is allowed to succeed. ELECT FREMONT AND THE FIRST BLOW TO THE SEPARATION OF THE UNITED STATES IS EFFECTED!"

ANTAGONISM BETWEEN THE OATH OF THE KNOW NOTHINGS AND THE CONSTITUTIoN OF THE UNITED STATES.

CONSTITUTION OF THE UNITED STATES.	KNOW NOTHING CONSTITUTION.
Art. VI.—" No *religious test* shall *ever* be required as a qualification to *any* office of public trust under this government."	Art. III.—" The object of this organization shall be to resist the insidious policy of the Church of Rome, and other foreign influence against the institutions of the country, *by placing in all offices in the gift of the people, or by appointment, none but native born* PROTESTANT *citizens*."

Compare it also with the act of religious toleration in the Constitution of Virginia, penned by Thomas Jefferson, the authorship of which is his epitaph on his tombstone:

16. That religion, or the duty which we owe to our Creator, and the manner of discharging it, can be directed only by reason and conviction—not by force or violence; and therefore, all men are equally entitled to the free exercise of religion, according to the dictates of conscience; and that it is the mutual duty of all to practise christian forbearance, love, and charity towards each other.

KNOW NOTHING OATH.

"You futhermore promise and declare that you will not vote nor give your influence for any man for any office in the gift of the people, unless he be an American born citizen, in favor of Americans ruling America, *nor if he be a Roman Catholic.*"

Again: "You solemnly and sincerely swear that, if it may be done legally, you will, when elected to any office, remove all foreigners *and Roman Catholics from office,* and that *you will in no case appoint such to office.*"

PROSCRIPTION OF ONE RELIGIOUS SECT WILL LEAD EVENTUALLY TO THE PROSCRIPTION IN TURN OF ALL.

The following, says the Trenton True American, is taken from a pamphlet written by a member of one of the American orders to prove that the Methodist Church ought not to be tolerated in a free country.

Recollect Methodists that this is from one of a faction that is endeavoring to get your aid to proscribe your Catholic fellow citizens.

"But again— the very organization of the Methodist Episcopal Church is dangerous to the liberties of a free people. Suppose a crisis to arrive in political action, in which the hierarchy of the Methodist Church is interested. From the dependence of all the parts on one great central power, it is easy to perceive how the suffrages of most of the members may be controlled by the bishops. Let the bishop suggest to the presiding elders that the interests of their ecclesiastical despotism will be subserved by the election of a certain set of men to office; the presiding elders use their influence over the preachers, the preachers over the class leaders, and the class leaders over their class members, and thus the balance af power in a political contest may rest in the hands of SEVEN EPISCOPAL METHODIST BISHOPS. There is as much danger of this, as there is of Romanism accomplishing a similar result; provided the occasion requires it. It may be said that the members of the Methodist Episcopal Church are too independent to be thus influenced; but, while they submit to the degradation to which I have shown they are subjected in Church matters, let them not speak of independence in political matters. Let them become ecclesiastically free, and then it may be hoped that they would *dare* to become *politically* free if the bishops undertook to prevent it.

"I have thus briefly shown that Episcopal Methodism is anti-American in its spirit and tendency, and that it is a dangerous foe to republicanism. I have shown that it had its origin in *usurpation*—that its very organization provides for the support and extension of *assumed power,* and that this power may be *oppressively exercised without re-restriction.* I have shown that Methodist Episcopacy contains in itself the very elements of an *absolute despotism,* and therefore must ultimately, unless checked, subvert and destroy our republican institutions.

A KNOW-NOTHING MAYOR vs. THE CONSTITUTION.

The Constitution says:

"SEC. II—ARTICLE III.—No person held to service or labor in one State, under the laws thereof, escaping into another, shall, in consequence of any law or regulation therein, be discharged from such service or labor; but shall be delivered up on claim of the party to whom such service or labor may be due."

Here is what a Know-Nothing Mayor, whose election was hailed in every section, even in the South, as a great American triumph, said:

"MAYOR'S OFFICE, PHILA., MARCH 6, 1835.

"MR. SAMUEL JOHNSON—DEAR SIR: *With the kindest feelings for you personally, and with great respect for your character as an officer, it is proper that I should inform you that if you act as the agent of Louisiana to return Warwick, charged with encouraging the escape of a fugitive slave to that State, I will consider it my duty to discharge you immediately from the police force of this city.*

"Yours, respectfully, R. T. CONRAD, MAYOR."

KENNETH RAYNER.

No man in the country pretends to be more afraid of the Pope, at this time than Kenneth Rayner. He is his terror by day as well as by night A Catholic, to his eyes, is a monstrum horrendum. He wants legislation against Catholics, although he knows that it is neither practicable or constitutional to do it. But let us exhibit the humbuggery of Know-Nothingism, by showing when Rayner had it in his hands to move to oppress them, what he then said. In the Constitutional Convention of North Carolina, in 1835, he, the said Rayner, thus spoke:

"I do not conceive that we have anything to do with the tenets of any particular creed. We have not to decide between the merits of contending sects. We have not to inquire whether the Pope of Rome is the legal custodian of the Keys of Christ's Kingdom, or whether, (according to the opinion of some,) he is the many-headed monster mentioned in the Apocalypse.

"But it is said, if the Catholic is excluded from office, that will not deprive him of the right of worshipping God according to the dictates of his own conscience. Sir, the right of worshipping God free from all personal pains and penalties, is a right which can now be enjoyed in any country in Christendom. An exclusion from the honors, the profits, and the emoluments of the State, is the highest persecution which public opinion will tolerate in any Christian country in this enlightened age. So that if you sanction the principle recognized in the 32d Article, you use the rod of persecution with as unsparing a hand as it is used in Spain, or the States of the Church. And if you exclude one sect, why not another and another, and finally all. except one?

"Retain that Article, and I assert it, the Catholic and Jew will be placed under the ban of proscription, no matter how great may be his merit; although he may love his country with a patriotism as pure as the first love of woman; although he may pour out his blood like water in her defence; yet, for daring to 'worship God according to the dictates of his own conscience,' you cut him off from all hope of political preferment and from all stimulus to ambition. Like the Israelites in Egypt, he will be oppressed by the land in which he lives, the soil on which he treads, and like them, he will have left no other resource but to turn back upon the graves of his fathers, and take up his march to a more tolerant clime. Sir, the exclusion from office for opinion's sake, in this enlightened age, proceeds from the same spirit of bigotry and superstition which has preyed upon mankind from the building of Babel to the present time."

Mr. Rayner concludes his defence of the Catholics in the following manner:

"Sir, is this convention ready to incorporate into our fundamental law the doctrine, that 'honesty, capability, and faithfulness to the Constitution,' is not a sufficient qualification for office, but that he who obtains it must abjure a certain particular faith? Sir, who constituted us judges of the hearts and consciences of men? What right have we to impugn the motives of our fellow men? It is asserting one of the attributes of the Deity himself, for it is the Lord alone that pondereth the heart. Sir, you may carry on this system of persecution, but there is one point beyond which you cannot go. You may snbject the body to privation and torture, but you cannot fetter the mind—fetters cannot bind it—tyrants cannot enchain it—dungeons cannot confine it—it will rise superior to the powers of fate, and aspire to Him who gave it."

For the correctness of the quotation (says the Fayetteville Carolinian) we refer the reader to the Debates of the Convention of 1835, pages 262–3–4.

Mr. Alex. H. H. Stuart, one of the Know-Nothing Electors in the State of Virginia, who was Secretary of the Interior under the administration of Mr. Fillmore, thus endeavored to blarney our Irish Fellow Citizens, when he was in hopes that his Master my Lord Fillmore would be the Whig nominee and would like to have their votes.

WASHINGTON, March 13, 1852.

Gentlemen:—I have been favored with the receipt of your invitation to attend a public dinner to be given in the city of Philadelphia on the 17th inst., in celebration of the anniversary of St. Patrick's day."

The occasion is an interesting one, and there is no portion of our citizens whom it would give me greater pleasure to meet around the social board. I have always regarded it as a happy omen of the perpetuity of our Government, that so large a portion of the emigration to our shores is of the Irish race—kindred to ourselves—and who *so readily become incorporated with us. I have been struck with the facility with which they adapt themselves to our institutions, rightly entering into their scope and spirit—becoming, in a word, thoroughly Americanized.* And I feel assured that, while the approaching festival will naturally call up hallowed recollections of old Erin, it will be with hearts full of attachments and devotion to the home of their adoption, and with sentiments that will do honor to the character of American citizens.

Regretting that official engagements will forbid my acceptance of your kind invitation, and wishing you all joy on this festive occasion. I am, very respectfully,

Your obedient servant,
ALEX. H. H. STUART.

EXTRACT FROM THE WILL OF GENERAL JACKSON.

"*I bequeath to my well-beloved nephew, Andrew J. Donelson, son of Samuel Donelson, deceased, the elegant sword presented to me by the State of Tennessee with this injunction, that he fail not to use it when necessary in support and protection of our glorious Union, and for the protection of the Constitutional rights of our beloved country, should they be assailed by foreign or domestic traitors.*"

Where was this sword and its owner during the Mexican War?

HUMPHREY MARSHALL AND FREMONT.

The Loudoun, Va., Democratic Mirror, speaking of a speech made by Humphrey Marshall, at Leesburg, r cently, says:

"He was also very severe upon Mr. Buchanan, charged him with being the squatter sovereignty candidate of the North, and declared that he would as leave see John C. Fremont, or the Devil himself made President as James Buchanan."

PRENTICE AN ABOLITIONIST.

In 1829, Prentice was the editor of a paper called the Weekly Review, printed at Hartford, Connecticut, and on the 27th of July, of that year, he published the following editorial in that paper. Read it slaveholders:

"The purchase of Texas must be opposed. Every man who does not wish to see the power of the Northern and Western States depart forever; every man who does not wish to see a dozen new slave States added to the Union, and to hear the cries of additional millions of wretched negroes going up to meet the Lord in the air and imprecate vengeance upon our land, will oppose the purchase of Texas with a deep and irresistible determination.

LAST BALLOT FOR SPEAKER OF THE HOUSE OF REPRESENTATIVES, 34TH CONGRESS.

On the 2d day of February, 1856, the House adopted a resolution, that on the third ballot, who ever received the highest plurality should be the Speaker. The third ballot resulted in the choice of Mr. Banks. It was as follows:

Nathaniel P. Banks received	108
William Aiken	100
Henry M. Fuller	6
Lewis D. Campbell	4
Daniel Wells	1

The following is the vote in detail:

For Mr. Banks—Messrs. Albright, Allison, Ball, Barbour, Henry Bennett, Benson, Billinghurst, Bingham, Bishop, Bliss, Bradshaw, Brenton, Buffington, Burlingame, Jas. H. Campbell, Lewis D. Campbell, Chaffee, Ezra Clark, Clawson, Colfax, Comins, Covode, Cragin, Cumback, Damrell, Timothy Davis, Day, Dean, De Witt, Dick, Dickson, Dodd, Durfee, Edie, Flagler, Galloway, Giddings, Gilbert, Granger, Grow, Robert B. Hall, Harlan, Holloway, Thomas R. Horton, Howard, Kelsey, King, Knapp, Knight, Knowlton, Knox, Kunkel, Leiter, Mace, Matteson, McCarty, Meacham, Killian Miller, Morgan, Morrill, Mott, Murray, Nichols, Norton, Andrew Oliver, Parker, Pearce, Pelton, Pennington, Perry, Pettit, Pike, Pringle, Purviance, Ritchie, Robbins, Roberts, Robison, Sabin, Sage, Sapp, Sherman, Simmons, Spinner, Stanton, Stranahan, Tappan, Thorington, Thurston, Todd, Trafton, Tyson, Wade, Walbridge, Waldron, Calwalader C. Washburne, Elihu B. Washburne, Israel Washburn, Watson, Welch, Wood, Woodruff, and Woodworth.

For Mr. Aiken—Messrs. Allen, Barksdale, Bell, Hendley S. Bennett, Bocock, Bowie, Boyce, Branch, Brooks, Burnett, Cadwalader, John P. Campbell, Carlisle, Caruthers, Caskie, Clingman, Howell Cobb, Williamson R. W. Cobb, Cox, Crawford, Davidson, Denver, Dowdell, Edmundson, Elliott, English, Etheridge, Eustis, Evans, Faulkner, Florence, Foster, Thomas J. D. Fuller, Goode, Greenwood, Augustus Hall, J. Morrison Harris, Sampson W. Harris, Thomas L. Harris, Herbert, Hoffman, Houston, Jewett, George W. Jones, J. Glancy Jones, Keitt, Kelly, Kennett, Kidwell, Lake, Letcher, Lindley, Lumpkin, Alexander K. Marshall, Humphrey Marshall, Samuel S. Marshall, Maxwell, McMullin, McQueen, Smith Miller, Millson, Mordecai, Oliver, Orr, Paine, Peck, Phelps, Porter, Powell, Puryear, Quitman, Reade, Ready, Ricaud, Rivers, Ruffin, Rust, Sandidge, Savage, Shorter, Samuel A. Smith, William Smith, William R. Smith, Sneed, Stephens, Stewart, Swope, Talbott, Trippe, Underwood, Vail, Walker, Warner, Watkins, Wells, Wheeler, Williams, Winslow, Daniel B. Wright, John V. Wright, and Zollicoffer.

For Mr. Fuller—Messrs. Broom, Bayard Clark, Cullen, Henry Winter Davis, Millward, and Whitney.

For Mr. Campbell—Messrs. Dunn, Harrison, Moore, and Scott.

For Mr. Wells—Mr. Hickman.

Messrs. Broom, Clarke, Fuller, Whitney, and Richardson who voted for Mr. Aiken the day before, did not vote for him on the last ballot. Messrs. Broome, Clarke, and Whitney voted for Mr. Fuller. Mr. Fuller was in the Hall and did not vote. It was stated that he had paired off with Mr. Barclay, who was also in the Hall. This Mr. Barclay denies. Messrs. Faulkner, Alexander K. Marshall, and Keitt, who were not present the day before voted for Mr. Aiken then. Mr. Richardson had to resume a pair with Mr. Emrie, of Ohio, which Mr. Faulkner had temporarily taken off his hands.

LAST DAY OF THE CALLED SESSION.

(*From the Daily Globe.*)

SATURDAY, AUGUST 30, 1856.

In the *House of Representatives* Mr. CAMPBELL, of Ohio, by leave, reported from the Ways and Means Committee another Army appropriation bill, with the proviso, that no part of the military of the United States, for the support of which appropriations are made by this act, shall be employed in aid of the enforcement of any enactment of the body claiming to be the Territorial Legislature of Kansas.

The previous question was seconded, and under the operation thereof, the bill was read a third time and passed, by the following vote:

YEAS.—Messrs. Albright, Allison, Barbour, Barclay, Henry Bennett, Benson, Billinghurst, Bingham, Bliss, Bradshaw, Brenton, Buffington, James H. Campbell, Lewis D. Campbell, Chaffee, Ezra Clark, Clawson, Colfax, Comins, Covode, Cragin, Cumback, Damrell, Henry Winter Davis, Timothy Davis, Dean, De Witt, Dick, Dickson, Dodd, Durfee, Edie, Edwards, Emrie, Flagler, Galloway, Giddings, Gilbert, Granger, Grow, Harlan, Haven, Holloway, Thomas R. Horton, Howard, Hughston, Kelsey, King, Knapp, Knight, Knowlton, Knox, Kunkel, Leiter, Matteson, McCarty, Morgan, Morrill, Mott, Murray, Norton, Andrew Oliver, Parker, Pelton, Pettit, Pike, Pringle, Purviance, Ritchie, Robbins, Roberts, Robison, Sabin, Sage, Sapp, Scott, Sherman, Simmons, Spinner, Stranahan, Tappan, Thorington, Thruston, Todd, Trafton, Tyson, Wade, Wakeman, Walbridge, Waldron, Cadwalader C. Washburne, Elihu B. Washburne, Israel Washburne, Welch, Wells, Williams, Wood, Woodruff, and Woodworth—99.

NAYS.—Messrs. Aiken, Akers, Barksdale, Bell, Hendley S. Bennett, Bocock, Bowie, Boyce, Branch, Burnett, Cadwalader, John P. Campbell, Carlile, Caskie, Clingman, Howell Cobb, Williamson R. W. Cobb, Cox, Craige, Crawford, Cullen, Dowdell, Dunn, Edmundson, Elliott, Etheridge, Florence, Thomas J. D. Fuller, Goode, Greenwood, Augustus Hall, J. Morrison Harris, Sampson W. Harris, Thomas L. Harris, Harrison, Hickman, Hoffman, Houston, Jewett, George W. Jones, J. Glancy Jones, Kennett, Kidwell, Lake, Letcher, Lumpkin, Mace, Alexander K. Marshall, Humphrey Marshall, Maxwell, McMullin, McQueen, Smith Miller, Millson, Mordecai Oliver, Orr, Pennington, Phelps, Powell, Puryear, Quitman, Ricaud, Rivers, Ruffin, Rust, Shorter, William Smith, William R. Smith, Stanton, Stewart, Talbott, Vail, Walker, Warner, Wheeler, Daniel B. Wright, and John V. Wrigit—77.

In the *Senate*, the bill having been taken up for consideration, Mr. HUNTER moved that the Kansas proviso be stricken out of the bill, which was agreed to by the following vote:

YEAS.—Messrs. Adams, Allen, Bayard, Bell of Tennessee, Bright, Brodhead, Brown, Butler, Cass, Clay, Crittenden, Douglas, Geyer, Houston, Hunter, Iverson, Johnson, Jones of Tennessee, Mason, Pratt, Pugh, Reid, Thompson of Kentucky, Toucey, Weller, and Wright—26.

NAYS.—Messrs. Durkee, Foot, Foster, Harlan, Trumbull, Wade, and Wilson—7.

The vote in the Senate on the passage of the bill as amended, was the same as the last except one less in the affirmative, Mr. Bell of Tennessee, who voted on the previous vote being absent.

IN THE HOUSE.

A message having been received from the Senate, announcing that that body had passed the Army appropriation bill with an amendment striking out the Kansas proviso, the House proceeded to consider the amendment; when it was agreed to by the following vote:

YEAS.—Messrs, Aiken, Akers, Barksdale, Bell, Bennett of Mississippi, Bocock, Bowie, Boyce, Branch, Burnett, Cadwalader, Campbell of Kentucky, Carlile, Caskie, Clingman, Cobb of Georgia, Cobb of Alabama, Cox, Craige, Crawford, Cullen, Davidson, Davis of Maryland, Denver, Dowdell, Edmundson, Elliot, Etheridge, Eustis, Evans, Faulkner, Florence, Fuller of Maine, Goode, Greenwood, Hall of Iowa, Harris of Maryland, Harris of Alabama, Harris of Illinois, Harrison, Haven, Hickman, Hoffman, Houston, Jewett, Jones of Tennessee, Jones of Pennsylvania, Keitt, Kelly, Kennett, Kidwell, Lake, Letcher, Lumpkin, A. K. Marshall of Kentucky, H. Marshall of Kentucky, Marshall of Illinois, Maxwell, McMullin, McQueen, Miller of Indiana, Milson, Oliver of Missouri, Orr, Packer, Peck, Phelps, Porter, Powell, Puryear, Quitman, Ricaud, Rivers, Ruffin, Rust, Sandidge, Savage, Seward, Shorter, Smith of Tennessee, Smith of Virginia, Smith of Alabama, Sneed, Stephens, Stewart, Swope, Talbott, Taylor, Tyson, Underwood, Vail, Walker, Warner, Wells, Wheeler, Whitney, Williams, Winslow, Wright of Mississippi, Wright of Tennessee, and Zolicoffer—101.

Nays.—Messrs. Allbright, Allison, Barbour, Barclay, Bennett of New York, Benson, Billinghurst, Bingham, Bliss, Bradshaw, Brenton, Buffington, Campbell of Pennsylvania, Campbell of Ohio, Chaffee, Clark of Connecticut, Clawson, Colfax, Comins, Covode, Cragin, Cumback, Damrell, Davis of Massachusetts, Dean, DeWitt, Dick, Dickson, Dodd, Dunn, Durfee, Edie, Edwards, Emrie, Flagler, Galloway, Giddings, Gilbert, Granger, Grow, Harlan, Holloway, Horton of New York, Howard, Hughston, Kelsey, King, Knapp, Knight, Knowlton, Knox, Kunkel, Leiter, Mace, Matteson, McCarty, Morgan, Morrill, Mott, Murray, Norton, Oliver of New York, Parker, Pelton, Pennington, Pettit, Pike, Pringle, Purviance, Ritchie, Robbins, Roberts, Robinson, Sabin, Sage, Sapp, Scott, Sherman, Simmons, Spinner, Stanton, Stranahan, Tappan, Thorington, Thurston, Todd, Trafton, Wade, Wakeman, Walbridge, Waldron, Washburne of Wisconsin, Washburne of Illinois, Washburne of Maine, Welch, Wood, Woodruff, and Woodworth—98.

Mr. Whitney, of New-York, now that the Army bill had passed, asked leave to bring in a bill repealing the obnoxious laws in Kansas. Mr. Washburne, of Illinois, and other Republicans objected, so leave was not granted.

ELECTORAL VOTE OF STATES.

State	Votes	State	Votes
Maine	8	Alabama	9
New Hampshire	5	Mississippi	7
Vermont	5	Louisiana	6
Massachusetts	13	Arkansas	4
Rhode Island	4	Texas	4
Connecticut	6	Missouri	9
New York	35	Kentucky	12
Pennsylvania	27	Tennessee	12
New Jersey	7	Iowa	4
Delaware	3	Illinoise	11
Maryland	8	Indiana	13
Virginia	15	Ohio	23
North Carolina	10	Michigan	6
South Carolina	8	Wisconsin	5
Georgia	10	California	4
Florida	3		

VIRGINIA RESOLUTIONS OF 1798,

PRONOUNCING THE ALIEN AND SEDITION LAWS TO BE UNCONSTITUTIONAL, AND DEFINING THE RIGHTS OF THE STATES.—DRAWN BY MR. MADISON.

IN THE VIRGINIA HOUSE OF DELEGATES,
Friday, Dec. 21, 1798.

Resolved, That the General Assembly of Virginia doth unequivocally express a firm resolution to maintain and defend the Constitution of the United States, and the Constitution of this State, against every aggression either foreign or domestic; and that they will support the Government of the United States in all measures warranted by the former.

That this Assembly most solemnly declares a warm attachment to the Union of the States, to maintain which it pledges its powers; and, that for this end, it is their duty to watch over and *oppose every infraction of those principles which constitute the only basis of that Union,* because a faithful observance of them can alone secure its existence and the public happiness.

That this Assembly doth explicitly and peremptorily declare, THAT IT VIEWS THE POWERS OF THE FEDERAL GOVERNMENT, AS RESULTING FROM THE COMPACT TO WHICH THE STATES ARE PARTIES, AS LIMITED BY THE PLAIN SENSE AND INTENTION OF THE INSTRUMENT CONSTITUTING THAT COMPACT, AS NO FARTHER VALID THAN THEY ARE AUTHORIZED BY THE GRANTS ENUMERATED IN THAT COMPACT; AND THAT IN CASE OF A DELIBERATE, PALPABLE, AND DANGEROUS EXERCISE OF OTHER POWERS, NOT GRANTED BY THE SAID COMPACT, THE STATES, WHO ARE PARTIES THERETO, HAVE THE RIGHT, AND ARE IN DUTY BOUND, TO INTERPOSE, FOR ARRESTING THE PROGRESS OF THE EVIL, AND FOR MAINTAINING WITHIN THEIR RESPECTIVE LIMITS THE AUTHORITIES, RIGHTS, AND LIBERTIES APPERTAINING TO THEM.

That the General Assembly doth also express its deep regret, that a spirit has, in sundry instances, been manifested by the Federal Government, to enlarge its powers by forced constructions of the constitutional charter which defines them;

and, that indications have appeared of a design to expound certain general phrases (which, having been copied from the very limited grant of powers in the former articles of confederation, were the less liable to be misconstrued) so as to destroy the meaning and effect of the particular enumeration which necessarily explains, and limits the general phrases, and so as to CONSOLIDATE THE STATES BY DEGREES INTO ONE SOVEREIGNTY, THE OBVIOUS TENDENCY AND INEVITABLE RESULT OF WHICH WOULD BE, TO TRANSFORM THE PRESENT REPUBLICAN SYSTEM OF THE UNITED STATES INTO AN ABSOLUTE, OR AT BEST, A MIXED MONARCHY.

That the General Assembly doth particularly protest against the palpable and alarming infractions of the Constitution, in the two late cases of the "Alien and Sedition Acts," passed at the last session of Congress; the first of which, exercises a power no where delegated to the Federal Government, and which, by uniting Legislative and Judicial powers to those of Executive, subverts the general principles of free government, as well as the particular organization and positive provisions of the Federal Constitution; and the other of which acts exercises, in like manner, a power not delegated by the Constitution, but on the contrary, expressly and positively forbidden by one of the amendments thereto; a power which, more than any other, ought to produce universal alarm, because it is levelled against the right of freely examining public characters and measures, and of free communication among the people thereon, which has ever been justly deemed the only effectual guardian of every other right.

That this State having by its Convention, which ratified the Federal Constitution, expressly declared, that among other essential rights, "the liberty of conscience and the press cannot be cancelled, abridged, restrained or modified by any authority of the United States," and from its extreme anxiety to guard these rights from every possible attack of sophistry and ambition, having with other States recommended an amendment for that purpose, which amendment was, in due time, annexed to the Constitution, it would mark a reproachful inconsistency, and criminal degeneracy, if an indifference were now shown to the most palpable violation of one of the rights, thus declared and secured; and to the establishment of a precedent which may be fatal to the other.

That the good people of this Commonwealth, having ever felt, and continuing to feel the most sincere affection for their brethren of the other States; the truest anxiety for establishing and perpetuating the union of all; and the most scrupulous fidelity to that Constitution, which is the pledge of mutual friendship, and the instrument of mutual happiness; the General Assembly doth solemnly appeal to the like dispositions in the other States, in confidence, that they will concur with this Commonwealth, in declaring, as it does hereby declare, that the acts aforesaid are UNCONSTITUTIONAL; and, that the necessary and proper measures will be taken *by each* for co-operating with this State, in maintaining unimpaired the authorities, rights, and liberties, reserved to the States, respectively, or to the people.

That the Governor be desired to transmit a copy of the foregoing resolutions to the Executive authority of each of the other States, with a request, that the same may be communicated to the Legislature thereof; and that a copy be furnished to each of the Senators and Representatives representing this State in the Congress of the United States.

Attest, JOHN STEWART.

1798, December 24th. Agreed to by the Senate.

H. BROOKE.

A true copy from the original deposited in the office of the General Assembly.

JOHN STEWART, Keeper of Rolls.

EXTRACTS

From the Address to the People, which accompanied the foregoing Resolutions.

FELLOW CITIZENS—Unwilling to shrink from our representative responsibility, conscious of the purity of our motives, but acknowledging your right to supervise our conduct, we invite your serious attention to the emergency which dictated the subjoined resolutions. Whilst we disdain to alarm you by ill-founded jealousies, we recommended an investigation, guided by the coolness of wisdom, and a decision bottomed on firmness but tempered with moderation.

It would be perfidious in those entrusted with the GUARDIANSHIP OF THE STATE SOVEREIGNTY, and acting under the solemn obligation of the following oath: "I do swear, that I will support the Constitution of the United States," not to warn you of encroachments, which, though clothed with the pretext of necessity, or disguised by arguments of expediency, may yet establish precedents, which may ultimately devote a generous and unsuspicious people to all the consequences of usurped power.

Encroachments springing from a government WHOSE ORGANIZATION CANNOT BE MAINTAINED WITHOUT THE CO-OPERATION OF THE STATES, furnish the strongest excitements upon the State Legislatures to watchfulness, and impose upon them the strongest obligation TO PRESERVE UNIMPAIRED THE LINE OF PARTITION.

The *acquiescence of the States* under *infractions* of the Federal *Compact*, would either beget a speedy consolidation, by precipitating the State Governments into impotency and contempt; or prepare the way for a revolution, by a repetition of these infractions, until the people are aroused to appear in the majesty of their strength. It is to avoid these calamities, that we exhibit to the people the momentous question, whether the Constitution of the United States shall yield to a construction, which defies every restraint, and overwhelms the best hopes of republicanism.

Exhortations to disregard domestic usurpations, until foreign danger shall have passed, is an artifice which may be forever used; because the possessors of power, who are the advocates for its extension, can ever create national embarrassments, to be successively employed to soothe the people into sleep, whilst that power is swelling, silently, secretly, and fatally. Of the same character are insinuations of a foreign influence, which seize upon a laudable enthusiasm against danger from abroad, and distort it by an unnatural application, so as to blind your eyes against danger at home.

The Sedition act presents a scene, which was never expected by the early friends of the Constitution. It was then admitted that the *State sovereignties were only diminished, by powers specifically enumerated*, or necessary to carry the specified powers into effect. Now Federal authority is deduced from *implication*, and from the existence of State law it is inferred, that Congress possess a similar power of legislation; whence Congress will be endowed with a power of legislation, in all cases whatsoever, and the States will be stript of every right reserved, by the concurrent claims of a paramount Legislature.

The Sedition act is the offspring of these tremendous pretensions, which inflict a death wound on the sovereignty of the States.

For the honor of American understanding, we will not believe, that the people have been allured into the adoption of the Constitution, by an affectation of defining powers, whilst the *preamble* would admit a construction which would erect the *will of Congress* into a power *paramount in all cases*, and therefore limited in none. On the contrary, it is evident that the objects for which the Constitution was formed were deemed attainable only by a particular enumeration and specification of each power granted to the Federal Government; reserving all others to the people, or to the States. And yet it is in vain we search for any specified power, embracing the right of legislation against the freedom of the press.

Had the States been despoiled of their sovereignty by the generality of the preamble, and had the Federal Government been endowed with whatever they should judge to be instrumental towards union, justice, tranquillity, common defence, general welfare, and the preservation of liberty, nothing could have been more frivolous than an enumeration of powers.

All the preceding arguments rising from a deficiency of constitutional power in Congress, apply to the Alien act, and this act is liable to other objections peculiar to itself. If a suspicion that aliens are dangerous, constitute the justification of that power exercised over them by Congress, then a similar suspicion will justify the exercise of a similar power over natives. Because there is nothing in the Constitution distinguishing between the power of a State to permit the residence of natives and aliens. It is, therefore, a right originally possessed, and never surrendered by the respective States, and which is rendered dear and valuable to Virginia, because it is assailed through the bosom of the Constitution, and because her peculiar situation renders the easy admission of artizans and laborers an interest of vast importance.

But this bill contains other features, still more alarming and dangerous. It dispenses with the trial by jury; it violates the judicial system; it confounds legislative, executive, and judicial powers; it punishes without trial; and it bestows upon the President despotic power over a numerous class of men. Are such measures consistent with our constitutional principles? And will an accumulation of power so extensive, in the hands of the Executive, over aliens, secure to natives the blessings of republican liberty?

If measures can mould Governments, and if an uncontrolled power of construction is surrendered to those who administer them, their progress may be easily foreseen and their end easily foretold. A lover of monarchy, who opens the treasures of corruption, by distributing emolument among devoted partizans, may at the same time be approaching his object, and deluding the people with professions of republicanism. He may confound monarchy and republicanism, by the art of definition. He may varnish over the dexterity which ambition never fails to display, with the pliancy of language, the seduction of expediency, or the prejudices of the times. And he may come at length to avow, that so extensive a territory as that of the United States can only be governed by the energies of monarchy; that it cannot be defended, except by standing armies; and that it cannot be united, except by consolidation.

Measures have already been adopted, which may lead to these consequences. They consist:

In fiscal systems and arrangements, which keep an host of commercial and wealthy individuals, embodied and obedient, to the mandates of the treasury.

In armies and navies, which will, on the one hand, enlist the tendency of man to pay homage to his fellow creature who can feed or honor him; and on the other, employ the principle of fear, by punishing imaginary insurrections, under the pretext of preventive justice.

In swarms of officers, civil and military, who can inculcate political tenets tending to consolidation and monarchy, both by indulgences and severities; and can act as spies over the free exercise of human reason.

In restraining the freedom of the press, and investing the Executive with legislative, executive, and judicial powers, over a numerous body of men.

And, that we may shorten the catalogue, in *establishing by successive precedents such a mode of construing the Constitution, as will rapidly remove every restraint upon Federal power.*

Let history be consulted; let the man of experience reflect; nay, let the artificers of monarchy be asked, what farther materials they can need for building up their favorite system?

These are solemn, but painful truths; and yet we recommend it to you, not to forget the possibility of danger from without, although danger threatens us from within. Usurpation is indeed dreadful, but against foreign invasion, if that should happen, let us rise with hearts and hands united, and repel the attack, with the zeal of freemen, who will strengthen their title to examine and correct domestic measures, by having defended their country against foreign aggression.

Pledged as we are, fellow-citizens, to these sacred engagements, we yet humbly and fervently implore the Almighty Disposer of Events, to avert from our land war and usurpation, the scourges of mankind; to permit our fields to be cultivated in peace; to instil into nations the love of friendly intercourse; to suffer our youth to be educated in virtue; and to preserve our morality from the pollution, invariably incident to habits of war; to prevent the laborer and husbandman from being harassed by *taxes* and *imposts;* to remove from ambition the means of disturbing the Commonwealth; to annihilate all pretexts for power afforded by war; to maintain the Constitution; and, to bless our nation with tranquillity, under whose benign influence, we may reach the summit of happiness and glory, to which we are destined by NATURE and NATURE'S GOD.

Attest, JOHN STEWART, C. H. D.

1799, January 23d. Agreed to by the Senate.

H. BROOKE, C. S.

A true copy from the original deposited in the office of the General Assembly. JOHN STEWART, Keeper of Rolls.

ANSWERS OF THE SEVERAL STATE LEGISLATURES.

STATE OF DELAWARE.

In the House of Representatives, February 1, 1799.—*Resolved*, By the Senate and House of Representatives of the State of Delaware, in General Assembly met, that they consider the resolutions from the State of Virginia as a very unjustifiable interference with the General Government and constituted authorities of the United States, and of dangerous tendency, and therefore not fit subject for the further consideration of the General Assembly.

ISAAC DAVIS, Speaker of the Senate.
STEPHEN LEWIS, Speaker of the H. of Rep's.

Test—John Fisher, C. S.—John Caldwell, C. H. R.

STATE OF RHODE ISLAND AND PROVIDENCE PLANTATIONS.

In General Assembly, February, A. D. 1799.—Certain Resolutions of the Legislature of Virginia, passed on 21st of December last, being communicated to this Assembly,

1. *Resolved*, That in the opinion of this Legislature, the second section of third article of the Constitution of the United States in these words, to wit: *The Judicial power shall extend*

to all cases arising under the laws of the United States, vests in the Federal Courts, exclusively, and in the Supreme Court of the United States, ultimately the authority of deciding on the constitutionality of any act or law of the Congress of the United States.

2. *Resolved,* That for any State legislature to assume that authority, would be,

1st. Blending together legislative and judicial powers.

2d. Hazarding an interruption of the peace of the States by civil discord, in case of a diversity of opinions among the State legislatures; each State having, in that case, no resort for vindicating its own opinions, but to the strength of its own arm.

3d. Submitting most important questions of law to less competent tribunals: and

4th. An infraction of the Constitution of the United States, expressed in plain terms.

3. *Resolved,* That although for the above reasons, this legislature, in their public capacity, do not feel themselves authorized to consider and decide on the constitutionality of the Sedition and Alien laws (so called:) yet they are called upon by the exigency of this occasion, to declare, that in their private opinions, these laws are within the powers delegated to Congress, and promotive of the welfare of the United States.

4. *Resolved,* That the Governor communicate these resolutions to the supreme executive of the State of Virginia, and at the same time express to him that this legislature cannot contemplate, without extreme concern and regret, the many evil and fatal consequences which may flow from the very unwarrantable resolutions aforesaid, of the legislature of Virginia, passed on the twenty-first day of December last.

A true copy, SAMUEL EDDY, *Sec'y.*

COMMONWEALTH OF MASSACHUSETTS.

In Senate, February 9, 1799.—The Legislature of Massachusetts having taken into serious consideration the resolutions of the State of Virginia, passed the 21st day of December last, and communicated by his excellency the Governor, relative to certain supposed infractions of the Constitution of the United States, by the government thereof, and being convinced that the Federal Constitution is calculated to promote the happiness, prosperity and safety of the people of these United States, and to maintain that union of the several States, so essential to the welfare of the whole; and being bound by solemn oath to support and defend that Constitution, feel it unnecessary to make any professions of their attachment to it, or of their firm determination to support it against every aggression, foreign or domestic.

But they deem it their duty solemnly to declare, that while they hold sacred the principle, that consent of the people is the only pure source of just and legitimate power, they cannot admit the right of the State legislatures to denounce the administration of that government to which the people themselves, by a solemn compact, have exclusively committed their national concerns: That, although a liberal and enlightened vigilance among the people is always to be cherished, yet an unreasonable jealousy of the men of their choice, and a recurrence to measures of extremity, upon groundless or trivial pretexts, have a strong tendency to destroy all rational liberty at home, and to deprive the United States of the most essential advantages in their relations abroad: That this legislature are persuaded, that the decision of all cases in law and equity, arising under the Constitution of the United States, and the construction of all laws made in pursuance thereof, are exclusively vested by the people in the judicial courts of the United States.

That the people in that solemn compact, which is declared to be the supreme law of the land, have not constituted the State legislatures the judges of the acts or measures of the Federal Government, but have confided to them the power of proposing such amendments of the Constitution, as shall appear to them necessary to the interests, or conformable to the wishes of the people whom they represent.

That by this construction of the Constitution, an amicable and dispassionate remedy is pointed out for any evil which experience may prove to exist, and the peace and prosperity of the United States may be preserved without interruption.

But, should the respectable State of Virginia persist in the assumption of the right to declare the acts of the National Government unconstitutional, and should she oppose successfully her force and will to those of the nation, the Constitution would be reduced to a mere cypher, to the form and pageantry of authority, without the energy of power. Every act of the Federal Government which thwarted the views or checked the ambitious projects of a particular State, or of its leading and influential members, would be the object of opposition and of remonstrance; while the people, convulsed and confused by the conflict between two hostile jurisdictions, enjoying the protection of neither, would be wearied into a submission to some bold leader, who would establish himself on the ruins of both.

The legislature of Massachusetts, although they do not themselves claim the right, nor admit the authority of any of the State governments, to decide upon the constitutionality of the acts of the Federal Government, still, least their silence should be construed into disapprobation, or at best into a doubt of the constitutionality of the acts referred to by the State of Virginia; and, as the General Assembly of Virginia has called for an expression of their sentiments, do explicitly declare, that they consider the acts of Congress, commonly called "the Alien and Sedition acts," not only constitutional, but expedient and necessary: That the former act respects a description of persons whose rights were not particularly contemplated in the Constitution of the United States, who are entitled only to a temporary protection, while they yield a temporary allegiance; a protection which ought to be withdrawn whenever they become "dangerous to the public safety," or are found guilty of "treasonable machination" against the government: That Congress having been especially entrusted by the people with the general defence of the nation, had not only the right, but were bound to protect it against internal as well as external foes. That the United States, at the time of passing the *act concerning aliens*, were threatened with actual invasion, had been driven by the unjust and ambitious conduct of the French Government into warlike preparations, expensive and burthensome, and had then, within the bosom of the country, thousands of aliens, who, we doubt not, were ready to co-operate in any external attack.

It cannot be seriously believed, that the United States should have waited till the poignard had in fact been plunged. The removal of aliens is the usual preliminary of hostility, and is justified by the invariable usages of nations. Actual hostility had unhappily long been experienced, and a formal declaration of it the government had reason daily to expect. The law, therefore, was just and salutary, and no officer could with so much propriety be entrusted with the execution of it, as the one in whom the Constitution has reposed the executive power of the United States.

The *Sedition act*, so called, is, in the opinion of this legislature, equally defensible. The General Assembly of Virginia, in their resolve under consideration, observe, that when that State by its convention, ratified the Federal Constitution, it expressly declared, "That, among other essential rights, the liberty of conscience and of the press cannot be cancelled, abridged, restrained or modified by any authority of the United States," and from its extreme anxiety to guard these rights from every possible attack of sophistry or ambition, with other States, recommend an amendment for that purpose: which amendment was, in due time, annexed to the Constitution; but they did not surely expect that the proceedings of their State convention were to explain the amendment adopted by the Union. The words of that amendment, on this subject, are, "Congress shall make no law abridging the freedom of speech or of the press."

The act complained of is no abridgment of the freedom of either. The genuine liberty of speech and the press, is the liberty to utter and publish the truth; but the constitutional right of the citizen to utter and publish the truth, is not to be confounded with the licentiousness in speaking and writing, that is only employed in propagating falsehood and slander. This freedom of the press has been explicitly secured by most, if not all the State constitutions; and of this provision there has been generally but one construction among enlightened men; that it is a security for the rational use and not the abuse of the press; of which the courts of law, the juries and people will judge; this right is not infringed, but confirmed and established by the late act of Congress.

By the Constitution, the legislative, executive and judicial departments of government are ordained and established; and general enumerated powers vested in them respectively, including those which are prohibited to the several States. Certain powers are granted in general terms by the people to their General Government, for the purposes of their safety and protection. The government is not only empowered, but it is made their duty to repel invasions and suppress insurrections; to guarantee to the several States a republican form of government; to protect each State against invasion, and, when applied to, against domestic violence; to hear and decide all cases in law and equity, arising under the Constitution, and under any treaty or law made in pursuance thereof; and all cases of admiralty and maritime jurisdiction, and relating to the law of nations. Whenever, therefore, it becomes necessary to effect any of the objects designated, it is perfectly consonant to all just rules of construction, to infer, that the usual means and powers necessary to the attainment of that object, are also granted: But the Constitution has left no occasion to resort to implication for these powers; it has made an express grant of them, in the 8th section of the first article, which ordains, "That Congress shall have power to make all laws which shall be necessary and proper for carrying into execution the foregoing powers, and all other powers vested by the Constitution in the government of the United States or in any department or officer thereof."

This Constitution has established a Supreme Court of the United States, but has made no provision for its protection, even against such improper conduct in its presence, as might disturb its proceedings, unless expressed in the section before recited. But as no statute has been passed on this subject, this protection is, and has been for nine years past, uniformly found in the application of the principles and usages of the common law. The same protection may unquestionably be afforded by a statute passed in virtue of the before mentioned section, as necessary and proper, for carrying into execution the powers vested in that department. A construction of the different parts of the Constitution, perfectly just and fair, will, on analogous principles, extend protection and security against the offences in question, to the other departments of government, in discharge of their respective trusts.

The President of the United States is bound by his oath "to preserve, protect and defend the Constitution," and it is expressly made his duty "to take care that the laws be faithfully executed;" but this would be impracticable by any created being, if there could be no legal restraint of those scandalous misrepresentations of his measures and motives, which directly tend to rob him of the public confidence. And equally impotent would be every other public officer, if thus left to the mercy of the seditious.

It is holden to be a truth most clear, that the important trusts before enumerated cannot be discharged by the government to which they are committed, without the power to restrain seditious practices and unlawful combinations against itself, and to protect the officers thereof from abusive misrepresentations. Had the Constitution withheld this power, it would have made the government responsible for the effects without any control over the causes which naturally produce them, and would have essentially failed of answering the great ends for which the people of the United States declare, in the first clause of that instrument, that they establish the same, viz: "To form a more perfect union, establish justice, insure domestic tranquillity, provide for the common defence, promote the general welfare, and secure the blessings of liberty to ourselves and posterity."

Seditious practices and unlawful combinations against the Federal Government, or any officer thereof, in the performance of his duty, as well as licentiousness of speech and of the press, were punishable on the principles of common law in the courts of the United States, before the act in question was passed. This act then is an amelioration of that law in favor of the party accused, as it mitigates the punishment which that authorizes, and admits of any investigation of public men and measures which is regulated by truth. It is not intended to protect men in office, only as they are agents of the people. Its object is to afford legal security to public offices and trusts created for the safety and happiness of the people, and therefore the security derived from it is for the benefit of the people, and is their right.

This construction of the Constitution and of the existing law of the land, as well as the act complained of, the legislature of Massachusetts most deliberately and firmly believe results from a just and full view of the several parts of the Constitution: and they consider that act to be wise and necessary, as an audacious and unprincipled spirit of falsehood and abuse had been too long unremittingly exerted for the purpose of perverting public opinion, and threatened to undermine and destroy the whole fabric of government.

The legislature further declare, that in the foregoing sentiments they have expressed the general opinion of their constituents, who have not only acquiesced without complaint in those particular measures of the Federal Government, but have given their explicit approbation by re-electing those men who voted for the adoption of them. Nor is it apprehended, that the citizens of this State will be accused of supineness or of an indifference to their constitutional rights; for, while on the one hand, they regard with due vigilance the conduct of the government; on the other, their freedom, safety and happiness require, that they should defend that government and its constitutional measures against the open or insidious attacks of any foe, whether foreign or domestic.

And, lastly, that the legislature of Massachusetts feel a strong conviction, that the several United States are connected by a common interest which ought to render their union indissoluble, and that this State will always co-operate with its confederate States in rendering that union productive of mutual security, freedom and happiness.

Sent down for concurrence.

SAMUEL PHILIPS, *President.*

In the House of Representatives, Feb. 13, 1799,

Read and concurred.

EDWARD H. ROBBINS, *Speaker.*

A true copy. Attest. JOHN AVERY, *Secretary.*

STATE OF NEW YORK.

In Senate, March 5, 1799.—Whereas, the people of the United States have established for themselves a free and independent national government: And whereas it is essential to the existence of every government, that it have authority to defend and preserve its constitutional powers inviolate, inasmuch as every infringement thereof tends to its subversion. And whereas the judicial power extends expressly to all cases of law and equity arising under the Constitution and the laws of the United States whereby the interference of the legislatures of the particular States in those cases is manifestly excluded. And, whereas, our peace, prosperity and happiness, eminently depend on the preservation of the Union, in order to which, a reasonable confidence in the constituted authorities and chosen representatives of the people is indispensable. And, whereas, every measure calculated to weaken that confidence has a tendency to destroy the usefulness of our public functionaries, and to excite jealousies equally hostile to rational liberty, and the principles of a good republican government. And, whereas, the Senate not perceiving that the rights of the particular States have been violated, nor any unconstitutional powers assumed by the General Government, cannot forbear to express the anxiety and regret with which they observe the inflammatory and pernicious sentiments and doctrines which are contained in the resolutions of the legislatures of Virginia and Kentucky—sentiments and doctrines, no less repugnant to the Constitution of the United States, and the principles of their union, than destructive to the Federal Government, and unjust to those whom the people have elected to administer it: wherefore, *Resolved*, That while the Senate feel themselves constrained to bear unequivocal testimony against such sentiments and doctrines, they deem it a duty no less indispensable, explicitly to declare their incompetency, as a branch of the legislature of this State, to supervise the acts of the General Government.

Resolved, That his excellency, the Governor, be, and he is hereby requested to transmit a copy of the foregoing resolution to the executives of the States of Virginia and Kentucky, to the end that the same may be communicated to the legislatures thereof.

A true copy. ABM. B. BAUCKER, *Clerk*.

STATE OF CONNECTICUT.

At a General Assembly of the State of Connecticut, holden at Hartford, in the said State, on the second Thursday of May, Anno Domini, 1799, his excellency the Governor having communicated to this assembly sundry resolutions of the Legislature of Virginia adopted in December, 1798, which relate to the measures of the General Government, and the said resolutions having been considered, it is

Resolved, That this assembly views with deep regret, and explicitly disavows, the principles contained in the aforesaid resolutions; and particularly the opposition to the "Alien and Sedition acts"—acts which the constitution authorised: which the exigency of the country rendered necessary: which the constituted authorities have enacted, and which merit the entire approbation of this assembly. They, therefore, decidedly refuse to concur with the Legislature of Virginia, in promoting any of the objects attempted in the aforesaid resolutions.

And it is further resolved, That his excellency the Governor be requested to transmit a copy of the foregoing resolution to the Governor of Virginia, that it may be communicated to the Legislature of that State.

Passed in the House of Representatives unanimously.

Attest, JOHN C. SMITH, *Clerk*.

Concurred, unanimously, in the Upper House.

Teste, SAM. WYLLYS, *Sec'ry*.

STATE OF NEW HAMPSHIRE.

In the House of Representatives, June 14, 1799.—The committee, to take into consideration the resolutions of the general assembly of Virginia, dated December 21st, 1798; also certain resolutions of the Legislature of Kentucky, of the 10th of November, 1798, report as follows:

The Legislature of New Hampshire having taken into consideration certain resolutions of the general assembly of Virginia, dated December 21, 1798; also certain resolutions of the Legislature of Kentucky, of the 10th of November, 1798,

Resolved, That the Legislature of New Hampshire unequivocally express a firm resolution to maintain and defend the Constitution of the United States, and the Constitution of this State, against every aggression, either foreign or domestic, and that they will support the Government of the United States in all measures warranted by the former.

That the State Legislatures are not the proper tribunals to determine the constitutionality of the laws of the General Government—that the duty of such decision is properly and exclusively confided to the judicial department.

That if the Legislature of New Hampshire, for mere speculative purposes, were to express an opinion on the acts of the General Government, commonly called "the Alien and Sedition bills," that opinion would unreservedly be, that those acts are constitutional, and, in the present critical situation of our country, highly expedient.

That the constitutionality and expediency of the acts aforesaid have been very ably advocated and clearly demonstrated by many citizens of the United States, more especially by the minority of the General Assembly of Virginia. The Legislature of New Hampshire, therefore, deem it unnecessary, by any train of arguments, to attempt further illustration of the propositions, the truth of which, it is confidently believed, at this day, is very generally seen and acknowledged.

Which report being read and considered, was unanimously received and accepted, one hundred and thirty-seven members being present.

Sent up for concurrence. JOHN PRENTICE, *Speaker*.

In Senate, same day, read and concurred in unanimously.

AMOS SHEPARD, *President*.

Approved, June 15th, 1799.

J. T. GILMAN, *Governor*.

A true copy. Attest, JOSEPH PEARSON, *Secretary*.

STATE OF VERMONT.

In the House of Representatives, October 30th, A. D., 1799. The House proceeded to take under their consideration the resolutions of the General Assembly of Virginia, relative to certain measures of the General Government, transmitted to the Legislature of this State, for their consideration: Whereupon,

Resolved, That the General Assembly of the State of Vermont do highly disapprove of the resolutions of the General Assembly of the State of Virginia, as being unconstitutional in their nature, and dangerous in their tendency. It belongs not to State Legislatures to decide on the constitutionality of laws made by the General Government; this power being exclusively vested in the judiciary courts of the Union: That his excellency the Governor be requested to transmit a copy of this resolution to the executive of Virginia, to be communicated to the General Assembly of that State: And that the same be sent to the Governor and Council for their concurrence.

SAMUEL C. CRAFTS, *Clerk.*

In Council, October 30, 1799. Read and concurred in unanimously.

RICHARD WHITNEY. *Secretary.*

KENTUCKY RESOLUTIONS OF 1798 AND 1799.

[The original draught prepared by Thomas Jefferson.]

The following Resolutions passed the House of Representatives of Kentucky, Nov. 10th, 1798. On the passage of the first Resolution, one dissentient; 2d, 3d, 4th, 5th, 6th, 7th, 8th, two dissentients; 9th, three dissentients.

I. *Resolved,* That the several States composing the United States of America, are not united on the principle of unlimited submission to their General Government; but that by compact under the style and title of a Constitution for the United States, and of amendments thereto, they constituted a General Government for special purposes, delegated to that Government certain definite powers, reserving, each State to itself, the residuary mass of right to their own self-government; and, that whensoever the General Government assumes undelegated powers, its acts are unauthoritative, void, and of no force; that to this compact each State acceded as a State, and is an integral party; that this Government, created by this compact, was not made the exclusive or final judge of the extent of the powers delegated to itself; since that would have made its discretion, and not the Constitution, the measure of its powers; but, that as in all other cases of compact, among parties having no common judge, EACH PARTY HAS AN EQUAL RIGHT TO JUDGE FOR ITSELF, AS WELL OF INFRACTIONS AS OF THE MODE AND MEASURE OF REDRESS.

II. *Resolved,* That the Constitution of the United States having delegated to Congress a power to punish treason, counterfeiting the securities and current coin of the United States, piracies and felonies committed on the high seas, and offences against the laws of nations, and no other crimes whatever; and it being true, as a general principle, and one of the amendments to the Constitution having also declared, "that the powers not delegated to the United States by the Constitution, nor prohibited by it to the States, are reserved to the States respectively, or to the people," therefore, also, the same act of Congress, passed on the 14th day of July, 1798, and entitled, "An act in addition to the act entitled an act for the punishment of certain crimes against the United States;" as also, the act passed by them on the 27th day of June, 1798, entitled, "An act to punish frauds committed on the Bank of the United States," (and all other their acts which assume to create, define, or punish crimes other than those enumerated in the Constitution) *are altogether void and of no force,* and that the power to create, define, and punish such other crimes is reserved, and of right appertains solely and exclusively to the respective States, each within its own territory.

III. *Resolved,* That it is true, as a general principle, and is also expressly declared by one of the amendments to the Constitution, that "the powers not delegated to the United States by the Constitution, nor prohibited by it to the States, are reserved to the States respectively or to the people;" and, that no power over the freedom of religion, freedom of speech, or freedom of the press being delegated to the United States by the Constitution, nor prohibited by it to the States, all lawful powers respecting the same did of right remain, and were reserved to the States or to the people; that thus was manifested their determination to retain to themselves the right of judging how far the licentiousness of speech and of the press may be abridged without lessoning their useful freedom, and how far those abuses which cannot be separated from their use should be tolerated rather than the use be destroyed; and thus also they guarded against all abridgment by the United States, of the freedom of religious principles and exercises, and retained to themselves the right of protecting the same, as this, stated by a law passed on the general demand of its citizens, had already protected them from all human restraint or interference: and, that, in addition to this general principle and express declaration, another and more special provision has been made by one of the amendments to the Constitution, which expressly declares, that "Congress shall make no laws respecting an establishment of religion, or prohibiting the free exercise thereof, or abridging the freedom of speech, or of the press," thereby guarding in the same sentence, and under the same words, the freedom of religion, of speech, and of the press, insomuch, that whatever violates either, throws down the sanctuary which covers the others; and that libels, falsehood, and defamation, equally with heresy and false religion, are withheld from the cognizance of Federal tribunals. That therefore the act of the Congress of the United States, passed on the 14th of July, 1798, entitled, "An act in addition to the act entitled an act for the punishment of certain crimes against the United States," which does abridge the freedom of the press, is NOT LAW, but is altogether VOID and OF NO FORCE.

IV. *Resolved*, That alien friends are under the jurisdiction and protection of the laws of the State wherein they are: that no power over them has been delegated to the United States, nor prohibited to the individual States distinct from their power over citizens; and it being true, as a general principle, and one of the amendments to the Constitution having also declared, that "the powers not delegated to the United States by the Constitution, nor prohibited to the States, are reserved to the States respectively, or to the people," the act of the Congress of the United States, passed the 22d day of June, 1798, entitled, "An act concerning aliens," which assumes power over alien friends not delegated by the Constitution, is NOT LAW, but is altogether VOID and OF NO FORCE.

V. *Resolved*, That in addition to the general principle as well as the express declaration, that powers not delegated are reserved, another and more special provision inferred in the Constitution, from abundant caution has declared, "that the migration or importation of such persons as any of the States now existing shall think proper to admit, shall not be prohibited by the Congress prior to the year 1808." That this Commonwealth does admit the migration of alien friends described as the subject of the said act concerning aliens; that a provision against prohibiting their migration, is a provision against all acts equivalent thereto, or it would be nugatory; that to remove them when migrated is equivalent to a prohibition of their migration, and is, therefore, contrary to the said provision of the Constitution, and *void*.

VI. *Resolved*, That the imprisonment of a person under the protection of the laws of this Commonwealth on his failure to obey the simple order of the President to depart out of the United States, as is undertaken by the said act, entitled, "An act concerning aliens," is contrary to the Constitution, one amendment in which has provided, that "no person shall be deprived of liberty without due process of law," and, that another having provided, "that in all criminal prosecutions, the accused shall enjoy the right to a public trial by an impartial jury, to be informed as to the nature and cause of the accusation, to be confronted with the witnesses against him, to have compulsory process for obtaining witnesses in his favor, and to have assistance of counsel for his defence," the same act undertaking to authorize the President to remove a person out of the United States who is under the protection of the law, on his own suspicion, without jury, without public trial, without confrontation of the witnesses against him, without having witnesses in his favor, without defence, without counsel, is contrary to these provisions also of the Constitution, is therefore NOT LAW, but utterly VOID and OF NO FORCE.

That transferring the power of judging any person who is under the protection of the laws, from the courts to the President of the United States, as is undertaken by the same act concerning aliens, is against the article of the Constitution which provides, that, "the judicial power of the United States shall be vested in the courts, the judges of which shall hold their office during good behavior," and that the said act is void for that reason also; and it is further to be noted that this transfer of judiciary power is to that magistrate of the General Government who already possesses all the executive, and a qualified negative in all the legislative powers.

VII. *Resolved*, That the construction applied by the General Government (as is evident by sundry of their proceedings) to those parts of the Constitution of the United States which delegate to Congress power to lay and collect taxes, duties, imposts, excises; to pay the debts, and provide for the common defence, and general welfare of the United States, and to make all laws which shall be necessary and proper for carrying into execution the powers vested by the Constitution in the government of the United States, or any department thereof, goes to the destruction of all the limits prescribed to their power by the Constitution: That words meant by that instrument to be subsiduary only to the execution of the limited powers, ought not to be so construed as themselves to give unlimited powers, nor a part so to be taken as to destroy the whole residue of the instrument: That the proceedings of the General Government under color of those articles, will be a fit and necessary subject for revisal and correction at a time of greater tranquillity, while those specified in the preceding resolutions call for immediate redress.

VIII. *Resolved*, That the preceding resolutions be transmitted to the Senators and Representatives in Congress from this Commonwealth, who are enjoined to present the same to their respective houses, and to use their best endeavors to procure at the next session of Congress a repeal of the aforesaid unconstitutional and obnoxious acts.

IX. *Resolved lastly,* That the Governor of this Commonwealth be, and is hereby authorized and requested to communicate the preceding resolutions to the legislatures of the several States, to assure them that this Commonwealth considers union for special national purposes, and particularly for those specified in their late federal compact, to be friendly to the peace, happiness and prosperity of all the States—that faithful to that compact, according to the plain intent and meaning in which it was understood and acceded to by the several parties, it is sincerely anxious for its preservation; that it does also believe, that to take from the States all the powers of self-government, and transfer them to a general and consolidated government, without regard to the special delegations and reservations solemnly agreed to in that compact, is not for the peace, happiness, or prosperity of these States; And that, therefore, this Commonwealth is determined, as it doubts not its co-States are, to *submit to undelegated* and consequently unlimited *powers in no man, or body of men on earth:* that if the acts before specified should stand, these conclusions would flow from them; that the General Government may place any act they think proper on the list of crimes and punish it themselves, whether enumerated or not enumerated by the Constitution as cognizable by them; that they may transfer its cognizance to the President or any other person, who may himself be the accuser, counsel, judge, and jury, whose suspicions may be the evidence, his order the sentence, his officer the executioner, and his breast the sole record of the transaction; that a very numerous and valuable description of the inhabitants of these States, being by this precedent reduced as outlaws to the absolute dominion of one man and the barriers of the Constitution thus swept from us all, no rampart now remains against the passions and the power of a majority of Congress, to protect from a like exportation or other grievous punishment the minority of the same body, the legislatures, judges, governors, and counsellors of the States, nor their other peaceable inhabitants who may venture to reclaim the constitutional rights and liberties of the States and people, or who, for other causes, good or bad, may be obnoxious to the view or marked by the suspicions of the President, or to be thought dangerous to his or their elections or other interests, public or personal; that the friendless alien has been selected as the safest subject of a first experiment; but the citizen will soon follow, or rather has already followed; for, already has a sedition act marked him as a prey: That these and successive acts of the same character, unless *arrested on the threshold,* may tend to drive these States into revolution and blood, and will furnish new calumnies against republican governments, and new pretexts for those who wish it to be believed, that man cannot be governed but by a rod of iron; that it would be a dangerous delusion were a confidence in the men of our choice to silence our fears for the safety of our rights; that confidence is every where the parent of despotism; free government is found in jealousy and not in confidence; it is jealousy and not confidence which prescribes limited constitutions to bind down those whom we are obliged to trust with power; that our Constitution has accordingly fixed the limits to which, and no farther, our confidence may go; and let the honest advocate of confidence read the Alien and Sedition acts, and say if the Constitution has not been wise in fixing limits to the government it created, and whether we should be wise in destroying those limits? Let him say what the government is, if it be not a tyranny, which the men of our choice have conferred on the President, and the President of our choice has assented to and accepted over the friendly strangers, to whom the mild spirit of our country and its laws had pledged hospitality and protection; that the men of our choice have more respected the bare suspicions of the President than the solid rights of innocence, the claims of justification, the sacred force of truth, and the forms and substance of law and justice. In questions of power, then, let no more be said of confidence in man, but bind him down from mischief by the chains of the Constitution. That THIS COMMONWEALTH DOES THEREFORE CALL ON ITS CO-STATES for an expression of their sentiments on the acts concerning aliens, and for the punishment of certain crimes herein before specified, plainly declaring whether these acts are or are not authorized by the federal compact. *And it doubts not that their sense will be so announced as to prove their attachment to limited government, whether general or particular, and that the rights and liberties of their co-States will be exposed to no dangers by remaining embarked on a common bottom with their own: But they will concur with this Commonwealth in considering the said acts as so palpably against the Constitution as to amount to an undisguised declaration, that the compact is not meant to be the measure of the powers of the*

General Government, but that it will proceed in the exercise over these States of all powers whatsoever. That they will view this as seizing the rights of the States and consolidating them in the hands of the General Government, with a power assumed to bind the States (not merely in cases made federal) but in all cases whatsoever, by laws made, not with their consent, but by others against their consent; that this would be to surrender the form of government we have chosen, and live under one deriving its powers from its own will, and not from our authority; and that the co-States recurring to their natural rights in cases not made federal, will concur in declaring these VOID *and of no* FORCE, *and will each unite with this Commonwealth in requesting their repeal at the next session of Congress.*

EDMUND BULLOCK, S. H. R.
JOHN CAMPBELL, S. S. P. T.

Passed the House of Representatives, Nov. 10, 1798.
Attest, THOS. TODD, C. H. R.

In SENATE, Nov. 13, 1789—Unanimously concurred in.
Attest, B. THURSTON, C. S.

Approved, November 19th, 1798.
JAMES GARRARD, Governor of Kentucky.

By the Governor,
HARRY TOULMIN, Secretary of State.

HOUSE OF REPRESENTATIVES, *Thursday, Nov.* 14, 1799.

The House, according to the standing order of the day, resolved itself into a Committee of the whole House, on the state of the Commonwealth, Mr. Desha in the chair; and, after some time spent therein, the Speaker resumed the chair, and Mr. Desha reported, that the Committee had taken under consideration sundry resolutions passed by several State Legislatures, on the subject of the Alien and Sedition Laws, and had come to a resolution thereupon, which he delivered in at the Clerk's table, where it was read and *unanimously* agreed to by the House, as follows:

The representatives of the good people of this Commonwealth, in General Assembly convened, having maturely considered the answers of sundry States in the Union, to their resolutions passed the last session, respecting certain unconstitutional laws of Congress, commonly called the Alien and Sedition Laws, would be faithless, indeed, to themselves and to those they represent, were they silently to acquiesce in the principles and doctrines attempted to be maintained in all those answers, that of Virginia only excepted. To again enter the field of argument, and attempt more fully or forcibly to expose the unconstitutionality of those obnoxious laws, would, it is apprehended, be as unnecessary as unavailing. We cannot, however, but lament, that, in the discussion of those interesting subjects, by sundry of the Legislatures of our sister States, unfounded suggestions, and uncandid insinuations, derogatory to the true character and principles of this Commonwealth, have been substituted in place of fair reasoning and sound argument. Our opinions of these alarming measures of the General Government, together with our reasons for those opinions, were detailed with decency, and with temper, and submitted to the discussion and judgment of our fellow-citizens throughout the Union. Whether the like decency and temper have been observed in the answers of most of those States, who have denied or attempted to obviate the great truths contained in those resolutions, we have now only to submit to a candid world. Faithful to the true principles of the Federal Union, unconscious of any designs to disturb the harmony of that Union, and anxious only to escape the fangs of despotism, the good people of this Commonwealth are regardless of censure or calumniation. Least, however, the silence of this Commonwealth should be construed into an acquiescence in the doctrines and principles advanced and attempted to be maintained by the said answers, or least those of our fellow-citizens throughout the Union who so widely differ from us on those important subjects, should be deluded by the expectation, that we shall be deterred from what we conceive our duty, or shrink from the principles contained in those resolutions—therefore,

Resolved, That this Commonwealth considers the Federal Union, upon the terms and for the purposes specified in the late compact, as conducive to the liberty and happiness of the several States: That it does now unequivocally declare its attachment to the Union, and to that compact, agreeably to its obvious and real intention, and will be among the last to seek its dissolution: That if those who administer the General Government be permitted to transgress the limits fixed by that compact, by a total disregard to the special delegations of power therein contained, an annihilation of the State Governments, and the creation upon their ruins of a General Consolidated Government, will be the inevitable consequence: THAT THE PRINCIPLE AND CONSTRUCTION CONTENDED FOR BY SUNDRY OF THE STATE LEGISLATURES, THAT THE GENERAL GOVERNMENT IS THE EXCLU-

SIVE JUDGE OF THE EXTENT OF THE POWERS DELEGATED TO IT, STOP NOTHING SHORT OF DESPOTISM—SINCE THE DISCRETION OF THOSE WHO ADMINISTER THE GOVERNMENT, AND NOT THE CONSTITUTION, WOULD BE THE MEASURE OF THEIR POWERS: That the several States who formed that instrument being sovereign and independent have the unquestionable right to judge of the infraction; and, THAT A NULLIFICATION BY THOSE SOVEREIGNTIES, OF ALL UNAUTHORIZED ACTS DONE UNDER COLOR OF THAT INSTRUMENT IS THE RIGHTFUL REMEDY: That this Commonwealth does, under the most deliberate reconsideration, declare, that the said Alien and Sedition Laws are, in their opinion, palpable violations of the said Constitution; and, however cheerful it may be disposed to surrender its opinion to a majority of its sister States, in matters of ordinary or doubtful policy, yet, in no momentous regulations like the present, which so vitally wound the best rights of the citizen, it would consider a silent acquiescence as highly criminal: That although this Commonwealth, as a party to the Federal compact, will bow to the laws of the Union, yet, it does at the same time declare, that it will not now, or ever hereafter, cease to oppose in a constitutional manner every attempt, at what quarter soever offered, to violate that compact. And, finally, in order that no pretext or arguments may be drawn from a supposed acquiescence, on the part of this Commonwealth, in the constitutionality of those laws, and be thereby used as precedents for similar future violations of the Federal compact—this Commonwealth does now enter against them its SOLEMN PROTEST.

Extract, &c. Attest, THOS. TODD, C. H. R.

In SENATE, Nov. 22, 1799—Read and concurred in.

Attest, B. THURSTON, C. S.

APPENDIX.

ORDINANCE OF 1787.

CESSION FROM THE STATE OF VIRGINIA.

Whereas the General Assembly of Virginia, at their session, commencing on the 20th day of October, 1783, passed an act to authorize their delegates in Congress to convey to the United States in Congress assembled, all the right of that Commonwealth to the territory northwestward of the river Ohio: and whereas the delegates of the said Commonwealth have presented to Congress the form of a deed proposed to be executed pursuant to the said act, in the words following:

To all who shall see these presents, we, Thomas Jefferson, Samuel Hardy, Arthur Lee, and James Monroe, the underwritten delegates for the Commonwealth of Virginia, in the Congress of the United States of America, send greeting:

Whereas the General Assembly of the Commonwealth of Virginia, at their sessions, begun on the 20th day of October, 1783, passed an act, entitled, "An act to authorize the delegates of this State in Congress to convey to the United States in Congress assembled, all the right of this Commonwealth to the territory northwestward of the river Ohio," in these words following, to wit:

"Whereas the Congress of the United States did, by their act of the sixth day of September, in the year one thousand seven hundred and eighty, recommend to the several States in the Union, having claims to waste and unappropriated lands in the western country, a liberal cession to the United States, of a portion of their respective claims, for the common benefit of the Union: and whereas this Commonwealth did, on the second day of January, in the year one thousand seven hundred and eighty-one, yield to the Congress of the United States, for the benefit of the said States, all right, title, and claim, which the said Commonwealth had to the territory northwest of the river Ohio, subject to the conditions annexed to the said act of cession. And whereas the United States in Congress assembled have, by their act of the thirteenth of September last, stipulated the terms on which they agree to accept the cession of this State, should the Legislature approve thereof, which terms, although they do not come fully up to the propositions of this Commonwealth, are conceived, on the whole, to approach so nearly to them, as to induce this State to accept thereof, in full confidence, that Congress will, in justice to this State, for the liberal cession she hath made, earnestly press upon the other States claiming large tracts of waste and uncultivated territory, the propriety of making cessions equally liberal, for the common benefit and support of the Union. Be it enacted by the General Assembly, That it shall and may be lawful for the delegates of this State to the Congress of the United States, or such of them as shall be assembled in Congress, and the said delegates, or such of them so assembled, are hereby fully authorized and empowered, for and on behalf of this State, by proper deeds or instrument in writing, under their hands and seals, to convey, transfer, assign, and make over, unto the United States in Congress assembled, for the benefit of the said States, all right, title, and claim, as well of soil as jurisdiction, which this Commonwealth hath to the territory or tract of country within the limits of the Virginia charter, situate, lying, and being, to the northwest of the river Ohio, subject to the terms and conditions contained in the before recited act of Congress of the thirteenth day of September last; that is to say, upon condition that the territory so ceded shall be laid out and formed into States, containing a suitable extent of territory, not less than one hundred, nor more than one hundred and fifty miles square, or as near thereto as circumstances will admit: and that the States so formed shall be distinct republican States, and admitted members of the Federal Union, having the same rights of sovereignty, freedom, and independence, as the other States.

That the necessary and reasonable expenses incurred by this State, in subduing any British posts, or in maintaining forts and garrisons within, and for the defence, or in acquiring any part of, the territory so ceded or relinquished, shall be fully reimbursed by the United States: and that one commissioner shall be appointed by Congress, one by this Commonwealth, and another by those two commissioners, who, or a majority of them, shall be authorized and empowered to adjust and liquidate the account of the necessary and reasonable expenses incurred by this State, which they shall judge to be comprised within the intent and meaning of the act of Congress, of the tenth of October, one thousand seven hundred and eighty, respecting such expenses. That the French and Canadian inhabitants, and other settlers of the Kaskaskies, St. Vincents, and the neighboring villages, who have professed themselves citizens of Virginia, shall have their possessions and titles confirmed to them, and be protected in the enjoyment of their rights and liberties. That a quantity not exceeding one hundred and fifty thousand acres of land, promised by this State, shall be allowed and granted to the then colonel, now general George Rogers Clarke, and to the officers and soldiers of his regiment, who marched with him when the post of Kaskaskies and St. Vincents were reduced, and to the officers and soldiers that have been since incorporated into the said regiment, to be laid off in one tract, the length of which not to exceed double the breadth, in such place, on the northwest side of the Ohio, as a majority of the officers shall choose, and to be afterwards divided among the said officers and soldiers in due proportion, according to the laws of Virginia. That in case the quantity of good land on the southeast side of the Ohio, upon the waters of Cumberland river, and between the Green river and Tennessee river, which have been reserved by law for the Virginia troops, upon continental establishment, should, from the North Carolina line bearing in further upon the Cumberland lands than was expected, prove insufficient for their legal bounties, the deficiency should be made up to the said troops, in good lands, to be laid off between the rivers Scioto and Little Miami, on the northwest side of the river Ohio, in such proportions as have been engaged to them by the laws of Virginia. That all the lands within the territory so ceded to the United States, and not reserved for, or appropriated to, any of the before mentioned purposes, or disposed of in bounties to the officers and soldiers of the American army, shall be considered as a common fund for the use and benefit of such of the United States as have become, or shall become, members of the confederation or federal alliance of the said States, Virginia inclusive, according to their usual respective proportions in the general charge and expenditure, and shall be faithfully and bona fide disposed of for that purpose, and for no other use or purpose whatsoever. Provided, that the trust hereby reposed in the delegates of this State shall not be executed unless three of them at least are present in Congress.

And whereas the said General Assembly, by their resolution of June sixth, one thousand seven hundred and eighty-three, had constituted and appointed us, the said Thomas Jefferson, Samuel Hardy, Arthur Lee, and James Monroe, delegates to represent the said Commonwealth in Congress for one year, from the first Monday in November then next following, which resolution remains in full force: Now, therefore, know ye, that we, the said Thomas Jefferson, Samuel Hardy, Arthur Lee, and James Monroe, by virtue of the power and authority committed to us by the act of the said General Assembly of Virginia, before recited, and in the name, and for and on behalf, of the said Commonwealth, do, by these presents, convey, transfer, assign, and make over, unto the United States, in Congress assembled, for the benefit of the said States, Virginia inclusive, all right, title and claim, as well of soil as of jurisdiction, which the said Commonwealth hath to the territory or tract of country within the limits of the Virginia charter, situate, lying, and being, to the northwest of the river Ohio, to and for the uses and purposes and on the conditions of the said recited act. In testimony whereof, we have hereunto subscribed our names and affixed our seals, in Congress, the first day of March, in the year of our Lord one thousand seven hundred and eighty-four, and of the Independence of the United States the eighth.

Resolved, That the United States in Congress assembled are ready to receive this deed, whenever the delegates of the State of Virginia are ready to execute the same.

The delegates of Virginia then proceeded and signed, sealed, and delivered the said deed; whereupon Congress came to the following resolution:

The delegates of the Commonwealth of Virginia having executed the deed,

Resolved, That the same be recorded and enrolled among the acts of the United States, in Congress assembled.

Resolved, That it be, and it hereby is, recommended to the Legislature of Virginia, to take into consideration their act of cession: and revise the same, so far as to empower the United States in Congress assembled, to make such a division of the territory of the United States, lying northerly and westerly of the river Ohio, into distinct republican States, not more than five nor less than three, as the situation of that country and future circumstances may require; which States shall hereafter become members of the Federal Union, and have the same rights of sovereignty, freedom, and independence, as the original States: in conformity with the resolution of Congress of the tenth October, 1780.*

According to order, the ordinance for the government of the territory of the United States northwest of the river Ohio, was read a third time, and passed, as follows:

An ordinance for the government of the territory of the United States northwest of the river Ohio.

Be it ordained by the United States in Congress assembled, That the said territory, for the purposes of temporary government, be one district; subject, however, to be divided into two districts, as future circumstances may, in the opinion of Congress, make it expedient.

Be it ordained by the authority aforesaid, That the estates both of resident and non-resident proprietors in the said territory, dying intestate, shall descend to, and be distributed among their children, and the descendants of a deceased child, in equal parts; the descendants of a deceased child or grandchild to take the share of their deceased parent in equal parts among them: and where there shall be no children or descendants, then in equal parts to the next of kin, in equal degree; and among collaterals, the children of a deceased brother or sister of the intestate shall have, in equal parts among them, their deceased parents' share; and there shall, in no case, be a distinction between kindred of the whole and half-blood; saving in all cases to the widow of the intestate her third part of the

* *Resolved*, That the unappropriated lands that may be ceded or relinquished to the United States, by any particular State, pursuant to the recommendation of Congress, of the sixth day of September last, shall be disposed of for the common benefit of the United States, and be settled and formed into distinct republican States, which shall become members of the Federal Union, and have the same rights of sovereignty, freedom, and independence, as the other States: that each State which shall be so formed shall contain a suitable extent of territory, not less than one hundred, nor more than one hundred and fifty miles square, or as near thereto as circumstances will admit: that the necessary and reasonable expenses which any particular State shall have incurred, since the commencement of the present war, in subduing any British posts, or in maintaining forts or garrisons within, and for the defence, or in acquiring any part of, the territory that may be ceded or relinquished to the United States, shall be reimbursed:

That the said lands shall be granted or settled at such times and under such regulations as shall hereafter be agreed on by the United States in Congress assembled, or any nine or more of them.—*Journals of Congress, October* 10, 1780.

real estate for life, and one-third part of the personal estate; and this law relative to descents and dower shall remain in full force until altered by the Legislature of the district. And until the governor and judges shall adopt laws as hereinafter mentioned, estates in the said territory may be devised or bequeathed by wills in writing, signed and sealed by him or her in whom the estate may be, (being of full age,) and attested by three witnesses; and real estates may be conveyed by lease and release, or bargain and sale, signed, sealed, and delivered, by the person, being of full age, in whom the estate may be, and attested by two witnesses, provided such wills be duly proved, and such conveyances be acknowledged, or the execution thereof duly proved, and be recorded within one year after proper magistrates, courts, and registers, shall be appointed for that purpose; and personal property may be transferred by delivery; saving, however, to the French and Canadian inhabitants, and other settlers of the Kaskaskies, St. Vincents, and the neighboring villages, who have heretofore professed themselves citizens of Virginia, their laws and customs now in force among them, relative to the descent and conveyance of property.

Be it ordained by the authority aforesaid, That there shall be appointed, from time to time, by Congress, a governor, whose commission shall continue in force for the term of three years, unless sooner revoked by Congress: he shall reside in the district, and have a freehold estate therein, in one thousand acres of land, while in the exercise of his office.

There shall be appointed, from time to time, by Congress, a secretary, whose commission shall continue in force for four years, unless sooner revoked; he shall reside in the district, and have a freehold estate therein, in five hundred acres of land, while in the exercise of his office; it shall be his duty to keep and preserve the acts and laws passed by the Legislature, and the public records of the district, and the proceedings of the governor in his executive department; and transmit authentic copies of such acts and proceedings, every six months, to the secretary of Congress: There shall also be appointed a court, to consist of three judges, any two of whom to form a court, who shall have a common law jurisdiction, and reside in the district, and have each therein a freehold estate, in five hundred acres of land, while in the exercise of their offices; and their commissions shall continue in force during good behavior.

The governor and judges, or a majority of them, shall adopt and publish in the district such laws of the original States, criminal and civil, as may be necessary, and best suited to the circumstances of the district, and report them to Congress, from time to time; which laws shall be in force in the district until the organization of the General Assembly therein, unless disapproved of by Congress; but afterwards the Legislature shall have authority to alter them as they shall think fit.

The Governor for the time being, shall be commander-in-chief of the militia, appoint and commission all officers in the same, below the rank of general officers; all general officers shall be appointed and commissioned by Congress.

Previous to the organization of the General Assembly, the Governor shall appoint such magistrates and other civil officers, in each county or township, as he shall find necessary for the preservation of the peace and good order in the same. After the General Assembly shall be organized, the powers and duties of magistrates and other civil officers shall be regulated and defined by the said Assembly; but all magistrates and other civil officers, not herein otherwise directed, shall, during the continuance of this temporary Government, be appointed by the Governor.

For the prevention of crimes and injuries, the laws to be adopted or made shall have force in all parts of the district; and for the execution of process, criminal and civil, the Governor shall make proper divisions thereof; and he shall proceed from time to time, as circumstances may require, to lay out the parts of the district in which the Indian titles shall have been extinguished, into counties and townships, subject, however, to such alterations as may thereafter be made by the Legislature.

So soon as there shall be five thousand free male inhabitants, of full age, in the district, upon giving proof thereof to the Governor, they shall receive authority, with time and place, to elect representatives from their counties or townships, to represent them in the General Assembly; provided that, for every five hundred free male inhabitants, there shall be one representative, and so on, progressively, with the number of free male inhabitants, shall the right of representation increase, until the number of representatives shall amount to twenty-five; after which the number and proportion of representatives shall be regulated by the Legislature; provided, that no person be eligible or qualified to act as a representative unless he shall have been a citizen of one of the United States three years, and be a resident in the district, or unless he shall have resided in the district three years; and in either case, shall likewise hold in his own right, in fee simple, two hundred acres of land within the same; provided also, that a freehold in fifty acres of land in the district, having been a citizen of one of the States, and being resident in the district, or the like freehold and two years' residence in the district, shall be necessary to qualify a man as an elector of a representative.

The representatives thus elected shall serve for the term of two years; and in case of the death of a representative, or removal from office, the Governor shall issue a writ to the county or township, for which he was a member, to elect another in his stead, to serve for the residue of the term.

The General Assembly, or Legislature, shall consist of the Governor, Legislative Council, and a House of Representatives. The Legislative Council shall consist of five members, to continue in office five years, unless sooner removed by Congress; any three of whom to be a quorum: and the members of the Council shall be nominated and appointed in the following manner, to wit: As soon as representatives shall be elected, the Governor shall appoint a time and place for them to meet together, and when met, they shall nominate ten persons, residents in the district, and each possessed of a freehold in five hundred acres of land, and return their names to Congress; five of whom Congress shall appoint and commission to serve as aforesaid: and whenever a vacancy shall happen in the Council, by death or removal from office, the House of Representatives shall nominate two persons, qualified as aforesaid, for each vacancy, and return their names to Congress; one of whom Congress shall appoint and commission for the residue of the term: And every five years, four months at least before the expiration of the time of service of the members of the Council, the said House shall nominate ten persons, qualified as aforesaid, and return their names to Congress; five of whom Congress shall appoint and commission to serve as members of the Council five years, unless sooner removed. And the Governor, Legislative Council, and House of Representatives, shall have authority to make laws, in all cases, for the good government of the district, not repugnant to the principles and articles in this ordinance established and declared. And all bills, having passed by a majority in the House, and by a majority in the Council, shall be referred to the Governor for his assent; but no bill or legislative act whatever shall be of any force without his assent. The Governor shall have power to convene, prorogue, and dissolve the General Assembly, when in his opinion it shall be expedient.

The Governor, Judges, Legislative Council, Secretary, and

such other officers as Congress shall appoint in the district, shall take an oath or affirmation of fidelity, and of office; the Governor before the President of Congress, and all other officers before the Governor. As soon as a Legislature shall be formed in the district, the Council and House assembled, in one room, shall have authority, by joint ballot, to elect a delegate to Congress, who shall have a seat in Congress, with a right of debating, but not of voting during this temporary Government.

And for extending the fundamental principles of civil and religious liberty, which form the basis whereon these republics, their laws and constitutions, are erected; to fix and establish those principles as the basis of all laws, constitutions, and governments, which forever hereafter shall be formed in the said territory; to provide, also, for the establishment of States, and permanent government therein, and for their admission to a share in the Federal Councils on an equal footing with the original States, at as early periods as may be consistent with the general interest:

It is hereby ordained and declared, by the authority aforesaid, That the following articles shall be considered as articles of compact, between the original States and the people and States in the said territory, and for ever remain unalterable, unless by common consent, to wit:

ART. 1. No person, demeaning himself in a peaceable and orderly manner, shall ever be molested on account of his mode of worship or religious sentiments, in the said territory.

ART. 2. The inhabitants of the said territory shall always be entitled to the benefits of the writ of habeas corpus, and of the trial by jury; of a proportionate representation of the people in the legislature, and of judicial proceedings according to the course of the common law. All persons shall be bailable, unless for capital offences, where the proof shall be evident, or the presumption great. All fines shall be moderate: and no cruel or unusual punishments shall be inflicted. No man shall be deprived of his liberty or property, but by the judgment of his peers, or the law of the land; and should the public exigencies make it necessary, for the common preservation, to take any person's property, or to demand his particular services, full compensation shall be made for the same. And, in the just preservation of rights and property, it is understood and declared, that no law ought ever to be made, or have force in the said territory, that shall, in any manner whatever, interfere with, or affect, private contracts or engagements, bona fide, and without fraud, previously formed.

ART. 3. Religion, morality, and knowledge, being necessary to good government and the happiness of mankind, schools and the means of education shall forever be encouraged. The utmost good faith shall always be observed towards the Indians; their lands and property shall never be taken from them without their consent; and in their property, rights, and liberty, they never shall be invaded or disturbed, unless in just and lawful wars authorized by Congress; but laws founded in justice and humanity shall, from time to time, be made, for preventing wrongs being done to them, and for preserving peace and friendship with them.

ART. 4. The said territory, and the States which may be formed therein, shall forever remain a part of this confederacy of the United States of America, subject to the articles of confederation, and to such alterations therein as shall be constitutionally made; and to all the acts and ordinances of the United States in Congress assembled, conformable thereto. The inhabitants and settlers in the said territory shall be subject to pay a part of the federal debts, contracted or to be contracted, and a proportional part of the expenses of government, to be apportioned on them by Congress, according to the same common rule and measure by which apportionments thereof shall be made on the other States; and the taxes for paying their proportion shall be laid and levied by the authority and direction of the Legislatures of the district or districts, or new States, as in the original States, within the time agreed upon by the United States in Congress assembled. The Legislatures of those districts, or new States, shall never interfere with the primary disposal of the soil by the United States in Congress assembled, nor with any regulations Congress may find necessary, for securing the title in such soil to the bona fide purchasers. No tax shall be imposed on lands the property of the United States; and in no case shall non-resident proprietors be taxed higher than residents. The navigable waters leading into the Mississippi and St. Lawrence, and the carrying places between the same, shall be common highways, and forever free, as well to the inhabitants of the said territory, as to the citizens of the United States, and those of any other States that may be admitted into the confederacy, without any tax, impost, or duty therefor.

ART. 5. There shall be formed in the said territory, not less than three, nor more than five States; and the boundaries of the States, as soon as Virginia shall alter her act of cession, and consent to the same, shall become fixed and established as.

follows, to wit: the western State in the said territory, shall be bounded by the Mississippi, the Ohio, and Wabash rivers; a direct line drawn from the Wabash and Post Vincents, due north, to the territorial line between the United States and Canada; and by the said territorial line to the Lake of the Woods and Mississippi. The middle State shall be bounded by the said direct line, the Wabash, from Post Vincents to the Ohio, by the Ohio, by a direct line drawn due north from the mouth of the Great Miami to the said territorial line, and by the said territorial line. The eastern State shall be bounded by the last mentioned direct line, the Ohio, Pennsylvania, and the said territorial line: provided however, and it is further understood and declared, that the boundaries of these three States shall be subject so far to be altered, that, if Congress shall hereafter find it expedient, they shall have authority to form one or two States in that part of the said territory which lies north of an east and west line drawn through the southerly bend or extreme of Lake Michigan. And whenever any of the said States shall have sixty thousand free inhabitants therein, such State shall be admitted, by its delegates, into the Congress of the United States, on an equal footing with the original States, in all respects whatever; and shall be at liberty to form a permanent constitution and State government: provided the constitution and government, so to be formed, shall be republican, and in conformity to the principles contained in these articles; and, so far as it can be consistent with the general interest of the confederacy, such admission shall be allowed at an earlier period, and when there may be a less number of free inhabitants in the State than sixty thousand.

ART. 6. There shall be neither slavery nor involuntary servitude in the said territory, otherwise than in the punishment of crimes, whereof the party shall have been duly convicted: provided always, that any person escaping into the same, from whom labor or service is lawfully claimed in any one of the original States, such fugitive may be lawfully reclaimed, and conveyed to the person claiming his or her labor or service as aforesaid.

Be it ordained by the authority aforesaid, That the resolutions of the 23d of April, 1784,* relative to the subject of this

* *Resolved*, That so much of the territory ceded or to be ceded by individual States to the United States, as is already purchased or shall be purchased of the Indian inhabitants, and offered for sale by Congress, shall be divided into distinct States in the following manner, as nearly as such cessions will admit; that is to say, by parallels of latitude, so that each State shall comprehend from north to south two degrees

ordinance, be, and the same are hereby repealed and declared null and void. Done, &c.

Whereas the United States in Congress assembled did, on the seventh day of July, in the year of our Lord one thousand seven hundred and eighty-six, state certain reasons, showing that a division of the territory which hath been ceded to the said United States, by this commonwealth, into States, in conformity to the terms of cession, should the same be adhered to, would be attended with many inconveniences, and did recommend a revision of the act of cession, so far as to empower Congress to make such a division of the said territory into distinct and republican States, not more than five nor less than three in number, as the situation of that country and future circumstances might require: and the said United States in Congress assembled have, in an ordinance for the government of the territory northwest of the river Ohio, passed on the thirteenth of

of latitude, beginning to count from the completion of forty-five degrees north of the equator: and by meridians of longitude, one of which shall pass through the lowest point of the rapids of Ohio, and the other through the western cape of the mouth of the great Kanhaway; but the territory eastward of this last meridian, between the Ohio, lake Erie, and Pennsylvania, shall be one State, whatsoever may be its comprehension of latitude. That which may lie beyond the completion of the 45th degree, between the said meridians, shall make part of the State adjoining it on the south; and that part of the Ohio, which is between the same meridians, coinciding nearly with the parallel of 39 degrees, shall be substituted so far in lieu of that parallel as a boundary line.

That the settlers on any territory so purchased and offered for sale, shall, either on their own petition or on the order of Congress, receive authority from them, with appointments of time and place, for their free males of full age, within the limits of their State, to meet together, for the purpose of establishing a temporary government, to adopt the constitution and laws of any one of the original States, so that such laws, nevertheless, shall be subject to alteration by their ordinary legislature; and to erect, subject to a like alteration, counties, townships, or other divisions, for the election of members for their legislature.

That when any such State shall have acquired twenty thousand free inhabitants, on giving due proof thereof to Congress, they shall receive from them authority, with appointments of time and place, to call a convention of representatives to establish a permanent constitution and government for themselves. Provided, that both the temporary and permanent governments be established on these principles as their basis:

1. That they shall for ever remain a part of this confederacy of the United States of America.

2. That they shall be subject to the articles of confederation in all those cases in which the original States shall be so subject, and to all the acts and ordinances of the United States in Congress assembled, conformable thereto.

3. That they, in no case, shall interfere with the primary disposal of the soil by the United States in Congress assembled, nor with the ordinances and regulations which Congress may find necessary for securing the title in such soil to the bona fide purchasers.

4. That they shall be subject to pay a part of the federal debts contracted, or to be contracted, to be apportioned on them by Congress, according to the same common rule and measure by which apportionments thereof shall be made on the other States.

July, one thousand seven hundred and eighty-seven, declared the following as one of the articles of compact between the original States and the people and States in the said territory, viz:

[Here the 5th article of compact, of the ordinance of Congress of 13th July, 1787, is recited verbatim. See ante, page 297.]

And it is expedient that this Commonwealth do assent to the proposed alteration, so as to ratify and confirm the said article of compact between the original States and the people and States in the said territory.

2. Be it, therefore, enacted, by the General Assembly, That the aforerecited article of compact, between the original States and the people and States in the territory northwest of Ohio river, be, and the same is hereby ratified and confirmed, any thing to the contrary, in the deed of cession of the said territory by this Commonwealth to the United States, notwithstanding.

5. That no tax shall be imposed on lands the property of the United States.

6. That their respective governments shall be republican.

7. That the lands of non-resident proprietors shall, in no case, be taxed higher than those of residents within any new State, before the admission thereof to a vote by its delegates in Congress.

That whensoever any of the said States shall have, of free inhabitants, as many as shall then be in any one the least numerous of the thirteen original States, such State shall be admitted by its delegates into the Congress of the United States, on an equal footing with the said original States; provided the consent of so many States in Congress is first obtained as may, at the time, be competent to such admission. And in order to adapt the said articles of confederation to the state of Congress when its numbers shall be thus increased, it shall be proposed to the legislatures of the States, originally parties thereto, to require the assent of two-thirds of the United States in Congress assembled, in all those cases wherein, by the said articles, the assent of nine States is now required, which, being agreed to by them, shall be binding on the new States. Until such admission by their delegates into Congress, any of the said States, after the establishment of their temporary government, shall have authority to keep a member in Congress, with a right of debating, but not of voting.

That measures, not inconsistent with the principles of the confederation, and necessary for the preservation of peace and good order among the settlers in any of the said new States, until they shall assume a temporary government as aforesaid, may, from time to time, be taken by the United States in Congress assembled.

That the preceding articles shall be formed into a charter of compact; shall be duly executed by the President of the United States in Congress assembled, under his hand, and the seal of the United States; shall be promulgated; and shall stand as fundamental constitutions between the thirteen original States, and each of the several States now newly described, unalterable from and after the sale of any part of the territory of such State, pursuant to this resolve, but by the joint consent of the United States in Congress assembled, and of the particular State within which such alteration is proposed to be made.—*Journals of Congress.*

Abstract of the Laws of Prussia of December 31, 1842, *on the subject of Emigration and of Military Service.*

PARAGRAPH 15.—*The quality of a Prussian subject is lost:*

1st. By discharge upon the subject's request:
2nd. By sentence of the competent authority:
3rd. By living ten years in a foreign country:
4th. By marriage of a female Prussian with a foreigner.

PARAGRAPH 16.

The discharge has to be asked from the police authority of the province in which the subject's domicil is situated, and is effected by a document made out by the same authority.

PARAGRAPH 17.—*The discharge cannot be granted:*

1st. To male subjects who are between seventeen and twenty-five years of age, until they have got a certificate of the military commission of recruitment of their district, proving that their application for discharge is not made merely to avoid the fulfilling of their military duty in the standing army:

2nd. To actual soldiers belonging either to the standing army or to the reserve, to officers of the militia, and to public functionaries, before their being discharged from service.

3rd. To subjects having formerly served as officers in the standing army or the militia, or having been appointed military employés with the rank of officers of civil functionaries, before they have got the consent of their former chief.

4th. To the persons belonging to the militia, not being officers, after their having been convoked for actual service.

PARAGRAPH 18.

To subjects wishing to emigrate into a State of the German confederacy, the discharge may be refused if they cannot prove that the said State is willing to receive them.—(See Act of the German Confederation, Art. 18, No. 2, letter A.)

PARAGRAPH 19.

For other reasons than those specified in Paragraphs 17 and 18, the discharge cannot be refused in time of peace. For the time of war special regulations will be made.

PARAGRAPH 20.

The document of discharge effects, at the moment of its delivery, the loss of the quality as Prussian subjects.

PARAGRAPH 21.

If there is no special exception, the discharge comprehends also the wife and the minor children that are still under the father's authority.

PARAGRAPH 22.

Subjects living in Foreign Countries may lose their quality as Prussians by a declaration of the police authority of Prussia, if they do not obey, within the time fixed to them, the express summons for returning to their country.

PARAGRAPH 23.

Subjects who either,

1st. Leave our States without permission, and do not return within ten years, or

2nd. Leave our States with permission, but do not return within ten years after the expiration of the term granted by the said permission, lose their quality as Prussian subjects.

PARAGRAPH 24.—*Entering into public service in a Foreign State.*

The entering of a subject into public service in a foreign State is allowed only after his discharge (see paragraph 20,) has been granted to him. Any body who has obtained it, is permitted to do so without restriction.

PARAGRAPH 25.

A subject who,

1st. Either takes public service in a foreign State with our immediate permission:

2nd. Or is appointed in our State by a foreign Power in an office established with our permission, as, for instance, that of Consul, Commercial Agent, &c., remains in his quality as a Prussian.

PARAGRAPH 26.—*General Disposition.*

Subjects who emigrate without having obtained their discharge, or violate, by their entering into public service in a foreign State, the disposition of Paragraph 24, are to be punished according to the laws existing in that respect.

Extract from the Constitution of Prussia of 1850.

Tit: II. Rights of the Prussians.

Art: 11. The right to emigrate cannot be restricted by the State, except with respect to the duty of military service.

Extract from Circular to Consuls and Commercial Agents of the United States, from Department of State, dated September 18, 1854.

Consuls and Commercial Agents, &c., are prohibited, under a heavy fine, by the 2d section of the Act of 28th of February, 1803, from granting a passport or other paper, certifying that an alien, knowing him or her to be such, is a citizen of the United States, and they should be careful not to be led into a violation of this Act by granting a passport as an American citizen to an alien who may have become domiciled in the United States, or to a foreigner who has merely declared his intention to become an American citizen. Both of these classes of persons, however, may be entitled to some recognition by this Government, and this can be afforded by merely certifying to the genuineness of their papers when presented for attestation, provided the Consul or Commercial Agent should have no reasonable doubts of their authenticity. Consuls and Commercial Agents are instructed, in no case to grant or visé passports to foreigners coming to the United States, as no such papers are required in this country, and to supply or visé them would only subject the applicants to an unnecessary expense.

The attention of Consuls and Commercial Agents located at ports where there is more or less emigration to the United States, is particularly called to the General Regulations, No. 34, issued on the 26th of August last by the Treasury Department; and they will not omit to report any violation, which may come to their knowledge, of the laws of the United States regulating passenger ships and vessels. They will, also, not omit, in cases of the intended shipment of paupers and pardoned convicts to this country, to give timely notice of the fact, both to this Department and to the Collector of the Customs at the port to which the vessel having them on board may be bound, furnishing the names of the parties, a description of their persons, the name of the vessel, the date of sailing, &c., in order that proper steps may be taken for the enforcement of such police regulations as may have been adopted by the several States upon the subject.

FREMONT—HIS SUPPORTERS AND THEIR RECORD.

THE OPINIONS OF OUR GREAT STATESMEN UPON THE MISSOURI RESTRICTION.

BY AN INDIANIAN.

The Black Republican candidate for the Presidency, though a senator of the United States for several months, was in his seat and participated in the proceedings of that body but twenty-one days; yet, during that time, he showed himself to be a most ultra pro-slavery man.

He is now the candidate of, and supported by, that class of abolitionists who demand that wherever Congress has the power, slavery shall be abolished.

When bill No. 226, "To suppress the slave trade in the District of Columbia," was under consideration, Mr. Seward moved an amendment, "To abolish slavery in the District of Columbia." Chase, Hale and Seward voted for the amendment, and FREMONT and DAYTON against it. (Senate Journal, 1st session 31st Congress, p. 627.)

Subsequently, when bill No. 347 was under consideration, the same amendment was proposed by Mr. Hale, and supported by Messrs. Hale, Chase and Seward, and opposed by Messrs. FREMONT and DAYTON. (Senate Journal, 1st session 31st Congress, p. 647.)

Under the responsibility of official duty, and the obligations of his senatorial oath, Mr. Fremont resisted the proposition to abolish slavery in the District of Columbia, although he conceded the power. Yet, he is now the candidate of the party with which that measure is first in importance. What brought about this change in his views of right and duty in relation to so important a measure? Has he abandoned a high principle to attain a high position? Has his gaze been so intent upon the White House, that he would send his principles to the auction block, that he might reach the Presidency? Let the unprejudiced mind answer.

The Senate on the 14th of September, 1850, resumed the consideration of bill No. 226, "To suppress the slave trade in the District of Columbia," the third section of which provided, that any person who should induce or entice a slave to run away from his master should be imprisoned in the penitentiary for ten years. Senator Badger, of North Carolina, moved to strike out the clause denouncing a penalty of ten years' imprisonment, and insert, "For any time not exceeding five years."

Mr. FREMONT voted against this amendment. (Senate Journal, 1st session 31st Congress, p. 632.)

He was the only senator representing a free State who voted against that wise and humane proposition, originating in the benevolent feelings of a southern senator. In his judgment, to persude a slave to leave his master was a crime of such magnitude, that nothing less than *ten years'* imprisonment in a southern penitentiary would be an adequate punishment; and so stern and harsh must the law be, that the court should be denied all discretion in imposing the penalty, nor allowed to take into consideration the character, age, or intelligence of the accused, nor any mitigating circumstance. The amendment was proposed by a southern senator, an enlightened and able defender of southern rights and institutions, but it was too liberal, too indulgent to secure the vote of Mr. Fremont, though he represented a free State. To satisfy his convictions of right, the man who might encourage a faithful slave to escape from a cruel master, must be crushed with a penalty more severe than is usually inflicted upon the perpetrators of high crimes and infamous felonies in the States. For crimes against the property and persons of the people, the courts and juries may, in most cases, reduce the imprisonment to a term of two years; but the misguided enthusiast, or blind fanatic, who should encourage a slave to flee for liberty, is denied the mercy of the court, and must suffer a fixed and certain penalty of ten years' imprisonment in the penitentiary. So voted Fremont—and in giving that vote he stood *alone* among the senators from the *North*. That record stands unchanged; but where stands the man who made it?—the man who was so ultra in his views that a southern measure was not sufficiently stringent—he who was so quick and valiant to draw his sword for the South? Six years have passed since that record, but in that short period the relative position and strength of the sections, North and South, have greatly changed. The North has become powerful and defiant—whilst the South, by calling into action every energy, is scarcely able to maintain her constitutional rights, and her equality in the Union. A sectional party in the North seeks to seize and control the government, and this late champion of the South, John C. Fremont, is their candidate for the Presidency. He is supported by Seward, Sumner, Giddings, Chase, Wade, Hale, and their compeers—the acknowledged leaders and mouth-pieces of the Abolition party of the United States.

John C. Fremont has made no political record since his brilliant senatorial career; therefore to ascertain the opinions and sentiments that will govern him in his administration of public affairs, if the American people shall, by their suffrage, place him in the highest office in the gift of a free people, we must recur to the avowed and published opinions and purposes of his political associates.

The leaders of his party have a record—a record of vituperation against the Democratic party, against the federal constitution, and against the federal Union; this record we submit to the American people, and ask them to decide, in November next, whether the diversified interests of this great country are to be subserved by committing them to the management of such men.

On the petition of John J. Woodward and others, praying that a plan might be devised for a '*dissolution of the Union*, the yeas were, SALMON P. CHASE, JOHN P. HALE, and WILLIAM H. SEWARD. (Senate Journal, 1st session 31st Congress, p. 129.)

These men are now the acknowledged leaders of Black Republicanism; they are of those who *profess* love for the constitution and the Union, whilst black and horrid treason has *possession* of their hearts; but when they nominated John C. Fremont, they declared to the world that "the constitution must and shall be preserved." This they did, only to deceive the confiding, and mislead the unwary. Their votes speak louder than their words. They use the language of patriotism and of love for the Union to secure the support of Union-loving men, whilst their votes, their acts, and their organization, lead only to a dissolution, and all the evils that must follow. They believe in the "higher-law" doctrine, first enunciated at a Black Republican (then called a Liberty) convention, held in the city of Buffalo in 1843, at which the following resolution was unanimously adopted, with Salmon P. Chase as chairman of the Committee on Resolutions:

"*Resolved*, That we hereby give it to be *distinctly understood*, by this nation and the world, that, AS ABOLITIONISTS, considering that the strength of our cause lies in its righteousness, and our hopes for it in our conformity to the laws of God, and our support of the rights of man, we owe to the sovereign Ruler of the Universe, *as a proof of our allegiance to Him*, in all our civil relations and *offices*, whether as friends, citizens, or as *public functionaries, sworn to support* the constitution of the United States, to regard and treat the third clause of the instrument, whenever applied in the case of a fugitive slave, as *utterly null and void*, and consequently as forming *no part of the constitution of the United States, whenever* we are *called upon*, or *sworn* to support it."

This doctrine was reiterated in June, 1853, at Ravenna, Ohio, by a mass meeting of Free-soilers, which was addressed by CHASE, GIDDINGS, SAMUEL LEWIS, and JUDGE SPAULDING, (all of whom are now the champions of the Fremont cause,) by the adoption of the following resolution:

"*Resolved*, That we cannot respect, nor can we confide in those *lower-law doctors* of divinity who hold human laws above the laws of God; nor can we concur in their teachings, that the divine law is subject to *Congressional compromises*."

And again announced by the Hon. Charles Sumner, in 1854, in the Senate of the United States.

Mr. Butler, of South Carolina, asked, "If we repeal the fugitive-slave law, will Massachusetts execute the provision of the constitution without any law of Congress?" Will this honorable senator [Mr. Sumner] tell me that he will do it?" To which Mr. Sumner replied: "Is thy servant a dog, that he should do this thing?" Mr. Butler continued: "Then you would not obey the constitution. Sir, standing here before this tribunal, where you swore to support it, you rise and tell me that you regard it the office of a dog to enforce it. You stand in my presence as a co-equal senator, and tell me that it is a dog's office to execute the constitution of the United States?" To which Mr. Sumner said: "I recognise no such obligation."

Welcome is Mr. Sumner to his senatorial honors, acquired by charging that only a "dog" could recognise or execute an express clause of the constitution of the United States, which, however, is in strict accordance with the Buffalo and Ravenna resolutions, and comports with the "higher-law" notions of the party who recently made Colonel Fremont their presidential candidate.

This doctrine, which makes the private notions or prejudices of each individual the paramount law of his political action, is but a practical development of the "higher-law" notions as applied to American politics by William H. Seward, who, in a speech delivered in the United States Senate in 1850, said:

"The constitution regulates our stewardship; the constitution devotes the domain to Union, to justice, to defence, to welfare, and to liberty. But there is a *higher law than the constitution*, which regulates our authority over the domain, and devotes it to the same noble purposes."

It is scarcely necessary to say that, with such ideas in the ascendant in any country, no government is practical, and anarchy and confusion, and brute force, must inevitably rule the hour. Bodies of men or individuals, maddened by sectional or party prejudices, will never want an excuse for the violation of unpalatable laws, so long as they are permitted to substitute the vagaries of their own distempered intellects as having a stronger claim to their obedience than the constitution of their country.

As a further development of this idea of individual sovereignty, Wendell Phillips, of Massachusetts, at a Free-soil meeting in Boston, in May, 1849, said:

"We confess that we intend to trample under foot the constitution of this country. Daniel Webster says: 'You are a law-abiding people;' that the glory of New England is, 'that it is a law-abiding community.' Shame on it, if this be true; if even the religion of New England sinks as low as its statute-book. But I say *we are not a law-abiding community*. God be thanked for it."

But the Black Republican platform says:

"The federal constitution, the rights of the States, and the Union of the States, must and shall be preserved."

In preservation of the "rights of the States," JOSHUA R. GIDDINGS, in the House of Representatives, in May, 1854, said:

"I look forward to the day when there shall be a servile insurrection in the South; when the black man, armed with British bayonets, and commanded by British officers, shall wage a war of extermination against the white man; when the master shall see his dwelling in flames, and his *hearth-stone polluted*; and, though I may not mock at their calamity, nor laugh when their fear cometh, yet shall I hail it as the dawn of a political millenium."

The man who uttered this *chaste* sentiment contributed more to the nomination of Fremont than perhaps any other man in the convention; he was the master-spirit of that convention, and was no doubt the author of that clause in the platform which declares "the rights of the States must and shall be preserved." Yes, such preservation "as the wolf gives to the lamb!"

But certainly that Black Republican party which *professes* so much love for the federal constitution and the union of the States must have a record in strict conformity to such professions. Let us, then, look to that record. Mr. Mann, of Massachusetts, in 1850, expressed his love for the constitution and the Union as follows:

"I have only to add, that, under a full sense of my responsibility to my country and my God, I *deliberately* say, better disunion, better a civil or a servile war, better anything that God, in his Providence, shall send, than an extension of the bounds of slavery."

At a celebration of the 4th day of July, 1854, by citizens of Massachusetts, in which the Rev. (?) Theodore Parker, Wendell Phillips, and others, took the lead, the constitution of the United States was thrown into a fire, built for that purpose, and burnt in derision of the American Union.

Senator Wade, of Ohio, in a speech to a mass meeting of the Black Republicans, held in the State of Maine in 1855, according to the Boston Atlas, said:

"There was no freedom at the South for either white or black, and he would strive to protect the free soil of the North from the same blighting curse. *There was really no Union now between the North and the South*, and he believed no two nations upon the earth entertained feelings of more bitter rancor towards each other than these two sections of the republic. The only salvation of the Union, therefore, *was to be found in divesting it entirely from all taint of slavery. There was no Union with the South.* Let us have a Union, said he, *or let us sweep away this remnant which we call a Union.* I go for a Union where all men are equal, or for no Union at all, and I go for right."

This speech was vociferously applauded by the constitution-union-loving people of Maine.

These disunion sentiments, and the man who uttered them, were endorsed by the Black Republican legislature of Ohio in 1856, by re-electing him to the Senate of the United States. The Black Republicans of the great State of Ohio, therefore, respond faithfully to the sentiment: "*Let us sweep away this remnant which we call a Union.*"

This same party, at a convention held in Boston in 1855, adopted, by a unanimous vote, the following resolutions:

"15. *Resolved*, That a constitution which provides for a slave representation and a slave oligarchy in Congress, which legalizes slave hunting and slave catching on every inch of American soil, and which pledges the military and naval power of the country to keep four millions of chattel slaves in their chains, is to be trodden under foot and pronounced accursed, however unexceptionable or valuable may be its other provisions.

"16. *Resolved*, That the one great issue before the country is, the dissolution of the Union, in comparison with which all other issues with the slave power are as dust in the balance; therefore, we will give ourselves to the work of annulling this 'covenant with death,' as essential to our own innocency, and the speedy and everlasting overthrow of the slave system."

This same party "loves this Union!" yet, at various meetings and processions in Indiana, during the month of July, 1856, flags and transparencies were carried with but *sixteen stars;* emblematic of a northern confederacy of the sixteen free States. The same thing has recently occurred in the State of Maine:

"Hannibal Hamlin, Lot M. Morril, and Charles W. Goddard, esq., of Danville, addressed a Fremont meeting at Norway on Monday, standing under an American flag, on which were only *sixteen stars!*

"The disunion flag, with sixteen stars only, still continues to float across the public highway in this village—an emblem of sectionalism, and a disgrace to the party who placed it there."—*Norway Advertiser.*

"The 'Portland State of Maine' has hung out a Fremont and Dayton flag, on which are only sixteen stars.

"A salute of sixteen guns was fired at Portland the day Hamlin was nominated for governor.

"Only sixteen States were represented in the convention which nominated Fremont and Dayton.

"These are significant signs of the disunion tendencies and feelings of the Black Republicans. They scarcely take any pains to disguise their hostility to the Union. Let those who love their country and desire to perpetuate the Union ponder these things, and then *do their duty.*"

Senator Sumner, of Massachusetts, in a speech delivered in Faneuil Hall, Boston, on the 2d November, 1855, said:

"Not that I love the Union less, but freedom more, do I now, in pleading this great cause, insist that freedom, AT ALL HAZARDS, shall be preserved. God forbid *that for the sake of the Union*, we should sacrifice the very thing for which the Union was made."

Our glorious Union was formed to promote the prosperity and happiness of the white race, and as a condition of the Union, expressed in the constitution, the rights of the slave States are recognised and guarantied. Shall it be sacrificed to a false philanthropy, a wild and fanatical sentimentality towards the black race? You respond "yes," when you, as sectional men, support John Charles Fremont.

Wade, Sumner, and their political associates, have long and openly declared their disunion sentiments; they have violated their constitutional obligations; they have defamed our glorious constitution; they have traduced their country, and have plotted treason against our beloved Union; they are the leaders of the black cohorts of Black Republicanism; whilst plotting treason, they are also plotting for the election of Fremont; and if successful in either, they will have accomplished their great first design, the disunion of these States.

Wendell Phillips issued a pamphlet in 1850, reviewing Mr. Webster's speech "on the constitutional rights of the States," in which is the following:

"We are disunionists, not from any love of separate confederacies, or as ignorant of the thousand evils that spring from neighboring and quarrelsome States, but we would get rid of this Union."

This man that uttered these delectable sentiments is a leading Black Republican of Massachusetts and New England, and his shrieks are loud and long for "free speech, FREE MEN, and Fremont."

The Black Republican-Know-nothing legislature of Massachusetts, in 1855, passed an act denominated the personal liberty bill, nullifying thereby an act of Congress, which, by the constitution, is a part of the supreme law of the land.

This "personal liberty bill," as has been well said, "menaces with *disfranchisement* any lawyer who appears for the claimant of the fugitive slave; menaces with *impeachment* any judge who issues a warrant or certificate, or holds even the office of commissioner under the federal law; and menaces with *infamous punishment* any ministerial officer or officer of militia who aids in its execution." And although Governor Gardner vetoed the bill because of its conflict with the constitution of the United States, yet this Black Republican and Know-nothing legislature passed it over the veto, and it became a law.

The legislature of Ohio, composed of the same material as the legislature of Massachusetts, at their session in 1856, passed laws nullifying the same acts of Congress.

Judge Spaulding, one of the leaders in the Black Republican convention from Ohio, said:

"In the case of the alternative being presented of the continuance of slavery or a dissolution of the Union, I am for dissolution, and I care not how quick it comes."

John P. Hale addressed the convention as follows:

"You have assembled, not to say whether this Union shall be preserved, but to say whether it shall be a blessing or a scorn and hissing among the nations."

Senator Wilson, on the 12th of June, 1855, in the Philadelphia Know-nothing convention, said:

"I am in favor of relieving the federal government from all connexion with, and responsibility for, the existence of slavery. To effect this object, I am in favor of the abolition of slavery in the District of Columbia, and the prohibition of slavery in all the Territories."

Mr. Wilson, by abolishing slavery in the District of Columbia, would perpetrate an act of bad faith, highly injurious to the peace and quietness of the States of Virginia and Maryland, from whom the cession was made to the general government. He would demand of a Congress, composed of members from all the States, to denounce and abolish an institution recognised and protected by fifteen States of this Union; yet what cares he for the peace and harmony of the Union, or the great wrong that he would inflict upon the South, so that his morbid appetite should be gratified? But the abolishment of slavery in the

District of Columbia, and the prohibition of slavery in the Territories, Mr. Clay said, were "but so many masked batteries, concealing the real and ultimate point of attack. That point of attack is the institution of slavery as it exists in the States. Their purpose is abolition—universal abolition—peaceably if they can, forcibly if they must."

Mr. Banks, the present Abolition-know-nothing Speaker of the House of Representatives, and who declined the nomination of the New York Know-nothing convention in favor of Mr. Fremont, said:

"I am not one of that class of men who cry for the perpetuation of the Union, *though I am willing, in a certain state of circumstances, to let it slide.*"

Mr. Josiah Quincy, of Boston, in a speech in August, 1854, said:

"The obligation incumbent upon the free States to deliver up fugitive slaves is that burden, and *it must be obliterated from that constitution at every hazard.*"

General James Watson Webb, a Black Republican leader, said, in the Philadelphia convention:

"Our people come together from all parts of the Union and ask *us* to give them a nomination which, when fairly put before the people, will unite public sentiment, and, through the ballot-box, will restrain and repel this pro-slavery extension and this aggression of the slaveocracy. What else are they doing? They tell you that they are willing to abide by the ballot-box, and willing to make that the last appeal. *If we fail there, what then?* WE WILL DRIVE IT BACK, SWORD IN HAND, *and, so help me God! believing that to be right, I am with them.*" [Loud and prolonged applause.]

Let the ballot-box fail to elect Fremont, and the cartridge-box is threatened against the American people. The idiosyncracies of the Black Republican party must prevail, or the fire and sword must follow. They are truly a constitution Union-loving party.

Mr. Burlingame, in the House of Representatives, in 1856, said:

"The times demand, and we must have, an ANTI-SLAVERY CONSTITUTION, AN ANTI-SLAVERY BIBLE, AND AN ANTI-SLAVERY GOD."

The following extract is from the "Boston Liberator," a paper now warmly supporting Mr. Fremont:

"Justice and liberty, God and man, demand the dissolution of this slaveholding Union and the formation of a NORTHERN CONFEDERACY, in which slaveholders shall stand before the law as *felons* and be treated as *pirates*. God and humanity demand a ballot-box in which the slaveholders shall never cast a ballot. In this, what State so prepared to lead as the Old Bay State? *She has already made it a penal offence to help to execute a law of the Union. I want to see the officers of the State brought into collision with those of the Union.*"

These benevolent and patriotic sentiments meet with a hearty response from the leaders of this Union-loving-Fremont party.

But of all the damnable sentiments that have ever met the public gaze were those uttered by that prince of Black Republicans, WILLIAM LLOYD GARRISON, who, in a speech made in New York on the 1st day of August, 1855, spoke thus:

"The issue is this: God Almighty has made it impossible from the beginning for liberty and slavery to mingle together, or a union to be founded between abolitionists and slaveholders—between those who oppress and those who are oppressed. THIS UNION IS A LIE; THE AMERICAN UNION IS A SHAM, AN IMPOSTURE, A COVENANT WITH DEATH, AN AGREEMENT WITH HELL, AND IT IS OUR BUSINESS TO CALL FOR A DISSOLUTION. LET THAT UNION BE ACCURSED WHEREIN THREE MILLIONS AND A HALF OF SLAVES CAN BE DRIVEN TO UNREQUITED TOIL BY THEIR MASTERS.

"I will continue to experiment no longer—it is all madness. LET THE SLAVEHOLDING UNION GO, AND SLAVERY WILL GO WITH THE UNION DOWN INTO THE DUST. If the church is against disunion, and not on the side of the slave, then I pronounce it as of the devil.

"I SAY LET US CEASE STRIKING HANDS WITH THIEVES AND ADULTERERS, and give to the winds the rallying cry, 'NO UNION WITH SLAVEHOLDERS, SOCIALLY OR RELIGIOUSLY, AND UP WITH THE FLAG OF DISUNION.'"

This party, with these leaders and this record, ask the Americau people to vote for their candidate for the presidency, John C. Fremont. Are you prepared to endorse the doctrine that, for our civil government, there is a "higher law" than the constitution? Are you prepared to say you owe no allegiance to that government which gives you protection in your person and property? that you "are not a law-abiding people?" Can you find it in your hearts to utter that this Union "is accursed," and that the great compact of your fathers is "a covenant with hell?" If you can deliberately do all this, then, indeed, are you a Black Republican, and you ought to cast your vote for John C. Fremont. But truly might you ask, "Is thy servant a dog, that he shall do this thing?"

For two years past the opponents of the Democratic party throughout the United States have waged a cruel and relentless war upon foreigners and members of the Roman Catholic church. These classes have been proscribed—commercial rights and political equality have been refused them—their fitness to participate in the affairs of government has been denied. They have been driven from the ballot-boxes, beaten and murdered in the streets, their homes sacked, their houses burned, and their wives and children cruelly murdered. That was the work of superstition, proscription, and bigotry. And whilst the rights of man were thus being crushed, and human blood made to flow, Abolitionism and Know-nothingism were allies—brothers in the field. Against them was arrayed the National Democracy. True to its mission, that party fought for the rights of man, and the freedom of religion. It has defeated and scattered the oath-bound forces of Know-nothingism. Democrats have fought the battle, and the foreigner is made secure in his social and political rights and privileges; and, strange to tell, the Abolitionists now ask him to turn against his friends.

His sympathies are invoked in behalf of the negro, and he is told that the war which they had waged for two years against him has ceased. Were not the legislatures of Massachusetts, Vermont, New Hampshire, and Connecticut, in 1855, composed almost entirely of Abolition-Know-nothings? Those legislatures passed laws to elevate, socially and politically, the negro, whilst they denied social or political equality to the adopted citizen. They denied their State courts to a foreigner, who should apply for naturalization; they hampered their law with conditions, so as to prevent the adopted citizen from exercising the elective franchise; they elevated the negro, and degraded the naturalized citizen; they are of the leaders of Fremont, and still shout "Down with the foreigners," "Up with the negroes," and "Americans must rule America." They are still of the Abolition party, and still against the Democracy; they hate the adopted citizen; they trample upon the constitution; they accurse the Union, and sing pæans of praise and love to the negro. Such is the Abolition-Know-nothing party of those States, and such are the supporters of John C. Fremont for the Presidency.

David Kilgore, in the Indiana Constitutional Convention in 1850, in speaking of our adopted citizens, said:

"A man, then, who has no feeling in common with us, who never felt the pulse of liberty till he set foot upon our soil, such a man is to enjoy the opportunity and the right to vote amongst us, whilst these rights are to be denied to the unfortunate black man, who has ten times more intelligence, and who has lived in the State of Indiana from his birth." [See debates in the Convention, vol. 1, p. 253.]

And at the Black Republican State Convention in 1856, he said:

"NO NOMINATION SHOULD BE MADE WHICH WOULD TREAD UPON THE TOES OF THE KNOW-NOTHINGS—neither should a nomination be made which would tread upon the toes of the Free-soilers—even the most ultra anti-slavery man. * * * * * * He was opposed to foreigners. They should be permitted to come to this country—to buy lands here—to till the soil, but they should be the horses, not the drivers. The Americans would hold the lines—the foreigners could draw the burdens. [This infamous sentiment was applauded.] The foreigner should not be allowed to make our laws. He might live under them and must obey them, but he should have no voice in the making of them."

This man is now the Know-nothing-Abolition candidate for Congress in the fifth Congressional district in the State of Indiana, regularly nominated by what they termed a "Republican Convention," and if elected, he is pledged to labor in Congress for the principles of his party—the elevation of the negro, and the degradation of the unfortunate victims of European oppression, who have sought an asylum in free America. To this work of self-debasement the foreigner himself is asked to give his influence and vote. Will he give his vote to such men, and prove to them and the world that what his enemies have asserted is true—that he cannot appreciate a free government—that he is unfit to be a freeman? Let the adopted citizen ponder well before he casts his vote for his enemies, lest they may hereafter point to this very act, as evidence of a want of intelligence and capacity to vindicate the rights of a freeman.

On the 19th day of June, 1856, John C. Fremont was nominated for the Presidency by a grand council of Know-nothings, in the city of New York, representing all the Know-nothings of the northern and some of the southern States. On the 30th day of June he accepted that nomination, and in his letter of acceptance he speaks of it as an honor conferred upon him, and tenders his "grateful acknowledgment" to the members of that council, and to "their respective constituencies," *for the "distinguished expression of their confidence."* The constituencies represented were the Know-nothing lodges and wigwams all over the country, in which, for two years before, the destruction or degradation of foreigners was planned and plotted—in which companies of men were armed, organized, and sworn to attack, beat, and murder the foreign-born citizen. From them Fremont accepts the nomination as an honor; and if he accepts their services to secure his election, must he not represent their sentiments, and give himself up to their work of hatred and destruction?

On the day after Fremont received this Know-nothing nomination, the New York Herald, a Fremont paper, made the following announcement:

"The sudden change which has taken place in the sentiments of the convention in regard to Mr. Fremont is attributable to the fact that that gentleman was waited on last night by a delegation from this party, with whom he had a long and earnest confabulation, extending into the small hours of the morning; that he then and there declared himself unreservedly in favor of the principles of the Know-nothing party, and would give them his entire and cordial adherence, and that he was perfectly convinced that if he did not receive the support of the American party throughout the Union, he had not the slightest prospect of being elected."

When Senate bill No. 343, making temporary provision for working the mines in California, was under consideration, Mr. Seward, of New

York, moved to extend to all persons "who shall have, in pursuance of law, declared their intention to become citizens," the same benefits and privileges conferred upon citizens of the United States relative to working the gold mines. Mr. Fremont voted against the proposition, (Sen. Jour., 1st ses. 31st Cong., p. 671.) The most bitter and proscriptive Know-nothings have conceded that the foreigner might come to our land and enjoy the profits of his labor, demanding only that he be socially and politically degraded. But Mr. Fremont would go further: by his vote in the Senate, he said, that among the thousands of adventurers in California the foreigner shall not mingle. Although he may have declared his intention to become a citizen of the United States, he shall not be allowed the only profitable labor in California, but shall stand by until his full term of five years shall have expired—the mines in the mean time being exhausted or wholly occupied. The labor was profitable, and therefore he should be excluded from it. That principle, thus supported by Mr. Fremont, goes further: it excludes the foreigner from our rich lands, where his labor would secure him a rich return in plentiful harvests, and says to him, social and political inferiority shall be your condition, and poor lands and unprofitable labor your portion in this land of plenty. The Know-nothing council of New York could well afford to nominate a man who has shown so unmistakably his sympathy with that order in its hostility towards the foreigner.

James Buchanan, the candidate of the democracy, proscribes no man because of his religion or birth-place, but, adopting the republican sentiment that each man shall be judged by his own conduct, he has supported wise, just, and equal laws; his political career has been a long and useful one; he has been tried, and proved himself an incorruptible patriot, qualified for all the high positions which he has filled; he is against sectionalism, and will maintain the Union—the whole Union—upon the firm basis of the constitution; and, to use his own language, he "will cultivate peace and friendship with all nations, believing this to be our highest policy, as well as our most imperative duty." With James Buchanan as the candidate of the national democracy, opposed to John C. Fremont, the nominee of the sectional Know-nothing and Black Republican conventions, can we doubt a glorious triumph for the Democracy and James Buchanan, of Pennsylvania?

The Black Republican party allege that the great excitement, now prevailing to such an alarming extent throughout the country, has legitimately resulted from the repeal of the so-called Missouri compromise; and, in their denunciation of the Kansas-Nebraska act, they appeal to the fathers for the justification of their action in resisting the passage of the bill; they invoke the names of Thomas Jefferson, James Madison, and James Monroe, to prove that the prohibition of slavery in the Territories by Congress was the settled doctrine of the early fathers. They would deceive you in the opinions entertained by those great statesmen, and would mislead you as to the cause of the excitement which is now almost wrecking this fair fabric. We quote from the fathers that they would invoke, to show that this excitement, properly and legitimately, is the consequence of the legislation of 1820; that the prohibition of slavery in the territory north of 36° 30′ was the first fire-brand to disturb the peace of the Union; that we are now realizing the almost prophetic language of that great states man, Thomas Jefferson, when he said he considered the Missouri question "as the knell of the Union," and that "every new irritation would mark it deeper and deeper." But let these great men speak for themselves. In reference to sectionalism and the Missouri question, Jefferson said:

"The question is a mere party trick. The leaders of federalism, defeated in their schemes of obtaining power by rallying partisans to the principle of monarchism—a principle of personal, not of local division—have changed their tact and thrown out another barrel to the whale. They are taking advantage of the virtuous feeling of the people to effect a division of parties by a geographical line; they expect that this will insure them, on local principles, the majority they could never obtain on principles of federalism; but they are still putting their shoulders to the wrong wheel; they are wasting jeremiads on the miseries of slavery *as if we were advocates of it.* Sincerity in their declamations should direct their efforts to the true point of difficulty, and *unite their councils with ours in devising some reasonable and practicable plan of getting rid of it."—Jefferson's Writings, vol. 7.*

In a letter to Mr. Adams, dated January 22, 1821, he says:

"Our anxieties in this quarter are all concentrated in the question, What does the holy alliance, in and out of Congress, mean to do with us on the Missouri question? And this, by the way, is but the name of the case; it is only the John Doe or Richard Roe of the ejectment. The real question, as seen in the States afflicted with this unfortunate population, is, Are our slaves to be presented with freedom and a dagger? For, if Congress has the power to regulate the conditions of the inhabitants of the States within the States, it will be but another exercise of that power to declare that all shall be free. Are we, then, to see again Athenian and Lacædemonian confederacies? To wage another Peloponnesian war to settle the ascendency between them? Or is this the tocsin of merely a servile war? THAT REMAINS TO BE SEEN; BUT I HOPE NOT BY YOU OR ME. SURELY THEY WILL PARLEY AWHILE AND GIVE US TIME TO GET OUT OF THE WAY. What a bedlamite is man!"

In a letter to Lafayette, dated November 4, 1823, Mr. Jefferson said:

"On the eclipse of federalism with us, although not its extinction, its leaders got up the Missouri question, under the false front of lessening the measure of slavery, but with the real view of producing a geographical division of parties, which might insure them the next President. The people of the North went blindfold into the snare, and followed their leaders for a while with a zeal truly moral and laudable, until they became sensible that they were injuring instead of aiding the real interests of the slaves; that they had been used merely as tools for electioneering purposes, and that trick of hypocrisy then fell as quickly as it had been got up."

In a letter to Mr. Short, dated April 13, 1820, Mr. Jefferson says:

"Although I had laid down as a law to myself never to write, talk, or even think of politics, to know nothing of public affairs, and had therefore ceased to read newspapers, yet the Missouri question aroused and filled me with alarm. The old schism of federal and republican threatened nothing, because it existed in every State, and united them together by the fraternism of party. But the coincidence of a marked principle, moral and political, with a geographical line, once conceived, I feared would never more be obliterated from the mind; that it would be recurring on every occasion, and renewing irritations, until it would kindle such mutual and mortal hatred as to render separation preferable to eternal discord. I have been among the most sanguine in believing that our Union would be of long duration. I now doubt it much, and see the event at no great distance, and the direct consequence of this question; not by the line which has been so confidently counted on—the laws of nature control this—but by the Potomac, Ohio, and Missouri, or more probably the Mississippi, upwards to our northern boundary. My only comfort and consolation is, that I shall not live to see it; and I envy not the present generation the glory of throwing away the fruits of their fathers' sacrifices of life and fortune, and of rendering desperate the experiment which was to decide ultimately whether man is capable of self-government. This treason against human hope will signalize their epoch in future history as the counterpart of the model of their predecessors."

"I thank you, my dear sir, for the copy you have been so kind as to send me of the letter to your constituents on the Missouri question. * * * But this momentous question, like a fire-bell in the night, awakened and filled me with terror. I considered it at once as the knell of the Union. It is hushed, indeed, for the moment; but this is a reprieve only, not a final sentence. A geographical line, coinciding with a marked principle, moral and political, once conceived and held up to the angry passions of men, will never be obliterated ; and every new irritation will mark it deeper and deeper. * * * If they would but dispassionately weigh the blessings they will throw away, against an abstract principle, more likely to be effected by union that by scission, they would pause before they could perpetrate this act of suicide on themselves and of treason against the hopes of the world."—*Letter to Jno. Holmes, dated Monticello, April* 22, 1820.

"I am indebted to you for your two letters of February 7th and 19th. This Missouri question, by a geographical line of division, is the most portentous one I ever contemplated. * * * * is ready to risk the Union for any chance of restoring his party to power, and wriggling himself to the head of it; nor is * * * * without his hopes, nor scrupulous as to the means of fulfilling them."—*Letter to Mr. Madison.*

"The banks, bankrupt law, manufactures, Spanish treaty, are nothing. These are occurrences which, like waves in a storm, will pass under the ship ; but the MISSOURI QUESTION is a breaker on which we lose the Missouri country by revolt, and what more, God only knows. From the battle of Bunker's Hill to the treaty of Paris, we never had so ominous a question. It even damps the joy with which I hear of your high health, and welcomes to me the want of it. I thank God I shall not live to witness its issue."—*Letter to John Adams, December* 10, 1819.

"The line of division lately marked out between different portions of our confederacy, is such as will never, I fear, be obliterated, and we are now trusting to those who are against us in position and principle, to fashion to their own form the minds and affections of our youth. If, as has been estimated, we send three hundred thousand dollars a year to the northern seminaries, for the instruction of our own sons, then we must have five hundred of our sons imbibing opinions and principles in discord with those of their own country. This canker is eating on the vitals of our existence, and, if not arrested at once, will be beyond remedy."—*Letter to General Breckenridge, February* 11, 1821.

"The Missouri question is the most portentous one which ever yet threatened our Union. In the gloomiest moment of the revolutionary war, I never had any apprehension equal to that I felt from this source."—*Letter to Mr. Monroe, March* 3, 1820.

Mr. Madison said:

"On one side it naturally occurs, that the right being given from the necessity of the case, and in suspension of the great principle of self-government, ought not to be extended further, nor continued longer, than the occasion might fairly require.

"The questions to be decided seem to be, first, whether a *territorial* restriction be an assumption of illegitimate power; or, second, a misuse of legitimate power ; and if the latter only, when the injury threatened to the nation from an acquiescence in the misuse, or from a frustration of it, be the greater.

"On the first point there is certainly room for difference of opinion ; though, for myself, I must own that I have always leaned to the belief the *restriction was not within the true scope of the constitution.*"—*Letter to Mr. Monroe in* 1820.

"Hearken not to the unnatural voice which tells you that the people of America, knit together as they are by so many cords of affection, can no longer live together as members of the same family—can no longer continue the mutual guardians of their mutual happiness—can no longer be fellow-citizens of one great, respectable, and flourishing empire. The kindred blood which flows in the veins of American citizens—the mingled blood which they have shed in defence of their sacred rights, consecrate their union, and excite horror at the idea of their becoming aliens, rivals, enemies. And if novelties are to be shunned, believe me, the most alarming of all novelties—the most wild of all projects—the most rash of all attempts, is that of *rending us in pieces* in order to *preserve our liberties and promote our happiness.*"

[*The Federalist, p.* 86.

"Should a state of parties arise, founded on geographical boundaries and other physical distinctions which happen to coincide with them, what is to control those great repulsive masses from awful shocks against each other?"—*Letter to Mr. Walsh, dated November* 27, 1819.

General Harrison said :

"I am, and have been for many years, so much opposed to slavery, that I will never live in a State where it exists But I believe that the constitution has given no power to the general government to interfere in this matter, and that to have slaves or no slaves depends upon the people in each State or Territory alone.

"But besides the constitutional objections, I am persuaded that the obvious tendency of such interferences on the part of the States which have no slaves with the property of their fellow-citizens of the others, is to produce a state of discord and jealousy that will in the end prove fatal to the Union. I believe in no other State are such wild and dangerous sentiments entertained on this subject as in Ohio."—*General Harrison in a letter to President Monroe in* 1821.

In reference to sectionalism, and the nullification of the acts of Congress, General Jackson said:

"The laws of the United States must be executed. * Those who told you that you might peaceably prevent their execution, deceived you; they could not have been deceived themselves. They know that a forcible opposition could alone prevent the execution of the laws, and they know that such opposition must be repelled. Their object is disunion; but be not deceived by names; disunion, by armed force, is TREASON."—*Message of General Jackson, in 1833, on Nullification.*

"Appeals, too, are constantly made to sectional interests, in order to influence the election of the Chief Magistrate, as if it were desired that he should favor a particular quarter of the country, instead of fulfilling the duties of his station with impartial justice to all; and the possible dissolution of the Union has at length become an ordinary and familiar subject of discussion. Has the warning voice of Washington been forgotten, or have designs already been formed to dissolve the Union?" * * * * "Mutual suspicion and reproaches may in time create mutual hostility; and artful and designing men will always be found who are ready to foment these fatal divisions and inflame the natural jealousies of different sections of the country. The history of the world is full of such examples, and especially the history of republics."

"And no citizen who loves his country would, in any case whatever, resort to forcible resistance, unless he clearly saw that the time had come when a freeman should prefer death to submission." * * * * "Rest assured that men found busy in this work of discord are not worthy of your confidence, and deserve your strongest reprobation.

"In the legislation of Congress, also, and in every measure of the general government, justice to every portion of the United States should be faithfully observed. No free government can stand without virtue in the people and a lofty spirit of patriotism; and if the sordid feelings of mere selfishness shall usurp the place which ought to be filled by public spirit, the legislation of Congress will soon be converted into a scramble for personal and sectional advantages."—*Jackson.*

"And solemnly proclaim that the constitution and the laws are supreme, and the Union indissoluble."—*Jackson's Message, Jan 16,* 1833.

In relation to the very questions now agitating the country, the Sage of Ashland said:

"Sir, I am not in the habit of speaking lightly of the possibility of dissolving this happy Union. The Senate know that I have deprecated allusions, on ordinary occasions, to that direful event. The country will testify that, if there be anything in the history of my public career worthy of recollection, it is the truth and sincerity of my ardent devotion to its lasting preservation. But we should be false in our allegiance to it if we did not discriminate between the imaginary and real dangers by which it may be assailed. Abolitionism should no longer be regarded as an imaginary danger. The abolitionists, let me suppose, succeed in their present aim of uniting the inhabitants of the free States, as one man, against the inhabitants of the slave States. Union on one side will beget union on the other, and this process of reciprocal consolidation will be attended with all the violent prejudice, embittered passions, and implacable animosities which ever degraded or deformed human nature. * * * One section will stand in menacing and hostile array against the other. The collision of opinion will be quickly followed by the clash of arms. I will not attempt to describe scenes which now happily lie concealed from our view. Abolitionists themselves would shrink back in dismay and horror at the contemplation of desolated fields, conflagrated cities, murdered inhabitants, and the overthrow of the fairest fabric of human government that ever rose to animate the hopes of civilized man."—*Speech of Mr. Clay in the U. S. Senate on the 7th of February,* 1839.

In the same speech Mr. Clay summed up what the abolitionists wanted, as follows:

"And the third class are the real ultra abolitionists, who are resolved to persevere in the pursuit of their object at all hazards. With this class the immediate abolition of slavery in the District of Columbia, the prohibition of the removal of slaves from State to State, and the refusal to admit any new State comprising within its limits the institution of domestic slavery, are but so many means conducing to the accomplishment of the ultimate but perilous end, at which they avowedly and boldly aim, are but so many short stages in the long and bloody road to the distant goal at which they would finally arrive. Their purpose is abolition—universal abolition—peaceably if they can, forcibly if they must."

The Fremont party of 1856 has assumed a position identical with the abolition party of 1839. How well the picture of abolitionism, drawn by Mr. Clay in 1839, suits the Republican party of the present day. They have but one common aim—the dissolution of this Union.

Mr. Clay, in speaking of our Catholic citizens, said:

"With regard to their superstition, they worship the same God with us. *Their prayers are offered up in their temples to the same Redeemer, whose intercession we expect to save us.* NOR IS

THERE ANYTHING IN THE CATHOLIC RELIGION UNFAVORABLE TO FREEDOM. All religions united with government are more or less inimical to liberty. All separated from the government are compatible with liberty."—*Speech in Congress, March 24, 1818.*

And in reference to our adopted citizens, he made use of the following language:

"The honest, patient, industrious GERMAN readily unites with our people, establishes himself on some of our fat lands, fills his capacious barns, and enjoys in tranquillity the abundant fruits which his diligence gathers around him, always ready to fly to the standard of his adopted country, or of its laws, when called by duties of patriotism.

"The gay, the versatile, the philosophical FRENCHMAN, accommodating himself cheerfully to all the vicissitudes of life, incorporates himself without difficulty in our society.

"But of all foreigners, none amalgamate themselves so quickly with our people as the NATIVES OF THE EMERALD ISLE. In some of the visions which have passed through my imagination, I have supposed that Ireland was originally part and parcel of this continent, and that by some extraordinary convulsion of nature it was torn from America, and, drifting across the ocean, was placed in the unfortunate vicinity of Great Britain.

"The same open-heartedness, the same generous hospitality, the same careless and uncalculating indifference about human life, characterized the inhabitants of both countries. Kentucky has sometimes been called the Ireland of America. And I have no doubt that if the current of emigration were reversed, and set from America upon the shores of Europe, every American emigrant to Ireland would there find, as every Irish emigrant here finds, a hearty welcome, and a happy home"—*Speech in the United States Senate in defence of the American System.*

The democracy now stand where Jefferson and Madison stood; they have restored our territorial policy as it existed prior to that violent and unconstitutional departure in 1820. The exigencies demanded, and the democracy, true to the rights of man and the equality of the States, gave the country the compromise measures of 1850. These were endorsed by the Baltimore convention, ratified by the people in 1852 by the election of Franklin Pierce, reaffirmed by the democracy in the Kansas-Nebraska act of 1854, re-endorsed by the Cincinnati convention, and will stand confirmed by the American people in 1856 by the election of James Buchanan to the presidency.

This vindication of the right of the people to form their own domestic institutions is a vindication of the instructions given by the colonies to their delegates to form a confederation—a vindication of the spirit and letter of the immortal Declaration of Independence—a vindication of our glorious constitution, and a vindication of the inalienable rights of an American citizen.

Our opponents have been uniform in their hatred and denunciation of the Democratic party; they opposed the election of Jefferson, of Madison, and of Jackson; they repudiated the Louisiana purchase; they denounced the war of 1812, and burnt blue-lights in their windows to light the enemys' ships into our harbors; they endeavored to defeat the purchase of the Floridas and the annexation of Texas, and would have welcomed our brave soldiers in Mexico "with bloody hands to hospitable graves;" they forced upon the people the restriction of 1820 by refusing to admit Missouri into the Union, and repudiated it in 1848 by opposing its extension to the Pacific. The legitimate consequence of such repudiation was the compromise of 1850, the passage of which they resisted by every parliamentary expedient, and by every appeal to a false and fanatical philanthropy. They counselled revolution on the floor of Congress, in resistance to the passage of the Kansas-Nebraska act, because it carried out the great principles embodied in the compromise of 1850. They would subvert, through emigrant aid societies and other appliances, the practical development of non-intervention by Congress, and the right of the people to govern themselves; they would counsel the incendiary torch and the assassin's knife against the most sacred rights of American freemen in the Territory of Kansas; they have a deep and profound hatred against, and denounce in unmeasured terms, the doctrine that the *bona fide* residents of Kansas should adjust their domestic affairs in their own way; they have sought foreign aid, and have carried foreign assistance into the Territory of Kansas for the express purpose of interfering in the domestic policy of the people of that Territory; they are the authors and instigators of, and before God and man are responsible for, all the outrages, the arsons, and the murders in Kansas.

The democracy, true to the great doctrine of the early fathers, true to the rights of the States, the constitution, the Union, and ever watchful of the peace, happiness, and prosperity of a free people, have sought, by wise and pacific legislation, to rescue the people of Kansas from the anarchy, the rapine, and murder brought upon them by the Black Republican party.

The democratic Senate, on the 3d of July, 1856, after a continuous session of twenty-one hours, passed, and sent to the Black Republican House, a great pacific measure, declaring null and void those acts of the Kansas Legislature repugnant to the bill of rights as embodied in our great charter of liberty—a measure which secures the freedom of speech, the freedom of the press, and the writ of habeas corpus—prohibits religious tests for office, or an established religion—protects the rights of conscience, the persons and property of the people, and their right to hold and bear arms—forbids excessive bail, excessive fines, and cruel and unusual punishments—declares that no test-oath, or oath to support any act of Congress or other legislative act, shall be required as a qualification for any office or trust, or for any employment or profession, or to serve as a juror, or to vote at an election—and that no tax shall be imposed upon the exercise of the right of suffrage, and guarantees to the people the free discussion of any law or subject of legislation, and in a free expression of opinion upon all questions whatever—provides for the appointment of five commissioners to arrange the preliminaries and superintend the election; for the registration of voters, and all other needful regulations necessary to a fair and impartial expression at the ballot-box of the *bona fide* residents of Kansas; and pledges the entire military force of the government to a pure and untrammelled ballot-box. If any resident shall have left the Territory, he is protected in his rights, provided he shall return by the 1st day of October, 1856. If any person is imprisoned for a violation of the obnoxious laws of Kansas, his prison-doors are opened, and he is restored to all his rights. But it also provides that the people, the *bona fide* residents of Kansas, shall regulate and form their domestic institutions in their own way, subject only to the constitution of the United States; and they shall be admitted into the Union on a footing with the original States whenever they shall present a constitution with a republican form of government. Every Black-Republican senator resisted the bill at its various stages, and voted against it on its passage. Let it be proclaimed to the people, let it be known in every town and hamlet, that the democracy have given a fair and honest bill—one that will restore peace to a distracted country, correct the outrages and murders in an unhappy Territory, vindicate the majesty of the law, and protect the American citizen in an inalienable right—that the democracy have given such a bill to the Black Republican House of Representatives for their action. If they desire tranquillity in the States, peace and happiness to Kansas, and a correction of the violent abuses and outrages committed, they will immediately pass the Senate bill; but if outrage upon outrage and blood upon blood is necessary to the accomplishment of their political ends, necessary to the election of John C. Fremont, then will they refuse to pass the bill or to give repose to Kansas.

THE ISSUE FAIRLY PRESENTED.

THE SENATE BILL

FOR

THE ADMISSION OF KANSAS AS A STATE.

DEMOCRACY,

LAW, ORDER, AND THE WILL OF THE MAJORITY OF THE WHOLE PEOPLE OF THE TERRITORY,

AGAINST

BLACK REPUBLICANISM,

USURPATION, REVOLUTION, ANARCHY, AND THE WILL OF A MEAGRE MINORITY.

PUBLISHED BY ORDER OF THE DEMOCRATIC NATIONAL COMMITTEE.

WASHINGTON:
PRINTED AT THE UNION OFFICE.
1856

TO THE PEOPLE OF THE UNITED STATES.

The Democratic National Committee—with the hope of allaying in some degree the wild excitement now prevailing in many sections of the country in reference to the unhappy state of affairs in Kansas, and also of disabusing the public mind upon the subject of the designs and principles of the democratic party with regard to the question of slavery in the territories—ask the attention of the public to a practical issue now made up between the two parties, in the course of recent congressional legislation. We propose fairly and fearlessly to appeal to the people, whether the bill passed by the democratic senators on the 2d of July instant, to admit Kansas as a State by a prescribed process, is not preferable to the adoption of the crude, partial, and revolutionary measure commonly called the Topeka Constitution. Other questions may be incidentally glanced at; but our main purpose on this occasion will be to show, by a distinct and definite appeal to the record, that (whether in or out of Congress,)

THE BLACK REPUBLICAN LEADERS DO NOT DESIRE PEACE IN KANSAS PRIOR TO THE PRESIDENTIAL ELECTION!

The question of human slavery has been a topic of partisan discussion ever since our government began; but it is in relation to the territories of the Union that it has presented itself in the most complicated and dangerous form.

To discuss this question at length, in any of its various aspects, is wholly foreign to our present purpose. We shall not undertake to determine why the God of nature made the African inferior to the white man; or why He permitted England to fasten the institution of slavery upon the colonies against their repeated and earnest remonstrances. Nor can we tell what Heaven in its wisdom may intend to work out of the relations of master and slave, as they now exist in several of the United States.

This, however, we do know, and will add, that when these States, as independent parties, agreed to come under a common Constitution and into a common Union—it was upon terms of perfect equality, for the mutual and equal benefit of all, and that African slavery was one of the recognized subjects of that compact. All power over it was expressly reserved to each member of the confederacy.

Nothing was yielded, and no new right in this respect was added, except that each State bound itself to return to any other, upon demand, fugitives from legal servitude. We know, too, in relation to any compact, it is always good faith and good morals to keep it in whole, as well as in part; in the spirit as well as to the letter; in regard to Territories as well as in reference to the States of this Union. An evasion of a promise or covenant is as immoral as a bold and open breach of it; and involves, in addition, the contempt which inevitably falls upon trickery or cowardice. It is obvious, then, that the success of any attempt practically to disregard a particular feature of the Constitution, whether relating to the rendition of fugitives from labor, or any other distinct guarantee to the citizens or the States, would operate as a virtual abandonment and demoralization of the whole instrument, an event which the Union could not long survive.

The ordinance of 1787, which seems to have been established without much objection at the time, adjusted the subject of slavery in the Northwestern Territory. Again in 1820, Congress, after an angry and exciting controversy, passed a law, excluding the institution from that part of the Louisiana territory which lies north of a certain parallel of latitude. In 1845, when Texas was admitted into the Union, this line of inhibition was also applied to that State.

But when the acquisition of territory from Mexico once more presented this subject, the mode of adjustment by a geographical line was considered, and finally rejected by Congress; and this mainly by the votes and influence of the very same brood of agitators who now affect to regret the abandonment of the principle! This result created the necessity of resorting to some other mode of settling the question. Finally, in 1850, after a period of great agitation throughout the country, the leading patriots and wise men of both parties, such as Clay, Webster, Cass, and others, decided upon leaving this question where it always ought to have been left, and where the true spirit of our institutions places it—*in the hands and under the control of the people of the Territories themselves*, restrained only by the Constitution.

The whole nation rejoiced in this wise adjustment, and all parties claimed it as a finality as to this principle of territorial organization. For once, the question of slavery in the Territories was settled upon the principles of our revolutionary fathers, who demanded a voice and a vote in regulating their own institutions; the same great fundamental principles of human government, which underlie and uphold our whole republican system—principles suited to all Territories and to all times, and as broad and enduring as eternal truth. This form of adjustment was denominated *non-intervention* by Congress—*self-government* by the people of the Territories.

In 1854, when it became necessary to organize the Territories of Kansas and Nebraska, it was deemed just and proper to extend these principles of self-government to those Territories, regardless of the restrictive Missouri line. It seemed manifestly unjust to accord such high privileges to citizens who might reside in the Territories of Washington, Utah, and New Mexico, and deny their enjoyment to those who should go to Kansas and Nebraska. Nor did it seem right to reject the practical use of a great principle, which had been so universally approved by all parties. The Kansas-Nebraska act accordingly became a law of the land.

Then it was that the abolition party renewed their schemes of agitation. Up to that hour, they had scarcely ceased to denounce the Missouri demarcation as unconstitutional, arbitrary, and unjust. Their indignation at its adoption had been unbounded. No public man who had sustained it, that was within their reach, escaped their vengeance. But no sooner had this arbitrary rule been superseded by one more republican and reasonable, than their admiration for the former suddenly burst forth in the strongest terms. They now affected to see in it the force and virtue of a solemn compact of good faith, justice, and liberty; and proceeded to denounce those who favored its repeal with as much bitterness as they had employed at an earlier day, against those who had sanctioned its adoption.

Reckless and inconsistent upon this subject to the very last, these desperate agitators are now engaged in charging the unhappy state of society in Kansas to the legislation of the Democratic party, and as consequent upon the incorporation of the principles of self-government into the organic law of Kansas Territory; forgetting, or wilfully overlooking the fact, that in Washington, Utah, and New Mexico, *all organized upon the same principle*, there is entire quiet and good order. It would be equally logical and true to say in reply and in defence, that they themselves became the authors of the evils in Kansas, by rejecting the extension of the Missouri line to the Pacific, as a final adjustment, when proposed by Judge Douglas in 1848. Some other mode of adjustment was thus, and by their own act, rendered absolutely necessary; and that applied to Kansas was devised by the wisest men of the nation, in 1850, to meet the exigencies then presented.

But the real purposes of the agitators cannot be concealed. Excitement on the slavery question is the very life-blood of their fanatical organization. Take this away, and there remains to them only a few minor and kindred topics, by the agitation of which they can hope to secure position and notoriety.

Upon the subject of Kansas, these leaders sanctimoniously, and with affectation of great humanity, claim before the public a desire only to advance the interests of peace, and to secure for the settler in that Territory a just and equal State government, of his own unawed and untrammelled choice. They have uniformly contended in Congress that the free State party were largely in the majority, and that all they desired was, that the popular will should be fairly reflected on the subject of slavery; and that the proper remedy for the evils in Kansas was her prompt admission as a State.

Mark, now, the progress of events in Congress, and judge of the sincerity of these professions. On the 23d day of July, Mr. Toombs, a southern senator, submitted a proposition for the early admission of Kansas as a State, by authorizing the present inhabitants, in a prescribed manner, to form a State constitution in November next. The main features of this measure, as finally passed by the Senate, are hereto appended, so that the reader can come to his own conclusion as to the fairness of its provisions.

A leading and vital idea of this bill, it will be seen, is to terminate at once all inducement on the part of outsiders to force temporary population into the Territory, with the view of controlling a decision on the question of slavery. The sole right to influence such decision is confined to citizens who may have already become *bona fide* inhabitants of the Territory; thus ending this angry struggle, and giving peace to the whole country. This movement produced a deep sensation in the Senate and throughout the Union, and no small share of consternation amongst the Kansas agitators, who saw in it the elements of destruction of their vocation. It struck all right-minded men as eminently just and wise in its provisions. Even Senator Hale, so distinguished for his aversion to everything emanating from a southern source, could not restrain his admiration, and almost involuntarily paid it the following just tribute:

"But, sir, I do not want to dwell on that subject, but to speak a very few words in reference to this bill which has been introduced by the Senator from Georgia. I take this occasion to say that the bill, as a whole, does great credit to the magnanimity, to the patriotism, and to the sense of justice of the honorable senator who introduced it. It is a much fairer bill than I expected from that latitude. I say so because I am always willing and determined, when I have occasion to speak anything, to do ample justice. I think the bill is almost unexceptionable."

After having been read in due course in the Senate, it was referred to the proper committee of that body; which subsequently returned it with amendments, accompanied by an elaborate and able report, in which the subject is thus treated:

"The existing government in the Territory of Kansas was organized in pursuance of an act of Congress approved May 30, 1850, instituting temporary governments for the Territories of Nebraska and Kansas, preliminary to their admission into the Union on an equal footing with the original States, so soon as they should have the requisite population. The organic law of Kansas is identical with that of Nebraska in all its provisions and principles. Each is based on that great fundamental principle of self-government which underlies our whole system of republican institutions, as promulgated in the Declaration of Independence, consecrated by the blood of the Revolution, and consolidated and firmly established by the Constitution of the United States. Each recognizes the right of the people thereof, while a Territory, to form and regulate their own domestic institutions in their own way, subject only to the Constitution of the United States, and to be received into the Union, so soon as they should attain the requisite number of inhabitants, on an equal footing with the original States in all respects whatever. These two Territories were thus organized in 1854, under the authority of the same act of Congress, with equal rights, privileges, and immunities, and with the same safeguards and guarantees for the quiet enjoyment of their liberties, without molestation by foreign interference or domestic violence.

"In Nebraska the inhabitants have enjoyed all the blessings which it is possible for a law-abiding people to derive from the faithful administration of a wise and just government. Life, liberty, and property have been held sacred, the elective franchise has been preserved inviolate, and all the rights of the citizen have been protected against fraud or violence, by laws of his own making. These are the legitimate fruits of the principle, the practical results of fidelity to the provisions of the Nebraska organic act. There was no foreign interference with their domestic affairs, no fraudulent attempts to control the elections by non-resident voters. Emigrant aid societies, with their affiliated associations and enormous capital, did not extend their operations to Nebraska, and hence there were no counter schemes formed to control the elections and force institutions upon the Territory regardless of the rights and wishes of the *bona fide* inhabitants. The principle of the organic law, the right of the people to manage their internal affairs, and control their domestic concerns in obedience to the Federal Constitution, was permitted to have fair play, and work out its natural and legitimate results. Hence, peace, security, and progress, in all the elements of prosperity in this Territory, have vindicated the wisdom and policy of the Nebraska act.

"Fortunate would it have been for the peace and harmony of the republic, and still more fortunate for the unhappy people of Kansas, had they been permitted, in the undisturbed enjoyment of their acknowledged rights, to derive similar blessings from the same organic law. Your committee can perceive no reason why the same causes would not have produced like results in Kansas but for the misguided efforts of non-residents of the Territory, citizens of different States, who had no moral or legal right to interfere with the elections and legislation of the Territory, to seize upon the legislative power through the ballot-box, and thus control the local and domestic institutions of a feeble and sparsely settled Territory."

This measure of peace and justice, so well described in the report, came up in the Senate for final passage on the 2d day of July, and was steadily resisted by the Republican Senators, during a prolonged session of twenty-one hours. Notwithstanding the declaration of Mr. Hale, that the proposition was a fair one—"almost unexceptionable"—it encountered the bitterest hostility. Objection after objection was presented, and promptly removed by the friends of the bill—*until it was made manifest that the Republican Senators had determined to accept no measure of peace.* Mr. Seward discarded all attempts to accommodate it to his views, and vauntingly declared that "*the day for compromises had gone by.*"

It was first objected, that the laws of the Territory restrain the free discussion of the question of slavery, and impose test oaths for suffrage and office, and consequently the pro-slavery party would have the advantage. The friends of the measure answered, that all such laws are in conflict with the Constitution and the organic act of Congress, and the bill may be made to provide for their repeal.

Then it was alleged that many of the free State men had been driven out of the Territory, and therefore the bill would make Kansas a slave State. This objection was promptly met by an amendment in the 11th section, giving all such an opportunity to return and have their names registered, and participate in the election for delegates to make a constitution.

It was next said that the penalties for abusing or obstructing the right of suffrage were too light, and these were immediately increased.

The last discovery was, that the President, with the consent of the Senate, had the right to appoint the commissioners, and they had no confidence in this appointing power. To meet this difficulty, General Cass rose in his place and gave them a pledge, on the part of the President and the Senate, that the commissioners should be selected from both political parties, and all be men of the highest integrity and ability.

Then they evinced their want of sincerity in all their objections to the details, by voting in a body for the proposition of Senator Wilson to strike out the entire bill, and insert, instead, a single section, repealing all the laws now in force in Kansas, and leaving the people in anarchy and confusion!

The senator from New Hampshire, (Mr. Hale,) having recovered from his right impulses under the party lash, came forward and moved to defer the effect of the bill to July, 1857, so that the struggle might last another year—in order *"that Kansas and liberty might bleed"* till after the presidential election; and in this he was sustained by the vote of every republican senator!

Mr. Seward, the file leader of the factionists, did his part by moving to strike out the entire bill, and inserting another admitting Kansas into the Union under the Topeka constitution, and was sustained in this by his entire party. Many other amendments were offered, all designed to defeat the object of the bill, or to force its friends to cast votes liable to misrepresentation.

But at last the test vote could no longer be avoided. They had said the remedy for the evils in Kansas was her prompt admission as a State; that the territorial laws were odious and oppressive, and must be repealed; that the elective franchise had been abused, and it must be protected; that the free State party were largely in the ascendancy, and the voice of the majority must be heard. The bill provided for all these things. What then did these black republicans do? Did they act up to their professions by favoring this measure of relief and pacification for Kansas? It is almost incredible that they did not. They resisted it to the bitter end. They deliberately voted against the repeal of the laws subversive of the liberty of speech and freedom of the press; against the prompt admission of Kansas as a State, and, virtually, in favor of the continuance of the present territorial government and laws! It is no justification to say that they preferred the Topeka constitution; *that* measure had already failed; and this Senate bill then came up as against the present government and laws of Kansas. These "*friends* of Kansas" decided in favor of the latter. From this record there is no escape. Failing to get the Topeka constitution, which they had claimed as the best thing that could be done, they were bound, as honest men and patriots, to go for the next best; but they have made their record.

What clearer evidence can we have that these agitators do not desire peace in Kansas than is furnished in this brief and true history? The proof amounts almost to demonstration.

But now for *their* remedy—the Topeka constitution. It was objected to by the democratic senators because it was the work of a party, and not of the whole people; because that work was commenced without authority of law, and prosecuted in open defiance and menace of the government and its authority, emanating from and partaking of a spirit of *rebellion* at every step; *because its recognition by Congress would furnish authority and precedent for revolution against the government, on the ground of alleged grievances, without any previous effort to gain redress by petition*—a step too hazardous, as we believe, for any government. A very brief history of the Topeka movement will be sufficient to convince all of the truth of these allegations.

ORIGIN AND AIM OF THE TOPEKA MOVEMENT.

Preparatory to the Topeka movement two conventions were held—the first at Lawrence on the 14th of August, and the second at Big Springs on the 5th of September. The proceedings of the Lawrence meeting are based on the declaration, "That the people of Kansas Territory have been since its settlement, and now are, without any law-making power," &c.

At the Big Springs convention the following resolutions were unanimously adopted:

"*Resolved*, That this convention, in view of its recent repudiation of the acts of the so-called Kansas legislative assembly, respond most heartily to the call made by the people's convention of the 14th ultimo for a delegate convention of the people of Kansas, to be held at Topeka on the 19th instant, to consider the propriety of the formation of a State constitution, and such matters as may legitimately come before it.

"*Resolved*, That we owe no allegiance or obedience to the tyrannical enactments of this *spurious legislature;* that their laws have no validity or binding force upon the people of Kansas; and that every freeman among us is at full liberty, consistently with his obligations as a citizen and a man, to defy and resist them, if he choose so to do.

"*Resolved*, That we will endure and submit to these laws no longer than the best interests of the Territory require, as the least of two evils, and will resist them to a bloody issue as soon as we ascertain that peaceable remedies shall fail, and forcible resistance shall furnish any reasonable prospect of success; and that, in the mean time, we recommend to our friends throughout the Territory the organization and discipline of volunteer companies, and the procurement and preparation of arms."

Addresses of the most inflammatory character were made by Governor Reeder and others, avowing their determination to resort to force in case their views were not adopted by the government; that "*they must conquer, or mingle the bodies of the oppressor with those of the oppressed in a common grave.*"

But all doubt on this point was settled by the action of the convention itself, immediately after it met on the 4th day of October, 1855, as can be seen by the proceedings.

A resolution was offered by Mr. Smith instructing the various committees to shape their proceedings with reference to an immediate organization of a State government, irrespective of any action of Congress. The proposition was adopted at the end of a long debate, in the course of which Mr. Delahay, who now claims a seat in Congress under the constitution made by that body, made a powerful appeal against it, on the ground that it made the convention "*an act of rebellion*" against the government; but he was answered by the *majority that "they should not, and would not, wait one day for the action of Congress.*"

The constitution framed by the revolutionary convention was submitted to a vote of the people, and it is a disputed point whether it received 700 or 1,700 out of the 6,000 then in the Territory! Its advocates only claim for it the sanction of 1,700 people, whilst the other side say it did not receive half that number.

Colonel James H. Lane, claiming a seat in the United States Senate, on behalf of the State erected by this constitution, was deputed to convey to Congress the memorial of the so-called legislature, praying for the admission of the State so constituted into the Union. The scene which followed its presentation in the senate will long be remembered. The document was handed to the venerable Senator from Michigan (Mr. Cass) within a few minutes of the opening of the session, with the request that he would present it, which he did. In the course of the debate, on a proposition to refer and print it, the discovery was made that the paper was not an original one; that the signatures were all in the same handwriting; that it was blurred on every page by erasures and interlineations. A closer examination proved that it was a virtual fraud; that it bore no evidence of authority; that the revolutionary ground on which the convention and members of the legislature had first based their action had been stricken from it, and that it had evidently *been recently shaped to suit the views of the republican members of Congress!* They had taken ground that the Topeka convention was "a peaceable assembling of the people to petition for redress," and the memorial was mutilated to suit their partisan ends. Like Mr. Delahay, they had not the courage to stand up to it if called "rebellion." It must be shaped to suit their partisan issue, though fraud and forgery became the agents of the work. This disfigured document, so imposed upon the Senate, was indignantly hurled back by a vote of 32 yeas to 3 nays, and has remained in silent oblivion ever since!

It is true that the minority of the Committee on Territories in the Senate made a very unfair, though futile attempt to redeem this movement from the odium cast about it by its rebellious and revolutionary aspect, claiming that it was only "a peaceable assembling of the people to petition for redress of grievances." To accomplish this end, the true import of the opinion of Attorney General Butler, in the Arkansas case, was deliberately perverted. Such portions only were used as answered the ends of the committee; and in this way many honest people have been misled as to the analogy between the Topeka movement and that of the people of Arkansas. Had the committee used the entire opinion it would have been fatal to their case. The Attorney General, it is true, conceded the right of the people peaceably to assemble and to make a written constitution, a report of their prayer to Congress for admission into the Union as a State, but he added, "*provided always, that such measure be commenced and prosecuted in a peaceable manner, in strict subordination to the territorial government, and in entire subserviency to the power of Congress to adopt, reject, or disregard them at pleasure.*" We submit to the people of the United States to determine, without further comment, whether it is fair or candid to pretend that the Topeka constitution falls within these rules and principles.

MICHIGAN VINDICATED AGAINST AN UNFAIR COMPARISON

Attempts have also been made to find a precedent for this lawless movement in the circumstances surrounding the admission of the State of Michigan. But the following remarks of General Cass, in reply to Mr. Sumner, on this point, and the views of his colleague, Mr. Stewart, presented in another part of this address, will settle the unfairness of that plea beyond cavil.

Mr. CASS. I have listened with equal regret and surprise to the speech of the honorable Senator from Massachusetts. Such a speech—the most un-American and unpatriotic that ever grated on the ears of the members of this high body—as I hope never to hear again here or elsewhere. But, sir, I did not rise to make any comments on the speech of the honorable Senator, open as it is to the highest censure and disapprobation. I rise for another purpose. The honorable Senator has so misunderstood and misapplied the case of Michigan, which he brings forward as a justification of the proceedings in Kansas, that, as I know the facts connected with it, I feel bound to say a few words—and but very few they will be—to the Senate upon the subject.

The honorable Senator has spoken of the right of the people to form conventions with a view to obstruct the authorized laws of the country. I deny such a right. I do not deny the right of any portion of the American people to form conventions; but conventions formed to obstruct the existing laws of the country, unless they succeed, are rebellion. The conventions to which the Senator alluded were held in times of revolution. He referred to the early proceedings in Virginia, while the country was in a state of revolution; when the people rose up to assert their rights; when the Government was opposed to them; and when they had to take measures in their own hands to put down British tyranny and oppression. These were acts of revolution, and justified conventions; but the American people now have no justification for acts of rebellion. Whom do they rebel against? Themselves. The majority always can control the elections, and give form and substance to their representatives to procure any measures they please—not, perhaps, to-day, or within a week, or a month; but the time must come shortly when they will be felt. So much for the States. And Congress is always ready to afford relief and protection to the Territories.

Michigan was guilty of no such crime as that, I am proud to say. The proceedings in that State have no analogy with the proceedings in Kansas. The convention in Michigan was not for the purpose of opposing the law. Let me explain the circumstances in a few words.

The ordinance of Congress of 1787 provided, as I have already said in the Senate, for three States certainly, and two more at the will of Congress, within the Northwest Territory. If the number was increased to five, the first three States were to be bounded on the north by a line running due east from the southern extreme of Lake Michigan. Congress made provision for the three States—Ohio, Indiana, and Illinois. When Ohio came into the Union, she proposed that her boundary, instead of being the east line, should, if it was found that that line would strike Lake Erie south of the north cape of the Maumee Bay, be a straight line from the southern extremity of Lake Michigan to the north cape of Maumee Bay.

When her constitution came before Congress for acceptance, a committee of the House of Representatives, at the head of which was John Randolph, took charge of this subject, and that committee reported that Congress ought not to change the line. Congress had, in the mean time, provided for the territory of Michigan, with the east line for its southern boundary. The Senate will recollect that the provision of the ordinance of Congress of 1787, with respect to the States to be formed in that region, was, that when they had sixty thousand inhabitants they should be admitted, by their delegates, into the Union. The words were, "should be entitled by their delegates to take a seat in Congress." It was contended, in early times, in that country, and, for myself, I think correctly, that the people, at any time when they numbered sixty thousand, under that ordinance, had the right themselves, through the action of the Territorial Legislature, to come forward and claim admission. That was the foundation of the proceedings of the State of Michigan based on the law which I now state.

Michigan had a population of sixty thousand, and came forward for admission into the Union. A convention was called, not by the act of the people—that is, not by the act of individuals—but by a law passed by the Territorial Legislature. Their convention assembled and formed a State constitution, and came forward claiming their boundary to the line established by the ordinance of Congress, and not acknowledging the Ohio line. My honorable friend from California, who was then a citizen of Ohio, I presume was in the State at the time. He knows there was almost civil war. He must remember that the militia of Ohio and Michigan were called out. I was here in the Cabinet of General Jackson. I knew his anxiety. We were all apprehensive that a war might break out.

In reply to Mr. Wade and Mr. Trumbull, who had argued that the admission of Michigan into the Union furnished a precedent for accepting Kansas on the Topeka constitution, Mr. Stewart submitted the following overwhelming argument:

"If the Senator will hear me, I will show him that he is mistaken in every particular. In the first place, the ordinance of 1787 authorized a certain number of States to be formed out of the Northwestern Territory, and authorized their admission into the Union whenever they should have sixty thousand inhabitants. Acting upon that authority, the Territorial Legislature of Michigan, after we had that number of inhabitants and more, passed a law to enable the people to elect delegates to a State convention to form a State constitution. Those delegates were elected, and they formed a State constitution, and submitted the adoption of it to the people of the Territory, and the people adopted the constitution. They elected a legislature under it, and they elected their senators to Congress. The people elected a representative to the other House. They came here, and demanded admission into the Union. All this was done in virtue of the territorial laws of Michigan, acting in virtue of the ordinance of 1787. When they came here, Ohio disputed the southern boundary. That boundary included the mouth of the Maumee river. It had, up to that time, been within the jurisdiction of the Territory of Michigan. It had not been within the jurisdiction of Ohio. All the officers, township and county, justices of the peace, and all others, were Michigan officers down to the southern boundary which we claimed; but Ohio claimed a right to that portion of the Territory. Congress took up the subject, and determined that Michigan should release that boundary, and carry it ten miles further north, as a condition of being admitted into the Union; and they determined that that consent should be given by 'a convention of the people.' That is the language of the law of Congress. They did not say how that convention should be called. They did not say that it should be called by the legislature. They did not say that there should be legislative consent; but they said a convention of the people of Michigan should consent to that boundary. The legislature afterwards called a convention, and that convention rejected the proposition. The people then took up the subject themselves, and they called a convention. That convention accepted the proposition, and that acceptance was sent to the President of the United States. He transmitted it to Congress; and Congress, after full debate, decided that that acceptance was within the terms of its own law. Therefore, you see, sir, that there was not a movement in Michigan, from the beginning to the end, that was not in accordance with the provisions of a law, either of the Territory or of Congress, or of both. Now, here is the Topeka constitution, formed throughout without law from its inception to its end, admittedly by its friends, and yet it is said to be a parallel case to Michigan. I submit that there is not a single circumstance, from its commencement to its end, that is parallel; and I hope (although I confess that I have no ground to hope, from past experience) that it will not be asserted, at least here again, that the case of Kansas and the case of Michigan are parallel."

There are also a few additional features of this Topeka movement which are not inappropriate at this point. They may serve to illustrate the sincerity and consistency of its advocates as the friends of the colored race and the opponents of laws not authorized by a majority of the people.

One is the 1st section of the 11th article of the constitution, to be found on page 631 of the report of the House committee to investigate Kansas affairs, which provides that the constitution shall not be amended or altered prior to the year 1865, nine years after its adoption. The black republicans have indulged in unlimited denunciations of the laws of Kansas, because a majority of the people did not authorize their adoption, and yet, at the same time, you see they insist upon the recognition of a constitution, *unalterable for nine years*, brought forth in the most informal mode, and unsustained by that great element of authority, the popular will.

Another is, that at the time the constitution was made it was determined to submit to a vote of the people the question of admitting or excluding free people of color from the State; the decision to be binding upon the legislature. The vote on this subject can be found in the report of the committee, between pages 718 and 755, inclusive, showing a decided majority in favor of "exclusion."

On page 645, under the ominous caption of "*Constitutional Proclamation,*" James H. Lane, as chairman of the executive constitutional committee, announces the result of the vote as follows, to wit:

> "And I do further proclaim and make known, that of the votes cast at the aforesaid election for and against the passage of a law, by the General Assembly, providing for the EXCLUSION OF FREE NEGROES FROM THE STATE OF KANSAS, the result of such vote to operate as instructions to the first General Assembly—*a majority are in favor of exclusion*, as ascertained by the returns of said election now on file in the office of the executive committee.
>
> "JAMES H. LANE, *Chairman Executive Committee*."

Here is a specimen of the humanity and liberality of those who are so constantly "shrieking for liberty in Kansas," who are daily shedding crocodile tears over the hardships of the down-trodden negro. They are the advocates of the same provision, resisted in 1819 by Mr. Adams and others, the insertion of which in the constitution of Missouri kept her out of the Union until she repealed it. These philanthropists mean to have Kansas free, indeed—free of colored freemen as well as of slaves! Expulsion of the colored race, bond and free, from the enjoyment of the rich valleys and pure air of free Kansas, is what *they* mean by liberty and equality—the hypocrites.

We have now, fellow-citizens, given you the history and character of the measure which the friends of Colonel Frémont wish you to sustain in preference to the wise and just law passed by a democratic Senate; and we shall await your verdict with confidence. We are entirely certain that you will never sanction a measure so fraught with mischief to our institutions—so tarnished with violence, insubordination, disorder, and fraud, and so unsustained by that great element of governmental power, the will of the people.

DEBATE IN THE SENATE.

We now ask you to read the following remarks of Mr. Toombs, delivered on the 2d of July, in explanation of the character and effect of his bill, and his views and purposes in presenting it. We are quite certain that you will agree with us that they are able, clear, and patriotic, and evince no want of courage or frankness in the author of this great measure of freedom and justice.

Mr. TOOMBS said:

Mr. President and Senators: It was not at first my purpose to add anything to the observations which I made when I gave notice of the bill which is substantially the one now before the Senate. I have never been under the necessity of making one speech to explain another. Though that was brief, it told plainly what I wanted, what I meant to do, and how I intended to do it. At the same time, I declared my willingness to accept suggestions from those who agreed with me, so as to do these things in the most effectual manner. With that view, I accepted with pleasure the few amendments to the bill proposed by the Committee on Territories, and was obliged to them for correcting my own errors in matters of detail with which they were much better acquainted than myself. Nor, sir, would the motion of the senator from Massachusetts (Mr. Wilson) have altered my determination but for its being seconded by the senator from New York, (Mr. Seward,) accompanied with the assignment of reasons so untenable and extraordinary for his position.

The senator from New York, in a speech delivered some two months since, after recounting the various grievances of the people of Kansas, (which had no other foundation than his own imagination, and the unreliable sources from which he usually derives his information, sustained not by proof but by intrepid assertions,) called upon the Senate, and upon the country, to give peace to Kansas by introducing her as a State, with the Topeka constitution. The foundation upon which he offered that constitution to the acceptance of the Senate and the country was, that it was the voice of Kansas, the will of her *bona fide* inhabitants. He assumed, enlarged upon it, and proclaimed it to the civilized world as a fact, that the voice of Kansas was smothered by invasion, that her true people were overrun and conquered by aliens, that their ballot-boxes were seized and their liberties were trampled under foot by foreigners, and he demanded that you should give justice to Kansas by allowing her people to make their own institutions. When he made that demand, though I admitted none of his assertions to be true, though I denied the truth of every single fact upon which he based his demand, I thought I saw in his demand a basis for a speedy and satisfactory adjustment of this question, if he were sincere in his demand. I had again and again avowed my purpose to allow the people of Kansas the right to make their own domestic institutions, under the organic law and the constitution. I stood pledged to that policy as a public man, a pledge which I have again and again, at this session and at previous sessions, reiterated my readiness to redeem.

Then there was a common point of agreement between us. It was not upon past grievances; for there we differed. It was not upon his allegation of frauds or injuries inflicted on the inhabitants; for those I denied to the extent stated by him and his friends. But we agreed that the people of Kansas should legislate for themselves, without the intervention of force, fear, or fraud. We had but one point to settle—what was the will of Kansas? That senator asserted that the Topeka constitution was the true exponent of that popular will, and as such he demanded its acceptance. He put it to the Senate, the country, and the civilized world, that such was the fact. I did not think he believed it; I do not think so now; but I determined to meet him fairly on that issue, to test the sincerity of these declarations. I was willing to give down-trodden Kansas, if she be down-trodden, a right to make her own institutions, under the constitution, according to her own will. This is the principle upon which I supported the Kansas-Nebraska bill. I stood upon it in no fraudulent or double sense, but as an honest man ready to maintain it in the Senate and before the country, at any time and at all times. I determined to give peace to the country, if this would do it. It was in affirmance and not in derogation of the principles advocated by the friends of the original Kansas bill. I only required one fact to be established: Is the Topeka constitution the voice of Kansas? This is the only question I asked; this is the sole demand I made; this is the sole difference between my proposition and that proposed by the senator from New York. I did not believe he wanted any settlement of this question, and he has since satisfied me abundantly of the truth of that belief. I believe he wanted grievances; I believe he wanted discord; I believe he wanted anything but peace; I believe he wanted nothing but revolution, or a state of things sufficiently near it as to give power to his party. I will offer the evidence of this belief to the Senate and the country. He and his associates told us this same story, with all its variations—the free-soilers, the abolitionists, the two senators from New York, the senator from Vermont, (Mr. Collamer,) and others repeated it. I believe the senator from Vermont went so far as to suppose that nineteen-twentieths, or some other large number, of the Kansas population were all on one side. He told us in his report that Kansas was down-trodden; that the laws made by the legislature were not the laws of Kansas, but were made by representatives of Missouri; that the majority of the people of Kansas abhorred them; that they were imposed on them by force and by fraud.

Mr. COLLAMER. Is the gentleman alluding to me?

Mr. TOOMBS. Yes, sir. In the senator's speech he said the laws were against the will of the real settlers.

Mr. COLLAMER. I said—and I produced my proof by reference to the returns—that the legislature was elected by Missouri votes.

Mr. TOOMBS. And did not represent the will of the people of the Territory?

Mr. COLLAMER. Yes.

Mr. TOOMBS. That is what I stated.

Mr. COLLAMER. I meant simply that a large majority of the votes which created the legislature were cast by people from Missouri.

Mr. TOOMBS. That is what I stated to be the gentleman's position. Then I am not mistaken in asserting that the senator set forth before the country, in an elaborate report, the position that the present government of Kansas was against the will of the people of Kansas; that a large majority of those people were opposed to the laws enacted by the legislature; that a majority wanted the Topeka Constitution; that the majority had been invaded, overridden, trampled under foot, ravished, plundered, imprisoned, murdered—as we have heard to-day. I did not believe a word of all this. I did not think those who said them believed them. I intended to apply a test to them which would show whether those senators would act as all reasonable men would who believed their statements; or whether I was sustained in my opinion of their objects, views, and purposes. I submit that point to the American people and the world. The senator from Massachusetts, now absent from his seat, [Mr. SUMNER,] told very much the same story. He spoke of down-trodden Kansas, overridden Kansas, plundered Kansas. He told us that her people had, by a foreign invasion, been deprived of the right which had been promised them—of being allowed to select their own institutions for themselves. However variously ramified, enlarged, painted, or bedaubed, this was the basis, the corner-stone, upon which were built all of their pretended grievances—all of their frantic agonies.

If these things were true, they demanded redress; but the facts being controverted, the first step towards any just measure of redress would be to ascertain the facts—to learn the truth, and then to act upon it—to act promptly, efficiently. The measure which I proposed was founded on that principle. I sought to ascertain the facts in the best possible mode that my own mind could suggest, to the end, that if these alleged wrongs were true, to remove them; and if they were not true, to demonstrate it to the thousands of honest men in the republic who have been deceived and deluded by falsehoods concocted in the Territory, and daily transmitted to the public through congressional speeches and reports, in order to conceal the base metal under the cover of official sanction.

I came forward to offer it, not in a spirit of compromise, as I said to the senator from New York, but in vindication of a principle. I offered it on principles which have been affirmed by the great body of the American people. I did not expect to satisfy bad men on any side. When, four years ago, the present Chief Magistrate was elected—and I believe most of these gentlemen voted for him, or his prominent opponent, General Scott—the people of the United States, with singular unanimity, declared it to be a sound fundamental principle that, when the people of a Territory came to be admitted into the Union, they should be admitted with or without slavery, as the *bona fide* inhabitants should determine. This was affirmed at Baltimore by the democratic and whig parties; it was affirmed by nineteen-twentieths of the American people. Then, without going into controverted questions, as these gentlemen demanded what the democrats and whigs declared to be correct—as they demanded what I held to be the true principle—I felt ready at any moment to grant it. But what did I require? Simply that the fact upon which it all turned should be truly ascertained. I said: "Gentlemen—you the senators from New York, you the senators from Massachusetts, you the senators from Vermont—(whom I had long known, and thought I could safely rely upon for a fair judgment)—if you say the voice of Kansas is for a free State, take what I offer; I present you a proposition to let her have her own free choice forever. If you have spoken truly for her, why do you not take the coveted prize?

When I make the annunciation, that I am willing to surrender Kansas precisely in conformity with the will of the nation—in conformity with your own declarations, how am I met? I offer you a pure and undefiled ballot-box. I protect it by all the means which law, backed by force, can give it. I offer the entire military force of this great country to secure to you that inestimable privilege—a free untrammelled, and uncontrolled ballot-box. How am I met? Instead of a pure ballot-box, the senator from Massachusetts and the senator from New York tender me the cartridge-box. Mr. President, if I believed those gentlemen represented the North, I would accept it and withdraw my bill now. If I believed the people of the free States were ready for that issue, before God and my country I would not shrink from it. I am content to accept it whenever the North offers it. I present no compromises; I present principles; but I do not know what claim either of those gentlemen has to speak for the North. I see around me able, patriotic, and venerable statesmen—some of whom have for fifty years, in peace and in war, been honored and trusted by the North, by the South, by mankind. They give me a different account of the North. The representatives of millions of northern freemen, from every State, county, and town in the non-slaveholding States, met in council with their countrymen of the South four short weeks ago. I consider them better witnesses of the feelings and wishes of the North than the black republican and abolition senators on this floor. In regard to the senator from New York, to my knowledge, for the last ten years, all parties have dreaded nothing he would do or say so much as the odium of his alliance. I deny their right to speak for the North.

* * * * * * * * * *

We next call your special attention to the following extracts from speeches delivered in the Senate on the 9th of July, pending the question on General Cass' motion to print twenty thousand copies of the Senate bill for circulation. They are selected in the order in which they were delivered, and will serve still further to illustrate the noble and just position of the democracy, as well as the inconsistencies and absurdities indulged in by the opponents of the bill:

Mr. Toucey. Mr. President, the House of Representatives has passed a bill for the admission of Kansas into the Union upon the so-called Topeka constitution. The Senate, not satisfied with that pretended constitution, on the ground that it was a mere partial revolutionary movement—that it was against law—that it was adopted by only a portion of a party which had no power to act for the people of Kansas, or to impose on them a constitution, have submitted a proposition and passed it, by which the question shall be submitted to the *bona fide* settlers of Kansas, and a constitution formed, if they see fit to form one. The bill which was passed by the House of Representatives, and sent to the Senate, has been amended by substituting the bill of the Senate, and sending that to the House; so that the issue is made between the majority of the Senate and the majority of the House of Representatives, upon one point only—namely: whether a constitution fairly formed by the whole people of Kansas, in the manner provided by the Senate's bill, is to be preferred over the revolutionary constitution which was attempted to be made at the Topeka convention.

Now, sir, I desire that this bill of the Senate—which is so just and fair in itself—which provides against every evil, so far as I can judge, that has been complained of—may be spread before the country in the fullest manner for the information of the public; and I know of no mode in which it can be done so effectively as by sending out the bill itself without note or comment. Let the people judge, from an inspection of the bill itself, whether we ought to have adopted it—whether we, who originally proposed to leave the whole subject of their domestic institutions to the people of Kansas, intend to carry out that measure in good faith. For one I was committed to that measure at the outset, and I intended that the people of Kansas, fairly and freely, without any external interference from any quarter, should, as every State does, and as every community has been accustomed to do from the first settlement of this country down to the present time—exercise the right of self-government, and decide for itself upon its own domestic laws and institutions.

Sir, I wish to appeal to the people of the country, by the bill which we have presented, and now again present to the House of Representatives, both as an original proposition, and as an amendment to their bill—whether we do not now propose to carry out that doctrine fairly and truly as we avowed? I desire no better vindication of my course than that the people shall read this bill. There was only one objection to it, and that was the want of numbers; but the House of Representatives has waived that objection, and we have waived it. We do so on the ground of the difficulties now existing in Kansas, and we apply a remedy. That remedy is, by the action of the *bona fide* settlers, forming a constitution for themselves without external interference, and we mean to uphold them in their right to form their own constitution, and to establish their own domestic institutions, as every State in the Union now does, and has hitherto been accustomed to do.

As I said before, I wish this bill to go to the American people. It has been misrepresented; it is now grossly misrepresented. Instead of taking the misrepresentation, I wish the bill to go to the people, that they may see what it is, and that intelligent men everywhere may understand what it is.

Mr. FESSENDEN. Will the honorable senator allow me to ask him in what particular it has been misrepresented?

Mr. TOUCEY. Misrepresented, sir! It is represented as a mere slave measure; it is represented as an unfair measure; it is denounced and misrepresented as designed for other purposes than to secure to the *bona fide* settlers of the Territory the right of self-government; and there are thousands who will never know, until it is too late, what is the true character of this bill and what are its provisions. I desire that the bill may go before the people at the north, and throughout the whole north, that they may see and know who they are who are disposed to leave it to the people of the Territory to govern themselves, to make their own laws, to establish their own institutions, and who propose a different and an opposite course. * * * * * *

Mr. WELLER. I do not desire to engage in the discussion of the merits of the bill; I only wish to say a word in regard to the publication of it. I am very glad to find that the senators from Ohio and Massachusetts are willing to print twenty thousand extra copies of the bill in order that the people may understand precisely the position which the majority of the Senate occupy on this question. The senator from Massachusetts certainly must know that this bill has been shamefully misrepresented—I do not say by any senators here, but by the public press of the country—and I am satisfied from what I have seen, that there are really some very intelligent editors in the country who do not comprehend this question, who do not understand this bill as it has been passed by the Senate. Why, sir, the misrepresentations of the public press are of such a character that no public man dare now go before an assembly and read a newspaper as authority. I grant you, this bill will be published in the newspapers; but where will you find a public man who will risk his reputation by reading a newspaper as authority to sustain any fact which he may affirm? I know that in the State of Ohio no public speaker dare allude to a newspaper as authority for any statement he may make. Therefore it is that I desire to get this bill in an official form. It will then be a document which cannot be controverted. The public press very often misrepresents senators. They have even gone so far as to say that the senator from Massachusetts the other day, in a public speech which he made in the city of Philadelphia, declared that Mr. Buchanan had affirmed that, if he had a drop of democratic blood in his veins, he would let it out. Now I am sure that it is a misrepresentation of the public press. The senator from Massachusetts is an intelligent man, and never could have uttered any thing so destitute of truth as that.

I only allude to this to show the misrepresentations of the public press, not only as to public men, but as to public measures. We desire, on this side of the chamber, that our position shall be understood. Let the people read the bill, and my word for it they will never give such a construction to it as has been given to it by the senator from Ohio, (Mr. Wade.) At all events, let it go out. We shall meet them at the ballot box; we shall argue this question there; and if the judgment of the people be against it, we shall submit. We shall not threaten revolution, as some of the leading newspapers on that side have done. We shall not threaten force and violence. We shall threaten another appeal to the ballot box at some other time.

Mr. BIGLER. Mr. President, I have listened to the remarks of the senator from Massachusetts with surprise. He has gravely inquired for the time and occasion when the bill (which it is proposed to print) was misrepresented. Why, sir, there can be no difficulty in answering that question. He has done so himself. Immediately after making the inquiry, the honorable senator asserted, with great earnertness of manner, that the intention and purpose of the bill is to carry out the work already commenced by the border ruffians of Missouri! Will the senator say that such statements are not a palpable misrepresentation of the measure? Will he pretend that the language of the proposed law justifies any such conclusion? What feature of the act has brought the senator to the belief, that the intention is to carry on the work of usurpation, fraud, arson, and murder, which he has told us has been begun in Kansas? What language in the bill looks to a work of that kind—that justifies, invites, or countenances it to the slightest extent?

Now, sir, when this measure was first under consideration, the senator made a statement similar to that which he has dropped this morning. He then said the intention was to bring Kansas into the Union as a slave State. Will not such statements be picked up by the press in his part of the Union, for the purpose of creating the impression that there is some hidden purpose in the bill calculated to do injustice to a portion of the people of Kansas? And yet the senator manifests surprise that misrepresentations should be anticipated.

Now, sir, I assert, unqualifiedly, that the bill intends no such purpose as that imputed to it by the senator from Massachusetts; and I ask him to point to the section or clause that justifies his assertion. Its language and purpose are clear, so much so, that the wayfaring man cannot misunderstand it. It simply intends that the people—the *bona fide* citizens, now in Kansas, shall, by the expression of their will, uncontrolled, decide the question of slavery for themselves—shall determine whether they will have the institution or not. Is this not fair? Have we not been told by both sides, that they ask nothing more? Is not this in accordance with the spirit of the organic law?

But we are next told by the senator from Ohio, that if a little more time had been given for the organization of the State under the bill, it would have been more acceptable. This is extraordinary logic to come from those who insist upon the admission of Kansas, immediately, on the Topeka constitution; a measure adopted when the population was far less than at present, and which, on the face of the proceedings connected with it, only purports to come from a portion of the people—those not content with the territorial government. Again, he alleges that a certain class of the inhabitants have been driven out. The honorable senator is certainly aware that the eleventh section of the bill, as passed by the Senate, makes a provision, that all those who at any time had been citizens of the Territory, and had left, temporarily, because of the bad condition of society, or for any other reason, shall have the right to return and participate in the election.

Mr. Wade. Does this bill give any additional right to the people to return there? Have they not a right to go there whether your bill passes or not? Is there anything gained by it?

Mr. Bigler. Certainly the people can return to the Territory, whether the bill passes or not; but that is not the point. The senator knows that the 4th day of July, 1856, is named as the time when the bill shall take effect. Those who are citizens at that time are to have the right to vote for delegates. The senator, and those acting with him, objected to this feature, alleging that the free State party had been driven out of the Territory, and therefore the tendency was to make Kansas a slave State. This objection was promptly met by a provision from the committee, which I have just described, that all who had left could return and participate in forming a State government. The commissioners appointed to superintend the election are directed to enter the names of all such on the list, and permit them to vote for delegates; so that all the qualified voters who were in the Territory at the time the Topeka Constitution was made, and all who have at any time made their residence there up to the 4th of July, 1856, will have a part in making the constitution. Surely, Mr. President, no man who advocates the Topeka constitution can consistently object to this bill on the ground that all the citizens are not to participate in carrying out its provisions. Any objection to the Senate bill on that point will apply with destructive force to the Topeka movement.

* * * * * * * * * *

It is most extraordinary, Mr. President, that we should be lectured—no, I will not say lectured—but edified from the other side, on the necessity of order and form in our movements—that we should not attempt suddenly to force a measure on the country which is not intended to accomplish the end which appears on its face, and at the same time be urged to sanction the Topeka constitution, a step which all must agree was taken, not only without authority of law, but in derogation of all law, and which progressed in menace of the government, at every step, and which has been marked by violence and disorder in every stage of its emanation.

Now, sir, I wish to say to the senators from Massachusetts and Ohio, very distinctly, that when they describe the tendencies of the bill as forcing slavery into the Territory, and as perpetuating the work of the border ruffians—if they mean to say that I seek to produce such consequences, they misrepresent my motives. I simply intend that the *bona fide* citizens of Kansas shall, without dictation from any quarter, decide the question of slavery for themselves. This is all the bill intends, or is calculated to produce. I have liked this measure from the beginning, because I thought it contained the elements of peace and quiet, together with those of perfect fairness to all; its leading idea being the prompt termination of the contest as to the local policy of the Territory touching the institution of slavery. We have been told by the other side that there was no remedy for the state of society in Kansas but her prompt admission into the Union as a State, and this is what the bill provides for. We have been told, also, by these gentlemen, that they had no confidence in the local government of Kansas—that it was controlled by the slave power entirely—that free State people were driven from the polls. In order to meet this objection, an independent organ has been provided, to administer the provisions of the law—a board of five commissioners, to be taken from both sides, and who, I trust, will be able and pure men, and who are to be clothed with ample power to protect the ballot-box against aggressions from Missouri or any other quarter. They can even call in the aid of the military to accomplish this end. Now, sir, I am not to be misunderstood on this subject of intrusions from Missouri. I countenance no such. I have uniformly discarded and condemned them. I seek only a fair and free expression of popular will.

* * * * * * * * * *

But we have been exultingly told that we have abandoned the doctrine of non-intervention by the bill. I do not intend to argue this point at length. The senator from Michigan, when the bill was under consideration put that allegation down. I certainly do not intend to impair the doctrine by any act of mine, for I intend it shall be a finality on this subject. But I can see a very clear distinction between annulling laws clearly unconstitutional, and in violation of the letter and spirit of the organic act, and a law of Congress dictating or interdicting a local institution—saying that the people should or should not sell ardent spirits—that they should or should not hold slaves. It should be observed, again, that the proposed action has special reference to the preparation of Kansas for admission as a State, and not to her policy as a Territory. I am aware, Mr. President, that some features of the bill look like interference; but the Kansas-Nebraska act declares that the action of the local legislature shall be confined to rightful subjects of legislation. Will it be pretended, then, that interfering with the right of free discussion is a rightful subject of legislation? I do not care to raise the question of congressional power, for I hold that, however the question may be decided, it is politic for Congress not to exercise the right to interfere with the question of slavery in the Territories.

* * * * * * * * * *

In conclusion, Mr. President, I wish to repeat that the vitality of this bill is found in that feature which so promptly terminates all motive, on the part of outsiders, to force a temporary population into the Territory for the purpose of shaping its policy on the subject of slavery. So soon, then, as the bill shall become a law, that feature will take effect. Thereafter it will be idle for the advocates of slavery on the one hand, and the enemies of the institution on the other, not residents, to continue their efforts and excitement. I seek to adopt a measure of peace; and much as I dislike the precedent for the admission of States with very small population, I am willing to forego this, because I think the exigencies demand extraordinary measures. But I cannot vote for the admission of Kansas on the Topeka constitution. It would be the recognition of violence—of usurpation, and because it would be unjust to a portion of the people—would countenance revolution, attempted without any previous application for redress—for the Topeka convention took the subject into their own hands, without asking redress at the hands of Congress at all. Both sides have invited the proposed measure by seeking early admission into the Union, and I have no fear of the result; the provisions of the bill will be embraced. The senator from Massachusetts [Mr. Wilson] has said that the consequences will be to bring Kansas in as a slave State; and yet that senator has uniformly claimed, as have all on the other side, that three fourths or nine tenths of the people of Kansas are for a free State, and I have shown that all who may have left have the opportunity to return. Up to the introduction of this bill we have been told by the other side that all they desired was a fair expression of the will of the people. This bill will afford an opportunity for such expression, and those who oppose it must take the responsibility. I shall vote for the motion to print.

Mr. Douglas. I shall not detain the Senate long. The excuse heretofore given for resisting the law and shooting down the officers of the law in Kansas, has been that the same legislature which made the Kansas code passed two or three statutes which the resistants did not like—statutes invading the liberty of the press and the freedom of speech, and imposing certain tests for voting and for jurors. It was said that these particular laws were barbarous and monstrous—that a free people should not submit to them, and that, whilst such laws stood on the statute book, they were justified in resisting the constituted authorities of the Territory. Well, sir, the Senate has passed a bill which declares all such obnoxious provisions or laws in the Territory null and void. Every statutory provision which has been given as an excuse for resistance to laws, has been blotted out. What excuse now have you for getting up rebellion, and riots, and bloodshed, and house-burnings in Kansas? If now you resist the law, you are resisting statutes that are acknowledged to be proper and wise—those which punish murder, and house-breaking, and robbery, and those crimes that are punished, and ought to be punished, in all civilized communities. What excuse have you now for resistance to the law? Do you say that the murderer should not be punished, because you do not believe that the legislature was fairly elected which made the law against murder? Are you going to rescue the thief because you do not like the legislature that passed the law against larceny? The obnoxious laws are gone, and the senator from Ohio [Mr. Wade] laments that they are gone. He laments it in his speech, and I have no doubt laments it in his heart. The material out of which political capital is to be made is gone.

Gentlemen have been kind enough to say that the object of this bill is to make a slave State in Kansas. I show them that by the provisions of the bill its object is to allow the people to make just such a State as they wish. The Senator from Maine (Mr. Fessenden) says he has a right to go a little behind the face of the bill, and give his opinion that the object is to make Kansas a slave State. Conceding that right, and acting upon it, I have a right to come to the conclusion, that all these gentlemen want is to get up murder and bloodshed in Kansas for political effect. They do not mean that there shall be peace until after the Presidential election. They sent their partisan agents to get up rebelion, to commit crime, to burn houses, and then their newspaper agents are to report these acts here, and charge them on the border ruffians. This whole game of violence there, and the publication of it here, is done by the one and same set of men—done for political effect. It is a part of their game. They do not mean that there shall be peace. Their capital for the Presidential election is blood. We may as well talk plainly. An angel from heaven could not write a bill to restore peace in Kansas that would be acceptable to the Abolition Republican party previous to the Presidential election (Laughter and applause in the galleries.)

The Presiding Officer, (Mr. Foot,) order.

Mr. Douglas. The Senate has passed and now propose to print a bill no man on earth can pretend is not fair, just, and equitable in all its provisions. Even the most hardened partisan does not pretend to say the bill is unfair. Then why not go for it? They say there is something beyond it. The Senator from Vermont (Mr. Collamer) says he must look at the cause of the difficulty, in order to provide the remedy. But if this bill is a fair one; if its provisions are such as will insure a true expression of the popular voice of Kansas, why not agree to it? You say you do not like the cause that produced the difficulty in Kansas. Nor do we. We believe that you originated all the difficulties, and are justly responsible for the consequences; we believe your Emigrant Aid Society was organized for such purposes. We believe there never would have been any trouble in Kansas but for your efforts, and that they were for political objects. Still, you have brought these difficulties upon Kansas, and we have to deal with the facts as they are. We have to deal with existing facts. Shall we refuse to remedy the evils because we feel and know that you produced them; or will you refuse to remedy the evils because you charge the origin of them on us? We are bound as honest men and patriots to apply a remedy to the evils, no matter from what quarter they may have originated.

Then, sir, if it be an evil to have laws in force infringing the freedom of speech in the Territory, why not join with us to pass this bill, which obliterates those laws? If it be an evil of such magnitude as to justify rebellion and bloodshed to have the test oaths in the Territory, why not join with us in blotting them out? If there be such evils as are portrayed in Kansas, why not join us in applying the remedy? No; you vainly hope that you can make the people believe that the Democracy are responsible for the consequences of your own acts, and thus gather political capital from the blood of your fellow-citizens, if violence can reign and the excitement last until the Presidential election. Hence, law must not prevail—life must not be safe—property must not be secure—peace must not be restored in Kansas, if the Abolition Republican leaders can prevent it until after the election. You mistake, if you suppose the people will not be able to understand this scheme.

When we present you with a fair bill designed and calculated to have a fair election, if you are willing that there should be a fair election, why not join us in passing the bill? Your excuse is, that the free State men have all left Kansas, and that there is no hope or expectation that they ever will return. If, for the sake of the argument, the truth of this position should be granted, would that fact furnish sufficient reason for denying to the actual inhabitants of Kansas—those who intend to remain and make it their home—the right of living under a constitution and laws of their own making? By the terms of the bill, all who have left have the right to return and vote at the election. If they do not return and make Kansas their home, and vote at the election, it will be their own fault or choice. But is it true, in fact, that the great body of the free State men have left Kansas? If they have, and if it be true that they will not go back, do you propose to give effect to a constitution which they made, and to which they will not return and live under? If your statement be true that they have all left, you have got a constitution which nobody in the Territory is in favor of—a constitution to govern a people, all of whom are against it—a constitution in the making of which nobody there participated. If your statement be true that those who made the Topeka constitution have left and gone to parts unknown, and cannot be induced to return, with what propriety or truth can you say that the constitution ought to govern a people who are opposed to it, and had no voice in making it? But why talk about the free State men, or any considerable portion of them, having been driven from the Territory? If the newspapers are to be believed, a few have left on both sides, and probably in about equal proportions in respect to numbers.

* * * * * * * * * *

Then, I ask, what cause of complaint is there, that the free State men have left the Territory? How long is it since this cry has been raised? The whistle was sounded by the leader (Mr. Seward,) and every one repeated it like a parrot. Up to the moment this bill was submitted to them—up to that very instant of the time—the leader said, and every one repeated it, that the free State men were in the ratio of ten or twenty to one to the pro-slavery men of Kansas. You all affirmed the statement, and repeated it over and over again in your speeches, as a reason why Kansas should be admitted with the Topeka constitution. You all averred that the Topeka party comprised a vast majority of the inhabitants of Kansas—some of you stating that a majority ten to one, while others estimated it at twenty to one; but all agreeing that there was an overwhelming majority in favor of a free State, and for that reason, insisted upon the admission of Kansas with the Topeka constitution. You affirmed the truth of this fact up to the very hour that the Senator from Georgia gave notice of his proposition to ascertain, by a fair election, the real opinions and wishes of the people of Kansas, when suddenly you all changed your tune, and declared that such a law would result inevitably in making Kansas a slave State. How could such a bill make Kansas a slave State, if a majority of the people were opposed it? It is admitted on all hands that the bill is just and equitable in all its provisions, and provides for a fair and impartial election. Your argument was, that Kansas should be permitted to speak; that her voice should be heard; her will obeyed, by allowing her people to have such a constitution as nineteen twentieths of them demanded. You said it was a great crime against Kansas, to compel the majority to submit to the minority; that a free people would not submit, and ought never to submit, to a system of laws forced upon them in opposition to their wishes, and regardless of their rights under the organic law to decide the slavery question for themselves.

Now, when we propose to permit Kansas to speak, and to speak her own voice, uninfluenced and unawed by any foreign power, or any other power than their own free will, your excuse for denying them the right of making their own fundamental law, is that your friends have been driven out, or they are imprisoned! Imprisoned! for what? You give us to understand that they are all in prison for violating the law abridging the freedom of speech and of the press. Bear in mind—and I have had to remind you of it several times this session—there has never been one of your men imprisoned for a violation of either one of the obnoxious laws of which you have complained. If it be true, as is now said, that they are in prison, and under arrest for a violation of any one of those laws, this bill abrogates those laws, and thus releases your prisoners. There is no lawyer who will deny that a bill repealing a penal law without a reservation as to pre-existing offences, dismisses the indictment, and releases the prisoner. It is a general jail delivery of the whole Territory as to any crime or alleged offence under any one of those obnoxious laws which you say ought not to be in force. Then what comes of your complaint that your men are all in prison? If they are in prison, they are not there for violating any one of those obnoxious laws. If they are in prison, they are there for larceny, for murder, for robbery, or for some other crime, punishment for which is usual and proper in all civilized communities. They are not in prison for violating any law abridging the freedom of speech, or the liberty of the press, or any other right held sacred in any Christian country. I repeat that all laws of which you complain have been declared null and void, as being contrary to the true intent and meaning of the organic law, and the Constitution of the United States.

Then what becomes of your objections to this bill? You are driven back to the flimsy pretext that it is a bill to make Kansas a slave State, and is so designed—yes, "designed" is the word. The bill provides that it shall be a free State, if there are a majority of the people for making it a free State, and a slave State, if a majority are in favor of its being a slave State; yet you say it is a bill to make Kansas a slave State. This allegation cannot be true, and you cannot believe it to be true, unless a majority of the *bona fide* inhabitants are opposed to the Topeka constitution, and in favor of making Kansas a slave State. Do you pretend that there is a majority there in favor of a slave State? If a majority of the *bona fide* inhabitants are in favor of a slave State, they have the right to make it so; and it is our duty to receive it into the Union either with or without slavery, as they shall determine. The will of that people fairly expressed, honestly embodied in their constitution, ought to be the fundamental law of the new State.

* * * * * * * * * *

I have a word to say on the subject of popular sovereignty, inasmuch as the gentleman from New Hampshire has brought it into the debate. He certainly could not have been here the other night, or else he is very forgetful, when he says the doctrine is now abandoned—that the legislature of a territory has the right to legislate on the subject of slavery, in obedience to the Constitution. Did not the senator from Michigan [Mr. Cass] affirm that right in debate the other night? Did not the senator from Connecticut [Mr. Toucey] vindicate that right in the same debate?

Did not the senator from Ohio [Mr. Pugh] avow and defend the same doctrine? Did I not do the same thing in that debate, in language so explicit and unequivocal that no man can be excused for misunderstanding? Did not every senator on this side of the chamber, without one exception, who spoke on the subject, distinctly avow and defend the same doctrine? And yet, in the face of all these avowals in the last debate which has occurred on the subject, we are told by the senator from New Hampshire [Mr. Hale] that the doctrine is abandoned. Abandoned! when, and by whom? Certainly not by its advocates. The doctrine was unanimously affirmed by the National Democratic Convention at Cincinnati, and now forms a fundamental article in the creed of the party as officially promulgated. This is all I have to say upon that point. The senator says he is in favor of popular sovereignty so far as to allow the people of each Territory to decide the slavery question for themselves when they form a constitution preparatory to their admission into the Union. I am glad to hear this avowal. I am sure it will astonish his political associates as much as it does his opponents. He complains that I should have intimated that he and his political friends were opposed to allowing the people to decide the question for themselves when they seek admission into the Union. I did suppose that the unanimous and determined opposition of the whole abolition party, including the senator himself, to the bill under consideration, justified such a declaration.

The whole object of the bill is to protect the people of Kansas in the undisturbed exercise of their right to form a constitution to suit themselves, and to come into the Union with slavery, or without it, as they shall determine in their constitution. If he and his party really believe in the doctrine which he now avows, he and they are bound to vote for the bill under discussion. Sir, if he is in favor of allowing each State to come into the Union with or without slavery, as it pleases, he belongs to a political party whose creed declares "no more slave States" in this Union under any circumstances. Your party is pledged never, "as long as the sun shall shine, or water shall run, or grass grow," to admit another slave State into this Union, whether the people want slavery or not. Is not that the position of your party?

You run a candidate pledged to do an act which you deem it unfair and unjust for us to charge on yourselves. You belong to and cooperate with a party unanimously pledged to do an act which you admit to be unconstitutional. Your party stands pledged, by every obligation which can bind men's honor, never to admit any more slave States, while you declare on the floor of the Senate that every new State has a right to come into the Union with or without slavery, as its own people shall determine for themselves. If you hold the sentiments which you now declare, you cannot and dare not vote for the Republican ticket, which is pledged against that very principle; nor could you be in favor of the restoration of the Missouri restriction, which prohibited slavery, not only while a Territory, but "forever," in the country over which it extended. So much for the views of the senator from New Hampshire on popular sovereignty!

But the senator says I have charged him with certain crimes, and he is grieved that I should have supposed he could be guilty of such grave offences. The charge consists in my having held him responsible for the natural consequences of every speech he has made in Congress during this session, if not for several years past. We were told yesterday, by the same senator, that it was but fair and legitimate to hold a senator responsible for the natural consequences of his own acts. Here is what he said:

"The senator from Illinois complains that it has been represented that there was an intention, a desire, a purpose, by the legislation of Congress, to make Kansas a slave State. Mr. President, I have been educated to believe in the wisdom of that maxim of the common law which says that a man intends the natural consequences of his act. It is not for a man to take a gun and fire into a crowd, and say he did not mean to hurt anybody. The law says he intended the natural consequences of his act."

Following that line of argument, the senator assumed the responsibility of charging me with the personal intention of creating a slave State in Kansas in direct contradiction to my own language on this floor. He had heard me deny that such was the intention of the bill, or of those who voted for it. He had heard me declare that the intention was to leave the people there free to form a slave State or a free State, as they should see proper; but in the teeth of my declaration, and in direct opposition to the terms of the bill, he took upon himself to charge me with an intent to do what he thought would be the result of the act. Now, when I, in turn, apply his own process of reasoning to him, and prove that if his reasoning be true he is guilty of every crime that has disgraced humanity in Kansas, he objects to the application of the rule. He is not willing to be held responsible for the natural consequences of his own action. He is not willing to be judged by the same rule which he professes to be fair when applied to others. Yet he must submit to the application of that rule to himself, or withdraw all he has said against us.

The senator from Maine, this morning, repeated the same declaration of his belief; so did the senator from Massachusetts. Do they expect that we will allow them to attribute designs to us in direct contradiction of our express language, and we refrain from holding them responsible before God and man for all the life that is taken, and the blood which is shed in pursuance of the line of policy they have worked out for the presidential campaign?

We show them that their intentions may be questioned, and motives impugned, as well as ours. This system of violating all the rules and usages of debate by impeaching senators' intentions, contrary to their declaration, they will find is not a pleasant business. I have never impugned a senator's motive except in self-defence, or just retaliation. In this sense I do say, without the least hesitation, that every crime committed in Kansas, every act of violence perpetrated in the Territory, has resulted naturally as the legitimate consequence of the speeches and action of the free-soil senators in this chamber. In your speeches you have told the people of Kansas that the legislature was an unlawful assemblage; that their enactments were not valid laws; that the people were under no obligation, moral or legal, to obey the local laws of the Territory; that the officers appointed to execute the laws had no rightful authority to do so; and that both officers and the laws might be resisted, even unto death, without incurring any responsibility or punishment.

That is the fair construction of every speech you have made. You have, by your speeches, advised bloody resistance to the law and its officers. You now complain that, in making that resistance, blood has been shed and life has been taken. If so, the blood has been shed and the life taken under your direct advice; it is the legitimate consequence of your own acts. Then, when I charge upon you as a party all the consequences of those bloody acts which have stained the history of Kansas, I only charge that which is and was the inevitable consequence of the speeches you have made and the course you have pursued.

Mr. FESSENDEN. Will the Senator state who has made any speech advising bloody resistance? I am not aware of any such. I have made no speech on the subject myself, and therefore the remark does not apply to me; but I have not heard any speeches of the kind.

Mr. DOUGLAS. Each one of the speeches which I have heard from your side of the Chamber has been calculated to encourage and excite resistance to the laws of the Territory.

Mr. FESSENDEN. That is your inference from the speeches.

Mr. DOUGLAS. Yes; and it must have been the inference, also, of every impartial man who has listened to the debates. Denunciations of the legislature of the Territory, and of its enactments, and of the officers of the law, together with eulogies upon the heroic people of Lawrence, and praises of the gallant free State party, have constituted the materials out of which nearly all of your speeches have been manufactured. The fact can neither be denied nor concealed, that the tendency of all such speeches was to stimulate and encourage rebellion against the laws, and resistance to the officers of the Territory. No crime has been perpetrated, no act of violence committed, which cannot find its justification in the speeches of senators. It is difficult to conceive for what purpose those speeches were made, unless it was to excite resistance to the laws of the Territory, and to convince the people of the United States that those laws ought to be successfully resisted. Thus you all counselled violence, and violence resulted from your counsels. It affords me no pleasure to speak in terms of severity of senators; but it is time they learned that they cannot assault me, or question my motives, with impunity.

Mr. President, the senator from New Hampshire has spoken of that great landmark of freedom, the Missouri compromise, which was so sacred that the denunciations of the Bible would rest upon any man who had ever committed the profane act of assisting in its removal. While the senator was pouring forth his eloquent denunciations on the heads of those who have removed the landmark, I sent one of the pages to get me a copy of a speech made by that senator during the discussions of the Compromise measures of 1850. I have the speech before me, and I will read what he then said of the Missouri compromise, and see how far it sustains the sacred character which he now attributes to that measure:

"Mr. Hale. I wish to say a word as a reason why I shall vote against the amendment. I shall vote against 36° 30′ *because I think there is an implication in it.* [Laughter.] I will vote for 37° or 36° either, just as it is convenient; but it is idle to shut our eyes to the fact that here is an attempt in this bill—I will not say it is the intention of the mover—to pledge this Senate and Congress to the imaginary line of 36° 30′, because there are some *historical recollections connected with it in regard to this controversy about slavery.* I will content myself with saying, that *I never will, by vote or speech, admit or submit to any thing that may bind the action of our legislation here to make the parallel of 36° 30′ the boundary line between slave and free territory.* And when I say that, I explain the reason why I go against the amendment."

When the question was presented for consideration whether 36° 30′ should be maintained as the dividing line between freedom and slavery, as the senator calls it, he represented such a dividing line as the worst of all modes of settlement that could be devised. Then he told us with eloquent tongue, and in bold language, appealing to God for the sincerity of his vow, that never would he, by act or speech, recognize the propriety of the line of 36° 30′. Now, when he thinks he can make a point on a political opponent, he speaks of that great covenant of peace, 36° 30′, and of the terrible condemnation threatened by Divine authority on men who remove the landmark, referring to 36° 30′, as a sacred monument between freedom and slavery. I ask him now, if he does not tremble lest the judgment of that just God, whose vengeance he has implored on us, will rest upon himself, for having first derided that measure, which for partisan purposes he now calls sacred? It does not become the senator from New Hampshire to arraign me for having abrogated the line 36° 30′.

While speaking of the territorial laws, condemning many of them, and conceding abuses in the elections for members of the legislature, Mr. Stuart, of Michigan, presented the following views as to the binding effect of the statutes, to wit:

I hold the doctrine in respect to those laws to be this: laws enacted by a legislature elected according to the forms of law, and placed upon a statute book by *courts* and be *executive officers* throughout this whole country, are to be regarded as binding laws, and it is their duty to execute them. It has been decided by the highest tribunals in thy States and the United States, that no court can go behind the law to see whether it was fairly passed or not, and no executive officer called on to execute the law can be permitted to determine for himself its validity. Then, when Senators on this floor have told the people of Kansas from this high place that they were justified in resisting those laws, they have told them what courts, acting in obedience to laws and constitutions, have determined to be criminal ever since civilization began. And yet they say they are not responsible! Men stand here in their places and say to the people of Kansas: "These laws have been forced on you by the people of Missouri; they are irregular; they are of no binding effect, and you are justified in their resistance;" and yet they "wash their hands of all the evils that exist in Kansas."

When it comes to a congressional question, in my judgment it is quite another affair. The authority of Congress put that Territory in a condition to be organized; and if Congress are satisfied that that organization has been irregular, fraudulent, and void, they possess the power clearly and beyond dispute to right the evil and afford a remedy. But, sir, the President of the United States and every executive officer, the Supreme Court of the United States and every judicial officer, is bound to regard those laws while they stand, as the existing *bona fide* laws of the Territory, and they are to be obeyed.

In reference to the character of the bill and the objections made to it, the same gentleman presented the following cogent remarks:

It is presented, therefore, in the existing excited condition of the country, and in the lamentable condition of Kansas, as the only remedy that it is possible to pass. And how is it objected to? Every Senator who has spoken on the other side has acknowledged that upon its face it is a good bill, and that if it could be carried out according to its own terms and provisions, it would execute a good purpose—it would heal the difficulties in Kansas, and reduce things to order and harmony throughout the country. Now, I say to my honorable friend's here—opponents as well as those who think with me—that whenever any man ventures opposition to a bill on the ground that it is to be dishonestly executed, it is an argument which subverts the foundation of all law. Human ingenuity cannot pass a law which is to be effective, if it is not to be honestly and completely executed. If you assume that the courts of the country, the President and the executive officers of the country, will not execute your laws, then you may abandon legislation upon this, and upon all other subjects. I go for this bill upon the belief and upon the expectation that, like all other laws, it will be honestly executed and carried out; and the surrounding circumstances of the country, so far from permitting me to leave them as they are, urge me to forgo the personal wishes which my friends know I had in respect to some amendments to that bill, and to give it my hearty and my full support.

Mr. Pugh concluded a very able discussion of the whole subject with the following cogent and convincing argument in favor of the Senate bill:

The Territory of Kansas is now convulsed by civil war. These Senators themselves proclaim the fact. They represent it as worse, much worse, than I have seen reason to believe. They tell us that the people—our fellow-citizens—men, women, children—are in a condition of horrible distress. What remedies are proposed? None sir, that can be effectual, or satisfactory, except the bill to which the Senate has given its approval. Will those senators defeat the bill? Will their partisans in the other House reject it? I adjure you to consider the consequences. Do you desire peace in Kansas? Do you wish to have a fair election? Do you intend to allow those inhabitants their undoubted rights as American citizens? Then assist in the adoption of the Senate bill. There is nothing else. If you do not assist—if you defeat that bill—if you prolong the sorrowful condition of Kansas—if you stimulate this unnatural controversy to greater lengths—then, I tell you, the curse of every crime which may henceforth be committed there—the blood of every man who may be slain—the honor of every woman who may be violated—will rise up in judgment against you. I will not now make the charge—although as a retort, it would be justifiable—that you desire a continuance of this anarchy, public distress, and civil war, in order that you may influence the results of the presidential election. That, however, is a question for the country at large; and I shall endeavor, in my humble sphere, to make the country understand and appreciate it.

Here is the substantive proposition: That with all the safeguards suggested in either House of Congress, an election is to be held in Kansas—a State government formed—and peace happily restored. What is proposed on the other side? First, the senator from Illinois [Mr. Trumbull] wishes to abolish all the laws of the Territory at once, and thus legitimate the outrages, the bloodshed, the anarchy, which he pretends to deplore. Second, he and his political associates offer to subjugate the citizens of the Territory to a constitution which they never ratified, which was formed without authority of law—and which modestly declares itself unalterable, in any particular for nine years.

Let the people of the United States consider such an issue—ay, sir, let them *decide* it. This involves everything connected with our government, which is worthy of consideration. If passion, prejudice, fanaticism—aided by all the modern arts and adjuncts of falsehood—can so mislead the American people that they will not distinguish good from evil—will no longer respect the fundamental principles of their own government—will rashly mutilate that sacred compact, THE FEDERAL CONSTITUTION, in which all the securities of our Union, our peace, our liberty, our happiness reside—it is of little consequence who may be the next President, and whether Congress should ever again assemble. The experiment of popular institutions will have utterly failed; for, without patriotism, intelligence, virtue, and self-command, a popular government must fall into confusion and despotism at last.

In any event, Mr. President, I can do nothing more. I have sacrificed every scruple, every minor consideration, to an ardent desire for peace. I have gone to the extremity of concession. I have agreed to whatever is honest and fair; and I am yet willing to vote for any amendment or scheme of that character which can be suggested. If the opposition will not meet us in this spirit—if the Senate pacification bill should be rejected by the House—I must discharge myself henceforth of all responsibility as a senator and a citizen. I shall have performed my duty to the uttermost; no blood will be upon my skirts, nor any reproach upon my conscience.

Judge Douglas, in his report of the 11th of August on the House bill for the reorganization of the Territory of Kansas, makes a number of telling points against the practical workings of the Topeka constitution, as adopted by the House of Representatives, which we deem proper to present in addition to those already given. They are substantially as follows, to wit:

First. It incorporates into Kansas a portion of the Cherokee country, which the United States has, by treaty, pledged the faith of the nation should never be incorporated into any State or Territory.

Second. It also incorporates into Kansas about 20,000 square miles of Mexico, establishes slavery therein until 1858, and prohibits it hereafter, in violation of the laws of the country, and of the compromise measures of 1850, which guarantied said Territory should come into the Union with or without slavery, as the people should determine.

Third. It legalizes and establishes slavery in Kansas and over a portion of New Mexico until 1858, and provides that children heretofore born shall be slaves for life, and their posterity after them, providing they are removed into a slave State or Territory prior to 1858.

Fourth. It recognizes the validity of the existing laws in Kansas, and provides for the faithful execution of them, except punishing murder, robbery, larceny, and other crimes.

Fifth. It provides no guard against illegal voting, frauds in conducting the elections, or violence at the polls; but legalizes all such outrages, by declaring that the law under which they could be punished shall not be enforced.

The report recommends the passage of the bill, which has twice passed the Senate, declaring all the obnoxious laws null and void, and allowing the people to form a constitution.

APPENDIX.

SYNOPSIS OF THE SENATE BILL.

The first section of the bill provides for the appointment of five commissioners, to be appointed by the President and confirmed by the Senate, and prescribes the oath to be taken.

SEC. 2. *And be it further enacted,* That it shall be the duty of said commissioners, under such regulations as the Secretary of the Interior may prescribe, to cause to be made a full and faithful enumeration of the legal voters resident in each county in the said Territory on the fourth day of July, eighteen hundred and fifty-six, and make returns thereof during the month of August next, or as soon thereafter as practicable, one of which returns shall be made to the office of the Secretary of the Interior, and one to the Secretary of the Territory of Kansas, and which shall also exhibit the names of all such legal voters, classed in such manner as shall be prescribed by the regulations of the Secretary of the Interior.

SEC. 3. *And be it further enacted,* That it shall be the duty of the Secretary of the Interior, immediately after the passage of this act, to prescribe regulations and forms to be observed in making the enumeration aforesaid, and to furnish the same with all necessary printed blanks to each of the commissioners as soon as may be after their appointment; and the commissioners shall meet without delay at the seat of government in Kansas Territory, and proceed to the discharge of the duties herein imposed upon them, and appoint a secretary to the board, and such other persons as shall be necessary to aid and assist them in taking the enumeration herein provided for, who must also be duly sworn faithfully, impartially, and truly to discharge the duties assigned them by the commissioners.

Section 4th provides for the division of the State into fifty-two representative districts on the basis of the census.

SEC. 5. *And be it further enacted,* That the said board, immediately after the apportionment of the members of said convention, shall cause a sufficient number of copies thereof and of the returns of the census (specifying the name of each legal voter in each county or district) to be published and distributed among the inhabitants of the several counties, and shall transmit one copy of the said apportionment and census, duly authenticated by them, to each clerk of a court of record within the Territory, who shall file the same, and keep open to the inspection of every inhabitant who shall desire to examine it, and shall also cause other copies to be posted up in at least three of the most public places in each voting precinct, to the end that every inhabitant may inspect the same, and apply to the board to correct any error he may find therein, in the manner hereinafter provided.

SEC. 6. *And be it further enacted,* That said board shall remain in session each day, Sundays excepted, from the time of making said apportionment until the twentieth day of October next, at such places as shall be most convenient to the inhabitants of said Territory, and shall proceed to the inspection of said returns, and hear, correct, and finally determine according to the facts, without unreasonable delay, under proper regulations to be made by the board for the ascertainment of disputed facts concerning said enumeration, all questions concerning the omission of any person from said returns, or the improper insertion of any name on said returns, and any other questions affecting the integrity or fidelity of said returns, and for this purpose the said board and each member thereof shall have power to administer oaths and examine witnesses, and compel their attendance in such manner as said board shall deem necessary.

SEC. 7. *And be it further enacted*, That as soon as the said lists of legal voters shall thus have been revised and corrected, it shall be the duty of said board to cause copies thereof to be printed and distributed generally among the inhabitants of the proposed State, and one copy shall be deposited with the clerk of each court of record within the limits of the proposed State, and one copy delivered to each judge of the election, and at least three copies shall be posted up at each place of voting.

SEC. 8. *And be it further enacted*, That an election shall be held for members of a convention to form a constitution for the State of Kansas, according to the apportionment to be made aforesaid, on the first Tuesday after the first Monday in November, eighteen hundred and fifty-six, to be held at such places and to be conducted in such manner, both as to persons who shall superintend such election and the returns thereof as the board of commissioners shall appoint and direct, except in cases by this act otherwise provided; and of such election no person shall be permitted to vote unless his name shall appear on said corrected lists.

SEC. 9. *And be it further enacted*, That the board of commissioners shall have power, and it shall be their duty, to make all needful rules and regulations for the conduct of the said election and the returns thereof. They shall appoint three suitable persons to be judges of the election at each place of voting, and prescribe the mode of supplying vacancies. They shall cause copies of the rules and regulations, with a notice of the places of holding elections and the names of the judges, to be published and distributed in every election district or precinct ten days before the day of election, and shall transmit a copy thereof to the clerk of each court of record, and one copy to each judge of election.

SEC. 10. *And be it further enacted*, That the judges of election shall each, before entering on the discharge of his duties, make oath or affirmation that he will faithfully and impartially discharge the duties of judge of the election according to law, which oath may be administered by any officer authorized by law to administer oaths. The clerks of election shall be appointed by the judges, and shall take the like oath or affirmation, to be administered by one of the judges or by any of the officers aforesaid. Duplicate returns of election shall be made and certified by the judges and clerks, one of which shall be deposited in the office of the clerk of the tribunal transacting county business for the county in which the election is held, and the other shall be transmitted to the board of commissioners, whose duty it shall be to decide, under proper regulations to be made by themselves, who are entitled to certificates of election, and to issue such certificates accordingly, to the persons who, upon examination of the returns and of such proofs as shall be adduced in case of a contest, shall appear to have been duly elected in each county or district: *Provided*, In case of a tie or contest, in which it cannot be satisfactorily determined who was duly elected, said commissioners shall order a new election in like manner as is herein provided. Upon the completion of these duties the said commissioners shall return to Washington, and report their proceedings to the Secretary of the Interior, whereupon the said commission shall cease and determine.

SEC. 11. *And be it further enacted*, That every white male citizen of the United States over twenty-one years of age, who may be a *bona fide* inhabitant of said Territory on the fourth day of July, eighteen hundred and fifty-six, and who shall have resided three months next before said election in the county in which he offers to vote, and no other persons whatever shall be entitled to vote at said election, and any person qualified as a voter may be a delegate to said convention, and no others; and all persons who shall possess the other qualifications for voters under this act, and who shall have been *bona fide* inhabitants of said Territory at any time since its organization, and who shall have absented themselves therefrom in consequence of the disturbances therein, and who shall return before the first day of October next and become *bona fide* inhabitants of the Territory with the intent of making it their permanent home, and shall present satisfactory evidence of these facts to the board of commissioners, shall be entitled to vote at said election, and to have their names placed on said corrected list of voters for that purpose; and to avoid all conflict in the complete execution of this act, all other elections in said Territory are hereby posponed until such time as said convention shall appoint.

SEC. 12. *And be it further enacted*, That the said commissioners, and all persons appointed by them to assist in taking the census, shall have power to administer oaths and examine persons on oath in all cases where it shall be necessary to the full and faithful performance of their duties under this act; and the secretary shall keep a journal of the proceedings of said board, and transmit copies thereof from time to time to the Secretary of the Interior; and when said commissioners shall have completed the business of their appointment, the books and papers of the board shall be deposited in the office of the Secretary of the Territory, and there kept as records of the office.

The 13th, 14th, and 15th sections impose severe penalties of fine and imprisonment for interrupting or abusing the right of suffrage.

Sec. 16. *And be it further enacted*, That the delegates thus elected shall assemble in convention at the capitol of said Territory on the first Monday in December next; and when so assembled, shall first determine by a majority of the whole number of members elected, whether it be or be not expedient at that time to form a constitution and State government, and if deemed expedient, shall proceed to form a constitution and State government, which shall be republican in its form, for admission into the Union on an equal footing with the original States in all respects whatever, by the name of the State of Kansas, with the following boundaries, to wit: beginning on the western boundary of the State of Missouri, where the thirty-seventh parallel of north latitude crosses the same, then west on said parallel to the one hundred and third meridian of longitude, then north on said meridian to the fortieth parallel of latitude, then east on said parallel of latitude to the western boundary of the State of Missouri, then southward with said boundary to the beginning; and until the next congressional apportionment the said State shall have one representative in the House of Representatives of the United States.

Section 17th provides for compensation of commissioners.

Sec. 18. *And be it further enacted*, That inasmuch as the Constitution of the United States and the organic act of said Territory has secured to the inhabitants thereof certain inalienable rights, of which they cannot be deprived by any legislative enactment, therefore no religious test shall ever be required as a qualification to any office or public trust; no law shall be in force or enforced in said Territory respecting an establishment of religion, or prohibiting the free exercise thereof; or abridging the freedom of speech, or of the press; or of the right of the people peaceably to assemble, and petition for the redress of grievances; the right of the people to be secure in their persons, houses, papers, and effects against unreasonable searches and seizures, shall not be violated; and no warrant shall issue but upon probable cause, supported by oath or affirmation, and particularly describing the place to be searched, and the person or things to be seized; nor shall the rights of the people to keep and bear arms be infringed. No person shall be held to answer for a capital or otherwise infamous crime, unless on a presentment or indictment of a grand jury; nor shall any person be subject for the same offence to be twice put in jeopardy of life or limb; nor shall be compelled in any criminal case to be a witness against himself, nor deprived of life, liberty, or property, without due process of law; nor shall private property be taken for public use without just compensation. In all criminal prosecutions, the accused shall enjoy the right to a speedy and public trial by an impartial jury of the district wherein the crime shall have been committed, which district shall have been previously ascertained by law, and to be informed of the nature and cause of the accusation; to be confronted with the witnesses against him; to have compulsory process of obtaining witnesses in his favor, and to have the assistance of counsel for his defence. The privilege of *habeas corpus* shall not be suspended, unless, when in case of rebellion or invasion, the public safety may require it. In suits at common law, where the value in controversy shall exceed twenty dollars, the right of trial by jury shall be preserved, and no fact tried by jury shall be otherwise re-examined in any court of the United States than according to the rules of the com mon law. Excessive bail shall not be required, nor excessive fines imposed, nor cruel and unusual punishment inflicted. No law shall be made or have force or effect in said Territory which shall require a test oath or oath to support any act of Congress or other legislative act as a qualification for any civil office or public trust, or for any employment or profession, or to serve as a juror or vote at an election, or which shall impose any tax upon or condition to the exercise of the right of suffrage by any qualified voter, or which shall restrain or prohibit the free discussion of any law or subject of legislation in the said Territory, or the free expression of opinion thereon by the people of said Territor

NATIONAL DEMOCRATIC COMMITTEE ROOMS,
August 1st, 1856.

TO JOHN C. RIVES, ESQ.,
Official Reporter and Publisher of Debates in Congress.

SIR: As a speech delivered by Mr. Buchanan in the Senate of the United States in 1840, on the Independent Treasury Bill, has been the subject of extensive misrepresentation, and has given rise to what is familiarly known as the "ten cent calumny," I desire you, on behalf of the National Committee, to publish in pamphlet form for general circulation the speech referred to, that the intelligent voters of the country may have the opportunity of reading it and of pronouncing their own judgment upon it. Yours,

CHAS. JAS. FAULKNER,
Chairman, Nat. D. R. C.

The following is the speech which is made the occasion of the charge against Mr. Buchanan. It was made in the Senate of the United States the 22d January, 1840, and may be found at page 129 of the Appendix to the Congressional Globe, 1st session of the 26th Congress.

Washington, 2d Aug., 1856.

JOHN C. RIVES,
Publisher of the Congressional Globe.

INDEPENDENT TREASURY.

SPEECH

OF

HON. JAMES BUCHANAN,

OF PENNSYLVANIA.

IN THE SENATE OF THE UNITED STATES, JANUARY 22, 1840, ON THE INDEPENDENT TREASURY BILL; IN REPLY TO MR. CLAY, OF KENTUCKY.

Mr. BUCHANAN said:

Mr. PRESIDENT: It is not my purpose, on the present occasion, to go very much at length into a discussion of the provisions of this bill. I intend, in a great degree, indeed almost exclusively, to confine myself to a reply, or at least to an attempt to reply, to the remarks of the Senator from Kentucky, [Mr. CLAY.]

In all discussions, if we desire to arrive at a satisfactory conclusion, it is absolutely necessary that we should distinctly understand what is the question to be discussed. Then let me ask, what is the nature and character of the Independent Treasury bill now before the Senate?

Since the origin of the Government, our own responsible officers have always collected the public revenue, and have always disbursed the public revenue. Heretofore, during the intermediate space of time between its collection and its disbursement, it has been deposited with banking corporations. The object of this bill is to provide that our own responsible officers shall be substituted as depositaries, instead of these banking corporations; and that these officers shall hereafter not only collect and disburse the public money as they have always done, but that they shall also have the custody of it between its collection and disbursement.

Under the provisions of this bill, every officer throughout the United States who receives public money is constituted a depository. But there are certain points where very large sums of public money are collected, or are disbursed, or both; and at these points, both the security of the revenue and the public convenience required that there should be depositaries distinct from, and independent of, the collecting officers. These points are Philadelphia, New Orleans, New York, Boston, Charleston, and St. Louis. Accordingly, the bill proposes to convert the Mint at Philadelphia and Branch Mint at New Orleans into places of public deposit, and intrusts the custody of the public money to the Treasurers of these institutions respectively; and it creates sub-treasuries, each to be under the contrôl of a receiver general, at New York, at Boston, at Charleston, and at St. Louis.

Thus far, sir, it will be perceived that this bill makes no change in the settled policy of the country except merely to provide that the public money, in the intermediate time, between its receipt in the Treasury and its disbursement, shall be intrusted to our own responsible officers, instead of irresponsible corporations.

In addition to these provisions the bill contains what has been commonly denominated the specie clause. This section provides that one fourth of the dues of the Government shall be collected in gold and silver, after the 30th of June, 1840; one half after the 30th of June 1841; three fourths after the 30th of June, 1842; and after the 30th of June, 1843, all the revenue of the Government shall be collected and all its disbursements shall be made in gold and silver coin.

Now, sir, when separated from the details necessary to carry these principles into execution. this is the bill, the whole bill, and nothing but the bill which has excited so much unnecessary alarm throughout the country.

In discussing this bill the Senator from Kentucky has divided his remarks into two general heads. He has first considered the bill according to what its friends say it is; and in the second place, has discussed it according to what he himself believes it to be. In my reply I shall invert this order, because it is necessary first to prove that the Senator himself has entirely mistaken the nature and effects of the measure, and that its friends entertain a just conception of its character.

The Senator held up the bill triumphantly to public view, and declared that it contained within its provisions a great Government treasury bank. Now, if I cannot make it manifest as the light of day that in this proposition he is entirely mistaken, I shall then agree to surrender the whole argument. The Senator has had an unsuccessful chase, through the provisions of this bill, after the lurking monster. Had he succeeded in dragging him into light I should have been one of the first men in the country to assist in putting him to instant death. But,

> "He must have optics sharp, I ween,
> Who sees what is not to be seen."

This, I think, has been the case with the Senator from Kentucky.

Now, sir, what is a bank? According to the usual acceptation of the word, in our country, it performs three offices. It receives deposits, it loans money upon discounts, and it issues a paper currency. I acknowledge that, in order to constitute a bank, it is not necessary that it should perform all these three functions. There are banks of discount and deposit merely, and there are also banks of deposit and issue only; and this latter class of banks are the most secure of any in the world, when the deposits are confined to the precious metals, and the issues, in the form of certificates, do not exceed the sums actually deposited. Such was the bank of Amsterdam, and such is now the bank of Hamburg. It would be difficult to form an idea of a bank of issue alone, without deposits or discounts, although I know, from the utter inability of the Bank of England to regulate the paper currency of that kingdom, the question has been seriously considered whether one bank of issue ought to be established, and whether all other banks ought not to be prohibited from emitting paper currency. It is certain that, at the present moment, a bank of issue, purely as a bank of issue, does not exist on the face of the earth. Now, sir, this bill does not authorize the public depositaries to receive money from individuals on deposit; and it not only does not authorize them to loan the public money entrusted to their care, but it makes such an act a felony, punishable by fine and imprisonment. This bill, then, clearly does not create a bank either of deposit or of discount, and the Senator has not contended for any such proposition. He has confined himself to prove that it will create a bank of issue; and I shall examine this proposition a little more in detail.

And, in the first place, if there be a bank lurking in the bill, then we have had a Treasury bank in full operation ever since the origin of the Government, without having the least idea of its existence until the Senator from Kentucky made the discovery. There has been no period of time, since General Washington was first inaugurated in 1789, until the present day, when the Treasurer of the United States did not draw his warrants, either on banks or receiving officers in favor of disbursing officers or creditors of the Government. Without this power the Treasury Department could not exist. Debts could not be paid to individuals, neither could the public revenue be applied to accomplish the objects contemplated by the Constitution. There is no other conceivable mode of conducting this branch of the public business. The bill makes no change whatever in this ancient and necessary practice, except to impose an important limitation upon it which has never heretofore existed; and yet, according to the Senator from Kentucky, it creates a bank of issue; and the drafts drawn by the Treasurer on the public depositaries in favor of public creditors and disbursing officers, are to be the paper currency which it will throw into circulation. This is the sum and substance of his whole argument on this point. He might with the same reason contend, that, if an individual in extensive business had deposits in several banks, and was in the habit of paying his debts and advancing money to his agents by drawing drafts upon these banks, that, therefore, he himself had established a bank of issue. The cases are precisely analogous.

In what part of this bill has the Senator discovered the charter of his bank? He has referred to one, and only one clause, for the purpose of proving its existence. This is to be found in the tenth section of the bill, and, as it is very brief, I shall read it to the Senate. It is as follows:

> "And for the purpose of payments on the public account, it shall be lawful for the Treasurer of the United States to draw upon any of the said depositaries, as he may think most conducive to the public interest, or to the convenience of the public creditors, or both."

There, sir, is the charter; and what is it but a mere recognition of the power which I have just been describing, and which has existed, and must necessarily have existed, ever since the origin of the Government. It requires the Treasurer of the United States to consult both the public interest and the convenience of the public creditor, or both, in selecting the depositary on which to draw his warrant. This he has always done. In the first place he must select a depositary with whom there is an amount of money sufficient to meet the draft; and among such depositaries he must, unless the public interest forbids, draw upon that one where it will be most convenient for the public creditor to receive his money. Why, sir, this clause, so terrific to the imagination of the gentleman, might be stricken from the bill altogether, without producing the slightest inconvenience. The practice which it prescribes, is that which must necessarily be pursued in paying the debts of the Government. And yet this simple and necessary power, is the only part of the bill on which the Senator relies to establish his great Treasury bank!

But I said that this bill contained an important limitation which had never heretofore existed. This was introduced at the special session of 1837, upon my own suggestion. It was then apprehended that the holders of these Treasury warrants might not present them for payment within a reasonable time; and that a large amount of them might remain outstanding, and be used as bills of exchange. As these outstanding drafts would necessarily represent an equal amount of gold and silver in the hands of the depositaries, it was apprehended that, unless they were speedily presented for payment, a mass of them might continue floating in the community, and thus produce an accumulation of specie in the hands of the depositaries which might prove injurious to the banks. To prevent this evil—to render the draft upon the banks for specie as light as possible—and to cause the gold and silver to flow out of the Treasury into general circulation, as rapidly as it had flowed into it, this amendment was adopted. It now constitutes the twenty-third section of the bill, and is as follows:

"SEC. 23. *And be it further enacted*, That it shall be the duty of the Secretary of the Treasury to issue and publish regulations to enforce the speedy presentation of all Government drafts for payment at the place where payable, and to prescribe the time, according to the different distances of the depositories from the seat of Government, within which all drafts upon them, respectively, shall be presented for payment; and, in default of such presentation, to direct any other mode and place of payment which he may deem proper. But in all those regulations and directions, it shall be the duty of the Secretary of the Treasury to guard, as far as may be, against those drafts being used, or thrown into circulation, as a paper currency or medium of exchange."

One might have supposed, from the extreme horror of the gentleman lest this bill might contain a Treasury bank, that he would have been delighted with the provisions of this section. Not so. On the contrary, he has declared, in the most solemn manner, that it confers a tremendous power on the Secretary of the Treasury, to which no people, jealous of their liberties, ought to submit. The Senator is hard to please. He first denounces, in the strongest terms, the tenth section of the bill, because the Treasury drafts issued under its authority will, in his opinion, become the circulating medium of his Treasury bank; and almost at the very next breath, he denounces, in terms equally strong, the very section which renders it impossible that they ever can become such a circulating medium.

And what is this tremendous power vested in the Secretary of the Treasury by the twenty-third section? Independently of postmasters, there are perhaps a hundred and fifty receivers of public money in the United States. These are scattered from Maine to Georgia, and from the Atantic to the far West. Some of them are at the distance of fifty miles, and others are a thousand miles from Washington. From the nature and necessity of the case, the discretionary power is conferred upon the Secretary to regulate the "speedy presentation" of these drafts, according to the different distances of the depositaries from the seat of Government; but even this is to be done in such a manner as to prevent them from being thrown into circulation as a paper currency or medium of exchange. And yet this is the tremendous power so much to be dreaded! No other provisions could have been made. It would have been a work of endless and unnecessary labor to have attempted to enumerate each of the depositaries in the bill, and to have prescribed the time within which drafts on each of them should be presented for payment. This is a mere matter of detail which must be yielded to the discretion of the Secretary.

And now what, in plain English, is this Government bank? It is no other than the power which has always been exercised by the Treasurer of the United States, to pay the public creditors, and to advance money to the disbursing officers by means of drafts on the public depositaries; with a new restriction, however, imposed upon the holders of these drafts, requiring their speedy presentation, for the express purpose of preventing the possibility of their ever becoming a circulating medium. Any man who can distinguish between a hawk and a handsaw, can discriminate between this simple provision and a great Government Treasury bank.

The Senator, feeling that he has no foundation on which to erect his Treasury bank in the bill as it is, has taxed his fancy—a never-failing resource—to alarm our fears as to what it will become hereafter. He leaves the present far behind and looks forward to the future. He predicts that in less than three years necessity will compel us to change the Independent Treasury into a bank of issue. Having given his fancy the reins, he tells us how this will be performed. The Secretary of the Treasury, instead of giving single drafts on the depositaries for the amount due to public creditors, and the sums to be advanced to disbursing officers, is to have drafts prepared upon bank paper, in the likeness of bank notes, of the denomination of twenty, of fifty, and of a hundred dollars. These drafts he is to pay out like bank paper. The restriction is to be repealed requiring their speedy presentation to the depositaries. They are to become the general circulating medium of the country. In less than ten years the receivers general are to have between forty and fifty millions of gold and silver in their vaults, to be represented by the same amount of Treasury drafts in circulation and in the possession of the banks. The Government then calculating that the demand upon these depositaries will not require them to keep this amount of specie on hand, will draw it out clandestinely for their own purposes, as was formerly done from the Bank of Amsterdam; and that some future President will, by means of this stolen money, subvert the Government and destroy the liberties of the people.

Now, sir, is not this the merest fancy picture that was ever sketched? It is all the offspring of the Senator's own prolific imagination. It is all prophecy, and no fact. Even by his own showing, there is no foundation for it in the bill. On the contrary, every precaution has been used to prevent the possibility of any such occurrences.

And what reason has he to predict that the friends of this measure will change all their principles and purposes in less than three years, and by new legislation convert the Independent Treasury into a government bank? Has not every Senator perceived the holy horror with which my friend from Missouri [Mr. BENTON] was inspired at the bare idea that the Government might ever issue "notes, bills, or paper," receivable in payment of the public dues? His lynx-eyed jealousy seized hold of these general expressions in the 19th and 20th sections of the bill, and although there was nothing on the face of the earth on which these words could operate, unless possibly on some straggling Treasury note which might remain unredeemed long after it became payable, yet he had them stricken from the bill. "He snuffed the tainted breeze" from afar; and although there was no present danger, yet he saw a possibility that these words might have a meaning hereafter; and that in future years the Government might be willing to issue "notes, bills, or paper," and therefore we all united with him in voting for his amendment. This was, in the phrase of the lawyers, the exclusion of any conclusion which might by possibility be drawn from these general words in favor of Government paper.

But again; did not the Senator from Kentucky perceive with what alacrity the friends of the bill supported the amendment of his colleague, [Mr. CRITTENDEN,] imposing it upon the Secretary of the Treasury as a solemn duty, to take care, in his regulations for the speedy presentation of Government drafts to the depositaries, that these drafts, as far as may be, shall never be used as a paper currency or medium of exchange?

Suppose it were possible that the Secretary of the Treasury, without authority, and in the very face of the provisions of this bill, and the known and avowed opinion of its friends, should, as the Senator supposes he might, circulate these Government drafts in the form of bank paper, and of the denomination of twenty, fifty, and a hundred dollars; what do you think would be the consequence? He would instantly be deprived of his office for this daring violation of law, and would be justly held up to public execration. In justice to that officer, I ought to say that I am not one of those who consider it possible that he could ever dream of pursuing such a course, without the express authority of Congress; and I may venture to predict, with unerring certainty, that such an authority will never be conferred upon him by the present party in power. But even if he should thus violate his duty, whilst the twenty-third section of this bill shall remain in force, these drafts never could become a general circulating medium; and, therefore, there could never be, as the Senator supposes, an accumulation of forty-five or fifty millions of dollars in the hands of the depositaries. But even if this miracle should be accomplished, and a future President should attempt to embezzle this money, for the purpose of subverting the Government, there would still be one most unpleasant obstacle in his way. He would then, under the provisions, of this bill, be guilty of felony, and would be transferred from the White House to the penitentiary. The truth is that, "these hydras, gorgons, and chimeras dire," exist only in the Senator's imagination.

The Senator, in a triumphant tone, exclaimed that, by the passage of the bill, the union of the purse with the sword will be consummated in the hands of the President. This, if true, would indeed be fearful. It would be the death-knell of civil liberty in this country. Wheresoever the power over the purse and the sword is united in the hands of one man, there the Government is despotic. If any Executive Magistrate, be he King, or be he President, possess the sole power to declare war, to raise armies, to impose taxes, and to expend the public money at his pleasure, there must be an end of civil liberty in that country. This, and this alone, is what I understand to be a union of the sword and the purse. But under our Constitution and laws the President neither has, nor ever can have, the power over either. Can he declare war? No, sir; the Constitution expressly confers this power upon Congress. Can he enlist soldiers? No, sir; he could not raise a single company to go to Florida, because Congress alone have the power to raise and support armies. Can he impose taxes upon the people, or borrow money? No, sir; Congress is exclusively vested with the power of laying taxes and borrowing money. But after this money shall have reached the Treasury, can he apply a dollar of it to any use, public or private? No, sir; no money can be drawn from the Treasury but in consequence of appropriations made by Congress. Nay, more; if the President were so far to forget the duties of his high station, as to enter into a collusion with any of the depositaries, and draw one dollar of public money out of their possession, he would, like any other citizen, subject himself to fine and imprisonment. And this is the union of the purse and the sword, which the Senator has so feelingly described! This phrase, I thought, had had its day, and had passed into oblivion; but the Senator has again conjured up the specter, for the purpose of alarming our fears.

The Senator tells us that he has been warring in vain for the last seven years against the extension of executive power and influence. Now, sir, if he had informed us that he had been warring against the Executive, but in favor of an increase of executive power and influence, in my humble opinion he would have come much nearer the mark. It is, perhaps, the strangest spectacle which has ever been presented on the face of the earth, that in this war between the Executive and the Senator's political party, he has been endeavoring to deprive himself of power, whilst they have been struggling to prevent him from making this self-sacrifice.

Let me remind the Senator of a few instances; and first, in regard to internal improvements. I happened to be a member of the other House during the administration of Mr. Adams. I do not intend now to cast any censure upon that Administration. I speak merely of historical facts. In those days, by virtue of an act of Congress, the President exercised the discretionary power of making as many surveys for internal improvements as he thought proper, all of which, it was hoped by those interested, would, at some future day, be constructed by the General Government. Splendid projects of such improvements were presented to dazzle the fancy, and excite the cupidity, of almost every man in the country. Our engineers were constantly traversing the Union from east to west, and from north to south; and before they were arrested in their career, the estimated cost of completing the improvements which they had surveyed or projected, if my memory serves me, amounted to more than one hundred millions of dollars. Here was a vast field for executive influence and power. The fat jobs which might have been bestowed on favorites; the actual expenditure of immense sums of money, and the alluring hope presented by the mere survey of any railroad, turnpike road, or canal, in which masses of people felt an interest; all, all contributed to swell the tide of executive influence. Now, sir, was there ever a lure more tempting to executive ambition than this power of pouring out the public treasure to benefit, and, in their estimation, to bless a large proportion of the people of this country? What was the conduct of the old Roman in regard to this question? For the good of his country, he sacrificed all this power and all this patronage. His veto of the Maysville road bill arrested the whole system; and, strange as it may seem, a portion of the gentlemen's seven years' war against the Executive, consisted in denouncing this voluntary surrender of executive power and influence, as ruinous to the best interest of the country.

Again: the very bill now before the Senate, against which the gentleman has been warring, is one of the strongest proofs which the present Chief Magistrate could give, that he is willing to abandon a large portion of executive influence. In 1837, there were between eighty and ninety Government deposit banks, scattered over every State in the Union. What an immense political power might have been exercised by the President, *through the agency of these banks!* We know, from letters read at the called session, that they were not very scrupulous, "where thrift would follow fawning." Affiliated as they were, if the President had been disposed to exert an improper influence over them, they might have been used with prodigious effect to accomplish his purposes. The selection of these depositaries, the amount of the public money which they should receive, how long they should retain it, and in what manner they should conduct their business—all, all was left to executive discretion. What a boundless field for executive influence is that which the present President now desires to abandon! And yet the Senator, both at the called session, and the session succeeding it, warred in favor of compelling him to retain in his hands this unbounded source of political patronage and power. He preferred then, and, such is his detestation for the present bill, would, I presume, even now prefer the deposit-bank system to the Independent Treasury.

Can any man, in sober earnest, compare the influence which the Executive will acquire, under this bill, by the appointment of four receivers general of public money with that over this affiliated league of State banks, which he now desires to abandon? Think ye, sir, that if any of the leading officers of Government, or any of the favored minions of executive power, had desired a loan from one of these banks, that he would have asked in vain? Under the Independent Treasury bill, such favors can never be extended without subjecting both the officer granting them, and the recipient, to punishment in the penitentiary.

The Senator complains that the power of removal from office should exist in the President, and says that he is not at all satisfied with the argument in the first Congress on which it was rested. This power has been exercised, without interruption, ever since 1789. It is not, then, a recent usurpation. The first Congress of the United States which ever assembled, by their construction of the Constitution, solemnly declared that the power of removal was vested in the President; and many of the members of this Congress had themselves been members of the Federal Convention. Since the gentleman addressed the Senate, I have examined the debate, and particularly Mr. Madison's remarks upon this subject, and I think they ought to prove satisfactory to every mind. He sketches the argument in favor of the power with a master's hand.

How could the President execute the laws at all, if this power did not exist? Suppose he should discover that one of the receivers general created by this very bill was applying the public money to his own use—if he were deprived of the power of removing him from office, he might be obliged to look patiently on and suffer him to embezzle millions. Suppose a foreign minister were violating his instructions, and betraying the best interests of his country abroad—what is to be done? Without the exercise of this power, the President would be compelled to wait until the mischief might be entirely consummated—until the country might be ruined—before he could recall this corrupt or wicked minister. I might present a hundred similar instances. This power is essential to the performance of the duty imposed upon the President of seeing that the laws are faithfully executed. Without it he would be deprived of the necessary means of executing this high trust reposed in him by the Constitution. It is, therefore, wonderful how the existence of this power could ever have been seriously contested.

If this power of removal did not exist in the President, it would follow as a necessary consequence that the Senate must remain in permanent session for the purpose of sanctioning removals from office, as they might become necessary, throughout this vast and growing country. The public interest imperiously demands that some power should always exist competent instantly to remove all officers the moment they are discovered to be betraying their trust. But the Constitution never contemplated that the Senate should be in session permanently. Heaven forbid that this should ever be the case! After having been in the political atmosphere of Washington for six months, it is necessary that we should go home to mingle with our constitutents, and to breathe the pure air of the country. The American people never will consent, and never ought to consent, that our sessions shall become permanent.

Having now replied to all the arguments adduced by the Senator under his second general head; and having, I think, demonstrated that the bill contains no Government Treasury bank, I shall proceed to reply to those which he urged under the first general head. It will be recollected that this was to consider the bill according to the construction placed upon it by its friends, which, I have endeavored to prove, is the true construction.

Before I address myself directly to the Senator's argument, allow me to indulge in some general observations.

What has been the financial history of this country for the last twenty-five years? I can speak with positive knowledge upon this subject during the period of eighteen years since I first came into public life. It has been a history of constant vibration—of extravagant expansions in the business of the country, succeeded by ruinous contractions. At successive intervals many of the best and most enterprising men of the country have been crushed. They have fallen victims at the shrine of the insatiate and insatiable spirit of extravagant banking and speculation. Starting at the extreme point of depression of one of these periods, we find that the country has been glutted with foreign merchandise, and it requires all our efforts to pay the debt thus contracted to foreign nations. At this crisis the banks can do nothing to relieve the people. In order to preserve their own existence, they are compelled to contract their loans and their issues. In the hour of distress, when their assistance is most needed, they can do nothing for their votaries. Every article sinks in price, men are unable to pay their debts, and wide-spread ruin pervades the land. During the first year of the cycle, we are able to import but comparatively little foreign merchandise, and this affords the country an opportunity of recruiting its exhausted energies. The next year the patient begins to recover. Domestic manufactures flourish in proportion as foreign goods become scarce. The industry and enterprise of our citizens have been exerted with energy, and our productions have liquidated the foreign debt. The third year, a fair business is done. The country presents a flourishing appearance. The banks, relieved from the drains of specie required for foreign export, begin once more to expand, and tempt the unwary to their ruin. Property of all descriptions commands a fair price. The fourth or the fifth year the era of extravagant banking and speculation returns again to be succeeded by another ruinous revulsion.

This was the history of the country up till 1837. Since then we have traveled the road to ruin much more rapidly than in former years. Before that period it had required from three to six years to get up an expansion and its corresponding explosion. We have now witnessed the astounding fact that we can pass through all these changes, and even from one suspension of specie payments to another, in little more than two years.

It is curious to observe with how much accuracy you can read the ever changing condition of this country in the varied amount of our importations. The year 1836 was one of vast expansion, and produced the explosion and suspension of specie payments in 1837. The imports were greatly diminished in 1837, being less than they had been in 1836, by nearly $50,000,000. In 1838, they had sunk down to $27,000,000 less than they had been in 1837, and nearly $77,000,000 less than they were in 1836. In 1839, we had another expansion, and our imports were $44,000,000 greater than they had been in 1838. This expansion preceded the explosion and suspension of specie payments in the month of October last. Thus we have become such skilful architects of ruin, that a single year was sufficient to prepare the late explosion.

There never has existed a nation on earth, except our own, that could endure such rapid and violent expansions and contractions. It is the buoyancy of youth; it is the energies of our population; it is the spirit which never quails before difficulties, which enables us to endure such shocks without utter ruin. Yes, sir, a difference in the amount of our imports between the years 1836 and 1838, of $77,000,000, is sufficient to excite the astonishment of the world.

What causes operated chiefly to produce this speedy recurrence of the second explosion and the second suspension of specie payments? Three may be mentioned. In the first place, after the bank suspension of 1837, every person who was friendly to well-regulated banks, if such a thing be possible under the present system, ardently desired that the different State Legislatures might impose upon them some wholesome restrictions. It was expected that they would be compelled to keep a certain amount of specie in their vaults in proportion to their circulation and deposits; that the foundation of a specie basis for our paper currency should be laid by prohibiting the circulation of bank notes at the first under the denomination of ten, and afterwards under that of twenty dollars; that the amount of their dividends should be limited; and, above all, that upon the occurrence of another suspension, their doors should be closed at once, and their affairs be placed in the hands of commissioners. The different Legislatures met. Much indignation was expressed at the conduct of the banks. They were severely threatened; but at last they proved too powerful for the people. Indeed, it would almost seem as if most of the State Legislatures had met for no other purpose than to legalize the previous suspension of specie payments. No efficient restrictions were imposed; and the banks were thus taught that they might thereafter go unpunished—unwhipped of justice. Past impunity prevented them from reducing their business and curtailing their profits in such a manner as to render them secure in the day of trial. They have fallen again; I fear again to enjoy the same impunity.

In the second place, the immense amount of money loaned to many of the States in England, a large portion of which was brought home in the form of foreign merchandise, afforded great facilities for over-trading, or, rather, over-buying.

And in the third place, the conduct of the Bank of the United States greatly tended to produce these excessive importations. That institution became the broker for the sale of all State bonds in Europe. It endeavored to monopolize the entire cotton trade of the country; and it drew bills of exchange on England most freely at moderate rates, against the proceeds of these bonds and of its cotton. Every temptation was thus presented to speculations in foreign merchandise.

These three causes combining have occasioned a second suspension of specie payments within two years after the first, and produced that bloated credit system, from the wreck of which our country is now deeply suffering.

I most heartily concur with the Senator from Kentucky in one of his positions. We certainly produce too little and import too much. Our expanded credit system is the great cause of this calamity. Confine it within safe and reasonable bounds, and this disastrous effect will no longer be produced. It is not in the power of Congress to do much towards a consummation so desirable. Still we shall do all we can; and the present bill will exercise some influence in restraining the banks from making extravagant loans and emitting extravagant issues.

What effect has this bloated system of credit produced upon the morals of the country? In the large commercial cities it has converted almost all men of business into gamblers. Where is there now to be found the old-fashioned importing merchant, whose word was as good as his bond, and who was content to grow rich, as our fathers did, by the successive and regular profits of many years of patient industry? Such men were the glory and pride of commerce, and elevated the character of their country both at home and abroad. I ask, where are they? Is not the race almost extinct? All now desire to grow rich rapidly. Each takes his chance in the lottery of speculation. Although there may be a hundred chances to one against him, each, eagerly intent upon the golden prize, overlooks the intervening rocks and quicksands between him and it, and when he fondly thinks he is about to clutch it, he sinks into bankruptcy and ruin. Such has been the fate of thousands of our most enterprising citizens.

If the speculator should prove successful, and win the golden prize, no matter by what means he may have acquired his wealth, this clothes him with honor and glory. Money, money, money, confers the highest distinction in society. The republican simplicity and virtue of a Macon would be subjects of ridicule in Wall street or Chestnut street. The highest talents, directed by the purest patriotism, moral worth, literary and professional fame, in short, every quality which ought to confer distinction in society, sink into insignificance when compared with wealth. Money is equivalent to a title of nobility in our larger commercial cities. This is the effect of our credit system.

We have widely departed from the economical habits and simple virtues of our forefathers. These are the only sure foundations upon which our republican institutions can rest. The desire to make an ostentatious display of rapidly acquired wealth, has produced a splendor and boundless expense unknown in former times. There is now more extravagance in our large commercial cities, than exists in any portion of the world which I have ever seen, except among the wealthy nobility of England. Thank Heaven, this extravagance has but partially reached the mountains and valleys of the interior. The people there, so far as their potential voice can be heard, are determined to put an end to this bloated credit system, which threatens to involve not only their private fortunes, but their political liberties in ruin.

After the revulsion in 1837—after the banks had blown up, and left the Government without a dollar, the President found it necessary to convene Congress. It then became indispensable to take a new departure. The course which ought to be pursued was the question. The banks had betrayed our trust; they had converted our money into rags, by a species of alchemy the very reverse of that which was attempted in former times, of converting baser things into gold. The President then recommended an absolute divorce between bank and State, and his political friends in Congress cordially responded to this recommendation. We then gave our banner to the breeze, with the motto of an Independent Treasury inscribed upon it. Have we not firmly and immovably maintained our position? Had we been the cormorants after office which our enemies have described us to be, we should have yielded our convictions, when we found one State after another abandoning our standard. Neither the love of power nor of place made us falter. We did not yield to the panic of the moment. We have ever since kept this issue distinctly before the people, honestly believing that a separation of the Government from banks was necessary to promote the best and dearest interests of the country. In the opinion of our political opponents, we stood self-immolated. But the people have at length gloriously come to the rescue. The Senator is entirely mistaken in supposing this bill to be unpopular. In every instance, during the elections of the last year, when the question of an Independent Treasury was distinctly made before the people, the result has been either the election of the Administration candidates, or a greatly increased number of votes in their favor. Is it not certain, that if the congressional elections in those States which elected their members in 1838, had been postponed until 1839, we should now be in a triumphant majority in the other House? The Whig party know this; and I am greatly mistaken in the signs of the times, if they have not determined that this bill shall pass. They will no longer give us the battle cry of an Independent Treasury. The bill is destined to become a law during the present session. I prophesy this result, and prophesy it solely upon my opinion of the sagacity of the Whig party. It is possible I may be mistaken, but if I should, I shall have one consolation in my disappointment. If my political existance depended upon the result, I should rather have the success of the Independent Treasury identified with the reëlection of Mr. Van Buren, than any other argument which can be used in his favor. It alone would be sufficient to defeat the hero of Tippecanoe.

Now, sir, great changes have taken place in public opinion since September, 1837. The prominent arguments then urged upon this floor against the Independent Treasury bill have nearly all vanished away. We now hear no more of a system of well-regulated specie-paying State banks to act as Government depositories. The half-way house has been abandoned. The accommodations there are no longer good. It is in a ruinous condition, and can no longer shelter those who formerly took refuge in it. The banks have blown up twice within little more than two years, and thus blown this argument of their friends sky-high. No statesman, after our recent experience, would now think of placing the people's treasure with the banks on general deposit for safe-keeping.

Far different is the independent Treasury. It presents every guarantee which can be afforded for the safety and security of the public money. It will be in the custody of officers appointed by the Government, responsible to the Government, and punishable as felons for every violation of their trust. In the day of danger, when the country is involved in war, the money will always be ready: and at such a crisis, the banks would almost certainly suspend specie payments. Besides they are mere State institutions, over which we have no control; and they may, when they please, convert our money into rags, and then place us at defiance. They are beyond the reach of punishment under our authority. The Federal Government cannot justly be considered independent if we must resort to State banks, or to any other power except our own, for the purpose of keeping the money raised from the people by taxation until it can be applied to execute the great powers conferred upon us by the Constitution.

Again: public opinion has annihilated another argument against the Independent Treasury. The Senator from South Carolina [Mr. Preston,] in March, 1838, in his tenderness towards the State banks, and for the purpose of enabling them to resume specie payments, proposed that we should, for a limited period, receive their irredeemable paper in the payment of dues to the Government. Much eloquence was also formerly wasted upon the extreme cruelty of having one currency for the Government and another for the people. Thank God! we hear no more of all this. No person now contends that, under any circumstances, the Government ought to receive depreciated bank paper. Such fantasies have proved too light for earth. They have risen to the moon, where it is said the crude notions of speculative politicians are still floating about, and have a local habitation and a name.

The Senator charges us with having employed the State banks as depositaries, and having commended their conduct in the highest terms. This was a grievous sin, and grievously have we answered it. The difference between him and us is this: that after they had shown themselves to be utterly unworthy of our confidence, we abandoned them; but at that moment he clasped them to his bosom. Admitting that there has been inconsistency on both sides, the state of the fact is this: we adopted the State banks; they betrayed us, and we cast them off forever. The Opposition denounced this system in the beginning, and prophesied that it would prove a failure; but at the very moment when their prediction was verified, they embraced these castaways themselves with all the ardor of lovers. These banks, as depositories of the public money, are now repudiated by all parties. Their day has passed, and we shall hear little more of them in connection with this subject.

All men are wise after the fact, but, to look back, it has often occurred to me as wonderful how we could ever have confided in the State banks as safe general depositories of the public treasure. Our system of banking is the very worst, and the most irresponsible that has ever existed on the face of the earth. The charters of these banks nowhere impose any efficient restraints upon the first instinct of their nature, which is to make as much money for their stockholders as possible. They will, therefore, always expand their credits and their issues in the day of delusive prosperity, without regarding the approaching storm. The immense deposits of the Government increased this fatal tendency; whilst the public money was freely loaned, and its security placed at hazard, for the benefit of their stockholders, but for the ruin of the country. The wonder, perhaps, ought rather to be that they held out so long, than that they should have finally exploded.

In 1836, the immense amount of these deposits had stimulated them almost to madness. The expansion was then great beyond all former example. Speculation reigned throughout the land. The suspicions of the country were aroused against the Government, and the banks were charged with granting peculiar favors to men high in office, and to influential partisans of the Administration. They were denominated "the pet banks." Such was the general sense of the insecurity of the public money, in their possession, and such the jealousy which existed among the people, in consequence of their connection with the Government, that I verily believe the present Chief Magistrate would never have been elected, had it not been for the passage of the deposit bill. The adoption of this measure was a choice of evils; but it was a much less evil than to have left nearly $40,000,000 of the public money in possession of the banks. Under the Independent Treasury system, we shall never again be placed in such a fearful dilemma.

I was very much astonished that he had no homily from the Senator against the specie clause of the bill. Even this seems to have lost much of its terrors. It is no longer the terrific monster which was to devour all the banks and establish a pure metallic currency for all the transactions of all the people of the United States.

There could be no Independent Treasury without this clause. If you were to receive bank notes in payment of the public dues, and retain them in your possession, you would, in this manner, encourage the banks as much to make extravagant expansions, as though you placed the same amount with them on general deposit. Besides, you would thus confer a dangerous power upon the Secretary of the Treasury, enabling him to favor some banks and to ruin others; and even if this power should not be abused, suspicion would always surround its exercise. You must separate from the banks in every particular. Evils, both to them and to the country, will follow from the least connection with them. Besides, if you receive bank notes at all, to the extent of the amount which you hold on hand, you incur the very same risk of having them converted into irredeemable paper by an explosion of the banks, as if they held them on general deposit.

The Senator commenced his speech by presenting us the most gloomy picture of national distress. He predicted that this distress would continue to increase during the present year, and that it would affect all classes of the community. The suffering, he thinks, will be peculiarly severe during the approaching summer. I might say to him,

"Thy wish was father, Harry, to the thought."

I do not believe, however, he would desire that the people should suffer in order to accomplish any political purpose. But if, without contributing to this result himself, it should be the will of the powers above to involve us in pecuniary distress between this time and the presidential election, he would doubtless bear the dispensation with Christian fortitude. It would furnish political capital for his friends, and might contribute greatly to verify his prediction, that General Harrison will take possession of the White House on the 4th of March, 1841.

In my opinion, the Senator has greatly exaggerated the extent of the existing distress. That all classes of the community have suffered in some degree is certain; but intense suffering has been chiefly confined to the large commercial cities, and those portions of the Union, such as the State of Mississippi, where the banks have so evidently ruined the people as to place all doubt of the cause at defiance. Where is there the country under the sun on which a bountiful Providence has poured out more blessings than on Mississippi? No population on the globe, in proportion to their number, produces a larger amount of wealth from the cultivation of the soil. And yet the bounty of Providence has been counteracted by her miserable banking system, and her people are now subjected to intense suffering. In this instance the effect flows so palpably from the cause, that every man sees and feels and knows it. What an astonishing fact was that stated by the Senator from Mississippi, [Mr. WALKER,] that in those counties of his State where banks do not exist, there is no suffering even at the present moment! If you wanted an illustration of the pernicious effects of the banking system, when it tempts farmers and planters to abandon their own proper business and embark on the ocean of wild speculation, you could not have one more striking than that presented by Mississippi at the present moment. I am not aware that there is much individual distress among the mass of the people in the interior of Pennsylvania. There it is chiefly confined to those who have been tempted, in the day of prosperity, to go beyond their means by the facility of obtaining bank accommodations.

But if I read the signs of the times aright, the crisis has passed, or rather is gradually passing away. We cannot return to a state of prosperity before the presidential election; but the condition of individuals, generally, will not be one of intense suffering. The resources of this vast country are so great, and the productive classes are so industrious, that with two years of fair play, they can produce as much wealth as the speculators have been able to squander in one. There will be no great suffering during the next summer, unless it may be in our large commercial cities.

After presenting in glowing colors the distress of the country, the Senator asks, what measure of relief have we proposed? I might ask him, in return, where he will find any clause in the Constitution conferring power upon Congress to regulate the banking and credit system of the respective States, and thus strike at the root of our calamities and embarrassments? The present Administration have not had the slightest agency in creating the existing distress, and can do but little to arrest it, or prevent its recurrence. This is a duty which devolves upon the States. Still we have proposed a measure which we believe will produce this effect to a limited extent. Our chief objects in adopting the Independent Treasury, are to disconnect the Government from all banks, to secure the people's money from the wreck of the banking system, and to have it always ready to promote the prosperity of the country in peace, and defend it in war. Incidentally, however, it will do some good in checking the extravagant spirit of speculation, which is the bane of the country.

In the first place, by requiring specie in all receipts and expenditures of the Government you will create an additional demand for gold and silver to the amount of five millions of dollars per annum, according to the estimate of the President. A large portion of this sum will be drawn from the banks, and this will compel them to keep more specie in their vaults in proportion to their circulation and deposits, and to bank less. This, so far as it may go, will strike at the root of the existing evil. I fear, however, that it will prove to be but a very inadequate restraint upon excessive banking.

In the second place, this bill will, in some degree, diminish our imports, especially after June, 1842. I most heartily concur with the Senator in desiring this result. What is the condition of the importing business at the present moment? It is almost exclusively in the hands of British agents, who sell all the manufactures they can dispose of in other portions of the world, and then bring the residium here to glut our markets. According to our existing laws they receive a credit from the Government for the amount of its duties. They sell the goods for cash; and this credit becomes so much capital in their hands to enable them to make fresh importations. The Independent Treasury bill requires that all duties shall be paid in gold and silver; and after June, 1842, the compromise law will take away the credits altogether. We shall then have a system of cash duties in operation, which will contribute much to reduce the amount of our importations, and to encourage domestic manufactures.

In the third place, this bill will make the banking interest the greatest economists in the country, so far as the Government is concerned. Their nerve of self-interest will be touched in favor of economy, and this will induce them to unite with the people in reducing the revenue and expenditures of the Government to the lowest standard consistently with the public good. They will hereafter abhor a surplus revenue, as much as they delighted in it formerly, when they used it for banking purposes. Any surplus which may exist in future will be locked up in gold and silver in the vaults of our depositaries; and, in proportion to its amount, will deprive the banks of so much of their specie. They will, therefore, become the partisans of reducing the revenue to the actual and necessary expenditures of the Government, so that the specie may flow out of the Sub-Treasuries with a rapidity corresponding with its influx. Nothing but a large surplus can seriously injure the banks. This was demonstrated to me by one of the most distinguished financiers which our country has ever produced, not himself, I believe, friendly to the Independent Treasury. These Treasury drafts, in the natural course of business, will find their way either into the banks at the very points where our depositaries are situated, or into the hands of individuals there having duties to pay to the Government. Take, for example, New York. A public creditor receives such a draft on the receiver general in payment of his debt. Will he carry it to New York, receive payment, and transport the specie from that city? Such instances will be rare. He will generally deposit it to his credit in the bank with which he transacts his business, wherever that may be. This bank, if not in New York, will transmit it for collection to one of the banks there; and thus these banks will draw the specie from our depositary as rapidly as it is drawn from them for the payment of the public dues. Thus the equilibrium will be preserved, so long as the Government is without a large surplus. In other instances, these drafts will be sought after and procured by individuals having duties to pay, and they will be presented to the receivers general, and accepted by them instead of gold and silver.

I now come to another, and the most important portion of the gentleman's argument. If the President had taken the Senator from Kentucky under his umbrella, and wrapped his India rubber cloak around him, and made him his Palinurus to steer the ship of State——

Mr. CLAY said this was not a possible case.

Mr. BUCHANAN replied, that all things are possible, and wonders will never cease. I admit that such an event is not very probable; but should it ever occur, true as the needle to the pole, the Senator would steer direct for a national bank. This is the Senator's sovereign panacea for regulating the currency of the country and restraining the extravagance of the State banks. I admit that the true issue now before the country is between an Independent Treasury and a national bank. "The Pet Bank" deposit system has been such an utter failure that another resort to it cannot be seriously contemplated by any considerable portion of the American people. I feel the utmost confidence in the success of the Independent Treasury, should the law be ably and efficiently executed; but should it fail, the next experiment will doubtless be another bank of the United States.

Waiving, at present, the constitutional question on which I have often expressed my opinion before the Senate, I propose to take up the Senator's argument, and prove that such a bank would not regulate the currency if it could; and that even if it felt the will to do so, it would be entirely destitute of the power.

Would such a bank, then, if it could, control and regulate the loans and issues of the State banks? In the affairs of human life, if you expect one agent to restrain another, you ought to render their interests conflicting. This proposition is emphatically true, when such agents are banking corporations, intent upon declaring the largest possible dividends among their stockholders. Now a bank of the United States, so far from feeling any interest adverse to the State banks, would have the very same inducements with them to make extravagant loans and issues. The duty of such a bank, as a regulator of the currency, would be directly at war with its interest as a banking institution. You cannot raise men above the selfish passions of their nature, by making them directors and stockholders in a bank of the United States. When their interest as bankers conflicts with their duty as regulators of the currency, the history of mankind points you to the probable result. Like the State banks, they will always extend their loans and their issues, whenever they can do so without endangering their own security. This is the powerful instinct of self-interest. It is absurd, then, to expect that the president and directors of a bank of the United States will ever become safe and efficient regulators of the currency, in the very face of their own interest as stockholders. It would be easy for me to prove, from historical facts, that neither the former nor the present Bank of the United States ever did exercise a regular and efficient control over the issues of the State institutions. On the contrary, whenever their interest impelled them to extend their own issues, they have pursued this course; and thus, instead of checking, they have given loose reins to the State banks. Both the Bank of the United States and these banks have thus together rushed on, and with united forces have ministered to that spirit of over-trading and extravagant speculation which has so often desolated our country. Time will not permit me to do more than refer to the vast expansions of this bank in 1817 and 1818, in 1823, in 1831, and 1834. These produced ruinous contractions and universal distress. I think I may affirm, with perfect safety, that at each of these periods, instead of restraining the State banks, it took the lead. Has it ever preserved the State banking institutions in a sound condition? Let Mr. Gallatin answer this question. He says that one hundred and sixty-five of our banks broke between 1811 and 1830; and during the greater part of this period, we all know that the present Bank of the United States was in active existence.

My great object, however, at this moment, is to prove, from the present condition of the Bank of the United States, how hopeless it is to expect that any similar institution can ever be relied upon as a regulator of the currency. That bank still exists, if its present condition may be called existence; and this is the first occasion on which I have ever known the Senator to be guilty of ungratefully abandoning an old friend in the hour of calamity. Before I take my seat, I shall endeavor to identify the gentleman and his party with this institution. "They were lovely in life, and in death they shall not be divided."

It is said that the Bank of the United States is now but a mere State institution. But is its character changed by changing the source whence it derives its charter? Is it not still the same institution that it ever has been, with the same capital, the same directors, the same stockholders, and, until very recently, has it not been governed by the same controlling will? Has it not been exultingly proclaimed by its former president, that it now has a much better charter from Pennsylvania than that which it had received from Congress? This is strictly the truth; for such a charter as that under which it now exists was never before granted to any banking corporation, either in England or this country. The United States, it is true, ceased to be a stockholder; but it enjoyed the privilege of selling their seven millions of stock, for which it could have procured, and doubtless did procure, a large advance.

From the very nature of things, this vast monopoly, with a capital of $35,000,000, could not have become a State Institution. A single State, with more than a sufficient number of State banks already in existence, could not have furnished employment for its immense capital. It would have starved within such narrow limits.

Did it, in point of fact, confine its operations to Pennsylvania? No sir; it aspired to regulate the currency and exchanges of the whole Union. This was the high political duty to the performance of which it proclaimed itself destined. To tell me that this bank all at once changed its character and became a mere State institution, simply because it had received a charter from the Legislature of Pennsylvania, is to deny the evidence of our own senses. Was not the currency issued under the new charter, as well as that under the old, declared, in 1836, to be the best currency which the world had ever seen? Did not the new notes command the same premium, all over the Union, with the old ones; and would they not still continue to command the same premium if it had not fallen—fallen from its high estate?

Why, sir, it became, in fact, more a Bank of the United States, after it received its Pennsylvania charter than it had ever been before. It bought up State banks and converted them into branches, in Louisiana and in Georgia; and it shot out its branch agencies over the whole Union. In New York it has established a branch bank, under their free banking law.

Since its new charter, not content with the whole United States, as the theater of its operations, it has established an agency in England, and aspired "to beard the lion in his den," and to become the rival of the Bank of England in London itself. It scorned to confine itself to banking operations alone; but has invaded the province of the merchant, and has attempted to monopolize and regulate the whole cotton trade between Europe and this country. And yet this bank is now said to be a mere Pennsylvania institution!

Now, sir, how has it succeeded in the task which it imposed upon itself—of regulating the bank issues, and the foreign and domestic exchanges of the Union? In little more than one year after its charter from Congress had expired, whilst in all respects it was under the same government, and continued to pursue the very same course of policy that it had done before, it became insolvent, and suspended specie payments with less than one million and a half of gold and silver in its vaults, or less than one dollar for twenty-three of its capital, to meet all its immense liabilities. Their amount at the time I do not recollect at present, nor have I the means of ascertaining it in my possession.

Now, sir, I would ask the Senator, is there the least reason to believe that if this bank had continued to be the depository of the public revenue until May, 1837, that its fate would have been averted, or that we should not then have had a general suspension of specie payments? Why, sir, the public deposits would only have added fuel to the flame; and would have tempted the bank to engage in still wider speculations. The overbanking and overtrading of 1836, which were conducted under its auspices, would have become still greater—the expansion would have been still more extravagant—the bloated credit system which enabled us in that year to import foreign merchandise to the value of nearly $190,000,000, might have raised our imports up to $250,000,000; and the catastrophe which followed would have been still more dreadful.

In order to repair its fallen fortunes, true to the law of its nature, this bank has since proceeded from one extravagance to another, until it is now almost a heap of ruins. Instead of controlling and regulating the other banks of the country, it has notoriously been the chief—nay, almost the only cause—of the existing suspension of specie payments. The glory of which its friends now boast is, that it has been able to borrow £800,000 sterling, at an extravagant rate of interest, from private bankers in England, to save it from immediate bankruptcy and ruin. Alas! how are the mighty fallen!

And it is by the creation of another such institution that the Senator seeks to regulate the currency, and control the bank issues of the country! Why, this is faith against fact; speculation against experience. This would be, to adopt as our grand regulator, an institution precisely similar to that which has been the great author of our vast bank expansions, and our bloated credit system: and which has fallen under the weight of its own extravagance. With all the experience which the people of the United States have had upon this subject, it will be long, I trust, very long, before they return to a bank of the United States.

But I proposed to prove that, even if a bank of the United States had the disposition to restrain the loans and issues of the State banks, it would not possess the power. I suppose a case for the sake of the argument, which can scarcely ever exist, because, as a regulator of the currency, it would have a duty to perform directly at war with the interest of its stockholders.

The only mode by which it has been thought that this object could be accomplished, was for the Bank of the United States, confining its own business within safe and proper limits, to receive the notes of the State banks on deposit and in payment, and to call upon them at short periods to pay the balances in specie. But, in the nature of things, it would be impossible for such a bank to receive the notes, and restrain the overissues of more than a very few of the eight hundred banks which are now scattered over this country. Each of these banks has its own limited sphere of circulation, and they are not compelled to receive the paper of each other. In point of fact, this is not generally done; nor could any bank of the United States be required to receive all the notes which these eight hundred paper manufactories are constantly pouring out upon the public. From the law which regulates currency, that which is the worst, has always the most extensive circulation. Individuals will always hold fast by the gold and silver, and pass away the bank notes; and of these notes, they will pay out the doubtful, and preserve those which are above suspicion. No bank of the United States, however great its capital, and extended its powers, could ever reach the evil. It could never transact business with one bank in ten, I might say in twenty, of the whole number.

But it is in vain to speculate upon this subject. Experience is the best teacher. One fact is worth one hundred arguments. Independently of the adverse experience of our own country, the experiment has been tried by the Bank of England under the most auspicious circumstances, and it has utterly failed.

The real capital of the Bank of England is about $70,000,000, and it has ten branches at the most commercial and manufacturing points of the kingdom. In 1836 the rate of foreign exchange was largely against England. The specie of the bank was, therefore, gradually drawn from its vaults for exportation. It became necessary, for its own salvation, that it should make a vigorous effort to diminish the amount of the circulating paper medium, and thereby restore the equilibrium of the foreign exchanges. The bank credits and currency of England had become so inflated, and, in consequence, the prices of all articles had advanced to such a standard, that, to use the language of one of their own statesmen, it had become the best country to sell in, and the worst country to buy in, throughout the world. It was profitable, therefore, to import every foreign production which could be admitted to entry, and on account of the high paper prices of their domestic productions their exports were greatly diminished. The consequence was a continued and ruinous drain of specie from the Bank of England to adjust the balance of the trade against that country. The bank well knew that, if it could limit the amount of the paper circulation, it would reduce the price of their home productions in the same proportion, and thus render it profitable for foreign merchants to export British manufactures instead of specie. For this purpose it contracted its loans and issues, in the vain hope that the joint-stock and private banks would be compelled to follow its example. In our slang, it put the screws upon them. What was the result? I shall not enter upon a detail of particulars. It is sufficient to say, that, as it contracted, the other banks of the kingdom expanded their loans and their issues; and that, too, in a greater proportion than its loans and issues were diminished. Prices still continued to rise, and bullion still continued to be drawn out of the bank for exportation. The utter impotency of this grand regulator of the currency to control the other banks and keep the paper currency of the kingdom within such limits as to arrest the exportation of gold and silver, has thus been so clearly demonstrated, that many of the ablest British statesmen despair of accomplishing the object in any other manner than by restricting the issues of paper money to a single bank, and regulating their amount by the agency of the Government. Here, then, is an important fact incontestibly established. If this be true—and there can be no question of its truth—I would ask the Senator how a national bank, even with a capital of $50,000,000, could regulate and restrain within proper limits, the loans and issues of eight hundred State banks, scattered over the whole extent of this vast country? The thing is impossible. It could not be accomplished by such a bank.

And what is the condition of the Bank of England at the present moment? According to the testimony of Mr. Horsley Palmer, its President, given before the secret committee of the House of Commons, previous to its re-charter in 1833, the principle on which it had proceeded in regulating its issues, was to keep as much coin and bullion in its coffers as amounted to a third part of its liabilities, including sums deposited, as well as notes in circulation. Experience had established the fact that this rule of one for three of circulation and deposits was the safe proportion. Its necessities have compelled it to depart widely from this rule of its own creation. Instead of being able to regulate the loans and issues of other banks, it has with difficulty been able to save itself. It has been going down and down, until, according to the last quarterly statement of its condition which I have seen, it had not one pound sterling in bullion for seven of its circulation and deposites. In this respect it is in a much worse condition than many of the banks in our own country. In order to save itself from utter ruin, British pride has humbled itself so much, that the Bank of England became a suppliant to that of France for a supply of bullion, which was graciously, though condescendingly, granted. This fact is the highest evidence it is possible to present of the advantages which a country, the basis of whose circulation is gold and silver, enjoys over another country whose paper currency is greatly expanded. The Bank of England will probably never see the day, under its present charter, when its bullion will again be equal to one third of its circulation and deposits. Indeed, one bad crop, in its present condition, would drain it of its gold and silver for the purpose of purchasing foreign grain, and compel it to suspend specie payments. Neither this bank, nor the Bank of the United States, can ever be relied upon as regulators of the loans and issues of the other banks of their respective countries.

The Senator from Kentucky would have "*a well regulated* Bank of the United States." He lays great emphasis upon the words "*well regulated.*" Does he mean to insinuate that the present Bank of the United States, under its charter from Congress, was not the best regulated bank which the world ever saw? I had thought that, in his opinion, this bank was perfection itself. The truth, however, is, that any regulations which you can prescribe in the charter of such an institution, will be disregarded, whenever a powerful interest dictates their violation. Like the strong man in the Scriptures, it will snap the chords by which it is bound, as if they were thread. It will calculate upon violating its charter with perfect impunity, because it well knows how unwilling Congress would be to inflict so much evil upon the country as would necessarily result from its sudden destruction. Once put such an institution into successful operation, and you can no longer regulate its motion by the restrictions of its charter. The present bank was ever a lawless institution, up until the day when it fraudulently seized upon the entire circulation of the old bank, illegal branch drafts and all, and compelled Congress to pass a law making it a penitentiary offense in its officers to reissue these "resurrection notes." Under its State charter, it has been true to its original character. Although it now has a charter such as no other banking institution ever had, it has already been guilty of several palpable violations of this charter, independent of having twice suspended specie payments. I shall not trouble the Senate with the enumeration of these violations. It is now at the mercy of the Legislature. It has pronounced its own doom under its own charter; and it now only remains for the Legislature or the Governor to carry this sentence into execution, through the agency of the judicial tribunals. Whether they shall enforce this forfeiture or not, is for them in their wisdom to determine, not me. I shall not, in this place, attempt to interfere with their high and responsible duties, although I should consider it the greatest of all bank reforms, if this bank could be blotted out of existence.

The Senator ridiculed the idea that the establishment of a new Bank of the United States could prove dangerous to civil liberty. Such a bank with a capital of from fifty to a hundred millions of dollars, with branches in every State of the Union, dirrcting, by its expansions and contractions, when prices should rise, and when they should fall, would be a most tremendous instrument of irresponsible power. It would be a machine much more formidable than this Government, even if the Administration were as corrupt as the fancy of some gentlemen has painted it. There is a natural alliance between wealth and power. Mr. Randolph once said, "Male and female created he them." Combine the moneyed aristocracy of the country, through the agency of a National Bank, with the Administration, and their united power would create an influence which it would be almost impossible for the people to withstand. We should never again see these powers in hostile array against each other. In the days of General Jackson we witnessed the exception, not the rule. Give any President such a bank as I have described, and we shall, hereafter, have a most peaceful succession. With all the power of the Executive, combined with all the wealth of the country, he would be the most arrant blockhead in the world if he were not able to re-elect himself, and to nominate his successor. All the forms of the Constitution might still remain. The people might still be deluded with the idea that they elected their President; but the animating spirit of our free institutions would be gone forever. A secret, but all-pervading, moneyed influence, would sap the foundations of liberty and render it an empty name.

The immense power of such an institution was manifested in the tremendous efforts which it made against General Jackson. Had he not enjoyed more personal popularity in this country than any man who ever lived, these efforts would have proved irresistable. As it was, the conflict was of the most portentous character, and shook the Union to its center. Indeed the bank, at one time, would, in all human probabilty, have gained the victory, had the election of President chanced to occur at that period; and we should then have witnessed the appalling spectacle of the triumph of the bank over the rights and liberties of the people. The Constitution of the country and the Democratic party would then have been prostrated together.

On Friday last, when I very unexpectedly addressed the Senate, I stated a principle of political enconomy which I shall now read from the book. It is this: "that if you double the amount of the 'necessary circulating medium in any country, 'you thereby double the nominal price of every 'article. If, when the circulating medium is fifty 'millions, an article should cost one dollar, it 'would cost two if, without any increase of the 'uses of a circulating medium, the quantity should 'be increased to one hundred millions." The same effect would be produced, whether the circulating medium were specie, or convertible bank paper mingled with specie. It is the increased quantity of the medium, not its character, which produces this effect. Of course I leave out of view irredeemable bank paper.

I do not pretend that, on questions of political economy, you can attain mathematical certainty. All you can accomplish is to approach it as near as possible. The principle which I have stated is sufficiently near the truth to answer my present purpose. From this principle, I drew an inference that the extravagant amount of our circulating medium, consisting, in a great degree, of the notes thrown out upon the community by eight hundred banks, was injurious to our domestic manufactures. In other words, that extravagant banking and domestic manufactures are directly hostile to each other.

I did not understand that the Senator from Massachusetts, [Mr. Davis,] contested the general proposition that an increase in the currency of any country, without any increase of the uses of a circulating medium, would, in the same proportion, enhance the price of all the productions of that country whose, value was not regulated by a foreign demand. He could not have contested this principle. If he had, all history and all experience would have been arrayed against him.

The discovery of the mines of South America, and the consequent vast increase of the precious metals put into circulation in the form of money, have greatly enhanced the nominal prices of all property throughout the world. Indeed, it is now a matter of curious amusement, to contrast the low prices of all articles three centuries ago, with their present greatly advanced rates. The Bank of England recognizes, and constantly acts upon this principle, though often without success. When prices become so high, in consequence of a redundancy of paper currency and bank credits, that it is more profitable to export the precious metals from the kingdom than its manufactures, this bank constantly diminishes its loans, raises the rate of interest, and reduces its circulation, with the avowed object of reducing prices to such a standard as will render it more profitable to export merchandise than bullion. It is in this manner that the Bank seeks to regulate the foreign exchanges.

But why need we resort to foreign nations for illustrations of the truth of this position when it has been brought home to the actual knowledge of every man within this country? Have we not all learned, by bitter experience, that when our periodical expansions commence, the price of all property begins to rise? It goes on increasing with the increasing expansion, until the bubble bursts; and then bank accommodations and bank issues are contracted, the amount of the currency is reduced, and prices fall to their former level. This is the history of our own country, and we all know it. A certain amount of currency is necessary to represent the entire exchangeable property of the country; and if this amount should be greatly increased, without a corresponding increase in the exchangeable productions of the country, the only consequence would be a great enhancement in nominal prices. I say nominal; because this increased price will not enable the man who receives it to purchase more real property or more of the necessaries and luxuries of life than he could have done before.

Let me now recur to the proposition with which I commenced; and I repeat that I do not pretend to mathematical accuracy in the illustration which I shall present. The United States carry on a trade with Germany and France; the former a hard-money country, and the latter approaching it so nearly as to have no bank notes in circulation under the denomination of five hundred francs, or nearly one hundred dollars. On the contrary, the United States is emphatically a paper-money country, having eight hundred banks of issue; all of them emitting notes of a denomination as low as five dollars, and most of them one, two and three-dollar notes. For every dollar of gold and silver in the vaults of these banks, they issue three, four, five, and some of them as high as ten, and even fifteen dollars of paper. This produces a vast but ever-changing expansion of the currency; and a consequent increase of the prices of all articles, the value of which is not regulated by the foreign demand, above the prices of similar articles in Germany and France. At particular stages of our expansions, we might with justice apply the principle which I have stated to our trade with these countries, and assert that, from the great redundancy of our currency, articles are manufactured in France and Germany for one half of their actual cost in this country. Let me present an example. In Germany, where the currency is purely metalic, and the cost of every thing is reduced to a hard-money standard, a piece of broadcloth can be manufactured for fifty dollars; the manufacture of which, in our country, from the expansion of our paper currency, would cost one hundred dollars. What is the consequence? The foreign French or German manufacturer imports this cloth into our country, and sells it for one hundred dollars. Does not every person perceive that the redundancy of our currency is equal to a premium of one hundred per cent. in favor of the foreign manufacturer? No tariff of protection, unless it amounted to prohibition, could counteract this advantage in favor of foreign manufactures. I would to Heaven that I could rouse the attention of every manufacturer of the nation to this important subject.

The foreign manufacturer will not receive our

bank notes in payment. He will take nothing home except gold and silver, or bills of exchange, which are equivalent. He does not expend this money here, where he would be compelled to support his family, and to purchase his labor and materials at the same rate of prices which he receives for his manufactures. On the contrary, he goes home, purchases his labor, his wool, and all other articles which enter into his manufacture, at half their cost in this country; and again returns to inundate us with foreign woolens, and to ruin our domestic manufactures. I might cite many other examples: but this, I trust, will be sufficient to draw public attention to the subject. This depreciation of our currency is, therefore, equivalent to a direct protection granted to the foreign over the domestic manufacturer. It is impossible that our manufacturer should be able to sustain such an unequal competition.

Sir, I solemnly believe that if we could but reduce this inflated paper bubble to any thing like reasonable dimensions, New England would become the most prosperous manufacturing country that the sun ever shown upon. Why cannot we manufacture goods, and especially cotton goods, which will go into successful competition with British manufactures in foreign markets? Have we not the necessary capital? Have we not the industry? Have we not the machinery? And above all, are not our skill, energy, and enterprise, proverbial throughout the world? Land is also cheaper here than in any other country on the face of the earth. We possess every advantage which Providence can bestow upon us for the manufacture of cotton; but they are all counteracted by the folly of man. The raw material costs us less than it does the English, because this is an article, the price of which depends upon foreign markets, and is not regulated by our own inflated currency. We, therefore, save the freight of the cotton across the Atlantic, and that of the manufactured article on its return here. What is the reason that, with all these advantages, and with the protective duties, which our laws afford to the domestic manufacturer of cotton, we cannot obtain exclusive possession of the home market, and successfully contend for the markets of the world? It is simply because we manufacture at the nominal prices of our own inflated currency, and are compelled to sell at the real prices of other nations. Reduce our nominal to the real standard of prices throughout the world, and you cover our country with blessings and benefits. I wish to Heaven I could speak in a voice loud enough to be heard throughout New England; because, if the attention of the manufacturers could once be directed to the subject, their own intelligence and native sagacity would teach them how injuriously they are affected by our bloated banking and credit system, and would enable them to apply the proper corrective.

What is the reason that our manufacturers have been able to sustain any sort of competition, even in the home market, with those of British origin? It is because England herself is, to a great extent, a paper-money country, though, in this respect, not to be compared with our own. From this very cause prices in England are much higher that they are upon the continent. The expense of living is there double what it costs in France. Hence, all the English who desire to nurse their fortunes by living cheaply emigrate from their own country to France, or some other portion of the continent. The comparative low prices of France and Germany have afforded such a stimulus to their manufactures that they are now rapidly extending themselves, and would obtain possession, in no small degree, even of the English home market, if it were not for their protecting duties. Whilst British manufactures are now languishing, those of the continent are springing into a healthy and vigorous existence. It was but the other day that I saw an extract from an English paper which stated that whilst the cutlery manfactured in Germany was equal in quality with the British, it was so reduced in price that the latter would have to abandon the manufacture altogether.

The Senator from Massachusetts, after all our experience, doubts whether our currency has been inflated beyond the proper degree; and to prove that it has not been, he says that the rates of exchange upon England have often been below par. This fact does not tend to prove that our paper currency is not inflated at home. Our foreign exchanges are regulated by the specie standard of the world, not by the amount of our bank issues at home; and whether they are above or below par depends upon whether we are the debtor or the creditor nation. We ought always to be, and would always be, the creditor nation, if it were not for our extravagant speculations in foreign merchandise, produced by the redundancy of our paper credits and circulation. Our immense exports of cotton ought always to produce a balance of trade in our favor; and yet this is rarely the case. There is generally a particular period, however, in the progress of each one of our expansions and contractions, when exchange is in our favor. This occurs after our cotton and other exports have paid the debt previously contracted to foreign nations, and before we have had the time and the ability to get fairly under way in a new career of extravagant importations. To say that this circumstance proves that our paper currency is not inflated is an argument which I cannot understand. It proves nothing but that Providence has provided us a resource in our vast production of cotton, which enables us to repair the injuries which we suffer from our extravagant speculations. It does not touch my argument to show the pernicious influence which our expanded currency exerts on our domestic manufactures. If it were not for this cause exchanges would not only be occasionally, but always, in our favor; and the Bank of England could not exercise that controlling influence over our banking institutions of which the Senator from Kentucky so loudly complains. This influence is derived solely from the fact that we are almost always the debtor nation, as we must continue to be until our wild speculations shall be arrested.

In addition to the reason suggested why foreign exchange has sometimes been in our favor, notwithstanding our extravagant importations, I might add another which has operated with vast power during the last two or three years. This is the immense amount of money which several of the States have borrowed from England within that period. This money constituted a fund on which bills were drawn to a large amount, and consequently reduced the rate of exchange. The payment of the interest on this debt, particularly as we shall probably not soon increase the principal, will operate hereafter in a contrary direction, and will tend to raise, not reduce, the rate of our foreign exchanges.

But the Senator from Kentucky leaves no stone unturned. He says that the friends of the Independent Treasury desire to establish an exclusive metallic currency, as the medium of all dealings throughout the Union; and also, to reduce the wages of the poor man's labor so that the rich employer may be able to sell his manufactures at a lower price. Now, sir, I deny the correctness of both these propositions; and, in the first place, I, for one, am not in favor of establishing an exclusive metallic currency for the people of this country. I desire to see the banks greatly reduced in number; and would, if I could, confine their accommodations to such loans or discounts, for limited periods, to the commercial, manufacturing, and trading classes of the community, as the ordinary course of their business might render necessary. I never wish to see farmers and mechanics and professional men tempted, by the facility of obtaining bank loans for long periods, to abandon their own proper and useful and respectable spheres and rush into wild and extravagant speculation. I would, if I could, radically reform the present banking system, so as to confine it within such limits as to prevent future suspensions of specie payments; and without exception, I would instantly deprive each and every bank of its charter which should again suspend. Establish these or similar reforms, and give us a real specie basis for our paper circulation, by increasing the denomination of bank notes first to ten, and afterwards to twenty dollars, and I shall then be the friend, not the enemy of banks. I know that the existence of banks and the circulation of bank paper are so identified with the habits of our people, that they cannot be abolished, even if this were desirable. To reform, and not destroy, is my motto. To confine them to their appropriate business, and prevent them from ministering to the spirit of wild and reckless speculation, by extravagant loans and issues, is all which ought to be desired. But this I shall say. If experience should prove it to be impossible to enjoy the facilities which well regulated banks would afford, without, at the same time, continuing to suffer the evils which the wild excesses of the present banks have hitherto entailed upon the country, then I should consider it the lesser evil to abolish them altogether. If the State Legislatures shall now do their duty, I do not believe that it will ever become necessary to decide on such an alternative

We are also charged by the Senator from Kentucky with a desire to reduce the wages of the poor man's labor. We have often been termed agrarians on our side of the House. It is something new under the sun, to hear the Senator and his friends attribute to us a desire to elevate the wealthy manufacturer, at the expense of the laboring man and the mechanic. From my soul, I respect the laboring man. Labor is the foundation of the wealth of every country; and the free laborers of the North deserve respect, both for their probity and their intelligence. Heaven forbid that I should do them wrong! Of all the countries on the earth, we ought to have the most consideration for the laboring man. From the very nature of our institutions, the wheel of fortune is constantly revolving and producing such mutations in property, that the wealthy man of to-day may become the poor laborer of to-morrow. Truly, wealth often takes to itself wings and flies away. A large fortune rarely lasts beyond the third generation, even if it endure so long. We must all know instances of individuals obliged to labor for their daily bread, whose grandfathers, were men of fortune. The regular process of society would almost seem to consist of the efforts of one class to dissipate the fortunes which they have inherited, whilst another class, by their industry and economy, are regularly rising to wealth. We have all, therefore, a common interest, as it is our common duty, to protect the rights of the laboring man; and if I believed for a moment that this bill would prove injurious to him, it should meet my unqualified opposition.

Although this bill will not have as great an influence as I could desire, yet, as far as it goes, it will benefit the laboring man as much, and probably more than any other class of society. What is it he ought most to desire? Constant employment, regular wages, and uniform reasonable prices for the necessaries and comforts of life which he requires. Now, sir, what has been his condition under our system of expansions and contractions? He has suffered more by them than any other class of society. The rate of his wages is fixed and known; and they are the last to rise with the increasing expansion and the first to fall when the corresponding revulsion occurs. He still continues to receive his dollar per day, whilst the price of every article which he consumes is rapidly rising. He is at length made to feel that, although he nominally earns as much, or even more than he did formerly, yet, from the increased price of all the necessaries of life, he cannot support his family. Hence the strikes for higher wages, and the uneasy and excited feelings which have at different periods, existed among the laboring classes. But the expansion at length reaches the exploding point, and what does the laboring man now suffer? He is for a season thrown out of employment altogether. Our manufactures are suspended; our public works are stopped; our private enterprises of different kinds are abandoned; and, whilst others are able to weather the storm, he can scarcely procure the means of bare subsistence.

Again, sir; who, do you suppose, held the greater part of the worthless paper of the one hundred and sixty-five broken banks to which I have referred? Certainly it was not the keen and wary speculator, who snuffs danger from afar. If you were to make the search, you would find more broken bank notes in the cottages of the laboring poor than anywhere else. And these miserable shinplasters, where are they? After the revulsion of 1837, laborers were glad to obtain employment on any terms; and they often received it upon the express condition that they should accept this worthless trash in payment. Sir, an entire suppression of all bank notes of a lower denomination than the value of one week's wages of the laboring man is absolutely necessary for his protection. He ought always to receive his wages in gold and silver. Of all men on the earth, the laborer is most interested in having a sound and stable currency.

All other circumstances being equal, I agree with the Senator from Kentucky that that country is most prosperous where labor commands the highest wages. I do not, however, mean by the terms "highest wages," the greatest nominal amount. During the Revolutionary war, one day's work commanded a hundred dollars of continental paper; but this would have scarcely purchased a breakfast. The more proper expression would be, to say that that country is most prosperous where labor commands the greatest reward; where one day's labor will procure not the greatest nominal amount of a depreciated currency, but most of the necessaries and comforts of life. If, therefore, you should, in some degree, reduce the nominal price paid for labor, by reducing the amount of your bank issues within reasonable and safe limits, and establishing a metallic basis for your paper circulation, would this injure the laborer? Certainly not; because the price of all the necessaries and comforts of life are reduced in the same proportion, and he will be able to purchase more of them for one dollar in a sound state of the currency, than he could have done, in the days of extravagant expansion, for a dollar and a quarter. So far from injuring, it will greatly benefit the laboring man. It will insure to him constant employment and regular prices, paid in a sound currency, which, of all things, he ought most to desire; and it will save him from being involved in ruin by a recurrence of those periodical expansions and contractions of the currency, which have hitherto convulsed the country.

This sound state of the currency will have another most happy effect upon the laboring man. He will receive his wages in gold and silver; and this will induce him to lay up, for future use, such a portion of them as he can spare, after satisfying his immediate wants. This he will not do at present, because he knows not whether the trash which he is now compelled to receive as money, will continue to be of any value a week or a month hereafter. A knowledge of this fact tends to banish economy from his dwelling, and induces him to expend all his wages as rapidly as possible, lest they may become worthless on his hands.

Sir, the laboring classes understand this subject perfectly. It is the hard-handed and firm-fisted men of the country on whom we must rely in the day of danger, who are the most friendly to the passage of this bill. It is they who are the most ardently in favor of infusing into the currency of the country a very large amount of the precious metals.

The Senator has advanced another position in which I am sorry I cannot agree with him. It is this: that a permanent high rate of interest is indicative of the prosperity of any country. Now, sir, a permanent high rate of interest is conclusive evidence of a scarcity of capital, and is indicative of anything but prosperity. I think, therefore, it would puzzle him, with all his ingenuity, to establish his proposition. To render a country truly prosperous, capital and labor must be so combined as each to receive a fair reward. In England, when the rate of interest was very high, the country was not at all in a flourishing condition; but as capital gradually accumulated, and the rate of interest consequently sunk, she became more and more prosperous, though she did not reach her highest elevation until money yielded considerably less than five per cent. But this subject is so little relevant to the question under discussion, that it is scarcely necessary to pursue it. If it were, it would be easy to show that a high rate of interest, generally, if not universally, enters into direct conflict with the wages of labor, which the Senator is so anxious to maintain. Suppose, for example, that it required a capital of $20,000 to put and to preserve an iron manufactory in successful operation. In one country the interest on this sum at ten per cent. would amount to $2,000; whilst in another it could be procured at four per cent., or $800. The difference would be $1,200; and, unless this amount can be saved either by a reduction in the wages of labor, or in some other manner, the manufacturer who pays the higher rate of interest cannot endure the competition. A higher rate of interest almost always presses upon the wages of labor.

If the gentleman's theory be correct, Wall street must be a perfect paradise of prosperity. *There*, the rate of interest for a long time has been permanently high, varying between two and four per cent. a month, or between twenty-four and forty-eight per cent. per annum. Post notes of the Bank of the United States have been discounted freely at two per cent. per month. With these facts before him, Mr. Jeffery would not now declare, as the Senator informs us he formerly did, "that this country was the heaven of the poor man and the hell of the rich." He might probably reverse the position, though it would be equally extravagant one way as the other. A country in which a rich man can realize from twenty-four to forty-eight per cent. for his money, would certainly be anything but a place of torment for him. But what is the condition of a poor man in such a country? When capital commands such an extravagant interest to liquidate commercial debts, it will no longer be used in the employment of labor; and hence poor men must necessarily be thrown out of employment. Such a condition is anything but a heaven for them.

The Senator exclaims with holy horror, "the Stuarts are still upon the throne, and Charles the Second has succeeded Charles the First." He has, I think, been very unfortunate in this historical allusion, if he intended to compare our Andrew with the first Charles. The enemies of Charles cut off his head, whilst our Andrew, politically speaking, cut the heads off all his enemies; and many of them were in such terror of him, that they dreaded he might turn the metaphor into a reality, and cut off their heads in earnest. Charles the Second did not succeed Charles the First. My Lord Protector intervened. Although he and the honorable Senator from Kentucky are as different in other respects as two able and brave men can be, yet whilst he was speaking, it struck me that there was one striking point of resemblance between them. And what, sir, do you think that was? My Lord Protector always begun and ended everything, as the Senator has begun and ended his speech—*with prayer*. Then, in regard to the Second Charles, I have a little to say. Of all men, the Senator ought to be the last to disparage our Martin. I have read of a great conquered general, who always pronounced his conqueror to be a very able and brave man, because, as the historian observes, it would have lessened the merits of the vanquished to have been overcome by a fool or a coward. The Senator, in speaking of Martin, ought rather to exclaim,

> "Great let me call him, for he conquered me."

If, in addition, the little magician should be victorious over the hero of Tippecanoe in the great battle to be fought the approaching autumn, and I have full faith that such will be the result, then he will go down to posterity with all "his blushing honors thick upon him."

Thanking the Senate for their patient attention, I shall now resume my seat.

READ AND REFLECT!

1. Let every lover of his country remember that during the present Congress, as will be shown by the following official records, the Republican (Fremont) party have voted to violate the most solemn treaties of the United States with the Indians.

2. That they have voted to violate the compact with Texas, by which the United States purchased all that part of Texas north of 36° 30′ and included it in New Mexico, with the guarantee "that when admitted as a State the said Territory, or any portion of the same, shall be received into the Union with or without slavery, as their constitution may prescribe at the time of their admission."

3. That they have, by their votes, repudiated the compromise measures of 1850, which contained the same guarantee in respect to the Territories of New Mexico and Utah, and to the support of which every Whig and every Democrat stood pledged by the platforms of the two great parties in 1852.

4. That they have voted to legalize and establish hereditary slavery in the whole of Kansas, and to introduce and establish slavery in a part of New Mexico, and to declare that children who shall be hereafter born to be slaves for life and their posterity after them, in violation of the great principles of self-government and State equality, which should leave the people of each State and Territory "perfectly free to form and regulate their domestic institutions in their own way, subject only to the Constitution of the United States."

6. That they have voted for a bill which recognizes the validity and binding force of all the laws enacted by the territorial legislature of Kansas at Shawnee Mission, and which, in their speeches, they have pretended to be illegal and void, inhuman and barbarous.

7. That they have voted in the same bill that all those Kansas enactments shall be enforced and carried into faithful execution, except the criminal code, which provides for the punishment of murder, robbery, larceny, arson, and other crimes punishable by the criminal codes of all civilized countries.

8. That they have voted to grant to all persons guilty of these crimes a general pardon for the past, and a full license to prosecute their bloody deeds with legalized impunity in the future, at the same time that they pretend that these crimes have all been perpetrated by organized bands of armed pro-slavery men and border ruffians upon unoffending and peaceable free State men.

9. That they provided in the same bill, in effect, that no person shall even be punished in Kansas for illegal voting, for violence at the polls, or for fraud in conducting the election, by declaring that the ONLY LAW which provides punishment for these offences shall never be enforced, while they pretend that large bodies of armed Missourians are in the habit of invading the Territory, seizing possession of the polls, driving away the lawful voters, and forcing a legislature upon the people contrary to their wishes.

5. That, while legalizing slavery in Kansas until 1858, which is probably beyond the period when it would become a State of the Union, they have voted to prohibit slavery therein forever from and

after that period, regardless of the wishes and in violation of the constitutional rights of the people to decide that question for themselves.

10. That they have refused to pass a bill which had been twice passed by the Senate, to declare inoperative and void all laws and enactments in Kansas in violation of the freedom of speech or of the press, or any other great principle of liberty and justice intended to be secured and protected by the Constitution of the United States and the organic act, at the same time that they advise their party in the Territory to resist the constituted authorities and raise the standard of rebellion against the territorial government established by Congress, and assign as their only excuse the existence of these same obnoxious laws, which they refuse to concur with the Senate in anulling.

11. That they have voted amendments on the general appropriation bills for the payment of the civil expenses of the government, intended to destroy the independence of the judiciary, and corrupt the judges, by making the payment of their salaries depend upon the particular way in which they should decide certain cases pending in their courts.

12. That they have voted amendments on the army appropriation bill, providing that the officers and soldiers of the army should not receive the pay, provisions, and clothing necessary for their subsistence, and to which they are entitled by law, when employed in aid of the enforcement of the enactments of the Kansas legislature, which they have recognized as valid and required to be enforced by the bill for which they all voted.

13. That they have, by their votes, instructed the President of the United States to proclaim martial law in the Territory of Kansas and on the national highways leading to it, and to protect persons and property with the bayonet and the sword, making his own will the law of the land for that purpose, at the same time that they say in their speeches and newspapers that the President has shown himself a traitor to all the free States, and forfeited the confidence of the whole country.

14. Let it be remembered and proclaimed everywhere that each of the above statements and specifications are established by the journals and archives of the two Houses of Congress, and are conclusively proven by the following official records, the truth of which no honest man will deny.

15. Let it also be remembered that when they discovered that these obnoxious and unconstitutional amendments to the appropriation bills must necessarily result in the defeat of those bills, and thus stop the wheels of government, (although they insisted their amendments to both bills were alike essential to the cause of freedom in Kansas,) they immediately took the back track, abandoned their amendments, and allowed the civil bill to become a law, which contained the appropriation for *their own pay* and the pay of all civil officers and employees who had votes to give at the ensuing elections, but at the same time insisted upon their amendments to the army bill, and thus defeated the pay of the officers and soldiers who had no votes to give.

Let these things be remembered, and read the following official cords in proof of the facts stated:

IN THE SENATE OF THE UNITED STATES, AUGUST 11, 1856

Mr. DOUGLAS made the following

REPORT.

[To accompany bill H. R. 75.]

The Committee on Territories, to whom was referred a bill from the House of Representatives, for "An act to reorganize the Territory of Kansas, and for other purposes," beg leave to report:

The first section of the bill provides, "That all that part of the Territory of the United States which lies between the parallels of thirty-six degrees and thirty minutes and forty degrees of north latitude, and which is east of the eastern boundary of the Territory of Utah to the southeast corner thereof, and east of a line thence due south to the said parallel of thirty-six degrees thirty minutes north latitude, and is bounded on the east by the western boundary of the State of Missouri, shall constitute one Territory, and shall be, and hereby is, constituted and organized into a temporary government, by the name of the Territory of Kansas."

By reference to the map it will be perceived that, in addition to all the country embraced within the limits of the present Territory of Kansas, it is proposed to include in the new Territory all the country between the southern boundary of the Territory, as now defined by law, and the parallel of 36° 30′, extending from the western boundary of the State of Missouri across more than twelve and a half degrees of longitude, and being about thirty-five miles in width at the eastern, and one hundred and five at the western extremity. The eastern portion of this strip of country, which it is now proposed to incorporate within, and render subject to the jurisdiction of, the Territory of Kansas, was ceded with other territory to the Cherokee Indians, by the treaties of the 6th of May, 1828, April 12th, 1833, and May 23, 1836, for "*a permanent home, and which shall, under the most solemn guarantee of the United States, be and remain theirs forever*—A HOME THAT SHALL NEVER, IN ALL FUTURE TIME, BE EMBARRASSED BY HAVING EXTENDED AROUND IT THE LINES, OR PLACED OVER IT THE JURISDICTION OF A TERRITORY OR STATE, *nor be pressed upon by* the extension *in any way of any of the* limits of any existing Territory or State."

In view of this "most solemn guaranty of the United States" to the Cherokees, your committee cannot refrain from the expression of the hope and belief that the House of Representatives, in passing a bill to extend around this Indian country the lines of Kansas, and render it subject to the jurisdiction of that Territory, acted without due consideration, and probably without a full knowledge of these treaty stipulations. When the organic act of Kansas was passed in 1854, the parallel of thirty-seven was fixed upon as the southern boundary of the Territory instead of the line of thirty-six degrees and thirty minutes, with the view to the preservation of faith on the part of the United States towards these Indians; and lest injustice might be done to other Indian tribes who held their lands under treaties with the United States, it was expressly provided, "That nothing in this act contained shall be construed to impair the rights of persons or property now pertaining to the Indians in said Territory, so long as such rights shall remain unextinguished by treaty between the United States and such Indians, or to include any territory which, by treaty with any Indian tribe, is not, without the consent of said tribe, to be included within the territorial limits or jurisdiction of any State or Territory; *but all such territory shall be excepted out of the boundaries, and constitute no part of the Territory of Kansas.*" In these considerations your committee find insuperable objections to that portion of the bill from the House of Representatives which proposes to include within the limits, and render subject to the jurisdiction of the Territory of Kansas, any part of the country which is thus secured to the Indians by solemn treaty stipulations.

Nor are the objections less formidable to incorporating within the limits of Kansas that portion of the Territory of New Mexico which lies north of the line of 36° 30′, and east of the Rio Grande, and subjecting it to the operation of the other provisions of the bill. That part of New Mexico, containing about 15,000 square miles, was purchased from Texas by one of the acts known as the compromise measures of 1850, and formed a part of the territory for which the United States paid the State of Texas ten millions of dollars. The second section of the act of Congress which contains the terms and conditions of the compact between the United States and Texas for the purchase of that Territory, incorporates the same in the Territory of New Mexico, with the following guarantee: "*And provided further, that when admitted as a State,* the said Territory, or any portion of the same, shall be received into the Union with *or without slavery, as their constitution may prescribe at the time of their admission.*"

After asserting this great principle of State equality as applicable to every portion of New Mexico under the Constitution, and as guarantied in the compact with Texas, by fair intendment, so far as the country was acquired from that State, the seventh section of the same act provides that the legislative power of the said Territory shall extend to all rightful subjects of legislation, consistent with the Constitution of the United States and the provisions of this act"—thus leaving the people perfectly free to form and regulate their domestic institutions in their own way, subject only to the Constitution. It is now proposed in the bill under consideration to repudiate these guarantees and violate these great fundamental principles, by annexing to Kansas all that portion of the country acquired from Texas which lies north of 36° 30′, and imposing upon it a prohibition of slavery forever, from and after the first day of January, 1858, regardless of the rights and wishes of the people who may inhabit the Territory.

The twenty-fourth section of the bill is in the following words:

SEC. 24. *And be it further enacted,* That so much of the fourteenth section, and also so much of the thirty-second section, of the act passed at the first session of the thirty-third Congress, commonly known as the Kansas-Nebraska act, as reads as follows, to wit: "Except the eighth section of the act preparatory to the admission of Missouri into the Union, approved March 6, 1820, which, being inconsistent with the principles of non-intervention by Congress with slavery in the States and Territories, as recognized by the legislation of 1850, commonly called the compromise measures, is hereby declared inoperative and void; it being the true intent and meaning of this act not to legislate slavery into any Territory or State, nor to exclude it therefrom, but to leave the people thereof perfectly free to form and regulate their domestic institutions in their own way, subject only to the Constitution of the United States: *Provided*, That nothing herein contained shall be construed to revive or put in force any law or regulation which may have existed prior to the act of 6th March, 1820, either protecting, establishing, prohibiting or abolishing slavery—be and the same is hereby repealed; and the said eighth section of said act of 6th March, 1820, is hereby revived and declared to be in full force and effect within the said Territories of Kansas and Nebraska: *Provided, however*, That any person lawfully held to service in either of said Territories shall not be discharged from such service by reason of such repeal and revival of said eighth section, if such person shall be permanently removed from such Territory or Territories prior to the 1st day of January, 1858; and any child or children born in either of said Territories, of any female lawfully held to service, if in like manner removed without said Territories before the expiration of that date, shall not be, by reason of anything in this act, emancipated from any service it might have owed had this act never been passed: *And provided, further*, That any person lawfully held to service in any other State or Territory of the United States, and escaping into either the Territory of Kansas or Nebraska, may be reclaimed and removed to the person or place where such service is due, under any law of the United States which shall be in force upon the subject."

In the opinion of your committee there are various grave and serious objections to this section of the bill. In the first place, it expressly repudiates and condemns the great fundamental principles of self-government and State equality which it was the paramount object of the Kansas-Nebraska act to maintain and perpetuate, as affirmed in the following provision: "It being the true intent and meaning of this act not to legislate slavery into any Territory or State, nor to exclude it therefrom, but to leave the people thereof perfectly free to form and regulate their domestic institutions in their own way, subject only to the Constitution of the United States."

Not content with repealing this wise and just provision, and condemning the sound constitutional principles asserted in it, the bill proceeds to legalize and establish, for a limited time, hereditary slavery, not only in the Territory of Kansas, (where there is no other local or affirmative law protecting it than the enactments of the Kansas Territorial legislature, which have been alleged to be illegal and void, and which the House of Representatives, by amendments to the appropriation bills, have instructed the President not to enforce,) but also in all that part of New Mexico which it is proposed to incorporate in the Territory of Kansas, and where slavery was prohibited by the Mexican law, and it is not pretended that there is any territorial enactment recognizing or establishing it. Having thus asserted and exercised the power of introducing and establishing slavery in the Territories by act of Congress, and declaring children hereafter born therein to be slaves for life and their posterity after them, provided they shall be removed therefrom within a specified period, the bill proceeds to affirm and exercise the power of prohibiting slavery in the same Territories forever from and after January 1, 1858, by enacting and putting in force the following provision, being the 8th section of the act passed March 6, 1820, to wit:

"SECTION 8. *And be it further enacted*, That in all that territory ceded by France to the United States, under the name of Louisiana, which lies north of thirty-six degrees and thirty minutes north latitude, not included within the limits of the State contemplated by this act, slavery and involuntary servitude, otherwise than in the punishment of crime, whereof the parties shall have been duly convicted, shall be, and is hereby, forever prohibited: *Provided always*, That any person escaping into the same, from whom labor or service is lawfully claimed in any State or Territory of the United States, such fugitive may be lawfully reclaimed and conveyed to the person claiming his or her labor or service as aforesaid."

It will be observed that this 8th section of the Missouri act (commonly called the Missouri compromise) by its terms only applied to the territory acquired from France, known as the Louisiana purchase, the western boundary of which was defined by the treaty with Spain in 1819, and subsequently by treaties with Mexico and Texas, to be the 100th meridian of longitude, while the bill under consideration, under the guise of reviving and restoring that provision, extends it more than seven degrees of longitude further westward, and applies it to that large extent of territory to which it had no application in its original enactment. Nor can it be said with fairness or t uth that this provision was applied to any portion of the territory in question by the "joint resolution for annexing Texas to the United States," for the reason that the whole territory embraced within the limits of the republic of Texas was admitted into the Union as one State, with the privilege of forming not exceeding four other States out of the State of Texas, "by the consent of said State," with the condition that "in such State or States as should be formed out of said territory, north of said Missouri compromise line, slavery or involuntary servitude (except forcri me) shall be prohibited."

It was left discretionary with Texas to remain forever one State, and to retain the whole of her territory as slave territory, or to consent to a division, in which case the prohibition would take effect, by virtue of the compact, from the date of the formation of a new State within the limits of the republic of Texas, north of 36° 30′. If, on the contrary, Texas should determine to withhold her assent, no such new State could ever be formed, and hence the prohibition would never take effect. All difficulty, however, on this point, has been removed by the act of 1850, purchasing from Texas all that portion of her territory lying north of 36° 30′, and incorporating it in the Territory of New Mexico, with the guarantee that "when admitted as a State, the said Territory, or any portion of the same, shall be received into the Union with or without slavery, as their constitution may prescribe at the time of admission." Hence all that territory, to which it is now proposed to apply the Missouri restriction for the first time, under the plea of restoring the Missouri compromise of the 6th of March, 1820, is protected from any such invasion of the rights of the inhabitants to form and regulate their own domestic affairs in their own way, by the solemn guaranties contained in the compromise measures of 1850, which blotted out the geographical line as a dividing line between free territory and slave territory, and substituted for it the cardinal principle of self-government, in accordance with the Constitution. But it will also be observed, that the bill under consideration does not propose to limit the restriction to the territory acquired from Texas, nor the country on the east side of the Rio Grande, but extend it across that river over a portion of the territory acquired from Mexico, which was never claimed by Texas nor embraced within the Louisiana purchase, and to which there is no pretext for asserting that the Missouri compromise ever applied. If, in the application of the 8th section of the act of the 6th of March, 1820, (commonly called the Missouri compromise,) over so large a district of country to which it never had any previous application, it be the policy of the House of Representatives to return to the "obsolete idea" of a geographical line as a dividing line in all time to come between slave territory and free territory, a perpetual barrier against the advancement of slavery on the one hand and free institutions on the other, the measure falls short of accomplishing the whole of their object in not extending the line to the Pacific ocean. Your committee can perceive many weighty considerations founded in policy, although wanting the sanction of sound constitutional principles, which might be urged in favor of such a measure, inasmuch as the barrier once erected from ocean to ocean—permitting slavery on the one side and prohibiting it on the other—if universally acquiesced in and religiously observed as a patriotic offering upon the altar of our common country, would put an end to the controversy forever, and form a bond of peace and brotherhood in the future. But, unfortunately, when this expedient was proposed by the Senate in 1848, it was indignantly repudiated by the House of Representatives, and as a consequence the whole country was plunged into a whirlpool of sectional strife and angry crimination, which alarmed the greatest and purest patriots of the land for the safety of the republic, and was only rescued from the impending perils by the adoption of the compromise measures of 1850, which abandoned the policy of a geographical line, and substituted for it the great principles of self government and State equality, in obedience to the federal Constitution. In view of the history of the past, your committee can perceive no safety in the future except in a strict and religious fidelity to the true principles of the Constitution as embodied in the adjustment of that unfortunate controversy, and adopted by the whole country as rules of action, to be applied in all future time, when in the progress of events it should be necessary to organize Territories or admit new States. The Kansas-Nebraska act was the logical sequence of the compromise measures of 1850, and rendered imperatively necessary in order to establish and perpetuate the principles of self-government and State equality in the organization of Territories and admission of new States. For these reasons your committee cannot concur with the House of Representatives in the proposition to blot out from the organic act of Kansas and Nebraska those essential provisions and cardinal principles, the faithful observance of which can alone preserve the just rights of the inhabitants of the Territories and maintain the peace, unity, and fraternity of the republic. The great object is to withdraw the slavery question from the halls of Congress and remand its decision to the people of the several States and Territories, subject to no other conditions or restrictions than those imposed by the Constitution of the United States. Those provisions of the bill under consideration which introduce and establish slavery, together with those which abolish and prohibit it, are alike obnoxious on the score of principle, inasmuch as they assert and exercise the right of Congress to form and regulate the local affairs and domestic institutions of a distant and distinct people without their consent and regardless of their rights and wishes. To avoid all misconstruction, however, upon this point, your committee deem it proper to remark that their objections do not apply to that part of the bill which extends the provisions of the fugitive slave law to the Territories of Kansas and Nebraska, and provides "that any person lawfully held to service in any other State or Territory, and escaping into either the Territory of Kansas or Nebraska, may be reclaimed and removed to the person or place where such service is due, under any law of the United States which shall be in force upon the subject." In this clause your committee are rejoiced to find a frank and conscientious acknowledgement of the duty of Congress to provide efficient laws for carrying into faithful execution the provision of the Constitution of the United States which provides for the rendition of fugitive slaves as well as all other obligations imposed by that instrument.

The preservation of our free institutions depend upon a faithful observance of the Constitution in all its parts; and the assurance thus furnished that the representatives of the people are ever ready to provide new and additional guarantees when supposed to be necessary for the faithful performance of that constitutional obligation, which has been the subject of the severest criticism in some portions of the country, cannot fail to gratify every true friend of the Union. In this case, however, no such legislation is necessary, inasmuch as the organic act of Kansas and Nebraska extended the provisions of the fugitive slave law to both of those Territories.

The fifteenth and sixteenth sections of the bill under consideration read as follows:

SEC. 15. *And be it further enacted,* That all suits, process, and proceedings, civil and criminal, at law and in chancery, and all indictments and informations which shall be pending and undetermined in the courts of the Territory of Kansas or of New Mexico, when this act shall take effect, shall remain in said courts where pending, to be heard, tried, prosecuted, and determined in such courts as though this act had not been passed: *Provided, nevertheless,* That all criminal prosecutions now pending in any of the courts of the Territory of Kansas, imputing to any person or persons the crime of treason against the United States, and all criminal prosecutions, by information or indictment, against any person or persons for any alleged violation or disregard whatever of what are usually known as the laws of the legislature of Kansas, shall be forthwith dismissed by the courts where such prosecutions may be pending, and every person who may be restrained of his liberty by reason of any of said prosecutions shall be released therefrom without delay. Nor shall there hereafter be instituted any criminal prosecution in any of the courts of the United

States, or of said Territory, against any person or persons, for any such charge of treason in the said Territory prior to the passage of this act, or any violation or disregard of said legislative enactments at any time.

SEC. 16. *And be it further enacted*, That all justices of the peace, constables, sheriffs, and all other judicial and ministerial officers, who shall be in office within the limits of said Territory when this act shall take effect, shall be, and they are hereby, authorized and required to continue to exercise and perform the duties of their respective offices as officers of the Territory of Kansas, temporarily, and until they, or others, shall be duly appointed and qualified to fill their places in the manner herein directed, or until their offices shall be abolished.

It will be observed that these two sections recognize the validity and binding force of the entire code of laws enacted at the Shawnee Mission, by the legislature of Kansas Territory, and provide for the faithful execution of all those enactments except the criminal code. All justices of the peace, constables, sheriffs, and all other judicial and ministerial officers, now in office are required to continue to exercise and perform the duties of their respective offices. All these officers, with the exception of the governor, three judges, secretary, and marshal, and district attorney, were elected or appointed under the laws enacted by the legislature of Kansas, while their powers, functions, and duties, are all prescribed by those laws and none others. These officers are all required to continue to perform the duties of their respective offices, by observing and enforcing all the laws enacted at the Shawnee Mission, except the criminal code. "All suits, process, and proceedings, civil and criminal, at law and in chancery, and all indictments and informations which shall be pending and undetermined in the courts of the Territory of Kansas or New Mexico, when this act shall take effect, shall remain in said courts where pending, to be heard, tried, prosecuted, and determined, in such courts, AS THOUGH THIS ACT HAD NOT BEEN PASSED." The election laws, and the laws concerning slaves and slavery, and all laws protecting the rights of persons and property, and affecting all the relations of life, are recognized as valid and required to be enforced, EXCEPTING CRIMINAL PROSECUTIONS, BY INFORMATION OR INDICTMENT, for violating or disregarding the laws of the legislature of Kansas. All such prosecutions are required to be forthwith dismissed, and the prisoners set at liberty, and no new prosecutions are to be commenced for "any violation or disregard of said legislative enactments at any time." Such is the legislation provided for in these two sections of the bill. They recognize the validity of the laws enacted at Shawnee Mission, and provide for the enforcement of all of them except in cases of criminal prosecution. Your committee are unable to perceive how the passage of such a bill would restore peace, quiet, and security to the people of Kansas. It has been alleged that there are in that Territory organized bands of lawless and desperate men, who are in the constant habit of perpetrating deeds of violence—murdering and plundering the inhabitants, stealing their property, burning their houses, and driving peaceable citizens from the polls on election day, and even from the Territory. The remedy proposed in the bill is to grant to the perpetrators of these crimes a general amnesty for the past, and a full license in the future to continue their bloody work.

There is no law in force in Kansas by which murder, robbery, larceny, arson, and other crimes known to the criminal codes of all civilized States, can be punished, except under the code enacted by the legislature of Kansas at the Shawnee Mission. The provisions of "an act for the punishment of crimes against the United States," approved April 30, 1790, is, by its terms, confined in its application to such crimes as shall be committed "within any fort, arsenal, dock-yard, magazine, or any other place or district of country under the sole and exclusive jurisdiction of the United States," and "upon the high seas and navigable waters out of the jurisdiction of any particular State," but has never been held or construed to apply to the Territories of the United States. The act of the 3d of March, 1817, "to provide for the punishment of crimes and offences committed within the Indian boundaries," extends the provisions of the said act of 1790 to the Indian country, but expressly restricts its application, as its title imports, to crimes committed "within any town, district, or territory *belonging to any nation or nations, tribe or tribes of Indians.*" Hence, the moment the Indian title is extinguished, and the country placed under the jurisdiction of a territorial government, it ceases to be "under the sole and exclusive jurisdiction of the United States," and is no longer subject to the provisions of either of the above cited acts. Thus it will be seen that if the bill from the House of Representatives should become a law with the provisions granting a general amnesty in respect to all past crimes, and unlimited license in the future to perpetrate such outrages as their own bad passions might instigate, there would be no law in force in Kansas to punish the guilty or protect the innocent.

Inasmuch as the House of Representatives, by the passage of the bill under consideration, and the Senate, by its bill for the admission of Kansas into the Union, have each recognized the validity of the laws enacted by the Kansas legislature at Shawnee Mission, so far as they are consistent with the Constitution and the organic act, and affirmed the propriety and duty of enforcing the same, except in certain specified cases, it becomes important to inquire into the extent of the differences of opinion between the House of Representatives and the Senate, in respect to the particular laws which ought not to be enforced. The Senate has already declared, in the bill for the admission of Kansas into the Union, that all laws and enactments in said Territory which are repugnant to, or in conflict with, the great principles of liberty and justice, as guarantied by the Constitution of the United States and the organic act, and embodied in the 18th section of that bill, shall be null and void, and that none such shall ever be enforced or executed in said Territory.

The said eighteenth section is in the following words:

"SEC. 18. *And be it further enacted*, That inasmuch as the Constitution of the United States and the organic act of said Territory has secured to the inhabitants thereof certain inalienable rights, of which they cannot be deprived by any legislative enactment, therefore no religious test shall ever be required as a qualification to any office or public trust; no law shall be in force or enforced in said Territory respecting an establishment of religion, or prohibiting the free exercise thereof; or abridging the freedom of speech, or of the press, or of the right of the people peaceably to assemble, and petition for the redress of grievances; the right of the people to be secure in their persons, houses, papers, and effects against unreasonable searches and seizures shall not be violated; and no warrant shall issue but upon probable cause, supported by oath or affirmation, and particularly describing the place to be searched, and the person or things to be seized; nor shall the right of the people to keep and bear arms be infringed. No person shall be held to answer for a capital or otherwise infamous crime, unless on a presentment or indictment of a grand jury; nor shall any person be subject for the same offence to be twice put in jeopardy of life or limb; nor shall be compelled in any criminal case to be a witness against himself, nor be deprived of life, liberty, or property, without due process of law; nor shall private property be taken for public use without just compensation. In all criminal prosecution, the accused shall enjoy the right to a speedy and public trial by an impartial jury of the district wherein the crime shall have been committed, which district shall have been previously ascertained by law, and to be informed of the nature and cause of the accusation; to be confronted with the witnesses against him; to have compulsory process of obtaining witnesses in his favor, and to have the assistance of counsel for his defence. The privilege of habeas corpus shall not be suspended unless, when in case of rebellion or invasion, the public safety may require it. In suits at common law, where the value in controversy shall exceed twenty dollars, the right of trial by jury shall be preserved, and no fact tried by jury shall be otherwise re-examined in any court of the United States than according to the rules of the common law. Excessive bail shall not be required, nor excessive fines imposed, nor cruel and unusual punishments inflicted. No law shall be made or have force or effect in said Territory which shall require a test oath or oath to support any act of Congress or other legislative act as a qualification for any civil office or public trust, or for any employment or profession, or to serve as a juror, or vote at an election, or which shall impose any tax upon or condition to the exercise of the right of suffrage by any qualified voter, or which shall restrain or prohibit the free discussion of any law or subject of legislation in the said Territory, or the free expression of opinion thereon by the people of said Territory."

By this provision of the bill, which has twice passed the Senate, and now remains on the Speaker's table of the House of Representatives unacted upon, and only awaits the favorable action of the House to enable it to become a law with the President's approval, all the obnoxious laws, which have been the subject of so much censure and complaint, are swept out of existence, leaving none in force in said Territory except such as are usual, proper, and necessary in all civilized communities for the protection of life, liberty, and property. Your committee have not yet relinquished the hope that the House of Representatives will concur with the Senate in the passage of that bill, and thus restore peace and security to the people of Kansas, by declaring all those obnoxious laws null and void, and providing for the faithful enforcement of the Kansas code, the validity of which has thus been frankly and solemnly acknowledged by the votes and action of each House of Congress. The two Houses of Congress having, by their action, each arrived at the conclusion that the Kansas code is valid, and that the obnoxious laws referred to ought to be declared inoperative and void, as being repugnant to the principles of liberty and justice intended to be secured by the Constitution of the United States and the Kansas-Nebraska act. it would seem, that the most serious and material point of difference between the two Houses which remains to be adjusted, is whether that part of the Kansas code which provides for the punishment of murder, robbery, larceny, and other criminal offences shall be enforced, or, whether all persons guilty of those offences shall be turned loose to prey upon the community with legalized impunity. It is true that there is, apparently, another point of difference between the two Houses, arising out of the question whether the people of Kansas shall be authorized to elect delegates to a convention, (with proper and satisfactory safe-guards against fraud, violence, and illegal voting,) and form a constitution and state government preparatory to their admission into the Union, or whether the Territory shall be reorganized in accordance with the provisions of the bill from the House and left, for some years to come, in that condition. While the House of Representatives has recently expressed its preference for the latter proposition, by the passage of the bill under consideration, your committee are not permitted to assume that they have insuperable objections to the admission of Kansas at this time, for the reason that a few weeks previous they passsed a bill to admit that Territory as a State, with the Topeka constitution. Hence the change of policy on the part of the House, in abandoning the State movement with the Topeka constitution, and substituting for it the proposition to reorganize the Territory and leave it in that condition, must be taken only as a strong expression of a decided preference on the part of the House for the bill under consideration, and not as conclusive evidence of insuperable objections to a fair bill, with proper and suitable guarantees against fraud and illegal voting, to authorize the people of Kansas to form a constitution and State government at this time. While the Senate bill, now pending before the House, is fair and impartial in all its provisions, with ample and satisfactory safe-guards against illegal and fraudulent voting, the bill from the House to reorganize the Territory contains no such provisions and affords no such assurances. It leaves the qualifications of the voters at the first election the same as they were under the Kansas-Nebraska act, with this difference, that it denies the privilege of voting and holding office to all men of foreign birth who shall have declared on oath their intention to become citizens, and who shall have taken an oath to support the Constitution of the United States, but who shall have failed from any cause to have completed their naturalization. The provision is, "that any white male inhabitant, being a citizen of the United States, above the age of twenty-one years, who shall have been a resident of said Territory at the time of the passage of this act, shall be entitled to vote at the first election." No penalties or punishments are provided for illegal voting; none for fraud in conducting the elections; none for violence at the polls; and none for destroying the ballot-boxes. All these things may be done with impunity; for, while the election must be held in pursuance of the existing laws of the Territory, which are recognized as being in force, the bill expressly provides that *no criminal prosecution shall hereafter be instituted* in any of the courts of the *United States or of said Territory for any violation or disregard of said legislative enactment at any time.* Under this bill any number of persons from Missouri or Iowa, from South Carolina or Massachusetts, or from any other part of the world, may enter the Territory on election day and take possession of the polls, and vote as many times as they choose, and drive every legal voter from the polls with entire impunity; for the bill declares that no criminal prosecutions shall ever be instituted in the courts of the United States or of said Territory for violating or disregarding the ONLY LAW which provides penalties and punishments for such outrages in the Territory of Kansas.

No measure can restore peace to Kansas which does not effectually protect the ballot-box against fraud and violence, and impart equal and exact justice to all the inhabitants. Under existing circumstances, your committee are unable to devise any measure which will more certainly accomplish these desirable objects than the bill which has twice passed the Senate, and now only awaits the concurrence of the House of Representatives, with the approval of the President, to become the law of the land.

For these reasons your committee recommend that the bill from the House of Representatives be laid on the table, as a test vote on its rejection, inasmuch as the objections apply to all the leading features and material provisions of the bill, and renders it incapable of amendment without preparing an entire new bill.

The following is the vote in the House of Representatives on the passage of the bill, the main provisions of which are set forth and explained in the foregoing report:

The yeas and nays were ordered.

The question was then taken; and it was decided in the affirmative—yeas 88, nays 74; as follows:

Yeas—Messrs. Albright, Allison, Ball, Barbour, Benson, Bishop, Bliss, Bradshaw, Brenton, Buffington, James H. Campbell, Lewis D. Campbell, Chaffee, Clawson, Colfax, Comins, Covode, Cumback, Damrell, Dean, Dick, Dodd, Dunn, Durfee, Edie, Edwards, Emrie, Flagler, Giddings, Gilbert, Granger, Grow, Robert B. Hall, Harlan, Harrison, Haven, Holloway, Thomas R. Horton, Valentine B. Horton, Hughston, Kelsey, King, Knapp, Knight, Knowlton, Knox, Kunkel, Matteson, McCarty, Killian Miller, Moore, Morgan, Morrill, Nichols, Norton, Andrew Oliver, Parker, Pelton, Perry, Pettit, Pringle, Purviance, Ritchie, Sabin, Sage, Sapp, Sherman, Simmons, Spinner, Stanton, Stranahan, Tappan, Thurston, Todd, Trafton, Wade, Wakeman, Walbridge, Waldron, Cadwallader C. Washburne, Ellihu B. Washburne, Israel Washburn, Watson, Welch, Wells, Wood, Woodruff, and Woodworth—88.

Nays—Messrs. Aiken, Barksdale, Bell, Bowie, Branch, Broom, Burnett, John P. Campbell, Carlile, Caruthers, Caskie, Howell Cobb, Williamson R. W. Cobb, Cox, Craige, Crawford, Cullen, Davidson, Henry Winter Davis, Denver, Dowdell, Edmundson, English, Faulkner, Foster, Goode, Greenwood, J. Morrison Harris, Sampson W. Harris, Thomas L. Harris, Houston, Jewett, George W. Jones, J. Glancy Jones, Kennett, Kidwell, Lake, Leiter, Lumpkin, Humphrey Marshall, Samuel S. Marshall, Maxwell, Smith Miller, Millson, Packer, Peck, Phelps, Powell, Puryear, Quitman, Reade, Ready, Ricaud, Rivers, Ruffin, Savage, Shorter, Samuel A. Smith, William Smith, Sneed, Stephens, Stewart, Swope, Taylor, Trippe, Underwood, Valk, Walker, Warner, Watkins, Winslow, Daniel B Wright, John V. Wright, and Zollicoffer—74.

So the bill, as amended, was passed.

Thus it will be seen, that while the entire republican party (with one solitary exception) voted for this odious measure, every democrat in the House voted against it. In the Senate it was referred to the Committee on Territories, where its provisions were carefully examined and thoroughly exposed in the foregoing report, which was concurred in by five of the six members of the committee. Mr. Collamer made a minority report, in which he attempts to palliate some of the monstrous provisions of the bill, but does not dispute the correctness of any one fact stated in the above report of the committee. After these two reports had been read to the Senate, and the subject had become thoroughly understood, the bill was laid on the table, with the distinct understanding that it should be deemed a test vote, on the rejection of the bill. The vote was as follows:

Yeas—Messrs. Adams, Allen, Bell, of Tennessee, Benjamin, Biggs, Bigler, Bright, Brodhead, Brown, Butler, Cass, Clay, Douglas, Evans, Fitzpatrick, Geyer, Houston, Hunter, Iverson, Jones, of Tennessee, Mallory, Mason, Pratt, Pugh, Reid, Sebastian, Slidell, Stuart, Thompson, of Kentucky, Thompson, of New Jersey, Toombs, Toucey, Weller, Wright, Yulee—35.

Nays—Messrs. Bell, of New Hampshire, Collamer, Fessenden, Fish, Foot, Foster, Hale, Harlan, Seward, Trumbull, Wade, Wilson—12.

Thus it appears that every Republican (all the supporters of Fremont) in the Senate voted against the rejection of this bill, or, in other words, every one of them declared by his vote that he was in favor of the passage of the bill, while every Democrat voted to kill the bill. But one friend of Fremont (Mr. Seward) expressed his dissent to any part of the bill; all the rest leaving it to be inferred that they were ready to vote for the bill as it stood.

VOTE IN THE HOUSE OF REPRESENTATIVES ON THE AMENDMENT MAKING THE SALARY OF THE JUDGES AND OTHER OFFICERS DEPENDENT ON THE DECISION THE COURT SHOULD MAKE IN CERTAIN CRIMINAL PROSECUTIONS.

The House then proceeded to consider the following amendment, as a proviso to the appropriations for Kansas, on which a separate vote had been asked:

Provided, That the money hereby appropriated shall not be drawn from the treasury, or any part thereof, and the same, or any part thereof, shall not be paid out of any other appropriation made by Congress, until all criminal prosecutions now pending in any court of the Territory of Kansas against any person or persons charged with treason against the United States, and all criminal prosecutions by information or indictment against any person or persons for any alleged violation or disregard of the professed laws of a body of men who assembled at the Shawnee Mission in said Territory, claiming to be the legislative assembly of the said Territory, shall be dismissed by the court; and every person who is, or may be, restrained of his liberty by reason of such prosecution or prosecutions, shall be released from confinement.

The yeas and nays were called for, and ordered.

FIRST VOTE.

The question was taken, and it was decided in the affirmative—yeas 84, nays 69, as follows:

Yeas—Messrs. Albright, Allison, Ball, Barbour, Barclay, Henry Bennett, Benson, Billinghurst, Bishop, Bliss, Bradshaw, Brenton, Buffinton, James H. Campbell, Chaffee, Ezra Clark, Clawson, Colfax, Comins, Covode, Cragin, Cumback, Damrell, Dean, Dick, Dodd, Durfee, Emrie, Flagler, Galloway, Giddings, Granger, Grow, Harlan, Holloway, Hughston, Kelsey, King, Knapp, Knight, Knowlton, Knox, Kunkel, Leiter, Matteson, McCarty, Killian Miller, Milward, Morgan, Morrill, Mott, Murray, Norton, Andrew Oliver, Parker, Pearce, Pelton, Pennington, Perry, Pettit, Pike, Pringle, Purviance, Ritchie, Robbins, Roberts, Sabin, Sapp, Sherman, Simmons, Spinner, Stanton, Stranahan, Tappan, Todd, Wade, Walbridge, Cadwalader C. Washburne, Elihu B. Washburne, Israel Washburn, Watson, Wood, Woodruff, and Woodworth—84.

Nays—Messrs. Aiken, Bocock, Bowie, Branch, Cadwalader, Lewis D. Campbell, Carlile, Caskie, Clingman, Williamson R. W. Cobb, Crawford, Henry Winter Davis, Dowdell, Dunn, Elliott, English, Eustis, Faulkner, Florence, Foster, Goode, Greenwood, Haven, Hickman, Valentine B. Horton, Houston, George W. Jones, J. Glancy Jones, Keitt, Kelly, Kidwell, Letcher, Lumpkin, Humphrey Marshall, Samuel S. Marshall, Maxwell, McMullin, Smith Miller, Millson, Moore, Phelps, Porter, Quitman, Reade, Richardson, Rivers, Ruffin, Rust, Sandidge, Savage, Seward, Shorter, William Smith, Sneed, Stewart, Swope, Taylor, Thurston, Tyson, Underwood, Valk, Warner, Watkins, Whitney, Williams, Winslow, Daniel B. Wright, John V. Wright, and Zollicoffer—69.

By the vote on this amendment it appears that the whole Republican or Fremont party attempted to destroy the purity of the judiciary and corrupt all the officers of the court, by making the payment of their salaries dependant upon their subserviency to the behests of a political party in the administration of justice.

ANOTHER ATTEMPT TO CORRUPT THE JUDICIARY FOR PARTY PURPOSES.

The following is the amendment and the vote on it, together with the vote on the passage of the bill after these amendments had been added to it:

The next amendment was read, as follows:

Add to the clause for defraying the expenses of the Supreme Court, &c., the following:

Provided, however, That no part of the money hereby appropriated shall be expended for prosecuting or detaining any person or persons charged with treason, or any other political offence in the Territory of Kansas.

Mr. PHELPS demanded the yeas and nays. The yeas and nays were ordered.

THIRD VOTE.

The question was taken; and it was decided in the affirmative—yeas 82, nays 60, as follows:

Yeas—Messrs. Albright, Allison, Ball, Barbour, Barclay, Henry Bennett, Benson, Billinghurst, Bliss, Bradshaw, Brenton, Buffington, James H. Campbell, Chaffee, Ezra Clark, Clawson, Colfax, Comins, Covode, Cragin, Cumback, Damrell, Dean, Dick, Dodd, Dunn, Emrie, Flagler, Giddings, Granger, Grow, Harlan, Hickman, Holloway, Valentine B. Horton, Hughston, Kelsey, King, Knight, Knowlton, Kunkel, Matteson, McCarty, Killian Miller, Millward, Morgan, Morrill, Mott, Murray, Norton, Andrew Oliver, Parker, Pearce, Pelton, Pennington, Perry, Pettit, Pike, Pringle, Purviance, Ritchie, Robbins, Roberts, Sabin, Sapp, Simmons, Spinner, Stanton, Stranahan, Tappan, Thurston, Todd, Trafton, Wade, Walbridge, Cadwalader C. Washburne, Elihu B. Washburne, Israel Washburn, Watson, Wood, and Woodworth—82.

Nay—Messrs. Aiken, Hendley S. Bennett, Bishop, Bowie, Branch, John P. Campbell, Lewis D. Campbell, Carlile, Caruthers, Caskie, Clingman, Williamson R. W. Cobb, Crawford, Henry Winter Davis, Dowdell, Edmundson, English, Florence, Foster, Goode, Greenwood, Thomas L. Harris, Haven, Houston, George W. Jones, J. Glancy Jones, Keitt, Kelly, Kidwell, Letcher, Lumpkin, Humphrey Marshall, Samuel S. Marshall, Maxwell, McMullin, Smith Miller, Millson, Phelps, Powell, Quitman, Richardson, Rivers, Ruffin, Rust, Sandidge, Seward, Shorter, William Smith, Sneed, Stewart, Taylor, Tyson, Underwood, Warner, Watkins, Williams, Winslow, Daniel B. Wright, John V. Wright, and Zollicoffer—60.

So the amendment was agreed to.

Pending the call of the roll,

Mr. CLINGMAN stated that Mr. EUSTIS and Mr. SHERMAN had paired off.

The bill, as amended, was then ordered to be engrossed, and read a third time; and being engrossed, it was accordingly read the third time.

Mr. PHELPS demanded the yeas and nays upon the passage of the bill.

The yeas and nays were ordered.

FOURTH VOTE.

The question was taken; and it was decided in the affirmative—yeas 84, nays 65; as follows:

Yeas—Messrs. Albright, Allison, Ball, Barbour, Barclay, Benson, Billinghurst, Bishop, Bliss, Bradshaw, Brenton, Buffinton, James H. Campbell, Lewis D. Campbell, Chaffee, Ezra Clark, Clawson, Colfax, Comins, Covode, Cragin, Cumback, Damrell, Dean, Dick, Dodd, Emrie, Flagler, Giddings, Granger, Grow, Harland, Hickman, Holloway, Valentine B. Horton, Hughston, Kelsey, King, Knapp, Knight, Knowlton, Kunkel, Leiter, Matteson, McCarty, Killian Miller, Millward, Morgan, Morrill, Mott, Murray, Norton, Andrew Oliver, Parker, Pearce, Pelton, Pennington, Perry, Pettit, Pike, Pringle, Purviance, Ritchie, Robbins, Roberts, Sabin, Sapp, Simmons, Spinner, Stanton, Stranahan, Tappan, Thurston, Todd, Trafton, Tyson, Wade, Walbridge, Cadwalader C. Washburne, Ellihu B. Washburne, Israel Washburn, Watson, Wood, and Woodworth—84.

Nays—Messrs. Aiken, Barksdale, Henry Bennett, Hendley S. Bennett, Bowie, Branch, John P. Campbell, Carlilie, Caskie, Clingman, Williamson R. W. Cobb, Crawford, Henry Winter Davis, Dowdell, Dunn, Edmunson, Elliot, Florence, Foster, Goode, Greenwood, Thomas L. Harris, Houston, George W. Jones, J. Glancy Jones, Keitt, Kidwell, Letcher, Lumpkin, Humphrey Marshall, Samuel S. Marshall, Maxwell, McMullin, Smith, Miller, Millson, Phelps, Powell, Quitman, Rivers, Ruffin, Rust, Sandidge, Seward, Shorter, William Smith, Sneed, Stewart, Taylor, Underwood, Warner, Watkins, Winslow, Daniel B. Wright, John V. Wright, and Zollicoffer—55.

So the bill was passed.

These provisions for bribing and corrupting the courts were forced on the civil appropriation bill by the republican or Fremont party, in opposition to the unanimous vote of the democracy, under the pretext that they were essential to the preservation of peace and freedom in Kansas, and that all who voted against these amendments were recreant to their duty in that respect. Fervent appeals were made to all the friends of Kansas to respond to "the shrieks for freedom," by standing by these amendments until the wheels of government should stop and anarchy reign; and they did stand firm until they discovered that the same bill contained the appropriations for their own pay and mileage, and that the Senate would refuse to pass the bill, and thus deprive the members of both houses of their pay unless these revolutionary amendments were stricken out. When these discoveries were made the republican or Fremont party were filled with consternation; they instantly became oblivious to the woes of suffering Kansas, turned a deaf ear to her shricks for freedom, and allowed enough of their own members to take the back track, vote against their own amendments, and pass the bill without any such revolutionary provisions. The potent argument of receiving *their own pay and mileage*, added to the consideration that all the persons provided for in the bill were voters at the elections, being in the employment of the civil departments of the government, could not fail to convince the supporters of Fremont that it would be wiser and more patriotic to abandon Kansas to her fate, and allow the courts to decide all cases before them, according to the law and evidence, than to stop the wheels of government by defeating *that particular bill*. Hence the civil bill became a law by the forbearance of the republican or Fremont party. It is to be hoped that the country will appreciate and reward their patriotism according to their merits.

THE ARMY BILL—AMENDMENTS—DEFEAT.

The following is the amendment which the republicans or Fremont men forced on the army appropriation bill in the House of Representatives, together with the vote on the same:

Provided, nevertheless, That no part of the military force of the United States herein provided for shall be employed in aid of the enforcement of the enactments of the alleged legislative assembly of the Territory of Kansas, recently assembled at Shawnee Mission, until Congress shall have enacted either that it was or was not a valid legislative assembly, chosen in conformity with the organic law by the people of the said Territory: *And provided,* That until Congress shall have passed on the validity of the said legislative assembly of Kansas, it shall be the duty of the President to use the military force in said Territory to preserve the peace, suppress insurrection, repel invasion, and protect persons and property therein, and upon the national highways in the State of Missouri, or elsewhere, from unlawful seizures and searches: *And be it further provided,* That the President is required to disarm the present organized militia of the Territory of Kansas, and recall all the United States arms therein distributed, and to prevent armed men from going into said Territory to disturb the public peace, or aid in the enforcement or resistance of real or pretended laws.

The question was taken, and it was decided in the affirmative—yeas 91, nays 86, as follows:

Yeas—Messrs. Albright, Allison, Ball, Barbour, Henry Bennett, Benson, Billinghurst, Bishop, Bliss, Bradshaw, Brenton, Buffington, James H. Campbell, Chaffee, Clawson, Colfax, Comins, Covode, Cragin, Cumback, Damrell, Day, Dean, Dick, Dodd, Dunn, Durfee, Edie, Emrie, Flagler, Galloway, Giddings, Gilbert, Granger, Grow, Robert B. Hall, Harlan, Harrison, Holloway, Thomas R. Horton, Valentine B. Horton, Hughston, Kelsey, King, Knapp, Knowlton, Knox, Kunkel, Leiter, Matteson, McCarty, Killian Miller, Moore, Morgan, Morrill, Mott, Nichols, Norton, Andrew Oliver, Parker, Pelton, Perry, Pettit, Pike, Pringle, Purviance, Ritchie, Sabin, Sage, Sapp, Sherman, Simmons, Spinner, Stanton, Stranahan, Tappan, Thurston, Todd, Trafton, Wade, Wakeman, Walbridge, Waldron, Cadwalader C. Washburne, Elihu B. Washburne, Israel Washburn, Watson, Welch, Wood, Woodruff, and Woodworth—91.

Nays—Messrs. Aiken, Barksdale, Bell, Bowie, Branch, Broom, Burnett, John P. Campbell, Lewis D. Campbell, Carlile, Caruthers, Caskie, Howell Cobb, Williamson R. W. Cobb, Cox, Craige, Crawford, Cullen, Davidson, Henry Winter Davis, Denver, Dowdell, Edmundson, English, Eustis, Faulkner, Foster, Henry M. Fuller, Thomas J. D. Fuller, Goode, Greenwood, J. Morrison Harris, Sampson W. Harris, Thomas L. Harris, Haven, Hoffman, Houston, Jewett, George W Jones, Kennett, Kidwell, Knight, Lake, Lindley, Lumpkin, Humphrey Marshall, Samuel S. Marshall, Maxwell, Smith Miller, Millson, Packer, Peck, Phelps, Powell, Puryear, Quitman, Reade, Ready, Ricaud, Rivers, Ruffin, Savage, Seward, Shorter, Samuel A. Smith, William Smith, William R. Smith, Sneed, Stevens, Stewart, Swope, Taylor, Trippe, Tyson, Underwood, Vail, Valk, Walker, Warner, Watkins, Whitney, Williams, Winslow, Daniel B. Wright, John V. Wright, and Zollicoffer—86.

So the amendment was concurred in.

The Senate refused to agree to this amendment for the following, among other reasons:

1st. It was irregular, unparliamentary, and revolutionary to put any such matter of legislation on a general appropriation.

2d. It undertook to deprive the President of the right to use the means authorized by the Constitution to perform his oath "to see the laws faithfully executed"—laws which the House of Representatives had recognized as valid and binding in the bill referred to in the report of the Committee on Territories, and which he was bound to use all lawful and constitutional means to enforce so long as they remained on the statute book, and so far as they were held to be constitutional by the courts of the country.

3d. It conferred on the President unlimited power—a power subversive of constitutional rights and dangerous to liberty—by substituting the military for the civil law, and making the discretion of the commander of the army the only law for the protection of persons and property in the Territory, and on the national highways in Missouri and elsewhere.

4th. It violated the following article of the amendments to the Constitution of the United States, by disarming the militia and depriving the people of the right to bear arms:

Art. 2. "A well regulated militia, being necessary to the security of a free State, the right of the people to keep and bear arms shall not be infringed."

In the Senate this Republican or Frémont amendment to the army bill was stricken out by a party vote, every Democrat voting to strike it out. The Republican or Frémont men in the House refused to allow the bill to pass as it went from the Senate, and consequently returned it to the Senate, with the following amendment:

The amendment was read, as follows:

Provided, nevertheless, and it is hereby declared, That no part of the military force of the United States, for the support of which appropriations are made by this act, shall be employed in aid of the enforcement of any enactment of the body claiming to be the Territorial Legislature of Kansas, until such enactment shall have been affirmed and approved by Congress, but this proviso shall not be so construed as to prevent the President from employing an adequate military force, but it shall be his duty to employ such force to prevent the invasion of said Territory by armed bands of non-residents, or any other body of non-residents acting, or claiming to act, as a *posse comitatus* of any officer in said Territory, in the enforcement of any such enactments, and to protect the persons and property therein, and upon the national highways leading to said Territory, from all unlawful searches and seizures; and it shall be his further duty to take efficient measures to compel the return of, and to withhold all arms of, the United States, distributed in, or to, said Territory, in pursuance of any law of the United States authorizing the distribution of arms to the States and Territories.

This amendment, being similar to the first in its objects, and obnoxious to nearly all the objections which had been found to exist to the other, was, of course, rejected by the Senate. Inasmuch as this bill contained no appropriation to pay the per diem and mileage of the members, and only provided for the payment of the officers and soldiers of the army—a class of persons who have no votes at elections—it met with no favor with the Republican or Frémont men, and they refused to allow it to become a law, and hence Congress adjourned without making any provision to pay, feed, and clothe the army.

Upon a full and careful revision of all the foregoing facts, every impartial mind is led irresistibly to the conclusion that the leading and paramount object of the Fremont party is to stop the wheels of government, stir up strife and discord in the country, and produce anarchy and violence in Kansas, with the hope of manufacturing political capital from all these sources of evil and mischief. The telegraph informs us that on the very day that the leaders of the Fremont party in Congress defeated the appropriation bill for the army, the notorious Jim Lane, their confederate, and acting under their advice and direction, and supported by money raised by subscription at their party meetings, invaded Kansas at the head of a band of lawless and marauding desperadoes, attacked and destroyed the town of Franklin, and robbed and murdered its unoffending inhabitants, for no other cause than their refusal to join the abolitionists and take up arms against the government of the Territory established by Congress. Peace, quiet, and security for life and property, prevailed in Kansas until these bands of desperadoes were sent there at the expense of the Frémont party to stir up strife and enact new scenes of violence and bloodshed, and to circulate false and exaggerated accounts throughout all the free States for political effect. These accounts, many of them manufactured to order without the slightest pretext of a foundation, and all of them distorted and colored to suit their own purposes, will increase and multiply each day until after the presidential election, when peace, and security, and law will prevail in that Territory, there being no more political capital to be made by violence, bloodshed and rebellion.

Let every fair minded man remember and reflect on these things, and be ready to expose these spurious and fraudulent accounts of the horrible deeds perpetrated in Kansas, as they shall be sent by telegraph for circulation in each State just before election. The last and only hope of the Fremont men consists in blood, violence, and murder in Kansas. If they shall fail through their agents and desperadoes to produce the sad reality upon the plains of Kansas, they will, at least, be able to fill the newspapers and flood the whole country with handbills, portraying black, bloody, and damnable deeds, with the hope of making the people believe them until after election. Let every friend of the Constitution and the Union be ready to expose the infamous fraud.

THE FEARFUL ISSUE

TO BE DECIDED IN NOVEMBER NEXT!

SHALL THE

CONSTITUTION

AND

THE UNION

STAND OR FALL?

FREMONT,

THE SECTIONAL CANDIDATE

OF THE

ADVOCATES OF DISSOLUTION!

BUCHANAN,

THE CANDIDATE OF THOSE WHO ADVOCATE

ONE COUNTRY! ONE UNION!

ONE CONSTITUTION!

AND

ONE DESTINY!

FREMONT AND HIS FRIENDS!

BEHOLD THE RECORD!

WE propose showing by indubitable testimony that John C. Fremont's leading friends are now the open enemies of the Federal Constitution; the enemies of the Union; the enemies of one-half of the States of the Union; the enemies of the laws of Congress; and the enemies to equality of the States.

THE BOSTON LIBERATOR—Garrison's organ—has finally decided to support John C. Fremont, as may be seen from the following paragraph announcing his nomination, which we copy from that paper of the 20th of June, 1856, and from other testimony which we subjoin:

"PRESIDENTIAL NOMINATIONS.—At the Anti-Fillmore American Convention, held at New York last week, Hon. Nathaniel P. Banks, of Massachusetts, was nominated for the Presidency, and Gov. Johnston, of Pennsylvania, for the Vice-Presidency. *Of course, Mr. Banks will decline this nomination. A small squad seceded, met in another hall, and nominated Com. Stockton, of New Jersey, and Kenneth Raynor, of North Carolina, for the same offices—a mere farce.* On Wednesday last, the National Republican Convention, at Philadelphia, nominated, on the first ballot, as the Republican candidate for the Presidency, Hon. John C. Fremont, of California. THE ENTHUSIASM WAS BOUNDLESS."

Banks, it will be seen, has withdrawn according to order; and all the Abolition Know Nothings are out for Fremont.

The same number of the same paper, The Liberator, holds the following language:

"*The United States Constitution is a covenant with death, and an agreement with hell.*"—See *Liberator*, June 20, 1856.

And now, from the same paper, observe the fearful issue involved in this Presidential contest. THIS IS THE ISSUE MADE PUBLIC IN THE LIBERATOR SINCE FREMONT'S NOMINATION:

"BUT ONE ISSUE—THE DISSOLUTION OF THE UNION.—See what the desperate and infernal spirit of the South is, by turning to the 'Refuge of Oppression,' and by reading the intelligence from Kansas in subsequent columns, and then sign and circulate this petition.

"*To the Senate and House of Representatives of the United States:*

"The undersigned, citizens and inhabitants of   State of respectfully submit to Congress:

"That as, in the nature of things, antagonistical principles, interests, pursuits, and institutions can never unite:

"That an experience of more than threescore years having demonstrated that there can be no real union between the North and the South, but, on the contrary, ever increasing alienation and strife, at the imminent hazard of civil war, in consequence of their conflicting views in relation to Freedom and Slavery:

"That the South, having declared it to be not only her right and purpose to eternise her slave system where it now exists, but to extend it over all the territories that now belong or may hereafter be annexed to the Republic, come what may; and having outlawed from her soil the entire free colored population of the North, made it perilous for any Northern white citizen to exercise his constitutional right of freedom of speech in that section of the country, and even in the national capital, and proclaimed her hostility to all free institutions universally:

"We, therefore, believe that the time has come for a new arrangement of elements so hostile, of interests so irreconcilable, of institutions so incongruous; and we earnestly request Congress, at its present session, to take such initiatory measures for the speedy, peaceful, and equitable dissolution of the existing Union as the exigencies of the case require—leaving the South to depend upon her own resources, and to take all the responsibility, in the maintenance of her slave system, and the North to organize an independent government in accordance with her own ideas of justice and the rights of man."—*Liberator, June* 20, 1856.

Since the above was written, the Boston Liberator, the infidel and disunion organ, through its editor, Garrison, *comes out still more openly for Fremont.*

In a speech delivered at the New England Anti-Slavery Convention on the 29th of May, 1856, by Wm. Lloyd Garrison, we have a flood of light shed on the relation between abolitionism and republicanism, which divests the subject of all doubt or uncertainty.

It would seem that some of the brothers or sisters in the Convention had spoken rather harshly of the Black Republicans, when Mr. Garrison rebuked them as follows:

"I come now to the Republican party; and while I do not forget its actual position under the Constitution and within the Union, I am constrained to differ in judgment from some of my respected friends here about the comparative merits of that party. I think that they do not always accord to it all that justice demands; *that they overlook the necessary formation of such a party as the result of our moral agitation;* and I marvel that they do not see that to quarrel with it, to the extent they are doing, is to quarrel *with cause and effect—with the work of our own hands.*"

When Mr. Garrison broached the idea that the Black Republicans were the offspring of the Abolitionists, and for that reason that they ought to be treated tenderly, Sister Foster could not restrain the instincts of her nature, and she spoke out in the meeting as follows:

"Mrs. Foster.—I admit that the party *is our own progeny;* but, as *every child needs a great deal of reproof* and constant effort to bring it up in the way it should go, this party, *which is the necessary offspring of our efforts, needs constant admonition and rebuke;* and, God giving me strength, *I will not spare it an hour until it is fully educated, reformed, and brought up to the high position of truth and duty.* [Applause.]"

At this point Brother Foster came to the relief of his spouse, and brought Mr. Garrison to the confessional by a very pertinent interrogatory:

"Mr. Foster.—Do you believe they can succeed?"

The Black Republican progeny of Mr. Garrison and Mrs. Stowe will not thank their great father for the candor of his reply to this question, but it is not the less truthful for the reason that it is disagreeable to them.

"Mr. Garrison.—*Certainly not!* But that is not the question. *They* believe that they can. They laugh at my incredulity because I do not believe it. I think that, ere long, they will be satisfied that I am right, and that they have been deluded; in which case, I expect then to hear them cry, 'EXCELSIOR—COME UP HIGHER!' *and to see many of them take their position under the banner of Disunion.*"

One more quotation from Mr. Garrison makes the record complete:

"I cannot, therefore, agree with such of our friends here as regard it as the worst or most dangerous party with which our movement has to contend. In its attitude toward the slave power, in the amount of conscience and humanity to be found in it, in its direct effort to baffle the designs of the slave oligarchy respecting the Territories of the country, it is a far better party than either of the others, and to that extent it is a sign of progress which we have no cause to lament. *I have said again and again, that in proportion to the growth of disunionism will be the growth of republicanism or free-soilism.* I think if you will examine the map of Massachusetts, for example, you will find this to hold true, with singular uniformity: *that in those places where there are the most abolitionists who have disfranchised themselves for conscience and the slave's sake, the heaviest vote is thrown for the free-soil ticket.* This is as inevitable as the law of gravitation. *The greater includes the less.* If we should begin our work over again, and try the same experiment ten thousand times over, we should have the same result in the formation of the same party. Why, then, should any one speak in a tone of despondency, or feel that our cause is in imminent danger of being wrecked? Is this to take a philosophical view of the subject? *Such, then, is my judgment of the Republican party.*"

The Liberator, of the last 4th of July, more boldly throws off the mask. Under the head of "The Great Fremont Meeting in New York," Garrison copies from the Herald and Tribune certain exaggerated extracts in favor of Fremont; and in his editorial column he thus pours out his feelings:

"INDEPENDENCE DAY.—This is the Eightieth Anniversary of American Independence. That Independence began in a spirit of compromise with the foul spirit of Slavery; it ends with every seventh person in the land a chattel slave,—the universal mastery of a slaveholding oligarchy,—the overthrow of all the constitutional rights of Northern citizens,—the reign of Lynch Law and Border Ruffianism throughout the entire South,—the subversion of the National Government by a clique of desperate and unprincipled demagogues, of which the President is a miserable and perjured tool,—the reign of violence, tyranny, and blood, on a frightful scale. *So much for disregarding the 'Higher Law' by our fathers! So much for entering into 'a covenant with death, and an agreement with hell!' Truly, God is just, and our national retribution another striking proof that, as a people sow, so shall they also reap.* A NEW REVOLUTION HAS BEGUN,—ANOTHER SECESSION is to take place,—and FREEDOM FOR ALL secured upon a sure basis. 'NO UNION WITH SLAVEHOLDERS!'"

How Seward hopes to Change the Constitution and to Dissolve the Union, beginning with Fremont's Election to the Presidency.

From Seward's speech at Albany, Oct. 12, 1855.

"Slavery is not, and never can be, perpetual. It will be overthrown either peacefully and lawfully under this Constitution or it will work the subversion of the Constitution together with its own overthrow. Then the slaveholders would perish in the struggle. The change can now be made without violence, and by the agency of the ballot-box. The temper of the nation is just, *liberal*, and forbearing. *It will contribute any money and endure any sacrifices to effect this great and important change; indeed, it is half made already.*"

William H. Seward was known at the Abolition Convention, at Philadelphia, first as a candidate, and afterwards as one of Fremont's warmest supporters. Indeed, it is well known that to Chase, Seward, and Greeley, Fremont is mainly indebted for his nomination: they defeated McLean. "When Henry Wilson mentioned the name of SEWARD, says the correspondent of the Pittsburg (Pa.) Gazette, *the whole Convention rose to its feet, gave the New York Senator three times three, and could not* have been warmer in their applause if he had just been nominated for President by acclamation."

Seward's Agitation after the Adoption of the Compromise Measures.

It is alleged by the Abolitionists that the Nebraska issue reopened the slavery agitation. To show how this is, it is only necessary to say that in April of 1851, when the cry of repeal was raised against the fugitive slave law as the Shibboleth of the party opposing the democracy, the Abolitionists of Massachusetts called a convention to assist in this repeal, and invited Mr. Seward to attend. He replied in a letter, of which the following is an extract:

"AUBURN, April 5, 1851.

"DEAR SIR: Your letter inviting me to attend a convention of the people of Massachusetts opposed to the fugitive slave law, and to communicate in writing my opinion on that statute, if I should be unable to attend the convention, has been received.

"While offering the pressure of duties here too long deferred as an apology for non-attendance, I pray you to assure the committee in whose behalf you act of my profound sense of their courtesy and kindness. It would be an honor to be invited to address the people of Massachusetts on any subject, but it might well satisfy a generous ambition to be called upon to speak to that great and enlightened Commonwealth on a question of human rights and civil liberty.

"I confess, sir, that I have earnestly desired not to mingle in the popular discussions of the measures of the last Congress. The issue necessarily involves the claims of their advocates and adversaries in the public councils to the confidence of the country. Some of those advocates have entered the popular arena, criminating those from whom they had differed, while others have endeavored by extraordinary means either to control discussion or to suppress it altogether, and thus they have shown themselves disqualified, by prejudice or interest, for practising that impartiality and candor which the occasion demanded.

"I am unwilling even to seem to imply, by reiterating arguments already before the public, either any distrust of the position of those with whom I stood in Congress or impatience for that favorable popular verdict which I believe to be near, and know to be ultimately certain.

"Nevertheless, there can be no impropriety in my declaring, when thus questioned, the opinions which will govern my vote upon any occasion when the fugitive slave law shall come up for review in the national legislature.

"I think the act signally unwise, because it is an attempt, by a purely federative government, to extend the economy of slave States throughout States which repudiate slavery as a moral, social, and political evil. Any despotic government would awaken sedition from its profoundest slumbers by such an attempt.

"*The attempt by the government has aroused constitutional resistance, which will not cease until the effort shall be relinquished.* He who teaches another faith than this, whether self-deceived or not, misleads. I think, also, that the attempt was unnecessary; that political ends—merely political ends—and not real evils resulting from the escape of slaves, constituted the prevailing motives to the enactment."

Disunionism in the House of Representatives.

Nathaniel P. Banks, Abolitionist and Disunionist, was elected Speaker of the House *by a solid sectional vote: he did not get one vote from the South.* He made the example now being followed by Fremont. His sentiments may be understood from the following unanswered extract from his speech to a Disunion meeting in New England:

"Although I am not one of that class of men who cry for the perpetuation of the Union, though *I am willing in a certain state of circumstances to let it 'slide,'* I have no fear for its perpetuation. But let me say, if the chief object of the people of this country be to maintain and propagate chattel property in man, in other words, human slavery, *this Union cannot and ought not to stand.*"

Mr. Banks is now actively leading the Abolition Know Nothings in support of Fremont.

But, before Banks was elected Speaker, Giddings had him instructed in the work of disunion. We copy from the Columbus (Ohio) State Journal, a Disunion paper. The following extract, taken from a Washington letter, dated the 5th of December, and appearing in the Journal, will throw considerable light upon the leading motives which instigated the opposition in the House of Representatives:

"On the 1st inst., at a very full meeting of the members opposed to the extension of slavery, the following resolution, offered by that vigilant, tried, and stern old man, Mr. Giddings, was adopted without a dissenting voice:

"*Resolved,* That we will support no man for Speaker who is not pledged to carry out the parliamentary law by giving to each proposed measure ordered by the House to be committed *a majority of such special committee, and to organize the standing committees of the House by placing on each a majority of the friends of freedom, and who are favorable to making reports on all petitions committed to them.*"

Giddings, in a letter to the Ashtabula (O.) Sentinel, dated Washington, December 6, 1855 (a letter which he subsequently admitted to be his on the floor of the House), spoke of this abolition triumph in the following strains:

"This unanimity of feeling was so strongly exhibited that my own mind ran back to other scenes and other times, the history of which is familiar to my readers; but the recollection is, perhaps, more vividly impressed on my own mind than that of any other man living. I will not, however, trust my pen nor my language to express the emotions which I then experienced.

"Our friends now appeared to feel that we had found a common sentiment and a common principle on which we could rally. Hope seemed to cheer them, and a firmer purpose to unite appeared to pervade the minds of all present."

The sentiments of Giddings against the South are those of Garrison, Greeley, and Phillips. No man has exhibited such ferocious hostility to the fugitive slave law, to the compromise measures, and to the Federal Constitution. His speeches, full of treason and of war, would fill a volume. We give the following specimens:

"I look forward to the day when there shall be a *servile insurrection* in the South; when the black man, armed with *British bayonets*, and led on by *British officers*, shall assert his freedom, and wage a war of extermination against his master; when the *torch of the incendiary shall light up the towns and cities of the South*, and blot out the last vestige of slavery. And though I may not mock at their calamity, nor laugh when their fear cometh, *yet I will hail it as the dawn of a political millennium*."

The following extracts are taken from a letter addressed by the Hon. J. R. Giddings, of the House of Representatives, to an anti fugitive slave law meeting held at Palmyra, Ohio, in 1850:

"The fugitive slave law commands us to participate in arresting and sending victims to this Southern immolation by torture a thousand times more cruel than ordinary assassination. I would be as willing to handle the scourge—to sink the thong into his quivering flesh, and to tear from him the life which God has given him—as to seize him and hand him over to his tormentors, with the full knowledge and conviction that they will do it. Nor is the crime of the slave-catcher less in the sight of God and good men than is the guilt of him who consummates the outrage by this final sacrifice of the victim.

"Yet we are told we must obey this law, and perpetuate these crimes, until a slave-ridden Congress shall see fit to reclaim us from such sin against God by repealing the law. '*Whether it be right to obey God rather than man, judge ye.*'

"From my innermost soul, I abhor, detest, and repudiate this law. I despise the human being who would obey it, if such a being has existence. I should regard such a man as a moral nuisance, contaminating the air of freedom, and would kick him from my door should he attempt to enter my dwelling.

"The authors of this law may take from me my substance, may imprison me, or take my life; but they have not the power to degrade me, by compelling me to commit such transcendent crimes against my fellow-man and against God's law.

"I rejoice exceedingly that the people of the free States comprehend and appreciate this insult to every freeman at the North. Public feeling is aroused; popular indignation is speaking trumpet-tongued to those servants of the people who dared thus degrade the American character by constituting us the catchpoles of Southern slave-hunters."

Giddings was the most prominent leader for Fremont in the Black Republican Convention of the 17th of June. See the testimony of the National Era, page 12.

Banks, having been instructed by Giddings, was elected. And how did he constitute the Committees of the House? BY SECTIONALIZING THE HOUSE! *Every leading committee has an Abolition Disunionist for chairman, and a Disunion majority!* There are some thirty-five committees in the House, and but one Southern Democrat was appointed chairman of a committee of the least consequence, Gen. Quitman, of Mississippi. Giddings, Grow, Campbell, of Ohio, Washburn, of Maine, Mace, Bennett, of New York, Benson, Simmons, of New York, Morgan, of New York, &c., &c., all Black Republicans, monopolized all the great committees. *Thus was the work of Disunion formally begun in the Congress of the United States!* This monstrous act, unprecedented in all our history, was the deliberate work of the men who now surround Fremont. Will he hesitate to carry out the baleful project, if elected? Will those who rule him be less bold than they are in Congress, when they lay hands on the Government and the Constitution? It would be madness to doubt them.

Fremont's Friends in Ohio.

The Abolitionist Convention, which nominated Salmon P. Chase, for Governor of Ohio, adopted the following resolutions. All these fanatics are now for Fremont:

"*Resovled,* That we cannot *respect,* nor can we *confide,* in those '*Lower Law*' doctors of Divinity, who hold *human* laws *above* the laws of God; nor can we concur in their teachings, that the *Divine* law is subject to *Congressional Compromise.*"—*Chase Convention, Ravenna.*

"*Resolved,* That we hereby give it distinctly to be understood, by this nation and the world, that, as Abolitionists, considering that the strength of our cause lies in its righteousness, and our hopes for it in our conformit to the laws of God, and our support for the rights of man, we owe to the *Sovereign Ruler of the Universe*, as a proof of our allegiance to Him, in all our civil relations and offices, whether as friends, citizens, or as public functionaries, sworn to support the Constitution of the United States, to regard and treat the third clause of the instrument, whenever applied in the case of a fugitive slave, as utterly *null* and *void*, and consequently as forming no part of the Constitution of the United States, whenever we are called upon or sworn to support it."—*Chase Convention.*

SALMON P. CHASE was at the Abolition Convention, at Philadelphia, on the 17th of June, by letter and originally as a candidate—afterwards a zealous supporter of Fremont for nomination. *He is an original old line Abolitionist, in favor of negro suffrage and negro equality; opposed to the Constitutional provisions for the rendition of fugitive slaves; in favor of excluding all slaveholders from office; believes that slavery in the States would not continue a year after the accession of the Anti-slavery party to power; and thinks that it ought to be abolished by the Constitutional power of Congress, and the State Legislatures.*

So BENJAMIN F. WADE, now a U. S. Senator from Ohio, is a supporter of Fremont, and a leader of the party. Hear him:

"He thought there was but one issue before the people, and that was the question of American slavery. *He said the Whig party is not only dead, but stinks.* It shows signs occasionally of convulsive spasms, as is sometimes exhibited in the dead snake's tail after the head and body have been buried.

"*There is really no union now between the North and the South*, and he believed no two nations upon the earth entertained feelings of more bitter rancor towards each other, than these two nations of the Republic. The only salvation of the Union, therefore, was to be found in divesting it entirely from all taint of slavery."

RUFUS P. SPAULDING was a member and leader of the Convention. Hear him:

"In the case of the alternative being presented of the continuance of slavery or a dissolution of the Union, I am for dissolution, and I care not how quick it comes."

HORACE MANN, formerly of Massachusetts, and now of Ohio, is the supporter of Fremont. Hear him;

"In conclusion I have only to add that such is my solemn and abiding conviction of the character of slavery, that, under a full sense of my responsibility to my country and my God, I deliberately say, *better disunion —better a civil or a servile war—better anything that God in his providence shall send—than an extension of the bounds of slavery.*"

What killed off Judge McLean at Philadelphia.

The public have long known Judge McLean as a man of learning and ability and firmness of character. When consulted by the "Republicans" on the subject of being a candidate for the Presidency, he made this distinct avowal:

"But my mind has been made up, if elected, I would reform the government and rest the executive power on the great principles of the Constitution, or fall in the attempt. On no other condition could I accept the office of President. This involves no sectionalism, except that which arises from the independence of State government and the fundamental law of the Union."

As the Philadelphia Convention was based on Sectionalism, its hopes of carrying the election resting almost wholly upon that ground, this repudiation by the Judge darkened his prospects. When he added that he would seek reform, instead of opening the treasury and means of the government to be plundered, his chance for a nomination became hopeless, and his name was withdrawn, and one believed to be more yielding and pliant on both points was promptly nominated. Sectionalism for a basis, and plunder for an object, were never more markedly displayed. Both are strikingly manifested in the selection of Fremont and Dayton.

Giddings in the Disunion Convention.

JOSHUA R. GIDDINGS was at this Convention, a leading spirit in all its acts, reeking as he is with the stench of twenty years of Abolitionism. What he did in that Convention, the National Executive Disunion organ at Washington will say. We copy from the Era of the 26th of June, 1856:

"Thank God! the movement has escaped this danger; the counsels of temporizing men have failed; to the bold, clear-sighted Joshua R. Giddings, sustained by the good sense of the Convention, are we indebted for the preservation of the Great Movement against the Slave Power, *free* from all entangling alliances."

The Friends of Fremont in Illinois.

The Abolition Know Nothings of Illinois, now all for Fremont, adopted the following resolutions, July 11, 1855. Their action since then is even more revolutionary.

"That the time has arrived when the American party of the United States are called upon to take open, fearless, and unreserved ground upon the great question of Slavery, that is now agitating the people of every section of this Union; and that the intense excitement and agitation which at the present time are distracting our country upon the subject of Slavery have been caused by the repeal of the Missouri Compromise; and that that repeal was uncalled for, a gross violation and disregard of a sacred compact, entered into between the two great sections of this confederacy, and in the highest degree destructive to the peace and welfare of this Union. That a restoration of the Missouri Compromise, as it will restore the territory for which it was originally made to the same situation in which it was before that line was unnecessarily destroyed, so it will restore peace and harmony to the country, without injury or injustice to any portion of the Union; that while it will only give to freedom that which with due solemnity and in good faith was long since conveyed to her under the contract, it will equally preserve the full and undisputed rights acquired under it by the South, and that therefore the Missouri Compromise should be restored, and that in all political national contests the American party in the State of Illinois will demand of its candidates for office, among other qualifications, their open and undisguised opinions upon this subject.

"The essential modification of the naturalization laws by extending the time of residence required of those of foreign birth to entitle them to citizenship. A total repeal of all state laws allowing any but citizens of the United States the right of suffrage. But a careful avoidance of all interference with rights of citizenship already acquired under existing laws.

"Resistance to the corrupting influences and aggressive policy of the Romish Church, unswerving opposition to all foreign influence, or interference of foreign emissaries, whether civil or ecclesiastical."

To this we may add the fact that every Black Republican in Congress from Illinois is for Fremont.

Fremont's Friends in New Hampshire.

Gov. Colby, Hale, Tuck, and all the Disunionists in New Hampshire, are under the Fremont flag. The following resolution passed the last Fremont Abolition Legislature of New Hampshire:

"*Resolved*, That the people of New Hampshire demand as a right the restoration of said Compromise, and the amendment of the Kansas and Nebraska bill, so called, so as to exclude Slavery from said Territories, and will never consent to the admission into the Union of any State out of said Territory with a Constitution tolerating Slavery."

John P. Hale, of New Hampshire, a delegate to the Black Republican Fremont Convention of the 17th of June, 1856, addressed that Convention, and said:

"Mr. Hale congratulated the Convention upon the spirit of unanimity with which it had done its work. *I believe*, said he, *that this is not so much a Convention to change the Administration of the Government, but to say whether there shall be any government to be administered. You have assembled, not to say whether this Union shall be preserved, but to say whether it shall be a blessing or a scorn and hissing among the nations.* Some men pretend to be astonished and surprised at the events which are occurring around us; but I am not more surprised than I shall be this autumn to see the fruits following the buds and the blossoms."

Fremont's Know Nothing Friends in Massachusetts.

In Massachusetts the Abolition column is a unit for Fremont, and this includes not only Wilson and Sumner, not only Garrison and Wendell Phillips, but, also, the Rockwell and Boston Atlas party.

Senator Wilson and Disunion.

In October, of 1855, Senator WILSON, of Massachusetts, made a speech at the Tabernacle, in New York, in which he said:

"Every generous impulse of the human heart is with us—every affection of the human conscience is with us; the great hopes of the human race are all with us, and we shall triumph in the end; we shall overthrow the slave power of the republic; we shall enthrone freedom; shall abolish slavery in the Territories; we shall sever the national government from all responsibility for slavery, and all connection with it; and then, gentlemen, then, when we have put the nation, in the words of Mr. Van Buren, openly, actually, and perpetually on the side of freedom, we shall have glorious allies in the South. We shall have men like Cassius M. Clay. [Loud applause.] We shall have generous, brave, gallant men rise upon the South, who will, in their own time, in their own way, for the interest of the master and bondsman, lay the foundations of a policy of emancipation that shall give freedom to three and a half millions of men in America. [Enthusiastic applause.] I say, gentlemen, these are our objects, and these are our purposes.

"We shall change the Supreme Court of the United States, and place men in that Court who believe with its pure and immaculate Chief Justice, John Jay, that our prayers will be impious to Heaven, while we sustain and support human slavery. We shall free the Supreme Court of the United States from Judge Kane. [Loud applause.] And here let me say there is a public sentiment growing up in this country that regards Passmore Williamson in his prison—[tremendous applause]—in his prison in Philadelphia, as a martyr to the holy cause of personal liberty. [Great applause.] There is a public sentiment springing up, that will brand upon the brow of Judge Kane a mark that will make him exclaim, as his namesake, the elder Cain, 'It is too great for me to bear.' [Loud applause.]"

Hear Henry Wilson, Senator, in the Philadelphia Know Nothing Convention, June 12, 1855:

"I am in favor of relieving the Federal Government from all connection with, and responsibility for, the existence of slavery. To effect this object I am in favor of the abolition of slavery in the District of Columbia, and the prohibition of slavery in all the Territories."

Garrison, Sumner, Banks, Rockwell, and Wilson.

We have already shown that Garrison has resolved to support Fremont; and it is known that Sumner, Banks, Rockwell, and Wilson, do so most heartily. The following exhibits the harmony of feeling between them:

"No union with slaveholders. Up with the flag of Disunion, that we may have a free and glorious Union of our own, &c."—*William L. Garrison.*

"Mark! How stands Massachusetts at this hour in reference to the Union? Just where she ought to be—*in an attitude of open hostility.*"—*The Liberator, Garrison's paper.*

"A northern confederacy, with no union with slaveholders. To this all is fast tending, and to this all must soon come. The longer it is delayed, the worse for the country, and for the cause of freedom. To this end all who love liberty will labor.

"Justice and liberty, God and man, demand the dissolution of this slaveholding Union, and the formation of a NORTHERN CONFEDERACY, in which slaveholders shall stand before the law as felons, and be treated as pirates are treated. God and humanity demand a ballot-box in which the slaveholders shall never cast a ballot. *In this, what State so prepared to lead as the old Bay State? She has already made it a penal offence to help execute a law of the Union. I want to see the officers of the State brought into collision with those of the Union.*"—*Liberator*, Sept. 1855.

This much for Garrison. He leaves no room for doubt as to what he means. He means dissolution, and nothing else. Let us see how these declarations harmonize with some others:

"The good citizen, as he reads the requirements of this act (the fugitive slave) is filled with horror. * * * Here the path of duty is clear. *I am bound to disobey this act.* * * * * *

"Sir, I will not dishonor this home of the Pilgrims and of the Revolution by admitting,—nay, I cannot believe—that this bill will be executed here."—*Charles Sumner, Oct.* 1850, *in Boston, and Aug.* 26, 1852, *in U. S. Senate.*

"Let us remember that more than three millions of bondmen, groaning under nameless woes, demand that we shall cease to reprove each other, and that we labor for their deliverance. * * * * * *

"I tell you here to-night, that the agitation of this question of human slavery will continue while the foot of a slave presses the soil of the American republic."—*Henry Wilson, United States Senator.*

"I am not one of that class of men who cry for the perpetuation of the Union, though *I am willing, in a certain state of circumstances, to let it 'slide.'* "—*Nathaniel P. Banks, Representative to Congress.*

"I will not stop to inquire whether or not the act is constitutional. If it is not, it ought to be. I view the act as the faithful expression of the moral sentiment of the people of Massachusetts."—*Mayor Chapin, of Worcester.*

"The object to be accomplished is this: *That the free States shall take possession of the Government by their united votes.* Minor interests and old party affiliations and prejudices must be forgotten. We have the power in number; *our strength is in union.*"—*Simon Brown, Massachusetts Freesoil Candidate for Lieutenant Governor.*

"Recognizing, therefore, *the paramount issue,* I recognize, as the only practical means of sustaining our position upon that issue, our co-operation with the masses of our friends in other States in the formation of the Republican party of the Union."—*Julius Rockwell, Massachusetts Freesoil Candidate for Governor.*

Hear James Watson Webb, another Fremont leader. (*We copy from Webb's New York Courier & Enquirer*)—

"We love (quoted) the Whig party, but we love its principles more. We dislike Abolitionism; but we would rather a thousand times vote for Garrison and Tappan as President and Vice President than tamely submit for an hour to the humiliation which the Senate has put upon us by the repeal of the Missouri Compromise.

"We are willing (quoted again) to consort with the most rabid Abolitionists in order to restore the Missouri Compromise, and thus redress a great wrong."

To which Garrison, in his Boston Liberator, thus affectionately responds:

"THE DISSOLUTION OF THE UNION ESSENTIAL TO THE ABOLITION OF SLAVERY.—But until we cease to strike hands religiously, politically, and governmentally with the South, and declare the Union to be at an end, I believe we can do nothing even against the encroachments of the slave power upon our rights. When will the people of the North see that it is not possible for liberty and slavery to commingle, or for a true union to be formed between freemen and slaveholders? Between those who oppress and the oppressed, no concord is possible. This Union—it is a lie, an imposture, and our first business is to seek its utter overthrow. In this Union there are three millions and a half of slaves clanking their chains in hopeless bondage. Let the Union be accursed! Look at the awful compromises of the constitution by which that instrument is saturated with the blood of the slave!"

General Webb's candidate for President has erected his platform!

Fremont's Friends in Massachusetts nullifying the Federal Constitution.

The celebrated Personal Liberty law, passed by the friends of Fremont in the Massachusetts Legislature, nullifying the fugitive slave law, a law based upon that provision of the Federal Constitution without which no Constitution could have been framed and adopted —is as follows:

"By the 10th section it is provided that 'any person who shall grant a certificate under the act of 1851 shall be deprived of any office he may hold under the Commonwealth, and shall be forever thereafter ineligible to any office of trust, honor, or emolument under the law of the Commonwealth.'

"Obedience to the laws of Congress is thus made a cause why a citizen should be deprived of all public confidence and offices of trust; in other words, rewards are held out for disobedience, while punishment is dealt out for fealty to the Constitution.

"The eleventh section declares that 'any person who shall act as counsel or attorney for any claimant under said act shall be deprived of any commission he may then hold under the laws of the Commonwealth, and shall be thereafter incapacitated to appear as counsel or attorney in the courts of the Commonwealth.'

"Any attorney who shall presume to pursue his chosen profession, and act as counsel in the United States Courts, to aid in the investigation of the rights of parties, and to give effect to the Constitution he was sworn to support when he became a member of the Massachusetts bar, and without which act he could not practise in said courts, is to be expelled from that same bar for doing what he was required to swear he would do when admitted.

"The 16th section forbids any member of the volunteer militia from aiding in the enforcement of the fugitive slave law, and provides that 'any member of the same who shall offend against the provisions of this section shall be punished by fine of not less than one thousand and not exceeding two thousand dollars, and by imprisonment in the State prison not less than one year and not more than two years.'

"Imprisonment 'not less than one year nor more than two years' is the moderate penalty attached to the criminal offence of aiding in the execution of the laws of the land. What language of nullification can be plainer? Well did Garrison assert that Massachusetts stands 'in an attitude of open hostility to the Union!'"

Now hear Josiah Quincey of Boston.

Josiah Quincey is the venerable head of a large class of men in Boston, who are constantly at work against the Union. During the late war with England he began his crusade against the Union, and surpassed its worst adversaries. He assailed Mr. Jefferson for his purchase of Louisiana, in 1803, because this was intended, in his opinion, to extend the area of Slavery. Though past eighty-five, he is still the enemy of the Democracy. *He is now in the field for Fremont.* What his views now are, may be seen from the following extract from his speech, at Boston, on the 18th of August, 1854.

"The Nebraska fraud is not that burden on which I intend now to speak. There is one nearer home, more immediately present and more insupportable. Of what that burden is, I shall speak plainly. The obligation incumbent upon the free States to deliver up fugitive slaves is that burden—*and it must be obliterated from that Constitution, at every hazard.*

"And such an obliteration can be demonstrated to be as much the interest of the South as it is of the North."

This man knows that we should have no Union or Constitution, but for this very provision!

Josiah Quincey is still in the land of the living; and though approaching his ninetieth year, is still as hostile to the Union as he was fifty-three years ago, while Jefferson was President, or at a later period, when Jackson was chief magistrate.

Fremont's Friends in New York.

Gen. JAMES WATSON WEBB was a delegate to the Black Republican Convention, at Philadelphia, and favored that body with his sage counsels. He delivered a speech, which is reported for the New York Times, and from which we make the following extract, and ask for it a careful perusal:

"Why, I ask, are we here? We are here because the country is in danger. We are here because a solemn compact, by which the curse of Slavery was limited forever to latitude 30 deg. 30 min. has been violently disruptured, torn asunder, and the people of the North told 'you shall have this matter forced upon you.' Now, what are the people doing? Our people, loving order and loving law, and willing to abide by the ballot-box, come together from all parts of the Union and ask us to give them a nomination which, when fairly put before the people, will unite public sentiment, and, through the ballot-box, will restrain and repel this pro-slavery extension, and this aggression of the slaveocracy. What else are they doing? They tell you that they are willing to abide by the ballot-box, and willing to make that the last appeal. *If we fail there, what then? We will drive it back, sword in hand, and, so help me God! believing that to be right, I am with them.* [Loud cheers, and cries of 'Good.'] Now, then, gentlemen, on your action depends the result. You may, with God's blessing, present to this country a name rallying around it all the elements of the opposition, and we will thus become so strong that through the ballot-box we shall save the country. *But, if a name be presented on which we may not rally, and the consequence is civil war—yes, nothing more, nothing less, but civil war—I ask, then, what is our first duty?*"

In another part of this pamphlet Mr. Seward's opinion may be found.

Horace Greeley was one of the most active advocates of Fremont, and now advocates him on the Disunion grounds.

James Gordon Bennett has also been hired to advocate Fremont, though on the 4th of April, 1856, he spoke of him in the following insulting terms:

"COL. FREMONT BROUGHT OUT.—The 'Cleveland Herald' (NIGGER WORSHIPPER), has hoisted the flag of Col. John C. Fremont, as the proper Presidential candidate of the Anti-slavery Holy Alliance. In the course of a lengthy glorification over him, this Cleveland organ says:

"'Col. Fremont, we feel authorized to say, does not acquiesce in the Kansas-Nebraska Act; in submission to the wrong perpetrated in violating the compact; in the atrocious iniquity of defeating the law thus substituted by force, when it was discovered that it would not subserve the purposes of the enemies of freedom; and the crime of the Government in upholding that usurpation, the most tyrannical in its laws of any since Draco's. When the proper occasion comes for an avowal of his principles and purposes on the leading questions of the day, we are assured, he will express them without reserve.'

"It thus appears, that our Cleveland abolition cotemporary speaks by authority. Fremont has caught the White House fever. He is in the hands of his friends. He is rich, exceedingly, and said to be liberal. Does Seward give way, to save expenses, this time? It looks very much as if Fremont were to be victimized to get the party organized. Let him consult Live Oak George."

The Avowed Abolitionist and Disunionist, H. Ward Beecher, of New York, on Fremont.

The reverend agitator, Ward Beecher, is out for Fremont, in the last number of his "Independent." He is, probably, next to Garrison and Phillips, the most profligate calumniator of the Constitution and the Union. Now for the opinions of this new captain of the Fremont forces:

On the 16th of January, 1855, Beecher said, in a lecture in New York, on the subject of cutting the North from the South:

"All attempts at evasion, at adjourning, at concealing and compromising, are in vain. The reason of our long agitation is, not that restless Abolitionists are abroad, that ministers will meddle with improper themes, that parties are disregardful of their country's interest. These are symptoms only, not the disease; the effects, not the causes.

"Two great powers that will not live together are in our midst, and tugging at each other's throats. They will search each other out, though you separate them a hundred times. And if by an insane blindness you shall contrive to put off the issue, and send this unsettled dispute down to your children, it will go down, gathering volume and strength at every step, to waste and desolate their heritage. Let it be settled now. Clear the place.

Bring in the champions. Let them put their lances in rest for the charge. Sound the trumpet, and *God save the right!*"

Rifles before Bibles.

At a public meeting held in his church to promote emigration to Kansas, the Rev. Henry Ward Beecher made the following remarks, as we find them in the report of the New York *Evening Post:*

"He believed that the Sharp rifle was truly *moral* agency, and there was more moral power in one of those instruments, so far as the slaveholders of Kansas were concerned, than in a hundred Bibles. You might just as well, said he, read the Bible to buffaloes as to those fellows who follow Atchison and Stringfellow; but they have a supreme respect for the logic that is embodied in Sharp's rifles. The Bible is addressed to the conscience; but when you address it to them it has no effect—there is no conscience there. Though he was a peace man, he had the greatest regard for Sharp's rifles, and for that pluck that induced those New England men to use them. In such issues, under such circumstances, he was decidedly in favor of such instrumentalities. General Scott had said it was difficult to get the New England men into a quarrel, but when they are waked up and have the law on their side, they are the ugliest customers in the world."

The *New York Observer*, a religious paper, of vast influence, copying the above, adds:

"We remember the time when, in the same church, the same minister of the Gospel of Christ presented a cannon-ball to a political agitator as the argument to which it was best to resort. That act, as inconsistent as it then appeared, and still appears to us, was innocent compared with the intemperate, not to say sacrilegious language of the extract made above."

WHAT A COMBINATION! Seward, Greeley, Bennet, Watson Webb, H. Ward Beecher, &c. There can be no doubt that this goodly company will speedily be increased by the addition of Fred. Douglass and his *black* republicans.

Every Black Republican in Congress, from New York, is now the earnest advocate of Fremont.

Another Disunion Witness for Fremont.

From the New York National Anti-Slavery Standard, June 21, 1856.

"THE ABOLITIONISTS AS PROPHETS.—Whoever has been an attentive reader of Anti-Slavery literature and journalism for the last fifteen or twenty years, cannot but have been struck with the spirit of prophecy that runs through it all. To be sure, the Abolitionists may be said to belong to that large class of prophets who help to bring about the accomplishment of their own predictions. But it is a proof that they have known what they wanted, and also how best to bring it about. They have had a clear vision from the beginning of the way in which they were to walk, and of the work which they had to do. They acted on certain fixed principles, basing their measures on the nature of things and the nature of man; and, as their principles were eternally right, and their views of man and his ways founded on reason and experience, and as their speculations and their practice had no taint of selfishness in them, it was almost inevitable that they should see clearly and act sagaciously. Only, they have not seen half that was to come to pass, and the times were hidden from them, so that they are astonished at the haste with which the procession of events hurries past, in spite of the second sight which discerned their coming shadows in the distant future.

"Among the many predictions which they have uttered, or rather the many statements they have made, as to what must come to pass, the one which five or six years ago, seemed the wildest, *was the necessary division of the nation into two parts—the Northern and the Southern—of which the principles should be Slavery and Anti-Slavery.* Five years ago, what seemed more unlikely than that the nation should be divided into strictly sectional parties as it is now? The Whigs were running up their bids for slaveholding support with a desperation which showed that they had abandoned any other hope of success. Daniel Webster had abandoned all hope of a North, and had flung himself and all he had at the feet of the Slave-masters, as his last and only chance for the eminence he sighed for. They spurned him away, to be sure, and sent him broken-hearted into his grave; but they appointed both the candidates and elected the one they loved the best.

"The idea of a Northern party, of a party which should not extend its ramifications into the Southern States, was regarded as something worse than a chimera, as a positive imagining of the death of the Republic, as a positive misprision of treason. What a change has come over the dreams of the people since then! The Whig party, five years ago in power, and with a reasonable prospect of maintaining it, now dispersed, is demolished and ground to powder. Their very name has vanished from the face of the earth—or exists only as a mockery and a laughing-stock. The Abolitionists foresaw that this must come to pass; but they did not dream of its accomplishing itself so soon." "That the National parties should sooner or later divide on the only real matter of dispute existing in the country, was inevitable."

"But the lines are now drawn and the hosts are encamped over against each other. The attempt to keep up a delusive alliance with natural enemies has been abandoned.

"The Abolitionists have been telling these things in the ears of the people for a quarter of a century. They have had a double part in what has come to pass, both by preparing the minds of the people of the North, and *by compelling the people of the South to the very atrocities which have startled the North into attention.* Nothing but the madness which ushers in destruction and the pride which goeth before a fall, on the part of the slaveholders, could have roused the sluggish North from its comfortable dreams of wealth, and made it put itself even into a posture of resistance."

"The North is in a state of excitement, temporary perhaps, but real for the time, and the widening lines of division between the North and South are growing deep and distinct.

"It is long since this paper took the ground that the *first thing, though by no means the only thing, needful was the formation of Sectional parties—of parties distinctly Northern and Southern, and, of necessity, Slavery and Anti-Slavery. We rejoice that our eyes behold the day of that beginning of the end.* Not that we have any very exalted hopes from the success of the Republican party, even if we considered its success a very likely thing. All that it proposes to itself is to keep Slavery out of Kansas, provided the actual settlers there do not want to have it in. This is a very small platform for a great party to stand upon, it must be owned; and in rejoicing to see it, we certainly are grateful for very moderate mercies. But it is not the platform that is significant—it is not the point nominally at issue that is the material thing. *The position is everything.* It is the attitude that is expressive and encouraging. *It is the entire separation of the party from all Southern alliance, and from all possibility of Slaveholding help, that gives it its encouraging aspect and makes it with all its shortcomings, a thing to thank God for.*

"We need hardly say that we do not look upon this new party as one that should supersede the Anti-Slavery Movement. *It has sprung from that movement, and whatever of strength and hope it has lies in the Anti-Slavery feeling of the Northern mind.* It is vain that servile men-pleasers *seek to separate this effect from its Anti-Slavery origin. The Slaveholders stamp it with its real character*, and DESCRIBE IT BETTER THAN IT LIKES TO DO ITSELF. It is true that the differing sagacities of the Slaveholders and the Abolitionists both discern that this must be the ultimate result."

The Disunion Organ at the seat of the National Government out for Fremont.

From the Washington National Era, of June 26, 1856.

"Having thus given an exposition of the action of the Convention, and defined our position, we shall henceforth do all that may lie in our power to bring about a perfect union of the friends of Freedom at home and of good faith and peace in our foreign relations, against the Cincinnati nominations, pledged as they are by the platform which accompanies them, and the majority who framed both, to Slavery at home and filibustering abroad. Like many others, we may have been vexed, disappointed, sometimes mortified, at the injudicious and unfair measures of men who ought to have known better; but, we place our great movement above men: it is the only movement which aims or is calculated to save Kansas, and put an end to the despotism which repealed the Missouri Compromise, and is perpetually seeking to subjugate the country to Slavery: its platform is clear, sound, and comprehensive: its nominations must represent it: by sustaining them, we sustain it: opposition to them will only tend to perpetuate the spirit and policy of an Administration which has brought the country to the verge of civil and foreign war. Will not patriotic men, whatever may have been their preferences, hesitate long before assuming such a responsibility as that?"

From the same paper of July 3, 1856.

"The Philadelphia Convention has defined the issues of the campaign, framed the platform, made the nominations, and respectfully called upon the People of the United States, without distinction of party, to sustain them. We shall be very happy to see North Americans and South Americans and all sorts of Americans rallying to the standard of Fremont, and uniting to put down the Slave Power, but let us have no talk of special arrangements with any particular class or party."

Fremont's Friends in Pennsylvania.

We aver that there is not an Abolitionist or Disunionist in Pennsylvania who is not an active and open friend of John C. Fremont for the Presidency. David Wilmot and William F. Johnston lead the motley crew, both recreants from the Democratic party, because the Democratic party respected the Constitution of the United States, and would not desert its injunctions. Ever since their recreancy, they have been busied in doing all within their power to destroy the efficiency of the Democracy, and to assist the worst fanatics of the day. Conservative men will not forget that Johnston, when the Legislature of Pennsylvania passed a law for the purpose of assisting the officers of the General Government to execute the fugitive slave law, put the bill in his pocket, while Governor of the State, and retained it, thus defeating the object of the majority of the Legislature. Wilmot has proceeded from bad to worse. At first, he was only in favor of the Wilmot proviso, and continued to profess to be a Democrat for some time. Now he is the companion and friend of men, whom, ten years ago, he would have regarded it as a personal insult to be associated with. We might enumerate a hundred others of the same way of thinking, but it is enough for us to mention Thaddeus Stevens, Passmore Williamson, and the officers of the Abolition and Anti-slavery Society in Philadelphia. The plotters of the Christiana outrage are all embarked in the cause which acknowledges John C. Fremont as its leader and its candidate.

The only candidate to arrest this tide of demoralization and sectionalism, is James Buchanan. It is against him and against the Constitution that this combination has been formed. It is in vain for a conservative citizen, of whatever politics, to close his eyes to the fact that the choice is narrowed down between Buchanan and Fremont, between the Constitution as represented by the one, and Disunion as represented by the other. The election of the latter would dissolve every tie binding these States together. It would convert the District of Columbia into the theatre of a civil war; it would alienate every Southern State through its representatives, and it would leave in each branch of Congress a fanatical representation committed to the worst doctrines that have ever been preached or practised in any country. It is also in vain for moderate order-loving citizens to deny to themselves that the combination which supports John C. Fremont is at the same time the representative of other factions, and that chief among these latter is the faction of Abolition Know Nothings. The national men in the North and South who still support Mr. Fillmore, are regarded already by Fremont and his friends as certain, in the end, to prove his willing or unwilling allies. Even now where there are Fremont and Fillmore tickets running in the free States, such men as Wm. F. Johnston, Thaddeus Stevens, and David Wilmot, of Pennsylvania, have prepared a plan by which the National friends of Fillmore and the Disunion friends of Fremont shall vote the same electoral ticket, though Fillmore himself has denounced in terms of withering eloquence the platform upon which Fremont stands, while in the South every vote thrown for Mr. Fillmore is more or less an aid to John C. Fremont, to the extent that it may weaken James Buchanan.

We would speak of Mr. Fillmore with entire respect. His speech at Albany was patriotic and forcible, but it cannot be denied that out of New York, in the North, all those who pretend to support him will be called upon in the State elections to unite against the Democratic party with the friends of Fremont, otherwise known as the Black Republicans. In the November election, when the Presidential candidates come to be voted for, a similar attempt will be made to bring his friends into the support of the same electoral ticket, which is pledged to the support of the candidate of Greeley, Seward, and Giddings.

SHORT ANSWERS

TO

RECKLESS FABRICATIONS,

AGAINST THE

Democratic Candidate for President,

JAMES BUCHANAN.

PHILADELPHIA:
WILLIAM RICE, BOOK AND JOB PRINTER,
PENNSYLVANIAN BUILDING, 46 S. THIRD STREET.
1856.

SHORT ANSWERS TO RECKLESS FABRICATIONS.

THE "DROP OF BLOOD" FALSEHOOD.

It must be a desperate calumny that Horace Greeley will not circulate against a political opponent. In his New York *Tribune*, of the 7th of June, 1856, he refuses to endorse the story, that Mr. Buchanan had once declared, that "if he had a drop of Democratic blood in his body, he would open his veins and let it out." Mr. Greeley says:

"There has long been a story current that, in his old Federal days, Mr. Buchanan once declared, that 'if he supposed he had a drop of Democratic blood in his veins, he would open them and let it out.' We do not think any one who knew Mr. Buchanan, can have ever credited this tale. There is not a man living more unlikely to make rash, silly speeches, than he is."

It is scarcely necessary to add refutation to this *amende honorable;* but as the accusation, contemptible as it is, may require some new authoritative contradiction, we give Mr. Buchanan's own words, in a letter to the Philadelphia *Courier and Enquirer*, introduced by the editor of the Harrisburg *Reporter:*

[From the Washington Union.]

THE "DROP OF BLOOD" CALUMNY.

We published yesterday the emphatic denunciation by the Lancaster *Intelligencer*, of the base calumny which attributed to Mr. Buchanan the declaration, that "if he had a drop of Democratic blood in his veins, he would let it out." It seems now that this falsehood originated in 1828, when Mr. Buchanan was a candidate for Congress as a Jackson Democrat. The charge was revived a few years afterwards, when Mr. Buchanan came forward with the characteristic straightforwardess and frankness of his nature, and denounced it as an unmitigated calumny. We copy from the Harrisburg (Pennsylvania) *Reporter*, the letter of Mr

Buchanan, with the single remark that, with such a refutation as we now present, no one can repeat the slander without knowingly giving currency to a falsehood:

[From the Harrisburg (Pa.) Reporter.]

We observe by the report of Congressional proceedings, in the *National Intelligencer*, of March 30th, that on the previous Friday evening, our Senator Buchanan was assailed by Mr. Morgan, of New York, and Mr. Cooper, of Pennsylvania, upon the floor of the House of Representatives, with the charge of once having said, in a 4th of July oration, "that if he thought he had one drop of Democratic blood in his veins, *he would let it out*." This charge was promptly contradicted by Messrs. Ramsey and General Keim, of the Pennsylvania delegation.

It is not our intention, at present, to make any comments upon this ridiculous story, which first originated in 1828, immediately preceding Mr. Buchanan's fifth election to Congress, but merely to re-publish the letter of that gentleman to the editor af the *Pennsylvania Inquirer and Courier*, dated February 27, 1838, contradicting the charge so explicitly and unequivocally, as to silence the slander, it was supposed, forever. This letter was elicited by a similar charge, made in debate by Mr. Cox, a member of the Convention for amending the Constitution of Pennsylvania, in May, 1837. It was then promptly repelled, before the Convention, by the present Judge Porter and Emanuel C. Reigart, both members of that body—the first a prominent Democrat, and the latter one of the anti-Masonic party in Pennsylvania. Had this sentiment, or anything like it, ever been uttered by Mr. Buchanan at a "political meeting in the court-house in Lancaster," these two gentlemen, from their position and character, must either have heard it themselves, or immediately heard it from others; both of them being residents of that city when it was alleged to have been uttered, and Mr. Reigart, residing there ever since. The charge would have specially attracted public attention at that time, as Mr. Buchanan was a successful candidate for the State Legislature both in October, 1814, and October, 1815.

Mr. Cox, not satisfied with the contradiction of Mr. Porter and Mr. Reigart, endeavored to obtain *proof* of the charge, and renewed, in a letter to the editor of the *Pennsylvania Inquirer and Courier*, dated February 24, and published in that paper of February 26, 1838, the testimony which he then adduced in support of it, and all which could be collected after a laborious search, consists of the certificate of a certain Anthony M'Glinn, and an extract of a letter from George Ford, Jr., both of which, it will be perceived, are referred to in the following letter of Mr. Buchanan:

To the Editor of the Pennsylvania Inquirer and Courier:

WASHINGTON CITY, February 27, 1838.

SIR:—I have this moment perused the letter of J. F. Cox, published in yesterday's *Inquirer*. His late official station, as a member of the Convention, induces me to notice the stale slander which he again repeats, and which *I now pronounce to be utterly and absolutely false, no matter from what source it may have proceeded or shall proceed.* I never did, upon any occasion, public or private, whether at the court-house in Lancaster, or elsewhere, declare that "if I knew I had a drop of Democratic blood in my veins, I would let it out," or any words to that effect. *This ridiculous story is without the shadow of foundation.*

The first version of the story was, that I had used the expression in an oration which I had delivered at the court-house in Lancaster, on the 4th of July, 1825. The oration itself disproved this assertion; and then, after Mr. Cox had made it a subject of debate before the Reform Convention, in May last, one of the papers at Harrisburg solemnly announced that the expression had been used by me on the floor of the House of Representatives, in this city, in reply to Gov. Floyd, of Virginia, and that it could be proved by a gentleman who had formerly been a Democratic representative in Congress from Pennsylvania. The scene is now again shifted to the court-house in Lancaster, and a certain Anthony M'Glinn is the witness. He states, that "a number of years ago, one evening," whilst I was addressing a political meeting there assembled, he had heard me use the expression already stated, "in an emphatic manner, with my right hand elevated above my head." He does not state the year when this expression was used, nor the name of any other person who was present at this public meeting.

It does not seem to have occurred to Mr. Cox, that if I had uttered such a sentiment as that attributed to me in the court-house at Lancaster, it would have been heard by hundreds of people; that it would immediately have become the subject of universal remark and universal condemnation, and that it would have been severely and justly commented upon in the newspapers of the day. Had it been true, there would have been no occasion to resort to Anthony M'Glinn to prove the charge, nor to a conversation alleged by Mr. Ford to have been held with Peter Shindle, who, although a respectable, is an aged man; and from a defect of memory, incident to that period of life, must have confounded what may have been stated to him by others with what he had heard himself. But, I repeat again, no matter who has been or shall be the witness, the tale is utterly and absolutely false.

Shortly after, the slander was made a subject of debate by Mr. Cox in the Reformed Convention; a number of the oldest and most respectable citizens of Lancaster, without distinction of party, signed a certificate disproving the charge, so far as it was possible for a negative to be proved, which was placed and still remains in the hands of one of my friends. After what had been said in reply to Mr. Cox by Mr. Porter and Mr. Reigart—who must either have heard the expression had it been used, or heard it immediately after—I deemed it wholly unnecessary then to publish this certificate. Yours, very respectfully,

JAMES BUCHANAN.

We have said, in the commencement of this article, that we would at this time publish nothing in refutation of this charge but Mr. Buchanan's own letter. We have, however, procured a copy of the certificate to which Mr. B. refers, and give it publicity below for the first time. In doing so, we will boldly assert, that the thirty subscribers to it are gentlemen of as much moral worth and respectability as can be found among the same number of individuals in any other community in the Union; and we venture to say, that NO RESPECTABLE MAN IN PENNSYLVANIA, OF ANY POLITICAL PARTY, after reading Mr. B's contradiction, endorsed by the cool and deliberate declaration of these gentlemen, will reiterate the charge, believing himself in its truth:

CERTIFICATE.

Several of the undersigned have known Mr. Buchanan ever since he first came to Lancaster to study law with the late James Hopkins, and the others for many years past. We are all convinced that, if at a public meeting at the court-house, or anywhere else in this city, he had ever used such an expression, or anything like it, as that which has been attributed to him by Mr. Cox in the Convention, to wit: "that he thanked his God he had not a drop of Democratic blood in his veins, and if he had, he would let it out," some of us would have heard it, and *all* of us would have heard of it, and it must have become a subject of general conversation throughout Lancaster. To the best of our knowledge, it never was mentioned by any person until the year 1828, immediately before Mr. Buchanan's last election to Congress on the Democratic Jackson ticket. As this election immediately preceded General Jackson's first election to the Presidency, (in November, 1828,) and as Mr. Buchanan had been for several years previously his ardent and active supporter, he was then opposed with much zeal and bitterness.

Ever since we first heard this story, referring back as it did to 1815, we have always believed, and still believe, that it was got up without any foundation in fact, for the purpose of operating against Mr. Buchanan's election to Congress in 1828. Indeed, we had never supposed that any person acquainted with his character could believe that at any period of life he would have made such a declaration as now seems to be seriously imputed to him.

Wm. Jenkins,	Jas. Humes,
Wm. B. Fordney,	Geo. H. Krug,
Reab Frazer,	Wm. Cooper,
F. A. Muhlenberg,	John N. Lane,
John Mathiot,	John Reynolds,
William Norris,	John R. Montgomery,
John Christ,	Henry Rogers,
George Musser,	Jacob Demuth,
William Frick,	Christian Bachman,
Samuel Dale,	John Bomberger,
Joseph Ogilby,	John Ross,
John F. Steinman,	John Evans,
Emanuel C. Reigart,	John Miller,
Adam Reigart,	Henry Keffer,
Benjamin Champneys,	George Messenkop.

The Harrisburg *Reporter* referred to, is not now published; but at the time the editorial above copied was written and printed, it was the Democratic State paper of Pennsylvania. The Mr. Cox, who made the charge against Mr. Buchanan, has been dead for some years; but before he died, he became a Democrat, and fully and repeatedly atoned for the wrong he did to Mr. Buchanan. Indeed, he became one of Mr. Buchanan's best friends. Of the signers to the card above quoted, a number have died. There were Democrats and Whigs on this list. Among those still living is Hon. E. C. Reigart, who was opposed to the Democracy in 1838, even while defending Mr. Buchanan against this aspersion. He is a distinguished politician and lawyer. He is now Mr. Buchanan's decided advocate for the Presidency.

FABRICATION NO. II.

MR. BUCHANAN AND THE WAR OF 1812.

Some of the opposition papers are re-publishing an oration alleged to have been delivered by Mr. Buchanan on the 4th of July, 1815; and he is falsely accused of having opposed the vigorous prosecution of the war of 1812. In 1847, after he was appointed Secretary of State by Mr. Polk, a similar charge was made against him in Tennessee, of which he was informed by Hon. George W. Jones, a leading member of the present Congress from that State. Mr. Buchanan replied by the following letter, which so clearly covers the whole ground, that all necessity for further comment is precluded:

WASHINGTON, April 23, 1847.

MY DEAR SIR:—I have this moment received your letter of the 15th inst., and hasten to return an answer.

In one respect I have been fortunate as a public man. My political enemies are obliged to go back for more than thirty years to find plausible charges against me.

In 1814, when a very young man, (being this day 56 years of age,) I made my first public speech before a meeting of my fellow-citizens of Lancaster. The object of this speech was to urge upon them the duty of volunteering their services in defence of their invaded country. A volunteer company was raised upon the spot, in which I was the first, I believe, to enter my name as a private. We forthwith proceeded to Baltimore, and served until we were honorably discharged.

In October, 1814, I was elected a member of the Pennsylvania Legislature; and in that body gave my support to every measure calculated, in my opinion, to aid the country against the common enemy.

In 1815, after peace had been concluded, I did express opinions in relation to the causes and conduct of the war, which I very soon after regretted and recalled. Since that period I have been ten years a member of the House of Representatives, and an equal time of the Senate, acting a part on every great question. My political enemies, finding nothing assailable throughout this long public career, now resort to my youthful years for expressions to injure my political character. The brave and generous citizens of Tennessee, to whatever party they may belong, will agree that this is a hard measure of justice, and it is still harder that, for this reason, they should condemn the President for having voluntarily offered me a seat in his Cabinet.

I never deemed it proper, at any period of my life, whilst the country was actually engaged in war with a foreign enemy, to utter a sentiment which could interfere with its successful prosecution. Whilst the war with Great Britain was raging, I should have deemed it little better than moral treason to paralyze the arm of the Government whilst dealing blows against the enemy. After peace was concluded, the case was then different. My enemies cannot point to an expression uttered by me during the continuance of the war, which was not favorable to its vigorous prosecution.

From your friend, very respectfully,

JAMES BUCHANAN.

Hon. George W. Jones.

FORMER OPPONENTS AND PRESENT OPPONENTS PAYING TRIBUTE TO MR. BUCHANAN'S INTEGRITY, AND REFUTING ATTACKS UPON HIS CHARACTER.

This pamphlet might be extended through many pages, by extracts from the speeches of former opponents, now acting with the Democratic party, and those supporting other candidates, bearing testimony either to Mr. Buchanan's spotless reputation and statesmanlike ability, or else contradicting the stories in circulation against him.

Let us take Andrew Jackson Donelson, now a candidate for the Vice-Presidency, on the Fillmore ticket, and we find that, while he was editor of the Washington *Union*, on the 5th of June, 1851, he defended Mr. Buchanan against an attack of the organ of Mr. Fillmore's administration, in the following language:

"But the special organ, instead of manfully acknowledging the error which has been committed by its party in the countenance it has given to political *anti-slavery organization—an error not denied nor even concealed by the President, or any one of his cabinet ministers, in the various speeches which they have addressed to the abolition districts of New*

York—imagines that it is its office to neutralize the force of such a fact, by reviving the stale charge of Federalism against Mr. Buchanan, who is one, amongst some eight or ten of the prominent men in the Democratic party, that may be brought before a National Convention, whose duty it will be to put some one of them in nomination for the Presidency. This gentleman has friends who will doubtless, in due season, make a more detailed vindication of his character than we have done in this hasty article. What we have said, is not a defence of Mr. Buchanan as a candidate for the Presidency, but as a member of the party in whose service he has acquired the high respect of his fellow-citizens, and has proved that he possesses the eminent ability and patriotism, which justified the confidence given to him by the State which he so long represented in the Senate of the United States, and afterwards by President Polk, who gave him the first place in his Cabinet."

The Hon. Oscar F. Moore, at present a representative in Congress from the Ross district, Ohio, a leading member of the Opposition party, in a letter to his constituents, defines his position as follows:

"With the announcement of the nomination of Fremont, as it spread with lightning rapidity over the land, expired the last hope that lingered around the Philadelphia Convention. What a fall! Judge McLean, with all his age, learning and experience, his fame, his stern integrity—the hopes of quiet, peace, purity, safety and glory to the country, concentrated in him—rejected! And a man, whose only merit, so far as history records it, is in the fact, that he was born in South Carolina, crossed the Rocky Mountains, subsisted on frogs, lizzards, snakes and grasshoppers, and *captured* a woolly horse, chosen as the person to control the destinies of this great nation! And this too, by the cool, deliberate, intellectual men of New England and the North!! But what shall we do! If Judge McLean had been nominated, no one could have hesitated. Nor can I now hesitate to take position. As warmly and as steadily as I have heretofore opposed the Democratic party, and as bitterly as I denounced the Cincinnati Platform now, with my respect for the ability, age and experience of Mr. Buchanan, and with my *contempt* for the claims of Fremont, and the *arrant folly*—to use no harsher term—of those who *dictated* his nomination, if I were *compelled* this day to choose between them, I should vote for Mr. Buchanan."

Thaddeus Stevens, with a full knowledge of Mr. Buchanan's position, (he resides in Mr. Buchanan's own county,) declared in the Philadelphia Black Republican Convention, that Mr. B. would carry the State of Pennsylvania by fifty thousand majority. He said:

Mr. Stevens saw what the current of the Convention was—he did not rise to resist it—but he admonished delegates to take care it does not sweep away friends as well as foes. [Applause.] Pennsylvania is embarrassed by the withdrawal of the only name he thought could save the

State. He would like to have time to consult his colleagues. He would be sorry to see Judge McLean's name introduced now; but he was assured that without that name, *Pennsylvania would be lost by* 50,000 *majority in the Fall!* In conclusion, he moved to adjourn until 10 o'clock next morning.

The *National Intelligencer*, the organ of the Fillmore opposition, at Washington, spoke of Mr. Buchanan's nomination, as follows:

"Mr. Buchanan is a man of character, of stainless private life, and of long and varied experience in public affairs. As a gentleman, we have nothing to object to him, save his party politics and party career; and although we trust that the anti-Democratic conservative power of the country will be able to beat him, yet, if they should fail, they may still hope that his success will give to the country a President, who will prove a friend to the Union, and more conservative in his administration, than is the political platform upon which he has been placed by the Convention."

As a comment upon the course of some of the opposition papers, we may add, that before the National Democratic Convention met, they were very confident that Mr. Buchanan would not be nominated, and many of them anticipating this result, spoke of him in the highest terms, some saying, that if nominated, it would be vain to make any opposition to him. No doubt much of this grew out of a desire to prepare the Democracy for a state of feeling consequent upon the unexpected defeat of Mr. Buchanan. An evidence of this is to be found in the following paragraph, which was telegraphed to the New York *Tribune*, from Cincinnati, on the 3d of June last:

An Early Surrender.—"If Mr. Buchanan's friends fulfil their confident expectations he will be nominated before this reaches the *Tribune*. He will not be nominated at all except by a divided Convention, after Thursday night. *His nomination has been generally deprecated by the Republicans as dangerous, if not* FATAL *to their success.*"

But probably the most complete answer to every charge against Mr. Buchanan, is to be found in the fact, that from Maine to Georgia, the most eminent minds heretofore opposed to the Democratic party are rallying in his support. Look at the list in Pennsylvania. There is Joseph R. Chandler, William B. Reed, Josiah Randall, Frederick Fraley, Eli K. Price, and hundreds of men who have heretofore been the light and the staff of the old Henry Clay party. In Maryland, there are Senators Pearce and Pratt, Reverdy Johnson, and hundreds of men of that class. In Louisiana, Senator J. P. Benjamin. In Missouri, Hon. Sam. Caruthers, and Mordecai Oliver. In Kentucky, Hon. Wm. E. Preston, and hosts of others. All these men with thousands at their backs agreeing with them, look down with ineffable contempt and scorn upon the calumnies which have grown so stale and so old, that Mr. Greeley himself has got tired and disgusted with them, and in a late number of his *Tribune*, speaks as follows:

"In opening the Presidential canvass of 1856—a canvass destined to form a memorable epoch in our Nation's history—we would impress on our compatriots in the support of Fremont and Dayton, and especially our brethren of the Republican Press, the wisdom and sound policy of refraining from all personal warfare. We believe all the candidates in nomination for President and Vice President have sustained fair reputations in all their relations as citizens; and, if it were possible to rake from the dust of oblivion some charge that would tend to the disparagement of one or another of them, we hold it unwise and improper to do so."

MR. BUCHANAN AND GENERAL JACKSON.—MR. BUCHANAN AND MR. CLAY.

Andrew Jackson Donelson, whose defence of Mr. Buchanan appears in another part of this pamphlet, has been ransacking some of General Jackson's *private letters*, to find reflections against Mr. Buchanan. A very brief answer only is necessary here. Two facts will go far to show that Mr. Buchanan bore a relation to General Jackson, such as no man ever maintained who did not secure the confidence of the old hero. After his ten years' service in the U. S. House of Representatives, Mr. B. retired to private life; and one of the first acts of General Jackson, after that, was to make a voluntary tender to him of the important mission to Russia. The other fact is that which defies denial—that Mr. Polk appointed Mr. Buchanan Secretary of State in his administration, after consultation with General Jackson, who was then residing at the Hermitage, and who recommended and approved the selection. On this latter point, the facts are alike ample and conclusive.

The following from the Washington *Union*, conducted by Hon. A. O. P. Nicholson, of Tennessee, and personally known to all the parties, is so full and complete on this subject, that we copy it entire:

[From the Washington Union.]

GEN. JACKSON.—MR. CLAY.—MR. BUCHANAN.

The friends of General Jackson will read the paragraph below, from the Nashville Union, with gratification. It is high time that Andrew Jackson should step forward to arrest the ruthless war of ingratitude and hyena-like malignity, which is being waged on the memory of his father. We trust that the son will be no longer restrained by feelings of delicacy from coming forward to shield the fame of his illustrious father, from the wicked abuse of the confidence which he reposed in such ingrates as Blair and Donelson. There is no lower deep of political degradation, than that to which the man has descended, who would take advantage of the speechless silence of the grave to abuse the confidence of his benefactor with impunity.

We suppose the late publication of what purports to be a part of a private letter of General Jackson, in which he refers to the connection of Mr. Buchanan with the charge of "bargain and intrigue," that involved General Jackson and Mr. Clay in an angry controversy, has induced Major Jackson to express the purpose indicated in the paragraph below. We understand the Nashville Union to intimate that Major Donelson has furnished this extract to his organ in Nashville, for publication. The object of its publication is to exhume from the graves of Jackson and Clay a quarrel which was buried with their bodies, under the hope of exciting the feelings of their respective friends against Mr. Buchanan. We know with how much ardor and earnestness the people of Tennessee and Kentucky contest the ascendancy in their political conflicts; but we know, too, that they are as generous, as brave, and as noble a people as live. We think, therefore, we risk nothing in predicting that the effort to revive a personal quarrel between the friends of the two men, whose memories are respectively dear to the two people, will cause both to turn with loathing and disgust from so unmanly a mode of warfare. It was our fortune to know something personally of General Jackson's feelings and opinions in respect to public men, as also to know from actual observation, the relations between Mr. Clay and Mr. Buchanan. Upon this knowledge, we have the most perfect conviction, that whatever feelings General Jackson and Mr. Clay carried to their graves towards each other, they carried none towards Mr. Buchanan, but those of earnest friendship. Before quoting the paragraph referred to, we commend to our readers, as a conclusive answer to the attempt to misrepresent the relations subsisting between General Jackson and Mr. Clay and Mr. Buchanan, the following extract from a late number of the Nashville Union:

"It is supposed that General Jackson and Mr. Clay knew more about this matter, and how far Mr. Buchanan was answerable, than any other two men that ever lived; and that, if General Jackson and Mr. Clay could excuse Mr. Buchanan of any wrongful intention, and honor him with their confidence, no one else can have proper cause of complaint against him. That Mr. Buchanan's explanation of the misunderstanding that had grown out of the conversation between himself and General Jackson, was entirely satisfactory to Mr. Clay, is a matter of history; many evidences of which could be given, but the following will suffice:"

MR. CLAY TO MR. BROOKE.

"Mr. Buchanan has presented his communication to the public; and although he evidently labors throughout the whole of it to spare and cover General Jackson, he fails in every essential particular to sustain the General. Indeed, I could not desire a stronger statement from Mr. Buchanan."

Ex-Governor Letcher, the bosom friend of Mr. Clay, writing from Lexington, Ky., August 25, 1827, says:

"With your letter of the 9th, Mr. Buchanan's response to the hero was received. This answer is well put together. As they say in Connecticut, 'there is a great deal of good reading' in Buck's reply. It is modest and gentle, yet strong and conclusive. I am truly delighted with the manner in which Mr. B. has acquitted himself."

We might also quote from Prentice's biography of Mr. Clay, written many years ago, in which he said that Mr. Buchanan had acquitted himself in this matter like "an honorable man." But the fact that Mr. Clay did not censure Mr. Buchanan, after being made to understand the facts, is too notorious for argument.

As to General Jackson, it is a matter interwoven with the history of the country—whatever scandalous betrayals of private confidence men may now make by parading letters shamefully perverted, and that were never intended to be published—that a warm and cordial intimacy and mutual regard and confidence existed between him and Mr. Buchanan to the last hour of the old hero's life.

All these old, unpleasant difficulties, rejuvenated by the Banner, through the aid of Maj. Donelson, were enacted from 1825 to 1827. Four years afterwards, upon retiring from Congress, in 1831, Mr. Buchanan received from Gen. Jackson, unsolicited, the high compliment and trust of the mission to Russia, in which capacity he rendered the country the important service of negotiating the first commercial treaty between the United States and Russia, which secured to our commerce the ports of the Baltic and the Black Sea.

Mr. Polk is known to have gone to the Hermitage, upon the eve of his departure, for the special purpose of consulting General Jackson on the subject of his Cabinet. Pennsylvania, led by James Buchanan, had contributed her electoral vote to his election. General Jackson had known Mr. Buchanan intimately for twenty years. The consequence was, Mr. Polk invited Mr. Buchanan to accept the portfolio of the State Department, the head of his Cabinet. It was in view of all these things, and the grave importance of the mission, that President Pierce sent him as Minister to England. And it is for his purity of public and private character, as attested by the confidence of Jackson, Polk, and Pierce, and the large and comprehensive statesmanship which he manifested in all these important public stations, filled at their solicitation, that the Democratic party have put him forward as their candidate for the Presidency.

If Mr. Clay "could not ask a stronger statement from Mr. Buchanan," and respected his great public worth, as he frequently attested when they were both members of the United States Senate in 1841—if General Jackson could so esteem him as to appoint him to an important foreign mission in 1831, recommend him to Mr. Polk as a Cabinet officer, and express regret for his defeat for the Senate as late as 1845—is it not the most contemptible twaddle for men who have been treacherous themselves to both the old parties, led respectively by Clay and Jackson, to be raising a hue and cry at this day, against so venerable a patriot and sage as James Buchanan? This is all we have to say on this branch of the subject.

It is in reference to the letter of Gen. Jackson, alluded to in the foregoing article, that the following paragraph appeared in a subsequent issue of the Nashville Union:

"We were much gratified a few days since, to receive a visit, from Mr. Andrew Jackson, the present occupant of the Hermitage. He expressed himself greatly mortified at the wanton and unauthorized use which has recently been made of the private letters of his father, Gen. Jackson—letters which the unworthy possessors of, would sooner stick their heads in the fire than to have published, if the old hero had been living. Mr. Jackson regards the use which has been made of these random letters as an outrage upon the memory of his revered father not longer to be submitted to in silence, and which he can and will effectually crush if persisted in."

MR. BUCHANAN'S OWN STATEMENT.

The following letter from the Hon. James Buchanan, to which both Mr. Clay and Mr. Letcher refer, is so candid, frank, and plain a statement, that we publish it entire. It was after the publication of this letter, that General Jackson offered to Mr. Buchanan the post of Minister to Russia, and recommended his appointment as Secretary of State to President Polk:

To the Editor of the Lancaster Journal.

The Cincinnati *Advertiser* was last night placed in my hands by a friend, containing an address from Gen. Jackson to the public, dated on the 18th ultimo, in which he announces me to be the Member of Congress to whom he had referred, in his letter to Mr. Beverly of the 5th of June last. The duty which I owe to the public, and to myself, now compels me to publish to the world, the only conversation which I ever held with Gen. Jackson, on the subject of the last Presidential election, prior to its termination.

In the month of December, 1824, a short time after the commencement of the session of Congress, I heard, among other rumors then in circulation, that Gen. Jackson had determined, should he be elected President, to continue Mr. Adams in the office of Secretary of State. Although I felt certain he had never intimated such an intention, yet I was sensible that nothing could be better calculated both to cool the ardor of his friends, and to inspire his enemies with confidence, than the belief that he had already selected *his chief competitor*, for the highest office within his gift. I thought General Jackson owed it to himself and to the cause, in which his political friends were engaged, to contradict this report; and to declare that he would not appoint to that office the man, however worthy he might be, who stood at the head of the most formidable party of his political enemies. These being my impressions, I addressed a letter to a confidential friend in Pennsylvania, then and still high in office, and exalted in character, and one who had ever been the decided advocate of General Jackson's election, requesting his opinion and advice upon the subject. I received his answer, dated the 27th December, 1824, upon the 29th, which is now before me, and which strengthened and confirmed my previous opinion.

I then finally determined, either that I would ask General Jackson myself, or get another of his friends to ask him—whether he had ever declared he would appoint Mr. Adams his Secretary of State. In this manner, I hoped a contradiction of the report might be obtained from himself and that he might probably declare it was not his intention to appoint Mr. Adams.

A short time previous to the receipt of the letter to which I have referred, my friend Mr. Markley and myself got into conversation, as we very often did, both before and after, upon the subject of the Presidential election, and concerning the person who would probably be selected by General Jackson, to fill the office of Secretary of State. I feel sincerely sorry that I am compelled thus to introduce his name; but I do so with the less reluctance, because it has already, without any agency of mine, found its way into the newspapers, in connection with this transaction.

Mr. Markley adverted to the rumor which I have mentioned, and said it was calculated to injure the General. He observed, that Mr. Clay's friends were warmly attached to him, and that he thought they would endeavor to act in concert at the election. That if they did so, they could either elect Mr. Adams or General Jackson at their pleasure; but that many of them would never agree to vote for the latter, if they knew he had predetermined to prefer another to Mr. Clay, for the first office in his gift. And that some of the friends of Mr. Adams had already been holding out the idea, that in case he were elected, Mr. Clay might probably be offered the situation of Secretary of State.

I told Mr. Markley, that I felt confident General Jackson had never said he would appoint Mr. Adams Secretary of State; because he was not in the habit of conversing upon the subject of the election; and if he were, whatever might be his secret intention, he had more prudence than to make such a declaration. I mentioned to him that I had been thinking, either that I would call upon the General myself, or get some one of his other friends to do so, and thus endeavored to obtain from him a contradiction of the report; although I doubted whether he would hold any conversation upon the subject.

Mr. Markley urged me to do so; and observed, if General Jackson had not determined whom he would appoint Secretary of State, and should say that it would not be Mr. Adams, it might be a great advantage to our cause, for us so to declare, upon his own authority; we should then be placed upon the same footing with the Adams men, and might fight them with their own weapons. That the western members would naturally prefer voting for a western man, if there were a probability that the claims of Mr. Clay to the second office in the Government should be fairly estimated; and that if they thought proper to vote for Gen. Jackson, they could soon decide the contest in his favor.

A short time after this conversation, on the 30th December, 1824, (I am enabled to fix the time not only from my own recollection, but from letters which I wrote on that day, on the day following, and on the 2d January, 1825) I called upon General Jackson. After the company had left him, by which I found him surrounded, he asked me to take a walk with him; and whilst we were walking together upon the street, I introduced the subject. I told him, I wished to ask him a question in relation to the Presidential election; that I knew he was unwilling to converse upon the subject; that therefore if he deemed the question improper, he might refuse to give it an answer. That my only motive in asking it, was friendship for him, and I trusted he would excuse me for thus introducing a subject, about which I knew he wished to be silent.

His reply was complimentary to myself, and, accompanied with a request that I should proceed. I then stated to him, there was a report in circulation, that he had determined he would appoint Mr. Adams Secretary of State, in case he were elected President: and that I wished to ascertain from him whether he had ever intimated such an intention. That he must at once perceive, how injurious to his election such a report might be. That no doubt, there were several able and ambitious men in the country, among whom I thought, Mr. Clay might be included, who were aspiring to that office; and if it were believed he had already determined to appoint *his chief competitor*, it might have a most unhappy effect upon their exertions, and those of their friends. That unless he had so determined, I thought this report should be promptly contradicted under his own authority.

I mentioned, it had already probably done him some injury, and proceeded to relate to him the substance of the conversation which I had held with Mr. Markley. I do not remember whether I mentioned his name, or merely described him as a friend of Mr. Clay.

After I had finished, the General declared he had not the least objection to answer my question. That he thought well of Mr. Adams; but had never said or intimated, that he would, or that he would not, appoint him Secretary of State. That these things were secrets he would keep to himself—he would conceal them from the very hairs of his head. That if he believed his right hand then knew what his left would do upon the subject of appointments to office, he would cut it off and cast it into the fire. That if he should ever be elected President, it would be without solicitation and without intrigue on his part—that he would then go into office perfectly free and untrammelled, and would be left at perfect liberty to fill the offices of government with the men whom at the time he believed to be the ablest and the best in the country.

I told him that his answer to my question was such an one as I had expected to receive, if he answered it at all; and that I had not sought to obtain it for my own satisfaction. I then asked him if I were at liberty to repeat his answer. He said I was perfectly at liberty to do so to any person I thought proper. I need scarcely remark that I afterwards availed myself of the privilege. The conversation upon this topic here ended—and in all our intercourse since, whether personally or in the course of our correspondence, Gen. Jackson never once adverted to the subject, prior to the date of his letter to Mr. Beverly.

I do not recollect that General Jackson told me I might repeat his answer to Mr. Clay and his friends; though I should be sorry to say he did not The whole conversation being upon the public street, it might have escaped my observation.

A few remarks more, and I trust I shall have done with this disagreeable business forever.

I called upon Gen. Jackson on the occasion which I have mentioned, solely as his friend, upon my individual responsibility, and not as the agent of Mr. Clay, or any other person. I never have been the political friend of Mr. Clay since he became a candidate for the office of President, as you very well know. Until I saw Gen. Jackson's letter to Mr. Beverly of the 5th ult., and at the same time was informed by letter from the Editor of the United States *Telegraph*, that I was the person to whom he alluded, the conception never once entered my mind, that he deemed me to have been the agent of Mr. Clay, or of his friends, or that I had intended to propose to him terms of any kind from them, or that he could have supposed me to be capable of expressing the "opinion that it was right to fight such intriguers with their own weapons." Such a supposition, had I entertained it, would have rendered me exceedingly unhappy; as there is no man upon earth whose good opinion I more value than that of General Jackson. He could not, I think, have received this impression until after Mr. Clay and his friends had actually elected Mr. Adams President, and Mr. Adams had appointed Mr. Clay Secretary of State. After these events had transpired, it may be readily conjectured, in what manner my communication might have led him into the mistake. I deeply deplore that such has been its effect.

I owe it to my own character to make another observation. Had I ever known, or even suspected that Gen. Jackson believed I had been sent to him by Mr. Clay or his friends, I should have immediately corrected his erroneous impression; and thus prevented the necessity for this most unpleasant explanation. When the Editor of the United States *Telegraph*, on the 12th of October last, asked me by letter for information upon the subject, I promptly informed him by the returning mail on the 16th of that mouth, that I had no authority from Mr. C. or his friends, to propose any terms to Gen. Jackson in relation to their votes, nor did I ever make any such proposition; and that I trusted I would be as incapable of becoming a messenger, upon such an occasion, as it was known Gen. Jackson would be to receive such a message. I have deemed it necessary to make this statement, in order to remove any misconception which may have been occasioned by the publication, in the *Telegraph*, of my letter to the editor, dated the 11th ultimo.

With another remark, I shall close this communication. Before I held the conversation with Gen. Jackson, which I have detailed, I called upon Major Eaton, and requested him to ask Gen. Jackson, whether he had ever declared or intimated, that he would appoint Mr. Adams Secretary of State, and expressed a desire that the General should say, if consistent with truth, that he did not intend to appoint him to that office. I believed that such a declaration would have a happy influence upon the election, and I endeavored to convince him that such would be its effect. The conversation between us was not so full as that with General Jackson. The Major politely declined to comply with my request, and advised me to propound the question to the General myself, as I possessed a full share of his confidence.

JAMES BUCHANAN.

Lancaster, 8*th August*, 1827.

MR. BUCHANAN AND THE LABORING MAN.

No public man has ever been more consistent in his defence of measures, in which the laboring classes have been interested, than Mr. Buchanan. While a Senator in Congress, he was probably the most effective advocate of all laws to liberalize and improve the Charter of the District of Columbia, particularly in his opposition to the circulation of small notes, that vitiated currency from which so many evils have sprung, and by which so many honest men and women have suffered. The explosions of the shin plaster shops, in the city of Washington, would never have occurred, had the laws for which Mr. Buchanan pleaded so earnestly in the Senate, been enforced. His speeches in favor of a liberal land policy, to enable the enterprizing poor man to settle upon the public lands, and be free from the clutches of those speculators, who so often take up millions of acres, for the purpose of coining fortunes out of the honest emigrant, are memorable. He was one of the earliest advocates of liberalizing the Constitution of Pennsylvania, so as to render it more popular in its character. In 1840, when everything seemed to be "fair in politics," a grand clamor was raised against Mr. Buchanan, on the ground that he had argued in the Senate, in his speech of 22d of January, 1840, in favor of paying the American laborer but ten cents a day. It teaches us a lesson now, when we see so many men (even among those who are at present supporting Mr. Fremont and Mr. Fillmore) coming forward and regretting and withdrawing this unjust accusation. This charge then rung from every stump; thousands of men were mislead by it; but time and reflection have done the work, and Mr. Buchanan is vindicated. A great revolution has taken place since he made the admirable speech from which this perverted statement was wrested. When he spoke, the country was suffering under the effects of a contraction in the money market, resulting from the explosion of the Bank of the United States, and every branch of industry was more or less affected by the condition of financial affairs. The Independent Treasury was then that great bugbear, which was to withdraw all the specie from circulation, and to ruin everybody, high and low. It was to prove the advantage of a sound currency, that Mr. Buchanan spoke against that multiplication of paper money, from which so many evils have sprung. But the objections to the Independent Treasury have been answered by results. Where is there now to be found, the man who doubts that the Independent Treasury has been of immense advantage to commerce and to trade; and where is the mechanic, or the laboring man, who sees for himself, how important it is to his interest to have sound banks or gold and silver, who will not look back upon the attacks upon Mr. Buchanan's Independent Treasury speech, in 1840, with something of confusion, that he should have permitted himself for a moment to be deluded by the accusations of the opposition? Mr. Greeley of the New York *Tribune*, again comes forward to make a clean breast of it. We copy from the *Tribune*, since Mr. Buchanan's nomination:

"The charge that Mr. Buchanan has advocated a reduction of laboring men's wages to ten cents per day, has but a very partial support in fact. He certainly never made any such proposition directly, nor anything, which he understood to have that effect."

Now, the editor of the *Tribune* should have been still more frank; he should have stated that no man did half so much as himself to keep alive sixteen years ago, the very falsehood which, at this late hour, he comes forward to clear his conscience of. Better late than never, however, and we congratulate the leading organ of the Fremont party upon the unconscious confession of its own sins, and the lesson it teaches those who are accustomed to believe in it.

FRANCIS P. BLAIR ANSWERING THIS CALUMNY.

The history of the gross and reckless misrepresentation of Mr. Buchanan's speech of January of 1840, has been written by Francis P. Blair, now one of the most active friends of Fremont. Mr. Blair, it will be recollected, was the editor of the Washington *Globe* in 1840, and at that time advocated the measures and the man that now encounter his extreme hostility. By degrees he has become so identified with the opposition to the Democratic party, that he has at last become the associate of Mr. Seward and Mr. Giddings. His testimony on the subject of the misrepresentation of Mr. Buchanan's speech is patent to the present attempt of the more reckless opponents of the Democratic party and expose them to ridicule and scorn. We copy from the *Globe*, of March 3, 1840, the following editorial from the pen of Mr. Blair:

[From the Washington Globe, March 3, 1840.]

We publish in this evening's *Globe* the remarks of Mr. Buchanan in the Senate on Tuesday last, in relation to the misrepresentations of his speech in favor of the Independent Treasury bill, contained in the published speech of Mr. Davis, (of Mass.) against that measure. It will be perceived that the charge made was, that this gentleman had, throughout his remarks, alleged that Mr. Buchanan had supported the bill on the principle that it would destroy the banking system, and restore an exclusive gold and silver currency, and would, as a necessary consequence, check importations, suppress credit, and reduce the wages of labor and the value of property to one-half their present prices. Such objections have heretofore been those chiefly urged by its enemies against the measure; but, by Mr. Davis, throughout his whole speech, they have been put into the mouth of Mr. Buchanan as arguments in its favor. Every one can perceive how much political capital might be made by circulating throughout the country, that the unfounded objections made to the bill by its open enemies, were not only admitted to exist by so distinguished a friend of the measure as Mr. Buchanan, but had been actually urged by him as arguments in its favor!

So far from this being the fact, the speech of Mr. Buchanan—and we heard every word of it—not only did not contain any such arguments as had been attributed to him by Mr. Davis, but his arguments were all of a contrary character. He ridiculed the idea which had been formerly urged by the opponents of the bill, that "it was to devour all the banks, and establish a pure metallic currency for all the tranactions of all the people of the United States," and while he proved conclusively that it would be of inestimable advantage by separating the banks from the Government, he rendered it clear that it would not injuriously affect the banks or the business of the country. How Mr. Davis could have put such arguments into his mouth, as he has done, we are utterly at a loss to conjecture.

A friend of Mr. Buchanan having called his attention to the published speech of Mr. Davis, the former brought the subject before the Senate on Tuesday last, in the remarks which we now publish. Mr. Buchanan conditionally applied the epithet "flagitious," which Mr. Davis had first used in his speech, to characterize the propositions which he said had been advocated by Mr. Buchanan, to the misrepresentations made by Mr. Davis, of Mr. Buchanan's argument. This produced some altercation; but, after the gentlemen had compared notes with each other, the subject seemed to have passed away without appearing to leave any very unpleasant feeling behind. On the next morning, (Wednesday,) Mr. Davis appeared in the Senate, said his remarks on the preceding day had been misunderstood by his friends, and desired a further opportunity of addressing the Senate on the subject; this was delayed by Mr. Grundy's speech, until Friday morning, when Mr. Davis rose and delivered a speech, marked throughout with strong and personally offensive expressions in regard to Mr. Buchanan's previous remarks, and concluded with the declaration, that "he repelled them with the scorn and contempt which they deserved."

Mr. Buchanan, who is proverbially mild and courteous to his opponents, was left without any alternative but that of treating Mr. Davis with severity. He was perfectly calm and collected in his manner. He commenced with stating what we copy from the notes of our reporter: "That when he had addressed the Senate a few days ago, he had endeavored to state what he believed to be his grievance in the mildest manner which the nature of the case admitted, and to treat the Senator from Massachusetts, so far as he could, with courtesy and respect. The remarks of that gentleman to-day, had, however, absolved him from any such obligation, and he should proceed to treat his misrepresentations as they deserved." We have never heard a more just and conclusive reply, or one more severe in its character. The Senator appeared altogether in a new light. Mr. Davis rejoined; the altercation became quite personal on both sides, and Mr. Buchanan, in conclusion, triumphantly declared that he had fixed the charge of grossly misrepresenting his remarks upon him, and there it should stick like the poisoned shirt of Nessus.

We have not met any candid and impartial man who was present, who does not believe that Mr. Buchanan made out his case clearly and triumphantly. It would have been better, much better, for Mr. Davis, at first, to have admitted the misrepresentations charged, and stated that they were unintentional mistakes, if such were the fact. From the result of the controversy, we entertain not a doubt that he is now of the same opinion. When the entire debate should be published, we have no doubt this will be the settled conviction of our readers.

We now come to a few extracts from the original speech, which has been so much misrepresented, referring those who want a full report of the speech, to the authentic copy, published by the Democratic National Committee, and to be found in the hands of most of the Democratic State and County Committees. We also append other extracts from Mr. Buchanan's subsequent speeches, exposing the misrepresentations of Davis:

Amongst others who undertook to answer Mr. Buchanan's speech, was the Hon. John Davis, of Massachusetts—he that was usually known as "honest John Davis." He assumed in his argument, directly in the teeth of the fact, that Mr. Buchanan had advocated the Independent Treasury on the ground that it would establish an exclusive metallic currency. Starting with this erroneous assumption, he argued to show that it would bring down the wages of labor to the standard of prices in countries where the currency is exclusively metallic. To this speech, when published, there was an appendix, in which he introduced a table, showing that in some of the exclusive metallic countries of Europe laborers only received ten cents a day. Putting the speech and the appendix together, the hint was taken, and a clamor raised that the Democrats were in favor of reducing the wages of labor to ten cents a day.

In a subsequent speech, made on the 3d of March, 1840, Mr. Buchanan denounced the charge against him in the strongest language, saying:

"Self-respect, as well as the respect which I owe to the Senate, restrains me from giving such a contradiction to this allegation as it deserves. It would surely not be deemed improper, however, in me, if I were to turn to the Senator and apply the epithet which he himself has applied to the proposition he imputes to me, and were to declare that such an imputation was a 'flagitious' misrepresentation of my remarks."

Mr. Buchanan repeated his real position as laid down in his original speech, as follows:

"In my remarks I stated distinctly what legislation would, I thought, be required to accomplish this purpose. In the first place, I observed that the banks ought to be compelled to keep in their vaults a certain fair proportion of specie compared with their circulation and deposits; or, in other words, a certain proportion of immediate specie means, to meet their immediate responsibilities. 2d. That the foundation of a specie basis for our paper currency should be laid by prohibiting the circulation of bank notes, at the first under the denomination of ten, and afterwards under that of twenty dollars. 3d. That the amount of bank dividends should be limited. 4th. And, above all, that, upon the occurrence of another suspension, the doors of the banks should be closed at once, and their affairs placed in the hands of commissioners. A certainty that such must be the inevitable effect of another suspension would do more to prevent it than any other cause. To reform, and not to destroy, was my avowed motto. I know that the existence of banks and the circulation of bank paper are so identified with the habits of our people, that they cannot be abolished, even if this were desirable.

"Such a reform in the banking system as I have indicated would benefit every class of society; but, above all others, the man who makes his living by the sweat of his brow. The object at which I aimed by these reforms, was not a pure metallic currency, but a currency of a mixed character; the paper portion of it always convertible into gold and silver, and subject to as little fluctuation in amount as the regular business of the country would admit. Of all reforms, this is what the mechanic and the laboring man ought most to desire. It would produce steady prices and steady employment, and, under its influence, the country would march steadily on in its career of prosperity without suffering from the ruinous expansions and contractions and explosions, which we have endured during the last twenty years. What is most essential to the prosperity of the mechanic and laboring man? Constant employment, steady and fair wages, with uniform prices for the necessaries and comforts of life which he must purchase, and payment for his labor in a sound currency."

After re-stating further his arguments, as presented in his original speech of January 22, Mr. Buchanan said, in reference to the reduction of the wages of laboring men:

"I contended that it would not injure, but greatly benefit, the laboring man, to prevent the violent and ruinous expansions and contractions to which our currency was incident, and, by judicious bank reform, to place it on a settled basis. If this were done, what would be the consequence? That, if the laboring man could not receive as great a nominal amount for his labor as he did 'in the days of extravagant expansion,' which must always, under our present system, be of short duration, he would be indemnified, and far more than indemnified, by the constant employment, the regular wages, and the uniform and more moderate prices of the necessaries and comforts of life. which a more stable currency would produce. Can this proposition be controverted? I think not. It is too plain for argument. Mark me, sir, I desire to produce this happy result, not by establishing a pure metallic currency, but 'by reducing the amount of your bank issues within reasonable and safe limits, and establishing a metallic basis for your paper circulation.' The idea plainly expressed is, that it is better, much better, for the laboring man, as well as for every other class of society, except the speculator, that the business of the country should be placed upon that fixed and permanent foundation, which would be laid by establishing such a bank reform as would render it certain that bank notes should be always convertible into gold and silver.

"And yet this plain and simple exposition of my views has been seized upon by those who desire to make political capital out of their perversion; and it has been represented far and wide, that it was my desire to reduce wages down to the prices received by the miserable serfs and laborers of European despotisms. I shall most cheerfully leave the public to decide between me and my traducers. The Senator from Massachusetts, after having attributed to me the intention of reducing the wages of labor to the hard-money standard, through the agency of the Independent Treasury bill, has added, as an appendix to his speech, a statement, made by the Senator from Maryland, (Mr. Merrick,) of the prices of labor in these hard-money despotisms; and it is thus left to be inferred that I am in favor of reducing the honest and independent laborer of this glorious and free country to the same degraded condition. The Senator ought to know that there is too much intelligence among the laboring classes in this highly favored land to be led astray by such representations."

Mr. Clay had charged that the friends of the Independent Treasury desired to reduce the wages of laboring men. As this is the charge which it is now sought to revive, we invite special attention to Mr. Buchanan's reply. It was as follows:

"We are also charged by the Senator from Kentucky with a desire to reduce the wages of the poor man's labor. We have been often termed agrarians on our side of the house. It is something new under the sun to hear the Senator and his friends attribute to us a desire to elevate the wealthy manufacturer at the expense of the laboring man and the mechanic. From my soul I respect the laboring man. Labor is the foundation of the wealth of every country; and the free laborers of the North deserve respect both for their probity and their intelligence. Heaven forbid that I should do them wrong! Of all the countries on the earth, we ought to have the most consideration for the laboring man. From the very nature of our institutions, the wheel of fortune is constantly revolving and producing such mutations in property, that the wealthy man of to-day may become the poor laborer of to-morrow. Truly wealth often takes to itself wings and flies away. A large fortune rarely lasts beyond the third generation, even if it it endure so long. We must all know instances of individuals obliged to labor for their daily bread, whose grandfathers were men of fortune. The regular process of society would almost seem to consist of the efforts of one class to dissipate the fortunes which they have inherited, whilst another class, by their industry and economy, are regularly rising to wealth. We have all, therefore, a common interest, as it is our common duty, to protect the rights of the laboring man; and if I believed for a moment that this bill would prove injurious to him, it should meet my unqualified opposition.

"Although this bill will not have as great an influence as I could desire, yet, as far as it goes, it will benefit the laboring man as much, and probably more than any other class of society. What is it he ought most to desire? Constant employment, regular wages, and uniform, reasonable prices for the necessaries and comforts of life which he requires. Now, sir, what has been his condition under our system of expansions and contractions? He has suffered more by them than any other class of society. The rate of his wages is fixed and known; and they are the last to rise with the increasing expansion, and the first to fall when the corresponding revulsion occurs. He still continues to receive his dollar per day, whilst the price of every article which he consumes is rapidly rising. He is at length made to feel that, although he nominally earns as much, or even more than he did formerly, yet, from the increased price of all the necessaries of life, he cannot support his family. Hence he strikes for higher wages, and the uneasy and excited feelings which have at different periods existed among the laboring classes. But the expansion at length reaches the exploding point, and what does the laboring man now suffer? He is for a season thrown out of employment altogether. Our manufactures are suspended; our public works are stopped; our private enterprises of different kinds are abandoned; and, whilst others are able to weather the storm, he can scarcely procure the means of bare subsistance."

The predictions of Mr. Buchanan have been wonderfully fulfilled. No reduction in wages has taken place, as a consequence of keeping the public money out of the banks, but a condition of things has succeeded to that great measure, which has assisted every branch of commerce and of labor.

It will appear that not one line, or syllable, in Mr. Buchanan's speech of January, 1840, or any other of his speeches, can be found to justify the allegation that he favored the reduction of wages. The whole false fabric falls to the ground.

In connection with this subject, we will here introduce an extract from the remarks of the Hon. C. J. FAULKNER, of Va., at the Ratification meeting held in Washington City:

I represent in Congress a district which abounds, perhaps, to a greater extent than any in Virginia, in laboring men—I mean men who live by their own toil, and by the daily, weekly, or yearly wages of hard and honest labor. National workshops, machine-shops, and manufacturing establishments may be seen at short intervals, from the time you enter that district at Harper's Ferry, until you leave it, some thirty miles west of Cumberland. When on my way to Cincinnati, towards the close of last month, and when I passed the principal points where these establishments are located—Harper's Ferry, Martinsburg, and Piedmont—these noble sons of toil, these brawny, hard-fisted men of labor, crowded around the cars to express their most anxious wishes for the nomination of James Buchanan. "For God's sake, give us Buchanan," was the impassioned cry of many of them. I dwelt upon this fact upon more than one occasion in Cincinnati. For, I thought when the popular instinct was thus so firmly directed, and the popular heart thus vividly aroused, it would, indeed, have been a most rash and dangerous experiment to have disregarded it. I do not believe there is now living in this country a public man more deeply enthroned in the hearts of the laboring men, than James Buchanan. [Great applause.] It would be quite an entertaining sight to see one of those advocates of the bank rags of 1839 and 1840—one of those champions of a false, spurious, and irredeemable paper currency—seek to insult the intelligence of such men as these by the cry of "Ten-cent Jemmy." I see that some of our leading Democratic editors are gravely occupied in vindicating Mr. Buchanan from this "ten-cent and low-wages" calumny. It is all waste time. The great mass of the people understand that subject far better than the Know-Nothing editors who publish such stuff. I have not met with a laboring man of ordinary intelligence in my district, who does uot understand the origin of this story about "low wages and ten cents," who cannot tell you how the lie was gotten up; what temporary purpose it was intended to serve; and how justly the whole affair deserves the scorn and contempt of every fair mind. They know that the very speech from which they pretend to derive this misrepresentation, is one of the noblest vindications of the rights and interests of the laboring man, and as such, it shall, as far as I am able, find its way into the hands of every artizan and mechanic in the country before November next. The laboring men of the country look upon the whole story as one that has passed into the sewer of forgotten calumnies, and not to be recollected, except as a scar received by Mr. Buchanan in his gigantic conflict with bank monopoly and bank corruption, or referred to as a memorial of those days when he stood up in the Senate house—and there were giants in those days—as the unflinching advocate of the interests of honest labor against the outside pressure of swindlers, shavers and speculators. [Immense cheering.]

MR. BUCHANAN AND THE NATIONAL ARMORIES.

A mechanic of the city of Baltimore, in a letter to the editor of the Baltimore *Argus*, of the 9th of July last, reproduces another evidence of Mr. Buchanan's attachment to the laboring classes. We copy as follows. The votes of Mr. Buchanan, as a member of the Senate, were consistently given in support of the Civil, and for the overthrow of the Military system, as the records of that body abundantly prove.

In 1841, the supervision of National Armories was changed from civil to military, the result of which became so odious by the petty military orders, rules and regulations, from time to time issued by the commanding officer, that indignation meetings were held, and a committee appointed to proceed to Washington from the armory at Harper's Ferry, for the purpose of restoring the old civil system, which had been the government of the armory from its foundation by Gen. Washington. I was one of that committee, and we enlisted all the force in the Senate and House we could for the restoration of a civilian. I called upon and afterwards addressed the Hon. James Buchanan, of Pa., and received in reply the following letter:

SENATE CHAMBER, July 12, 1842.

Dear Sir:—The pressure of public business has prevented me from acknowledging the receipt of your letter at an earlier day. I cheerfully espouse your cause. I am clearly of opinion that the workmen at our armories ought to be placed under a civil, and not military superintendance; and I sincerely regret that a majority of the Senate have thought differently. In what manner the question may be decided by the House, I cannot anticipate, yet I fear the result.

Yours, sincerely,

JAMES BUCHANAN.

I trust, Mr. Editor, that my fellow-workmen will not be so silly as to believe that Mr. Buchanan, in any shape or manner, is opposed to our best interests. It is wrong, it is unjust to believe otherwise than that he is the friend of labor and its reward. EIGHTEENTH WARD.

MORE EVIDENCE ON THE SUBJECT OF MR. BUCHANAN AND THE WAGES OF LABOR.

In looking over an old file of the *Army and Navy Chronicle*, says the *Boston Daily Times*, we came across the following letter, written by Mr. Buchanan, then a U. S. Senator from Pennsylvania, to the Hon. Mahlon Dickerson, then Secretary of the Navy. Although written nearly twenty years ago, it is another of the many evidences of the sympathy of James Buchanan for the laboring classes. We cannot find on record anything that would show Mr. Buchanan's want of feeling to the colored men, whom some of our rampant Black Republicans are wont to call "men and brethren;" nor can we find anything which would go to show that Mr. Buchanan, in his proverbial benevolence, gave preference to the negro over the men of his own color and blood. A constitutional democrat, and a friend of the Union, he looks upon the South as equal with the North, and he will sustain the rights of each under the Constitution. As a statesman, he regards this as a government of white men, and not a government of colored men. As a philosopher, he feels that the condition of the three millions of blacks in our Southern States, is incomparably better, in being well fed, well housed, well clothed, and well cared for, in every moral and physical detail, than any other three millions of negroes that ever have existed, or now exist, in any part of the world. But read the letter of Mr. Buchanan, and the white laborers and mechanics of the North will perceive that his feelings are not intensified upon a race upon whom God has placed his mark, distinguishing them from a superior creation, created for a distinct purpose.

WASHINGTON, Dec. 26, 1837.

My Dear Sir:—Permit me to address you on a subject which has excited much feeling throughout the city and county of Philadelphia, and has enlisted my warmest sympathies.

Five hundred mechanics have been suddenly thrown out of employment in the Navy Yard in Philadelphia, at this inclement season of the year. Most of them depending on their daily labor for their daily bread, you can easily appreciate what must be their sufferings. Their large families (as a friend informs me) are in a most lamentable condition, and God only knows what will become of them unless government gives them employment.

Now, sir, allow me to remark, that nothing short of necessity ought to compel a paternal government to place such a body of mechanics, who have faithfully performed their duty, in such deplorable circumstances. I know that the feelings of your heart will respond to this sentiment. Why not, then, make an effort for their relief? They ask no favor, but to be permitted to give, in their labor, an equivalent for bread for themselves, their wives, and their children. I understand there is now a frigate at the Navy Yard, on which they might be employed.

Even if the department, under other circumstances, should deem it more advisable, for the present, to delay completion, still a mere question of a few months in point of time, becomes comparatively insignificant, when weighed in the balance against humanity and justice. Besides, unless the Navy Yard at Philadelphia is to be abandoned—which I trust is not contemplated by the department—it is of great importance to the government to prevent such a body of faithful and skilful mechanics from dispersing.

I therefore appeal to you, with confidence, to grant them employment—and I almost envy you the power of conferring blessings upon so many industrious and meritorious citizens, without doing injury to the Government.

I feel confident you will pardon me for requesting as early an answer to this communication as may be consistent with your convenience.

Yours, very respectfully,

JAMES BUCHANAN.

Hon. MAHLON DICKERSON, *Secretary of the Navy*.

MR. BUCHANAN'S CHARACTER AT HOME.

It is said that no man is a prophet in his own country; but, after all, the good opinion of one's neighbors is a jewel above price. Mr. Buchanan has resided in the town of Lancaster forty odd years, man and boy. If he had been guilty of any offences against propriety, they would have appeared in that long time. He has had his share of political abuse; he has been a lawyer of great prominence; but throughout, no man has ever been found to question his integrity, or to insinuate a whisper against his reputation in public or private life. He has been a model of uprightness, quiet dignity and gentle deportment, scorning the arts of the demagogue, and discharging all his duties to his fellow-citizens conscientiously. Mr. Buchanan's fortune, which is not very large, has been the result of hard study, persevering toil, and fair dealing in his profession. He has always given freely in works of charity, and has shown much public spirit. In his own family, his kindness, his gentleness, and his hospitality, are proverbial. The memoir written and published by the Democratic State Central Committee, makes the following allusion to Mr. Buchanan "at home."

At this day, after more than half a century's intercourse as man and boy with the people of his own immediate district, and with the people of Pennsylvania; after having figured prominently in the conflicts of parties; after having shared the confidence of successive Democratic administrations; after having contributed his energies to the overthrow of political heresies without number, he might leave his case to thousands and tens of thousands, who have at various times antagonized his opinions, but now, with the annals of his life before them, stand ready to pay their tribute to his consistency and to his integrity as a public man, by uniting with his political friends in placing him in the Presidential chair! What nobler monument could be raised in commemoration of any American patriot? What more significant refutation of all the accusations of heated party combatants? What more conclusive proof could be given to the nation at large, of the fitness and the merits of a statesman who, after such a lifetime, finds his endorsers in the hearts of the people among whom he has lived, and his warmest supporters among men who have for more than forty years stood in opposition to his opinions?

Let a stranger go to Lancaster now, and he will be surprised to find that hundreds of the leading Whigs of that old county are enrolled among the supporters of James Buchanan—are his active friends, and deem it a pleasing duty, a duty to their State and their country, to support their distinguished fellow-citizen. The old Germans, whom he has defended at the bar, come forward to give their suffrages to the honest and conscientious lawyer; and hundreds whom he served during his Congressional career, are eager to render him their support. The young men are enthusiastically at his side; and the public press, with a single infamous exception, has been glad to bear voluntary testimony to his virtues, his abilities and his deservings.

Two or three instances of Mr. Buchanan's benevolence may as well appear in this connection:

[From the Pittsburg Post.]

BUCHANAN AND PITTSBURG.

On the 10th of April, 1845, a large portion of Pittsburg was laid in ashes by the great fire. There was no telegraph to Pittsburg in those days, and the news of our calamity could only reach Washington by the

14th of April. Mr. Buchanan was then Secretary of State. On that day the following document left Washington for Pittsburg, addressed by Mr. Buchanan to Wm J. Howard, then mayor of our city. Comment is unnecessary, even to those maligners who would represent Mr. Buchanan as cold and selfish:

$500.] WASHINGTON, April 14, 1845.

Cashier of the Bank of Metropolis: Pay to the order of W. J. Howard, mayor of the city of Pittsburg, for the use of the sufferers by the late fire, five hundred dollars. JAMES BUCHANAN.

Dear Sir:—Will you please to accept and apply the above towards the relief of the sufferers in the late dreadful calamity. My feelings of sympathy and compassion have never been so strongly excited upon any similar occasion. But let the people be of good cheer, and exert their accustomed energy, and, under the blessings of Providence, all will yet be well, and Pittsburg will arise more glorious than ever from its ashes. JAMES BUCHANAN.

W. J. HOWARD, Esq.

WHAT HIS NEIGHBORS SAY OF HIM.

It is no matter of trifling consideration and importance that those who know a man best should eulogise him most. More especially is praise to be valued when it is extorted from a political opponent. The Lancaster (Pennsylvania) *Express*, a Know-Nothing Republican paper, published in the immediate neighborhood of Mr. Buchanan's residence, is compelled to bear testimony to his unbending integrity and blameless life. After a few introductory remarks, the editor proceeds, and says:

"We know the man as one of our most respected fellow-citizens; a gentleman of unblemished personal integrity and unusually agreeable manners in his social intercourse with all classes. We know him as the friend of the poor, as a perpetual benefactor of the poor widows of this city, who, when the piercing blasts of each successive winter brought shrieks of cold, and hunger, and want, in the frail tenements of poverty, could apply to the 'Buchanan Relief Donation' for their annnal supply of wood, and sitting down with their orphaned children in the cheerful warmth of a blazing fire, lift their hearts in silent gratitude to God, and teach their little ones to bless the name of James Buchanan. As a citizen, a neighbor, a friend, in a word, as simply James Buchanan, we yield to no man in the measure of our respect and esteem; and were he still before us as *simply* James Buchanan, as he was a few years, and he and we occupied the same broad Jeffersonian republican platform, when at least one of the editors of this paper voted with him year after year the same Democratic ticket, then ours would be the more pleasing duty of supporting instead of opposing the election of our esteemed fellow-citizen and neighbor to the highest office in the gift of the American people, and the highest position of political distinction in the world."

A STRIKING TRAIT IN MR. BUCHANAN'S CHARACTER.

In his long intercourse with public men, why is it that Mr. Buchanan, whom his opponents now call "a cold-hearted man," can point to such an army of enthusiastic and devoted friends? He has them not only at home, but in every State in the Union. He finds them not merely in the higher walks of public life, but in every class and station of society. While a member of the House of Representatives and of the Senate, a period something over twenty years, he made friends who adhered to him through life, many of whom are still living. While in the Cabinet of President Polk, he was a favorite of his associates, without exception. He can recall, with pleasure, his companionship with Lewis F. Linn, of Missouri, and with Ambrose H. Sevier, of Arkansas, gallant spirits, now gathered to their fathers. He was the friend of Levi Woodbury, the companion of Wm. R. King, of Roane, of Silas Wright, of John C. Calhoun, of Felix Grundy, and of all that sterling race of men who adorned the era in which he was an actor. At the present moment Bancroft, the historian, William L. Marcy, Robert J. Walker, Nathan Clifford, Isaac Toucey, John Y. Mason, and Cave Johnson, his associates during the memorable administration of Mr. Polk, are all advocating his election, and nearly all ardently preferred him before all others as a candidate for the Presidency.

It cannot be a cold-hearted man who can retain such men at his side through so many years. It proves fidelity to his friends, truth in his dealings with them, and a readiness at all times to respond to a generous action.

The following is from the pen of a very distinguished old line Whig in Philadelphia:

MR. BUCHANAN AND THE OSTEND MANIFESTO.

The self-styled neutral press—of that class who are loud in vaunting their perfect independence of politics—of which the "*Evening Bulletin*" is a malignant type, are busy and constant in their efforts to misrepresent the purport of this celebrated paper. I am a Whig—a Whig of the Clay, Webster and Sergeant school. I was a Whig when what is now Black Republicanism was fanatical abolitionism—resisted as ably and strenuously by our great leaders as it was by the Democratic party. I am a Whig still, and think I stand on the same platform with reference to the only issues before the country that Clay and Webster stood. They were opposed to *Sectionalism*, to abolitionism—so am I. And were they alive, I doubt not they would cast their vote as I intend to vote in November next—for James Buchanan. I shall vote for him, because he is the only candidate who represents fully the principle with reference to the slavery question, that I think vital to the safety of the country, and the permanence of the union of the States; because he represents the only party that is national in its character, and has positive and governing strength in every section of the confederacy, North, South, East and West. I shall vote for him because the platform of the party which has nominated him, proposes to remove the Slavery agitation from the halls of Congress entirely, where it has always been, and always will be, a cause of discord and strife, and to let the people of the Territories or States decide for themselves the character of their domestic institutions. I shall vote for him, because he is a statesman of enlarged experience, conservative in his character, and who, apart from the impregnable position occupied by himself and his party on the Slavery question, upon which the Union depends, is eminently qualified to conduct the affairs, both foreign and domestic, of Government, with honor in these difficult times. I shall vote for him, because I think his position with reference to Cuba, as laid down in the "Ostend Manifesto," eminently wise and sound, and if understood properly, will meet with a hearty response from every true American citizen. It is fortunate for Mr. Buchanan that his real position on the Cuban question is susceptible of an elucidation so clear and certain, that no apology for misconstruction or misrepresentation can exist. The "Ostend Manifesto" itself furnishes a triumphant answer to the charge so flippantly made, "that Mr. Buchanan does not hesitate to say that we *must have Cuba at all risks*. If Spain refuses to sell, then take it (Cuba) by force!" I undertake to prove from the paper itself, that no such doctrine or sentiments are entertained or found in it. The argument of the Ostend paper is clear, concise, and to the point—that we should not acquire Cuba *without the consent of Spain*, UNLESS JUSTIFIED BY THE GREAT LAW OF SELF-PRESERVATION.

The Ostend document holds this language:

"It must be clear to every reflecting mind that, from the peculiarity of its geographical position and the considerations attendant on it, Cuba is as necessary to the North American republic as any of its present members, and that it belongs naturally to that great family of States of which the Union is the providential nursery.

"From its locality it commands the mouth of the Mississippi, and the immense and annually increasing trade, which must seek this avenue to the ocean.

"On the numerous navigable streams, measuring an aggregate course of some thirty thousand miles, which disembogue themselves through this magnificent river into the Gulf of Mexico, the increase of the population, within the last ten years, amounts to more than that of the entire Union at the time Louisiana was annexed to it.

"The natural and main outlet to the products of this entire population, the highway of their direct intercourse with the Atlantic and the Pacific States, can never be secure, but must ever be endangered, whilst Cuba is a dependency of a distant power, in whose possession it has proved to be a source of constant annoyance and embarrassment to their interests.

"Indeed, the Union can never enjoy repose, nor possess reliable security, as long as Cuba is not embraced within its boundaries.

"After we shall have offered Spain a price for Cuba far beyond its present value, and this shall have been refused, it will then be time to consider the question: Does Cuba in the possession of Spain seriously endanger our internal peace and the existence of our cherished Union?

"Should this question be answered in the affirmative, then by every law, human and divine, we shall be justified in wresting it from Spain, if we pos sess the power—and this upon the very same principle that would justify an individual in tearing down the burning house of his neighbor, if there were no other means of preventing the flames from destroying his own home.

"Under such circumstances, we ought neither to count the cost nor regard the odds which Spain might enlist against us. We forbear to enter into the question whether the present condition of the island would justify such a measure.

"Our past history forbids that we should acquire the island of Cuba without the consent of Spain, *unless justified by the great law of self-preservation*. We must, in any event, preserve our own conscious rectitude and our own self-respect.

"But if Spain, deaf to the voice of her own interest, and actuated by stubborn pride and a false sense of honor, should refuse to sell Cuba to the United States, then the question will arise, what ought to be the course of the American government under such circumstances.

"Self-preservation is the first law of nature, with States as well as with individuals. All nations have at different periods acted upon this maxim. Although it has been made the pretext for committing flagrant injustice, as in the partition of Poland, and other similar cases which history records, yet the principle itself, though often abused, has always been recognised."

Mr. Buchanan's position is, that if Spain refuses to sell, then (not that our government shall take it by force) will be the time to consider the question: Does Cuba, in the possession of Spain, seriously endanger our internal peace and the existence of our cherished Union?

Let us be specific on this matter. Mr. Buchanan lays down the great law of self preservation as applicable to States as well as individuals. Will any one dispute the truth of that position? He says that, as important as Cuba is to our peace and prosperity, we should not think of acquiring it without the consent of Spain, *except* in the last resort, as a means of saving our own nation from ruin. Will any one venture to take issue with him on this position? He says that, before considering the question whether the acquisition of Cuba is essential for our preservation, we should offer to buy the island, and even to offer more than its value. Will anybody come forward to dispute this position? He says that if Spain refuses to sell at such price, it will then be time for our government to consider the momentous question whether Cuba is essential to our self-preservation; and if it shall be decided in the affirmative, then, to save ourselves from ruin, we should take Cuba at any cost or peril. Who can successfully gainsay this proposition? Who will say that "an individual would not be justified in tearing down the burning house of his neighbor, if that were the only means of saving his own home?"

I have no fears that the people, the sound conservative, right-thinking, right-minded people, will be misled by the misrepresentations of partizan zealots; in this age of steam-presses, no public man of the country has perhaps so little to fear from a dispassionate examination of his record—which can be found on almost every page of our history for the last thirty years.

Nominated by his party for the highest office in the world, without any seeking either by word or deed from him—thousands and thousands of his old political opponents are flocking to his standard, as the only means of saving the institutions of the country from civil discord and strife. His election in November next is certain.

The men and the papers now engaged in misrepresenting the Ostend Manifesto, and especially those who think it will arouse the animosity of Spain, should know that the manifesto, when received in Spain, so far from being hurtful, was succeeded by a state of feeling among the Spanish statesmen, of the most satisfactory character. Its reasoning and conclusions are such as no upright man, especially no American, could then, or can now, conscientiously resist or refute.

MR. CLAY SPEAKS—HEAR HIM!

We find in the Lexington *Observer and Reporter*, a letter copied from the Kentucky *Statesman*, which we publish with great satisfaction. It is from James B. Clay, a son of Henry Clay, the great American Statesman, whom all men delight to honor.

This letter is the best refutation that could be made of the stale slanders now attempted to be revived by a venal partizan press, relative to the unfounded charges against Mr. Buchanan—charges denied by Henry Clay himself, by his biographer, and now by the public generally. The high personal regard which these distinguished statesmen ever entertained for each other, also effectually disproves these malicious fabrications.

Mr. Clay, in announcing his determination to vote for Mr. Buchanan, assumes a position which is alike honorable to himself and the powerful party of which his honored father was the acknowledged leader.

[From the Kentucky Statesman.]

Mr. Editor:—I desire, through your courtesy, to correct a statement made in the *Statesman* of the 4th inst., which does great injustice to two of my friends, and political brothers, the Hon. Joshua F. Bell, of Boyle, and the Hon. William B. Kinkead, of Kenton, and which moreover is untrue. The article to which I refer, states "that resolutions expressing the confidence of the Whigs of Kentucky in Mr. Fillmore, and saying he was worthy of their support as in 1848," were rejected by the votes of sixteen counties to one, in the State Convention held at Louisville, on the 3d inst., *and that Mr. Bell and Kinkead advocated them.*

It is undeniably true that such resolutions were offered in the Convention by Col. Hopkins, of Henderson, and it is also true that they were laid upon the table by a vote of sixteen counties to one. But it is not true that either Mr. Bell or Mr. Kinkead voted for them; on the contrary, both gentlemen opposed them, as I have reason to believe they would have done, resolutions to endorse any one but a true old line Whig for the office of President. It was, also, at the express desire and request of Mr. Kinkead that Mr. Adams withdrew his motion, to the effect "that the Whigs of Kentucky have undiminished confidence in Millard Fillmore." It is, however, but candid to say, that every member of the Convention understood that Mr. Bell and Judge Kinkead preferred Mr. Fillmore to either Mr. Buchanan or Mr. Fremont; neither of them made any attempt to do so gross and unjust a thing, as to commit an old line Whig Convention to the endorsement of anybody but a Whig.

There is also a statement copied into the *Observer and Reporter* of the 5th inst., "that I had been heard to say, that I was not for Buchanan." I may have said that Mr. Buchanan was not my candidate, or was not my choice for the Presidency; but I have not said that I should not vote for him. I prefer Mr. Fillmore personally, and if he stood on the same principles he did in 1850, I would vote for him in preference to any man I know. But I expect to cast my vote for that candidate who, in my opinion, may have the best chance to defeat the candidate of the Black Republican party; and, at present advised, I think Mr. Buchanan has the best chance to do so. I wish it, nevertheless, to be distinctly understood, that if I shall think it my duty to vote for Mr. Buchanan, I shall vote as an old line Whig, making a choice of what he believes to be evils, for the good of the country; and that whenever the Whig standard shall again be raised, adhering always to the principles which I have been instrumental in asserting at Lexington, and at Louisville on the 3d July, I shall be ready, fairly, honestly and fearlessly to battle against those principles and practices of the Democratic party which conflict with our own views.

I feel sure, Mr. Editor, that your readers will not do me the injustice to attribute to me too great a desire to force myself before their notice, in venturing to corrrect misrepresentations affecting my friends and myself, however well I may know the little importance that may be attached to any opinions of mine. I hope the *Observer and Reporter* will also do me the favor, as well as justice, to copy this letter I am sir, respectfully, &c.,

Your obedient servant,

JAMES B. CLAY

Ashland, July 8, 1856.

WHERE ARE HENRY CLAY'S FAMILY AND FRIENDS?

All of Mr. Clay's immediate family, with a single exception, are in the same position as the gentleman above referred to, and some are openly out for Buchanan. The sons of the old Henry Clay leader, John Sergeant, of Philadelphia, are out for Buchanan, and in the Senate, Henry Clay Whigs, like Benjamin, of La., Pratt, of Md., Pearce, of Md., and J. C. Jones, of Tenn., have taken open ground in favor of Buchanan's election.

INFIDELITY AND ABOLITIONISM.

AN OPEN LETTER

TO THE FRIENDS OF

RELIGION, MORALITY, AND THE AMERICAN UNION.

No nation has ever long existed which did not repose, as upon a rock, upon the principles and teachings of the Holy Scriptures, as understood and practised by the civilized races of man. It is no less true, that never since the world began have these teachings and principles been so deeply fixed and so widely disseminated as since the erection of the American Republic. Hand-in-hand with the growth of our government, and the increase of our population, and our territory, the moral virtues have increased, and the followers of Bible faith have multiplied. Free institutions have secured perfect religious equality; the Union of the States has been the bond between different denominations; and the fountain of patriotism has so mingled the sacred memories of the labors of the sages of the past and the sufferings of the holy men who toiled with them, that it has become a common belief that Providence holds us in his most special keeping.

It is a rude contrast to this agreeable retrospect to say that the attempt now making to destroy the Union, and the sacred interests involved in its existence, is a serious attempt. It is more than this: it is a bold and flagrant attempt; a widely-extended conspiracy; a deeply-laid and profoundly-concerted plot. A few plain facts will show whether these assertions are reasonable or not.

John C. Fremont is the candidate for the Presidency of conjoined fanaticisms, one of which assails all true religion, and the other of which assails the Union of the States. They go together in a body; they cannot be separated. We assert and defy contradiction, that every organization boasting infidel doctrines is now an organization in favor of Fremont; and we assert also, that all those desiring a dissolution of the Union are openly co-operating with these organizations. The best way to prove this is to show what the leaders of these united factions have repeatedly announced to the world. We ask the close attention of our readers to the following authentic declarations of the leading friends of John C. Fremont:—

The American Tract Society, an organization of immense usefulness, is assailed with great violence by the Abolitionists, because it will not unite in this disunion, infidel movement. We could multiply extracts to prove this statement, but the religious public is well aware of it. One authority is sufficient to show how infidels and disunionists unite. We copy from a Fremont Abolition organ, the New York Standard, April 19, 1856, a paper of great circulation. An influential religious journal, the Christian Messenger, having said with great truth, that "Infidelity strikes at the root of social order, domestic purity, and national security," and "*Infidelity fans the flame of sectional jealousy and hate.*" This advocate of Fremont, the Standard, says:

"The only question which, at the present day, can possibly be said to excite *sectional* jealousy and hate is the Slavery question, and this is the flame which the American Tract Society declares is fanned by infidelity. If it be true that infidelity is raising its voice against the iniquities and abominations of American bondage, it has in fact become more Christian than cotton divinity, which insults the Almighty, revokes his precepts, and degrades his Holy Word by making it the warrant for the foulest injustice, the vilest cruelty."

Another Fremont leader is the notorious Theodore Parker, who in the course of an anti-slavery speech in New York, last March, said,

"The North has a duty to perform—to put slavery down, 'peaceably if it can, forcibly if it must.' There are two ways to go to work to do this: one is, dissolve the Union, and leave the South to settle the matter for herself.

"There are many things that look that way; and there are some who think this the true system. Among them is my friend Johnson, *who so handsomely introduced me as an infidel.* But he meant such an infidel as loves the good God and his fellow-man. Mr. Garrison is in favor of the dissolution of the Union. He is a great and good man, and I love him."

The following extract from a sermon of the same Rev. Theodore Parker, is a fair sample of the line of argument used by Fremont's reverend supporters:

"I do not believe in the miraculous origin of the Hebrew Church, or the Budhist Church, or of the Christian Church, nor of the miraculous character of Jesus. I take not the Bible for my master, nor yet the Church, nor even Jesus of Nazareth for my master. He is my best historical dial of human greatness, nor without the stain of his times and, I presume of course, not without sin, for men without sin exist only in the dreams of girls."

Let Garrison talk for himself.

From the Boston Liberator, Garrison's paper, June 20, 1856—a paper that supports John C. Fremont:

"*The United States Constitution is a covenant with death and an agreement with hell.*"

The same number of the Liberator contains an editorial article indorsing Fremont's nomination; and a petition to Congress which *demands the dissolution of the Union.*

Garrison's infidelity is so strongly marked, that in his paper of March 21, 1856, we find it stated by himself that he attended an anti-Bible Convention at Hartford (Conn.), at which, we use his own language, "he offered a series of resolutions *in opposition to the popular dogma respecting that volume!*" The Convention met under the following call:

☞ TO THE FRIENDS OF FREE DISCUSSION. The undersigned hereby invite all who are friendly to free discussion, to attend a Convention to be held at Hartford (Ct), on Thursday, Friday, Saturday, and Sunday, 2d, 3d, 4th, and 5th of June next, for the purpose of freely and fully canvassing the ORIGIN, AUTHORITY, AND INFLUENCE OF THE JEWISH AND CHRISTIAN SCRIPTURES.

This invitation is not given to any particular class of Philosophers, Theologians, or Thinkers, but it is in good faith extended to all who feel an interest in the examination of the question above stated. There are many who believe that a supernatural revelation has been given to man; many others who deny this, and a large number who are afflicted with perplexing doubts—trembling between the silent skepticism of their reason and the fear of absolute denial. In issuing a call for a Convention, we have in view the correction of error, *by which party soever entertained*, and the relief of those who stand between doubt and fear, from their embarrassing position.

Some may have no doubt that the Jewish and Christian Scriptures have subserved an important end, and yet believe their mission is nearly completed, and must be superseded by a new dispensation; some may believe that their influence has been prejudicial in every respect, and that they have been a curse rather than a blessing to mankind; others may believe them a perfect record of the Divine will to man—good in the past and for all time to come; and others still may deny the plenary inspiration of the Bible, discarding much of the Old Testament, and receiving most or all of the New. Still, such diversity of opinion, instead of prejudicing the interests and good results which ought to attend such a Convention, will rather tend to increase its interest and enhance its value to the cause of truth.

Doubtless a free interchange of thought is the best mode of exciting inquiry, and of arriving at the truth.

"He who has a truth and keeps it,
Keeps what not to him belongs;
But performs a selfish action,
And his fellow-mortal wrongs."

We invite, therefore, all who feel an interest in this question, without distinction of sex, color, sect, or party, to come together, that we may sit down like brethren in a communion before the altar of intellectual and spiritual freedom.

In the same number of this paper, dissolution of the Union is ably advocated, and three months later, as we have shown, John C. Fremont was advocated by Garrison as the true man to commence *the good work*.

In the same paper, of the 4th of May, 1855, we find a communication conspicuously published, and signed by Francis Barry, Berlin Heights, Ohio (no doubt if living a Fremont advocate), which contains the following extract:

"I have carefully looked over my last article (see Liberator, Feb. 2), and I can but find a single expression that begins to compare, in point of "profanity," with the above extracts. I said, if God had the power to abolish slavery, and would not, he was "a very great scoundrel." Now, did I recognize the *existence* of an infinitely holy being, and then should speak of him in such a manner, you might call it profanity; but as I believe in no God, my statement amounts simply to this: Any being whatever, having the power to strike the chains from the limbs of the slave, and should refuse to exercise it, is a scoundrel—I should have said, *devil.* And if there is a man, not a fiend in human shape, who does not respond to this sentiment, it is because his humanity is swallowed up in his 'theology.' No doubt you would agree with me, that the *man* who will not do all in his power for the abolition of slavery, has more of the devilish than of the divine in his nature; but *God* may be deaf to the cry of despair, may even command his serviles to rob, ravish, and murder, as did fabled "Israel's God," and yet we must yield to this omnipotent fiend unlimited reverence. This is one of the pernicious effects of belief in a God. He may do whatever he pleases, whether it be right or wrong, angelic or devilish, and it is right, because *he* does it! The immutability of *Justice* is not recognized. Right, justice, truth, are arbitrary affairs—the present will or opinion of a changeable being—now one thing, now another. Belief in a being whose word, whatever it is, is recognized as truth, and whose will, however unreasonable or tyrannical, is recognized as law, involves a contempt for the eternal, immutable principles of justice and truth."

Horrible as this is, we defy contradiction, and stand ready to prove that the above is a true extract from a leading Abolition Disunion and Fremont paper, the "Boston Liberator."

At Boston, in May 29, 1855, and the same has lately been repeated—the following resolution against the "American Tract Society" and other Christian organizations, was adopted by the Anti-Slavery Society:

"4. Resolved, That the multiplication of converts to such a religion, instead of indicating any progress in the cause of justice, freedom, and Christianity, or furnishing any occasion for congratulation, is a sure sign of moral degeneracy, judicial blindness, and pharisaical malignity, to be denounced as an imposture; and that such a 'revival' is only a device of time-serving hirelings, to withdraw attention from the reforms of the age, and especially from the anti-slavery movement—to affect a zeal for God for the benefit of their craft—and to shield themselves from the condemnation they deserve for their treachery to the rights of man."

Wendell Phillips says:

"It is the first Sectional party ever organized in this country. It does not know its own face, and it calls itself National; but it is not national, it is sectional. It is the North arrayed against the South. Henry Wilson said to me, 'We must get every Northern State in order to elect Fremont. Even in imagination he did not count upon a single Southern State. It was a distinct recognition of the fact that the Republican party is a party of the North pledged against the South. Theodore Parker wanted to know once where Disunion would begin. I will tell him: Just where that party divides. That is a Northern party against the Southern. I do not call it an Anti-Slavery party; it has not risen to that yet. It is a Northern party against the Southern. They made the first little breach. The first crack in the iceberg is visible; you will hear it go with a crack through to the centre. Its first distinct recognition was Bank's election. He was elected by Northern men—not a man from the South voting for him. That is the value of that party. I hail it as a sign—as a great gain. I did not hope to see it for ten years; it has come unexpectedly early." —*Wendell Philipps, a Boston Infidel.*

"The times demand and we must have an ANTI-SLAVERY CONSTITUTION, AN ANTI-SLAVERY BIBLE, AND AN ANTI-SLAVERY GOD."—*Anson Burlingame, member of Congress from Massachusetts.*

In one of the churches of Detroit, "a fearless and faithful minister of Christ"—as the *Tribune* terms him—preached an Abolition sermon, in which he remarked as follows:

"Before I would see popular sovereignty wrested by force from the people of the Territories (referring to the determination of the authorities to enforce obedience to the laws), *I would have the plains of Kansas silent with universal death.* Before I would have the lips of our Senators and Representatives sealed in craven silence by the hand of Southern violence (referring to the castigation bestowed upon Sumner by Brooks for *personal*, not political reasons), *I would see the halls of Congress ankle deep in blood!*"

The New York Tribune is the chief party organ of these infidel disunionists. That journal has been the reservoir, for years, of all the levelling, anti-religious, and revolutionary doctrines of European ultraists and destructives. It is controlled by a corps among whom are notorious infidels. It has opened its columns to the revolting doctrines of "free love," to Fourierism, and to the scarcely less dangerous dogma of "spiritualism." All the wild, monstrous, and absurd theories of the day, including the political equality, and the certain and consequent social equality of blacks and whites, have found favor in its sight. It is this dangerous paper whose editor, Horace Greeley, has assisted at public meetings of blacks and whites in the City of New York, where both God and the Constitution have been reviled; it is he who has co-operated with the advocates of woman's rights in the same city, where unsexed females have delighted in addressing mobs of men in strains of vulgar violence. And it is his associate, Fry, who, at a late meeting in Camden, New Jersey, compared John C. Fremont to Jesus Christ, and declared that he wished an earthquake would swallow up the Christian Churches that did not join in present disunion phrensy. Greeley leads and stimulates the Fremont party in every Free State.

The next organ of the Infidel movement against the Union is the infamous James Gordon Bennett, of the New York Herald, a man whose vast fortune has been coined by ministering to the worst vices of human nature, and whose daily columns, from the editorials to the advertisements, so groan with offers to depravity, and with proclamations of premiums for prostitution, that no decent citizen admits it into his family.

It is easy to say: you would not hold Mr. Fremont's party responsible for these atrocious sentiments and examples. We reply, not if those who uttered and gave them countenance were not his leaders. Greeley is his accepted and leading organ; and Greeley's Fourierism, Free-Loveism, Spiritualism, *are parts of that platform of which Sectionalism is the soul.* Col. Fremont's platform is Greeley's Sectionalism; and this Sectionalism is to the Infidels and Traitors whom we have quoted an acceptable substitute for their hatred of the Bible, and their contempt for the Constitution and the Union. *They know that if Sectionalism succeeds, with Fremont at its head, the Christian Religion and the American Union, are hopelessly impaired, or utterly destroyed*, and this is the key to the whole movement.

We believe and admit that many good men have expected to vote for Fremont, who will reject all such sentiments as those asserted and adopted by his organs and friends; but still he can no more escape than he can successfully deny the fearful responsibility. *The moment he consented to inflict the curse of Sectionalism upon the land, he became the instrument of vice, and the foe of God and of Freedom.*

Despotism views the greatness and wealth of our happy Union with envy and fear, and gloats upon the prospect of Disunion with song and exultation.

Infidelity is no less eager in its desire to overthrow religion; and to this end Disunion will contribute the only swift and ready weapon!

What is Liberty without the Union?

What would Religion be without a Constitution?

Both would be a mockery and a desolation.

Oppression and Tyranny would follow after the dissolution of the Union, and Religion would expire amid the clang of arms, or become the slave of the military despot.

Ask History for evidence of the truth of this picture; and, then, open the gates of servile and civil war, IF YOU DARE!

Do you tell us, O Christian minister, that these influences are not strong enough to divide the American Union?

We answer that they have already divided highly respectable Christian congregations.

If they could defy the law of God, what heed will they pay to the hopes and prayers of man?

At the two last General Conferences of the Methodist Episcopal Church, the question of Slavery was introduced, and all will remember the grateful prayers and the joyous expressions of the members of that great Church, at the success of peaceful counsels, after a long and painful debate; and the consequent dejection of the Abolitionists.

What is more soul-harrowing to the truly sincere patriot, to the honest believer in the Bible, to the moral and upright citizen, than to hear a political preacher hurling his anathemas against his fellow man, for their political opinions, from the pulpit, reared as an altar to the ever-living God? How often have we not seen it! How many happy communities has it not divided! How many bitter words has it not called out between brothers and friends! How has it not rejoiced Infidelity to see those evidences of expiring morality and blighted religion!

Look at your own experience, reader, and you will find that this is not a fancy sketch.

Remember your own sorrows, oh, faithful minister of Christ, whilst you have witnessed these humiliating scenes.

Recall the language of those Christian newspapers who have implored in vain that these degradations should cease.

Yesterday, it was Religious Intolerance which called out these too saddening exhibitions.

To-day, it is Disunionism, or in other words, devotion to "Fremont and Human Freedom," the shameless jargon by which traitors seek to dull the ears of our countrymen to the tocsin of alarm that proclaims a fatal peril to Religion and the American Union.

What will it be to-morrow? What if Fremont should be elected in November? God grant the veil of the future may never be lifted upon that catastrophe!

We appeal, finally, to the humane and honest classes of our countrymen. If you regard the Southern people as your brothers, and not your enemies, if Southern men are not accursed by heaven in your eyes, if you believe this Constitution of ours worth preserving, if you think your Christian Churches worth protecting, even those of the Free States; if in a word, you have any veneration remaining for those who lived and died to serve and save the Republic, put your heel upon this double-headed serpent, this monster of Infidelity and of Abolition. There is but one way left to do it, and that is to oppose John C. Fremont's election to the Presidency.

CONCLUSION.

The Hon. J. K. Paulding, of New York, clearly and forcibly states the position of the parties in the present struggle in the following extract of a letter, dated on the 25th of June.

> The two great parties have never been arrayed in direct opposition to each other on questions exclusively referring to political opinions, but moral, social, and religious principles, which form the basis of the entire standing of society, and the removal of which would produce a complete revolution, moral, social, and religious. In the words of one of the lecturers of this new school of ranting philosophy, now a member of Congress, "We must have an Anti-Slavery Bible, and an Anti-Slavery God."
>
> What also distinguishes the approaching Presidential election from all preceding ones, is, that it involves not merely a construction of certain provisions of the Constitution, but the existence of the Constitution itself. Whatever may be the names which the parties in opposition to the Democracy choose to adopt for purposes of deception, it must be obvious to all observers, that its entire mass is pervaded by the leaven of Abolition, without which it would be inert and comparatively lifeless. To conciliate that dangerous faction, it is absolutely necessary to adopt its principles; and they are sufficiently notorious, having been repeatedly avowed at conventions and lectures and anniversary meetings.
>
> They denounce the Bible, because it is an Anti-Slavery Bible; they denounce Christianity, because it tolerates a state of society which existed at the time, and has ever since been recognized; they denounce all laws inconsistent with the great dogma which constitutes their religious, moral, and political creed; and, finally, they denounce the Constitution "as a gross violation of the law of God and the rights of nature."
>
> It must be evident to every mind that can follow out principles to their inevitable consequences, that were a party holding such doctrines to wield the powers of this government, it must necessarily lead to a revolution, not political, but religious, moral, and social. It would not be merely reform but complete subversion. It would uproot the very foundation of the great system of whose beneficent operation the people of the United States have hitherto enjoyed a degree of prosperity and happiness without a parallel in the history of the world. We shall be out adrift from all our safe moorings, to float on the wide ocean of untried experiment, without rudder or compass, without any pilots, but mad-brained fanatics, and visionary reformers, who can neither comprehend their own vagaries nor make them comprehensive to others.

OFFICIAL PROCEEDINGS

OF THE

NATIONAL

Democratic Convention,

HELD IN

CINCINNATI,

JUNE 2-6, 1856.

PUBLISHED BY ORDER OF THE CONVENTION.

CINCINNATI:
ENQUIRER COMPANY STEAM PRINTING ESTABLIS
T. WRIGHTSON, Superintendent.
1856.

PROCEEDINGS

OF THE

DEMOCRATIC CONVENTION.

MONDAY, June 2, 1856.

Pursuant to the call of the Democratic National Committee, the Delegates to the National Convention assembled in Smith & Nixon's Hall in Cincinnati, Ohio, at 12 o'clock, noon, on the second day of June, 1856.

Robert McLane, of Maryland, as Chairman of the National Democratic Committee, called the Convention to order.

W. A. Richardson, of Illinois, arose and proposed that the Convention, for temporary organization, should elect Samuel Medary, of Ohio, President *pro tem.*, (Loud applause), which was unanimously adopted.

On motion, A. B. Clitherall, of Alabama, and W. F. Ritchie, of Virginia; were appointed Secretaries pro tem.

Mr. B. F. Hallett, of Massachusetts, asked that before further proceedings, the call of the Convention should be read, which was done by the Secretary. It is as follows:

Voted, That the next Democratic National Convention be held at Cincinnati, in the State of Ohio.

Voted, That in constituting the future National Convention, the Democratic Committee, in order to secure the respective rights of the States, each State shall be entitled to twice the number of delegates it has in the Electoral College, and no more; and the Democratic Committee, in making arrangements for the next Democratic Convention, provide such number of seats, and secure the same to the delegates elect.

Hon. A. P. Edgerton, of Ohio, Chairman of the Committee of Arrangements, handed to the President a list of the Delegates elected where seats were not contested, which was as follows:

List of Delegates to the Democratic National Convention,

Held at Cincinnati, June 2d, 1856.

MAINE.

Wyman B. S. Moor,	Waterville,	A. B. Chase,	Dover,
William K. Kimball,	Paris,	Isaac Tyler,	Farmington,
John C. Talbot, jr.,	Lubec,	Israel R. Bray,	Kingfield,
Samuel Watts,	Thomaston,	F. T. Lally,	Gardiner,
Dudley F. Leavitt,	Bangor,	Andrew Masters,	Hallowell,
Benjamin Wiggin,	Bangor,	A. G. Chandler,	Calais,
Jonathan Smith,	Portland,	Israel Chadbourne,	York,
John Babson,	Wiscasset.	George Parcher,	Ellsworth.

NEW HAMPSHIRE.

Harry Hibbard,	Bath,	Henry B. Rust,	Wolfeboro',
Joseph H. Smith,	Dover,	George Bowers,	Nashua,
John H. George,	Concord,	Horatio Kimball,	Keene,
B. F. Ayer,	Manchester,	Jonas Livingston,	Claremont,
Chas. Levi Woodbury,	Portsmouth.	Robert Ingalls,	

VERMONT.

D. A. Smalley,	Burlington,	Tappan Stevens,	Newbury,
J. P. Kidder,	West Randolph,	John Cain,	Rutland,
C. G. Eastman,	Montpelier,	Lyman P. White,	Whiting,
Bradley Barlow,	Fairfield,	Isaac B. Bowdish,	Swanton,
Robert Harvey,	Barnet.	P. S. Benjamin,	Wolcott.

MASSACHUSETTS.

Benjamin F. Butler,	Lowell,	James Cheever,	Boston,
Charles G. Greene,	Boston,	George B. Loring,	Salem,
N. J. Lord,	Salem,	Albert J. Currier,	Newburyport,
Whiting Griswold,	Greenfield,	Chas. H. Peaslee,	Boston,
S. B. Phinney,	Barnstable,	W. W. Pierce,	Charlestown,
James D. Thompson,	New Bedford,	Fisher A. Hildreth,	Lowell,
Alden S. Loud,		W. Fessenden,	Townsend,
E. P. Hathway,	Abington,	Isaac Davis,	Worcester,
Ezra S. Conant,	Randolph,	George W. Gill,	Worcester,
Henry P. Henshaw,	Newton,	Stephen C. Bemis,	Springfield,
Patrick Riley,	Boston,	Calvin Tincey,	Palmer,
Isaac Adams,	Boston,	James S. Whitney,	Springfield,
Benjamin F. Hallett,	Boston.	Henry H. Childs,	Pittsfield,

RHODE ISLAND.

Wm. B. Lawrence,	Newport.	H. J. Burroughs,	Providence,
Ariel Ballou,	Woonsocket,	Wm. J. Miller,	Bristol,
Peleg W. Gardiner,	Providence,	Elisha R. Potter,	Kingston,
Alfred Anthony,	Do.	Albert S. Gallup,	Providence.

CONNECTICUT.

James T. Pratt,	Rock Hill,	James Gallagher,	New Haven,
Colin M. Ingersoll,	New Haven,	Sam'l. Ingham,	Essex,
Joel W. White,	Norwich,	John P. C. Mather,	New London,
E. A. Phelps,	Nh. Colebrook,	Peleg C. Child,	Nh. Woodstock,
Heman H. Barbour,	Hartford,	John C. Smith,	Sharon,
Alvan P. Hyde,	Tolland.	Wm. D. Bishop,	Bridgeport.

NEW JERSEY.

Wm. Cook,	Bordentown,	Wm. D. Davis,	Freehold,
Alfred Hugg,	Camden,	Arch. Osburn,	Asbury,
J. S. Darsey,	Newark,	Ingham Coryell,	Lambertsville,
E. R. V. Wright,	Hudson City,	Jacob Vanatta,	Morristown,
Wm. Hanna,	Camden,	John Hooper,	Paterson,
Ephraim E. Sheppard,	Bridgeton,	Simeon Harrison,	Orange,
Garrett S. Cannon,	Bordentown.	Charles Fink,	Jersey City.

PENNSYLVANIA.

Arnold Plummer,	Franklin,	John G. Brenner,	Philadelphia,
Henry D. Foster,	Greensburg,	Orrin Jones,	
D. R. Porter,	Harrisburg,	Thomas J. Roberts,	Philadelphia.
James L. Reynolds,	Lancaster,	John Rutter,	West Chester,
Edward G. Webb,	Philadelphia.	Charles D. Manley,	Media, Del. Co.
John McCarthy,	Do.	John D. Stiles,	Allentown,
Jas. C. Vandyke,	Do.	Ed. Nicholson,	Bucks County,
C. McKibben,	Do.	J. Glancy Jones,	Reading,
John Robbins, jr.,	Kensington,	P. K. Miller,	Do.
Chas. W. Carrigan,	Philadelphia,	Jacob Forney,	Kittanning,
Joseph Lippincott,	Do.	John L. Dawson,	Brownsville,
Andrew Burke,	Pittsburg,	C. L. Ward,	Towanda,
Samuel W. Black,	Pittsburg,	W. F. Packer,	Williamsport,
M. C. Trout,	Sharon,	John H. Morrison,	
J. L. Gillis,	Ridgway,	Henry Welsh,	York,
J. Porter Branley,	Meadville,	John Stuart,	Carlisle,
A. S. Wilson,	Lewistown,	A. P. Lusk,	
H. B. Swan,	Lancaster,	John Cessna,	Bedford,
Joseph B. Baker,	Gap,	John C. Everhart,	Martinsburg,
John Weidman,	Lebanon,	Richard White,	Hemlock,
J. M. Kreister,	Harrisburg,	Alex. McKinney,	Greensburg,
Wm. L. Dewar,	Sunbury,	William Hopkins,	Washington,
C. M. Straub,	Pottsville,	Charles Barnett,	Pittsburg,
H. B. Wright,	Wilkesbarre,	James A. Gibson,	Allegheny Co.
J. G. Montgomery,	Danville,	John N. McGuffin,	New Castle,
John N. Hutchison,	Easton,	J. Y. James,	Warren,
H. B. Beardsly,	Honesdale,	Wilson Laird,	Erie.
W. E. Piolett,	Wyson.		

DELAWARE.

George Riddle,	Wilmington.	Wm. H. Ross,	Seaford.
Gove Salisbury,	Dover.	James A. Bayard,	Wilmington.
Willard Salisbury,	Georgetown.	H. Ridgley,	Dover.

MARYLAND.

R. B. Carmichael,		James M. Buchanan,	Baltimore.
Walter P. Snow,	Snow Hill.	William Byrne,	Baltimore.
William D. Merrick,	Allen's Fresh,	Rob't M. McLane,	Baltimore.
Nathaniel Cox,	Baltimore.	C. J. M. Gwinn,	Baltimore.
Cathill Humphreys,	Salisbury.	J. Thompson Mason,	Annapolis.
James A. Stewart,	Cambridge.	S. Lewis Lowe,	Frederick City.
John A. J. Creswell,	Elkton, Cecil Co.	Edward Hammond,	Ellicott's Mills.
Otho Scott,	Belle Air.	John A. B. Leonard.	Poolesville,

VIRGINIA.

T. S. Bocock,	Appomatton c.h.	Eppa Hunton,	Brentsville,
E. W. Hubbard,	Curdsville,	Thomas M. Isbell,	Rippon, Jeff. co.
W. H. Clark,	Scottsburgh,	J. Randolph Tucker,	Winchester,
W. P. Thompson,	Retreat,	Chas. W. Russell,	Wheeling.
John P. Barbour, Jr.,	Alexandria.	James Nelson,	Fairmount.
B. W. Jackson,	Parkersburg.	J. L. Carr,	Kanawha c. h.
J. G. Jenkins,	Green Bottom.	Eustace Conway,	Fredericksburg
M. R. H. Garnett,	Loyds, Essex Co.	James A. Seddon,	Goochland Co.
Paulus Powell,	Amherst c. h.	R. A. Banks,	Madison c. h.
R. K. Meade,	Petersburg.	Lewis E. Harris,	Mattoac Depot.
Wm. B. Shands,	Southampton.	W. H. Edwards,	Baileysburg.
H. T. Hopkins,	Macon, Powhatn	M. W. Fisher,	Eastville.
George Booker,	Hampton.	Archibald Graham,	Lexington.
Samuel C. Williams,	Woodstock,	A. A. Chapman,	
Fayette McMullen,	Rye, Scott Co.	John B. Floyd,	Abington.

NORTH CAROLINA.

Wm. S. Ashe,	Wilmington.	W. W. Avery,	Morgantown.
R. R. Heath,	Edonton.	Bedford Brown,	Locust Hill.
Wm. Sloan,	Dallas.	H. G. Williams,	Hubbardstown.
J. T. Granberry,	Woodville.	F. A. Thornton,	Macon Depot.
M. Silby,	Lake Landing.	John Morrison,	Carthage.
Wm. J. Yates,	Fayetteville.	A. J. Stafford,	Winston.
T. D. McDowall,	Elizabethtown.	J. W. Neal,	Lawsonville.
Burton Craige,	Salisbury..	J. B. Gordon,	Wilkesboro.
Thos. L. Clingman,	Asheville.	J. T. Lewis,	Faulkner.

SOUTH CAROLINA.

F. W. Pickins,	Edgefield c. h.	B. H. Brown,	Barnwell.
J. Gadberry,	Unionville.	J. L. Manning,	Fulton.
B. H. Wilson,	Georgetown.	J. D. Allen,	Barnwell.
C. W. Dudley,	Bennettsville	James Farrow,	Spartanburg.
W. D. Porter,		F. J. Moses,	Sumpterville.
C. McBeth,	Charleston.	E. G. Palmer,	Winnsboro.

GEORGIA.

J. W. H. Underwood,	Rome.	James Gardner,	Augusta.
M. J. Wellborn,	Columbus.	L. Stephens,	Sparta.
John E. Ward,	Savannah.	A. H. Colquitt,	Newton.
R. F. Lyon,	Albany.	Hugh Buchanan,	Newnan.
W. K. DeGraffenried,	Macon.	J. W. Lewis,	Cartersville.
Charles Murphy,	Decatur.	Wm. H. Hull,	Athens.
Aug. R. Wright,	Rome.	A. E. Cochran,	Brunswick.
H. Strickland,	Hightower.	J. T. Irvin,	Washington.
A. S. Atkinson,	Langsbury.	R. J. Conout,	Atlanta.
John J. Cary,	Macon.	J. L. Rowland,	Cartersville.

ALABAMA.

John Forsyth,	Mobile.	James R. Powell,	Montgomery.
R. Chapman.	Huntsville.	James B. Martin,	Talladega.
David Hubbard,	Kenlock.	J. W. Portiss,	Suggsville,
John Cochran,	Eufala.	A. L. Milligan,	Geneva,
Julius Hessee	Mobile.	J. B. Tate,	Uchee,
Bolling Hall,	Montgomery.	R. H. Clements,	Tuscaloosa,
A. B. Clitherall,	Carrollton.	Thos. H. Hobbs,	Athens,
H. D. Smith,	Florence.	W. Acklin,	Huntsville.
T. J. Burnett,	Greenville.	H. W. Nelson,	

LOUISIANA.

E. LaSere,	New Orleans.	A. Derbis,	New Orleans.
P. Soule,	New Orleans.	Thos Cottman,	Donaldsonville.
W. W. Pugh,	Assumption.	F. H. Hatch,	Darlington.
Chas. G. McHatton,	Baton Rouge.	Alexander Mouton,	Vermillionville.
P. A. Moise,	Natchitoches.	O. D. Block,	
W. S. Parham,	Richmond.	John L. Lewis.	Minden.

MISSOURI.

W. A. Harris,	Bowling Green.	Thomas B. English,	Jackson.
E. D. Bevitt,	St. Charles.	Joseph Coffman,	St. Genevieve,
James S. Greene,	Canton.	Thomas B. Hudson,	St. Louis.
A. W. Lamb,	Hannibal.	D. D. Berry,	Springfield.
P. H. McBride,	Columbia.	Ferdinand Kennett,	Old Mines.
William Shields,	Lexington.	W. Watson,	Georgetown.
R. H. Stevens,	Bellemonte.	James Craig,	St. Joseph.
S. R. Shrader,	Liberty.	John S. Phelps,	Springfield.
John S. McCracken,	Jefferson City.	Stark Manzey.	Brownville.

INDIANA.

Wm. Rockhill,	Fort Wayne.	James Osborn,	Fairfield.
John Pettit,	Lafayette.	Alex. F. Morrison,	Indianapolis.
Jos. W. Chapman,	Madison.	Franklin Hardin,	Glenns Valley,
John L. Robinson,	Rushville.	G. T. Cookerly,	Terre Haute.
Turner Nelson,	Mt. Vernon.	Wm. M. Franklin,	Spencer.
John C. Hebertt,	Vincennes.	S. W. Telford,	Lafayette,
P. M. Kent,	New Albany.	M. D. Manson,	Crawfordsville.
D. S. Huffstetter,	Orleans.	A. A. Whitlock,	
R. W. Aiken,	Bloomington.	N. O. Ross,	Peru.
S. P. Mooney,	Brownstown.	G. W. McConnell,	Angola.
C. O'Brien,	Lawrenceburg.	J. W. Borden,	Fort Wayne.
A. Davidson.	Greensburg.	J. R. Slack,	Huntington.
James Elder,	Richmond.	W. Ryan,	Anderson.

OHIO.

Samuel Medary,	Columbus.	L. W. Safford,	Chillicothe.
Henry B. Paine,	Cleveland.	Wm. Medill,	Lancaster.
James B. Stedman,	Toledo.	B. P. Hewitt,	McArthur.
C. L. Vallandigham,	Dayton.	Lewis Evans,	Newark.
Washington McLean,	Cincinnati.	W. A. Delaplaine,	Circleville.
J. L. Vattier,	Cincinnati.	H. C. Brumback,	Mt. Gilead.
J. J. Quinn,	Cincinnati.	John Mack,	Shelby.
Joseph Cooper,	Glendale.	D. B. Austin,	
M. C. Ryan,	Hamilton.	J. A. Marchand,	Wooster.
R. S. Cunningham,	Eaton.	M. Hoagland,	Millersburg.
G. V. Dorsey,	Piqua.	Eli Miller,	Mt. Vernon.
J. Counts,	Sidney.	H. J. Jewett,	Zanesville.
J. G. Haley,	Napoleon.	Amos Layman,	Marietta.
M. C. Whitley,		Wm. Lawrence,	Washington.
John W. Bell,	Hillsboro.	Jas. R. Morris,	Woodsfield.
George W. Hamer,	Georgetown.	Geo. W. Belden,	Canton.
J. M. Smith,	London.	R. O. Hammond,	Akron.
T. L. Carothers,	Wilmington.	Arthur Hughes,	Cleveland.

John A. Corwin, Urbana.
James Wood,
M. P. Bean, Bucyrus.
George W. Glick, Tremont.
J. W. Davis, Portsmouth.
D. R. Paige, Madison.
R. P. Ranny, Warren.
S. W. Gilson, Canfield.
W. H. Gill, New Lisbon.
Geo. W. McCook, Steubenville.

MISSISSIPPI.

Powhattan Ellis, Natchez.
E. Barksdale, Jackson.
O. R. Singleton, Canton.
James Drane, Bankston.
G. F. Neill, Carrollton.
Jacob Thompson, Oxford.
A. G. Brown, Newtown,
W. W. H. Linn, Houston.
W. L. Balfour, Vernon.
G. A. Sykes, Austin.
J. A. Orr, Houston,
Wm. A. Stone, Monticello.
Sampson Parks,
A. M. Clayton, Marshall Co.

TEXAS.

R. B. Hubbard, Tyler.
Matt Ward, Jefferson.
W. C. Pollock, Nacogdoches.
Wm. Fields, Galveston.
Wm. S. Oldham, Austin.
H. P. Bee, Laredo.
Jacob Wallder. San Antonio.
Guy M. Bryan, Brazona.

FLORIDA.

C. E. Dyke, Tallahassee.
J. R. Brooks, Pensacola.
D. L. Yulee, Homasassa.
John H. Parkhill, Tallahassee.
S. St. George Rodgers, Ocola.
J. T. Maybee, Tampa.

TENNESSEE.

Thomas C. Lyon, Knoxville.
E. L. Gardenhire, Sparta.
W. E. Travis, Manleyville.
W. M. Lowrey, Greeneville.
J. D. Goodpasture, Livingston.
H. M. Colquitt,
Lewis Shepherd, Chickamanga.
Austin Miller, Bolivar.
B. M. Moore, Lawrenceburg.
E. G. Eastman, Nashville.
Jacob Miller, Yellow Stone.
W. W. Ferguson, Carthage.
W. B. Bate, Gallatin.
T. W. Newham, Winchester.
J. H. Thomas, Columbia.
Thomas M. Jones, Pulaski.
S. P. Allison, Nashville,
M. A. Quarles, Clarksville.
T. J. Freeman, Trenton.
B. F. Lamb, Paris.
J. Knox Walker, Memphis.
L. C. Waggoner, Franklin.
John C. Ramsey, Knoxville.
A. J. Vaughen, Madisonville.

KENTUCKY.

J. P. Bates, Glasgow,
Jas. H. Garrard, Danville,
C. A. Wickliffe, Bardstown,
J. P. Martin, Prestonsburg,
Levy Tyler, Louisville,
B. L. Clarke, Franklin,
J. C. Breckinridge, Lexington,
Beriah Magoffin, Harrodsburg,
Wm. Preston, Louisville,
T. C. McCreery, Owensboro',
L. Desha,
Nath'l. S. Strange, Smith's Grove.
B. Spalding, Lebanon,
Luther Branner, Boonville,
German Baker, Shelbyville,
L. B. Dickerson, Georgetown,
E. Whitaker, Maysville,
J. C. Mason, Owingsville,
J. W. Stevenson, Covington,
G. B. Cook, Princeton,
John Chapeze, Greenville,
R. B. J. Twyman, Paducah,
S. Garfield, Paris,
W. E. Frazer, Columbia.

ILLINOIS.

J. A. Mattison,	Springfield,	John S. Hacker,	Cairo,
Wm. A. Richardson,	Quincy,	T. R. Young,	Marshall,
T. L. Harris,	Pettesburg,	W. B. Ficklin,	Charleston,
J. W. Singleton,		H. W. Dorsett,	Waukegan,
H. B. L. Steward,	Chicago,	Wm. R. Morrison,	Waterloo,
J. C. Walker,	Bloomington,	J. B. Danforth, jr.,	Rock Island,
L. F. Ross,	Lewiston,	B. F. Fredley,	
J. L. McCormier,	Jacksonville,	J. M. Campbell,	Macomb,
R. W. English,	Alton,	C. H. Lamphier,	Springfield,
S. Y. Baldwin,	Decatur,	T. S. Hick,	New Haven,
W. Cockle,	Peoria,	C. J. Houseman,	Rockford.
C. T. Gibbs,	Griggsville.		

WISCONSIN.

Nelson Dewey,	Cassville,	Sam'l. Crawford,	Mineral Point,
Paul Juneau,	Juneau,	Horace T. Saunders,	Racine,
James B. Cross,	Milwaukee,	M. J. Thomas,	Fond du Lac,
Satterlee Clarke,	Green Lake,	W. J. Gibson,	La Crosse,
H. J. Shultyes,	Schlersingerville,	Beriah Brown,	Madison.

IOWA.

T. S. Wilson,	Dubuque,	D. H. Solomons,	Glenwood,
W. F. Coolbaugh,	Burlington,	A. T. Walling,	Keokuk,
C. J. McFarland,		R. M. Evans,	Iowa City,
J. C. Ramsey,	Agency City.	Bernhart Henn,	Fairfield.

MICHIGAN.

W. F. Story,	Detroit,	Wm. Hale,	Detroit.
F. C. Whipple,	Howell,	J. S. Barry,	Constantine,
John P. Cook,	Hillsdale,	J. G. Thurber,	Monroe,
A. E. Campbell,	Battle,	Jacob Beeson,	Niles,
C. C. Chatfield,	Eaton Rapids,	Geo. W. Peck,	Lansing,
M. E. Crofoot,	Pontiac.	Ebenezer Warren,	Saut St. Marie.

ARKANSAS.

R. M. Gaines,	Gaines Landing	John Hutt,	Little Rock,
J. N. Embree,	Pine Bluff,	John S. Roame,	Pine Bluff,
C. A. Carroll,	Fort Smith,	T. B. Flournoy,	Laconice,
R. E. Jackson,	Valley Grove,	C. Caldwell,	Madison,
J. P. Johnson,			

CALIFORNIA.

P. C. Rust,	Marysville,	P. L. Solomon,	Sonora,
Sam'l. H. Dosh,	Shasta,	J. Lancaster Brent,	Los Angelos,
D. E. Buel,	Colema,	J. N. Dawley,	Nevada,
J. H. Hill,	Sonoma,	S. W. Inge,	San Francisco.

Mr. McLane said: "I have been requested by the Committee of Arrangements to place in the hands of the Temporary Chairman of this Convention a list of the delegates elected. I have also been requested to state that two papers have been presented to that Committee by two different delegations from the State of New York. The gentlemen composing the Committee of Arrangements desire to communicate to the Convention that they have regarded all papers which on their face bear *prima facie* evidence of the regular election of the person presenting them, as entitling those persons to seats in this hall. They considered it their duty to issue tickets to all delegates who presented themselves with such *prima facie* evidence of election by the people. By this rule, when the State of Missouri presented itself the Committee issued tickets to those who presented this *prima facie* evidence that they were delegates elect. Another set, also claiming seats, presented themselves from the State of Missouri; but as in the opinion of the committee they did not present the necessary *prima facie* evidence of election, tickets were refused to them. The same governed in the case of New York, as in that of others bearing prima facia evidence of election. The New York delegations could not but be regarded as in the same position as the delegations from other States which presented the names of more than two delegates for each electoral vote. The same thing was, therefore, required of New York as was required of the Mississippi delegation—that the delegation should select the proper number to take seats on this floor. Mississippi complied with that requirement.

There are now here the proper number of delegates to occupy the seats assigned to Mississippi, though there are in the city over sixty members elected delegates from that State.

A Member—Eighty.

It was the pleasure of the delegations from New York to intimate that such an arrangement would not be altogether satisfactory, though the committee does not understand that the arrangement was peremptorily declined. I am requested by the committee to state it would with great pleasure have given tickets to the whole of the one hundred and forty delegates presenting themselves from the State of New York, if the committee could in any way have selected seventy members to occupy the seats assigned to New York. I desire only to say in conclusion, from the Committee of Arrangements, that both sets of delegates from New York are without, and demand admission to this hall. (Applause).

Samuel Medary was then escorted to the chair, amid much applause; and addressed the Convention in the following terms:

I can only return thanks to the Convention for the temporary honor it has conferred upon me by selecting me to preside over its preliminary deliberations. All that I can offer in return for the honor of the position in which you have placed me, will be to the best of my ability, to preserve that order which is so necessary on such occasions. While I am not a new visitor to conventions of this kind, I am yet new to the position in which your kindness has placed me. I have been a delegate to National Conventions, when the Republic extended but little beyond the city in which we are now assembled, I was a delegate to the first Convention that nominated General Jackson for the Presidency. I was then, as now, one of the representatives of the Democratic party of the nation. It is now a grand party, grasping in its arms the shores of the two oceans of the world. In this Convention delegates are present from the Atlantic slope and the shores of the wide Pacific—thus manifesting in an unmistakable form, the progress of Democratic institutions and constitutional government. These are the institutions and this the government which it is our mission to defend and maintain. I repeat, that as long as we are governed by written constitutions and written laws, we should observe that deportment both personal and political, which will justify the expectation that we are capable of self-government. It is true that in governments like ours, we may expect temporary ebulitions of popular excitement. Like the great ocean, they cannot always be still. There cannot be a perpetual calm. We may sometimes expect the storms which purify the atmosphere.

Gentlemen, I will not detain you. I can only say that my highest purpose in accepting this unexpected promotion, is to perform the duties which it imposes on me, faithfully and impartially to all.

And now, while there is a brief silence and calm, allow me gentlemen, to introduce the Reverend Mr. Nicholson, who will address the Throne of Grace in behalf of the Convention.

The Reverend Mr. Nicholson, of the Episcopal Church, offered up the following

PRAYER;

O Eternal God, we, Thy helpless creatures, desire to make our supplications unto Thee. Thou art glorious in holiness, fearful in praises, doing wonders. While Thy tender mercies are over all Thy works, Thou art of purer eyes than to behold iniquity, and Thou puttest away the wicked like dross. The very heavens, we are assured, are not clean in Thy sight. Wherewith, then, shall we come before the Lord, and bow ourselves before the High God? For we have erred and strayed from Thy ways like lost sheep. We have followed too much the devices and desires of our own hearts. We have offended against Thy holy laws. We have left undone those things which we ought to have done, and we have done those things which we ought not to have done, and there is no health in us. But oh! what infinite love Thou hast manifested towards us! for Thou hast revealed to us the way of salvation through the death and sacrifice our of Lord Jesus Christ, Thine Eternal Son; in whom whosever believeth with the heart shall not die eternally. Oh, Lord God, for the sake of Thine only Son, have mercy upon us, miserable offenders. Spare Thou those who confess their faults. Restore Thou those who are penitent, according to Thy promises declared unto mankind in Christ Jesus our Lord. And grant, most merciful Father, that hereafter we may lead a holy, righteous and sober life, to the glory of thy holy name.

We approach Thee, O Lord God, at this time in an especial manner, as the universal Ruler of men and things. Thou conductest both in heaven and on earth after the counsel of Thine own will. Thou settest up one and Thou pullest down another. Thou art the Avenger of Thy truth on the nations that depart from Thy ways; while Thou art the Rewarder of all such as diligently seek Thee. O God, bless our beloved land! bless our beloved land! Let it not be said of us, Ah, sinful nation,a people laden with iniquity, a seed of evil-doers, children that are corrupters; they have forsaken the Lord, they have provoked the Holy One to anger, they are all gone away backward. But let integrity, jusice and the fear of God prevail in all our high places of authority. Rebuke, throughout the land the daring spirit of infidelity insubordination, and of an excessive worldliness. Let truth and righteousness flow down all our streets, and the songs of the righteous be heard from all the habitations of the land.

Most gracious God, we humbly beseech Thee, as for the people of these United States in general, so especially for those who, having come from all parts of our country, are here in convention assembled, that Thou wouldst be pleased to direct and prosper all their consultations to the advancement of Thy glory, the good of Thy Church, the safety, honor and welfare of Thy people; that all things may be so ordered and settled by their endeavors, on the best and surest foundations; that peace and happiness, truth and justice, religion and piety, may be established among us for all generations. To these representatives of the views and interests of so large a proportion of our fellow-citizens throughout the land, give a readiness of mind to follow the counsels of wisdom and experience; take from them all self-conceit, and shield their virtue from the assaults of the world, the flesh and the devil. These and all other necessaries for them, for us and Thy whole Church, we humbly beg in the name and mediation of Jesus Christ, our most blessed Lord and Savior.

Almighty God, unto whom all hearts are open, all desires known, and from whom no secrets are hid, cleanse the thoughts of our hearts by the inspiration of Thy Holy Spirit, that we may perfectly love Thee and worthily magnify Thy holy name, through Christ our Lord.

Direct us, O Lord, in all our doings, with Thy most gracious favor, and further us with Thy continual help, that in all our works begun, continued and ended in Thee, we may glorify Thy holy name, through Jesus Christ our Savior.

Our Father, who art in heaven, hallowed be Thy name, Thy kingdom come, Thy will be done on earth as it is in heaven. Give us this day our daily bread; forgive us our trespasses as we forgive those who trepass against us; lead us not into temptation, but deliver us from evil, for Thine is the kingdom and the power, and the glory for ever and ever.

The grace of our Lord Jesus Christ, the love of God, and the fellowship of the Holy Ghost be with us all evermore. Amen.

Mr. Brown of Mississippi, offered a resolution that seats be tendered to the delegates and alternates more than the several States are entitled to, and have allotted to them without the bar. He stated that there were vacant places within the Convention, and it was desirable that the delegates should have an opportunity of consulting their friends, and that all who came should participate in the great patriotic object for which they were assembled.

Mr. Thomas L. Harris, of Illinois, suggested that there would not be seats enough for them, and proposed to modify the motion so as to refer the selection of such as should have seats, to the Committee of Arrangements.

After some discussion, on motion, the resolution was for the present laid on the table.

Thomas L. Harris, of Illinois, then proposed that a Committee of Credentials, to be composed of a delegate from each State in which there is no disputed delegation, to be designated by the delegation, be appointed, whose duty it shall be to report to the Convention the delegates that present the proper credentials, and are entitled to take their seats in this body. Adopted.

The several delegations then gave in the following names for the Committee on Credentials:

Benjamin Wiggin, of *Maine*,
John H. George, of *New Hampshire*,
Bradley Barlow, of *Vermont*,
James S. Whitney, of *Massachusetts*,
G. S. Cannon, of *New Jersey*,
Edward A. Phelps, of *Connecticut*,
R. R. Heath, of *North Carolina*,
Wm. Acklin, of *Alabama*,
J. Lancaster Brent, of *California*,
G. F. Neal, of *Mississippi*,
G. M. Bryan, of *Texas*,
F. H. Hatch, of *Louisiana*,
James B. Stedman, *Ohio*,
John W. Stevenson, of *Kentucky*,
James H. Thomas, of *Tennessee*,
H. B. Wright, of *Pennsylvania*,
James A. Bayard, of *Delaware*,
Otho Scott, of *Maryland*,
Henry J. Burroughs of *Rhode Island*,
M. R. H. Garnett, of *Virginia*,
Samuel W. Telford, of *Indiana*,
Calvert Caldwell, of *Arkansas*,
Albert W. Lamb, of *Missouri*,
James Gardiner, of *Georgia*,
Franklin J. Moses, of *South Carolina*,
Thomas L. Harris, of *Illinois*,
William Hale, of *Michigan*,
David L. Yulee, of *Florida*,
Bernhardt Henn, of *Iowa*,
Paul Juneau, of *Wisconsin*,

Immediately after the election of President *pro tem*, a number of persons without tickets of admission, had thrust aside the door-keeper and rushed into the hall, claiming that they were delegates from Missouri. They had taken possession of the vacant seats assigned to New York.

When the members to compose the Committee on Credentials were announced, one of those claimants from Missouri arose and said that he had not heard Missouri called.

Mr. Richardson, of Illinois, said: Mr. President, I have no desire to interfere in the affairs of another State, but I must maintain, sir, that this Convention owes it to its dignity and self-respect that no person should be permitted to enter this hall, or take seats on this floor who has entered in defiance of the power of the door-keeper. I have no desire, sir, to enter into a discussion of the matter, but I declare it as my sentiment and opinion that this Convention owes it to itself, and to its dignity, to protect itself from insult.

The President—I would inform the gentlemen from Missouri, with all kindness, but with all determination, that according to the rules of the Convention, seats have been provided for the delegations from each State, and that only such as have tickets from the Committee of Arrangements are admitted to seats on this floor. The delegates having tickets have quietly and peaceably taken their seats. The temporary chairman cannot recognize any gentleman who is not entitled to a seat under these rules.

The claimant from Missouri—Mr. President—

[Cries of "Order! order!"]

The President—Let me say a few words, and if I am out of order some one will doubtless correct me. I hope the claimants that have gained admission to the Convention, from Missouri, without tickets, will listen to the voice of an individual who certainly has no wish to injure them or prejudge their case. These gentlemen must apply to the Committee on Arrangements. That is the only application they can make as the Convention is at present organized. I hope they will abide by this rule.

The Missouri claimant—The delegation from Missouri cheerfully bows to the decision of the Convention. And the whole contesting delegation arose and retired from the Convention.

Mr. Bocock, of Virginia, called attention to the terms of the resolution offered by Mr. Harris, whereupon the Missouri delegation to whom seats had been given, withdrew the name of Mr. Lamb, as a member of the Committee on Credentials, until the Convention should pass upon the contested seats from that State.

C. A. Wickliff, of Kentucky, renewed the resolution, similar to that offered by Mr. Brown, of Mississippi, to allow alternates seats in the body.

After some discussion said resolution was withdrawn.

Mr. Stedman, from Ohio, presented an invitation from the Young Men's Mercantile Library Association, tendering the use of their hall and library to the delegates of the convention.

Mr. McCook, of Ohio, offered the following resolution:

Resolved That a committee of one from each State be selected by the respective delegations, and whose duty it shall be to select permanent officers of the Convention. Adopted.

The respective delegations announced the members to act as said Committee as follows:

Maine, J. C. Talbot, jr.
New Hampshire, H. B. Rust.
Vermont, Robert Harvey,
Georgia, Alfred H. Holford.
Massachusetts, Isaac Davis.
Alabama, John Forsyth.
Rhode Island, A. S. Gallup,
Mississippi, E. Barksdale,
Connecticut, P. C. Childs,
New Jersey, Charles Fink,
Pennsylvania, John L. Dawson,
Delaware, Dr. C. Caldwell,
Louisiana, P. A. Moise,
Ohio, G. V. Dorsey,
Kentucky, B. L. Clarke,
Tennessee, J. K. Walker,
Maryland, James M. Buchanan,
Virginia, Paulus Powell,
North Carolina, James B. Gordon,
South Carolina, Charles McBeth,
Indiana, P. M. Kent,
Illinois, T. R. Young,
Missouri, John S. Phelps,
Arkansas, R. M. Gaines,
Michigan, J. G. Thurber,
Florida, Charles E. Dyke,
Texas, R. P. Hubbard,
Iowa, James C. Ramsey,
Wisconsin, Wm. J. Gibson,
California, P. C. Rust.

Mr. McCook, of Ohio, offered the following resolution:

Resolved, That the Committee on Organization be instructed to report rules for the Government of this Convention; and that in the meantime the rules of the last Convention be the rules of this body. Adopted.

Mr. Hallett, of Massachusetts, offered the following:

Resolved, That a Committee, of one delegate from each State, to be selected by the delegation thereof, be appointed to report resolutions, and that all resolutions in relation to the Platform of the Democratic Party, be referred to said Committee, on presentation, without debate.

Mr. Bayard, of Delaware, moved to lay the resolution on the table. Carried.

Mr. Butler of Mass., demanded that the vote to lay the resolution, offered by him, on the table, be taken by States, and the States voted as follows:

YEAS.—Connecticut, 6 ; New Jersey, 7 ; Pennsylvania, 27 ; Delaware, 3 ; Maryland, 8 ; South Carolina, 8 ; Mississippi, 7; Arkansas, 4; Michigan, 6 ; Texas, 4; Iowa, 4 ; Wisconsin, 5. Total, 84.

NAYS.—Maine, 8; New Hampshire, 5; Vermont, 5; Massachusetts, 13 ; Rhode Island, 3 ; Virginia, 15 ; North Carolina, 10 ; Georgia, 10 ; Alabama, 9 ; Louisiana, 6 ; Ohio, 23; Kentucky, 12 ; Tennessee, 12 ; Indiana, 13 ; Illinois, 11 ; Missouri, 9 ; Florida, 3; California, 4. Total, 177.

The chair decided the motion to lay on the table lost. On motion the resolution was then adopted, and the following delegates were selected for the Committee on Resolutions :

Maine, A. G. Chandler,
New Hampshire, B. F. Ayer,
Vermont, Charles G. Eastman,
Massachusetts, Benjamin F. Hallett,
Delaware, W. Salisbury,
Maryland, C. J. M. Gwinn,
Virginia, A. A. Chapman,
North Carolina, W. S. Ashe,
South Carolina, C. W. Dudley,
Georgia, A. R. Wright,
Alabama, John Cochran,
Mississippi, Jacob Thompson,
Louisiana, Pierre Soule,
Ohio, C. L. Vallandigham,
Kentucky, B. Magoffin,
Rhode Island, Wm. B. Lawrence,
Connecticut, A. B. Hyde,
New Jersey, E. R. V. Wright,
Pennsylvania, J. G. Jones,
Tennessee, W. A. Quarles,
Indiana, J. L. Robinson,
Illinois, O. B. Ficklin,
Missouri, Thomas B. Hudson,
Arkansas, John Hutt,
Michigan, W. F. Story,
Florida, S. St. George Rodgers,
Texas, H. P. Bee,
Iowa, Thomas S. Wilson,
Wisconsin, S. Clarke,
California, S. W. Inge.

Mr. Black, of Pennsylvania, moved to reserve the front seats in the galleries for the use of the ladies.

On motion of Mr. Pettit, the motion was laid on the table.

And then the Convention adjourned until ten o'clock, A. M., tomorrow.

SECOND DAY'S PROCEEDING.

CINCINNATI, June 3, 1856.

The Convention was called to order precisely at ten o'clock, by the *pro tem.* President, Samuel Medary. Excellent order prevailed at the opening of the session, and the temper of the members appeared calm and sedate.

The President—The first thing in order will be the report of the Committee on Permanent Organization. If ready to report, the Convention will now receive it.

J. L. Dawson, of Pennsylvania—The Committee appointed to recommend suitable persons for permanent officers of this Convention, respectfully report the following :

FOR PRESIDENT OF THE CONVENTION,

HON. JOHN E. WARD, of Georgia.

FOR VICE-PRESIDENTS,

Jonathan Smith, of *Maine*,
Charles L. Woodbury, *New Hampshire.*
Jefferson P. Kidder, *Vermont.*
Henry H. Childs, *Massachusetts.*
Peleg W. Gardner, *Rhode Island.*
James T. Pratt, *Connecticut.*
John S. Darsey, *New Jersey.*
Arnold Plummer, *Pennsylvania.*
Wm. H. Ross, *Delaware.*
C. Humphries, *Maryland.*
Robert A. Banks, *Virginia.*
Bedford Brown, *North Corolina.*
B. H. Brown, *South Carolina.*
Dr. John W. Lewis, *Georgia.*
David Hubbard, *Alabama.*
Wm. L. Balfour, *Mississippi.*
Alex. Mouton, *Louisiana.*
George W. Belden, *Ohio.*
Levi Tyler, *Kentucky.*
Thomas C. Lyon, *Tennessee.*
William Rockhill, *Indiana.*
Joel A. Mattison, *Illinois.*
John S. Roame, *Arkansas.*
M. E. Crofoot, *Michigan.*
J. T. Maybee, *Florida.*
Matthew Ward, *Texas.*
P. H. McBride, *Missouri.*
C. J. McFarland, *Iowa.*
Nelson Dewey, *Wisconsin.*
J. H. Hill, *California.*

FOR SECRETARIES.

Wm. K. Kimball, *Maine.*
H. Kimball, *New Hampshire.*
Isaac B. Bowditch, *Vermont.*
J. C. Abbott, *Massachusetts.*
Wm. J. Miller, *Rhode Island.*
Wm. D. Bishop, *Connecticut.*
Wm. Hanna, *New Jersey.*
John N. Hutchison, *Pennsylvania.*
Amos Layman, *Ohio.*
Samuel Williams, *Kentucky.*
Jacob Miller, *Tennessee.*
James Elder, *Indiana.*
C. H. Lamphier, *Illinois.*
Daniel D. Berry, *Missouri.*
R. E. Jackson, *Arkansas.*
W. P. Snow, *Maryland.*
Wm. F. Ritchie, *Virginia.*
H. G. Williams, *North Carolina.*
B. H. Wilson, *South Carolina.*
H. Buchanan, *Georgia.*
Julius Hessee, *Alabama.*
A. Derbis, *Louisiana.*
W. W. H. Dixon, *Mississippi.*
C. C. Chatfield, *Michigan.*
J. R. Brooks, *Florida.*
W. C. Pollock, *Texas.*
A. T. Walling, *Iowa.*
A. T. Gray, *Wisconsin.*
J. N. Dawley, *California.*

The Committee further recommends that the rules and regulations adopted by the National Democratic Convention in 1852, be adopted by this Convention for its government.

JOHN L. DAWSON, *Chairman.*

J. KNOX WALKER, *Secretary.*

On motion of Mr. Bordan, of Indiana, the report was unanimously adopted.

The Chair then appointed Mr. Dawson, of Pennsylvania, and Mr. Yulee, of Florida, to conduct the President elect to the chair.

Before taking his seat, the President addressed the Convention as follows:

Gentlemen of the Convention: The summons to preside over your deliberations is as unexpected as it is grateful to me. The distinguished gentleman who yesterday presided, the connecting link between the past and the present, carried us back to that period in our history when the Democratic party assembled to give into the hands of its favorite son, its standard to go forth to battle against a noble and gallant party. That party, with the issues which then divided us, have passed away. Many of its leaders, one by one, have stolen to their silent resting place, filled with years and honors, mourned by political friends and political foes.

> "How sleep the brave, who sink to rest
> With all their countries' honors blest,
> When Spring, with dewey fingers cold,
> Returns to deck their hallowed mold,
> She there shall find a sweeter sod
> Than Fancy's feet have ever trod.
> There Honor comes, a pilgrim gray,
> To deck the mold that wraps their clay;
> And Freedom for a while repair
> To dwell a weeping hermit there."

Many of that noble party who still survive are with us to-day. They are with us in our deliberations, and they are prepared to go forth with us to battle in behalf of the Constitution and the Union. Why, why, then, gentlemen of the Convention, with this party passed away, and these issues settled, why are we environed with difficulties, and surrounded with dangers before unknown? Our land is convulsed with factions. The one, recreant to the Constitution, would build a wall around our country, and give a home to the exile who seeks our shores, only on condition that he renounce all the privileges which are dear to freemen; a party which, in the pride of power, assumes to dictate to the consciences of men, and which would allow no man to be fit to serve his country who bowed not with them at the same altar.

The other faction—more dangerous only because it is more numerous—has liberty emblazoned on its banners and deadly treason festering in its heart. It is engaged in an unholy crusade against the Constitution, which has so long maintained its hold on the affections of the people, in the fond hope that they may involve in one common ruin all the glorious recollections of the past, and all our proud anticipations of the future. Insignificant and contemptible in itself, it is formidable only for its tendency to unite with all other factions in their opposition to a party which makes no concessions, courts no alliances, asks no affiliations.

From the shores of the Pacific, from the mountains of the North, from the plains of the South, from the valleys of the West, delegates have come up to-day to present a platform and to select a standard bearer in the great contest against these factions. Uniting as a band of brothers around the altar of our common country, let us lay upon that altar, as a willing sacrifice, our personal aspirations, our sectional prejudices, and above and beyond all, our private friendships.

With an abiding confidence that the kindness which has summoned me to this place, will sustain me in the performance of its duties, and will generously pardon my errors, I assume the trust committed to me.

The Vice Presidents and Secretaries were then invited to take seats on the stand.

Mr. J. A. Bayard, of Delaware, submitted the following:

REPORT OF THE COMMITTEE ON CREDENTIALS.

Your Committee proceeded yesterday, after the adjournment of the Convention, in the performance of the duty assigned to them, and find that all the States of the Union, except the State of New York, are represented in the Convention by delegates duly elected in the several States, by State or District organizations of the Democratic party, and they append to this report, as part thereof, full lists of the delegates so elected.

There were contesting claimants of the seats held by the delegation from Missouri, who claim to be admitted either in part or in whole as delegates from the same State.

The following gentlemen, claiming to be the regular delegation from the Democracy of Missouri, had, on *prima facia* evidence, been assigned seats in the Convention by the Committee of Arrangements viz:

Wm. A. Harris, E. D. Bevitt, James S. Green, A. W. Lamb, P. H. McBride, Wm. Shields, R. H. Stephens, S. R. Shrader, John S. McCracken, Thos. B. English, Joseph Coffman, Thomas B. Hudson, D. D. Berry, Fred. Kennett, Dr. W. Watson, James Craig, John S. Phelps, and were represented before the committee by Messrs. Green and Phelps.

The contesting parties who claimed seats were B. Gratz Brown, Barton Able, P. J. McSherry, Stephen Rice, S. J. Lowe, Jacob Hall, Logan Clarke, John M. Richardson, A. McCoy, John D. Stevenson, Thomas L. Price, John C. Walker, Patrick H. Davis, Madison Miller, P. Harney, J. S. Foy, George Smith and Samuel Simmons, and were represented before the committee by Messrs. Price and Brown.

The committee deem it unnecessary to recapitulate the arguments and statement of facts of either side, and confine themselves to the conclusion to which they have arrived.

After hearing fully the representatives of each contesting delegation, the following resolution was *unanimously* adopted:

Resolved, That the Democratic delegates from the State of Missouri, represented before the Committee by Messrs. Green and Phelps, are the duly elected delegates of the Democracy of Missouri, and are entitled to their seats in the National Convention, to the exclusion of the contesting claimants, represented by Messrs. Price and Brown.

The length of time occupied in hearing the parties to the contested seats in Missouri has prevented any hearing of the two sets of delegates from New York, who claim respectively to represent the Democracy of New York, but that hearing has been commenced this morning, and will be concluded as speedily as justice to the parties will permit, and be made the subject of a further report.

All of which is respectfully submitted.

June 3, 1856. J. A. BAYARD, *Chairman.*

On motion of Mr. C. T. McFarland of Iowa, the report of the Committee was, amid great applause, *unanimously* concurred in, and the delegates from Missouri holding seats were declared entitled to the same, to the exclusion of their contestants.

Mr. Bayard asked, in behalf of the Committee on Credentials, that they be allowed to sit during the session of the Convention, which was granted.

Mr. Green, of Missouri, moved that the name of A. W. Lamb be now added to those of the Committee on Credentials. Adopted.

A delegate from Alabama moved a resolution to admit the delegates from the District of Columbia into the Convention, to participate in the deliberations and action of the Convention.

Mr. Twyman, of Kentucky, was opposed to the delegates from the District of Columbia, who had no votes for the Presidency, participating in the action of the Convention. He had no objection to their admission, as lookers-on, in the hall. He moved to lay the resolution on the table.

Mr. Thomas L. Harris, of Illinois, endeavored to address the Convention on this question, but the Chair decided that he was not in order.

Mr. Harris said that he did not wish to discuss the question; he merely wished to read a telegraphic despatch which he held in his hand, announcing that the Democracy of the District of Columbia had carried the election in Washington by a handsome majority. (Great applause and hurrahs.)

The motion to lay upon the table the resolutions admitting the delegates from the District of Columbia, was then put and adopted by a large majority.

Mr. Brown, of Mississippi, offered the following resolution:

Resolved, That the seats in the galleries of this hall be declared vacant, and that the National Democratic Convention divide them, *pro rata*, among the States and Territories, and issue tickets accordingly and deliver them to the delegations from the several States; *Provided*, that no more persons be admitted than can be conveniently and safely accommodated.

Mr. Mickle of New Jersey offered the following amendment:

Resolved, That the galleries on the right of the President be appropriated exclusively for the use of the ladies, and gentlemen accompanying them.

Mr. Avery, of North Carolina, moved to lay the resolution and amendment on the table. The votes by States being called for, resulted as follows:

Yeas.—Massachusetts, 13; Rhode Island, 4; Connecticut, 6; New Jersey, 7; Pennsylvania, 21; Delaware, 3; North Carolina, 10; South Carolina, 8; Georgia, 6; Louisiana, 6; Ohio, 12; Tennessee, 12; Indiana, 13; Illinois, 11; Arkansas, 4; Michigan, 6; Texas, 4; Iowa, 4; Wisconsin, 5; California, 4. Total, 159.

Nays.—Maine, 8; New Hampshire, 5; Vermont, 5; Pennsylvania, 6; Maryland, 8; Virginia, 15; Georgia, 4; Alabama, 9; Mississippi, 7; Ohio, 12; Kentucky, 12; Missouri, 9; Florida, 3. Total, 103.

And the resolution and amendment were laid on the table.

Mr. Meade, of Virginia; moved that a ticket of admission be issued to Mr. D. B. Layne, a delegate to the Convention, whose ticket had been lost. Adopted.

Judge Mason, of Maryland, offered the following resolution:

Resolved. That the galleries be cleared, and that the Committee on Organization be instructed to issue three tickets to each delegate of the Convention, for distribution.

Mr. Mason modified the resolution by inserting one instead of three.

Mr. Hubbard, of Iowa, moved to lay the resolution on the table. A call by States being made, resulted as follows:

Yeas.—New Hampshire, 5; Massachusetts, 13, Rhode Island, 4; Connecticut, 6; New Jersey, 7; Pennsylvania, 27, Delaware, 3; North Carolina, 11; South Carolina, 8; Georgia, 6; Louisiana, 6; Illinois, 11; Missouri, 9; Michigan, 6; Texas, 4; Iowa, 4; Wisconsin, 2; California, 4. Total, 136.

NAYS.—Maine, 8; Vermont, 5; Maryland, 8; Virginia, 15, Georgia, 4; Alabama, 9; Mississippi, 7; Ohio, 24; Kentucky, 12; Tennessee, 12; Indiana, 13; Arkansas, 4; Florida, 3; Wisconsin, 2. Total, 126.

And the resolution was laid on the table.

Mr. Singleton, of Mississippi, offered the following resolution:

Resolved, That the galleries of this hall be declared free to all spectators.

Mr. Wilson, of Iowa, offered the following amendment: That the question of admission of persons to seats in the galleries, be referred to the Committee on Organization, with directions to adopt some equal and just plan for the admission of persons from the several States; and that said Committee report to the Convention as early as practicable.

On motion the resolution and amendment were laid on the table.

Mr. Moore, of Maine offered the following resolution:

Resolved, That the Committee of Arrangements be instructed to issue no more tickets of admission to this hall, without the special order of this Convention.

Mr. Pettit, of Indiana, moved that the galleries be cleared, which motion was lost.

Mr. Vallandigham, of Ohio, moved to refer the resolution of Mr. Moore, of Maine, and all other resolutions on the subject, to the Committee of Arrangements.

Mr. McMullen, of Virginia, moved to lay the resolution on the table. Carried.

Mr. Thompson, of Mississippi, offered the following resolution:

Resolved, That the Committee on Arrangements be instructed to admit Mr. J. W. McDonald to his seat as reporter from Mississippi. Adopted.

After several motions to amend, and considerable debate with reference to the galleries,

Mr. McLane, of Maryland, said—Gentlemen of the Convention, I desire to say, on behalf of the Committee of Arrangements, that in this hall it is absolutely impossible to seat a number of persons greater than the number that has been provided for. I will state further, that it was not the design of the Committee originally to apply the galleries to the use of the press. It was designed to seat the reporters for the various newspapers on the platform on each side of the President. That was the arrangement made for the press. If gentlemen will look at the platform and consider that, in the plan of organization now adopted, room must be made for three Vice-Presidents, and thirty-one Secretaries, they will see that the press had as large a space as possible devoted to their use. I would remark that over three hundred applications were made for tickets by gentlemen, under the style of reporters for the press. In very few cases was it believed that these were efficient reporters of the proceedings of this Convention. In very few cases did they profess to be so. They simply professed to be attached to corps of reporters. The Committee of Arrangements, of which I am not a member, but which I have been requested to represent on this floor, deemed it proper that these gentlemen should be admitted as reporters, and have seats in the galleries as such. The Committee did not think it ought to take the responsibility of saying to these gentlemen who professed to be reporters of the press, that they could not have seats when there was a place for them. But they understood very well that it was the right of the Convention when organized to appropriate the galleries to its own use. It is idle to suppose that the Convention has no such right. But it is the misfortune of this Convention that there is no hall in the city of Cincinnati suitable for its accommodation.

With these views I have suggested to the honorable member from Mississippi, and to the Convention, that this resolution be withdrawn, and that the Committee of Arrangements be instructed to issue new tickets for the galleries, under the direction of the President. The present gallery tickets will be cancelled after to-day. This suggestion was adopted, and the Committee so instructed.

D. C. Buel, of California, moved that the Convention appoint one Seargant-at-Arms, and two deputies, for the Convention.

Dr. Cottman, of Louisiana, suggested that the Committee of Arrangements appoint these officers.

Some one else proposed that the President make these appointments. Adopted.

Mr. McMullen, of Virginia, moved that the Convention, when it adjourns, adjourn to to-morrow at 10 o'clock, A. M. Adopted.

A letter of invitation to use their hall, was read from the Young Men's Democratic Association; also, a letter from the Horticultural Society of Ohio, inviting the members to attend their exhibition on Elm street, on Thursday next.

Judge Clitherall, of Alabama, moved a resolution that each delegate, when addressing the Convention, should proceed to the stand and address the body from that place. Rejected.

On motion of Hon. J. L. Dawson, of Penn., the Convention took a recess until four o'clock.

AFTERNOON SESSION.

At 4 o'clock the President called the Convention to order.

Hilliard Salisbury, of Delaware—Mr. President, I desire to state that, as I am informed, there are now in Cincinnati fifteen or twenty members of the Senate and House of Representatives of the United States, who have come here with the expectation of witnessing, or participating in this Convention, I offer this resolution:

Resolved, That the Democratic members of the Senate and House of Representatives of the United States, who may be in Cincinnati during the session of the Convention, are invited to take seats on the platform and floor of the Convention.

Mr. Chapman, of Alabama—I move to amend, by inviting the members of the different State Legislatures who may be now in the city.

After some debate, Mr. Avery of N. C., said—As this Convention has no time to send out and collect the balance of mankind, I move to lay the resolution and amendments on the table.

The motion to lay them on the table was carried.

Mr. Petit, of Indiana—I desire to inquire, for I have been informally informed that such is the case, whether the Committee on Resolutions is ready to report. If they are ready I desire to move that they be permitted to report.

Mr. Wilson—The Chairman of the Committee on Resolutions, is absent from his seat, and, therefore, cannot answer. I am informed, however, that the Committee will not be prepared to report till to-morrow morning at 10 o'clock.

Mr. P. C. Child of Connecticut, said—Mr. President, I wish members of this honorable body, assembled from all sections of the country, to set apart a short period for communing with each other, and telling each other their experience in the Democratic church. Certainly, the time not devoted to the business which has called us hither, could not be more usefully or profitably employed. I stand here, sir, in this National Convention, composed of delegates from the democracy of every State of our glorious confederacy, a representative of the State of Connecticut—a representative from the county of Wyndham, more commonly called "Wolf Den" county, the county which was the residence of that ever-to-be-remembered hero who fought shoulder to shoulder with the patriots of North Carolina, and the patriots of South Carolina, in that revolutionary struggle by which was achieved the freedom we now enjoy. It will be remembered here, on this occasion, when we have again assembled in a spirit of harmony and fraternity, in the defense of a common cause, and the pursuit of a common object, that South Carolina was one of the immortal Thirteen. It will also be remembered Connecticut, the State which I have the honor to represent was also one of the immortal Thirteen. My object in introducing this resolution is for the purpose of allowing time for the different delegations from the various parts of this great Union, to compare notes with each other. I hope, as there is nothing else to occupy the time and attention of this body, that an opportunity will be presented for the accomplishment of this purpose, and for allowing members to tell their experience in the different States of the confederacy."

Mr. Child's resolution was one of invitation to the delegates from the various States, to give their views on the present state of parties. The resolution was not acted on.

Mr Phelps, of Missouri, proposed a resolution that the Committee on resolutions be authorized to have their report printed so that it could be laid before all the members, and made the order of the Convention to-morrow.

Mr. Hallett, of Massachusetts, stated that there would be one more meeting of the Committee, that the resolutions were nearly all agreed upon, and that steps had already been taken to have the resolutions printed, and that they would be reported to-morrow at 10 o'clock.

On motion of Mr. Petit, of Indiana, the Convention then adjourned till to-morrow, Wednesday, June 4, at 10 o'clock, A. M.

THIRD DAY'S PROCEEDINGS.

MORNING SESSION, JUNE 4, 1856.

At ten o'clock the Convention was called to order by the President, General Ward.

After waiting some time, Mr. Stewart, of Maryland, called the attention of the Convention to the necessity of transacting business in its regular order, and as speedily as possible. He supposed the report of the Committee on Resolutions was first in order, and if so, he would now call for it.

Mr. Hallett, (who had ascended the platform) said—He would state that the Committee is prepared to make its report as soon as the Convention is ready to receive it.

[Voices.—Now! Now!]

The President.—The Convention must come to entire order before the Chairman will proceed to read the resolutions.

The Convention having come to order, Mr. Hallett said:

I have been instructed, as the Chairman of the Committee on resolutions, to report to this Convention the platform of resolutions which they have adopted. I am also instructed by the Committee to say that the portion of the resolutions which relates to Kanzas and Nebraska, and those propositions concerning the administration of the General Government, have been adopted by the Committee with entire unanimity, every member from every State having signified his perfect acquiescence in these resolutions.. There is another and very important class of resolutions, relating to the foreign policy of the country. While these resolutions have been recommended by the Committee as as a portion of the platform, it is proper to state that they were not adopted with entire unanimity. I am also instructed to report a resolution, as recommended by the Committee, concerning communication between the Atlantic and Pacific oceans.

With these explanations I shall proceed to read the resolutions:

REPORT OF THE COMMITTEE ON RESOLUTIONS.

The Committee on Resolutions, by their Chairman, Mr. Hallett, of Massachusetts, submit the following Report:

Resolved, That the American Democracy place their trust in the intelligence, the patriotism, and the discriminating justice of the American people.

Resolved, That we regard this as a distinctive feature of our political creed, which we are proud to maintain before the world, as the great moral element in a form of government springing from and upheld by the popular will; and we contrast it with the creed and practice of Federalism, under whatever name or form, which seeks to palsy the will of the constituent, and which conceives no imposture too monstrous foı the popular credulity.

Resolved, therefore, That, entertaining these views, the Democratic party of this Union, through their Delegates assembled in a general Convention, coming together in a spirit of concord, of devotion to the doctrines and faith of a free representative government, and appealing to their fellow-citizens for the rectitude of their intentions, renew and re-assert before the American people, the declarations of principles avowed by them when, on former occasions in general Convention, they have presented their candidates for the popular suffrages.

1. That the Federal Government is one of limited power, derived solely from the Constitution; and the grants of power made therein ought to be strictly construed by all the departments and agents of the government; and that it is inexpedient and dangerous to exercise doubtful constitutional powers.

2. That the Constitution does not confer upon the General Government the power to commence and carry on a general system of internal improvements.

3. That the Constitution does not confer authority upon the Federal Government, directly or indirectly, to assume the debts of the several States, contracted for local and internal improvements, or other State purposes; nor would such assumption be just or expedient.

4. That justice and sound policy forbid the Federal Government to foster one branch of industry to the detriment of any other, or to cherish the interests of one portion to the injury of another portion of our common country; that every citizen and every section of the country has a right to demand and insist upon an equality of rights and privileges, and to complete an ample protection of persons and property from domestic violence or foreign aggression.

5. That it is the duty of every branch of the Government to enforce and practice the most rigid economy in conducting our public affairs, and that no more revenue ought to be raised than is required to defray the necessary expenses of the Government, and for the gradual, but certain extinction of the public debt.

6. That the proceeds of the public lands ought to be sacredly applied to the national objects specified in the Constitution; and that we are opposed to any law for the distribution of such proceeds among the States, as alike inexpedient in policy and repugnant to the Constitution.

7. That Congress has no power to charter a national bank; that we believe such an institution one of deadly hostility to the best interests of the country, dangerous to our republican institutions and the liberties of the people, and calculated to place the business of the country within the control of a concentrated money power, and above the laws and the will of the people; and that the results of Democratic legislation in this and all other financial measures upon which issues have been made between the two political parties of the country, have demonstrated to candid and practical men of all parties, their soundness, safety, and utility, in all business pursuits.

8. That the separation of the moneys of the Government from banking institutions is indispensable for the safety of the funds of the Government, and the rights of the people.

9. That we are decidedly opposed to taking from the President the qualified veto power, by which he is enabled, under restrictions and responsibilities amply sufficient to guard the public interests, to suspend the passage of a bill whose merits cannot secure the approval of two-thirds of the Senate and House of Representatives, until the judgment of the people can be obtained thereon, and which has saved the American people from the corrupt and tyrannical domination of the Bank of the United States, and from a corrupting system of general internal improvements.

10. That the liberal principles embodied by Jefferson in the Declaration of Independence, and sanctioned in the Constitution, which makes ours the land of liberty, and the asylum of the oppressed of every nation, have ever been cardinal principles in the Democratic faith, and every attempt to abridge the

privilege of becoming citizens and the owners of soil among us, ought to be resisted with the same spirit which swept the alien and sedition laws from our statute books.

And, WHEREAS, Since the foregoing declaration was uniformly adopted by our predecessors in National Conventions, an adverse political and religious test has been secretly organized by a party claiming to be exclusively American, it is proper that the American Democracy should clearly define its relation thereto, and declare its determined opposition to all secret political societies, by whatever name they may be called.

Resolved, That the foundation of this union of States having been laid in, and its prosperity, expansion, and pre-eminent example in free government, built upon entire freedom in matters of religious concernment, and no respect of person in regard to rank or place of birth; no party can justly be deemed national, constitutional, or in accordance with American principles, which bases its exclusive organization upon religious opinions and accidental birth-place. And hence a political crusade in the nineteenth century, and in the United States of America, against Catholic and foreign-born, is neither justified by the past history or the future prospects of the country, nor in unison with the spirit of toleration and enlarged freedom which peculiarly distinguishes the American system of popular government.

Resolved, That we reiterate with renewed energy of purpose, the well considered declarations of former Conventions upon the sectional issue of Domestic Slavery, and concerning the reserved rights of the States.

1. That Congress has no power under the Constitution, to interfere with or control the domestic institutions of the several States, and that such States are the sole and proper judges of everything appertaining to their own affairs, not prohibited by the Constitution; that all efforts of the abolitionists, or others, made to induce Congress to interfere with questions of slavery, or to take incipient steps in relation thereto, are calculated to lead to the most alarming and dangerous consequences; and that all such efforts have an inevitable tendency to diminish the happiness of the people, and endanger the stability and permanency of the Union, and ought not to be countenanced by any friend of our political institutions.

2. That the foregoing proposition covers, and was intended to embrace, the whole subject of slavery agitation in Congress; and therefore, the Democratic party of the Union, standing on this national platform, will abide by and adhere to a faithful execution of the acts known as the Compromise measures, settled by the Congress of 1850; "the act for reclaiming fugitives from service or labor," included; which act being designed to carry out an express provision of the Constitution, cannot, with fidelity thereto, be repealed, or so changed as to destroy or impair its efficiency.

3. That the Democratic party will resist all attempts at renewing, in Congress or out of it, the agitation of the slavery question under whatever shape or color the attempt may be made.

4. That the Democratic party will faithfully abide by and uphold, the principles laid down in the Kentucky and Virginia resolutions of 1798, and in the report of Mr. Madison to the Virginia Legislature, in 1799: that it adopts those principles as constituting one of the main foundations of its political creed, and is resolved to carry them out in their obvious meaning and import.

And that we may more distinctly meet the issue on which a sectional party, subsisting exclusively on slavery agitation, now relies to test the fidelity of the people, north and south, to the Constitution and the Union—

1. *Resolved*, That claiming fellowship with, and desiring the co-operation of all who regard the preservation of the Union under the Constitution as the

paramount issue—and repudiating all sectional parties and platforms concerning domestic slavery, which seek to embroil the States and incite to treason and armed resistance to law in the Territories; and whose avowed purposes, if consummated, must end in civil war and disunion. The American Democracy recognize and adopt the principles contained in the organic laws establishing the Territories of Kansas and Nebraska as embodying the only sound and safe solution of the "slavery question" upon which the great national idea of the people of this whole country can repose in its determined conservatism of the Union--NON-INTERFERENCE BY CONGRESS WITH SLAVERY IN STATE AND TERRITORY, OR IN THE DISTRICT OF COLUMBIA.

2. That this was the basis of the Compromises of 1850—confirmed by both the Democratic and Whig parties in national Conventions—ratified by the people in the election of 1852—and rightly applied to the organization of Territories in 1854.

3. That by the uniform application of this Democratic principle to the organization of territories, and to the admission of new States, with or without domestic slavery, as they may elect—the equal rights of all the States will be preserved intact—the original compacts of the Constitution maintained inviolate—and the perpetuity and expansion of this Union insured to its utmost capacity of embracing, in peace and harmony, every future American State that may be constituted or annexed, with a republican form of government.

Resolved, That we recognize the right of the people of all the Territories, including Kansas and Nebraska, acting through the legally and fairly expressed will of a majority of actual residents, and whenever the number of their inhabitants justifies it; to form a Constitution, with or without domestic slavery, and be admitted into the Union upon terms of perfect equality with the other States.

Resolved, finally, That in the view of the condition of popular institutions in the Old World (and the dangerous tendencies of sectional agitation, combined with the attempt to enforce civil and religious disabilities against the rights of acquiring and enjoying citizenship, in our own land)—a high and sacred duty is devolved with increased responsibility upon the Democratic party of this country, as the party of the Union, to uphold and maintain the rights of every State, and thereby the Union of the States; and to sustain and advance among us constitutional liberty, by continuing to resist all monopolies and exclusive legislation for the benefit of the few, at the expense of the many, and by a vigilant and constant adherence to those principles and compromises of the Constitution, which are broad enough and strong enough to embrace and uphold the Union as it was, the Union as it is, and the Union as it shall be, in the full expansion of the energies and capacity of this great and progressive people.

1. *Resolved*, That there are questions connected with the foreign policy of this country, which are inferior to no domestic question whatever. The time has come for the people of the United States to declare themselves in favor of free seas and progressive free trade throughout the world, and, by solemn manifestations, to place their moral influence at the side of their successful example.

2. *Resolved*, That our geographical and political position with reference to the other States of this continent, no less than the interest of our commerce and the development of our growing power, requires that we should hold as sacred the principles involved in the Monroe Doctrine: their bearing and import admit of no misconstruction; they should be applied with unbending rigidity.

3. *Resolved*, That the great highway which nature, as well as the assent of the States most immediately interested in its maintainance, has marked out

for a free communication between the Atlantic and the Pacific oceans, constitutes one of the most important achievements realized by the spirit of modern times and the unconquerable energy of our people. That result should be secured by a timely and efficient exertion of the control which we have the right to claim over it, and no power on earth should be suffered to impede or clog its progress by any interference with the relations it may suit our policy to establish between our government and the Governments of the States within whose dominions it lies. We can, under no circumstance, surrender our preponderance in the adjustment of all questions arising out of it.

4. *Resolved*, That, in view of so commanding an interest, the people of the United States can not but sympathize with the efforts which are being made by the people of Central America to regenerate that portion of the continent which covers the passage across the Interoceanic Isthmus.

5. *Resolved*, That the Democratic party will expect of the next Administration that every proper effort be made to insure our ascendancy in the Gulf of Mexico, and to maintain a permanent protection to the great outlets through which are emptied into its waters the products raised out of the soil, and the commodities created by the industry of the people of our Western valleys, and of the Union at large.

B. F. HALLETT, *Chairman.*

The following is the resolution with respect to overland communication with the Pacific:

Resolved, That the Democratic party recognizes the great importance, in a political and commercial point of view, of a safe and speedy communication, by military and postal roads, through our own territory, between the Atlantic and Pacific coasts of this Union, and that it is the duty of the Federal Government to exercise promptly all its constitutional power for the attainment of that object.

The reading of the resolutions on Know-Nothingism and the Kansas-Nebraska question was followed by long continued and enthusiastic applause ; in which every delegation joined in the most earnest manner.

Mr. Hallett—I am instructed by the Committee to lay these resolutions before the Convention.

W. F. Packer, of Pennsylvania—I move that this report and resolutions be unanimously adopted, without the crossing of a *t* or the dotting of an *i*.
[Great applause.]

Mr. Conway, of Virginia—I move that there be a division of the question, and that the Convention first act upon the resolutions relating to the domestic policy of the Nation. There were delegates here, especially from the State which he in part represented, who were not prepared to adopt all these resolutions; and it would be necessary to divide the body on the resolutions.

B. F. Butler, of Massachusetts—As this report is the unanimous result of the labors of a committee composed of delegates from all the States, and I believe embodies principles which have obtained the acquiescence of all the Democrats in every part of our Union, I shall move the previous question.

M. R. H. Garnett, of Virginia—I rise to a point of order. A division of the question has been asked by my colleague, that takes precedence.

Mr. Garnett: Before such resolutions are forced upon us—before they are forced upon the Democracy of the Old Dominion, which has steadily opposed the doctrines embraced in one of them—that Old Dominion which has never faltered in defense of the Democratic faith —before you force such resolutions upon us, I ask for a division of the question.

Several members here arose and called to order, and insisted that there could be no debate pending a call for the previous question.

Mr. Hibbard, of New Hampshire, said that the call for a division of the main question, under the rules of the House of Representatives, was in order after the previous question was demanded and sustained, and that any one member was entitled to have the main question divided.

The President said that the previous question having been demanded, the question first in order was, shall the call for the previous qeestion be sustained? Then, if it was sustained, the question should be, shall the main question be now put? And if that was decided in the affirmative, the gentleman from Virginia was entitled to have the main question divided.

Mr. Phelps, of Missouri—Mr. President, I desire to suggest that the right of a delegation from a State, which casts thirty-five votes upon this floor, to be admitted, has not been settled, and I would ask whether it is not premature to adopt the resolutions just read before New York is heard. I think it is, and I appeal to the gentleman from Massachusetts to withdraw the call for the previous question, that I may move to postpone the further consideration of this platform until the New York contested case is decided.

Mr. Butler refused to withdraw the call for the previous question.

Mr. Avery, of North Carolina, moved that the Convention should first consider the resolutions reported, and acted upon by the committee, disregarding the extra resolution relative to a public road.

The Chair, however, would not entertain the motion, but the previous question being seconded, was put to the body, and the body sustained it by a large majority. The order was that the Convention would now vote upon the resolution relating to the domestic policy of the country.

The call was for a vote by States.

The States were severally called, and each delegation unanimously voted aye in favor of the resolutions. The Virginia and Mississippi delegations alone retired to consult, but returned with their unanimous approval of the resolutions.

When the North Carolina vote was announced, Mr. Avery, who was the organ of the delegation, remarked, "North Carolina gives ten votes for the resolutions, and will give ten thousand in November." [Applause.]

When Alabama was called, Gov. Chapman cried out, "Alabama votes nine votes for the resolutions, and in November, as usual, she will roll up her fifteen thousand Democratic majority." [Cheers.]

When Kentucky was called, the Hon. C. A. Wickliffe announced that Kentucky gave her twelve votes for the resolutions, and all she could promise would be a majority in November next. [Loud applause.]

The President then announced that the several delegations had voted unanimously, to-wit: two hundred and sixty-one votes in favor of the resolutions reported by the committee relating to the domestic policy of the country.

Mr. Wickliffe—Before we are called on to vote on the remaining portions of the resolutions, I think we should have time from now till three o'clock, in order that in a pure air and a clear atmosphere we may look at them with some degree of deliberation, and appreciate the importance of our action in either accepting or rejecting them. I ask for my State a recess until 4 o'clock. Rejected.

Mr. Phelps, of Mo., moved to adjourn to 4 o'clock. Lost, ayes 78, nays 193.

Mr. Meade, of Virginia, moved a recess for one hour. If the vote was taken on the other resolutions without a recess, he should ask leave for the Virginia delegation to retire, to consult for at least that time. Lost.

Mr. Ingersoll, of Connecticut, demanded that under the division of the question, the remaining resolutions should be voted on separately.

The President said that a vote upon each would be so taken.

Mr. Meade, of Virginia, asked leave for the delegation to retire for the purpose of consultation as to their action upon the remaining resolutions.

Leave was given by the Convention; and the same was requested for the like purpose by the delegations of Maryland and Missouri, which was acceded to.

On motion of Mr. Barksdale, of Mississippi, the Convention took a recess until two o'clock.

AFTERNOON SESSION—JUNE 4TH.

The Convention met at two o'clock, and was called to order by the President.

In conformity with the resolution empowering the President to appoint a Sergeant-at-arms and two assistants, the following appointments were made: principal Sergeant-at-arms, George W. Palmer; assistants, John R. Johnson and Stephen S. Ayres.

Mr. Hibbard, of New Hampshire, moved to reconsider the vote on the first part of the report of the Committee on Resolutions, and that said motion be laid on the table. The motion prevailed unanimously.

The Chair then proceeded to take the vote on the questions relative to foreign policy. The first resolution was as follows:

1. *Resolved*, That there are questions connected with the foreign policy of this country which are inferior to no domestic questions whatever. The time has come for the people of the United States to declare themselves in favor of free seas and progressive free trade throughout the world, and, by solemn manifestations, to place their moral influence at the side of their successful example.

The vote by States being called, the following States voted unanimously in the affirmative:

Maine 8, New Hampshire 5. Vermont 5, Massachusetts 13, New Jersey 7, Pennsylvania 27, Virginia 15, North Carolina 10, South Carolina 8, Louisiana 6, Ohio 23, Indiana 13, Illinois 11, Missouri 9, Arkansas 4, Michigan 6, Florida 3, Texas 4, Iowa 4, Wisconsin 5, Kentucky 12.

The following States divided: Connecticut—1 aye, 5 nays; Tennessee—11 ayes, 1 nay. The following States voted in the negative: Rhode Island 4, Delaware 3, Maryland 6, Georgia 10.

The Chair proclaimed the resolution adopted, by 230 ayes, 29 nays.

The second resolution, which is as follows, was then voted on by States:

2. *Resolved*, That our geographical and political position with reference to other States of this continent, no less than the interest of our commerce, and the development of our growing power, requires that we should hold as sacred the principles involved in the Monroe doctrine; their bearing and import admit of no misconstruction; they should be applied with unbending rigidity.

The following was the vote:

AYES—Maine, New Hampshire, Vermont, Massachusetts 12, Connecticut, New Jersey, Pennsylvania, Virginia, North Carolina, South Carolina, Georgia 6, Alabama, Mississippi, Louisiana, Ohio, Kentucky, Tennessee 11, Indiana, Illinois, Missouri, Arkansas, Michigan, Florida, Texas, Iowa, Wisconsin, California—239.

NAYS—Massachusetts 1, Rhode Island 4, Delaware, Maryland, Georgia 4, Tennessee 1—21.

C. A. Wickliffe, of the Kentucky delegation, asked leave to change their vote on first resolution from the negative to the affirmative. Granted. [Applause.]

The Mississippi delegation asked leave to change their vote to the affirmative, which was granted. [Applause.]

The vote was then taken on the following resolution:

3. *Resolved*, That the great highway which nature, as well as the assent of the States most immediately interested in its maintenance, has marked out for free communication between the Atlantic and the Pacific Oceans, constitutes one of the most important achievments realized by the spirit of modern times and the unconquerable energy of our people. That result should be secured by a timely and efficient exertion of the control which we have the right to claim over it, and no power on earth should be suffered to impede or clog its progress by any interference with the relations it may suit our policy to establish between our government and the governments of the States within whose dominions it lies. We can, under no circumstances surrender our preponderance in the adjustment of all questions arising out of it.

Ayes—Maine 7, New Hampshire, Vermont, Massachusetts. Connecticut 4, New Jersey, 7, Pennsylvania 27, North Carolina 10, Georgia 10, Alabama 9, Mississippi 7, Tennessee 7, Indiana 13, Illinois 11, Missouri 9, Arkansas 4, Michigan 6, Florida 3, Texas 4, Iowa 4, Wisconsin 5, California 4, Louisiana 6, Ohio 23—180.

Nays—Maine 1, Rhode Island 4, Connecticut 2, Delaware 3, Maryland 6, Virginia 15, South Carolina 8, Kentucky 12, Tennessee 5—56.

The vote by States was then taken on the following resolution:

Resolved, That in view of so commanding an interest, the people of the United States cannot but sympathize with the efforts which are being made by the people of Central America to regenerate that portion of the continent which covers the passage across the Interoceanic Isthmus.

Ayes—Maine 8, New Hampshire 5, Vermont 5, Massachusetts 13, Connecticut 4, New Jersey 7, Pennsylvania 27, Virginia 15, North Carolina 9, Georgia 10, Alabama 9, Mississippi 7, Louisiana 6, Ohio 23, Tennessee 10, Indiana 13, Illinois 11, Missouri 9, Arkansas 4, Michigan 6, Florida 3, Texas 4, Iowa 4, Wisconsin 5, California 4—221.

Nays—Rhode Island 4, Connecticut 2, Delaware 3, Maryland 6, North Carolina 1, South Carolina 8, Kentucky 12, Tennessee 2—38.

The vote was then taken by States, on the following resolution:

Resolved, That the Democratic party will expect of the next administration that every proper effort will be made to insure our ascendency in the Gulf of Mexico, and to maintain a permanent protection to the great outlets through which are emptied into its waters the products raised out of the soil, and the commodities created by the industry of the people of our Western valleys and the Union at large.

Ayes—Maine 7, New Hampshire 5, Vermont 5, Massachusetts 11, Connecticut 4, New Jersey 7, Pennsylvania 27, Virginia 15, North Carolina 9, Georgia 10, Alabama 9, Mississippi 7, Louisiana 6, Ohio 23, Kentucky 12, Tennesssee 9, Indiana 13, Illinois 11, Missouri 9, Arkansas 4, Michigan 6, Florida 3, Texas 4, Iowa 4, Wisconsin 5, California 4—229.

Nays—Maine 1, Massachusetts 2, Rhode Island 4, Connecticut 2, Delaware 4, Maryland 8, North Carolina 1, South Carolina 8, Tennessee 3—33.

The following resolution then coming up, H. Salisbury, of Delaware, moved to lay it on the table:

Resolved, That the Democratic party recognizes the great importance, in a political and commercial point of view, of a safe and speedy communication by military and postal roads, through our own territory, between the Atlantic and Pacific coasts of this Union, and that it is the duty of the Federal Government to exercise promptly all its constitutional powers for the attainment of hat object.

On this motion the vote was as follows :

Ayes---Maine 1; New Hampshire 4, Massachusetts 17, Rhode Island 4, Connecticut 6, New Jersey 7, Pennsylvania 27, Delaware 3, Virginia 15, North Carolina 10, South Carolina 8, Georgia 6, Alabama (under protest of Judge Clitherall) 9, Mississippi 7, Ohio 16, Kentucky 8, Tennessee 3, Florida 3—154 yeas.

Nays—Maine 7, New Hampshire 1, Vermont 5, Massachusetts 12, Maryland 6, Georgia 4, Louisiana 6, Ohio 6, Kentucky 4, Tennessee 9, Indiana 13, Illinois 11, Missouri 9, Arkansas 4, Michigan 6, Texas 4, Iowa 4, Wisconsin 5, California 4—120 nays.

So the resolution was laid on the table.

Mr. Colquitt, of Georgia, moved to reconsider the vote on the three last resolutions on the foreign policy of the Government, and G. W. Peck, of Michigan, moved to lay on the table the motion to reconsider.

On this motion the vote was as follows :

Yeas.—Maine, 8 ; New Hampshire, 5 ; Vermont, 5 ; Massachusetts, 5 ; New Jersey, 7 ; Pennsylvania, 27 ; Maryland, 1 ; North Carolina, 10 ; Mississippi, 7 ; Louisiana, 6 ; Ohio, 23 ; Tennessee, 10 ; Indiana, 13 ; Illinois, 11 ; Missouri, 9 ; Arkansas, 4 ; Michigan, 6 ; Florida, 3 ; Texas, 4 ; Iowa, 4 ; Wisconsin, 5 ; California, 4 —171.

Nays.—Massachusetts, 4 ; Rhode Island, 4 ; Connecticut, 6 ; Delaware, 3 ; Maryland, 7 ; Virginia, 15 ; South Carolina, 8 ; Georgia, 9 ; Alabama, 9 ; Kentucky, 12 ; Tennessee, 2—79.

So the motion to reconsider was laid on the table.

Mr. Meade, of Virginia, offered the following resolution :

Resolved, That the resolutions in regard to the foreign policy of this Government are the expressions of opinion of this Convention, and are not to be exacted as articles of party faith.

G. W. Peck, of Michigan, objected that this resolution could not be entertained, but must, under the rules, go to the Committee on Resolutions.

Mr. Meade—after in vain asking to be heard on the resolution, the Chair deciding that the question could not be debated, but must go to the committee—moved that the rules be suspended.

A vote by States was called for and resulted as follows :

Ayes.—Delaware, 3 ; Maryland, 7 ; Virginia, 15 ; South Carolina, 8 ; Kentucky, 12 ; Tennessee, 9 ; Missouri, 9 ; Arkansas, 4 ; Florida, 3 ; Texas, 4—74.

Nays.—Maine, 8 ; New Hampshire, 5 ; Vermont, 5 ; Massachusetts, 13 ; Rhode Island, 4 ; Connecticut, 6 ; New Jersey, 7 ; Pennsylvania, 27 ; Maryland, 1 ; North Carolina, 10 ; Georgia, 10 ;

Alabama, 9; Mississippi, 7; Louisiana, 6; Ohio, 23; Tennessee, 3; Indiana, 13; Illinois, 11; Michigan, 6; Iowa, 4; Wisconsin, 5; California, 4—171.

So the motion to suspend was lost, and the resolution was referred to the Committee on Resolutions.

Mr. Lowe, of Maryland, sent to the Chair the following resolution, adopted by the Maryland Delegation, which he had been instructed to present, as explanatory of the vote of that State, and to ask that the same be spread on the records of the Convention. No objection being made, it was so ordered:

Resolved, That without expressing any opinion in regard to the principles involved in the last five resolutions of the proposed platform, we deem it inexpedient to adopt said resolutions as part of said platform, and that the Chairman of this Delegation be directed to cast its vote in the negative upon said resolution, and that he is further instructed at the proper time to request the reading of this resolution to the Convention, as the ground upon which the action of this Delegation is based.

Judge Borden, of Indiana, moved the following resolution:

Resolved, That a committee of one from each State, to be selected by the Delegates thereof, be appointed to report the names of persons to constitute the Democratic National Committee, and the mode of constituting and calling the next Democratic Convention. Adopted.

The following names were proposed under this resolution by the various delegations:

Maine, Dudley F. Leavitt.
New Hampshire, J. H. Smith.
Vermont, John Cain.
Massachusetts, Whiting Griswold.
Rhode Island, William J. Miller.
Connecticut, J. P. C. Mather.
New York,
New Jersey, John W. Mickle.
Pennsylvania, H. D. Foster.
Delaware, Henry Ridgely.
Maryland, E. Hamilton.
Virginia, Archibald Graham.
North Carolina, Burton Craige.
South Carolina, B. H. Wilson.
Georgia, John H. W. Underwood.
Alabama, James R. Powell.
Mississippi, O. R. Singleton.
Louisiana, W. W. Pugh.
Ohio, Wm. Lawrence.
Kentucky, T. C. McCreery.
Tennessee, T. M. Jones.
Indiana, G. T. Cookerly.
Illinois, W. Cockle.
Missouri, William Watson.
Arkansas, Jordan N. Embree.
Michigan, A. E. Campbell.
Florida, C. E. Dyke.
Texas, William Fields.
Iowa, D. H. Solomons.
Wisconsin, M. J. Thomas.
California, D. E. Buel.

A delegate, calling attention to the quantity of work already done, and that the Committee on Credentials not being ready to report on the New York controversy, moved that the Convention adjourn.

Mr. Hibbard, of Texas, was enforcing the necessity of having a full vote on the great question of selecting the Presidency, when he was interrupted by Mr. Petit, of Indiana, who said:

Mr. President—If the New Yorkers are not ready to come into the Convention and participate with us in its labors, there are other States that are ready, and I move that we proceed to vote for the candidate for the Presidency and Vice Presidency.

Mr. Hibbard resumed—The motion is to proceed to vote for a candidate for President and Vice President. In the Baltimore Convention of 1852, when there were contested votes from New York and Georgia, the Convention decided that it would not proceed to the nomination of a candidate for the Presidency, until the contested elections were determined. New York sends two sets of delegates, whose claims are under consideration by the Committee on Credentials. Whatever may be the decision, at least one of the delegations will be entitled to a seat, and perhaps both. New York has a right to be heard on the momentous question of the nomination of a candidate for the Presidency. We thought that there was sufficient soundness in the Democracy of New York to recognize the platform adopted by the Convention without the formality of their voting. But on the nomination of the candidates we have no right to deny them a hearing. I trust that the gentleman will withdraw his motion.

Mr. Petit withdrew his motion.

H. Salisbury, of Delaware—Sir, we have done more to-day than has generally been done by Democratic Conventions. We have gone, in the adoption of our resolutions, beyond the precedents of previous Conventions. It would be wise for us not to proceed further and too rapidly, but to act calmly and discreetly; and he was therefore in favor of adjourning to hear the Committee on Credentials.

H. B. Wright, of Pennsylvania, said he was one of the Committee on Credentials, and the committee had been much engaged in hearing the parties in the contested case of New York, but that it would be prepared to make a report on to-morrow at two o'clock.

Mr. Wilson, of Iowa, was in favor of adjourning, but he added that he was against waiting any longer on those gentlemen who could not settle their quarrels at home. He would not wait a day longer for them than to-morrow. If they were not prepared to come into the Convention and arrange their difficulties after a reasonable time he hoped that the other States would proceed to perform their duty, and discharge the trust for which they were sent here.

The vote to adjourn to to-morrow 10 o'clock, A. M.. was then taken and carried.

FOURTH DAY'S PROCEEDINGS.

MORNING SESSION, June 5th, 1856.

At 10 o'clock the President called the Convention to order.

Mr. J. W. Stevenson, of Kentucky, after some preliminary remarks, offered, on the part of a majority of the Committee on Credentials, the following resolutions:

Resolved, That it is the duty of the entire Democracy of New York to unite; and, as a beginning of that union, that the two delegations from that State be now consolidated.

Resolved, That that portion of the Democracy of New York represented by the delegation, of which the Hon. Horatio Seymour is chairman, are entitled, on the score of numbers, to forty-four delegates, and that portion of the Democracy represented by the delegations, of which the Hon. Samuel Beardsley is Chairman, is entitled on the score of numbers to twenty-six delegates in the Convention, and that said delegation be admitted in proportion aforesaid to seats in the Convention, the persons so to be admitted to be designated by the respective delegations, and that, in counting the vote of the State of New York in the Convention, the minority shall not be subject to the majority without their consent.

Resolved, That the delegation from New York, when admitted, be permitted to record their votes upon the resolutions adopted yesterday by the Convention.

Mr. James A. Bayard, on behalf of the minority of the Committee on Credentials, offered the following resolution as a substitute for those presented by Mr. Stevenson:

Resolved, That the two delegations from New York be authorized to select each thirty-five delegates, and that the seventy delegates thus selected be admitted as the delegation of the two sections of the New York Democracy to this Convention, and that they be allowed one hour to report their selections. The two delegations to vote separately, each to be entitled to seventeen votes, the remaining vote of this State to be cast alternately by the two delegations, the Softs casting it the first time.

Mr. Butler, of Massachusetts, moved the adoption of the majority resolutions and called for the previous question.

At the request of Mr. Richardson, said motion was withdrawn.

Mr. McLane, of Maryland, rose to a point of order, and submitted that the gentleman from Massachusetts had not the power to demand the previous question upon the majority resolutions. The resolution of Mr. Bayard, of Delaware, being an amendment, the vote on that must he first taken.

Mr. Meade, of Virginia, concurred in this view and he had before risen to say so. As the resolution of Mr. Bayard would be first voted upon, he would move the previous question.

The Convention sustained the call for the previous question, and the President decided that the main question should now be put, first upon the minority resolution of Mr. Bayard, of Delaware.

Pending the call of the roll, Mr. Robinson, of Indiana, moved to lay the whole subject on the table.

The President entertained the motion, it being to lay the whole subject upon the table.

The vote being taken on this motion by States, resulted as follows:

AYES.—Massachusetts 2; New Jersey, 4; South Carolina, 8; Louisiana, 6; Ohio, 1; Kentucky, 7; Indiana, 13; Arkansas, 3. Total, 44.

NAYS.—Maine, 8; New Hampshire, 5; Vermont, 5; Massachusetts, 11; Rhode Island, 4; Connecticut, 6; New Jersey, 3; Pennsylvania, 27; Delaware, 3; Maryland, 8; Virginia, 15; North Carolina, 10; Georgia, 10; Alabama, 9; Mississippi, 7; Ohio, 22; Kentucky 12; Tennessee, 5; Arkansas, 1; Illinois, 11; Missouri, 9; Michigan, 6; Florida, 3; Texas, 4; Iowa, 4; Wisconsin, 5; California, 4. Total, 217.

The motion being lost, the question came upon the adoption of the minority resolution of the Committee on Credentials, reported by Mr. Bayard, and the vote being called by States, resulted as follows :

AYES.—Maine, 6; Massachusetts, 3; Rhode Island, 1; Connecticut, 6; New Jersey, 6; Pennsylvania, 27; Delaware, 3; Maryland, 6; Virginia, 15; Georgia, 4; Ohio, 10; Kentucky, 6; Tennessee, 10; Indiana, 13; Missouri, 6; Arkansas, 2; Texas, 3; Wisconsin, 5; California, 4. Total, 137.

NAYS.—Maine, 2; New Hampshire, 5; Vermont, 5; Massachusetts, 10; Rhode Island, 3; New Jersey, 1; Maryland, 2; North Carolina, 10; South Carolina, 8; Georgia, 6; Alabama, 9; Mississippi, 7; Louisiana, 6; Ohio, 13; Kentucky, 5; Tennessee, 2; Illinois, 11; Missouri, 3; Arkansas, 2; Michigan, 6; Florida, 3; Iowa, 4. Total, 123.

The President proclaimed the resolution of the minority, reported by Mr. Bayard, as adopted.

Mr. Preston, of Kentucky, moved to reconsider this vote, and that the motion lay on the table. Adopted.

The question was then put on the adoption of the resolution as amended, and the same was carried.

Mr. Preston moved to reconsider this vote, and that the motion lie on the table. Adopted.

Mr. Preston moved that a committee of seven of the Convention be appointed to wait upon the New York delegations, and inform them of the decision of the Convention.

The Chair announced the following as the committee to wait on the New York delegations and acquaint them with the decision of the Convention :

Preston, of Kentucky; Butler, of Massachusetts; Richardson, of Illinois; Gardner, of Georgia; Meade, of Virginia; Wickliffe, of Kentucky; Pickens, of South Carolina.

George McCook of Ohio, moved the following resolution:

Resolved, That at two o'clock P. M., this day, this Convention will proceed, by a call of the States, to nominate a candidate for the Presidency. [Adopted.

On motion the Convention then took a recess until two o'clock, P. M.

AFTERNOON SESSION, JUNE 5, 1856.

Mr. Preston, of Kentucky, reported from the committee to acquaint the New York Delegations of the decision of the Convention in the New York contest, that the committee had performed their duty, and that the contesting delegations had declared their acquiescence in the decision, and would be prepared to comply with it.

The following is the list of Delegates, from New York, as reported to the Convention by the respective delegations from that State.

The delegation of which Hon. Horatio Seymour was at the head was

Horatio Seymour, *of Utica*,
Nicholas Hill, Jr., *Albany*,
Wm. H. Ludlow,
Samuel E. Johnson,
Thomas Byrns,
George H. Purser,
Stephen H. Feeks,
John Cochran, *New York*,
Lorenzo B. Shepherd, *do.*,
Daniel F.
J. N. Fowler, *New York*,
John C. Holley,
Thomas R. Westbrook,
Dean Richmond, *Buffalo*,
Charles L. McArthur,
John V. L. Pruyn, *Albany*,
Lemuel L. Jenks,
Timothy Hoyle,
William C. Crain,
John C. Wright,
Horatio Bullard,
John Stryker,
Horace G. Prindle,
Sands N. Kenyon,
DeWitt C. West,
Dennis McCarthy,
Elmore P. Ross,
William C. Dyer,
John J. Taylor,
William C. Rhodes,
Simon B. Jewett,
L. P. Weatherby,
William Vandervert,
Israel T. Hatch,
N. Sackett.

The delegation of which the Hon. Samuel Beardsley was at the head, was

Samuel Beardsley, *Utica*,
George W. Clinton, *Buffalo*,
Legrand G. Capers,
Henry C. Murphy,
Joseph Blackburn,
Thomas Wheeler,
Robert W. Allen,
Augustus Schell, *New York*,
Elijah Ward,
Daniel B. Taylor, *New York*,
Robert H. Ludlow,
Samuel Fowler,
William F. Russell,
George W. Petton,
David L. Seymour, *Troy*,
David Hamilton,
Orville Clark, *Sandy Hill*,
Putnam B. Fisk,
Charles Gray.
Thomas B. Mitchell,
Samuel S. Brown,
John Rice,
Ausburn Birdsall, *Binghampton*,
Delos DeWolf,
Lysander H. Brown,
John J. Peck,
Charles W. Pomeroy,
Wm. Clark,
Erastus Evans,
John A. Vanderlip,
Nicholas E. Pain,
James G. Shepherd,
Harvey Goodrich,
Henry A. Rogers, *Buffalo*,
Benjamin Walworth.

Mr. Inge, of California, moved that the resolution relative to the establishment of a public road across our territory be reconsidered.

Mr. Thompson, of Mississippi, insisted that the motion was not in order; that by the decision of the Convention this morning, the order of the hour was to ballot for the Presidency.

The President so decided.

Mr. Callehan, of Pennsylvania, arose to a privileged question. The New York delegation had been admitted, but they had not yet signified their acquiescence in the platform, and they ought to be permitted to do so. [Applause. Yes, yes.]

Mr. Meade, of Virginia, then moved that New York be now permitted to vote on the resolutions constituting the platform, which motion was unanimously adopted.

New York was then called for her vote on said resolutions, and by her respective Chairmen, cast her entire *thirty-five* votes in the affirmative, which was received with *great applause.*

Mr. Inge, of California, moved for a suspension of the rules, with a view to reconsider the vote laying upon the table, the resolution in favor of an overland communication between the Atlantic and Pacific coasts—and he called for a vote by States.

Ayes:—Maine, 1, Vermont 5, Massachusetts, 11, New York 35, Maryland 8, Georgia 1, Louisiana 6, Ohio 6, Tennessee 5, Illinois 11, Missouri 9, Michigan 6, Texas 4, Iowa 4, Wisconsin 5, California 4—121.

Noes:—Maine 7, New Hampshire 5, Massachusetts 2, Rhode Island 4, Connecticut 6, New Jersey 7, Pennsylvania 27, Delaware 3, Virginia 15, North Carolina 10, South Carolina 8, Georgia 9, Alabama 9, Mississippi 7, Ohio 17, Kentucky 12, Tennessee 7, Iowa 13, Arkansas 4, Florida 3—175.

So the motion to suspend the rules was lost.

Mr. Ludlow, of New York, alluding to the conciliatory spirit which had influenced the Convention in its action on the question so happily adjusted, asked that in the same spirit the Convention would not suffer some seventy good Democrats, who had been sent here as delegates, to wander through the streets of Cincinnati without permission to enter the hall.

The President decided that the gentleman was out of order.

The Chair then announced that the order of the hour was the vote on the nomination for Presidency.

R. Kidder Meade, of Virginia—I am charged by my delegation with the duty of presenting to this Convention, as a candidate for the Presidency, the name of that honest and eminent statesman, James Buchanan. [Applause.]

Harry Hibbard, of New Hampshire—In the name of the Democracy of New Hampshire I present the name of Franklin Pierce. [Applause.]

Mr. Inge, of California—I am unanimously instructed by the delegation from California to put in nomination the great champion of American progress, Lewis Cass, of Michigan. [Applause.]

Mr. Richardson—I propose Stephen A. Douglas, of Illinois, for the nomination for the Presidency. [Applause.]

The Convention then proceeded to vote for a candidate for President. The first ballot was as follows:

1st BALLOT FOR PRESIDENT.

States.	James Buchanan.	Franklin Pierce.	Stephen A. Douglas.	Lewis Cass.
Maine,............	5	3		
New Hampshire,..		5		
Vermont,.........		5		
Massachusetts,.....	4	9		
Rhode Island,.....		4		
Connecticut,......	6			
New York,........	17	18		
New Jersey,......	7			
Pennsylvania,.....	27			
Delaware,.........	3			
Maryland,........	6	2		
Virginia,..........	15			
North Carolina,...		10		
South Carolina,...		8		
Georgia,..........		10		
Alabama,.........		9		
Mississippi,.......		7		
Louisiana,.........	6			
Ohio,..............	13½	4½	4	1
Kentucky,........	4	5	3	
Tennessee,........		12		
Indiana,..........	13			
Illinois,...........			11	
Missouri,.........			9	
Arkansas,.........		4		
Michigan,.........	6			
Florida,..........		3		
Texas,............		4		
Iowa,.............			4	
Wisconsin,........	3		2	
California,........				4
	135½	122½	33	5

There being no choice the Chair ordered a 2d ballot.

2d BALLOT FOR PRESIDENT.

States.	James Buchanan.	Franklin Pierce.	Stephen A. Douglas.	Lewis Cass.
Maine,............	5	3		
New Hampshire,..		5		
Vermont,.........		5		
Massachusetts,.....	4	9		
Rhode Island,.....		4		
Connecticut,......	6			
New York,........	18	17		
New Jersey,.......	7			
Pennsylvania,.....	27			
Delaware,.........	3			
Maryland,........	6	2		
Virginia,..........	15			
North Carolina,...		10		
South Carolina,...		8		
Georgia,..........		10		
Alabama,..........		9		
Mississippi,.......		7		
Louisiana,.........	6			
Ohio,..............	13	3½	4½	2
Kentucky,........	5	4	3	
Tennessee,........		12		
Indiana,..........	13			
Illinois,...........			11	
Missouri,.........			9	
Arkansas,........		4		
Michigan,.........	6			
Florida,..........		3		
Texas,............		4		
Iowa..............	2		2	
Wisconsin,........	3		2	
California,........				4
	139	119½	31½	6

There being no choice, a 3d ballot was ordered.

3d BALLOT FOR PRESIDENT.

States.	James Buchanan.	Franklin Pierce.	Stephen A. Douglas.	Lewis Cass.
Maine,............	5	3		
New Hampshire,..		5		
Vermont,.........		5		
Massachusetts,.....	4	9		
Rhode Island,.....		4		
Connecticut,......	6			
New York,........	17	18		
New Jersey,......	7			
Pennsylvania,.....	27			
Delaware,.........	3			
Maryland,.........	6	2		
Virginia,..........	15			
North Carolina,...		10		
South Carolina,...		8		
Georgia,..........		10		
Alabama,.........		9		
Mississippi........		7		
Louisiana,........	6			
Ohio,..............	13½	3	5	1½
Kentucky,........	4	3	5	
Tennessee,........		12		
Indiana,..........	13			
Illinois,...........			11	
Missouri,.........			9	
Arkansas,.........		4		
Michigan,.........	6			
Florida,...........		3		
Texas,............		4		
Iowa,.............	2		2	
Wisconsin,........	5			
California,........				4
	139½	119	32	5½

A 4th ballot was then had.

4th BALLOT FOR PRESIDENT.

States.	James Buchanan.	Franklin Pierce.	Stephen A. Douglas.	Lewis Cass
Maine,............	5	3		
New Hampshire,..		5		
Vermont,.........		5		
Massachusetts,.....	4	9		
Rhode Island,.....		4		
Connecticut,......	6			
New York,........	18	17		
New Jersey,......	7			
Pennsylvania,.....	27			
Delaware,.........	3			
Maryland,........	6	2		
Virginia,..........	15			
North Carolina,...		10		
South Carolina,....		8		
Georgia,..........		10		
Alabama,.........		9		
Mississippi,.......		7		
Louisiana,.........	6			
Ohio,..............	13½	3	5	1½
Kentucky,........	5	4	3	
Tennessee,........		12		
Indiana,..........	13			
Illinois,...........			11	
Missouri,.........			9	
Arkansas,.........		4		
Michigan,.........	6			
Flor ida,..........		3		
Texas,............		4		
Iowa,.............	2		2	
Wisconsin,........	5			
California,........				4
	141½	119	30	5½

A 5th ballot was then directed.

5th BALLOT FOR PRESIDENT.

STATES.	James Buchanan.	Franklin Pierce.	Stephen A. Douglas.	Lewis Cass.
Maine,	5	3		
New Hampshire,		5		
Vermont,		5		
Massachusetts,	5	8		
Rhode Island,		4		
Connecticut,	6			
New York,	17	18		
New Jersey,	7			
Pennsylvania,	27			
Delaware,	3			
Maryland,	6	2		
Virginia,	15			
North Carolina,		10		
South Carolina,		8		
Georgia,		10		
Alabama,		9		
Mississippi,		7		
Louisiana,	6			
Ohio,	13½	3	5	1½
Kentucky,	3½	4½	4	
Tennessee,		12		
Indiana,	13			
Illinois,			11	
Missouri,			9	
Arkansas,		4		
Michigan,	6			
Florida,		3		
Texas,		4		
Iowa,	2		2	
Wisconsin,	5			
California,				4
	140	119½	31	5½

A 6th ballot was then had.

6TH BALLOT FOR PRESIDENT.

STATES.	James Buchanan.	Franklin Pierce.	Stephen A. Douglas.	Lewis Cass.
Maine,	5	3		
New Hampshire,		5		
Vermont,		5		
Massachusetts,	5	8		
Rhode Island,		4		
Connecticut,	6			
New York,	18	17		
New Jersey,	7			
Pennsylvania,	27			
Delaware,	3			
Maryland,	6	2		
Virginia,	15			
North Carolina,		10		
South Carolina,		8		
Georgia,		10		
Alabama,		9		
Mississippi,		7		
Louisiana,	6			
Ohio,	13½	3	5	1½
Kentucky,	5½	5½	1	
Tennessee,	12			
Indiana,	13			
Illinois,			11	
Missouri,			9	
Arkansas,		4		
Michigan,	6			
Florida,		3		
Texas,		4		
Iowa,	2		2	
Wisconsin,	5			
California,				4
	155	107½	28	5½

A 7th ballot was then taken.

7TH BALLOT FOR PRESIDENT.

STATES.	James Buchanan	Franklin Pierce.	Stephen A. Douglas.	Lewis Cass.
Maine,	5	3		
New Hampshire,		5		
Vermont,		5		
Massachusetts,	6	7		
Rhode Island,		4		
Connecticut,	6			
New York,	17	18		
New Jersey,	7			
Pennsylvania,	27			
Delaware,	3			
Maryland,	6	2		
Virginia,	15			
North Carolina,		10		
South Carolina,		8		
Georgia,	3		7	
Alabama,		9		
Mississippi,		7		
Louisiana,	6			
Ohio,	13	4	4½	1½
Kentucky,	3½		8½	
Tennessee,			12	
Indiana,	13			
Illinois,			11	
Missouri,			9	
Arkansas,			4	
Michigan,	6			
Florida,		3		
Texas,		4		
Iowa,	2		2	
Wisconsin,	5			
California,				4
	143½	89	58	5½

The States were then called for the 8th ballot.

8TH BALLOT FOR PRESIDENT.

STATES.	James Buchanan.	Franklin Pierce.	Stephen A. Douglas.	Lewis Cass
Maine,	6	2		
New Hampshire,		5		
Vermont,		5		
Massachusetts,	6	7		
Rhode Island,		4		
Connecticut,	6			
New York,	18	17		
New Jersey,	7			
Pennsylvania,	27			
Delaware,	3			
Maryland,	6	2		
Virginia,	15			
North Carolina,		10		
South Carolina,		8		
Georgia,	3		7	
Alabama,		9		
Mississippi,		7		
Louisiana,	6			
Ohio,	13	4	4½	1½
Kentucky,	5½		6½	
Tennessee,			12	
Indiana,	13			
Illinois,			11	
Missouri,			9	
Arkansas,			4	
Michigan,	6			
Florida,		3		
Texas,		4		
Iowa,	2		2	
Wisconsin,	5			
California,				4
	147½	87	56	5½

After the result of the 8th ballot Mr. Yulee moved an adjournment, which was lost, and the 9th ballot ordered.

9TH BALLOT FOR PRESIDENT.

STATES.	James Buchanan.	Franklin Pierce.	Stephen A. Douglas.	Lewis Cass.
Maine,..	6	2		
New Hampshire,		5		
Vermont,........		5		
Massachusetts,...	6	7		
Rhode Island,...		4		
Connecticut,....	6			
New York,......	17	18		
New Jersey,.....	7			
Pennsylvania,...	27			
Delaware,.......	3			
Maryland,......	7	1		
Virginia,........	15			
North Carolina,.		10		
South Carolina,.		8		
Georgia,........	3		7	
Alabama,.......		9		
Mississippi,.....		7		
Louisiana,.......	6			
Ohio,...........	13	4	3	3
Kentucky,......	4		8	
Tennessee,......			12	
Indiana,........	13			
Illinois,.........			11	
Missouri,.......			9	
Arkansas,.......			4	
Michigan,.......	6			
Florida,.........		3		
Texas,..........		4		
Iowa...........	2		2	
Wisconsin,......	5			
California,......				4
	146	87	56	7

The 10th ballot was then taken.

10TH BALLOT FOR PRESIDENT.

STATES.	James Buchanan.	Franklin Pierce.	Stephen A. Douglas.	Lewis Cass.
Maine,..........	6	2		
New Hampshire,		5		
Vermont,........			5	
Massachusetts,...	6	7		
Rhode Island,...		4		
Connecticut,....	6			
New York,......	18	17		
New Jersey,.....	7			
Pennsylvania,...	27			
Delaware,.......	3			
Maryland,.......	7	1		
Virginia,........	15			
North Carolina,.		10		
South Carolina,.		8		
Georgia,.........	3		7	
Alabama,........		9		
Mississippi,.....		7		
Louisiana,.......	6			
Ohio,...........	13	3½	5	1½
Kentucky,......	4½		7½	
Tennessee,......			12	
Indiana,........	13			
Illinois,.........			11	
Missouri,.......			9	
Arkansas,.......			4	
Michigan,.......	6			
Florida,........		3		
Texas,..........		4		
Iowa,..........	2		2	
Wisconsin,......	5			
California,......				4
	147½	80½	62½	5½

The 11th ballot was then taken.

11TH BALLOT FOR PRESIDENT.

STATES.	James Buchanan.	Franklin Pierce.	Stephen A. Douglas.	Lewis Cass.
Maine,.........	6	2		
New Hampshire,		5		
Vermont,.......			5	
Massachusetts,...	6	7		
Rhode Island,...		4		
Connecticut,....	6			
New York,......	17	18		
New Jersey,.....	7			
Pennsylvania,...	27			
Delaware,.......	3			
Maryland,......	8			
Virginia,........	15			
North Carolina,.		10		
South Carolina,.		8		
Georgia,........	3		7	
Alabama,.......		9		
Mississippi,......		7		
Louisiana,.......	6			
Ohio,...........	13	3	5½	1½
Kentucky,......	4½		7½	
Tennessee,......			12	
Indiana,........	13			
Illinois,.........			11	
Missouri,.......			9	
Arkansas,.......			4	
Michigan,.......	6			
Florida,.........		3		
Texas,..........		4		
Iowa,..........	2		2	
Wisconsin,......	5			
California,......				4
	147½	80	63	5½

The States were called for the 12th ballot.

12TH BALLOT FOR PRESIDENT.

STATES.	James Buchanan.	Franklin Pierce.	Stephen A. Douglas.	Lewis Cass.
Maine,..........	6	2		
New Hampshire,		5		
Vermont,........			5	
Massachusetts,..	6	7		
Rhode Island,...		4		
Connecticut,....	6			
New York,......	18	17		
New Jersey,.....	7			
Pennsylvania,...	27			
Delaware,.......	3			
Maryland,......	8			
Virginia,........	15			
North Carolina,.		10		
South Carolina,.		8		
Georgia,........	3		7	
Alabama,.......		9		
Mississippi,......		7		
Louisiana,.......	6			
Ohio,...........	12½	3	6	1½
Kentucky,......	4½		7½	
Tennessee,......			12	
Indiana,.........	13			
Illinois,.........			11	
Missouri,.......			9	
Arkansas,.......			4	
Michigan,.......	6			
Florida,.........		3		
Texas,..........		4		
Iowa,..........	2		2	
Wisconsin,......	5			
California,......				4
	148	79	63½	5½

After the 12th ballot Mr. Burnett, of Alabama, moved an adjournment; but objection being made, it was withdrawn and the 13th ballot called for.

13TH BALLOT FOR PRESIDENT.

STATES.	James Buchanan.	Franklin Pierce.	Stephen A. Douglas.	Lewis Cass.
Maine,..........	6	2		
New Hampshire,		5		
Vermont,.......			5	
Massachusetts,..	6½	6½		
Rhode Island,...	2	2		
Connecticut,.....	6			
New York,......	17	18		
New Jersey,....	7			
Pennsylvania,...	27			
Delaware,.......	3			
Maryland,......	8			
Virginia,........	15			
North Carolina,.		10		
South Carolina,.		8		
Georgia,.........	3		7	
Alabama,.......		9		
Mississippi,......		7		
Louisiana,.......	6			
Ohio,...........	13	3	5½	1½
Kentucky,......	4½		7½	
Tennessee,.......			12	
Indiana,........	13			
Illinois,.........			11	
Missouri,........			9	
Arkansas,.......			4	
Michigan,........	6			
Florida,..........		3		
Texas,..........		4		
Iowa,...........	2		2	
Wisconsin,,.....	5			
California,.......				4
	150	77½	63	5½

AFTER THE 13TH BALLOT, Mr. McMullen, of Virginia, moved an adjournment. The vote by States being called for, resulted as follows :

YEAS.—New Hampshire, 5 ; Vermont, 5 ; Rhode Island, 4 ; New York, 17 ; North Carolina, 5 ; South Carolina, 8 ; Georgia, 10 ; Alabama, 9 ; Mississippi, 7 ; Ohio, 8 ; Kentucky, 5 ; Tennessee, 12 ; Illinois, 11 ; Missouri, 9 ; Arkansas, 4 ; Florida, 3 ; Texas, 4 ; Iowa, 2 ; California, 4—Total, 132.

NAYS.—Maine, 8 ; Massachusetts, 13 ; Connecticut, 6 ; New York, 18; New Jersey, 7 ; Pennsylvania, 27 ; Delaware, 3 ; Maryland, 8 ; Virginia, 15 ; North Carolina, 5 ; Louisiana, 6 ; Ohio, 15 ; Kentucky, 7 ; Indiana, 13 ; Michigan, 6 ; Iowa, 2 ; Wisconsin, 5. Total, 164. So the motion was lost.

14TH BALLOT FOR PRESIDENT.

STATES.	James Buchanan.	Franklin Pierce.	Stephen A. Douglas.	Lewis Cass.
Maine,.........	6	2		
New Hampshire,		5		
Vermont,.......			5	
Massachusetts,...	7	6		
Rhode Island,...	4			
Connecticut,....	6			
New York,.......	17	18		
New Jersey,....	7			
Pennsylvania,...	27			
Delaware,.......	3			
Maryland,......	8			
Virginia,........	15			
North Carolina,.		10		
South Carolina,.		8		
Georgia,........	3		7	
Alabama,........		9		
Mississippi,.....		7		
Louisiana,.......	6			
Ohio,...........	13	3	5½	1½
Kentucky,.......	4½		7½	
Tennessee,.......			12	
Indiana,........	13			
Illinois,.........			11	
Missouri,.......			9	
Arkansas,.......			4	
Michigan,.......	6			
Florida,.........		3		
Texas,.........		4		
Iowa,...........	2		2	
Wisconsin,......	5			
Cailfornia,.......				4
	152½	75	63	5½

AFTER THE 14TH BALLOT, Mr. Flournoy, of Arkansas, moved that the Convention do now adjourn until to-morrow morning at 9 o'clock. A call for votes by States being made, resulted as follows :

YEAS.—Maine, 1 ; New Hampshire, 5 ; Vermont, 5 ; Massachusetts, 8 ; Rhode Island, 4 ; New York, 17 ; New Jersey, 7 ; Pennsylvania, 27 ; Delaware 5 ; Virginia, 15 ; North Carolina, 10 ; South Carolina, 8 ; Georgia, 9 ; Alabama, 9 ; Mississippi, 7 ; Louisiana, 6 ; Ohio, 15 ; Kentucky, 12 ; Tennessee, 6 ; Indiana, 13 ; Illinois, 11 ; Missouri, 9 ; Arkansas, 4 ; Florida, 3 , Texas, 4 ; Iowa, 4 ; Wisconsin, 5 ; California, 4 Total, 231.

NAYS.—Maine, 7 ; Massachusetts, 5 ; Connecticut, 6 ; New York, 18 ; Maryland, 8; Georgia, 1; Ohio, 8; Tennessee, 6; Michigan, 6. Total, 65.
The Convention adjourned until to-morrow morning at 9 o'clock.

FIFTH DAY'S PROCEEDINGS.

MORNING SESSION, JUNE 6, 1856.

The Convention was called to order precisely at nine o'clock. The President said that they would now proceed to the fifteenth ballot.

Mr. Hibbard, of New Hampshire, arose and said :

Mr. President—New Hampshire has thus far given her votes for Franklin Pierce, in accordance with the wishes of the entire body of the democracy of our State. In common with other friends, tried and true, she has supported him steadfastly and earnestly. But, sir, strong as is her preference for her own distinguished son, abiding as is her confidence in his patriotism and statesmanship, warm as is her attachment to him personally, she is willing to defer even these considerations for what may seem the more practicable method of advancing cherished principles. She lays them all as an offering upon the altar of our common cause. In so doing, she acts in accordance, not only with the dictates of her political duty, but with his own expressed desire. The unanimous adoption by this Convention of our noble platform, is the most comprehensive and emphatic sanction of the administration of President Pierce. Beyond this, there needs no tongue to speak his eulogy. I therefore withdraw his name from the present contest. And, sir, by the unanimous instruction of our delegation, I cast the five votes of our State for the man we regard as the next best exponent of the principles and measures so nobly illustrated by the administration of Franklin Pierce—the bold, efficient and ever faithful statesman of Illinois, Stephen A. Douglas. [Great Applause.]

15TH BALLOT FOR PRESIDENT.

States.	James Buchanan.	Franklin Pierce.	Stephen A. Douglas.	Lewis Cass.
Maine,	7	1		
New Hampshire,			5	
Vermont,			5	
Massachusetts,	10		3	
Rhode Island,	4			
Connecticut,	6			
New York,	17		18	
New Jersey,	7			
Pennsylvania	27			
Delaware,	3			
Maryland,	8			
Virginia,	15			
North Carolina,			10	
South Carolina,			8	
Georgia,	3		7	
Alabama,			9	
Mississippi,			7	
Louisiana,	6			
Ohio,	13½	2½	6½	½
Kentucky,	4		7	
Tennessee,	12			
Indiana,	13			
Illinois,			11	
Missouri,			9	
Arkansas,			4	
Michigan,	6			
Florida,			3	
Texas,			4	
Iowa,	2		2	
Wisconsin,	5			
California,				4
	168½	3½	118½	4½

There being no choice, the 16th ballot was called for.

16TH BALLOT FOR PRESIDENT.

States.	James Buchanan.	Franklin Pierce.	Stephen A. Douglas.	Lewis Cass.
Maine,	8			
New Hampshire,			5	
Vermont,			5	
Massachusetts,	10		3	
Rhode Island,	4			
Connecticut,	6			
New York,	18		17	
New Jersey,	7			
Pennsylvania,	27			
Delaware,	3			
Maryland,	8			
Virginia,	15			
North Carolina,			10	
South Carolina,			8	
Georgia,	3		7	
Alabama,			9	
Mississippi,			7	
Louisiana,	6			
Ohio,	15		6	2
Kentucky,			12	
Tennessee,	12			
Indiana,	13			
Illinois,			11	
Missouri,			9	
Arkansas,			4	
Michigan,	6			
Florida,			3	
Texas,			4	
Iowa,	2		2	
Wisconsin,	5			
California,				4
	168		122	6

No choice being made, the 17th ballot was had.

When Mr. Preston, of Kentucky, said; Mr. President—As one of the friends of Mr. Douglas, I have become sufficiently satisfied by the evidences presented here, that it is the wish of this Convention that James Buchanan should be the nominee for President of the United States; I believe that Judge Douglas himself, and the friends of Judge Douglas, and when I say this, I speak with some degree of knowledge on the subject—I believe that the friends of Mr. Douglas will be among the first to come forward, and in a spirit of liberality, put an end to the useless contest. I will now give way to the gentleman from Illinois, the friend of Mr. Douglas.

During Mr. Preston's remarks there were loud expressions of dissatisfaction and cries of "No, no!" "Don't withdraw!" "Don't withdraw!"

Here W. A. Richardson, of Illinois, arose, and waiving his hand, there was immediate and general silence. In a solemn and impressive manner that gentleman proceeded to address the Convention as follows:

Mr. Richardson—Mr. President and gentlemen of the Convention: Before undertaking to advise any gentleman on this floor what he ought to do, I consider that I have a duty which I owe to my constituents, and which, since it is now imposed on me, I feel it is due to the Democratic party and friends of Stephen A. Douglas, that I should discharge. Whatever may be the opinion of the gentleman as to the contest, I am satisfied that I cannot advance his interests or the interests of the common cause, or the principles of the Democratic party, by continuing him in this contest. I will, therefore, state that I have a dispatch from Judge Douglas, which I desire, may be permitted to be read, and I shall then withdraw his name from before the Convention. I desire, gentlemen, after that, to decide on what course they may deem it proper to pursue. [Tremendous applause—profound sensation.]

The dispatch was sent to the Chair to be read, and is as follows:

LETTER OF S. A. DOUGLAS TO W. A. RICHARDSON, OF ILLINOIS.

WASHINGTON, June 4, 1856.

Dear Sir: From the telegraphic reports in the newspapers, I fear that an embittered state of feeling is being engendered in the Convention, which may endanger the harmony and success of our party. I wish you and all my friends to bear in mind that I have a thousand fold more anxiety for the triumph of our principles than for my own personal elevation.

If the withdrawal of my name will contribute to the harmony of our party or the success of our cause, I hope you will not hesitate to take the step. Especially it is my desire that the action of the Convention will embody and express the wishes, feelings and principles of the Democracy of the Republic; and hence, if Mr. Pierce or Mr. Buchanan, or any other statesman who is faithful to the great issues involved in the contest, shall receive a majority of the Convention, I earnestly hope that all my friends will unite in insuring him two thirds, and then in making his nomination unanimous. Let no personal considerations disturb the harmony or endanger the triumph of our principles.

S. A. DOUGLAS.

To Hon. W. A. RICHARDSON, Burnet House, Cincinnati, Ohio.

The reading of this dispatch was interrupted by frequent and tremendous applause. It was some time before order could be restored. When the Convention had subsided into something like order, the Prasident announced that they would proceed with the seventeenth ballot.

Mr. Preston—I move that James Buchanan be nominated as the candidate of the democratic party, for President of the United States, by acclamation.

Voices—Go on with the call—go on with the call!

The roll was then called for the seventeenth ballot:

Maine cast her eight votes for James Buchanan.

When New Hampshire, was called, Mr. Hibbard said:—Mr. President: New Hampshire has steadily supported the favorite of her people, until it was apparent that he was not the choice of the convention. She then withdrew his name and went heartily for the champion of the North West. The ballottings have shown a like disposition with regard to him. His name, too, is now withdrawn. It is apparent that Mr. Buchanan is the candidate of the Convention. The will of the majority becomes now the choice of all. New Hampshire, sir, bows most respectfully to that decision. She will support the great statesman of Pennsylvania with the same fidelity and determination she has devoted to the cause of her own cherished son. She throws her five votes for James Buchanan, and she will roll down for him her majority of thousands in November next, like an avalanche from her granite hills! [Great applause.]

Vermont being called, Mr. Smalley rose and said:—Vermont cast her unanimous vote for nine successive ballots for Franklin Pierce, because they regard his Administration, both in its domestic and foreign policy, as entitled to the entire confidence and approbation of every true Democrat. He has, in a perilous crisis, maintained firmly our honor abroad, fearlessly confronted all the intestine factions that have for the last three years distracted our Republic, and nobly sustained the constitutional rights of every part of our common country. He is our neighbor, and we *know* him to be a man, a patriot, and a statesman without reproach. But we became convinced that he was not the choice of this Convention, and therefore Vermont gave her five votes for a favorite son, who was born and educated amid her Green Mountains—the bold, the eloquent, and the successful champion in the United States Senate of the great principle of Popular Sovereignty—Stephen A. Douglas. But his name has been, for the purpose of conciliation, harmony and unity of action, at his request, withdrawn from the Convention. Vermont now comes cordially and earnestly to the support of the ripe, able and accomplished statesman of Pennsylvania. And though her Democracy can promise but little, will yield to none in the fidelity and zeal with which they will battle for his election. I am unanimously instructed to cast the five votes of Vermont for James Buchanan. [Loud cheers.]

Massachusetts was next called, when Mr. Butler answered as follows: Massachusetts has heretofore shown that she reposes faith and confidence in the distinguished statesman of her own section of the country; yet she has no factious opposition to make to the wishes of the great Democratic party, as indicated in this convention. And though, sir, she cannot promise much, yet, when the nomination is made, she will say, in the language of one of her gallant sons at Lundy's Lane, when ordered to take a British battery—"We will try." I am instructed to cast the thirteen votes of Massachusetts for James Buchanan. [Applause.]

When the vote of Rhode Island was called for, Mr. Lawrence said: Mr. President: Rhode Island, during twelve ballots, manifested her approval of the administration of our distinguished President, whose nomination—which she ratified by her electoral vote—her delegates four years ago were among the first to sustain. She would have continued to cast the same vote had she not been convinced that General Pierce could not unite the requisite support in this Convention. She therefore, last evening transferred her votes to the eminent citizen of Pennsylvania, who, I am free to declare, is, under existing circumstances, the only one of the candidates that have been before us that can redeem our State, and it is with the greatest satisfaction that the delegation of Rhode Island congratulate their fellow citizens that the nomination of James Buchanan is now unanimously responded to.

Connecticut then cast her six votes for James Buchanan.

New York was next called, whereupon Mr. Horatio Seymour rose and said: The State of New York, in many respects divided, has at last become united on one point, the moral necessity of confining the nomination within the circle of the three distinguished gentlemen whose names were first presented to the people as candidates for the Presidency. Speaking, in this convention, for one section of the Democratic party of the State of New York, I have felt it to be my duty—I state that we have felt it our duty to cast our votes for Franklin Pierce. So long as his name continued before the convention, we unfalteringly adhered to him. When his nomination became impossible, we felt it our duty to give our support to the nomination of Stephen A. Douglas, of Illinois. His name is now formally withdrawn by the person authorized to speak for him; indeed, he has spoken for himself. While we have the strongest desire to continue our support for him, we feel that we should be recreant to ourselves and to those whom we represent, if the State of New York should go beyond the limits of the three names originally presented to the people of the United States for nomination. At this stage of the proceedings, in view of this statement, in view of the exigencies of the case, in view of the position in which we are now placed, I ask that we may be permitted to retire and consult, in order that this nomination may go forth with that moral force and influence which we have so much at heart.

Hereupon that part of the delegation from New York, of which Mr. Ludlow was chairman, withdrew for consultation, and on returning to the Convention,

Mr. Ludlow of New York, said—Mr. President, The wing of the Democratic party of the State of New York, represented by the delegation of which I have the honor to be chairman, has come into this Convention under great disadvantages. It has, Sir, ever been a strong distinctive feature of our Democracy of New York, to stand with reliable truth and firmness by those whom we have reason to regard our friends, and Sir, in this view having had no candidate of our own to present, and without any pledges to others, we have been content and pleased to support the nominees of our friends. We have done so, honorably and honestly, and now that those nominees are withdrawn from the further consideration of this Convention, we shall assume no factious attitude, and I take pleasure in following out the sentiment of this Convention, as now indicated, and give eighteen votes from New York, for James Buchanan.

New Jersey then casts her seven votes for James Buchanan.

When Pennsylvania was called,

Hon. John L. Dawson, said—Mr. President, The venerable chairman of our delegation, Gov. Porter, not much accustomed to public speaking, has devolved upon me the duty of expressing to this Convention our high appreciation of the honor conferred upon our State in the selection of its distinguished citizen as the nominee of the Democratic party. [Great applause.] We are more than gratified that the time has arrived in the deliberations of this body, when the sacrifice of personal preferences and predilections becomes a virtue. Ardent attachment to distinguished, able and well-tried leaders is a noble characteristic of our people, and is only to be waived at the call of patriotism and necessity. [Cheers.] In this case that harmony and unanimity which is essential to our action, and the surest harbingers of success, has generously secured this surrender.

The chiefs of the Democracy present many honored names, either of whom would worthily have supported the banner upon which are inscribed the principles to which we own allegiance—that banner now reared to be borne by the distinguished son of our own State, the far beaming effulgence of its legend will penetrate the remotest retreats of the land, and quickly rally around it an invincible host, filled with the enthusiasm inspired by a great cause and by the memory of former triumphs and glories. [Great cheering.]

Mr. Buchanan is a man upon whom all can unite, and in doing so there is no expectation that there will be any surrender of the confidence in or admiration of those whom we pass by.

There is not a heart in this Convention that does not glow with full and grateful recognition of the eminent services, to the Democratic party, of Cass, Hunter, Douglas, Bright, Pierce and others whose names have been mentioned.

The first is, indeed, a mighty name which was long since voluntarily withdrawn from the contest, and whose brilliant efforts in patriotic devotion to the national interest will forever brighten the pages of our country's history. [Tremendous cheers.] In Mr. Hunter we recognize the model Senator, the distinguished Statesman, a chivalric son of old Virginia, he has been nurtured in the school of her sages who laid the foundation and shaped the superstructure of the confederacy. [Applause.]

The clear-sighted boldness, the skilful battle for the right that has marked the public career of Douglas, would have made him a gallant leader in the contest, whom we should all have delighted to follow; [renewed applause;] while in Bright we recognize those high qualities that mark the rising statesmen of the West, and see in him the true representative of her gigantic and advancing power. [Great applause.]

4

The Administration of General Pierce requires no eulogium from me. True to the Constitution, to the principles and policy of the Democratic party, we say in a spirit of justice: "Well done, good and faithful servant." [Loud cheers.]

As Pennsylvanians, the representatives on this floor of a State, which, in all the elements of greatness, we claim in a spirit of patriotic attachment, is inferior to none in the Union—one of the "Old Thirteen"—are proud that the towering greatness of her son has secured to her the well-merited and distinguished honor. [Loud and long continued applause.] His nomination is a guaranty to the country of an administration of the Constitution in its purity, with a just regard to all sections, and without partial and modern constructions of its spirit and provisions. [Renewed applause.] His election will restore confidence, secure peace to a restless people, and kindle anew the fires of patriotism and love of the Union in bosoms where those sentiments had begun to smoulder. He will receive a large and overwhelming majority in the Keystone State. [Enthusiastic cheers.] A majority demanded by her numerical power consistent with the integrity of her people and their loyalty to the Constitution and the Union of the States. Her gallant sons will rally from the Delaware to the Ohio; on the loftiest summit of her mountain range they will fling our banner to the breeze, bearing upon it the inscription of the honored name of "James Buchanan, our country and the Constitution," and victory as certain as that which attended the American arms upon the immortal battle fields of our national history will brighten in letters of living light upon its broad and ample folds as it will wave so gracefully and gallantly in triumph over the land. [Hearty and long-continued applause.]

Delaware casts her 3 votes for James Buchanan, Maryland 8, and Virginia 15.

When North Carolina was called,

Mr. Avery, Chairman of the North Carolina delegation, said—Mr. President, The delegation of North Carolina appeared in this Convention, with the view to battle for great principles, not for men. The platform adopted by the Convention commanded their most hearty approval; it is broad enough to hold every national man within the limits of the republic; nothing can be taken from it without impairing its symmetry; nothing can be added to it without marring its fair proportions. Under these circumstances we have been prepared to sustain the nominee who may be placed upon that platform with no ordinary zeal. We adhered to Franklin Pierce through many ballotings, not only as a matter of choice as being preferred by us above all others at this time, but because we conceived it a duty imposed upon the South to support him in view of the bold and manly stand taken by his Administration in maintaining the laws under the Constitution, and upholding the rights of all the States in this Union. When the State of New Hampshire, in a spirit of conciliation, abandoned her favorite son, we felt it a duty to pay a tribute of respect and gratitude to the distinguished son of Illinois, Stephen A. Douglas. And, General

Pierce out of the way, we could not have returned to our constituents without having manifested in some way our high appreciation of the eminent services rendered to his country by the author of the Kansas and Nebraska bill.

We have sustained by our votes thus far these two eminent men, in no factious spirit; and as it is apparent that the feeling of this Convention is in favor of the distinguished son of the Keystone State, we acquiesce in that manifestation of preference made by our political brethren here assembled. The Hon. James Buchanan was the first choice of North Carolina for President four years ago. He has undergone no change in political sentiments since that time, and our confidence in him has not been in any wise impaired, for the Democracy of North Carolina loves James Buchanan still. Pending his stay in Europe, events transpired which identified Messrs. Pierce and Douglas more prominently than others with certain leading issues before the country, and according to the views we entertained respecting their services in that behalf, we could not consistently abandon them while the name of either of them was before the Convention; *they* are now both withdrawn, and we come a united delegation with a hearty good will to the support of the man for whom North Carolina did battle four years ago. On behalf of the North Carolina delegation I cast ten votes for James Buchanan, of Pennsylvania. [Applause.

When South Carolina was called, Governor Manning addressed the President as follows:—

South Carolina, determined as she is to support the candidates placed upon the platform of principles erected by this Convention, has given that support in the first instance to Franklin Pierce of New Hampshire, and then to Stephen A. Douglas of Illinois, and she would have continued to yield to them an unfaltering support as long as their names were presented by their friends to the Convention. But there is something else that South Carolina has at heart, as much as her attachment to persons or friends in this contest—the preservation of the Constitution and the Union. By the action of this Convention, and by the presence here of South Carolina, the bond of brotherhood among all the States of this Union is undivided. South Carolina, Sir, casts her eight votes for James Buchanan, of Pennsylvania. [Loud applause.]

The State of Georgia being then called, Mr. Gardner said: The Georgia delegation, Sir, came here pledged to the support of the gentleman for whom her vote was first cast, and for whom her warm and cordial sympathies were enlisted. Next to him, the delegation, or at least a large portion of them, thought it their duty to come to the support of Judge Douglas, of Illinois. They considered it their duty to do so, in view of the fact that this gentleman had manfully battled for great constitutional and conservative principles. But we love not Pierce and Douglas alone; we have a warm and cordial Southern heart for James Buchanan. From the broad ocean's shore—from the midland counties of the State—from its mountains and its valleys, with a loud and exulting shout of triumph, the Democracy will come forward in support of James Buchanan; and we pledge to him the ten electoral votes of Georgia. [Applause.]

The State of Alabama was then called by the Secretary. Mr. Chapman, of Alabama, said: I hope, Sir, I shall be indulged by the Convention while I make a brief statement in regard to the position of Alabama. The delegation from that State came here united in support of Franklin Pierce. After he was withdrawn, they voted for Stephen A. Douglas. These votes, Sir, were not given on account of any hostility to the distinguished son of Pennsylvania, but because those gentlemen were, in our opinion, more immediately identified with the new question which has recently arisen. There is no State in the Union where the son of Pennsylvania is held in higher esteem and honor than the one from which I come. We still have confidence in him; he is still a favorite of Alabama. We have seen the unanimity with which the delegation from Pennsylvania have come to the support of our platform of principles, and this alone would be sufficient to impart confidence in the candidate they have presented to the Convention. We remember, too, that in the last Convention, James Buchanan was the first choice of Alabama; we remember that he was the favorite candidate of the lamented William R. King, who was associated on the same ticket with Franklin Pierce. And, humble as I am, I claim that no one excels me in confidence and esteem for the eminent statesman for whom Alabama is about to cast her vote. Not reluctantly, but with pleasure she gives her votes to James Buchanan, of Pennsylvania. [Cheers.]

The Secretary then called Mississippi, when Mr. Clayton, for the Mississippi delegation, said that by the vote of Mississippi, now about to be given, she desired to give one more evidence of her devotion to Democratic principles. She had thus far voted first for Pierce, next for Douglas, because she regarded them as the exponents and embodiment of her principles; but she never had any opposition to Mr. Buchanan. Four years ago she had voted for him twenty-seven times in the Baltimore Convention. She now again casts her vote for him, with a pledge that her people will ratify it by six thousand majority.

Mr. Matthews, of Mississippi, added: I desire to state, Sir, that Mississippi, in casting her vote first for Franklin Pierce, and then for Judge Douglas, wishes not to be understood as having any opposition to Pennsylvania's favorite son. She voted for those gentlemen as representatives of that great principle which claims to lie at the very foundation of American liberty. She did not for a moment suppose Mr. Buchanan to be opposed to that principle; but she considered Mr. Pierce and Mr. Douglas to be more intimately identified with it. Mississippi will support the nominee. With pride and pleasure she will take up the banner which the Democracy have entrusted to the hands of James Buchanan, and carry it in triumph through nearly every county in the State. Mississippi casts her seven votes for James Buchanan. [Loud cheering.]

President.—Let Louisiana be called.

Secretary.—Louisiana.

Gov. Marston.—Louisiana, as heretofore, casts her six votes for James Buchanan.

Ohio was next called, and she answered by Mr. Medary: It is with great pleasure, I announce to you, Mr. President, and the honorable delegates to this Convention, that Ohio has no longer to cast fractional votes. With the platform that you have given us as a bond of union for the Democracy of this great country, we are willing to fight under any leader that this Convention may select for us. I assure you, Mr. President, that as a personal friend of that Little Giant of the north-west, for whom so many of us have cast our votes, or for whom I am willing to do battle even single-handed, that no one will yield more pleasantly to the decision of the Convention; and I can speak also for the whole of the delegation with which I am associated, and that none will more readily and zealously support the nominee presented to us to-day. I pledge you, in behalf of the Democracy of Ohio, that as they have been so exact in casting their vote here, they will be equally exact in casting their whole vote for James Buchanan, and though divided here, they will be united at the polls, and will not consider their duty discharged till they have deposited their whole vote in the ballot box; and they will carry the State next November by at least twenty-five thousand majority. They will unite not only with their neighbors in Pennsylvania, but will stretch out their hands to the extreme South, the West and the East, to meet their Democratic brethren, and to assist in giving the death-blow to fanatacism in this country. Ohio casts her twenty-three votes for James Buchanan, of Pennsylvania. [Tremendous cheers.]

Kentucky, when her name was called, through Gov. Wickliffe, said: Kentucky, though she cannot promise her thousands in November next, yet she says to the Democracy of the Union now, that when the hour of battle arrives, she will give a majority to James Buchanan, for whom she now casts her 12 votes.

The Secretary then called Tennessee, and Mr. Bate, of Tennessee, said: We came here, gentlemen of the Convention, representing the spirit of the Democracy of Jackson and of Polk. I wish to state, on behalf of the Democracy of Tennessee, that they voted for the distinguished individual who now occupies the Executive chair, as the representative of the great principle which now presents the prominent issue before the country, and afterward, for the same reason, testified their appreciation of the eminent gentleman who introduced the measure. Tennessee, Sir, has not cast her vote for a Democratic candidate for the Presidency, since she voted for her own son, the illustrious Jackson. But standing here now, the representative, in part, of the Democracy of Tennessee, I promise that she will give for the nominee of this Convention, a Democratic majority of ten thousand votes. While here, we have cast the vote of Tennessee as a unit. There has been some division of opinion in the delegation. We now, however, give a heartfelt and entire vote to James Buchanan, of Pennsylvania.

Secretary.—Indiana.

Judge Borden.—Thirteen votes for James Buchanan, of Pennsylvania, now, and the same in November next.

Illinois was then called for, and Col. Richardson rose, in behalf of that State, and responded as follows: I am instructed by the delegation from the State of Illinois, to return to this Convention their heartfelt acknowldgements for the complimentary vote their distinguished son has received; and above and beyond all to return their thanks that while he has received one hundred and twenty-two votes as a candidate for the Presidency, before the highest tribunal known to the Democratic party; the adoption of the great principle embodied in that platform, which received the assent of every member of the Committee on Resolutions, and of every member of the Convention, has endorsed the political opinions of Stephen A. Douglas. While he has been complimented by that vote, the fact that the principles for which he has battled in the Senate and before the whole country, are made by the Democratic party the leading principles of its political faith, is a still higher compliment, which might excite sentiments of pride in the bosom of any man. We have come here, Sir, animated by no sectional spirit. We have come here in the full belief that the spirit of the Democratic party resides in its principles more than in its men. We have come to say to the Democratic party all over this Union that, as in times past, the Democratic banner has never been torn in Illinois, so it will not be torn in November next. Illinois joins her voice to the voices of the delegates of the other States, and casts her eleven votes for James Buchanan, of Pennsylvania.

Missouri was then called, and Mr. W. A. Harris answered: That before he cast the vote of his State, he was instructed to offer a few words of explanation. He said that it was known to the Convention that although the vote of Missouri had been cast as a unit for Judge Douglas, that there were on that delegation many friends of President Pierce, and also a large minority who preferred Mr. Buchanan as their first choice. Yet, having determined among themselves not to depart from the list of names before the Convention, they had from the beginning decided to vote for Mr. Pierce, or Mr. Douglas or Mr. Buchanan, till the one or the other was nominated. Mr. Douglas has endeared himself to the State of Missouri and to the whole country, in manfully standing up for all the great principles of the Constitution, in justly interpreting and enforcing all its guarantees and powers, with a constancy and fidelity never surpassed by any statesman of the country. But it was by his authorship of the Kansas-Nebraska bill, and his arguments of transcendent ability and eloquence in its support, and the moral heroism with which he has constantly met and vanquished the enemies of our peace, and the enemies of our Union, that he has established himself in the hearts and affections of the people. But, in a spirit of manly self-denial, he has directed his friends to withdraw his name from the list of those now before the Convention for nomination. We surrender him, therefore, to be warmed and cherished in the hearts of the people, to still further add to his glorious record of sound statesmanship, until his countrymen call upon him for the performance of still greater duties in higher spheres.

Thus, then, we are free to cast our united vote for him who, from the beginning and for many years, was the honored and long-cherished first choice of a large minority of us—a statesman of the greatest talents and ability, the most enlarged experience, and the most pre-eminent qualifications for the high office of President of the United States. His record of forty years is but the record of his wisdom and services as a statesman, his ability and sagacity as a diplomatist, and his devotion to the Union and the rights of the States. It is a record without a blemish and without a stain. The hearts of his countrymen are warmed and drawn to him with a force and a fervor which will bear him with shouts and acclamations into the Presidential chair. Being one of his original, ardent and long-devoted friends, my delegation has kindly accorded to me the grateful pleasure of casting our unanimous vote for that noble son of a noble State, James Buchanan, of Pennsylvania.

President—Call *Arkansas*.

Secretary—Arkansas !

Mr. Flournoy, of Arkansas—It is known, sir, to this Convention, that the delegation from Arkansas came here instructed to cast their vote for the present Executive, Franklin Pierce, of New Hampshire. In accordance with those instructions, they faithfully adhered to him until they saw he no longer had a chance to obtain the nomination of the Convention. They then came enthusiastically and harmoniously to the support of the Little Giant of Illinois. They have voted for him since that time, and wherever his banner was seen to float, there were we seen to battle. But, sir, we have had no factious opposition to make to any candidate. Our vote was merely the expression of a personal preference. It was well known to us, and well appreciated, that James Buchanan was a pure patriot and a great man, and that he was in every way worthy of our support and our vote. While, for a time, we did battle against him, we never meant our vote to go beyond the circle of the three names which were originally presented to this Convention, and we always intended, whenever there should be a firm and decided majority in favor of Mr. Buchanan, to show that we were animated by no factious spirit of opposition, and to add our vote to those of his supporters. We are now as enthusiastic friends of Mr. Buchanan as can be found on this floor. There is, sir, an anecdote in history which would well illustrate the position of Arkansas. When the Prince and Princess of Armenia were captured by Cyrus, and led out to receive the sentence of death or of banishment that might be imposed on them by the conqueror, and the Prince was asked what he had to say why sentence should not be pronounced, he answered that for himself he had nothing to say, but for the Princess he asked that she might be permitted to return to her own country—"as for me," he said, "do with me as you please." After she had returned, when all were expressing admiration for Cyrus, who was said to be the man of most gallant bearing in the world, the Princess was asked what she thought of him. She replied that she had never seen him. When surprise was manifested that she, who had been in his presence, had not seen him, she answered that she had no eyes except for the man who had been willing to sacrifice his own life to save hers. Thus, sir, it is with Arkansas. From this time till November, she will have no eyes except for James Buchanan. I pledge myself that, in November next, she will give for him in proportion to her vote a larger majority than any other State in the Union. And, sir, as I am always willing to back my judgment, I will bet a banner, to be worked by the fairest hands in Arkansas, that such will be the case.

Many members—We take the bet.

Mr. Flournoy—Well, sir, the banners will be ready to send to the States that win them, and I predict that after the election, we shall be overwhelmed with flags from every State in the Union. As I have said, we have hitherto been opposed to the nominee of this Convention, but our opposition has been guided by dignity and moderation. We expect—and we have some reason to expect it—that we shall meet with noble and generous conquerors, and that some little favor will be extended to us when we express a choice for the second office in the gift of the Convention. I now cast the four votes of Arkansas for James Buchanan, of Pennsylvania.

Secretary : Michigan !

Mr. ——— : Michigan still casts her six votes for James Buchanan.

Secretary : *Florida !*

Response : Florida casts her three votes for James Buchanan.

When the vote of Texas was called, Mr. Waelder, of Texas, said :

Mr. President : In 1852, when the final vote of the National Convention was taken, Texas had no speech to make, neither does she desire to impose a long speech upon the Convention of 1856 ; but, sir, as chairman of the Texas delegation, I desire to say these few words :

Heretofore the State of Texas has cast her four votes, first for Franklin Pierce, next for Stephen A. Douglas. In thus casting her vote, she did not regard James Buchanan as less pure, as less true to our common Constitution; but, sir, she voted for Franklin Pierce and Stephen A. Douglas, because they had been more actively engaged in the struggle which has of late convulsed every section of our country.

We heartily concur in the nomination of James Buchanan. As the Democracy of Pennsylvania have heretofore done battle for the constitutional rights of the South, and of every section of the Union, so the Democracy of the "Lone Star" do battle for that favorite, noble son of the "Keystone of the Arch." Sir, from the flowered prairies of the South-west we extend the Democratic hand of fellowship to the Democracy of every section of this Union.

As to the vote of Texas on the first Monday of November next, I will make no pledges. But that our majority for the Democratic cause will out-rival even that of the native State of the nominee, in proportion to the population of the two States, I have no doubt.

I now cast the four votes of the State of Texas (and I do so with great pleasure) for James Buchanan, of Pennsylvania.

Iowa next cast her four votes for James Buchanan.

Wisconsin being called : Five votes for James Buchanan.

The Secretary then called for California, when she answered as follows :

Mr. Inge, of California—Mr. President : California came here for the purpose of giving a frank, loyal and united support to the eminent statesman who is now receiving by general acclaim from this Convention the enthusiastic tribute of generous hearts, vindicating him as their unanimous choice for a position higher in moral grandeur than the loftiest of the imperial thrones of this Earth.

The expression of preference for Mr. Buchanan, on the part of our State Convention, left the delegation in no doubt as to the course proper for them to pursue. But the State Convention, at the same time that it expressed, in distinct terms, its preference for Buchanan, virtually instructed us to obtain from this National Convention of the great Democratic party, a full endorsement of the policy of a safe and speedy communication, through our own territory, between the Atlantic and Pacific coasts of this confederacy. It must be conceded that no achievement of American arms or diplomacy, has redounded more to the prosperity and glory of our country than the acquisition of California. [Here Mr. Inge was called to order by the President, who remarked, that he was traveling beyond the record, and could not proceed without the unanimous consent of the Convention. Cries of leave ! leave ! accompanied with applause, from all parts of the hall, invited the Speaker to proceed with his remarks, who continued as follows :

I am deeply grateful to this Convention for the consideration accorded to the distant State of California. This Convention remembers, Mr. President, that we have traveled six thousand miles, traversing two oceans, and braving the fiery sun and the deadly malaria of the tropics, to meet our democratic brothers here, and to aid in this glorious consummation. [Applause.] The acquisition of California, as I have said, was justly regarded as the most brilliant achievement of the American arms. To accomplish it much of the most precious blood of the republic has been shed. and millions of treasure have been lavishly expended. From the year 1800, from the days of Jefferson to the treaty of Guadalupe Hidalgo, the acquisition of that territory, has been a paramount object of American diplomacy. It has ever been the dream of our statesmen, and an object dear to the hearts of our people to make America an ocean-bound republic. [Applause.]

Well sir, that country has been acquired. She is now a member of our ocean-bound confederacy—the brightest star in the glorious constellation of American States. [Applause.] There she lies before you sir, filled with an industrious and energetic population; with her vast commercial and agricultural resources ; and with a climate, whose geniality attests, more than any other creation of Omnipotent power, the beneficence of God to his creatures. Above all she is distinguishable from her sisters, by the golden treasures, sparkling in exhaustless profusion upon her surface, and which lie embedded in her snow-capped mountains. But with all these facts entitling California to the favorable consideration of the federal government, after having been a sovereign member of the confederacy for nearly six years, after contributing five hundred millions of dollars to the wealth of the country. What has been done to facilitate communication between the Atlantic and Pacific coasts of the confederacy ? California, at this day, remains isolated in position, and practically out of the Union, by the failure of Congress to establish the means of an overland communication. On this subject the masses of the American people are united. State legislatures, mass meetings, the press of the country with its thousand tongues, have urged upon Congress prompt and efficient legislation, for the attainment of this great national object. Look, for a moment, at her present condition. The route across the plains, infested with hostile Indians, is no longer open to the adventurous march of the emigrant. In Nicaragua civil war rages ; in the midst of which there is no protection to life or property. The emigrant can only pass there, between files of contending soldiers, and with feet stained with human blood. At Panama, the brutal and savage negro, animated by the hope of plunder, have recently assailed our unarmed countrymen, inflicting death indiscriminately. Upon both the Isthmus routes, danger, disease and death stand in frightful array along the pathway of the emigrant. Sir, we ask that the federal government may exercise all its constitutional power, to provide a safe and speedy communication over our own territory between the Atlantic and Pacific coasts of this Union. A resolution embracing that policy, has been laid on the table by a vote of this Convention, the delegation from Pennsylvania, voting aye upon the motion to lay upon the table. With the vote of Pennsylvania, thus recorded, against a policy so vital to the interests of our State, the delegation from California have not felt it consistent with their own self respect, or with the dignity of the State which they have the honor to represent, to cast their votes for James Buchanan. But they have assurances now, that Mr. Buchanan does not concur in the opposition to that measure, indicated by the votes of the Pennsylvania delegation, and we therefore cordially acquiesce in his nomination, and pledge our State to his support. Sir, we do more, we pledge her to an overwhelming majority. When the shouts of victory from the East boom across the plains and ascend the lofty summits of the Cordilleras, they will be met by responsive shouts of triumph from the golden valleys of the Pacific State. [Tremendous applause.]

[Subsequently the proposition for an overland communication, within our own territory between the Atlantic and Pacific, was voted upon, directly, by the Convention, the Pennsylvania delegation voting unanimously against laying the same on the table; and, on its final passage a portion of said delegation voted for, and a portion against its adoption; said proposition having been carried; ayes 205, noes 87.]

The President of the Convention—Gentlemen: The result of the seventeenth ballot is as follows: James Buchanan has received 296 votes, which being the whole vote cast, and the entire vote of the Convention, I announce with pleasure, that James Buchanan, of Pennsylvania, is unanimously nominated as the Democratic candidate for President of the United States. [Vociferous cheering; long continued.]

Here shouts were raised for Col. Black, of Pennsylvania; whereupon after silence was restored, the Hon. Samuel Black rose and spoke as follows:

Col. Samuel W. Black, of Pennsylvania—Mr. President: At the unanimous request of the Pennsylvania delegation, I rise to express their thanks for the high honor conferred upon our State, in the unanimous vote of this Convention, now recorded for James Buchanan. I do not design, sir, to weary the well tried patience of this assembly with a set speech. Your labors have been protracted and severe. It is desirable and just that we should bring them to a speedy and harmonious conclusion. Pennsylvania, in whose name and stead I am permitted to speak, offers from her heart, to every other state of the confederacy, this public acknowledgment of deep and sincere gratitude. Every portion of our country is here represented. I do not say section, for, sir, with the Democracy of Pennsylvania that term is abhorred, and the spirit of sectionalism is a by-word and reproach. We recognize, and will forever maintain and defend every several right of every sovereign State of the American Union. And we will vindicate, with the same spirit that leads us to assert the sovereign rights of our own State, the rights of the people of every territory to settle for themselves their own form of Government—to choose their own Democratic institutions and to manage them according to the council and pleasure of their own will—they, like as we do, submitting in all things to the guidance and control of the Constitution of the United States. We believe that sentiments similar to these will form amongst the American people a prevailing aud perpetual bond of Union. Universal confidence and kindness will take the place of distrust and jealousy. It is only by an open and manly recognition of the rights that belong to every State and Territory, that we can hope for a peaceful perpetuity to our Union.

That we may attest our earnestness, Pennsylvania, in the presence of her country's star-lit flag, and in his presence who is the pattern of his country and the father also to the Constitution, though not its author, we renew our vows of fidelity to the Union and the Constitution. (A portrait of Washington, festooned with flags, was directly in front of the speaker).

If the evil day should come, which God mercifully avert, when we should see the rights of any State abused or crushed, her appeal to Pennsylvania will not be in vain. If she is feeble, her weakness will strengthen our attachment and love. Our beloved State will say from the heart to the heart—"Entreat me not to leave thee, nor to return from following after thee; where thou goest I will go, where thou lodgest I will lodge, thy people shall be my people, and thy God my God. Where thou diest I will die, and there will I be buried. The Lord do so to me and mine also, if aught but death part thee and me." (Great emotion and applause).

But, sir, I have wandered from my duty, and returning to it I renew our thanks to every State represented in this Convention. Before I close allow me to vindicate Pennsylvania's favorite son against the charge of having failed in that higher duty which every man owes to himself, to society and to the sweeter sex. Mr. Buchanan, we confess, is a bachelor. But the reason is a complete vindication as will, I am sure, satisfy every gentleman here present. It is this—as soon as James Buchanan was old enough to marry, he became wedded to the Constitution of his country, and the laws of Pennsylvania do not allow a man to have more than one wife.

For some time the cheers, long and loud, from without, and the roar of cannon, had announced that along the telegraphic wires the glad news was streaming to every part of the Republic that James Buchanan was the unanimous choice of the American Democracy for President of the United States.

After the vote had been duly recorded, there was such a general sensation, that it was difficult to proceed with other business.

B. F. Hallett, from the Committee on Resolutions, reported the following :

Resolved, That the administration of Franklin Pierce has been true to the great interests of the country. In the face of the most determined opposition it has maintained the laws, enforced economy, fostered progress, and infused integrity and vigor into every department of the government at home. It has signally improved our treaty relations, extended the field of commercial enterprise, and vindicated the rights of American citizens abroad. It has asserted with eminent impartiality the just claims of every section, and has at all times been faithful to the Constitution. We therefore proclaim our unqualified approbation of its measures and its policy.

Adopted, with long and rapturous applause, and unanimously.

The Committee on Resolutions, to whom was referred the resolution submitted by the delegation for Virginia, have instructed their Chairman to ask that they be discharged from its further consideration.

June 5, 1856. B. F. HALLETT, *Chairman.*

Which Report was concurred in.

H. B. Wright, of Pennsylvania, with remarks, offered the following resolution:

Resolved, That the proceedings in this Convention, relating to the conflicting delegations from the State of New York, be stricken from the record thereof, and that we earnestly recommend to both delegations here present to unite in a call for a single State Convention to nominate an electoral ticket and ticket for State officers.

The following are the remarks of Mr. Beardsley, Mr. Ludlow and Governor Seymour, of New York, upon the resolution offered by Mr. Wright, of Pennsylvania, to expunge from the reports of the Committee on Credentials all but the resolutions in the New York case:

Mr. Beardsley rose deliberately and said—For the representatives of our section of the Democracy of New York, I am ready to avow here, that they have every wish to unite the Democracy of New York on sound principles, and to sustain the nomination made here and all who stand firmly on the platform which has been erected by the Convention. They, sir, have no reproaches to make. They honestly agree to act as they believe to be the wish of their brethren throughout the Union, and they entertain the firm conviction that the vote of New York will exhibit a glorious Democratic victory at the coming election. I have said enough to show what we feel, and I do not mean to imply a doubt that our brethren in New York will participate in these feelings, and act in accordance with the pledge we have given.

Mr. Ludlow—On behalf of the delegation which I have the honor to represent, I most cordially and most heartily reciprocate the sentiments avowed by the Chairman of the other delegation. Sir, I congratulate the Democracy of New York; I congratulate the Democracy of Pennsylvania; I congratulate the Democracy of the whole Union, that the proposition has been introduced by the gentleman who has been representing Pennsylvania on this floor. The introduction of that resolution is a pledge on the part of the friends of Mr. Buchanan that whatever differences may have grown up, are eradicated forever. By the adoption of that resolution, New York stands pledged next fall to elect the Democratic nominee. As an accompaniment to that resolution, not as an amendment, but I hope it will be accepted by the mover of the resolution now before the Convention, I have one in my hand, which I wish to offer. Divided as we have been, it may give rise to some embarrassment in New York to choose a member of the National Committee. I propose that the election of that member may be referred to the next State Convention held under that resolution.

Which proposition being opposed by Mr. Beardsley, of N. Y., was, at the request of Horatio Seymour, of N. Y., and others, withdrawn by Mr. Ludlow, and the original resolution unanimously adopted.

Thereupon the Convention adjourned until 2 o'clock, P. M.

AFTERNOON SESSION, JUNE 6, 1856.

At 2 o'clock the Convention was called to order.

Mr. Shields, of Missouri, rose and said—Mr. President, I have been unanimously instructed by the Delegation from Missouri to offer in their name, the resolution which I now send to the Clerk's table to be read, and I ask this Convention to adopt the same, not only as an act of justice to the Great West and our Pacific brethren, but as a measure to bind more closely together our wide-spread Union in enduring bonds. It has been framed with a view to secure, if possible, the unanimous approval of this body. The President decided that under the rules, the resolution must go, without debate, to the Committee on Resolutions. The resolution was as follows:—

Resolved, That it is the duty of the Federal Government to construct, so far as it has constitutional power so to do, a safe overland communication within our own territory between the Pacific and Atlantic States.

Mr. Saunders of Wisconsin—I offer the following amendment to the resolution of the gentleman from Missouri, and I move that the Committee on Resolutions be instructed to report it back to the Convention with the recommendation that the same be adopted.

Resolved, That the Democratic party recognizes the great importance, in a political and commercial point of view, of a safe and speedy communication through our own territory between the Atlantic and Pacific coasts of the Union, and that it is the duty of the Federal Government to exercise all its constitutional power to the attainment of that object, thereby binding the Union of these States in indissoluble bonds, and opening to the rich commerce of Asia an overland transit from the Pacific to the Mississippi River, and the great lakes of the North.

Here Gov. Chapman raised a point of order, viz.: that under the special order of the Convention we must now proceed to the nomination of Vice President.

President—There is no such special order.

Mr. Thompson, of Mississippi, moved to lay the whole subject on the table.

Mr. Shields accepted the resolution of the gentleman of Wisconsin, as an amendment of his own.

On the motion to lay on the table, the votes by States being taken, resulted as follows—Ayes 74, nays 220.

AYES—New Hampshire 4, Massachusetts 1, Rhode Island 2, Connecticut 4, New Jersey 7, Delaware 1, Virginia 15, North Carolina 10, South Carolina 8, Georgia 7, Mississippi 7, Ohio 6, Tennessee 1, Florida 3—74.

NAYS—Maine 8, New Hampshire 1, Vermont 5, Massachusetts 12, Rhode Island 2, Connecticut 2, New York 35, Pennsylvania 27, Delaware 2, Maryland 8, Georgia 31, Alabama 9, Louisiana 6, Ohio 17, Kentucky 12, Tennessee 11, Indiana 13, Illinois 11, Missouri 9,

Arkansas 4, Michigan 6, Texas 4, Iowa 4, Wisconsin 5, California 4—220.

So the motion to lay on the table was lost.

Mr. Phelps of Missouri—If my friend from Michigan will withdraw his motion, which is out of order, I will move to suspend the rules, which will bring the Convention to a direct vote on the resolution itself.

President—The motion of the gentleman from Wisconsin is out of order—does he give way for the gentleman from Missouri.

Mr. Saunders—I withdraw my motion, and make that suggested by the gentleman from Missouri—that the rules be suspended.

The vote was called for by States, and was as follows :—

Ayes—Maine 8, New Hampshire 1, Vermont 5, Massachusetts 11, Rhode Island 2, Connecticut 3, New York 35, Pennsylvania 6, Delaware 2, Maryland 8, Georgia 3, Alabama 9, Missouri 7, Louisiana 6, Ohio 19, Kentucky 12, Tennessee 11, Indiana, 13, Illinois 11, Missouri 9, Arkansas 4, Michigan 6, Texas 4, Iowa 4, Wisconsin 5, California 4—208.

Nays—New Hampshire 4, Massachusetts 2, Rhode Island 2, Connecticut 3, New Jersey 7, Pennsylvania 21, Delaware 1, Virginia 15, North Carolina 10, South Carolina 8, Georgia 7, Ohio 4, Tennessee 1, Florida 3—88.

So the rules were suspended, by a vote of two-thirds.

Mr. Inge, of California, then moved the adoption of the resolution, and on this motion called for the previous question.

The call for the previous question being sustained, the vote was taken on the resolution, and resulted as follows :—

Ayes—Maine 8, New Hampshire 1, Vermont 5, Massachusetts 11, Rhode Island 2, Connecticut 3, New York 35, Pennsylvania 6, Delaware 1, Maryland 8, Georgia 6, Alabama 9, Mississippi 7, Louisiana 6, Ohio 14, Kentucky 12, Tennessee 11, Indiana 13, Illinois 11, Missouri 9, Arkansas 4, Michigan 6, Texas 4, Iowa 4, Wisconsin 5, California 4—205.

Nays—New Hampshire 4, Massachusetts 2, Rhode Island 2, Connecticut 3, New Jersey 7, Pennsylvania 21, Delaware 1, Virginia 15, North Carolina 10, South Carolina 8, Georgia 4, Ohio 6, Tennessee 1, Florida 3—87.

So the resolution was adopted by the Convention.

Mr. Phelps, of Missouri—I now move to reconsider the vote adopting the resolution, and move further that said motion be laid on the table, so as to clinch the passage of said resolution. Adopted.

The President then announced that the next business in order was the nominations for Vice President.

Mr. C. A. Wickliffe, of Kentucky, arose and said, I am instructed unanimously by the delegation to present to the Convention, for the second office in the gift of the Democracy, that tried Democrat of their own State, Linn Boyd, of Kentucky. [Loud applause.]

Thomas L. Harris, of Illinois.—Mr. President: By the unanimous vote of the delegation from Illinois, I present to the Convention for the Vice Presidency the name of a gentleman who, though born on the banks of the Hudson, now lives on the banks of the Mississippi. He was a gentleman of whom the whole nation was proud; who was equally distinguished for the boldness, as for the goodness of his heart; whose nature was as warm and affectionate as it was true and gallant. I have had the honor to serve under him in the perilous scenes of a fierce conflict in a hostile and distant land, and I can bear personal testimony to his patriotism, his fidelity to duty, his dauntless bravery—he was ever foremost where danger and duty called. He it was who so nobly led the gallant volunteers of his country through such appalling dangers into the very heart of the enemy's capital, and there first, on one of the loftiest citadels of the Montezumas, planted the banner of the Republic. This name, which Illinois, with her unanimous voice and all her heart, presented to the Convention for the Vice Presidency, was John A. Quitman, of Mississippi. [Immense and prolonged applause.]

Gen. J. L. Lewis, of Louisiana, was instructed by his delegation to present the name of John C. Breckinridge, of Kentucky, for the Vice Presidency. [Applause.]

Mr. Breckinridge arose amid great applause. It was some time before the cheering ceased and he could be heard. He said:

Mr. President: How can I adequately express my gratitude to the noble State of Louisiana, for this flattering manifestation of their good will? But, Sir, I have always held that promotion should follow seniority. Besides, I am already a candidate for the votes of the people, having been designated by the Democracy as the elector in my district, and expect soon to enter upon an active campaign—to traverse the valleys and climb the mountains of my native State, in behalf of the distinguished and noble candidate we have already selected for the Presidency, and, in advocacy of the glorious State Rights Platform, which we have adopted with such signal unanimity. There is still another reason why my name should not be pressed for this high post. The delegation of my own State, with which I cordially concur, have already presented the name of one of her sons—a tried and able champion of Democracy—for this very office. I can never consent that my name should be placed in opposition to, or my merits in competition with his. I beg, therefore, with grateful acknowledgements for the high compliment offered me by the delegation from Louisiana, that my name may be withdrawn. [Great applause.]

Mr. Chapman, of Alabama—Mr. President: In behalf of the Alabama delegation, I am proud to present for the consideration of the Convention, the name of one of her tried and talented statesmen; one who has already—in the high office he so worthily fills—evinced his fidelity to the faith of the Democracy; I name Benjamin Fitzpatrick. With such a name associated with that of Pennsylvania's great and wise statesman, Alabama, in the next contest, will roll up a majority of fifteen thousand. In answer to the objection that the last Vice President was taken from Alabama, I would remind the Convention of the melancholy event by which the nation was deprived of the services of that distinguished statesman, so long the intimate and confidential friend of James Buchanan. [Applause.]

A delegate from Tennessee nominated A. V. Brown, and spoke of his fidelity to the Democracy for thirty years; his intimacy and cordial co-operation with Jackson and Polk, and declared that, with his name, the Democratic party would, in the next election, achieve one of the most brilliant triumphs in the history of political victories.

Mr. Wilson, of South Carolina—Mr. President: In behalf of the delegation of South Carolina, I beg to present to the Convention the name of one of the distinguished sons of the Old Dominion, whom genius, eloquence and sound Democracy commend him to the people, as the man for the high position for which we are now about to nominate the candidate. Sir, I allude to James A. Seddon. [Great applause.]

Jas. A. Seddon of Virginia—Mr. President, I appreciate profoundly the honor conferred by the nomination just made, and am especially gratified by the source whence it has proceeded. To receive the approving plaudits of the "gallant Percy of the South" is inestimably grateful to my feelings, and till my heart's last throb must be borne in indelible remembrance. I must, however, decline the nomination tendered, and beg the honorable gentleman to withdraw my name from the candidacy. The Virginia delegation, with my entire assent, have concurred in the sentiment that, considering the circumstances under which she has acted and the position she has occupied in relation to the nomination for the Presidency, it would be more consistent with her dignity and honor that no son of hers should be placed in nomination for the Vice-President. In addition, I may add as my private judgment, that it would be more judicious and disinterested that no nomination for the Vice-Presidency should be made from among the delegates to the nominating body. In deference, therefore, both to the ascertained sentiment of my co-delegates and to my personal conviction, I beg, with all respect to the gallant State proposing me, that my name be withdrawn, and I am happy to be able to illustrate in my own case the principle of disinterestedness commended by my State and my own judgment.

Mr. Avery, of North Carolina—I am instructed by the delegation of North Carolina to call the attention of the Convention to the merits and qualifications of one of her distinguished sons, whose ability and high administrative talents have been so conspicuously displayed in that department of the Executive Government which is most intimately connected with the interest and feelings of the people. North Carolina was a modest State; she rarely obtruded her pretensions on her brothers of other States; but the great attainments, eminent services and wide popularity of her son, induced her delegation now to present his name for the second office in the gift of the Democracy. North Carolina presented the name of James C. Dobbin. [Loud cheers.]

Mr. Underwood, of Georgia—Mr. President: Since the Government was established, Georgia has had but three Cabinet or excutive offices in the Government. Her recent brilliant triumphs for the Democracy give some claims to be considered in the choice of the candidate for at least the second office in the Government, I will, therefore, present the name of one of her sons who, in two of the severest political battles ever fought in the State, bore with his stalwart arm and dauntless heart the flag of Democracy to glorious victory, that man who had met one of the fiercest and most dangerous factions that ever raised its grim front in the land, and sent it howling back to its den.

I propose the name of Herschell V. Johnson. [Loud applause.]

Mr. Moore, of Maine, presented the name, and gave the eight votes of his State for Thomas J. Rusk, of Texas.

A delegate from Texas said that, while the delegation from Texas felt highly honored in having her favorite son named for the Vice-Presidency, they felt it their duty to that distinguished citizen to beg that his name be withdrawn. General Rusk had recently received the unanimous vote of the Legislature of his State for the United States Senate, and he felt it to be his duty to remain at his post and fulfill the wishes and guard the honor and interests of his State in that important sphere.

Mr. G. Salisbury, of Delaware, nominated Jas. A. Bayard, of his State, for the Vice-Presidency.

Mr. W. Salisbury, of Delaware—I nominate that eminent son of Delaware, and distinguished Democrat of Missouri, the standard-bearer of its gallant Democracy, Trusten Polk.

Mr. Phelps, of Missouri: Missouri highly appreciates this compliment to her distinguished citizen, coming as it does from his native State; but that gentleman had already been placed in nomination by the Democracy of Missouri for the Governorship of the State. He was already in the field, and the Democracy of Missouri could not spare him for any other post. He begged, therefore, that his name might be withdrawn.

In that State the contest is a peculiar one. Our geographical position and the strange effort made there by those upon whose pretensions this Convention has already passed, demands that the eloquent voice of our nominee for Governor shall continue to be heard, arousing her true Democracy as by a trumpet blast to the great battle, in which all friends of the Constitution and Union are now to engage under the national championship of the honored son of Pennsylvania. The Democracy of Missouri, by acclamation, put their standard into his hands—they mean to respond with enthusiasm to his appeals. Only a few weeks are to elapse before the election. It is too late for them in that vast State to change front now, by substitution of a new Gubernatorial candidate. Knowing his devotion to the cause, as manifested in the self-sacrifice he made, in consenting to bear our State banner, notwithstanding the situation of his private affairs, and knowing that his pure patriotism always beats exultant to the call of duty, regardless of self, the Missouri Delegation, profoundly thankful for the warm regard expressed by his native State, as well as others, beg his friends from Delaware to withdraw his name. Missouri, in her State election, must meet the first shock of the conflict. It is important that she should meet it triumphantly. The Democracy of the Union need Trusten Polk where he now is, and where Missouri has placed him. [Cheers.]

The President.—The Convention will now proceed to ballot for a candidate for the Vice Presidency. The Secretary will call the States.

Maine.—Rusk, 8 votes.

New Hampshire.—Quitman, 1; Fitzpatrick, 2; Dobbin, 2.

When Vermont was called, Mr. Smalley said—The delegation of Vermont believing that no Democrat has a right to refuse his services when his country calls, have instructed me to cast the five votes of Vermont for the talented, accomplished and eloquent son of Kentucky, John C. Breckinridge. [Loud applause.]

John C. Breckinridge, 5.

Massachusetts—Quitman, 1; Fitzpatrick, 2; Brown, 6; Johnson, 1; Bayard, 1; Rusk, 2.
Rhode Island—Johnson, 4.
Connecticut—Johnson, 6.
New York—Quitman, 7; Bayard, 18.
New Jersey—Boyd, 2; Polk, 5.
Pennsylvania—Butler, 27.
Delaware—Bayard, 3.
Maryland—Johnson, 8.
Virginia—Breckinridge, 15.
North Carolina—Dobbin, 10.
South Carolina—Quitman, 8.
Georgia—Johnson, 10.
Alabama—Fitzpatrick, 9.
Mississippi—Quitman, 7.
Louisiana—Breckinridge, 6.
Ohio—Quitman, 8; Boyd, 6; Johnson, 2; Breckinridge, 7.
Kentucky—Boyd, 12.
Tennessee—Brown, 12.
Indiana—Boyd, 13.
Illinois—Quitman, 11.
Missouri—Bayard, 9.
Arkansas—Quitman, 4.
Michigan—Brown, 6.
Florida—Dobbin, 4.
Texas—Quitman, 3; Brown, 1.
Iowa—Breckinridge, 4.
Wisconsin—Rusk, 5.
California—Brown, 4.

Before the vote was announced, Maine changed her 8 votes from Rusk to Breckinridge; and New Hampshire changed her 5 votes, and cast them also for Breckinridge.

Total.—Quitman, 59; Boyd 33; Fitzpatrick, 11; Brown, 29; Dobbin, 13; Johnson, 31; Breckinridge, 51; Bayard, 31; Polk, 5; Butler, 27; Rusk, 7,

On the second ballot, Maine, New Hampshire and Vermont led off for Breckinridge—Massachusetts followed with eleven out of thirteen votes—Rhode Island followed with her four, then the New York Softs gave him eighteen. Delaware, Maryland and Virginia voting in the same way, it became quite obvious that he was the choice of the body, and though several of the remaining States voted for other candidates, they quickly, one by one, changed their votes; the several delegates making neat and appropriate speeches in announcing the change of the vote. The entire vote being polled for John C. Breckinridge, of Kentucky.

Then commenced the withdrawal.

Mr. Salisbury withdrew the name of Bayard, and threw the vote of Delaware for Breckinridge.

When Connecticut was called, P. C. Childs said: Mr. President— Let the South say whom they desire for this office, and we will put him through in a minute. If they don't agree, Connecticut will put Isaac Toucey in the field.

Another delegate from Connecticut—Oh, no: we will keep Toucey for some higher game.

Chapman, of Albama, withdrew Fitzpatrick and threw the vote of that State for Breckinridge.

Col. Bates, of Tennessee, withdrew A. V. Brown, pledging his cordial support of the ticket and declaring the vote for Breckinridge.

Governor Matthews, of Mississippi, after returning thanks to Illinois for placing Mississippi's favorite son in nomination, withdrew the name of Quitman.

All the other candidates were severally withdrawn by the gentlemen who had nominated them.

Quickly all the other States changed their votes, wheeled into line, and before the roll was concluded there was a solid column of all the delegations, and TWO HUNDRED AND NINETY-SIX votes were given for John C. Breckinridge. (Immense cheering, long continued, enthusiastic and overwhelming.)

The whole Convention rose, and with waving of handkerchiefs and and the loudest calls, directed its gaze upon the tall and graceful delegate from Kentucky, who had been so unexpectedly nominated for such an exalted post.

It was long before these demonstrations subsided so as to allow a word to be heard. At last the manly form of Mr. Breckinridge stood above the surrounding crowd, and silence and profound attention marking the aspect of the vast assembly, he spoke as follows:

Mr. President, and gentlemen of the Democratic National Convention: The result just announced is quite as unexpected to me as it could be to any gentlemen on this floor. In the inferior and personal aspect of the matter, I beg you to consider all said that ought to be said on such an occasion. I am truly and sincerely without words to convey to you my profound gratitude for such an unexpected and signal testimonial of your confidence and favor. I may say sincerely, and call upon my associates in this body to bear witness to its truth, that in my course as a member of this body, I have made no concealments of my preferences, nor used any art or taken one step toward bringing about this result.

But it is not my purpose to make a speech. I merely arose to express to you the thanks of a true heart. I may add, too, the declaration of my high appreciation of the association of my humble name with that of the distinguished and tried statesman of Pennsylvania. I have always regarded Mr. Buchanan as the last survivor of that noble band of American statesmen and orators, whose names are associated with the brightest glories of our country, and whose deeds constitute its most cherished memorials. He has come down from that generation to transmit and guide us of the present. He has lived down calumny and detraction, and now stands forth the peerless champion of Democracy. Honored and beloved by all his countrymen, and only waiting a few months to be clothed with the highest dignity the nation and the people can confer.

The platform you have so unanimously adopted I need not, as a State-Rights man, say I cordially approve and indorse. With these true Jeffersonian principles, and with the temper of Jackson to enforce and maintain them, Democracy will enter the contest with the determination to add another to the brilliant victories which have so often crowned their efforts. It would not be appropriate to discuss any general principle or enter further upon the issues which will be involved in this contest. I will therefore conclude by expressing my purpose to devote all my heart and mind to the great duty which has been so unexpectedly conferred upon me, and to strive to justify the confidence which you have manifested. [Immense applause. Loud cheers within and without the hall.]

During the delivery of the speech of Mr. Breckinridge, the cannon of the Empire Club were thundering their approval of the nomination, and the Convention was boisterous in its applause.

When Mr. Breckinridge resumed his seat, there was a loud call for Mr. Preston of Kentucky, when that gentleman came forward and addressed the Convention in an eloquent off-hand speech, which produced the most thrilling effect.

Wm. E. Preston, of Kentucky said: Mr. President and Gentlemen of the Convention, I am at present laboring under much physical debility, but I can not feel insensible to the honor you have done me, by thus unexpectedly calling me to the stand. Although by this expression of your esteem, so genially given, I feel as much surprised as my friend and comrade must have been, by the great testimonial which you have but just now given by his selection —I will not say nomination—for the office of Vice-Presidency of the United States. For myself, I stand here comparatively a stranger amongst you; but he had a right by inheritance to the favorable opinions of the Democracy, and his elevation to the second office in the Government, is an auspicious augury of the return of Kentucky to the Democratic faith of her fathers. (Great applause.) It is the preliminary announcement of the return of my native State to the honored principles of the past, those principles which were in the ascendant, when John Breckinridge of Kentucky, the grand-father of the nominee, asserted with all the strength of a virtuous purpose and signal ability the celebrated resolutions of 1798, the foundation upon which yet repose the principles of the Democratic party, and their theory of the Constitution. I do not appropriate to myself personally the loud acclaims which have greeted me in this assembly, but I regard it as a generous earnest of that magnanimous regard which the Democracy have exhibited for all that true and loyal band of old Whigs whose honorable existence as a party having closed are now compelled to choose between the factions,—I will not flatter them with the name of parties,—that are struggling in unprincipled confusion for political ascendancy, and the great party of the national Democracy. I am proud to avow that I belong to those old Whigs who, revering the Constitution of our country, look alone to its principles as the true safeguard of the Union, rather than to the bigoted and trenchant rituals of a secret organization. You know, Mr. President, the glories of the men to whom I allude. They have come forward animated alone by love of Rebublican freedom, and disdaining the senseless mummeries of the Know Nothng order, and the treasonable doctrine of the Black Republican party, as honorable auxilliaries, to swell the ranks that to-day array themselves under the banner of the National Democracy, and under the brilliant leadership of Buchanan and Breckinridge. (Cheers.) I feel, sir, a profound satisfaction that we came to the aid of the party now assembled, and joined its standard in the hour of darkness and peril, without terms or compromise, neither asking honors, no longer as enemies but as friends determined to stand by that party which did not hesitate to sustain the Union and the Constitution. In many an honorable field, in many a tough contest, the old Whig party, led by its venerated statesmen, have encountered the Democracy, and sometimes with success. The policy of both were based on the Constitution, and were patriotic and comprehensive, but different. No blush of shame rose either to the cheek of the victor or the vanquished party when the fight was over but a manly acquiescence in the verdict of the people was yielded to the successful party. No oaths to proscribe the friendless, no obligations to infringe religious freedom stain their history, no treasonable dogmas like those of the Black Republicans, impairing, if carried into effect, the equality of the States and violating the Constitution, marked the race, but a free and honorable difference of opinion as to the commercial, financial and domestic policy which should be pursued by the nation. Against such factions, however, it now becomes the duty of the Whig party to do battle or send in servile capitulation. It is between them and the Democracy that the old Whigs of the country are compelled to decide. My choice is made, (cheers) and when I see around me the numbers of delegates who once were members of that organization—when I see them seeking refuge in the unshaken battalions of the Democracy—when I know that two or three hundred thousand of the old Whig party share our sentiments, I cannot doubt result. It would be unjust in me, to refuse the testimony I offer to the gallant and patriotic stand made by the Democracy during the last two years of the darkest hours that threatened the country. Standing as it does this day, it is more glorious far, than at any former period of its history. It occupies a grander position than when by the foresight of Jefferson, it secured the bright and fertile plains of Louisiana, or when it added the beautiful savannahs of Texas to the Union, or when it planted in triumph our standard upon the turrets of Mexico, or when it completed the continental breadth of the empire, by giving it an ocean boundary on either side, or when it impressed the arts, the arms, the civilization and the free institutions of our people upon the golden shores of California. (Applause.) Yes, Mr. President, grander by far stands the Democratic party of to-day, than at either of those proud epochs; because in the day of gloom and disaster it courageously confronted domestic dissentions, trampled under foot the foul theory of factions, and now prepares, in this hall, by these principles, and under the leaders to-day chosen, to maintain to the last extremity those principles upon which rest the prosperity of our country and the peaceful union of these States. It is true that, remembering rather the animosities of the past than the emergencies of the present, there are some of the old Whig guard that, like John Bunyan's pilgrims, yet halt at Doubting Castle; but when the telegraph bears upon its wings the result of this day's deliberations, their cheeks will no longer be sicklied with irresolution, but they will rush to your standard and join you for the common cause of their country. (Great applause.)

Permit me to add another remark: There were in the States of the North a company of gallant men feeling the full force of constitutional obligations and recognizing the sovereign right of the States of the Confederacy both to regulate their own internal affairs and to lend the impress of our institutions to the common territory of the country, without sectional distinction, who, when Douglas, with the intrepidity of genius and the foresight of a statesman sought to remove forever the irritating causes which for thirty years, had produced festering discontent at the North and the South, came forward as a forlorn hope, in the passage of the Nebraska-Kansas act. I shall never forget the deep emotions of respect and admiration with which I saw them repair to resist the sectional prejudices of the people they represented. It exhibited a moral grandeur worthy of the best days of the Republic. They prepared to execute at once and forever an act which was the logical consequence of the compromise of 1850, and to remove forever from the domination of Congress to the tribunals of the territories, the decision of the only great question which has disturbed the fraternal love of our country. All knew that the act was of such magnitude that it could not be performed without hearing a loud outcry of fanatics, mal-contents and demagogues, but they proved themselves equal to the occasion. The tempest burst forth with all its fury; every foul element of religious rancor and hatred of race, was invoked to increase its strength. The treasonable wave of the Black Republican party united with the fierce fanatacism of the miscalled American order, swept over the land, and few were able to withstand the shock. I see many around me who were the victims of the misguided vengeance of the people. Let such men be remembered in your coming hour of victory. If they should never arise from their prostrate position, they have fallen because of their patriotism and courage, and the epitaph which marked the spot where the immortal three hundred fell at Thermopylæ, might well be inscribed to commemorate their deeds: "Go, stranger, and at Lacedæmon tell that here, obedient to her laws, we fell." But I can not believe that such injustice would ever mark the history of the Democracy. I believe that the people, when the public reason is restored, will again lift them in their arms, bind up their wounds, and amid the clangor of the approaching Presidential contest, will hail them as leaders in the greatest battle which it has ever been the fortune of the Democracy to offer in behalf of the Constitution and the union, against all comers. *The first duty of the Democracy is to restore those to honor who who were the first to maintain, at all hazards, the principles and honor of the Democratic party*, and whom the enemies of the Democracy first ovewhelmed.

In conclusion, I return thanks, Mr. President, once more for the high kindness with which I have been signalized by this Convention; and, in tendering co-operation and allegiance to the Democratic party, I shall attempt, as far as lies within my humble power, to ride deep into the ranks of our adversaries, and win my spurs in the approaching battle. I shall do this in no inimical spirit, but I trust with all the fervor and sincerity of a man who appreciates the priceless blessings that our Union confers, believes that they can only be preserved by regarding all our people as equal without respect to institutions or sections, and is determined while his heart beats to know no friends or political associations which do not struggle to attain this end and preserve the Union by the only means it can be preserved, which is by a strict observance of the Constitution under which we live. I thank heaven that while I stand here to-day and gaze across at the hills of my native Kentucky, I stand with a party which by the unanimous voices of the delegates of thirty-one States, has emblazoned its policy upon its banner, by the party which, by a unanimous voice, has selected its leaders—leaders of known worth, ability and patriotism, as the exponents of its ideas, and a party which is the same, both in principles and in candidates, from the Atlantic to the Pacific, from Canada to the Gulf—a party that stands majestic in its strength and simplicity, divided by no chain of mountains, severed by no river, while all the other contending factions that hover around it, find that Southern institutions are the boundaries of their patriotism, and the Ohio river the frontier of their nationality. (Tremendous cheering.)

Mr. Petit, of Indiana, said—Mr. President, I thank you for the honor you have done me in calling me up on this occasion. There is in the history of the past of our party but little to bring a blush mantling upon the cheek; while if we look forward there is much to beckon onward, and invite us to new hopes, new trials, new victories and rewards. With the platform you have presented, you will march to victory, and give repose to the country.

You have crushed out the viper of a secret organization which disseminated itself through the land, poisoning the springs of liberal and virtuous political action; and you stand upon a firm foundation with your candidates before the country, certain to triumph in the approaching contest. [Mr. Petit spoke further, but in consequence of confusion upon the floor we were unable to catch his remarks.]

Mr. Richardson, of Illinois, moved that the Chair appoint a committee of nine to officially inform Messrs. Buchanan and Breckinridge of their nomination. Carried.

The President appointed the following gentlemen to constitute said Committee:—

Richardson of Illinois, Hibbard of New Hampshire, Lawrence of Rhode Island, Brown of Mississippi, Tucker of Virginia, Forsyth of Alabama, Manning of South Carolina, Preston of Kentucky, Horatio Seymour, of New York.

At the unanimous and earnest request of the Convention, the name of the President, John E. Ward, was added to the Committee as Chairman thereof.

The Special Committee appointed to select a National Committee submitted the following report:—

Resolved, That the next Democratic National Convention, be held at Charleston in the State of South Carolina.

Resolved, That the rule adopted by the Convention of 1852, and acted upon in this Convention, be the rule for the number of delegates each state shall be entitled to in the next Democratic National Convention, and that the National Committee, in calling the next Convention, shall provide seats therein for each State equal to twice the number of its electoral votes, and no more.

Resolved, That the time of holding the next Convention be designated by the Democratic National Committee, and that, in their call, the resolutions of 1852, providing for the number of delegates, be inserted as the rule for choosing delegates.

Resolved, That the National Democratic Committee cause an official report of the proceedings of this Convention to be prepared, published and distributed among members, for their respective States, and that said report shall contain a list of the names of and the post office address of each delegate, and the number of electoral votes of each State.

Resolved, That the first State Convention to be held in New York under one undivided Democratic organization, be authorized by this Convention to appoint a member of the National Committee from that State.

(Signed,)

THOS. McCREERY, *Chairman*.

W. M. Pugh, *Secretary*.

After reading the report Mr. McCreery said:—

In selecting a place for holding the next Convention, the Committee was divided between New York and Charleston. The Democracy of both have been recently distracted and divided; let this be received by them as an offering and incentive to union and continued exertion in the great Democratic cause. In the name of the Committee he presented the report.

Judge Beardsley would make an explanation as to New York with regard to this matter. It will be understood by the Convention that until quite recently the Democracy of New York to which I belong, did not comprehend that proposition by which it is intended to send the question of the selection of a National Committeeman to the next State Convention to be held in New York. We are prepared to live up to the arrangement into which we have entered. I hope that it may have the effect of producing that harmony among us which is so much to be desired; but I hope this Convention will not send to New York for decision the trivial matter of selecting a Committeeman. It would be a thorn in the side of the Democracy there, and likely to cause fresh irritation and disagreement. He would move that all that part of the report relating to the New York National Committeeman be stricken out.

Mr. Ludlow opposed this motion. If the matter was so trivial of itself, why should it be stricken out? This matter relating to New York, should be sent to New York for decision. He assured them that New York had been out of communion with the Democracy of the Union too long, and they did not desire to have no committeemen for four years longer, but wished to be in communication with other States in the National Committee.

On motion of Mr. Meade, of Virginia, the following resolution was offered for the one reported by the committee on the subject:

Resolved, That each delegation report a name to the Chairman to be placed by him in a hat, and that he draw one of the names, the same to be declared duly elected a member of the Committee.

The resolution was adopted and the report was then agreed to.

Thereupon, the President requested each delegation from New York to send one name to the President's table, so that the choice might be made. The delegation represented by Judge Beardsley, submitted the name of Augustus Schell. Mr. Ludlow said those whom he represented would yield to the other members of the New York delegation the member of the committee for that State, rather than trouble the Convention with such a matter. And the President then announced that Augustus Schell was selected as the member of said committee on the part of New York.

The National Democratic Committee, as chosen, was composed of the following gentlemen:

NAMES OF NATIONAL COMMITTEE.

STATE.	NAME.	POST OFFICE.
Maine	John Babson	Wiscasset.
New Hampshire	John H. George	Concord.
Vermont	David A. Smalley	Burlington.
Massachusetts	James Cheever	Boston.
Rhode Island	Elisha R. Potter	South Kingston.
Connecticut	James T. Pratt	Rocky Hill.
New York	Augustus Schell	New York City.
New Jersey	Jacob Vanatta	Morristown.
Pennsylvania	C. L. Ward	Towanda.
Delaware	Wm. D. Ochiltree	New Castle.
Maryland	Richard B. Carmichael	Centreville.
Virginia	Wm. H. Clark	Halifax Court House.
North Carolina	Thos. D. McDowell	Elizabethtown.
South Carolina	Benjamin H. Wilson	Georgetown.
Georgia	Wm. K. DeGraffenried	Macon.
Alabama	Henry D. Smith	Florence.

Mississippi......................Wm. R. Cannon..............Columbus.
Louisiana.........................Thomas E. P. Cottman......Donaldsonville.
Ohio...............................C. L. Vallandigham.........Dayton.
Kentucky.........................George A. Caldwell.........Louisville.
Tennessee........................Randal W. McCavock......Nashville.
Indiana............................James R. Stack..............Huntington.
Illinois.............................Thomas Dyer..................Chicago.
Missouri...........................John M. Krum................St. Louis.
Arkansas..........................Albert Rust....................El Dorado.
Michigan..........................Jacob Besan...................Niles.
Florida..............................A. E. Maxwell................Pensacola.
Texas................................Wm. S. Oldham..............Austin.
Iowa.................................Wm. Thompson...............Burlington.
Wisconsin.........................Geo. B. Smith.................Madison.
California..........................Sam'l H. Dosh................Shasta.

Mr. White, of Connecticut, offered a resolution pledging the exertions of the Democracy to bring about the single term system.

Referred to the Committee on Resolutions without debate.

On motion of Mr. Riddle, of Delaware, it was

Resolved, That the unanimous thanks of this Convention, be and are hereby extended to the Hon. John E. Ward, the presiding officer, and his able assistants, and also to the Hon. A. P. Edgerton, and associates, Committee of Arrangements, and all other officers, for the able, dignified and efficient manner in which they have discharged their respective duties.

The resolution was adopted unanimously.

On motion of S. W. Inge, of California,

Resolved, That the thanks of this Convention are due, and are hereby specially tendered to Mr. Julius Hessee, of Alabama, and to Alex. F. Gray, of Wisconsin, principal Secretaries, for their energy, zeal, and attention to the laborious duties of the Convention.

Adopted unanimously.

A vote of thanks to the citizens of Cincinnati for their hospitality and kindness during the session of the Convention, was also passed.

On motion, the Convention then adjourned *sine die*.

JOHN E. WARD, President.

WM. K. KIMBALL.	W. H. H. DIXON.
H. KIMBALL.	AMOS LAYMAN.
ISAAC B. BOWDITCH.	SAMUEL WILLIAMS.
J. C. ABBOTT.	JACOB MILLER.
WM. J. MILLER.	JAMES ELDER.
WM. D. BISHOP.	C. H. LAMPHEIR.
WM. HANNA.	DANIEL D. BERRY.
JOHN N. HUTCHISON.	R. E. JACKSON.
W. P. SNOW.	C. C. CHATFIELD.
WM. F. RITCHIE.	J. R. BROOKS.
H. G. WILLIAMS.	W. C. POLLOCK.
B. WILSON.	A. T. WALLING.
H. BUCHANAN.	A. T. GRAY.
JULIUS HESSEE.	J N. DAWLEY.
A. DERBIS.	

Seretaries.

After the motion to adjourn was declared to be carried, the President, on the enthusiastic and repeated call of the Convention came forward and spoke, in substance, as follows :

I have occupied too much of your time to trespass longer on your patience. I came among you an unknown stranger, without a herald to announce me. I have been received by you in a manner, and honored by you with a position far beyond what my fondest hope could have anticipated. New as I was to the duties which belong to that station, I have found you ready and willing, at all times, to forget my errors, and to sustain me in the discharge of those duties. I have made errors which appear as facts on the record ; but I trust I have no faults to be fastened on your recollections. The struggst here has been nobly and manfully contested. Three of the greatest names that adorn our country have been presented to this Convention. They came before it with ardent, noble, devoted friends. Our enemies said in their hearts, like the foes of David, " Ah ha ! Ah ha ! So we would have it." They anticipated what they classically termed a fight of the Kilkenny cats. But what was the result ? The moment the Convention designated a man as the choice of the majority, the minority stepped forward and offered on the altar of their country, a sacrifice of their friendship—the strongest feeling that can animate a man. Though the contest has been warm, it has not been an embittered one ; and when we pass beyond these walls, and go forth to rally around the standard which is borne aloft by that glorious old son of Pennsylvania, and beneath whose mighty shade this whole nation will find repose from the distractions which have agitated it, let us forget the past, and let our quarrels be like those between man and wife—violent while they last, but tending to a closer and sweeter communion.

These remarks were received with loud cheers, after which the crowd of delegates and other spectators separated.

CORRESPONDENCE.

LANCASTER, June 13th, 1856.

SIR:—The National Convention of the Democratic party, which assembled at Cincinnati, on the first Monday in June, unanimously nominated you as a candidate for the office of President of the United States.

We have been directed by the Convention to convey to you this intelligence, and to request you, in their name, to accept the nomination for the exalted trust which the Chief Magistracy of the Union imposes.

The Convention, founding their action upon the time-honored principles of the Democratic party, have announced their views in relation to the chief questions which engage the public mind; and, while adhering to the truths of the past, have manifested the policy of the present in a series of resolutions, to which we invoke your attention.

The Convention feel assured, in tendering to you this signal proof of the respect and esteem of your countrymen, that they truly reflect the opinion which the people of the United States entertain of your eminent character and distinguished public services. They cherish a profound conviction that your elevation to the first office in the Republic, will give a moral guarantee to the country, that the true principles of the Constitution will be asserted and maintained; that the public tranquility will be established; that the tumults of faction will be stilled; that our domestic industry will flourish; that our foreign affairs will be conducted with such wisdom and firmness as to assure the prosperity of the people at home, while the interests and honor of our country are wisely but inflexibly maintained in our intercourse with other nations; and, especially, that your public experience and the confidence of your countrymen, will enable you to give effect to Democratic principles, so as to render indissoluble the strong bonds of mutual interest and national glory which unite our confederacy and secure the prosperity of our people.

While we offer to the country our sincere congratulations upon the fortunate auspices of the future, we tender to you personally, the assurances of the respect and esteem of

Your fellow-citizens,

JOHN E. WARD.
W. A. RICHARDSON.
HARRY HIBBARD.
W. B. LAWRENCE.
A. G. BROWN.
JNO. L. MANNING.
JOHN FORSYTH.
W. PRESTON.
J. RANDOLPH TUCKER.
HORATIO SEYMOUR.

HON. JAMES BUCHANAN.

MR. BUCHANAN'S ACCEPTANCE.

WHEATLAND, (near Lancaster,)
June 16, 1856.

GENTLEMEN:—I have the honor to acknowledge the receipt of your communication of the 13th instant, informing me officially of my nomination by the Democratic National Convention, recently held at Cincinnati, as the Democratic candidate for the office of President of the United States. I shall not attempt to express the grateful feelings which I entertain towards my Democratic fellow-citizens for having deemed me worthy of this—the highest political honor on earth—an honor such as the people of no other country have the power to bestow. Deeply sensible of the vast and varied responsibility attached to the station, especially at the present crisis in our affairs, I have carefully refrained from seeking the nomination either by word or by deed. Now, that it has been offered by the Democratic party, I accept it with diffidence in my own abilities, but with an humble trust, that in the event of my election, I may be enabled to discharge my duty in such a manner as to allay domestic strife, preserve peace and friendship with foreign nations, and promote the best interests of the Republic.

In accepting the nomination I need scarcely say that I accept in the same spirit, the resolutions constituting the platform of principles erected by the Convention. To this platform I intend to confine myself throughout the canvass, believing that I have no right, as the candidate of the Democratic party, by answering interrogatories, to present new and different issues before the people.

It will not be expected that in this answer, I should specially refer to the subject of each of the resolutions; and I shall therefore confine myself to the two topics now most prominently before the people.

And in the first place, I cordially concur in the sentiments expressed by the Convention on the subject of civil and religious liberty. No party founded on political or religious intolerance towards one class of American citizens, whether born in our own or in a foreign land, can long continue to exist in this country. We are all equal before God and the Constitution; and the dark spirit of despotism and bigotry which would create odious distinctions among our fellow-citizens, will be speedily rebuked by a free and enlightened public opinion.

The agitation on the question of Domestic Slavery has too long distracted and divided the people of this Union and alienated their affections from each other. This agitation has assumed many forms since its commencement, but it now seems to be directed chiefly to the Territories; and judging from its present character, I think that we may safely anticipate that it is rapidly approaching a "finality." The recent legislation of Congress respecting domestic slavery, derived, as it has been, from the original and pure fountain of legitimate political power, the will of the majority, promises ere long, to allay the dangerous excitement. This legislation is founded upon principles, as ancient as free government itself, and in accordance with them, has simply declared that the people of a Territory, like those of a State, shall decide or themselves, whether slavery shall or shall not exist within their limits.

The Nebraska-Kansas Act does no more than give the force of law to this elementary principle of self-government; declaring it to be "the true intent and meaning of this act not to legislate slavery into any Territory or State, nor to exclude it therefrom; but to leave the people thereof perfectly free to form and regulate their domestic institutions in their own way, subject only to the Constitution of the United States." This principle will surely not be controverted by any individual of any party professing devotion to popular government. Besides how vain and illusory would any other principle prove in practice in regard to the Territories! This is apparent from the fact admitted by all, that after a territory shall have entered the Union and become a State, no Constitutional power would then exist which could prevent it from either abolishing or establishing slavery, as the case may be, according to its sovereign will and pleasure.

Most happy would it be for the country if this long agitation were at an end. During its whole progress it has produced no practical good to any human being, whilst it has been the source of great and dangerous evils. It has alienated and estranged one portion of the Union from the other, and has even seriously threatened its very existence. To my own personal knowledge, it has produced the impression among foreign nations that our great and glorious confederacy is in constant danger of dissolution. This does us serious injury, because acknowledged power and stability always command respect among nations, and are among the best securities against unjust aggression and in favor of the maintenance of honorable peace.

May we not hope that it is the mission of the Democratic party, now the only surviving conservative party of the country, ere long to overthrow all sectional parties and restore the peace, friendship, and mutual confidence which prevailed in the good old time, among the different members of the confederacy. Its character is strictly national, and it therefore asserts no principle for the guidance of the Federal Government which is not adopted and sustained by its members in each and every State. For this reason it is everywhere the same determined foe of all geographical parties, so much and so justly dreaded by the Father of his Country. From its very nature it must continue to exist so long as there is a Constitution and a Union to preserve. A conviction of these truths has induced many of the purest, the ablest and most independent of our former opponents, who have differed from us in times gone by upon old and extinct party issues, to come into our ranks and devote themselves with us to the cause of the Constitution and the Union. Under these circumstances, I most cheerfully pledge myself, should the nomination of the Convention be ratified by the people, that all the power and influence, constitutionally possessed by the Executive, shall be exerted in a firm but conciliatory spirit, during the single term I shall remain in office, to restore the same harmony among the sister States which prevailed before this apple of discord, in the form of slavery agitation, had been cast into their midst. Let the members of the family abstain from intermeddling with the exclusive domestic concerns of each other, and cordially unite, on the basis of perfect equality among themselves, in promoting the great national objects of common interest to all, and the good work will be instantly accomplished.

In regard to our foreign policy, to which you have referred in your communication,—it is quite impossible for any human foreknowledge to prescribe positive rules in advance, to regulate the conduct of a future administration in all the exigencies which may arise in our various and ever changing relations with foreign powers. The Federal Government must of necessity exercise a sound discretion in dealing with international questions as they may occur; but this under the strict responsibility which the Executive must always feel to the people of the United States and the judgment of posterity. You will therefore excuse me for not entering into particulars; whilst I heartily concur with you in the general sentiment, that our foreign affairs ought to be conducted with such wisdom and firmness as to assure the prosperity of the people at home, whilst the interests and honor of our country are wisely but inflexibly maintained abroad. Our foreign policy ought ever to be based upon the principle of doing justice to all nations, and requiring justice from them in return; and from this principle I shall never depart.

Should I be placed in the Executive Chair, I shall use my best exertions to cultivate peace and friendship with all nations, believing this to be our highest policy as well as our most imperative duty; but at the same time, I shall never forget that in case the necessity should arise, which I do not now apprehend, our national rights and national honor must be preserved at all hazards and at any sacrifice.

Firmly convinced that a special Providence governs the affairs of nations, let us humbly implore his continued blessing upon our country, and that he may avert from us the punishment we justly deserve for being discontented and ungrateful whilst enjoying privileges above all nations, under such a Constitution and such a Union as has never been vouchsafed to any other people.

Yours, very respectfully,

JAMES BUCHANAN.

Hon. John E. Ward, W. A. Richardson, Harry Hibbard, W. B. Lawrence, A. G. Brown, John L. Manning, John Forsyth, W. Preston, J. Randolph Tucker, and Horatio Seymour, Committee, &c.

BLACK REPUBLICAN

IMPOSTURE EXPOSED!

FRAUD UPON THE PEOPLE.

FREMONT AND HIS SPECULATIONS.

How he employed public money to buy a large estate.

How he employed public money to buy breeding cattle to stock it with.

How he stood for some years as a defaulter for the same upon the books of the Government.

How he sold the Government its own beef cattle to pay the balance due to itself.

WASHINGTON:
PRINTED AT POLKINHORN'S STEAM JOB OFFICE.

1856.

GOVERNOR FREMONT'S FINANCIAL OPERATIONS.

We have, in a previous number, examined the accounts of Col. Fremont as a disbursing officer, and established the charge of extravagance and want of care and judgment in his management of the public accounts.

We shall next take up the pecuniary obligations incurred by him whilst contending for the appointment of Governor of California, against the order of the President, conferring that authority upon General Kearney. For this usurpation of office, and insubordination as a soldier, he was tried and broke by court-martial.

The obligations incurred by Col. Fremont on behalf of the United States, during the brief term for which he claimed to hold the office of Governor, consist of three principal items.

THE HUTTMAN DRAFTS.

[*From the Washington Union.*]

On the 18th March, 1847, "Governor" Fremont borrowed of F. Huttman fifteen thousand dollars, and gave him four drafts for $6,000, $5,000, $4,000, and $4,500, (*the latter for premium,*) making an aggregate of $19,500. The drafts were drawn on the *Secretary of State*, and *were protested for non-acceptance*, as the "Governor" had no authority to draw upon the department. Nothing now was said about the non-payment of the drafts until the 18th August, 1848, when "Governor" Fremont, being then in Washington city, transmitted his accounts for disbursements in California during the years 1847 and 1848. In his general account, he charged himself with moneys received by him from Purser Speiden and Captain Gillespie of the marine corps, amounting to.......... $23,199 40
And he claimed credit for disbursements and advances amounting to....... 42,861 15

Leaving a balance due him of.. $19,661 75

The whole of the above balance was paid to him or his agent as follows: On the 7th September, 1848, $9,056.07 was paid; on the 5th April, 1850, $1,673.74 was paid, and the remainder of the balance, amounting to $8,931.94, was placed to his credit as a *set-off to balances against him.*

Appended to the above account rendered by "Governor" Fremont, and settled as above stated, was the following note to which particular attention is called, as it affords *proof positive* that "Governor" Fremont recognised an individual responsibility to Huttman for the amount of the drafts:

"In addition to the sums above credited, I drew *two* drafts on the State Department in 1847—*one* in favor of F. Huttman, *a Ciudad de los Angeles*, for $19,000, (less the amount of 30 per cent. premium paid,) and the other for $1,000, (less a premium of 25 per cent.,) in favor of William Wolfs Knott; *which drafts having been protested and not recognised by the government, I don't consider them chargeable to my account.* J. C. FREMONT."

We italicise the *number* of the drafts, as the description therein given is inaccurate, and furnishes evidence of the *carelessness* of a disbursing officer of the government, which has heretofore been held to be reprehensible. The amount drawn in favor of Huttman is stated by him to be *nineteen thousand dollars, in one draft.* There was only one transaction with Huttman—namely, for *four* drafts, amounting, in the aggregate, to nineteen thousand *five hundred* dollars. The original drafts are on file in the department, subject to the examination of searchers after truth. From the 21st of March to the 6th of October, 1847, "Governor" Fremont disbursed to Major Redding and others the sum of $14,696.12, which was allowed by the department as a set-off to the Huttman drafts; though, on the other hand, over and above the amounts paid "Governor" Fremont on settlement in 1848, the following debits were charged to him:

In the 2d Auditor's Office (moneys received)........................	$731 85
3d........do......... ....do...	810 00
4th........do......money received from Major A. G. Gillespie (military contributions)............................	4,846 00
	$6,387 85

In 1852, "Governor" Fremont went to England, and was arrested on a writ from her Britannic Majesty's Court of Exchequer, at the suit of A. Gibbs & Son, of London, (the assignees of F. Huttman,) on the four several bills of exchange or drafts above spoken of. As soon as the news of his arrest reached Washington, a bill was introduced in Congress for his relief. The claim was laid, in the name of F. Huttman, before a board of army officers, composed of Brev. Col. Smith, 2d artillery, Maj. Lee, commissary department, and Lt. Col. Thomas, quartermaster's department, who were appointed by a special act of Congress to examine into *California claims.* The board recommended payment of the claim in the following words:

"The board is of opinion that the claim is just, and recommends it to the favorable consideration of Congress."

The grounds of the opinion so reported were not set forth. It was not stated whether the claim of Huttman was *just*, simply because *he was the holder of the drafts of an accredited officer of the government, or because the money was*, in the opinion of the board, *due* from the United States to "Governor" Fremont. The board did not have before it the accounts of "Governor" Fremont or others, or *other evidence* which *was and is* in the departments, having a bearing upon Huttman's or other claims presented to it—the reasons of which are set forth as follows, in the letter transmitting the report to Congress:

"The *very limited* powers conferred upon the board by Congress *restricted* it in the examination of the claims presented to simply receiving such *explanations* and *testimony* as *might* be offered by the claimants, or their agents or assigns, and *not to seek the same from any other* than official sources, such as the records of the Treasury and other departments of the government might furnish."

From the above report it will be seen that the board had no authority, under the act of Congress, to go into the departments for evidence.

When the report was made to Congress it was supposed that the amount proposed by the bill would not exceed $19,500, the amount of the drafts. The bill passed ordering the money to be paid, without leaving any discretion with the Secretary of the Treasury, except that he should be satisfied that the amount obtained on the drafts had been expended for the benefit of the public service.

The facts were "that *it had been expended for the public service*," and, further, that *long prior* to the passage of the appropriation bill he (Fremont) had drawn the money from the treasury; and it was his duty to have paid the debt to Huttman, as it had *become an individual debt on the part* of Fremont *the moment he drew the money* from the treasury, and consequently not a debt due by the United States.

In carrying out the provisions of the act, the proper officer of the Treasury Department reported, July 7, 1853, to the Secretary, after enumerating the facts, as follows:

"Thus it appears—

"1st. That, in a *liberal sense*, the proceeds of the drafts referred to were expended for the benefit of the public service.

"2d. That the amount of said expenditure *has been refunded to and settled with* Col. Fremont.

"3d. That Col. Fremont is, over and above, and on other accounts, *now indebted* on the books in the sum of $6,337.85, to which is to be added, if the *present payment is made*, the amount of said drafts less the premium of $4,500—say $15,000—making an aggregate indebtedness of $21,337.85."

On the 9th of July, 1853, the Secretary of the Treasury, having no discretion, ordered payment to be made to A. Gibbs & Son, on the four drafts, under the act passed March 3, 1853—Statutes at large, vol. 10, pp 759 and 760. Under said act and order of the Secretary there was paid to the plaintiffs the sum of FORTY-EIGHT THOUSAND EIGHT HUNDRED and FORTY-THREE DOLLARS and THIRTY-THREE CENTS.

To this large amount the drafts had swelled in reaching a judgment in the English courts. After the payment above made, the Secretary directed that the sum of fifteen thousand dollars should be charged to Fremont, with interest from the date of his settlement in 1848, and that he should be called on to settle this and *other balances* against him. The balances, however, stood against the "Governor" until July 29, 1854, when his *cele-*

brated bill for BEEF *furnished* to the Indians in California (not one pound of which, save the entrails, horns, hides, and hoofs, was ever issued to the Indians, as can be proven by thousands of miners who purchased it at from twenty-five to fifty cents a pound, and also by the affidavits forwarded to the Indian Department by Lieut. Beale, of Brooks, and others who butchered and sold the beef) was passed.

The act (Statutes at Large, vol. 10, p. 804) appropriated $242,036.25, from which was deducted by the Secretary of the Treasury the following amounts overdrawn and due by Col. Fremont, most of which had been standing against him for several years:

Balance due Second Auditor's office..............................	$771 85
Balance due Third Auditor's office, (Huttman's draft and interest)...	15,945 88
Balance due Fourth Auditor's office, received from Gillespie in 1847	4,846 00
	$21,563 73

The act of March 3, 1853, provided for the payment of the debt due by Fremont, and "*also for such necessary expenses as he*, Fremont, *may have incurred in defending the suit*"—*his own*. Under that proviso, "Governor" Fremont presented a *claim for expenses incurred* for the sum of $2,150.49, which was allowed and placed to the credit of a "*balance*" against him on the books of the Third Auditor, and *there still* remains a *balance* against him of 1,986.51.

By all the rules of equity and justice, "Governor" Fremont is indebted to the government on account of the Huttman drafts as follows:

Amount paid in England..	$48,843 33
Amount paid for expenses..	2,150 49
Cr..	50,993 82
By amount stopped out of beef account...............................	15,945 88
Balance due, with interest from date of payment,....................	$35,047 94

Shades of Galphin and Gardiner! where are ye gone? Come back and take lessons.

THE TEMPLE CASE.

On the 25th January, 1847, Col. Fremont, by virtue of his office as Governor of California, borrowed of Mr. John Temple, of Angeles, fifteen hundred dollars, according to the following specialties executed by him:

Received of Mr. John Temple the sum of fifteen hundred dollars in cash, for the use of the United States, for which sum I promise (in the name of the United States, as governor of California) to pay two per cent. per month until paid, said per centage being customary in this Territory.

J. C. FREMONT,
Gov. of California.

ANGELES, capital of California, Jan. 25, 1847.

We, the undersigned, merchants residing in California, certify that the customary price paid for the use of money in this Territory is two per cent per month, and frequently more.

TALBOT H. GREEN,
W. D. M. HOWARD,
ABEL STEARNS.

ANGELES, Upper California, Jan. 25, 1847.

This money was obtained for the service of the Cal. battalion, and expended accordingly.
$1,500.
J. C. FREMONT.
July 11, 1853.

I certify that I have compared the above signature with original signatures in this office, and to the best of my belief pronounce it to be genuine.

S. COOPER,
Adj. Gen'l.

ADJ. GEN'L'S OFFICE, Oct. 8, 1852.

This bill having been forwarded for acceptance and collection to Messrs. Curtis & Peabody, of Boston, they addressed letters of inquiry to the Secretary of War, and received the following reply:

WAR DEPARTMENT,
Washington, December 7, 1848.

GENTLEMEN: I have the honor to acknowledge the receipt of your letter of the 4th September and 30th ultimo, respecting the draft which you hold of J C. Fremont, for the money borrowed by him in California. Mr. Fremont memorialized Congress on the subject of the liabilities he had incurred in California. But the bill in regard to them, which was introduced as stated in my letter to you of the 8th of August, did not become a law. I am unable to say what further action may be expected, if any, at the present session. As no officer of this department is authorized to borrow money on the faith of the United States, the department cannot recognise any such contract. Mr. Fremont, individually, it is presumed, has received credit at the Treasury for all disbursements he thus made in the public service, whether from money received by him from the treasury or raised on his own account.

Very respectfully, your obedient servant,
W. L. MARCY,
Secretary of War.

Messrs. CURTIS & PEABODY, Boston, Mass.

It will be observed that the Secretary of War says "that no officer of this Department is authorized to borrow money on the faith of the United States," and refuses to "recognise any such contract."

Upon an examination, the Board directs the sum of $1,500, without the interest, to be charged to the account of Colonel Fremont.

Board for the examination of claims contracted in California under Lieut. Col. John C. Fremont.

[Opinion on the claim of John Temple. No. 1.]
Cash $1,500.

On the additional testimony produced, the board deems the claim reasonable and just, including the interest, as stated, to the date at which Lieut. Col. Fremont settled his account at the Treasury, say the first of October, 1848; and accordingly recommends it to the favorable consideration of Congress: *Provided*, That, on the payment of the claim, the amount thereof, deducting the interest, be charged to Col. Fremont.

[Vote unanimous—see page 208, journal.]

C. F. SMITH, Col. U. S. Army,
President of the Board.

DECEMBER 3, 1853.

THE COT LOAN.

On the 4th February, 1847, Colonel Fremont borrowed of Jose Cot, merchant of Angeles, two thousand dollars, and, a short time subsequently, the further sum of one thousand dollars, for which he executed the following obligation:

[Translation.]

I, the undersigned, Governor of California, for the United States of North America, do acknowledge having received, from Don Antonio Jose Cot, merchant of this city, two thousand dollars in hard cash, which he has furnished this Government for the wants of the service; and, in the name of the Government of the United States, I bind myself to return said sum within the term of two months from this date, with the interest of three per cent. per month, or one hundred and twenty dollars.

But if, at the expiration of this period, I should see fit still to make use of said two thousand dollars, said Mr. Cot agrees that the interest shall run for four months longer at 2 per cent. for month, or one hundred and sixty dollars for the four months; and to the fulfilment of these stipulations I bind myself as Governor of California.

For $2,000.

J. C. FREMONT,
Governor of California.

ANGELES, February 4, 1847.

I have likewise received from said Mr. Cot the sum of one thousand dollars on the terms expressed on the other side.

J. C. FREMONT, Governor of California.

ANGELES, February 20, 1847.

I have received from Sr. Fremont the sum of one hundred and eighty dollars for two months' interest on the three thousand dollars expressed in this obligation.

ANTONIO JOSE COT.

ANGELES, April 12, 1847.

The Board of Commissioners allowed the claim, with instructions to charge the principal sum to the account of Col. Fremont.

Board for the examination of claims contracted in California under Lieutenant Colonel John C. Fremont.

[Opinion on the claim of Antonia Jose Cot. No. 153.]
Cash, $3,240.

The board deems the claim just, including the interest as stated for four months, and accordingly recommends it to the favorable consideration of Congress.

Provided, That, on the payment of the claim, the amount thereof, deducting the interest, be charged against Lieut. Col. Fremont.

[Vote unanimous—see journal, page 255.]

C. F. SMITH, Col. U. S. Army,
President of the Board.

JANUARY 26, 1854.

It will be observed that two thousand dollars of this money was borrowed on the 4th of February, and one thousand dollars a few days afterwards. The Temple loan, of $1,500, was effected on the 25th January. Now observe: The biographer of Col. Fremont describes how, "by a ju‑'dicious investment of about $3,000, in 1847, he (Col. Fremont) had be‑'come the proprietor of one of the most valuable tracts of land in the 'world, the Mariposas;" and, in an abstract of the title to this valuable grant, he adds, "ON THE 10th OF FEBRUARY, 1847, Alvarado executed 'a deed of the property, as described in his own grant to Col. Fremont, 'with a general warranty of title." THE CONSIDERATION STATED IN THE CONVEYANCE WAS 3,000!

Col. Fremont was an officer without ostensible means, distant from home, engaged in a tedious campaign against a disaffected people. Two questions arise: 1. How did he get the money to pay for the valuable tract of land? 2. How did he apply the money obtained from Cot and Temple?*

We are aware that the advocates of Mr. Fremont will pretend great indignation, and protest against being required to account for the derivation or application of his private means. But we submit that the co-incidence of his having received three thousand dollars on the credit of the United States and the payment of three thousand dollars for the valuable tract of land, is so remarkable that, in justice to Col. Fremont, his

*NOTE.—The debit items, $1,500, $3,000, and $350, were advanced to Colonel Fremont in cash, for the use of the battalion of volunteers in California, by John Temple, on January 25th, 1847, and by Antonio Jose Cot, on February 4, 1847, and T. H. Green, on November 16, 1846.

These sums were recommended for allowance by the Army Board, and were afterwards paid to the parties making the advances from the Treasury of the United States, and charged to Colonel Fremont until he should satisfactorily show when and how he applied the same properly to the public service. This he has not yet done.—Sen. Ex. Doc., 1st session, 34th Congress, page 53.

friends should exonerate him from the imputation of having employed the public money for purposes of private speculation.

THE CONTRACT WITH CELIS.

On the 3rd March, 1847, Colonel Fremont, claiming to be Governor of California and legal agent of the Government of the United States, borrowed the sum of two thousand five hundred dollars from Eulojio de Celis, according to the following specialty:

Eight months after date, J. C. Fremont, Governor of California, and, thereby, the legal agent of the Government of the United States of North America, in consideration of the sum of two thousand five hundred dollars being borrowed, or advanced to me, for the benefit of the said Government of the United States, by Eulojio de Cel s, hereby promise and oblig- myself, in my fiduciary character as governor aforesaid, and my successors in office, to pay to said Eulojio de Celis, and his heirs, executors, administrators, and assigns, the aforesaid sum of two thousand five hundred dollars without defalcation. It is agreed and understood that if the aforesaid sum of two thousand five hundred dollars is not paid on or before maturity, it is to draw interest at the rate of two per cent. per month from the time it falls due. In testimony whereof, I have hereunto set my hand and have caused the seal of the Territory to be affixed, at the city de los Angeles, the capital of California, this 3d day of March, in the year 1847.

J. C. FREMONT,
Governor of California.

On the same date Colonel Fremont, in the same capacity, purchased of the same person a lot of beef cattle according to the following agreement:

A.

This article of agreement, made and entered into this third day of March, in the year 1847, by and between Eulojio de Celis, a resident of the City de Los Angeles, capital of Upper California, of the first part, and J. C. Fremont, Governor of California, and lega representative of the Government of the United States of North America, of the second part, witnesseth, that the said Eulojio de Celis has sold to J. C. Fremont, GOVERNOR of California aforesaid, a lot of six hundred head of cattle, of good merchantable kind, and suitable for beef, to be delivered to the commissary of the troops, under the immediate command of Governor Fremont, in number corresponding with the requisition of the commissary; and the said Governor Fremont binds himself and his successors in office to pay to said Eulojio de Celis, his heirs, executors, administrators, or assigns, at the expiration of eight months, the sum of six thousand dollars, without defalcation. It is expressly understood, between the above contracting parties, that if the said Eulojio de Celis fails to deliver good merchantable cattle, when required to do so by the commissary, the contract is to be considered null and void by the said Governor Fremont—he paying to Eulojio de Celis ten dollars per head for the number delivered; and it is further understood that the hides of the above cattle are to be delivered, on application, to the said Eulojio de Celis, to whom they belong by agreement.

In testimony of the above, the said parties have hereunto set their hands and affixed their seals, at the city de Los Angeles, the capitol of California, the day and year before written.

EULOJIO DE CELIS, [L. S.]
J. C. FREMONT, [L. S.]
Governor of California.

In acknowledgment that Celis had complied with this contract, Colonel Fremont executed the following receipt:

I do hereby certify that Don Eulojio de Celis has complied to the within obligation and contract on his part, by delivering the number of cattle as specified; and in payment thereof, I have this day executed to said Celis my note for the sum of six thousand nine hundred and seventy-five dollars, including the hides of the whole number of cattle.

J. C. FREMONT,
Lieut. Col. U. S. Army.

ANGELES, April 26, 1847.

In fulfilment of this transaction, Colonel Fremont executes this note as of the same date, as follows:

ANGELES, CALIFORNIA, *April* 26, 1847.

This is to certify that there is due, from the United States to Don Eulojio de Celis, the sum of six thousand nine hundred and seventy-five dollars, on account of *supplies furnished by him for subsisting* United States' troops in service in this Territory, and under my command. The above sum, for which this obligation is given, shall be subject to an interest of two per centum per month, after the expiration of eight months from the 18th April, 1847, until paid.—Rep. No. 817, page 16.

J. C. FREMONT,
Lieut. Col. U. S. Army.

On the 1st of May, 1847, appears the following receipts:

ANGELES, *Mayo* 1, *de* 1847.

Recibi de Don Eulogio de Celis cuatro cientos ochenta y un reses, par cuenta de Don J. C. Fremont, teniente-colonel del ejercito de los Estados Unidos, cayo ganado existe en mi poder.

Son 481 reses. ABEL STEARNS.

LOS ANGELES, *June* 18, 1847.

I certify the above to be a true copy of the original.

J. W. DAVIDSON,
Lieut. U. S. Army.

I have received from Don Eulojio de Celis four hundred and eighty-one head of cattle on account of Mr. J. C. Fremont, Lieutenant Colonel of the Army of the United States, which cattle exist in my possession.

481 head of cattle.
Certified as true. ABEL STEARNS.

I have received from Don Eulojio de Celis one hundred and nineteen head of cattle, on account of Mr. J. C. Fremont, Lieutenant Colonel of the Army of the United States, and said cattle remain in my possession according to agreement.

ABEL STEARNS.

ANGELES, July 7, 1847.

We extract from the *Washington Union* the following just and pungent comments upon these transactions.

[*From the Washington Union.*]

* * * * * * * * * * *

This same document, at page 370, shows that Fremont bought, in March, 1847, six hundred head of cattle for six thousand dollars, of one Celis, of Los Angeles, at ten dollars a head, for which he gave an obligation, as Governor of California, for six thousand dollars, which he never paid, but which has since been discharged by Government under a special law. These cattle, as appears by said document, at pages 367–8, were delivered to one Stearns, who certified: "I hold these cattle by agreement, and for the term of three years; to return the same number and class at the end of the term, with one-half of increase, excepting such as may be lost, in any way whatever, and not for want of care on my part. *I consider the cattle as the private property of Lieutenant Colonel Fremont, not being instructed by him to the contrary.*" Colonel Mason, in his letter at page 3[illegible]2, shows that not one of these cattle was ever slaughtered or used for the United States, and that, at the date of the transaction, another officer was present having charge of the commissary department. It does not appear that Fremont has ever accounted for these cattle, or paid for them in any way whatever. Afterwards, when Beale became Indian superintendent, Fremont furnished cattle for Indian supplies at some *sixty dollars per head*, for which he has been fully paid by special act of Congress. From the papers heretofore presented to the Indian Office, we understand that there is ample evidence to prove that, through Beale, Fremont sold these very Celis cattle, or many of them, to the Government for Indian beef, and received for them about *six times* as much as they originally cost. From these extraordinary financial performances, we can well understand how those men who are bankrupt themselves, and who have contributed to bankrupt their States, and would bankrupt Uncle Sam if they could, were so enthusiastic in cheering for Fremont.

If elected, could he well deny his leading supporters privileges at money-making corresponding with those formerly enjoyed by himself? If they should follow the precedents set by him, would not the speculations prove splendid? It is certainly natural that such prospects should rejuvenate the dilapidated, and inspirit the decayed politician to the greatest possible exertions. Fremont was mainly nominated by this class. What will those who sustain themselves by honest industry say to the Mariposa and cattle speculations? *Will* they give either their approval?

But the long recognized tests of official fitness are repudiated and rejected by the friends of Colonel Fremont. If he is charged with being a Roman Catholic, the whole brood of Republican organs rush to his defence, and crowd their columns with affidavits, certificates, and editorials to relieve him of what they seem to regard as a horrible crime! If he is charged with being the owner of slaves, all Black Republicandom is shocked at the enormity of the injustice, and is prompt to repel the libellous imputation! But when official records are produced, tending to excite suspicion as to Colonel Fremont's integrity an d fidelity in the discharge of his official duties, while acting in a fiduciary character in California; when those official documents raise the presumption that he used the crd it attaching to his official position to borrow money for his individual speculations; when they make out a *prima facie* case of buying property ostensibly for the use of the Government, when, in fact, the purchase was for his individual benefit; when they show that hundreds of thousands of dollars claimed from the Government upon the strength of his official certificates have been rejected by the accounting officers of the Government for illegality; when such charges as these, based upon authentic public documents, are brought forward, and the friends of Fremont are asked to explain these transactions, and thus vindicate his character for honesty, fidelity, and capacity, the only answer given is, that *Colonel Fremont will dignify no libel by a personal contradiction, but commit his character to the generous appreciation and clear discernment of the American people.*

Is it possible that Colonel Fremont has so little care about his reputation, or labors under the delusion that his character is so far above assault that for more than five years he has allowed charges so grave to remain on the public records and in the public archives, without a word of explanation; and now, when they are brought to his attention, does hespresume to meet them by throwing himself on his dignity, and trusting to the generout appreciation of the people? It was not in this way that he met the insinuation of Mr. Clay in the Senate when he understood his personal character to be impeached. It was not by dignified silence that he allowed Mr. Foote to indulge in personal reflections in the Senate. But now, when he is presented as a candidate for the most elevated and responsible position in the Government, and when charges, resting upon official documents, are made, which, if true, are wholly irreconcilable with integrity, fidelity, or capacity, the only response made is that *Colonel Fremont trusts to the generous appreciation and clear discernment of the American people* We know that the American people are *generous*, and that they have a *clear discernment*, but at the same time they regard no man as so eleva ed by a mere nomination for the Presidency as to be placed beyond the test to which all applicants for their suffrages are subjected. When they see Colonel Fremont nervously sensitive about being suspected of Roman Catholicism and of being the owner of slaves, they will have "clear discernment" enough to conclude that his refusal to repel charges that really involve an impeachment of his character for honesty and fidelity, is a virtual confession that they are well founded.

PUBLIC PROPERTY TAKEN FOR PRIVATE USE.

We come now to the full *denouèment* of this matter. Fremont left California in June, 1847; nothing was heard of the cattle by the commissary nor by Colonel Mason, until application was made by the holder of the agreement to know whether the amount would be paid at maturity. This elicited an inquiry into the character of the transaction. Colonel J. D. Stephenson addressed two letters to Abel Stearns, the recipient of the cattle, inquiring how he held them and to whom they belonged. The following are his answers:

No. 7.

Angeles, August 20, 1845.

Dear Sir—In reply to your official letter of yesterday I would observe that I hold in my possession six hundred head of cattle, (the major part of them breeding cows,) received from Don Eulojio de Celis, on account of Lieutenant Colonel J. C. Fremont. I hold these cattle by agreement, and for the term of three years, to return the same number and class at the term, with one-half the increase, excepting such as may be lost in any way whatever, and not for want of care on my part. I consider the cattle as the private property of Colonel J. C. Fremont, not being instructed by him to the contrary.

I have the honor to be, &c.

ABEL STEARNS.

Col. J. D. Stephenson, *Commanding Southern Military District, California.*

No. 10.

Angeles, September 20, 1847.

Sir: I have the honor to acknowledge the receipt of your official note of the 17th instant, with an extract from an official letter to you from W. S. Sherman, Acting Assistant Adjutant General, requiring from me further information relative to a contract by which I hold a certain lot of cattle received from Don E. Celis, for account of Lieutenant Colonel J. C. Fremont, and whether I have a written contract or a verbal one; if the latter, to furnish you with the evidence to prove my right to the trust. In answer to which I have to observe that I hold the cattle by verbal contract; witness to the same, Mr. Samuel Hensly Captain in the late California battalion, to whom I refer you particularly. He resides near Nueva Helvetia; also, to Midshipman John K. Wilson, and Lieutenant A. H. Gillespie, United States Marines. Both, I think, were present and knowing to the contract. As the above gentlemen are not here, I cannot furnish you with their certificates relative to the contract.

Very respectfully,

ABEL STEARNS.

To Col. J. D. Stephenson, *Commanding Southern Military District, California.*

Can there be any rational doubt on the perusal of the above official papers, that Fremont intended to make a speculation for his own benefit? The fact that on the 26th of April, 1847, he executed the obligation marked No. 2, in which the sum of $975 is added to the price agreed to be paid, being a compensation for the hides of the cattle, and this, too, before a solitary cow had been delivered, shows that it was not then the intention of Fremont that the cattle should be used for the army. It shows that the idea of leasing out the cattle on shares was not merely an after-thought but a part of his original design. But why resort to such inferences when we have the damning fact that instead of cattle "suitable for beef," as named in the original contract, "breeding cows" were delivered, and that, too, with the evident concurrence of Fremont in the fraud.

We need do no more than add the letter of Colonel Mason which was sent to the War Department, accompanied by the foregoing documents. It is unnecessary to add that, at the time this information was sent, Colonel Mason, being Governor of California, was the proper person to make a report of such conduct. It arrived at Washington city after the court martial on Colonel Fremont had commenced its sittings. It is impossible to read this letter and the collateral proof without coming to the conclusion that Colonel Fremont was guilty of a deliberate attempt to defraud the Government which he represented.

Headquarters, Tenth Military Department,
Monterey, California, October 9, 1847.

Sir—I have the honor herewith to enclose to you the papers relating to a certain contract entered into on the 3d day of March, 1847, by Lieutenant Colonel Fremont, mounted rifleman, with a Don Eulojio de Celis, a resident of Cuidad de los Angeles, California. The paper marked A is a copy of this contract, with Lieutenant Colonel Fremont's certificate bearing date April 26, 1847, that the contract had been complied with on the part of Don Eulojio de Celis, and that he, Fremont, had executed to him in payment a note for the sum of six thousand nine hundred and seventy-five dollars.

Lieutenant Colonel Fremont left California in the month of June, 1847, giving no notice to General Kearney or myself of the existence of such a contract, or that he pledged the faith of his Government for the redemption of it by the payment of $6,975. Nor had I the least idea of this obligation, until applied to by Colonel Stevenson, whether I would recognize the contract, and redeem the bond at maturity. This letter was accompanied by others, which show that, in fact, notwithstanding the certificate of Lieutenant Colonel Fremont, Mr. Celis never delivered to the commissary of the California battalion one single head of beef cattle under this contract, and that not one of these six hundred head of cattle was slaughtered for the use of that battalion; but, on the contrary that they have been delivered to a Mr. Stearns, of Los Angeles, in two parcels; one of four hundsed and eighty-one, on the first day of May, and another of one hundred and nineteen, on the sixth day of July, 1847, both of which dates are subsequent to the discharge of the California battalion commanded by Lieutenant Colonel J. C. Fremont. There is no doubt that these cattle are the same six hundred contracted for by Lieutenant Fremont on the 3d of March, 1847. Mr. Celis stated it positively in the letter marked D; and the receipts for them by Stearns, marked B and F especially state that he (Stearns) receipts for them in the name and order of Lieutenant Colonel Fremont.

These deliveries occurred at a time *when* a garrison was stationed at Los Angeles, with a commissioned agent of the commissary department of the army, Lieutenant Davidson, to take charge of subsistence stores intended for public use; yet these cattle, furnished by a formal contract, are delivered to a private individual upon a special agreement (as he Stearns, says) to breed on shares for a term of three years. I have endeavored to procure from Mr. Stearns a copy of the agreement he has made with Lieutenant Colonel Fremont to take care of these cattle, but his letters (marked 7 and 10) positively assert that he regards those cattle as the private property of Lieutenant Colonel Fremont, but that the agreement by which he holds them is a verbal one, witnessed by a Mr. Hensly and Lieutenant Gillespie of the United States Navy. Thus stand the facts, and I am applied to to know whether payment will be made upon the paper marked 2, which is a certificate that the sum of $6,975 is due to Mr. Celis for supplies furnished the California battalion, which supplies are clearly and plainly the lot of six hundred breeding cows now in the hands of a private individual, not one of which has been used for public purposes. This note becomes due on the 18th day of December, 1847, and bears an interest of twenty-four per centum per annum, after that date.

In connection with this subject, I call your attention to the paper marked 3, wherein Lieutenant Colonel Fremont has bound himself and future Governors of California to pay the sum of $2,500 at the expiration of eight months after the date of March 3, 1847, or in default thereof, that the note shall bear an interest of twenty-four per cent. per annum; this, too, when the acting assistant quartermaster at Monterey had been more than a month in the country, with a supply of money applicable to the proper expenses of the army in California.

Mr. Celis states that it was partly to secure this loan of money that Lieutenant Colonel Fremont made with him the liberal bargain for cattle, which the price is about forty per cent. higher than the market price at the time. Both of these notes are soon due, and Mr. Celis is going to make application for payment, as he claims to have fulfilled his part of a contract, for the redemption of which the good faith of the Government of the United States is pledged by an officer thereof; but the whole transaction, as shown by the accompanying papers, appears to me of *such a character* that I shall not order payment of the money to Mr. Celis, but refer all the papers to the department, for such action as they may consider proper in the case. I have the honor to be &c.

R. B. MASON, *Colonel 1st Dragoons Commanding.*

To GEN. R. JONES, Washington City.

HEADQUARTERS 10th MILITARY DEPARTMENT,
MONTEREY, CALA., June 21, 1847.

A claim has to-day been presented to me against the United States, of so extraordinary a nature that I deem it proper to send it to you for the information of the Department.

You will perceive that it is for money borrowed at an enormous rate of interest by Lieutenant Colonel Fremont from one Antonio Jose Cot, and, too, in the official (character) of "governor" of California, when he knew that General Kearney, his superior and commanding officer, was here in the country.

In the same manner, the Lieutenant Colonel gave orders and caused the collector of customs at San Pedro to receive in payment of custom-house dues a large amount—say about one thosand seven hundred dollars—of depreciated paper signed by individuals in no way responsible to the government.

The object I now have in view is the request that Lieutenant Colonel Fremont may be required to refund immediately the seventeen hundred dollars that the treasury of California has thus lost by his illegal order.

I am, &c., R. B. MASON,
Col. 1st Dragoons commanding.

To Brig. General R. JONES,
Adj. Gen. U. S. Army, Washington city.

Translation of the original obligation given by Fremont to Cot, and now on file in the Department.

ANGELES, February 4, 1847,

I, the undersigned *governor* of California for the United States of North America, acknowledge that I have received from Don Antonio Jose Cot, merchant of this city, two thousand dollars in hard cash, which he has furnished this government for the public service. And I bind myself, in the name of the United States Government, to return the said sum within the term of two months from this date, paying for interest three per cent. per month, or one hundred and twenty dollars. But if, at the expiration of this term, the government should see fit still to make use of these two thousand dollars, Mr. Cot agrees that the interest shall run for four months longer at two per cent. per month, or of one hundred and sixty dollars for four months. And for the fulfilment of what has been stipulated, I bind myself, as *governor* of California.

For $2,000. J. C. FREMONT.

ANGELES, February 10, 1848.

I have furthermore received from the said Mr. Cot the sum of one thousand dollars in the terms expressed above.

For $1,000 J. C. FREMONT.

THE FRAUD UPON THE PEOPLE PROVEN.

The word Governor is italicized by us, and needs no further comment. From the first invasion of California by the American troops, a large portion of the leading citizens of California, among whom I may mention Don Pedro C. Corrillo, Don Jose Corrillo, Pedrorena, Cot, and Celis, welcomed our troops with open arms, and willingly furnished material aid in establishing the supremacy of our flag in the El Dorado of the West. In consequence of their sympathy in our success, *any one professing* to be the agents of our Government, could have obtained the last dollar that any of those gentlemen possessed ; hence the facility by which "our Governor" was enabled to borrow this and other sums from other individuals.

The claim of Don Cot was not allowed by the Treasury Department, and it was presented to the army board, organized under the 6th section of the appropriation act passed August, 1852, who, on the 26th of January, 1854, recommended the allowance in full, with two hundred and forty dollars additional for four months' interest at two per cent. per month. Congress having made the necessary appropriations, the claim was allowed by the accounting officers of the Treasury on the 31st October, 1854, and was paid on a power of attorney from Cot to Corcoran & Riggs, into whose hands the claim had passed.

The board was induced to allow the claim, not on account of its legality, but from the fact that Don Cot loaned the money believing that it was for the use of the Government of the United States, and the board thought it unjust that he should be the victim of his own patriotism, though he must doubtless have suffered considerable loss in having it discounted. Colonel Fremont was called upon, but being *unwilling or unable* (or at least neglecting to do so) to show *how* the money *thus borrowed* by him *was applied to the service* of the Government, it was charged to him upon the books of the Department, and has remained wholly unaccounted for by him up to this time. On the 30th of January, 1856, a claim was allowed Colonel Fremont by the Secretary of the Treasury, and it was placed to his credit upon the before mentioned debt against him, which, being deducted, leave a balance of $1,986 51 of the $3,000 (and interest) still unaccounted for and standing against the "gallant" candidate for President on the books of the Department. It is more than probable that the story current in California will account for the *disbursement* of the money borrowed of Don Cot, which is, that it went to pay for the celebrated humbug "Mariposa claim," of, and about which, so much has been said and written the past four months.

[D.]

The undersigned certifies that the governor and commandant of this Territory, Mr. J. C. Fremont, finding himself short of resources for the support of the armed force which, under his command, co-operated toward the pacification of the country, solicited from various individuals a loan for the object indicated ; and the undersigned having been requested, through the medium of Mr. Chas Flugge, to furnish provisions and cash, the accompanying contract took place, the cash having been delivered immediately, without interest, for the term of eight months, and the cattle were to be delivered when they might be wanted ; it being understood that the terms of payment should run on from the day of the contract, on account of the cattle being movable property which could not be consumed in two or three months, and, besides, was augmenting daily, it chiefly consisting of cows. It is likewise added that the contract was complied with on the part of the declarant to the satisfaction of the "*Governor*," who, not having time to consume said cattle on account of having received a superior order to deliver up the command and *disband the force, he ordered said cattle to be delivered to* Mr. Abel Stearns, as I understand, in the quality of a deposite, until the Government should dispose of them.

EULOJIO DE CELIS.

ANGELES, July 8, 1847.

Accompanying the above document are the letters and certificates of Col. J. D. Stevenson, colonel commanding the southern military district of California ; Dr. S. C. Foster, at present Mayor of Los Angeles; J. M. Davidson, Lieutenant United States Army; A. J. Smith, lieutenant 1st dragoons; W. G. Sherman, 3d artillery, and a number of others, all tending to corroborate and establish the authenticity of the papers, which I omit on account of the space they would occupy. That there is evidence of intention on the part of the "Governor," or Lieutenant Colonel Fremont, to defraud the Government, must be clear to every unprejudiced person who reads the charges, and the opinion is strengthened when it is known that the charges were known to Colonel—no, "*Governor*" Fremont, and he has never made any effort to disprove them. Unless there was a consciousness of guilt, would not any individual, however humble, have made an effort to explain or disprove the charges. The only effort on the part of *Governor* Fremont, that I ever heard of, was threats, in Washington City, to kill Governor Mason in California, who, in laying the facts before the Department, was merely performing a duty which, as an officer of the Government, he was sworn to perform."

As "Governor" Fremont is the candidate for the office of President of the United States, his official acts are public property: if meritorious, they should be rewarded, and if discreditable they should be made public. I intend to furnish additional proofs of the skill of the "Governor" in financial affairs, though I fear they will only give him additional *eclat* with his party, a leader of which (Ford, of Ohio,) lately boasted in a speech that "in case of a division of the Union, Ohio would *steal* all the negroes in the South." That being a cardinal virtue with them, of course proof of fraud on the part of their candidate would only elevate him in their estimation.

At the date of the operations of Colonel Fremont, Brigadier General Kearney was the only recognised Governor of California—that is by the Departments at Washington.

Gen. Kearney arrested Col. Fremont in August; and he was arraigned before a court-martial, composed of the ablest officers of the United States army, on the 27th September, 1847, at Washington city, to answer the following charges: 1st. Mutiny—11 specifications. 2d. Disobedience of the lawful commands of his superior officers—7 specifications. 3d. Conduct to the prejudice of good order and military discipline—5 specifications. The court on the 31st of January, 1848, found Col. Fremont guilty on each of the charges, and *every one* of the specifications. On the 16th February, 1848, President Polk, in pursuance of the finding of the court-martial, dismissed Col. Fremont the service. The charges made by General Mason, the successor of Kearney, were received too late, or there would have been a *fourth* and a *fifth* charge, for fraud and peculation. A fitting subject for a President!

N. B.—By reference to Executive Documents, 1st session 31st Congress, 1849 and 1850, volume 5, Document No 17, pages 329 and 330, and pages 363 to 373 inclusive, it will be seen that the charges contained in the above article were reported to the House of Representatives on the 21st January, 1850, by President Z. Taylor, in answer to a resolution of the House of the 31st December, 1849.

From the facts cited in connection with the financial operations of Col. Fremont, it would appear:

1. That he resisted the orders of the Federal Government, and usurped the office of Governor of California. That he employed that office to borrow money upon the credit of the United States. That simultaneonsly with the reception of a particular sum from that source, he purchased and paid a similar sum for valuable private property. That he had no ostensible means of his own. That he has never accounted for the money received from the United States.

2. That Colonel Fremont purchased a lot of cattle in the name and for the use of the United States. That he acknowledged the receipt of these cattle on the 26th May, 1847. That he then executed an obligation for the value of the cattle. That the cattle were not delivered by the contractor for two months *after Colonel Fremont had acknowledged their delivery*, and that then they were delivered to the agent of Colonel Fremont, to be kept for his own use, and for another purpose.

3. That whilst the Government paid for these cattle, Colonel Fremont never accounted for them, but kept them as his own. That he afterwards sold the Government a part of its own cattle to feed the Indians, but that the Indians got no part of the Government beef, except the offal, be-

cause the California miners finally eat the beef, and paid Colonel Fremont for it.

ANOTHER BEEF CONTRACT.

The following letter from E. W. Barbour, Commissioner of California Indians, will with the aid of a few italics, explain how Colonel Fremont paid off the balance of $21,563.73, which had been standing for some years against him on the books of the Treasury Department.

Extract from a communication of the 5*th January*, 1852, *from G. W. Barbour, commissioner for the Indians in California, to Hon. Luke Lea, Commissioner of Indian Affairs.*

After separating with my colleagues, many proposals were made by different persons to supply the amount of beef, &c., necessary to carry out the treaties that had or might be made by me. *I invariably answered such propositions by an assurance that I had no direct authority to make such contracts.* On the 25th of May I received from Col. J. C. Fremont a letter, containing a proposition to supply beef, &c., a copy of which is herewith enclosed. After consulting with some of the officers in command of the escort, and reflecting on what had been done, and knowing as well as I did the necessity for something to be done to secure the peace of the country, and save not only the lives and property of the citizens, but the Indians from destruction, *I determined on the 28th of May to make a conditional contract with Fremont; but he having arrived in camp, I would make no contract with him until I had shown to him my letter of appointment, instructions, &c., assuring him at the time that I did not believe that I was authorised by my instructions to make such contracts;* and that if made at all, they would not be paid until Congress passed upon them, and provided a fund out of which they could be paid, besides the approval or rejection of such contracts by your department. After examining those papers, he professed an entire willingness to "take the chances" under all the circumstances. I then addressed him a note, under date of the 28th of May, a copy of which I herewith enclose, concluding with him a conditional contract, as you will perceive; of all which I in due time informed your department.

Colonel Fremont in a few days started for Los Angelos, in the vicinity of which place he contemplated purchasing cattle to fulfil said contract. I afterwards met with him in Los Angelos in the last days of June or the first of July, and informed him that I had received a letter from Colonel McKee of the commission, in which he stated that only the sum of $25,000 had been appropriated for the object of our mission, and that your department had instructed the commissioners to make no further stipulations for feeding the Indians during the year 1851 in any treaties that we might make after the receipt of that letter. *He, Colonel, Fremont, then went on to furnish those tribes with whom treaties had already been concluded with beef only, to the amount of the drafts drawn by me on the Secretary of the Interior*, (say $183,825.)

After the delivery of a portion of the beef, Colonel Fremont called upon me, and requested as a favor that I would draw on the Secretary of the Interior three several drafts—one for $5,000, one for $3,000, and one for $2,000—to enable him to carry out his contract. *I objected to doing so, telling him that I had no authority for so doing.* He replied that he could not get along without, unless at a great sacrifice; that if the drafts were drawn, he had friends who knew the difficulties in the way of the probable honoring of the drafts, but who would nevertheless aid him if it was put into that shape, knowing *that if I drew the drafts as desired by him, it would make no difference so far as the government was concerned, in the contract or transaction*, and at the same time be of essential service to him as he stated. I consented, and drew accordingly. Subsequently, and after the delivery of the remainder of the beef, I drew according to his (Colonel Fremont's) request, the other drafts on the same department or officer.

In doing so, *I knew I was acting without any direct authority*, and could only justify the act by the *pressing and urgent necessities of the case*, and in the absence of direct instructions.

From the letter it appears:

That Mr. Barbour refused "many proposals to supply the amount of beef, &c.," because he had no direct authority to make such contract.

Yet he made a private contract with Colonel Fremont, without any farther authority from the Department.

That Mr. Barbour made the contract with Colonel Fremont because it was necessary "to secure the peace of the country."

Yet the contract with Colonel Fremont was not only made to feed the Indians, but to supply them with "brood mares and brood cows." That Mr. Barbour made this contract from the necessity of the case, and because he was unable to wait for the action of the Department. Yet the contract runs through the years 1851 and 1852.

That Mr. Barbour contracted with Colonel Fremont because he considered him the only "responsible" bidder. Yet at the request of Colonel Fremont he draws upon the Government for the full amount of his contract, although he knew he was "acting without any direct authority."

Col. Fremont, as in the cases of Col. Temple and Huttman, cornered the Government; the beef had been delivered upon the authority of an Indian agent, who declared he had "no authority." The beef had been eaten, and it had to be paid for. So the Government paid the account of Col. Fremont, with interest to the 1st. August, 1854, amounting to $242,036.25

Out of this beef account, created without warrant or authority, the balance standing for years on the books of the Government, against Col. Fremont, was deducted.

Up to this date Col. Fremont had been technically a defaulter, and but for that fortuitous and audacious speculation, he might have continued in arrears to the present day.

In this transaction the leading features of Col. Fremont's character are obvious. A majority of the Indian commissioners are opposed to making contracts to supply the Indians. Congress has cut down the application made by the Indian Department for Indian supplies to $25,000. Col. Fremont persuades one of the commissioners to make the contract; and although aware of the obstacles and the want of authority, he agrees, in the language of the commissioners, "to take the chances of being paid."

Having made the contract, he persuades the commissioners to do as he had himself done in similar cases—to draw upon the Government without authority. Although he had represented himself as perfectly responsible, he now says that these drafts are necessary to enable him to carry out his contract.

The whole transaction evinces a reckless and speculative nature, wholly unfit for the representatives of a constitutional government, and convey imputations of personal rapacity utterly incompatible with the character of an honest and honorable nation. We have stated these transactions impartially and from the records. We shall offer no comments upon them. We will not say that Col. Fremont borrowed money on the credit of the United States to buy land and cattle for himself, but we will say, that the inference is irresistible that he has done so.

It is difficult to anticipate whether the mines of Mariposa will prove the prolific source of wealth anticipated by the sanguine proprietors, but we must say, that if Col. Fremont will only work those mines to the same advantage that he appears to have *worked* UNCLE SAM, his associates in interest will have no reason to complain, but must realise very handsome dividends upon their speculation.

BLACK REPUBLICAN

IMPOSTURE EXPOSED!

FRAUD UPON THE PEOPLE!

THE ACCOUNTS OF FREMONT EXAMINED;

SHOWING

AN ASTOUNDING DISREGARD OF THE PUBLIC INTEREST, ONLY TO BE ACCOUNTED FOR BY EXTRAVAGANCE, RECKLESSNESS, OR AN UTTER WANT OF JUDGMENT!

WASHINGTON:
1856.

FREMONT NO STATESMAN.

In the pursuance of the painful duty of exposing the impositions attempted by the Black Republican party, by presenting for the Presidency the name of an individual utterly unfit for the discharge of its responsible duties, we proceed to examine the pretensions of Colonel Fremont as a STATESMAN; and, as one of his biographers has said that he "resembles Washington," we will see how far he resembles that man, whom it is profanation to compare with any other, in that first official attribute—accuracy and fidelity in his pecuniary transactions. In doing so, we mean no imputation upon the personal character of Colonel Fremont. We shall state recorded facts, and leave the people to judge for themselves of his motives and merits.

COLONEL FREMONT AS A DISBURSING OFFICER.

The chief dealings of Colonel Fremont as a disbursing officer arose during the campaign in California whilst he commanded the volunteers. The obligation of the government to pay all the expenses of the military occupation and conquest of California, was properly held to relate back to the beginning of the revolution. The term of service of the California volunteers began about the 19th July, 1846, when they were received into the service of the United States, and ended when they were discharged from its service about the 19th April, 1847.(1.) The California volunteers were then in the service of the United States ten months.(2.)

The whole amount of claims for the support of these volunteers, filed before the board appointed to audit them, amounted to $960,614.

The whole amount allowed by the board was $157,317. The immense proportion of $803,297 was disallowed(3) or suspended.

From the authorities to which we have referred, it will appear that Colonel Fremont's command consisted for five months of 160 men, and for five months more of 450 men. This was an average command of 205 men. They cost the government the sum stated, and required for their transportation about 3,500 horses, and for their support about 3,000 cattle*—being at the rate of seventeen horses and fifteen cows per

---

(1.) Report of board at p. —, in MS.

(2.) This was not a battalion. The use of the term is calculated to deceive. "A battallion is a body of infantry, consisting of from 500 to 800 men." This was a mounted company, consisting, during much the largest term of its military service, of less than 200 men, never more than 450. It consisted on the 19th July, 1840, of 160 men, and continued at that number until about the 1st November, 1846, when it was increased by recruits from new immigrants, 250 of whom, says Colonel Russel, enlisted.—[Ex. Doc. Ho. Reps., No. 175, 1st sess. 33d Con., p. 51.] It then numbered 450, which was the maximum up to the date of its discharge.

(3.) Doc. No. 13, 33d Congress, 2d session.

* Colonel Fremont's deposition.—[Sen. Rep. Com., No. 75, 1st sess. — Con.]

man, besides other supplies, and not estimating that they were at sea some six weeks of the time, and it is to be supposed subsisted upon the ship stores.

This statement of facts will fully justify the imputation that Colonel Fremont manifested in this campaign great extravagance in the use of public money.

We will next publish some of these claims to show that

Colonel Fremont evinced either a want of care, judgment, or integrity, as a disbursing officer.

On the 31st August, 30th September, and 11th November, 1852, Messrs. Corcoran & Riggs, bankers, Washington city, addressed the letters which follow to the Secretary of War:

Letters of Messrs. Corcoran & Riggs referred to.

[Note to report on claim No. 8.]

WASHINGTON, August 31, 1852.

DEAR SIR: We beg to enclose the following accounts of Mariano G. Vallejo for supplies furnished to the United States troops under the command of Captain John C. Fremont, and which please place on file for payment to us, as we have the necessary power to collect the same:

One account for	$82,625
One.... do	24,750
One.... do	500
	107,875

Yours respectfully, CORCORAN & RIGGS.

Hon. C. M. CONRAD, *Secretary of War, &c.*

WASHINGTON September 30, 1852.

SIR: At the request of Hon. Rob. M. McLane we enclose the following accounts for supplies furnished to the United States troops under the command of, and certified by, Captain J. C. Fremont, which we request may be filed for examination and payment to him, in virtue of the powers of attorney in his possession:

Julio Carullo	$17,500
Victor Purdon	7,390
Damasa Rodrigues	2,675
Jose de la Rosa	5,040
Cayetano Juares	10,520
Mariano G. Vallejo	143,300
Salvador Vallejo	53,100
	239,525

Very respectfully, your obd't ser't, CORCORAN & RIGGS.

Hon. SECRETARY OF WAR, *Washington.*

WASHINGTON, November 11, 1852.

DEAR SIR: Under date of 30th September last, certain accounts were transmitted by us, at the request of Hon. Rob. M. McLane, for supplies furnished to the United States troops under the command of Captain J. C. Premont; among these accounts was one of Mariano G. Vallejo for $143,500, which ought to have been filed, as explanatory of the accounts to you, *August* 31, 1852, amounting to $107,875—both accounts being for the same supplies, but the latter having been stated at reduced prices *in consequence of Colonel Fremont's having refused to certify to the value of the articles as charged in the original account transmitted in our letter of* 30*th September*. [Our italics.]

Yours respectfully, &c., CORCORAN & RIGGS.

Hon. C. M. CONRAD, *Secretary of War, &c.*

As the claims of Vallejo were at first presented, they consisted of the three separate accounts which follow:

The United States, Dr.

To Mariano G. Vallejo.

For the following property taken from the ranchos and stores of Mariano G. Vallejo, for the use of the United States troops under the command of Captain John C. Fremont, in the month of August, A. D. one thousand eight hundred and forty-six:

To five hundred head of first-quality horses, at $100 each	$50,000
To three hundred and nine head of horses, at $75 each	23,175
To two hundred and fifty head of wild mares, at $25 each	6,250
To forty saddles, complete, at $50 each	2,000
To forty pairs of spurs, at $5 each	200
To two hundred blankets, at $5 each	1,000
Total	82,625

M. G. VALLEJO.

SONOMA, August 30, 1856.

I certify, on honor, that the foregoing account is substantially correct and just; that the animals and other property enumerated were taken from General Mariano G. Vallejo for the use of the United States troops under my command serving in California during the year 1846; that this property was lost and expended in said service, and no portion of it returned to General Vallejo; and that he has received no compensation whatever for the same. I do further certify that the prices charged are reasonable, not exceeding the value of the property at the time it was furnished for the use of the United States troops under my command in California.

JOHN C. FREMONT.

In explanation of this amount, it is proper to state that I considered the stock owned by General Vallejo to be of superior quality, and that I was directed by this knowledge in admitting the higher prices set out herein. It is further proper to state that in Sonoma, and generally throughout California, the stock found upon farms was driven off, as much in the view of preventing it from falling into the hands of the enemy as for the use of the troops, to which latter purpose only a comparatively small portion was appropriated. Great numbers of the stock so driven off by us were scattered over the country, and were, consequently, lost and perished. And it is in this extended sense that the words "consumed and expended" in the service of the United States were intended to be understood.

JULY 11, 1853. JOHN C. FREMONT.

The United States, Dr.

To Mariano G. Vallejo.

For the following property taken from the ranchos of General Mariano G. Vallejo, for the use of the United States troops under the command of Captain John C. Fremont in the month of August, A. D. 1846:

To eight hundred head of cows and large cattle, at $15 each	$12,000
To six hundred head of second class cattle, at $12 each	7,200
To six hundred head of third-class cattle, at $8 each	4,800
To one hundred head of sheep, at $5 each	750
Total	24,750

M. G. VALLEJO.

SONOMA, August 30, 1846.

I certify, on honor, that the foregoing account is substantially correct and just; that the property enumerated and charged was taken from General Vallejo for the use of the United States troops under my command serving in California during the year 1846; that this property was consumed and expended in said service, and no portion of it returned to General Vallejo; and that he has received no compensation whatever for the same.

I do further certify, that the prices charged are reasonable, not exceeding the value of the property at the time it was furnished for the use of the United States troops under my command in California.

JOHN C. FREMONT.

The explanatory remarks of this date, appended to claim No. 9, I consider as applicable to this case.

JULY 11, 1853. JOHN C. FREMONT.

[A small account of $500 allowed, omitted.]

These accounts, it will be seen, amount, in the aggregate, to $107,875. They are all certified by Colonel Fremont as correct.

On the 11th November, 1852, the bankers, in explanation of these accounts, present to the board one inclusive account, as follows:

The United States

To Mariano G. Vallejo, Dr.

For the following property taken from the ranchos and stores of Mariano G. Vallejo by the troops under the command of Captain J. C. Fremont in the month of June, July, and August, A. D. 1846:

To 500 head of number one horses, at $150 each	$75,000
To 309 head of horses, at $100 each	30,900
To 800 head of cows and large cattle, at $15 each	12,000
To 600 head of second-class cattle, at $12 each	7,200
To 600 head of third-class cattle, at $8 each	4,800
To 150 head of sheep, at $5 each	750
To 250 head of wild mares, at $25 each	6,250
To 40 saddles, at $100 each	4,000
To 40 pair of spurs, at $10 each	400
To 9 rifles, at $100 each	900
To 1 pair of pistols	100
To 200 blankets, at $5 each	1,000
Amounting to	143,300

SONOMA, August 30, 1846.

I certify that the above account is generally correct. The property described was taken by the troops under my command, and used in the service of the United States. From the nature of the operations which have been carried on in this country, it has not been possible for me to keep myself exactly informed of the quantity of property taken from individuals; but in the present instance it was taken under my more immediate personal direction, subject to my inspection. I therefore believe the above account to be substantially correct, and accordingly acknowledge and approve it.

J. C. FREMONT.

Now, will any friend of Colonel Frémont explain to us how it was, that on the 30th August, 1846, Colonel Fremont certified the items of which the account amounting to $143,300 is composed, "as substantially correct, and accordingly acknowledge and approve it," and subsequently, on the 11th July, 1853, certified "on honor" the same items when scaled and reduced in the aggregate by the sum of $35,425, or thirty per cent., as being "substantially correct and just," and "not exceeding the value of the property at the time it was purchased for the use of the United States troops?"

Colonel Fremont has also certified, at the same dates, the claim of Salvador Vallejo, amounting to $53,100, of Antonio Carrillo, amounting to $14,010, and others, at the same extravagant figures, and some of them are represented by the same solicitors:

[Claim No. 246.]

United States, Dr.

To Carlos Antonio Carrillo.

For supplies furnished United States troops under command of Col. John C. Fremont:

1847. January 5.	To 38 mules, at $100	3,800
	To 20 mares, at $50	1,000
	To 75 horses, at $100	7,500
	To 35 cows, (milch,) at $30	1,050
	To 100 fanegas corn, at $3	300
	To 60 fanegas beans, at $4	240
	To 4 saddles, at $30	120
		14,010

I certify that the above account is correct, and that the supplies enumerated in the bill were furnished to the troops under my command, and applied accordingly to the use of the United States forces.

JOHN C. FREMONT.

United States, Dr.

To Julio Carrillo.

For the following property taken from the ranchos and stores of Julio Carrillo, by the troops under the command of Capt. J. C. Fremont, in the months of June, July, and August, A. D. 1846:

To 40 head of second-quality horses, at $100 each	$4,000
To 80 head third-quality horses, at $80 each	6,400
To 80 mares, at $80 each	6,400
To 4 saddles, at $100 each	400
To 3 rifles, at $100 each	300
Total	17,500

The within account approved.

J. C. FREMONT.

[Claim No. 16.]

United States, Dr.

To Salvador Vallejo.

For the following property taken from the ranchos and stores of Salvador Vallejo, by the troops under the command of Captain J. C. Fremont, in the months of June, July, and August, A. D. one thousand eight hundred and forty-six:

To two hundred head of first-quality horses, at one hundred and thirty dollars each	26,000
To two hundred and forty head of second-quality horses, at one hundred dollars each	24,000
To fifteen saddles, at one hundred dollars each	1,500
To four rifles, at one hundred dollars each	400
To one rifle, at two hundred dollars	200
To two pair of pistols, at one hundred dollars each	200
To ten mares, at eighty dollars each	800
Total—fifty-three thousand one hundred dollars	$53,100

The remarks of this date, appended to claim No. 11, are appllicable to the present case, except that it is proper further to say that the arms specified herein were of a superior quality.

JOHN C. FREMONT.

July 11, 1853.

Sworn to by claimant, and endorsed: Approved.

J. C. FREMONT.

United States, Dr.

To Jose De La Rosa.

For the following property taken from the stores of Jose de la Rosa, in Sonoma, by the troops under the command of Captain J. C. Fremont, in the months of June, July, and August, A. D. 1846:

To 21 mares, at $80 each	1,680
To 28 tame cows, at $30 each	1,100
To 11 horses, at $100 each	1,100
To 9 horses, at $80 each	720

To 4 mules, at $100 each 400
To 3 rifles, at $100 each 300

Total $5,040

Endorsed on the back: The within account approved.

J. C. FREMONT.

[Claim No. 230.]

The United States

To William D. Phelps, Dr.

For services for himself, crew, and boats of the barque Moscow, of Boston, of which he was part owner and in command, and being agent for all other owners, and for the risk and hazard incident to such service, in transporting Captain J. C. Fremont and a detachment of men under his command to a fort on the opposite side of the bay and entrance to the port of San Francisco, in Upper California, in July, 1846, and aiding him in capturing and dismantling the said fort, and spiking the guns thereof, consisting of three brass and seven iron cannon, of heavy calibre, and a part of which was afterwards taken on board the United States ship Portsmouth, by order of Captain J. B. Montgomery, United States navy, $10,000.

E. E. WILLIAM PHELPS.

Sworn to by the claimant.

I certify that Captain William D. Phelps did transport a party of men under my command to the fort near the Presidio, at the entrance of the bay of San Francisco, under the circumstances narrated in the above deposition; that he aided in dismantling the fort, and that I have always considered his services on that occasion to have been very valuable to the United States.

JOHN C. FREMONT.

WASHINGTON CITY, August 5, 1853.

I certify that in July, 1846, Captain W. D. Phelps did transport a party of men under the command of Captain J. C. Fremont from Sancelito across the bay of San Francisco (seven miles) to the fort at Yerba Buena, commanding the entrance to the harbor, for the purpose of spiking the guns of the fort, which was in a very dismantled condition, and could not have been occupied without having been almost entirely rebuilt. There was no enemy present, and the sole object Captain Fremont had in view was to prevent the Californians from using the guns at any future time. There was no risk or personal danger incurred, and the service would be well paid for at fifty dollars.

ARCHI. W. GILLESPIE,
Bvt. Major U. S. M. Corps.

WASHINGTON, September 19, 1853.

Board for the examination of claims contracted in California under Lt. Col. John C. Fremont.

[Opinion on the claim of Wm. D. Phelps, No. 230.—Services of boats' crew and use of boat, $10, 000.]

The board deems a part of this claim, amounting to fifty dollars, ($50.) just, and accordingly recommend so much of it in amount to the favorable consideration of Congress; the balance, nine thousand nine hundred and fifty dollars, ($9,950,) being disallowed.

[Vote unanimous—see journal, page 302.]

C. F. SMITH,
Col. U. S. Army, President of the Board.

FEBRUARY 8, 1854.

Here is a claim of ten thousand dollars, certified by Colonel Fremont to be just, which a competent witness says would be "well paid for at $50," and the board of sworn commissioners disallows nine thousand nine hundred and fifty dollars! The claimant, backed by Colonel Fremont's certificate, recovers just five per cent. of his demand! The public escapes the payment of nine thousand nine hundred and fifty dollars! Shade of Nathaniel Macon, rise and protect a plundered treasury!

How can these extravagant allowances, and these accommodating certificates; be explained? We ask a reply.

But the board of commissioners differed very greatly with Colonel Fremont and the great banking solicitors in their opinion of the value of horses in California, and therefore abated the claims immensely. Speaking of that portion of the claim represented in the first demand by an account of $82,625, the board says:

Board for the examination of claims contracted in California under Lieut. Col. John C. Fremont.

[Opinion in the claim of Mariano G. Vallejo, No. 9.—Horses, cattle, &c., $82,625.]

On the additional testimony produced, the board is of opinion that a part of this claim, amounting to thirty-two thousand six hundred and twenty-five dollars, ($32,625,) is just, and accordingly recommend so much of it in amount to the favorable consideration of Congress; the balance, fifty thousand dollars, ($50,000,) being disallowed. This amount is arrived at by allowing the undermentioned rates, the price affixed for the first quality of horses appearing to be the highest that was paid by the quartermaster, or any other official, for horses for the California batallion, viz:

500 horses, 1st quality, at $40	$20,000
309 do 2d do at $25	7,725
250 wild mares, at $10	2,500
40 saddles, complete, at $30	1,200
40 pairs of spurs, at $5	200
200 blankets, at $5	1,000
	$32,625

[Vote unanimous—see journal, page 226.]

JANUARY 17, 1854.

C. F. SMITH,
Colonel U. S. Army, President of the Board.

The moderate little sum of $50,000, certified by Colonel Fremont "as just and correct" is certified by the board to have been an improper demand.

And so in the cases of Salvador Vallejo and C. A. Carrillo, both of which were "approved" by Colonel Fremont. This inexorable board made the following awards:

Board for the examination of claims contracted in California under Lieut. Col. John C. Fremont.

[Opinion on the claim of Salvador Vallejo.—Horses, arms, &c., $53,100. No. 16.]

On the additional testimony produced, the board is of opinion that a part of this claim, amounting to eleven thousand seven hundred dollars ($11,700) is just, and accordingly recommend so much of it in amount to the favorable consideration of Congress; the balance, forty-one thousand four hundred dollars ($41,400) being disallowed.

This amount is arrived at by allowing the undermentioned rates, viz:

200 horses, first quality, at $30	$6,000
240 horses, second quality, at $20	4,800
15 saddles, at $30	450
4 rifles, at $50	200
1 rifle, at $50	50
2 pair pistols, at $50	100
10 mares, at $10	100
	11,700

[Vote unanimous—see journal, page 230.]

C. F. SMITH,
Colonel U. S. Army, President of the Board.

JANUARY 19, 1854.

REMARKS AND ACTION OF THE BOARD IN THE CASE OF JULIO CARRILLO.

It does not appear from this account—the only testimony before the board—when, where, or by whom, the property was taken.

The board is of the opinion that the prices charged are extravagant, and taking into consideration other claims, for supplies of a similar nature, that the number of animals is disproportionate to the force in service; on which points it deems additional testimony necessary. The board also deems additional proof or explanation requisite with respect to the number or quantity of the articles or supplies taken.

Board for the examination of claims contracted in California under Lieut. Col. John C. Fremont.

[Opinion on the claim of Carlos Antonio Carrilo, No. 246.—Horses, &c., $14,010.]

The board deems a part of this claim, amounting to four thousand and thirty-five dollars, ($4,035,) just, and accordingly recommend so much of it in amount to the favorable consideration of Congress; the balance, nine thousand nine hundred and seventy-five dollars, ($9,975,) being disallowed. This amount is arrived at by the allowing the undermentioned rates, viz:

38 mules, at $25	$950
20 mares, at $10	200
75 horses, at $25	1,875
35 cows, at $10	350
100 fanegas corn, at $3	300
60 do beans, at $4	240
4 saddles, at $30	120
	4,035

[Vote unanimous—see journal, page 305.]

FEBRUARY 9, 1854.

C. F. SMITH,
Colonel U. S. Army, President of the Board.

In this last case there is the sum of more than fifty thousand dollars out of sixty-four thousand dollars, "approved" by Colonel Fremont as a proper charge upon the public treasury, disallowed and cast out as an attempted fraud and imposition by the claimants or those who represent them; and as a final and conclusive condemnation of these accounts so certified by Col. Fremont, and presented by Messrs. Corcoran & Riggs, the board made the following recapitulatory report:

F.

Claim No. 5—J. A Sutter	$7,200	not allowed.
" 7—Mariano G. Vallejo	500	"
" 8— do. do.	24,700	"
" 9— do. do.	82,625	"
" 10— do. do.	143,300	"
" 11—Julio Carrillo	17,500	"
" 12—Victor Prudon	7,390	"
" 13—Damasa Rodriguez	2,675	"
" 14—Jose de la Rosa	5,040	"
" 15—Cayetano Juarez	10,520	"
" 16—Salvador Vallejo	53,100	"

[Report of board on Claims No. 11, 12, 13, 14, 15, 16.]

It does not appear from this account—the only testimony before the board—when, where, or by whom the property was taken.

The board is of opinion that the prices charged are extravagant, and, taking into consideration other claims for supplies of a similar nature, that the number of animals is disproportionate to the force in service, on which points it deems additional testimony necessary.

The board also deems additional proof or explanation requisite with respect to the number or quantity of the articles of supplies taken.

[Report of board on No. 10.]

Withdrawn, and submitted "as explanatory" to claims Nos. 7, 8, and 9.

Now, lest it may be said that these prices were too low, or that in the case of the reduced accounts that prices had declined thirty per cent. within the period that intervened between the first and second certificates of Colonel Fremont, let us examine a few other accounts for supplies of the same description, furnished during the same campaign. The evidence which we shall adduce will vindicate the board from any imputation of injustice.

The first testimony which we shall offer will be that of one of Colonel Fremont's witnesses, Captain Hensley, who says, under the caption of "the average prices of military supplies of all descriptions in California, before and during the war:" "Horses and mules from $25 to $35. Beef cattle, from $8 to $10 per head."*

The reader will now examine the following accounts for horses furnished the volunteers, all of which were approved by Col. Fremont:

[Claim No. 97.]

This is to certify that Don Antonio German has delivered for the service of the United States volunteers, the following horses, &c., &c.

One tortello horse, feine de Thodora Areanes, valued at	$25 00
One rolento horse, feine del rancho [ ] valued at	25 00
One segno horse, feine del rancho [ ] valued at	25 00
One rosello horse, feine del rancho [ ] valued at	25 00
One baym blanco, feine del rancho [ ] valued at	25 00
One curselano, feine del rancho [ ] valued at	25 00
One pinto, feine del rancho [ ] valued at	25 00
One rosello, feine del rancho [ ] valued at	25 00
One tortello, feine del rancho [ ] valued at	25 00
One callote, feine de dos riandos del rancho [ ] valued at	15 00
One mare, callo blanco del rancho [ ] valued at	12 00
One crulla horse, del rancho [ ] valued at	25 00
One new saddle, valued at	25 00
One pair spurs, valued at	8 00
One bridle, valued at	5 00
One riada, valued at	1 00
One carbine, valued at	8 00
Two pair spurs, taken at the house	16 00
Two bridles	10 00
Three hundred and fifty dollars in full	350 00

PUEBLA, SAN JOSEPH, November, 1846.

CHAS. M. WEBER,
Commanding U. S. Charge, Puebla.

Approved:

J. C. FREMONT,
Lieut. Col. U. S. A., commanding California battallion.

The board is of opinion that the claim is reasonable and just, and accordingly recommends it to the favorable consideration of Congress.

---

* Ex. Doc. House of Reps. 817, 1st sess. 30th Cong., p. 37.

[Claim No. 95.]

The United States government, Dr.

To Tomaso Hernandez.

To	1 saddle, complete with spurs and bridle	$30 00
	1 tortello horse	25 00
	1 grullo horse	30 00
	1 grullo mare	10 00
		95 00
	1 shot-pouch, and two powder horns	5 00
		100 00

Puebla, San Jose, February 26, 1847.

Approved:

CHAS. M. WEBER,
Commanding U. S. Charge, Puebla.

Approved:

JOHN C. FREMONT,
Lieut. Col. U. S. A. commanding California batallion.

The board is of opinion that the claim is reasonable and just, and accordingly recommends it to the favorable consideration of Congress.

[Claim No. 96.]

Received of Don Miguel Castro, de San Juan, for the service of the United States forces in California, the following horses, &c:

5 horses, with his own mark, valued at $20 each	100 00
5 mares .... do .... do.... $10 each	50 00
1 saddle, bridle, and one spur	24 00
Valued in full, one hundred and seventy-four dollars.	174 00

CHAS. M. WEBER,
Commanding U. S. Charge of Puebla.

Approved:

J. C. FREMONT,
Lieut. Col. U. S. A., commanding California batallion.

The board is of opinion that the claim is reasonable and just, and accordingly recommends it to the favorable consideration of Congress.

[Claim No. 94.]

Receipt of Charles M. Weber, dated Ranch Pinola, ——— 1846, ——— of D. Jose Martinez, eight horses (five horses and three mares) for the service of the United States troops—their value is $15 a head, $120 00.

Approved:

J. C. FREMONT,
Lieut. Col. U. S. A., commanding California batallion.

The board is of opinion that the claim is reasonable and just, and accordingly recommends it to the favorable consideration of Congress.

[Claim No. 83.]

Receipt of L. W. Hastings, commanding the United States volunteers en route for Monterey, dated November 13, 1846, of Wm O. Conner, one fat cow, for the use of the United States volunteers under his command, valued at $8 00

Approved:

J. C. FREMONT,
Lieut. Col. United States Army.

The board is of opinion that the claim is reasonable and just, and accordingly recommend it to the favorable consideration of Congress.

[Claim No. 82.]

Receipt of L. W. Hastings, commanding the United States volunteers at Pueblo, dated November 12, 1846, of S. Finley, one rifle gun, for the use of the United States volunteers under my command, valued at $15 00

Approved:

J. C. FREMONT,
Lieut. Col. United States Army.

The board is of opinion that the claim is reasonable and just, and accordingly recommend it to the favorable consideration of Congress.

[Claim No. 80.]

This is to certify that a sorrel horse, belonging to Dr. James Stokes, was taken into the United States service, and has not by me been receipted for or otherwise accounted for—said horse was worth $30 .... $30 00

L. W. HASTINGS.

SAN FRANCISCO, *February* 27, 1847.

Approved:

J. C. FREMONT,
Lieut. Col. United States Army.

The board is of opinion that the claim is reasonable and just, and accordingly recommend it to the favorable consideration of Congress.

[Claim No. 67.]

Due-bill of Jacob R. Snyder, quartermaster, dated Angeles, January 28th, 1847: due to Wm. B. Elliott, from the United States quartermaster's department, for one horse, furnished California batallion United Ssates forces $30 00

Approved:

J. C. FREMONT,
Lieut. Col. U. S. Army, commanding California batallion.

The board is of the opinion that the claim is reasonable and just, and accordingly recommend it to the favorable consideration of Congress.

[Claim No. 65.]

Receipt of Jacob R. Snyder, quartermaster, California batallion United States forces, dated Monterey, November 20, 1846, of Mrs. Modesta Castro, the following described property for the use of the California batallion:

40 horses	$400
30 mares	210
20 horses	260
	876

Approved:

J. C. FREMONT,
Lieut. Col. United States Army.

The board is of opinion that the claim is reasonable and just, and accordingly recommend it to the favorable consideration of Congress.

It is not the least extraordinary feature of this transaction that those three thousand five hundred horses should have dwindled down at the close of the campaign to less than two hundred, and that when turned over to the United States they were scattered about and abandoned, and "a great part of them, and the pick and choice of them, sold for a trifle, say some three thousand dollars."*

We have cited a few of the numerous claims presented to the board and allowed. From these it will be seen that, whilst the rich and powerful family of the Vallejos, whose claims were subsequently stated by influential bankers, *were allowed to make out their accounts at prices four and five hundred per cent. above those charged by others for the same supplies during the same campaign*, and were, moreover, allowed to vary their charges 30 per cent., with the certificate of Colonel Fremont for both sets of prices, the humble and friendless settlers, and the helpless Mexican widow, received but from one-fifth to one-fourth of the prices allowed them for the same articles. Look at the claim of Antonio German for 12 horses, at from $12 to $25; of Wm. B. El-

* Question by Col. Fremont's counsel. Sen. Ex. Doc. No. 33, 1st sess, 30th Cong., p. 145.

liott for 1 horse, at $30; of Mrs. Castro for 40 horses, at $10 each; for 30 mares, at $7 each; and for 20 horses, at $13 each. Was their stock less valuable than that of Messrs. Vallejo? Unhappy widow! unfortunate settlers! you were poor; you had no rich bankers to back your little claims; *your* horses were not worth one-fourth as much as if they had been raised on the ranchos of General Vallejo!

Let not our readers think that the horses and cattle of Gen. Vallejo brought the high prices solicited and certified for them, because they had become more valuable by an increasing demand. Gold was not discovered in California for nearly two years after the conquest, and the horses bought of Vallejo, and Çarillo, and de la Roso, were bought at the *beginning* of the revolution. The prices allowed the other claimants were for horses taken near the *end* of the revolution; yet the price of horses declines with the demand, and are worth less *after* an enemy has been foraging the country for ten months, than *before* he entered it!

We have no right to say that Colonel Fremont was in any manner interested in the claims represented by these wealthy bankers. We have no right to say that he favored these wealthy and influential Californians, that he might take an interest in their recovery from his own government. What his motives were we do not know, and therefore will not intimate. But this we will say fearlessly, because we are borne out by the recorded documents of the government in doing so, that Colonel Fremont certified one man's horses to be worth $150 each, and the horses of others to be worth, at the same time and under the same circumstances, but from $10 to $25 each. That claims for horses and other stock were reduced more than thirty-five thousand dollars, with the certified approval of Colonel Fremont, and that the commissioners scaled these particular accounts more than eighty-four thousand dollars!

Here are the specifications. Carelessness, recklessness, favoritism, and connivance with the claimants. The friends of Colonel Fremont may defend themselves against any or all. We cite the facts, without any other comment than this, that Colonel Fremont was either no judge of horse-flesh himself, or thought nobody else was. That is all.

We shall offer but one other evidence of his want of judgment, or of his reckless indifference to the public interest.

THE

IMMIGRATION INTO THE UNITED STATES OF AMERICA,

FROM

A STATISTICAL AND NATIONAL-ECONOMICAL POINT OF VIEW.

BY

LOUIS SCHADE, OF WASHINGTON, D. C.

WASHINGTON:
PRINTED AT THE UNION OFFICE.
1856.

IMMIGRATION INTO THE UNITED STATES.

The subject of the immigration of foreigners into the United States has become one of the gravest questions of the day. To show the importance of that immigration, from a statistical and national-economical point of view, is what is intended by this work.

Emigration is as old as mankind. The first history of men is nothing but a narration of events which befell individuals or whole nations whilst migrating from one country to another, pictured by single deeds of gallantry or depravity of prominent men. In general, emigration has always flowed from east to west. The ancient Greeks established colonies in almost every section of the coast of the Mediterranean and Black seas. Among them only freemen, but no slaves were permitted to emigrate. Greek arts and science, especially on the Asiatic shore, flourished in the midst of barbarians for centuries. Homer himself was born in one of these colonies. The same was the case with the Phœnicians and Carthagenians. The Romans conquered, but did not colonize in the same sense. The great migrations of nations at the end of the Roman empire, 376 after Christ, were nothing but warlike expeditions, incited by victories of others, and the imbecility, effeminacy, and consequent weakness, of the western European nations. Of the mediæval age, the expeditions of the Normans, the Crusades, the settlements of the Teutonic and other orders in Prussia and Livonia, were half expeditions for adventures, half colonizations—a desire of actions, which, especially after the discovery of the route around the Cape of Good Hope to the East Indies, and, a few years later, of America, we meet with in southern Europe; however, the greater part of the southerners returned to Europe, after having made a fortune, or having otherwise been either successful or disappointed in their expectations, and therefore it was more speculation than emigration in our sense. After the Reformation, religious persecutions drove a good many persons from their homes. But emigration in the American sense was unknown to the ancient and middle ages. The emigrants to this country came not as conquerors fighting for their native sovereign, or to increase, by their labor, his finances and revenues, but for the purpose of founding a new home, a new fatherland. They came to the land of their choice as freemen, with the expectation to die also as such.

In the catalogue of "injuries and usurpations" on which the immortal signers of the Declaration of Independence based their resolution to defy the power of the king of Great Britain, the following stands conspicuous:

"He has endeavored to prevent the population of these States; for that purpose obstructing the laws for naturalization of foreigners; refusing to pass others to encourage their migration hither, and raising the conditions of new appropriations of lands."

These, amongst others, were enumerated as evidences of a direct object on the part of the British king to establish "an absolute tyranny over these States." The founders of our republic, therefore, favored immigration, and to that end denounced the obstructions to naturalization, and the refusal to "encourage migration hither" by George the Third, as acts of tyranny. The illustrious patriots who framed the constitution introduced into it a clause empowering Congress to adopt a "uniform rule of naturalization." The first Congress which assembled under the constitution, composed in a great degree of the same sages and statesmen who had signed the Declaration of Independence and framed the constitution, enacted a law by which any free white alien, who had resided two years within the United States, might become a citizen. This law was passed in March, 1790. In January, 1795, the term of residence, prior to admission as a citizen, was increased to five years. Such was the legislation during President Washington's two terms. In June, 1798, after John Adams became President, and when federalism held sway in the government, the term of residence, prior to admission to citizenship, was increased to fourteen years. It so continued until April, 1802, when, Mr. Jefferson being President, and democracy in the ascendant, the term was reduced to the Washington standard of five years, and so it has remained down to the present day.

It is now proposed by the modern order of patriots, who delight in the name of know-nothings, to prevent the further immigration of foreigners by repealing the naturalization laws entirely, if that is found practicable, and, if not, to obstruct it as much as possible by extending the term of residence to twenty-one years. Their first proposition is substantially the policy of the king of Great Britain, which the signers of the Declaration denounced to the world as tyrannical; their alternative proposition is substantially the policy of the federalists of 1798, except that it is worse by just one-half. The democrats stand upon the platform first erected under Washington, and re-established under Jefferson, for carrying into practical effect the policy proclaimed by the signers of the Declaration of Independence.

I propose now to vindicate the wisdom and patrotism of the fathers of the republic against the reckless and factious attacks of the modern federal advocates of the policy of king George the Third. Upon the principle which these model patriots now promulgate, they would have been on the side of the British king in 1776, and in 1798 they would have passed as acceptable federalists. *If immigration is wrong now, it was wrong then; if obstructions to naturalization are right now, they were right then.*

We are not without reliable data on which to determine whether know-nothings are wiser and more patriotic than Washington, Jefferson, Madison, and the host of sages and statesmen who have concurred with them in encouraging immigration and facilitating naturalization. We have the fruits of their policy, and by that standard we will judge of its wisdom. With the exception of four years, the democratic policy, as to immigration and naturalization, has been in force from the beginning of the government to the present time. We commenced with thirteen States and a free population of less than three millions and a half. We have now thirty-one States, with a free population of more than twenty millions. Population and territory are prominent elements in national strength, prosperity, and greatness. Our revenues have increased from a few millions to more than fifty annually. Immense empires of new territory have been acquired and paid for, and now furnish homes and happiness to millions of enterprising and productive citizens. Our progress, in all that gives power and greatness to a nation, has filled the world with wonder and admiration, whilst it has filled our own people with a spirit of national pride which they have abundant cause to indulge. All this, and manyfold more, will be readily conceded even by our know-nothing patriots; but, in their simplicity, they will ask, what has our amazing progress, in all the elements of national prosperity and grandeur, to do with the policy of immigration and naturalization? We will endeavor to enlighten them by the irresistible logic of facts and figures.

If the know-nothings had controlled the government in 1789, when the constitution went into operation, instead of encouraging immigration and enacting liberal naturalization laws, their policy would have been a total exclusion of all foreigners. They would have acted upon the doctrine which they now advocate, "Americans must rule America;' and to that end no foreigner would have been allowed a resting place within the limits of the Old Thirteen. Let us see how that policy would have worked.

In 1790 the population of the United States, including whites and free colored persons, was 3,231,930. If all increase from immigration had been cut off, in pursuance of the know-nothing doctrine, the surplus of births over deaths would have constituted the only growth in our population. A very interesting problem then presents itself. Upon the know-nothing policy, if adopted in 1790, what would be the present population of the United States? Fortunately, the census table furnishes us with the data for solving this proposition, and of illustrating the wonderful wisdom of the know-nothing policy. If we take the census returns for 1850, we find the number of births to be 548,835, and the number of deaths 271,890—confining ourselves to the white and free colored population. The difference, being 276,945, was the increase of population for 1850 from excess of births over deaths. The whole population in 1850, of whites and free-colored persons, was, 9,987,573. The increase, therefore, from the excess of births over deaths, was one and thirty-eight hundredths per cent. We take 1850 as an example to ascertain the per-centage of increase from the only source of growth in our population which the know-nothing policy recognises wise and patriotic. As the know-nothings are using the United States Census Report as far as it favors their purpose, but repudiate it as false as soon as, in accordance with veracity, it speaks in favor of the immigrants; and to show that the per-centage furnished by the returns of 1850 is reliable, I furnish a table carefully made out, showing the per-centage in a number of countries from which I have official statistical returns. The table is as follows:

TABLE No. 1.—*Showing the increase of population by the surplus of births over deaths.*

Year.	Name of the country.	Number of inhabitants.	Number of births in the respective year.	Numb. of deaths in the respective year.	Per cent. of increase of the total population.
1850	United States	19,987,573*	548,835*	271,890*	1.38*
1850	England and Wales..............	17,927,609	593,422	368,986	1.25
1851	France	35,783,170	943,061	784,433	0.44
1835	Russia............................	59,000,000	2,173,055	1,731,834	0.74
1849	Prussia	16,331,187	691,562	498,862	1.17
1850	Holland	3,056,591	105,338	67,568	1.23
1850	Belgium...........................	4,426,202	120,107	92,820	0.81
1849	Portugal..........................	3,473,758	114,331	88,992	0.72
1852	Saxony............................	1,987,832	80,322	58,739	1.08

*The United States Census of 1850 gives the *births* and *deaths* of the white and free colored population in one column, without any separation; therefore, it has become necessary to include the free colored population in all other tables hereafter given. As to the slave population the writer sees, for his purpose, no necessity to mention any thing of it at all, as it has no connexion whatever with the immigration.

As would be expected, it is seen that the excess of births over deaths in the United States is larger than in any other country; and hence I have no hesitation in adopting the per-centage of annual increase of one and thirty-eight hundredths as reliable. This furnishes us a rule to solve the problem before stated. The population in 1790 was 3,231,930. Excluding all immigration, the increase of population each year would be at the rate of 1.38 per cent. This increase added each year to the aggregate of the preceding year, down to 1850, will give us the population of the United States in 1850 as it would have been upon the know-nothing policy of excluding all immigration. In the following table will be also shown what our population in 1850 would have amounted to if immigration had been stopped in 1800, 1810, 1820, 1830, or 1840, taking the actual population of those years as starting point. The calculation is a long and tedious one, but the result is mathematically certain. It is this: The population in 1790 being 3,231,930, and being increased alone by the surplus of births over deaths, would in 1850 amount to 7,555,423 whites and free colored persons, including 200,000 for Louisiana, Florida, California and those territories which were acquired since 1790. But upon turning to the actual returns of the census of 1850, we find the number of whites and free colored persons to be 19,987,573. It appears, then, that if the know-nothing policy had been adopted in 1790, our present population would be 7,555,423, instead of its actual number of 19,987,573—a difference in population between the know-nothing and the democratic policy of 12,432,150.

TABLE No. 2.—*Showing the increase of the white and free colored population of the United States, if without immigration since the respective yeas 1790 to 1840, after the ratio of increase in 1850:*

Year.	Annual increase of the white and free color'd population if without immigration since 1790	Annual surplus of births.	Annual increase of the white and free color'd population if without immigration since 1800.	Annual surplus of birth
1790...........................	3,231,930	....	....	....
1791...........................	3,276,530	44,600	....	....
1792...........................	3,321,746	45,216	....	....
1793...........................	3,367,586	45,840	....	....
1794...........................	3,414,058	46,472	....	....
1795...........................	3,461,172	47,114	....	....
1796...........................	3,508,936	47,764	....	....

Table No. 2—Continued.

Year.	Annual increase of the white and free color'd population if without immigration since 1790.	Annual surplus of births.	Annual increase of the white and free color'd population if without immigration since 1800.	Annual surplus of births.
1797	3,557,359	48,423	....	....
1798	3,606,450	49,091	....	....
1799	3,656,219	49,769	....	....
1800	3,706,674	50,455	4,412,884	....
1801	3,757,826	51,152	4,473,781	60,897
1802	3,809,684	51,858	4,535,519	61,738
1803	3,862,257	52,573	4,598,109	62,590
1804	3,915,556	53,299	4,661,562	63,453
1805	3,969,590	54,034	4,725,991	64,329
1806	4,024,358	54,768	4,791,209	65,216
1807	4,079,895	55,537	4,857,327	66,118
1808	4,136,197	56,302	4,924,358	67,031
1809	4,193,276	57,079	4,992,314	67,958
1810	4,251,143	57,867	5,061,207	68,893
1811	4,309,808	58,665	5,131,051	69,844
1812	4,369,283	59,475	5,201,859	70,808
1813	4,429,579	60,296	5,273,644	71,785
1814	4,490,707	61,128	5,346,409	72,765
1815	4,552,678	61,971	5,420,189	73,780
1816	4,615,504	62,826	5,494,990	74,801
1817	4,679,197	63,693	5,570,820	75,830
1818	4,743,769	64,572	5,647,697	76,877
1819	4,809,233	65,464	5,724,733	77,036
1820	4,875,600	66,367	5,803,734	79,001
1821	4,942,883	67,283	5,883,825	80,091
1822	5,011,094	68,211	5,965,021	81,196
1823	5,080,247	69,153	6,047,338	82,317
1824	5,150,354	70,107	6,130,791	83,453
1825	5,221,428	71,074	6,215,295	84,504
1826	5,293,473	72,055	6,301,066	85,771
1827	5,366,522	73,049	6,388,020	86,954
1828	5,440,580	74,058	6,476,174	88,154
1829	5,515,659	75,079	6,565,545	89,371
1830	5,591,775	76,116	6,656,149	90,604
1831	5,668,941	77,166	6,748,003	91,854
1832	5,747,172	78,231	6,841,125	93,122
1833	5,826,482	79,310	6,935,532	94,407
1834	5,906,887	80,405	7,031,242	95,710
1835	5,988,402	81,515	7,128,273	97,031
1836	6,071,041	82,639	7,226,643	98,370
1837	6,154,821	83,780	7,326,470	99,727
1838	6,239,757	84,936	7,427,576	101,106
1839	6,325,865	86,108	7,530,076	102,500
1840	6,413,161	87,296	7,633,991	103,915
1841	6,501,662	88,501	7,739,340	105,349
1842	6,591,384	89,722	7,846,142	106,802
1843	6,682,345	90,961	7,954,418	108,276
1844	6,774,561	92,216	8,064,188	109,770
1845	6,868,049	93,488	8,175,473	111,285
1846	6,962,828	94,779	8,288,294	112,821
1847	7,059,115	96,287	8,402,672	114,378
1848	7,156,530	97,415	8,518,628	115,956
1849	7,255,300	98,770	8,636,185	117,557
1850	7,355,423	100,123	8,755,364	119,179

Table No. 2—Continued.

Year.	Annual increase of the white and free color'd population if without immigration since 1810.	Annual surplus of births.	Annual increase of the white and free color'd population if without immigration since 1820.	Annual surplus of births.
1810	6,048,450	....	....	....
1811	6,131,918	83,468	....	....
1812	6,216,538	84,620	....	....
1813	6,302,326	85,788	....	....
1814	6,389,298	86,972	....	....
1815	6,477,470	88,172	....	....
1816	6,566,859	89,389	....	....
1817	6,657,481	90,622	....	....
1818	6,749,354	91,873	....	....
1819	6,842,495	93,141	....	....
1820	6,936,921	94,426	8,100,093	....
1821	7,032,650	95,729	8,211,874	111,781
1822	7,129,700	97,050	8,325,197	113,323

Table No. 2—Continued.

Year.	Annual increase of the white and free color'd population if without immigration since 1810.	Annual surplus of births.	Annual increase of the white and free color'd population if without immigration since 1820.	Annual surplus of births.
1823	7,228,089	98,389	8,440,184	114,987
1824	7,327,836	99,747	8,556,658	116,474
1825	7,428,960	101,124	8,674,739	118,081
1826	7,531,479	102,519	8,794,449	119,711
1827	7,635,413	103,934	8,915,802	121,353
1828	7,740,781	105,368	9,038,840	123,038
1829	7,847,603	106,822	9,163,575	124,735
1830	7,955,899	108,296	9,290,032	126,457
1831	8,065,691	109,792	9,418,234	128,202
1832	8,176,997	111,306	9,548,205	129,971
1833	8,404,238	114,399	9,678,970	130,765
1834	8,520,216	115,978	9,812,539	133,569
1835	8,637,794	117,578	9,947,952	135,413
1836	8,756,995	119,201	10,085,233	137,281
1837	8,877,841	120,846	10,224,409	139,176
1838	9,000,355	122,514	10,365,505	141,096
1839	9,124,559	124,204	10,508,548	143,043
1840	9,250,477	125,918	10,653,565	145,017
1841	9,378,133	127,656	10,800,584	147,019
1842	9,507,551	129,418	10,949,632	149,048
1843	9,638,755	131,204	11,100,727	151,104
1844	9,771,769	133,014	11,253,917	153,190
1845	9,906,619	134,850	11,409,221	155,304
1846	10.043,330	136,711	11,566,668	157,447
1847	10,182,927	138,597	11,726,288	159,620
1848	10,323,451	140,524	11,888,110	161,822
1849	10,465.914	142.463	12,052,165	164,055
1850	10,610,343	144,429	12,218,484	166,319

Table No. 2—Continued.

Year.	Annual increase of the white and free color'd population if without immigration since 1830.	Annual surplus of births.	Annual increase of the white and free color'd population if without immigration since 1840.	Annual surplus of births.
1830	10,856,977	...	...	...
1831	11,006,803	149,826	...	...
1832	11,158,696	151,893	...	...
1833	11,312,686	153,990	...	...
1834	11,468,801	156,115	...	...
1835	11,627,070	158,269	...	...
1836	11,787,523	160,453	...	...
1837	11,950,190	162,667	...	...
1838	12,115,102	164,912	...	...
1839	12,282,290	167,188	...	...
1840	12,451,785	169,495	14,581,998	...
1841	12,623,619	171,834	14,783,229	201,231
1842	12,797,824	174,205	14,985,237	202,008
1843	12,974,333	176,509	15,192,03[illegible]	206,796
1844	13,153,378	179,045	15,401,683	209,650
1845	13,334,874	181,496	15,614,226	212,543
1846	13,518,895	184,021	15,829,702	216,476
1847	13,705,455	186,560	16,048,151	218,449
1848	13,894,590	189,135	16,269,615	221,464
1849	14,086,335	191,745	16,494,135	224,520
1850	14,280,726	194,391	16,721,674	227,539

To these are to be added the results for Louisiana, (1803); Florida, (1821); California, New Mexico, Texas, and Oregon. Louisiana had in 1803, 77,000 inhabitants, of which 53,000 were slaves. Florida, in 1821, had about 10,000. California and New Mexico, at the time of their acquisition, had about 60,000. Texas and Oregon only brought back into the Union citizens who had emigrated thither but a short time before. If we put them down in 1850, after the above scale, with 200,000 white and free colored persons, the writer thinks he has done them more than ample justice.

Table No. 3.—*Recapitulation.*

The United States would have in 1850—		Total white and free colored population.
If without immigration since 1790	7,355,423	
Addition for Louisiana, Florida, &c	200,000	7,555,423
If without immigration since 1800	8,755,364	
Addition for Louisiana, Florida, &c	200,000	8,955,364
If without immigration since 1810	10,610,343	
Addition for Florida, &c	100,000	10,710,343
If without immigration since 1820	12,218,484	
Addition for Florida, &c	100,000	12,318,484
If without immigration since 1830	14,280,726	
Addition for New Mexico and California	50,000	14,330,726
If without immigration since 1840	16,721,674	
Addition for New Mexico and California	50,000	16,771,674
They had actually, however		19,987,573

This will be to many an astonishing result; but I am well assured of the correctness of this statement.*

As I have shown above that the mean (1.38 per cent.) by which I have made up these tables corresponds well with that of other countries, I will also compare the result. It will be found that no European country has *actually* increased in the same period so much as the United States would have, if, instead of a population of 19,987,573, they had in 1850 only 7,555,423. The figures in the following table are taken from official returns.

Table No. 4.—*Increase of various European nations since the last decennium of the 18th century.*

England and Wales	in 1790	8,675,000	Increase .. = 2.06
Do.........do.	in 1851	17,922,768	
Austria	in 1792	23,500,000	do...... = 1.55
Do.	in 1851	36,514,466	
France	in 1789	26,000,000	do...... = 1.37
Do.	in 1851	35,783,170	
Prussia	in 1797	8,660,000	do...... = 1.88
Do.	in 1849	16,331,187	
Spain	in 1797	10,351,075	do...... = 1.33
Do.	in 1849	14,216,219	
Sweden	in 1790	2,150,493	do...... = 1.54
Do.	in 1849	3,316,535	
Sardinia, (Island)	in 1790	456,990	do...... = 1.19
Do........do.	in 1848	547,948	
United States*	in 1790	3,231,930	do...... = 2.33
Without immigration since 1790	in 1850	7,555,423	

* White and free colored.

This table clearly proves the above estimate of the population of the United States, without immigration since 1790, to be not only a correct one, but even exhibiting a higher increase than any other country. England, the highest among them, is still, with one year more increase, twenty-seven on the hundred behind the United States. Some persons may think doubtful that the actual increase of England and Wales is so close to that of the United States, as there has been every year a

*An abstract of these statistics I published in a small pamphlet last June. The principal papers of the United States took notice of it, and commented, with one insignificant exception, as far as I know, very highly on it. Of statistical authorities, De Bow's Review published it in September, Hunt's Merchants' Magazine in December; in which later month it was also read before the American Geographical and Statistical Society of New York. I have constantly been on the alert to hear that its correctness and reliability its attacked, the more, as I took the liberty to beg the statisticians of this country to honor it with a thorough examination; but till now, at least to my knowledge, there has been no such attack.

large emigration. But it must be remembered that England has had in return a considerable immigration from Ireland, Scotland, and even from the continent of Europe, invited by the enormous rise of her manufactures and commerce. England is not only a very healthy country, but also inhabited by a healthy people. Besides, it is a known fact that the population of manufacturing districts increases more than that where agriculture is the principal branch of occupation.

But there is another point of great importance, and in favor of my problem. The people of the United States, left without immigration, would not have increased 1.38 per cent. every year. Proof hereof is found in Massachusetts. This State had, in 1850, 830,066 native and 164,448 foreign born inhabitants, or *one* foreigner to *five* natives. The marriages were, during the years 1849 to 1851, Americans 18,286, or 220 in 10,000 of their own race; foreigners 7,440, or 450 in 10,000. This is 104.5 per cent. of foreign over native ratio. The births were in Massachusetts in the three years 1849, '50, and '51, of American parents 47,982, or 578 in 10,000 of their own race; foreign 24,523, or 1,491 in 10,000 of their own race. In Boston there were, American 7,278, or 966 in 10,000; foreign 13,032, or 2,053 in 10,000 of their own race, Of the 32,000 born in Massachusetts in 1854, 16,470 were of American parentage, while some 14,000 were of parents one or both foreigners; and the increase from foreign parents was more than twice what it was from native parents. At the same rate shortly we shall have more children born in Massachusetts from foreigners than from natives; for in five years the American births have not increased 1,000, while the foreign have increased more than 5,000. In Suffolk county already the births in foreign families are more than twice as numerous as in American, being 3,735 in the former, and 1,737 in the latter. Of the parents of Boston children, in 1854, the largest number was from Ireland, 2,824 fathers and 2,957 mothers, while there were but 410 fathers and 524 mothers natives of the city, and 533 fathers and 475 mothers natives of Massachusetts, out of Boston, or of other States. Cambridge had born of foreign parents 422 children to 208 Americans; Fall River, 223 to 88; Lawrence, 322 to 146; Lowell, 596 to 427; Roxbury, 383 to 168; Salem, 344 to 120; Taunton, 221 to 142; and Worcester, 421 foreign to 320 American. The foreigners in Massachusetts are chiefly of Celtic origin. In twenty years from the present time, one-half of the young men and women in the State will be of direct Celtic descendency, and there is no doubt that they also will brag and boast of their Pilgrim fathers, their revolutionary ancestry, and especially of their Anglo-Saxon blood in their Celtic veins. And why should not they? They will have the same right to do so as is possessed by at least two-thirds of our know-nothings. As the traces of a negro descendency disappear already in the third or fourth generation, I should think that in Massachusetts the Pilgrim and revolutionary blood, if it is not already so, must, in very short time, become at least very thin.

The cause of the large increase of foreign births is simply that, whilst of the native population in 1850 there were only 49.07 per cent. over the 15th year of age, the average amount of foreigners, of the same age, who arrived in 1854 and 1855, was 77.63 per cent.

Number of white inhabitants of the United States in 1850 under 15 years........	8,002,715 = 40.93	pr. cent.
Do...............do...............do...............over 15 years........	11,550,353 = 59.07	"
	19,553,068 = 100.00	"
Number of immigrants in 1854 under 15 years....	100,013 = 21.72	"
Do...............do.........over 15 years.....................................	360,461 = 78.28	"
	460,474 = 100.00	"
Number of immigrants in 1855 under 15 years...	53,045 = 23.02	"
Do...... ....do.........over 15 years.....................................	177,431 = 76.98	"
	230,476 = 100.00	"

Suppose that there are now five millions of foreigners in this country, they will, from this cause, produce just as much, and increase in the same degree, as 6,610,169 natives. Before the mortality tables of the United States were published, statisticians and political writers usually believed that the foreign born died in a greater proportion than the natives. But I always doubted it from the reason that over one-half of the deaths occurs under the age of twenty. Of the foreigners living in this country, however, only one-fourth is below that age, and especially the children are wanting, amongst which the mortality is always proportionally the greatest. The census has shown that I was not in error. According to a statement therein contained, the per-centage of native deaths, excluding slaves, was 1.494, whilst that of the foreign was only 1.469. I take only the aggregate ratio of the total number of deaths in the United States, without going into details, as I do not believe in its correctness, being convinced that the ratio is too high in favor of the natives and against the foreigners. According to this mortality report, there died in New York, one out of 32 foreigners; in Massachusetts, one of every 60; in New Jersey, one of every 110; and in Maryland, one of every 116. These discrepancies are too great to bear any similarity to truth. But it matters nothing for my purpose, as it yet shows that, contrary to former supposition, the foreigners have at most the same and not a greater ratio of deaths than the native population.

According to the above calculation the immigrants and their descendants number in 1850:

Since 1790..............................	12,432,150
" 1800..............................	11,032,109
" 1810..............................	9,277,230
" 1820..............................	8,669,089
" 1830..............................	5,656,847
" 1840..............................	3,215,899

At the first glance it will seem almost incredible that the excess from immigration should alone amount in the single decade of 1840 to 1850 to 3,215,899. But it must be remembered that the immigration within these years, as given by the custom-house reports, amounted to not less than 1,677,330, without those of which the custom-houses give no returns, and which Dr. Chickering, in his essay on immigration, puts down at 50 per cent. of the total number. Should their natural increase resemble that of the foreign population in Massachusetts, as stated above, none will find my hypothetical statement out of reach of probability.

These astounding results enable us to discuss intelligibly the effects of immigration upon our national progress in the great elements of strength and greatness, and wealth and prosperity. If immigration had been cut off in 1790, our population in 1850 would have been about what it actually was in 1820. Immigration, then, has put us thirty years forward in this important element of national prosperity. Our increase in all the departments of national progress has been in the exact ratio of our increase in population. Whilst the latter has increased sixfold, our commercial exports have increased, in the same period, eightfold, and our imports threefold.

YEAR.	Value of imports.	Value of exports.	Commercial fleet.	Revenues.
			Tons.	
1789-91	$52,200,000	$19,012,041	502,146	$4,399,473
1800	91,252,768	70,971,780	972,492	10,624,997
1810	85,400,000	66,757,974	1,424,783	9,299,737
1820	74,450,000	69,691,699	1,280,166	16,779,331
1830	70,876,920	73,849,508	1,191,776	24,280,888
1840	131,571,950	104,805,891	2,180,764	16,993,858
1850	178,136,318	151,898,720	3,535,454	43,375,798
1855	261,468,520	275,156,846	5,212,001	65,203,930

None can fali to see in these figures the great benefit this country has derived from the increased immigration. Enormous is the increase of shipping, revenues, and commerce, from 1840 to 1855. Our imports increased 200 per cent., our exports 300 per cent., our commercial fleet 100 per cent., and our revenues more than 300 per cent. Since 1840, immigration has been chiefly directed to this country. Compare, again, 1850 with 1855, and the blindest man will perceive that the sudden rise of wealth and power this country owes chiefly to immigration. But for the influence of immigration, the wonderful works of improvement, which have added so much to our national wealth and prosperity, could not have been accomplished. To this we are indebted, in an eminent degree, for the thousands of miles of railroad and canal communication which now cover our vast domain like a net-work, and furnish ready and profitable facilities for realizing the benefits of the productive energies and enterprise of every industrial pursuit. To this we are indebted for the reduction of the vast wilderness of the west and northwest to the dominion of civilization and industry, swelling the amount of our annual revenues, increasing to an almost limitless extent our commercial wealth, and placing us in the front rank of nations as an agricultural, manufacturing, and commercial people. To immigration we are indebted in no small degree for the rapid addition of State after State to the confederacy, until we have spanned the continent with more than double our original number. But it cannot be necessary to dwell upon results so astounding to foreign nations, and so flattering to our own national pride. To appreciate them, we have but to imagine twelve millions of our population withdrawn, and reflect upon the amazing contrast that would now be presented with a population little more than one-third of its present number! This contrast will be better appreciated, if we imagine the following eighteen of the bright stars which now illustrate the galaxy of States expunged from our national banner: Alabama, Arkansas,

California, Florida, Illinois, Indiana, Iowa, Kentucky, Louisiana, Michigan, Mississippi, Missouri, Ohio, Tennessee, Texas, Wisconsin, Virginia, and New York. These States have a free white population of twelve millions, the amount of increase resulting from immigration. Instead of setting up a just claim to being the most happy, and prosperous, and powerful nation on the earth, able to command respect all over the world, to maintain our rights on sea and land against any foreign combination, and by the moral power of our republican example to shake the hoary thrones of monarchs in the Old World, we should be a fourth rate national power, subject to constant dangers of foreign invasion, and poorly able to defy the aggressions of a foreign enemy. These results prove the wisdom of the fathers of the republic in resisting the attempts of the British king to prevent immigration into the colonies, and illustrate the soundness of the policy which has enacted liberal naturalization laws and given encouragement to foreign immigration.

Men do not come here merely for the purpose of improving their physical condition. This is especially shown by the sudden decrease of immigration since the political ascendancy of the know-nothings. Exactly one hundred per cent. less have arrived in 1855 than in the preceding year 1854.

In 1854, landed - - - -	460,474
In 1855 " - - - -	230,476
Decrease - - -	229,998

In order to have an idea of the loss this country has sustained hereby, it will not be amiss to state that the population of Delaware and Florida together is yet far below the number of persons the know-nothing policy has kept away in 1855. Rhode Island had, in 1850 only 147,545, and may have now about 180,000. Only imagine that *one* year of know-nothing reign has cost us already more than the present population of two States like Delaware and Florida! How much will it cost us if this sway should be extended to four years more? This is the real and true standard with which to measure the prudence of the principles of the know-nothings, and the depth of their love to this country. It is more than probable that the immigration of 1856 will be even far behind that of 1855, if one may judge after the comparatively small number who have arrived in the first quarter of this year. After that rate the whole immigration will hardly exceed 50,000. This shows sufficiently that the immigrants come to this country just as much for political freedom as material well-being. It is true, the people of the United States, as a power, can use means to prevent immigration, and prohibit it if they will. But, in doing so, an original and distinguished principle of the government must be abrogated; and, having done this, we descend to a level with the arbitrary and proscriptive thrones o Europe. But the loss of the laborious immigrant will soon be felt. As already stated, the most of the immigrants wended their way to the prairies of the Far West, buying from the government with their own money the public lands, in order to wrest a livelihood from the bosom of mother earth. Their labors have enriched not only the cultivator, but the country and the native-born citizen. Others again remained in the great Atlantic cities, where their herculean energies have been employed in the erection of public works. Men of genius, artists, scholars, came with this tide of immigration; and, while they have been able to find employment for themselves, they have also vastly contributed to the intellectual stores of this country. A remarkable instance of the public spirit and generosity of foreign-born citizens may be seen in the fact that the three leading scientific or educational institutions in the United States were founded by men born in other lands. I allude to the great Astor Library, of New York, endowed by the German, John Jacob Astor; the Girard College, in Philadelphia, endowed by the Frenchman, Stephen Girard; and the Smithsonian Institution, at Washington, endowed by the Englishman, John Smithson.

It is not a high estimate if we put down the immigration in five years, from 1850 to 1855, at about two and a half millions. Suppose this number brought with them in value only 30 dollars per head, which is the very lowest estimate; and they have enriched the country in the very short space of five years, by an amount equal to $75,000,000. It is also a very safe calculation to say that these immigrants have paid $150,000,000 into the treasury of the United States for public lands. The revolutions of 1848 gave emigration a vast impulse, and drove masses of men of excellent quality to our shores. Whether we consider the amount of money, principally specie, brought with them, or the amount paid into the treasury for public lands, or the advantages conferred upon the native population by their industry and their skill, we may well hesitate in alarm and surprise, that any movement looking to the arrest or curtailment of the tide of immigration should for one moment have been encouraged by any portion of the American people. The principles of the know-nothings carried out would degrade the emigrant to the low position of an East Indian pariah, or a Russian serf, excepting only that he could not be sold. They would doom him to a fate far worse than the hardest despotism of the Old World. There, at least, he would have the consciousness of not suffering alone, as the whole population, and not a part of it, would have no more rights than himself. Here he would be marked out as an inferior, useful only to dig canals and build railroads, to fight like the Helots of old, to act as hewer of wood and drawer of water to those who falsely call themselves superior beings. And not this only. While this is sought to be made the lot of the white adopted citizens—while the laboring classes are appealed to deny equal privileges to the foreign-born fellow-being of their own race—behold their efforts making in the free States to elevate the negro to the political rights and privileges of the whites!

"Americans must rule America!"—that is the constant war-cry of the know-nothings. There are at present in the United States twenty-seven millions of inhabitants, of which five millions are foreigners. The Senate contains 62 and the House 234 members. Should the five millions be equally represented in their specific qualification as foreigners, of the Senators 14 and of the House 53 should be foreign-born citizens. But there is not a single foreign-born member in Congress. Are the democratic members for whom foreign-born citizens have cast their votes, not as good, intelligent, and wise as those who have been elected by a mere native vote? The know-nothings speak constantly of their revolutionary inheritance, their "glorious sires of '76." Will they inform me how many of them can trace back their lineage to the time of the Revolution? Are not at least two-thirds of their number descendants of those who arrived in the country since 1790? Was not, in New York, even their candidate for governor a son of a foreigner? Are not, with the only exception of *two*, all the 148 or 149 know-nothings of the New York State legislature sons of foreign parents? The answer to these questions will put to shame the warfare which know-nothingism is waging upon the policy of the founders of this republic. It is not simply a warfare upon the foreign-born citizens diffused throughout the Union, identified in interest with our institutions; connected by the closest ties with native-born citizens; engaged in industrial pursuits which add to the national wealth and prosperity; levelling mountains and filling up valleys for our great internal improvements; felling the forests, and spreading the area of productive agriculture in the Far West; shouldering their muskets when the tocsin of war sounds; and fighting and dying bravely on the battle field by the side of native Americans. A warfare upon such a body of men is bad enough in all conscience; but the warfare of know-nothingism is against the principles on which our Revolution was started and was consummated—against the policy engrafted upon our constitution, and carried out by liberal naturalization laws in Congress; and against the prosperity of the nation, which has received one of its chief impulses from this policy.

OLD LINE WHIGS

FOR

BUCHANAN & BRECKINRIDGE

LETTERS

FROM

HON. JAMES ALFRED PEARCE,

AND

HON. THOMAS G. PRATT,

TO THE WHIGS OF MARYLAND.

SPEECHES

OF

HON. J. W. CRISFIELD, of Maryland,

AND

HON. JAMES B. CLAY, of Kentucky.

LETTER OF HON. JAMES A. PEARCE.

WASHINGTON, JULY 31, 1856.

MY DEAR SIR: You ask what part I mean to take in the coming Presidential election, and what I think should be done by old Whigs who have never been attached to any other party, and who do not desire to enter into new political connexions.

I am well aware of the embarrassments to such persons which attend a choice among the candidates for the Presidency now before the country. In my own case this embarrassment is sensibly felt. My inclinations point one way, a sense of the duty arising from the present dangerous condition of domestic politics, leads me another way.

My past relations, political and personal, with Mr. Fillmore, the confidence I have always reposed in his integrity and ability, the wisdom of his Administration, and the conviction I entertain that he is a just national man and free from sectional prejudice, would induce me to prefer him to his competitors. Neither do I object to the sentiment of American nationality, properly limited and restrained. Indeed I think that our present system has made American citizenship too cheap. But I did not approve the mysterious system under which the American party, of which he is now the representative, was organized; the oaths administered to members on initiation, and the discipline of the order, by which secrecy and obedience was secured. How far all this has been dispensed with I do not know. The original plan of their organization I could not but condemn, as I do the adoption of any principle which founds a rule of political exclusion upon a diversity of religious faith. However modified in these respects their plan may now be, it is not necessary for me to inquire. The Northern wing of the party came into it, as I think with purposes very different from those entertained by the rest. They adopted it as a cloak to schemes which all of us in Maryland condemn and detest. The necessary affiliations of that wing of the party were with the anti-slavery men; and accordingly we find the mask now thrown off by the most of them, and see the development of their plans in such a measure as the personal liberty bill of Massachusetts, which nullifies a law of Congress, violates the constitutional guarantee for the recovery of fugitive slaves, and creates the fiercest and most dangerous discord between the north and the South. Their members of Congress have for the most part been consolidated with the pernicious party miscalled Republican, and many of their delegates to their Presidential Convention have deserted to that motly alliance, whose triumph would be the saddest calamity that has ever befel our Union. The comparatively small portion of the American party which remained after this transfer to the anti-slavery men, and which has nominated Mr. Fillmore, is without power to elect him, even with the assistance of Southern Whigs or National Northern Whigs. These, however great their personal respect for and confidence in Mr. Fillmore, are under no party obligation now to give him their support, seeing tha he has become a member and accepted the nomination of a party which repudiates the Whigs; and while they would be willing in a contest with their old opponents to stand by all their political opinions to the last, they find ample reason in the present condition of parties, in the political anarchy which prevails, and in the fear of a sectional and anti-slavery triumph, leading to ulterior consequences of the worst sort, to consider whether it is not their duty to sacrifice all personal feeling and party prejudice for the sake of the Union, and to sustain the nominations of the democrats as the only means of defeating the schemes of the mad agitators who rule the Republican party.

The contest it seems to me, lies between Mr. Buchanan and Mr. Fremont. Mr. Fillmore's friends indeed claim a great reaction in his favor; but I have taken much pains to ascertain what his strength is in the free states, and so far I have not been able to satisfy myself that he can carry a single one of them. His wise and patriotic conduct while President, which recommended him so strongly to the Whigs of the South, is regarded by the majority at the North as a fatal objection to him. It is not moderation and conciliation they desire; they think as one of their leaders said, that the time for compromise has passed. They want, in the President, an instrument to punish the South for what they fancy or pretend to be the aggressions of the "slave power" upon the North. Mr. Fillmore is too national for this purpose, and he must indeed be credulous or sanguine in the extreme who supposes that the politicians who have misguided and inflamed the Northern majority, will abandon their designs and renounce the spoils for which they hunger and thirst, just at the moment when, for the first time, they are confident of the success of the one and the enjoyment of the other. Mr. Fillmore's strength lies in the Whig States of the South. If all the Southern States should give him their votes, he would fail in the election without such assistance from the free States as it would be vain to look for. The choice, then, is between Mr. Buchanan and Mr. Fremont, and what Maryland Whig, believing as I do, can hesitate?

I am not so unjust as to charge all the Northern men who join in the support of Mr. Fremont with being abolitionists. There are men among them whom I hold in much respect, while deploring the error of judgment into which they have fallen; but the most active and influential of their leaders are men who, from perverted judgment or inflamed passion, or what is worse, from deliberate calculation, have determined to build up a sectional party, reckless of its peril to the Union, once so justly valued, but now estimated far less at the North than at the South. Mr. Greeley is at this moment more potential with his party than any other of its members. He has the benefit of Mr. Giddings' co-operation. Governor Chase, Mr. Seward, and Mr. Wilson are active and influential leaders. Their presses teem with the fiercest abuse of Southern men and Southern institutions, with the grossest perversions of the truth, wickedly made to inflame the Northern mind. Their orators denounce us equally, and some do not hesitate to say that they intend or desire not only to restore Kansas to he operation of the Missouri restriction, but to repeal the fugitive slave bill, to abolish slavery in the District of Columbia, to interdict the interstate slave trade, so as to prevent the owner from migrating with his domestics from one slave State to another, to prevent forever hereafter the admission of any new State which tolerates domestic servitude, and to hem in and confine slavery within its present limits; thus continually increasing the political power of their section, until we shall be too weak to resist their future efforts to impair the value of our peculiar property and, finally to destroy it. We do not indeed find all these objects laid down in the platform of their party; and there are men associated with them whose designs by no means extend so far, and who, if they knew the probable consequences of their success, would recoil from the evil associations into which they have fallen. But, then, more moderate men are not the master spirits in this league of agitation, and will be powerless to stop the mischievous measures, which I think certain to follow the success of the combinations which they are now aiding. The tone of the press in their interest, the speeches of many members of Congress and of the amateur orators of the party, all clearly evince a determination to unite all the people of the free States, if possible, in fierce and relentless hostility to those of the South. It is in the strife of sections in which they hope to succeed; and in what would their success result? Not in forming a more perfect union, not in establishing justice or ensuring domestic tranquility, all of which are among the declared objects of that Constitution which Washington and the other Fathers of the Republic gave to us; but in the jealousies, discord, and hatred inseparable from party "characterized by geographical discriminations." It was against this that the Father of his Country warned us in his farewell address—the last legacy of the spotless patriot, to the country he had loved and served so well.

Some years ago, (in 1830,) when the danger of this sectional organization was less than it is now, Mr. Clay gave us his advice in the following words:

"Abolitionism should no longer be regarded as an imaginary danger. The Abolitionists, let me suppose, succeed in their present aim *of uniting the inhabitants of the free States as one man against the inhabitants of the slave States. Union on the one side will beget union on the other, and this process of reciprocal consolidation will be attended with all the violent prejudices, embittered passions, and implacable animosities which ever degraded or deformed human nature.* Virtual dissolution of the Union will have taken place, whilst the forms of its existence remain. * * * *One section will stand in menacing and hostile array against the other. The collision of opinion will soon be followed by the clash of arms.* I will not attempt to describe scenes which now happily lie concealed from our view. Abolitionists themselves would shrink back in dismay and horror at the contemplation of desolated fields, conflagrated cities, murdered inhabitants, and the overthrow of the fairest fabric of human government that ever rose to animate the hopes of civilized man."

It will be said perhaps that this is mere declamation; that Mr. Clay's fervid spirit gave too warm a coloring to the picture; but we need only remark the passionate violence which characterizes men who have lately yielded to this sectional phrenzy, to satisfy ourselves what is the temper natural to such an organization. At the Convention in Philadelphia, held by those who nominated Mr. Fremont, a conspicuous and distinguished gentleman heretofore considered moderate and conservative, made a speech, in which, amidst cheers and cries of "good" he spoke as follows:

They (meaning those who appointed the members of the convention,) ask us to give them a nomination, which, when fairly put before the people, will unite public sentiment, and through the ballot-box, will restrain and repel this pro slavery extension and this aggression of the slave-ocracy. What else are they doing? They tell you they are willing to abide by the ballot-box and willing to make that the last appeal. If we fail there, what then? We will drive it back sword in hand, and so help me God, I'm with them."

It is true that the author of these remarks has since publicly avowed that he alone is responsible for this rhapsody. But it cannot be doubted that the feeling which prompted him was the same which animated the preacher who proposed to supply the brethren in Kansas with bread and *powder* too, and which has stimulated other preachers and their congregations to subscribe Sharpe's rifles as the most efficacious instrument in the adjustment of the controversies in that Territory, which all good men deplore, however they may differ as to the causes of the unhappy anarchy which prevails there. For myself I acknowledge my duty to redress, so far as I can, all the real grievances complained of in that region; and I have supposed that the bill recently passed by the Senate was calculated to remedy them, because it proposes to enact that no law shall be made or have force or effect in said Territory which shall require a test oath, or oath to support any act of Congress or other legislative act, as a qualification for any civil office or public trust, or for any employment or profession, or to serve as a juror or vote at an election, or which shall impose any tax upon or condition to the exercise of the right of suffrage by any qualified voter, or which shall restrain or prohibit the free discussion of any law or subject of legislation in the said Territory, or the free expression of opinion thereon by the people of said Territory; and secures, as far as law can secure, the operation of the public will in the formation of a State government. That this bill was sincerely meant to effect its avowed purpose I am quite confident; and I believe that there are conservative men at the North, who do not yield to prejudice or passion, who will credit this assertion. Unfortunately they are not the majority. At all events, in the most of the free States the masses of the Republican party are led by men who do not mean to be satisfied with any legislation which is not to result in placing the Government under their control; by men who say that the framers of the Constitution "made a compromise that cannot be mentioned without shame;" who say of Mr. Fillmore, in allusion to his signing the fugitive slave bill, "better far had he never been born—better for his memory, and for the name of his children, had he never been President;" who declare that bill to be "one of the immortal catalogues of national crimes" and that he who signed it thereby "sunk into the depths of infamy;" who pronounce the fugitive slave to be "one of the heroes of the age," and the master who demands him a "vile slave-hunter," whom all men should look upon with contempt, indignation and abhorrence; men who do not regard the Constitution, and the laws made in pursuance of it, as the supreme law of the land; who disregard the decisions of that high tribunal whose office it is to decide the constitutional questions; who claim to set up their individual opinions against the official ones of the judicial authorities, and refer their obligations, not to the instrument which they have sworn to support, which is at once the bond and the principle of our Union, but to some "higher law," whose foundations are to be found in their own *fanatical imaginations*. Some of the leaders go further still, and consider slavery as a wrong so transcendant that it must not only be limited to its present bounds, but, must be abolished altogether. We see the effects of this in the increasing restiveness of a part of our population, in the often repeated escapes of our servants from the mildest form of servitude ever known, and in the ready acceptance of the recommendation not to hesitate at theft, robbery and murder, if need be, to accomplish their flight. From this condition of things we can expect no relief if the anti-slavery party succeed in the election of Mr. Fremont. To defeat their nomination seems to me to be our first duty and greatest interest, and therefore I am ready to adopt that candidate who appears most likely to accomplish this purpose. I add as showing the extreme designs of the anti-slavery zealots the following remarks, reported as having been made lately by Mr. Wendell Phillips. Speaking of the Republican party, he says:

"It is the first sectional party ever organised in this country. It does not know its own face. It calls itself national; but it is not national; it is sectional. It is the North arrayed against the South. Henry Wilson said to me, 'We must get every Northern State in order to elect Fremont!' It was a distinct recognition of the fact that the Republican party is a party of the North pledged against the South. Theodore Parker wanted to know once where disunion would begin? I will tell him—just where that party decides; that is, a Northern party against the Southern. I do not call it an anti-slavery party; it has not risen to that yet. Its first distinct recognition was Banks' election."

I have no idea that this is to be considered as showing the general purpose of the Republican party, but I am well satisfied that such opinions are growing in the North, under the constant teachings of such apostles as Mr. Phillips, and this speech shows the tendencyf of present events.

I have been politically opposed to the Democratic party for so many years that I cannot without reluctance contemplate the necessity of supporting their nominee. Yet it must be admitted that he is a man of abilities and large public experience; that he has been just to the South, though not assuming to be a Northern man with Southern principles; that his inclinations ar generally conservative; that he numbers among his prominent supporters many gentlemen of talents and patriotic character entitled not only to the confidence of their party, but to influence with the country at large; and that many of the old issues between the Whigs and the Democrats are obsolete. Two objections to him are much relied on by his opponents in the South. It has been alleged that he countenanced and promulgated the charge of bargain and corruption against Mr Clay in the election by the House of Representatives in 1825. I should denounce him for this as readily and as severely as any one if I thought this allegation just. But I remember that this charge against Mr. Clay was made without any direct testimony until 1827, when the Carter Beverly letter led to Mr. Buchanan's being named as a witness; and that he then promptly denied the statement which he was relied on to prove, and at the risk of losing Gen. Jackson's favor and that of his party, exonerated Mr. Clay. From the letter which he then published I extract the following passage:

"I owe it to my own character to make another observation. Had I ever known or even suspected that Gen. Jackson believed I had been sent to him by Mr. Clay or his friends, I should have immediately corrected his erroneous impression, and thus prevented the necessity for this most unpleasant explanation. When the editor of the United States Telegraph, on the 12th of October last, asked me by letter for information upon this subject, I promptly informed him by the returning mail, on the 19th of that month, that I had no authority from Mr. Clay or his friends to propose any terms to General Jackson in relation to their votes, nor did I ever make any such propositions; and that I trusted I would be as incapable of becoming a messenger upon such an occasion as it was known Gen. Jackson would be to receive such a message. I have deemed it necessary to make this statement in order to remove any misconception which may have been occasioned by the publication in the Telegraph of my letter to the editor, dated the 11th ultimo."

Again, in 1828, in a speech delivered in the House of Representatives, Mr. Buchanan declared that he had no knowledge of the bargain and corruption charged on Mr. Clay. These disavowals may be considered as merely cold justice to the great and incorruptible Whig leader, but surely they contradict most flatly the charge of being his "traducer and defamer." If further proof were needed it may be found in the following remarks recently made in Kentucky, by Mr. Jas. B. Clay, his son.

"Mr. Clay then proceeded to urge upon his old Whig friends, the companions and constituents of his father, to rally around that banner which he had *spent his life in upholding*—the banner of the Union. He was ready to follow the Whig standard as the Douglass followed the heart of Bruce—as long as it waved. But that flag was no longer to be seen on the battle-field. It might yet be unfurled. After death there was the resurrection. But at present there was no whig organization, and the only party of the Union was that of which Buchanan and Breckinridge were the candidates.

"Mr. Clay referred to the attempt to implicate Mr. Buchanan in the charge of bargain and corruption. On that subject he proposed to take the testimony of his own father, and he read from Mr. Clay's letter to show that Mr. Buchanan had conducted himself in that affair as a man of truth and honor. He should believe what his father said before others. Besides the evidence he had read, there was other testimony bearing on the same point. In feeling and eloquent terms he referred to the heavy weight of that charge against his father, and how gallantly and bravely he had borne it. Thank God, it died before his father! and now he was proud to say that there lived not the man who would whisper it. But Mr. Buchanan was free from all connection with the matter.

"Mr. Clay concluded with an eloquent appeal to his fellow citizens, especially Old-Line Whigs, to give their cordial support to the Union ticket—to Buchanan and Breckinridge.

The next great object is that Mr. Buchanan would be unsafe in his management of foreign affairs. I readily admit that I do not like the Ostend paper, and I do not approve certain resolutions adopted by the Cincinnati Convention, notwithstanding the unaminous opposition of the Virginia and Maryland delegates, and I believe of others; and if he should adopt the aggressive policy supposed to be prescribed by that paper and the resolutions, I should be as ready and as earnest in my opposition to him as any one. But he is a man of known caution, which, with his intelligent comprehension of the true interests of the United States, and the responsibility of the Presidential office, which he could not but recognise, would forbid his urging the country upon a course of aggression inconsistent with the spirit of our Government, faithless to treaties, violative of the rights of other nations, and destructive of our own peace, honor, and concord. I know that many of the leading men of his own party are sound and reliable in this respect; and I believe that their conservative influence would harmonize with his own disposition. I am the more assured of this because I observe that in his letter of acceptance there is no recognition of the resolutions, (which were not considered by the Convention as forming a part of the platform,) but, on the contrary, a prudent and conservative tone, which met with the approbation of even the judicious and experienced Editors of the National Intelligencer—themselves, *par excellence*, the foes of all fillibustering. In an additional article noticing Mr. Buchanan's letter of acceptance, they said:

"We may say, however, that Mr. Buchanan's official letter of acceptance, while not expressly repudiating the extreme and exceptionable doctrines foisted into the Democratic confessions of faith by the Cincinnati Convention, does not, by its spirit and tenor, incline us to hope that he means if elected, so to construe those doctrines as to disarm them of their mischievous significance and evil tendency. Indeed we can give no other meaning than this to Mr. Buchanan's declaration when he says that he accepts the 'resolutions constituting the platform of the principles erected by the Convention' in the same spirit as that which prompts his acceptance of the nomination tendered to him by his party, namely, a desire so to discharge the duties of the high office to which he aspires as 'to allay domestic strife, *preserve peace and friendship with foreign nations*, and promote the best interests of the Republic."

At present the prospects is that the conservative Whig vote will be so divided as to defeat a popular election and throw the decision upon the House of Representatives—at all times an event to be deprecated, but at this period peculiarly pernicious and dangerous, and threatening the rudest shock to our system. What the result will be I will not venture to predict, but I will say that I do not see the least probability of Mr. Fillmore's election by the House of Representatives. I think, therefore, it would be the part of wisdom and patriotism in the Whigs (by which I mean those who have affiliated with no other party,) to throw their votes for Mr. Buchanan as the strongest of the candidates opposed to the Northern Sectional party. This they may do without renouncing their old political faith, without stain of honor or suspicion of apostacy. The motive being the integrity of the Union, the defeat of a party which is founded on geographical discriminations and bound together by dangerous sectional schemes, the act will be vindicated by disinterested patriotism.

For my part, I shall not abjure my political creed, and, having in view but the one object which I have stated, I shall hold myself ready to take any other course which may be necessary to effect that object. Should the hopes of Mr. Fillmore's friends be realized; should it appear that he is more likely to carry the great body of the patriotic, but quiet people, who generally come to the rescue in times of public peril; that he is, in short, the best able to subdue this storm of sectional passion and prejudice, I shall rejoice to see him again filling the chair of State. But I will not affect an unalloyed gratification; for I cannot forget that he is the candidate of a party which has proscribed Whigs who were not members of "the order"—of a party which boasted that it had risen on the ruins of the Whig and Democratic parties, and which has pronounced both of them corrupt.

Whatever the result, I shall be content if the dangerous excitement which threatens our peace and union can be calmed down, so that the extreme opinions which have their roots in prejudice and passion may wither away. Then a liberal forbearance and kindly toleration of different sentiments may resume their influence. If this cannot be done, if the South and the North are to regard one another as enemies, then sooner or later our "house, divided against itself," must fall. Then we shall have to say, with Pantheus—

Venit summa dies et ineluctabile tempus
Dardaniæ.

But ours will be a sadder fate than that of Priam's empire; for it was not the Dardanian people by whom the inevitable doom of Troy was fixed. A foreign foe beat down her lofty walls and destroyed the high renown of Teucer's race; but we shall fall by our own suicidal hands; we will kindle the flames which shall destroy the edifice of our constitutional Union; ourselves will break the bonds of harmonious interest and fraternal concord which have held us together as one people. May Heaven inspire us with wisdom to avert so sad a catastrophe!

Very truly, my dear sir, your friend,

JAS. ALFRED PEARCE.

To the Hon. J. R. FRANKLIN,

Snow Hill, Maryland.

P. S. I add a letter of Mr. Clay to Rev Walter Colton, which shows his opinion in 1843, of the effect of the abolition movements of that day:

ASHLAND, Sept. 2, 1843.

MY DEAR SIR:—Allow me to suggest a subject for one of your tracts, which, treated in your popular and condensed way, I think would be attended with great and good effect. I mean abolition.

It is manifest that the ultras of that party are extremely mischievous, and are hurrying on the country to fearful consequences. They are not to be conciliated by the Whigs. Engrossed with a single idea, they care for nothing else. They would see the administration of the government precipitate the nation into absolute ruin before they would lend a helping hand to arrest its career. They treat worst and denounce most those who treat them best, who so far agree with them as to admit slavery to be an evil. Witness their conduct towards Mr. Briggs and Mr. Adams in Massachusetts, and towards me.

I will give you an outline of the manner in which I would handle it: Show the origin of slavery; trace its introduction to the British Government. Show how it is disposed of by the Federal Constitution; that it is left exclusively to the States, except in regard to fugitives, direct taxes, and representation. Show that the agitation of the question in the free States will first destroy all harmony, and finally lead to disunion, perpetual war, the extinction of the African race, ultimate military despotism.

But the great aim and object of your tract should be to arouse the working classes in the free States against abolition. Depict the consequences to them of immediate abolition. The slaves, being free, would be dispersed throughout the Union; they would enter into competition with the free laborer—with the American, the Irish, the German—reduce his wages, be confounded with him, and affect his moral and social standing. And, as the ultras go both for abolition and amalgamation, show that their object is to unite in marriage the laboring white man and the laboring black woman; to reduce the white laboring man to the despised and degraded condition of the black man.

I would show their opposition to colonization; show its humane, religious, and patriotic aims; that they are to separate those whom God has separated. Why do the abolitionists oppose colonization? To keep and amalgamate together the two races, in violation of God's will, and to keep the blacks here, that they may interfere with, degrade, and debase the laboring whites. Show that the British Government is co-operating with the abolitionists for the purpose of dissolving the Union, &c. You can make a powerful article that will be felt in every extremity of the Union. I am perfectly satisfied it will do great good. Let me hear from you on this subject.

HENRY CLAY.

LETTER OF HON. THOS. G. PRATT.

In response to the communications received from many of my brother Whigs, I deem it my privilege, in this manner, to counsel with all in relation to the course which patriotism and duty would seem to indicate as proper in the present political crisis.

No lover of his country whose judgment is unbiased by party zeal and uncontrolled by Northern or Southern fanaticism, can fail to see the pending danger to the Union.

The first duty of every man who loves his country and her institutions, is to provide for their safety. The life of the nation is in danger. It must be saved; then, and not till then, will it be permissable to us to discuss our differences of opinion upon minor subjects.

I say that the life of the Union is in danger, because, for the first time in our history, a party has been formed composed exclusively of citizens of one section of the country, bound together by the single bond of an alliance for offensive warfare against the other section. That the success of such a party would imperil the Union has been recently demonstrated by an address of Mr. Fillmore, and will, it is submitted, be apparent to all who will bestow a moment's consideration upon the existing posture of political affairs.

The value of the slave property at the South, is not less than two thousand millions of dollars, a sum equal to the value of all the other property in the United States, as shown by the last census. This property is not only recognized, but so far guaranteed by the Constitution as to impose upon the Federal Government the duty of restoring to his owner the slave who may escape into another State or Territory of the United States. For years past this constitutional obligation has been not only repudiated by *some* of the non-slaveholding States, but political parties have been organized in *all* with the avowed object of liberating the slaves, and thus not only depriving the South of this vast amount of property, but subjecting it to all the horrors which would necessarily result from such a consummation. In addition to all this, whilst the abolitionists on the one hand openly avow their opposition to the Constitution and their desire to destroy a government which imposes obligations repudiated by them, on the other hand, many Southern men, goaded by the incessant attacks of their Northern fellow citizens upon their feelings, their property, and their constitutional rights, express the belief that the interests of the South would be more effectually protected by a separation of the slave from the non-slaveholding States, and, therefore, rather promote than interpose to prevent a result so calamitous. We have hitherto disregarded the danger which such a state of feeling and such a course of action would indicate as most imminent, because we have assumed that such sentiments and action could only be attributed to a small minority of our Northern brethren. But now, when this sectional exasperation has been made available for the inauguration of a party calling itself Republican, under whose banner, for the first time in the history of the country, this sectional opposition to Southern rights and interests have *united* in nominating, with alleged probabilities of success, a purely sectional ticket for the Presidency and Vice Presidency of the United States, we can no longer shut our eyes to the reality of the threatening danger; we cannot but feel that the success of such a party would be the death knell of the Union. The unpatriotic purposes of this sectional party are but too manifest. Many of its supporters avow their object and purpose to be disunion, and have even gone so far in the madness of their fanaticism as to desecrate the flag of our country by obliterating from its constellation the fifteen stars which represent the slaveholding States, and displaying *as their party banner* that flag with but sixteen of its stars remaining to represent the sixteen non-slaveholding States. It is manifest that those who disavow the object are not ignorant of the inevitable result.

The Whigs of Maryland whom I have the honor to address, need no proof to convince *them* that calamitous consequences would flow from the success of this sectional party. They each and all *know* that the election of Mr. Fremont, and the administration of the Government by him upon the principles of *his* party, would necessarily occasion a dissolution of the Federal Union, to which *they* have been taught to look as the source of national strength and of individual prosperity and happiness.

I have known the Whigs of my State too long, I estimate their patriotism too highly, I have associated with them too intimately, to suppose it necessary for a moment to offer an argument to *them* in behalf of their country. They appreciate, as fully as I could depict, the horrors of disunion; they will see the loss of national strength, the internal dissentions, the fatal check to civilization and freedom, the contempt of the world which would be the consequences of such a calamity. The Whigs of Maryland, who have followed the lead of such patriots as Clay and Webster, "will never keep step to any other music than that of the Union."

It, therefore, only remains to inquire what course shall be taken to rebuke sectional fanaticism and preserve our country from the dangers of its success.

You are aware that this Republican party, which we all agree must be put down at all hazards, is opposed by two other party organizations: the American, headed by Messrs. Fillmore and Donelson, and the Democratic, led on by Messrs. Buchanan and Breckinridge. You will recollect that Mr. Fillmore, prior to his recent visit to Europe, abandond the Whig party and became a member of the former of these organizations, which boasted that it had risen upon the downfall of the Whig party, and which proclaimed that the corruptions of the Whig and Democratic parties constituted the necessity of its existence. You know that he and Andrew Jackson Donelson have been nominated by this party (not by the Whig party,) for the Presidency and Vice Presidency, and you will admit that the principles of proscription because of religious opinions, and other repudiated tenets of this new party, are in direct antagonism with the principles of that good old Whig party to which *we* are still attached, and which has been abandoned by Mr. Fillmore. It is not my object in referring to these facts to deny to the American party, since the secession of its abolition adherents, a fair claim to nationality; nor to deny the patriotism and virtue of Mr. Fillmore, nor his eminent qualification for the office of Chief Magistrate. But I do deduce from them the necessary conclusion that as Whigs, we owe no party allegiance to Messrs. Fillmore and Donelson, members and nominees of the American party. I deduce the conclusion that, as Whigs, we are not only at liberty, but that as patriots we are bound, by every obligation to our country and posterity, to throw aside, on the one hand, the feelings of hostility which Mr. Fillmore's desertion of our party would be calculated to engender, and, on the other hand, to forget for the time our former battles with the Democratic party, and to ask ourselves but one question—*which* of the *two* national organizations offers the *best guarantee* of success in crushing out of existence this new and monstrous sectional party which threatens the life of your country? I do not propose to examine the relative claims of the two national parties or their nominees to our support. It is not, in my judgment, permissable in the present crisis to interpose our individual differences of opinion upon minor questions. It is sufficient for us to know that the election of either national nominee would secure the Union; and the only question permitted by patriotism is, whether our support of the one or the other would more certainly prove successful?

But before I proceed to this inquiry, having shown that no political allegiance to Messrs. Fillmore and Donelson will interpose to prevent the fair exercise of our judgment on that side, I propose briefly to inquire whether there is anything to prevent our support of the Democratic nominees, if after investigation, we shall believe that our vote in their favor would more certainly secure the safety of our country. It cannot have escaped your observation that the political principles upon which the Whig and Democratic parties have battled for thirty years, with varied success, have been for the most part settled by the fiat of the people, and that such as have not been so definitely disposed of have been either abandoned by the one or adopted by the other of those parties; so that now the representatives of the people in the halls of State and Federal legislation are found indiscriminately advocating and opposing the same principles and measures. Not only is there no principle of political antagonism which should prevent Whigs and Democrats acting together for the benefit of their common country, but it is confidently submitted that upon the only vital question, that which now agitates and endangers the country, the two parties fully accord. The Whig and Democratic platforms upon the slavery question in eighteen hundred and fifty-two were identical; and there being no Whig nominees before the people, it *might* be suggested that consistency would rather require than oppose the support of the Democratic nominees by Whigs. The controlling inquiry to the patriot now recurs, *which of the two national organizations can by his vote be made most certainly successful?*

Every Maryland Whig will be bound by every tie of duty to vote as his judgment shall decide this question.

It may not be immaterial to observe that neither of the national nominees will obtain throughout this broad land any votes which will not be cast by national conservative citizens, and it is to be regretted that in this crisis that vote should be divided between *two national* candidates whilst the entire anti-national vote will be concentrated upon the sectional nominee. To judge of the relative strength of the two national organizations it is unnecessary to trace minutely the origin of the American party. It is sufficient to bring to your recollection that it was originally composed, North and South, of the dissatisfied members of the two parties, and that in the North its original members were chiefly those who opposed the conservative principle upon the slavery question avowed in the platforms of the two old parties. It must not escape your recollection that upon the nomination of Messrs. Fillmore and Donelson a large majority of the Northern delegates seceded from the Convention, declared their intention not to support those nominees, and subsequently united in the nomination of Mr. Fremont. This separation of the sectional from the national portion of the American party has occurred in every Northern State in the Confederacy. I deduce from these facts the nationality of the supporters of Messrs. Fillmore and Donelson, and I submit the inquiry for the honest decision of those to whom this paper is addressed, *what non-slave-holding* State can this *national branch* of the American party, thus shorn of the larger portion of its original strength, *promise its nominees?* Let the Whigs of Maryland ponder upon the view of this subject I have endeavored to present to their consideration, and no one of them will say that a single non-slave-holding State is certain for Fillmore and Donelson. Time, *I think*, will develop the fact that Messrs. Fillmore and Donelson will be left without an electoral ticket in most of the free States, and it is at any rate the deliberate conviction of my judgment that they will not carry a single non-slaveholding State in the Union. If I am right, or even approximate the truth in the view I have taken, it will necessarily follow that any conservative vote for the American nominee North will be equivalent to a vote for Mr. Fremont, as it will be a vote taken from Mr. Buchanan, his only real competitor.

It is clear, then, that to the South alone can the friends of Messrs. Fillmore and Donelson look for the probable chance of an electoral vote; and it is to the States of Maryland, Tennessee, Kentucky and Missouri that they profess to look with the greatest hope of success. It is manifest that if this hope were realized, it might indeed prevent the election of Messrs. Buchanan and Breckinridge by the people, but it would only throw the election of President into the *present House of Representatives*, composed as that House now is. Does not the election of this same House, after a contest of two months, of a Black Republican Speaker admonish us of the danger of such an experiment? Who can doubt that our political fabric would be shaken to its very foundations by this election of President being thrown upon the present House of Representatives? On the other hand, it is not certain beyond the contingency of a doubt, that the vote of the States indicated for Mr. Buchanan, when added to that of the other Southern States, would *secure* his election and the consequent safety of the Union? It is obvious that in this condition of the canvass the only serious contest is that between Fremont and Buchanan; that the only possible result that the most sanguine of the friends of Fillmore and Donelson can hope to obtain is to carry the contest into the House of Representatives. Who can conceive any thing more fatal to the peace of the country, more insane in political action, than such a course of conduct leading to such a result? Suppose Mr Fillmore to reach the House of Representatives with the votes of four or five States, (his utmost possible strength,) no man can seriously contend that he would be elected President, and assuredly few will be found bold enough to assert that, under such circumstances, he ought to be. The only effect, then, of giving the electoral vote of any portion of the South to Mr. Fillmore would be to transfer the contest between Mr. Buchanan and Fremont from the hustings to the House of Representatives; and the danger to our country, now sufficiently menacing, would, in that event, be appalling indeed. Who can contemplate the occurrence of such a contingency without feeling that he would be a traitor to his country if he failed to exert every possible effort to avert so awful a calamity?

I deem it, then, to be *my* duty, as well as that of all who believe with me that the election of Fremont would be the death-knell of the Union, to unite in the support of Messrs. Buchanan and Breckinridge; and I shall sustain their election to the best of my ability. Whilst I concede that there are certain principles hitherto professed by the party which nominated them that cannot receive our support, yet on the great issues of the constitutional rights of the South, the platform on which they stand meets my cordial approval, and is in accordance with that of the party which I now address, and to whose kind favor I owe the honor of holding the seat I now occupy, and which I shall cease to hold after the 4th of March next by the fiat of that party to which Mr. Fillmore has attached himself, and which is now dominant in the Legislature of my native State.

Let Maryland Whigs remember that the political battle now being fought is one of the deepest interest to them; that the maintenance of the constitutional rights of the South is the issue tendered to the American people by the Democratic party, and (as the Whigs have no candidate) by that party alone; that upon this issue the Republican party have staked the Union, and in such a battle, upon such an issue, they must be true to those who are doing battle in our behalf. It would be indeed sad, if, in such a contest, the conservative strength of the country should not be united: it would be as strange as sad, if, in such a contest, Southern men should not be found battling shoulder to shoulder for the maintenance of their own constitutional rights.

In thus accomplishing what I believe to be a

duty, I shall be inexpressibly gratified if I shall find myself sustained by the approval of my fellow Whigs, who have refused to abandon either the party or the principles in support of which we shall remain at perfect liberty to reorganize as soon as our common efforts shall have succeeded in averting the perils that now threaten our beloved country.

THOMAS G. PRATT.

SPEECH OF HON. JNO. W. CRISFIELD.

Mr. Crisfield, after acknowledging the compliment their presence and call implied, which, he said, was as unexpected as it was unmerited, and expressing his thanks, proceeded, in substance to say: That they all knew his antecedents; that it was well known he had always been a Whig, and under all circumstances, as well in the darkest hours of defeat as in the hour of triumph, had stood under the banner of tha party, proud to do battle in its support. He had done so, because the leading principles of that party and the doctrines it proclaimed were just and patriotic, and had the unqualified approval of his heart and judgment. These principles, in his opinion, so just, so conservative, so consistent with the Constitution, had been so long cherished, and so ardently loved, that he could no more shake them off or change them than he could change his opinions of religion or of morals. And he felt sure that no one expected him to do it. He reavowed them, and declared that as they had been the rulers of his political conduct in the past, so they would be in the future, whenever, from the state of parties and the condition of the country, those principles should be in issue. But unfortunately that was not now; the Whig party was not a party to this fight; Whig principles are not in issue; and Whig candidates were not, and would not be in the field. New parties had been formed, new issues had been joined, and upon these all Southern men could stand side by side. The real contest now was between Southern rights and Northern fanaticism. In this state of circumstances, he felt it to be his solemn duty to lay aside ancient prejudices, and fraternize with that party now organized, and in the field, which in his judgment, offers the best guarantee of its own success and of safety for our national and domestic institutions; and in the performance of this duty, after dispassionately examining the whole subject, he had come to the determination now for the first time publicly announced, to give his support—his cordial and energetic support—to the *nominees of the Cincinnati Convention.*

Mr. C. said he would briefly assign some of the reasons which had brought him to this determination.

He could not support Mr. Fillmore. He was a supporter of his administration; he thought it one of the purest and best which had transpired in his time; and if it could be restored, as he thought it was, he would prefer it over all others. He had, too, been an ardent admirer of Mr. Fillmore personally, and if he could regard him now as he formerly had, he would perhaps prefer him for the high office which he once filled, over all others. But he had changed. The painful conclusion had been forced upon him that Mr. Fillmore was not now what he had been. He had become a member of a secret political organization, dangerous in its tendency, destructive of the freedom of political opinion, and at war with the theory of man's capacity for self-government—an organization proscriptive in its character and intolerant of religious freedom, which enforced its jesuitical policy by oaths not authorized by law and demoralizing in their tendency. He is, as we are informed, "a member in good standing of Council No. 177," in western New York. If this be so, as few will doubt, it is a sad truth. Its discovery crimsoned his cheek with shame. In allowing himself to be placed in this position, Mr. Fillmore has been unjust to himself, and reckless of his own fame. But this is not all; he has unwhigged himself; he has become a member of an organization which boasts of having arisen upon the ruins, and in spite of the opposition, of the Whig party, and proclaims, in its well considered confession of faith, that it is not responsible for the obnoxious errors and violated pledges of that party. He consorts with Andrew Jackson Donelson, the defamer of his Administration and the reviler of the Whig party, a Democrat of the stamp most odious to Whigs; and he now demands of us, as Whigs, our support of this extraordinary and anomalous association. At this moment he is carrying the banner of those who conspired for the destruction of the Whig party. With these facts before him, he could not recognize Mr. Fillmore as a Whig; he had disrobed himself of that title; he is an alien from the fold, and had not a shadow of a claim, based on old party associations, to the support of the few who still remain constant to the ancient faith.

But if he were willing, in consideration of his services, to overlook these serious objections to Mr. Fillmore, he could not support him without also supporting Mr. Donelson. The two are indissolubly blended; and he would not vote for Mr. Donelson. He had not a single qualification to recommend him for the high place for which he is nominated; and to old Whigs, he is perhaps the most objectionable man who could be named. For his own part, he was not willing to vote for any man for Vice President whom he would be unwilling to trust as President. He had not forgotten the blasted fruits of the Whig triumph of 1840. Who would be willing to see Mr. Donelson President? No one, he would venture to say; and yet, if the Fillmore ticket prevails, he may, and probably will, be. Twice have the Whigs carried the Presidential election, and on both occasions, scarcely had the shout of triumph ceased to re-echo before they were called upon to mourn the death of their President. What right have we to calculate upon exemption from a like calamity in the next Presidential term? What guarantee have we that Mr. Fillmore will not also be taken? and if he should be, who is not appalled at the idea of the duties of that high station devolving on Mr. Donelson? Who does not tremble at the thought of entrusting him with the whole power of this Government; of placing in his hands its army and its navy; of committing to his management its foreign policy; and of leaving to his charge the settlement of the perilous questions of domestic policy which at this moment are rudely agitating the Union of these States, and threatening dissolution? He could not vote for Mr. Donelson; and if any one should twit him for supporting Mr. Buchanan because he is a Democrat, Mr. C. would just remind him that Mr. Donelson, also, is a Democrat, with the stain of Know-nothingism and incapacity superadded.

But if he waved these considerations, there were other reasons, still more conclusive, which obliged him at this crisis to give his support to Mr. Buchanan. The contest in which we are engaged, unhappily, is a contest between the North and the South—between abolitionism and free-soilism on the one side, and the preservation of southern rights and the Union on the other. This was the real issue, and he might say the only issue now to be decided—and one of more overwhelming importance was never presented for decision to the American people. On the one side we find the Republicans, led on by Mr. Fremont, sustaining the ultra northern view. The objects of this party are unmistakable; they are humiliating to the South, and destructive of her constitutional rights and material interests. The Republicans deny to her her just share of political power; negative those constitutional guarantees which were intended for protection, and without which she would never have entered the Union. And is there no danger that they may triumph? Already have they obtained control of nearly every State legislature north of Mason and Dixon's line; they have a majority in the House of Representatives, which elects the President in case of the failure of the people to elect; and to preside over the deliberations of that body, they have elected Mr. Banks, who boldly avows, that sooner than abolition and free-soil measures should fail, he would "let the Union slide." The people of the Free States, burning with fanaticism, inflated by these successes, and heedless of constitutional restraints and of consequences, are madly rushing into the Republican ranks with a unanimity hitherto without example; and it may well be feared that even the united energies of all southern men and the conservatives of every section may be too feeble to resist the overwhelming power. The Union trembles under the blows of this sectional strife; God grant that the fearful catastrophe of its dissolution may be averted! The election of Fremont would be its death-knell. If his supporters are strong enough to elect him, they are also strong enough to consummate their designs of sectional aggrandizement and southern humiliation; and in spite of the Constitution they will assume the power of Congress to legislate our Slavery in the Territories of the United States; they will exclude the South from its just rights in the national domain, abolish slavery in the District of Columbia, repeal the fugitive slave bill and refuse to admit new States into the Union unless they repudiate slavery. That these measures would follow the election of Fremont he had no doubt; and when they did, the Union would, and ought to be, dissolved. These measures, and each of them, negative important provisions of the Constitution inserted for the security of the South, and if persisted in are just grounds of separation.

Fellow citizens, do you appreciate the dangers which encompass you? He feared we were on the verge of dissolution. Gloom and apprehension shroud the future; our very existence as a nation—as one united people—in all probability depends upon the result of this election. Our institutions are assailed in their most vulnerable part. The torch of the incendiary is blazing; the citadel of the Union is besieged; and this is no time for the garrison to be wasting the time and strength, which should be given to the common enemy, in the indulgence of old antipathies and vain disputes; but regardless of the past, and with patriotic devotion, sacrificing, on the altar of our common country our ancient prejudices and preferences, we should rally under the standard of that leader who give the best assurance of his ability to preserve the common safety.

If we concede Mr. Fillmore's entire nationality, and that, if elected, his energies would be devoted in good faith to preserve the Union, and quell all sectional discord, what assurance have we that he can be elected? Does any one believe that he can be? He who thinks he can be is blind to the signs of the times. Mr. C knew very well that in certain quarters studied efforts had been made to produce the impression that his election was certain, and it is quite possible that there are those whose vision does not reach beyond the narrow horizon of Somerset, or even of the State of Maryland, who may think so; but the man who comprehends within his view the whole country, and the present state of parties, who has observed for the last half-year the varied and manifold indications of popular sentiment, and is familar with the spirit of the American press, and can think there is the remotest probability of the election of Mr. Fillmore by the people, has become insensible to evidence. Where is he to get the votes? He is the nominee of the American party, which, if it was even a national party, has long since ceased to be so by the defection of its own members. A large portion of the members from the free States of the convention which nominated him at that time seceded, and went over to the Republicans; and from that time to this the work of secession has been going on, until now it may be truthfully affirmed that the American party, distinct from, and unconnected with, the Republicans, has ceased to exist in those States. True, individual members remain firm; but, as a party, capable any where in those States, unless it be in the city of New York, of effecting anything, it does not exist. Nor can he expect any important aid in those States from other parties. The Whig party there, for the most part, lost itself in Americanism, and as part of the American party has gone over to the Republicans. Except Choate and Winthrop, and probably Everett, of Massachusetts, he could not name a Whig of New England, of national reputation, who was not now a Republican. Even the most active and able supporters of Mr. Fillmore's administration have enlisted in the Republican ranks. Dayton, of New Jersey, is the Republican candidate for Vice President; Collamer, of Vermont, is the chosen advocate of Republicanism in the United States Senate, and Corwin, of Ohio, his Secretary of the Treasury, is stumping Indiana for Fremont; and the same may be said of many others of like stamp.

In the free States nearly every Whig of national reputation may now be found among the Republicans. The legislatures of those States are either Republican or Democratic—not Fillmore Americans; in the House of Representatives there are scarcely enough members from the free States who favor Mr. Fillmore's election to fill the cabinet appointments, even if they were of the right material; and if there is one member from those States in the Senate of the United States who favors his election, Mr. C. could not name him. Of the anti-democratic press of those States the same may be said. Out of 91 anti-democratic journals from the free States which exchange with the New York *Herald*, 78, as we learn from that paper, are for Fremont, and 11 for Fillmore and 2 for Buchanan. Shut their eyes, as the friends of Mr. Fillmore may, the fact is nevertheless true that the whole North and West are either Republican or Democratic; and no reasonable ground exists justifying the belief that he can get a single electoral vote in the free States, unless it be in California, of which he did not pretend to speak. These States will vote for Buchanan or Fremont. Mr. C. greatly feared a majority of them would go for the latter. In the South, Mr. Fillmore may do better. His friends last year carried Delaware, Maryland and Kentucky; if these be accorded to him now, they will not elect him. Can he get any more? Few, if any, think he can; but suppose he gets Tennessee, North Carolina and Louisiana—and his most sanguine friends claim no more in the South—still he is greatly in the minority. Then, he cannot be elected by the popular vote; and every vote thrown for him, with that view, is a vote thrown away. But votes for him may have a different and very mischievous effect. If he carries the States referred to, or even a considerable portion of them no election probably will be effected by the people, and the election will be referred to the House of Representatives. Will that benefit him?

Certainly not. His strength in that House is the Fuller squad; which after a two months' struggle could not get a Speaker. But in a Presidential election, when the vote is cast by States. it would have even less effective strength, for they are in the majority in three States only, (Delaware, Maryland and Kentucky,) which would give him three votes only. Then it is equally certain that he cannot be elected by the House. If it goes to the House, Fremont will be elected, or there will be no election. The Republicans were strong enough to elect Banks Speaker; and is there any reasonable ground to doubt their ability to elect Fremont President? They have, it is feared, already fourteen States, and it requires but sixteen to elect. Starting with this immense odds in his favor, and with the patronage of the government at his disposal, in the event of success, his friends will have no difficulty in procuring the additional votes required. He considered, then, all votes given for Fillmore for the purpose of defeating the election by the people, and of throwing it into the House, as votes given to promote Fremont's election; and that those who, under existing circumstances, and with such an object, cast their votes, are unfriendly to the South, and responsible for all the consequences which may follow.

If the friends of Mr. Fillmore could reasonably calculate on his election, or if the contest was between him and Buchanan, he would have nothing to say. He should vote in silence according to his convictions of propriety, feeling assured that, whether the one or the other succeeded, the substantial interests of the country—above all, the safety of the Union—would be preserved. But the contest is not between them; and his being in the field, at least in the Southern States, can be productive of mischief only. While the Freesoil interests are all combined and combining, the South presents a divided front; defeat and humiliation are the certain consequences of these tactics, if persevered in. The real contest is between Mr. Buchanan and Mr. Fremont; one or the other of these must succeed; and, as between them, he held it to be the duty of every Union-loving man—of every man who cherished the honor of the South, and desired her to be preserved in the enjoyment of her constitutional rights and authority—to give the former a cheerful and unreserved support. For one, he intended to do it. The ground Mr. Buchanan occupied on this great question was the true, constitutional and only safe ground; it corresponded with Mr. C's long-cherished and oft-repeated opinions; and he should be false to those opinions if he hesitated, at this time, in giving him and them his support. He thought that the duty of all, Southern men especially. He regretted that many of those with whom he had long acted, his cherished and familiar friends, thought differently; he regretted not to see them around him to-night, and hear their familiar voices cheering him onward—the separation pained him. He conceded to them an equal degree of intelligence and patriotism which he claimed for himself; and could only regret that they would not think with him. He believed he was right, he knew he was sincere, and he should act up to his duty, painful though it be. Possibly he might be denounced; better men had been denounced, and he knew of no reason why he ought to expect exemption; but he should not hesitate or falter, he should act up to his principles, and according to his sense of duty, in the face of all denunciation. He was not afraid to do his duty. He would leave consequences to take care of themselves.

Mr. Crisfield, after having told an anecdote illustrative of his own position, again tendered his thanks to the audience, bid them good night, and retired.

SPEECH OF JAMES B. CLAY,

DELIVERED AT THE UNION MEETING IN MASON COUNTY, KENTUCKY.

Mr. Clay being called for was introduced to the assemblage as an Old-Line Whig, and said:

Ladies and Gentlemen, Fellow-Citizens of Mason County: I present myself before you on this occasion under circumstances peculiar and extraordinary. A candidate for no office in the gift of the people, in bad health, I have left my home and my occupation as an humble, plain farmer, at the request of those in whose names I recognize old Whigs and Democrats, to come here to-day to cast in my mite and to strike one blow for the Union. In all this vast assemblage there are perhaps not more than half a dozen persons who have ever seen me before, and not that number with whom I have the least personal acquaintance. You have all of you, however, heard my name; and all of you have heard the vilest charges made against me, designed and calculated to destroy whatever little influence I might happen to possess as an individual, and to take from me the confidence and respect of my fellow men. I have been denounced as false to the memory of my father, and as a renegade to his principles. Fellow-citizens, I was born within stone's throw of the Capitol, in the very house in which my father died. Educated under his care, the same shades of Ashland in which he so much delighted, and under which he had some of his noblest inspiration, gave shelter to me in my youthful days. I thank God that, by my own exertions, I have been able to preserve that spot in his family. In my more mature manhood I was the companion, the partner, the trusted friend of my father. Thus educated and thus associated, to be a Whig became a part of my nature. I am now a Whig; and I expect to die a Whig, as I have lived.

Fellow-citizens you have heard the charges and calumnies against me. I am now before you, face to face, and you can judge for yourselves whether I have the countenance of a false and insincere man. There is not one drop of false blood coursing through my veins. Numbers of you here present are old enough to remember the River Raisin, and that bloody day, when all Kentuckey was clothed in mourning One of my race, on that disastrous occasion, poured out his life's blood for his country. All of you have heard of Buena Vista, and how my noble brother, covered with a hundred wounds, upon his back, surrounded by enemies, so long as his feeble arm could raise his sword, battled for the honor and glory of the Union and of his native Kentucky. None of you can have forgotten that funeral cortege, which, leaving Washington City, passing through half the Union, arrived at Ashland, amid the nation's tears and grief—a patriot was brought home to be laid under the green sod of the land which had so honored him, and upon which he had reflected so much honor. Fellow-citizens, this is my race—these were my people—and with their memories always present and clustering around me, I appeal to you to know whether it is possible for me to be false or insincere.

Early in the last year, fellow-citizens, it was apparent to all men that the Whig party, as an organized party, was gone. The seeds of its fall were sown in 1840, when the plume of a military chieftain was permitted to dazzle men's eyes. But in 1848, when adopting the doctrine that availability and success were rather to be looked to than right, in lieu of the noble idea that it was better to be right than be President, the Convention of Philadelphia set the seal upon the fate of the party. Refusing to reassert a platform of Whig principles, it selected General Taylor as its candidate for the Presidency upon the single idea of his availability. The hand-writing was as plainly upon the wall as at Belshazzar's feast. The Whig party broken up, disorganized, and apparently hopelessly so, Old Line Whigs began to ask themselves the question which once the immortal Sage of Marshfield propounded himself, "Where am I to go?" Rumors came to us of a party which was said already to have attained vast strength, even while many doubted its very existence. Secret and mysterious, it was repeated, like Minerva from the brain of Jove, to have sprung forth fully armed. Its purposes were said to be the introduction of a purer and better state of things in politics, and the good only of the country.

Seeing many of my old Whig associates attaching themselves to it, I was told it was but Whiggery in disguise, and that it only differed from the old Whig party in seeking a modification of the naturalization laws. I had myself always thought that some modification ought to be made of those laws, and that greater safeguards ought to be placed around the elective franchise. I was told that its secrecy, which was abhorrent to my nature, was only to continue until the party got fairly underweigh, when everything would be made open and public. Deceived by men in whom I had every confidence, I thought it to be my duty to join this new party. I presented myself for admission into the order. Do not be deceived—I did not get in. The first questions that were propounded to me astounded and startled me. They were in substance these; I do not pretend to quote the very words: Where was I born? The place of my residence? Was I twenty-one years of age? Was I a Roman Catholic? Were my parents Protestant? Was my wife a Roman Catholic? Was I willing to oppose for all offices of honor, trust or profit in the gift of the people, all foreigners and Roman Catholics?

Fellow-citizens, I am not telling you untruths. I declare to you upon my honor, and in the presence of God, that I believe these to be substantially the questions which were proposed to me; and I appeal to those members of the so called American party, who may be present, to answer whether I have not stated truly the obligations under which they placed themselves in the early part of 1855, whatever may now be the doctrines of their party, which I do not pretend to know. I do not expect them to answer me, but I do expect them, when they go to their own homes, to make answer to their own consciences whether I have not spoken the truth. Shocked and startled, I requested the presiding officer to read again the obligation against foreigners and Catholics. It was done, and an attempt made to explain away the force of the clear meaning of the words of the obligation. I observed that I had been mistaken and deceived as to the purposes of the party, or my shadow would never have darkened their door. I took my hat and wished them good morning.

Fellow-citizens, there was once in the middle ages a political society in Europe, and especially in Germany, called the *Illuminati ;* one of its practices was that when an individual became partially or fully initiated, and afterward disclosed any of its secrets, two alternatives were offered to the wretched victim—a cord and a dagger were secretly placed by his bed-side, and he might either hang himself or put himself to death with the dagger; if he chose neither of the delightful alternatives, his nearest relation, even his own brother, if a member of the society, was bound to take his life. Fellow-citizens, all secret political societies are alike. In this age, since letters and the press are come about, the cord and the dagger are no longer used; a venal press affords a far more potent weapon and more vindictive punishment. By falsehood, by calumny, by libel and detraction, not only may the heart of the victim himself be torn in pieces, but the feelings of his wife, his mother, his children, of his whole family are reached and lacerated for vengeance sake. Fellow-citizens, such persecution I myself have undergone, and you know it.

I could not reconcile it to my conscience to become a Know-Nothing, because I believed the principles of the party to be antagonistic to civil and religious liberty, and dangerous to our republican institutions. Throwing out a banner inscribed, "Americans only shall rule America," they appeared to me like the vailed Prophet of Khorassan, who, concealing his horrible visage behind a silver vail, erected shrines

"Where faith may mutter o'er her mystic spell,
Written in blood, and bigotry may swell,
The sail he spreads for Heaven with blasts from Hell."

I could not become a Know-Nothing—"where shall I go?" Fellow citizens, I turned my thoughts back to the old party of my father. I knew its principles to be true; some of its practices had been bad; but I believed its principles, once true, they must always be so, for truth cannot die. They told me that the party was dead, but I believed that the party was only after the death that the resurrection could come. In concert with some of my Whig brethren, we determined to strive after its resurrection. There was no meeting calling itself Whig in all my region of country, which I did not attend. There was no Convention at which I was not present. Every effort to resuscitate the old party, which could be made was made. The result was the Convention at Louisville on the 3rd of July. It was then resolved to be inexpedient to present Whig candidates for the highest offices for the suffrages of the people; and it was determined that, having asserted our old principles, it was proper that each individual should be left free to make his own choice according to his own conscience and his own principles, for the good of his country.

Fellow-citizens, I have followed the Whig standard so long as it fluttered in the breeze. I would have followed it always, and I always expect to maintain Whig principles. Like an eloquent Old-Line Whig of Missouri, now acting with the Democrats, "I have surveyed the whole battlefield ,but I find no Whig banner under which to fight." Like him, I am forced to the conviction that the old Whig flag lies furled upon the tomb of my father.

Fellow-citizens, the country is in danger. In 1820 our wisest and best statesmen told us there was great danger from the question of slavery. For the purpose of putting it at rest the so called Missouri Compromise was made, but it did not settle the question. Again, in 1819-50, it raised its horrid front. Fortunately for the country, at that time there were then at Washington, men of giant race, who could see and appreciate the danger, and warn the country of it. Do you not recollect how the black cloud sat like a leaden pall upon the hearts of men—how the bravest trembled for the Union? Do you not remember with what anxiety all eyes were turned to Washington—with what trembling eagerness you listened for every scrap of news? At last the tidings came that the Compromise measures of 1850 had been passed, although in detail. Have you forgotten the rejoicings throughout the whole land? How the bells rung, and the glad shouts went up to Heaven in gratitude that the country was safe? How vain and how futile were the hopes of the best and wisest of men. Scarcely are some of the principal actors in those noble scenes cold in their graves, when again the black cloud is upon us. The country is in danger. The Black Republicans of the North, determined to carry out their designs against the South at all hazards, and at every risk, have nominated purely sectional candidates for the Presidency and Vice Presidency. North against South—union or disunion—this is the question now before you, and you cannot avoid it. It is not I alone who tells you so. Americans, as you choose to call yourselves Old-Line Whigs, it is Mr. Fillmore also who tells you so. Hear what he says in his Albany speech, recently delivered—a speech so patriotic and honorable to him.

"Sir, you have been pleased to say that I have the union of these States at heart. This, sir, is most true, for if there be one object dearer to me than any other, it is the unity, prosperity and glory of this great Republic; and I confess frankly, sir, that I fear it is in danger. I say nothing of any particular section, much less of the several candidates before the people. I presume they are all honorable men. But, sir, what do we see? An exasperated feeling between the North and South, on the most exciting of all topics, resulting in bloodshed and organized military array.

"But this is not all, sir. We see a political party presenting candidates for the Presidency and Vice Presidency, selected for the first time from the free States alone, with the avowed purpose of electing these candidates by the suffrages of one part of the Union only to rule over the whole United States. Can it be possible that those who are engaged in such a measure, could have seriously reflected upon the consequences which must inevitably follow in case of success? [Cheers.] Can they have the madness or folly to believe that our Southern brethren would submit to be governed by such a Chief Magistrate? [Cheers.] Would he be required to follow the rule prescribed by those who elected him in making his appointments? If a man living south of Mason and Dixon's line, be not worthy to be President or Vice President, would it be proper to select one from the same quarter as one of his Cabinet Council, or to represent the nation in a foreign country? Or, indeed, to collect the revenue or administer the laws of the United States? If not, what new rule is the President to adopt in selecting men for office?

"These are serious, but practical questions, and in order to appreciate them fully, it is only necessary to turn the tables upon ourselves. Suppose that the South, having a majority of the electoral votes, should declare that they would only have slaveholders for President and Vice President, and should elect such by their exclusive suffrages to rule over us at the North, do you think we would submit to it? No, not for a moment. [Applause.] And do you believe that your Southern brethren are less sensitive on this subject than you are, or less jealous of their rights? [Tremendous cheering.] If you do, let me tell you that you are mistaken. And, therefore, you must see that if this sectional party succeeds, it leads inevitably to the destruction of this beautiful fabric, reared by our forefathers, cemented by their blood, and bequeathed to us as a priceless inheritance.

"I tell you, my friends, that I speak warmly on this subject, for I feel that we are in danger. I am determined to make a clean breast of it. I will wash my hands of the consequences, whatever they may be; and I tell you that we are treading upon the brink of a volcano that is liable at any moment to burst forth and overwhelm the nation. I might by soft words hold out delusive hopes, and thereby win votes, but I never can consent to be one thing to the North and another to the South. I should despise myself if I could be guilty of such evasion."

I believe every word that Mr. Fillmore says. *As surely as the sun shines the country is in danger.* I have a high respect for Mr. Fillmore, and if he stood precisely where he did in 1850, I should prefer him to any man for the Presidency. Even as it is, personally I prefer him to either of the other candidates. But, fellow-citizens, there is no living man whom I love so well as I do that great union of States—my country—for which my father gave his life. Mr. Fillmore has given us good advice—advice which accords with my own judgment; he tells us that the Union is in imminent danger; he leads us to believe that the probabilities are that if Mr. Fremont is elected, the Union will be dissolved; and not into two parts, but shivered into fragments! Old-Line Whigs, what is our duty? It lies with us to save the Union. The candidates of the Black-Republican party must be defeated, else, as Mr. Fillmore tells us—as we have been told by the greatest statesmen since 1820—the Union is in dire and imminent peril. For me, I am for the preservation of the Union. Destroy all the parties now in existence, but for God's sake—for the sake of human liberty—save the Union. I have no faith in the sincerity of that man who, with his mouth full of protestations of love for his country, and for the memory of my dead father, cannot lay his personal prejudices and predilections upon the altar, a willing sacrifice for the salvation of his country.

How are we to defeat Fremont? We cannot elect both his opponents. Neither of them—neither Mr. Fillmore nor Mr. Buchanan—is presented for the suffrage of Old-Line Whigs, upon a pure Whig platform. There are principles avowed and maintained by both the parties of which they are representatives, which we do not approve. It is necessary for us to choose between them, whichever is most likely to defeat the Black-Republican candidate; and in making the choice it is not necessary for us to indorse or to give in our adhesion to the principles which either represent. I believe that the Union would be safe with either; and it is our duty to save the Union if we can. The question for us is resolved into a mere question of chances, which is the most likely to succeed according to our best light, Mr. Fillmore or Mr. Buchanan?

Fellow-citizens, I have made my choice. Looking over the whole country, not confining my view to my own State, or to my own locality, not suffering myself to be influenced by partisan journals or by partisan orators—I am deliberately convinced that Mr. Fillmore has not the least chance of success, and that if it be at all possible to defeat Fremont, the Democratic party, with their candidates Buchanan and Breckinridge, with the aid of the Union-loving Old-line Whigs, is the only party which has the least chance to do so. Show me a State certain or nearly certain for Fillmore, and I will show you two for Buchanan. I hold in my hand authentic results of the last elections, from which alone we can form reliable conclusions. From these it appears that, while twelve of the Southern States are almost certain for Buchanan, Mr. Fillmore has, at the best, but doubtful chances for the remaining three. Thus, Mr. Buchanan presents himself with almost the whole South in solid phalanx. At the North his count of States is to the full as good, and in my opinion much better, than Mr. Fillmore's; besides, we Whigs know well, and to our cost the wonderful tenacity of the Democratic party—how it has held together and had success when we most confidentially expected its defeat.

I know, fellow-whigs, how difficult it is for you to get rid of old prejudices, either of attraction or repulsion. I have not forgotten, however, that upon a question of mere availability, the Whigs of Kentucky were able, through their delegates at Philadelphia in 1848, to give up their idol, the man whom they loved, and who loved them and who had done so much for the honor of Kentucky, that whenever Kentucky's name was mentioned, at home or abroad, his name at once arose before the mind's eye, and whenever his name was mentioned Kentucky appeared. Fellow-whigs, do you love Mr. Fillmore so much better than you did Henry Clay that you cannot make the same sacrifice of your predilections for one that you did for the other upon much less occasion?

But, fellow-citizens, I am often asked how it is possible that I, my father's son, can reconcile it to myself to vote for Mr. Buchanan, who, they say, had so seriouly injured and wronged my father by originating, or, if not originating, by being complicated with and mixed up in some way or other with that vile old charge of bargain and intrigue betwixt him and Mr. Adams. In nine cases out of ten the persons who in my presence refer to that affair, know absolutely nothing about it, and when I refer them to authentic records, they are too much prejudiced, and love to be prejudiced too well, to allow them to make the most ordinary examination. I have fully and carefully studied the whole history of the bargain and intrigue slander, with the express purpose of ascertaining the truth or the falsity of the charges made against Mr. Buchanan, and the result of my research has been, that as an honest man I am bound to acquit him of having had any part in the original slander, or having done my father any wrong, when he was summoned before the public as a witness against him. I am bound to acquit him upon the testimony of the very person whom he is said to have wronged and slandered, and however little partisan editors and partisan orators may esteem the evidence of my father himself, it is abundantly sufficient for me his son. The charge of bargain and intrigue was first made by Mr. Kremer, in an anonymous letter, subsequently reiterated by Carter Beverly, in his celebrated Fayetteville letter, and finally asserted by General Jackson, who assumed the responsibility of it, and to prove its truth, summoned Mr. Buchanan before the public as his only witness. Mr. Buchanan promptly responded to the call for his testimony. Did he sustain Mr. Kremer, Carter Beverly and General Jackson, the last of whom had summoned him? On the contrary, his evidence was clear and distinct, and fully exculpated Mr. Clay from the charges made against him. So Mr. Clay regarded it himself, and he, the person accused, testified, publicly and privately, that he considered Mr. Buchanan had done him no wrong. I read to you from *Colton's Private Correspondence* of my father, his private letter to his old friend, Judge Brooke, of Virginia—the friend of his life-time—a letter never intended for publication, dated August, 1827, in which, referring to Mr. Buchanan's Lancaster letter, he says; "I could not desire a stronger statement." Again in public, upon the occasion of a dinner given him in Washington on his retirement from the office of Secretary of State, he said:

"That citizen (General Jackson) has done me great injustice. It was inflicted, as I must ever believe, for the double purpose of gratifying private resentment and promoting personal ambition. When, during the late canvass, he came forward in the public prints, under his proper name, with his charge against me, and summoned before the public tribunal his friend and only witness, Mr. Buchanan, to establish it, the anxious attention of the whole American people was directed to the testimony which that witness might render. He promptly obeyed the call, and testified to what he knew. He *could* say nothing, and he *said nothing*, which cast the slightest shade upon my honor or integrity. What he *did* say was the reverse of any implication of me."

Thus, fellow-citizens, we have the private and public opinion of my father respecting the testimony of Mr. Buchanan upon the charge of bargain and intrigue. I know that my father would not have expressed such opinions unless he believed them to be true. He was satisfied with Mr. Buchanan, and so expressed himself privately and publicly; that is enough for me, and so far as I am concerned, it is of the smallest possible consequence what may be the opinion of those partisans who are now endeavoring to strike down their political opponent with weapons dragged from the tomb.

Fellow-citizens, you are aware you cannot vote for Fillmore alone. You must know that in voting for the electoral ticket of Mr. Fillmore, you also vote for Andrew Jackson Donelson; as in voting for that of Mr. Buchanan, you vote for John C. Breckinridge. Mr. Fillmore himself became President by one of those dispensations of Providence which may likewise cause Mr. Donelson to fill the chair, if their ticket were successful. Between Donelson and Breckinridge I could not hesitate for a single instant. I know Major Breckinridge well; he is not only my fellow-Kentuckian, but my fellow-townsman also. We have differed in politics, but I have never heard but one opinion expressed of him—that he is an honorable, high-toned Kentucky gentleman. It affords me very great pleasure to relate to you an incident which occurred in my presence, and which afforded as much gratification to my father as it was honorable and creditable to Major Breckinridge. Very soon after his first election to Congress, Major Breckinridge called upon my father, and I was present at the interview. "Mr. Clay," said Major Breckingridge, (of course I can only give the substance,) "I have been elected from your old district, and am about to go, quite a young man, to Washington City. We have always differed, sir, in politics, but I have ever entertained the highest respect for you. I have no doubt but I shall often have occasion for good advice, and if you will allow me, sir, to do so, it will afford me great satisfaction to call freely upon you at Washington, and to be enabled to avail myself of your wisdom and great experience."

Between such a man as this and Andrew Jackson Donelson, I, at least, fellow-citizens, would have no difficulty in making a choice.

Fellow-citizens, I have already occupied more of your time than I had any right to expect would be given so attentively to every word that I have addressed to you. I thank you from the bottom of my heart. I trust that you will allow me, on taking my leave of you, to indulge the hope that my effort to direct your attention to the imminent danger which threatens our glorious Union may not be wholly without avail, and that you will, at any rate, fellow-citizens, believe me in what I have said to you, to have been perfectly and entirely sincere.

SPEECH

OF

HON. ALEXANDER H. STEPHENS,

OF GEORGIA,

ON

THE BILL TO ADMIT KANSAS AS A STATE

UNDER THE TOPEKA CONSTITUTION.

DELIVERED IN THE HOUSE OF REPRESENTATIVES, JUNE 28, 1856.

WASHINGTON:
PRINTED AT THE CONGRESSIONAL GLOBE OFFICE.
1856.

ADMISSION OF KANSAS.

The House having under consideration the bill reported from the Committee on Territories, providing for the admission of Kansas into the Union as a State, with the constitution prepared at Topeka by the free-State party.

Mr. STEPHENS said: I propose, Mr. Speaker, before I proceed to what I have arisen mainly to say on this occasion, to ask the consent of the House to allow me now to offer the amendment which I stated yesterday I wished to propose to the bill now before us.

Mr. WASHBURN, of Maine. If the gentleman asks that consent now, I shall object to it, as I shall at all times.

Mr. STEPHENS. On the motion to commit the bill to the Committee of the Whole on the state of the Union, the amendment is not in order, unless by unanimous consent.

Mr. WASHBURN. I understand that to be a side measure, intended to destroy the bill, and I shall object to it now, and at all times.

Mr. STEPHENS. I state to the gentleman that I have no *side blows* for this bill, nor is my amendment intended as any *side measure*. I wish my proposition to come distinctly before the House as a substitute for the pending bill. I am opposed out and out to this bill as it now stands. I want no misunderstanding on that point. I will, however, vote for the substitute; and what I want is a direct vote between the bill now pending, and the substitute offered as an amendment. But as the gentleman from Maine will not allow me to offer my proposition as an amendment, I now move to amend the motion to commit this bill to the Committee of the Whole on the state of the Union, by adding to it, "With instructions to report this amendment in lieu of the original bill;" in other words, with instructions to strike out all in the original bill, and to insert my amendment in lieu thereof. That is the motion which I submit to the House, and upon it I shall proceed with what I have to say.

It is immaterial to me, Mr. Speaker, if I can get a vote in the House on the proposition submitted by me, whether it goes to the Committee of the Whole on the state of the Union, or not. I am myself prepared to vote on it to-day, either in the House or in the Committee of the Whole on the state of the Union. But I am inclined to think that it had better go to the committee. We can then take up this amendment, and consider it in detail. It may be some gentlemen would suggest modifications, which I would accept. We can then discuss the merits of the original bill. Its friends can amend that, if they wish. My amendment can be put in such form as a majority of the committee may desire, if a majority be favorable to its objects. I therefore shall vote for the reference. But the gentleman from Ohio [Mr. Campbell] the other day said, that the motion to refer or commit, made by the gentleman from Indiana, [Mr. Dunn,] and which is now pending, was equivalent, if successful, to a defeat of the bill. The gentleman from Maine [Mr. Washburn] also followed in the same line. Now, I told these gentlemen, day before yesterday, and I state it again to the House, that I do not consider the motion to commit the bill to the Committee of the Whole on the state of the Union, if carried, as equivalent to a defeat of the measure at all. By no means, sir. What is the argument of those who say a reference of the bill is tantamount to its defeat? Nothing better than this, as argued by the gentleman from Maine, to wit: that all the friends of the Kansas bill, two years ago, when that bill was referred to the Committee of the Whole on the state of the Union, considered it as equivalent to its defeat. That is his argument, and the authority adduced by him to sustain it. Sir, it is immaterial to me what certain friends of the Kansas bill may have thought would be the effect of its reference, when it was referred. If they considered that reference as equivalent to its defeat, the sequel showed that they were in error. That is all. It was referred. It was considered two weeks in committee, and it was then passed.

Mr. WASHBURN. Will the gentleman allow me to say that that was simply because they broke down the rules of the House in two instances. If they had not they never could have got that bill out of committee.

Mr. STEPHENS. Will the gentleman state what two instances?

Mr. WASHBURN. In the first place, by deciding that under the 119th rule you might strike out the enacting clause of the bill. In the second place, by rising and reporting the bill to the House when there was no quorum voting, as every body knows.

Mr. RICHARDSON. The gentleman from Maine is totally mistaken when he says there was no quorum.

Mr. STEPHENS. I hope the gentleman from Illinois will let me proceed. The gentleman from Maine is mistaken in both his instances. The record shows that the tellers, Mr. CLINGMAN and Mr. SAPP, reported 103 in favor of the motion, and 22 against it. That is more than a quorum—one hundred and eighteen was a quorum—one hundred and twenty-five voted. Though a great many present refused to vote, more than a quorum, however, did vote on the motion to strike out. It does not require a quorum to vote on a motion to rise, as every one knows. And as far as the violation of the 119th rule is concerned, I have this to say to the gentleman—as I said the day before yesterday—that nothing can be clearer than that everything done in the committee on the passage of the Kansas bill under the 119th rule, was legitimate and proper; and that no rule of this House was violated or overrode on that occasion. This I intend to show beyond cavil or doubt. The charge that there was no quorum voting is answered by the record, as I have stated; then as to the two other charges—for besides the charge relating to the 119th rule now made, the gentleman from Maine, [Mr. WASHBURN,] or some other gentleman, said, two days ago, that there was another rule violated. What one I do not know—for no one was mentioned—but the statement was, that the committee had violated the rules of the House by setting aside other bills having priority in the order of business on the Calendar to the Kansas-Nebraska bill. That was one statement; and I think it was also said that upwards of a hundred bills were thus set aside to reach this one. Now, Mr. Speaker, I have the rules of the House before me, and ask the attention of the House to the 135th rule:

"In Committee of the Whole on the state of the Union the bills shall be taken up and disposed of in their order on the Calendar; but *when objection* is made to the consideration of a bill a *majority of the committee shall decide, without debate*, whether it shall be taken up and disposed of, or laid aside; provided, that general appropriation bills, and, in time of war, bills for raising men or money, and bills concerning a treaty of peace, shall be preferred to all other bills at *the discretion of the* committee; and when demanded by any member the question shall *first be put in regard to them*."

Even in times of war, appropriation bills, and bills relating to treaties of peace, have no other preference, except that the question of taking them up first shall be first put. A majority may lay even them aside.

Sir, could a rule be written more plainly? Can language be more clear or more distinct than this—that when the House goes into the Committee of the Whole on the state of the Union, and when the first bill in order is read by the Clerk, and a gentleman objects to taking it up, it is then submitted to the committee whether it will be taken up or not; and a *majority of the committee have the expressly-granted power to determine, without debate*, whether they will then act on it, or lay it aside for other business; and so on to the second, and so to the third, and to the fourth, and to the one hundred and fiftieth, if you please? Was it not perfectly competent for a majority of the Committee of the Whole on the state of the Union, when the Kansas bill was in committee, to pass over other bills, and take up that bill when they wished to do so?

This they did. Each bill was laid aside as it was reached. They had a right to do it. They violated no rule in doing it. The number of bills laid aside to reach it was only eighteen, I think. But if the number had been legion—if there had been one hundred, or five hundred, or a thousand, it would have made no difference.

Sir, the rule in this case is as clear as it could be made; and the action of the committee on that occasion was strictly in order. This I maintain, and defy an answer or reply to it.

Now, then, sir, as to the 119th rule.

When the committee on that occasion had laid aside the first bill, and the second bill, and the third bill, and so on, until they had come to the Kansas bill, the eighteenth in order—which they had a right to do—they took it up for consideration; and after it had been discussed for two weeks in committee, which was as long as was thought proper by the House, the 119th rule was resorted to, to stop debate in committee and bring the subject before the House for a vote. That rule is as follows:

"A motion to strike out the enacting words of a bill shall have precedence of a motion to amend; and, if carried, shall be equivalent to its rejection."

Under this rule, a motion was made by myself in committee to strike out the enacting words of the Kansas bill—a motion which *took precedence of all motions to amend*, as the rule says. The motion was properly put; and it was carried by a vote of one hundred and three for it, to but twenty-two against it, as I have said. Where, then, was there any violation of the rules in this? But the gentleman from Ohio, [Mr. CAMPBELL,] who says he wishes to reply to what I say, insisted the day before yesterday that this 119th rule never was intended to apply in committee.

The rule, in its language, was too clear, too overwhelming, too unanswerable; but to avoid its conclusiveness against him, he said *it was made to apply to the House, and not to the Committee of the Whole, &c.* Well, sir, let us see how this subterfuge will avail the gentleman. The history of this rule, as given in our Manual, is as follows:

"In 1814, a Committee of the Whole struck out the first and only section of a bill, and so reported to the House. Mr. Speaker Cheves refused to receive the report, on the ground that it was tantamount to a rejection of the bill, which the committee had not power to do." Just as the gentleman now says. "After this, that the merit of questions might be tested in Committee of the Whole, rule 119 was adopted."

This history clearly shows that it was expressly *adopted for the Committee of the Whole, &c.*

I have produced this additional authority to show that there was *no violation of the rule on the occasion alluded to*—that the Committee of the Whole on the Kansas bill did just exactly what the rule intended that they might do, and fully empowered them to do. But gentlemen say, if this rule was *intended* to be applied to the Committee of the Whole, why has it never been put in practice before? That was the argument of the gentleman from Maine.

Well, Mr. Speaker, my reply to him is, that it has been put in practice before. It was adopted in 1822. Ten days after its adoption, on the 2d of March, 1822, first session of the Seventeeth Congress, I find the Journal of the House record thus:

"The House took up and proceeded to consider the bill for the relief of Benjamin Freeland and John M. Jenkins; and the amount reported thereto from the Committee of the Whole House, on the 14th instant, being read as follows: '*striking out the enacting clause of said bill,*'

"The question was put on concurring with the Committee of the Whole House in the said amendment,

"And passed in the affirmative."

Here the committee did the very same thing, ten days after the rule was adopted, that was done on the Kansas bill. What did the House do? Did they say that the Committee of the Whole had acted improperly? No, sir. The Journal says: "the question was taken upon concurring with the Committee of the Whole on said amendment, and it passed in the affirmative."

I find in the first session of the Eighteenth Congress, on the 22d of May, this record:

"The question was then taken to concur with the Committee of the Whole House on striking out the enacting words of the bill from the Senate, entitled 'An act relative to the Patent Office and to the salary of the superintendent thereof,'

"And passed in the affirmative."

Again, sir, in the first session of the Twenty-First Congress, I find on the Journal this record:

"The House resolved itself into a Committee of the Whole House on the bill (No. 127) for the relief of Walter Livingston, deceased, and after some time spent therein, the Speaker resumed the chair, and Mr. Storrs, of New York, reported the same, with the *enacting clause stricken out.*"

"The question was then put, that the House do concur with the Committee of the Whole House in striking out the enacting words of said bill,

"And passed in the affirmative—yeas 84, nays 59."

I find in the same Congress, in the action of the House on the bill for the relief of John Robinson, that

"The question was then put to concur with the Committee of the Whole House in striking out *the enacting words of the bill* (No. 175) for the relief of John Robinson,

"And passed in the affirmative.

"So the land bill was rejected."

Sir, I shall not go on with this record. It is sufficient for me to state to those gentlemen who complain of my motion under this rule, that their not knowing that such a motion had ever been made before does not seem to me to be an argument of much merit or force. I show you, Mr. Speaker, the House, and the country, the rule. No man can question that. I show you, also, its history; and from that, that it was made for just such a purpose as the one I applied it to. No man now can gainsay that. I go further, and show you the *practice* of the House under it. No man can any longer question that. Then, sir, how can gentlemen rise up here, and say that the passage of the Kansas and Nebraska bill was accomplished by overriding the rules of the House? Gentlemen may have been surprised and astonished at the parliamentary tactics practiced under the rule; they may never have dreamed of how the friends of a measure, in committee, could vote to strike out the enacting words—thus apparently defeating it—and then, when it was so reported to the House, reverse their position, disagree to the report of the committee striking out the enacting words, and then pass it. They may not have understood the process by which a bill might be temporarily apparently killed by its friends in Committee of the Whole, for the purpose of getting it out, and then revived again in the House, by disagreeing to the report of the committee; but this is the whole of it. This is the ground of all this clamor about the violation of the rules of the House, in the passage of the Kansas bill—for it is nothing but clamor.

The charge of a violation of rules has not the semblance of a fact to rest upon. And let no man hereafter say that sending a bill to the Committee of the Whole is equivalent to its defeat. Our rules requiring this committee, and directing how business shall be disposed of in it, are wise and proper. And the rules, when properly administered, work harmoniously for the perfection and dispatch of legislation. It is only those who do not understand them who see confusion and mystery in them. Where, then, was the wrong or the fraud perpetrated on the rules in the passage of the Kansas bill? It exists only in the fancy of gentlemen who declaim so violently on the subject. I said, sir, I intended to vindicate the action both of the committee and the House on that occasion, and put the matter beyond all future cavil or doubt. This, I think, I have done. Now, sir, I intend also, with the same confidence, to vindicate the principles of that bill against the equally unfounded assaults which have been made upon them. What, sir, are those assaults?

The gentleman from Ohio [Mr. CAMPBELL] said the other day, and again says, that the passage of the Nebraska bill was the origin of all the troubles in the country. Sir, what troubles does he allude to? What troubles have we upon us? Standing in my place in the Hall of the Representatives of the United States, I ask to-day, what troubles is the country laboring under? Were any people of the world ever more prosperous than the people of the United States now are? We are at peace with all other nations; we hear of no complaint about Federal taxes or high tariffs; we hear of no disarrangement of the currency or of the finances of the country; we hear of no clamor against banks; our tables are not loaded down with petitions or remonstrances against grievances of any sort; thrift and plenty seem to be smiling over the land from one extent to the other. Our commerce was never more flourishing; agriculture never yielded a more bountiful supply from the bosom of the earth to the tillers of her soil than it now does, nor was the average value of products ever higher. Industry, in every department of business, whether upon the ocean or the land, never had more inducements to ply its energies, not only for competency and comforts, but for the accumulation of riches and wealth. Never did labor, in all its branches, receive more readily than it now does fair and justly compensating wages. Our internal and foreign trade was never in a more flourishing condition. What are the troubles, then, of which the gentleman speaks? Why, sir, if one could cast his eye over this wide Republic at this time, and see the thrift and prosperity in every department of industry, arising from our benign institutions, he would almost be compelled to exclaim, that all the troubles of which we hear grow out of nothing but that exuberance of liberty and multitude of blessings which seem to be driving us on to licentiousness. This we see in the mobs at Cincinnati, Louisville, New Orleans, in this city, and in San Francisco. The laws have been set aside; force has been resorted to; arms have been used; and men have been slain. But the absorbing theme now is the "civil war," as it called, in Kansas. This is the announcement made in a neighboring city, the commercial metropolis of this Union, the other night, according to a report of their proceedings which I find in a newspaper, to a large crowd of people there assembled. I see it was proclaimed that civil war was raging in Kansas; and that that assembly gave shouts of applause at the announcement! These are the troubles I suppose of which the gentleman speaks — troubles produced not by this Kansas bill, but by the mischievous designs and reckless purposes of those who, in their efforts to defeat the quiet and peaceful operation of the sound purposes of that bill, have for some time been engaged in their unholy work of attempting to get up civil war in the country, and can now shout in applause at even the most distant prospect of success.

This, sir, is the work of that class of restless malcontents, who have for years been endeavoring to produce a sectional conflict in this country; who have no regard for the constitutional equality of the States of this Union; who repudiate the most sacred obligations of that compact which binds us together, and who have proclaimed that the Constitution itself is a league with death and a covenant with hell! How far they shall be permitted to go on with their work until checked by a sound reactive public sentiment—how far they shall get sympathy and coöperation from those whom they are now attempting to mislead —how far they may be successful in their long cherished wish for civil strife, I cannot say. That is a problem for the future to settle; that depends upon the virtue, intelligence, and integrity of the people. But that they ought not to succeed—that they ought not only to be discouraged, but rebuked and condemned in every part of this country, and by every man who has a spark of patriotism in his bosom, as well in the North as in the South, I this day maintain. But the gentleman from Ohio says all this comes from the Kansas bill. How? In what way?

What is there wrong in that Kansas measure? It has been said that it is a fraud. It has been said that it is the greatest of iniquities. It has been said that it is a crime against God. It has been said that it is a crime against nature. Well, sir, what is this fraud, this iniquity, this crime against nature and against God? It is the simple declaration of the principle that the people of the Territories of Kansas and Nebraska—the pioneer freemen there—our own brothers in flesh and blood—going there from every State of the Union, for the purpose of settling that distant frontier—there to build up new homes for themselves and their posterity—should have the right, without limitation or restriction from any quarter, save the Constitution of the United States, to form and mold just such institutions for their own government as they pleased—a right which lies at the foundation of all our State governments, and upon which the whole Republic, in its several parts, is built and established. This is the fraud, this is the iniquity, this is the great crime of crimes, the security to the people of the Territories of the right of self-government under the Constitution. The amount of the crime is, that freemen shall be permitted to make such constitutions, republican in form, for their own government, without dictation or control from any other power, as they please. Tell it wherever you go, that this was the monstrous outrage committed by an American Congress in 1850, the middle of the nineteenth century, on the Territories of Utah and New Mexico, and repeated by the same body in 1854, on the Territories of Nebraska and "bleeding Kansas!" This is the whole of it—nothing more and nothing less. These troubles we now hear of—these efforts to get up civil war—these shouts at the announcement that civil war has already commenced—are but part and parcel of that spirit which animated a portion, and only a portion, of the opposition to the Kansas bill, during the pendency of that measure in this House. That same spirit at the North that had so bitterly opposed the establishment of this great principle of territorial policy in 1850 could not bear the idea of its being carried out in the future.

I recollect very well, sir, that while the Kansas bill was progressing here, a newspaper in the city of New York, edited by a man of great ability, untiring energy and industry, and who is now the head and front—the animating spirit of the present opposition, and civil war champion's undertook to lecture this House as to our duty in regard to that bill. We were told then by him what an enormous wrong it would be; and when the measure was about to pass an editorial in that paper reached here, from which I wish to present some extracts, to show that it is the same spirit now at work:

> "We urge, therefore, unbending determination on the part of the northern members hostile to this intolerable outrage, and demand of them, in behalf of peace—in behalf of freedom—in behalf of justice and humanity—resistance to the last. Better that confusion should ensue—better that discord should reign in the national councils—*better that Congress should break up in wild disorder—nay, better that the Capitol itself should blaze by the torch of the incendiary*, or fall and bury all its inmates beneath its crumbling ruins, than that this perfidy and wrong should be finally accomplished."

This is the language of the New York Tribune in reference to the Kansas bill a few days before it passed. Yes, sir, even then that editor declared that it was better that this Capitol should be burnt by the torch of an incendiary—better that the Government should go into dissolution, than that the people colonizing and settling Kansas and Nebraska should be just as free as the people of New York, or, as he states it, than that this act of perfidy and wrong should be finally accomplished. What wrong did the act contain? Wrong to whom? to whom was there anything in it either wrong or unjust? Was it wrong to the people of the South, one large section of the Union, to permit them to enjoy an equal and fair participation of the public domain purchased by the common blood and common treasure of all? Was it wrong or unjust to permit the people of New York, Massachusetts, and other States of the North going into a new Territory, to be as free there as they were in their native homes? Was it wrong or unjust to allow all from all the States, who might be disposed to quit the old States, and seek to better their fortunes by cutting down the forests of the West, turning up its virgin soil, and making the wilderness to blossom as the rose, to enjoy the same rights which their fathers did in the early formation of all our present State constitutions and governments? Whom, I say, did the bill wrong? To whom did it deal any injustice? Was it the slave, the African, whom his southern master might take there? How could it be unjust even to him? Is not his condition as much bettered by new lands and virgin soils as that of his master? Is not expansion of that portion of southern population quite as necessary for their comfort and well-being as it is for the whites? Would you keep them hemmed in in their present limits, until subsistence shall fail, and starvation shall effect the objects of a misguided humanity?

Without stopping here to say a word upon the subject of southern society, and the relation which the negro there sustains to the white man, either as to the necessity of that relation, or its wisdom or propriety, does it work any wrong or injury to the slave to take him from old lands to new lands? Is not his condition bettered by the change? And have we not new lands enough for all? Your Topeka convention, which formed the pretended free-State constitution now before us, proposed to exclude the negro and mulatto forever from that country. Upon the score of humanity, then, even towards the "poor negro" about whom so much sympathy is attempted to be excited, I ask, which does him the greater wrong, the Kansas bill, or the project of your free-State constitution? Who, to him, is the Good Samaritan in this case? The Free-Soil Levite, who would leave him to starve without land to work? or his humane southern master, who is willing to provide both land and shelter, food and raiment? Where, then, is the wrong of this bill? It consists in nothing but permitting the freemen of our own race to settle this question of the *status* of the African amongst themselves, as they in their wisdom and patriotism may think best for the happiness of both races, just as the freemen of our own race did in each of the old thirteen States of the Union.

But, sir, the House did not heed this lecture of the editor. The bill passed this body; it passed the Senate; it received the constitutional approval of the Executive, and became the law of the land. The revolutionary spirit, however, which invoked the burning of the Capitol, did not stop with defeat in all three of the departments of legislation. Members of Congress with others, beaten in the House of Representatives, beaten in the Senate, failing in their threats and denunciations of the Executive, betook themselves forthwith to plotting schemes to defeat the will of the people as constitutionally expressed. Societies were formed, one of them by members of this House, immediately after the bill passed; money was raised; circulars were issued,—all with the avowed purpose of sending people to Kansas to prevent the peaceful and quiet operation of the wise and beneficent principles of the territorial law—movements having a direct tendency to kindle this civil war of which we now hear.

The Capitol fortunately was not burnt—that suggestion did not take. Disorder did not reign here—that suggestion did not take. But bodies of men were organized—not allowing the legitimate laws of nature, of climate, and of soil to determine the character of the pioneer population from all the States alike who might choose to make settlement there. Men were sent out in large companies, with arms and munitions of war; Sharpe's rifles were sent; artillery was sent. What for? Did these colonists go to Kansas as our forefathers sought homes at Plymouth, St. Mary's, Jamestown, and Savannah? Or did they not rather go as the train-bands of Cortes and Pizzaro went forth thirsting for the conquest of the Montezumas and the Incas? Was not their sole object to effect by force and violence what they had failed to do by legislation? What other meaning can be put upon the following manifesto which was published in the "Herald of Freedom," their organ at Lawrence, the head-quarters of these emigrants in the Territory:

> "Come one, come all, slaveocrats and nullifiers; we have rifles enough, and bullets enough, to send you all to your (and Judas's) 'own place.' 'If you're coming, why don't you come along?'"

Was not this a direct invitation to arms? And whatever troubles or disturbances exist in Kansas, let them not be charged to the Kansas bill, but to those who have sworn in their wrath that that bill never shall work out its natural and legitimate results, if they can prevent it. As well might the wars about points of doctrine and religious creeds which have disgraced Christendom, be charged upon the heavenly principles of the gospel. Christ himself said that it was impossible but that offenses in this world of wickedness would come. When bad men are at work, they cannot be prevented. The principles of that bill are in no way responsible for any outrages or trampling upon rights by parties on the other side of the controversy, got up and provoked in that Territory by designing men outside, for mischievous purposes. A[illegible]riends of that bill—those who stand ple[illegible]ts principles—condemn outrages [illegible] ei[illegible]th sides alike.

But a word, [illegible], as [illegible]ature and extent of these difficulties. Ar[illegible]y not greatly exaggerated and magnified? Let us look at the facts. Some men, it is true, have been killed—some on both sides. And what else could have been expected? What other result could have been looked for by those instigating the movements I have alluded to? The first man killed in the Territory was Davis. He fell by the hands of those calling themselves free-State men. Then Dow, a free-State man, was killed by Coleman; but the quarrel between them arose about a land claim. It was a private and personal matter. Coleman immediately gave himself up to the legal authorities, claiming to have acted in self-defense. Whether he did or not, I do not know, and will not pretend to say; but a friend of Dow, of the name of Branson, having made threats of avenging his death, was arrested under a peace warrant, and, while in the hands of an officer, was rescued by a party of free-State men. Warrants were taken out for these, and they took shelter in Lawrence, where they put themselves in defiance of the civil authorities. The posse was called out to aid in the arrest, and this led first to the seige of Lawrence, and then to the capitulation of December last. In this war, no lives were lost. Two or three other homicides had been committed in the Territory; but in all, from the organization of the Territory, up to the attempted assassination of Sheriff Jones, I think not exceeding half a dozen! In what part of the United States, sir, in the same length of time, with the same population they have in Kansas, have there been fewer murders or deaths by violence? How many were killed in the riots last year in Cincinnati? How many in Louisville, Kentucky?

I venture to say to-day, that with all this clamor about civil war in Kansas, more lives have not been lost there, since the organization of the Territory, than have been in several of the large city elections of the United States within the last twelve months. It is not my wish to make light of these things, but to take a calm and dispassionate view of them. A strong and general tendency to disregard law and order is one of the most lamentable evils of the day. It is not confined to Kansas, but it is seen and felt everywhere. And our object, and that of all good men, should be to check it rather than excite it.

Then, sir, as to the election in Kansas and the laws passed by their Legislature. One word upon this point. The first election was held there for a Delegate to Congress in November, 1854. That there were illegal votes on both sides I have no doubt; but I believe it is admitted by every one that, notwithstanding the efforts of the emigrant aid companies to prevent it, General Whitfield had much the larger number of the legal votes of the Territory, and was duly elected. In March afterwards greater efforts were made to carry the Legislature. The result was the commission or certificate of election by Governor Reeder himself to a large majority [illegible] both branches of that body. They were theref[illegible]lly constituted as a [illegible]gislative body. T[illegible]y have been illegal voting on both sides[illegible]s [illegible]btless in all our elections. But up[illegible]well [illegible]ettled and fixed principles on which [illegible]our representative institutions rest, and without a maintenance of which there can be neither "law nor order," that is now a closed question. The laws, therefore, of that Legislature must be observed and obeyed until repealed or modified by legislative power, or set aside by the courts as void. And upon the character of these laws I wish to make but a passing remark. The gentleman from Indiana [Mr. Colfax] pointed out quite a number of them the other day, which he said were very bad ones. Well, sir, I am not going to discuss their respective merits. Perhaps some of them are bad; it would be an extraordinary code if it were otherwise. I know the advocates of the present government in the Territory—the law-and-order party there—do not themselves approve of all of them. I will read what they say on the subject:

> "The law for the protection of slave property has also been much misunderstood. The right to pass such a law is expressly stated by Governor Reeder in his inaugural message, in which he says: 'A Territorial Legislature may undoubtedly act upon the question to a limited and partial extent, and may temporarily prohibit, tolerate, or regulate slavery in the Territory, and in an absolute or modified form, with all the force and effect of any other legislative act, binding until repealed by the same power that enacted it.' There is nothing in the act itself, as has been charged, to prevent a free discussion of the subject of slavery. Its bearing on society, its morality or expediency, or whether it would be politic or impolitic to make this a slave State, can be discussed here as freely as in any State in this Union, without infringing any of the provisions of the law. To deny the right of a person to hold slaves under the law in this Territory is made penal; but, beyond this, there is no restriction to the discussion of the slavery question in any aspect in which it is capable of being considered. We do not wish to be understood as approving of all the laws passed by the Legislature; on the contrary, we would state that there are some that we do not approve of, and which are condemned by public opinion here, and which will no doubt be repealed or modified at the meeting of the next Legislature. But this is nothing more than what frequently occurs, both in the legislation of Congress and of the various State Legislatures. The remedy for such evils is to be found in public opinion, to which, sooner or later, in a Government like ours, all laws must conform."

Mr. COLFAX. What is the date of that?

Mr. STEPHENS. Last November. Now, sir, I have examined this whole code of laws, and as a whole, some few exceptions out, I say that no State in the Union has got better ones. There are some in it I do not approve—there are some in all the codes I have ever seen that I do not approve. I will not go to the gentleman's State, or to any other gentleman's State, to find laws that I do not approve. We have plenty of them in my own State. And the gentleman ought to feel highly blessed if he has none in Indiana that he disapproves. We have a great many in Georgia I do not approve. There is one in particular which I fought in the Legislature and opposed before the courts with all the power that I had. It was a law making it penal to bear concealed deadly weapons. I am individually opposed to bearing such weapons. I never bear weapons of any sort; but I believed that it was the constitutional right of every American citizen to bear arms if he chooses, and just such arms, and in just such way, as he chooses. I thought that it was the birthright of every Georgian to do it. I was defeated in our Legislature. I was defeated before our courts. The question went up to the highest judicial tribunal in our State, the Supreme Court, which sustained the law. In that decision all had to acquiesce. Sir, the people in all the States have to obey the laws as pronounced and expounded by the courts. The difference between a republic and a monarchy is, that the one is a government of laws, subject to be changed by the people; the other is a government dependent upon the caprice or whim, and arbitrary will of one man. And when the people of a Republic array themselves against their laws, the first step is into anarchy, and then comes monarchy. The speech of the gentleman from Indiana is sufficiently answered by the address of his own party adopted at Pittsburg, though those who issued it seemed not to be conscious of the effect of the admission. That address, after specifying the same objectionable laws in the Kansas code which he has, says:

"That these despotic acts, even if they had been passed by a Legislature duly elected by the people of the Territory, would have been null and void, inasmuch as they are plainly in violation of the Federal Constitution, is too clear for argument. Congress itself is expressly forbidden by the Constitution of the United States to make any laws abridging the freedom of speech and of the press; and it is absurd to suppose that a Territorial Legislature, deriving all its power from Congress, should not be subject to the same restrictions."

The latter is a very clear proposition, to my mind. Neither Congress nor a Territorial Legislature can pass any law abridging the freedom of speech or of the press. This is, indeed, too clear for argument. I indorse that part of the Pittsburg platform. But not a single disturbance in the Territory has grown out of either of these laws complained of as despotic. But if there had—if these laws be so clearly unconstitutional and so manifestly violative of the freedom of speech and of the press, why should not any party aggrieved refer the question to the judicial tribunals? If the case is so clear, why not go to the courts? There are Federal courts in the Territory; and an appeal can be taken to the same high tribunal that all of us in such matters have to appeal to in the last resort—the Supreme Court of the United States.

Mr. CAMPBELL, of Ohio, (interrupting.) I rise to propound a question, if it is entirely agreeable to the gentleman from Georgia, and not otherwise.

Mr. STEPHENS. Perfectly agreeable; but I hope the gentleman will not take much of my time.

Mr. CAMPBELL. I was similarly responded to on a former occasion, and I shall take warning, and occupy but a moment of the gentleman s time. Why did not you, and those who sought to disturb the time-honored compromise of our fathers of 1820, if they regarded the eighth section of the Missouri act as unconstitutional, resort to the courts to test its constitutionality?

Mr. STEPHENS. There is a case of that sort now before the Supreme Court.

Mr. CAMPBELL. Why, instead of bringing all this trouble on the country, did he not then resort to the courts?

Mr. STEPHENS. Why, Mr. Speaker, it was first my duty as a legislator, believing it to be wrong, to vote to repeal it, and I did so, [laughter;] and if the Congress of the United States had not repealed it, and I had been personally affected by it in the Territory, then I might have resorted to the courts.

Mr. CAMPBELL. Did not the gentleman vote to repeal it because of its unconstitutionality?

Mr. STEPHENS. Standing as it did, I did, for that and other reasons. As long as it stood as a regulation founded on the principle of a division of the Territory, I was willing to abide by it; but when it was abandoned and repudiated as such, it was, in my judgment, an odious and unjust restriction. But I do not wish the gentleman to divert me from the line of argument I was pursuing.

Mr. CAMPBELL. If the gentleman voted to repeal it in 1854 because it was unconstitutional, why did he vote to fasten it upon Texas in 1846, unless, in the meanwhile, there was a change in the Constitution?

Mr. STEPHENS. For the very reason that I have just stated. In 1845, on the annexation of Texas, I voted for it, upon the principle of a division of the Territory. Congress has a right to pass all needful laws and regulations for the Territory, as *property;* so said Mr. Madison; this includes the power to divide, if necessary or needful for public peace and harmony. When I voted for it, it was upon that principle. And, sir, it was in 1850, after the gentleman's party had repeatedly—in 1846, 1847, 1848, 1849, and 1850—denied, repudiated, and scouted at what they now call the time-honored compromise of our fathers of 1820, that I voted for the reëstablishment of the old principle in our territorial policy—of leaving the public domain open for the free and equal settlement and colonization of the people from all the States alike, without congressional limitations or restrictions upon any. This principle was reëstablished in 1850—after the one proposed in 1820 had been abandoned—and this principle I voted to carry out in 1854, in the Territories of Kansas and Nebraska.

Mr. CAMPBELL. Will the gentleman explain to the House and to the country, how it is that a measure may be constitutional which excludes slavery on one side of a given line, in a Territory belonging to the people of the States in common, and unconstitutional on the other?

Mr. STEPHENS. My explanation of the point the gentleman makes is this: Upon the principle of a division of the Territory as public property between the two sections, it might be constitutional to set aside a portion to one by fixed lines and boundaries, while the appropriation of the whole of it to that section would be manifestly wrong, unjust, and therefore unconstitutional. Just as in the case of the division of the surplus revenue—public property—among the States—the part assigned to each, on division fairly and justly made, was constitutionally held; but if some States had taken all to the exclusion of the rest, that would have been manifestl[illegible]ust, and therefore unconstitutional. But [illegible]ven my views at large upon this subjec[illegible]re this session.

Mr. CAMPBELL. [illegible]en——

Mr. STEPHENS. I [illegible] wish the gentleman to divert me from my argument by a continuation of questions upon other subjects.

Mr. CAMPBELL. I hope I may be fortunate

enough to get the floor at the expiration of the gentleman's hour, and therefore will not press my inquiries now on this interesting point.

Mr. STEPHENS. Now, sir, just here I wish to say a word more about "that time-honored compact of our fathers," which it is said has been violated. Mr. Speaker, I say that the fathers who made this Republic, from the beginning of it—from the date of the Constitution and up to 1820, never in a single instance exercised the power of excluding the migration of slaves from any of the States of this Union to the common territory. The gentleman now claims to follow the fathers of the Republic. Well, I suppose General Washington, Mr. Madison, and Mr. Jefferson, are as eminently entitled as any others to occupy that position. Mr. Jefferson especially is often quoted by those holding seats on this side of the House. Mr. Jefferson, it is said, was against slavery. I grant that. But how? Mr. Jefferson was in favor of every State retaining and exercising jurisdiction over the subject for itself. Mr. Jefferson was himself opposed to the passage of that restriction in 1820, now called a time-honored compact. I do not care as to what his abstract opinions were. I believe he was for providing for the gradual abolition of slavery in Virginia. But his plan was for the people of Virginia to do it for themselves, without any interference from abroad or influence from this Government—I mean after the present Constitution was formed and adopted. I have Mr. Jefferson's sentiments here before me on this particular Missouri restriction, when it was passed. It is immaterial what his opinions of slavery were—what did he think of that measure? The author of the Declaration of Independence is often appealed to as authority by the gentleman's party. Sir, if the departed Jefferson could return from the realms above—if the seals of the tomb at Monticello could be broken, and that spirit could be permitted to revisit the earth, believe you that he would speak a different sentiment to-day from that he uttered then?

Here is the letter which Mr. Jefferson wrote. It is too long to read the whole; but in this letter to Mr. Holmes, of Maine, dated the 29th April, 1820, after strongly condemning the establishment of a geographical line, and the attempt to restrain the "diffusion of slavery over a greater surface," he says:

"An abstinence, too, from this act of power would remove the jealousy excited by the undertaking of Congress to regulate the condition of the different descriptions of men composing a State. This, certainly, is the *exclusive right* of every State, which *nothing in the Constitution* has taken from them and given to the General Government. Could Congress, for example, say that the now freemen of Connecticut should be freemen, and that they shall not emigrate into any other State?"

This is plain and explicit, and on the very question.

Again, in a lett[illegible]Mr. Madison on the sa[illegible]e subject, he says[illegible]

"I am indebted t[illegible]your two letters of February 7 and 19. This Misso[illegible]stion, by a geographical line of division, is the most p[illegible]ntous one I have ever contemplated." * * * "Is ready to risk the Union for any chance of restoring his party to power, and wriggling himself to the head of it."

The allusion here is evidently to Rufus King, who was the first mover of the restriction. Such, sir, were the sentiments of him who was not only the author of the Declaration of Independence, but the author of the ordinance of 1787, under the old Confederation. This is what he said of the restriction of 1820, under our present Constitution.

Here is also Mr. Madison's emphatic opinion against the same measure. I cannot take up my time in reading it. I state the fact, and challenge contradiction. Jefferson was against the restriction of 1820. Madison was against it, and Jackson was against it. No man can deny these facts. It was reluctantly accepted by the South, however, as an alternative, and only as an alternative, for the sake of peace and harmony. And who are those now who call it a sacred compact? Those very men, the gentleman and his party, who denounced every man from the North as "*a dough-face*," who from 1846 to 1850 were in favor of abiding by it for the sake of union and harmony. Not a man can be named from the North who was willing to abide by that line of division during the period I have stated who was not denounced by the gentleman and his party as "a dough-face." Who now are the "dough-faces?" And if the gentleman wishes to know what tree brought forth that better fruit of which he spoke the other day, I will tell him. It was not the Kansas tree, but that old political upas planted by Rufus King in 1820. It grew up; it flourished, and it sent its poisonous exhalations throughout this country till it came well nigh extinguishing the life of the Republic in 1850.

Mr. CAMPBELL. That tree was planted when—[Cries of "Order!" "Order!"]—when slavery was first brought to the shores of America. [Cries of "Order!" "Order!"]

Mr. STEPHENS. Well, then, Mr. Speaker, it is much older than the Kansas bill. It was planted before the Government was formed. The Constitution itself was grafted upon its stock. The condition or slavery of the African race, as it exists amongst us, is a "fixed fact" in the Constitution. From this a tree has indeed sprung—bearing, however, no troubles or bitter fruits. It is the tree of national liberty, which, by the culture of statesmen and patriots, has grown up and flourished, and is now sending its branches far and wide, ladened with no fruit but national happiness, prosperity, glory, and renown.

Mr. CAMPBELL. Will the gentleman from Georgia read the preamble to the Constitution?

Mr. STEPHENS. Yes; and I believe I can repeat it to him. It is "in order to form a more perfect union, establish justice, *insure domestic tranquillity*."

Mr. CAMPBELL. "And secure the blessings of liberty to ourselves and our posterity."

Mr. STEPHENS. Yes, sir, to themselves and *their posterity*—not to the negroes and Africans—and what sort of liberty? Constitutional liberty; that liberty which recognized the inferior condition of the African race amongst them; the liberty which we now enjoy; the liberty which all the States enjoyed at that time, save one, (for all were then slaveholding, except Massachusetts.) That is the sort of liberty. None of your Socialism liberty. None of your Fourierism liberty. Constitutional liberty—"law and order" abiding liberty. That is the liberty which they meant to perpetuate.

Now, Mr. Speaker, to return from this digression—I was on the subject of the Kansas laws—I had a good deal to say on that point I must now omit; for I have a good deal I wish also to say on the measure immediately before us, and the amendment which I have submitted, and my time is rapidly passing away. I shall proceed, then, to the bill and the amendment.

The bill under consideration proposes to admit Kansas as a State at once under the Topeka constitution. I am opposed to it; because that constitution was formed without any authority of law, either from the territorial authorities or from Congress. It was formed in open opposition to law; it was formed by men in open rebellion, with arms in their hands, against the only legally-constituted government in the Territory. The leaders most conspicuous in getting it up are now under arrest for treason. Whether they are guilty or not, I will not even express an opinion. That is a question for the courts—the Federal courts—not the courts created by the Territorial Legislature, but the United States courts, with an appeal to the Supreme Court of the United States—to determine. I do not wish in any way to interfere with that judicial question. Let these gentlemen stand or fall according to their guilt or innocence, as it may be made to appear before the proper tribunals, at the proper time. Let us not, in the mean time, prejudge the case either for or against them. The man who claims to be Governor under this Topeka constitution is now in custody awaiting his trial for the highest offense known to the laws and Constitution of the United States.

I am opposed to this bill, because we have no evidence that a majority, or anything like a majority, of the people of Kansas are in favor of this pretended Topeka constitution. It is an *ex parte* proceeding from beginning to end. It was got up by a party. It was contrived by Governor Reeder; and though he and his associates now place the whole grounds of their justification upon the plea that the Territorial Legislature was composed of usurpers—that the election was carried by an invasion of non-residents, who passed laws that they cannot submit to, yet it must be recollected by all fair-minded men that this Legislature, however elected, was organized under the auspices of Governor Reeder himself. He was the judge of the election returns of its members in the first instance, and he duly commissioned a large majority of both branches of it, and gave his own official certificate that they were duly elected. If what is now asserted by him and others be true, why did he not at the proper time arrest it? Why now lay a complaint at the door of the President for not preventing an invasion of Kansas, or setting aside the legislative election, while he, as Governor, made no complaint to the President? He was the sentinel placed upon the watch-tower in Kansas. The only cry heard from him by the President or the country, during this now-pretended invasion, and for several long months afterwards, was, "All's well!" He recognized this Legislature after it was organized, and after he knew full well how it was elected. I must therefore receive with many grains of allowance what he now asserts, all tending towards nothing more strongly than the impeachment of his own official integrity. His position is not such as to warrant me, as a fair man, now to back him in his present revolutionary movement. I see no sufficient grievance even alleged to justify me in doing it.

Grant that some of the laws passed by the Legislature that Reeder certified to as having been duly elected were bad laws—not a single case of oppression, growing out of any one of these laws, has arisen. I was on this point when interrupted by the gentleman from Ohio, [Mr. CAMPBELL.] How does it appear but that the courts would pronounce these laws unconstitutional, as some on this floor maintain that they are? Why resort to revolution until the courts fail? Nay, more: if a majority of the people of Kansas are opposed to these laws, as is so boldly asserted on this floor, why can they not have them repealed by the next Legislature, soon to be elected, even if the courts should sustain them? The next Legislature is to be chosen in October. Why not settle that question at the ballot-box? Is not that a fair and just way of settling such questions? Is it not the way we have to do in all our States? Are those who press this *ex parte* constitution upon us afraid of the ballot-box? Whatever else may be said of the acts of the Kansas Legislature, they certainly secured the purity of the fountain of political power. Here is a part of their election law:

"SEC. 24. If any person, by menaces, threats, and force, or by any other unlawful means, either directly or indirectly, attempt to influence any qualified voter in giving his vote, or to deter him from giving the same, or disturb or hinder him in the free exercise of his right of suffrage, at any election held under the laws of this Territory, the person so offending shall, on conviction thereof, be adjudged guilty of a misdemeanor, and be punished by fine not exceeding five hundred dollars, or by imprisonment in the county jail not exceeding one year.

"SEC. 25. Every person who shall, at the same election, vote more than once, either at the same or a different place, shall, on conviction, be adjudged guilty of a misdemeanor, and be punished by fine not exceeding fifty dollars, or by imprisonment in the county jail not exceeding three months.

"SEC. 26. Every person not being a qualified voter according to the organic law and the laws of this Territory, who shall vote at any election within this Territory, knowing that he is not entitled to vote, shall be adjudged guilty of a misdemeanor, and punished by fine not exceeding fifty dollars.

"SEC. 27. Any person who designedly gives a printed or written ticket to any qualified voter of this Territory, containing the written or printed names of persons for whom said voter does not design to vote, for the purpose of causing such voter to poll his vote contrary to his own wishes, shall, on conviction, be adjudged guilty of a misdemeanor, and punished by fine not exceeding five hundred dollars, or by imprisonment in the county jail not exceeding three months, or by both such fine and imprisonment.

"SEC. 28. Any person who shall cause to be printed and circulated, or who shall circulate, any false and fraudulent tickets, which upon their face appear to be designed as a fraud upon voters, shall, upon conviction, be punished by fine not exceeding five hundred dollars, or by imprisonment in the county jail, not exceeding three months, or by both such fine and imprisonment.

"This act to take effect and be in force from and after its passage."—Chap. 52, p. 281.

Does any free man want a better security for his sovereign right of suffrage than is here given? Does this look like the work of "border ruffians" who were looking to carry elections by fraud or violence? But it is said that in the same law it is provided that no man shall be entitled to vote who has been guilty of a violation of the fugitive slave law passed by Congress! Well, sir, is this an onerous restriction? Ought men who set themselves up in open violation of the laws of our country to complain of being deprived of the right of having a voice in making laws? Are not certain offenses in all our States grounds of denying suffrage? But the great question is, cannot this provision of the election law be repealed by the next Legislature if a majority of the honest people there are against it? The case then presented by the Governor and his associates in the Topeka movement is not such as to justify, in my judgment, this revolution which they have set on foot, and now ask Congress to approve and sanction. Besides this, Mr. Speaker, the evidence is very strong to my mind, if not conclusive, that this Topeka constitution does not meet the approval of a majority of the people of Kansas. When it was submitted to popular vote, only about seventeen hundred in the whole Territory approved it. Now, sir, I am for no such judgment either way—I am for fair dealing in this matter on both sides.

I wish for nothing but a fair expression of the will of the *bona fide* residents of Kansas upon this subject. When I voted for the Kansas bill, I did so, not for the purpose of making it a slave State, unless a majority of the white freemen there desired it; and if they did desire it, I was for permitting them to exercise the same power over the subject that the freemen of the other States of the Union exercise over the same subjects within their respective limits. I never regarded the success of that measure as a triumph of the South over the North, further than it was a triumph of this great constitutional principle of equality over that sectionalism of a party at the North, which denied it. Whether Kansas or Nebraska would be slave States or free States, I did not know. I left that to time, climate, soil, and the people, to settle. And now, sir, though upon general principles I am opposed to the admission of any State into the Union without population sufficient to entitle them to a member on this floor, according to the ratio of representation, yet, in the present case, if gentlemen are so anxious to press the admission of Kansas, I am willing to forego the usual inquiry into the exact amount of population there. I will waive that point. I do not know the number of people there. Gentlemen on the other side vary in their estimates from sixty thousand to ninety thousand. I think it would be best first to ascertain the facts. Still I will, I say, waive that point; and if gentlemen are so anxious for the admission of the people of that Territory, whatever may be their numbers, as a State, I meet them, and offer the substitute to this bill which I have submitted. Mine is an alternative proposition. If Kansas is to be admitted, let it be done in a fair, just, and proper way, and not at the instance of an irregular, illegal, and revolutionary convention of only a portion, and a very small portion at that, of the people of the Territory. The plan I submit is the same offered by my colleague [Mr. Toombs] in the Senate. I suppose gentlemen have read it. I cannot now read it. Its main features are to provide for the admission of Kansas, under such constitution as her people may form, at as early a day as is practicable.

It provides, first, for the taking of a census. This is to be done by five commissioners, to be appointed by the President, and ratified by the Senate.

It provides, secondly, for an election to be held in the Territory on the first Tuesday after the first Monday in November next, (the day of the Presidential election in the States,) for delegates to a convention to form a State constitution.

Representation in this convention is to be according to the number of voters in the several counties and districts, as shall appear from the census, which is, amongst other things, to exhibit the names of all the actual residents of the Territory at the date of the passage of the bill.

These commissioners are to appoint the officers to conduct the election. Returns are to be made to them, and they are to judge and determine all questions relating to the election, and to give certificates of the same.

Three months' residence in the county is required to entitle any one to vote.

And to guard the purity and sanctity of the ballot-box, so that the untrammeled voice of the people may be heard, let it be as it may, these stringent provisions are inserted:

Sec. 10. *And be it further enacted*, That every white male citizen of the United States, (including Indians of like description qualified by existing laws to vote,) over twenty-one years old, who may be a *bona fide* inhabitant of said Territory at the pasage of this act, and who shall have resided three months next before said election in the county in which he offers to vote, and no other persons whatever, shall be entitled to vote at said election; and all persons qualified as voters may be elected delegates to said convention, and no others.

Sec. 11. *And be it further enacted*, That, if any person, by menaces, threats, or force, or by any other unlawful means, shall directly or indirectly attempt to influence any qualified voter in giving his vote, or deter him from giving the same, or disturb or hinder him in the free exercise of his right of suffrage, at the election provided for by this act, the person so offending shall be adjudged guilty of a misdemeanor, and be punished by fine not exceeding five hundred dollars, or by imprisonment not exceeding one year, or by both, at the discretion of the court.

Sec. 12. *And be it further enacted*, That any person not being a qualified voter, according to the provisions of this act, who shall vote at the election herein provided for, knowing that he is not entitled to vote, and any person who shall, at the same election, vote more than once, whether at the same or at different places, shall be adjudged guilty of a misdemeanor, and punished by fine not exceeding two hundred and fifty dollars, or by imprisonment not exceeding six months, or both, at the discretion of the court.

Sec. 13. *And be it further enacted*, That any person whatsoever who may be charged with the holding of the election herein authorized to be held, who shall willfully and knowingly commit any fraud or irregularity whatever, with the intent to hinder or prevent, or defeat a fair expression of the popular will in said election, shall be guilty of a misdemeanor, and punished by fine not exceeding one thousand dollars, and imprisonment not exceeding two years, or both, at the discretion of the court.

But, sir, my time will not allow me to go more into details. The object of the bill, from the beginning to the end, is to provide for as fair an expression of the popular will of the Territory as human ingenuity can devise. By the expression of that will, when thus made, I shall abide, let it be which way it may. For your bill as it stands, I can never vote. Against the substitute I offer, who can raise any objection that is in favor of disposing of this question upon principles of fairness, of justice, of law, of order, and of the Constitution? I present the distinct issue between these two measures to the House and the country.

I am constrained, Mr. Speaker, to believe that all this clamor we hear about "free Kansas," and "down-trodden Kansas," and "bleeding Kansas," arises much more from a desire and hope of exciting by it sectional hate and the alienation of one portion of the Union from the other, than from any wish to have even "free Kansas" admitted into the Union, or from any conviction that a majority of the people there are in favor of this Topeka constitution. The object, I am constrained to believe, is not so much to get another State added to the Union, as it is to use the question to produce a severance of those States now united. Why these violent denunciations against one whole section of the Confederacy? Why is such unbridled vituperation indulged in towards southern men and southern institutions? Why these shouts of joy in New York on the announcement that "civil war" was raging in Kansas? What other construction can be put upon the movement of a late sectional convention held in Philadelphia to nominate party candidates for President and Vice President? What is the meaning of all these appeals to the passions and prejudices of the people of the northern States, exciting them to rise up against their southern brethren? Is it not part and parcel of that same spirit which proclaimed that it were better that the Capitol should blaze by the torch of an incendiary, and wild disorder ensue, than that the free people of Kansas and Nebraska should regulate their own domestic institutions in their own way? That is all that the advocates of the Kansas bill asked; that is all it was designed to effect; and that is all I this day ask this House to join me in carrying out in good faith to the letter and spirit.

To show the House and the country some of the grounds for my belief touching the ulterior objects of some of those who are joining in this "Kansas cry" at the North, I ask attention to an editorial of the New York Courier and Enquirer of the 26th instant. In this, that editor says:

"We are in the midst of a revolution, the origin of which is *sectional*, and its avowed object to gratify the grasping ambition of the slave power; and a civil war waged in behalf of freedom and in resistance of slavery extension is a fitting accompaniment of an attempt on the part of the South and their co-laborers of the North, to trample on the principles and guarantees of the Constitution, by the extension of slavery into free territory through the direct legislation of the General Government."

Here it is announced that we are in the "midst of a revolution, the origin of which is *sectional*." But most strange to say, the cause of it is charged upon the South; and stranger still, that cause is asserted to be an attempt on the part of the South to "trample on the principles and guarantees of the Constitution, by the *extension of slavery into free territory through the direct legislation of the General Government*." Was ever accusation more groundless and utterly unfounded, than this against the South? The South never asked Congress, by legislation, to extend slavery; nor has it ever been done by any such legislation. All that the South ever asked, or now asks, is, to leave the question to be settled by those who are to be affected by it.

General James Watson Webb, the editor of this paper, (the Courier and Enquirer,) was a delegate to the late Philadelphia convention, the object of which was to embody this sectional movement of the North against the South. In that convention he made a speech. From that speech, as reported in the New York Times, we are not left to inference as to what is the design and intention of the leading spirits controlling it. In speaking of the people the convention represented, he says:

"They ask us to give them a nomination which, when put fairly before the people, will unite public sentiment, and, through the ballot-box, will restrain and repel this pro-slavery extension, and this aggression of the slaveocracy. What else are they doing? They tell you that they are willing to abide by the ballot-box, and willing to make that the last appeal. *If we fail there, what then? We will drive it back, sword in hand, and so help me God! believing that to be right, I am with them.* [Loud cheers, and cries of 'Good!']"

This was in no common town or city meeting. But it was in that great northern sectional convention lately assembled at Philadelphia, that these sentiments received such bursts of applause. There is, I say, no mistaking the object of the leaders of this movement. They evidently intend to use this Kansas question to make as much political capital out of it as they can to aid them in carrying the election, by which means they hope to get power to "crush out" the South, as they suppose; but, if they fail in the election, then they are, sword in hand, to join the revolutionists in Kansas.

In the first editorial I read from, in this mammoth sheet, (the Courier and Enquirer,) issued the 26th instant, and written, doubtless, by General Webb himself, who seems to be the Magnus Apollo of the Black Republican hosts, are these significant, as well as studied, words:

"The remedy is, to go to the polls, and through the ballot-box repudiate the infamous platform put forth at Cincinnati, and over which the black flag of *slavery* waves with characteristic impudence; *and failing in this*, do as our fathers did before us—stand by our inalienable rights, and *drive back with arms* those who dare to trample upon our inheritance. There is no boasting and no threat in this. It is the calm language of honest, conscientious, and determined freemen, wafted to us by every breeze from the West; and they are already acting in strict conformity with their avowed determination."

Now, sir, I care as little for these belligerent manifestoes of this redoubtable general of the Courier and Enquirer, as I did two years ago for the "*blazing*" and "*incendiary*" bulletins of his cotemporary of the Tribune. I refer to them only to show the purposes at work; and I put the question directly to this House: Are you going to allow this subject to be used for any such purposes? If you want Kansas admitted as a

State, do I not offer you a fair, liberal, and just proposition for accomplishing that object? Do you wish to go before the country with the question, to inflame the public mind at the North, to move their passions, to stir up their blood, and prepare their hearts for a war of extermination against their southern brethren?—"*to drive them back, sword in hand, in case you fail in the election?*" If so, then be it so. But be it known to you, that you will have to take the question with the issue this day joined. Between you and me—between these two propositions, I am willing that the people North, as well as the South, may judge. Nothing would afford me more pleasure than to argue the question with you before any intelligent constituency in the Republic.

Patriotism, as I have heretofore found it, is the same everywhere. Nor has it in days past been confined to any locality in this broad land. It is, I believe, indigenous wherever the national flag floats. In the forests and ship-yards and market towns of Maine it is to be found; in the factories, workshops, and commercial houses of the old Bay State it is to be found. In State street and Faneuil Hall its voice has often been heard. So on the White Mountains of New Hampshire and the Green Mountains of Vermont; on the hills and valleys of Connecticut, Rhode Island, New York, Pennsylvania, and New Jersey. It is a plant that heretofore has grown with as much vigor on the most sterile soil of the East as it has upon the fairest plains of the South or the richest prairies of the West. I cannot believe that a change of political climate has rendered it an exotic in any part of this country yet. Upon nothing, however, should I rely in presenting this issue everywhere, but upon the reason, justice, intelligence, virtue, integrity, and patriotism of the people; upon these all our republican institutions must rest; when they fail, all that we hold dear must go with them. And if the North shall decide to follow General Webb, let the responsibility rest upon him and them.

I cannot believe that the great body of honest business people of the North are prepared to join a set of reckless leaders in this crusade against the South, or will lend their *influence* and aid in kindling a civil war in Kansas which may extend until it involves the whole country. This I cannot believe, and will not believe for the present at least. It is for them to determine whether they will or not. That question they will have to meet, not only on this issue, if the majority of this House so determine, but upon that other, and at this time more absorbing, issue of the Cincinnati platform. That platform bears no black flag, as this "sword-in-hand" general asserts. Black flags belong to those who think more of black men than they do of the white man, and who exhibit more sympathy for the well-provided African race than they do for the suffering and oppressed poor of their own. The flag of the Cincinnati platform on this subject bears no principles ascribed upon its broad folds but those of the Constitution. The friends of the Union under the Constitution must and will approve them everywhere; while none but the enemies of one or the other of these, or both, can denounce them. Upon this great sectional question all national men, I care not of what party—all true hearted patriots, who look from the bright history of the past with hopes to a brighter future before us, must and will give those principles, announced at Cincinnati, their sanction and approval. The issue on this subject presented at Cincinnati is *nationalism* against *sectionalism*—the issue presented at Philadelphia is *sectionalism* against *nationalism.*

Are we, Mr. Speaker, to remain a united people? Are we to go on in that high career of achievement in science, in art, and in civilization, which we have so conspicuously entered upon? Or are we to be arrested in our upward course long before reaching the half-way point towards ultimate culmination? Are our deeds of glory all numbered? Are the memories of the past to be forgotten, and the benefits and blessings of the present to be derided and rejected? Is the radiant orb of day brightening the morning of our existence to be darkened and obscured, and with it the light of the world extinguished forever? And all this because Congress, in its wisdom, has thought proper to permit the free white men of Kansas to determine for themselves whether the negro in that Territory shall be the same nondescript outcast, neither citizen nor slave, amongst them, that he is in sixteen States of the Union, or whether he shall occupy the same condition there in relation to them which a Christian philanthropy has assigned him in the other fifteen States. I say Christian philanthropy, notwithstanding the remarks of the gentleman from Indiana [Mr. Dunn] and the gentleman from Ohio, [Mr. Giddings,] the other day, denouncing slavery as a violation of the laws of nature and of God! To those remarks, though my time is short, I wish very briefly to reply before I close.

Even, however, if slavery be sinful, as they affirm, or their language implies, permit me here to ask, is not the sin the same whether the slave be held in Georgia, Carolina, or in Kansas? Is it any more sinful in one place than another? But are these gentlemen correct? Is African slavery, as it exists in the South, either a violation of the laws of nature, the laws of nations, or the laws of God? I maintain that it is not. It has been recognized by the laws of nations from time immemorial. The highest court in this country, the Supreme Court of the United States, has so decided the laws of nations to be. And where do we get the laws of nature but in nature's works about us? Those general rules and principles by which all things in nature, according to their kinds respectively, seem to be regulated, and to which they seem to conform, we call laws; and in the handiwork of creation nothing is more striking to the philosophic observer than that order is nature's first great law.

Gradation, too, is stamped upon everything animate as well as inanimate—if, indeed, there be anything inanimate. A scale, from the lowest degree of inferiority to the highest degree of superiority, runs through all animal life. We see it in the insect tribes—we see it in the fishes of the sea, the fowls of the air, in the beasts of the earth, and we see it in the races of men. We see the same principle pervading the heavenly bodies above us. One star differs from another star in magnitude and luster—some are larger, others are smaller—but the greater and superior uniformly influences and controls the lesser and inferior within its sphere. If there is any fixed principle or law of nature it is this. In the races of men we find like differences in capacity and development. The negro is inferior to the white man; nature has made him so; observation and history, from the remotest times, establish the fact; and all attempts to make the inferior equal to the superior is but an effort to reverse the decrees of the Creator, who has made all things as we find them, according to the counsels of his own will. The Ethiopian can no more change his nature or his skin than the leopard his spots. Do what you will, a negro is a negro, and he will remain a negro still. In the social and political system of the South the negro is assigned to that subordinate position for which he is fitted by the laws of nature. Our system of civilization is founded in strict conformity to these laws. Order and subordination, according to the natural fitness of things, is the principle upon which the whole fabric of our southern institutions rest.

Then as to the law of God—that law we read not only in his works about us, around us, and over us, but in that inspired Book wherein he has revealed his will to man. When we differ as to the voice of nature, or the language of God, as spoken in nature's works, we go to that great Book, the Book of Books, which is the fountain of all truth. To that Book I now appeal. God, in the days of old, made a covenant with the human family—for the redemption of fallen man: that covenant is the corner-stone of the whole Christian system. Abram, afterwards called Abraham, was the man with whom that covenant was made. He was the great first head of an organized visible church here below. He believed God, and it was accounted to him for righteousness. He was in deed and in truth the father of the faithful. Abraham, sir, was a slaveholder. Nay, more, he was required to have the sign of that covenant administered to the slaves of his household.

Mr. CAMPBELL. Page, bring me a Bible.

Mr. STEPHENS. I have one here which the gentleman can consult if he wishes. Here is the passage, Genesis xvii., 13. God said to Abraham:

"13. He that is *born in thy house* and he that is *bought with thy money* must needs be circumcised; and my covenant shall be in your flesh for an everlasting covenant."

Yes, sir, Abraham was not only a slaveholder, but a slave dealer, it seems, for he bought men with his money, and yet it was with him the covenant was made by which the world was to be redeemed from the dominion of sin. And it was into his bosom in heaven that the poor man who died at the rich man's gate was borne by angels, according to the parable of the Savior. In the 20th chapter of Exodus, the great moral law is found—that law that defines sin—the ten commandments, written by the finger of God himself upon tables of stone. In two of these commandments, the 4th and 10th, verses 10th and 17th, slavery is expressly recognized, and in none of them is there anything against it—this is the moral law. In Leviticus we have the civil law on this subject, as given by God to Moses for the government of his chosen people in their municipal affairs. In chapter xxv., verses 44, 45, and 46, I read as follows:

"44. Both thy bondmen and thy bondmaids which thou shalt have shall be of the heathen that are round about you; of them ye shall buy bondmen and bondmaids.

"45. Moreover, of the children of the strangers that do sojourn among you, of them ye shall buy, and of their families that are with you which they begat in your land: and they shall be your possession.

"46. And ye shall take them as an inheritance for your children after you, to inherit them for a possession; they shall be your bondmen forever; but over your brethren, the children of Israel, ye shall not rule one over another, with rigor."

This was the law given to the Jews soon after they left Egypt for their government when they should reach the land of promise. They could have had no slaves then. It authorized the introduction of slavery amongst them when they should become established in Canaan. And it is to be noted that their bondmen and bondmaids to be bought, and held for *a possession and an inheritance* for their children after them, were to be of the heathen round about them. Over their brethren they were not to rule with rigor. Our southern system is in strict conformity with this injunction. Men of our own blood and our own race, wherever born, or from whatever clime they come, are free and equal. We have no castes or classes amongst white men—no "upper tendom" or "lower tendom." All are equals. Our slaves were taken from the heathen tribes—the barbarians of Africa. In our households they are brought within the pale of the covenant, under Christian teaching and influence; and more of them are partakers of the benefits of the gospel than ever were rendered so by missionary enterprise. The wisdom of man is foolishness—the ways of Providence are mysterious. Nor does the negro feel any sense of degradation in his condition—he is not *degraded*. He occupies and fills the same *grade* or rank in society and the State that he does in the scale of being; it is his natural place; and all things fit when nature's great first law of order is conformed to.

Again: Job was certainly one of the best men of whom we read in the Bible. He was a large slaveholder. So, too, were Isaac and Jacob, and all the patriarchs. But, it is said, this was under the Jewish dispensation. Granted. Has any change been made since? Is anything to be found in the New Testament against it? Nothing—not a word. Slavery existed when the Gospel was preached by Christ and his Apostles, and where they preached: it was all around them. And though the Scribes and Pharisees were denounced by our Savior for their hypocrisy and robbing "widows' houses," yet not a word did He utter against slaveholding. On one occasion, He was sought for by a centurion, who asked him to heal his slave, who was sick. Jesus said he would go; but the centurion objected, saying: "Lord, I am not worthy that thou shouldst come under my roof; but speak the word only, and my servant shall be healed. For I am a man under authority, having soldiers under me; and I say to this man, go, and he roeth; and to another come, and he cometh; and to my *slave*, do this, and he doeth it." *Matthew* viii., 9. The word rendered here "servant" in our translation, means *slave*. It means just such a servant as all our slaves at the South are. I have the original Greek.

[Here the hammer fell. Mr. STEPHENS asked that he might be permitted to go on as long as the gentleman from Ohio [Mr. CAMPBELL] had taken up his time. He had but a little more to say. Mr. GIDDINGS, of Ohio, objected; and what follows is the substance of what he intended to say, if he had not been cut off by the hour rule.]

The word in the original is *doulos*, and the meaning of this word, as given in Robinson's Greek and English Lexicon, is this—I read from the book: "In the family the *doulos* was one *bound to serve, a slave*, and was the property of his master—'a living possession,' as Aristotle calls him." And again: "The *doulos*, therefore, was never a *hired servant*, the latter being called *misthios*," &c. This is the meaning of the word, as given by Robinson, a learned doctor of divinity, as well as of laws. The centurion on that occasion said to Christ himself, "I say *to my slave, do this, and he doeth it*, and do Thou but speak the word, and he shall be healed." What was the Savior's reply? Did He tell him to go loose the bonds that fettered his fellow man? Did He tell him he was sinning against God for holding a *slave*? No such thing. But we are told by the inspired penman that:

"When Jesus heard it he marveled and said to them that followed: Verily, I say unto you, I have not found so great faith, no, not in Israel. And I say unto you that many shall come from the east and west and shall sit down with Abraham, and Isaac, and Jacob, in the kingdom of Heaven. But the children of the kingdom shall be cast out into utter darkness; there shall be weeping and gnashing of teeth. And Jesus said, unto the centurion, Go thy way, and as thou hast believed so be it done unto thee. And his servant [or *slave*] was healed in the selfsame hour."

Was Christ a "*doughface*?" Did He quail before the slave power? And if he did not rebuke the lordly centurion for speaking as he did of his authority over his slave, but healed the sick man, and said that he had not found so great faith in all Israel as he had in his master, who shall now presume, in His name, to rebuke others for exercising similar authority, or say that their faith may not be as strong as that of the centurion's?

In no place in the New Testament, sir, is slavery held up as sinful. Several of the Apostles alluded to it, but none of them—not one of them, mentions or condemns it as a relation sinful in itself, or violative of the laws of God, or even Christian duty. They enjoin the relative duties of both master and slave. Paul sent a runaway slave, Onesimus, back to Philemon, his master. He frequently alludes to slavery in his letters to the churches, but in no case speaks of it as sinful. To what he says in one of these epistles I ask special attention. It is 1st Timothy, chapter 6th, and beginning with the 1st verse:

"1. Let as many servants [*douloi*, slaves in the original, which I have before me] as are under the yoke [that is, those who are the most abject of slaves] count their own masters worthy of all honor, that the name of God and his doctrine be not blasphemed.

"2. And they that have believing masters, [according to modern doctrine there can be no such thing as a slaveholding believer; so did not think Paul,] let them not despise [or neglect and not care for] them, because they are brethren; but rather do them service, because they are faithful and beloved, partakers of the benefit. These things teach and exhort.

"3. *If any man teach otherwise* and consent not to wholesome words, *even the words of our Lord Jesus Christ*, and to the doctrine which is according to godliness:

"4. He is proud, [or *self-conceited*,] *knowing nothing but doting about questions and strifes of words*, whereof cometh envy, strife, railings, evil surmisings,

"5. Perverse disputings of *men of corrupt minds*, and destitute of the truth, supposing that gain is godliness: *from such withdraw thyself*."

This language of St. Paul, the great Apostle of the Gentiles, is just as appropriate this day, in this House, as it was when he penned it eighteen hundred years ago. No man could frame a more direct reply to the doctrines of the gentleman from Ohio, [Mr. GIDDINGS,] and the gentleman from Indiana, [Mr. DUNN,] than is here contained in the sacred book. What does all this strife, and envy, and railings, and "civil war" in Kansas come from, but the TEACHINGS of those in our day who teach otherwise than Paul taught, and "do not *consent to wholesome words, even the words of our Lord Jesus Christ*?"

Let no man, then, say that African slavery as it exists in the South, incorporated in, and sanctioned by, the Constitution of the United States, is in violation of either the laws of nations, the laws of nature, or the laws of God!

And if it "must needs be" that such an offense shall come from this source as shall sever the ties that now unite these States together in fraternal bonds, and involve the land in civil war, then "wo be unto them from whom the offense cometh!"

SPEECH

OF

HON. ALEXANDER H. STEPHENS,

OF GEORGIA,

ON THE

REPORT OF THE KANSAS INVESTIGATING COMMITTEE,

IN THE CASE OF

REEDER AGAINST WHITFIELD.

DELIVERED IN THE HOUSE OF REPRESENTATIVES, JULY 31, 1856.

WASHINGTON:
PRINTED AT THE CONGRESSIONAL GLOBE OFFICE.
1856.

KANSAS CONTESTED ELECTION.

Mr. STEPHENS said:

Mr. SPEAKER: If I were to consult my feelings to-day, my strength and physical ability, I should not trespass upon the patience of the House. If I were to consider the temperature of the day, the heat—the sweltering heat by which we are almost overpowered, I should certainly say nothing on this occasion. If I were to look to what is the apparent temper and tone of this body upon the subject before us, as indicated by the vote taken two days ago, I should feel constrained to let this question now be decided without a word from me. I should despair of all hope of being able to change what seems to be a fixed determination of a majority of the House by any effort I could make. Day before yesterday I saw a majority on this floor, in order to reach a purpose similar to that which they now seem bent on, vote to confer the most unlimited and dangerous power on the President of the United States. No subservient party in the British House of Commons ever yielded more power to the Crown by a vote of confidence, than this House on the occasion I refer to, conferred upon our Chief Magistrate, whom they have been wont so generally to mistrust, and unjustly to censure and upbraid. I allude to the vote on the amendment offered by the gentleman from Ohio [Mr. SHERMAN] to the Army bill. It is in these words:

"*Provided, nevertheless*, That no part of the military force of the United States herein provided for shall be employed in aid of the enforcement of the enactments of the alleged Legislative Assembly of the Territory of Kansas, recently assembled at Shawnee Mission, until Congress shall have enacted either that it was or was not a valid Legislative Assembly, chosen in conformity with the organic law by the people of the said Territory: *And provided*, That until Congress shall have passed on the validity of the said Legislative Assembly of Kansas, it shall be the duty of the President to use the military force in said Territory to preserve the peace, suppress insurrection, repel invasion, and protect persons and property therein, and upon the national highways in the State of Missouri, or elsewhere, from unlawful seizures and searches: *And be it further provided*, That the President is required to disarm the present organized militia of the Territory of Kansas, and recall all the United States arms therein distributed, and to prevent armed men from going into said Territory to disturb the public peace, or aid in the enforcement or resistance of real or pretended laws."

The President, by this provision, which received the sanction of a majority of this House, is created sole dictator over Kansas. His will, should the Senate concur—which I feel confident they will not do — would be more omnipotent there than that of Cæsar's ever was over the Roman legions, before he crossed the Rubicon. Gentlemen on this side of the House, in their misguided zeal for what they call *freedom*, have conferred on the President a power that I myself would confer on no living man. Not only this: they have conferred a power in direct violation of the Constitution of the United States. They have authorized the President to *disarm the militia of Kansas!* The second amendment of the Constitution is in these words——

Mr. PURVIANCE. I rise to a question of order. Is it in order to refer to the action of this body on a former occasion?

The SPEAKER. The Chair thinks that the gentleman from Georgia is in order so far as he has proceeded.

Mr. STEPHENS. The gentleman may keep quiet. This is not the only vote of the majority I intend to allude to. Another one I have in store may disturb him even more than this. The second article of the amendment to the Constitution of the United States is as follows:

> "A well-regulated militia being necessary to the security of a free State, the right of the people to keep and bear arms shall not be infringed."

That is the language of the Constitution we have all sworn to support. The right of the people—the militia—to *keep and bear arms shall not be infringed*, says the Constitution; but this House, in the face and teeth of the Constitution, has said that this right shall be infringed!—that the militia of Kansas shall be disarmed, and that the wheels of Government shall be stopped, unless this unconstitutional behest of theirs shall be complied with. And now, since I have seen the majority of this House thus arraying themselves against the Constitution, and striking down this great bulwark of liberty, and the safeguard of the rights of the free white people of this country, to answer an unhallowed purpose of party, under a false idea of "*negro freedom*," am I not justified in saying that I almost despair of effecting anything by what I may say in behalf of right, truth, justice, law, order, and the Constitution?

But, sir, that vote was given without argument —without full debate. On the subject now before us, we are not yet trammeled with the previous question. It is my purpose, therefore, to-day—notwithstanding my bodily weakness, notwithstanding the heat of the weather, and notwithstanding this unfavorable indication of the tone and temper of the House—to make an appeal to whatever good sense and sound judgment may be left in the House. I do not yet despair of the cause of truth. I shall never despair so long as men will hear and lend a listening ear to reason. I intend to-day to argue this question on principles, fixed, immutable, and as unassailable as those of the Constitution itself; and I approach the subject with the feelings of one thrice nerved for the argument, with the consciousness that his cause is bottomed upon truth and right.

The first resolution upon your table declares that JOHN W. WHITFIELD, the sitting Delegate of the Territory of Kansas, is not entitled to his seat, as such, on this floor. And I state, in the outset of what I shall say in opposition to this resolution, that the question has not changed in the slightest degree since the subject was here before. The report of the investigating committee sent out to Kansas has not changed the merits of the case an iota. There is no fact, no circumstance, collected in the mass of testimony that I now have before me, which changes the merits of the question in the smallest particular. How stood the case before the committee was instituted? The sitting Delegate presented himself, with the certificate, under the seal of the Governor of the Territory, as duly elected under the territorial law, passed in conformity with the law of Congress. By virtue of the certificate he was sworn in, and took his seat. What was the objection filed to his holding his seat as such? An allegation on the part of the contestant, not that he did not have a majority of the legal voters at the election, but that the *law passed* in the Territory, under which the sitting Delegate was elected, was *invalid*, and the election under it therefore *void*, *because* of the illegality of the organization of the Territorial Legislature that enacted it. This statement covers the whole merits of the case, as it stood when the committee was raised. I said then, and I say now, that the subject of the *legality* or *illegality* of the organization of the Territorial Legislature of Kansas is a question over which this House has no jurisdiction. The proper return and election of the members of that Legislature were questions to be settled and determined by the Governor and the Houses of the Legislature respectively, themselves. This was my position then, and it is the same now. I shall not, at this time, repeat the argument then submitted; but I throw down the gauntlet, and defy any gentleman to answer or controvert it. No man can get over it or around it, but by overriding principles as old as Magna Charta, and which lie at the foundation of all American representative institutions. The right of every legislative body to settle and determine *absolutely* the election of its own members, is a necessary incident of its own organic functions. In England, the House of Lords cannot question any decision of the Commons touching the election of its members; neither can the Commons question a like decision on the part of the Lords touching the qualifications of a peer; neither can the King, by his prerogative, interfere with the decision of either House on such subjects. These principles are laid down as the "*lex parliamentari*," by Sir Edward Coke, sustained by Blackstone, Mr. Justice Story, Kent, Rawle, and all writers upon the subject. They are incorporated in express terms in the Constitution of the United States, so far as the rights of both Houses of Congress are concerned, and in the constitutions of all our State governments, defining the powers of their legislative bodies.

The same principle is recognized and affirmed by the Supreme Court of the United States in the case of Borden and others, growing out of the Dorr rebellion in Rhode Island in 1842. It lies at the foundation of all legitimate political power as recognized in this country. Without it there can be no certainty in legislation; and without its maintenance, nothing but disorder, confusion, and the wildest anarchy may be expected to ensue. We cannot have a representative Government administered on any other principle. If you can inquire into the legality of the election of the members of the Legislature of the Territory of Kansas, in the question now before us, you can do the same thing with regard to the States. If you can judge of the returns and qualifications of members of that Legislative Assembly, you can also upon the same principle inquire into and judge of the legality of the elections, returns, and qualifications of members of the several State Legislatures that passed the laws under which all the members of this House were elected. The Senate may do the same in their body. Where is the difference? And where is this matter to end? In judging the qualifications and elections of the members of this House, we sit as a court; and in passing judgment upon the validity of such laws as come before us in our investigations, we are to be governed by the same rules and principles as those of all other courts in like cases. If the law of Kansas under which the sitting Delegate was elected, has anything in it inconsistent with the Constitution of the United States, or the organic act of the Territory, you have a right to that extent to pronounce it *invalid* and *void*, as any other court would have; but questions relating to the organization of the law-making power, courts will never inquire into, and we cannot properly do it either. No case can be found where it has ever been done, either in this country or England.

The Legislature of Kansas was elected in pursuance of a proclamation of the Governor of the Territory, under the organic act passed by Congress. It was made the duty of the Governor to supervise that election, prescribe the mode and manner of holding it, and to declare who was properly and legally elected. You passed another bill day before yesterday, for the reorganization of that Territory, and directing another election to be held in the same way. In that bill the same identical words are used—"that the Governor shall declare who are legally elected to the Legislature." Suppose that bill should become a law, and the Governor appointed under it should order a new election, and after the returns made should declare a majority to be duly elected, just as in the case of the Legislature whose laws are now brought in review, would this House again untertake to set aside that judgment, if it should so turn out that the new Legislature under the new act should pass any laws that the majority of this House might not like? Where is to be the end of this business?

Now, sir, I maintain that, if the bill which has just passed this House, shall become a law, and the Governor to be appointed under it shall order an election for another Legislature, and in pursuance of his directions an election shall be held for members of a House of Representatives and a Council as provided, and the Governor, upon canvassing the returns, shall declare, as it will be his duty to do, who may be duly and legally elected, and shall give certificates accordingly, and the two houses of the Legislature, thus constituted, shall, after being duly sworn, enter upon their legislative duties under a law thus passed by Congress, and shall hear and determine, each House for itself, all matters pertaining to the election of its members, outside of the *prima facie* certificate of the Governor; all such matters and questions so pertaining to the election of the members, and the *legality* of the organization of the Legislature so constituted, will be forever closed by that determination. This House would have no right or power to reopen the question.

And just so in the case before us, Congress passed a law organizing a territorial government. The Governor appointed was authorized to order an election for members of a Legislature at such time, and such places, and in such manner as he thought proper. The returns of the election were to be made to him, and he had power to declare who was duly elected. The House of Representatives was to consist of twenty-six members, and the Council of thirteen. The Governor ordered an election on the 30th of March, 1855. He divided the Territory into ten council districts, fourteen representative districts, and eighteen election districts, or voting precincts. He appointed the judges of election at each poll, and directed how their places thould be filled in case those appointed should fail or refuse to act. The judges were all to be sworn. The rules and regulations for conducting the election were exceedingly rigid. The election was so held. The returns were made to him as required; and out of the twenty-six members of the House of Representatives, he declared seventeen were duly elected, and awarded certificates accordingly. Of thirteen Councilmen, he declared nine were duly elected, and awarded them certificates accordingly. The election of four councilmen and nine representatives to the House he set aside. In these cases he ordered new elections. This took place on the 22d of May, and he awarded certificates to those whom he declared to be duly elected at that election. The members of the House and Council, thus declared to be duly elected by him, were convened by him on the 2d day of July, 1855. Every member, of both the Council and House of Representatives, in that Legislature so convened, took his seat by virtue of the Governor's certificate. These are admitted facts. Nothing brought to light by the investigating committee assails or impeaches any one of them in the slightest degree. Each House, after being thus constituted, inquired into, heard, and determined all questions of contested seats in their respective bodies, as all other legislative assemblies do. The right to do this was inherent in them. On this point Judge Story says, in his Treatise on the Constitution of the United States, volume 2, page 295:

"The only possible question on such a subject is as to *the body* in which such a power shall be lodged. If lodged in any other than the *legislative body itself*, its independence, its purity, and even its existence and action, may be destroyed or put into imminent danger. No other body but itself can have the same motives to perpetuate and preserve these attributes; no other body can be so perpetually watchful to guard its own rights and privileges from infringement, to purify and vindicate its own character, and to preserve the rights and sustain the free choice of its constituents. *Accordingly, the power has always been lodged in the legislative body by the uniform practice of England and America.*"

Such, too, is the doctrine of Coke, of Blackstone, of Kent, and all writers upon the subject, as I showed before. Each House, therefore, of the Kansas Legislature was the proper tribunal to settle all questions pertaining to the election of its own members; and their decision, when made, was just as final in law as that of ours upon a similar question here. There was, however, no contest over the election of but seven members of the House, and two of the Council. Two members of the Council, and two of the House, whose election was set aside at the first election, were declared duly elected at the second election. Every one of the thirteen members of the Council, therefore, except two, held his seat without any contest whatever; and nineteen of the twenty-six members of the House of Representatives held their seats without any contest. And after the Houses were thus organized in pursuance of law, and compliance with every legal form, they were recognized as a legally-constituted, law-making body by the Governor. He addressed them official communications as such.

In his first message, in pointing out to them their duties, amongst other things the Governor named the duty of passing some such law as that under which the sitting Delegate was elected. He vetoed some of their acts; but not upon any grounds touching the *legality of their election or organization*. All questions, therefore, of that character, I maintain, upon the soundest principles of constitutional law, are now closed. It is too late to open them; and not one of these great, leading and controlling facts, in this case, is even assailed by any testimony taken by the investigating committee. They are all confirmed and established by that testimony; and if the sitting Delegate shall be voted out upon grounds assumed in the report of the majority of the Committee of Elections, it will establish not only a novel, but a most mischievous precedent. It will be taking one long step towards that revolution which a party in this country seems to be aiming at. This House will but be doing what *it is said* the people of Missouri did in Kansas. It is said they carried the election there by *illegal voting;* and what else will you be doing here? Where do you get the power or authority to say that Governor Reeder did not act right in giving certificates of election to the members of the Legislature whom he adjudged to be duly elected? Where do you get the power, under the Constitution, or under the organic law, or under any other law, to vacate his judgment in this case? The right to judge in the first instance was expressly given to him. The right to judge finally and absolutely necessarily devolved upon the houses of the Legislature respectively. Congress reserved no supervisory power over the subject. Where, then, do you derive your power of annulling a judgment of another department of Government having exclusive and absolute power and jurisdiction over the subject-matter?

If it were true that the greatest frauds had been practiced in the election in Kansas—if any amount of illegal voting had been resorted to, and the people *waived their right* to inquire into it at the *proper time* and before the *proper tribunal*—if they made *no complaint to the Governor* when they *ought to have done it*—if they made *no protest* within the *time prescribed*—if defeated candidates *failed to contest* the returns of their competitors until after the term of office of the members of the Legislature expired, it is, as I maintain, now too late to file any such complaints before this or any other body. The question of the legality of the organization of that Legislature, so elected, so constituted, so recognized by the Governor, so discharging the functions of a law-making power, is, in my judgment, a closed question forever. And this is certainly the private opinion of Governor Reeder himself; for in the mass of testimony, collected by the committee, (pages 1152, 1153, and 1154,) I find two letters written by him in this city last winter to a friend of his in Kansas. I will read to the House an extract of one of these, bearing date the 12th February, 1856. It was in relation to the movements in Kansas, in opposition to the territorial laws. In this letter he says:

"As to putting a set of laws into operation in opposition to the territorial government, my opinion is confirmed instead of being shaken; my predictions have all been verified so far, and will be in the future. *We will be, so far as legality is concerned, in the wrong; and that is no trifling matter, in so critical a state of things, and in view of such bloody consequences.*" * * * * * "I may speak my plain and private opinion to our friends in Kansas, for it is my duty. But to the public, as you will see by my published letter, I show no divided front."

This admission covers the whole ground. In it he distinctly asserts, and gives it as his own candid judgment, that, "*so far as legality is concerned,*" he and his friends were in the wrong. The truths acknowledged in this admission are the same which I have been endeavoring to enforce. The whole merits of this case turn, in the report of the Committee of Elections, upon the simple question of the *legality* of the organization of the Legislature that passed the law under which the sitting Delegate was elected. That, in my judgment, is a closed question. That, in the private judgment of Governor Reeder also, was a closed question. Out of his mouth he stands condemned in this movement.

But, Mr. Speaker, strong as these positions are—unassailable as they are—impregnable as they are—I do not intend to rest the argument solely upon them. I intend to take up the report of the committee of investigation referred to by the gentleman from Maine, [Mr. Washburn.] I intend to examine it, and exhibit to this House and the country the character of some of the *facts* reported by them. I intend to examine some of their conclusions, too. The gentleman from Maine [Mr. Washburn] says, "that all the conclusions as to matters of fact arrived at by the said special committee are clearly and incontrovertibly established by the testimony in the case." Now, sir, I join issue with the gentleman from Maine, [Mr. Washburn.] I join issue with the majority of the Committee of Elections. I join issue also with the investigating committee as to the matters of fact arrived at by them in the conclusions to which they come in their report; and I defy the gentleman from Maine, [Mr. Washburn,] or either gentleman on the investigating committee, or anybody else in this House or out of it, to maintain the correctness of the conclusions as to matters of fact arrived at by them. I shall show that what has been proclaimed "official proof," is nothing but *reckless assertion*. The first of these conclusions is in these words:

"That each election in the Territory, held under the organic or alleged territorial law, has been carried by organized invasion from the State of Missouri, by which the people of the Territory have been prevented from exercising the rights secured to them by the organic law."

Now, sir, the gentleman from Maine, [Mr.

WASHBURN,] and the majority of the Committee of Elections, assert in their report that this conclusion, as a matter of fact, is incontrovertibly established by the testimony taken. I say that the testimony taken establishes no such fact. I say that the testimony taken establishes a fact in direct contradiction to this statement. I say that the evidence abundantly and conclusively establishes the fact that General Whitfield was duly elected by the actual and legal resident voters of the Territory, at the election on the 29th of November, 1854. This fact appears not only from the testimony, but it is admitted by the committee of investigation themselves in their own report. Then how can it be true that every election there has been carried by an organized invasion from Missouri?

I will read from the document itself. Here on page 8 is what purports to be an abstract of the vote cast on the 29th of November, 1854, from which it seems that Whitfield got 2,258 votes; Flenniken 305; Wakefield, which (I believe) was a mistake for Whitfield, 248, and 22 scattering. These 305 for Flenniken, and 22 scattering, were all the votes cast against Whitfield in the entire Territory.

Mr. SHERMAN. The gentleman is entirely mistaken. The abstract shows that 2,258 votes were cast for Whitfield; 248 for Wakefield; 305 for Flenniken, and 22 scattering, but that 1,729 of those votes were illegal, and only 1,114 were legal. Of the legal votes cast General Whitfield had a plurality, having received 537 legal votes.

Mr. STEPHENS. I tell the gentleman I am not mistaken; and his statement, that 1,729 of the 2,258 cast for Whitfield were illegal, is not sustained by proof. There is a wide difference between assertion and proof, and this table exhibits the truth of this most forcibly. The table states that there were 1,729 illegal votes cast; but where is the proof of the fact of these 1,729 votes being illegal? The table is not proof. The table also states that there were only 1,114 legal votes cast at that election. Where is the proof of that? But suppose there were only 1,114 legal votes cast. Take from that number 305 votes cast for Flenniken, and 22 scattering, and it would leave Whitfield elected by a large majority; or, if the 248 for Wakefield were not intended for Whitfield, and if all the votes for that name, and the 327 for Flenniken, and scattering, were legal votes, as is assumed, but without proof, then, Whitfield, having 537 admitted legal votes, was duly elected, having received a greater number than any other candidate. How, then, can it be said that his election, in this instance, was carried by an organized invasion from Missouri?

But, sir, I call for the proof upon which this exhibit of *legal* and *illegal* votes is made! The exhibit of Whitfield's, Wakefield's, and Flenniken's votes, and the scattering votes, is copied from the official return, but the *addenda* touching the *legal* and *illegal* votes, and the number of voters under the census taken three months after, have been put to it by the committee. It is in their statement, not in the testimony, and I ask for the proof to warrant it? But, even according to the gentleman's own showing, now made, after deducting from his count one thousand seven hundred and twenty-nine without proof, Whitfield was certainly duly elected *at that election* by the legal voters of the Territory. Indeed, the committee of investigation say, in reference to this election, on page 8 of their report: "Of the legal votes cast, General Whitfield received a plurality." This settles the question. If Whitfield got a plurality of the legal votes of the Territory, of course he was duly elected. Now, sir, I ask the gentleman upon my right [Mr. WASHBURN] to tell me, and this House, and the country, how he and a majority of the committee of elections can say that it is established by "*incontrovertible proof*" that "*each election* in the Territory, held under the organic or alleged territorial law, has been carried by an *organized invasion* from the State of Missouri?" &c. This matter of fact, arrived at by the special committee, "as clearly and incontrovertibly established by the testimony," cannot stand a moment's handling. It falls at the first blow. It is the first conclusion arrived at by the committee of investigation, and incorporated in the report of the Committee of Elections, as the foundation, the very corner-stone of the fabric of their report in this case. This corner-stone, sir, I knock from under the fabric, and the whole superstructure must fall with it, if there be nothing more solid or firm for it to rest upon.

But, sir, I do not intend to stop here. This conclusion of the committee is but a sample of all the rest. I have read the whole of this document of one thousand two hundred and six pages, and I assert that there is not a single one of the conclusions of the committee arrived at as matters of fact, which is sustained by the testimony, massive, voluminous, and contradictory as it is. I repeat, however, here again, that there is not a fact or statement contained in it, by the most prejudiced, one-sided witness sworn, which goes to assail or impeach in the slightest degree the great leading facts upon which the merits of this case rest. These are the elections held in pursuance of the Governor's proclamation under the organic law—his judgment upon the returns of the election of the members—the large majority of both branches of the Legislature holding their seats during their whole term under the certificates of the Governor, without a word of complaint from him or anybody else—that he, as Governor, recognized them as a legislative body—that he did not question the legality of their organization. The testimony of Governor Reeder himself was taken, and none of these facts are denied by him. No word of complaint was ever heard about the legality of the organization of the Legislature, or about an invasion from Missouri, for several long months after the election; nor until after he was turned out of office. During all this time, before he was removed by the President, the only cry heard from him, as the sentinel upon the watchtower of the rights of the people of Kansas, was, "All's well!"

But, sir, I will proceed. I intend to take up this mass of testimony, and sift it a little further, to see how far it warrants the conclusions of the committee touching the elections of the members of the Legislature on the 30th of March, 1855. The testimony is all we have anything to do with. The conclusions of the committee are nothing. They were not authorized to give us any of their conclusions; and I have shown you what their conclusions are worth, taking one as a sample. To collect and report the facts was all they had to do. Then, sir, what fact is sworn to by a single witness, upon which the election, in a single district, held on the 30th of March, could be legally set aside if we were now sitting in judgment upon it? The greater part of this testimony, taken with the view to impeach the election of 30th of March, is nothing but long-winded stories, as pointless as they are evidently prejudiced, founded in many instances upon bare hearsay, and altogether establishing nothing. The statements of most of the witnesses are all on the same line, speaking of an invasion, companies of men coming over from Missouri in hundreds, in wagons, armed with guns, pistols, knives, &c., *but not one of them* swears that a *single man* in the Territory, at a *single election precinct*, was *prevented* from voting by the use of these arms, or any other violence. The testimony of all the witnesses sworn does not establish the fact, that one hundred known residents of Missouri voted in the whole Territory, or that the result at a single poll would have been different if all the votes proven to be illegal be rejected in the count. There were but three or four fights throughout the Territory on the day of the election, and not one of these about voting. All this general vague rumor and statement, therefore, about an invasion from Missouri, and the election having been carried by fraud, force, and violence, I shall pass over. To set aside an election upon the grounds of illegal voting, the names of the voters must be stated, and the illegality of the votes proved. There is nothing of this kind in this testimony. Nor is the bare fact of illegal voting at an election sufficient to set it aside. If this were so, there are very few of us entitled to seats upon this floor, I suspect. To set aside an election on such grounds, it must be shown that the result would be different by a rejection of the illegal votes.

I wish, however, to call the attention of the House and the country to some real, substantial facts collected by the committee, of much weightier import than these loose sayings of one-sided and swift witnesses. Amongst these facts of substantial character is a copy of the census taken in February, 1855, which is to be found commencing on page 72 of the committee's report. This census gives the name of each resident legal voter in the Territory, thirty days before the March election. It also gives the State from which the settler migrated. The committee do not seem to have given much attention to the important facts disclosed by this official document. They have made no analysis of these facts. I have. I have counted every name on the census roll, and noted the section of country from which the settler migrated, and I find that of those who were registered as legal voters of the Territory in February, a month before the election, 1,670 were from the southern States, and only 1,018 from the entire North! There were 217 from other countries. That makes the 2,905 *resident legal voters* in the Territory, a month before the election. I have compiled a table setting forth the number of settlers from the North, and settlers from the South, as given in the census report, for each district in the Territory. Here it is:

	Settlers from the North.	*Settlers from the South.*
First district	280	88
Second district	67	132
Third district	49	37
Fourth district	24	23
Fifth district	129	295
Sixth district	83	155
Seventh district	32	21
Eighth district	12	26
Ninth district	27	10
Tenth district	29	27
Eleventh district	-	28
Twelfth district	50	49
Thirteenth district	22	55
Fourteenth district	42	286
Fifteenth district	37	206
Sixteenth district	125	192
Seventeenth district	10	40
	1,018	1,670

In the first election district, there were 280 legal voters, emigrants from the northern States, and 88 from the southern. That is the Lawrence district. In the second district, there were 67 from the North, and 132 from the South. In the third district, there were 49 from the North, and 37 from the South. In the fourth district, there were 24 from the North, and 23 from the South. In the fifth district, there were 129 from the North, and 295 from the South. In the sixth, there were 83 from the North, and 155 from the South.

Mr. SHERMAN. Will my friend read again the numbers from the fifth district?

Mr. STEPHENS. In the fifth district, there were 129 from the North, and 295 from the South. The fifth district had an overwhelming majority of residents from the South, and that is the only district, I believe, in which the committee have taken the testimony of witnesses to prove that the Abolitionists were in a majority on the day of election.

Now, sir, from these facts—facts of record, and indisputable, I deduce an argument which, to my mind, is much more incontrovertible and irresistible than any inference the majority of the committee may draw from the vague sayings of witnesses, about a multitude of strangers being at the polls in wagons, &c. This inference, which I draw from these facts, is, that there was a decided majority of anti-Free-Soilers in the Territory, and in a large majority of the districts, in the month of February, if there had been no immigration after that time. But the evidence is abundant and conclusive that there was a large immigration of legal voters from the South after the census was taken, and before the election, much larger than at any other time. (A. B. Wade, page 159, and others.) One witness, Mr. Banks, on page 164, swears, that "betwixt two and three hundred settlers moved into the district (the first) in which he lived, which was after the census was taken, and before the election." His testimony related to only part of the district, where he was acquainted. Another witness swears that, to the best of his knowledge and belief, there were four hundred actual residents and legal voters of the pro-slavery party in this first district on the day of election, (page 1159.) The testimony shows that, in most of the districts, there was a large immigration of actual residents, legal voters from the South, after the census was taken, and before the day of election. It shows, further, that the immigration during that time was much larger from the South than the North. But the facts disclosed by the census show that there was a majority of six hundred and fifty-two of legal voters from the South over those from the North, in February. Now, sir, with these facts before us, I call the special attention of the gentleman from Ohio [Mr. Sherman] to the following statement in his report, on page 34:

"If the election had been confined to the actual settlers, undeterred by the presence of non-residents, or the knowledge that they would be present in numbers sufficient to outvote them, the testimony indicates that the council would have been composed of seven in favor of making Kansas a free State, elected from the first, second, third, fourth, and sixth council districts. The result in the eighth and tenth, electing three members, would have been doubtful; and the fifth, seventh, and ninth, would have elected three pro-slavery members.

"Under like circumstances the House of Representatives would have been composed of fourteen members in favor of making Kansas a free State, elected from the second, third, fourth, fifth, seventh, eighth, ninth, and tenth representative districts.

"The result in the twelfth and fourteenth representative districts, electing five members, would have been doubtful; and the first, sixth, eleventh, and fifteenth districts would have elected seven pro-slavery members.

"By the election as conducted, the pro-slavery candidates in every district but the eighth representative district received a majority of the votes."

In this statement the committee say that the testimony indicates that, if the election had been confined to the actual settlers, the council would have been composed of seven in favor of making Kansas a free State, elected from the first, second, third, fourth, and sixth council districts.

Now, sir, I join issue with the gentleman and the committee on this point. The census, which the committee seem not to have consulted, is the best testimony on it. Let us then see what *indications* it affords. The first council district consisted of the first, fourth, and seventeenth election districts. In these, according to the census, the legal voters, emigrants from the North, according to the census, was 314, from the South 151; making the number of legal resident voters in that council district 465, in February, without taking any count of immigration afterwards; but the evidence shows that many of the residents coming from the North, and even some of the acknowledged free-State men, voted for those called pro-slavery candidates, because they did not like the candidates put up by their party. They were too ultra in their abolitionism, (page 160.) The testimony shows, also, that the whole number of votes cast for the Free-Soil candidates in that council district, was but 254, (page 31.) This would give 43 majority for them, if the 254 cast for them were all *legal votes*. But the testimony of Mr. Ladd, Governor Reeder's own witness, who was a candidate on that ticket for councilman, establishes the fact that at least *fifty* of these votes were illegal, cast by emigrants from New England, just arrived—some of them forty-eight hours before the election. This will be seen on page 118 of this huge volume. His language is as follows:

"I know some of those who had recently arrived voted; I can only approximate their numbers—I should think there were from fifty to sixty. I think there were some who arrived within forty-eight hours; I cannot say as to whether they made settlements in the Territory at that time."

If, then, these fifty or sixty acknowledged illegal votes be deducted from those cast for the Abolition ticket, it would leave a majority for the candidates on the other side, of the *actual residents in February*, even in Lawrence, the great rendezvous of New England emigrants, and without any reference to the emigration from the South after the census was taken. There is no evidence, by any witness sworn, that any man, even in Lawrence, was prevented from voting by force, violence, or intimidation. Some witnesses swear that they did not vote because of the crowd; but not one swears that he could not have voted if he had wanted to, in consequence of any violence, force, or threat; and there was no crowd about the polls in the afterpart of the day. Therefore, in this first district, the testimony in connection with the census does not indicate that, if the election had been left to the *actual residents* alone, the Free-Soil ticket would have been elected. This, however, was one of the elections set aside by the Governor, and another was held there on the 22d of May.

But, sir, how is it in the other council districts mentioned by the committee? I have a paper before me which I have compiled, exhibiting the organization of all of the council districts, with the number of settlers in each from the North and South, according to the census as far as can be ascertained. The seventh, eighth, ninth, and tenth council districts were formed by dividing the districts in which the census was taken, in such a way that the exact number of settlers from each section cannot be accurately arrived at in them; but it is apparent, from the census returns, that they could not have been divided so as not to have had a large majority of settlers from the South in each. Here is the exhibit:

COUNCIL DISTRICTS.

Number of Council District.	Election Districts.	Settlers from the North.	Settlers from the South.	No. of Council.
1st, composed of	1st 4th 17th	280 24 10	88 23 40	2
		314	151	
2d " "	2d	67	132	1
3d " "	3d 7th 8th	49 32 12	37 21 26	1
		93	84	
4th " "	5th	129	295	2
5th " "	6th	83	155	1
6th " "	9th 10th 11th 12th	27 29 - 50	10 27 28 49	1
		106	114	
7th " "	18th and parts of 14th and 15th	-	Large majority from the South.	1
8th " "	Part of 14th,—Burr Oak precinct.	-	Large majority from the South.	1
9th " "	Part of 15th	-	Large majority from the South.	1
10th " "	16th and part of 13th	-	Large majority from the South.	2

I have already shown what the testimony indicates in the first council district. Then how is it in the second? The census shows that there were 67 resident legal votes in it from the North, and 132 from the South. The evidence of witnesses shows that this majority from the South was largely increased by actual residents before the election, (page 1157.) In the third council district the census showed a majority of 9 only from the North. The evidence of witnesses shows that this majority was overcome before the election by actual settlers from the South. The fourth shows only 129 from the North, against 295 from the South. The sixth district shows a majority of 8 from the South. In the districts mentioned by the committee, the census returns, by themselves, *clearly indicate* that but two of them had a majority of settlers from the North, while no witness states any fact to the contrary; but many confirm this indication. The eighth and tenth districts, they say, would have been doubtful, while the census shows a large majority of the settlers in those districts were emigrants from the South.

In reply to what is said in the extract read from the report touching the character of the House I have also made an exhibit from which it will be seen upon what sort of foundation that statement rests.

REPRESENTATIVE DISTRICTS.

Number of Representative districts.	Election districts.	Settlers from the North.	Settlers from the South.	No. of Reps.
1st composed of	17th 4th	10 24	40 23	1
		34	63	
2d " "	1st	280	88	3
3d " "	2d	67	132	2
4th " "	3d	49	37	1
5th " "	7th 8th	32 12	21 26	1
		44	47	
6th " "	6th	83	155	2
7th " "	5th	129	295	4
8th " "	9th 10th	27 29	10 27	1
		56	37	
9th " "	11th 12th	- 50	28 49	1
		50	77	
10th " "	13th	22	55	1
11th " "	7th Council district; viz: 18th and parts of 14th and 15th.	-	Large majority from the South.	2
12th " "	Burr Oak precinct in the 14th.	-	Majority from the South.	2
13th " "	Part of 15th	-	Majority from the South.	2
14th " "	16th and part of 13th	-	Majority from the South.	3

From this table, based upon the census, it is clearly established that there was a majority of the actual settlers from the North in the Territory in but three of the fourteen representative districts. These were the second, fourth, and eighth—electing in all but five members out of the twenty-six.

But I cannot dwell upon these exhibits. No man can gainsay the facts they disclose. They are based upon the census, and the organization of the districts by Governor Reeder; and these two exhibits show conclusively to my mind, and as I think to all candid minds, that if the vote in the Territory had been confined exclusively to the *actual resident registered voters in February*, the result of the election would not have been different from what it was! The census shows that there were then a majority of 652 residents in the Territory from the South, over those from the North; and it is well known that great numbers of the emigrants from the North voted with the southern settlers against the Free-Soil party at the election. Four of the members elected to the Legislature, voted for by southern men, were from the North. Mr. Banks, a member of the House, went from Pennsylvania; Mr. Waterson, from Ohio; Mr. Lykins, a member of the Council, was from Indiana, and Mr. Barbee from Illinois. These men, though emigrating from the North, were members of the Legislature, and belonged to what the gentleman styles the pro-slavery or "border ruffian" party in Kansas. The whole "Free-Soil vote," or "free-State" vote, as the gentleman calls it, in the entire Territory on the 30th of March, amounted to less than 800, as appears from the exhibits of the committee's report, (pages 31 and 32.) This is more than 200 less than the number of emigrants from the North in the Territory, according to the census, and less than one third of the legally-registered voters in February.

Now, as no witness swears that any man of that party was prevented from voting, the whole evidence taken together clearly indicates, if it does not establish, the fact conclusively, that the Free-Soil party in Kansas was largely in the minority at the March election, and that all this cry about an invasion, and the election having been carried by Missourians, is nothing but clamor. It is an after-thought. As to the statement of old man Jordan, it is sufficient to say, in reply to it, that there was no Free-Soil ticket run at the election where he was, in the third district. There was no reason, therefore, for any attempt to keep him from voting.

It is very possible, Mr. Speaker—it is even probable, and I do not mean to say but what it is altogether true, that a great many illegal votes were cast at the election. It is certainly admitted, also, that great numbers of the citizens of Missouri went into the Territory on the day of the election, but there is no proof that any great numbers of them voted. They went, according to the testimony, to see that illegal voting should not be allowed by parties sent out by the eastern emigrant aid societies, barely for the purpose of voting and returning. The main point, however, I am now presenting is, that if every vote be rejected and cast out of the count but those of the *actual resident registered voters in the Territory in February*, the result, upon all reasonable and rational grounds of calculation and conclusion, would have been the same as it was. These views are founded upon fixed and ascertained facts—upon a registry of the legal voters, with the places from which they went, and not upon loose statements of one-sided witnesses about the polls being crowded with strangers, and great multitudes of people coming upon the ground in wagons, &c. Why, Mr. Johnson (one of the judges of election, too, at a precinct in the seventh district) swears, on page 261, that "a great many of the people in that district, whom he considered legal voters, came to the polls in their wagons, I have no doubt, as I came there myself in my wagon. *It is the habit of the people in the Territory to go to gatherings in their wagons.*" And in this immediate connection, too, he states, "and as a judge of election, I am willing now to swear that we allowed no man to vote that we did not consider had a right to vote."

The tale told by all the witnesses examined by Governor Reeder amounts to nearly the same thing. They all had their "story pat." A great crowd was assembled about the polls. Some had guns, pistols, and knives. Well, sir, when and where was there ever an election held at which the people did not crowd about the polls? And is it not strange, that this army of invasion, with flags, banners, and music—guns, pistols, and knives, did so little mischief? Not a man was hurt by them in the whole Territory! Not a homicide committed! Not even an assault and battery about voting in the whole Territory! For from all the testimony taken it appears that there were but three or four fights in all Kansas on the day of election; and these fights were not about voting! Why, sir, in the municipal election in this city, the other day, at one precinct alone, there were half a dozen men knocked down—some were shot—one has since died of the wounds received in the affray; and one man, two or three days afterwards, was killed in the streets merely for hurrahing for his candidate! But in the invasion and subjugation of Kansas on this memorable election day, no man was killed—no man was even whipped for, or on account of, his voting! Strange invasion and subjugation was that! A subjugation without a life lost, a bone broken, or a bruise given, and about which no complaint was raised until months afterwards! And why, Mr. Speaker, was it got up afterwards? Why do we hear so much of it now? What is the real cause of all this clamor at this time, in this House and out of it, about the illegality of the election of the Legislature in Kansas, and these pretended grievances of a pretended down-trodden majority there crying out for redress against a system of laws imposed upon them by the people of a neighboring State? I understand it, sir, very well, and you, too, doubtless, understand it. We all understand it. There is a party in this country determined to "*rule or ruin*"—not only in Kansas, [illegible] throughout the Republic. It is a party formed [illegible] geographical lines against the warning in the Farewell Address of the Father of his Country.

I may be permitted, in this connection, to allude to this true and real cause of all these difficulties; for, but for this cause, I venture to say, such a case as that now presented before this House would not have received one hour's consideration. The true cause, then, lies in no real grievance in Kansas, but in the aims, objects, and purposes of this party. They are against allowing the people of the Territories of the United States to exercise the right of self-government, as provided in the Kansas bill. The elections in Kansas did not go to suit that party. They call themselves Republicans, and their republicanism amounts to about this: they acknowledge the right of the people to govern themselves, provided they do it according to their notions. They make loud professions, and utter "shrieks" for the "freedom of the Africans" amongst us, while they will not grant the freedom of making their own laws to their own countrymen, of their own race and blood, unless it is exercised in conformity to their will. These men were opposed originally to the Kansas-Nebraska act, because it granted the right to the free white men there to assign the negro to that *status*, in their political systems, which they, in their wisdom and patriotism, might determine to be best for both them and him. They wish to govern Kansas, not according to the wishes of the people there, but as they please.

Sir, I profess to be a republican of the old school, of the school of Madison and Jefferson and Washington. It was upon the principles of that school I was in favor of the Kansas bill, and am still; and I am in favor of adhering to it and carrying it out in good faith, both in letter and spirit. I justify no wrongs that may have arisen under it, if any have, coming from any quarter whatever; and I am compelled to believe, from all the testimony taken in this case, that whatever wrongs may have been committed by any portion of the people of Missouri, they were retaliatory in their character. The first wrong was committed by those whose sole object was to defeat the peaceful and quiet operation of the principles of that bill. Whatever ills may have befallen these intermeddlers, have been clearly of their own seeking; and we seldom see a man going out of his way to get into a difficulty who makes much by it. I am, however, sir, for applying all proper remedies for existing difficulties, and for quieting all disturbances which have arisen in Kansas, in any proper and legitimate way. This I have shown by my advocacy of the Senate's bill, which still sleeps upon your table, and which you will not touch: that is a fair and a just mode of pacification. If pacification is what you want, that is one way in which it can be accomplished. It cannot be done by *ignoring* their laws, and voting their Delegate out of a seat on this floor. It cannot be done by making the President supreme dictator over them. It cannot be done by withholding appropriations and stopping the wheels of the General Government, and throwing us all into anarchy, unless the will of a majority of this House, upon the subject of African slavery, shall be the law in that Territory. It cannot be done by sixteen States of this Union setting themselves up to govern not only Kansas, but the other fifteen separate and independent coequal States in this Confederacy. It can only be done by leaving this question, in some form or another, just where the Kansas bill put it. This is the only ultimate, peaceful solution of the whole matter, and it will be so found in the end.

The people of Kansas, I take it, are capable of governing themselves, just as wisely, peacefully, patriotically, and as safely, without dictation from, or control by you, as they were in the States from which they migrated. They lost none of their intelligence, virtue, patriotism, or sovereignty, I trust, by a change of residence. They can judge better of the character of their laws than you can. If they do not suit the wishes of a majority of the people there, they doubtless will be changed in due time and in a proper way. The day for a new election, if the Senate bill is not to pass, is near at hand. In October a new Legislature is to be elected. Why should the people there be encouraged to acts of revolution, or this House be induced to take steps leading to revolution here, when the constitutional and peaceful remedy of the ballot-box is so near at hand? Why cannot all these questions be left to the people of Kansas to settle at their next election? If the Free-Soil party are in the majority, as you say it is, why shrink from that test? I question if any State in the Union has got a better election law—one more rigidly guarding the free exercise of the elective franchise—than the people of Kansas have, which is that very law you are now about to be called upon to declare invalid and void. Amongst other provisions, it contains the following, which I called the attention of the House to once before on this floor:

"SEC. 24. If any person, by menaces, threats, and force, or by any other unlawful means, either directly or indirectly, attempt to influence any qualified voter in giving his vote, or to deter him from giving the same, or disturb or hinder him in the free exercise of his right of suffrage, at any election held under the laws of this Territory, the person so offending shall, on conviction thereof, be adjudged guilty of a misdemeanor, and be punished by fine not exceeding five hundred dollars, or by imprisonment in the county jail not exceeding one year.

"SEC. 25. Every person who shall, at the same election, vote more than once, either at the same or a different place, shall, on conviction, be adjudged guilty of a misdemeanor, and be punished by fine not exceeding fifty dollars, or by imprisonment in the county jail not exceeding three months.

"SEC. 26. Every person not being a qualified voter according to the organic law and the laws of this Territory, who shall vote at any election within this Territory, knowing that he is not entitled to vote, shall be adjudged guilty of a misdemeanor, and punished by fine not exceeding fifty dollars.

"SEC. 27. Any person who designedly gives a printed or written ticket to any qualified voter of this Territory, containing the written or printed names of persons for whom said voter does not design to vote, for the purpose of causing such voter to poll his vote contrary to his own wishes, shall, on conviction, be adjudged guilty of a misdemeanor, and punished by fine not exceeding five hundred dollars, or by imprisonment in the county jail not exceeding three months, or by both such fine and imprisonment.

"Sec. 28. Any person who shall cause to be printed and circulated, or who shall circulate, any false and fraudulent tickets, which upon their face appear to be designed as a fraud upon voters, shall, upon conviction, be punished by fine not exceeding five hundred dollars, or by imprisonment in the county jail not exceeding three months, or by both such fine and imprisonment.

"This act to take effect and be in force from and after its passage."—Chap. 52, p. 281.

Are not these provisions ample to secure a full and fair expression of the popular will in the choice of those who shall make laws for them, or to change and alter any obnoxious ones that may now be in force? What objection is there to it? The only one I have heard is, that another clause denies the right of suffrage to those who may be guilty of a violation of the fugitive slave law, and requires a voter, on being challenged, to purge himself by what is called the "test oath." This is the provision to which the gentleman from Vermont [Mr. Meacham] alluded the other day, I suppose, when he applied to it the term "scandalous." But, sir, I do not see how that gentleman and his friends generally can object strongly even to that feature, since their vote, two days ago, upon the bill introduced by the gentleman from Indiana, [Mr. Dunn.] That bill expressly affirms the fugitive slave law, notwithstanding all that has been said by them against it, and their denunciations of those by whose votes it was passed. In order to get a restoration of the Missouri restriction over Kansas, this side of the House voted for this very fugitive slave law; and nothing but a "*pair*" prevented the gentleman from Vermont [Mr. Meacham] from voting for it himself. Here is a clause, for which all on this side of the House voted:

"*And provided further*, That any person lawfully held to service in any other State or Territory of the United States, and escaping into either the Territory of Kansas or Nebraska, may be reclaimed and removed to the person or place where such service is due, under any law of the United States which shall be in force upon the subject."

This is an indorsement in express terms of the fugitive slave law, as it now exists upon the statute-book, for which I say all on this side of the House voted a few days ago.

Mr. LEITER. I did not vote for that provision.

Mr. STEPHENS. I beg the gentleman's pardon; he did vote against it, I believe.

Mr. BENNETT, of New York. The gentleman must make another exception. I did not vote for the fugitive slave provision.

Mr. STEPHENS. I believe the gentleman did not vote at all. I intended to speak only of those who did vote. The gentleman from Ohio [Mr. Leiter] is the only one on the Free-Soil side who voted against it. All the others who voted at all voted for it; and I allude to the fact to show that, for the purpose of accomplishing a favorite object, those who have been so loud in their denunciations of this law have been willing to give it their sanction. Even the senior gentleman from Ohio, [Mr. Giddings,] who some time ago arraigned his colleague, [Mr. Campbell,] the chairman of the Ways and Means Committee, for bringing forward a bill containing items of appropriation to pay officers for the discharge of their duty in the execution of this law, has, by his vote, not only sanctioned its constitutionality, but the propriety of its enforcement.

Mr. GIDDINGS. Will the gentleman from Georgia allow me to ask him a question? I understand he is in favor of the fugitive slave law; but I ask him whether he voted for the fugitive slave law to which he alludes, the other day?

Mr. STEPHENS. I did not.

Mr. GIDDINGS. Then the gentleman and I disagree.

Mr. STEPHENS. Yes, we disagree in many things, but not on that point in that bill, if the gentleman was really in favor of what he voted for. The gentleman voted for the bill, I suppose, notwithstanding it contained the fugitive slave clause, because it contained an arbitrary and absolute restriction upon the *free will* of the *free white men* in Kansas. It was upon that point we disagreed. The fugitive slave law is already in force in that Territory by the original Kansas bill, for which I voted. But how can that gentleman and others, who gave the vote they did the other day, ever hereafter raise their voices against the *constitutionality* of this law, and in denunciation of those who voted for it in 1850? I recollect a member from Michigan, (Mr. Buel,) who was literally run down in his State for voting for it at that time. Pictures were got up, I was told, representing him with a slaveholder in pursuit of his fugitives. He was beaten before the people in his election for giving that vote. Perhaps some one who aided in that defeat is present. If so, and if he was in his place and voted two days ago, he reaffirmed by his vote the very same law. Let this be made known to his constituents. It is but due to the character and worth of a noble and true man, who fell a victim to the Moloch of party in the discharge of a public duty, and in the maintenance of his constitutional obligations.

But, sir, the point I was on is this: How can gentlemen raise such objections to that feature in the Kansas election law, which denies the right of suffrage to those who are guilty of a violation of a statute of the United States, which they, by their votes, have affirmed shall subject them to the pains and penalties of felony? Crimes of certain grades, in many of the States, deprive men of the right of voting. Why may not felony in Kansas be a disqualification as well as anywhere else? Why not leave this matter to a majority of the honest people in the Territory to settle for themselves at the next election? The reason, sir, is obvious. The party to which I have alluded are opposed to the principle of the people in each State and community attending to their own internal affairs, and of allowing those in other States and communities to do the same. All our American systems rest upon this principle; yet they are opposed to it. Men in Massachusetts, New York, and Ohio, are not content with looking after the well-being of their own States, but they wish to set themselves up as supervisors, legislators, and rulers of the people in other places beyond their jurisdiction. And these are the men who are so constantly *prating* about the slave power—its aggressions, its insolence, and its dictation. When, sir—when did the slave power ever assume such insolence, put on such arrogance, use such dictation, or claim such prerogatives, as this class of men do in this instance? When did southern statesmen ever seek to impose their institutions upon any other State or Territory? I know it is said that they have endeavored to extend slavery by Congress.

The gentleman from Indiana [Mr. CUMBACK] the other day said the object of the Kansas bill was to make Kansas a slave State by act of Congress. No such thing, sir. The object of the Kansas bill was neither to make it a slave State nor a free State; but, after taking off the restriction of 1820, to leave that matter without any interference, dictation, or control on the part of Congress to the people there to settle for themselves, subject only to the Constitution of the United States. The object is clearly set forth in the bill itself. Here are its words:

"That the Constitution and all laws of the United States, which are not locally inapplicable, shall have the same force and effect in the said Territory of Kansas as elsewhere within the United States, except the eighth section of the 'Act preparatory to the admission of Missouri into the Union,' approved March 6, 1820, which, being inconsistent with the principle of non-intervention by Congress with slavery in the States and Territories, as recognized by the legislation of 1850, commonly called the compromise measures, is hereby declared inoperative and void; it being the true intent and meaning of this act not to legislate slavery into any Territory or State, nor to exclude it therefrom, but to leave the people thereof perfectly free to form and regulate their domestic institutions in their own way, subject only to the Constitution of the United States."

The difference between southern statesmen and northern Free-Soilers upon this subject is, that the former are willing, and ever have been, to leave the question of the domestic institutions in the new States to the people to settle for themselves; while the latter are seeking to mold and fashion them according to their peculiar prejudices. All that the South asked in the annexation of Texas, and all the guarantee she got was, simply, that the people in certain States, hereafter to be formed out of Texas, might come into the Union either with or without slavery, as the people may determine for themselves. This is what Free-Soilers call an aggression of the slave power. We at the South consider it nothing but the establishment of the great principle of self-government which was the germ of the American Revolution. Free-Soilers hold the position towards the Territories and new States, which Lord North and his ministry in the British Parliament did, towards the colonies. He and they, in adhering to their policy of governing the colonies in all cases whatsoever, severed one empire. It may be that their imitators on this continent, by pursuing a similar policy, may sever a far more glorious, prosperous, and happy Confederacy of States. Southern statesmen on this question occupy the grounds of the old Whigs, the old Democrats, and the old Republicans, of the days of the Revolution. They say it is not only unjust, but anti-republican, for the Representatives on this floor from the various States of the Union, to attempt, arbitrarily, to impose laws and institutions upon the people of the distant Territories, who have no representation by votes upon this floor.

When I addressed this House some time ago, I called attention to some remarks made by Mr. John Quincy Adams, at Pittsburg, in November, 1843, upon the subject of abolishing slavery in this District. These remarks are pertinent to the present question. His anti-slavery sentiments were quite as strong, perhaps, as those of any man now present; but he was opposed to the abolition of slavery in this District by Congress, because it was anti-republican. These are his words:

"As to the abolition of slavery in the District of Columbia, I have said that I was opposed to it—not because I have any doubts of the power of Congress to abolish slavery in the District, for I have none. But I regard it as *a violation of republican principles* to enact laws at the petition of *one people* which are to operate upon *another people against their consent.*"

Mr. Adams said it was a "*violation of republican principles* to enact laws at the petition of *one people* which are to operate upon *another people against their consent;*" and for the same reason I say to you, who have assumed the title of Republicans, you violate every principle consecrated by the name you bear, by attempting to force institutions upon the people of Kansas against their consent. If a majority there see fit to assign the negro the same condition he occupies in the southern States, let them do it. If a majority of them shall prefer that he shall be an outcast amongst them, without the franchise of a freeman, or the protection of a master, as he is in many States of the Union—a vagabond, in a worse condition than that of Cain—for he had a mark on him that no man should hurt him—let them so determine. This is our position.

Mr. STANTON. Does the gentleman hold that the Territorial Legislatures have power to exclude slavery?

Mr. STEPHENS. I say that, if Congress has the power, so has the Territorial Legislature. The gentleman, I believe, holds that Congress has the power, I do not; and consequently I do not hold that the Territorial Legislatures can rightfully exclude slavery. I hold that the public domain being public property, purchased by the common blood and common treasure of all, should be left free and open for settlement and colonization equally by the citizens of all the States alike until they come to form their State constitution; but I repeat what I have said before, that if a majority of the people of the Territory, upon a fair expression of the popular will in due form of law, shall decide against slavery, I am willing to abide by that determination. Now is the gentleman willing to do this? He is silent. By his votes he has said that he is unwilling to do it. That is the difference between us.

Now, I say, again, that southern statesmen have never asked Congress to impose their institutions upon an unwilling people. They have always believed in the ability and capacity of the men of their own race to govern themselves wisely, and for the best interests of themselves and their posterity, in each State and community for itself. The party to which I have alluded is arrayed against this principle. It is nothing but a shoot, a sprout, a *rattoon* from the buried roots of the old Rufus-King, Hartford-convention party, which was always against this principle of self-government—of popular sovereignty—upon which all our American institutions rest.

Mr. GIDDINGS. The gentleman from Georgia says that the South has always held to the capability of man for self-government. I would inquire whether it is a part of that self-government to flog their slaves?

Mr. STEPHENS. It is a part of all kinds of government to punish offenders, whether white or black, bond or free. This may be done, according to the grade of the offense, either by flogging, imprisoning, branding, or hanging, as the law-making power may determine. The principle of self-government which I advocate applies to men of our own race—free white men. I do not believe that the African race is capable of self-government, either in the South or North. They never have been from the earliest days of history. In the gentleman's own State they are not acknowledged to be within the principle. They are not acknowledged as equals either socially or politically. They take no part in the government under which they live. Whether they are flogged there I do not know, but great numbers of them are in jails, according to the census. The constitutions of most of what are called "*free States*" in this Union show that they are not even there considered capable of self-government.

Mr. GIDDINGS. Does the gentleman believe that the Africans who captured American Christians, and made slaves of them, were capable of self-government?

Mr. STEPHENS. They were of a different race. I allude to the black, woolly-headed negroes. [Laughter.]

Mr. GIDDINGS. The gentleman knows there are descendants of Jefferson and others here whose blood is tinctured with that of the African. Now, how much African blood must they have to be incapable of self-government?

Mr. STEPHENS. One eighth part or degree by our law. [Renewed laughter.] Has the gentleman any further question? Now, sir, notwithstanding we at the South hold this incapacity in the negro of self-government, and notwithstanding we deny him social and political equality, I maintain that he is better off there, better provided for, better taken care of, and is more prosperous and happy in his condition amongst us, than he is in any other part of the world—not excepting the gentleman's own State. This the last census showed. The negroes with us, sir, even under the restraints of power over them, enjoy not only more comforts of life, but more rational liberty than they do anywhere else. They enjoy quite as much as they are fit for. All rational liberty is founded on restraints. "Bonds make free." To constitutional and legal bonds we are all indebted for whatever liberty any of us enjoy. Liberty without bonds of some sort is nothing but licentiousness. And those bonds in which the negro is placed with us are only such as are necessary for the largest liberty he is capable of enjoying. Dependence and subordination is his natural and normal condition; but socially, the position of this people is better at the South than it is at the North, so far as my observation has extended. At the North they are excluded, and shunned as a leprous *caste.* At the South they look to their masters as guardians for protection, and they are treated with that respect and kindness due to their condition. But, sir, I must return from this digression.

I have shown you the utter groundlessness of the assumed facts upon which the first resolution before us, proposing to vote the sitting Delegate out of his seat, is founded. I have also shown that the real and true reason of this unheard-of proceeding is not the one assigned, but that it is to be found in the purposes of that great sectional, abolition party, which is now seeking to govern as they please, not only the common Territories, but the whole fifteen southern States of this Union.

It is now for me briefly—for I have but a few moments of time left—to allude to the second resolution before us, which is even more monstrous than the first. This proposes to assign a seat on this floor to Andrew H. Reeder, as a Delegate from Kansas, not by virtue of his being entitled to it, but because it is supposed there is a majority here willing to do it. It is not pretended that he has the shadow of a claim of legal right to it. The majority of the Committee of Elections who have reported this resolution, do not venture to say that he is *entitled* to a seat. The resolution is an anomaly of its character. It simply says:

Resolved, That Andrew H. Reeder be admitted to a seat on this floor as a Delegate from the Territory of Kansas.

He presents no certificate of election, or credentials from any quarter, except the report of the Kansas committee. This committee, on page 67, say, "That Andrew H. Reeder received a greater number of votes of resident citizens than John W. Whitfield for Delegate." This is his whole case, and this statement by them is unsustained by proof. The majority of the Committee of Elections have adopted it; and I now call upon the chairman, [Mr. WASHBURN, of Maine,] who will conclude this argument, to show the evidence upon which it is founded. I make the demand of him in the presence of the House and the country. He cannot respond to it; for this is one of the bold assertions of this investigating committee, which there is no testimony to warrant. Reeder was not a candidate at the election when Whitfield was elected. He was not a candidate at any election held in pursuance of any legal authority. He was voted for, it is said, on the day that delegates were elected to a convention under the Topeka movement; and on page 58 of the report, there appears what is styled an abstract of the number of votes received by him; but this is nothing but a statement by the committee. There is not a particle of evidence to show where it came from, or what credit is to be given to it; and I call upon the gentleman from Ohio [Mr. SHERMAN] to show the facts upon which this statement—this abstract is based. There is not a particle of evidence in this whole volume to sustain it. The only evidence showing the number of votes that Reeder got is to be found on pages 670, 682, and 683. On page 670 it appears that he received at the third and seventh precincts of the third district, 24 votes. On page 682, it appears that he received at the house of Richard J. Farqua, in the sixth district, 12 votes; and on page 683, it appears that he received at Columbia precinct, in the same district, 20 votes—making 56 in all, and all told! If there is any evidence, or any proof that he received another vote in the Territory, I call upon the gentleman to point it out. If there be any such, it has escaped me; while it appears from a copy of the official records, to be found on pages 45 and 46, that Whitfield received upwards of 2,700 votes. How, then, could the Kansas committee say that Reeder received a larger number of the votes of resident citizens than Whitfield did? And yet this is one of the incontrovertible facts which the Committee of Elections say have been established by the proof.

Mr. Speaker, I can say no more upon the subject. If Whitfield is to be ousted because he was not elected in pursuance of any valid law, upon what principle can Reeder be put in by this House, when in his case there was neither law nor votes. There is but one principle upon which it can be done, and that is, "*Sic volo, sic jubeo*"—I so will it, and I so order it. It is the principle of all tyrannies, and the beginning of all usurpations; but I will not permit myself to believe that this House will commit such an outrage. I will not believe it until I see th perpetration of the deed.

KANSAS—THE TERRITORIES.

SPEECH

OF

HON. LEWIS CASS, OF MICHIGAN,

DELIVERED

IN THE SENATE OF THE UNITED STATES, MAY 12-13, 1856.

The Senate, as in committee of the whole, resumed the consideration of the bill (S. No. 172) to authorize the people of the Territory of Kansas to form a constitution and State government, preparatory to their admission into the Union, when they have the requisite population.

Mr. CASS proceeded to address the Senate. He said:

Mr. PRESIDENT: The bill under discussion relating to Kansas presents itself in a double aspect to the consideration of Congress. It involves not only the present condition of that Territory, and the measures proper to be taken with reference to it, but it involves also the general principles connected with the Territories of the United States, and the extent, as well of their rights, as of the constitutional power of Congress over them. I propose to submit to the Senate some remarks upon both these topics, but principally upon the latter—not only on account of the importance of the subject, but also on account of the many and discordant views, and the elaborate discussions, to which it has given rise in this body, and in the co-ordinate branch of the national legislature I shall commence with the relations between the United States and their Territories, but shall endeavor first to redeem from obloquy a cherished American principle, which lies at the foundation of free institutions.

This principle has been designated as popular sovereignty, squatter sovereignty, territorial sovereignty, and marked by other sneering terms, used contemptuously as nicknames, rather than descriptively as definitions, and which has served to cast reproach, and often designedly, upon a great element of human freedom, and to bring it into discredit.

This system of tactics originated during the progress of the controversy concerning the admission of California, when it was contended that the government established there in self-defence, by the people, ought not to be recognised; and, among other reasons, because they were squatters—that was the cant phrase—and did not own the land: as though American citizens, borne by the accidents of life to a part of the national domain without the limits of an organized State or Territory, are destitute of all rights, and, in the absence of established law, can establish no law for themselves; and, as a corollary, that the only true sovereignty is landlord sovereignty. Sir, this is strange doctrine for this great republic, boasting of its political equality, and for this middle of the nineteenth century, boasting of its political progress and intelligence. It carries us back to the worst periods of the world, when man was nothing, and lands, and trees, and rocks, were everything.

On a former occasion I adverted to the happy manner in which this artificial and unjust state of society was ridiculed by Dr. Franklin, in one of his practical apologues, more powerful than argument; but it is so appropriate to this discussion, that I am tempted again to call it into the service of human rights. A property qualification is required (said the American parable-maker) to entitle any one to enjoy political privileges. To-day a man possesses a jackass, and is therefore a voter. To-morrow the ass dies, and the vote dies with him. To whom did the vote belong, to the ass or to his owner? I am not political casuist enough to answer the question; I leave its solution to him who believes in the necessary connexion between the money-box and the ballot-box. One hundred thousand American citizens found themselves without law in California, soon after its cession to the United States. Congress refused or neglected to make any arrangement for their government, leaving them exposed to the terrible evils of anarchy. By all the laws of God and nature they were justified, as a measure of self-defence, which is as incident to communities as to individuals, in providing for their own safety—existence, indeed—by the institution of a government. They did so, and came here for admission, and were met by reproaches, and harsh epithets, and delays, almost refusal, and were characterized as landless and lawless adventurers. That they were landless was neither their crime nor their fault; that they did not continue lawless, they owed to their own firmness and intelligence, not to our justice or sympathy. They did, as the self-exiled adventurers had done centuries before them, when they landed upon this continent, and "combined themselves together (these are memorable and historic words) in a civil body-politic;" and never did human government rest upon a truer basis than did these political systems in the infancy of the settlements upon the coasts of the Atlantic and the Pacific oceans.

The misapprehension or misrepresentation, which has prevailed respecting the doctrine of those who maintain that American citizens, thrown as waifs upon an unoccupied strand, have a right, in the absence of law, to provide it for themselves, and have at all times other natural rights, of which they cannot be deprived without their own consent, except by the authority of the constitution of the United States, serves to show that strong prejudices have been at work, mingling themselves with the investigation of this interesting subject. The proposition that our citizens are not political slaves, and have rights which Congress neither gave nor can take away, was first called squatter sovereignty by way of derision, and yet receives the same appellation, but now in sober earnest; and if not with the purpose, certainly with the effect, of identifying the name with absurd or dangerous doctrines. I heard it said here, after the imposition of this *sobriquet*, that squatter sovereignty was a claim to divest Congress of its rights over the public land. Six years have passed away, and no such pretension has been advanced; and he who should seriously advocate it would hardly need the certificate of a physician to prove his qualification for a mad-house.

This principle of self-government is confounded with revolution, and it is charged with making that extraordinary remedy an ordinary legal right. Sir, no true believer in the doctrine, that American citizens possess rights in the Territories, includes in that proposition the right of revolution. That is an extraordinary resource against oppression, belonging to all political communities, and to be resorted to by each at its discretion, and upon its responsibility. Free as our government is, I can foresee cases, not probable, scarcely possible even, in which this great measure of self-defence might become necessary and justifiable. If a Territory, having passed legally into a State, should apply for admission into the Union, and the application should be rejected, unless with the imposition of conditions destructive of its true equality—such as a requisition to exclude slavery, or to do any other act not prescribed by the constitution—a State, under these circumstances, would have a right, in the words of the Declaration of Independence, to *dissolve the political bands which connect it with an unjust government*, and to claim admittance, as a distinct member, into the family of nations.

It seems also to be supposed by many that the advocate of squatter or popular sovereignty, assuming the name as an established one—and for myself I shall not quarrel with it, considering the doctrine so good that it could survive a much more powerful assault than this baptismal one—advocates also the right of the people of a Territory to change the government at their pleasure; and I have heard it maintained that the recent attempt to establish a State government in Kansas must be supported by every advocate of this doctrine, if he would preserve his own consistency. Sir, I believe in no such pretension. I never advanced or defended it, nor shall I defend it now. Although cases have occurred where the measures for the establishment of a State government have had their initiation in the local legislature, yet they originated in, and were justified by, peculiar circumstances. But an attempt to change the government by a partial popular interference, without the intermediation of Congress, or of the Territorial legislature, finds no support in any views I have ever presented upon this subject. And the dangers attending the public tranquillity, which must necessarily accompany a voluntary effort like that among an excited people, divided in opinion, are enough to deter me from favoring it.

In brief, sir, this is my creed upon this subject:

1. I believe that American citizens have rights in the Territories, whether they own land or not.

2. Those rights are independent of Congress, and neither derived from nor granted by that body.

3 It is the duty of Congress to organize governments for the Territories; and if that duty is refused, it is the right of the people to do it for themselves.

4. The change from a Territorial to a State government should not be undertaken without the vote of the majority of the people, authorized by law to be taken; for without such authority it is obvious that the whole transaction becomes a spontaneous one, which will be supported by its partisans only, and in which those who are opposed to it will take no part, and the result, therefore, will be no indication of the true views of the people. And the foundation will be laid for bitter dissensions, and the resisting and the intruding governments will each find partisans and enemies.

Sovereignty is, in no proper acceptation of the word, applicable to the Territories of the United States. They are dependencies of the general government, and possess no attribute of independence.

But the question is, what political relation do they bear to that government, and what powers can it constitutionally exercise over their inhabitants? Are these inhabitants destitute of all rights, and subject to the uncontrolled will of Congress? And can that body "sell them into slavery," as coolly asserted in the House of Representatives by a member from Indiana?

Those who maintain that the people of the Territories have certain inalienable rights, maintain just what our fathers contended for, first by argument, and then by arms, in opposition to a similar assumption of uncontrolled power of legislation by the British Parliament, which declares that HIS MAJESTY IN PARLIAMENT HAS THE RIGHT BY STATUTE TO BIND THE COLONIES IN ALL CASES WHATSOEVER.

What rights have the people of the Territories?

They possess all those natural rights, "written,"—as Lord Chatham said, when he nobly advocated their existence and obligation in the House of Lords—"written in the great volume of nature," which are not taken from them, and intrusted to Congress by the constitution of the United States.

The inquiry, then, is, not into the rights of the people, but into the constitutional power of Congress to interfere with them; and this, too, under a government not only of limited but of granted powers, and which can exercise no authority not conferred by express provision, or by *necessary and proper* implication, for these are the words of the BOOK.

And still more: a government whose very corner-stone is the inseparable connexion between power and representation, and which seeks to extend its jurisdiction—and one, too, which penetrates into the most hidden recesses of private and domestic life, over distant communities, which have no participation in this far away legislation—no means to keep a foreign law-giver from its hearthstone.

What power, then, has the federal legislature over the territories of the United States? To THE LAW AND TO THE TESTIMONY.

The word "territory" is not to be found in the federal constitution as applicable to a political community. It occurs there but once, and in the following clause:

> "The Congress shall have power to dispose of and make all needful rules and regulations concerning the territory or other property of the United States."

(Not shall have power to make laws to govern people)

The Supreme Court has decided, and the meaning is undeniable by any one possessing but a slight knowledge of the laws of English syntax, even without such decision, that "the term 'territory,' as here used, is merely descriptive of one branch of property, and is equivalent to the word 'land;' and Congress has the same power over it as over every other property of the United States."

The clause, by this construction, may be thus read: The Congress shall have power to dispose of and make all needful rules and regulations concerning the *land* and other property of the United States. Here is no grant of political power, no jurisdiction over the lives and persons and property of American citizens, but only an authority to take care of and sell the public land—such an authority as a land-owner may properly exercise. If the word "territory" means a political community, and not land merely, it follows that, as Congress may dispose of it, they may sell every territory, people and all; and this, too, though the whole land may have been previously disposed of to purchasers, and not an acre left to the United States. And this tremendous, unlimited power over American citizens, involving all the issues of life and death, is derived from a simple grant to regulate and sell land. And this regulation must be "needful," says the constitution. Needful for what? For the regulation and sale of the property. Not needful for the constitution of the United States, nor for any of the ends for which that compact was formed—such as the general welfare, the establishment of justice, and others, as Mr. Adams contended some years since; for such a construction is not only in the very face of any just rule of interpretation, but it would prostrate the barriers of the constitution, leaving all powers to be considered needful which any party might desire to exercise. This is the very consequence foreseen and foretold by the legislature of Virginia in their memorable resolutions of 1799, as the result of this indefensible latitude of construction: "That it would have the inadmissible effect of rendering nugatory or improper every part of the constitution."

And, in this connexion, I may ask, what has the relation of husband and wife, or of parent and child, or of master and servant, to do with the property of the general government? Or how does that government acquire any jurisdiction over these conditions of society, under the pretence that it is needful for the management of their property? And I may ask as much respecting a note of hand, or any of the infinite variety of the concerns of life, for the protection of which governments are instituted. Can construction be further construed?

I desire to know, if this clause is the foundation of the authority exercised by Congress over the Territories, how it happens that this authority has been exercised over thousands of square miles in the various Territories, not one foot of which was ever the "territory"—meaning the property—of the United States; as in the State of Ohio, when a part of the Northwestern Territory, over a superficial extent equal to one-fourth part of the State, being the Connecticut western reserve, extending one hundred and twenty miles east and west, and the Virginia military reservation, embracing the whole country between the Sciota and the Little Miami rivers, both of which districts of country were reserved by those States respectively, when they made their cessions, and never belonged, not the smallest portion of them, to the United States; and in the State of Tennessee, when the Southwestern Territory, over more than seven-eighths of its area, disposed of by the State of North Carolina before its act of cession, and never conveyed to the United States; and over vast regions in Florida, Louisiana, Arkansas, Missouri, and almost every other territory where rights to land had been acquired by individuals before the cession of the country, and were held independent of the United States. As in these cases there was no "territory," or land, to dispose of or regulate, there was nothing on which the constitutional provision could operate. And the inquiry is equally pertinent as to the continuance of this power after the public land *is disposed of*—how it carried with it legislative authority over the extensive districts—sold to the Ohio Company, and to John C. Symmes, in that part of the Northwestern Territory, now the State of Ohio, before the general government went into operation; and how it happens that, when a tract is sold and thus ceases to make a part of the public domain, the power of government over it does not cease, if that power is derived from the constitutional authority to regulate, *not private*, but public property? In such a case, the power passes with the object; and this clause is just as applicable to private property in the State of New York as to private property in a political Territory.

I have heretofore shown, upon this floor, that there were twelve principles or provisions of the constitution from which this uncontrolled power of congressional legislation over the people of the Territories is deduced. I have no purpose to re-examine them upon this occasion, and shall do little more than enumerate them, adding three auxiliary powers since discovered; and I do so merely to call attention to this multitude of derivative clauses, each with its advocates, as a significant fact, furnishing a powerful presumption against the existence of a despotic authority—a foundling wandering about the constitution in search of its true parentage.

These assumed provisions and principles—for there are both—are as follows:

1. The land regulating and selling power, to which I have already referred.
2. The war and treaty making power.
3. The right to admit new States.
4. The implication clause of the constitution, attaching itself to the right to sell the public land.
5. The rights of ownership.
6. The right and duty of settlement.
7. The attribute of sovereignty.
8. The nature of government.
9. Nationality.
10. The principle of agency and trust.
11. That provision of the constitution which declares that "all debts contracted or engagements entered into before the adoption of the present constitution, shall be as valid against the United States under this constitution as under the confederation."
12. There are those who admit that the ordinance of 1787 was "passed by the old Congress of the confederation, without authority from the States;" and among these was Mr. Adams, late President of the United States, who contended, not that the clause respecting debts and engagements confirmed the former, but that it "had been tacitly confirmed by the adoption of the present constitution of the United States, and the authority given to Congress to make needful rules and regulations for the territory." Surely it cannot be necessary to investigate such a foundation of power under a government which derives all its authority, not merely from express grants, but which is still further restricted in its operation by the emphatic declaration that "the powers not delegated to the United States by the constitution, nor prohibited by it to the States, are reserved to the States respectively, or to the people." Never was the abuse, I might almost say the use, of power more jealously guarded; and we yet here find the sixth Chief Magistrate, in the very infancy of the Republic, maintaining, as a ground of congressional jurisdiction, that its exercise had been "tacitly confirmed" by the adoption of the constitution, and by the authority to regulate and sell the public land; not by a grant of power, but by the usurpation of it—by "tacitly" assuming that the engagement clause confirms the authority, while expressly admitting that it does not. I leave, without further comment, this rule of interpretation to those who can find either wisdom or safety in its application.

I have said that three new sources of power have recently been discovered to justify congressional interposition, and I now add that these are:

13. The right and duty of guardianship.
14. The transmissible power, by which the constitution of another country is substituted for that of the United States.
15. What may be called the paternal power, which places the general government *in loco parentis*.

Mr. President, I repeat that I have no design to enter into an investigation of the reasons which are urged in support of these various derivations whence the power of government is deduced, or rather whence it is not deduced, contenting myself with leaving them where I left them upon a former occasion. I shall depart from this determination in one or two cases only, and I do this in consequence of the presentation of new views, or of views presented with new force.

The majority of the Committee on the Territories, in their recent inquiry into the true foundation of the power to establish Territorial governments, have sought it, and seem to believe they have found it, in the provision of the constitution, that "new States may be admitted by the Congress into the Union," &c. I can trace no such grant to such an authority. It proceeds upon the inadmissible pretension that the federal legislature may take any appropriate means, not merely to enable it to exercise a granted power, but to exercise an independent power over which it has no control.

Mr. President, some years since this whole subject of the right of congressional jurisdiction over the Territories was learnedly and laboriously investigated in both wings of the capitol. It was then maintained, as now, among various sources of authority, that the right to admit new States carried with it the power to establish governments. "There are two purposes for which territory is held," said one of the most able and experienced members of the Senate, "the disposition of the soil and the erection of new States. Now, the right of governing new territory is necessary to the efficient exercise of both objects." And yet one power is expressly given and the other withheld; and we are called upon to assume the latter, as if it were actually granted, for reasons as numerous almost as the speakers, but which would render a written constitution a plastic instrument, to be *formed and moulded* at the will of its creature, the legislative authority.

"The purpose," (of the right of government,) said another distinguished Senator, "is to train up a nation of freemen, and to fit them to share in the privileges of this Union." And the doctrine is pushed to as latitudinarian an extent as the loosest constructionist can desire. "Whatever," said the speaker, "is necessary to this object, Congress is authorized to do."

The majority of the Committee on Territories, and the two members of the Senate whose opinions I have quoted, equally derive the authority to govern our colonial establishments from the power to admit new States into the Union. Whether with the same views to justify the action of Congress, or, in other words, with the same views as to the connexion between the power of government and the power of admission, so as to render the former a true constitutional auxiliary of the latter, I am at a loss to determine. The senatorial predecessors of the committee, in the annunciation of the origin of the power, trace it to the duty or necessity of *training up freemen, and fitting them to share in the privileges of the Union*, and to the *training up of these infant communities under such institutions as may fit them to become members of our great confederacy*.

The following paragraph contains the position assumed and maintained by the committee; and, in whatever light it is viewed, it appears to me equally erroneous in theory and dangerous in practice:

> "Is not the organization of a Territory eminently necessary and proper as a means of enabling the people thereof to form and mould their local and domestic institutions and establish a State government under the authority of the constitution, preparatory to its admission into the Union? If so, the right of Congress to pass the organic act for the temporary government is clearly included in the provision which authorizes the admission of new States."

I do not understand these views of the committee. When analyzed, it will be found that the power of instituting a Territorial government is claimed in a double capacity—first, as a means to enable Congress to enable the people to form and mould their institutions; and, second, to establish a State government. The forming and moulding of political institutions is a figurative expression—a dangerous process of reasoning in strict investigations; but it seems here to imply their adoption, and then their change, from time to time, till the work is completed by its adaptation to the wants or will of the community. In another part of the report it is declared, that the people must be left "entirely free" in the exertion of the rights of self-government; *entirely free to regulate their domestic institutions and internal concerns in their own way*. for such is substantially the proposition. This is a full measure of self-government; and, if the doctrine is correct, whatever provision in the organic law interferes with it interferes also with the constitution, and is void. The people, therefore, upon this political theory, must be left free to regulate, "in their own way," the election of governor, the appointment of judges and other officers, and the nature and extent of their duties, as well as the system of jurisprudence, or they are deprived of this "true freedom."

Experience is certainly desirable in the work of establishing a new system of laws for a new country—a state of things designated as "preparatory" to that permanent condition which admission to the Union brings with it. How far the committee consider this chrysalis state a kind of school in which the knowledge of self-government is to be acquired does not distinctly appear; whether the people are to be enabled to form and mould their institutions with a view to their practical operation during their subordinate condition, or as a means of learning how to exercise the rights and privileges which are to become their heritage. We have seen that distinguished senators have heretofore maintained upon this floor that the last object is the one which really confers upon Congress this disputed power. And the process of the committee would seem to indicate somewhat kindred views in the application of the power, as it indicates an identity of views in its derivation. For it is worthy of observation—perhaps, indeed, a significant fact—that the protection of life and property and the preservation of order, the great objects of human governments, are not even alluded to by the committee as reasons for congressional interposition, nor is the necessity of legal organization for any such purposes sought to be derived from any express grant of power. There are those, and Judge McLean is among them, who, while they deny the authority to establish Territorial governments as directly included in the power to dispose of and regulate the public land, yet derive it as an incident from that provision, because the establishment of order among the emigrants would facilitate the sale and settlement of the land. Mr. Rhett also maintained that doctrine in the House of Representatives. But the committee, while claiming the same power, do not attempt to show in what manner it is an incident, or, in other words, how its exercise is necessary and proper to the exertion of the right to admit new States. They say, indeed, that the organization of a Territory is necessary and proper as a means of enabling the people thereof to form and mould their institutions, but there they stop. What bearing this work of *forming and moulding* has upon the act of admission, so as to render it a just incident of that great power, we may in vain search the report to discover.

The doctrine is repeated, though in somewhat different language, in another part of the report; but with the same defect in the process. We are told that "the organic act" "must leave the people entirely free to form and regulate their domestic institutions and their internal concerns in their own way," "to the end that, when they attain the requisite population and establish a State government, they may be admitted into the Union," "on an equal footing," &c. But we are not told how this "end," admission, is reached by the means indicated, the regulation of internal concerns; and I cannot supply this hiatus in the argument by maintaining that the power of government may be assumed, in order, by the establishment of law, that the prosperity of those remote communities may be promoted, and their population augmented with a view to their admission into the Union, because the adoption of such a principle might lead to very fearful consequences. It proceeds upon the assumption that Congress may, by virtue of the power to admit new States, take such measures as it may judge best calculated to facilitate their formation, and application and admission. A large discretion would be the result of the establishment of this doctrine, and how it might be used or abused it were presumptuous to foretell.

The right to exclude slavery from each Territory, as an avowed means of promoting its growth and prosperity, would soon find friends and advocates in Congress, and perhaps, ere long, enough of them to make that measure a permanent one; and, as it is, the theory of the committee places the denial of this power of exclusion upon no very safe foundation; for it is urged upon the ground that the State must be admitted into the Union upon an equal footing with the original States. The proposition is incontrovertible; but its application to the intermediate condition of Territorial existence is not so clear. It would render all previous congressional interference void upon the formation of a new State; all prohibitions of slavery would fall before the will of the people. But if the true reason for the restraint upon the action of Congress is given by the Committee—to wit: equal admission after the formation of a State constitution—it is difficult to see how this condition of things is to operate until the arrival of the period of political sovereignty. That the exercise of such an act of intermediate authority might have the effect to encourage the settlement of the country by a population favoring the restriction, there can be no doubt. But the question does not touch the effect upon emigration to the Territory, but upon the admission of the State. If the people composing it at the time of application for admission become free from all restraints but those imposed by the constitution upon sovereign States, then this great principle can hardly be said to have been violated, whatever circumstances may have preceded this last condition. That they are thus free is maintained, and justly, by the committee, because this equality is one of the fundamental principles of our institutions. Those who believe that civil government is essential to the new Territories, and that the right of Congress to establish it—the duty rather—is the result of necessity, whether arising from implication or otherwise, hold opinions which are free from this difficulty and danger, as Congress can exert its power no further than the necessity extends, and cannot reach the domestic relations of the people. In fact, if the view of the committee be the true one, it is not easy to prescribe boundaries to congressional legislation.

I have already said that the power to establish these temporary governments was not claimed by the committee as a means of securing public order; nor, if it were so claimed, do I see what effect such a measure could have upon the power of admission, which does not come into operation till the temporary organization is terminated, unless, indeed, the inadmissible one to which I have alluded, of controlling the condition of the country.

As to the exercise of political rights by any portion of the American people as a means of improving their capacity for self-government, and of fitting them for any change before them, it is a principle of organization unknown to our institutions. Governments are not established as schools, where "free men are to be trained," and "fitted to become members of our great confederacy." And nothing but an entire misapprehension of the true functions of the general government could lead to this fundamental error, as to the nature of its just operation. This whole subject has been made the victim of false analogies instead of the object of constitutional inquiries; nor has the heresy been more prevalent in any branch of the controversy than in the derivation of the power of government from the necessity of political instruction. Our Territories are settled by our citizens, who all their lives have enjoyed the privilege of self-government. A man knows as much in a Territory as in a State, and is just as capable of discharging his political duties. He does not pass the boundary to learn the lesson of a freeman, but he passes it in order, by a life of industry and enterprise, to improve his condition, and to grow with the growth of the country.

I have said that the power of congressional government is claimed by the committee, not only as a means of enabling the people to form and mould their institutions, but also as a means of establishing a State government, preparatory to admission into the Union. I am here at fault again, and it is as to the "necessary and proper" connection between the institution of a government and its avowed purpose, which is to justify the action of Congress—namely, the establishment of a State government. Assuming that the power to establish States is among the granted powers which carry "necessary and proper" incidents with them, is the machinery of Territorial government an incident necessary to the exercise of this power by Congress? I confine the inquiry to this single purpose, leaving out of view the necessity of civil organization for the wants of society, because the latter is ignored by the committee, and the former constitutes the only ground on which they place this congressional right of interposition. I repeat, is the means constitutionally adapted to the end? The postulate is, that Congress may establish Territorial governments, in order to enable the people to establish State governments. But how? The only means known to our system is by the election of conventions. And how are these bodies to be elected? Cases have occurred, though they are the exceptions, which have been justified by the circumstances, in which the local authority has taken the initiative in calling conventions But this is not a proceeding which the committee would sanction as an established one. The "means" to which they refer is the action of Congress authorizing the election and the convocation of a convention. And what, then, is left to the agency of a Territorial government in this change of political condition? The power to petition Congress, or, instead of that measure, the power to call upon the people to do so, either by vote or by direct application. And this interference, which is an assumed authority, exhausts the whole power of these Territorial legislatures. And we are now brought to this inquiry, is this intermediation, confined to this single object, such a necessary means as to justify the creation of a Territorial government with a jurisdiction extending over all the concerns of life? Why is any intermediation necessary? Why cannot Congress exercise the power itself, if it possess it, and receive the application of the people, and then provide for the election of a convention? Or, why not make early and previous provision, by which the wishes of the people can at any time be ascertained, thus rendering any other interference, either general or local, unnecessary?

This principle was once adopted by the Congress of the confederation. It was in 1784, in an ordinance, the predecessor of that of 1787, and in some respects it superior, for it avoided the contested points which have made the latter a subject of long and bitter controversy; such as the articles of compact and the want of power to regulate governments, &c. It authorized the people upon any Indian cession to establish temporary governments for themselves; and it went still further, indicating the course for the Congress of the constitution to take, proper, not only in itself, but also, if all its authority over this subject is derived, as the committee intimates, from a power to enable the people of a Territory to establish a State government That seems to have been the opinion in 1784 of the Congress of the confederation respecting the extent of its own authority. The ordinance provided:

> "That when any such State shall have acquired twenty thousand free inhabitants, on giving due proof thereof to Congress, they shall receive from them authority, with appointments of time and place, to call a convention of representatives to establish a permanent constitution and government for themselves."

If, then, Congress has the constitutional power to enable the people of a Territory to establish a State government, it can exert that power without intermediation, and no other agency is required for that purpose. Still less is it necessary, or constitutional—if other means are resorted to—that they should far exceed the necessity which can alone call them into being. If Territorial governments are required only as the means of enabling the people to apply to Congress to call a convention, how happens it that such governments are not confined to the object of their institution? Judge McLean lays it down as a principle—

> "That implied powers can only be exercised in carrying into effect a specific power; and this implication is limited to such measures as shall be appropriate to the object. This is an admitted and safe rule of construction. It is believed to be the only one which has been sanctioned by statesmen and jurists. Powers exercised beyond this are not derived from the constitution, but must depend upon unlimited discretion, and this is despotism."

This principle, in effect, receives the sanction of the committee, who admit that the organic law, deriving its validity from the power to admit new States, must be exercised with reference only to that end, and that "beyond that point the authority cannot extend." Then, sir, the constitutional power is to admit new States The necessary means, for using the implied power, is an authority to enable the people to establish a State government; or, in other words, to form a State, by providing for the calling of a convention. What, then, becomes of the principle of limitation laid down by Judge McLean, and by the committee, that an implied power must be exercised, so far only as is necessary to carry into effect a granted power?—a principle by which the committee except from the jurisdiction of Congress the subject of slavery, and which, if carried to its legitimate conclusion, would except every power but the one which touches the convocation of a convention. How, then, are all the issues of life and death, all the social and political relations, all the objects for which governments are instituted—how are they brought within the jurisdiction of a local legislature, instituted for a single constitutional purpose, and that purpose connected with the action of the people in the formation of a new State? Is not this the "diffusive and ductile interpretation" of Mr Madison? Does the power to admit new States create, in the words of Mr. Jefferson, a necessity, "invincible by any other means" than the complete organization of Territorial governments? I content myself with proposing these questions asked by two of the great expounders of constitutional law, avoiding the embarrassment of answering them.

Mr. President, the Senator to whom I first referred, as tracing the right to establish Territorial governments to the power to admit new States, calls the act of admission the *erection* of a new State This is a grave error, and certainly much of the reasoning of the committee indicates their participation in it. The erection or formation of new States, and their admission into the Union, are separate and independent acts; the former belonging to the people, the latter to Congress. Congress may rightfully pass any laws, *necessary and proper*—these are the words on the TABLET, for carrying into effect its granted power. What is the granted power touching new States? It is to admit them, and by virtue of that high trust to make legislative provision for all the measures which justly belong to that step in the career of self-government, such, perhaps, as ascertaining the wishes of the inhabitants, the taking of a census, and other proceedings having a direct bearing upon the act of admission. Congress cannot precede its exercise, for an almost indefinite period of time, by a series of measures relating not to the act itself, but to the government and institutions of a country over which the national legislation has no just control. Does not such a boundless latitude of construction, to quote the expressive language of Mr. Jefferson, "swallow up all the delegated powers," and leave to Congress to substitute its own will, under the name of discretion, for all the safeguards of the constitution? I find myself no clear power even to pass laws for the assembling of conventions, but it has often been done, though not always; and as its exercise calls for no interference with the rights of the people, but is designed to aid them in their progress to State sovereignty, I am not disposed to censure the practice.

In reviewing the history of our legislation over the Territories, it is obvious that the moulding of their own institutions by the people, whether with a view to knowledge or to admission, has constituted neither the motive for the action of Congress, nor the object it has sought to attain. It is numbers, not political intelligence, which have regulated the entrance of States into the Union. When the system was commenced each State had one vote in Congress; and there would have been neither justice nor policy in permitting these small communities, with their sparse population, to take their places as coequals in the confederacy. They had, therefore, to occupy subordinate positions, till their numbers should enable them to share the duties and expenses, as well as the rights of the Union. If this condition is considered a school for the acquisition of political knowledge, to "fit them to become members of our great confederacy," then there was much injustice done to some of the scholars, or they did great injustice to themselves, as is shown by their respective periods of tuition; for while the school of Ohio, under the name of a Territorial government, continued fourteen years, that of Tennessee occupied but six years, Louisiana seven years, and Iowa nine years; and while Alabama, the most precocious of the family, underwent but two years' "training," Michigan, it would appear, the least gifted of the sisters, required thirty years in order to be prepared for the full rights of "majority." I need not say, sir, that all this analogical illustration is a mere effort of the imagination, and that the change was the result of numbers depending, for their augmentation, upon the rapidity of emigration. And as to the agency of the people in moulding their institutions, as the foundation of civil government, the idea is a pleasant one, but it will hardly bear a close scrutiny. From the first Territorial government in 17‑7 to the last in 1854, there has not been one where the people have had the actual control of their institutions, so as to be able to "mould" them agreeably to their will. In all the earlier Territories, till within a few years indeed, there was a period called the first grade of government, when the laws were passed by the governor and judges, and during which the people had no more concern in the administration of their public affairs, executive judicial, or legislative, than they had in those of China. When the free white male population, above the age of twenty-one years, reached the number of five thousand, then a legislature was organized, consisting of a house of representatives, elected by the people, and of a council appointed by the President from a list furnished by the house.

I need not pursue this investigation to show how limited was the participation which the inhabitants had in the management of their political interests. After the cession of Louisiana an act of Congress was passed giving authority to the President, (Mr. Jefferson,) to prescribe the manner in which all powers, "civil, military, and judicial," should be exercised. A poor school this for the people, but a good opportunity for a one-man "moulding" of institutions. The power, however, could not have been in safer hands. I am well aware, sir, that these harsh examples of congressional interference settle no questions of constitutional law. I refer to the course of our legislative proceedings with relation to the Territories, to show that the reason given by the committee for the institution of these governments will not fully bear out the exercise of the authority in a single instance. Certainly a favorable change, for some time, has been going on in our system of Territorial administration. The interference of the general government has been relaxing, and the political condition of the people improving. And I am happy in being able to render a tribute of justice to the honorable Senator of Illinois, the chairman of the Committee on the Territories, by saying, that he has lent his powerful influence to these meliorations. The latest Territorial acts—those for the government of Kansas and Nebraska—introduced and most ably advocated by the Senator, are marked by this feature. They are more liberal, more just I should say, than any organic laws that preceded them. They surrender the absolute veto of the governor, and the supervisory power of legislation by Congress. But even in these, and still more in other late acts—those for the government of Oregon, New Mexico, Utah, and Washington—there are provisions incompatible with the power of the people to form and mould their institutions at their own pleasure, and which make it undeniable that some other foundation than this must be resorted to as a justification for congressional action. In fact, it is difficult to see why this principle, if the true one, does not carry with it the entire right of government, uncontrolled by any external dictation; as, without exemption from interference, both in the Territory and elsewhere, the attainment of the very object alleged to be the justification for the establishment of a government may be defeated, and their institutions prevented from being formed and moulded by the people.

I propose to review, very briefly, the reasons which have recently been offered in favor of the derivation of the power of governing the Territories from that clause of the constitution which rendered the new government responsible for the engagements of the old. During the last autumn there was quite a flourish of trumpets, either at the fancied discovery of this origin of congressional authority, or at the powerful arguments by which it was vindicated. This laudation was behind the time; for years ago this branch of the subject was fully considered and fairly exhausted. But the honorable Senator from Georgia, [Mr. TOOMBS,] in his able and interesting remarks upon these Kansas difficulties, to which we all listened with so much interest and pleasure, a short time since, presented views of this question upon the interrogatory of the Senator from New Hampshire, [Mr. HALE,] which met, like everything which falls from him, the careful attention of the Senate. I think the Senator was led into error; and as that error materially affects the positions he reached, I consider it important to examine it with a view to correct some of the conclusions.

In the first place, it is evident to me, not less from the subject-matter than from the words and the context, that the phrase, "debts contracted and engagements entered into," was never intended to touch the exercise of political power.

In the next place, the "engagements" referred to in the constitution must be "valid," in order to be obligatory by virtue of this clause. This self-styled compact never had any claim to validity—none whatever; it was void from its initiation.

1. Because the Congress of the confederation never had, as Mr. Madison said, "the least color of constitutional authority to establish Territorial governments," much less to make irrepealable compacts to regulate their destiny in all time to come. From the first word to the very last of the articles of confederation, there is not one which looks even to this power, or has the remotest reference to it. Let him who doubts this position examine the constitution of the confederation, and he will soon find his doubts removed.

2. A compact is an agreement—nothing more, nothing less; "a mutual appointment," as Johnson says, "between two or more to do or to forbear something."

There was evidently in the minds of the framers of that ordinance an impression of their want of legislative power; and they sought to supply this defect of authority by endeavoring to convert what should have been an act of legislation into a compact or contract. Now, a contract must have two or more parties, each assenting to the instrument of agreement. But it is all idle to talk about the compacts in this ordinance of 1787. The articles so designated are destitute of the very first elements of reciprocal obligation. This arbitrary declaration is unilateral; it never had more than one party. That party was the Congress of the old confederation "overstepping its power," to borrow again the authority of Mr. Madison. The other party should have been the "people and States" (these are the descriptive words) of this new Territory, where there were then no States, and very few people. No assent was ever asked, none was ever given, either then or since, either expressly or by the most remote implication. Had the land been sold to the settlers upon condition that they should be considered as yielding their assent to this perpetual and unchangeable obligation, such an attempt to extort an unwilling obedience, and to barter great political rights and State equality for an unworthy consideration, though not defensible, might yet have been less reprehensible than this open attack upon the will of the people, the fundamental principle of the institutions of our country. But there was no resort to this expedient. The land was sold without condition, and the compact depends for its efficacy upon its own arbitrary authority. It must be recollected that, at the time this ordinance was passed, there were many thousands of people living in this Territory, settlers upon the Wabash, in the Illinois country, in the Detroit country, at Green Bay, at Prairie du Chien, and elsewhere, little colonies scattered over this extensive region, mostly relics of French enterprise; and they were all entitled by the treaty of peace to the privileges of American citizens. And still more it was declared in the deed of cession of Virginia; and as one of the conditions, that they should be "protected in the enjoyment of their rights and privileges." A precious kind of protection that, which inaugurated a new government by a falsely-styled compact, perpetually binding this transferred population to the most solemn obligations, without their assent, and even without their knowledge. These ancient inhabitants of the country constituted the counter party then actually existing; and this compact, by a kind of legislative legerdemain, was made forever binding upon them and their descendants. Why, sir, if there had been but one man in that country, instead of the thousands who occupied it, he would not have been bound by a contract he knew nothing of, and to which his assent was never asked. As to making a contract with unborn States and millions, by the simple act of a foreign body constituting itself one of the parties, and acting for the other, and without demanding its assent, now or hereafter, for all time to come, had we not witnessed the zeal with which this utter contempt of all the principles of law and ethics is maintained and defended, we might well doubt whether a single man could be found to contend for such a monstrous usurpation.

Mr. President, the honorable Senator from Georgia, in discussing this branch of the subject, and in alluding to the transfer of the Territorial governments from the confederation to the constitution, remarked that "by that constitution Congress was bound by all the contracts of the old government." He then quotes the first act of Congress, extending the new power over the Territories, and making some necessary changes in the provisions of the ordinance to accommodate it to the changed state of things, and thus continues: "The ordinance purports on its face to be a contract between the people of Virginia, the inhabitants of the Northwest Territory, and the government of the United States, perpetual and unchangeable, except by consent of all parties." The error to which I have already referred lies in the view here presented, and it is sufficiently important to require correction. Sir, the ordinance of Congress of July 13, 1787, for the government of the Northwestern Territory, is no compact so far as respects that government, nor does it purport to be one. There is a prevalent misapprehension upon this subject, and the sooner it is cleared up the better. That ordinance contains twelve clauses, or sections, providing for the establishment of a government, and eventually of additional governments over the extensive region north of the Ohio river. All the arrangements, including those for the appointment of officers, the definition of their duties, the qualification of voters, and various other details necessary to this new political condition, are amply provided for. And all this is done in the ordinary form of legislation, claiming no peculiar sanctity, and repealable at any time by the existing law-making power. After making these arrangements for temporary governments, the only legitimate object of congressional legislation over a distant people deprived of representation, the ordinance proceeds with the declaration, that "it is hereby ordained by the authority aforesaid, that the following articles shall be considered as articles of compact between the original States, and the people and States in the said Territory, and forever remain unalterable unless by common consent;" and then follow six sections purporting to be those far-famed articles of compact.

1. The first insures the freedom of religious worship.

2. The second guaranties certain principles of the English common law, such as the trial by jury, and other well-known features of that code, which are ingrafted into our system. In the progress of political improvement, should the northwestern States deem it important to introduce changes into their jurisprudence by attempting to meliorate some of these provisions, they would find themselves deprived of the first attribute of sovereignty, and would be compelled to ask the consent of Congress, if this doctrine of the perpetual obligation of the ordinance is the true one.

3. The third section recommends the encouragement of schools, and the preservation of good faith towards the Indian.

4. The fourth declares that the Territory shall forever form part of the Union, and regulates its duties in relation to it.

5. The fifth provides for the establishment of boundaries, and for the admission of these new States.

6 The sixth prohibits the introduction of slavery.

These are the articles of compact, and all of them; and it will be seen they have no relation, none at all, to the establishment of Territorial governments. And it follows beyond contradiction, that, so far as concerns those temporary organizations, this ordinance is no compact; nor does it derive any vital force from that clause of the constitution which provides for the immunity of engagements, thus conferring a power of legislation which would otherwise be destitute of any validity.

The Senator from Georgia will now perceive the misapprehension to which he has lent his high authority. The six sections of the ordinance, called articles of compact, did not purport to be, as he supposes, "a contract between the people of Virginia, the inhabitants of the Northwestern Territory, and the government of the United States." They assume to be a contract "between the original States, and the people and States in the said Territory;" and so far from its "having been accepted by all three of the parties," it was never accepted by the original States, unless the passage of the law is called an act of acceptance; and as to the people and States of that new region, they were never asked for their consent, and of course never gave it. What is meant in these declaratory clauses by the States, as contradistinguished from the people, as I do not know, I shall not attempt to explain. The State of Virginia was no party to this contract, except in her capacity as one of the members of the confederacy, and therefore could not accept it. In her deed of cession to the United States, she provided that the expense of subduing the country should be refunded to her, and made arrangements for the reservation of land for her troops; and declared, as a condition of the grant, that the country should be divided into States, not less than one hundred nor more than one hundred and fifty miles square, providing, at the same time, for their admission into the Union. Congress enlarged the size of the States, and reduced the number to three, with power to increase that number to five; and it thus became necessary to ask the assent of Virginia to this change in the political organization of the country. That assent was given, and this is all the participation that Virginia had in the ordinance of Congress of 1787. She never acted on the subject of the Territorial governments, nor was she, as an independent State, any party to the exclusion of slavery from that region.

3. To pursue the investigation, I observe, in the third place, that this perpetual compact—constitution, in fact—has been declared invalid by the Supreme Court of the United States.

4. And, in the fourth place, admitting its validity and its operation as a constitutional "engagement," confirming the action of Congress over the Northwestern Territory, what becomes of the vast territorial regions since acquired by the United States, and where there have been no "compacts," followed by "engagements," to carry jurisdiction with them? Whence is derived the power to govern, among others, the Territories of Kansas and Nebraska, and to

regulate their internal affairs, including all the relations of life? I turn over this question to those who advocate the extensive operation of the word "engagements" in the constitution.

5 And, in the last place, this inviolable compact has been coolly violated by Congress, without the slightest objection, and after a full report upon the subject to the Senate.

Among the irrepealable clauses of that compact is one, which provides that there shall be not less than three, nor more than five, States in the Northwestern Territory. Congress, after providing for five States, now Ohio, Indiana, Illinois, Michigan, and Wisconsin, made provision for another, at its pleasure, in the country north of Wisconsin and east of the Mississippi—forming part of the territory over which the ordinance of 1787 extended. So much for the irrepealable compact.

I now return to the three new sources of power, the reward of recent investigations, and which are, as I have said:

13. The right and duty of guardianship.

14. The transmissible power, by which the constitution of another country is substituted for that of the United States.

15. What may be called the paternal power, which places the general government *in loco parentis.*

The first of these has been recently urged in the House of Representatives, and the latter in the Senate. I leave them both without argument—epitaphs, I may say, for they will soon need them, as their tenure of life must be a brief one—contenting myself with suffering the Senator from Iowa, [Mr. HARLAN,] to whom we owe the discovery of the second, to state his proposition in his own language. Illustrating it by the annexation of Louisiana, he said that "the United States, by a direct purchase, succeeded to all the rights and sovereignty possessed by the grantor, and hence became the actual, full, complete, and exclusive sovereign of the Territory." And afterwards: "It was a part of the dominions of France; she was its absolute sovereign. Hence the government of the United States must have succeeded to the same unrestricted rights, and may hold, exercise, and enjoy them, until she chooses to confer them upon another sovereignty."

I am not going to employ my time, and that of the Senate, so badly as to argue this point; to undertake to refute the proposition, that the Congress of the United States may seek its authority, not in our constitution, but in that of a foreign government, and thus transfer to a republic the powers of an absolute monarchy. The error of the speaker is obviously in deducing the power of Congress from the attribute of sovereignty, as I trust a few remarks I propose to make will show. For the third of these sources of power we are indebted to one of the most experienced and intelligent Senators who ever occupied a seat among us. He said upon that occasion, "the Territories are the children of the States—they are minors, under twenty-one years of age, and it is the business of the States, through their delegations in Congress, to take care of these minors until they are of age—until they are ripe for State government—then to give them an equality with their fathers." And, he added, with characteristic emphasis, "that is the law and the sense of the case." And thus the constitution is not to be merely interpreted, but it is to be interpolated, and its supposed omissions are to be supplied by useless analogies, drawn from youth and age, and applied with equal rashness and confidence where there is no reason for application Analogy is not only utterly erroneous as a foundation of the means of construction even, but here it is destitute of any point of similitude; for the duration of a Territorial government has no connexion with the years of its organization, as that depends wholly on the amount of population; a Territory being entitled to admission into the Union as soon as it possesses sixty thousand inhabitants, according to the original arrangement, even if that event occur within six months after the establishment of its temporary government.

No reflecting person, sir, who reads in the annals of mankind the story of the never-halting tendency of every government to increase its power, can contemplate, without some anxiety, the additional proof which we are contributing to the experience of the world upon this subject. Analogies derived from physical, are transferred to political life, and become the foundation of some of the highest operations of government; and because a parent may rule a child, therefore Congress may rule the Territories. Attributes of national independent existence, like sovereignty, which carry with them coequal rights among the Powers of the world, but which confer no authority upon any department of our government, unless written down in the constitution, are appealed to as grants of substantive power, to be exercised at the will of Congress. There is no general grant of the right of legislation in the constitution. Its provisions on that subject are as cautious as they are wise and clear. "All legislative power HEREIN GRANTED," says our charter, "shall be vested in a Congress;" and then follows the enumeration of its powers, with the declaration that all powers not granted are reserved, &c.

The word "sovereign" is not to be found in the constitution, and yet it is pressed into hourly and daily service in the investigation of our relations with the Territories, on one side to justify the exercise of unlimited congressional power, and on the other to prove that, as the Territories are not sovereign, the people living there have no political privileges. Strange deductions these, in a government of limited powers and of equal rights! And the Committee on the Territories, in their report, speak of the "sovereignty of a Territory remaining in abeyance, suspended in trust for the people till admitted," &c.; and, if I understood correctly the honorable Senator from Mississippi, [Mr. BROWN,] in his remarks the other day, he approved and adopted these positions; and perhaps I should do so too, if I comprehended them; but as I do not, my incredulity may be pardoned. It seems to me, that this transfer to our government of some of the technical niceties of the English common law, which gladdened the hearts of Coke and his school in the days of legal metaphysics, is to mistake equally our age and our country. The simple fact repels all these subtleties. That fact is, that no one claims sovereignty for the Territories; or, in other words, no one claims that they are independent nations. That attribute, with respect to them, is not in abeyance; it is not in existence, any more than their membership of the Union or any other power depending ultimately on admission. When admission comes, it confers these powers and conditions; until that time it is a mere act of fancy to suppose they are existing, and must be held by somebody, in trust for somebody else, lest they perish. They may never come into existence, for that depends on a state of things which may not happen; such as the amount of the population, the wishes of the people, &c. All these nice and learned distinctions give no jurisdiction to Congress. If they did, they would make that body what the constitution has not made it, a kind of reservoir, holding all that is given, and all that can be taken. There is no such power in the book. You can find in the constitution no recognition of sovereignty in Congress; nor, if there were, is any grant of power attached to that condition. That instrument grants authority to Congress to declare war. If that authority were not thus delegated, will any man venture to assert that Congress might assume it by virtue of the sovereignty of the nation?

In the people of the United States resides the sovereignty of this country; and we may go to the elementary writers to ascertain what rights that high attribute gives to us among the Powers of the world; but we must go to the constitution of the United States to ascertain what department of the government, if any, can exercise those rights; and if we do not find it written down there, the power belongs to the States or to the people. And I have recently seen speculations in some of the public journals which show that this constitutional fallacy has "increased, is increasing, and ought to be diminished." The following extract furnishes proof of its extent:

"We cannot conceive how any doubt can arise as to the full, perfect, unlimited, and sovereign power of the federal government over the Territory of Kansas as the agent or trustee of the existing States." * * * "These States can only exercise their sovereign, administrative, and governmental rights through the instrumentality of the Territorial governments."

Full, perfect, unlimited sovereign power! Large words these, and large would be their extent. They carry with them Wilmot provisoes, and every other tyrannical infliction it may please the calculation or the caprice of Congress to visit upon the people; and all this power comes not from the constitution, but "from the purchase of Louisiana, and the subsequent extinction of the Indian titles," which gave us the territory "to dipose of and govern as we pleased for the common benefit of all the States." I suppose the constitution gives the right of foreign acquisition, and that it is derived from the treaty-making power. When territory is acquired, it comes under the operation of the constitution, and Congress must go to that expressed will of the American people to ascertain its powers before it can exercise them. This annotator maintains that acquisition gives Congress the power of disposal and of government. It gives the title, but the power to dispose of the "property" is expressly given by the constitution; and had it not been so given, it could not have been exercised while the power of government is an omitted case, unless, indeed, it is an incident to a granted one, and is not to be supplied by attributes and analogies.

These views, sir, previously announced, as we have seen, by the Senator from Iowa, [Mr. Harlan,] and as establishing the right of Congress to prohibit slavery in the Territories, are also announced in one of the most respectable and justly-esteemed journals in our country, though certainly with no concurrence in that conclusion. But how it is to be avoided I know not, and cannot conjecture.

In the days of the patriarchs of the Democratic faith—of the great teachers in the school of strict construction—such a derivation of the authority of the general government would have been denounced as a dangerous heresy. Jefferson, and Madison, and Taylor, and Mason, and their political coadjutors, went to the constitution for the powers of Congress, and not to the code of Napoleon, nor to the code of Powhatan, or Pontiac, or Tecumseh. And these, and other pretensions I have not time to examine, to enumerate even, and which hardly need refutation, abound in the debates and discussions which this subject, prolific in heresies, has called forth. I leave them, not in their strength, but in their weakness, and proceed to say that, if the power to regulate and sell land—for this is the grant, and all the grant—conveys full legislative authority over this property, and over all persons living not only upon it, but in the same region of country, making man the mere incident of property—never were words more unhappily chosen, and never was a character for clearness and perspicuity, which has been heretofore universally accorded to the phraseology of the constitution, more unjustly acquired. The Senator from New Hampshire [Mr. Hale] has attempted, as others have attempted before him, to derive full legislative power from the words "rules and regulations," because, being enacted by legislative authority, they are, in effect, laws. I am not going, sir, into the subtlety of this investigation. All I have to say is, that the very fact that the convention provided for the adoption of rules and regulations respecting the public land is a strong presumption that there was something different from the ordinary exercise of legislative power. When they provided for legislation over the District of Columbia, and the reservations of the United States, they did not call it rules and regulations, but they called it by the proper term, legislation, conveying, as it did, full jurisdiction over American citizens, and all the concerns of life. The convention used the terms "rules and regulations," because they did not grant general powers of legislation, but power to govern and regulate the property of the United States. The inteligence of the convention would be but little esteemed, if, at the commencement of the constitution, instead of the present provision, that "all legislative powers herein granted shall be vested," &c , they had said that all the powers to make *rules and regulations* herein granted shall be vested, &c.; or if, instead of the enactment of the eighth article, that "this constitution and the laws of the United States which shall be made." &c., "shall be the supreme law of the land," it had been declared that this constitution, and the rules and regulations which shall be made, &c., shall be the supreme rule and regulation of the land.

I will merely add, Mr. President, that the word "territories," inserted in the eighteenth clause of the eighth section of the first article of the constitution, which grants legislative power to Congress over the District of Columbia, and over the reservations or cessions for forts, &c., in the several States, would have conveyed all the rights of government, and would have placed the relations between these political communities and the national legislature beyond doubt or dispute; and so would seven words, "Congress shall exercise legislation over the Territories," to adopt the phraseology of the clause just referred to and used by the convention, when it intended to grant the power of government in exceptional cases. But the constitution contains no such clause nor words, and their place is not to be supplied by forced constructions, founded upon no just principle of interpretation, and at war with the first elements of human freedom. As Judge McLean well remarks, "Such a power was given in relation to the District of Columbia, and it was equally necessary in regard to other Territories;" but it is not there, and no power but that of the people can place it there.

The cause of the failure of the convention to make provision in the constitution for the government of Territories was well explained by the senator from Missouri [Mr. GEYER] in his powerful and interesting discussion of this general subject. The ordinance of 1787, which preceded the signing of the constitution, had exhausted the territorial possessions then belonging to the United States. It provided for the political organization of the whole western territory, as it was called, being the country north of the Ohio and east of the Mississippi, making both temporary and permanent arrangements for its condition. And this accounts for the fact that the proposition of Mr. Madison, to make provision for a power of government, was negatived in the convention, evidently under the conviction that the whole subject had been disposed of by the ordinance of 1787; but the power of regulation and sale, making part of the proposition, was accepted and adopted into the constitution, because the title yet remained in the United States.

Much of the confusion which accompanies this subject has obviously arisen from confounding the word "territory," as used in the constitution, with the word "territories," as applied by law and by custom to political communities, as the term "colonies" is applied in England; and to such an extent has this gone, that we find the phrase often quoted as a constitutional provision, that Congress shall have power to regulate the Territories of the United States.

Mr. Venable said in the House of Representatives:

"Sir, the constitution provides for Territories as property, and authorizes Congress to dispose of and make all needful rules and regulations."

And what is less excusable is the commission of the same error by Chancellor Kent, who, in his Commentaries on the Constitution, equally misquotes that instrument, making it read:

"Congress shall have power to dispose of and make all needful rules and regulations respecting the *Territories* or other property of the United States."

Had we retained the appellation "colonies" this confusion would have been avoided, and this claim of political jurisdiction never have arisen under the power to sell land, for then we should have had no double meaning attached to the same word.

The political organization of the Territories is not provided for in the constitution any more than it was provided for in the old articles of confederation. With respect to the latter Mr. Madison said that, in creating temporary governments over the Territories, *Congress had acted, without the least color of constitutional authority.* He justified the act by "the public interest, the necessity of the case, [which] imposed on them the task of overleaping their constitutional limits." And he added: "yet no blame has been whispered."

And such is precisely the condition of the relation between Congress and the Territories under the constitution; and such, and no other, is the justification, excuse rather, as far as it goes, for congressional action—what Mr. Jefferson calls "an excess of authority, for which a representative is responsible, when," as he says, "he must throw himself upon his country for his excuse for doing the act." And such act must extend no further than to comply with the necessity which calls it into being. I call the attention of the senator from New York to the language of Mr. Madison, which I have quoted.

The following extract is from an able review of the subject by Judge McLean:

"The true construction of the constitution is, that implied powers can only be exercised in carrying into effect a specified power, and this implication is limited to such measures as shall be appropriate to the object. This is an admitted and safe rule of construction. It is believed to be the only one which has been sanctioned by jurists and statesmen. Powers exercised beyond this are not derived from the constitution, but must depend upon unlimited discretion, and this is despotism. Now there is no specific power in the constitution which authorizes the organization of Territorial governments. Such a power was given in relation to the District of Columbia, and it was equally necessary in regard to the other Territories. But if this power is implied from the specific power given to regulate the disposition of the public lands, it must, under the above rule, be limited to means suitable to the end in view. If Congress go beyond this in the organization of a Territorial government, they act without limitation, and may establish a monarchy. Admit that they may organize a government which shall protect the land purchased, and provide for the administration of justice among the settlers, it does by no means follow that they may establish slavery. This is a relation which must be created by the local sovereignty. It is a municipal regulation of limited extent, and necessarily of an equally limited origin. It is a domestic relation over which the federal government can exercise no control."

Judge McLean lays down the proper boundary of congressional interposition. It should be confined to the *organization of governments*, leaving untouched the domestic relations, whether of husband and wife, of parent and child, of master and servant, or of any other of the social conditions "over which the federal government can exercise no control." And this is in conformity with the views of Mr. Madison, who said:

"This power of governing the people without representation is in suspension of the great principle of self-government, and not to be extended further, nor continued longer, than the occasion might fairly require."

The power, then, however derived, is confined to the establishment of Territories, and to the organization of their governments, leaving the inhabitants in possession of the rights of internal administration, to be exercised at their pleasure, subject only to the constitution of the United States.

Beyond this establishment and organization there is no necessity for the action of Congress, as the people are fully competent to administer their own domestic affairs, and the power, being derived from necessity, stops where the necessity ceases. In a written constitution like ours, where we have a perpetual standard, to which legislative powers may be applied, and by which their obligation may be tested, the authority of precedent is entitled to far less weight, than where political institutions depend upon tradition for their organization. There is no doubt but that the constitutional government early placed itself, with respect to the Territories, in the relation previously occupied by its confederated predecessor, and went on with the same legislative and executive work; but, so far as we know, this process provoked no investigation. There is not the slightest reason to believe that, for many years after the adoption of the constitution, the constitutional principles involved in this exercise of power were made the subject of examination. The cotemporaneous debates reflect no light upon this subject. It seems to have been conceded, or silently acquiesced in, without direct concession, that Congress should proceed and fulfil the functions, which had been discharged by the legislature of the confederation; and it was not till 1820, upon the approach of the Missouri controversy, that this question underwent a searching investigation. Certainly, the *sub silentio* assumption of jurisdiction is but a sandy foundation for the exercise of power under the constitution as vigilantly guarded as ours. It wants something far more solid than that to justify the superstructure of authority which we have seen erected upon it. In this uncertainty we are left without the means of judging what different clauses of the constitution were relied upon by different members of the legislature, each in support of his own opinion, whether the land-disposing power, the State-admitting power, the treaty-making power, or any other power, through the long catalogue of enumerated grants, including the action from necessity, as the grant which conferred this jurisdiction upon the national legislature. Opinions then may have been as various as they are now. Surely the assumption of the right of legislation under these circumstances carries with it no such weight of opinion as would give any authority to the interpretation of a doubtful constitutional principle The fact is, that thirty years of legislation are lost, so far as regards the effect of precedent; and till the Missouri compromise there was no such contest of mind as, when continued, is sure to separate truth from error, and to establish the ascendency of the just principles of the constitution.

So far as respects my own personal views, I beg leave to say that my opinion of the want of constitutional power in Congress to exercise political jurisdiction over the Territories has been long entertained and expressed. In the Washington Globe of March 31, 1832, may be found a review of the decision of the Supreme Court upon the Cherokee question, in Georgia, which was written by me, and read to and approved by General Jackson, and by my colleagues of the cabinet, and in which I said:

"The power to dispose of and make needful rules and regulations respecting the property of the United States, and the power to exercise general jurisdiction over persons upon it, are essentially different and independent. The former is general, and is given in the clause referred to. The latter is special, and is given in another clause, and confined to the federal district, and to places purchased by consent of the legislature of the State in which the same shall be, for the erection of forts, magazines, arsenals, dock-yards, and other needful buildings."

The principle of the establishment of local governments by a metropolitan authority, and the administration of such governments by those over whom they operate, is familiar to every American. It forms a memorable chapter in our colonial history, its violation by the British Parliament having constituted the great political oppression, which led to the war of independence. It was announced in the declaration of the Continental Congress of 1774, in these words: The English colonists "are entitled to a free and exclusive power of legislation in their several provincial legislatures, where their rights of representation can alone be preserved in all cases of taxation and internal polity," &c.

From the preceding considerations it follows that, when Congress establishes a Territory and organizes its government, it has exhausted its power, and the people of such Territory have the right to adjust every question of their "internal polity," to use words rendered dear by the patriarchs of the Revolution, in the mode most acceptable to themselves, subject only to the constitution.

In these days of political metaphysics it has been objected to this view of the relations subsisting between the general government and its Territories, that there is not a fixed tangible boundary between the power of the superior authority and that of the dependent one; that in the organization of these temporary governments Congress have assumed many powers incompatible with Territorial self-government; and those thus objecting would, therefore, test the existence of a principle of human freedom by its liability to abuse. No doubt but these organic acts have gone too far in interfering with the rights of people deprived of representation in the body assuming to govern them. Those legislators who find in the constitution a direct grant of unlimited power, have only their own discretion to consult in its exercise; but those who deduce such an authority from the necessity of the action of Congress to preserve social order, or to carry into effect any granted power, are bound not to exceed the limits prescribed by their own principle, but to leave to the people the enjoyment of all rights compatible with this duty of organization. Certainly there may be honest differences of opinion as to the necessary extent of these paramount regulations, providing the rules of administration, touching the appointment of officers, the qualifications of voters, and various other points relating to the institution of a government. For myself I believe that the federal legislature has gone too much into detail in this exercise of a power which, as Mr. Madison said, is in suspension of human freedom, and that the management of all their concerns, after setting the government in operation, should be left to the people themselves. But, after making allowance for these different views, when we come to the internal affairs of a remote Territorial people—to those sacred domestic relations, which no foreign authority can touch without an act of unmitigated despotism—we reach a practical boundary which no Congress of Washington or of Westminster should overstep. There is no necessity to justify such interference, and therefore no rightful power to assume it. Our revolutionary fathers were too clear-headed to lose themselves in the mazes of such subtile logic, and admitted the principle of organization, even with the doubts which might sometimes arise in its practical application.

The people of the Territories do not derive this attribute of self-government—the power of internal legislation—as a boon from Congress. All they derive from that body is the opportunity of exercising it; and even this they may rightfully assume by their own act, whenever the national legislature refuses, or unreasonably delays, measures of organization; as in the case of California, where the people were driven, in the maintenance of social order, to those first principles of self-defence, which belong not less to communities than to individuals, and which neither predicates nor copulas, nor all the apparatus of verbal logic, can wrest from them. I do not speak of a revolution. That is the ultimate resort for oppression. I speak of rights and necessary acts within the proper allegiance of a colonial community to a paramount authority.

The just foundation of local legislation is laid down in the Declaration of Independence, wherein it is said: "Legislative powers, incapable of annihilation, have returned to the people at large for their exercise." RETURNED to the fountain whence they issued—to the people to whom they belong—not to king, Congress, nor Parliament.

It will be observed that in this analysis I have examined the question as a general one, within the constitution, of the legislative power of the people of the Territories under acts of organization, where no specific objects are enumerated over which legislation may extend. The Kansas-Nebraska acts, however, render a decision of the general question unnecessary, for they contain an express grant—recognition rather—of the right of the people of these Territories to regulate the condition of slavery for themselves, unless prohibited by the constitution of the United States. Is there such a prohibition? I believe there is not; and I submitted my views upon the subject in this body at some length on the passage of these acts. I will not go over the question again at this time, for I feel that I am already trespassing too much on the indulgence of the Senate.

But I will add, sir, that the honorable senator from Mississippi [Mr. BROWN] mistakes the position of the two distinguished gentlemen, to whom he alluded in his remarks the other day, if, as I understood him, he supposes that in their opinion the people of a Territory ought not to have the right to regulate the question of slavery for themselves. These gentlemen are the President of the United States, and the chairman of the Committee on Territories, the member from Illinois, [Mr. DOUGLAS.] I am gratified in being able to assure the senator from Mississippi that they have both announced their adhesion to this American principle of self-government. The former calls it "the true principle of leaving each State and Territory to regulate its own laws of labor according to its own sense of right and expediency." The latter, when the Kansas and Nebraska acts were under discussion, took the opportunity of referring to and reaffirming the sentiments on this subject which he had avowed and supported while the bills for the establishment of governments in Utah and New Mexico were under consideration. When a proposition was pending at that time, prohibiting the local legislatures from legislating on the subject of slavery, he observed:

"I wish to say one word before this part of the bill is voted upon. I must confess that I rather regretted that a clause had been introduced into this bill providing that the Territorial governments should not legislate in respect to African slavery. The position that I have ever taken has been that this and all other questions relating to the domestic affairs and domestic policy of the Territories ought to be left to the decision of the people themselves, and that we ought to be content with whatever way they may decide the question, because they have a much deeper interest in these matters than we have, and know much better what institutions suit them than we who have never been there can decide for them."

And again:

"I do not see how those of us who have taken the position which we have taken, (that of non-interference,) and have argued in favor of the right of the people to legislate for themselves on this question, can support such a provision without abandoning all the arguments which we urged in the presidential campaign, and the principles set forth by the senator from Michigan in that letter which is known as the Nicholson letter. We are required to abandon our platform. We are required to abandon those principles and to stultify ourselves, and to adopt the opposite doctrine, and for what? In order to say that the people of the Territories shall not have such institutions as they shall deem adapted to their condition and their wants."

And yet again:

"But I do say, that if left to myself to carry out my own opinion, I would leave the whole subject to the people of the Territories themselves, and allow them to introduce or abolish slavery as they may prefer. I believe that is the principle on which our institutions rest."

Mr. FOOT. The usual hour for adjournment having arrived, if the senator from Michigan will yield the floor I will move an adjournment.

Mr. CASS. I yield to the senator's suggestion.

TUESDAY, *May* 13, 1856.

This morning the further consideration of the subject was resumed at the usual hour, and the honorable senator from Michigan thus concluded:

Mr. President, yesterday I submitted to the Senate a view and review of the constitutional principles which regulate the relations between the United States and their Territories, and of the course of legislation with regard to those dependencies; and to-day I propose to submit some remarks upon the state of things in Kansas, and upon the measures which Congress is called upon to adopt.

Mr. President, I am not going into a detailed examination of the occurrences in that Territory which render our interposition necessary, especially after the investigation which they have undergone, and which we have read in reports and listened to in debates. I shall deal only in general facts, with a view to general conclusions.

In the first place, sir, allow me to observe, that whatever unjustifiable proceedings have taken place in Kansas—and there have been too many of them—they have not shaken, in the slightest degree, my conviction of the right of man to govern himself, nor my confidence in the salutary operation of that true principle of human authority. I have read and heard sneering remarks upon the so-called failure of the experiment of popular sovereignty, preposterously called an experiment, after our experience of generations—remarks made, I have no doubt, by those who desire a failure. Even were it so, it would not touch the question, unless we are prepared to test the truth of a great principle by its accidental abuse. The political organization of our country is the history, as well as the exemplification of popular sovereignty for a long series of years. Glorious has been its work, and more glorious will it be hereafter; and yet there is scarcely a State in the Union in which, at some period of its existence, commotions have not broken out, and the laws been resisted, and sometimes the most alarming consequences threatened. But these have all happily passed away; and while leaving their memory a warning, leaving it also a proof that free institutions carry with them the power of self-conservation and the means of safety. And in all this time, and during many a day of trial and danger, not one human life has been sacrificed to avenge the law, or to restore its supremacy! What other country can say as much since the first institution of governments after the dispersion of the descendants of Adam upon the plains of Shinar? I am satisfied, from some examination, that there was a greater waste of human life and treasure in the riots of London, in 1780, than there has been in this country in all the acts of resistance to the public authority which are found in our history, colonial or independent. Does the experience of the world show that man is fitter to govern others than himself, and that power is safer with the few than with the many? Let history answer this question, and answer also the indignant interrogatory of Mr. Jefferson, "Have we found angels in the form of men to govern us?"

There were peculiar circumstances attending the institution of government in Kansas to which, and not to the principles that regulated it, are the lamentable proceedings to be traced. Those principles were wise and just, and not a voice has been raised in their condemnation among the people over whom they were to operate. From the 4th of July, 1776, to this day, they have been the American guides of political organization; but at this time they were applied to a country beset with external, rather than internal, difficulties and dangers. These arose out of the question of slavery, which seems destined by its opponents to be an eternal subject of agitation—a subject which, though never sleeping, becomes quadrennially more violent as the presidential term approaches its renewal. This is its recurring season, and time and experience teach us no lesson of wisdom or forebearance. My sentiments on the general subject of this slavery excitement are already before the country, and events as they pass by serve but to strengthen my convictions. I listened with deep interest the other day to the masterly effort of the senator from Alabama, [Mr. CLAY,] who, while doing justice to his constituents, did honor to himself and to the Senate. Though I dissented from some of his remarks and conclusions, yet in the general scope of his observations there was great force and justice—considerations of the gravest character, appealing to every true-hearted American. While I listened to the complaints he spread before us in behalf of the South against the North, I wished I could deny their justice, but felt that I could not; and as he proceeded with his recapitulation, I felt also that this eternal warfare against one half of the Union had become as disgusting by its repetition as it was unjust in itself and dangerous in its consequences. I begin to have as little charity for many of those engaged in this crusade as sympathy with the movement itself. The South intermeddles not with the social institutions of the North; let the North exhibit the same spirit of toleration, and we shall be the strongest and the most contented, as we are the freest, nation on the face of the globe. We have been told here, time and again, recently and formerly, that there is no design to interfere with slavery in any of the States of the Union. The power is disavowed as well as the purpose; but the disavowal is contradicted by events that are hourly passing before our eyes. He who believes in a higher law, of whose extent and obligations he is the judge, and which justifies him in disobeying a human law, is prepared to follow the fantasies of the wildest imagination. What is the constitution to him who has a constitution of his own, overruling and overriding the laws of his country? Why, sir, in the House of Representatives during the present session of Congress, a member from New York maintained that "slavery in the United States is unconstitutional, and therefore unlawful" "The constitution, both in spirit and express terms, repudiates slavery, and bars its existence."

And even now we are just told, by a resolution of the "American Anti-Slavery Society," "that the right to enslave a human being, on any pretence whatever, is not a debatable question, any more than is the right to commit adultery, burglary, highway robbery, or piracy."

And we are told, in another resolution, "that they are struggling to drive slavery out of the land." It requires a good deal of moral courage, in the face of such declarations, to contend that no one entertains a design to interfere with slavery in the States. No man of ordinary sagacity can doubt the tendency of the doctrines which are disseminated in high places and in low places upon this whole subject, and that are addressed to passions more easily excited than allayed. Among other dangerous signs, a spirit of fanaticism is evoked, before which the guarantees of the constitution may be prostrated, as easily as the marks on the sand are obliterated by the incoming tide of the ocean. It is already doing its work, and this is the most alarming symptom in this terrible national malady. It is fostered and encouraged by men professedly servants of the Most High, and ministering at His altar. It prostrates the judgment and almost paralyzes the conscience, and prepares the excited mind for strange delusions and dangerous deeds. The scene which lately passed at New Haven, when God's day and God's house were desecrated by appeals to fierce passions to stimulate men to action, instead of being devoted to their true purpose of guiding and restraining them, was a spectacle to be contemplated with regret, with indignation indeed, and alarm. The temple at Jerusalem was defiled by the money-changers, who converted it into a bank of that day, and made it a scene of abominations. Our Saviour drove them out, saying, "It is written, my house shall be called the house of prayer, but ye have made it a den of thieves." The house of prayer is now made an armory for the collection of weapons to arm Americans against their countrymen: and clergymen are not indeed money-changers, but gatherers and distributers of carnal, not of Christian weapons, to fight the battles of the flesh, and not the battles of the faith, forgetting that "all they that take the sword shall perish by the sword;" and that they are warned by the apostle of the Gentiles that "the weapons of their warfare are not carnal," &c.

Mr. President, to preach the gospel of Jesus is work enough for any human heart and intellect. He who devotes himself to this duty and then goes after strange gods, entering the field of politics and mingling in its strife and bitterness, does more injury to the cause of true religion within the sphere of his labors, than the writings of Voltaire and Hume, and all the other infidel authors who ever sought, by their sneers and malign influence, to destroy human confidence in the most precious gift of God to man. And it is a consolatory proof of the reality of revealed religion, that it is equally triumphant over the assaults of its open enemies and the indiscretion, or something worse, of its professed friends.

I have already remarked that the intention to interfere with slavery in the States is disavowed, and therefore the more immediate theatre of these labors of strife is the Territories, over which there is no constitutional grant of power in relation to this subject; and if there were, there would be no justice in its exercise, because it is a question which the people are competent to determine for themselves, and which cannot be determined for them by a foreign body, where they have no representation, without violating a great principle of self-government, the very foundation of our institutions, in defence of which our fathers engaged in a contest with the mightiest nation on the face of the globe. I have no patience with Americans who thus condemn the patriots of the Revolution, casting dirt on their fathers, as the eastern phrase is, and seek, to exercise a power over another which they would suffer no man to exercise over themselves. Upon the very first attempt they would indignantly resist at home the interference they so loudly call for elsewhere. Their consciences, which now dictate violent action, where self is not concerned, would soon learn their true duties when their own rights were in question. And the zeal, violence, indeed, with which this claim to govern others, without their own consent or co-operation, is asserted and prosecuted in the very face of our whole history, is a moral phenomenon, betokening some strange hallucination.

And it is a part of the prevailing system of aggression to excite and nourish prejudices against the South by making slavery the perpetual theme of denunciation, and too often of misrepresentation, as though, if it were all its enemies say of it, the present generation, of whose social system it makes an essential part, were responsible for its introduction, or could terminate its existence. It came to them by inheritance, not by their own co-operation; and when or how it is to cease is known only to Him who holds nations, not less than individuals, in the hollow of His hand, for it is beyond the sagacity of man to discover. The emancipation of nearly four millions of human beings of a different caste and color and condition, living in a state of servitude, among a superior race—superior in numbers, in power, in intellect—is a fearful question, which no right-minded man can contemplate without the deepest solicitude. I am not presumptuous enough to say how it could be done. But of this I am certain, that it is a matter which should be left to those whom it vitally interests, and who alone can decide it. If it were in my power to set free, to-morrow, every slave in the United States, I would not do it. I think the act would be followed by fearful convulsions, the apprehension of which should cause the wisest to pause and the firmest to tremble. The result of the experiment which England made in the Antilles, has not been such as to encourage other countries to follow the example. The standard English historian, Allison, in a new volume of his great work, which has just issued from the press, tells the story in melancholy terms. He says:

"The effect of the emancipation of the negroes has been to ruin our own planters, stop the civilization of our own negroes, and double the slave trade in extent, and quadruple it in its horrors."

He repeats:

"Disastrous as the results of the change have been to British interests, both at home and in the West Indies, they are as nothing to those which have ensued to the negroes themselves."

To emancipate a comparatively small number of slaves in a West Indian island, which may be covered by the troops and surrounded by the fleets of the mother country, is one thing. To do the same deed of liberation in a far-spreading region, measured not by miles, but almost by great circles of the globe, and destitute of a military force to restrain the revengeful promptings or the dangerous suggestions of suddenly-acquired freedom, is another and quite a different thing. Believing that slavery is a misfortune to any country, I hope that it will come to an end in ours; but it must be in God's good time, and in some far away day, when master and slave are prepared for it.

In the prosecution of this warfare against the character, the tranquillity, and the rights of the South, the press, not less than the pulpit, has been made an active coadjutor, and the world has been inundated with log-cabin books, and other productions of equal fairness and value, and about as worthy of credit as the travels of the renowned Gulliver, too often drawing their facts from the imagination, and their conclusions from the dictates of a wild or false heart, or of a disordered head. Sir, I am no defender of the South. It needs not my aid. It has powerful advocates here and elsewhere, able to assert its cause: and the latest among them, who has volunteered in this commendable work—the member from Louisiana, [Mr BENJAMIN]—in his address to the Senate a few days ago, made an appeal to American justice and patriotism which I have never heard surpassed in vigor or of intellect, or in true eloquence. The undivided attention of this high body was a just tribute to the effort of the gifted speaker. As a man loving my country, and jealous of her name and fame among the nations of the earth, I feel indignant at these atrocious calumnies upon a large portion of my countrymen, and I have no disposition to conceal nor to repress that feeling. I know something of the condition of the slaves; and I believe, as I have before said in this place, that they are treated with all the humanity which can reasonably be expected in their situation—with a humanity honorable to the proprietors as a class, and, to say the least of it, quite as well as they would be in the northern States, had this kind of servitude survived till this day, and far better than by many, whose philanthropy is shown by the railing and reproachful words they utter, and not by the relief they contribute to human misery.

I know something also of the condition of the poverty-stricken population of Europe, of a large portion of the inhabitants who lie down in sorrow and get up in care, and who pass their lives in want, and many of them in a state of destitution utterly unknown in this country. And I have seen more misery in the proudest capitals of Europe than I ever saw in our own favored land, among white or black, bond or free. The condition of slavery has existed since the earliest ages of the world, and regretted as it is, and must be, by the moralist, it is a great practical question, which every established community must arrange for itself. The Revolution found it in most of the States, and there it was at the adoption of the constitution, and in many it yet remains, making part of the rights and guarantees of the confederation. To touch it by the general government would be to shake to its corner-stone our whole political edifice. And disavowed as that purpose is by many of those who are engaged in this warfare, and who take counsel from discretion, seeing the full time has not yet come, it should be obvious to the most superficial observer that the inevitable tendency of this state of *quasi* hostilities is to weaken the fealty and attachment to the Union; to create a morbid excitement, by which the mind and the heart are intently fixed upon one object, the abolition of slavery to the exclusion of many a true work of charity, and to the extinction of many a kindly and patriotic sentiment, and also to the imminent hazard of following the institution, with hostile views, wherever it exists, as regardless of the rights of others as of the constitutional securities which protect it. It would almost appear as though the whole stock of philanthropy—of talking philanthropy I mean—in portions of the country were exhausted upon the black man, and that the men of our own race were out of the circle of human sympathy. All this would be but regretable were it not rendered serious by its danger. Its effect is but too palpable in the heart-burnings it has created on each side of the line of separation. This condition of the public mind excites my apprehension, and ought to awaken the attention and arouse the exertion of every true patriot before the evil day is upon us, and the deed of disunion shall be done.

When the Kansas act was passed it was hoped that the great principle of self-government embodied in it would lead to the tranquil adjustment of much of this controversy. It was looked upon as the olive branch, announcing the recession of the waters of bitterness. And such would it have proved had the people of the Territory been left to regulate this subject for themselves. The times indeed were not as propitious as they would have been had a better spirit prevailed at the North. The fugitive slave law had been opposed, and its operation vilified and obstructed. Laws had been passed incompatible with the provisions of the federal constitution, and confessedly from hostility to the South, and other acts were done, and sentiments avowed, of the most unfriendly character, which are too fresh in general recollection to require recapitulation. And under these circumstances commenced the settlement and the government of Kansas.

I have said that I had no purpose minutely to recall the untoward events which accompanied the progress of this movement. I have read with care the narrative compiled by the senator from Illinois in his report, and while it is marked with signal ability, it seems to me to be marked also with a commendable regard to the truth. I have rarely read a more powerful State paper, and in my opinion it entitles its distinguished author to the thanks of the country.

It is easy to trace the disturbances in Kansas to their true source—to external interference. That portion of the Union connected with slavery, and where it is not merely a question of servitude, but also of safety, were in much and just excitement at the unconstitutional assaults upon this element of their social system. And this moment was chosen by the partisans of abolition in the northern States to organize emigrating parties, supplying them with assistance described by a learned professor at New Haven "as moral encouragement and material aid in money or arms." And these new implements, not of agriculture, but of death, were designed for human bodies, instead of a virgin soil; and, as the same literary gentleman said, while defending this *charitable contribution*, they "were to be wielded by strong hands and directed by courageous minds." And "this material aid" was commended to the precaution of the emigrants, who were advised to hasten on to the promised land, not for their own sakes, looking forward to the reward of industry and enterprise in a new country, but as soldiers, to fight a political battle, with such weapons, whether of law or of iron, as circumstances might render expedient. It is not surprising that the approach of these new adventurers, avowing designs peculiarly obnoxious to the neighboring State of Missouri, should excite alarm, and lead the people to combine in order to resist combinations.

I am accounting for this state of things, not justifying it—and the solution is found in the ordinary principles of human nature. Confederations, to bring about great public purposes by those who seek them, are sure to be met and resisted by antagonistic unions. I think there was no justification for the interference of persons in the northern States who did not intend to emigrate to Kansas, with a view to control the political course of the emigrants, and to pledge them to a particular line of policy, stimulating their feelings while supplying the means; and it is my deliberate opinion, that those who planned and promoted this scheme are morally responsible for many of its deplorable consequences. At the same time, I think that the emigrant who went to Kansas to become a *bona fide* settler, was in the exercise of his constitutional right, when he proclaimed his purpose by lawful means to oppose the introduction of slavery, and when he followed that purpose to its consummation at the polls. But I cannot say the same of the irruption of citizens from Missouri, some armed and some unarmed, who entered Kansas, with no design to become residents, but to control the political power of the Territory with a view to political action. I believe the extent of this unfortunate movement has been overrated; but, after making all reasonable deductions for exaggeration, enough yet remains to excite regret, and to call for condemnation. The sanctity of elections is the very palladium of our liberty. The places where they are held should be holy ground, where neither fraud nor violence should be permitted to enter. And, above all, they should not be entered by armed parties, with a view to subject this living element of freedom to lawless violence—thus bringing dishonor upon our institutions, and weakening respect for the laws, and impairing their obligations. I cannot be restrained by any considerations from this expression of my regret and disapprobation.

Passing now, sir, from these topics, I shall briefly refer to the occurrences in Kansas connected with the organization of its government, in order to ascertain how far the Executive is justly liable to the censures we have heard proclaimed, and what course it becomes Congress to adopt in the present conjuncture of affairs there. The majority and minority reports of the committee afford all the facts necessary to a just appreciation of the circumstances. I shall therefore deal mostly with results.

The organic law made provision for the institution and operation of the government. The principal agent was the governor, and under his directions the preparatory measures were all taken, and the elections held. Evil passions were abroad, and in some of the districts irregular and violent proceedings took place, of which the committee reports give us the history. But the necessary returns were made, and both branches of the legislature were declared constituted, and were recognised by the proper authority Some of the returns were contested, but the seats of the majority of both bodies, forming a legal quorum for each, were not disputed, so that there was no just pretence for denying the legal organization of the legislature. There is no need, for any purpose I propose to myself, to pass in review the local controversy concerning the first election, the setting aside of the returns by the governor, the second election held by his order, or the ultimate decision of the council and house as to the persons entitled to the contested seats in those respective bodies: because, after the convocation and organization of the legislature, the qualification of its members was a subject within its own jurisdiction, as an incident of its existence; as much so as the power to preserve order. And that jurisdiction could not be rightfully disputed without the interposition of Congress, however it may have been exerted, unless made a question before a judicial tribunal. This principle is universal; and the proceedings of a legislature cannot be invalidated by any allegation of erroneous decisions respecting the qualification of its members.

In the progress of this inquiry we are now brought to the accusations against the Executive. What are they, and how are they prosecuted and maintained? But before proceeding to the consideration of this branch of the subject, I must request the attention of the Senate to an episode in the progress of our investigation, which comes to relieve the monotony of the work. The honorable senator from New York [Mr. SEWARD] has placed himself prominently among those who seek to charge the occurrences in Kansas to the President; and he tells us, in advance, that those who do not adopt the course which he recommends—that is, the immediate admission of Kansas—will reject it in "the hope of carrying African slavery into that new Territory." His speech was heralded before delivery, and applauded after it; and it is evidently considered by those who concur in his opinions as the test and standard of their views and purposes. It has been carefully prepared, and is an elaborate assault upon the President, "an elaborate misconception," to borrow the language applied to him by the senator, and an unsparing denunciation of the course of the administration and of the views of a majority of the Senate, while it is made the vehicle of opinions peculiar to the senator, some of which are rather shadowed forth than distinctly announced. These considerations, not less than the high character of the speaker, give special importance to his effort; and I propose, therefore, to examine it with some attention, in order to condemn and correct portions of his statements and doctrines more particularly obnoxious to animadversion.

But while I shall do this plainly, as the importance of the subject demands, I shall do it, I trust, in a proper spirit, and with kind personal feelings towards the Senator. I shall apply to him no allusion nor epithet—for it is not my habit—that ought to offend even fastidious delicacy, except such as is applied in his speech to the President of the United States; and I mean to make my application more just than his. And I shall do this in the hope that this lesson of the return of the chalice—not poisoned, but vituperative—may be profitable. That it is just, no one will question who considers that these assaults, not of argument but of language—of offensive language, upon the President, are not the result of hasty impulse, yielded to in the heat of debate, but of cool premeditation, prepared in the closet and recited in the Senate. In thus dealing with hard and bitter words and personal imputations towards the Chief Magistrate of the country in relation to the performance of his official duties, if the senator forgot the respect due to that high functionary as well as to himself, he should have recollected the respect due to the Senate, and, still more, to the country. There is no excuse for his having spoken of what he calls the President's defences as "indirect," "irrelevant," "ill-tempered," "sophistical," and "evasive;" of the President's "disingenuousness," "distortion of the constitution," "false and impertinent issue," "ambitious imbecility," "betrayal of his trust," "obscure and unfair statement," and for having made use of other harsh language, heard then with regret and surprise by almost all, and now recalled by me with pain.

"Believe the prophets of God," said the King of Judah, when all the men of the kingdom, with their wives and their children, had taken refuge in Jerusalem, dismayed at the invasion of the Moabites. "Believe the prophets of God, so shall ye prosper." And the senator from New York, more emphatic than impassioned, has read this portion of Jewish history, and pressed it into his service "Senators of the free States," said he, "I appeal to you: believe ye the prophets? I know ye do." And what is the application of this oratorical apostrophe? I grieve at the lamentable descent—at the fall from the dignity of style and subject. "You know, then" he continued, "that slavery neither works mines nor quarries;" nor do other deeds of utilitarian value, which he enumerates. To believe the prophets in the days of old was the safety of Israel: to believe the prophets in the days that are upon us is the safety of mines, of quarries—and of abolition. We were warned, in the time of our Saviour, that false prophets should come to seduce "even the elect" They are already upon us May the God of our fathers and our own God incline the hearts of the American people to reject their evil counsels, and to hold on to our precious heritage of Union!

I consider the senator's address upon that occasion one of the most extraordinary displays of legislative oratory it has ever been my fortune, good or bad, to listen to. How he ventured upon some of his statements, upon many of his assertions and conclusions—upon the personal imputations which abound in his speech, and upon a new edition of the higher law doctrine, freshly enunciated, but not amended, I confess my inability to comprehend. Instead of a full commentary upon this effusion, "this studied, partial, and prejudicial history," to borrow again from the senatorial vocabulary prepared for the President, I shall restrict myself to transferring from it to the Senate some of its most salient passages, leaving them, almost without remark, to tell their own story and the objects of their author, and to carry with them their own refutation.

The speech of the senator must be yet vivid in the recollection of the Senate. However intended, it came upon us with a kind of theatrical effect. Instead of being a grave and severe discussion, befitting the subject and the place, much of it took on the appearance of scenic representation; and we had an impeachment, in a "comedy of errors," rather than a dispassionate statesmanlike investigation. And in this contribution—whether to justice or party, let the country decide—the honorable senator performed all the parts necessary to the success of the piece. First, the author; he then assumed the various and incongruous characters of prosecutor, of witness, of defendant, and of judge, with due gravity and dignity, "citing the President" to the bar of the Senate, conducting the trial, and pronouncing the condemnation.

If the failure has been a signal one, those who know the Senator will be sure to attribute it to the weakness of the cause, which could not be saved even by the acknowledged power of the advocate.

After giving his version of the troubles in Kansas, connected with the organization and proceedings of the legislature, and "an obscure and unfair statement it is"—this is another extract from the speech, and spoken of the President—the senator enters upon his principal object, the inculpation of the President, without fear and without reserve, as he says, but with the self-confidence of one who declares he is aware of the gravity of the charges—with the self-confidence, indeed, of the great Roman orator, when he arraigned the proconsular robber of Sicily before the Roman senate. He prefers what he calls his charges, which are made up of his version of the transactions transferred to the President. Here they are:

Armed bands from Missouri seized the polls, overpowered or drove away the inhabitants, usurped the elective franchise, deposited false and spurious ballots, procured official certificates by fraud, &c.

The legislature established a complete and effective foreign tyranny over the people of the Territory.

These high-handed transactions were for the express purpose of establishing African slavery in the Territory by force, &c.

Then come the application and the guilt.

The President has been an accessory to these political transactions, with full complicity in regard to the purpose for which they were committed.

He has adopted the usurpation, and made it his own, and is now maintaining it with the military arm of the republic.

And thus are the charges against the President prepared, and thus is he shown to be guilty.

A plain tale will put this down.

The President was officially informed that danger of resistance to the law was to be apprehended in Kansas; and in conformity with his duty he directed the military force in that Territory, when called on by the proper Territorial authority, to aid in the maintenance of the laws. This is the head and front of his offence. And all the epithets, profusely employed on this occasion to describe the tyranny on one side and the abuse and oppression on the other, and to create a corresponding public reprobation and indignation, have reference to this single act—nothing more, nothing less. The matter lies within the narrowest compass, and may be summed up in two propositions:

First, the legislature of Kansas being organized, clothed with legal forms, recognised by the officer, to whom that duty was assigned by law, and in full operation, the President had no more right to interfere with that body than the legislature had to interfere with him.

Secondly, it was the legal duty of the President to direct the military force of the United States to aid in enforcing the law in Kansas, when properly informed there was danger of resistance.

So much for the sophism (another extract) of an accusation. And now for the sophism of a defence. The senator speaks and respeaks of the President's defences—that is the word—as though a formal indictment had been found against him, and he had as formally defended himself against many charges.

On the 31st December, 1855, the President, in his annual message to Congress, made a brief allusion to the affairs of Kansas, and made some very just and opportune remarks on the political agitation arising out of the assaults upon the southern States; and on the 24th of January succeeding he communicated in another message a detailed statement of the origin, progress, and condition of the troubles in the Territory.

And these executive documents, laid before Congress and the nation in obedience to the requisition of the constitution, the senator designates as the President's defences, thus imposing on the unwary the impression of a real trial and defence instead of a rhetorical exhibition. And with such pertinacious gravity does he follow out his system of tactics that one of his first complaints against the President is that he did not wait till his accuser, the youngest born of the republic, as he rather facetiously denominates Kansas—a State born before its birth—had appeared at the Capitol to prosecute him, but unfairly made his DEFENCES to Congress before the proper time. That is, when divested of all tropes, the President actually communicated to Congress and to his constituents, the American people, two messages, containing his views of the state of affairs in Kansas, and rendering an account of his stewardship, before the new candidate for admission into the Union had appeared here by her "two chosen senators and one representative." Unheard-of "tyranny," "suppression," "usurpation," "oppression," "subjugation," "submission," "disfranchisement," "mockery," and whatever other obnoxious epithets industry can collect or ingenuity can apply to excite opprobrium against the President for the "impertinence" and guilt of communicating messages to Congress.

The "disingenuous views" (another loan) taken by the senator of the powers and duties of the President are among the strangest constitutional heresies to which this claim to rule Americans without representation, and in contempt of their feelings and rights, has given birth. I comprehend clearly enough his object, which is to excite political indignation; but I fail entirely to comprehend how he fixes upon the President, even to his own satisfaction, any neglect of duty, still less any charge of a determination to introduce slavery into Kansas; for that is distinctly asserted, and without the shadow of proof. There is one portion of his speech which is mystical—indeed, almost a myth—where, personating the *speechless* people of the Territory—the word is his—he comes forward in a theatrical manner, stretching forth the *wand of New York*, and, holding in his hand the impeachment of George the Third by the Congress of 1776, impeaches, in the words of the Declaration of Independence, the President of the United States.

He then goes on to apply to the President the complaints made against the King of England, arranging eleven clauses in formal succession, each with its charge of omission or of commission, in the very language of that immortal State paper, substituting Kansas for the colonies, and the Republican Chief Magistrate for the anointed Potentate, beginning:

"He has refused to pass laws for the accommodation of the people," &c.

"He has called together legislative bodies at a place unusual, uncomfortable," &c., "for the purpose of fatiguing them into compliance with his measures."

"He has prevented legislative houses from being elected," &c., "because they would oppose, with manly firmness, his invasion on the rights of the people."

"He has created a multitude of new offices, and sent hither swarms of officers to harass our people and eat out their substance," &c.

"He has kept among us in time of peace standing armies," &c., "to compel our submission to a foreign legislature," &c.

And so on to the end of the chapter of colonial grievances against Great Britain.

Really, Mr. President, I can hardly treat this subject with the decorum due to our position and functions. Has the Senator from New York formed so poor an estimate of the intelligence of his associates here, or of his countrymen anywhere, as to suppose that one man can be found who believes that the President of the United States possesses the same powers in our Territories as the sovereign of England possesses in her colonies?—for hers they are in the eye of the law. With the exception of the appointment of some five or six officers, and the authority to remove them, the President has as little legal power in the Territories as the Senator from New York, unless, indeed, there is violent opposition to the laws; when, if he is legally informed of the danger, he must use the force the law places at his disposal to preserve and restore public order and tranquillity. And yet an American Senator dares, in his place, to say that "Kansas is to-day in the very act of revolution against the tyranny of the President of the United States;" thus identifying the constitutional action of the Executive with that tyranny which gave birth to the American Revolution. And after this startling proposition the Senator indulges in some rather incomprehensible reflections on "the profound philosophy of revolutions," the value of which escapes my penetration. And the profundity of this ethical sentiment is illustrated by the discovery that "the President is assumed, by the people of Kansas, to entertain a resentment which can never be appeased, and his power must, consequently, be wholly taken away;" that is, the Kansas public, or a portion of them, believe the President is displeased with them, and therefore they must have a revolution—and therefore "they have constituted themselves a State," and come here asking admission into the Union. And all this is "the profound philosophy of revolution."

The Senator is quite didactic in his speech, and passes happily and readily from one topic to another—from the philosophy of revolution to the philosophy of propagandism; and condemns the President for censuring the "propagandist attempt to colonize the Territory with opponents of slavery." The President censures, and justly, the external interference in the affairs of Kansas, by which efforts were made, in various States, to propagate "their social theories" in that Territory. And this is reproved by the Senator as *launching severe denunciations against what he says the President calls "propagandist attempts."* And then follows a eulogy upon that "*great element of colonization which has peopled the western continent;*" as though the adventurers who fled from civil and religious tyranny, and sought refuge here, came not to enjoy their opinions, but to disseminate them, and to live the lives of missionaries; and still more, as though the pious men who devote themselves to spreading the Gospel of Jesus, are but co-laborers with the political partisan who stays at home and stimulates others to carry agitation abroad, and to propagate secular opinions dangerous to the peace and tranquillity of another community.

There is a school of social, or rather anti-social, propagandism, composed of zealous and active disciples, followers of Proudhon, who maintain that *property is robbery*. They have faithful coadjutors in this country, whose industrial congress, as it was called, in laying down their creed, resolved, among other things, "That, by the land reform, we understand the entire abolition and annulment of all property value or ownership in the soil," &c.

I do not accuse the Senator of participating in these sentiments. He has powerful motives, from his success in life, for abjuring them; but I recollect that in a speech he made not long since in the city of New York, when he commenced by HAILING the city, as he commenced here by SALUTING the Senate—a fashion of salutatory introduction, preluding one's self or one's topic, more honored by the breach than by the observance—he supported views which, it appears to me, originate in the same kind of obliquity of moral vision, or in something not as pardonable. He announced that there was an aristocracy in this country; that aristocracies are created by privileged classes; that slaveholders constitute one of these classes. And why this attempt to excite popular indignation against a portion of our fellow-citizens by conferring upon them an obnoxious designation? The slaveholder owns slaves because the law permits it. Conscience and sound policy, said the Senator, prohibit it. The landholder owns land as he is allowed to do by law. Proudhon and his school say that conscience and sound policy prohibit it, for it is robbery.

Here is the same principle, differing only in its specific application. All who come within it are equally aristocrats. A privileged class is created by the Senator from New York, and is made a kind of raw-head and bloody-bones because it holds one species of property. But there are neither peculiar privileges nor exclusive rights attached to its tenure; for every man in a slave State may by law, without distinction, possess it. And why does not the denunciation equally apply to the holders of every species of property—to the holders of real estate, of money, of stock, of manufacturing establishments, which concentrate and control labor, and to every other article which constitutes the wealth of society, and the object and the reward of laudable industry and enterprise? It is easy to raise prejudices upon this subject. It is easy to conceive their operation upon the human mind, and how the man who has a coat is considered an aristocrat by him who has none. It is an old story in human experience, as the Senator knows, for he has studied the history of Rome, and referred us to the conduct of her tribunes. The office does not exist in this country; but one of the abuses which made it memorable—that of pandering to popular prejudices—is among us carefully cherished and often faithfully practised.

Now, sir, according to the Senator, he who goes abroad to teach "his social and political theories," is a missionary of propagandism, and his character is not changed by the nature of his doctrine; and he who censures his ill-timed zeal or wicked purpose casts reproach *where never prince, king, emperor, or president*, cast reproach before. The dissemination of the Gospel of Jesus Christ is brought down to the level of these political agitators. "The only common element of all these forms was propagandism." He exemplifies these forms by the various settlements in this country, attributing some to a zeal for religion, others to a zeal for slavery, and others to a zeal for free labor. The injunction of the risen Saviour, "Go ye forth, therefore, and teach all nations, baptizing them in the name of the Father, and of the Son, and of the Holy Ghost," is degraded by such an association. And I can discover no other motive for this desecration, but a desire to represent the President as condemning a great principle of human action. The Senator's test of the right to teach and preach anything is shown by the inquiry, "Does any law of nature or nations forbid?" The great law in the everlasting code of the Gospel, of doing as you would be done by, forbids every American from such propagandist interference with the internal affairs of another State or Territory as will tend to raise agitation, or to endanger the public peace and tranquillity. Leave to others the liberty you claim for yourself—the liberty to conduct their own affairs in their own way—and there will be no need of the perversion of the true principles of propagandism to justify unjustifiable acts.

In the pleasant town where the Senator resides is a dishonorable home provided by retributive justice for unfortunate outcasts, whose crimes, if not expiated, are justly punished there. I doubt not but that many a man has gone there, and will yet be followed by many another, victims of false and dangerous theories, who have been taught that there are aristocrats in the land—privileged classes; that property is robbery, and that what God made for all, the few have no right to appropriate to themselves; and that he who wants may justly take his share, wherever he finds it, of which another has unjustly deprived him. The Senator from New York has not yet reached the full measure of his faith, though his denunciations against one kind of property necessarily lead to the whole doctrine. A little spark kindleth a great fire. It is dangerous to tamper with human passions. Better is it to instruct than to stimulate them. And the Senator, by devoting his acknowledged talents to this work and withdrawing from his present field of excitement, will acquire more permanent fame than ever followed political agitation.

When the senator proceeds to establish, as he says, the truth of his conclusions, he gives us an inkling of the philosophy of evidence, asking what kind he must bring forward to support the impeachment, and finally falls back upon what he dignifies as presumptive proofs. And presumptuous, indeed, it is to endeavor to fortify such grave charges by idle—I might say, following his example, "impertinent"—suggestions, at once so feeble in themselves and so remote in their application. There are no less than thirty of these barren suggestions, spread out in formidable array, and they constitute about as curious an exhibition of judicial "distortion" as the whole history of evidence affords. I shall stop neither to recapitulate nor to digest them, limiting myself to garnering a few from the abundant harvest-field, but sample enough to establish the true character of the whole crop.

He begins by observing that such presumptive evidence is derived from the nature and character of the President's defences, again intimating that the President had actually come forward to defend himself from the senator's accusations. And then follow the thirty interrogatories, or, in other words, the thirty proofs. Here they are, or rather specimens of them:

"Why did the President plead at all on the 31st of December last, when the new State of Kansas was yet unorganized, and could not appear here to prefer her accusations until the 23d of March?"

Divested of mysticism, this means, as I have before said, why did the President presume to communicate to Congress the state of affairs in Kansas? I have too much respect for the Senate to do more than to let the senator ask this question—and such a question. Again:

"Why, if he must answer so prematurely, did he not plead a general and direct denial?"

Say guilty or not guilty in his message. This rather smells of the shop. It is too technical.

"Why did he interpose the false and impertinent issue whether one State could intervene by its laws or by force to abolish slavery in another State?"

To borrow an expression from the senator, this certainly "clinches conviction."

"Why did he arraign so unnecessarily and so unjustly, not one, but all of the original States?"

"Why did he drag into this case, where only Kansas is concerned, a studied, partial, and prejudicial history of the past enlargements of the national domain?"

"Why did he submit a second plea in advance?"

Translated—"Why did he render an account to Congress of the state of matters in Kansas?"

Why did he "denounce Massachusetts?" Another "misrepresentation." This denunciation was the expression of regret as to the course of some of the northern states and their citizens.

On what evidence does he say that there were "mutual complaints," &c., in Kansas, as though it were not a fact universally known? Why does he argue that Governor Reeder alone had power to receive and consider the returns of elections, &c., "when he knows that the governor, being his own agent," &c. A less profound statesman would say that officer was the agent of the law.

"Why was Governor Reeder replaced by Mr. Shannon, who immediately proclaimed" the legislature as legal, &c.?

"The President virtually confesses" his guilt, by presenting a system of maxims and principles invented to justify him.

There are yet other exhibitions attending this rare process, and resulting from the peculiar views of the senator, or from the sextuple capacity of accuser, prosecutor, witness, defendant, jury, and judge, in which he presents himself, that are not unworthy of passing notice.

Because the President enforces the laws of the United States in Kansas, by that act "he adopts the usurpation and makes it his own."

Kansas has thus been revolutionized, (by being prevented from making a revolution,) and "is prostrated at the foot of the President."

Because the President says, in his annual message to Congress, that if there should be obstructions to the federal law, or organized resistance to the Territorial law in Kansas, assuming the character of insurrection, it would be his duty to suppress it, therefore, "he menaces the people of Kansas with a threat that he will overcome and suppress them." This is no menace; it is only a warning to the law-breaker, whoever he may be.

"The President's mind was oppressed; was full of something too large and burdensome to be concealed, and yet too critical to be told," and, therefore, he told it to Congress and to the country.

One of the most reprehensible passages in the whole speech of the senator is that where he draws a parallel between Christianity and abolition, anticipating for the latter the miraculous progress which proves the divinity of the former. "Abolition," he says, "is a slow but irrepressible uprising of principles of natural justice and humanity," &c. "I may, however, remind slaveholders that there is a time when oppression and persecution cease to be effectual against such movements," &c. "Christianity, blindly maligned during three centuries by prætors, governors, senators, councils, and emperors, towered above its enemies in a fourth; and even the cross on which its founder had expired, and which, therefore, was the emblem of its shame, became the sign under which it went forth evermore thereafter conquering and to conquer. ABOLITION IS YET IN ITS FIRST CENTURY." To which I add, may it be its last—the last of external interference in the domestic concerns of other communities.

He who runs may read that the purpose of all this irreverence is to elevate this fanatical and political firebrand to an equality with the Gospel of Jesus Christ.

The President laments that the election of a delegate to Congress could not have been held early enough to enable the House of Representatives to judge of the election, and thereby decide the question of qualification of voters; therefore, the President regretted that there was not a merely formal election of the legislature, "in fraud of the organic law, and of the people of Kansas, and of the course of natural justice and humanity." And this great injury would have been the result of the judgment of the House of Representatives of the United States.

Because the President can see no legal power possessed by him to examine into the validity of the election in Kansas, therefore it is "ambitious imbecility." What condition of the human mind is described by this phrase I leave to the adept in ambitious rhetoric to explain.

The President openly lent his "official influence and patronage to the slaveholders of Missouri;" the proof of which is, that he knew their purposes, as the senator says, and did not interfere to prevent them; or, in other words, to assume powers the law has not conferred upon him.

The President is forcibly introducing and establishing slavery in Kansas.

"The Congress of the United States can refuse admission to Kansas only on the ground that it will not relinquish the hope of carrying African slavery into that new Territory."

This is another bold assertion, sir, but that is its only claim to concurrence. I shall vote to refuse admission to Kansas; and, at the same time, I hope that neither African slavery, nor any other kind of slavery, will be established there; and I believe, if the senator and his political friends will cease their agitation, that Kansas will eventually be a free State. At the same time, whether slavery is to be established there or not, my course will be the same. I shall maintain the principle which leaves that question to the people, and I shall rest satisfied with their decision, trusting that the question may be determined by them, uninfluenced by any external interference, whether from Missouri or Massachusetts.

But, sir, I have not time to follow the senator in his "extraordinary inconsistency"—another phrase coined by him for the President. I must hasten on, and leave that task to those who consider it a useful one. The Kansas legislature, under its panoply of legal form, was as independent of the Executive as the Executive was of that body. The only case which admitted legal interference was the case that occurred when, there being danger of opposition to the law, and that danger having been duly made known, the President promptly took legal measures for the preservation of the public peace. For that act of wise precaution he is entitled to the commendation of the country. It has probably prevented a civil war among the people themselves, and perhaps an insurrection against the United States. After the organization of the Kansas legislature there were two modes of proceeding open to all those who considered themselves aggrieved. One was to resort to the judicial tribunals, and the other to appeal to Congress. Neither measure was adopted. In the mean time the legislature went on with its work of law-making; and its labors have been exposed to severe criticism, as well as to grave censure—whether justly or not does not affect the inquiry we are engaged in, which turns upon the legal powers of the legislature, and not upon the wisdom or the folly of their exercise. Though I am free to confess that, while the great body of the code they enacted is marked with wise and salutary provisions, and may favorably compare with the legal systems of our older States, offences are created, and prohibitions and penalties provided, irreconcilable with the first principles of human freedom, and revolting to American feeling. Determined to examine this whole subject dispassionately, I determined also to express my opinion frankly, and to condemn or approve, as justice should seem to me to require; and in the condemnation I am now pronouncing I am acting in that spirit. I am not to be led—misled rather—by opinions like those we have heard putting constructions on these laws inconsistent with their plain import, and declared when public sentiment had pronounced them indefensible. Those entertaining such opinions speak for themselves; but I read the terms employed by the legislature, and judge for myself. They are unequivocal, and the proceeding is a reproach to American jurisprudence.

Disregarding the two legal remedies within their power, the citizens of Kansas opposed to the action of the legislature resorted to a revolution. This is what the senator from New York calls the movement, while he approves it; and this is what it would have been if carried into operation. A convention was elected, and quickly convened, and it as quickly formed a constitution, making provision for its operation, without the sanction of Congress, as soon as approved by a popular vote. This vote it received; and if wiser counsels finally prevailed, and the constitution was not forcibly carried into operation during the existence of the government instituted by Congress, and a collision thus avoided, the result formed no part of the original plan. That constitution is now before us.

And why this precipitate act of revolution, which, if consummated, would have brought those participating in it into direct collision with the government of the United States? Why not ask Congress for a redress of grievances arising out of a law enacted by itself? No man can doubt the power of Congress to watch the operation of its own laws, and to provide all necessary remedies for their mal-administration. Nor ought any man to doubt that if this whole matter had been properly presented by petition from the people at the commencement of the session, there would have been an impartial and rigid inquiry, followed by such measures as justice might have required. Instead of that course, we are now asked to give our sanction to these revolutionary proceedings by confirming them, and thus to establish a principle incompatible with future tranquillity in the Territories, and holding out encouragement for future resistance.

Now, sir, this application will not receive my vote. I will agree to set no such example. The immediate effect would be to render operative a constitution for Kansas, the work of but one portion of a people divided by internal dissensions, being a portion arraying itself against the law, instead of appealing for redress to this high tribunal of the nation, competent to administer it. The course proposed by the Committee on the Territories is free from objection, and I shall vote for it. It is to submit to the whole people, and by legal authorization, the question of the institution of their own government, and not subject one portion to the work of another, thus perpetuating divisions, which it is the interest of the country to terminate as soon as possible. Warned by the past, I think we should provide for the future by adequate penalties in the organic laws against all unlawful external interference in the affairs of the Territories, and especially against the entrance of armed persons or parties to control or overawe the elections; and I submit for consideration, whether some provision of that nature is not now required at our hands; whether it would not be a just measure in itself, and a proper tribute to the purity of elections—a great conservative principle, dear to every right-minded American. Let us have no more armed invasion from without, nor insurrection within.

Mr. President, many and signal have been the interpositions of Providence in our favor since the commencement of our national existence. We have been carried forward in a career of prosperity unexampled in the history of the world. Difficulties and dangers have beset us upon the right hand and upon the left; but we have safely passed through them, gathering strength in our progress till we have nothing to fear but ourselves and the just judgments of God. A question is around us, among us, exciting angry passions, and arraying one portion of the country against another—a sectional question, the most difficult and delicate with which we have to deal. And a way has been found to deal with it which requires no sacrifice of principle, of pride, or of opinion, by one part of the confederation to the other, but their mutual submission of the controversy to the operation of the great doctrine of the right of man to govern himself, the only solid basis of republican governments. And the dispensations of Providence towards us have never been marked with more kindness than in inclining the hearts of the American people to seek refuge from impending danger in this, the only means of averting it. There is no other ground on which we can stand together. The wisdom of man can discover no other. But this is holy ground, sanctified by a living principle, and rising above a world of waters, which has been spreading out over the land. I trust it will yet stay the flood, and rescue us from the only peril which the patriot contemplates with doubt and apprehension.

THE SPURIOUS KANSAS MEMORIAL.

DEBATE

IN THE

SENATE OF THE UNITED STATES,

ON THE

MEMORIAL OF JAMES H. LANE,

PRAYING

'HAT THE SENATE RECEIVE AND GRANT THE PRAYER

OF THE

MEMORIAL PRESENTED BY GENERAL CASS, AND AFTERWARDS WITHDRAWN;

EMBRACING

THE SPEECHES OF SENATORS DOUGLAS, PUGH, BUTLER, TOUCEY, RUSK, &c.

WASHINGTON:
PRINTED AT THE UNION OFFICE.
1856.

THE SPURIOUS KANSAS MEMORIAL.

Debate in the Senate, April 14, 1856, *on the memorial of* James H. Lane, *praying that the Senate receive and grant the prayer of the memorial presented by General* Cass, *and afterwards withdrawn, embracing the speeches of Senators* Douglas, Pugh, Butler, Toucey, Rusk, *&c.*

The debate was opened by Mr. HARLAN, who presented the memorial of Colonel Lane, and proceeded to pass a high eulogium upon him for his services as a politician and a soldier. After detailing Colonel Lane's services, Mr. Harlan proceeded :

But, Mr. President, I desire to remind the democracy of the country, so ably represented on this floor, who had conferred on him so many distinguished honors, that when he came to his own his own knew him not. They seemed to have entirely forgotten his distinguished services in days of yore. It was not remembered with sufficient vividness to be a voucher for his personal honesty. The honorable senator from Louisiana (Mr. Benjamin) said of the paper which he presented to the Senate of the United States, in the name of the members of the Senate and House of Representatives :

"I believe, upon the face of this petition and upon scrutinizing its statements and the signatures which are attached to it, that it is an impudent forgery, attempted to be palmed off upon the Senate of the United States through the hands of the venerable senator from Michigan. I do not believe this to be the petition of the men from whom it purports to emanate. I want to know how this petition got here under such circumstances as to call for such observations as it has elicited from all sides of the house."

But no one answers. No one knows. No one seems to remember who James H. Lane is. The honorable senator from Connecticut, (Mr. Toucey,) who, I believe, was a member of the cabinet organized by Mr. Polk, whose election was aided very materially by the stump speeches of Mr. Lane, does not seem to know who he is. The honorable senator from Ohio, (Mr. Pugh,) his companion in arms, too, seems to have forgotten him.

Mr. PUGH. Mr. President, I desire that the Senator from Iowa shall not misrepresent me. I made no remark whatever, not a syllable, in reference to the gentleman who brought this petition here. I abstained carefully from anything of the sort, and the senator will so find in the report of my remarks.

Mr. HARLAN. If the remark which I made does misrepresent the honorable senator from Ohio, no one will more gladly stand corrected than myself.

Mr. TOUCEY. I beg leave to correct the senator.

Mr. HARLAN. I think, if honorable senators will suffer me to proceed, they will find that I do not differ with them as to what they did state.

Mr. TOUCEY. I did not say one word in regard to Colonel Lane. I did not allude to him.

Mr. HARLAN. It is this death-like silence [laughter] that, I suppose, caused the honorable senator from South Carolina to inquire of the Senate who was the bearer of the petition. All his friends had forgotten him. The honorable senator from South Carolina asked, Who is this James H. Lane? He told us he did not know him. The honorable senator from Ohio made no response.

Mr. PUGH. I heard no such question. If the Senator himself, or any one else, had asked me who was Colonel Lane, I should have given all the information in my power ; and if the senator desires me to give it, I will do so now.

Mr. HARLAN. Fortunately now, by reference to the records and the history of the country, I am tolerably well posted up. If the information had been given on Thursday last it would have been very acceptable.

Mr. PUGH. Then the senator does not wish to hear from me.

Mr. BUTLER. I never mentioned Lane's name.

Mr. HARLAN. By reference to the printed speech of the honorable senator from South Carolina, he will find that he propounded the question, How did this petition get here? and he told us that he did not know. The honorable senator from Michigan, too, who presented the petition, was unable to answer the question. It seemed just at that time that his memory was oblivious, and that he had forgotten the author of the letter addressed to himself at Paris, dictated and drawn up, I believe, by this James H. Lane.

Mr. CASS. Does the senator mean to say that I made any allusion to him at all?

Mr. HARLAN. I meant to say that the question of the honorable senator from South Carolina was not answered by any one of these honorable senators.

Mr. CASS. Allow me to say one word to the gentleman. He assumes that a question was put which was not answered. Why, sir, you have no right to require every man to get up here and answer every question put in that way. If a senator, in the course of his remarks, says that a fact is not so, am I bound to contradict it? You may allude to what a senator himself says, but you can draw no inference from his failure to notice or answer a question that is not addressed to him; there is no ethics in that.

Mr. BUTLER. I do not intend to detain the Senate by making any reply to the senator from Iowa—very far from it; but I do not wish the senator from Iowa to make an issue for me which he cannot understand.

Mr. HARLAN. Will the honorable senator state his remark again.

Mr. BUTLER. I say that I do not wish you again, as you have attempted heretofore, to make an issue for me before the country which you cannot understand.

The *gravamen* of my argument against the printing of this memorial last week was that the motion to print it was in violation of a rule of the Senate. Why do I say it was a violation of the rules of the Senate? Because it came in here with the intrusive title marked upon it that it was a paper that was presented by the senators and representatives of the State of Kansas. I did ask the question who has presented this petition that can be invested with any of the attributes or the dignity of senators or representatives of Kansas, when we knew there was no such State? That is the way in which I stated my proposition. I did not allude to Colonel Lane. I do not know that the mere person was in my mind. I asked officially who was it that presented it here—in what capacity; and how did it get to the Senate of the United States? Did it come here through the straight gate, or over the wall, or under it? That is what I said, and I confine myself always to the proposition before the Senate. The gentleman, I have no doubt, is very willing to take a great advantage of the fact that sometimes I illustrate the few remarks which I make by some allusion to the Iliad. I did not know before that Lane was the hero of Buena Vista. I have no doubt hereafter this oration will be put in verse and will be called the *Lanead*. [Laughter.]

The *gravamen* of my proposition was as I have stated; and I now state that the rule requires every petition coming to the Senate of the United States to have signatures attached to it. My friend from Illinois will take care of that. I have used the word *gravamen*. I hope the gentleman will forgive me, for I understand about as much of Latin as he does of English. [Laughter.]

Mr. DOUGLAS. Mr. President, I propose to raise the question of the reception of this memorial, and to give the reasons why it ought not to be received. Colonel Lane now presents a paper here in his own name, claiming to be entitled to a seat in the Senate of the United States from the State of Kansas, and sets forth in the memorial——

Mr. HARLAN. I hope the honorable senator will allow me to state the proposition. He claims to be entitled to a seat on this floor from the State of Kansas when that State shall have been received into the Union.

Mr. DOUGLAS. He puts the form of expression in that way to avoid the objection which was taken to the memorial the other day, purporting to be from the senators and representatives of the legislature of the State of Kansas. It shows clearly that it is an evasion to change the phraseology, and yet affirm his right to a seat in this body. He makes it an individual memorial, and then annexes to it the obnoxious paper which was rejected by the Senate the other day. Inasmuch as he annexes that paper, and makes it a part of his memorial, it is liable to all the objections which were urged to that, together with others of a still more serious character.

Now, sir, what is the explanation which he gives for having presented the paper the other day, through the senator from Michigan, with a declaration that it was a memorial from the members of that legislature then in session? The excuse is, that the paper then presented was copied from an original memorial reported to the legislature of the self-styled State of Kansas from a committee by Mr. Hutchinson, its chairman, and which was first adopted, and then referred to a committee of revision. This fact is verified by the oath of Colonel Lane, drawn in language so equivocal and evasive as to raise a doubt in regard to the fairness of the explanation. His oath is, that that paper was drawn up and adopted, and was referred to a committee of revision, from which the present revised copy is taken. By whom was it taken? I will show you that it is a totally different document, and not a true or even substantial copy of the one which he alleges was adopted in Kansas.

Here I may be permitted to remark that I do not see what connexion it has with the genuineness of the paper to prove that Colonel Lane was in the Mexican war. I do not see the force of that fact to elucidate the point in dispute. Great pains have also been taken here to prove that this could not have been a fraud, because Colonel Lane was a democrat! I admit that is a pretty fair presumption. I admit there is great weight in that position.

The senator from Iowa also assumes that this could not have been a fraud because Colonel

Lane voted for the Nebraska bill. That fact, too, ought to have its full weight in his favor, and may raise the presumption that he is an honest man, and incapable of perpetrating a fraud upon the Senate.

But are these satisfactory proofs on the point in dispute? I have known men to claim to be democrats before who had about as good a title and as good a record as Colonel Lane. I I suppose that Mr. Francis P. Blair could prove a good record during the lifetime of General Jackson, and a volume could be written to show his services and his devotion to the democratic cause. But if you will trace his history a little further, you will find him president of a black republican convention at Pittsburg. In the face of that fact, would you deem it fair to quote him as a democrat at the present time? I suppose that one Andrew Jackson Donelson could show a record representing him as private secretary to the old hero, with the false claim put forth by his new friends that he was entitled to claim the honors of an adopted son. He, too, is a candidate for the vice presidency of the United States on the know-nothing ticket! Does this fact prove that he is a democrat now?

I suppose it will not be denied by his new political associates that Colonel Lane now is as essentially identified with the black republican party as Mr. Blair himself is, or as Mr. Donelson is with the know-nothing party. Is the mere fact that they once belonged to the democratic party conclusive evidence that they could not have done anything wrong since their apostacy? Is there so much virtue in democratic associations that it protects a man's reputation from all injurious imputations after having fallen from grace? I admit the virtue so long as they are faithful to democratic principles, but I deny that they have a right to claim, as a saving grace, sufficient to exculpate them for subsequent sins that they were once democrats, and apostacized from the true faith. That, sir, is all I have to say of the democracy of Colonel Lane, and all that class of modern politicians whose chief claim to popular favor consists in the fact that they were once democrats, and have betrayed those who have reposed confidence in them and heaped honors on them.

I have to deal with this paper as I find it. Now, is the paper which was presented the other day a copy, or not, of the paper now presented as the original? The first three pages of the original are not to be found at all in the paper presented by the senator from Michigan I will read some portions of those three pages. On the second page will be found this paragraph:

"The Constitution of the United States guaranties to every State a republican form of government, and delegates to Congress no power to establish any laws over any State, except such as are national, and affect the States alike for the common good. The people of any Territory or State, over whom the Constitution extends, although not admitted into the Union as a sovereign State, have reserved to themselves the same inherent and inalienable rights as belonged to the people of the several States of the Union. The Constitution declares that powers not delegated to the United States by the Constitution, nor prohibited by it to the States, are reserved to the States respectively or to the people. Therefore, since the Constitution delegates to Congress no power to establish a government over the new Territories, the same inherent rights are reserved to the people of a Territory over which the Constitution extends, as are reserved to the people of the several original States."

Thus the memorial, which, as it is said, was adopted by the Kansas legislature, declared their right to form a State constitution because the Nebraska bill was unconstitutional; because, being unconstitutional, it was a nullity; because there were no constituted authorities in the Territory; because Congress had no power over them; and hence they would not submit to the power of Congress. That is the ground on which this memorial adopted by the Kansas legislature puts their case. It is the very point asserted in the majority report, and denied by the senator from Vermont (Mr. Collamer) in the minority report—the very point in controversy between us and our opponents. Colonel Lane comes here standing on the revolutionary right, with a memorial that denies the power of Congress, and defies its authority; he finds his friends backing out, saying that it is not their position; and then he sits down and makes what he calls a copy, and omits that fundamental principle on which their whole action rested. It is not an immaterial point. It is not a mere surplusage as pretended. It is striking at the fundamental principle upon which they rest all their action. It is a change in a vital part of the memorial, for the purpose of avoiding the issue which the majority of the Committee on Territories had made with the minority, for the purpose of avoiding the weight of the blows under which the defenders of this rebellion were staggering and tottering, until they found that they could not maintain their position.

In order to enable them to change the position in which they had been beaten in argument, somebody took their own memorial and struck out the very ground on which they justified their whole action, and brought forward a different thing altogether, as a justification of their conduct. I submit whether this does not make it a totally different document, affirming entirely different principles, in order to place their action in a totally different light. The Kansas legislature, in the original document, said they justified their acts because Congress had no power over them. The memorial came in the other day recognizing the power of Congress. I ask, then, if it is not a forgery, thus to change the document in the most vitally important point upon which the whole proceeding rests? I do not say by whom the forgery was committed—I care not. The taint runs through this whole proceeding, and the affidavit does not cure or remedy it. Here are other parts of this original memorial, which were omitted or suppressed in the paper presented the other day, purporting to be a memorial signed by all the members of this bogus legislature:

I doubt whether Judge McLean has authority to administer such an oath; but let that pass. Now, Mr. President, what does the affidavit declare? Is this the memorial of the general assembly, so called, of the State of Kansas? No, sir; by Colonel Lane's own statement, it is not. This is the mere draft, adopted by a committee, and read to the so called legislature. That body, we are told, has agreed to it in substance, but never has ordered it to be engrossed and signed. Neither the members nor the officers, in fact, ever affixed their signatures. They gave it no sort of authentication.

What did the members of the self-styled legislature direct? They referred it to *another* committee for revision, intending that it should be put into shape before its final adoption and signature; but this committee of revision, instead of performing the duty enjoined—instead of revising the memorial, and reporting it to the legislature, so called, for consideration, has given the paper to Colonel James H. Lane, and devolved on him, not a member of the legislature at all, the duty and the authority of revision. That is what Colonel Lane here affirms, and that, I presume, is the case. The committee of revision never reported the memorial. The draft of it was handed to Colonel Lane, and Colonel Lane has revised it. He assumes to be the spokesman for all these provisional legislators. They have only to swear in his words, and follow in his footsteps; whatever he chooses to say, I suppose, they are to be considered as having indorsed, upon faith, beforehand. Yet, sir, we are told that this is the memorial of men acting themselves in a delegated and representative character; speaking for others who have confided in their special discretion—of men assembled in the high capacity of a State legislature!

Mr. President, if it were not for the great question which is behind—if it were not for the agitation which now prevails in all quarters of the Union—if no terrible controversy, political and sectional, had arisen—there is not a senator in this chamber who would vote to receive this paper—not one. It is an imperfect undertaking at best. If the self-styled general assembly of Kansas should ever hold another session—if the members can succeed in escaping grand juries, and indictments, marshals, and writs, and the issues of solemn judicial investigation, and then assemble for the transaction of business—it may be that this document will be reported regularly from the committee on revision, and authenticated as well as adopted in due form. When such an event shall have happened—if happen it possibly can—and the memorial is again presented here for our consideration, I will decide what becomes me as a senator toward the petitioners and the country at large.

Now, sir, as we have heard so much lately about the right of petition, let us see how far this paper conforms to the rules established in ancient times, and written down for our instruction. I read from one of the Secretary's books, "Laws, Privileges, Proceedings, and Usages of Parliament," page 303:

"The petition should be written upon parchment or paper, for a printed or lithographed petition will not be received; and at least one signature should be upon the same sheet or skin upon which the petition is written. It must be in the English language, or accompanied with a translation which the member who presents it states to be correct; it must be free from interlineations and erasures; it must be signed; it must have original signatures or marks, and not copies from the original, nor signatures of agents on behalf of others; and it must not have letters, nor affidavits, or other documents annexed. Petitions of corporations aggregate should be under their common seal. To these rules another may be added, that, if the chairman of a public meeting signs a petition on behalf of those assembled, it is only received as the petition of the individual, and is so entered on the journals, because the signature of one party for others cannot be recognized.

"It may be a useful caution to state that any forgery or fraud in the preparation of petitions, or in the signatures attached, will be punished as a breach of privilege. By a resolution of the House of Commons, 2d of June, 1774, it was declared:

"'That it is highly unwarrantable, and a breach of the privilege of this House, for any person to set the name of any other person to any petition to be presented to this House.'

"And there have been frequent instances in which such irregularities have been discovered and punished."

That is the English rule. We are not quite so strict in the United States. Here is what Mr. Jefferson says:

"Petitions must be subscribed by the petitioners, unless they are attending, or unable to sign, and averred by a member. But a petition not subscribed, but which the member presenting it affirmed to be all in the handwriting of the petitioner, and his name written in the beginning, was on a question (March 14, 1800) received by the Senate. The averment of a member, or of somebody without doors, that they know the handwriting of the petitioners, is necessary, if it be questioned."

I do not ask even this strictness. I simply ask that the paper should express the sentiments of the persons from whom it purports to emanate, in their own language, or in language which they have considered and adopted.

I do not agree that these men, whether you call them a legislature, or by some other title, can deputize Colonel Lane to put the recital of their grievances into form. I do not agree to receive any paper from him at all, unless it be his own petition, in his individual character, and upon his responsibility as a citizen.

But, sir, this is not the only objection. I find another rule worthy of notice, on page 304 of the book which I first quoted :

"The language of a petition should be respectful and temperate, and free from offensive imputations upon the character and conduct of parliament, or the courts of justice, or other tribunal, or constituted authority. It may not allude to debates in either house of parliament, nor to intended motions."

Now, Mr. President, I wish to call the attention of the Senate to a few paragraphs in this paper :

"The undersigned have witnessed, with astonishment and deep regret, the coarse insinuation on the character and conduct of the people of Kansas contained in the recent special message of the President of the United States."

Again, sir, on a subsequent page :

"Toleration of such outrages is but an enslavement of the people of Kansas, and a breach of faith, and a dereliction of duty on the part of the Federal Executive."

Mr. President, whatever my relations to a citizen so eminent as he must be who is exalted to the office of Chief Magistrate—if I were ever so much opposed to him in political sentiment—I could not vote to receive any petition which thus reflected upon his character and motives. What right have we to receive such a petition? This, sir, is not the House by which the President can be impeached. This is the House which must try the President whenever he has been impeached ; and shall we permit any accuser, except the House of Representatives, to drag him before us? Shall we dignify or affirm charges of so gross a character, in advance of any trial, in advance of any impeachment, by enjoining on our committees the duty which attends the reference of a petition? Sir, the grossest act of usurpation ever practiced in this body, as I believe, was when President Jackson was condemned by resolution without a trial. I will not agree—knowing that among the duties devolved on me, in virtue of my official oath, is that of delivering judgment upon the Chief Magistrate whenever he shall have been properly arraigned—I will not agree that Colonel Lane and his associates shall assume the office and authority of the grand inquest of the nation, which now sits at the other end of the Capitol.

I told the Senator from Iowa, when he first referred to me by name, that I had not made any charge or insinuation against the character of Colonel Lane. I did not think it necessary to the maintenance of my position. I make no charges now. I cannot imagine what we have to do with that gentleman. I do not see the propriety of thrusting his praises into this discussion. The senator from Iowa has related his biography at great length, his public services, and his partisan services, and then appeals to me, in a sneering manner, as his companion in arms, his political confederate, and what not, that I was under some obligation to support Colonel Lane's pretensions or endorse his behavior. I violated my duty, forsooth, because I did not answer some general question propounded by my honorable friend from South Carolina, (Mr. Butler,) which I did not hear, and which I told the Senator from Iowa distinctly I did not hear. Besides, sir, I agree with my honorable and distinguished friend from Michigan, (Mr. Cass,) that I was under no obligations to answer a rhetorical question, general in its character, if I had heard it. I have other duties here and other tastes than to rehearse the biography of individuals, living or dead, at the mere solicitation of a senator. I am not one of Colonel Lane's witnesses. He has not asked me to be his witness ; he has not asked me to present any of his papers ; he has not asked me to give a recital of his services, his sufferings, or his sacrifices ; and, indeed, the senator from Iowa has dispensed with the necessity of all that.

My colleague says that the citizens of Ohio feel a deep interest in the affairs of Kansas Territory. I believe that is true ; I believe the citizens of every State in the Union feel such an interest. He declares, furthermore, that it shall be a part of his duty to extend a special protection over those who have emigrated from the State of Ohio into the Territory of Kansas, and established their residence in it. Sir, I disclaim such duty, for my part. I disclaim all charge over them, or partisanship for them, except as they are citizens of the United States, and entitled to the protection of the Constitution and the laws. There sits before me, sir, a gentleman who once held a prominent position in the State which I have the honor to represent, but who has since become a citizen of the State of California, (Mr. Weller,) and she has showered honors upon him. I should like to know if my colleague imagines that he and I are to exercise guardianship over the honorable senator from California? Those men who emigrated from Ohio to Kansas have gone from his care and mine. They abandoned our State and all allegiance to it. They are no longer citizens of Ohio in any sense. And whenever the State, by any of her authorities—her legislature, her governor, or either of her senators—shall assume to dictate for the Territory of Kansas, upon such a pretence as that, it will be an act of unwarrantable and inexcusable usurpation.

I understand, perhaps, to what my colleague alludes. I know the fact—he knows it—others know it—that the gentleman who now holds the chief executive office in Ohio has addressed a message to the general assembly of the State upon the subject of Kansas affairs—advising that the State should intervene, in its sovereign capacity, for the settlement of certain controversies between the territorial legislature upon the one side, and the insurgents at Lawrence upon the other. It was a proposition to engage the State in rebellion and civil war. Thereupon, sir, one member of the legislature—a representative of the county, perhaps, in which my colleague resides—introduced a resolution that five regiments of soldiers should be enlisted and sent to Kansas for the purpose of waging a war upon the territorial authorities.

I am happy to inform the Senate, however, that the proposition was not adopted. Yet the legislature has passed resolutions which, in my judgment, are almost as objectionable—resolutions which indicate, as do some of their statutes, the design of urging our citizens to a choice, finally, between their allegiance to the Union and their allegiance to the State government. The resolutions will be presented here, I suppose, in a few days. Sir, it is this intervention from abroad in the affairs of Kansas Territory—intervention by States, by municipal and private corporations, by organized bands of factions and parties, by the arts of ambitious men stimulating the passions of our people, north and south, with falsehoods, clamors, and every species of plausible appeal—which prevents the fair adjustment of all controversies in the Territory and elsewhere, and which, worse than even that, has induced throughout the republic an anxiety, and horrible fear and distrust for the perpetuity of the Union. I give my colleague notice, once for all, that I engage in no such enterprises; that I shall resist them, here and elsewhere, with whatever zeal and ability God has bestowed on me. In their true character, as citizens of the United States inhabiting the Territory—citizens who have gone thither, in good faith, to enjoy the protection of the Constitution under the guarantees of the organic law—all who have emigrated from Ohio, and all who have emigrated from other States, are entitled to whatever attention and respect for their wishes—whatever redress for their grievances—it may be in my power to grant. But, sir, I will not take upon myself, directly or indirectly, the regulation of domestic affairs or local institutions for the Territory further than to restore peace and silence rebellion, to maintain the supremacy of the laws, to protect every individual—high and low, rich and poor—from all outrages and all oppression.

"By the provisions of the organic act a government was established over the Territory, and officers were appointed by the President to administer said government. This form of government is unknown to the Constitution, is extra-constitutional, and is only the creature of necessity awaiting the action of the people, and cannot remain in force contrary to the will of the people living under it. It may be regarded as a benevolent provision on the part of Congress thus to provide a government for a sparsely settled people, too few in numbers to support a government of their own; *but when it becomes oppressive, or when the people become sufficiently strong to establish a government of their own, in accordance with the Constitution of the United States, it is their right so to do and thereby throw off that extended over them.*"

Here their revolutionary right is again asserted to throw off the government established over them by Congress. Here they again affirm the precise position taken by the Committee on Territories, and denied by their advocates here. In running through the whole document, you find that every passage that would tend to sustain the argument of the majority of the committee and to controvert the positions of the minority, is stricken out. This shows that the plan of campaign on that side of the House has been changed since this memorial was got up. The mode of defence here has been changed; and official documents must be garbled and modified, added to or subtracted from, in order to conform to that change of policy.

Why, sir, to show what free use has been made with the sacred right of petition of these people of Kansas, I will refer to another fact. It had been contended in argument, in the minority report, that the Arkansas case was a case in point to justify Kansas, because Mr. Attorney General Butler there said that the territorial legislature could give no authority for forming a State constitution without the consent of Congress. They took the same position in this report, stating the Arkansas case as interpreted by the minority of the committee; but when I, in my first speech, showed that, in the same opinion, Mr. Butler had said that unless the proceeding was had in subordination to the territorial government, it was revolutionary and criminal, this memorial was changed, in order to avoid the force of my exposure, by obliterating the passage, striking out all reference to the Arkansas case.

I can take up this memorial and show that, as I have exposed one heresy after another of their pretensions, they took the pen and ran through this memorial to get rid of the objection. It has been changed from time to time in material points, striking out and inserting, until it has hardly a vestige of its original form. The very comparison which is here challenged between the pretended copy, presented the other day, and the original now, proves conclusively that such is the case. I then submit whether here was not evidence of the most glaring fraud ever attempted to be perpetrated upon a legislative body. After that fraud has been once detected and exposed, the question is whether a second one is to be perpetrated upon us by taking the same spurious document and attaching it to a memorial and thus dragging it into the Senate.

Again, the original memorial does not pretend that the legislature was in session. Take the copy which they brought here the other day, and you find interlined the words, "now in session." I can show you the different handwritings in which various interlineations have been made from time to time.

Further, the memorial, as presented to us the other day, had the signatures of all the members of the legislature attached to it. Look at the original here ; it has no signatures a all ; and there is no certificate that it was adopted in either house ; no mode of authentication, and no date. How do they account for that? By saying that a committee of revision was appointed to revise the memorial, and that the members left three copies of their names to be appended. It is pretended that the committee revised the paper, and delivered it to Colonel Lane and Governor Robinson without any signatures to it ; and that they brought it to Washington and revised it again, and chang d it into its present shape, ready for appending the signatures, when it was discovered that they had lost them ! And then, because they had lost them, they sat down and wrote the names of the members of the legislature, and attached them to the new document which they had thus manufactured. How did they get the names? Why, they find a memorandum book, belonging to Colonel Lane, which he exhibits to the Senate, but is not willing that we should read, because it contains private matters!

Why exhibit the book unless we are permitted to examine it? Of what use is it to us to see the outside of the book if he will not let us see the inside, and read the writing in it? Does this contain authority to him to change the memorial and sign their names to it? This is not pretended. Why this formality of shaking in our faces a memorandum-book containing these names? He says they are original signatures. That may be, but we have no curiosity to see the autographs of these illustrious legislators, unless they are signed to the memorial. Their names in the memorandum-book are of no authority unless it contains a power of attorney to Mr. Lane to make a memorial for them. No such authority is pretended!

Then we find that there is no authentication of this document, except the affidavit of Mr. Lane, made this day, and sworn to before Judge McLean of the Supreme Court. I will read the affidavit:

" District of Columbia,

" *County and City of Washington, ss :*

" Personally appeared before the undersigned, duly authorized by law to administer oaths, James H. Lane, Senator elect from Kansas "—

—he swears in that capacity—not as an individual—

" who, being duly sworn, upon his oath, states: that the twenty-four half sheets of paper hereunto annexed contain the original draft of the memorial from the members of the general assembly of Kansas, which convened at Topeka on the 4th of March last, to the Congress of the United Sates as reported to the said assembly by John Hutchinson, esq., chairman of the committee appointed to draft said memorial ; as adopted by both branches of said assembly ; as referred to the committee on revision, and intrusted by said committee to this affiant, and from which the revised copy was prepared which was submitted to the Senate of the United States by General Cass, and which was the subject of remark on Thursday last."

Dated Washington city, the 14th day of April, 1856.

J. H. LANE.

Sworn and subscribed before me this 14th day of April, 1856.

John McLean,
Justice Supreme Court United States.

" From which it was prepared ! " By whom " prepared ? " Not by that revising committee, for his memorial shows that it was prepared in the city of Washington. The paper on which it is written shows that it is paper of the House of Representatives—entirely different from that on which the original was written, and which could not have been had in Kansas.

I submit, then, Mr. President, whether we ought to receive the memorial at all, with these badges of fraud running through every line of it. I object to its reception, and hope that the Senate will wash its hands of this spurious paper, and of all proceedings that are connected with it.

Mr. WADE said he saw nothing wrong in the conduct of Colonel Lane. His affidavit explained the matter satisfactorily. He says the original paper was prepared by the legislature that convened at Topeka just as they adjourned. They had no time to draw it up and prepare it with all the particularity of language with which they would be glad to clothe their ideas. Conscious of this, and having entire confidence in certain gentlemen of the legislature, they referred it to them, and entrusted them with a discretionary power to alter it, so far as they thought it might be altered without altering the sense.

Mr. PUGH. Mr. President, I agree with my colleague (Mr. Wade) that whether we receive this document or reject it can have no influence upon the decision of the questions relating to the Territory of Kansas. I do not rise to speak with that view, but I must complain of the senator from Iowa (Mr. Harlan) for the language and the tone which he has employed toward me.

When one of these papers was before the Senate on Thursday last, I desired to be rid of the discussion raised upon it, and, as the record will show, voted to proceed to the consideration of the orders of the day, and allow the subject to remain where the decision of the chair left it. But when I saw upon the other side of the chamber a resolution to force us into the debate of very serious questions, when I discovered the purpose of certain gentlemen to raise a controversy upon the right of petition, to invent a collateral and colorable issue for the sake of adding to the disputes which already agitate the nation, I felt bound to give the paper a careful and deliberate examination. I stated the results of my examination to the Senate. I said that the petition and its signatures were written by one hand; no senator denies that. I said there were important interlineations in the document, such as changed its sense to some extent; that is not denied. I said there were erasures in it, not merely of words, not merely of sentences, but of whole paragraphs, as if the person who had it in charge, after listening to our discussion here, had abandoned some propositions as untenable, and altered the petition accordingly. I said that whenever the original should be produced, if there was any original, it would be time enough to decide upon my course. For having said that, sir, the senator from Iowa has arraigned me this morning in the course of his reiterated discussion of the general subject.

I should think the senator ought to be satisfied. When a proposition was made to print extra copies of the documents submitted to us by the President of the United States, in order that the country might be informed on these questions from Kansas, that, instead of irresponsible paragraphs in the newspapers, appeals to passion and to prejudice, our common constituents—the constituents of that senator as well as my constituents—might see the original and authentic reports transmitted to the Senate by the executive head of the government—when that proposition was made, senator after senator on the other side claimed the right to be heard, and thus postponed any discussion. The question has not yet been taken, sir, although a period of more than two months has elapsed. The senator from Iowa gave us notice that he desired to return home, and asked the privilege of being heard on the subject, as an act of courtesy. His request was granted, and he addressed the Senate for several hours.

Mr. HARLAN. I think the senator, on reflection, will find that he is mistaken. He makes a mistake when he says that I stated to the Senate that I intended to return home, and gave that as a reason. The gentleman must be thinking of some other senator.

Mr. PUGH. Sir, I appeal to the record. When two reports were made from the Committee on Territories, and senators on the other side challenged us to allow the reports to be printed together, and thus sent before the country, I moved that a certain number of copies should be so printed; and the motion went to the Committee on Printing, under the rules. I then stated that, by this system of debating immaterial motions, we had been prevented from printing extra copies of the President's Kansas message, and urged the Senate to decide the question at once, and agree to proceed with the discussion upon the bill of which the committee had given notice. I was answered by the senator from New York, (Mr. Seward,) that the senator from Iowa claimed the floor upon the motion to print the President's special message, and that he wished to be heard. Accordingly, sir, the motion was laid over from day to day, from week to week, until the senator had made his speech. I missed him then from the chamber, and supposed that he had gone home.

Now, sir, there are some others of us who feel bound, by the emergencies of our position, to express the opinions which we entertain with reference to these Kansas troubles. I desire, at a proper time, to express my opinions; but I do protest that when a senator has been heard, hour after hour, upon the question, he ought not, on the mere presentation of a memorial, to obstruct the progress of business in the Senate by repeating his speech; and especially should he avoid calling in question the conduct or the motives of other Senators.

Mr. President, I made no reflection upon the gentleman who brought this paper here—none I did not feel bound to give the Senate his biography; I did not know it. I knew that he was once a citizen of the State which you represent; I knew that he had been promoted to important offices by the nomination of the democratic party in your State; but I have heard, whether it be true or not, that, four or five months ago, in the Territory of Kansas, he publicly expressed a full adhesion to the republican party and platform. He is not the first man who has enjoyed the confidence of the democratic party, and then abandoned us for some other political organization. But I tell the senator from Iowa this: Whenever a man joins the republican party (so called) he is a democrat no more; and the sooner he parts with that title the better for himself and for all concerned.

Now, sir, the question is upon the reception of another pretended memorial. It is produced here as the original of the petition which we rejected on Thursday last, and, as I understand, in compliance with a demand then made for the original. Is it anything of the sort? What senator so pretends? It is not the same petition in any conceivable sense. It does not resemble the other in beginning or in conclusion. Shall we, then, receive this paper? That is the question. To the other paper, I have said, all the signatures were subscribed by one hand. This has an advantage; there are no signatures to it, and no attestation. Whence it comes, sir, we know not, except from the assertions of senators, and from the affidavit which I shall now read:

"District of Columbia,
"*County and city of Washington, ss:*

"Personally appeared before the undersigned, duly authorized by law to administer oaths, James H. Lane, senator elect from Kansas, who, being duly sworn, upon his oath, states: that the twenty-four half sheets of paper hereto annexed contain the original draft of the memorial from the members of the general assembly of Kansas, which convened at Topeka on the 4th March last, to the Congress of the United States, as reported to the said assembly by

John Hutchinson, esq., chairman of the committee appointed to draft said memorial; as adopted by both branches of said assembly; as referred to the committee on revision, and intrusted by said committee to this affiant, and from which the revised copy was prepared which was submitted to the Senate of the United States by General CASS, and which was the subject of remark on Thursday last.

"Dated Washington city, the 14th day of April, 1856.

"J. H. LANE.

"Sworn and subscribed before me this 14th of April, 1856.

"JOHN McLEAN,
"*Justice Supreme Court United States.*"

Mr. HALE thought the true question was not as to the reception of the memorial for the admission of Kansas, but the reception of Colonel Lane's petition for redress of a grievance growing out of imputations cast upon his character.

Mr. PUGH. I appeal to the candor of the senator from New Hampshire, when he had that document in his hand, and I wish the Senate to take notice what is its real meaning. The prayer of that document was as I stated, that the Senate would receive the former memorial. That is the prayer of the petition. The senator from New Hampshire says that if we refuse that prayer, we refuse this gentlemen an opportunity of explanation. I say again, that if Colonel Lane presents a petition here, stating that he considers himself injured or aggrieved by the language of the senator from Virginia—which is a matter with which I have no concern—I will vote to receive the paper; but, if he only uses his own memorial as the machinery by which he brings these papers again before the Senate, I shall not vote to receive it.

Mr. DOUGLAS. As I trust this is the last time that the question of the genuineness of these papers will be presented, I have another point to which I wish to call the attention of senators. The agents of this mock legislature presented to the honorable senator from Michigan, and got him to present to the Senate, the constitution of this pretended State of Kansas. I have kept my eye on the history of that document, and the proceedings connected with it; and it is well known to the country that there was a clause adopted by a separate vote of the people, and made a part of that constitution, making it a duty of the legislature never to permit negroes (free or slave) to enter the State of Kansas—a provision similar to the one in the constitutions of Illinois and Indiana, and some other States, which have been so severely condemned and denounced by those who have become the special champions of Kansas. Look into the constitution, as they furnish it, and as the senator from Michigan has presented it here, and you will find that clause is suppressed; that important, material provision is not to be found in the document which they bring here. I know, from the history of the transaction, that it was voted in by a majority of the persons who voted for the adoption of the Kansas constitution. Am I mistaken? I ask, was it not adopted at the same election at which the constitution of the pretended State of Kansas was adopted, as a part of the constitution?

Mr. WILSON. If the senator will allow me I will answer, by saying that it was not to be a part of the constitution. Such a vote was given in Kansas, but not making it a part of the constitution of the State.

Mr. DOUGLAS. There was a separate vote upon it.

Mr. SEWARD. Mr. President——

Mr. DOUGLAS. I will hear the senator from New York.

Mr. SEWARD. It is no favor to me; but I hope the honorable senator likes to be right.

Mr. DOUGLAS. I do.

Mr. SEWARD. I beg to tell the honorable senator that I speak of no knowledge of my own; but Colonel Lane, senator elect from that State, leaned over, as the senator from Illinois was making his statement, and gave me his account of the transaction; which was, that this provision, such as the honorable senator from Illinois describes, was submitted to the people for their consideration and approval or rejection, by a provision which directed that it should not be a part of the constitution, but should be in the nature of instructions to the first legislature of the State of Kansas. That is all of it.

Mr. DOUGLAS. Now we come to the point. It is admitted that such a provision was submitted to the voters at the same election with the constitution, and was adopted as an instruction to the legislature, commanding them to pass such a law. Hence it was adopted in precisely the same way that a similar provision was adopted in Illinois, and was in like manner submitted to the people as a distinct provision, to be voted on separately, and when ratified become a part of the constitution. But the senator from New York says this was not to be a part of the constitution! Such is not my recollection of the provision. I do not believe that the provision did declare that it was not to be a part of the constitution as stated by Colonel Lane. I deny his statement, and call for the production of the instrument. It will show, when produced, that that was a part of the constitution, as well as an instruction. What does he mean by an instruction to the legislature? Was it not adopted as a part of the supreme law of the land? He admits that it was. He tells us that it was an instruction to the legislature, and hence binding on them. What is that called which instructs the legislature, and commands certain things to be done, and forbids others to be done? Do we not call it a constitution? What is the constitution, unless it be the supreme law of the land adopted by the people to instruct and control the action of the legislature? This provision was adopted as an instruction to the legislature; it was submitted at the same time, and adopted at the same election, with the other portions of the constitution; it has the same validity and binding force over the legislature as any other clause of the constitution; it will become the supreme law of the land whenever Kansas shall be admitted into the Union with that constitution.

You might as well deny that any other provision of that instrument is a part of the constitution, as to deny that this is a part of the constitution, when you admit that it is the supreme law of the land, binding on the legislature the moment Kansas shall be admitted with the Topeka constitution. I care not by what name you call it, so long as you admit that it is obligatory on the legislature. Call it a constitution; call it a fundamental law; call it the supreme law; call it an instruction; call it what you please—the name does not change its substance, so long as you admit that it compels the legislature to keep the negroes out, and not allow them to live or breathe in Kansas. You cannot avoid the force of my argument by calling a provision of the supreme law by a different name. The point I make is that you have presented here a paper purporting to contain the supreme law of Kansas, omitting and suppressing at least one material provision of that supreme law. You profess to have presented the whole of the supreme law, while you have withheld a part of it. You withheld the part which you dare not defend! I drove the senator from New York to the wall on this point the other day. After various attempts to evade the point, he acknowledged that he did not approve and would not defend the provision. He cannot destroy its validity by calling it an instruction, or by any other name. If his bill passes to admit Kansas with her Topeka constitution, that provision will become the supreme law of the land. The only way he can avoid that result is to vote against his own bill.

Call the provision by what name you will, you cannot escape the responsibility of having suppressed a material provision of the supreme law, which was formed at Topeka for the government of the proposed State of Kansas. The criminality of the act is not extenuated by the fact that the provision thus suppressed was one which you dare not attempt to justify. All these attempts at evasion and equivocation are calculated to raise the presumption that the act of suppression was premeditated and fraudulent on the part of those who felt an interest in concealing from the public a provision which they were not willing to defend, at the same time that they were endeavoring to put it in force and give it vitality, by admitting Kansas with the Topeka constitution.

I have a right to call on those who brought the constitution here to produce the provision which has been suppressed. We have a right to know whether any other provisions, instructing the legislature to pass particular laws, have been suppressed. It is not an unusual thing, in making a constitution, to submit particular clauses or provisions to the people separately. When we adopted the new constitution in Illinois in 1847, two provisions were thus submitted to the decision of the people, and both adopted—the one like this in Kansas to exclude negroes from the State, and the other to impose a tax for the payment of the State debt, which should be irrepealable so long as any portion of the debt should remain unpaid.

These provisions, like the one in Kansas, when adopted, became perpetual instructions to the legislature, and hence are held to be essential parts of the constitution, or supreme law of the land. They can no more be erased or suppressed than any other or every other part of the constitution. No member of the legislature is at liberty to violate or disregard either of these instructions, as the senator from New York now calls them, than he is to violate or disregard every other portion of the constitution. I am informed that the new constitution of New York contains several provisions or instructions which were submitted and adopted by the people separately. I do not know how the fact is; the senator from New York will correct me if I am in error upon that point. Will the senator from New York contend that he has a right to evade or suppress those provisions in the constitution of his own State, upon the plea that they were adopted by the people separately, and intended as perpetual instructions to the legislature?

This excuse will not be satisfactory to any fair-minded man. The pretext is too flimsy to deceive anybody. The fact can no longer be concealed, that an imperfect and incomplete copy of the constitution of the State of Kansas (so called) has been palmed off on the Senate; that a material portion of it has been suppressed—a portion so material and vital that the champions of the Topeka movement dare not defend it, and hence have an interest in suppressing it. I call upon them to produce the original document without any mutilations. Let us have it complete as it came from the hands of those who made it. We have been imposed upon sufficiently by garbled and mutilated papers. Let there be an end of this system of fraud. Let the truth, and the whole truth, be laid before the Senate and the country, and let our action be based on the facts as they really and truly exist.

Mr. WADE. I do not propose to detain the Senate long, but I certainly cannot sit here and permit any senator to look me in the face and talk to our side of the chamber as having suppressed papers. It is an imputation of motives which should not be permitted in the Senate.

First of all, the senator from Illinois assumes to know a great deal more about the constitution of Kansas than those who made it; and he asks for proof. I demand the proof from the senator from Illinois. On what does he found the statement that such a clause was incorporated into the constitution of Kansas? Where is his evidence of it? They who helped to make it are here to negative all that he says upon that subject; and it hangs upon his *ipse dixit* merely, unsupported by any proof whatever. Standing upon that frail foundation, he turns round and charges that one side of this chamber has suppressed something for the purpose of committing a fraud on the Senate.

Mr. DOUGLAS. Does the senator from Ohio say that there is any man here claiming to be an honest man, or a decent man, who denies that the convention which framed the constitution of Kansas submitted a separate provision to keep negroes out, which was to have the force of instruction binding on the legislature, and that that was adopted by the people of Kansas? Is that denied?

Mr. WADE. Mr. President, it is perfectly well known on what I found my statement, and the gentleman shall not evade the issue in that way. I demand the proof of you, sir, for what you state. On what authority, and on what evidence do you charge that there ever was such a clause in the constitution of Kansas? You have heard from a senator on this floor that Mr. Lane has stated that there is no such thing.

Mr. DOUGLAS. I will state my evidence. In the first place, I have talked with Governor Reeder, and he told me so. In the next place, I have talked with General Whitfield, and he told me so. In the next place, I spoke to Colonel Lane on the subject the other night at my house, and he told me so. In the next place, I charged it on the senator from New York the other day, and he admitted the fact. In the next place, no man ever did deny it before, and the senator from Ohio now will not deny that such a separate provision was submitted and adopted as instruction to the legislature, whether you call it constitution or ordinance; that there was such a provision submitted separately, to be voted on by the people, and that if a majority was in its favor, and the constitution was adopted, it should become binding on the legislature, the senator from Ohio will not now deny. Will he?

Mr. WADE. Mr. President, the explanation is a very long and a very roundabout one. The senator says he has conversed with a great many people; but that is very loose evidence to prove what a constitution contains. He says the constitution of Kansas provides so and so, and he has talked with divers gentlemen whose character he stands here to impeach. In one breath he says he does not believe a word they say, and accuses them, perhaps, of perjury; but in the next breath he comes forward and says that their testimony is sufficient to establish a clause in the constitution.

Mr. DOUGLAS. I hardly ever knew a judge to refuse to receive the plea of guilty from a murderer or a thief when he asks to enter it.

Mr. JONES, of Tennessee. Mr. President, I do not propose to take any part in this debate, but I think I can correct the position which was assumed by the senator from New Hampshire. He changes the tactics of this fight a little by assuming that we are not called upon to-day to receive the memorial coming from the self-styled legislature of Kansas, but that we are simply to act on the reception of the memorial of an individual citizen who feels himself aggrieved by the action of the Senate. If this were the real position of the question, I might possibly vote to receive his memorial; but there is no such separation between the two as the senator from New Hampshire assumes. They are presented as parts of the same thing; and if you receive the one you necessarily receive the other. If you receive the petition of Mr. Lane you not only receive the memorial which was withdrawn and sent out of the Senate the other day, but you receive another paper, which he is pleased to term the original; and from which the document presented to the senator from Michigan purports to be an extract or an identical copy. Let me read from Mr. Lane's memorial:

"Herewith, and as part of this memorial, is appended the original draft, authenticated, of the memorial referred to, as reported by the chairman of the committee, Mr Hutchinson; adopted by the general assembly; referred to the committee on revision; entrusted to your memorialist, and from which the revised copy which was submitted to your honorable body was prepared."

No man can doubt for a single moment that the original is a part of this memorial. The memorialist states it in terms. He says "herewith, and as part of this memorial, is appended the original draft," which I now hold in my hand. Then what becomes of the other draft, which he says is a fair transcript of the original, being a part of his memorial? You have to receive that if you receive his. He says:

"With this explanation and exhibit, which your memorialist trusts will be satisfactory, he, on behalf of the provisional legislative bodies of Kansas, prays you to receive again the memorial with which he is charged by them, being the one which was submitted by General CASS, and grant the prayer therein expressed, to admit Kansas into the Union with her present constitution, on an equal footing with the other States."

Now, I submit to the senator from New Hampshire himself, and to every man, if we receive the one paper, do we not receive the others at the same time? He sets it out here, and prays you to receive it. He says the original is part of his memorial. He sends the transcript, and asks you to receive it, and grant the prayer therein contained. If you receive the one I think you are bound to receive all.

Mr. TOUCEY. Mr. President, I think that the device which is resorted to in order to introduce again the petition which was rejected on Thursday last, is not the least extraordinary thing that has been done in reference to this subject. A memorial was presented which, by an almost unanimous vote of the Senate, was virtually rejected; and after that vote of the

Senate the memorial was withdrawn by the honorable senator who presented it. Now, if I understand, a private gentleman has made a written request that we shall receive that memorial and grant its prayer. Suppose this device should succeed, and a memorial should be presented here to-day, and rejected unanimously, and any gentleman to-morrow, outside, should present a written request to the Senate that it would receive that memorial and grant its prayer. According to the argument on the other side of the house the Senate is bound to receive it. If it is received and referred to the committee, what is the question before the committee? Is it whether that memorial shall be received? It is a part of the petition now presented. It is a part of the prayer of that petition that Kansas may be admitted as a free State.

Why, sir, it is a mere evasion of the decision of the Senate by an almost unanimous vote. What does Colonel Lane ask the Senate to do? Is it anything more or less than to grant the prayer of his petition, the substance of which is, that, upon receiving this pretended memorial from the so called State of Kansas, we shall admit Kansas as a free State? It is not the memorial of the State of Kansas, or of the Territory of Kansas. If it were, I should be entirely opposed to it, because it assumes that Kansas is a State, and is ready to be admitted into the Union, when the fact is not so.

Sir, senators on the other side of the chamber feel oppressed by this question. When the so called constitution of Kansas is presented here, they say it is a provisional constitution. On looking at it, however, you find there is not a syllable in it making it a provisional constitution. On its face it purports to be adopted by the people of the State of Kansas. The convention ordered it to be submitted to the people, and they say it has been submitted to the people and adopted by them. They ordered the pretended legislature elected under it to assemble on a particular day. They did assemble. Now, I say, that when gentlemen on the other side of the chamber contend that this is a provisional constitution, it is their own language only. The instrument itself is absolute and purports to overturn the existing government. It is in defiance of the law of Congress; in defiance of the constituted authorities of the Territory; and upon its face is insurrection and rebellion against the existing government. I should on that ground object entirely to this petition; but as to treating it as the petition of Colonel Lane, that he may ask that the memorial which we have rejected may be received and its prayer granted, I say, it would be a mere evasion of the decision which the Senate made on Thursday, when the question was fully considered.

Mr. WILSON said a separate proposition was submitted to the people of Kansas, whether free negroes ought to be admitted into the State or not; but if adopted, it was not to be a part of the constitution, but was to operate as instructions to the first legislature. He was opposed to such a provision in any State. We consider it anti-democratic, unchristian, and inhuman, a violation of the Declaration of Independence and the Constitution of the United States. He said he and his friends were against the extension of slavery, but not in favor of interfering with it in the States. He complained of the use of the terms black republican and abolitionist. Mr. Wilson said he should vote for the reception of the memorial. It was imperfectly drawn, because the legislature at Topeka were in haste, and they authorized Colonel Lane to revise and modify it, and he had done so; and that was the whole case. He was proud that the men who stood by Andrew Jackson and the doctrines proclaimed in the Senate on the Michigan question by Silas Wright, by James Buchanan, and by the chiefs of the democracy, are now acting with him in regard to Kansas. He referred to the statement in some of the papers that General Atchison had demanded of Mr. Douglas to introduce a clause into the Nebraska bill repealing the Missouri restriction. He alluded, also, to the remark of Mr. Douglas about "subduing us." He said his friends might be voted down but not subdued; they would live to fight another day.

Mr. DOUGLAS.

"He who fights and runs away
May live to fight another day."

Mr. WILSON. We shall not run away to live; we shall live to run away. He proceeded to boast of the progress of abolitionism within the last quarter of a century, and predicted that his friends would yet have a majority in the Senate, in the House, and would elect one of their class to the Presidency.

Mr. DOUGLAS. Mr. President, I regret that the senator from Massachusetts (Mr. Wilson) should so far have forgotten what was due to the proprieties of the Senate, as to have quoted a vile slander from the columns of a filthy newspaper, published in New York, whose editor is known only as a disgrace to humanity for his mendacity and blackguardism, and becomes responsible for it by its repetition here He has represented me as having said, in debate, to those who differ with me on the other side of the chamber, "we will subdue you;" in the sense that we were going to subdue by force all opponents who differed with us in opinion on the slavery question. Every man here knows, and the published debate shows, that I was speaking of the rebellion in Kansas, and the attempts to put the Constitution and laws at defiance, when I said we will reduce you to subjection to the Constitution and laws. That is what I said then, and what I am prepared to repeat here and everywhere, now and at all times. If there is any disposition to take issue on what I did say, let those who choose to try the experiment commit the overt acts of treason or rebellion, and I say to them now, we will reduce you to subjection to the Constitution and laws. I was vindicating the great principles to which my life has been devoted—that the Constitution must be respected and obeyed in all its parts, as the supreme law of the land ; that the supremacy of the laws must be maintained ; that treason must be rebuked, and rebellion crushed, and all lawless men subdued and reduced into subjection to the Constitution and laws. This is what I did say. No man who heard me has any excuse to represent me otherwise.

I am aware that what I did say on that occasion, as what I do and say from day to day, is purposely misrepresented and sent abroad to be repeated in all the abolition papers for partisan advantage. The author of that falsehood has published what purports to be an abstract of the bill which I reported from the Committee on Territories to enable the people of Kansas to form a constitution and State government when they have the requisite population, which abstract contains a falsehood in every line, with no one provision of the bill truly stated. I am not in the habit of noticing these misrepresentations, and should not do so now but for the fact that they are repeated by a senator in my presence. I wish senators would quote me as I speak, and not as their organs elsewhere may choose to report me.

The senator complains that I designate those composing the party with which he acts, Black Republicans. I will tell the gentleman why I used the term. It is necessary to have some distinguishing name for political parties. Some years ago, when I first came into public life, there was a National Republican party in the country, and my first political speeches were in opposition to the National Republicans. In the course of events new questions came up, and that title was changed to the name of Whig. Since the dismemberment of the Whig party, that portion of its adherents who have abandoned its principles and become Abolitionists, have formed a coalition or fusion with all the other isms of the day, under the name of the "Republican Party." They no longer claim to be *national* men, and hence drop the word "*national*" as a prefix to the name Republican.

There was a good reason for omitting the word "national" as a part of their name. The old national republican party, of which Clay and Webster were the distinguished leaders, held that the Constitution was the supreme law of the republic, and should be obeyed as such with equal fidelity in all its provisions. They proclaimed and advocated national principles upon the subject of banks, finance, revenue, public lands, and upon all questions of a public nature. They proclaimed their principles alike in the north and the south, in the east and the west, wherever the Constitution reigned; whether their measures were expedient it is not now necessary to inquire; it is sufficient to show that their creed was national and uniform. This new republican party has abandoned the creed as well as the name of the old one, so far as it relates to its nationality. The new creed abjures and ignores every question which has for its object the welfare and happiness of the white man—every question which does not propose to put the negro on an equality with the white man, politically and socially. It is a purely sectional party, with a platform which cannot cross the Ohio river, and a creed which inevitably brings the north and the south—the free and slave States—into hostile collision. What are the objects to which they stand pledged?

First, no more slave States.

Second, the repeal of the fugitive slave law.

Third, the abolition of the slave trade between the States.

Fourth, the abolition of slavery in the District of Columbia.

Fifth, the restoration of the Missouri compromise.

Sixth, no more territory to be acquired unless slavery is first prohibited.

Every plank in their platform rests on a black basis—every clause relates to the negro—and hence consistency requires that the word "black" should be substituted for the word "national," in the name of this new "republican party." I wish to call things by their right names—the name should be significant of the nature and object of the organization. For these reasons the whole country seem, by common consent, to recognize the propriety of calling this new party the "black republican party."

Mr. WILSON. I hope the senator will allow me to interrupt him.

Mr. DOUGLAS. Certainly.

Mr. WILSON. The senator says our principles are sectional, and that none of us dare advocate them in portions of the Union—in the slave States. I will say to the senator that last Friday evening I addressed a large meeting in the city hall, in Wilmington, Delaware, with the city hall packed and crowded, and the doctrines of the republican party were laid down fairly and squarely, and generally assented to. We claim that our principles are national, and we shall advocate them in every section of this Union.

Mr. DOUGLAS. I trust we shall find in the south that they will avow them as explicitly and boldly as they do in the north. There is no question but that I have stated their platform truly, as laid down when they organized their party. The senator says now there shall be no dodging of the issue ; that the question shall be met boldly and fairly. I trust it will thus be met. I am in favor of coming directly to the issue. The Nebraska bill contains, in substance, a negative on each and all of their propositions. It affirms the equality of the States. It declares the right of each State to come into the Union, with or without slavery, as it pleases, in opposition to their doctrine of "no more slave States." It declares the principle of non-intervention. It incorporates the principle of the fugitive slave law in the act. It declares, in substance, the negative of each of their issues. Where their issues are not embraced in the Nebraska bill, we accept the negative of them. We want to see them come to the very points in dispute ; and when you tell us that there shall be no wavering on your part, give us some proof of it by your acts. By the fusion or coalition of abolitionism, freesoilism, and know-nothingism, under the name of anti-Nebraskaism in the northern States, you have formed this black republican party. No man knows better the nature and the extent of the fusion and coalition between northern know-nothingism and freesoil and abolitionism, than the senator from Massachusetts. He has enjoyed all its advantages and honors, and incurred all its responsibilities. It was that amalgamation which brought him into this chamber, and carried an anti-Nebraska majority into the House of Representatives.

It has been a matter of boast to-day, that you have increased the other side of the chamber and thinned this a little. In every case it was the result of a coalition between abolitionism and northern know-nothingism that supplied the recruits of which you now boast. In the House of Representatives, where you got a majority on pledges to repeal the fugitive slave law, have you a man there who has dared to bring forward a bill to redeem the pledge? You promised to restore the Missouri compromise; have you a man there with courage to bring forward a bill to redeem the pledge? You promised that you would prohibit slavery in the District of Columbia; where is your bill to redeem the pledge? You promised to abolish the slave trade between the States; where is the bill to redeem that pledge?

I told you the other day that rumor said you had determined that it was not safe, in view of the presidential election, to hazard these issues by redeeming your pledges and carrying out your principles. I have received no answer on that point. It suits your policy better to talk about dodging issues than it does to pass your bills to redeem your pledges. You have the affirmative. Bring forward your measures. We accept your issues. You have got your organization You have got your speaker, who is both a freesoiler and a know-nothing, and thus represents your party exactly. If he is not now a know-nothing, he certainly was one when he was elected. Perhaps you change names so often that I may not be correct in the name; but it is well known that he made the first know-nothing speech ever made in the House of Representatives. You have got committees of your own appointing. Why not bring forward your measures?

Mr. WADE. If the gentleman will allow me, I will say that I believe there is a bill now pending in the other House to apply the Jefferson proviso to the territory south of 36° 30′. In due season you will see one after another of our measures as fast as you will want to take them.

Mr. DOUGLAS. Is that what you call redeeming your pledges? Your pledge was to restore the Missouri compromise line, which did not prohibit slavery south of 36° 30′; but the way you redeem your pledge is by bringing forward a bill to do precisely what you said you would not do, and omit to do precisely what you said you would do. Is that the way to redeem your pledges? A prohibition of slavery south of the line is a violation of your compromise. You bring that proposition in lieu of the redemption of your pledge until after the election. I ask you to bring forward your bills to redeem your pledges. If the Missouri compromise was a sacred compact, as you have asserted—if its repeal was a violation of a compact, and if faith and honor require that it should be restored, bring forward your bill to restore it.

Mr. President, I do not intend to prolong this debate. I wish to bring these gentlemen to the test. When they taunt us with being cut down, one by one, gradually but certainly diminishing until we shall have been swept away, all we ask of you is to bring your men up to the line; stand up to your principles; redeem your pledges. You need not trouble yourselves about finding a man as the standard-bearer on our side, who is not thoroughly committed to our creed on all points. You need not fear that our candidate will not stand firmly and immovably upon the Nebraska bill. You need not have any fear that he will not take issue with you on every one of the points which you tender—"no more slave States," "the repeal of the fugitive slave law," "the abolition of the slave trade between the States," and "the abolition of slavery in the District of Columbia." Upon each and all of them you need have no fear that our candidate will not stand firmly, immovably and unequivocally, upon the democratic platform.

Give us a man for your standard-bearer who is in like manner identified with your side of each of these issues. Do not take a man uncommitted, with the hope of getting votes from both sides, and then cheating somebody. Why point to the deserters from the democratic ranks who have become your leaders, as evidence that you are democrats? You might as well talk of the Christianity of Omer Pasha because he was a Christian before he apostatized and turned Turk. By this pretension you confess that you are in the wrong. You claim as a merit that the deserters from our ranks to yours were once as pure and patriotic as we now are. I wish to understand the precise position. Does the merit consist in the fact that you were once democrats? Or does it consist in the fact that you have since betrayed your party and your principles? Is it the democracy which you once had, but have since lost, or is it the desertion, which constitutes your high claims to popular favor? It seems, even now, that you are more proud of what you once were than what you now are.

That is the argument. I was in hopes that you had faith enough in the justice of your own cause and consciousness of its strength and inherent truth, to be able to stand upon that, and to make it a matter of pride and boast, as the senator from New York did the other day, when he said he was an abolitionist. The senator, however, gave us an illustration which, perhaps, may be satisfactory to him, but I am afraid will not be entirely so to all the members of his party. He reminded us that, while it took Christianity three centuries to be recognized by the princes of Europe, and while he argued that abolitionism was as certain to triumph as

Christianity, yet this was but the first century of abolitionism. Allow me to tell the senator from New York, that he disappointed the expectations of some of his followers, when he intimated to them that they must wait two hundred years longer before they triumphed and got possession of the spoils of government. [Laughter.] If the senator is aiming at the reputation of being a martyr to his cause, I think he is adopting the proper course; and when I am sure it is only at the honors of martyrdom that he is aiming, I shall be better reconciled to his position. Although I have no ambition to be considered a martyr, I have respect for those who cherish such a hope; and I wish all these modern martyrs to remember that it is a fundamental principle of martyrdom, that no man shall seek his reward until two hundred years after his death! [Laughter.]

In that sense the senator from New York did not object to be called an abolitionist. He was looking to the honors of martydom, and fancying to himself how much he should enjoy them at the time when they should be thrown upon him; but the senator from Massachusetts seems to claim that they are to reap their reward now. I like that mode of fighting better.

Let us have a fair issue now—an issue on principles and on men. Let there be no endeavor to cover up the main issues under the irregularities which may have occurred at the election in Kansas. Let there be no equivocation upon the plea of disturbances of a temporary character that may have arisen here and there; but give us an issue on the great undying principles involved in the contest—the equality of the States—the right of self-government everywhere under the Constitution—the right of each State to come into the Union, with slavery or without it, as it pleases—the right of the citizens of each State holding slaves to insist upon the return of fugitives, in obedience to the Constitution—the right of every man to enjoy every privilege, and insist upon the fulfilment of every obligation conferred or imposed by the Constitution.

Again, let us have no equivocation in meeting the issue, whether a clause in the constitu- of a new State, directing the legislature to pass a particular law, is to be called a constitutional provision, or by some other name. The senator from Massachusetts tells us (following the lead of the senator from New York the other day) that he is opposed to that clause which declares that a free negro shall never go into the new State of Kansas. He does not deny but that there was a provision submitted for decision at the time when the constitution was adopted, whether negroes should be admitted to go there or not, and it was decided in the negative by those who voted at that election. He does not deny, therefore, but that that clause becomes a part of the constitution of Kansas in the event that Kansas is admitted with the Topeka constitution. But, he says, that clause is a barbarous provision, and he would like to know my opinion of it. I gave my opinion the other day. I stated that Illinois had a similar clause in her constitution; she had a right to put it there; it was our business, and not yours; and if Massachusetts does not like it let her do as she pleases within her own limits, so that she does not violate the Constitution of the United States. We do not believe in the equality of the negro, socially or politically, with the white man. You may practice it, but do not try to force the negro on an equality with us in our State. Our people are a white people; our State is a white State; and we mean to preserve the race pure, without any mixture with the negro. If you wish your blood and that of the African mingled in the same channel, we trust that you will keep at a respectful distance from us, and not try to force that on us as one of your domestic institutions. [Laughter, and applause in the galleries.]

Now, sir, I am willing that the people of Kansas shall decide that question for themselves, as they will have a right to do when they form their constitution. I hold that it is their right to do as they please, so that they do not violate the Constitution of the United States, and to come into the Union with such a constitution as they please. You say no. You say it is your right and duty, under the Constitution of the United States, to inspect the constitution of Kansas; and if you find slavery there, or any other obnoxious provision which creates an inequality between the negro and the white man, you will vote to exclude such State.

When you look into the constitution of Kansas, you find a provision standing as a perpetual instruction to the legislature, in all time to come, commanding that legislature never to allow the negro to tread the soil, or breathe the air of Kansas. By your doctrine, you are responsible for it. Abandon your abolition notions that you are to fix the local and domestic institutions of a new State, instead of leaving it to the people to do so, and you will have no difficulty. Hence I say, give us a fair issue in this campaign that shall settle the question forever between the true principles of the Constitution—the equality of the States, the right of each State to manage its own affairs—non-interference with slavery on the one side, and slavery agitation and foreign interference on the other. We are not aiming at a triumph on immaterial side issues. What we want is, to bury abolitionism, with all its allies, in a common grave at this election, and thereby restore peace and quiet and good order to a constitution-loving people. That is the kind of issue which we desire you to give us—an open one on principle, with men identified with the platforms.

The senator from Massachusetts has referred to that stale abolition libel that Senator Atchison said he had given me twenty-four hours to say whether I would bring in the Nebraska bill, or resign to him the chairmanship of the Committee on Territories. That is a vile abolition libel. General Atchison has on more than one occasion denounced it as a libel. I thus brand it here as being without a shadow of truth You know, Mr. President, (referring to Mr. Bright, in the chair,) that that bill was prepared before any southern man was consulted, and that you, together with another northwestern senator, were the first who were consulted on the subject. Then, after you had indorsed it, as I take pleasure in saying you did, promptly and fearlessly, we consulted our southern friends. I trust, therefore, that I have put an end to that foul slander, invented for partisan and malicious purposes, and which has been repeated so often and so wide spread over the whole country.

The senator from Georgia (Mr. TOOMBS) has been represented as being the author of the bill, and the man who dragooned me into bringing forward that bill. The New York Evening Post, which the senator from Massachusetts (Mr. WILSON) quotes with so much admiration, has said a hundred times that "Mr. TOOMBS, of Georgia, was the man that stood over Mr. DOUGLAS, and forced him to bring it in," when the senator from Georgia knows that, up to that time, he had never planted his foot in the Senate, and did not arrive in the city until after the bill was prepared and introduced.

Mr. TOOMBS. That is true.

Mr. DOUGLAS. He was not here, and never set eyes on me nor I on him, nor exchanged a word with me, directly or indirectly, until the thing was done, and he came here to engage in fighting the great battle. So it is with these other things. I have failed to notice them before, for the reason that I had such a contempt for this system of making side issues. Heretofore I have not noticed such charges; but when they are thrust in my face in the Senate, I feel it to be my duty to repel them, on the supposition that they have acquired dignity enough by being repeated here to justify me in noticing them. I am not in the habit of noticing the many misrepresentations and assaults which are made on me. I am willing to trust my character and reputation on the result of the great principles involved, and upon the judgment that shall be pronounced on them when passion shall have passed away, and the sober reason of the country shall have returned.

Mr. WILSON, in reply, read what purported to be a report of a speech of General ATCHISON, in the "Parkville Luminary," in which he was reported as speaking harshly of Messrs. BELL and HOUSTON,

Mr. RUSK. The senator has made a declaration in regard to my colleague which, in his absence, I desire to correct He says that General Atchison made a speech, in which he denounced my colleague. That is a mistake. There was a false or erroneous report in a newspaper, purporting to be what General Atchison had said, that did reflect on my colleague and the senator from Tennessee. General Atchison, as soon as he saw the erroneous report of his speech, wrote a letter promptly correcting it, and stated what he did say, in which there was no denunciation of the senator from Tennessee, (Mr. BELL,) or of my colleague. I have known Gen. Atchison for a long time, and I am sure he would not state what was not true. He told me that he made no such charges against them; he had previously sent me a paper containing the correction of the errors in the false report of his speech, made by some one no doubt for the purpose of raising mischief. The senator from Massachusetts has fallen into another error, which I may as well correct now. He says that, at the session of 1853, Gen. Atchison came into this body, and directed that the first Nebraska bill should be defeated. He represents all of us here as having obeyed this great chieftain. His statement is incorrect. On the contrary, General Atchison supported and sustained that bill. I had almost a personal quarrel with him and the senator from Illinois in regard to it. I opposed that bill for various reasons, which will be found spread on the records at the time. I asked that the bill should not be taken up when I was absent. It came here at the last hours of the session of 1853, while I was out on a committee of conference. I asked the senator from Illinois and General Atchison not to allow the bill to be taken up in my absence. I came back from a committee of conference, and found the bill under discussion.

Mr. DOUGLAS. The discussion was on a motion to take it up. The bill was not taken up in the Senate.

Mr. RUSK. I believe the senator is correct. I felt indignant; and I charged both the senator from Illinois and General Atchison with acting in bad faith towards me; strong words passed betweeen us; but I found I was in error; both had acted fairly towards me in the matter. To show General Atchison's position I will appeal to the record. I will read it to the senator from Massachusetts, so that he may correct his recollection on the subject. At page 321, of the Senate journal for the second session of the thirty-second Congress, this will be found:

"On motion by Mr. DOUGLAS that the Senate proceed to consider the bill (H. R. No. 353) to organize the Territory of Nebraska—

"A motion was made by Mr. BORLAND that it lie on the table; and it was determined in the affirmative—yeas 23, nays 17.

"On motion by Mr. WELLER, the yeas and nays being desired by one-fifth of the Senate present, those who voted in the affirmative are:

"Messrs. Adams, Bayard, Bell, Borland, * * * Houston, * * * Rusk. * * *

"Those who voted in the negative are:

"Messrs. Atchison, Bright, Cooper, Dodge, of Wisconsin, Dodge, of Iowa, Douglas," &c.

I merely wished to correct the senator from Massachusetts.

Mr. WILSON spoke of his willingness to meet the issue on the Kansas question, and said:

The honorable senator wishes the issue distinctly made. He will have the issue as distinct as he can desire. We will make our own platform. We do not allow that senator to make it for us, or define it for us. We shall make it for ourselves; and, as he says, we will nominate a candidate committed, fully committed, to its doctrines. If we fail, we will cheerfully submit; if we triumph, we shall embrace in our policy the whole country, and guard the rights of every section of our common country. Threats have been thrown out that, if the "black republicans" triumph in 1856, the Union will be dissolved. Sir, we heard these idle threats when the election of Speaker was pending in the other House; but, when the contest closed by the election of the "black republican" from Massachusetts, his chivalrous competitor from South Carolina, claimed the honor of escorting him to the chair. Sir, you cannot kick out of the Union the men who utter these impotent threats. They know the words of the brilliant Sheridan are true, that—

"Out of oppression is squeezed retribution;"

that "wherever the heel of oppression is raised, trodden misery springs up and glares around for vengeance." They know that they live in a section of this Union where there are nearly four millions of an oppressed race; that there is not a mother in the south who would not clasp her babe closer to her bosom if she believed this Union would be dissolved. The men who fling out these idle threats know that they sleep peacefully at night because the Union does stand, and they have the power of this government to protect them.

Mr. STUART. Mr. President, nominally, the Senate is engaged in the consideration of one of the most important questions which was ever addressed to it in the exercise of its duties—that is, the question of receiving a petition. Upon that question I have settled convictions, undisturbed, I think, by any argument that can be addressed to me; and they are simply these: that if a petition comes from anybody, addressed in respectful terms, in relation to a subject which is or can be under discussion in the Senate, I will receive it, and treat it with all proper respect. Applying that doctrine to this case, if any man, or any set of men, in the Territory of Kansas, representing themselves as they choose, should address a petition to this body of the character I have just described, my vote would be to receive it, to give it its appropriate reference, and to endeavor to pass upon it a respectful and sound judgment. But, Mr. President, it is obvious that this is what I denominated it when I rose, but the nominal question before the Senate.

Five hours and more I have sat here to-day, in the vain hope that this great question would be brought to an issue; but the memorial has not even been read at your desk.

Now, Mr. President, is any man so blind as not to see the reason of this movement? Is any man so blind as not to see its consequences? This subject occupied all day on Thursday last. It was discussed in every point of view; and what was the result? Why, sir, an illustration of the suggestion of the honorable senator from Massachusetts, who has just taken his seat, that—

"He who fights and runs away,
May live to fight another day!"

But three votes were found sustaining the position that was taken, and the vote of that honorable senator was not among the number. Therefore, he lives to fight another day. [Laughter.] Now, what in fact is the question?

Mr. SUMNER. I hope the senator will allow me to interrupt him.

Mr. STUART. Certainly.

Mr. SUMNER. I do not observe my colleague in his seat at this moment, and therefore I reply for him that he was absent from the city on that day.

Mr. STUART. I watched that proceeding; it is not a new one. If I speak somewhat strongly I hope I shall be excused, for I belong to that portion of the Senate who desire to do business. What is the history of to-day? I wish it recorded so that the people of the United States may look at it when they choose. There has not been an opportunity to offer a memorial or to make a report. The special orders which involve the interests of the country have been postponed—for what? To be enlightened on the right of petition? To investigate the subject that is presented to the Senate in the memorial now asked to be received? Not at all; but to endeavor to do what the senator from Massachusetts says his party are going to do—to seize the reins of government. Yes, sir; this delicate subject, upon which the people in various sections of the Union are so sensitive; this one which ought to be abjured from consideration at any and at all times, except when it demands serious and respectful legislation, is thrust in here and seized with the avidity with which hungry hounds seize a carcass—for what purpose? That certain gentlemen may raise into power because of their sympathy for the black man? None of it. Because of a desire to interfere with slavery in the States? That is denied. Is it to secure quiet in Kansas? It is the last object desired. What then, sir? Why, the Senate of the United States is turned into a theatre, exciting applause from the galleries, that a party may ride into power; and that, too, by making a bantling of the most delicate subject that exists under our institutions.

At proper times, upon proper occasions, before the people, in elementary meetings, I have sometimes discussed this question; I expect to do it again—never, sir, to raise the hydra-headed form of agitation. This question I have not discussed in the Senate of the United States; I will discuss it, whenever there shall be a legitimate subject for discussion before us, to the extent of my ability; but that discussion shall be for peace, for harmony. If I were clothed with the power to spread over the Territory of Kansas the mantle of peace, and quiet, and harmony, until it should react on the States of this Union, I would consider it a prouder day than to occupy a position in the White House. He who has no aspirations above the paltry feeling of power, and is willing to attain that power by hazarding the interests of thirty millions of free people, has an ambition that I desire not to imitate.

Sir, is not the history of this day one which ought to arrest the attention of the Senate and of the country? Every senator was ready to give his vote on this question within five minutes after it was presented. But we have had a biography of Colonel Lane; we have had the history of the campaigns in which he has been engaged, both political and warlike, in the country; we have had everything here except a vote on the question. It is—not humiliating, because that would be a term which would be improper to use in the Senate; but it grieves me to see the business of the country—that business which demands action—thrust aside, day after day, that the wheel may turn and this old subject be drawn into the arena to be kicked and cuffed for five or six long hours. What good can grow out of it? None. Is any expected? None. Is any desired? I am afraid not, sir—I am afraid not. I would rather see a remark made years ago by my distinguished colleague have full force here, and throughout this country, that the subject to which the honorable senator from Massachusetts referred, the dissolution of this Union, should be an unspeakable phrase. I would join heartily in that other remark of his, and I would ask that every man should cling to the Constitution as the wrecked mariner to the last plank, when night and the tempest surround him. Sir, if there be a man that can utter, against north or south, a sentiment even indicating that that section cannot be kicked out of the Union, I beg him to reserve that sentiment for some place other than the Senate of the United States.

Mr. WILSON. Will the senator from Michigan allow me to ask him a question?

Mr. STUART. Certainly.

Mr. WILSON. Did the senator understand that I said that the south could not be kicked out of the Union?

Mr. STUART. I did.

Mr. WELLER and others. Certainly.

Mr. WILSON. I made no such declaration. I said that those gentlemen who made the threats to which I alluded could not be kicked out of the Union; that men who threatened that they would dissolve the Union if a certain party should obtain power, could not be kicked out of the Union. I believe we shall never have any trouble about kicking any section or State out of this Union.

Mr. STUART. I cannot consent to repeat all the language which the senator used on that subject. So far as he has repeated it, he is correct; but he cannot forget that he connected with it certain other remarks which gave it a locality. But, sir, I repeat what I said before, I care not to what section of the country it is addressed, or to what man in any section of the Union, I am happy to believe that the people are for maintaining it in its integrity, and if they are ever driven from their position, it will be by accidentally placing men in position who say things and do things so tantalizing as to drive others mad.

Now, Mr. President, I am anxious to get rid of this subject. I am desirous that the legislation of the country shall proceed, and I will join with my fellow senators here in any amount of labor to facilitate the legislation of the country; and, if the Senate believe it will answer their purpose as well, I should like to move to lay this whole subject on the table.

Mr. CLAYTON and others. Certainly; we will agree to that.

Mr. STUART. I think it will essentially carry out our views, and in it we shall say that by taking this bantling away from here on Thursday last, and giving it a new shape without its living long enough to get any feathers on it, has not at all helped the question; that it is no such subject as this individual has a right here to present. I move, therefore, to lay the motion to receive the petition on the table.

The PRESIDENT. That motion is in order.

Mr. HARLAN addressed the chair.

The PRESIDENT. The question is not debatable.

Mr. SUMNER. I call for the yeas and nays.

The yeas and nays were ordered; and being taken resulted—yeas 30, nays 11; as follows:

YEAS—Messrs. Adams, Allen, Benjamin, Biggs, Bigler, Bright, Brown, Butler, Cass, Clayton, Dodge, Douglas, Evans, Fitzpatrick, Hunter, Iverson, James, Jones of Iowa, Jones of Tennessee, Pugh, Reid, Rusk, Sebastian, Slidell, Stuart, Toombs, Toucey, Weller, Wright, and Yulee—30.

NAYS—Messrs. Collamer, Durkee, Foot, Hale, Hamlin, Harlan, Seward, Sumner, Trumbull, Wade, and Wilson—11.

So the motion to receive the petition was ordered to lie on the table.

From the Washington Union of April 26.

THE DOUGLAS AND LANE CORRESPONDENCE.

The false rumors which have been put afloat in regard to an alleged correspondence between Colonel Lane and Judge Douglas in relation to the debate on the spurious Kansas memorial, have induced several of Judge Douglas' friends to ask his consent to give the correspondence publicity. The letters will be found in our paper this morning; and we risk nothing in saying that Judge Douglas' letter places Colonel Lane in a worse predicament even than he was in before. We observe, by the New York Times which reached us last night, that Colonel Lane has published a card in that paper of yesterday, in which he introduces his own letter to Judge Douglas, with the exception of the concluding sentence, but fails to accompany it with Judge Douglas' reply. He undertakes to give the points of Judge Douglas' reply, but he does it so imperfectly that it is grossly unjust. Without dwelling on the card of Colonel Lane, we deem it due to Judge Douglas to say, upon authority, that the statements that when Colonel Lane's letter was handed to Judge Douglas he "*asked until one o'clock to reply, which was granted,*" and that "he then asked until four o'clock, and afterwards until Monday," which were "cheerfully granted," are a total perversion and misrepresentation of the facts. Judge Douglas asked no time to reply, and none was granted. When Mr. Watson called on Saturday and delivered Colonel Lane's letter Judge Douglas had company, and he informed Mr. Watson that he would be ready to reply in an hour or two, which would be one o'clock. Mr. Watson said he would be engaged for several hours, and probably until four o'clock. Judge Douglas then fixed four o'clock for his reply. After his company left he read the letter, and found that it would take more time than until four o'clock to make such a reply as his judgment dictated as proper. He immediately requested Colonel Orr to see Mr. Watson, and notify him that his reply would be made on Monday morning. Colonel Orr, not finding Mr. Watson, left a note for him giving the notice. These are substantially the facts, and they show how grossly Colonel Lane has perverted and misstated them:

CORRESPONDENCE.

House of Representatives, *April* 25, 1856.

Sir: You will please publish the enclosed correspondence. The letter of Judge Douglas to Hon. C. K. Watson was delivered by me to him on Monday last. After reading it, Mr. Watson said to me, verbally, that he was not aware, when he delivered Colonel Lane's note, that it could be construed as hostile in its character, and that it was his determination not to prosecute further the correspondence.

It is due to Mr. Watson to say that his manner and conversation in relation to this matter have been courteous and friendly, holding that no rule or technicality should induce him to do anything that his judgment could not approve. This met the approval of my own judgment.

Very respectfully, your obedient servant,

JOSEPH LANE.

Editor Union.

Washington City, *April* 25, 1856.

Dear Sir: It has been announced in the newspapers that a hostile message had been sent to you by Colonel James H. Lane, of Kansas Territory, and your course in regard to that matter has been most grossly misrepresented. We, as friends whom you consulted, and who advised the course which you pursued on that occasion, request your permission to publish the correspondence now in our hands, in order that the *facts* may be understood.

Very truly, your obedient servants,

R. TOOMBS,
JOHN B. WELLER,
J. D. BRIGHT,
JAMES L. ORR,
JOSEPH LANE.

Hon. S. A. Douglas.

Washington, *April* 25, 1856.

Gentlemen: In reply to your note of this date, I take pleasure in saying that you have my permission to make such disposition of the correspondence referred to as you may think the circumstances require.

Very truly your friend,
S. A. DOUGLAS.

Messrs. R. Toombs, J. B. Weller, J. D. Bright, J. L. Orr, Joseph Lane.

WASHINGTON, D. C., *April* 18, 1856.

SIR: One day last week I placed in the hands of General Cass, with a request to lay it before the Senate, the memorial of the general assembly of Kansas, praying for her admission into the Union as a sovereign State. I gave that direction to the memorial from the fact that the convention which framed the constitution of Kansas, with great unanimity, had before selected General Cass as the medium by which to present the constitution to the Senate, deeming him, on account of seniority, the more proper person to introduce into the new applicant.

On Thursday of that week that memorial was the subject of severe criticism, and in connexion with it charges of the most grave character were preferred against me.

On Monday last in a paper read in your hearing and by yours, I frankly avowed myself the reviser of that memorial; stated distinctly that it was prepared under my direction, in conformity with the authority vested in me; that no human being was consulted in the preparation of it, the instructions of my principals faithfully carried out; the explanation was as full as the avowal was frank, nothing being withheld. After this, in connexion with the memorial, you repeat the charge in a form much more objectionable than before. Believing, as I do, that neither the Constitution of the United States nor the rules of the Senate were intended to justify or sanction so gross an attack upon the character of an American citizen, I respectfully ask for such an explanation of your language upon that occasion as will remove all imputation upon the integrity of my action or motives in connexion with that memorial.

When you are reminded that although I have a certificate of election to a seat in the body of which you are a member, and so far your peer, yet I am not permitted to speak in my own defence; when you are reminded of the friendship, personal as well as political, which has heretofore existed between us; that I came here your friend confidently expecting to find you on the Kansas application where you stood in '44 on the Texas question, in '50 on the California question, in favor of recognizing the people's government, and extending over American citizens the protecting arm of the general government, I feel confident you will, without hesitation, tender the explanation requested, and thereby render a simple act of justice toward one who has faithfully discharged his duty to his constituents in all the relations which have given rise to the existing controversy.

My friend, Hon. C. R. Watson, will deliver this to you and receive your answer.

Respectfully,

J. H. LANE.

Hon. STEPHEN A. DOUGLAS, *Washington city.*

SATURDAY, *April* 19, 1856.

SIR: I have examined the letter signed by your friend, James H. Lane, which you placed in my hands to-day, and will now give you my reasons for responding to you as its bearer, instead of him as its author.

The letter is so equivocal in terms, and portions of it so irreconcilable with other portions, that it is impossible to determine, with any certainty, whether it is intended as a hostile message or a friendly note. It is true that the city is full of rumors that your friend, Colonel Lane, intended to challenge me, and the letter-writers for those newspapers in the eastern cities most friendly to the revolutionary movements in Kansas and most hostile to myself not only announced the fact some three or four days ago, but actually fixed the time when your friend intended to send the hostile message. The object of your friend in causing his intentions to be made known to the world and published in the newspapers is not for me to explain, when he and every one must have known that the effect would inevitably be to have both parties arrested the moment he succeeded in making the public believe that he intended to invite a hostile meeting.

In the National Intelligencer of this morning I find a "Card," published by your friend, in which he attempts to assail me personally, and to raise a question of veracity between us upon a point in reference to which he admits, and affirmatively asserts, the truth of my statement, but denies that he gave me or any other person a "shadow of *authority* for making any such statement." Having selected his tribunal and removed his complaint from the jurisdiction to which public letter-writers in his confidence had declared he would bring it, and appealed to the public through the columns of the newspaper press, he is at liberty to prosecute it in that forum as long as he pleases. Since the publication of this "Card" in the newspapers, your friend, in a letter of which you are the bearer, and in which you are designated as his friend to receive my answer, referring to the debate on Monday last in the United States Senate on the fraudulent memorial of the spurious legislature of Kansas, makes the following request of me: "I respectfully ask for such an explanation of your language upon that occasion as will remove all imputation upon the integrity of my action or motives in connexion with that memorial."

The reasons assigned for calling upon me to vindicate "the integrity of his action and motives in connexion with that memorial" are, that "on Thursday of that week (*the week previous to the debate of which he now complains*) that memorial was the subject of severe criticism, and in connexion with it CHARGES OF THE MOST GRAVE CHARACTER WERE PREFERRED AGAINST ME," [your friend, Colonel Lane.] It is not pretended that I made those charges against him in *that* debate. The published debate shows that "on Thursday of that week" no less than three or four senators did denounce that memorial as "an impudent forgery, attempted to be palmed off upon the Senate of the United States, through the hands of the venerable senator from Michigan;" as "a paper which has reached the Senate through fraud, which has stamped upon it every mark of forgery;" as "a forgery which has been palmed off on the Senate;" and various other denunciations of a like character, all tending to stamp the memorial with fraud and forgery. I did not endorse these grave charges, on the one hand, nor repel them, on the other, for the reason that while all the facts then known to the Senate seemed to justify a strong suspicion, and, indeed, raise the presumption, that they were true, yet the circumstances were not such as to render it my duty to do more than to reject the memorial upon the facts disclosed in the debate. In fact, I followed the lead of the illustrious senator from Michigan, who presented the memorial under the impression that it was a genuine paper by expressing a willingness to vote for his motion to print, as a matter of courtesy to him, so long as it involved no other consideration than the amount of money which the printing would cost. But when its reception and printing become the test of a principle which was to recognize and sanction the revolutionary proceedings in Kansas, I announced my purpose to vote against it for that reason. Subsequently such disclosures were made as to create doubts in the mind of General Cass in respect to the authenticity of the paper, and he, after an interview with Colonel Lane, from whom he had received it, made the following announcement to the Senate, and voted for the resolution rescinding the action of the Senate whereby the memorial was received and referred, and therefore withdrew it. General Cass said:

"Within a few minutes I have had an interview with the gentleman who presented me with the petition, *and I am bound to say to the Senate*, that I am not *satisfied that this paper is one which ought to be acted on by the Senate. This is all that it is necessary for me to say. I shall vote for the resolution of the senator from Virginia.*"

After the "memorial" had been denounced by several senators as a fraud and a forgery, and after General Cass had thus announced his purpose to vote for its rejection for the reasons stated, Mr. Seward rose and said that he had just conversed with Colonel Lane upon the subject, and he added:

"He tells me, and authorizes me to say, and requests me to say to the Senate, as I do in his behalf, that before he left the State of Kansas he saw this paper, the same paper—he does not say that it is the identical paper in chirography—but he saw the memorial of which this is the substance and text signed by all the members of the provisional legislature of Kansas, and that this is a true copy of that paper, as he had before stated to the honorable senator from Michigan, and I suppose the original is within his reach and available. This is in no substantial respect different."

Mr. Seward also further said that "this statement is due to him; and this statement is all that I need say in justice to myself."

In reply to Mr. Seward a senator arose and said:

"I think, Mr. President, this debate will not be without its advantage to the country. We are beginning now to get at the truth of this matter slowly, but it would seem securely.

"Where do we stand? A paper has been presented here, palmed upon the senator from Michigan, purporting to be a memorial from certain persons in Kansas, who claim to be the senators and representatives of the State of Kansas. It is questioned; its authenticity is doubted; it is denounced as a forgery and a fraud. We learn now that it reached the honorable senator from Michigan at the hand of one who is sent here as a senator from Kansas We learn from the senator from New York that that paper, thus denounced on this floor as a forgery, and fraudulently done, came to the hands of the senator from Michigan by one of those men who is sent here as a senator for the *pseudo* State of Kansas; and yet there is no man whom I have heard who undertakes to vindicate him. There is no gentleman who stands on this floor and says that the man who brought the paper here is what he claims to be—an honorable man—and that he brought a fair and honest paper. I do not understand the senator from New York to do that. Where are the gentlemen who claim to be here speaking for the oppressed people of Kansas? Sir, *noscitur sociis* is a safe maxim—the man is known by the company he keeps If it be true that the man is known by the company he keeps, the company is known by the man who helps them."

After further discussion of a similar character, the resolution of Mr. Mason was adopted by a vote of thirty-two in the affirmative to three in the negative, by which the orders to refer the fraudulent paper to the Committees on Territories and Printing were rescinded, and the paper was then withdrawn by General Cass and returned to Colonel Lane.

I have been thus minute in tracing the outline of the debate which occurred on the first presentation of this fraudulent memorial in order to show that I took no part in the discussion which questioned the authenticity of the paper, or the conduct of Colonel Lane in connexion with it. Yet it will be observed that, in the letter which you bore from Colonel Lane to me, it is stated, as the first cause of grievance, that "on Thursday of that week that memorial was the subject of severe criticism, and in connexion with it charges of a most grave character are preferred against me," [Colonel Lane.]

We have seen what those charges were: They were no less than that of FRAUD and FORGERY! These charges were made and repeated by several senators in the course of that debate, and received the sanction of the Senate by a vote of 32 to 3 in the adoption of Mr. Mason's resolution. Your friend, Colonel Lane, rested under these charges until the next week, when he attempted to exculpate himself, not by calling on the senators who made the charges for explanation, but by presenting a petition signed by himself, with the original memorial made a part of it, praying that the pretended copy, which had been rejected on the previous Thursday, might also be received, and inviting a comparison between the two, with a view of enabling the Senate to determine whether the one which the Senate had rejected was a copy or a forgery. As the chairman of the committee having charge of territorial affairs, it became my appropriate duty to institute the comparison which had been invited by Colonel Lane in his petition, and to give the Senate the result of my investigation. I found that while the rejected copy purported to be authenticated by the signatures (all in one handwriting) of the members of both houses of that spurious legislature, the original, from which it was pretended to have been copied, had no signatures at all attached to it, and no authentication whatever, except an evasive affidavit taken that day before Judge McLean. I also found that the first three pages of the original were entirely suppressed in the pretended copy. I also found many other material omissions and suppressions, many interpolations and alterations running all through the paper, and changing its whole character, not only in form, but in substance and principle. I exposed these things to the Senate in plain and unmeasured terms, as it was my right and duty to do. I did not go out of my way to criminate or exculpate any one. I dealt with the fraudulent paper as it came before me in the line of my duty, and left the anthors of the iniquity free to pursue their own course. I showed that the original memorial, which it is alleged was adopted by the spurious legislature of Kansas, was based on the fundamental idea or principle that Congress had no power to establish governments for the Territories; that the Kansas-Nebraska act was unconstitutional and void for that reason; that the people of the Territories owed no allegiance to the governments which had been or should be established by Congress in the Territories; and hence they had an inherent right to take the steps which they had taken to overthrow the territorial government without the consent and in defiance of the authority of Congress. I also showed that in the pretended copy all this had been suppressed since the issue was made up between the two parties by the reports of the majority and minority of the Committee on Territories, and in lieu of it had been inserted an humble petition to Congress recognising its authority and praying for its interposition. In short, I showed and proved by a comparison of the two papers that the pretended copy was *not* a copy in any sense of the word—that it was a spurious, fraudulent paper; in other words, that it was a base and impudent forgery. No senator did no man in or out of the Senate can, vindicate the paper from this just condemnation. The severest judgment which I pronounced on this transaction is contained in the following extracts from my speech, which I now repeat as the only explanation I have to make of the matters to which they refer:

"I submit whether this does not make it a totally different document, affirming entirely different principles, in order to place their action in a totally different light. The Kansas legislature, in the original document, said they justified their acts because Congress had no power over them. The memorial came in the other day recognising the power of Congress. I ask, them, if it is not a forgery thus to change the document in the most vitally important point upon which the whole proceeding rests? I do not say by whom the forgery was committed—I care not. The taint runs throu h this whole proceeding, and the affidavit does not cure or remedy it.

Again:

"I can take up this memorial and show that, as I have exposed one heresy after another of their pretensions, they took the pen and ran through this memorial to get rid of the objection.

"It has been changed from time to time in material points, striking out and inserting, until it has hardly a vistige of its original form. The very comparison which is here challenged between the pretended copy, presented the other day, and the original now proves conclusively that such is the case. I then submit whether here was not evidence of the most glaring fraud ever attempted to be perpetrated upon a legislative body. After that fraud has been once detected and exposed, the question is, whether a second one is to be perpetrated upon us by taking the same spurious document and attaching it to a memorial, and thus dragging it into the Senate?"

It should be borne in mind, that the first time this fraudulent paper was presented to the Senate I pronounced no judgment upon the question of its authenticity, or the means by which it found its way to the Secretary's table Other senators did denounce it as "a fraud and impudent forgery." I remained silent on these points, not from any sympathy with the perpetrators of the fraud, but from my profound respect for the feelings of the illustrious senator from Michigan, whose confidence had been abused so far as to induce him to present it under the impression that it was an authentic memorial. When he discovered his mistake,

I joined him in that vote of condemnation which the Senate pronounced by 32 to 3 in the adoption of Mr. Mason's resolution.

The next week Colonel Lane comes to the Senate, through Mr. Harlan, of Iowa, and presents a memorial, in which he asks and challenges a comparison of the two papers, with the view of inducing the Senate to reverse the judgment which had been so emphatically pronounced upon the conduct of the authors of that fraud, at the same time avowing himself to be the person who perpetrated the act. I did make the comparison in pursuance of the request contained in his memorial, and stated the facts to the Senate as I found them to exist, together with my opinions upon them. The Senate ratified those opinions in the rejection of the memorial by a vote of 30 to 11.

In the face of these facts, your friend, Colonel Lane, calls upon me "for such an explanation of my language upon that occasion as will remove all imputation upon the integrity of his action or motives in connexion with that memorial." My reply is, that there are no facts within my knowledge which can "remove all imputation upon the integrity of his action or motives in connexion with that memorial."

For the reasons which I have stated, I can have no correspondence with Colonel Lane, and therefore address this note to you.

Your obedient servant,

S. A. DOUGLAS.

Hon. C. R. WATSON.

From the Union, April 19.

Mr. Douglas' bill for the admission of Kansas as a State.—Abolition misrepresentations corrected.

Falsehood and misrepresentation are the order of the day amongst the opponents of the Nebraska-Kansas law. This system, which has served so successfully in enabling the agitators to keep the country in a continued state of excitement since the passage of that law, is now resorted to and persisted in with undiminished impudence and pertinacity in regard to the bill lately reported by Mr. Douglas, providing for the early admission of Kansas into the Union as a State. Horace Greeley has located himself in Washington to "oversee" the black republican forces, and to act as their "driver" on questions calling for the "crack of his whip." He is faithfully seconded and supported in his humane undertaking by the prompt counsels and co-operation of James Watson Webb and Francis P. Blair, who are always ready to act as an advisory board. Day by day Mr. Greeley issues his edicts by letter and by telegraph, and thus entitles himself to be regarded as supreme dictator of black republicandom. He was at his post when Mr. Douglas brought forward his report on the Kansas question, accompanied by his bill "to authorize the people of Kansas Territory to form a constitution and State government, preparatory to their admission in the Union when they have the requisite population." He was equally prompt and vigilant when Mr. Douglas opened the debate on the question, and when he explained in clear and explicit terms the provisions of his bill. Faithful to the system of misrepresentation and falsehood, which has marked the entire opposition to the Kansas measure, Mr. Greeley assailed the bill of Mr. Douglas, and grossly falsified and perverted its provisions. He announced to his followers that by the bill the question as to who are qualified voters in Kansas is left where the code of laws enacted by the Missouri "border ruffians," assembled at Shawnee Mission, left it, and, therefore, that, according to that code, an oath of obedience to the fugitive slave law, and the production of certificate of the payment of a dollar as a tax, were conditions precedent to the exercise of the elective franchise. At a subsequent day Mr. Douglas alluded to this perversion of his bill and denounced it as its recklessness deserved. Mr. Greeley was forced to make an apology, but in so lame and reluctant a manner that it was an aggravation of his original offence. His excuse for his misrepresentation was that he had not read the bill, that he does not think it had been printed when he wrote the falsehood, and that he presumed upon the correctness of his statements from the supposition that the bill had adopted the provisions of the Kansas code!

As was to be expected, this lame apology had no other effect on the black republican corps of organs, except it was to instigate them to increased industry in giving currency to the misrepresentation. The New York Evening Post, as late as the 15th instant, contained nearly a column of comments on what it calls "the Douglas process"—which means the bill before alluded to. Instead of avoiding the misrepresentation of Mr. Greeley, which Mr. Douglas had publicly corrected and denounced, and which Mr. Greeley himself had half-way admitted and apologized for, the Post repeats, in explicit terms, the same false statements, and upon this misrepresentation bases its only objection to the bill. Before we proceed to nail this falsehood, like base coin, to the counter, we quote the language in which it is repeated by the Post, as follows:

"By the bill which he has introduced in the Senate, and which both he and the Senate seem already to have forgotten, a new constitution is to be framed for Kansas as soon as the inhabitants of the Territory shall have reached a certain number—a constitution agreed upon by delegates elected by the 'qualified voters' of the Territory—and with this constitution she is to be received into the Union. Who is to be regarded as a qualified voter is not expressed in the bill; that question is left where the code of laws enacted by the Missourians assembled at Shawnee Mission left it. The qualifications of a voter, according to that code, are, an oath of obedience to the fugitive slave law and the production of a certificate that a dollar has been paid to an officer who holds his appointment from the spurious government constituted at the Shawnee Mission. Be the person who offers to vote a resident or not, if he submits to the test, and produces the certificate, he is to be admitted. If he have lived in the Territory from the time it was organized, yet if he cannot conscientiously take the test, he is excluded from voting.

"The free State party cannot, and will not, submit to a test of this kind, passed by a legislature whose authority they deny. The greater number, probably, could not conscientiously take it. We could not, even if the legislature which enacted the test sat with a legal and undisputed commission; there are provisions in the fugitive slave law which nothing could induce us to obey. Mr. Douglas' process, therefore, shuts out from the elective franchise all the free State residents of Kansas. Their places will be easily supplied if it be thought necessary to import voters from Missouri, to give the semblance of a popular election to the choice of delegates. A dollar will make a voter; for a thousand dollars you may have a thousand voters fresh from Missouri; or, if that be too dear, the tax collector appointed by Stringfellow and his associates will, of course, make no scruple to grant the certificates gratuitously. After the constitution is framed, the same set of qualified voters, with the same exclusion of the real residents, must adopt it, and Kansas will then be ready for admission into the Union. This is what the Union calls Mr. Douglas' process. It is quite worthy of the framer of the Nebraska bill."

If the reader has any suspicion that we have dealt too harshly in denouncing the false statements contained in the foregoing, we beg him to turn back and read the extract again, and remember that it is a repetition in an enlarged form of a fabrication from the mint of Horace Greeley, and that its circulation is persisted in under circumstances that give peculiar aggravation to the offence. It will be observed that the only objection urged by the Post against Mr. Douglas' bill is based upon the assertion that the qualifications of voters who are to take the initiatory and preparatory steps for the early introduction of Kansas as a State is not provided for in Mr. Douglas' bill, but is left to the code of laws passed by the late Kansas legislature. If we remove this objection, black republicanism will stand unmasked and without an excuse for further opposition to the bill. We proceed to do this upon documentary proof, which, whilst it will expose thoroughly the misrepresentations of the Post, will also fully vindicate the wisdom of the bill so grossly abused and falsified.

We begin with the opening remarks of Mr. Douglas in the Senate on the 20th of March, when he sustained his majority report against the attacks of his colleague, Mr. Trumbull, and replied to the minority report of Mr. Collamer. We quote as follows:

Mr. Douglas said:

Mr. President: I will ask the indulgence of the Senate for such length of time as the subject may require, provided my strength do not fail me, while I submit some views in vindication of the majority report, and in answer to that of the minority of the Committee on Territories upon the Kansas question.

In the first place, however, as we have taken up for consideration the bill reported by the Committee on Territories to authorize the people of that Territory to form a constitution and State government, preparatory to admission into the Union, it is due to the subject that I should give a brief exposition of the provisions and principles of the bill.

The first section provides that whenever the Territory of Kansas shall contain 93,420 inhabitants, to be ascertained by a census taken in conformity with law, (that being the present ratio for a member of Congress,) a convention may be called by the legislature of the Territory to form a constitution and State government, preparatory to its admission into the Union as a State.

The second section provides that the convention shall be composed of twice the number of delegates which each district in the proposed State has representatives in the territorial legislature. At the election of those delegates it is proposed that all the white male inhabitants who shall have attained the age of twenty-one years, and who shall have resided six months in the Territory, and three months in the district, may vote, provided they possess the qualifications required by the organic act of the Territory. By examination of the precedents, I find that it has been usual to prescribe the qualifications of the voters in the acts of Congress authorizing the people of the Territories to hold conventions and form constitutions preparatory to their admission into the Union.

The several acts of Congress preparatory to the admission of the following States prescribed a residence varying from three to twelve months as a condition of voting, to wit: Illinois, six months; Indiana, twelve months; Ohio, twelve months; Mississippi, twelve months; Missouri, three months; Louisiana, twelve months; Alabama, three months. Most of the other new States formed their constitutions under the authority of their territorial legislatures, without the preliminary action of Congress. In preparing this bill I have adopted the medium according to the precedents running through our whole territorial history—six months' residence in the Territory, and three months in the district in which the vote may be given.

The third and only remaining section of the bill provides for the usual grants of land to be made to the State of Kansas on the same terms upon which they have been made to most of the other new States.

If there is anything objectionable in the details of the bill they will be open to amendment, and I shall be ready to accept any amendment which my judgment approves.

After reminding the reader that this speech was made more than a month ago, that more than a hundred thousand copies in pamphlet form have been circulated, and after it has been the subject of comment throughout the country for several weeks before the Post penned its misrepresentation of the bill, we proceed next to quote the two first sections of the bill itself, which contain all that relates to the matter in hand. They are as follows:

"A bill to authorize the people of the Territory of Kansas to form a constitution and State "government, preparatory to their admission into the Union when they have the requisite "population.

"*Be it enacted by the Senate and House of Representatives of the United States of America in "Congress assembled*, That whenever it shall appear, by a census to be taken under the direc- "tion of the governor, by the authority of the legislature, that there shall be ninety-three "thousand four hundred and twenty inhabitants (that being the number required by the pre- "sent ratio of representation for a member of Congress) within the limits hereinafter de- "scribed in the Territory of Kansas, the legislature of said Territory shall be, and is hereby, "authorized to provide by law for the election of delegates by the people of said Territory, to "assemble in convention and form a constitution and State government, preparatory to their "admission into the Union on an equal footing with the original States in all respects what- "soever, by the name of the STATE OF KANSAS, with the following boundaries, to wit: Be- "ginning on the western boundary of the State of Missouri where the thirty-seventh parallel "of north latitude crosses the same, thence west on said parallel to the one hundred and "third meridian of longitude, thence north on said meridian to the fortieth parallel of latitude, "thence east on said parallel of latitude to the western boundary of the State of Missouri, "thence southward with said boundary to the place of beginning.

"SEC. 2. *And be it further enacted*, That the said convention shall be composed of dele- "gates from each representative district within the limits of the proposed State, and that "each district shall elect double the number of delegates to which it may be entitled to rep- "resentatives in the territorial legislature; and that, at the said election of delegates, all "white male inhabitants who shall have arrived at the age of twenty-one years, and shall "have been actual residents in said Territory for the period of six months, and in the district "for the period of three months, next preceding the day of election, and who shall possess "the other qualifications required by the organic act of the Territory, shall be entitled to "vote, and that none others shall be permitted to vote at said election."

It is seen from the bill itself that Mr. Douglas has not left the question as to who are qualified voters to the code of laws passed by the Kansas legislature, but that he enumerates and defines expressly that the voters must be white male inhabitants, of the age of twenty-one years, actual residents of the Territory for six months, and of the district for three months, next preceding the day of election, "*and who shall possess the other qualifications required by the organic act of the Territory.*" By the organic act of the Territory, all citizens, whether native or naturalized, and all foreign born who have filed their application for naturalization and taken the necessary oaths under the naturalization laws, are qualified voters. Not one word of reference is found in the bill to the code of laws passed by the Kansas legislature; no oath required to support the fugitive-slave law; no payment of a dollar as a condition precedent to qualification as a voter It is, therefore, clearly shown that the original statement of Mr. Greeley was a bold and bald misrepresentation, and that its repetition by the Post, under all the circumstances, is an aggravation of the offence. And now we ask, with earnestness, what valid objection can even black republicans have to the bill? It provides for the early admission of Kansas as a State, with a constitution to be adopted by a convention, to be chosen by voters whose qualifications are clearly defined, and it provides for the immediate expulsion from Congress of any further cause of sectional agitation. Mr. Seward's substitute provides for the immediate admission of Kansas, with a constitution adopted by an unofficial and revolutionary assembly, chosen by voters with no legally prescribed qualifications, held in open defiance of the laws of the Territory, and ratified by the irregular votes of a mere party, and that party in a state of rebellion. If a desire of continued agitation for bad political purposes does not control the councils of the opponents of Mr. Douglas' bill, we are unable to comprehend the motives which superinduce conduct so unreasonable and criminal.

Extracts from Mr. Douglas' reply to Mr. Collamer, April 4, 1856.

Mr. President, I have said enough to bring back the points to the position in which I left them in my former speech. I am not going to follow the senator from Vermont through all his criticisms on the majority report. They are not of a character which call for a reply at this time, nor would it be fair to detain the Senate for that purpose at this late hour.

The senator from Vermont has explained what he meant by the word "experiment" in his minority report—the natural, and perhaps unavoidable, consequence of which would be violence and bloodshed. He says he alluded to the experiment of the Nebraska bill, by which the question of slavery was, for the first time in our history, left to the decision of the people. What is the objection to leaving the decision of that, as well as all other local and domestic questions, to the people who are immediately interested in it?

His objection is that it has a tendency to bring opposing elements and inflammable materials into collision from which violence may be apprehended. Does not the same objection apply to all other questions which involve the interests and excite the passions of men as well as the question of slavery? Does it not apply to the Maine liquor law, to railroad controversies, to taxation, to schools, to the location of county seats, to the division of counties? in short, does it not apply to all questions of legislation which affect the property and enlist the feelings and passions of the community? If the objection be a valid one against the Nebraska bill in respect to the slavery question, it applies in a greater or less degree to every other subject of legislation in proportion as it affects the interests and feelings of the people. It is an objection to the fundamental principles upon which all free governments rest, and which, when admitted to be valid, drives us irresistibly to despotism. The argument is that the people should not be permitted to vote upon a question involving their social and domestic systems, lest there might arise a diversity of opinion which might possibly degenerate into quarrels and controversies, and terminate in violence! Hence, it would seem to follow, that if the people were allowed any voice in making their own laws it should be confined to those insignificant questions in which they feel no interest, and in regard to which there could be no probability of a diversity of opinion! Precious boon—to allow the people to vote when they feel no interest in the question, and deny them the privilege when they do, for fear they will differ in opinion and become excited about it! This is "the experiment"—"the vice of a mistaken law"—to which the senator from Vermont traces all the difficulties in Kansas! He seems to be under the impression that this "experiment" is now introduced into our legislation for the first time in respect to the slavery question by the Nebraska bill! He makes the Nebraska act a far more important measure—one reflecting infinitely more credit upon its author than I ever claimed for it! I was under the impression that the same principle, or experiment, as he prefers to call it, was involved and affirmed in the compromise measures of 1850, and incorporated into the platforms of the whig party and of the democratic party at Baltimore in 1852, as a rule of action by which each party pledged itself to be governed in all future controversies upon the slavery question. Did not the acts for the organization of the Territories of Utah and New Mexico try the same "experiment?" Were not those acts based on the same principle? Did not those acts "leave the people perfectly free to form and regulate their domestic institutions in their own way, subject only to the Constitution of the United States," with the guarantee that, when admitted into the Union, they should be received "with or without slavery," as their constitution should provide at the time of admission? Did violence and bloodshed result as the natural, and perhaps unavoidable, consequences of this experiment in 1850? Have any such consequences resulted from the same experiment in Nebraska in 1854? If violence and bloodshed are the natural consequences of such an experiment, why have not the same causes produced like effects elsewhere as well as in Kansas? I would like to have this inquiry answered by the senator from Vermont, or by the senator from New York, (Mr. SEWARD,) who has endorsed his report and pledged himself to make good its positions. I will give them the benefit of my answer now. There were no Emigrant Aid Societies in 1850. There were no organized systems of foreign interference in either of those Territories? The Emigrant Aid Societies have not extended their operations to Nebraska! The "experiment" of self-government—that "vice of a mistaken law"—has had fair play in Nebraska; hence nothing has occurred in that Territory to disturb the peace and quiet of the inhabitants. On the contrary, in Kansas, where there has been organized foreign interference—where the Emigrant Aid Societies concentrated all their efforts to control the domestic institutions and local legislation of the Territory—violence and bloodshed have resulted as the natural consequence, not of the "vice of a mistaken law," but of their experiment of foreign interference with the domestic concerns of a distant Territory!

But the senator from Vermont has made one concession for which I return him my acknowledgments. He admits that, by the Constitution of the United States, each State has a right to decide the slavery question for itself, and that this right could have been exercised by the people of Kansas when they should form a constitution, preparatory to their admission into the Union, even if the Nebraska bill had not repealed the Missouri compromise. I thank him for this admission. I hope those with whom he acts will endorse the proposition. Then I would like to have him and them explain what harm the repeal has done, and why they desire to have it restored? If Kansas could have become a slave State before as well as now, what is the use of restoring the Missouri compromise?

Mr. SEWARD. The honorable senator will excuse me for calling his attention to a misapprehension under which he labors with regard to the remark of the senator from Vermont, who is now absent, which is the only reason why I interpose.

Mr. DOUGLAS. I yield the floor with pleasure.

Mr. SEWARD I heard a large portion of the senator's speech, and I did not understand him to say that a State would have the right to come into the Union with or without slavery, as her people pleased, if the compromise act had not been repealed. I understood him to say that, after coming in, it would have the right to establish or prohibit slavery.

Mr. TOOMBS and several other senators. No, no.

Mr. DOUGLAS. On the contrary, he took the distinct ground that a State, when its people assembled to form a constitution, preparatory to admission, had the right to come in with or without slavery, even under the Missouri compromise.

Mr. SEWARD. I did not hear that.

Mr. DOUGLAS. My colleague came to the same conclusion the other day in his speech. We seem to be making converts to the true doctrine. It is a sound constitutional principle. If we get men to admit that a State has the right when she forms her constitution either to have slavery or not, to adopt or reject it, as she pleases, it is a pretty good step towards the doctrine of the Nebraska bill. When that admission is made, I want to know what you all mean when you talk about a breach of faith in the repeal of the Missouri compromise? You have all been in the habit of saying on the stump, and wherever else you had the opportunity, that by the Nebraska bill we had broken a covenant which dedicated Kansas and Nebraska to freedom "FOREVER." We are now told that "forever" means "hereafter," and lasts only until there are people enough to form a State, and that no partiular number is required for that purpose.

The senator from Vermont attempts to ridicule the Nebraska bill because it contains a provision declaring the Constitution of the United States to be in force in the Territory. He desires to know who ever doubted that such would be the case without that provision? Who was ever silly enough to suppose that the constitution could be extended by law over a Territory which it did not reach without such law? I will answer his question. I will tell him the man. It was no less a person than Daniel Webster—New England's great statesman, whom she delighted to call the great expounder of the constitution. Senators who were then members of this body have not forgotten, and will not soon forget, the debate between Mr. Webster and Mr. Calhoun upon this very point, in which the former contended that the Constitution of the United States did not extend over the Territories without an act of Congress to that effect; while, on the other hand, the great Carolinean insisted that the constitution was coextensive with the limits and covered all the Territories pertaining to the republic. Without endorsing the peculiar opinions of Mr. Webster on this point, Mr. Clay did not hesitate, in deference to them, to adopt, in the Compromise of 1850, the identical provision which the senator from Vermont now attempts to ridicule, under the supposition that I introduced it into the Nebraska act for the first time in our legislation. I copied the provision from the compromise measures of 1850 for the same reasons which induced Mr. Clay to adopt it, although it is but fair to say that I never did concur in the opinion of Mr. Webster that the constitution did not apply to the Territories without an act of Congress carrying it there.

Mr. President, I have a few words to say to the senator from New York [Mr. Seward] before I close my remarks. On the day I presented to the Senate the report of the Committee on Territories, and immediately after the minority report was read at the Secretary's desk, he rose and volunteered the pledge that he would make good every position affirmed by it. As he has the floor for the next speech upon this question, he will be expected to redeem this pledge, or acknowledge his inability to do so. One of these positions is, that the "experiment" of allowing the people to settle the slavery question for themselves in Territories preparatory to their admission into the Union was introduced into our legislation for the first time in the history of this republic in the Kansas-Nebraska act; and that, if violence resulted from this experiment as a natural, and perhaps unavoidable, consequence, it was the "vice of a mistaken law." I call on the senator from New York to sustain the truth of this allegation. I desire him to answer specifically whether the compromise measures of 1850 did not leave the people of New Mexico and Utah perfectly free to decide the slavery question for themselves, and guaranty their admission into the Union with or without slavery, as their constitution should provide at the time of admission? I ask him if he did not oppose the bills for the organization of those Territories at that time, for the reason that they did not contain the Wilmot proviso, prohibiting slavery, and for the reason that they did contain the guarantee that they should be admitted with or without slavery, as they should decide for themselves? When he answers this question, I would like to have him explain at the same time whether he did not stand pledged in 1852 to sustain the whig Baltimore platform, and to support General Scott, standing on that platform "with the resolutions annexed," to use his emphatic language; and whether those resolutions did not bind General Scott, and the party supporting him, to carry out in good faith the compromise measures of 1850 "in substance and in principle?" I desire a direct answer on these points, in order that the Senate may judge how far he redeems his pledge to make good the positions of the minority report. I would like to have him explain the difference between the "experiment" of the compromise measures of 1850 and of the Kansas-Nebraska act of 1854, in allowing the people to decide the slavery question for themselves, and whether that principle in each case was equally the "vice of a mistaken law?" If he shall answer that he did regard both measures in the same light, I should be gratified if he will explain how it was that he united with the whig party in 1852 to sustain the "vice of that mistaken law," and now calls upon all the odds and ends, fragments and portions, of parties and isms, to merge all differences on other points, and form a *fusion* with him on the isolated point of eradicating this "vice of a mistaken law" in the name of freedom and humanity? While he is portraying the beauties of negro freedom and equality, and demonstrating the propriety of sacrificing the political and constitutional rights of 20,000,000 of white people for the benefit of 3,000,000 of negroes, I would be glad if he would point out the advantages which the negro will derive from the admission of Kansas with the Topeka constitution. That constitution provides that as long as Kansas shall be a State, as long as water runs and grass grows, no negro, FREE or *slave*, shall ever live or breathe under that constitution.

Mr. SEWARD. Does the senator wish me to answer now?

Mr. DOUGLAS. Yes, sir.

Mr. SEWARD. Then, my answer is, that, such being the constitution, he is wrong in his premises that I am desirous to admit the State of Kansas for the benefit of the negro. It must be for the benefit of the white man.

Mr. DOUGLAS. Am I to understand the senator that he has abandoned the cause of the negro upon the ground that his freedom and equality are inconsistent with the rights of the white man? What has become of his professions of sympathy for the poor negro? What are we to think of the sincerity of his professions upon this subject?

Mr. SEWARD. That is another thing.

Mr. DOUGLAS. That is the very thing. If all other considerations are to be made to yield to the paramount object of prohibiting slavery in Kansas upon the ground that the inequality which it imposes is unjust to the negro, will that injustice be removed by adopting a constitution which in effect declares that the negro, whether free or slave, shall never tread the soil, nor drink the water, nor breathe the air of Kansas? The senator from New York admits that the constitution with which he proposes by his bill to admit Kansas contains such a provision. Under the code of laws enacted by the territorial legislature of Kansas, which the senator, in common with his party, professes to consider monstrous and barbarous, a negro may go to Kansas and be protected in all his rights, so long as he obeys the laws of the land. In order to get rid of those laws, the senator from New York proposes to give effect to a constitutional provision which is designed to prevent the negro forever from entering the State!

I should like to hear from the senator from Massachusetts on this point. I believe he took particular pains a few years ago to arraign the State of Illinois for inserting a similar clause in her constitution.

Mr. SUMNER. Never.

Mr. DOUGLAS. Well, perhaps it was his predecessor, [Mr. Winthrop.] Upon reflection, I think it was. I recollect that it once became my duty to vindicate the right of my own State to insert such a clause in her constitution against the assaults of a Massachusetts senator. Had the present senator been here at that time, and found it necessary to have spoken on the subject, is it assuming too much to venture the opinion that he would have joined in that condemnation?

Mr. SUMNER. I should condemn it, certainly.

Mr. DOUGLAS. Then, will the senator approve in the constitution of Kansas what he condemns in the constitution of Illinois? I would like to hear the senator's response to this inquiry. If such a provision was wrong in Illinois, is it right in Kansas? Had not the democratic State of Illinois as good a right to adopt such a provision as the free-soil party of Kansas? Will the senator from Massachusetts vote for the bill introduced by the senator from New York to admit Kansas, at a time when she has not one-third of the requisite population, with such a constitution?

I do not wish to be misunderstood on this point. I object to the admission of Kansas at this time, and under existing circumstances, on entirely different grounds. I affirm the right of Illinois to put such a clause in her constitution. The people of Illinois had a right to do as they pleased on that subject. We tried slavery while a Territory, notwithstanding the ordinance of 1787, until we found that in our climate and with our productions it was not good for us to retain it, and for that reason we abolished and prohibited it. When we decided that Illinois should be a free State we also determined that it should be a white State. We did not believe in the equality of the negro with the white man, and hence were opposed to a mixture of the races. The constitution of Illinois was made by white men for the benefit of white men. The same principle of State rights and State equality which authorized Illinois to abolish slavery secured to each other State the privilege of retaining it if it chose. The same principle which authorized Illinois to exclude the free negro allows each other State to receive him if agreeable to her tastes and consistent with her interests. We are perfectly content with the practical operation of this great principle, which teaches the people of each separate community to mind their own business, and accord the same right to their neighbors. Hence I should have no controversy with the senator from New York, or his political associates, in regard to this particular clause in the Kansas constitution, did they not claim the right, and insist that it is their duty, to examine the provisions of the constitution of each State applying for admission, and then either to admit or reject the application, according as they may approve or disapprove the constitution. It is on this ground that they claim the right to inquire whether the constitution prohibits or protects slavery, and to vote for a free State and against a slave State. It was on this ground that the northern States voted against the admission of Missouri in 1821—one year after the adoption of the Missouri Compromise—because the constitution had a similar provision against free negroes to the one in the Kansas constitution. Hence I desire to learn from the senator from New York whether he and his sympathizing associates do really approve of a constitutional provision which shall deny to the negro forever, not merely the right to enjoy the same liberty accorded to the white man, but also the right to live and breathe within the limits of the proposed State of Kansas?

Mr. SEWARD. Will the honorable senator allow me to answer now?

Mr. DOUGLAS. Yes, sir.

Mr. SEWARD. I need scarcely inform the honorable senator that I do not approve of any such provision in any constitution in the world. I never did, and I never shall, vote to approve or sanction in any constitution, or in any law, a provision which tends to keep any man being, any member of the human family to which I belong, in a condition of degradation below the position which I occupy myself except for his own fault or crime.

Mr. DOUGLAS. The senator does not approve of this provision, and never can, for the reason that it does not put the negro on an equality with himself! Then, will he vote for admitting Kansas in this irregular manner, and without the requisite population, merely because her constitution has a provision which keeps slaves from going into the Territory, together with another clause "which tends to keep a man being a member of the human family to which he belongs—in a condition of degradation below the position which he occupies himself?" Yet, if he votes for his own bill to admit Kansas with the Topeka constitution, according to his own doctrine he does vote to saction a provision to keep the negro out altogether; he will not allow a negro to come in a condition either below him or above him!

Mr. SEWARD. You can take it either way—above or below.

Mr. DOUGLAS. Yes; he will exclude the negro absolutely if he is below or above him! He will insist upon having the negro upon a footing of entire and perfect equality with himself. Yet, if his bill passes, and Kansas is admitted with the constitution which has been formed and presented here, all negroes, both free and slave, are forever prohibited from entering the State of Kansas by the terms of the instrument. He cannot escape the responsibility of this result on the plea that he does not vote directly to endorse and sanction the constitution in all its parts; for his doctrine, and the doctrine of his party, is that they not only have the right, but that it is their duty, to examine the constitution in all its parts, and vote for it or against it, according as they approve or disapprove of its provisions, and especially those provisions which degrade the negro below the level of the white man. He must abandon all the principles to which his life has been devoted; he must abandon the creed of the party of which he is the acknowledged leader before he can vote for his own bill. The black republican party was organized and founded on the fundamental principle of perfect and entire equality of rights and privileges between the negro and the white man—an equality secured and guaranteed by a law higher than the Constitution of the United States. In your creed, as proclaimed to the world, you stand pledged against "the admission of any more slave States;"

To repeal the fugitive slave law;

To abolish the slave trade between the States;

To prohibit slavery in the District of Columbia;

To restore the prohibition on Kansas and Nebraska; and

To acquire no more territory unless slavery shall be first prohibited.

This is your creed, authoritatively proclaimed. I trust there is to be no evading or dodging the issue—no lowering of the flag. Let each party stand by its principles and the issues as you have presented them and we have accepted them. Let us have a fair, bold fight before the people, and then let the verdict be pronounced.

Mr. SEWARD. You will have it.

Mr. DOUGLAS. I rejoice in this assurance. I trust the senator will be able to bring his troops up to the line, and to hold them there. I trust there is to be no lowering of the flag—no abandonment or change of the issues. There are rumors afloat that you are about to strike your colors; that you propose to surrender each one of these issues, not because you do not profess to be right, but because you cannot succeed in the right; that you propose to throw overboard all the bold men who distinguished themselves in your service in fighting the anti-Nebraska fight, and to take a new man, who, in consequence of not being committed to either side, will be enabled to cheat somebody by getting votes from both sides! Rumor says that all your veteran generals who have received scars and wounds in the anti-Nebraska campaign are now considered unfit to command, and are to be laid aside in order to take up some new man who has not antagonized with the great principles of self-government and State equality. Rumors says that, in pursuance of this line of policy, you dare not allow your committees in the House of Representatives to bring in bills to redeem your pledges and carry out your principles; that there is to be no bill passed in your fusion House to repeal the Kansas-Nebraska act—none to repeal the fugitive-slave law—none to abolish the slave trade between the States—none to abolish slavery in the District of Columbia—none to redeem any one of your pledges, or carry out any one of your principles, upon which you secured a majority in the House by a fusion with northern know-nothingism. Rumor says that your committees were arranged with the view of keeping all these questions in the back ground until after the presidential election, in order that the agitation may be reopened with better prospects of success when power shall have been obtained under the auspices of a new man, who has not been crippled in the great battle. Would it not be a curious spectacle to see this great anti-Nebraska or black republican party—which, less than eighteen months ago, proclaimed a war of extermination, in which no quarter was to be granted or received, and no prisoners to be taken—skirmishing to avoid a pitched battle, and get an opportunity to retreat from the face of those whom they determined ,to hang and burn and torture with all the refine . ents of cruelty which their vengeance could devise? Are the offices and patronage of government so much more important to you than your principles that you feel it your duty to sacrifice your creed, and the men identified with it, in order to get power? Are you prepared to ignore the material points in issue for fear that they will compromit you in the presidential election?

Mr. WADE. We will whip you then.

Mr. DOUGLAS. That remains to be seen. We are prepared to give you a fair fight on the issues you have tendered and we accepted. Let the presidential contest be one of principle alone; let the principles involved be distinctly stated and boldly met, without any attempts at concealment or equivocation; let the result be a verdict of approval or disapproval so emphatic that it connot be misunderstood. One year ago you promised us a fair fight in the open field upon the principles of the Kansas-Nebraska act! You then unfurled your banner and bore it aloft in the hands of your own favorite and tried leaders, with your principles emblazoned upon it? Are you now preparing to lower your flag—to throw overboard all your tried men who have rendered service in your cause—and issue a search warrant in hopes of finding a new man, who has not antagonized with anybody, and whose principles are unknown, for the purpose of cheating somebody by getting votes from all sorts of men? Let us have an open and a fair fight. [Applause in the galleries.]

The CHAIR. The galleries will be cleared if these demonstrations are renewed.

Mr. DOUGLAS. I will not pursue the subject further.

THE GREAT FRAUD

BY WHICH

Pennsylvania is Sought to be Abolitionised

IN OCTOBER AND NOVEMBER.

THE ABOLITION STATE TICKET AND THE ABOLITION ELECTORAL FILLMORE TICKET.

Early in July, Millard Fillmore, the candidate of the American party, reached the city of Albany, New York, and in reply to an address of Mayor Perry, who welcomed him to his native land, he delivered the following animated speech. This speech has been made the platform of the Fillmore party in New York, Pennsylvania, Ohio, Indiana, and throughout the Northern, Western and Southern States. It will be seen that Mr. Fillmore does not hesitate to express his earnest apprehension that the present agitation of the slavery question, resulting in a geographical or sectional party, must end, unless it is resisted, in a dissolution of the American Union. *He goes so far, it will be seen, as to charge moral treason upon those engaged in the cause of Fremont.*

MR. FILLMORE'S RESPONSE.

MR. MAYOR AND FELLOW-CITIZENS:—This overwhelming demonstration of congratulation and welcome almost deprives me of the power of speech. Here, nearly thirty years ago, I commenced my political career. In this building I first saw a legislative body in session; (cheers) but at that time it never entered into the aspirations of my heart that I ever should receive such a welcome as this in the capital of my native State. (Cheers.)

You have been pleased sir, to allude to my former services and my probable course if I should again be called to the position of Chief Magistrate of the nation. (Applause.) It is not pleasant to speak of one's self, yet I trust that the occasion will justify me in briefly alluding to one or two events connected with my administration. (Cheers.) You all know that when I was called to the Executive chair by a bereavement which shrouded a nation in mourning, that the country was unfortunately agitated from one end to the other upon the all-exciting subject of slavery. It was then, sir, that I felt it my duty to rise above every sectional prejudice, and look to the welfare of the whole nation. (Applause.) I was compelled to a certain extent to overcome long cherished prejudices, and disregard party claims. (Great and prolonged applause.) But in doing this, sir, I did no more than was done by many abler and better men than myself. I was by no means the sole instrument, under Providence, in harmonizing these difficulties. (Applause.) There were at that time noble, independent, high-souled men in both Houses of Congress, belonging to both the great political parties of the country—Whigs and Democrats—who spurned the dictation of selfish party leaders, and rallied around my administration, in support of the great measures which restored peace to an agitated and distracted country. (Cheers.) Some of these have gone to their eternal rest, with the blessings of their country on their heads, but others yet survive, deserving the benediction and honors of a grateful people. By the blessings of Divine Providence, our efforts were crowned with signal success, (cheers) and when I left the Presidential chair, the whole nation was prosperous and contented, and our relations with all foreign nations were of the most amicable kind. (Cheers.) The cloud that hung upon the horizon was dissipated. But where are we now? Alas! threatened at home with civil war, and from abroad with a rupture of our peaceful relations. I shall not seek to trace the causes of this change. These are the facts, and it is for you to ponder upon them. Of the present administration I have nothing to say, for I know and can appreciate the difficulties of administering this government, and if the present executive and his supporters have with good intentions and honest hearts made a mistake, I hope God may forgive them, as I freely do. (Loud and prolonged applause.) But, if there be those who have brought these calamities upon the country for selfish or ambitious objects, it is your duty fellow-citizens, to hold them to a strict responsibility. (Cheers.)

The agitation which disturbed the peace of the country in 1850, was unavoidable. It was brought upon us by the acquisition of new territory, for the government of which it was necessary to provide territorial organization. But it is for you to say whether the present agitation, which distracts the country and threatens us with civil war, has not been recklessly and wantonly produced, by the adoption of a measure to aid in personal advancement rather than in any public good. (Cheers.)

Sir, you have been pleased to say, that I have the union of these States at heart; this, sir, is most true, for if there be one object dearer to me than any other, it is the unity, prosperity, and glory of this great Republic; and I confess frankly, sir, that I fear it is in danger. I say nothing of any particular section, much less of the several candidates before the people. I presume they are all honorable men. But, sir, what do we see? An exasperated feeling between the North and the South, on the most exciting of all topics, resulting in bloodshed and organized military array.

But this is not all, sir. We see a political party, presenting candidates for the Presidency and Vice Presidency, selected for the first time from the free States alone, with the avowed purpose of electing these candidates by suffrages of one part of the Union only, to rule over the whole United States. Can it be possible that those who are engaged in such a measure can have seriously reflected upon the consequences which must inevitably follow, in case of success? (Cheers.) Can they have the madness or the folly to believe that our Southern brethren would submit to be governed by such a Chief Magistrate? (Cheers.) Would he be required to follow the same rule prescribed by those who elected him, in making his appointments? If a man living south of Mason and Dixon's line be not worthy to be President or Vice President, would it be proper to select one from the same quarter, as one of his Cabinet Council, or to represent the nation in a foreign country? Or, indeed, to collect the revenue, or administer the laws of the United States? If not, what new rule is the President to adopt in selecting men for office, that the people themselves discard in selecting him? These are serious, but practical questions, and in order to appreciate them fully, it is only necessary to turn the tables upon ourselves. Suppose that the South, having a majority of the electoral votes, should declare that they would only have slaveholders for President and Vice President, and should elect such by their exclusive suffrages to rule over us at the North. Do you think we would submit to it? No, not for a moment. (Applause.) And do you believe that your Southern brethren are less sensitive on this subject than you are, or less jealous of their rights? (Tremendous cheering.) If you do, let me tell you that you are mistaken. And, therefore, you must see that if this sectional party succeeds, it leads inevitably to the destruction of this beautiful fabric reared by our forefathers, cemented by their blood, and bequeathed to us as a priceless inheritance.

I tell you, my friends, that I feel deeply, and therefore I speak earnestly on this subject, (cries of "you're right!") for I feel that you are in danger. I am determined to make a clean breast of it. I will wash my hands of the consequences, whatever they may be; and I tell you that we are treading upon the brink of a volcano, that is liable at any moment to burst forth and overwhelm the nation. I might, by soft words, inspire delusive hopes, and thereby win votes. But I can never consent to be one thing to the North and another to the South. I should despise myself, if I could be guilty of such duplicity. For my conscience would exclaim, with the dramatic poet

"Is there not some chosen curse,
Some hidden thunder in the stores of heaven,
Red with uncommon wrath, to blast the man
Who owes his greatness to his country's ruin?"

In the language of the lamented, but immortal Clay: "I had rather be right than be President!"

It seems to me impossible that those engaged in this can have contemplated the awful consequences of success. If it breaks asunder the bonds of our Union, and spreads anarchy and civil war through the land, what is it less than moral treason? (Cries of "nothing—nothing less!") Law and common sense hold a man responsible for the natural consequence of his acts, and must not those whose acts tend to the destruction of the government, be equally held responsible? (Cries of "yes! yes!")

And let me also add, that when this Union is dissolved, it will not be divided into two republics, or two monarchies, but be broken into fragments, and at war with each other. (Sensation.)

But, fellow-citizens, I have, perhaps, said all that was necessary on this subject—(cries of "go on! go on!")—and I turn with pleasure to a less important but more agreeable topic. It has been my fortune during my travels in Europe, to witness the reception of royalty, in all the pomp and splendor of military array, where the music was given to order and the cheers at the word of command. But for myself, I prize the honest, spontaneous throb—(great cheering)—of affection with which you have welcomed me back to my native State—(renewed cheering)—above all the pageants which royalty can display. (Cheers.) Therefore, with a heart, overflowing with grateful emotions, I return you a thousand thanks, and bid you adieu."

As Mr. Fillmore concluded, the vast multitude raised their voices in repeated cheers, waving their hats and handkerchiefs, making all possible enthusiastic demonstrations, which were continued some minutes.

Mr. Fillmore then stepped back, and received the congratulations and welcomings of a large number of citizens of Albany and other cities.

There is a Fillmore party in Pennsylvania, and the writer of this paper claims to be a member of it. Some months ago, a Convention which, as the result has proved, was controlled by Thaddeus Stevens, David Wilmot and William F. Johnston; indeed, which was called under the joint influences of these Abolition leaders, assembled at Harrisburg, to place in nomination a State ticket, and the result of their labors was to select as candidates for the three offices to be voted for in October, the following persons: THOMAS E. COCHRAN, for Canal Commissioner; DARWIN PHELPS, for Auditor General, and BARTHOLOMEW LAPORTE, for Surveyor-General.

On the evening before this Convention, Wilmot and a few others held a caucus at Buchler's Hotel, Harrisburg, and placed in nomination the persons above named, and carried them through the Convention next morning.

But little or no attention was paid to this assembly by the old line Whigs, and the ticket selected was allowed to pass as one of the many tricks played off upon that body of citizens, by Johnston and Stevens. But it appears that the managers of the Convention were careful to place no one in nomination who might be called the representative of Whig principles; and since the selection of John C. Fremont as the Abolition and disunion candidate for the Presidency, and the nomination of Millard Fillmore for the same office, *it appears that all three of these men are opposed to the latter, and two of them openly committed to the former;* Mr. Cochran reserving himself for opposition to Fillmore and Buchanan.

Laporte was formerly a Democrat. Under the guidance of Wilmot, however, he was elected to the Legislature of Pennsylvania for two sessions, where he became so offensive an Abolitionist, that all connection between him and the Democratic party was severed, and he soon took position under the Black flag of Seward and Greeley. He is *now*, as he has ever since been, the obsequious instrument of Wilmot, a slanderer of Clay, Webster and Fillmore; and, as the reader who is curious to know, can readily inform himself, by writing to

Bradford county, is probably the most fanatical opponent of national principles in that region, excepting Wilmot. On the 4th of July last, he appeared at a Fremont meeting in Asylum, Bradford county, and participated in the proceedings with great activity. Indeed, in the county of Bradford, in which Laporte resides, there is no Fillmore organization except that which is under the management of the HON. JOHN C. ADAMS, an old line Whig, who is, at the same time, an adversary of this very man Laporte, and his neighbor Wilmot. *Laporte is therefore the representative of Wilmot on the fusion ticket.*

Darwin Phelps, the second Abolitionist on the list, is *per se* the reprsentative of William F. Johnston. It is scarcely necessary that I should call the attention of the Fillmore men to the career of William F. Johnston, a man who has done more to break down the Whig party than any other man in Pennsylvania, excepting Stevens. *He only favored the American party to use it for Abolition purposes.* Johnston deserted the Democratic party sixteen or seventeen years ago, and has ever since been a shameless advocate of the worst Abolition doctrines. His treason to Clay, his anxiety to postpone the claims of the great Kentucky leader, in favor of available candidates for the Presidency, is familiar to all true Whigs. Until he got position in the Whig ranks, the charge of Abolitionism against the Whigs of Pennsylvania was made in vain. At war with all the old line National Whigs of Philadelphia and the State, we now witness the effect of his policy, in seeing the most of these gentlemen in the ranks of the Democratic party, advocating there the doctrines which they can no longer advocate in their own. Had he signed the bill which repealed the State law prohibiting the use of our jails to Southern citizens for the detention of their fugitives, that blot upon the escutcheon of the Whig party would not have been placed there; and had he and Stevens sunk their personal feelings and their Abolition proclivities, there is no doubt a Whig party would still be in existence. We are indebted to him, and to such as him, for the most unfortunate nomination of Nicholson, in 1855, for Canal Commissioner, a man who ran in the West as the Republican and anti-American candidate, and in the East as the American candidate, deceiving both sides; at the same time, causing our defeat, and leaving nothing on his record after his overthrow, but shame and disgrace. Mr. Phelps resides in the county of Armstrong, and represented it last year in the Legislature. Armstrong was long the residence of Johnston, and Phelps is his instrument on the Abolition State ticket. Like Laporte, he is an avowed Abolitionist, one of long standing, coming from the Eastern States, and an advocate of all the fanaticisms of that region; and like him, an advocate of John C. Fremont for the Presidency. In Armstrong county, the Fillmore party has no organization, a fact which proves beyond doubt that Mr. Phelps, who is the leader of the Fremont party in that region, is committed and pledged to the Seward, Greeley, Giddings and Garrison candidate.

Mr. Cochran who resides in the town of York, is distinguished for his bitter opposition to the American party, and for his avowed hostility to Millard Fillmore. This fact challenges contradiction, and can be ascertained by any person doubting it, who may address intelligent gentlemen at York.

This plain statement should satisfy all Whigs who have a spark of nationality remaining in their composition, what course they should take in the coming October election. If it needs any further proof to establish the charge, that the State ticket is an out-and-out Abolition State ticket, we find it in the fact that it is now openly advocated by every Abolitionist, and every public enemy of Fillmore, who has come into Pennsylvania from other parts of the Union. Greeley is in favor of it, as the columns of his newspaper will show, the same paper in which Mr. Fillmore is daily vituperated. Burlingame is in favor of it, as his speeches in this State will prove. The notorious Ford, of Ohio, one of the worst Abolitionists living, *a deserter from Fillmore*, has been paid to traverse our State and advocate it; and you will soon be called upon to witness the presence of Giddings, L. D. Campbell, Collamer and Trumbull, and doubtless Seward himself, in Pennsylvania, to push on the column in favor of Phelps, Laporte and Cochran. *All these men are Mr. Fillmore's personal enemies.*

Thaddeus Stevens himself, whose hostility to Fillmore is unceasing and unscrupulous, through his organ at Lancaster, has raised this ticket, and advocates it with much earnestness. George Earle, of Philadelphia, an ultra Abolionist, advocates it. The Anti-Slavery Society advocates it. Passmore Williamson supports it. Samuel Aaron, of Montgomery county, bold and rancorous in his animosity to the Union of the States, supports it with the utmost zeal. Aaron is known to be a fanatic of the worst Abolition type, and Mr. Fillmore's insolent enemy. Wherever there is a Fremont Abolitionist,—whether Williams, of Allegheny, Bowen, of Chester, Caleb N. Taylor, of Bucks, John Allison, of Beaver, Duffield, of Fulton, or Deacon White, of Pittsburg,—you will find him eager and anxious for the election of this ticket. Should it be elected, it will be hailed as an Abolition triumph all over the Union; not merely over Buchanan, but a triumph over every National Whig who supports Fillmore, and over Fillmore himself. It will be regarded in the South as the knell of Millard Fillmore. Even the Democratic papers there are charging that the Fillmore men of Pennsylvania intend voting this ticket. Those who assist in supporting it, therefore, will do so with their eyes open. I am determined, for one, that all the facts shall be known to the friends of Fillmore, so that no excuse can be left for their conduct, should they vote this ticket.

The next trick of Stevens and Johnston, is to be found in the manner in which the Fillmore State Convention, held at Harrisburg, on the 5th of August, put in nomination a so-called electoral ticket, pledged to Millard Fillmore. The honored name of Joseph R. Ingersoll, was placed at the head of the ticket in company with the name of Andrew Stewart, for Senatorial Electors. There can be no doubt that Mr. Ingersoll will repudiate all connection with this ticket, as soon as he perceives the base purposes which it is expected to subserve. There is also, no doubt, that Andrew Stewart entered into this bargain, after conference with Stevens and Johnston, in order that the ticket might be turned to the election of John C. Fremont. His history shows that he is always willing to make a good bargain when he can, and how far he has shown this disposition, in the construction of this electoral ticket, will be seen from the fact, that since the selection of that ticket, a number of those upon it, *have been proved to be rank Fremont men*, four of them having come out openly in favor of the Seward and Giddings candidate for the Presidency. Caleb N. Tayor, of Bucks county, one of the so-called Fillmore electors, appeared at a late Fremont meeting, in that county, and took ground in favor of Fremont; and Dr. S. E. Duffield, another of the so-called Fillmore electors, has in terms done the same thing. Duffield resides in Fulton county, and has been traversing that region, with the man Ford, the Ohio Abolitionist, who has already been referred to, who was publicly committed to Fremont in the New York North American Convention—a convention which, professing to be American, was called to destroy Mr. Fillmore, and ended its proceedings by placing in nomination John C. Fremont and William F. Johnston.

On Tuesday evening, the 9th of August, 1856, this same Dr. S. E. Duffield, Fillmore Elector, at an American meeting held in the Court-house, at McConnelsburg, showed his extreme anxiety to establish a fusion with Abolitionism, by offering the following resolution, which was unanimously adopted. (We copy from the proceedings published in the Fulton *Republican*, an American newspaper, printed at McConnelsburg, Fulton county, Pa., where this same Duffield resides.)

The following resolution was offered by Dr. S. E. Duffield, and was unanimously adopted:

"*Resolved*, That in the event of a satisfactory Union of the anti-Administration vote in Pennsylvania, (brought about as hereinbefore expressed,) the American party at Fulton county are willing to subscribe to such arrangement provided they are not called upon to abandon their principles."

Another fact is stated by two correspondents as follows:

"Attleboro', Bucks Co., Pa., Aug. 13, 1856.

"*Dear Sir*:—On Wednesday evening last, C. N. Taylor, Fillmore elector for the District, addressed a *Fremont* Club in this place, *advocating the claims of the Black Republican candidate for the Chief Magistracy*. He made no allusion whatever to Fillmore, or to the fact of being himself a Fillmore elector. Some of the Fremonters are quite jubilant at the idea of a fusion with the Fillmore men. While some of the Fillmore men say, 'Buchanan before Fremont.'"

"Yardleyville, Bucks Co., Pa., Aug. 15.

"That notorious abolitionist, Caleb N. Taylor—the Fillmore Elector from the Bucks and Lehigh districts—is stumping the district for Fremont. He addressed a Fremont meeting on Wednesday evening last in Attleborough, this county. This said Caleb N. Taylor attended the Black Republican County Convention at Doylestown, in June, made a speech, and was elected a delegate to the Black Republican Convention, which assembled at Philadelphia on the 17th of June. It can be seen that while they have passed resolutions against any coalition with the Black Republicans, they have nominated C. N. Taylor as the Elector of the district—a Black Republican of the deepest dye."

A correpondent from Lycoming county furnishes the following account of the Fillmore (?) elector of the Fifteenth District:

It is quite certain that the Know-Nothings have been sold and transferred to the Abolitionists, both in the sham Union ticket and the selection of electors. We can produce the evidence to clinch the assertion, at least as far as this district is concerned. G. W. Youngman, (a nomination fit to be made for such a purpose,) was selected and placed on the Fillmore electoral ticket in this district. It is notoriously understood that the *private opinion and taste of the gentleman is in favor of mule-pie and grasshopper soup.* But all doubts upon that subject were cleared away, when the fact became notorious that he has been distributing Abolition documents, and no later than yesterday gave a man (supposed to be a Fremonter) *a large bundle of Heralds and Tribunes for distribution.* This explains the reason why the Convention adjourned and refused to take any action upon the usual motion made, that the electors pledged themselves to support Fillmore and Donelson. G. W. Youngman will not, and dare not, deny the above."

We have also full report of the proceedings of a Fremont and Dayton meeting held at Waynesburg, Greene county, Pa., on the evening of Wednesday, August 15, 1856, at which all the proceeding were of the most ultra Black Republican character. J. H. Wells, the Fillmore (?) Elector of the District, reported the preamble and resolutions. We have not space for them all. The preamble sets out with this declaration:

"Two candidates for the Presidency are now presented to the American people for their consideration and determination. These candidates are James Buchanan and John C. Fremont."

This statement of course entirely ignores Mr. Fillmore, and the following resolution fully endorsing Fremont was then reported:

"*Resolved*, That we have the fullest confidence in John C. Fremont, and that in him we behold a man possessing in an eminent degree, the Jeffersonian qualifications of honesty and capacity, who 'asks nothing but what is clearly right, and submits to nothing that is wrong.' And that he will enter upon the execution of the duties of the Presidency with a single-hearted determination to promote the good of the *whole country.*"

Of course there can no longer be any doubt of the position of Mr. Wells.

It will thus be seen that one of the chief leaders of Fillmore, advertises his willingness to sell out to Fremont, and three others openly go for the disunion candidate. Was there ever a more corrupt and scandalous proceeding than this!

I now call upon all Fillmore men in Pennsylvania, after reading this plain statement of facts, this unanswerable exposure of the tricks of Stevens, Johnston and their allies, to read over the speech of Mr. Fillmore at Albany, copied at the beginning of this pamphlet, and answer, how can they reconcile their regard for the doctrines there laid down, with the idea of supporting a State ticket composed of these three enemies of Fillmore, and two of them loud and unscrupulous advocates of Fremont; and how can they submit to allowing such men as Taylor, of Bucks, and as Duffield, of Fulton, and Wells, of Lycoming, and Youngman, of Greene, to remain upon the Fillmore ticket? No doubt there are others; Andrew Stuart's history proves him to be one. In due time they will be exposed. Meanwhile, we should remember that Millard Fillmore is in the field, resolved to remain there to the last.

The facts stated in this communication challenge contradiction. They have been repeatedly made before and have never been denied.

☞ Read and hand to your Neighbor.

WORDS OF COUNSEL

TO

MEN OF BUSINESS.

BY A MAN OF BUSINESS.

WORDS OF COUNSEL.

THE object of this little tract—simply and intelligibly written—is to show reflecting men, and especially citizens of Pennsylvania and the North, why they should vote for Mr. Buchanan as President of the United States. It is addressed to men of business and practical industry. It is written by a man of business, who understands the work he has had to do in life better than politics; and who was born and bred and has earned his living, and whatever success he has had, here in Pennsylvania. Nor is it at all material—and so end these words of preface—whether the writer is a merchant or mechanic of Philadelphia, a farmer of Lancaster or Berks, a collier from Schuylkill, or Luzerne, or Lehigh, an iron-master from Centre or Columbia, or a manufacturer from Pittsburg—if the reader will realize the actual truth that he *is* a man of work, mental and bodily. Among all trades and occupations, especially here in Pennsylvania, penetrated in every nook and corner by the nerves of internal commerce, and more dependent than any other State on domestic tranquillity, there is the closest sympathy and communion. The question of the next Presidency is a question of practical interest to all, and so it ought to be regarded.

THE TRUE QUESTION.

Let us see how it presents itself, under what aspect of novelty, and with what portents for the future—not the remote future which is to dawn upon our children, but the immediate future in which we living, working-men are interested. It may be well to look at this question without reference to individuals. Let us then so consider it—and let him who reads meditate on each proposition that is stated, and if he questions any matter of fact, let him scrutinize it for himself. This is no appeal to passion or to prejudice, but an honest effort to convince.

It is now, or will be next September, sixty-nine years since the Constitution of the United States was formed. They have been years of tranquillity and prosperous progress. With brief spasms of war, lasting in the aggregate but some half dozen years out of the sixty-nine—and of occasional commercial distress, trade and industry, except when experiments with the currency have interfered with them, have wonderfully prospered, but never have they more prospered than within the last ten years. Yet during this long period of steady progress, there have been periodical political contests and changes, marked with ordinary party acrimony. One side has succeeded to-day—and another succeeded to-morrow, and yet national prosperity, social and economical, has not been disturbed. In truth, the revolutions in national politics, especially those which have occurred since 1836, have seemed to exercise a salutary influence by the very change of administrative routine which they involved. Questions of politics ran through the whole Union. The Southern Democrat or the Southern Whig had close sympathy with his Northern or Eastern or Western brother. The four Presidents of the last sixteen years were sometimes Northern and sometimes Southern men, but whatever they were, there was nothing in the victory their party gained, to force on them the necessity of proscribing, in their administrative arrangements, the public men of any portion of the country. All was harmonious, and the government, with apparent rather than real change of policy, continued to protect and sustain the great interests of the whole country. That which was the great element of success with government, and contentment with the people, was the absence of sectional party spirit. Throughout the last half century there has been not only a political union in form, but a sympathy that transcended and overcame all territorial divisions—and it is not in the capacity of language to describe how conducive this has been to the business interests of the country. Every now and then, a spirit of sectionalism broke out, as a pestilence is apt to do, in a certain spot, but it raged with violence only round that spot, and the rest of the Union put it in strict quarantine and kept it out. In 1844, "sectionalism," or to use a more familiar term, "abolitionism" (or under its new name "republicanism"), prevented the election of Mr. Clay, determining by the Birney votes, that of the State of New York. In 1848, sectionalism in a new guise reappeared in certain localities as before, and took the same vote from General Cass. But then, and till now, sectionalism was what the doctors call sporadic: very bad in certain places, but easily managed and controlled elsewhere. How is it going to be now? This is the question for men of business, for national men, for patriots, for lovers of the Constitution—without whose protection business interests cannot exist—to ponder over well. The Union has been before now supposed to be in danger, and anxious and nervous, and in some instances, judicious men have become alarmed about its permanence. This was the case in 1819, in the agitation of the Missouri Question, when the real point at issue before the people was evaded, and the palliative was resorted to of a territorial prohibition for posterity, to postpone the evil day. It was the case again in 1832, when General Jackson's resolute patriotism (and how thoroughly and gallantly the whole nation sustained him!) repressed Nullification in a single Southern State, and a compromise postponing tariff pregnant of future trouble was the remedy. And again was there anxiety and alarm in 1850, when local irritation in the form of Wilmot provisoes, and Prigg decisions, and evasions and resistance of fugitive slave laws in the North—and jealous irritability and perhaps disappointment in the South, led to apparent conflict and disturbance, and to the compromise measures of 1850. The almost dying words of a Whig President, in the only message he sent to Congress, yet linger in the heart of this nation—for, Southern man as he was, he loved the Union with a simple faith and loyalty that shames the treasonable denunciations of fanaticism.

"For more than half a century," said General Taylor in his message to the 31st Congress, "during which kingdoms and empires have fallen, this Union has stood unshaken. The patriots who formed it have long since descended to the grave; yet still it remains the proudest monument to their memory, and the object of affection and admiration with every one worthy to bear the American name. In my judgment, its dissolution would be the greatest of calamities, and to avert that should be the study of every American. Upon its preservation must depend our own happiness and that of countless generations to come."

But all these were superficial irritations and transient alarms, for through them all, in the darkest and most threatening hours, there was nothing like sectional politics. There were Southern and Northern Whigs, and Southern and Northern Democrats—and fanatics and sectionalists stood aloof, in little knots by themselves. No Abolitionist, as such, ventured to raise his voice or show his face in a Democratic or a Whig meeting or Convention. If abolitionism, or sectionalism, or intrusive fanaticism, had opened its lips in the whig city of Philadelphia, the merchants, and manufacturers, aside from all patriotic sentiment, feeling how deeply their business interests were involved in the peace of the Union, would have sternly rebuked it—if in the Democratic counties of Berks, or Schuylkill, or Westmoreland or Centre, the voice of treason or even disaffection to the Union had been heard, the result would have been the same.

But now, in this year 1856, for the first time in the history of the nation, the politics of the country have, by the acts of one party alone, become intensely sectional. Every calculation of chance which fanaticism makes is founded on sectionalism. One candidate, and he the candidate, not of the patriotic, but of the fanatic North, expects to get none but Northern votes, and thus to gain a sectional triumph.

Let us see how this has come about, and what it must end in. The answer is to be found in the action of two political conventions, one of which met at Cincinnati, and nominated James Buchanan, and the other of which met at Philadelphia, two weeks later, and nominated John C. Fremont. It must be borne in mind that in this relation we are not speaking of individuals, or of candidates, except as representatives.

In the Cincinnati Convention, every State of the Union, North, South, East, and West, was fully represented, and the choice was a Northern man. In the Philadelphia Convention no Southern State had an actual representation. Virginia had a few straggling representatives, but they felt themselves degraded, and were silent. It was, in its component parts, sectional from first to last.

But what spirit directed its action and controlled its choice? In what spirit was it convoked?

On the 16th of May, 1856, thus spoke a Senator from Massachusetts in his place in the Senate.

"The slave power with its loathsome folds is now coiled over the whole land." "It shall be swept into the charnel-house of defunct tyrannies." "Hirelings picked from the drunken spew and vomit of an uneasy civilization—in the form of men—leagued together by secret signs and lodges, have renewed the incredible atrocities of the Assassins and of the Thugs; showing the blind submission of the Assassins to the Old Man of the Mountain, in robbing Christians on the road to Jerusalem, and showing the heartlessness of the Thugs, who, avowing that murder was their religion, waylaid travellers on the great road from Agra to Delhi; with the more deadly bowie-knife for the dagger of the Assassin, and the more deadly revolver for the noose of the Thug."

So spoke one Massachusetts man in an atmosphere already heated and explosive.

Mark, American reader—mark, you who love the Union, and feel how much the Union does for you and yours—the words of another Massachusetts man—one who was found worthy to be Daniel Webster's first successor in the Senate. On the 2d of June, but a few days before the Philadelphia Convention met, Robert C. Winthrop wrote these words of wise and gentle counsel:

"I have no hope that violent speeches, angry resolutions, or inflammatory appeals will do anything towards accomplishing a good result. It is no time for indulging in sweeping denunciations, indiscriminate and insulting reproaches, towards other sections of the Union. On the contrary, beyond almost all other periods of our history, since we had a history as a united nation, unless we are willing to see that history brought to a bloody close and the volume closed forever, it is the time for the calmest, wisest, most collected words of which any man is capable."

To these words of gentle wisdom, while "licentious grossness of language and personal violence" were desecrating the Capitol and preparing for the outburst of fanaticism at Philadelphia, there came an answer from Virginia, from one of the most distinguished and most tolerant and conservative of her statesmen, living in retirement within sight of Jefferson's grave.

"We have been," writes William C. Rives, of Virginia, "of late rapidly and fearfully drifting into that geographical antagonism of parties, which all good and wise men have so earnestly deprecated; and in which, when it shall have been consummated, what, Mr. Madison impressively asks, is to 'control those great repulsive masses from awful shocks against each other?' Passing events have given a solemnity to this prophetic warning, which it is no longer possible to disregard, and which calls upon patriotic and reflecting men everywhere to unite in a strenuous and determined effort to exclude from the arena of national politics a question so fruitful of sectional strife."

At the same time, as if in further warning, Millard Fillmore wrote from the Old World to his friends here, that he was returning home, "if possible to aid in quieting that alarming sectional agitation which, while it delights the monarchists of Europe, causes every true friend of our own country to mourn."

Thus stimulated on the one hand and warned on the other—in the city where the Constitution was framed, and where were uttered Washington's farewell words of warning against "Geographical Parties," a Convention met, and named a sectional candidate for President of the United States, and urged his election on sectional grounds. This, no human being doubts. No longer were abolitionists localized. They—the most violent and fanatical of the name—were the leaders of the Convention. The orators were Giddings and Wilmot and Elder and Lovejoy—the slanderers of Clay and Webster, the defiers of the Constitution, the exhorters of resistance to statutes of the United States.—When the name of John M'Lean, of Ohio, was suggested and urged, the memory that as a Federal Judge, sworn to support the Constitution of the United States, he had sustained and enforced the Fugitive Slave Law, rose up, and he was rejected, almost in scorn, as unsuited to sectional purposes.

One speaker (J. Watson Webb) said, embodying in his words the worst spirit of violence, "If we fail at the election, we must drive back the slaveocracy with fire and sword;" and another (O. J. Lovejoy) used plainer language still, and he was cheered and applauded. These are the significant words:

"The American people have a mission to carry out—this mission was understood in the days of the Pilgrim fathers, and in the days of Jefferson. It was not to chase negroes—it was indicated in the Declaration of Independence. The question now to be decided is, whether we will fulfil our mission. *I proclaim myself an Abolitionist—I think the party has that disease, and, before the campaign is through, it will break out all over.*"

Now, with these words fresh in recollection, authenticated and acknowledged, will any reflecting man, North or South, hesitate in believing that the issue thus presented to the people is a sectional one, and that the worst prophecy of evil as to geographical parties has at length been realized? To vote for candidates thus named and thus sustained is to endorse the principles of disunion enunciated. And, supposing for a moment that such candidates could be elected, and an Executive Administration inaugurated on a narrow sectional basis, what four years of strife, and bickering, and domestic turmoil would ensue—and in such strife and turmoil that which would be soonest sacrificed is the great business interests of the Nation. All past distraction would be as nothing compared with this.

Let any man of practical and successful industry realize, if he can, the dreary waste which civil strife produces. There have been imaginings heretofore. The inauguration of sectionalism would work awful realities. They need no rhetoric to paint them.

It is a fearful truth, that there is greater danger at this moment to the Union than ever in the history of the country. It is more alarming because the feeling, which this sectional nomination creates, is silent and suppressed.

There is no railing, there is no violence—but the conviction forced on the mind of the South, that the North, or any portion of the North, excludes them, and as it were marks them off, sinks deep into the heart.

The election of an Abolition President breaks the Union into pieces, and Pennsylvania becomes a frontier, with the ragged edges of a frontier, with questions of boundary, of runaways, of aggression and resistance, of trouble of every kind; and Philadelphia and Pittsburg, neither of them fifty miles from the dividing line, not as they now are, great circulators of trade and manufactures through the South and West, reduced to doubtful frontier towns, with markets dependent on foreign and uncertain legislation.

The difficulty is to make people believe all this possible. We have been so long used to peace and domestic concord that we can hardly imagine a disruption of the actual ties of political union.

Yet, to repeat again Mr. Madison's question, in such a state of things as now exists, with the fearful antagonism of geographical parties—"what is to control these great repulsive masses of North and South from awful shocks against each other"—and when was this antagonism more likely to produce these results than now? In order to make a practical application of this, let us contemplate an inevitable practical effect. Mr. Fremont is elected on the principles enunciated by Mr. Giddings and the Philadelphia Convention—the principles of ultra, offensive Abolition—the disease, which it is foretold, is to break out throughout the party, before the victory is won—how is he to carry on the Government? His cabinet must be formed of men bred in the school, and faithful to the principles he espouses. To suppose that, if elected by such men, he would repudiate and abandon them, is to impute personal dishonor. He goes into office bound hand and foot by express promises and close sympathy with men who do not scruple to avow they recognize, as citizens, a higher law than the Constitution, and are willing, in contingencies which are carelessly regarded as probable to let "the Union slide."

Now, it is a matter of no conjecture, but of absolute assurance, that a government thus inaugurated cannot be peacefully or contentedly administered. There will be no repose. There will be no harmony of local interests. There will be aggression, and there must be resistance. Four years of such disturbance is a long period in the lives of us all. Its convulsions and excitements leave traces behind them on the business interests of the people that cannot soon be obliterated. He is at this moment the avowed candidate of the party and of the individual men (their names are on the record of the Republican Convention), whom, in 1838, Henry Clay thus described and thus denounced:

"With them the rights of property are nothing; the deficiency of the powers of the General Government is nothing; the acknowledged and incontestable powers of the States are nothing; civil war, a dissolution of the Union, and the overthrow of a government, in which are concentrated the fondest hopes of the civilized world, are nothing; a single idea has taken possession of their minds, and onward they pursue it, overlooking all barriers, reckless and regardless of all consequences. Their purpose is abolition, universal abolition, peaceably, if it can, forcibly, if it must. One means and a most lamentable one, to which they resort, is that which this class of men is endeavoring to employ, of arraying one portion against another portion of the Union. They try to excite the imaginations and stimulate the rage of the people of the Free States against the people of the Slave States. They infuse a spirit of detestation and hatred against one entire section of the Union."

Let it be understood that it is under this influence that the Republican Candidate is nominated, will be supported, and, if elected, will administer, or try to administer, the Government. Who can doubt the mischievous result?

JAMES BUCHANAN NO SECTIONALIST.

Turning from this scene of violence, and sectionalism, and certain discord, we invite the working and business man to note the contrast. Let him observe the words of peaceful and conservative wisdom with which JAMES BUCHANAN speaks of this hateful subject of slavery and sectional discord. They are earnest. They are emphatic. They are precise. They reflect the deliberate intent with which he approaches the discharge of the great duty upon him—that of a National President of the United States.

"The agitation on the question of Domestic Slavery," says Mr. Buchanan, "has too long distracted and divided the people of this Union, and alienated their affections from each other.

"Most happy will it be for the country, if this long agitation were at an end. During its whole progress it has produced no practical good to any human being, whilst it has been the source of great and dangerous evils. It has alienated and estranged one portion of the Union from the other, and has even seriously threatened its very existence. To my own personal knowledge, it has produced the impression among foreign nations, that our great and glorious confederacy is in constant danger of dissolution. This does us serious injury, because acknowledged power and stability always command respect among nations, and are among the best securities against unjust aggression and in favor of the maintainance of honorable peace."

Now, in these few words of plain and direct truth, is the promise which this nomination gives to the industry of the nation, that they shall have, on this exciting topic, at least during Mr. Buchanan's Administration,—what industry most needs,—what the merchant and farmer, the mechanic and manufacturer, most require—stability, steadiness, repose. What a blessing beyond calculation it will be, to have an administration for four years, during which, by the mere force of personal example, no word of acrimony shall be uttered on the subject of Domestic Slavery, and the nation's evil passions may be at rest!

So much for the claims and merits of each party on the one absorbing question of Sectionalism and Nationalism. It will be well now to inquire,—keeping steadily in view the business, practical interests of the nation—what else the administration of a public man like James Buchanan promises to the people.

HIS PRIVATE CHARACTER.

Let us, in no spirit of adulation (for the day for idolizing great men has happily passed by), look back on his career, as illustrated in forty years' history of his country, and see what assurance it gives.

Chief of all his claims on public confidence (and let no technical politician depreciate the praise) is his gentle temper, and the unblemished purity of his private life. Of that high honor, not even ungenerous adversaries can deprive him; and if the attempt were made, there would arise from the neighborhood where his whole life has been spent, a voice of indignant, hearty vindication. The life of a public man has its private trials and temptations. There beset the path of an American Statesman, extending in this instance from youth to age, not a few perils to which the private character of many a one has been sacrificed. It is only he who, guarded and protected by kind and gentle influence generated in his own heart, walks steadily that walks securely. More than two thousand years ago an orator of freedom wisely said that it was impossible for a man whose private character was bad to be a faithful leader of his country; or that private depravity could consist with public virtue; or that he could be the Nation's friend, who was, in truth, the friend of no man there—that he could be strenuous in his country's cause, who slighted the charities

> "For whose dear sake
> That country, if at all, must be beloved!"

It is the truth yet—and the private character of the Pennsylvania Statesman, thus unstained and spotless, is the highest and strongest of the links that bind him around the hearts of his countrymen.

Nor is this an austere, forbidding virtue, for it is ennobled and harmonized by a gentle, genial temper, and this too will be the testimony of those who know him best, of h s Lancaster County neighbors, his friends and associates of fifty years—and of those public men who through all the vehemence of party strife (and our country has known heated times within the last brief century) have always acknowledged his gentleness, his liberality, his devoted courtesy. And here, too, we may well say, let no rude caviller deride this gentle virtue; it helps to make the career of any public man happier. Mr. Buchanan's words have never stung to resentment. His personal demeanor has never made his friends for a moment blush for passion or indiscretion. There has been no vehemence, no intemperance in anything he ever uttered.

Ours is the day of vehement passions and heated sectional animosities. It is the day too when the legislation of the country is believed to be threatened with insidious dangers. It is, therefore, the time of all others when there is needed at the head of affairs a Statesman of pure character, unsuspected integrity, and of conciliatory, gentle, but resolute temper.

HIS PUBLIC CAREER.

Now let us, in the same spirit of candor, see what assurance for the future his long public life, chequered by few reverses, gives his countrymen.

That future—our immediate future—at the moment these words are written—is swelling with events of perilous significance. To some affecting internal peace allusion has been made. To others threatening our friendly relations with the world abroad, it is not necessary further to refer than by saying how clearly they admonish us to trust the Executive administration to safe, discreet, and resolute hands. Well might the man of business tremble for his fortune or his credit if there were danger that sectional intolerance and undisciplined enthusiasm so kindred to weakness should at a crisis like this usurp the government.

THE STATE LEGISLATURE.

It is now forty-two years since Mr. Buchanan entered public life. His first step was on the modest platform of the State Legislature, where in Pennsylvania so much talent has been unostentatiously developed, but from which till now, to our shame be it spoken, there has been so little preferment. James Buchanan learned his earliest political lessons in the best school for public men, the Legislature of his native State. He was there during a foreign war, voting steadily to sustain the measures of that war, and enabling Pennsylvania to attain the real honor for which other States are now fiercely contending of contributing (as she did in the Revolution) most men and most money to the public service.

He became a national man in 1821, having that year entered the House of Representatives.

THE MISSOURI QUESTION.

It was a period of lull after a momentous storm; for the Missouri question had just been decided, and the compromise line of arbitrary division adopted. The public mind was relieved from an impending danger, and all were glad to have repose at any cost.

Mr. Buchanan came into national public life just as this struggle was over—the danger of sectionalism removed—the pretension of Congress to take from a State with a republican constitution the right to regulate for itself its own domestic institutions once and forever repudiated, and that question at last settled.

THE WAR OF THE CURRENCY.

Then came—and Mr. Buchanan was in it from first to last—the great twenty years' warfare about currency and trade. It began as early as General Jackson's first administration, and it ended on the permanent establishment of a revenue tariff and the utter separation of the Government and its resources from banking institutions and their resources, whatever they may claim to be. In all this wild warfare Mr. Buchanan has been steady and consistent, and moreover, has been proved to be in the right. For if at this moment of substantial prosperity, there is one thing on which the public mind of this nation is settled—it is that freedom of commercial intercourse, that a tariff for revenue, and above all restriction, vigilant and suspicious, of all contrivances for expanded credit, are the true secret of sound economical administration. There is not, it may safely be affirmed, a sane man in the country, who desires to see restored a high tariff—a Bank of the United States—or an expansion of paper currency. There is not a farmer, or a collier, or a miner, or a mechanic, from one end of the United States to the other, who is not at this moment content with what he earns, and with the coin in which he is paid for his daily labor. Yet it was for this that during twenty years, for the triumph was slowly won, James Buchanan and the Democratic party labored. Who shall say after watching this struggle, and this great result, that the party of the people is not after all the conservative party of the country.

And who shall say—and this is the moral to which we call the attention of the working business men—that the commercial and industrial interests of the nation are not safer in the guardianship of public men thus trained and thus conservative, than in the hands of any light-headed, inexperienced adventurer, sprung from the diseased soil of commercial speculation. The Pennsylvania statesman who has all his life seen the same results of steady labor operating on the generous but not luxuriant soil of our fertile valleys, or winning by patient industry sure wages from our coal-mountains and iron-mines, is a safer guardian of the great interests, social and economical, of this hard-working people, than any gold-digger or land operator that ever became rich by luck.

And this training—this discipline in the right school of finance —it is which makes JAMES BUCHANAN the very man for the times, looking at the election in its relations to mere business interests—the interest of the merchant, the farmer, or the manufacturer. For industry, the great blessing is stability and repose.

This review of Mr. Buchanan's life is not meant to be biography. It is but the rapid recapitulation of leading incidents, or rather the retrospect of a long career of public service, which it is believed has tended to form the character of a conservative statesman—a safe man for the times.

National, then, in his views of our conflicting domestic institutions—resolute in his convictions on the great questions of finance and currency, what assurance do his life and character of mind give as to our foreign policy?

FOREIGN POLICY.

The anxious wish of the American people—let mischievous traducers say what they please—is for honorable peace with all the world, and strict neutrality in the conflicts of foreign nations. Never did this wish more strongly move the people than at this very moment. Commerce, and manufactures, and agriculture, and the mechanic arts, never more prosperous than now, need and will exact, a peaceful policy from our rulers. The nomination at Cincinnati was hailed by all thoughtful men at home, and will be so regarded abroad, as the triumph of the principles and policy of peace. It is, however, especially the triumph of the best sort of peaceful influences and sentiment—those which are consistent with jealous maintenance of national honor and national interests. Nothing can more tend to maintain peace with foreign nations—and especially that great nation from whom we inherit so many virtues and some peculiarities—than such concord and united counsels as the Convention at Cincinnati presented, united on all questions of internal policy, and united in the choice of their candidates. What could more stimulate the aggressions of foreign nations, especially those whose commercial interest it may seem to be to divide us, than the prospect that, for four years to come, there are to be domestic bickerings and discordant counsels—the North arrayed against the South, and the South against the North—an accidental and inexperienced Executive, in turmoil with Congress, and looked upon as an enemy worse than a foreign foe by a large portion of the people. The most hostile Englishman or Frenchman that ever railed at our free institutions never breathed harsher or more envenomed words—amounting to moral treason—than were familiarly uttered and vehemently applauded in the assemblage which lately met in Philadelphia. The peace which they must expect from the world is only the peace which pity might vouchsafe to grant—not the peace which union and strength demand.

In the Democratic Convention there was no word of sectional discord. The spectacle there exhibited was the representation of a united, high-spirited, and yet peace-loving nation. The only word of dissent that was whispered came from Southern lips and they were words (and this the calumniators of the South would do well to remember) of caution and circumspection on the side of peace. For it is a fact worthy to be meditated on even by fanatics, and certainly by Northern men of business, that more than once in the history of our country, have Southern statesmen saved us from the calamities of actual war, or those hardly less annoying inflictions of commercial anxiety whether there will be war or not. The much-reviled South has sometimes saved us from the follies and passions of the North. They are our friends and brothers yet.

And most of all did the nomination, by cordial unanimity, of JAMES BUCHANAN say to the world that the United States desires honorable peace.

"The nomination of Mr. BUCHANAN," writes Fremont's father-in-law, to the citizens of Missouri, "determines my course. I consider him the safest chance for preserving the peace of the country, now greatly endangered both at home and abroad; and believing him to be the best chance for peace, I hold it to be the duty of all to support it."*

The American people so regard it. Mr. BUCHANAN has exactly that experience which fits him for the crisis, whether it be one of peace or war, or the anxious, doubtful, crisis of peace or war, when a rash word or a timid look may precipitate an impending evil. He has been under varied circumstances our representative abroad. First, at the court of that great power of the North of Europe, whence more than once, out of the thick darkness of apparent despotism, have issued gleams of friendly feeling to our American interests and our country; then and lately, and during a period of grave responsibility, at the metropolis of Great Britain, the seat of intelligence and high civilization more formidable in the rivalry of friendly nations than ruder elements of power. To meet and appreciate actual kindness, and yet not to be swayed too much by it—to assert rights with firmness—to repulse the first signs of indignity—to conduct controversy with ability and courtesy—and to make strangers, and especially Englishmen (who, to their credit and not to their

* Colonel Benton's Letter, June 7, 1856.

shame be it spoken, are always watching and promoting English interests all the world over), to make them understand that American interests are dear to American statesmen, and will at all hazards, or at any sacrifice, be maintained;—these were the duties and this the success of our Pennsylvania statesman during the three years he has, with so much honor to himself and us, represented this nation abroad.

Nor is this all—four years of Mr. BUCHANAN'S life, from 1844 to 1848, were passed as the chief adviser of an executive administration, during a period of hostile diplomatic controversy with more nations than one, and at last of actual war. He was Secretary of State during that brief but perilous conflict with Mexico, which severely tried the spirit of the Nation and settled forever the doubt whether a Republic could wage a war in a distant country. The war was waged and the victory was won. The great executive trial was withstood. The flag of the Union was carried by our gallant soldiers to the centre of an enemy's country. It was magnanimously withdrawn when the victory was won—and it is part of Mr. BUCHANAN'S fame, one of the elements of strength he now has at home and abroad, that he was one of that Cabinet which carried the war to its wonderful result.

Who then gives better assurance for peace than he does? Who could more safely administer the Government in the trial of war, should Providence in its inscrutable wisdom thus afflict us?

RELIGIOUS TOLERANCE.

Thus then stands, in these leading relations, the question before the people of the United States. There is one other, though lower point of view in which it must be regarded. It is a painful and degrading one. Still it must be recalled.

Sixty years ago, in the month of January, 1793, GEORGE WASHINGTON wrote these memorable words:

"We have abundant reason to rejoice that in this land the light of truth and reason has triumphed over the power of bigotry and superstition, and that every person may here worship God according to the dictates of his own heart. In this enlightened age and in the land of equal liberty, it is our boast that a man's religious tenets will not forfeit the protection of the laws, nor deprive him of the right of attaining and holding the highest offices in the United States."

On the 16th June, 1856, JAMES BUCHANAN said to the people of the United States words not unlike those of WASHINGTON:

"I cordially concur in the sentiments expressed by the Convention on the subject of civil and religious liberty. No party founded on religious or political intolerance towards one class of

American citizens, whether born in our own or in a foreign land, can long continue to exist in this country. We are all equal before God and the Constitution; and the dark spirit of despotism and bigotry which would create odious distinctions among our fellow-citizens, will be speedily rebuked by a free and enlightened public opinion."

And we may well pause and ask why in this day of toleration and intelligence, it is necessary for a public man thus to speak. Why, have Washington's words of warning against religious intolerance gained new significance?

The answer, humiliating as it is, is at hand. Less than two years ago, there sprang up in darkness and secrecy—literally the growth of night—a political organization banded together by fearful and dishonest obligations, having two leading objects,—the political and social proscription of naturalized citizens and of the professors of one form of religious belief. It had for a time an ominous success. It seduced into its ranks many an honest and misguided man who saw not the path designing men were tempting him to tread. It had its attractions in mystery and mummery. It made its appeals to the worst passions of humanity, those endurating influences which have hardened the persecutor's heart in every age. The leading idea of its discipline was disingenuous evasion. It was the only party ever known whose fidelity was falsehood. Still, it grew, and strengthened, and, in its mystery and its intolerance, became one of the political parties of the country. It usurped a sacred name "American," just as "Abolitionism" tries to wear the uniform of "Republicanism." But the moment of its apparent triumph was that of its discomfiture, for, as soon as it abandoned its secresy and renounced the sectarian sentiment, it withered and perished. So low did it sink, so fallen did it become, that its candidates have been thrust aside, and, when its principles were hinted at in the Convention, which now seeks to raise Republicanism on its ruins, it was derided and insulted. Nay, further, as if to degrade this once powerful organization still more, the leaders of the sectional agitation movement—those, who, in Convention, at first faintly cajoled the accredited Americans, are now indirectly trying to court the very voters, who, a year ago, were persecuted and proscribed. Mark the words in which a leading Republican appeals to the emigrant from other lands. Mark the enormity, with which he compares our Southern brethren, one and all, to the butchers and despots of Austria and Italy.

"Our Declaration (of Abolition) appeals to the foreign born, who, rejoicing in the privileges of American citizens, will not hesitate to join in this holy endeavour to vindicate them against the aggressions of an oligarchy worse than any tyranny from which they have fled. In this contest there is every motive to union, and also every motive to exertion. 'Now or never, now and forever!' Such was the ancient war cry which, embroidered on the Irish flag, streamed from the Castle of Dublin and resounded through the whole island, arousing a generous people to a new struggle for their ancient rights; and this war cry may be fitly inscribed on our standard now. Arise now, or our inexorable slave-driving tyranny will be fastened upon you; arise now, and liberty will be secured forever."*

Is it possible that this is an American citizen speaking of his own country and his own countrymen? Is it conceivable that "Americans" can forgive such insults? Who can imagine that the naturalized or Catholic citizen can be misled by an appeal so disingenuous and indecent?

The Democratic party and their candidate profess no new-born zeal for religious freedom and equality of rights. They stand where they have always stood, and stand there more proudly now, surrounded and supported by gallant and honorable men of other parties who were glad to join them on the great platform which Washington helped to build, and which rests on the granite of the Constitution.

Hence it is, that JAMES BUCHANAN utters, on this vital topic, with new emphasis, the precepts and almost the words of Washington.

THE PENNSYLVANIA SPIRIT.

These are the national aspects in which the question of the next Presidency is submitted to the people. There is one other view, more narrow, but still very impressive, which must be taken of it.

It is a Pennsylvania nomination, and as such is commended to Pennsylvanians. To them the appeal is directly made. Why should the local sentiment be disowned? Why should it not be stimulated?

When, on his return from England, Mr. Buchanan was welcomed back by his fellow-citizens of Maryland, he told them that, at the outset of his professional life, he had once thought of removing and living in Baltimore; but early association, love for the soil which gave him birth, the memory of childhood,—all those ties which, operating on generous and patriotic hearts, bind us to our birth-place, were too powerful. He could not, and he did not desert Pennsylvania. Nor will Pennsylvania now withhold her support from him.

The old Thirteen States,—of which Pennsylvania was the central and controlling one,—have given birth to twelve Presidents

* Letter of the Hon. Charles Sumner on Fremont's nomination.

of the United States (Virginia, six; Massachusetts, two; North Carolina, two; New York and New Hampshire each one); and yet never till now has a nomination been made from Pennsylvania. Pennsylvania by her vote has decided every Presidential election, yet her claims have never been regarded. She has yielded, and been postponed, and no voice of murmur or complaint has ever escaped her lips. Her fidelity to the Constitution and the Union,—her deference to national duty,—her submission to national policy, has been manifested at all times, and in every crisis. Her loyalty to a common country was proved long ago amid the trials of the Revolution; and justice, slow but sure, is now done to her patriots of that day. "Pennsylvania," wrote Washington in the darkest hour of the war, "Pennsylvania is our chief dependence;" and our commonwealth did not fail him. It was on her shoulder, and not on that of Massachusetts and Virginia (as has been claimed) that the hand of Washington rested most heavily in hours of the greatest gloom and perplexity. When, in March, 1780, she abolished slavery within her limits, as she had a right to do, it was done temperately, delicately, and with tender regard for the rights of others bound at least in social union with her. As has been well said by one of her own historians, "No Southern State, no Southern statesman complained of her example. Obtrusive fanaticism had not then alienated the sympathies of our Southern brethren. The Pennsylvania statesmen of the Revolution thought and acted in their treatment of this perilous subject on principles of moderate and practical wisdom. Abolition was with them no wayward freak of headlong enthusiasm." What a profanation of history it is, to compare the temperate, loyal spirit which then reigned in Pennsylvania with the vituperative disloyalty of our times! It is quite as unjust as to call sectarian intolerance and proscription "Americanism," or to dignify abolitionists as republicans.

When the Constitution of the United States was formed, the first State which adopted it was our neighbor Delaware, the next Pennsylvania, and the third New Jersey. The three middle states of the Old Thirteen, then as ever, were quickest in their loyalty. And they have been steadfast ever since. In 1819, the Legislature of Pennsylvania instructed its representatives to support the Missouri restriction; but when Congress, reflecting the popular feeling throughout the land, decided adversely, Pennsylvania acquiesced, and welcomed Missouri cordially as she chose to come,—with or without slavery, as her people determined for themselves,—into the family of States. No Pennsylvania Legislature ever approved the Missouri compromise. When, in 1847, designing and excited men,—the very same who now are fomenting sectional excitement again,—tore down part of the fabric of legislation, which our ancestors erected sixty-seven years before, and sought to declare a paltering, timid war against the United States, by denying facilities to its officers, the sober loyalty of the people revolted, and the Democracy of Pennsylvania never rested till this vexatious statute was abrogated. Governor Johnston's defeat in 1851 was mainly attributable to his adherence to this reprobated legislation; and now, let it be observed, his reward is, being a Pennsylvanian, to be scornfully repudiated and disowned by the very men and the very party which led him into error. The Democracy on this and on kindred subjects, in its loyalty to the Union and the Constitution, has known no shadow of turning.

And now that, thus national in its feelings, a national man of her own, like Mr. Buchanan, is put forward for the first office in the people's gift, who shall say that an appeal to the state pride of Pennsylvania will be vain? It has been truly said by a loyal Pennsylvanian:

"Local exultation in honors rendered to our own public men, is not an illusory sentiment. No one will think the worse of us for indulging it. It is that which has made Virginia the mother of Presidents. She nurses her children like a loving mother, and does not bind them out or cast them off without care as to what becomes of them. It was that which made Massachusetts cling to Mr. Webster; North Carolina to William Gaston, one who, according to the new standard of politico-religious intolerance, was not fit to be trusted in public office; and South Carolina to Mr. Calhoun; and which bound Kentucky, by devotion that never abated, to Mr. Clay. And now, when, for the first time for seventy years, a Pennsylvania Statesman is named for the highest honor in the Nation's gift, have we not a right, nay, is it not our duty to avow the throbbing of the same sentiment in our hearts? If the habit of easy self-sacrifice, the readiness to be content with small honors and subordinate offices, which has been so long the discredit and shame of Pennsylvania, if all this have not chilled to absolute indifference every natural emotion of honest pride in our bosom, this commonwealth will speak out now in tones which will not soon die away to silence."

Nor is this all,—and we regret to take a still narrower view of the subject,—as a matter of fair State competition, what would the interests of Pennsylvania gain by sustaining a candidate selected as John C. Fremont was, even aside from sectional feelings? The main influences which sustained him then, and which sustain him now, are Northern fanaticism and the wild spirit of speculative adventure, stimulated by the satanic and fanatic Press (those which have been well described as "the percussion presses of the country"),—the organs, by mutual crimination and confession, of venality and fanaticism. The nomination of Fremont was a victory over Pennsylvania. The power of speculative wealth,—the sympathy of operators in distant land scrip, puffed up to-day and depressed to-morrow, swayed the convention which made this nomination, and even there the Pennsylvania spirit was trampled down with insult.

This is not rhetoric—not declamation—but simple and precise truth. It is a fact which cannot be controverted, that this nomination is, at least partly, due to the speculative sympathy we have spoken of—in mines, and land scrip, and the worst of credit—and that if successful under such auspices, it would inaugurate a new era of commercial adventure and latitudinarian administration, such as no rational or conservative man can fail to deplore.

What can Pennsylvania—her moderate hard-working men—her modest but substantial enterprises—her farmers and miners and mechanics,—what can the merchants and traders of Philadelphia and Pittsburg, those who have contributed so many millions to our local improvements, gain from an ascendency like this?

It is their interest, then, as well as their duty, to support a statesman whose whole life and every thought is devoted to Pennsylvania, and no one out of Pennsylvania will think the worse of him for this. "The older I grow," said Mr. Buchanan, once, in his place in the Senate, "the more am I inclined to be a State Rights man."

Pennsylvania, surely, will thank him for this.

Such is the question which the American people must decide. If any fact has been here stated which history does not record, let it be disproved. If any inference has been drawn which fair reasoning does not authorize, let it be pointed out. The truth has been sought for anxiously and conscientiously. The issues for good or for evil are most momentous, and cannot be avoided or concealed in any spurious excitement which may be attempted. The election of a sectional President by a strictly geographical vote can lead to but one result,—the practical breaking down of the Executive Department of the Government, or a dissolution of the Union. And who, in his sober meditations, can decide which is the most fearful. It is no idle fear—no rhetorical prophecy of evil—but the statement of a certain result.

May these "Words of Counsel," written by no alarmist, but by a temperate and reasoning student of his country's history,—by one who has been taught from early boyhood to reverence as his highest social law the Constitution of the Union, and never believed before, that, in defiance of Washington's farewell and solemn words, sectional and geographical parties would divide this country and endanger the Union. May these words of friendly and earnest counsel, addressed to reasoning men, help to avert these sad results!

SPEECH

OF

HON. A. P. BUTLER, OF SOUTH CAROLINA,

ON THE

DIFFICULTY OF MESSRS. BROOKS AND SUMNER,

AND THE CAUSES THEREOF.

DELIVERED IN THE SENATE OF THE UNITED STATES, JUNE 12-13, 1856.

WASHINGTON:
PRINTED AT THE CONGRESSIONAL GLOBE OFFICE.
1856.

MR. BROOKS AND MR. SUMNER.

Mr. BUTLER. Mr. President, the occasion and the subject upon which I am about to address the Senate of the United States, at this time, have been brought about by events over which I have had no control, and could have had none—events which have grown out of the commencement of a controversy for which the Senator from Massachusetts (not now in his seat) [Mr. SUMNER] should be held exclusively responsible to his country and his God. He has delivered a speech the most extraordinary that has ever had utterance in any deliberative body recognizing the sanctions of law and decency. When it was delivered I was not here; and if I had been present, what I should have done it would be perfectly idle for me now to say; because no one can substitute the deliberations of a subsequent period for such as might have influenced him at another time and under different circumstances. My impression now is that, if I had been present, I should have asked the Senator, before he finished some of the paragraphs personally applicable to myself, to pause; and if he had gone on, I would have demanded of him, the next morning, that he should review that speech, and retract or modify it, so as to bring it within the sphere of parliamentary propriety. If he had refused this, what I would have done I cannot say; yet I can say that I would not have submitted to it. But what mode of redress I should have resorted to, I cannot tell.

I wish I had been here. I would have at least assumed, as I ought to have done on my responsibility as a Senator, and on my responsibility as a representative of South Carolina, all the consequences, let them lead where they might; but instead of that, the speech has involved his own friends, and his own colleague. It has involved my friends. It has involved one of them to such an extent that, at this time, he has been obliged to put his fortune and his life at stake. And, sir, if the consequences which are likely to flow from that speech hereafter shall end in blood and violence, that Senator should be prepared to repent in sackcloth and ashes.

Now, I pronounce a judgment on that speech which will be adopted by the public. I am as certain as I am speaking that it is now condemned by the public mind, and by posterity it will be consigned to infamy, for the mischievous consequences which have flowed from it already, and such as are likely yet to disturb the peace and repose of the country.

I said nothing, Mr. President, at any period of my life—much less did I say anything in the course of the debate to which the Senator from Massachusetts purports to have made a reply—that could have called for, much less have justified, the gross personal abuse, traduction, and calumny, to which he has resorted.

When I was at my little farm, enjoying myself quietly, and as I thought had taken refuge from the strifes and contentions of the Senate, and of politics, a message was brought to me that my kinsman had been involved in a difficulty on my account. It was so vague that I did not know how to account for it. I was far from any telegraphic communication. I did not wait five minutes before I left home to put myself within the reach of such information—and garbled even that was—as was accessible. I traveled four days continuously to Washington; and when I arrived I found the very subject under discussion which had given me so much anxiety; and it has been a source of the deepest concern to my feelings ever since I heard of it, on many accounts—on account of my country, and on account of the honor and the safety of my kinsman. When I arrived here, I found the subject under discussion. I went to the Senate worn down by travel; and I then gave notice that, when the resolutions from Massachusetts should be presented, I would speak to them, as coming from a Commonwealth whose history, and whose lessons of history, had inspired me with the very highest admiration — I would speak to them from a respect to a Commonwealth, whilst, perhaps, the Senator who had been the cause of their introduction ought not to deserve my notice, and would not have received it.

Well, sir, days passed, and those resolutions

were not presented. Now, they have been presented, and presented in a different way from any that I have ever known to be submitted from any Commonwealth before. They were not presented by one of its Senators, but were sent directly to the President of the Senate, and the Speaker of the House of Representatives. I waited for some time with the expectation that, when these resolutions should come, I would acquit myself of the painful task which circumstances had devolved upon me. They did not come until yesterday—more than two weeks after their adoption.

In the mean time — on Monday last — I gave notice that I would address the Senate to-day, under the confident belief, not that the present Senator [Mr. WILSON] would be here—because I have nothing to do with him—but that the Senator who has been the aggressor, the criminal aggressor, in this matter, would be present; and if I give credence to the testimony of Dr. Boyle, I see no reason why he should not be present. For anything that appears in that testimony, if he had been an officer of the Army, and had not appeared the next day on the battle-field, he would have deserved to be cashiered.

Sir, I am at a loss to know why he has aimed his assaults at me individually, and at my State on more occasions than one; but I am willing to adopt the clew afforded by the Rev. Mr. Beecher; and, as it is a clew upon the subject, I rely on it. I wish nothing of mine to go out that I do not intend to be entirely consistent with the convictions of my mind. I ask to have Mr. Beecher's remarks read. I adopt them, and they will acquit the Senator—or they will go very far to acquit him.

The SECRETARY read as follows:

"The only complaint which I have ever heard of Senator SUMNER has been this: that he, by his shrinking and sensitive nature, was not fit for the 'rough and tumble' of politics in our day. He would have held himself back, and avoided giving the slightest offense, had it not been that he was reproved and goaded into it by, as I think, the injudicious criticism of friends."

Mr. BUTLER. Sir, I believe it, and it will acquit his motives to some extent. Instead of making his speech here his own, as a Senator, under the obligations of the Constitution, and the highest sanctions which can influence the conduct of an honorable man — instead of making it the vehicle of high thoughts and noble emotions that would become a man and a Senator, it is obvious now that he has made that speech but the conduit —I will use a stronger expression—the fang, through which to express upon the public the compound poison of malignity and injustice. This is confirmed by his remarkable exordium; for, in many respects, this is the most extraordinary speech that has ever found its way in any book, or upon any occasion, ancient or modern. I have never before heard of proem or exordium by proclamation; and yet, before the delivery of his speech, by a telegraphic proclamation to Theodore Parker, he uttered this remarkable sentence: "Whilst you are deliberating in your meeting I am about to pronounce the most thorough philippic that was ever heard in the Senate of the United States." This is in conformity with Mr. Parker's opinion. He was a flexible conformist invoking the spirit of Theodore Parker as his muse to sustain him in the strife for which, by his nature and his talents, he was not fit. Sir, it was the tribute and deference of a flexible conformist, willing to be a rhetorical fabricator to carry out the views and subserve the purposes of a man who, as I understand, is of an iron will and robust intellect; who loves controversy, and has abilities which more fit him, perhaps, for that, than for worshiping the lamb as the emblem of innocence, and as the prototype of that Christ whose doctrines he has professed. To conciliate Parker, the Senator must make war upon South Carolina and upon myself. If he supposed that he would gain laurels by any attack on me because I was a "foeman worthy of his steel," I might feel complimented; but there was no such purpose. It was to pander to the prejudices of Massachusetts, or a portion of Massachusetts—for God forbid that I should say anything which is not proper of Massachusetts—to pander to a portion of Massachusetts by assailing South Carolina. Before I finish I shall say what I think, and if he were here in his place I would make him hang his head in shame; for I will demonstrate, before I conclude, that, in what he has said of South Carolina, he has aspersed the nearest and dearest comrade of his mother. Yes, sir, a degenerate son, incapable of appreciating the relations which subsisted between Massachusetts and South Carolina at a time when there was something more of peril to be encountered than exhibitions of rhetoric in the Senate of the United States; when men placed their lives and their fortunes on the issue which had been made. I will prove him a calumniator. While he has charged me with misstating history, law, and the Constitution, let me say that "he who lives in glass houses should not throw stones." I here say, and I pledge myself to it, that I will convict him, and shall demand of the Senate a verdict of guilty.

But, Mr. President, there is one result of this speech which I think may be regarded as good. He has shown, as Mr. Beecher says, that he is unfit for the war of debate. He has no business to gather the glories of the Senate Chamber and fight with orators, unless he is prepared to maintain the position of an honorable combatant. Though his friends have invested him with the dress of Achilles and offered him his armor, he has shown that he is only able to fight with the weapons of Thersites, and deserved what that brawler received from the hands of the gallant Ulysses.

I must say, Mr. President, that I was utterly disappointed in the body of the speech. Independent of the personalities which have distorted and disgraced it, there is nothing in the speech to distinguish it from pretty nearly all the speeches which he has made upon this subject—and I believe he has scarcely made any speeches on any other. He is one of those one-idea men who always go one way. Whilst this speech has much of the identity of former efforts, it has none of the freshness of their originality. If there is anything that varies it at all and distinguishes it from the others, it is the calico pictures impressed upon the "warp and woof" of his former speeches in the form of quotations; some of which—I say it as a moralist and as a Senator—stain the cloth upon which they are impressed, more by their obscenity than he can adorn it with the glare of their coloring.

I have made these remarks upon the character of the speech. He may regard them as criticism. Whether my criticism be one that will be adopted by the public, or such as will address itself to the good taste and good sense of this audience, I know not. I have given the convictions of my mind.

After these remarks upon the character of the speech, I come to make my points; and I will maintain them, not by general charges without specifications; not by that proclivity to error and falsehood which the Senator so decently imputed to me; not by general declamation from which he can take refuge in his own authority; but I will prove them by documents beyond all question.

In the first place, I say that what the Senator said of me and of the State of South Carolina was dragged into the debate by no law of legitimate association or connection; but it was injected into his speech positively in disregard of the tone and spirit of mine—neither in reply to, nor in recognition of, the kindness and forbearance which pervaded my speech. Sir, I am now passing through the last chapter of my public life. When I came here this year, I said to friends, "The last thing I would wish is, to have my name or reputation, if I have any, associated with party strife, much less with party contentions." My speech upon the Kansas question was the most guarded and remarkable for its forbearance of any that I have ever delivered. I commenced it by this declaration:

> "It may be said that I have passed through the ordeal of experience, and perhaps of time, and that they have had their influence on my temper; but, sir, I look on anything like a rupture in civil government, and especially such a one as would throw us into the horrors of anarchy, with not the same view as others who may be more intrepid, and who may think they can come out of it without hazard to themselves. There is nothing so mischievous to society as any movement affecting its stability, uncontrolled by responsibility and unregulated by intelligence."

Upon another occasion I remarked that I would be the last man to do or to say anything that would commit the issue in Kansas to the arbitrament of the sword in the hands of youth. Mine was a warning and a kind voice.

Before I proceed with the argument of my main points further, I will make a suggestion which may, perhaps, appear parenthetical. When the Senator from Massachusetts took his seat near me, I knew that he was a Free-soiler, or Abolitionist, as it was termed; but notwithstanding that, I had read some of his productions, and he was introduced to me, or perhaps, I to him. I had known many who came into the Senate of the United States, reeking with prejudices from home, who afterwards had the courage to lift themselves above the temporary influences which had controlled them. I supposed that a man who had read history could not be a bigot. I believed that one who was imbued with the literature which that Senator's mind had imbibed, could not sin in the face of light, and truth, and the lessons of history. With these views, I did not hesitate to keep up what my friends complained of, an intercourse with him, which was calculated to give him a currency far beyond what he might have had if I had not indulged in that species of intercourse. My friends here and everywhere know it. When I made my reply to him on the Nebraska and Kansas bill, I complimented him. I did not hesitate to compliment him, and he was gratified at it, for he said so. His opinion of me as a lawyer was very different then, (if I may be allowed to speak of what he then said,) not only on this floor, but to other persons. I did not hesitate to forbear a proscriptive judgment on any man because he happened to differ with me to-day or to-morrow; for life, sir, is but a span anyhow. I thought the time might come when the tide of events would bring to him the awful certainty of the doctrines which he held, and which in the first instance, when he came here, he was not disposed to propagate.

Things stood in this way until one day when it was proposed here to repeal the fugitive slave law. I said that I had no great confidence in that law, and turned to him with an honest purpose, with no design whatever to provoke anything like a personal or sectional issue, and asked of the Senator from Massachusetts whether, if there were no fugitive slave law, Massachusetts would be willing to carry out the provision of the Constitution. Then it was, in excitement, or as he said, "impulse"—an impulse, as I characterized it then, of the drawer—he rose and asked me if "he was a dog to do this thing?" I treated this answer with ridicule; it absolutely did not touch my heart; and after that I spoke to him.

Three days afterward he came in with a labored philippic touching me more deeply than he had before; but he then made, for the first time, a charge affecting the revolutionary history of South Carolina, by saying that John Rutledge, who was honored by Washington and all his countrymen, and who is a historical character, had offered, in 1779, in a negotiation with Prevost, at the gates of Charleston, that South Carolina should be neutral during the war of the Revolution. I did not wait until the next morning to reply to him. I responded at once, and I have no doubt I replied with indignation. I have no doubt that my heart threw the words upon him. Mortified vanity has no conscience; it may be that he did not think he came out of that controversy with as much credit as he should—at least his friends may have thought so. I gave him notice, however, that after that I should have no communication with him whatever—the bridge had been cut down—and I never have had.

Two years elapsed; and, during that time, I am bound in justice here to say, I have scarcely spoken to, of, or about him; and, perhaps, when I did speak about him, I said something which he would have been gratified to hear. My friends think that sometimes I did. Whatever the temptation of my resentment may be, I have passed, and shall pass, through life with one determination: if I cannot do justice, I will not do injustice to any man. I have exhibited here in debate, on more occasions than one, impatience and excitability. These are peculiarities which have followed me from the cradle. Perhaps, sometimes, anger, in its ebullitions, may have found an expression from me; but, thank God, I can say it was but a transient feeling, which at the time gushed from the heart; it was a feeling which subsequently was suppressed by reason and repentance. That, however, is a failing which cannot inhabit the same mind with treachery and malignity.

Now, sir, I proceed to make my points; and I

shall show that what the Senator said of myself, and South Carolina, was not in response to anything which I said; that he has gone outside the record to bring into the debate matters which did not legitimately belong to it by association or connection.

I will maintain these three propositions so certainly that, in my opinion, there will not be one mind here, unless it be disposed to morally perjure itself, which will not acquiesce in them. I will show that his remarks upon me and South Carolina were untrue and unjust; the language used was licentious; the spirit which prompted it was aggressive; and the whole tenor and tone of the speech was malignant and insulting.

In no speech which I have made during this session did I name Massachusetts or South Carolina. This is a most remarkable thing considering the nature of the debate. I have culled what I said, and I have not introduced South Carolina by name into the debate, nor have I brought in Massachusetts. Yet, sir, this Senator alludes to me in two paragraphs. I should like to know why he did not finish my picture in one sketch on the first day, when he spoke of me as being "Don Quixote in love with slavery as a mistress, because she was a harlot." I dislike to repeat the obscenity of his illustration. When he had me under review then, why did he not finish me in that general sketch? He took another night; and during that night the chaotic conceptions either emanated from his own mind or were suggested to it by those busy people who seem to have control over him; and then it was that he made this celebrated attack on me, assailing my reputation as a gentleman of veracity:

"With regret, I come again upon the Senator from South Carolina, [Mr. Butler,] who, omnipresent in this debate, overflowed with rage at the simple suggestion that Kansas had applied for admission as a State; and, with incoherent phrases, discharged the loose expectoration of his speech, now upon her representative, and then upon her people. There was no extravagance of the ancient parliamentary debate which he did not repeat; nor was there any possible deviation from the truth which he did not make, with so much of passion, I am glad to add, as to save him from the suspicion of intentional aberration. But the Senator touches nothing which he does not disfigure—with error, sometimes of principle, sometimes of fact. He shows an incapacity of accuracy, whether in stating the Constitution or in stating the law, whether in the details of statistics or the diversions of scholarship. He cannot ope his mouth, but out there flies a blunder. Surely he ought to be familiar with the life of Franklin; and yet he referred to this household character, while acting as agent of our fathers in England, as above suspicion; and this was done that he might give point to a false contrast with the agent of Kansas—not knowing that, however they may differ in genius and fame, in this experience they are alike: that Franklin, when intrusted with the petition of Massachusetts Bay, was assaulted by a foul-mouthed speaker, where he could not be heard in defense, and denounced as a 'thief,' even as the agent of Kansas has been assaulted on this floor, and denounced as a 'forger.' And let not the vanity of the Senator be inspired by the parallel with the British statesmen of that day; for it is only in hostility to freedom that any parallel can be recognized.

"But it is against the people of Kansas that the sensibilities of the Senator are particularly aroused. Coming, as he announces, 'from a State'—ay, sir, from South Carolina—he turns with lordly disgust from this newly-formed community, which he will not recognize even as 'a body-politic.' Pray, sir, by what title does he indulge in this egotism? Has he read the history of 'the State' which he represents? He cannot surely have forgotten its shameful imbecility from Slavery, confessed throughout the Revolution, followed by its more shameful assumptions for Slavery since. He cannot have forgotten its wretched persistence in the slave trade as the very apple of its eye, and the condition of its participation in the Union. He cannot have forgotten its Constitution, which is republican only in name, confirming power in the hands of the few, and founding the qualifications of its legislators on 'a settled freehold estate and ten negroes.' And yet the Senator, to whom that 'State' has in part committed the guardianship of its good name, instead of moving, with backward treading steps, to cover its nakedness, rushes forward, in the very ecstasy of madness, to expose it by provoking a comparison with Kansas!"

Now, Mr. President, I am going to state a proposition which will startle the Senate: what he here undertakes to quote as the constitution of South Carolina, in reference to the eligibility of members of the Legislature, is not to be found in it at all. How did he bring it in in response to any speech of mine? He has sworn in his affidavit that what he said was fairly in response to the speeches which I had made. I put the question to Senators, and I shall pause for their sentence: how dare he, from anything in my speeches, put his finger—his profane finger—upon the constitution of South Carolina? Is that a response to anything which I said? My speeches heretofore delivered are upon record, and can be referred to. I neither alluded to the constitution of South Carolina, nor did I mention South Carolina in the whole debate; and yet in his affidavit he says that all these are fairly referable as a response to the remarks of the Senator from South Carolina! What he has quoted here is not in the constitution of South Carolina; and when he undertakes to subject me to the severity of his criticisms, as a blunderer in the statements of law and constitution, let him stand convicted of one of two things—either that he did not read the constitution of South Carolina himself, and adopted it from others, or that, if he read it, he could not understand it. I intend to dwell upon this point with a view to convict him—not that I am going to vindicate the constitution of South Carolina, but I will convict this rhetorical jurist—this man who undertakes to sit on the tripod, and publish the oracles of Delphi, to sit upon me as a lawyer! My God, what have I come to! A man who never managed a case (as far as I know) in court, to sit on myself who have been thirty-five years engaged in law, either in appearing at the bar, or expounding it on the bench!

I have never delivered a judgment on a question of law here, as a member of the Committee on the Judiciary, whether I have made the majority or the minority report, when that Senator has not concurred with me; or if he differed it has been on sectional questions on which he has been overruled by the overwhelming authority of the Senate. Yet, a man who has agreed with me always—and that is the only bad sign about it [laughter]—undertakes to sit in judgment on my legal attainments! If his authority is worth anything, it is with me, for he has concurred with me. On all the contested-election cases, we have agreed, except, perhaps, in the Phelps case. There he may have differed from me; but if he did the Senate overruled him.

That, however, is not the question which I was approaching. I said that what he stated in reference to the constitution of South Carolina was not in response to anything which had fallen from me, and that there was no such thing to be found in the constitution of South Carolina as he has quoted. I will read the clause:

"No person shall be eligible to a seat in the House of

Representatives, unless he is a free white man, of the age of twenty-one years, and hath been a citizen and resident of this State three years previous to his election. If a resident in the election district, he shall not be eligible to a seat in the House of Representatives, unless he be legally seized and possessed, in his own right, of a settled freehold estate of five hundred acres of land, and ten negroes; or of a real estate of the value of one hundred and fifty pounds sterling, clear of debt. If a non-resident, he shall be legally seized and possessed of a settled freehold estate therein of the value of five hundred pounds sterling, clear of debt."

I venture to say that nearly half of the members of the Legislature of South Carolina, particularly those who come from the towns and cities, do not own a negro at all; and very few of them, as my colleague knows, own five hundred acres of land. Merchants do not want it; lawyers do not want it. The tenure by which they hold their offices is mainly by the latter clause, which the Senator left out, that a man to be eligible to a seat in the House of Representatives must own property to the amount of one hundred and fifty pounds sterling, clear of debt. That is a little over seven hundred dollars. Now I have got him; I call on Senators to convict him. There is but one verdict which can be rendered. He has gone out of the way to assail the constitution of South Carolina, and, in assailing it, he is guilty of the worst of all faults. I cannot conceive of a worse predicament than his, who, professing pedantic accuracy, and sitting in judgment on the quotations of others, is reduced to the alternative of admitting that he never read what he quoted, or, if he had read it, could not understand it, or garbled it.

Again, sir, he says the constitution of South Carolina is republican only in form. I say there is no State in the Union whose constitution gives a more enlarged right of suffrage. I have not the provision now before me, but I can state what my colleague knows to be the fact, that every free white man of South Carolina, of the age of twenty-one, has a right of suffrage, provided he pays seventeen shillings of tax. I may be mistaken, perhaps, in the amount.

Mr. EVANS. There is no tax at all required, if he is a resident, and has resided six months in the election district. Then he is entitled to vote without property qualification.

Mr. BUTLER. If he has resided there for six months, no property qualification is required; but, if he has not resided so long, he must have a very small amount of land. Our people do not even pay a poll-tax. Here is the provision of the South Carolina constitution:

"Every free white man of the age of twenty-one years, being a citizen of this State, and having resided therein two years previous to the day of election, and who hath a freehold of fifty acres of land, or a town lot of which he hath been legally seized and possessed at least six months before such election, or, not having such freehold or town lot, hath been a resident in the election district in which he offers to give his vote six months before the said election, and hath paid a tax the preceding year of three shillings sterling towards the support of this government, shall have a right to vote for a member or members to serve in either branch of the Legislature, for the election district in which he holds such property, or is so resident."

The Senator has presumed to characterize her constitution as republican only in form, when it has the freest and most enlarged right of suffrage of any State in the Union. I grant you that, when the Legislature comes into operation under the constitution, there are conservative elements which, I thank God, have withstood the wild feeling of what is called the progress of the times; but it does not become me to allude to them now.

I come next to an allegation which, if the Senator were here, I think he would not look me in the face when I repeat, and that is, his insolent and untrue charge of the "shameful imbecility" of South Carolina during the war of the Revolution in consequence of slavery. Sir, ingratitude is the monster of vices, and when it is associated with injustice, it ought to be condemned by the consuming indignation of even those who may to-morrow be our adversaries. What are the facts? The news of the battle of Lexington was carried to Charleston by express; and the very day they received the intelligence the Liberty men, as they were called, broke open the arsenals and distributed the arms. It was but a few days afterwards before Boston sent a vessel to South Carolina for bread and wine. We sent them, I think, $3,500 worth of provisions, and seventy barrels of wine—the Maine liquor law did not prevail in Boston at that time. [Laughter.] We gave them bread; and, I answer for it, South Carolina has never asked pay for her hospitality. She would never brook the thought of asking pay for the bread she poured out upon her countrymen—countrymen they were, sir. Massachusetts was without powder then, and we furnished her with it.

Here I will say, lest I forget it, that the battles of Lexington and Bunker Hill in the Revolution, I regard as the battles of Marathon and Salamis. They gave the Commonwealth of Massachusetts an immortality for commencing the glorious contest which has resulted in the independence of these United States; and I shall be the last man to touch the laurel crown which grows from the blood that enriched the soil upon which those battles were fought. The very powder that was used after the battle of Bunker Hill was furnished by South Carolina. Here is the entry, not only in the history of South Carolina, but in the history of Massachusetts. In Ramsay's History of the Revolution in South Carolina, volume 1, page 43, you will find:

"At the time all these military preparations were making, the whole quantity of powder in the province did not exceed three thousand pounds. The people not originally designing a military opposition, no care was taken to provide stores; but now, reduced to the alternative of fighting or submitting, extraordinary methods were taken to obtain a supply. The inhabitants of East Florida having never joined in measures of opposition to Great Britain, the ports of that province were open for the purposes of trade.

"Twelve persons, in which number were included Captains Tempirere, Cochran, Statter, Tufts, Joyner, Messrs. Tebant, Williamson, and Jenkins, authorized by the Council of Safety, sailed from Charleston for that coast, and, by surprise, boarded a vessel near the bar of St. Augustine, though twelve British grenadiers of the 14th regiment were on board. They took out fifteen thousand pounds of powder, for which they gave a bill of exchange to the captain; and, having secured a safe retreat to themselves, by spiking the guns of the powder vessel, they set sail for Carolina. Apprehending that they should be pursued, they steered for Beaufort. From that place they came by the inland navigation, and delivered their prize to the Council of Safety, whilst their pursuers were looking for them at the bar of Charleston. This seasonable supply enabled the people of South Carolina to oblige their suffering brethren in Massachusetts, who, though immediately exposed to the British army, were in a great measure destitute of that necessary article of defense."

In a book published in Boston, entitled "Dealings with the Dead," I find these entries:

"Our southern confederates are entitled to *civility*, because they are men and brethren; and they are entitled to *kindness and courtesy from us of Boston*, because we owe them a debt of gratitude, which it would be shameful to forget. Since we, of the North, have presumed to be *undertakers* upon this occasion, let us do the thing '*decenter et ornate*.' Besides, our friends of the South are notoriously testy and hot-headed; they are, geographically, children of the sun. John Smith's description of the Massachusetts Indians, in 1614, Richmond edition, 2, 194, is truly applicable to the southern people, '*very kind, but, in their fury, no less valiant*.'

"I am no more inclined to uphold the South, in the continued practice of a moral wrong, because they gave us bread when we were hungry, as they certainly did, than was Sir Matthew Hale to decide favorably for the suitor who sent him the fat buck." * * * *

"June 24, 1774. Twenty-four days after the port bill went into operation, a public meeting was held at Charleston, South Carolina. The moving spirits were the Trapiers and the Elliots, the Horries and the Clarksons, the Gadsdens and the Pinckneys, of that day; and resolutions were passed full of brotherly love and sympathy for the inhabitants of Boston." * * * * * *

"New York, August 15, 1774. Saturday last Captain Dickerson arrived here, and brought three hundred and seventy-six barrels of rye from South Carolina, to be sold, and proceeds remitted to Boston, a present to the sufferers; a still larger cargo is to be shipped for the like benevolent purpose." * * * * * * *

"Let the work of abolition go forward in a dignified and decent spirit. Let us argue; and, so far as we rightfully may, let us legislate. Let us bring the whole world's sympathy up to the work of emancipation. But let us not revile and vituperate those who are, to all intents and purposes, our brethren, as certainly as if they lived just over the Roxbury line, instead of Mason and Dixon's. Such harsh and unmitigated scoffing and abuse, as we too often witness, are equally ungracious, ungentlemanly, and ungrateful."

The Senator says that the southern States, in consequence of slavery, betrayed during the revolutionary war a "shameful imbecility." I challenge him to the truth of history. There was not a battle fought south of the Potomac which was not fought by southern troops and slaveholders, even if you choose to exclude Pennsylvania, which was at that time a slaveholding State. Muhlenberg's continental regiment was always with them, and I love to allude to it; but not a New England squad, company, or regiment ever passed the Potomac; and yet the Senator says that but for northern aid the southern States could not have sustained themselves.

Sir, who fought the battle of King's Mountain? It was not fought by anybody in pay. Patriots fought it, but they never received a dollar. That battle made an impression, perhaps, the most remarkable of any during the war. It turned the tide of events. Who fought the battle of Cowpens? There was none in that battle from the north of Maryland. The commander in that battle was Daniel Morgan; the hero of the day was, perhaps, John Eager Howard. Colonel Washington, commander of the cavalry, and Pickens, a citizen of South Carolina, and one of the heroes of the war, commanded the militia, and they never shrank from their duty. It has been said of the South Carolina militia, during the revolutionary war, that they were only raw troops, who stood to their guns and position, whenever they were mustered into the service, and called upon to perform duty. Who fought the battle of Hobkirk's Hill? General Greene was the commander; and he afterwards became a slaveholder, and, of his own choice, lived and died in a southern State, among friends and comrades in arms. Who fought the battle of Eutaw? Was there any New England regiment, or company, or squad there? Not one. That battle, the most distinguished which has ever been fought in the southern portion of the Confederacy, was fought by southern slaveholders from Maryland, Virginia, South Carolina, North Carolina, and Georgia. They were exclusively southern troops. In the face of these facts, the Senator said the imbecility of the South, arising from slavery, was such that they could not fight their battles without aid.

Shame! I call upon the shade of Hancock and Adams to look down and reprove a degenerate son who can thus invade the very sanctuary of the history which has given them immortality.

Do you think that, sir, by this remark I reproach the troops of New England? No, sir. When Yorktown surrendered, there was not a New England regiment there; I have a list of the troops who were present. But because I say that southern troops and those from Pennsylvania alone engaged in these distinguished battles, do I reproach the troops of Massachusetts? God forbid! They were under the command of Washington at the time when he went to Yorktown, and, as was his duty, he sent them to defend the vulnerable points of New York and Boston.

Now I will make a remark which I hope the Senate will remember: Notwithstanding their relative numbers compared with the pay list of New England, you may take the fighting days—if you have a mind to compute it as you would labor—you may take the fighting days during which the troops of South Carolina were engaged, and in the computation the balance will be found greatly against Massachusetts. If you have a mind to draw some other test—if you wish to test the question of sacrifice, and measure it by blood, South Carolina has poured out hogsheads of blood where gallons have been poured out by Massachusetts.

In proof of this I give a list of battles fought in South Carolina, and each was a bloody battle:

Battle of Fort Moultrie.
Battle of Stono.
Siege of Charleston.
Battle of Camden.
Battle of Hanging Rock.
Battle of Musgrove's Mill.
Battle of Blackstocks.
Battle of Georgetown, and the battle at Black Wings; by Marion.
Battle of King's Mountain.
Battle of Cowpens.
Battle of Fish Dam Ford; by Sumpter.
Battle at Ninety-six.
Battle at Fort Galphin.
Battle at Fort Watson.
Battle at Fort Mott.
Battle at Hobkirk's Hill.
Battle of Granby.
Battle of Cedar Spring.
Battle of Hammond's Store.
Battle of Quinby.
Battle of Eutaw.
Battle of Rocky Mount.
Battle of Port Royal.
Battle of Tulafinny.
Battle of Coosahatchie.
Battle of Waxham settlement; between Beaufort and Tarleton.
Battle of Cloud's Creek.
Battle at Hays's station.
Bloody battle of Kettle Creek; fought by General Pickens.

Battle of Houck's defeat.

Bloody battle of Twelve-mile Creek; in which Salvadore fell.

These were all fought in South Carolina, and in which South Carolinians were engaged, and were bloody battles. In addition there were almost daily skirmishes fought by Marion and Sumpter.

But I do not blame Massachusetts, for I have said she had glory enough, and she was covered with glory enough by taking the bold stand which she did in putting the ball of revolution in motion; but, when the Senator undertakes to cast reproaches on the history of South Carolina, he will have to take hard comparisons. She got bread from her comrade. The man who now reproaches South Carolina, as I said a little while ago, is a degenerate son reproaching the dearest and nearest comrade of his mother. You cannot get over the errors he has committed in history; you cannot obviate the malignity with which the arrow has been shot. Whether he shot it with the reckless aim of one who had his hand upon the bow, and directed the shaft conscious that it had been dipped in the poison of others, I know not; but I have unmasked him; I have detected and exposed the man who charges me with error, and such a proclivity to error that I cannot observe the line of truth without such deviations as to bring on me the censure, not of one intentionally guilty of falsehood, but one who, under the gust and whirlwind of passion, cannot observe the line of truth. I have detected him; I have exposed him; and now I demand of the Senate a verdict of guilty. I pause, sir.

But now, since he has given his testimony, I will ask that the testimony of another man may be read—the opinion of Daniel Webster with regard to the revolutionary history of South Carolina and Massachusetts.

The Secretary read the following extract from Mr. Webster's reply to Mr. Hayne, delivered January 21, 1830:

"Then, sir, the gentleman has no fault to find with these recently-promulgated South Carolina opinions. And, certainly, he need have none; for his own sentiments, as now advanced, and advanced on reflection—as far as I have been able to comprehend them—go the full length of all these opinions. I propose, sir, to say something on these, and to consider how far they are just and constitutional. Before doing that, however, let me observe, that the eulogium pronounced on the character of the State of South Carolina, by the honorable gentleman, for her revolutionary and other merits, meets my hearty concurrence. I shall not acknowledge that the honorable member goes before me in regard for whatever of distinguished talent, or distinguished character, South Carolina has produced. I claim part of the honor—I partake in the pride, of her great names. I claim them for countrymen—one and all. The Laurenses, the Rutledges, the Pinckneys, the Sumpters, the Marions—Americans all—whose fame is no more to be hemmed in by State lines than their talents and patriotism were capable of being circumscribed within the same narrow limits. In their day and generation they served and honored the country, and the whole country; and their renown is of the treasures of the whole country. Him, whose honored name the gentleman himself bears—does he esteem me less capable of gratitude for his patriotism, or sympathy for his sufferings, than if his eyes had first opened upon the light of Massachusetts, instead of South Carolina? Sir, does he suppose it in his power to exhibit a Carolina name so bright as to produce envy in my bosom? No, sir, increased gratification and delight, rather. I thank God that, if I am gifted with little of the spirit which is able to raise mortals to the skies, I have yet none, as I trust, of that other spirit which would drag angels down. When I shall be found, sir, in my place here, in the Senate, or elsewhere, to sneer at public merit, because it happens to spring up beyond the little limits of my own State or neighborhood; when I refuse, for any such cause, or for any cause, the homage due to American talent, to elevated patriotism, to sincere devotion to liberty and the country; or, if I see an uncommon endowment of Heaven—if I see extraordinary capacity and virtue in any son of the South—and if, moved by local prejudice or gangrened by State jealousy, I get up here to abate the tithe of a hair from his just character and just fame, may my tongue cleave to the roof of my mouth!

"Sir, let me recur to pleasing recollections—let me indulge in refreshing remembrance of the past—let me remind you that, in early times, no States cherished greater harmony, both of principle and feeling, than Massachusetts and South Carolina. Would to God that harmony might again return! Shoulder to shoulder they went through the Revolution—hand in hand they stood round the administration of Washington, and felt his own great arm lean on them for support. Unkind feeling, if it exist, alienation and distrust, are the growth, unnatural to such soils, of false principles since sown. They are weeds, the seeds of which that same great arm never scattered."

Mr. BUTLER. Sir, Daniel Webster is a Doric statue upon a colossal pedestal raised by the hands of patriots—raised by the hands of statesmen, a pedestal which is imperishable as long as the achievements of heroes, patriots, and statesmen can be transmitted to posterity by history. His tribute to South Carolina is worth something. It is the tribute of a statesman and an orator—of a man who could lift himself above the bigotry, and even prepare to be crushed under the wheel of wild fanaticism. It is such a tribute as was paid by an orator like Pericles, who had guided the helm of State, who had an Athenian spirit of patriotism, who was an orator and a statesman. Who is he that now gives a different opinion of South Carolina? Is it not a Cleon—one whose warfare is to assail his antagonist by crimination, calumny, and private slander—a man who draws his similes from obscene sources, and always thinks he has conquered when he has mortified and hurt the feelings of his adversary?

Sir, when I look at the evidence to which I have adverted—when I allude to the opinions pronounced between the two gentlemen—between Mr. Webster and the Senator from Massachusetts, who is absent—I can well say,

"Look upon *that* picture, and then upon this"—

I will not finish the quotation; I shall say nothing in this debate but what I believe to be true. If I were to undertake to compare the Senator from Massachusetts with the coarseness of Cleon in some of his similes and his grossness in some of his attacks on his adversary—I mean in point of taste—I might do injustice to my own criticism, because I believe the Senator is a man who understands the use of language—a gentleman who has gone back to classic fountains, and in that respect I separate him from Cleon, but otherwise not at all. Let the young men and boys who hear me go and read the life of Cleon, and, when they do, let them read the notice which even Grote attaches to it, the author who has taken the most favorable view of that demagogue—who could never lift himself above the local prejudice that surrounded him, and always pandered to it in order to obtain a conquest over his rival, who was in power, and was maintaining the honor and dignity of his country.

Now, I come to another branch of the subject, and it is, I confess, the sorest one of all. The Senator has made a very grave charge upon John Rutledge—not upon South Carolina in that point of view. The facts in relation to that transaction are these: When General Lincoln was called to the command of the southern army, Prevost was in possession of Savannah, and Georgia in fact was under British authority. When Lincoln took command of the southern troops, he conceived the bold experiment of crossing the Savannah river and reclaiming Georgia. His wily adversary, who was in Savannah, took advantage of his being at Augusta, about one hundred and fifty miles above, crossed the river at Savannah, and made his way to the gates of Charleston. When he reached Charleston, there were but about six hundred troops under the command of Moultrie, and as many under Pulaski. He had about four thousand. The militia, and, I believe, even the women, kept watch the whole night for fear the town would be stormed. In order to gain time, a parley was proposed the next day. Rutledge sent three different commissions. He knew that Lincoln would be upon the British if he could only detain them for a day. That parley was regarded by his friends as a stratagem. Some of his enemies were disposed to assail him for it. Whilst they were on that very parley, Moultrie said that Rutledge had no right to touch the garrison; he himself was commander-in-chief, and Rutledge could do nothing as Governor to comply with the terms which, for appearance sake, he had proposed. Here is the notice of it by the historian:

"It was presumed by the garrison that General Lincoln, with the army under his command, was in close pursuit of General Prevost, but his precise situation was unknown to every person within the lines. To gain time in such circumstances was a matter of great consequence. A whole day was therefore spent in sending and receiving flags. Commissioners from the garrison at Charleston were instructed to propose 'a neutrality during the war between Great Britain and America; and that the question, whether the State shall belong to Great Britain or remain one of the United States, be determined by the treaty of peace between these Powers.'"—*Ramsay's History*, vol. 2, p. 27.

Whilst they were upon that parley, it happened that Lincoln came up and drove off Prevost. That very proposition of Rutledge resulted in the safety of Charleston. Some of his enemies have said that the terror of his situation was so great, the women and children being in the town, with only twelve hundred troops to defend it, that he was willing to capitulate on such terms as would save innocence from the dangers of a storm. His friends have given it a different complexion. Be that as it may, everybody knows that the Governor of South Carolina at that time had no power to make such an engagement. Prevost knew it just as well as anybody else. If he had agreed to it, I presume Rutledge could have drawn out of it the next day, on the ground that there was no authority to make the stipulation. It was during the time when this matter was under consultation, that Lincoln came up and drove off Prevost, and fought the celebrated battle of Stono, so much spoken of in the southern country.

But suppose that John Rutledge could have subjected them to the terms which the gentleman has censured—for he is not only a superior lawyer to sit in judgment on everybody else's law knowledge, but it appears he is a military man, though I never heard of it before—suppose that John Rutledge had stipulated, as far as he could stipulate, that the people of Charleston should be remitted to British protection as long as they observed their parol, was it anything more than his own countryman, General Lincoln, did, on the 22d of May of the following year? General Lincoln was severely censured for his act; but it was done from feelings of humanity. He could have evacuated the city of Charleston, and saved his army, as Washington did at Philadelphia, but, instead of that, he agreed to stand by the houses of the women and children in Charleston at all hazards, and run the risk of the censure pronounced on him by military men. He capitulated; and what were the terms of the capitulation? That the militia should be under British protection, and should not be disturbed, in person or property, as long as they observed their parol. That was the act of Lincoln. He could do no more. The military men who were under his command were subject to be exchanged as prisoners of war. The Senator has gone out of his way to pronounce a judgment against Rutledge, to which his own countryman has been actually liable. I will give you an incident to show the difference between the taunting injustice and malignity which prevail now, and the chivalry which prevailed then. When they came to the terms of capitulation, Lincoln, with the proud spirit of a military man, insisted that he should leave Charleston beating the American march, with his colors unfolded, his flag furled. Clinton told him, "No, sir; we have reduced you to our own terms, and we intend to degrade you; you are rebels, and deserve none of these honors at our hands."

When Yorktown was taken, who was delegated to prescribe the terms of capitulation? John Laurens, of whom it has been said that a daring courage was the least of his accomplishments, and an excess of it his greatest fault. When Laurens was called upon by General Washington, who behaved on that occasion with a delicacy and propriety which history and poetry ought to commemorate, he told Laurens, "Sir, as your city surrendered to Clinton, I delegate to you the authority to prescribe the terms on which this surrender shall be made." Cornwallis said to him, "These are hard terms to require us to go out with folded colors, and to beat the Turk's march, a neutral march." Laurens said, "There shall not be a dot of an *i* or a cross of a *t* in the terms of capitulation at Yorktown which was not observed at Charleston." To make it more delicate to Lincoln, on whom the shade of censure had somewhat passed for his conduct at the siege of Charleston, Laurens said that it was proper to select Lincoln to receive the sword from Cornwallis, as he had surrendered the sword to Clinton. You will see him in the foreground of the picture in the Rotunda. There was chivalry, sir—a chivalry peculiar to the days in which it was exhibited. Is such conduct as that to be under the censure of a rhetorical fabricator at this day? It is hard to bear—it is unjust in itself.

Now, sir, I have done with these topics. I have not vindicated the history of South Carolina. I ask the Senate to bear me testimony, that I have not gone into this matter with a view to vindicate her. She does not need it. Adopting the language of Daniel Webster, I may say: "There is South Carolina; there she stands; she speaks for herself; she needs no eulogy;" she cannot be injured by the detraction of one who is under an influence not of justice, truth, or honor.

Having finished with these thrusts at the constitution of South Carolina, and at her history and character, I come now to another matter in relation to myself. He says that I have such a proclivity to error in my statistics, that I have as many words of error as I utter. What a wholesale assertion is that! Strange to say, I resorted to no statistics at all on the occasion to which he alluded. When I interrupted the Senator from New Hampshire, [Mr. Hale,] I had on my table returns from the Charleston custom-house. I alluded to them in general terms, to prove what he cannot dispute—that the slave trade was carried on in northern, and English, and Scotch vessels; that the profits of it redounded to them; and that, when the slave trade was opened, it gave them the regulation of commerce. The venerable grandfather of my friend from Virginia, [Mr. Mason,] in the Convention, had inserted into the Constitution a provision that a two-thirds vote of Congress should be necessary for the passage of any measure to regulate commerce.

I say here, that for South Carolina and Georgia it was a short-sighted policy when they gave up the regulation of commerce to the navigation interest, in consideration of their having the slave trade remain open until 1808, with the certainty before them that New England mainly gained the profits of that trade. If the sin of the slave trade is to be imputed to anybody, let it be imputed to the hand that took the child from under the tree, separated it from its mother in Africa, and brought it to this country under circumstances that, I confess now, are shocking. If I were to dwell on some of the circumstances of that slave trade, as I have heard them from Africans, and believe them to be true, they would shock the Senate. The slave trade threw its profits into New England. As a friend of mine from South Carolina [Mr. Keitt] said in the other House, if New England will to-day come back and return all the money she has got out of the slave trade, we will strike a balance with her and let her buy them; but she would not take them. This time, when the condition of the slave is better than it ever was at any other, is the very occasion when they are making war upon the institution. It is the common practice in my district—I cannot answer beyond my neighbors—to give the laboring hands three and a half pounds of good bacon every week, and as much bread as they can eat. It is the interest of their owners to clothe them. They are a happy, contented, intelligent, and reformed people

But, sir, the Senator undertakes to say that, because I have advocated here the constitutional rights of the South and the equality of these States, I subjected myself to an imputation which I shall not read myself. It bears his own handiwork. Mr. Secretary, I beg your pardon for asking you to read such a thing as this, but it is your duty, not mine.

The Secretary read the following extract from Mr. Sumner's speech of May 19:

"But, before entering upon the argument, I must say something of a general character, particularly in response to what has fallen from Senators who have raised themselves to eminence on this floor in championship of human wrongs; I mean the Senator from South Carolina, [Mr. Butler,] and the Senator from Illinois, [Mr. Douglas,] who, though unlike as Don Quixote and Sancho Panza, yet, like this couple, sally forth together in the same adventure. I regret much to miss the elder Senator from his seat; but the cause, against which he has run a tilt, with such activity of animosity, demands that the opportunity of exposing him should not be lost; and it is for the cause that I speak. The Senator from South Carolina has read many books of chivalry, and believes himself a chivalrous knight, with sentiments of honor and courage. Of course he has chosen a mistress to whom he has made his vows, and who, though ugly to others, is always lovely to him; though polluted in the sight of the world, is chaste in his sight—I mean the harlot Slavery. For her, his tongue is always profuse in words. Let her be impeached in character, or any proposition made to shut her out from the extension of her wantonness, and no extravagance of manner or hardihood of assertion is then too great for this Senator. The frenzy of Don Quixote, in behalf of his wench Dulcinea del Toboso, is all surpassed. The asserted rights of Slavery, which shock equality of all kinds, are cloaked by a fantastic claim of equality. If the slave States cannot enjoy what, in mockery of the great fathers of the Republic, he misnames equality under the Constitution—in other words, the full power in the National Territories to compel fellow-men to unpaid toil, to separate husband and wife, and to sell little children at the auction block—then, sir, the chivalric Senator will conduct the State of South Carolina out of the Union! Heroic knight! Exalted Senator! A second Moses come for a second exodus!

"But not content with this poor menace, which we have been twice told was 'measured,' the Senator, in the unrestrained chivalry of his nature, has undertaken to apply opprobrious words to those who differ from him on this floor. He calls them 'sectional and fanatical;' and opposition to the usurpation in Kansas, he denounces as 'an uncalculating fanaticism.' To be sure, these charges lack all grace of originality, and all sentiment of truth; but the adventurous Senator does not hesitate. He is the uncompromising, unblushing representative on this floor of a flagrant *sectionalism*, which now domineers over the Republic, and yet with a ludicrous ignorance of his own position —unable to see himself as others see him—or with an effrontery which even his white head ought not to protect from rebuke, he applies to those here who resist his *sectionalism* the very epithet which designates himself. The men who strive to bring back the Government to its original policy, when Freedom and not Slavery was national while Slavery and not Freedom was sectional, he arraigns as *sectional*. This will not do. It involves too great a perversion of terms. I tell that Senator, that it is to himself, and to the 'organization' of which he is the 'committed advocate,' that this epithet belongs. I now fasten it upon them. For myself, I care little for names; but since the question has been raised here, I affirm that the Republican party of the Union is in no just sense *sectional*, but, more than any other party, *national;* and that it now goes forth to dislodge from the high places of the Government the tyrannical sectionalism of which the Senator from South Carolina is one of the maddest zealots."

Mr. BUTLER. Now, Mr. President, how any man, who has not been excluded from society, could use such an illustration on this floor, I know not. I do not see how any man could obtain the consent of his own conscience to rise in the presence of a gallery of ladies and give to slavery the personification of a "mistress," and say that I loved her because she was a "harlot." I beg pardon for repeating it. What in the name of justice and decency could have ever led that man to use such language? That is the language of Cleon. It is a somewhat remarkable thing, that in the speech which I delivered here in reply to the Senator from New Hampshire, I used the word "slavery" but in one paragraph, and that was in response to a remark of his speaking of the Supreme Court as the citadel of slavery. I rebuked him. I said I would rather regard that court as the defender or as the promontory of the Constitution; and that he was at too great a distance ever to reach it by any arrow which he could discharge from his bow. Sectionalism was not in the speech itself. When I spoke of individuals in a particular section, I did not speak in terms which would imply or convey the idea that I meant the public of the slaveholding and non-slaveholding States. I confined it to that section who are suffering at this time, I hope to a limited extent, and who are burning their fires until they will be reduced to the caustic ashes of disappointment and disgrace. I did not speak of sectionalism in any other point of view. Sir, there are men on this floor who I believe honestly differ from me. I would not make any personal allusion to them. Far from widening this controversy, the object of my speech was to appease public sentiment. In the course of it I ventured to say, what I had never said before, that the man does not live who could look without concern at the consequences of a separation of these States effected in blood. I remarked that I would not say there was not intelligence enough ultimately to form new governments and make them a union of confederacies. Sir, in that speech I attempted to throw oil upon the troubled waters. My friends in some measure blamed me for the tone of my remarks. The so-called reply was already in the sap, the poisonous sap behind, and the Senator had to use his speech as a conduit to pour it out on me and on the country, when he had less occasion than was presented by any speech which I ever before made. Anybody who says we are incapable of preserving free institutions, I should be inclined, to consider a slanderer on free institutions; but I will never agree to live in any Government that has not some operative and enforcible provisions of a constitution to preserve my rights. If the Government were as it formerly was, South Carolina and Massachusetts having a common interest, do you think the Senator could arise as an adversary to be applauded by his people? There was a time, sir, when his people would have disgraced him for that very speech. At this day, I do not say they will acquit my kinsman; I dare say they will not; but the time is coming when there will be but one opinion—that that is the most mischievous speech which has ever been delivered in this country, and has involved more innocent persons. If the contest goes on upon such issues as it makes, blood must follow. I do not look on any such scenes with pleasure. I have not temper for them, though when a young man I might, perhaps, not have been indisposed to embark in the hazards of contests.

Whilst upon this point, I may remark that Josiah Quincy, for whom I have heretofore had a great respect, says the Senator has not gone a hair's breadth beyond the line of duty and truth. After my explanations here I hardly think he will say so. He is the only man of high respectability whom I have yet seen or heard make such a declaration. He made it, too, with a reproach that I was sorry to see escape from such a man. He said, alluding to the fracas in the Senate-house, not in the Senate, that it is only a part of that tribe who carry bowie-knives and revolvers. Sir, I never wore a secret weapon in my life. I am not going to discuss the fact that I have used open weapons; and that is the only way I choose to deal, but that is not the way we can get them to deal with us.

Unfortunately, I have had scenes of that kind which I have regretted all my life to some extent. I am mortified to hear such a man as Quincy making a charge upon a whole section, when I question if there is a southern man in this House with a pistol or bowie-knife in his pocket. He has gone out of the way gratuitously to say that we are of a "breed" who wear them as part of our dress. I am sorry to see such things creeping into the public mind. They mortify me; they annoy me.

But now I come to the resolutions of Massachusetts. I ask that they be read.

The Secretary read them as follows:

COMMONWEALTH OF MASSACHUSETTS. *In the year* 1856.

Resolves concerning the recent assault upon the Hon. Charles Sumner, at Washington.

Resolved by the Senate and House of Representatives of the Commonwealth of Massachusetts, That we have received with deep concern, information of the recent violent assault committed in the Senate Chamber at Washington, upon the person of the Hon. Charles Sumner, one of our Senators in Congress, by Preston S. Brooks, a member of the House of Representatives from South Carolina;—an assault which no provocation could justify—brutal and cowardly in itself—a gross breach of parliamentary privilege—a ruthless attack upon the liberty of speech—an outrage of the decencies of civilized life, and an indignity to the Commonwealth of Massachusetts.

Resolved, That the Legislature of Massachusetts, in the name of her free and enlightened people, demands for her representatives in the National Legislature entire *freedom of speech,* and will uphold them in the proper exercise of that essential right of American citizens.

Resolved, That we approve of Mr. Sumner's manliness and courage in his earnest and fearless declaration of free principles, and his defense of human rights and free territory.

Resolved, That the Legislature of Massachusetts is imperatively called upon by the plainest dictates of duty, from a decent regard to the rights of her citizens, and respect for her character as a sovereign State, to demand, and the Legislature of Massachusetts hereby does demand, of the national Congress, a prompt and strict investigation into the recent assault upon Senator Sumner, and the expulsion by the House of Representatives of Mr. Brooks, of South Carolina, and any other member concerned with him in said assault.

Resolved, That his excellency the Governor be requested to transmit a copy of the foregoing resolves to the President of the Senate, and Speaker of the House of Representatives, and to each of the Senators and members of the House of Representatives from this Commonwealth, in the Congress of the United States.

HOUSE OF REPRESENTATIVES, *May* 29, 1856.

Passed. CHARLES A. PHELPS, *Speaker.*

IN SENATE, *May* 30, 1856.

Passed. ELIHU C. BAKER, *President.*

MAY 31, 1856.

Approved. HENRY J. GARDINER.

SECRETARY'S OFFICE,
BOSTON, *May* 31, 1856.

I certify the foregoing to be a true copy of the original resolves.

Attest: FRANCIS DEWITT,
Secretary of the Commonwealth.

Mr. BUTLER. These resolutions give rise to more serious reflection than anything which has occurred to me in my time. I have been in the Senate for ten years, and this is the first occasion that I have ever seen one of the sovereign States of the Union taking cognizance of matters which occurred in Congress, with a view to influence the judgment of Congress in relation to one of their members. This is the first occasion of the kind in the history of the country. It has been done from an *ex parte* view of the subject; for it is now very apparent that the resolutions of Massachusetts were introduced and passed without regard to the evidence. These resolutions anticipated and asserted what may not be true—what the public may not think true—what the Senate may not think true—what the House of Representatives may not think true; and yet the sovereign State of Massachusetts, before there was any evidence, indicted my relative upon rumor—a measure which would have taken Stafford to the gallows. What! sir; indict a man in the language of these resolutions upon the rumor of newspapers? These resolutions—I say it more in sorrow than in anger—betray a temper and precipitancy of judgment that do not look like having a regard to that dignity which is associated with justice. I shall speak respectfully. So far as I have spoken of Massachusetts hitherto, no exception can be taken; but, when I speak of Massachusetts now, it must be of Massachusetts as she has sent forth these resolutions—under the influence of a feeling which pervades her—under the influence of a sentiment which denied Daniel Webster the right to speak in Faneuil Hall, and threw off the coffin of Lincoln because he had fallen in performing his professional duties in the cause of his country. Boston now is not the Boston that she was when Hancock wrote, and Adams spoke, and Otis thought, and Warren fell. They would not recognize her. She is no more the same. Yet, from that very hotbed of bitter feeling to the South, and especially to South Carolina, have I to look for the feelings which dictated these resolutions. I have to meet an indictment—for what? It is said that the liberty of speech has been violated. Upon that point I intend to deliver some remarks which, whether they be correct or not, I shall throw out. Our ancestors were a people of hardy morality. Generally, when they spoke, they spoke directly from the heart. Such a thing as printing speeches beforehand, or having them printed without being uttered in the Senate, was unheard of in their day. They were men who stood on their legs, and spoke out. They had hearts and mouths. They did not resort to the appliances of paper and printing before they brought their speeches here. If the Senator from Massachusetts were present, and would answer me, I would put the question to him, "Was not that speech of yours printed and published before you spoke it in the Senate of the United States?" What is the meaning of that provision of the Constitution, which says that a Senator, or a member of the House, for any speech or debate in either House, shall not be questioned in any other place? Does it mean to give the Congress of the United States the power of deciding what is privilege without the courts questioning it? If so, it goes far beyond the settled doctrine in Great Britain at this day, which was maintained by Chief Justice Denman, in the case of Stockdale *vs.* Hansard; and that case has much to do with the matter now under consideration. Hansard had undertaken, under the authority of Parliament, to publish a book which contained a libel. Without such license or privilege, all agreed that he was responsible. The English House of Commons said that having granted him the license, it was their privilege. Chief Justice Denman took cognizance of the case, on the broad ground that the courts could determine what was privilege under the Constitution of England. He said: "as a common law judge, I will show the Parliament whether I am not capable of deciding on my responsibility as one of the great departments of this Government. Can it be maintained"— and it is one of the most eloquent decisions I ever read—"that the House of Commons, by claiming a privilege, shall thereby appropriate it to themselves, and screen a villain from the consequence of his libel?" The judge said that although by the law of Parliament newspapers were passed through the country under the frank of members without paying postage, that privilege did not give them the right to make use of a newspaper as a libel. He uses the strong expression: "God forbid that Parliament should afford such a pretext for doing wrong." I say the same thing now.

Will you tell me that a member rising here and handing a speech to the reporter, and telling him to print it, comes within the purview of the Constitution? Has he uttered words in debate? Will you tell me that a member who has made a speech of five sentences may append to it a newspaper like the Tribune, which has libeled me, and has the right to send through the post offices of this Government, and have folded by the persons employed in the folding-room at the public expense, into my daughter's parlor, that which would cost him his life if he told it to me? Has it come to this, that a Senator upon this floor can claim such an extensive privilege, under the law of Parliament, that he can send off, by the twenty thousand, speeches to England and to the four corners of the globe, where I am not known, and then claim protection upon the ground that he has a privilege which precludes him from being questioned elsewhere for words spoken in debate?

Sir, the difference is an obvious one. Perhaps not more than five hundred or a thousand people heard the Senator on the occasion when he assailed me; and I venture to say that, of the number who were present and knew me, not one believed a word of what he said. It is a different thing when he has printed a package of twenty thousand of the documents, franked them, and sent them to England, where, I suppose, he will be highly praised. He will be fed with the oil which kindles English fires, to encourage him to walk in the light of his path. If I were to go to England, they might point at me and ask, "is that the man so monomaniacal in regard to slavery that he cannot tell the truth?" I am not accustomed to make comparisons, but I will say that there is not a parent or a husband on this floor who can approve the language of that Senator. Though I may have bitter enemies here—no doubt I have some, but I do not see why I have incurred their enmity—I venture to say that I do not think a single man on this floor would, if he were put on his oath, say that he believed what the Senator said of me. When spread abroad in the form of a libel it becomes of a very different character.

I say that this privilege under the Constitution is the subject of judicial inquiry. The courts may say where privilege ends, and where libel begins. He has been guilty of a libel. I know, sir, how sacred is the liberty of speech. I know what has been said by Mr. Erskine on this subject—his language has often been praised for its beauty—in the celebrated trial against Tom Paine. Mr. Erskine quoted language which he supposed had been used by Lord Chesterfield. Lord Kenyon said to him:

"Lord KENYON. That very speech which did Lord Chesterfield so much honor is supposed to have been written by Dr. Johnson.

"Mr. ERSKINE. Gentlemen, I believe it was so, and am much obliged to his lordship for giving me a far higher authority for my doctrine; for, though Lord Chesterfield was a man of great wit, he was undoubtedly far inferior in learning, and what is more to the purpose, in *monarchical* opinion, to the celebrated writer to whom my lord has now delivered the work by his authority. Dr. Johnson then says"—

Gentlemen may avail themselves of this, if they choose, when I come to another part of this matter. Dr. Johnson says, in the language put in the mouth of Lord Chesterfield:

"One of the greatest blessings we enjoy—one of the greatest blessings a people, my lords, can enjoy, is liberty; licentiousness is the alloy of liberty; it is an ebullition—an excrescence; it is a speck upon the eye of the political body, but which I can never touch but with a gentle, with a trembling hand, lest I destroy the body—lest I injure the eye upon which it is apt to appear.

"There is such a connection between licentiousness and liberty, that it is not easy to correct the one without dangerously wounding the other; it is extremely hard to distinguish the true limit between them; like a changeable silk, we can easily see there are two different colors, but we cannot easily discover where the one ends, or where the other begins."

In a subsequent part of this celebrated forensic speech, delivered by Lord Erskine, he goes on to show what is the liberty of speech, and what is its limit. He says, by way of illustration, what is exactly apposite to this case:

"I expect to hear, in answer to what I am now saying, much that will offend me. My learned friend"—

I do not call the Senator "my learned friend;" I make this periphrasis on that point—

"My learned friend, from the difficulties of his situation, which I know from experience how to feel for very sincerely, may be driven to advance propositions which it may be my duty, with much freedom, to reply to; and the law will sanction that freedom; but will not the ends of justice be completely answered by my exercise of that right, in terms that are decent, and calculated to expose its defects? or will my argument suffer, or will public justice be impeded, because neither private honor and justice, nor public decorum, would endure my telling my very learned friend, because I differ from him in opinion, that he is a fool, a liar, and a scoundrel, in the face of the Court?"

If the Senator had said, in respectful language, "We have been adversaries on this subject; I differ from you; I think you have been guilty of great errors which deserve the censure of a parliamentary speaker; and I intend to pronounce a censure, believing that I am right and you are wrong; I will detect you in the fallacies of your history; I will detect you in the errors of your law; I will expose those errors"—he would have had a right to do this, and in as strong language as he chose; but when he said almost in so many words, that my proclivity to error was such that I deviated from the truth in all these particulars, it is a libel in the very language of Mr. Erskine. If he were indicted for a libel to-morrow, could he claim his privilege under the Constitution, and would the courts be precluded from deciding the question whether it was a libel or not? There is no one, perhaps, who has a higher ideal admiration for the liberty of speech and the liberty of the press than I have.

The liberty of speech and of the press is the great conservative element of a Republic; it is to the political, what fire is to the material world, a subservient and affluent minister, when under the control of prudence and intelligence; but, when unchecked and unregulated, a consuming foe, withering and blasting everything along its pathway of ruin. Render freedom of speech tributary to the proprieties, decencies, and restraints of social life, and you may crown it with all the ministries and supremacies of intellect and liberty, but release it from them, and it becomes a blind and maddened giant of evil, tearing down the bulwarks of social order, and desecrating the very sanctuary of republican liberty. What would you think of a reckless man who should set fire to his own house, or should go about claiming the privilege of throwing his fire wherever he could among the most combustible materials, and say he had the right to do so, on the ground that he was a freeman, and could do as he pleased. Away with such liberty! Liberty that is worth anything must be in the harness of the law.

Liberty of speech and liberty of the press must have two restraints. The first is the highest, which will always govern a class of men who cannot violate it—the obligations of honor, decency, and justice. Another restraint upon licentiousness is that a man may publish and speak what he pleases with a knowledge that he is amenable to the tribunals of the law for what he has done. Congress cannot pass any statute to say that men shall not write against religion, or against the Government, or against individuals. Neither can Congress pass a law, nor can any State pass a law depriving the tribunals of the country of the right of saying whether you have gone beyond the limits of liberty, and have used your power, under that name, with criminal recklessness, with a licentious indifference to the feelings of individuals and the consequences upon society. I do not wish to live in any community where it is otherwise.

The press is losing its power, and it ought to lose it; for it is now beginning to be an engine of private revenge, and individual expression, instead of being a responsible organ of public opinion. Suppose I were to go to New York, and indict one of the editors there whom I could name, for the most atrocious libel that has ever been uttered upon the South. I will not name the editor, but he has uttered a sentiment akin to one which has been expressed by the Senator from Massachusetts. I saw in a New York paper—I have alluded to it heretofore—a statement that the southern States are too feeble and weak to take any part in a war—that all they can do is to take charge of their negroes! It said that if a war should take place between England and the United States, the English fleet would only have to go to the capes of the Chesapeake, and the effeminate masters would be kept at home. Fifty thousand slaves, inured to toil, could be mustered into service, and they would have the power to put their masters to the sword; and when the declaration of peace should come, the result would be the freedom of the slaves and the proscription of the masters! Suppose I should go into the community where this libel was uttered, and indict a man for such a sentiment as this, what would be the consequence in the present state of public opinion? It is idle, worse than idle, to talk about that as a remedy.

Liberty of the press! Sir, that man has franked twenty thousand of his speeches; and some of them, if I am not misinformed, were printed long before it was delivered. To bring him within the privileges of parliament is a mockery—a perfect mockery.

Now, Mr. President, I approach another most

painful part of this case, and I come to it in no bad temper; for, God knows, if my heart could be read, there is no one who would sooner than myself have averted the state of things which now exists, if I could, consistently with my honor and the honor of the gentleman to whom I shall allude. The resolutions of Massachusetts undertook, before any evidence was heard, to pronounce sentence on Mr. Brooks. Sir, I will tell you who Mr. Brooks is, and why he felt so deeply in reference to these abominable libels. I do not allude to him now as my hereditary kinsman; I think that is the smallest view to take of the matter; but I am his constituent. I live in "Ninety-six"—a district through which, if you pass, you will read upon the tombstones epitaphs which would reproach him for tame and ignominious submission to wrong and to insult.

He has as proud and intelligent a constituency as are to be found in any part of the globe. I am his constituent. But more than that, he has worn the epaulet and the sword; he has marched under the Palmetto banner, and his countrymen have awarded to him a sword for his good conduct in the war with Mexico. That sword was in some measure committed to him, that he might use it, when occasion required, to maintain the honor and the dignity of his State. When he heard of this speech first, and read it afterwards, this young man, in passing down the street, heard but one sentiment, and it was, that his State and his blood had been insulted. He could not go into the drawing-room, or parlor, or into a reading-room, without the street commentary reproaching him. Wherever he went, the question was asked, "Has the chivalry of South Carolina escaped, and is this to be a tame submission?" What advice I would have given him I do not now undertake to say.

But, sir, when this was said to this gentleman wherever he went, he felt that if something was not done he could not face his constituents without losing his usefulness, and without there being a taint on his honor and on his courage. He may have been mistaken in some respects. His coming into the Senate house was no option of his. When he formed his determination, as I am informed,—and I have kept aloof from conversation with him,—I judge from the evidence he had no purpose to profane the Senate house. I say the Senate house had been profaned before. I had rather to-morrow take ten blows inflicted on my body, than have the gas of the rhetorician poured out upon my character and State.

The Senator from Massachusetts chose to make his place here one from which to assail the history and reputation of South Carolina, and to assail an absent constituent of the gentleman who has taken redress into his own hands. In such a condition of things who could be placed in a situation more difficult? Surely, Mr. President, something is to be pardoned to the feelings of a man acting under sensibility, and under the dictates of high honor. If any one was here, placed in a situation to feel the touching appeal made by the ghost to Hamlet, "If thou hast nature in thee, bear it not," he was the man. Now, I ask the Secretary to read the extract which I have marked in the book which I send to him, and I do not intend to say where it comes from till it is read.

The Secretary read as follows:

"Do not believe that I am inculcating opinions, tending to disturb the peace of society. On the contrary, they are the principles that can preserve it. It is more dangerous for the laws to give security to a man, disposed to commit outrages on the persons of his fellow-citizens, than to authorize those, who must otherwise meet irreparable injury, to defend themselves at every hazard. Men of eminent talents and virtue, on whose exertions, in perilous times, the honor and happiness of their country must depend, will always be liable to be degraded by every daring miscreant, if they cannot defend themselves from personal insult and outrage. Men of this description must always feel, that to submit to degradation and dishonor is impossible. Nor is this feeling confined to men of that eminent grade. We have thousands in our country who possess this spirit; and without them we should soon deservedly cease to exist as an independent nation. I respect the laws of my country, and revere the precepts of our holy religion; I should shudder at shedding human blood; I would practice moderation and forbearance, to avoid so terrible a calamity; yet, should I ever be driven to that impassable point, where degradation and disgrace begin, may this arm shrink palsied from its socket if I fail to defend my own honor!"

Mr. BUTLER. Who uttered that sentiment? It is the sentiment of a gentleman whose speeches have always commended him to me. It is a sentiment worthy of the ancient days of Boston when Dexter spoke. This is a northern man speaking; and I adopt his language. I say with him that, when things "tend to that impassable point where degradation and disgrace begin, may my arm shrink palsied from its socket if I fail to defend my own honor!"

Sir, that sentiment was uttered at a time when clergymen confined themselves to the pulpit, and preached against crime and vice; when they did not use the pulpit as a recruiting station to issue Sharpe's rifles, and to mingle in all the bitter strife of the forum and the Agora. It was uttered when Boston knew how to respect the feelings of others. I concur in all that is said by Mr. Dexter. I deprecate blood and violence. I will not utter all that my heart prompts me to say, for fear of encouraging young men; but this I will say, that no son of mine should ever submit to insult without satisfaction.

[The honorable Senator, at this point, yielded the floor at the suggestion of Mr. Clay, on whose motion the Senate adjourned.]

Friday, *June* 13, 1856.

Mr. BUTLER. Mr. President, whilst I am indebted to my friend from Alabama [Mr. Clay] for asking that this debate should be adjourned over until to-day, I regret very much that I did not finish my remarks yesterday; for I do not wish to detain the Senate on this subject longer than justice and propriety, and a regard to the questions involved require.

Of course, Mr. President, it is obvious that I have become involved in this controversy in such a way as to make me, I hope, justly sensible to all the consequences which may grow out of the issue—not that I hold myself at all, directly or indirectly, responsible for the consequences which have followed the extraordinary speech which was delivered by the Senator from Massachusetts; but there are questions which have grown out of the assault that followed the speech, of a graver import than at one time I had thought the subject could assume. I think the resolutions from Massachusetts will present questions here for the consideration of the Senate, and I may say for the consideration of Congress, of a character never presented before.

I had yesterday spoken of those resolutions only in one point of view—so far as they denounced the assault of my friend and relative, Mr. Brooks, as a violation of the freedom of debate. I had not ventured to speak of the resolutions as I intend to do before I have closed my remarks. From conversation with others, as well as from my own reflections, I am satisfied that they are resolutions of dangerous import and precedence, utterly unknown in the history of this country before. I think they show that one State of the Confederacy may make a fearful issue in the Congress of the United States, under the immunities and privileges which by courtesy are sometimes extended to States, but would not otherwise grow up. If it is in the power of Massachusetts or South Carolina, or in the province of any one State in the Union—Wisconsin or Texas—to make such a quarrel as must necessarily result in an angry controversy that may array the different sections of the Union against each other, it is one of the most dangerous views in which the power of a State Legislature can exercise the privilege or courtesies which have been awarded to it.

Sir, I have intimated this much with a view to show that I intend to denounce those resolutions—to denounce them strongly—not that I denounce the individuals who passed them. I hope that I can go higher than the resentment to the mere individual who may assault the history of my State, or who may impugn my character. This is a question that goes deeper and higher—very far beyond anything which is involved in a mere personal controversy. I will reserve those remarks on the resolutions until after I shall have finished what I intended to say yesterday in relation to the actual state of things growing out of the speech delivered by the Senator from Massachusetts.

I said yesterday that my friend, my representative, my relative, one who is associated with me by more ties than either of these—had taken redress in his own hands—had resorted to his own mode of redress. I said that there were considerations connected with the occasion which, though they could not justify him before a legal tribunal, would excuse any man of his character and position, representing such constituents as he represented, and bound in some measure to sympathize with the opinions of the section with which he is associated. It was impossible that he could separate himself from those conclusions which others might not appreciate, and some could not understand. But I say that gentleman dare not—I do not say I would have advised him—but in his estimation he could not go home and face such a constituency without incurring what is the worst of all judgments—the judgment of the country against a man who is placed as a sentinel to represent it.

If, in the course of these proceedings and the events which have grown out of the speech which has been made by the Senator, it shall be said that Massachusetts can be justified by falling back on an opinion which will justify her Senators and Representatives, it is, I must be permitted to say, one of the unfortunate symptoms of the times in regard to which we have no common tribunal to decide between us. Sir, it seems to indicate a crisis when the opinion of the constituency of one portion of the Confederacy applauds one whilst it is ready to consume and put to the stake another. We have always supposed that public opinion would be right; and sir, I distinguish public opinion very much from popular prejudice. Popular prejudice is that which would consume in ignorance to-day, what it would repent of to-morrow. Public opinion is the judgment of an intelligent community, not formed under the excitement of the moment. It is not the sentiment of an irresponsible multitude; it is not the sentiment of an *ex parte* decision; it is not the judgment which can find its way into the history of the country, or which posterity will adopt as that which ought to be pronounced on the occasion. Public opinion is the highest, the gravest, the most solemn judgment to which any of us can defer. I would not give one cent for what is called public opinion, if it depended upon *ex parte* views of any subject. And I say that the resolutions which have been sent here from the Legislature of Massachusetts, are not only *ex parte*, but I am sorry to say that I fear their counselors were prejudice and malignity, even giving their counsels through the darkness of ignorance. I do not mean ignorance so far as regards the body individually, for I have no doubt it is intelligent enough; but I mean ignorance, so far as regards pronouncing a judgment without understanding the facts on which that judgment ought to turn. I say that my friend has been condemned without a hearing. He has been condemned by a judgment which, if suffered to go into history uncontradicted, unexamined, and unrefuted, would consign him to a fate which his character does not deserve, and shall not receive as long as I can stand here as his friend and advocate.

But, sir, before I approach the constitutional and legal view of these resolutions, I must acquit myself of the duty which I in some measure assumed yesterday evening, of presenting to the public the circumstances under which the fracas, as it is termed, or the assault, on the Senator from Massachusetts, occurred.

I said that my friend and relative was not in the Senate when the speech was being delivered, but he was summoned here, as I have learned from others. He was excited and stung by the street rumors and the street commentaries, and by the conversations in the parlors, where even ladies pronounced a judgment; and, sir, woman never fails to pronounce a judgment where honor is concerned, and it is always in favor of the redress of a wrong. I would trust to the instinct of woman upon subjects of this kind. He could not go into a parlor, or drawing-room, or to a dinner party, where he did not find an implied reproach that there was an unmanly submission to an insult to his State and his countrymen. Sir, it was hard for any man, much less for a man of his temperament, to bear this.

I intended to reserve a commentary which was at once made on the speech of the Senator from Massachusetts as the most important part of my conclusion; but I find that I can apply it at no better time than this. I allude to the commentary which was pronounced at the time; not when a controversy had arisen; not when it was supposed that the temptations of an adversary, or even the public mind, had so far made an issue that he was obliged to take one side or the other; but it was pronounced by a gentleman of distinguished position, a sage, a patriot, a man who had won laurels in the field, and justly deserved to be considered the Nestor of the Senate. Sir, the remarks made by the member from Michigan [Mr. CASS] struck me as the most consuming piece of criticism; and I think, taking it all into consideration, it would be more terrible to me than all the arguments of an advocate, and all the array that could be brought on one side or the other. It was the testimony of voluntary justice.

"I have listened"—said that distinguished gentleman, [Mr. CASS,] who had worn the sword and the robes of the Senate, with distinction and dignity—"with equal regret and surprise to the speech of the honorable Senator from Massachusetts. Such a speech—the most un-American and unpatriotic that ever grated on ears of the members of this high body—as I hope never to hear again, here or elsewhere. But, sir, I did not rise to make any comments on the speech of the honorable Senator, open as it is to the highest censure and disapprobation."

I am not as young a man as Mr. SUMNER, nor do I pretend to be in a condition to defy or place myself against the testimony which would put into operation a current of public opinion, such as was pronounced by the honorable Senator from Michigan in his place; but, sir, I can say, that, with my nature, I could not have slept that night on my pillow with such a censure and such a criticism pronounced in the Senate of the United States. I should have been ready to send a message to make atonement in some way. I should have wiped out, as far as I could, by repentance and atonement, the unmanly aggression and insult which had been offered, and was condemned by the highest authority. I do not undertake to say what was the opinion of that Senator, but I can quote from his State the most consuming judgment I ever heard pronounced. The sentiments expressed in the paragraph to which I allude, and in others, show that when the effervescence of popular prejudice shall have subsided, this case might be tried, even in Massachusetts itself. I should not be afraid to try it there. They are not slaves to be governed by fanatical madness. One of the journals there, in a remarkably well-written article, which I adopt, says:

"Charles Sumner's recent speeches in the United States Senate have not in any respect enhanced his reputation as a man, as a debater, or as a statesman. It is impossible, it seems to us, for any fair-minded man, who loves truth and regards honor and decency, to read these effusions, all reeking with falsehoods, bitterness and wrath, and indecency, without feeling that Massachusetts has been disgraced by an unworthy son in the Senate Chamber, before the country and in the face of the world. We venture the assertion that no parallel to these vituperative outbursts of Sumner can be found in the annals of Congress, nor in the records of any legislative assembly in the world. Overpowering passion, madness itself, seems to have bereft him of his senses, and left him oblivious of truth and honor, of the courtesies of intelligent and dignified debate, and of the proprieties of civilized life.

We do not, we cannot, use terms too strong in relation to this matter. It is not the character of Charles Sumner alone that is involved. The fair fame of Massachusetts suffers. Whatever may have been the political errors of Massachusetts, she has ever, heretofore, been represented in the Senate of the United States, and we might also say in the House of Representatives, by men, statesmen—Webster, Winthrop, Everett, Choate, Davis, and Bates—who knew their rights, and knowing dared to maintain, and maintained them with courtesy, dignity, and ability, in such a manner as to command the respect of their opponents, the applause of their friends, and the admiration of all their countrymen."

I knew some of the gentlemen here named, and I should never be afraid to meet them in debate anywhere, because with them I should never apprehend the assaults of calumny and slander. I cannot be reduced to such an issue that I must discount calumny and slander by the language of a blackguard. If it be the theory of gentlemen that when one uses language in debate transcending the sphere prescribed by propriety and justice, we are to resort to the same mode for redress and satisfaction, I am a non-combatant; I cannot enter into a controversy with gentlemen in which they are to bandy words.

These remarks are not without their direction. I have used them to show what was the impression on the public mind at the time when the assault was committed. Mr. BINGHAM, a friend of Mr. SUMNER I presume, says in his testimony that on hearing the speech he anticipated something. It was the general impression of the whole community that he deserved to receive a chastisement; or, at least, that he was bound to make atonement in some way for the insults and the wantonness of his insults to a gentleman (as I hope I am) then absent. This was the common sentiment pervading the public mind at Washington. What was my friend to do? Sue him? Indict him? If that was the mode in which he intended to take redress, he had better never go to South Carolina again. Was he to challenge him? That would have been an exhibition of chivalry having no meaning. Although he has been upon the field, both in open war and in a private affair, I should be very sorry to see any crisis requiring it again. A challenge would have been an advertisement to the world of his courage, when there was not a probability of its being tried. He would have made himself contemptible, and perhaps might have been committed to the penitentiary for sending a challenge.

Then, what course was left to him to pursue? Mr. SUMNER had opportunities enough to make an apology. God knows I could not have resisted the admonitory criticism of the distinguished Senator from Michigan, perhaps the most imposing authority in the Senate. He paid no regard to him, and for a very good reason: his speech was written, and had gone out, and he could not contradict what he had sent forth to the public with malice aforethought.

Well, sir, what did Mr. BROOKS do? It is said he sought Mr. SUMNER in the Senate Chamber. It is the last place in which he wished to seek him. He would have met him in an open combat, on a fair field, and under a free sky, at any time. And when the Legislature of Massachusetts chooses to say that his conduct is cowardly, let her try him in any way she chooses. [Applause.]

Mr. STUART. I hope the Chair will enforce the rules. I think, sir, what we have just witnessed has been repeated this session quite too often. If the amenities and proprieties of the Senate cannot be kept by gentlemen, they should not enter its Chamber.

The PRESIDENT *pro tempore*. Does the Senator desire the galleries to be cleared?

Mr. STUART. I shall not make any motion now; but I hope it will be understood by everybody who visits this Chamber, that the proprieties of the place shall be observed.

The PRESIDENT *pro tempore*. Persons in the galleries will distinctly understand, that if there be any further demonstration, the galleries will be cleared of all except ladies.

Mr. FESSENDEN. In justice to the galleries, I will suggest that the impression on this side of the House is, that the disturbance came from the floor of the Senate Chamber, and not from the galleries. I hope the galleries will not be punished for the act of persons on the floor.

Mr. BUTLER. Well, sir, I will go on in such a way that nobody shall be disturbed—not that I intend to suppress any single sentiment of mine; but I shall express it in the severity of truth. I can tell the Senator from Maine, with whom I have always been on good terms, that I shall say nothing out of the way.

Sir, a man who occupies a place in the Senate, representing a great Commonwealth like Massachusetts, or representing any State, as one of her Senators, occupies a very high position, from which he can send forth to the public what may affect the character of almost any man, except General Washington, or some one upon whose character the verdict of history has been rendered. There is scarcely any man who can withstand the slander which may be pronounced from the Senate Chamber of the United States. For this reason I would never look, and I never have looked, beyond the public position of a member here, to go into his private and personal character. I would not do it, because by so doing I should do a wrong which I could not redress. Even a word escaping my tongue in this Chamber, as a Senator, might go far to injure a man where he could not correct it. We are in a position which requires high considerations for the regulation of our conduct. I agree thoroughly with General Jackson, that the slanderer who involves third persons in difficulty and danger, is an incendiary, against whom we should guard more than any one else, in a parliamentary point of view. I will quote General Jackson's language. He said: "Over the doors of each House of Congress, in letters of gold, should be inscribed the words, 'The Slanderer is worse than the Murderer.'" A single murder is horrible. It may take a single individual from society. But when I look at the mischievous influence of slander, I find that it pervades a whole community; makes war in society; sets family against family; individual against individual; section against section. It is the most cowardly mode in which a war can be conducted.

With the state of opinion to which I have alluded prevailing, what did Mr. Brooks do? Of course he did not undertake to challenge Mr. Sumner to a fist fight, or a stick fight, or any other kind of fight. He thought Mr. Sumner deserved a castigation, and he undertook to give it to him according to the old-fashioned notion, by caning him. I have not heard Mr. Brooks detail the circumstances. I have not conversed with him in regard to the matter; I take my information from the published testimony. Mr. Brooks, not finding him anywhere else, came to him while he was sitting in his seat here, after the Senate had adjourned. He came to him in front—different from the statement made to the Massachusetts Legislature. He was half a minute in his proem or explanation. He said: "Mr. Sumner, I have read your speech. I have read it carefully, with as much consideration, and forbearance, and fairness as I could; but, sir, I have come to punish you now for the contents of that speech, which is a libel on my State, and on a gray-haired relative."

Instinct would have prompted most men to rise immediately. Mr. Sumner did rise. In the act of rising, Mr. Brooks struck him across the face—not, as has been represented, over his head, for that is not the truth, nor is it borne out by the testimony. On the second stroke the cane broke. It is the misfortune of Mr. Brooks to have incurred all the epithets which have been used in regard to an assassin-like and bludgeon attack, by the mere accident of having a foolish stick, which broke. It broke again; and it was not, as I understand, until it came very near the handle, that he inflicted blows which he would not have inflicted if he had an ordinary weapon of a kind which would have been a security against breaking. His design was to whip him; but the stick broke, and that has brought upon him these imputations.

It has gone through the country that Mr. Brooks struck him after he was prostrate on the floor. None who know this young man could entertain such an idea. I have known him from childhood. I used to have some control over him; but the scholar has become the master, and I suppose he would not care much about my advice now. By an hereditary tie our families are more closely united than any two with whom I have been acquainted. But that is far apart from the question. Independent of his filial feelings for me, and his regard for me as his constituent and Senator, I have no doubt that a personal feeling of regard for myself individually influenced him.

He approached that man with no other purpose than to disgrace him as far as he could; but the stick broke. After it broke he was reduced to a kind of necessity—a contingency not apprehended at all in the original inception of the purpose of making the assault. Notwithstanding all that has been said of his brutality, he is one of the best tempered fellows I ever knew—impetuous, no doubt, and quick in resentment, but he did not intend what has been assigned to him.

After all that has been said and done, on a *post bellum* examination, what is it? A fight in the Senate Chamber, resulting in two flesh wounds, which ought not to have detained him from the Senate. Being rather a handsome man, perhaps he would not like to expose himself by making his appearance for some time; but if he had been in the Army, there was no reason why he should not go to the field the next day; and he would deserve to be cashiered if he did not go. What does his physician say? He says that there were but two flesh wounds; that he never had a fever while under his care and attendance, and that he was ready to come into the Senate the next day, but for his advice; and his advice was, that he should not come into the Senate, because it would aggravate the excitement already too high. He did not recommend him not to go into the committee room to be examined on the ground that his wounds had enfeebled him, but for other considerations, because it might aggravate the excitement already prevailing to an extent which might lead to mischievous consequences.

This, then, is the mode of redress to which Mr. Brooks resorted. I do not say what I should have advised him to do, but perhaps it was fortunate that I was absent in one respect, for I certainly should not have submitted to that insult. Possibly it might not have been offered if I were present, though I do not know the fact, because I cannot say exactly what would be the course of one of those persons who have a way of fabricating speeches. Perhaps, being in his speech, he would have had to read it; but I think it possible that on the appeal which I would have made on my discretion, his friends might have induced him to reform it in some way so as to conform at least to the requirements of common decency in public opinion. If he had not done so, I do not know what would have been my course.

For this transaction, as I have detailed it, and without the intelligence which I have detailed being before them, the Legislature of Massachusetts have sent their resolutions here. These resolutions are without a precedent in the history of this country. I hope other Senators will speak to them, for they are not only an insult to South Carolina and her representatives in Congress, but I think they assail the Constitution of the country. Before commenting on them, I may be permitted to allude to the first precedent of a congressional fight, which was between two members from New England.

This affair is said to be an evidence of southern violence and southern ruffianism. Some papers speak of the bowie-knife and the revolver of southern blackguards. Why, sir, the first fight which took place in Congress was between Matthew Lyon and Roger Griswold, from Connecticut. Our ancestors in those days looked upon a fight with very little of the importance which is now attached to it. They said it was so unimportant, that they were vexed that so much of the time of the House was occupied in considering it.

It seems that Matthew Lyon, originally an officer in the Army, had been cashiered and awarded a wooden sword. He then lived in Connecticut. At that time, and at this, too, in Connecticut, there was a pretty pressing opinion against a low man, and he could not stand it. He had to move over into Vermont, a new State, then the frontier of the country. He was elected a member of Congress from Vermont. He was one of the Democrats. I suppose he was one of the Red Republicans of that day against John Adams's administration. Was he a Democrat?

Mr. FOOT. Yes, sir; he was a Democrat.

Mr. BUTLER. It was before the gentleman from Vermont taught school there, and Lyon assumed to be a kind of apostle of liberty and Democracy. Not satisfied with instructing the people of Vermont, he went to Mr. Griswold of Connecticut; stood behind his seat and told him, "Sir, you do not represent Connecticut correctly; I know these people; they are mean people; they will take $1,000 as soon as $9,000 for a salary." Griswold stood it for a great while. Finally Lyon said, "I will go over to Connecticut; I will talk to these people, and I will have an influence upon them; I will show whether you ought to occupy your seat or not." Griswold said, "I hope you will not go with your wooden sword." He repeated this twice; and after somebody suggested to Lyon that the third time was too much, he spit in Griswold's face. A great hubbub was raised, and Lyon was brought up, I suppose, to his perfect delight, to be tried as to whether he should be expelled from the House of Representatives or not. On the following day, Griswold involved himself in a difficulty without any consideration. He took a good hickory stick and went to Lyon. He did not give him any notice at all. They fought with hickory sticks, and spit-boxes, and tongs, all over the House of Representatives, while the House was in session. Our hardy ancestors at that time did not think a fight of so much importance that they should take it into serious consideration. They said, let them both go. They refused to expel either of them.

When Mr. Randolph struck Mr. Allstine, the matter was brought before the House; but none of these things were considered of a sufficient magnitude to invoke the high function of a Legislature sending its missive to Congress to tell them what to do. Massachusetts is the first to set the example. She has not only administered a reprimand to Mr. Brooks without any evidence; she has not only assumed to pronounce judgment before hearing the evidence, like a judge passing sentence on a criminal before hearing his defense; but she has undertaken indiscriminately to say, that she demands of the Congress of the United States to carry out her behests in regard to what she considers to be an outrage upon the privileges of the Senate.

Can anything be more insulting to the Congress of the United States than the spectacle of a State sending down a message to its "faithful Commons"—a message that they are to pronounce this or that judgment? Are we to submit to this? I did not wish to make the contest; but, in my opinion, these resolutions, in the terms they import, ought not to have been received by the Senate.

Taking all these things into consideration, indicted as Mr. Brooks has been by an *ex parte* accusation, without evidence, without even the finding of a grand jury, what is his position? If his case could go before any impartial tribunal, and I could employ counsel such as I would select, probably I would choose my friend from California, [Mr. Weller,] who lives in a free State, who is an impartial man, an advocate, a gentleman, a man of honor and courage.

If a civil action were brought by Mr. Sumner against Mr. Brooks for assault and battery, I pledge myself that, with all the resources he could bring to his command, he would be able to reduce the verdict to a penny damages. What would be the state of the pleadings? Mr. Brooks struck Mr. Sumner, would be the allegation. It would be admitted that he struck him, and inflicted two flesh wounds. Mr. Sumner would reply, "I am a Senator of the United States; and although the Senate was not in session, I was in that sacred temple, and my character is so sacred under the privileges of the Senate, that I am not to be assailed." What would Mr. BROOKS's counsel rejoin? The rejoinder would be, "Sir, you had profaned and disgraced the seat you occupied, before you were struck."

Then the question would be, what is this privilege so much spoken of—freedom of debate? The court would examine the question, whether what was said was privileged within the rules of the Senate, or whether it was a libel. If it should be pronounced to be a libel, and I were the judge before whom an action were brought—if a man brought before me could show that another insulted his mother, or his father, or his sister, or himself, or his country, I would say to the man who inflicted the blow, "My duty is to fine you; you are not justified by the law; but it is my privilege to say that, whilst I will enforce the law and maintain its dignity, I shall fine you as small a sum as I possibly can within my discretion."

Now let me state the testimony in such an action. It would be that, in the absence of the Senator from South Carolina, Mr. SUMNER rose in his seat, and pronounced what northern papers themselves say is an unparalleled insult, not only to the State of South Carolina, but to her absent Senator. It is one for which I cannot account. I ought to thank one of the Boston editors—I think the editor of the Courier—for a beautiful, perhaps an undeserved compliment, which he has paid to my speech. I ought to thank him here publicly, as one who has independence enough to express his opinions in opposition to the tide prevailing in his part of the country. In my absence, language was used of me which, I venture to say, no one who knew me believed. I might put that question to the Senator's colleague. I know nothing against either of the Senators from Massachusetts personally or privately. I dare say, as neighbors and individuals, I should not have the least right to complain of their judgment outside of the influences which operate upon them publicly and politically. They have no right here to attack any man's private character. I never transgressed the limits of propriety to reach over and look at any man's private character. I do not know that I have anything against Mr. SUMNER's private character; but that has nothing to do with the matter. Here, in his place, *in colore officii*, as a Senator from Massachusetts, he undertook to traduce and calumniate the revolutionary history of South Carolina, and to make remarks in regard to one of her Senators on this floor, a coequal with him, to which no one could have submitted. It happens that that Senator was the constituent of a member of the House of Representatives, who was his friend. That friend, finding that his own blood was insulted by an insult to his absent relative, was goaded on by the necessity of circumstances to take some measure of revenge. As I said yesterday, surely under such circumstances much is to be pardoned to the feelings of a man acting under such motives.

With these remarks I dismiss the resolutions of Massachusetts, hoping that somebody else besides a Senator from South Carolina will say something of them, for I do not wish to identify myself too much with them as a personal matter. I have attempted to keep aloof from that.

The Senator from Massachusetts, in his speech, made one or two allusions which I must incidentally notice to show how erroneous he is whenever he touches any subject. He says I indulged in licentious abuse of the people of Kansas. When he speaks of the people of Kansas I suppose he means those who were sent there by the aid societies. I presume he considers nobody as the people of Kansas except those who have the impression upon them of the people whom he designates to choose and comprehend within the term, "people of Kansas." He has no regard for the people of Kentucky, of Missouri, of Iowa, of Virginia, of South Carolina, who may have gone into that Territory, but he says I have abused its people. I never did abuse them. I did say that the man who came here with the so-called petition of Kansas in his hands without signatures, was attempting to come into the fold of this Federal Government by a fraud. I did not use as strong an expression as my friend from Louisiana, [Mr. BENJAMIN,] my friend from Virginia, [Mr. MASON,] and others. I did not say that the petition was a forgery. I denounced it as a violation of the rules of the Senate to print a paper of that kind, or to give it the dignity of a paper coming from a State. This is all that I said. I did not abuse the people. But what does Mr. SUMNER say of the portion, my portion, if he chooses to call them so, though I do not wish so to characterize them, of the people of Kansas? He speaks of them as "hirelings, picked from the drunken spew and vomit of an uneasy civilization—in the form of men—

> "'Ay, in the catalogue ye go for men ;
> As hounds and grayhounds, mongrels, spaniels, curs,
> Shoughs, water-rugs, and demi-wolves, are called
> All by the name of dogs.'"

Sir, he could not have provoked me in the spirit of controversy to say that. I have no doubt many worthy individuals have gone there under the influence of aid societies; I have not compared them, as the Senator has those who have gone there from Arkansas, Missouri, and Virginia, to the genus of wolves, dogs, and hirelings from the spew of an uneasy civilization. All are dogs, in his estimation, that do not come under the impression of his indorsement. This is language which I could not use of any set of men with whom I was not acquainted. If I were to settle in Kansas to-morrow among those very people, I think it probable that I should be on good terms with them; for I have never had a dispute with a neighbor. I do not think these people would disturb me. But what think you of this denunciation—this rhetorical bombardment from the Senate of the United States, of a class of individuals, as honorable and brave a set of men, I doubt not, as any other, though, perhaps, reckless to some extent. I regret the issue pending in Kansas. I said before, and now repeat, that the very last fate to which this country should be reduced, would be to commit the arbitrament of great questions to the issue of the sword in the hands of youth willing to contend and pleased with the pride of engaging in arms, and having bestowed on them all the fascination which can be imparted by danger and trial.

There is another part of his speech to which I must allude, which evinces—I do not like to use the word, but I cannot help it—the charlatan more than any production of his that I have ever seen. I was surprised when I saw it, and I venture to say there is not a person who hears me read it but will share my surprise. On a former occasion I spoke of serving the common-law process upon Sharpe's rifles. The Senator from Massachusetts undertook to say that I maintained the opinion that it was the duty of the Government to take the rifles out of the hands of those who had them. Who ever understood anything of that kind from my remarks? I used "Sharpe's rifles" as I would use the name of a corporation to serve process upon, but I had no idea of going and taking the rifles out of the hands of individuals. Let me read that part of his speech in which he treats of it:

"Next comes the *Remedy of Folly*, which, indeed, is also a Remedy of Tyranny; but its Folly is so surpassing as to eclipse even its Tyranny. It does not proceed from the President. With this proposition he is not in any way chargeable. It comes from the Senator from South Carolina, who, at the close of a long speech, offered it as his single contribution to the adjustment of this question, and who thus far stands alone in its support. It might, therefore, fitly bear his name; but that which I now give to it is a more suggestive synonim.

"This proposition, nakedly expressed, is that the people of Kansas should be deprived of their arms. That I may not do the least injustice to the Senator, I quote his precise words:

"'The President of the United States is under the highest and most solemn obligations to interpose; and if I were to indicate the manner in which he should interpose in Kansas, I would point out the old common-law process. I would serve a warrant on Sharpe's rifles, and if Sharpe's rifles did not answer the summons, and come into court on a day certain, or if they resisted the sheriff, I would summon the *posse comitatus*, and would have Colonel Sumner's regiment to be a part of that *posse comitatus*.'

"Really, sir, has it come to this? The rifle has ever been the companion of the pioneer, and, under God, his tutelary protector against the red man and the beast of the forest. Never was this efficient weapon more needed in just self-defense than now in Kansas, and at least one article in our national Constitution must be blotted out, before the complete right to it can in any way be impeached. And yet, such is the madness of the hour, that, in defiance of the solemn guarantee, embodied in the Amendments to the Constitution, that 'the right of the people to keep and bear arms shall not be infringed,' the people of Kansas have been arraigned for keeping and bearing them, and the Senator from South Carolina has had the face to say openly, on this floor, that they should be disarmed—of course, that the fanatics of Slavery, his allies and constituents, may meet no impediment. Sir, the Senator is venerable with years; he is reputed also to have worn at home, in the State which he represents, judicial honors; and he is placed here at the head of an important committee occupied particularly with questions of law; but neither his years nor his position, past or present, can give respectability to the demand he has made, or save him from indignant condemnation, when, to compass the wretched purposes of a wretched cause, he thus proposes to trample on one of the plainest provisions of constitutional liberty."

His conclusion is that I intended to send a posse there to take away the rifles from those who owned them. I simply said that there was an organized body whose *pronomen* was Sharpe's rifles, and that I would serve such process as to bring them before the court. This was the plain meaning of my language. I would not take them unless they resisted. If they were disposed to answer in court I would let them answer; I would indict them for resistance to the law, and have a fair and open trial before a jury. This was my meaning. He has gone off with a beautiful conception which may suit the meridian—no, sir, I will not say it, for I believe it suits no meridian where intelligence, and good sense, and honor, and justice prevail.

There is one point upon which I have no doubt the Senator will be more sore under my criticism than in regard to almost anything else, though it does not affect his honor, nor do I know that it affects his popular reputation. He has chosen to go out of his way to make a fling at me, by saying that I never can be right in my statements of law or Constitution, or even in the diversions of scholarship. Now, what did I see the other day? I do not believe that the Senator is guilty of meanness, but his papers are full of the idea—and they have almost made a caricature of it—that when I wanted a Latin quotation I had to hand it over to him, and then bring it back and put it before the public. When Mr. SUMNER and myself sat near each other, I did not hesitate to talk to him about Latin. I believe the only time I ever asked him for a quotation was for one which I intended to insert in my obituary notice of Mr. Webster; and I recollect that on one occasion I made a quotation from Juvenal, and he gave me the Latin, for which I was very much obliged to him. I do not pretend to compete with Mr. SUMNER in the attainments of scholarship; but I must say of him, whatever may be his attainments as a scholar, I very much fear he is like one of those who has a full supply of water in his mill-pond, but does not know how to turn it on a wheel so as to move the machinery; or, rather, it is such an even current that it runs upon a gentle declivity, and has no fall to turn any wheel at all. He has enough of it, and it is always running, but what good it has done I do not know. I said on one occasion that he had not made it subservient to the judgment of a statesman; nor do I believe he has used it as an orator would do on a high theme.

The best part of his late speech is a periphrasis of Demosthenes—almost a servile imitation of the apostrophe of Demosthenes. I never saw such a remarkable resemblance. When I said yesterday that this speech had an identity with his former ones, I should have excepted this passage which adopted the language and the sentiments of Demosthenes. I do not say it is a plagiarism; but it is a remarkable imitation, as far as one man incapable of comprehending the true spirit of Demosthenes could imitate him. Let me give you the two passages. Here is Demosthenes upon the crown speaking to the Athenians upon the responsibility of a man who was contending for his reputation and his administration:

"It cannot be that you have acted wrong in encountering danger for the liberty and safety of all Greece. No! By the generous souls who were exposed at Marathon! By those who stood arrayed at Platæ! By those who encountered the Persian fleet at Salamis—who fought at Artemisium! By all those illustrious sons of Athens whose remains lie deposited in the public monuments!" * * * "What belongs to gallant men they all performed—their success was such as Providence dispensed to each."

Here is Mr. SUMNER, speaking of Massachusetts:

"But it cannot be that she acts wrong for herself and children, when in this cause she thus encounters reproach. No! By the generous souls who were exposed at Lexington—by those who stood arrayed at Bunker Hill—by the many from her bosom who, on all the fields of the first great struggle, lent their vigorous arms to the great cause of all—by the children she has borne, whose names alone are national trophies, is Massachusetts now vowed irrevocably to this work. What belongs to the faithful servant she will do in all things, and Providence shall determine the result."

Here you have Lexington substituted for Marathon, and Bunker Hill for Platæa; and he has named Lexington and Bunker Hill, for they, I believe, are the only battles of the Revolution fought in Massachusetts, and they are glorious fields. This, as I have said, is a remarkable imitation. It is the best part of the speech. It is the only thing, except those polluting personalities to which I have alluded—but I will not use that term, because they hurt nobody—which distinguishes it from his former efforts.

Mr. President, I have convicted the Senator of making a speech which was not in response to anything I said. I have convicted him of such historical errors as no man can mistake. I have convicted him of making allegations against me of being ignorant of law and of Constitutions, and yet when he undertook to quote and expound the constitution of South Carolina, I have shown that he either never read that constitution, or he could not understand it, or, if he did understand it, he willfully misrepresented it. He has been guilty of the *suppressio veri* and the *suggestio falsi*. He cannot escape from these propositions.

I have a copy of the Senator's speech before me, and now I am going to turn his gun upon him. I ask the Senate to see if I do not turn it upon him to such an extent as to allow me to apply the apposite quotation of which I have often made use:

> "Mutato nomine, de te
> Fabula narratur."

Here is what he says of me:

> "With regret I come again upon the Senator from South Carolina, [Mr. Butler,] who, omnipresent in this debate"

Why, sir, I have counted the Congressional Globe, and my remarks make but twelve pages, while his are thirty-two. I have not gone into the subject at as great length as my friends from Alabama, [Mr. Clay,] Georgia, [Mr. Toombs,] and others. My speeches all put together on this subject are but twelve pages, and his are thirty-two; while those of his coadjutors amount, I suppose, to a hundred more. Yet he said I was omnipresent in this debate! I will not say that he is omnipresent in this debate, but he is omnipresent everywhere *out* of the debate. He says that I "overflowed with rage at the simple suggestion that Kansas had applied for admission as a State, and, with incoherent phrases, discharged the loose expectoration of his speech, now upon her representatives, and then upon her people." I said it was a fraud, and the Senate said so. Why did he single me out? Again, alluding to me, he said:

> "There was no extravagance of the ancient parliamentary debate which he did not repeat; nor was there any possible deviation from truth which he did not make, with so much of passion, I am glad to add, as to save him from the suspicion of intentional aberration."

I do not know that I have ever been an imitator in my life. Those who know me best say that I am rather *sui generis*. I never borrow from Demosthenes, and palm it off as my own. As for my deviation from the truth, let me ask, did he tell the truth when he quoted the constitution of South Carolina, and there was no such clause in it as he stated? Did he tell the truth when he undertook to say, that her imbecility was shameful during the Revolution? I have shown that she absolutely sent bread to Massachusetts. Did he tell the truth when he meant to impute to me what he has charged here? I retort upon him everything that follows.

I retort on him the very language which he applies to me. He accused me of such a proclivity to error that I could not conform to the line of truth, or was continually deviating from it. I have convicted him before the Senate, by the evidence which I have adduced, of calumniating the history and character of South Carolina, and of misrepresenting her constitution. He has done this, not in response to anything I had said, or anything which was legitimately connected with the debate. He has undertaken to charge me with ignorance of the law and the Constitution, which is perfectly independent of his arbitrary *dictum*—the *dictum*, allow me to say, of a man who has never conducted a great law case in this country. I believe no one would buy an estate worth $10,000 upon his opinion of the title. I would not engage him to conduct a cause, not that he is not a clear man, but I would not trust him as a lawyer. And yet he undertakes to be my judge. What right has he to pronounce judgment on me as a lawyer? I am reduced to a pretty predicament at this time of life, if I am to be subjected to such a judgment! It is a judgment about which I care little; and I do not suppose any man would give fifty dollars for it even in Massachusetts.

> "He cannot ope his mouth but out there flies a blunder."

I sincerely hope that what he has said is a blunder. I do not know but that he may have thought he would escape scrutiny and exposure. I hope that, when he opened his mouth and said what he did in reference to these matters, it was a blunder. He said of me, "the Senator touches nothing which he does not disfigure." I can say of him he has touched nothing which he has not misrepresented, except it be in his general declamation, and there is no detecting a man in that; it is a matter of taste. I appreciate highly the compliment I received this morning in the Boston Courier as to the merit of my speech. The Senator says of me, that "the Senator touches nothing which he does not disfigure—with error sometimes of principle, sometimes of fact." I apply this to him with this exception: I say error nearly always of principle, sometimes of fact. I leave the Senate to decide between us in that respect. Again he said of me:

> "He shows an incapacity of accuracy, whether in stating the Constitution or in stating the law—whether in the details of statistics or the diversions of scholarship."

I shall not compete with him in scholarship, for I should be vulnerable there; but "men who live in glass houses should never throw stones." Of all the things which that Senator ventured to do, I think he exposed his house most when he made that assertion, with the detection which I have fixed upon him of error, injustice, and malignity. It is nailed upon him, and he cannot get rid of it. I care not how far fanaticism may undertake to influence the judgment of public opinion, it cannot alter the truth. Truth is sometimes slow in making its impression on the public mind, but, when made, it is evidence which produces a belief that cannot be resisted. That belief will grow out of my statements, my remarks, and my references, and is just as certain as the truth of the evidence, and he cannot escape from it.

Mr. President, I have detained the Senate much longer than I wished. When I gave notice that I should speak to the resolutions of Massachusetts, it was with perfect confidence that the Senator would be in his seat. Finding that these resolutions were not here, on Monday last I gave notice that I should speak on Thursday, still confident that he would be here? Yesterday, having heard that perhaps he would not be present, I inquired in as delicate a manner as I could when he would be here? Although our relations are not friendly, I did not wish to assume a position which would be even apparently inconsistent with fair chivalry and bearing. I inquired whether he would be in the Senate within a fortnight, and, if so, I said I would postpone my remarks. Finding that it was his purpose to go, in a few days, to Massachusetts, and that he would not be likely to return for three or four weeks, I could not allow the opportunity to pass. I have stated these facts to show that I do not stand here taking advantage of his absence. I was willing to wait any reasonable time, but I could not allow error to prevail longer in relation to my State, my friend, or myself. This is my position.

Sir, if there is any one individual who more than another regrets the occasion on which I have spoken, it is myself. I have no temper for strife. I am passing through the last chapter of my public life, and I have no wish to identify my name with anything like a personal controversy. I have never sought it. When the question comes to be examined and solved, Who was the aggressor? it will be found that it was not I on any occasion. I admit that I have three peculiarities of manner—impatience, excitability, and perhaps absent-mindedness. They are peculiarities which have followed me from the cradle. But, sir, I hope I have never known the time when reason and repentance would not suppress even a temporary injustice. If injustice is done to me, or a wrong or insult offered, I never stop to parley in words. I ask justice, and if it is not given, I never would be in the wrong if I could help myself; but when I am in the right I do not think any man can blame me for vindicating my principles.

Now, sir, I appeal to the good sense of this country. I appeal to the lessons which its grave history inculcates. I appeal to the position which it occupies in relation to the history of the world, and to the high responsibilities which now rest on this Confederacy, not to allow it to be dissolved in blood. If we are to separate, let us have common sense enough to do it in a way becoming intelligent men, who have learned their lessons from the highest sources of intelligence and wisdom. If we are to live together, let it not be upon the terms prescribed or intimated by the tone and temper of the licentious and aggressive language of the speech delivered by the Senator from Massachusetts. It is impossible for self-respect to allow me to sit here and listen quietly to such a speech. If there were separate confederacies to-morrow, he dare not utter it without subjecting himself to a peril which he will not encounter now. He would then put his section in a position to make war, and he would be responsible to a higher tribunal than that of those who have erected themselves into it under an influence which I think must perish; and I hope the day is fast coming when the fires of that limited sectionalism will burn out, or will be reduced to the ashes of disappointment and disgrace.

MONDAY, *June* 16, 1856.

Mr. BUTLER. I desire to present a communication from Dr. Boyle, who feels that the certificate given the other day by Dr. Lindsley, in relation to the condition of Mr. Sumner, has done him injustice; and as it is a part of the *res gestæ* connected with the subject under discussion at our last meeting, I ask that it may be read.

The Secretary read as follows:

WASHINGTON CITY, *June* 14, 1856.

DEAR SIR: The note read in the Senate Chamber by the Hon. Mr. Wilson, of Massachusetts, from Dr. Lindsley, renders it necessary in justice to myself that I should make the following statement:

I was in attendance upon the Hon. Charles Sumner from the 22d to the 28th of May, inclusive. On the 27th of May I gave the principal part of my evidence before the House committee of investigation, which has been published, and on the 28th I received the following note from Mr. George Sumner:

SIXTH STREET, *Wednesday, p. m.*

DEAR SIR: Owing to the very critical situation of my brother, Dr. Perry has consented to remain in Washington to attend him.

In justice to you and to Dr. Perry, I must state that he does this at the request of myself and of many of my brother's friends.

Be so good as to send, Dr. Boyle, me your bill, and to accept my thanks for the attention shown to my brother.

I am, dear sir, truly yours, GEORGE SUMNER.

On the morning of the 30th of May, in conversation with Dr. Lindsley, he informed me that he had been called to see Mr. Sumner. I inquired of his condition, and Dr. Lindsley replied, "Not much the matter." I then asked how the wounds looked, and the doctor replied, "I did not examine them." On the same day I called to make a friendly visit to Dr. Perry, who had done me full justice in his published testimony, and was informed by the clerk at Willard's Hotel that Dr. Perry had left the city at six o'clock that morning, notwithstanding the "very critical" condition of Senator Sumner, as represented by his brother, Mr. George Sumner.

Since the note of Dr. Lindsley was read in the Senate by the Hon. Mr. Wilson, I have called upon Dr. Miller, who was consulting physician with Dr. Lindsley, and he has kindly furnished the following reply to interrogatories which I propounded to him:

WASHINGTON CITY, *June* 14, 1856.

DEAR DOCTOR: In reply to your inquiry as to the condition of the Hon. Charles Sumner at the time I visited him, I with pleasure furnish you with the following statement:

On the 30th ultimo I visited Mr. Sumner at his rooms on Sixth street, Dr. Harvey Lindsley (who was called the previous night) being in attendance. We examined the case together. When we entered the room, Mr. Sumner was in bed; he got up, and sat in a chair, that we might dress his wounds. Mr. Sumner was as cheerful as usual, a little pale, and somewhat reduced in flesh; attributable, no doubt, to loss of blood and confinement. He said he had passed a good night. He was free from fever; pulse seventy-four; complained of a little soreness of the scalp.

The wound on the left side of the head was healed; that on the right side had suppurated, and the pus being confined had burrowed under the scalp for about half an inch each way from the lips of the wound. We readily broke up the adhesion of the lips of the wound, and gave vent to the pus. He was much relieved by this. The absorbent vessels and a few of the glands of the right side of the neck were a little inflamed, and tender to the touch. We did not deem anything necessary except a mild poultice, quiet for a few days, and better diet.

Neither of us deemed Mr. Sumner in any danger.

Dr. Lindsley and myself visited Mr. Sumner, together, the next morning, at ten o'clock. He was doing so well that a consulting surgeon was considered unnecessary. I was therefore discontinued by Mr. George Sumner, with the understanding, that if his brother should become more unwell I should be again called.

Hearing nothing more of Mr. S., I presume his case progressed favorably.

Very respectfully, your obedient servant,

THOMAS MILLER.

Dr. CORNELIUS BOYLE, *Washington, District of Columbia.*

I address this communication to you, with a view to justice to all concerned; and for the further purpose of having myself appear right on the record; and authorize you to use it at your discretion.

I have the honor to be, &c.,

CORNELIUS BOYLE.

Hon. A. P. BUTLER.

APPENDIX.

Remarks of Mr. BUTLER *in the Senate, March* 5, 1856, *on affairs in the Territory of Kansas, and in vindication of General Atchison, of Missouri, to which Mr.* SUMNER, *in his affidavit before the Investigating Committee, said his speech of* 19*th and* 20*th May was a reply.*

The Senate resumed the consideration of Mr. WELLER's motion to print ten thousand extra copies of the President's message of February 18, with the accompanying documents, relative to affairs in the Territory of Kansas.

Mr. HUNTER. My friend from South Carolina, who has the floor on this question, is not very well to-day, and therefore I suggest that it should be postponed until to-morrow.

Several SENATORS. Say Monday. There is a special order for to-morrow.

Mr. WELLER. I desire to give notice that on Monday I shall ask the Senate to take up the bill to appropriate $3,000,000 for the purchase of arms for fortifications.

Mr. BUTLER said: Mr. President, I prefer to go on now. When I obtained the floor the other day upon this question, it was with a view to make a very few remarks in order to relieve the Senate from any impression which might be made on it by the statements made here on the responsibility of Senators, or by newspaper communications, in relation to the part which my friend, General Atchison, has acted in Kansas affairs. I intended no more; and I shall endeavor to discharge that duty before I conclude the remarks which I propose now to submit.

The debate on this subject, Mr. President, has brought many things within its scope, and has, in my opinion, been made the occasion of fearful indications for the future. What the developments of the future may disclose I know not; but this much I will say, before I approach the main subject on which I intend to deliver my views—that we are reduced, by the issue which has been made in Kansas, to the alternative either of suffering the President, under the message which he has sent to us and the proclamation which he has issued, to exercise his high office to preserve the peace which is threatened to be disturbed in Kansas, or subject ourselves to the usurpation of squatter sovereignty and the discretion of an uncalculating fanaticism; raising a whirlwind on which it may not be able to ride. This is the issue which is presented to us. For if the President does not interpose his authority to preserve peace, I have no reason to conclude but that the conflict between the two parties in Kansas may result in the shedding of blood; and, sir, my word for it, one drop of blood shed in civil strife in this country, in which parties have been distinctly arrayed, so far as they can be arrayed by their advocates, will have more effect on civilization and on society than all the blood shed in all the battles of antiquity, or in the struggle at Borodino and the battles which followed it. Sir, I am entirely persuaded that, if we are to approach what has been threatened—a rupture of this Union—or if we are to preserve the Union, it is the duty of every man, as far as he can, to throw his influence into the public opinion which will justify the course of the President, so as to be free from the consequences which may otherwise grow out of this fearful issue. Yes, sir; if the South is forced to take her destiny in her *separate* keeping, let us do all we can to justify our conduct before the tribunal of history; let us do all we can in the way of explanation to dispel delusion and rebuke the mad spirit which has infused itself into the public mind in a portion of this Confederacy. Danger may speak with a loud trumpet to the ear of Reason and Justice.

It may be said that I have passed through the

ordeal of experience, and perhaps of time, and that they have had their influence on my temper; but, sir, I look on anything like a rupture in civil government, and especially such a one as would throw us into the horrors of anarchy, with not the same view as others who may be more intrepid, and who may think they can come out of it without hazard to themselves. There is nothing so mischievous to society as any movement affecting its stability, uncontrolled by responsibility and unregulated by intelligence. Bigotry, fanaticism, and prejudice, are fatal counselors; and under the Sharpe's rifle influence they have exercised their influence on the issues of the day.

Now, before I approach the main point, I must dispose of some of the remarks made by the Senator from New Hampshire, [Mr. Hale.] I reply to his remarks because he has been in this Chamber for a longer period than the Senator from Massachusetts, [Mr. Wilson,] and has had associations here which I think ought at least to have tempered some of his expressions. I do not intend to use the language of asperity in this debate, if I can avoid it; but allow me to say to the Senator from New Hampshire that I think, when he used some expressions, not only in relation to the President of the United States, the Chief Magistrate of this Confederacy, but in relation to the Supreme Court, and other departments of this Government; and when he allowed himself to read from a newspaper, under the signature of an anonymous writer, statements in reference to a distinguished gentleman with whom he had been associated here—I will do him the justice to say that I hardly think he consulted the dictates of his own nature; for I believe that generally he has rather shown a temper that would lift him above such things, except when he acts as the committed archer pulling the arrow under the behests of his urging huntsmen. The Senator from New Hampshire is a committed advocate to a sectional, fanatical organization; and perhaps he is not at liberty to deny the authority under which he has entered the Senate.

Sir, what did I hear him say? That the Supreme Court of the United States was the citadel of slavery. He did not know, when he made that remark, how far it extended, and what it might not embrace. Is he not associated with a class of politicians in this country who have said that the Constitution of the United States—the fundamental law of their country—was the citadel of slavery? Yes, sir, I have had pamphlets within the last week laid on my desk, maintaining that the Constitution of the United States itself is the citadel of slavery; and that, unless it is broken down, and the institution of slavery thereby reached in all the States, it is a Constitution which ought to have no validity and obligation. I think I have seen the same statements in a paper called the Radical Abolitionist. When the Senator speaks of the Supreme Court as the citadel of the institution of slavery, he might better have designated them as opposed to those who have called the Constitution of their country the citadel of slavery. Sir, I would prefer regarding the Judges of the Supreme Court, as far as I know anything of their decisions, as the sentinels and defenders of the Constitution—a Constitution recognizing the equality of the States, and at least imposing on them such obligations as that they are not permitted to transfer their judgments into another jurisdiction, prescribed, I suppose, by what is technically called the higher law—a jurisdiction of discretion and *prejudice*.

They have not gone down or up—as gentlemen may choose to consider it—to the higher law. As far as I know the court—and I have had intercourse with its venerated and venerable Chief Justice, from my official position as chairman of the Committee on the Judiciary—I do not believe I have ever known a body of men more honestly disposed to do their duty under the obligations of the power which gave them the right to discharge judicial functions. I believe, when our first parents were driven out of Paradise, it was under the suggestions of the higher law. The Devil went in and suggested to Eve that there was a higher law; and, disregarding the law under which she was placed in Paradise, she and her posterity have suffered the penalties of disobedience: transgression is sin. I wish to recognize no tribunal and no set of opinions which will attempt to rule the country except by some prescribed law and a constitution laid down for them by those who give them their official existence. I believe that the Supreme Court has committed errors, though not intentionally. I believe their decision in the case of Prigg and Pennsylvania has led to mischievous consequences not intended by the court. When the court undertook to say that the States themselves might be absolved from the duty imposed on them by the Federal compact of returning fugitives from labor, I think they made a decision tending to absolve the States from the honor of compacts. They did not say it in so many words, nor do I think their decision is of that import, but the non-slaveholding States have so construed it. Instead of that decision being a judgment from the citadel of slavery, it has redounded entirely in its consequences to the non-slaveholding States of this Union; or rather to let their accommodating morality take refuge in it—to excuse them for disregarding the obligations imposed upon them as coöperative agencies, &c.

I would rather regard that high tribunal as one which could look abroad upon the vast and beautiful horizon of truth and justice. I should not wish to see them governed by that popular agitation which is threatening to undermine the institutions of the country, and to destroy, not only the present form of our Union, but to wash away the very landmarks of our forefathers. In such a case I would be glad to see the Supreme Court, like the proud promontory of the deep,

> "Let the fretful ocean surge upon its base,
> Let storms assail its summit."

I wish it to stand firm at least as the type of the duration of the institutions of this country, and as an emblem of eternal justice. I at least wish that, amidst the agitation of the time, it shall maintain its identity. Let not the Senator from New Hampshire suppose that he can assail or touch that promontory by any shaft that he may aim at it. The hand that shoots the arrow may belong to one more willing to wound than it can be able to hurt. It has certainly been discharged by an archer occupying too great a distance from his object to do harm. Let me hope there is more of the hand than the heart that has been exhibited in the shot. The weapon has fallen harmless.

After the Senator from New Hampshire had disposed of the Supreme Court under this denunciatory epithet, he approached the President. I am not one of those who undertake to defend the President on all occasions; but, sir, he is the Chief Magistrate of this Confederacy, and whilst I am in the Confederacy, I will see at least that a neighbor's hand, moved, perhaps, by resentful rivalry, shall not wound the Chief Magistracy of the whole country. The Senator from New Hampshire took exception to the course which the President has taken, by saying that he had committed himself to a different judgment and a different course of conduct by receiving Dorr when he was a refugee from justice from Rhode Island, and then sustained him by resolutions which were passed while he was chairman, I think, of some Democratic association. Mr. Pierce is arrayed against President Pierce. Does the Senator suppose that the Chief Magistrate of this Confederacy, after he has attained the high position which he now occupies, is to administer his trust as a common trustee for all the people of the United States, according to any opinions which he may have entertained on any former occasion, when he was chairman of a Democratic society? Why, sir, you might as well say that one ascending a mountain should stop half way and consult the vision which he then had, rather than the certainty of the more extended vision which he would have after attaining the summit, where the horizon would be more distinct, and where he would have a large and more extended view. The Chief Magistrate of the United States is the trustee of the whole Union. He is not the organ of any portion of New Hampshire; nor is he subject to any latitude. With the vigilance and even solicitude of a guardian, he must protect the interests and rights of all who are committed to his care. He is not now a party in the controversies of a former day, but a *judge* of all the parties before him.

Sir, the last thing to which I can ever consent is, that any man who goes abroad shall wound the home of his residence. I am not specially interested in the history of New Hampshire, but I say that this is not the place to expose her infirmities; nor is this the place to take occasion, because a gentleman gets a seat on this floor, to bring under proscription the conduct of one of his fellow-citizens, who is now the Chief Magistrate of the Confederacy. I shall not justify Mr. Pierce for receiving Dorr at the time, but I will say in relation to him, that he was then comparatively a young man, and that having cultivated the lessons of liberty which his ancestor had taught him, much, in the language of Mr. Burke, is to be pardoned to the spirit of liberty. Another thing is to be said, that the judgment in relation to Dorr had not then been formed. It was then passing through the ordeal of trial, and I know that that deluded young man had *many distinguished* sympathizers. Mr. Pierce gave Dorr shelter: this is the head and front of his offending.

Sir, I have always regarded it as one of the most odious acts of the British Government, when Napoleon Bonaparte went on board the Bellerophon, claiming the rights of hospitality, that they changed his condition into that of a prisoner of war. His reputation and position in the world entitled him to the rights and honors awarded to Themistocles. If Dorr, instead of going to New Hampshire, had gone to South Carolina, perhaps, at that time, I myself, to this deluded young man, would have been the last to have seen him sacrificed to his delusions; and I believe much may be pardoned to the spirit of liberty, guided by the ardor of youth.

I come now to another personage in this affair, a distinguished friend of mine, General Atchison, who has also received the notice both of the Senator from New Hampshire and the Senator from Massachusetts. I have known General Atchison long and well. They have attributed to him a ferocity and vulgar indifference and recklessness in relation to the affairs in Kansas, which is refuted by every confidential letter which he has written to me, and which is not in conformity to the truth. I will not say that General Atchison is the enemy of any one. I will not say that he is the enemy of the emigrants in Kansas who have been sent there by the aid societies; but I say that I know of no man, within the range of my acquaintance, who could be invested more effectually with the attributes of the conqueror of that class of people. And how do you suppose he would exercise that high power? Let those who now asperse him settle around him as neighbors, and if their houses were burned down and assistance were required, he would be the first man to render them assistance, and he would conquer them by his kindness, by his justice, by his good sense, and by his generosity. There never was a better illustration of his character than the conduct he displayed in the expected tragedy at Lawrence. I know the fact, and I state it on my authority, as a truth not to be disputed, (because I have his letters in my drawer,) that, when that controversy arose, General Atchison was absolutely called upon to attend General Richardson's command, and he went with a positive pledge on the part of those with whom he was associated that he should rather be the Mentor than the leader; and he has written to me that, but for his mediatorial offices, the houses of the people of Lawrence would have been burnt and the streets drenched in blood. An appeal was made to him under circumstances which his magnanimous nature could not resist. He had the courage to do a duty which in its performance might even offend his comrades and associates—a courage much higher than that of meeting an open enmy in the field. He effectually exerted his influence, under the appeal made to him, to save from fire and sword the village of Lawrence, the stronghold of the aid society emigrants. But for the gentle advice, and, perhaps, controlling influence of Atchison, the houses of the settlement would have been burnt and its highways drenched with blood.

When these people were suppliants, how differently they felt *then* from what their calumnies have evinced since! The generous person who saved them is to be converted into their ferocious persecutor; Atchison is to be immolated on the altar of fanatical vengeance; and that, too, through the medium of anonymous writers in newspapers, under the sanction of speeches made in this Chamber. Well, sir, is this to be his requital? Are aspersion and misrepresentation to pervert the truth of history? Gentlemen have attributed to him a ferocity of unexampled character—an attribute that cannot assimilate to his nature. Throughout the whole contest he has always said that he was in favor of—to use his own expression—"the competition of preëmption settlers." He believed that if that competition had been left to itself, and if there had been no hostile demonstration on the part of the northern societies, Kansas would have been settled by neighbors knowing each other, and who would have less objection because they did know each other; and that in the end, perhaps, there might be a few negroes, probably an "old mammy," or some favorite servants for household purposes, or some field-laborers, contented in and bettered by their condition. He supposed that there might have been a population of that sort, and such as the masters would not like to desert, and such as they would not commit to the Abolitionists. It would have been, in technical phrase, perhaps, a population with some *masters*, but with some servants, and scarcely any slaves. Those *called* masters would have been more like guardians, and those *called* slaves would have been better off for their protection. In this relation they become objectionable to the Abolitionists, who are willing to set them free, that they may become vagabonds, and be destroyed under the *philanthropy* of proscription and rivalry.

Under the current of this settlement, Kansas would likely have become a *quasi* community, with many white men and few negroes—with labor capable of being usefully and profitably employed—a community of farmers, using labor as they thought proper. In this way, by accretion, Kansas might have become a State.

Sir, I am not going to put on an equality, or anything like an equality, the movements and conduct of those who have gone to Kansas with Sharpe's rifles in their hands, and the Missouri "border ruffians," as they have been termed. They are not in *pari delictu*. The difference between the population of a portion of the two sections has never been so well illustrated, as in that very demonstration. The western people, of daring gallantry, of open hospitality, trust to the occasion, and when they draw the sword, it is rather under the influence of heat and passion than malice—but with a fertility of expedients that is equal to craft; and if they commit homicide under such circumstances, it is reduced at least to the grade of manslaughter. When, however, I see an organization at a distance of a thousand miles from the Territory, sending out men who go, not with fowling-pieces or the ordinary rifles, or common weapons of defense which they might use, but all going with one uniform gun—Sharpe's rifle—let me not be told that they were going there for merely the innocent purpose of settling the Territory themselves. It is evident they were going there to drive off others, if it became a contest, which the Missouri "border ruffians," as they are called, never anticipated. The crime of those who are designated by that name, if homicide should be committed, would be much nearer the character of manslaughter, whilst the blood shed by their opponents would much nearer approach a mercenary homicide.

Now, sir, I suppose this controversy may be regarded as a great ejectment case—perhaps the greatest that was ever tried—to try the title of the two different sections to the public domain, the common domain belonging to the whole Union. I suppose the emigrant aid societies' settlers may be regarded as one party, and what they choose to call the "border ruffians" the other party—one the John Doe, the other the Richard Roe, in this lawsuit. I am perfectly willing that the suit shall be tried by justice and truth, and not under the heated declamation of gentlemen who intend to inflame the public mind of their own section, without regard to the dictates of the truth of history. Now, what are the facts in relation to this case? As I have them, from authentic sources, they are not such as can give John Doe much credit.

In my opinion, Governor Reeder will have to answer, more than any other human being for the blood which will be shed—if any shall be shed—for he occupied an important position to control events. I suppose none will doubt now, that when the Missouri line was adopted, it was done by a mere legislative power, and therefore could be wiped out by the same competent authority. Missouri was admitted against the consent of the North, as a body; but the South, in a sprit of compromise, agreed to that line. How has she been treated? Since I have been a member of the Senate, no opportunity has been offered when some northern man has not, on the occasion of territory being acquired south of that line, made a motion to exclude the slaveholder. There has not been a single occasion, when the opportunity has been presented, when they have not violated the implied pledge contained in the obligations of that line. I ring it in their ears. If I had no other cause to wipe out the line, I could find it in the fact that they have not regarded it in good faith, but have violated their public honor and plighted faith, as expressed on the statute-book. When Oregon was organized into a Territory, this feeling so far prevailed that it would not allow southern men to vote for it, upon the ground that inasmuch as the Territory lay north of 36° 30′, it might be organized under the intendment of the Missouri compromise.

Sir, you will remember the occurrences of the war with Mexico. Day after day many of us went to the War Department expecting to hear, what many did hear, the dreadful results of battle to friends and relatives. I suppose we may consider the war with Mexico as having been fought to a certain extent to acquire the territory which followed its termination through the medium of negotiation. At that time, when the South contributed as many men, and as much money, for the prosecution of the war as the North—the South sending forth many more men—did I not hear a Senator from New York [Mr. Dix] rise in his place and say that he intended to maintain the Wilmot proviso on the ground mainly that it would create a cordon of free States around the slaveholding States, and with the assertion of the superior civilization of the free States? Was that no violation of the Missouri compromise? I put it now fairly to the men who speak in this heated language, if territory were to be acquired to-morrow would they not propose the same Wilmot proviso? Do they think that no violation of the Missouri compromise? They claim positively all that was conceded to them, and deny the benefit of its provisions to the South that made the concession. Now, I am willing to propose a game of *fair play. Let the opinion of the people, as it may be formed in the process of territorial existence,* determine the character of the State, and, whether the State presenting herself for admission shall admit or exclude slavery, be no bar to her admission.

Sir, that compromise, as it has been called, has never been observed. There never has been an opportunity offered when those who cry out about its abrogation have not been willing to violate its true intendment. I say its true intendment, because south of that line it was always understood that the people should have a right to hold slaves or not, according to their own option. In regard to the Territory of Kansas, I think it might well have been left a debatable ground—neither to call in a slaveholding nor a non-slaveholding State. It was an occasion when we might have cemented, in some measure, the bonds of the ancient brotherhood; but no, sir, we find that gentlemen come in with the Bible in one hand to preach against slavery, and the torch in the other. That is the attitude in which they present themselves in the temple of our common deliberations—the torch in one hand and the Bible in the other—the pulpit and Sharpe's rifle. Under the banner of theology, incendiaries march, with torches in their hands, proclaiming God's will, but doing their own.

I have stated one reason why the Missouri line should have been disregarded by the southern people. Now, I go further; and I say, in regard to the immediate issue on which the President has made the proclamation, he is justified. How was it brought about? I said before, that Governor Reeder was responsible for it. I say so now. By what authority did Reeder go to Kansas? He went there under the authority of a law regularly constituting a territorial government. He went there to be its Governor, and to carry out the provisions of that law, just as much as if the Missouri line had not been repealed. Reeder received his commission as a tenant under a landlord; and I have always said that it was one of the wisest provisions of the common law that no tenant should be allowed to dispute his landlord's title. He was placed there as a sentinel; but what was his course? He first assembled the Legislature at Pawnee City. They were not long there before they adjourned to the Shawnee Mission. He refused to sanction the adjournment; and the very first bill brought to him afterwards was one chartering the Kickapoo Ferry Company, I think. He refused to sanction the bill, and refused to maintain the authority which had been conferred on him, and without which he would have been a criminal intruder. As he was there under the color of law, he was in a position to do much evil or to do much good. He was the trusted officer on the quarter-deck in a storm, and by his judgment might save the vessel. He refused to continue with his trust, and has given rise to a fearful trial.

Well, sir, when Reeder would not do his duty and carry out the provisions of the law, what was the President to do? Remove him, of course. When he was removed, what was the next step? Those who call themselves free-State settlers, emigrants sent out by the aid societies, assembled at Big Springs, and nominated as their Governor (perhaps I may be mistaken, as their Delegate to Congress) this man, who was in open rebellion to his own authority—a man who had disputed the title under which he entered the Territory. They not only did that, but they instituted proceedings for establishing a government to invest themselves, under the name of squatter sovereignty, with, I suppose, the right of usurpers. They had a second meeting at Topeka, and adopted a constitution in convention, and under that constitution elections have been held, and a Governor, judges, and members of the Legislature have been elected. That Legislature was to assemble yesterday. God knows what may be the tragedy growing out of the 4th of March, 1856. Sir, the news of what occurred in Kansas on the 4th of March, 1856, may bring us the intelligence which will be the knell of the institutions—I will not say of the Union—of this country; for I hope there is wisdom enough left to preserve republican institutions in durable form, should the present Union be no more.

What was the President to do under these circumstances? Who brought about this catastrophe? What is the attitude of these men? They have taken the laws into their own hands, and when they did so they implored David R. Atchison for mercy, and he saved them. Here I will do him the justice to say that he has not heretofore passed the Rubicon, with the spirit of an ambitious ruler; but if hereafter he ever passes that Rubicon, all his benevolence—and it is very large—will not enable him to overlook the taunts and insults which have been heaped upon him. If David R. Atchison shall ever pass the line again, and say as Cæsar did, "I have passed the Rubicon, and now I draw the sword," I should dread the contest, for the very reason that he who goes into matters of this kind with reluctance is most to be feared. Remember, sir, that Hector, at the siege of Troy, was the last to espouse the cause of one who had done dishonor to Priam's house, and he was the last to desert it. He perished for the coward who got him into the difficulty. The proud patriot was averse to the quarrel of effeminate Paris—but once in, he was the last to yield up the honor of the house of Priam.

Sir, this subject enlarges itself very much in the estimation of gentlemen who have spoken upon it. I shall use no epithets towards the Senator from New Hampshire. I have thus far attempted to avoid them. I have characterized his speech, but I have used no epithets. The Senator from New Hampshire undertakes to say that, throughout the whole of the controversy in relation to the public domain of the United States, the South have been the aggressors. "Southern aggression" was the term on his lips—southern aggression—southern insolence and dough-face treason on the part of his own countrymen! Both statements are untrue. I do not impute to him personal untruth. I make the remark in a historical and parliamentary debate, and I am speaking of transactions. Let the Senator answer me one question. When Virginia ceded the North-western Territory, out of which five free States have been created, was it southern aggression? When she parted with that domain, and gave it over to the non-slaveholding population of the

North, was it southern aggression? She parted with her domain and bestowed it as a bounty upon those who have enjoyed it. I will not say who is the Cordelia or the Regan in the sisterhood, but I can say who has been the Lear. It was the Old Dominion. Little did Virginia think, when she planted those States by her own hand, that they would give rise to a controversy in which an opinion would be inculcated by which she should be reproached for her decrepitude. She can well say:

"How sharper than a serpent's tooth it is
To have a thankless child."

Hostile allies have availed themselves of the power thus acquired, and, like a cockatrice, are willing to sting the bosom that gave them life. The nurses, however, are much worse than the children, some of whom I have reason to know are true-hearted, and are willing to maintain good faith, but for the intermeddling of fanatical influence that regards no restraint of law and compact.

Do you call that southern aggression? The South then parted with her power, and now it is regarded as southern aggression when she resents the insults of those who have availed themselves of it. At least, this much may be fairly said—the fanatical portion of the North are willing to use all the advantage thus given to assail the southern section.

Now, look at the acquisition of the Territory of Louisiana. There the South agreed to exclude herself from all that portion of it north of 36° 30′, and one free State (Iowa) has been formed out of that portion of the Territory. The Senator from New Hampshire quoted the opinions of many Senators to the effect that Kansas is not to be a slave State. Sir, I do not know that it will be a slaveholding State. I say, however, that, when the southern portion of the United States parted with that dominion which we rightfully possessed, and allowed ourselves to be excluded from the Louisiana territory, we played the part of a generous parent who has only met with the scorn and contempt which a want of wisdom justly deserves. It was putting a rod in the hands of others, without knowing who they were, under the hope that it would be used as a weapon of common defense, but which has been used against the donor as a means of controlling his authority.

When we obtained California, by whose treasure and whose arms was it acquired? Sir, I will not imitate the example of the Senator from New Hampshire. I will not in my place allow myself to say that it was not acquired by northern as well as by southern arms, and by northern as well as by southern treasure. A protest was made that that acquisition was to redound to the South. Let me ask where the $300,000,000 which it is said have been collected from California have been poured out like the dew of heaven, which arises in one place and descends on another. I will not say, in this connection, that I might emblazon the fame and gallantry of southern heroes and generals. I might be as proud of the gallantry of my own section, as antiquity was of the heroes of Greece and of Rome, and the heroes of Marathon. I will not refuse a common grave to the gallant Ransom, and the equally gallant Dickerson, who fell in the same battle. I would not deny to them the mingled wreath of the laurel and the cypress. Sir, in the face of the truth of history, when we had shed our blood in a common contest, and when we acquired a territory by common treasure, what is the fact? Has it not been appropriated to the non-slaveholding portion of this Confederacy, under a non-slaveholding constitution? That is southern aggression!

Did the honorable Senator from New Hampshire think that he could satisfy any one who heard him on these points? No, sir; but it looks as if he intended to feed the flames which are burning, but which he, in his benevolence, ought to extinguish. The *gravamen* of his argument, however, is, that Texas was annexed with a view to pander to southern insolence and pride. Now, I intend, in that connection, to propound some questions which those who agree with him will find it very difficult to swallow. They have been so much used to eating dainty things at the North, that their stomachs are not quite strong enough for the wholesome food which I might offer them, and which their sentimental stomachs might reject. I will put my questions, however, to the Senator from New Hampshire, for I am better acquainted with him, and I suppose he is the organ, and stands at the head, of those who agree with him in opinion. Would he consent that Texas should have become a British province, with the certainty that England would place that province in the same condition as its West India islands, and with the certainty that her policy would be to make war on the institutions of Louisiana and other southern States? Would he take the part of England in such a controversy, sooner than of those who have given us our liberties and our rights? Would he consent that Great Britain should take possession of Texas, and make war, like a roaring lion, seeking whom it may devour among its neighbors? Would he consent to that, on an acknowledged condition only that it should not have slaves, and should be pledged to make war on the institutions of the southern States? Would he agree to make war on his southern confederates on such conditions and through such agencies?

The next question which I have to propound on that point is, whether they would consent that Texas should, up to this time, have retained her separate existence as an independent Republic upon our borders, carrying on, in a commercial point of view, a competition with us, which would have redounded to the advantage of the South; because, if Texas had opened her ports under the doctrine of free trade, she would have conciliated her southern neighbors both by propinquity, consanguinity, interest, and trade; and she would have had a right to do it. The North would have suffered more by her separate existence than the South, because they would have brought goods to Galveston, and when they got there all the Sharpe's rifles and the pulpits of the North could not prevent them from going wherever the people chose to carry them. I say nothing about smuggling. Let those do it who are accustomed to it. I wish to make no invidious distinctions; but I may remark that the Yankee is a very keen fellow, and I think he is the pioneer at bargain-making and trade wherever there is an opportunity.

The next question I put to the gentleman is, whether they would consent now to remit Texas to her original condition, and let her assume a separate existence as a rival republic? They would do none of these things if they would consult the public mind of their constituents. They might say so, but they would be rebuked about as effectually as any public men could be rebuked whenever they appealed to that judgment. These are hard questions, I admit. I ask them, would they agree that England should take Texas and exclude slavery, or that Texas should continue to be a separate republic; or would they expel her now from the Union if in their power? Why talk of these things when they do not intend to do what they speak about? They would do no such thing. They would not dare to do it. Still they resort to the safety-valve of rhetoric to get rid of these difficulties, and to pour out its effusions on a deluded constituency. They make an *ex parte* motion, and do not expect a judgment on it.

Now, sir, I have disposed of most of the topics which have been introduced into this debate, and I come to the main *gravamen* of the matter before us, and that is, what is the President to do? Suppose the so-called Legislature assembled in Kansas on the 4th of March, absolutely hoisting the banner of treason, rebellion, and insurrection, what is the President to do? I tell you, sir, as much as the gentlemen to whom I allude denounce the President, if he should not interpose his peace-making power in Kansas, that Legislature will be opposed, and opposed by men as brave as they are, with weapons in their hands, and the contest will be decided by the sword. If it was only to involve them, perhaps it would not be of serious consequence; but the feeling which they have engendered is pervading the Republic. Even in my own State I perceive that parties are being formed to go to Kansas—adventurous young men, who will fight anybody. Sir, let me caution you, do not hold out to the youth of this country a temptation to go into scenes of blood. If you do this, you will commit the gravest of all controversies on earth, and the most important concerns of society, to the youth of the country, for they will go there; and the cause of a republic may be decided by the judgment of youthful impulse.

Will gentlemen tell me that the President was not to interpose and save them from such a contest? Sir, he would be guilty of a criminal dereliction of duty if he were not to interpose; for, by interposing, he can save them from the consequences of this issue. I do not advise him to fire the Federal gun, of which the Senator from New Hampshire spoke. God knows, as I have said, one drop of blood shed in civil strife in this country may not only dissolve this Union, but may do worse. Sir, I have such confidence in the good sense of the country that I believe republican institutions might survive the present Union. Really it is broken already; for the spirit which cherished it has been extinguished, and the very altars upon which we ought to worship have been profaned by false fires. I have been accustomed only to look at this Union to be preserved by observing the obligations of the Federal Constitution, and the honor of compacts, and as to be maintained by the good faith of that old Puritan school which formed the Constitution, and did not have quite as much sentimentality as some of their successors. I do not say what kind of successors they are. Sir, the men of those days had a hardy morality, which dealt with events as they were. They had a wisdom which knew how to accommodate itself to circumstances, and did not lift themselves so high that they saw more than others, and sought ethereal regions because the earth was too good for them. Sir, it is not the purest bird which always seeks the highest regions of air. The vulture, it is said, lives in the regions of eternal snow, and yet it can descend from its ethereal height to live on garbage below.

The President of the United States is under the highest and most solemn obligations to interpose; and, if I were to indicate the manner in which he should interpose in Kansas, I would point out the old common law process. I would serve a warrant on Sharpe's rifles, and if Sharpe's rifles did not answer the summons, and come into court on a day certain, or if they resisted the sheriff, I would summon the *posse comitatus*, and I would have Colonel Sumner's regiment to be part of that *posse comitatus*. The men in Kansas may be deluded. There may be good men among them. I do not wish for an outbreak. I think there are many men among them who on reflection will give over their delusions. I am not among those who hate any man because he differs from me; but I do despise those who are willing to commit others to a contest in which they themselves will escape the consequences.

Mr. President, I shall not pursue this subject further. I have reviewed what has been said so far as I thought proper to allude to it, and now I conclude with this remark—that if we are to be drifting in this way into a dissolution of the Union, I would rather that it should be dissolved to-morrow—I wish my words measured—in preference to living in a Union without the protection of a Constitution which gives me an equality. I should tell my people so to-morrow. Yes, sir, the moment you say this Union is not under the control, and the influence, and the operative influence of the Constitution of the country, I say to South Carolina, "Go out of the Union, and make arrangements with others to form such a government as you can live in with honor and dignity."

Extract from a Speech delivered by Mr. Butler, *in the Senate, January 24, 1850, on the bill providing for the recovery of fugitives from labor.*

"How it has happened I cannot tell, but from some cause—not certainly deserved—Massachusetts and South Carolina have been made to take opposite positions in Federal politics; nay, more, to be made ostensibly bitter adversaries. It would be strange if those who had a common history should be the parties to destroy the bonds of a Union formed in a spirit of cordial confidence. The quarrel of Boston was espoused without calculation by the people of Charleston. There is something in the historical fact that John Hancock and Arthur Middleton, two of the wealthiest men of their day, seemed to have bound their respective States together by the strongest of personal pledges and associations. They tenanted the same house, ate at the same table, and worshiped at the same altar; and pledged their lives and their property in a common cause, and that common cause was maintained by the ommon blood and treasure of the States. My State was favorite colony of the mother country, and became the heater of the deciding contest. There is scarcely a path r a rivulet in her borders that was not crimsoned by the lood of patriots and soldiers fighting in a common cause. And there is scarcely a hill that was not a camp-ground, n which floated the banner of a northern general, for ommon rights, without regard to sectional institutions. Greene, at Ninety-Six and Camden, recognized Sumter, Marion, and Pickens, as his equals; and when he concluded o settle and live among us, he gave evidence that he was no sectional bigot. His ashes are now mingled with the soil of Georgia, and the epitaph on his tombstone will each a lesson of liberty and self-respect. These lessons are written in our earlier history, and they will not be disregarded; they cannot, without incurring an imputation of degeneracy. If I knew at this moment that all political connection was to cease between the North and the South, I would, as a matter of choice, hang up in my parlor the portraits of such men as Adams, Hancock, and Sherman! One lesson they especially teach—never to submit to a wrongful and oppressive exercise of authority. They would inculcate a lesson to maintain the rights that you were born to.

"The southern States have a common destiny; but some are more particularly concerned, from geographical position, than others may think themselves.

"Diomedes was the youngest hero at the siege of Troy. His courage was marked by promptness and intrepidity, and compared well with the sagacious and, perhaps, selfish courage of Ulysses. Georgia was the youngest sister of the thirteen. She has made her pledge in the spirit of Diomedes. And, sir, she will, with her sisters, maintain her motto—'Equality or Independence.'"

SPEECH

OF

HON. ROBERT M. T. HUNTER,

OF VIRGINIA,

ON THE

RESOLUTIONS OF THE MASSACHUSETTS LEGISLATURE

CONCERNING

THE ASSAULT ON MR. SUMNER.

DELIVERED IN THE SENATE OF THE UNITED STATES, JUNE 24, 1856.

WASHINGTON:
PRINTED AT THE CONGRESSIONAL GLOBE OFFICE.
1856.

ASSAULT ON MR. SUMNER.

On motion of Mr. BUTLER, the Senate, as in Committee of the Whole, resumed the consideration of the bill (S. No. 172) to authorize the people of Kansas to form a constitution and State government, preparatory to their admission into the Union when they have the requisite population.

Mr. HUNTER said: Mr. President, it was with deep regret that I first saw the announcement of the passage of those resolutions by the Legislature of the State of Massachusetts. I was concerned to see that great State interpose for the purpose of converting what seemed to me to be a personal dispute into the magnitude of a public quarrel. In the history of the two Houses of Congress since the institution of this Government, there have been many instances of personal collisions in which members have been engaged, arising out of words spoken in debate; but so far as I am acquainted with their history, this is the first case in which any State has interposed for the purpose of taking part in such quarrels. When Mr. John Quincy Adams, of Massachusetts, was President of the United States, his Secretary of State challenged a Senator from Virginia for words spoken in debate, and the quarrel thus made was not settled until two shots had been exchanged on the ground. The Legislature of Virginia did not interpose for the purpose of demanding of the Senate to protect the privileges of its Senator, or to shield him from the consequences of his speech; but, on the contrary, it was content to leave him to meet all his personal responsibilities, under the belief that he would be able to defend himself. There have been cases in which members have fallen at the hands of each other for disputes arising out of debates; and yet I know of no instance before, in which the Legislature of any State has stepped forward to prejudge the case, and to pronounce the sentence which is to be given.

I can see no consequence so likely to flow from this attempt, in the present instance, as that of exasperating the unfortunate sectional dispute which is now raging in the country. But, sir, that was not the only thing in these resolutions which excited pain and regret in my mind. I was concerned to see that, when the State of Massachusetts sat in judgment on this case, it had nothing to say by way of rebuke to its Senator for the offensive language which he uttered, not merely towards a majority of the members of this body, or towards certain individuals who were in it, but towards all the slave States, and particularly towards the States of South Carolina and Virginia. Not only did she have no word of rebuke to offer for such a speech—a speech which called out from the venerable Senator from Michigan [Mr. CASS] the declaration that it was the most unpatriotic and un-American speech he had ever heard on this floor—not only, I say, did she have no word of rebuke to utter for the offensive personalities of such a speech, but she actually indorsed and encouraged them, for she returned him her thanks for having made them; for in no other light can we regard her resolution "approving" of Mr. SUMNER's manliness and courage in his earnest and fearless declaration of free principles, and his defense of human rights and free territory.

Mr. President, so long as the attacks on my State emanated from a single individual, I had nothing to say. Virginia can live under the taunts of any individual, I care not who he be; and portentous indeed would be the day, if it should ever arise, when can be said, the

> "Falcon, tow'ring in her pride of place,
> Was by a mousing owl hawk'd at, and kill'd."

But when a State of this Confederacy comes forward to indorse the attack, and to thank the person who has uttered what I conceive to be a slander, it appears to me that I owe it as a duty to my constituents and to myself, as well as to others who may be concerned, to examine into the foundation upon which this accusation has been so unnecessarily and unprovokedly made against my State.

I pass over the personalities towards friends of mine on this floor—towards myself even, so far as I am included in that majority who voted for the Kansas-Nebraska bill, and towards the slaveholding States in the generality, to which I belong; and

I come to the specific attack on the State of Virginia, which I understand the State of Massachusetts to indorse and approve. The Senator from Massachusetts, [Mr. SUMNER,] speaking of my colleague, said:

"He holds the commission of Virginia: but he does not represent that early Virginia, so dear to our hearts, which gave to us the pen of Jefferson, by which the equality of men was declared, and the sword of Washington, by which independence was secured; but he represents that other Virginia, from which Washington and Jefferson now avert their faces, where human beings are bred as cattle for the shambles, and where a dungeon rewards the pious matron who teaches little children to relieve their bondage by reading the Book of Life. It is proper that such a Senator, representing such a State, should rail against free Kansas."

The foundation upon which this accusation rests—and it has not even the poor merit of originality with him who has last made it, is the fact that slavery, and as a consequence of it the slave trade, exists in the State of Virginia—that is to say, slaves are not only held in bondage, but, being treated as property, it follows as a consequence that they are sold from one to another. These are the facts upon which the attack is based. The coloring in which it is dressed up depends on the fancy or the taste of him who may happen to use the brush. I say it has not even the poor merit of originality, but it is a stale and hackneyed reproach in the cant of all the abolition newspapers. It was made by a distinguished scholar and rhetorician on the other side of the water, who assailed the States of Virginia and North Carolina for what he called the domestic slave trade—a man who, though distinguished for his felicity in picture writing, too often mars its effect by the extravagance of the coloring which he uses—I mean the celebrated Macaulay. The foundation on which this rests is, that owing to the fact of the juxtaposition of these two races on our soil, slavery has flowed from it as a necessary incident. These are circumstances of long standing, and for which we are no more responsible than those who accuse us. History proves that, so far as Virginia was concerned, this institution was fastened upon her against her remonstrance by the British Government. History also shows, and the Senator from Massachusetts confesses, the complicity of his State in his speech, that the slave was sold to us in great part by the men of Old England and New England; and surely the buyer could not have been more responsible than he who sold to him.

Now, sir, out of the fact that these races have been standing together side by side in great numbers in the relation of master and slave, it has followed that the happiness of both races requires that this relation should be kept up. This has been proved by the experience of the British Government itself; and if there were no such experience, it could be proved by any one who knew how to reason upon the principles of human nature. Turn them loose to-morrow side by side, and you would see the black race perishing in the fierce competition which would ensue with the superior and white race, which was dominant around it. You would see either that, or you would see that as they increased in numbers, and population began to press upon the means of subsistence, the white man would leave the country and abandon some of the fairest portions of this continent to the occupation of the negro. We know that from the experiment which has already been tried. I may say that human nature and the experience of States around us both teach us that, although the slave would be nominally emancipated, he would in fact be in far worse bondage than he was held before. He would have not one, but many masters; and instead of having some one person who was responsible for his protection, who was linked to him, as all persons are who inherit slaves, by the ties of a certain sort of family connection, he would belong to every white man, and nobody would be responsible for the treatment by which he was crushed. I say this is proved, too, by the experiment which has been tried by the English Government itself in the West India Islands. We know that if a similar experiment were tried here, its effect would be to substitute barbarism for civilization, and that the wilderness and waste would begin to encroach at once upon the cultivated field.

We know, on the other hand, that under this institution of slavery we can present more than three millions of African negroes who exhibit a greater degree of progress and improvement, of happiness and virtue, than the same number of that race who can be found under any other Government or in any other clime. I say, then, that we can point to all these things to prove, and to show, that the holding of these men in bondage is the necessary result of those circumstances which originated out of the action in part of Old England and of New England herself. Now, if we can show that the preservation of this relation inures to the benefit both of the white and the black race, and that to destroy it would effect a cruel injury to each, do we not show what justifies us in holding them in that condition? Do we not give reasons which prove that it is our duty to do so?

By what right, then, does any man reproach us for doing that which places the society of our country in the very best possible position? Sir, the statesman is not responsible for not attaining the greatest ideal good. He is responsible for not doing the best under the circumstances; and he who has done that has discharged his full duty to his race and to his principles. Are we to say, we will put down any organization, social or political, in which we find individual cases of evil and injustice? What social system or institutions would stand?—what government on the face of the earth could endure for a minute, under such a doctrine? We know that in the great scheme of creation itself, framed by an all-powerful, all-wise, and all-good Being, evil exists. He permits it, and why, we do not understand; but he does not destroy the works of his creation on this account. We know that, in any form of society which could be organized, evil must exist; and to reproach a statesman or a people because in their institutions they may not have attained perfection, is to demand of them more than is possible for human nature. All that they can be required to do is what is best under the circumstances. He who demands more, and makes war upon all Governments in which more is not effected, is an enemy of his race, and a disturber of the peace of mankind—a man to be ranked, not with the statesmen, but with the madmen of the world.

Now, sir, I ask if both reason and experience do not prove that to retain these two races in that relation on our own soil is the very best thing which can be done for them? But, Mr. President, the mischief of the attempt to turn these slaves loose, for the not doing of which we are thus reproached both abroad and at home, would not be confined to the two races on our soil; it would extend to those very countries which hurl these reproaches at us, and to the whole civilized world. There are probably as many people outside of the slave States who derive profit and existence from the proceeds of slave labor, as are to be found within them. On the great staple of slave-grown cotton, it is now estimated that nearly, or quite, three million British subjects depend for their subsistence. I take this from the recent declaration of the Manchester Peace Society, and I have seen a similar declaration before. When we come to add the number who depend on the other slave-grown staples, not only in Great Britain but in all Europe, and in the free States of our own Confederacy, we should find, I believe, that there were more depending for their existence on the institution of slavery, and its profits, outside of our slaveholding States than within them. We should find, probably, if we could pursue the inquiry strictly and accurately, that Massachusetts herself is more interested in the profits of slave labor, and subsists a larger number of people upon it, than do, perhaps, the States of Maryland or Missouri, or even some other slave States which I might enumerate.

Not only this; but those who thus make slavery profitable by creating the demand for the products of slave labor, are as much responsible for the institution as we are who own the slaves. The deadliest blow that could be dealt to slavery would be to refuse to receive the products of slave labor. Do that, and you destroy the demand which makes it profitable. Do that, and, so far as Old England or New England are concerned, you would do it at only a pecuniary expense; but it would cost us not merely money, but our social and political happiness. They could do that at a mere pecuniary expense; but will they do it, or have they done it? Why, sir, it is a little remarkable that, in this very philippic which Macaulay uttered against the institution of slavery in Virginia and North Carolina, he was engaged in the work, in which he succeeded, of repealing the discrimination against slave-grown sugar, which had been made for the benefit of their own colonies, upon whom they had forced emancipation. He not only made it to force the repeal of that discriminating duty, but he succeeded; and England did repeal it, notwithstanding the obligations which she owed to her colonies, on whom she had forced this harsh measure, to give them, at least, that advantage in her own markets.

If we examine the history of the institution, we find, as I have just endeavored to show, from its commencement to the present period, that those who now reproach us are as responsible as we. In the first instance, they sold the slave and we bought him. Now, we sell the products of his labor and they buy it. The complicity is the same; the process is reversed. It has been said, sir, and well said, that the judgment of him was to be commended,

> "Who sent the thief that stole the gold away,
> And punished him who put it in his way."

Upon that principle, I submit that, if there be guilt and if there be wrong in maintaining this relation, they are as responsible for it as we are. But in point of fact there is no guilt either in the one or in the other. The wrong is in converting that into a matter of reproach against us which is not properly the subject of reproach, and for which, if it were, they are as much responsible as we are.

Mr. President, it is said that slaves are sold as chattels and as property from one to another in the States in which the institution is tolerated. I know that this presents a splendid field for declamation; and if I had not known it before, I should have known it after following Macaulay in his display upon this subject. I know that individual cases may be selected, some of which are real, and some of which are imaginary, in which hardships and misery may be shown; but notwithstanding all that, I say the practice of selling them from one to another, and the slave trade itself, is the very safety-valve of the institution, so far as both races are concerned, in the South. It is owing to this that the slaves have been able to make the progress which they have done. It is through this process that they acquire the means and facilities for emigration which are necessary for the improvement of every race that has ever made any improvement in the history of man. The stronger races satisfy this necessity of their condition by armed emigration; the weaker are made to do it by forced emigration; and history shows that the African has performed his share of that process, from an age beyond the date of the pyramids, in the caravan of the slavetrader. Some of the very routes which he then traveled are pursued by him now for the same purposes and objects as if they had been traced out for him by some inexorable law of nature.

We know from experience that in the southern States it is this which has mitigated the institution and ameliorated his condition; because it is under this, that, when population begins to press on the means of subsistence, he is removed from a place where his labor pays but little to one in which it pays more, not only to the master but himself. Although it may seem to be hard that he should be thus forced to emigrate at the will of another instead of his own, yet, when we come to scrutinize closely the process, we find that the line of emigration which he pursues according to the laws of trade, is precisely that line which he would take if he were to follow only his own interests. Should we not find, if we were to examine it, in the history of the emigration of whites, as many individual instances of misery and suffering, as many cases of separation between members of the same family, as we do amongst the slaves who are thus sold from one State to another? I believe that, if we could trace the matter, we should find that the emigration from the Sutherland property, in Scotland, (Mr. Macaulay's own country,) was as involuntary in its movement and as sad in its consequences to those who made it, as any that ever took place from Virginia or North Carolina to the cotton States south of them. In the crowded population of the Old World, I believe we could find instances of emigration forced by circumstances which would harrow the heart fully as deeply as any that could be referred to in our States.

Why, Mr. President, under the operation of this trade, the effect has been that the moment the negro's labor becomes cheap in one region, and he gets a smaller share of the profits of his labor, he is transferred to another where the profits of his labor are greater, and where, of course, he gets a larger share, and where, in the end, he receives more consideration. Stop that trade to-morrow, and I believe you would inflict the greatest curse on the slave in the South that could be inflicted upon him. Pen him up in the old States, and the consequence must be, either that he must perish under the sufferings of a collision with the stronger race, when population presses too hard upon the means of subsistence, or else the whites will abandon the country, and leave it to the negro and his original barbarism.

Under these circumstances, if this process be one of relief and amelioration to the slave, I ask how is it that it should be the subject of so much reproach to those who permit it, and who find it necessary for the improvement of this very race that they should do so? If in truth it did deserve the reproaches which have been cast upon it—if in truth Virginia did accusations deserve the which have been thus made, I ask if it lies in the mouth of Old England, and New England, to utter them? I ask if it was out of their quivers that she had a right to expect such an arrow to be directed at her? Have I not shown that they were as responsible as we for the circumstances which make this institution necessary; that if we were the buyers they were the sellers; and that if we sell the product of slave labor they buy it, and contribute their full share to the maintenance of the institution? If they would destroy all trade from which there may be possible evil, why do they continue this, upon which the institution of their attacks depends for its existence?

Sir, in regard to Massachusetts, she was not only glad to receive our assistance in the Revolution, when we both held and sold slaves, but she was willing to admit us into the same family with herself. The men of that day—the men of the revolutionary generation who covered the name of Massachusetts with glory, the generation which produced the heroes of Concord, and Lexington, and Bunker Hill, and gave birth to the sages that illustrated the revolutionary councils, was not only willing but glad to receive Virginia into a family alliance. They were willing to enter into an association by which they bound themselves to put down insurrection in the States—by which they bound themselves to give a certain representation for the slaves—by which they bound themselves to restore the fugitive slave. And here it is to be remembered, that the covenants which they entered into the men of that day always kept. Under these circumstances, after they invited us into that family alliance, I ask if it is fair, if it is rightful, if it is honorable in their descendants to use the common Hall provided for our common deliberations for the purpose of abusing and vituperating us on account of that very state of things of which they had knowledge and cognizance when they entered into this union with us? I ask if they are not estopped by their own deed?

Now, Mr. President, we hear a new doctrine. We are told that the men of the present day are not to be held responsible for the men of that generation, which is branded by one of their descendants with turpitude. It is the Senator from Massachusetts who says, "Is the acknowledged turpitude of a departed generation to become an example for us?" Thus they are not content with hurling accusations against us, but they brand with turpitude the memory of their ancestors who entered into those bonds by which they became members of the great family of States, to which Virginia, too, belongs. Sir, if I am to choose between the generation which gave birth to the heroes and sages of whom I have spoken, and the men who now cast shame on their graves, I say, let me rather commune with the memories of those than walk in the living presence of these. If I am to choose between those heroes and sages, as I said before, who entered into a covenant to restore the fugitive slave, and who kept it, and these latter-day saints, who, whilst they claim all the benefits of the bond for themselves, refuse to execute their part of the compact, because they have discovered some law of higher obligation, which dispenses with the obligation of their oaths to support the Constitution, and discharge its duties, I say, let me associate with the men who made that covenant, and kept it, in preference to those who are breaking it. If I am to choose between the generation of men who, under the guarantee of treaties, under the sanction of laws, transferred the African from a worse to a better condition, and those who, in violation of law and of the Constitution, steal away the southern slave, and transfer him from a better to a worse condition, let me live with the first rather than with the last. If we have enjoyed the respect and affection of that generation which covered the name of Massachusetts with glory, we may live under the taunts of those who strike at the very memories of their fathers, because it is only through them that they may aim a blow at us.

Turpitude, sir! to talk of the turpitude of the generation of men who gave to Massachusetts the fair inheritance of glory which some of their descendants are now wasting so rapidly! When I hear such charges, I pause before the majesty of the silent shadows of those mighty dead, and wonder that a voice is not given to them to speak to those of their descendants who are thus violating their engagements, trampling on their ancient friendships, and casting shame on their names and graves. But, sir, why do I wonder?

If such a voice could be evoked from the tombs, and were it to charm ever so wisely, it would fall unheeded on the ear of the fanatical Abolitionist. He will not hear Moses and the Prophets; nor would he hear their voices, even if they could be permitted to speak to him.

But these are not the only charges. We are told of the dungeon to which the pious matron is consigned in Virginia who teaches the slave to read. Sir, I have seen in the State of Virginia thousands of slaves who could read and write; and if there ever was any matron, pious or otherwise, who was imprisoned for teaching them, I have yet to hear the history of the case. I have never known such a case; I do not believe that one exists. I think I have been told, that in one of the States of this Union there is a law making it penal to keep Christmas; but does any man suppose such a law has ever been enforced within the last quarter of a century? Suppose it were so; suppose some such enactments as these charged upon Virginia were to be found upon our statute-book, who are responsible for them? Are not those responsible who say to us, "Educate your slave at your peril; give him light and intelligence if you dare; and, if you do, we will make these gifts the means of applying the knife to your throats, and the torch to your dwellings?" Are not these the persons who would be responsible, and not we, if such things were to be found on the statute-book? I will say, however, not to them, not to those who have nothing to do with it, but to my countrymen in the South, that I believe it is our duty to remove whatever may cumber unprofitably the statute-book, whatever is improper or unjust. I believe that the progress of light and intelligence in both races is not incompatible with the institution of southern slavery. I believe that we are responsible for the happiness of all who are committed to our charge, whether they be white or black; and I say, let us do right in despite of the Abolitionist, however he may throw himself in the path of the improvement of the slave. We are strong enough within the Union, or without the Union, to defend ourselves, and with the blessing of Providence let us do right, and leave the consequences to God. To him who intrudes his opinion upon us—to him who has no right to make an inquiry as to our domestic affairs, I have only to say, "There is the southern slave; he speaks for the institution of slavery in our section; produce to us the same number of African negroes in bondage or otherwise, and in any other country, who have made the same progress in improvement, and then we may acknowledge your right to reproach us; but, until you do that, we are entitled rather to the voice of approbation and the hand of sympathy.

Mr. President, in taking the floor upon this occasion, it was my object in part to defend the State of Virginia against the aspersions which have been so unjustly cast upon her. I do not mean to say, for perhaps it does not become me to do so, anything by way of eulogy upon her. If I were to attempt such a thing, it might be thought that my partiality disturbed my judgment. She has taken her place in the great Pantheon of history. Posterity will pronounce its judgment on her present, as public opinion has given it upon her past. I speak the judgment thus pronounced when I say that the Virginian was the first great pioneer of the Anglo-American race upon this continent; that, upon the waters of the James he laid the first stone in the foundation of its empire; that he was the first to plant the banner of its civilization in the great valley of the West; and as the tide of population poured onward from the rising to the setting sun, the smoke of his camp-fire was ever seen far away in the distant wilderness as a pillar of cloud to guide the march of the coming column, and as an emblem of the presence of man to dispute the mastery and the empire, where nature had hitherto held its wild estate, and where silence and solitude had reigned supreme. Still onward as he passed, he left behind him institutions of government and the foundations of human society. He may have had his faults, and doubtless he did have them, and has them now; but amongst those faults covenant-breaking is not to be reckoned. He loves the Constitution and the Union of his country. He reveres the names of those who made that Constitution and Union, whether they came from Massachusetts or from Virginia; and so far from casting shame on their names or their graves, he would take off his shoes and walk silently and softly into the sanctuary which was hallowed by the ashes of those mighty dead.

But, Mr. President, as I said before, it is not my purpose to eulogize my native State. Neither the Senator from Massachusetts nor I, by taking thought, can diminish or increase, by a single cubit, the proportions of her stature. There she stands; and it is for History, not for me, to speak of her.

I come now, Mr. President, to another branch of this case, and another part of these resolutions. I pass away from that in which Massachusetts expresses her approbation of this unparalleled attack on States and their representatives, and come now to the other resolutions, in which she undertakes to sit in judgment on a case here pending, and not merely to request her Representatives, and to instruct her Senators, as other States do, but to "demand" of us that we should carry out her *fiat* and execute her judgment. I am willing to admit that Massachusetts is fully the equal, and has all the rights, of any other State in this Confederacy; but I cannot concede to her that she has more than all the rest besides. I cannot agree that she can come here and demand that her opinions shall be our law, and that her judgment is to be executed by us.

What gives her the right to claim this preëminence? Has she shown any superior fidelity to the laws and to the Constitution of the country? Has she shown that, in this regard, she is more entitled to have her opinions respected and enforced than the other States of the Union? She can make no such claim, whilst the personal liberty bill stands upon her statute-book. While she claims all the benefit conferred on her by this Union and its Constitution, she is bound by an honorable obligation to carry out the duties which it imposes on her in return. Every man who lives under this Constitution and enjoys its benefit, is bound, so far as he is able, to carry out its obligations, and to discharge the duties which it imposes on him.

I know it has been said by some of them that they did not believe Congress had the right to pass any law in regard to fugitive slaves. Those persons, or some of them, believe then that it is the duty of the State; and it was their duty to endeavor to adopt some State law for the purpose of discharging the obligation which is imposed by the common compact. Can such persons acquit their consciences of blame unless they make some effort to perform this duty to which they are bound? And yet no such attempt has been made. But there are others again who say that they believe there is yet a higher law, whose obligations restrain them from carrying out this part of the Constitution. I say to them that, whilst I admit, when the laws of God and man come into conflict, you must obey those of God rather than of man, at the same time it follows as a consequence that this law of God would forbid you to take an oath to support the Constitution which contained a provision contrary to its obligation. If your obligations to God forbid you to discharge the duties required by the society whose government protects you, nothing is left for you but to abandon that society if it will not change the government. You can have no right to enjoy the benefits and protection of that Government, and then refuse to perform the conditions upon which those advantages are extended to you.

Now, sir, if it be an individual who is in this unhappy case, there is nothing left for him but to expatriate himself at once, or else make up his mind to meet the penalties of the violated law. So, too, if a State finds itself unable, from conscientious scruples, to discharge its written obligations, and perform the conditions upon which the Union was formed, there is nothing left to it but to leave that Union. It cannot be right to treat the covenant as binding in all that is beneficial to yourself, and void and invalid so far as you have promised to discharge certain duties towards others. Is she not bound either to say "We will carry out the whole instrument; we will perform our part of the consideration?" or else, "Our conscience forbids us to remain in the same family of States with you, so long as this provision is in your Constitution, to which we object, and against which we have scruples?"

I say Massachusetts cannot justify herself in resisting the obligation of this law, and claiming, at the same time, all the benefits, both general and special, which the Constitution confers upon her. There is, probably, no State in this Union which has derived as much benefit from it as the State of Massachusetts. The navigating and manufacturing interests which have given her the immense wealth of which she boasts, have been the special creatures of legislation and of protection. Whilst she enjoys all these, is she not bound to make some effort, in some way, to carry out the reciprocal duty which the Constitution imposes upon her?

Then, Mr. President, if the claim which she has to be heard, more than all the residue of the States together, does not rest upon her superior fidelity to the obligations of the Constitution and the law, upon what does it rest? Does it repose upon the peculiar calmness of the judicial temperament which she brings to the task of deciding upon this delicate case? She begins her resolutions with a railing accusation against the offender; she characterizes him with all sorts of epithets; and then ends by pronouncing judgment before he has been heard, or before a trial has been had by the competent and proper authorities. This judgment she pronounces upon the ground that in this case there has been a breach of the privileges of the Senate.

I am willing to admit that for that opinion Massachusetts has probably the sanction, as the case first appeared in the papers, of some of the old precedents of the two Houses of Congress, and that also she has the authority of a written report on this very case which passed the Senate a short time since. I have a right to speak of that report, because I, for one, acquiesced in it. At the time, I believed that it was right and proper; and it was only on subsequent investigation that I came to the conclusion that we were claiming, in fact, a privilege which did not exist. Sir, I do not believe that, so far as we were concerned, it was a breach of privilege. I believe there was neither precedent nor authority for us to send a message to the House of Representatives on the subject, and take the position of prosecutor before it. I believe it was a case for the courts, and for the courts alone; and upon that point I beg the Senate for a few moments to give me their attention.

Suppose this had been the case, not of a member of the House of Representatives, but of some citizen of the District, who had made the assault upon a Senator. I say, if it were, I think I can show that you could do nothing with him, and would have no power to punish him, but that the sole power which exists is in the courts, and that there a Senator has the protection which every other citizen possesses—a protection ample and full—an independent tribunal to judge the case, fully armed with jurisdiction and powers for the case and for the occasion; but, beyond that, I do not believe the Senate could have punished an individual for an occurrence which took place when it was not in session, and not within its view.

If I were called upon, disembarrassed of the precedents which have been quoted, to give, *a priori*, a theory of privilege as it might be derived from the Constitution, I should say that the Constitution itself had defined the special privileges which it designed to give to members of Congress. In the first place, it provided that a member should not be held answerable elsewhere for words spoken in debate—that is, that he should not be held answerable under any legal prosecution for words spoken in debate, because, if it meant that he was not to be questioned at all, he would be exempted from criticism by the press, or by public speakers before popular assemblies, for the very reasons which are assigned to protect him against other assaults upon account of his speech; for such criticism would be more likely to deter some from the open expression of their opinions than any fears of personal violence.

Unless, then, you restrict this grant of privilege as I have done, it must be carried to a length utterly inconsistent with the spirit of the Constitution.

The other special privilege which it provided for him was, that he should be exempted from arrest, except in case of treason, felony, or breach of the peace. Here, again, is a privilege which is to be executed, not through either House of Congress, but through the courts of law; because it is to be remembered that the history of the formation of this Constitution shows that the Convention refused to permit each House to be the judge of its own privileges. A proposition was made (3 Madison Papers, 1365) that "each House shall be the judge of its own privileges, and shall have authority to punish by imprisonment every person violating the same, or who in the place where the Legislature may be sitting, and during the time of its session, shall threaten any of its members for anything said or done in the House; or who shall assault any of them therefor; or who shall assault or arrest any witness, or other person, ordered to attend either of the Houses, in his way going or returning; or who shall rescue any person arrested by their order." To this Mr. Madison objected, (*Ibid.* 1493,) who "distinguished between the power of judging of privileges previously and duly established, and the effect of the motion which would give to each House a discretion as to the extent of its own privileges. He suggested that it would be better to make provision for ascertaining by *law* the privileges of each House, than to allow each House to decide for itself." The sense of the convention was against this provision, and these privileges, in my opinion, were for the most part defined. The Constitution has said what should be the privileges of Senators and Representatives, and they are privileges which can be plead and used in courts of law alone.

Suppose an officer were to arrest a man who was privileged by the Constitution from arrest. The remedy against him would be, that the man thus arrested could plead that privilege in order to be released, and he could sue the officer for false imprisonment; but could this House take up the officer and punish him? Surely not. The Constitution itself provides that no man shall be punished either in life, liberty, or property, except by due process of law. The theory of our Constitution is one of law and of equal rights; and when any one is endowed with a special privilege, it is designated and specially given. If anything could be implied beyond this, it would be in regard to the privileges of the two Houses themselves in their corporate capacity. In Dunn's case (6 Wheeler) it has been decided that each House may claim such privileges upon the implication that it is necessary to protect their own existence, and to preserve the functions which were given them. This admission, it is said, puts an end to the argument, that the privileges of Congress are defined by the Constitution. Not at all. There is a law of nature which precedes that of man, and that is the right of self-preservation, which pertains to all bodies, artificial as well as natural.

Now, if this implied power exists until protection is afforded by law, what is its extent? The Supreme Court has said, in regard to the extent of the power to punish in such cases, that "it was the least possible power adequate to the proposed end." The same may be said of the privilege thus to be claimed, which, as it seems to me, would limit either House to what might be necessary to prevent intrusion or contempts within its presence and within its own view. Beyond that, nothing can be claimed for it by way of implication; and I doubt if these cases are not such as might be better provided for by law than by the exercise of an arbitrary discretion on the part of the two Houses of Congress.

Mr. President, so far I have been speaking only of the privileges of members of either House, or of the Houses themselves, in regard to others than their own members. In relation to their own members, each House has discretionary powers, which were given it to enable it to control its own proceedings, and to enforce its orders within the body itself. Of these I shall speak hereafter: they are not involved in the question of the extent of the power of either House to punish *others than its own members* for breach of privilege.

How, then, sir, have these claims been extended beyond what the Constitution has allowed? How have these precedents originated, which have been relied upon and referred to? They have originated in analogies attempted to be sustained between the English Parliament and our Congress. The sources from which these two bodies derive their powers are as different as possible. There, precedent makes the law; here, it is made by positive grant. There, their privileges were the slow accretion of ages, gathered and wrested, one by one, from the Crown. There, each House is the judge of its own privileges; here, the Federal convention expressly refused to make each House the judge of its privileges; and if questions arise, they have to be decided in the courts of law. To show that we cannot claim power here upon analogies drawn from the practice of the British Parliament, I need only refer to many of the cases in which privileges have been claimed and acted upon by the House of Commons. It can hardly be necessary to refer to Hatzel for them, as the recollections of the Senators themselves will doubtless supply the instances. But if any one desires to see a *resumé* of some of the most absurd, he may refer to the argument for the plaintiff in Stockdale's case, (2 Perry and Davidson,) where he would see powers exercised in the name of privilege which, if attempted to be exercised here, would bring down upon our proceedings shouts of derision and execration from the American people. They punished trespassers who fished in the pond of a member of the House of Commons; or who dug Lord Gage's coal; or plowed Mr. Bowles's land; or killed Lord Galway's rabbits; or who rode Mr. James's horse; or who assaulted the servant of a member. A thousand offenses, so trivial and so absurd, have been thus summarily disposed of, that it would be impossible for any man to maintain that we should be justified in the attempt to exercise such power upon precedents drawn from the British Parliament.

Sir, if we claim any privilege beyond what the Constitution has specially given, it is only under the implication that we may punish things done within our own view, and may preserve our own existence by expelling an intruder and preventing contempts. Beyond that there can be no claim of privilege by implication.

I believe that it will be found, if ever the precedents which have been relied upon here should come to receive a judicial criticism, that some of them will not stand the test of such an investigation. It will happen here, as it happened in England, that so long as the Houses were permitted to go on, and judge of their own privileges, they claimed them fast enough; but when the common law courts began to take jurisdiction, and submit them to the criticism of public opinion, these privileges have been abridged and reduced in their extent. So it will happen here. If ever we attempt to exercise privileges to the extent which is claimed across the water, enforce them against any individual citizen, and he chooses to refer to the courts, it will be found that they will restrict that claim in the decision which they will give upon it. The privileges given by the Constitution are ample and sufficient. They protect the House against everything against which it is necessary to protect it, and they protect the members, through the courts of law, against any assaults which may be made upon them.

In regard to the assaults on the person of a member: why should he be more privileged to seek redress in two tribunals than any other individual? The judiciary, which is independent; the judiciary, which can reach the person or the property of the offender, is sufficient in the case of the citizen. Is it not sufficient in the case of anybody, whether he be a member or not, who lives under the jurisdiction of our law? Is it not against the spirit of the Constitution to say that he shall be answerable twice—answerable not only in a court of law, which may decide as to his person and his property, but answerable here also?

I acknowledge that, in regard to its own member, the House has discretionary privileges, so as to make him respect its order, and to keep quiet in its proceedings. It may punish him for disorderly conduct, and may, by a vote of two thirds, expel him. That is a power which extends to *the member* of that very body, not to any other individual. We cannot claim that it be exercised in regard to the member of another House, any more than we could claim to inflict punishment in the case of an indifferent person—such a case as that to which I have referred.

This power of expulsion was given as an extreme remedy for extreme cases. It was vested in a body where it was supposed it would be used with the utmost reserve and caution; because it must have been foreseen that if it should be used under the influence of sectional or party feeling, the act itself would become one of political suicide. We find, as we approach the seat and the center of life, that the cases increase for which the physician cannot prescribe, and for which he must trust to the silent action of the vital forces. In the great scheme of life, the safeguards are provided rather against the assaults of other persons upon the vital organs, than against any injury which the possessor himself might inflict upon them. Against that danger, the instincts of self-preservation are supposed to afford a sufficient protection, except in the case of a frenzied or misguided will. As it is in the natural, so it is in the artificial body; for if ever this power, which is given over the very organs of life, should come to be exercised rashly and intemperately, from that moment political dissolution will become imminent.

But, Mr. President, happily, in presenting the arguments upon this case, it is not necessary to determine whether the precedents to which I have referred—and referred because I thought it was proper to notice them in this connection—be binding or not, because in truth they do not apply. This case, even if it had occurred in England, would not have been considered a breach of privilege; for there a distinction is drawn between speeches which are printed and published and circulated, and what is said in debate. There it has been established in more cases than one, and particularly in Stockdale's case that, although you shall not be held to be answerable for words spoken in debate, and although you shall not be held to be answerable for those words if published by order of the House of Commons, when the circulation is confined to the members of the House; yet, if you publish and circulate them, even by order of the House, abroad, you do become answerable in a suit for libel. That was decided in Stockdale's case by Lord Denman. So, indeed, it was decided before, in the King against Creevy, before Lord Ellenborough, (1 Maule and Selwyn, 275.) It is indeed an old decision, and not one of late days. As far back as the days of James II., there were two cases in which it was decided. For the publication of Dangerfield's case, two suits for libel were maintained; one against the Speaker, who signed the order for its publication by the House of Commons, and the other against Dangerfield, who circulated it generally. Lord Denman said, in Stockdale's case, (Perry and Davidson, vol 2, p. 121,) "The King against Williams was ill decided, because he was questioned for what he did by order of the House, within the walls of Parliament. The King *vs.* Dangerfield is undoubted law, because he sold and published beyond the walls of Parliament, under an order to do what is unlawful."

The principle of that decision has been recently maintained, and it is now the law of the land in England; so that if the House of Commons were to authorize a man to publish and circulate defamatory matter, he could be sued for a libel, if the courts of law were to adjudge that it was defamatory. That is the principle settled after long argument in the case of Stockdale *vs.* Hansard.

It cannot be said that the case is different here, because we have a provision in the Constitution, which says that no member shall be questioned in any other place for any speech or debate in either House. They have a similar provision in their Bill of Rights; but their courts have decided that this protection extends only to words spoken in debate, or to publications made by order of the House for the use of the House only, and does not cover cases where the publication was made and extensively circulated abroad. The same decision, I believe, will be given here, if ever the case should come up in court, because the same reasons which existed there exist here also.

In Creevy's case, it was well said by Mr. Justice Bayly:

"A member of Parliament has undoubtedly the privilege, for the purpose of producing parliamentary effect, to speak in Parliament boldly and clearly what he thinks conducive to that end. He may even, for that purpose, if he thinks it right, cast imputations in Parliament against the character of any individual, and still he will be protected. But if he is to be at liberty to circulate those imputations elsewhere, the evil would be very extensive. No member, therefore, is at liberty so to do."—*Maule and Selwyn*, p. 280.

Now, I say, inasmuch as it is manifest that this is a case which arose out of the publication and the circulation of a speech, it is no more a breach of privilege here to question a man for having done it, than it would be in England. I say, too, that, inasmuch as it arose out of the publication, the precedents upon which we have relied do not apply; that this is quite a different case; and that the point now and here made was never made in those other cases. Of course I argue upon the principle that the alleged breach of privilege is founded upon the constitutional provision as to words spoken in debate. I show enough, if I prove that this provision can in no way extend to a speech published and circulated. No one can allege, as it seems to me, that a mere assault upon a Senator is a breach of his parliamentary privilege. It is a violation of his legal rights, and for that wrong the courts afford a remedy.

If this be so, the Legislature of Massachusetts, had no right to pronounce this to be a breach of privilege, or to demand such summary punishment; neither had we the right to send to the House of Representatives and ask that they should take cognizance of the case. I know that such precedents exist in England, because they claim greater privileges there than we do here; and because, too, there each House is the judge of its own privileges; here that authority and that power are denied to us. There can be no necessity for such a practice here. If the constitutional privilege of a member of either House is violated, the remedy, as I think I have shown, is in the courts of law, which are alike open whether the defendant be a member of Congress or a private citizen. If the case be one of intrusion or contempt within the view of the Senate, the remedy must be used by that body itself, because, to be efficacious, it must be prompt, whether the offender be a member of the other House or not. There, if the case be one of breach of privilege, it is to be judged by the one House or the other; and courtesy has required that if a member were the offender his own House should judge him. But experience even there has shown that such a remedy has generally proved to be *brutum fulmen*, and Hatsell has some useful remarks upon that subject.

I say then, sir, that, so far from being governed by law in the course which we have taken, I respectfully suggest that we have departed from the true view of the power which the Constitution has given us; that we have acted upon the false light of precedents, whose principles do not apply to our case; and that we have made a mistake in the course which we have pursued. At any rate, I will say that surely we have no right to invoke the exercise of an arbitrary jurisdiction of any extreme discretionary power which may be lodged in the other House. We know that the free States of this Confederacy constitute a majority of it. Suppose they were all of them to act in the spirit of these Massachusetts resolutions; suppose they were to encourage their Senators to insult the members from the slave States; suppose they were to say: "If this is resented, you must expel him if you can find two thirds to do it; and if you cannot, you must annoy him by the power of your majority until you make his seat intolerable to him:"—I ask, under such circumstances, how long would it be before there would be a dissolution of such an assembly? I ask, what southern man would be willing to sit here if he was thus to be governed by such a power, exercised in such a manner?

Mr. President, I know it may be said, on the other side, is there not danger that freedom of speech will be abridged, if men undertake to resent or punish its excesses? I admit that evils may occur on that side, but not so great on that horn of the dilemma as on this; because it is always to be remembered that, in the other alternative, the courts of law are open, where you may sue by private action for damages, where you may indict for assault, and where the court has power and jurisdiction to punish for the offense, in either person or property; so that there is a full remedy and an impartial tribunal for any such injury. Besides that, we must further remember that one man is about as able to defend himself as another is to assail him, and that in such contests there are two to be engaged, so the probability is that, in the end, no very great mischief can ensue. At any rate, if scenes did occur which were to be deplored, if events did take place which were to be condemned, still we know there is not near so much danger on that side as there would be in employing the arbitrary and discretionary power of the House, vested in it only for extreme occasions, in cases where the judgment might be attributed not so much to the sense of right as to sectional feeling, or to party bias. I think that, under such circumstances as these, it is always best to transfer such feuds from the Houses of Congress to the courts of law—from a tribunal which must of course be, to some extent, prejudiced and partial, to one which is unprejudiced and impartial.

I give this counsel for the sake of peace. I advise such a measure, as one which seems to me to afford a solution by which we may escape from some of those difficulties that seem to threaten us with so much exasperation and strife. I believe that the merits of the whole case may thus be reached, and thus, too, we may save ourselves from the agitation which, rely upon it, is doing great mischief here and abroad. I think the Senate ought to reverse its position. Indeed, it would be but acting under the precedent in the case of Gunn, (a Senator who challenged a member of the House of Representatives,) if we were to withdraw our application after the apology of the member from South Carolina. In that case the proceedings were dropped the moment the Senator declared his contrition for what had happened. I believe that if this were done here, and the case were left to the courts, we should save both Houses from a scene of strife and exasperation which every patriot and every lover of his country must deplore.

Suppose that two foreign nations were mutually to instruct their representatives to insult and abuse each other: how long would peace be maintained? Suppose that the members of the same family were to use their opportunities of daily intercourse for the purpose of mutual vituperation: how long would harmony exist? Suppose that States which belonged to the same Union should use the common hall of their deliberations for the purpose of mutual crimination and recrimination: how long would that Union be maintained? Sir, "in the letter which killeth" it might endure for a while, but in "the spirit which giveth life" it would soon be gone and lost forever.

Now, sir, I ask if these are not considerations which should be impressed upon all? Our institutions rest not upon parchment securities, but upon the broad basis of public affection. Who shall measure the crime of him that disturbs the waters of the stream of public opinion which to us are the very waters of life—of him who troubles the stream at its fountain that he may defile it through the whole length of its course, until we turn loathing away from its waters, although our thirst may be almost unto death itself? Sir, the laws and the Constitution and the ordinances of our country, to have efficient force and life and being, must be engraved upon the hearts of the people. Once erase or obliterate that inscription, and it will not be long before the lawgiver himself, in some fit of exasperation, will shiver into fragments the tablets upon which they are written, as mere unspeaking stone.

In view of all these circumstances, does it not behoove us to do something to appease this strife, to settle these difficulties, to allay this bitterness? Who could have the heart, at such a moment as this, to engage in the work of crimination and recrimination amongst the States of the Confederacy? We all belong to the same family, and the character of the whole family is disparaged if we injure the reputation of one of its members. What pleasure or what profit should I derive by injuring the reputation of Massachusetts? by dimming the luster of her revolutionary glory? by taking a leaf from that chaplet of immortal flowers with which she is crowned? Sir, so far as I am concerned, instead of taking one stone from the Bunker Hill monument, I would add another to it. Let it tower to the skies, bearing upwards from earth to heaven whatever message of love and admiration may be transmitted from the living to the dead. Let it stand through the flight of ages, and carry down the story of those men and their deeds to the last syllable of recorded time. I will raise no sacrilegious hand against a single stone on that altar; and if there be any who has a heart for such a deed, he can find no sympathy from me.

Who can have the disposition to disparage the reputation and the military glory of any of the Old Thirteen? If there be any man who can have a heart for such a work, he can have but little feeling in common with me. I will not aid in such a work. What materials are these that we are collecting for history? What weapons are we placing in the hands of those who wish us ill, and who delight in every opportunity to disparage ourselves and our institutions?

Mr. President, it has been said by wise and good men, "give us peace abroad." I sympathize with them in that wish; but it may not always be in our power to secure that peace. It may require the will of another as well as of ourselves; but I say, give us what we can secure if we choose—give us peace at home. We want its opportunities to work out our destiny, and to crown with the glory of success the most wonderful experiment in human happiness that has ever been attempted in the history of man. We must have peace at home if we would wish to inspire either fear or respect abroad. Is there nothing in the condition of things around us—is there nothing in the condition of things abroad, to induce us to do something to compose these differences, to allay this excitement, to settle these feuds? Can any man reconcile it to his conscience to feed high the hot fires of sectional strife on such an occasion as this? Are the doors of our Chamber, are the doors of the Congress of the United States, like those of the temple of Janus, to be opened only for war, for civil war, for domestic strife? or may we not rather close them upon such scenes, or else open them to send forth once more the message of peace and good will, and to proclaim throughout the land a vow to devote ourselves to the common good of a common country, and to bury, as far as we can, the recollection of these unhappy disputes?

Mr. President, I do believe that the time has arrived when we should look at the state of circumstances around us, coolly and dispassionately, and when every man should come to the settlement of these differences with the will to sacrifice much of feeling, anything of the pride of opinion, everything that he can, consistently with duty and conscience, to settle and quiet them. Senators, I say to you that you hold in your hands the issues of life and death to this mighty Republic, to this great Union. On your souls, I charge you to take heed how you deal with them.

SPEECH

OF

JOSIAH RANDALL, ESQ.,

OF PHILADELPHIA,

Delivered at Chambersburg, August 6, 1856, *at the request of the Democratic State Convention, of Pennsylvania.*

IN obedience to the request of the Democratic State Convention, of Pennsylvania, I claim the attention of my fellow-citizens for a short time. I am aware that I have received this courtesy because I have heretofore been a member of the Old Line Whig party.

In 1824–5, the Democratic and Whig parties were separated by no principle, but were divided upon the question, whether Gen. JACKSON was entitled to be elected President of the United States. In the progress of time, during the thirty years of the existence of the Whig party, several important principles were presented, and the two parties became distinct and independent of each other upon questions of public policy. These were:

1. The renewal of the Charter of the Bank of the United States.
2. The Sub-Treasury.
3. The Distribution of the Proceeds of the Public Lands.
4. The Tariff.

A "National Bank" was abandoned by the Democratic party, under the veto of Gen. Jackson in 1832, and by the Whig party in 1844.

"The Sub-Treasury," the cardinal measure of Mr. Van Buren, was opposed by the Whig party, has fought itself into public favor, and now no one wishes to disturb it.

"The Distribution of the Proceeds of the Public Lands," has been superceded by the debt created by the Mexican war.

"The Tariff" no longer remains either a political or geographical question. During the last Congress, the "State Rights" men of the South and the Republican Abolitionists of the North, united against Pennsylvania, without distinction of party, to reduce the tariff below its present standard.

I do not include in this category the question of Internal Improvement by the Federal Government, or the Acquisition of New Territory. All parties in the West are in favor of the exercise of the first power; the second was determined by the election of Mr. Polk, in 1844, when a new feature in the Republic was developed, that our people collectively are anxious to increase the public domain in the same manner as individuals are anxious to increase their private property.

If there remains any practical disputable principle, which constituted an issue between the Democratic and the old Whig parties, I do not know it.

The Whig party has performed its duty, and has had its day. It has been prostrated by the organization of the American party, or the KNOW-NOTHING ORDER. They, and not the Old Line Whigs, have been the *executioners*. They have renounced their old *cognomen*, laid aside their old principles, and substituted in their place a new name and a new creed never before recognized by CLAY, WEBSTER, SERGEANT, or their noble compeers.

I know there are many intelligent and patriotic men who cherish the hope that the Whig party can again be resusciated, but the hope is delusive, and it is pernicious, because it deprives the country of a large portion of intellect and worth, which ought to be brought into public service. In the history of our republic, no party broken down has ever yet been re-organized. The fate of the Federal and Anti-Masonic parties establishes this fact. There is not, at this time, a Whig member of the popular branch of Congress elected by a Whig vote. There is not a member of the Legislature of Pennsylvania elected by a Whig vote. There is not a member of the Councils of the City of Philadelphia elected by a Whig vote. For the last two years, with but two exceptions, wherever the scattered members of the Whig party have met in council, they have felt their position, and have, therefore, wisely abstained from forming a ticket to be voted for at the polls. In New Hampshire and Massachusetts they rallied at the polls, and the result was paucity of numbers and total defeat. But what good would be derived from the re-organization and triumph of the old Whig party? They do not want a National Bank. They do not desire the repeal of the Sub-Treasury. The most ardent friends of the tariff do not ask for the re-establishment of the high tariff of 1828, or even of 1842; but all they ask is, that the tariff shall stand where it was placed in 1846 by the casting vote of the Vice President, Mr. DALLAS. All the old issues have been settled, and, as a natural consequence, new parties have sprung up, and new issues have been formed. The Order of Know-Nothings have violated the letter and spirit of the VI. Article of the Constitution of the United States, which declares that "*no religious test shall ever be required as a qnalification to any office or public trust under the United States.*" They have established secret societies, secret oaths and obligations. With these principles the Whig party, in its days of power and numerical strength, had no sympathy or affiliation, and there is no part of the Union where the Whigs were more inflexible in opposing these political heresies than in the State of Pennsylvania.

In 1845, when the Whig party met in the City of Philadelphia, after the defeat of Mr. CLAY, the duty of opening the meeting and setting forth their principles was committed to me. I held in my n ɑat that meeting, the charter of Rhode Island, granted to Roger Williams, a Baptist minister, which contains the broadest and most comprehensive declaration of religious LIBERTY AND EQUALITY ever yet penned. I read its eloquent and energetic platform and said, "THIS IS THE DOCTRINE OF THE WHIG PARTY," and pointing to the ruins of the Roman Catholic Church of St. Augustine, burnt during the disgraceful riots of 1844, and which lay within a few yards of the place of meeting, I added, "THERE IS ITS DESECRATION." There is not a nook nor corner in the vast region of our country which does not contain old line Whigs who are willing to stand by the Constitution and the Union. But their numerical strength is far exceeded by their patriotism, talents, and public spirit. This is the body to which I have been attached, and I feel the deepest interest in the course they shall pursue.

The Republican party is SECTIONAL, and its success must, in my judgment, lead to a severance of the Union. I do not believe that the great mass of that party anticipate this result; but if it should be consummated, their regret will be no equivalent for the damning injury thereby inflicted upon this great Republic. I appeal to every old line Whig in the Union to avert this calamity. The South cannot and will not remain in the Union, unless their rights shall be guaranteed to them. If we were in the same situation, we would demand our rights in tones as imperative and mandatory as those which are now used by our Southern brethren.

How is this great evil to be avoided? I answer, by the election of Mr. BUCHANAN. Every vote given to him is a check to the progress of the Republican party. I know there are many Whigs who approve of the administration of MILLARD FILLMORE, and are willing to trust him again. Every vote given to Mr. FILLMORE increases the danger of the success of Mr. FREMONT. Every vote given to Mr. BUCHANAN potentially seals the fate of Mr. FREMONT. But MILLARD FILLMORE in 1848, '50, and '52, is not the MILLARD FILLMORE of 1856. When he was elected Vice President in 1848,—when he became the acting President in 1850,—and when he was a candidate for re-nomination by the Whig Convention in Baltimore, in 1852, he professed to be a Whig—nothing more, nothing less. The Native American party at that time was in existence and proclaimed principles in terms far less exceptionable than those now avowed by the Know-Nothing party. But Mr. Fillmore then had neither part nor lot with them, he stood upon the ground occupied by CLAY, WEBSTER and SERGEANT. What is he now? He has been initiated into the Order of Know-Nothings, taken upon himself its secret oaths and obligations, and this at a time when his friends were presenting his claims to be elected President of the United States. He has since become the candidate and accepted the nomination of the American or Know-Nothing National Convention. In a correspondence between the Order of the United Americans of the State of New York and him, under the date of July 25th, 1856, they say:—

"Both from your past official acts, and from the assurances and views expressed by you on many occasions, as having similar sentiments in reference to those subjects, to them of so much seeming importance, the successful establishment of these principles, as the fundamental rules of our Government, they believe essential for its tranquillity, and a continued progress in the development of all its greatness."

Mr. Fillmore in his answer, dated 29th of July, 1856, acquiesces in this statement and replies—

"My position before the country is well known, admitting neither of disguise nor equivocation. I am the candidate of the American party."

Mr. FILLMORE here proclaims himself the American candidate, and adopts the creed, oaths and obligations of that party without "disguise or equivocation." In the Secret Lodge of the Order of Know-Nothings he has sworn that he will neither vote for nor appoint a Roman Catholic to office. If elected and inaugurated President of the United States, he would be compelled to swear that he would require "*no religious test as a qualification to any office or public trust under the United States.*" I ask, under such circumstances, which oath would he keep, and which oath would he violate? I desire to treat Mr. Fillmore fairly, but all experience tells us, that in such cases, the candidate if elected will preserve his political allegiance and forget his Constitutional injunction. Are the Old Line Whigs prepared to endorse Mr. FILLMORE, thus presented by himself for their suffrages? I know no difference between an individual joining the Order and giving his vote to sustain its candidate, except that the latter course is more effective in carrying out the tenets of this party.

The friends of Mr. Fillmore have assailed Mr. BUCHANAN for his Ostend communication. Without admitting or denying the soundness of the doctrine therein contained, I would remark that the correspondence of Mr. Everett, as Secretary of State under Mr. Fillmore, after the death of Mr. Webster, relative to Cuba, is more offensive, and ought to be more obnoxious to the criticism of conservative men than the Ostend Letter; and it should be remembered that the diplomatic manifesto of Mr. Everett was issued under the immediate supervision of Mr. Fillmore and his Cabinet.

Mr. Everett is probably the best educated statesman now living; he is an erudite scholar and a sound patriot. When in Congress, he took higher ground in favor of the South on the subject of slavery, than any Northern statesman had ever done before, or has ever done since. One thing is certain, any opinion upon International Law promulgated by him, is entitled to respect. Mr. Buchanan has been in public life upwards of forty years, he has filled the highest offices which his own State could confer upon him. He has occupied the first seat in the Cabinet during a most eventful epoch; and he has twice represented his country at the Courts of the two first nations in Europe. His private character stands without blot or blemish and beyond rebuke or reproach; and it is a high eulogium upon his public life, that the "*Ostend Letter*" is the only act which is designated by his opponents as the ground of attack.

On the subject contained in these diplomatic documents, I have not changed my former sentiments. I desire, ardently, the acquisition of Cuba; no child can look at the map without seeing it ought to belong to those who own the Gulf of Mexico; but unless we can honestly obtain it, I would leave it where it is. We have paid for every foot of ground that we have ever acquired, and unless Cuba can be obtained in the same manner that Louisiana, Florida, the recently acquired Territory from Mexico, and Texas, I am utterly opposed to any other mode of bringing it into the Union. The mother country who taunts us with the charge of being anxious to increase our Territory, is the most insatiate cormorant among the nations of the earth, has never paid for a foot of ground that she ever held, but has always wrested it from the weak and powerless who have been unable to protect their dominions.

There are many Old Line Whigs who are attached to their cognomen, and dislike changing it—this is an overscrupulous nicety. They must change their name—they must recognize the title of an American Know-Nothing, Republican, or a Democrat. If they refuse to elect either of these names, they must retire from all participation in public affairs. Gov. SEWARD is reported to have said in caucus, during the present session of Congress, that he cared nothing for names, but that he looked to principles alone. This remark showed he had a clear head and a sound judgment, and was worthy of a better cause.

I hold that the Territory ceded to us by Mexico was purchased by common treasure. The fifteen Slave States contributed their portion of the fund as well as the *then* fifteen Free States. Territory should stand on the same footing as admitted States, and the right of the people to hold Slaves or not, as they please, in the Territory, ought to be commensurate with the right of the people as they exist in the thirty-one States. There can be no just ground for any discrimination between the two cases. New Territory is surely not more sacred than the old thirteen States, or the present thirty-one States. The will of a majority prevails in the cases last enumerated, and the same orthodox principle should prevail in the newly-acquired Territory.

What is the doctrine of the Wilmot Proviso? It is the sixteen Free States declaring to the fifteen Slave States—you are part owners of this Territory; you have shed your blood and expended your treasure in acquiring it, but you shall have no share in its enjoyment or profits. Strip it of its trappings, and it amounts to this: there are thirty-one stockholders in a corporation, and sixteen say to fifteen, it is true you are part owners and have contributed to the purchase of our common property, but you shall have no share in the enjoyment of its privileges or the receipts of its profits. Such a doctrine is subversive of every principle of justice and equality, and cannot be sustained.

I am not the advocate of opinions that are new to the Whig party of Pennsylvania. At a Whig meeting held in September, 1850, at the Chinese Museum, in Philadelphia, I offered a resolution congratulating the Nation upon the restoration of peace and quietude to the country by the passage of the Compromise Acts of that year. It was unanimously adopted, and I then laid down the same principles which I am now endeavoring to inculcate.

In November, 1850, the great Union Meeting was held at the same place, over which John Sergeant presided. Among others, I again enforced the same principles. On the 27th of February, 1851, a pure Whig meeting was called to request the repeal of the Act of the Legislature of 1847, which closed the public jails of this Commonwealth against the custody of Fugitive Slaves. At that meeting Samuel Breck, second to no man in the country in intelligence and patriotism, presided. I again promulgated the same doctrines, and they were again endorsed by the Whig party assembled on that occasion.

In 1819–20 when the Missouri Compromise was adopted, the North, without distinction of party, held different sentiments. There is no real discrepance between the two attitudes when rightly understood. In 1820 the South adopted the Missouri Compromise, and never abandoned it until after 1850, when it was abrogated by what is generally understood as the Compromise Acts of Congress of that year. During the discussion of those measures, the South upon the amendment of Mr. Turney, of Tennessee, endeavored to continue that Compromise, by extending it to the Pacific, but the North rejected it. On the other hand, the Free-soil party have never abided by the Compromise of 1820. They opposed in 1821 the admission of Missouri, and in 1825, the admission of Arkansas. They now go back, and proclaim the Wilmot Proviso as their standard, which is a direct abrogation of the Missouri Compromise, and declares all territory whether North or South of 36 degrees 30 minutes, shall be free.

If the South were now willing to prohibit Slavery in the newly-acquired territory, I would rejoice at the declaration; but they are not willing. They assert *their rights*, and I am in favor of an enre and cordial recognition of those rights. If Maryland or any other Slave State should abolish slavery, it would give me unalloyed pleasure; but it does not follow, that I would therefore be in favor of compelling such Slave States against their will to abolish it.

These are some of the reasons why I invoke every Old Line Whig in Pennsylvania to support Mr. Buchanan. The triumph of the Democratic party in Pennsylvania, in October next, would place his election beyond doubt. It would remove the last glimmering hope of the opposition, restore peace and quietude to the country, and for one generation at least, put at rest the present agitation on the question of slavery. The Old Line Whigs of Pennsylvania possess the power to accomplish this great result; the responsibility rests upon them, and I have no doubt but that the draft which is made upon their patriotism will be promptly accepted, and that the great Keystone State will once more come to the rescue, and do as she has done heretofore, put down all sectional feeling, and at the ballot-box perpetuate the Union, which has so long been the pride and admiration of every friend of civil and religious liberty throughout the world.

IN SENATE. TUESDAY, AUGUST 6TH, 1850.

Admission of California.

Mr. TURNEY moved to strike out all after the enacting clause, and insert as follows:

"When it shall be made to appear to the President of the United States, by satisfactory evidence, that the people inhabiting the Territory of California, (or so much of said Territory, as is comprised within the limits proposed by this bill as the boundaries of the State of California,) assembled in Convention, have agreed to a line not further South than the parallel of 36° 30′ North latitude, as the Southern boundary of said State, and limited the representation of said State to one Representative until after the next census of the inhabitants of the United States, the said State of California may be admitted into the Union, upon the Proclamation of the President, upon an equal footing with the original States.

"SEC. —. *And be it further enacted*, That the line of 36° 30′ of North latitude, known as the Missouri Compromise line, as defined by the eighth section of an Act, entitled 'An Act to authorize the people of the Missouri Territory to form a Constitution and State government, and for the admission of such State into the Union on an equal footing with the original States, and to prohibit slavery in certain Territories,' approved March 6th, 1820, be, and the same is hereby declared to extend to the Pacific Ocean: and the said eighth section, together with the Compromise therein effected, is hereby revived, and declared to be in full force and binding for the future organization of the Territories of the United States, in the same sense and with the same understanding with which it was originally adopted."

The question was stated to be upon the amendment of Mr. TURNEY, and, being taken by yeas and nays, was rejected by the following vote:

YEAS—Messrs. Atchison, Badger, Barnwell, Bell, Berrien, Butler, Clemens, Davis, of Mississippi, Dawson, Downs, Foote, Houston, Hunter, King, Mangum, Mason, Morton, Pearce, Pratt, Rusk, Sebastian, Soule, Turney, and Yulee—24.

NAYS—Messrs. Baldwin, Benton, Bradbury, Bright, Cass, Clarke, Cooper, Davis, of Massachusetts, Dayton, Dickenson, Dodge, of Wisconsin, Dodge, of Iowa, Douglas, Ewing, Felch, Greene, Hale, Hamlin, Jones, Norris, Phelps, Seward, Shields, Smith, Spruance, Sturgeon, Underwood, Upham, Wales, Walker, Whitcomb, and Winthrop—32. *Congressional Globe*, 1*st Sess.* 31*st Cong.*, *Vol.* 21, *Part 2nd, page* 1532.

When this vote was taken Mr. Clay was absent from indisposition, Mr. Webster had been appointed Secretary of State and Mr. Winthrop was substituted in his stead. Both Mr. Clay and Mr. Webster had acted with the majority, and from their known sentiments would, if present, have voted against Mr. Turney's amendment.

NATIONAL POLITICS.

SPEECH

OF

HON. CHAS. JAS. FAULKNER,

OF VIRGINIA,

AT READING, PENNSYLVANIA,

SEPTEMBER 4, 1852.

WASHINGTON:
A. O P. NICHOLSON, PRINTER.

[*From the Pennsylvanian of Monday, September* 6, 1852.]

THE GREAT MEETING OF THE DEMOCRACY AT READING.

30,000 FREEMEN IN COUNCIL!

THE DEMOCRACY OF THE OLD KEYSTONE AROUSED!

Buchanan, Douglas, Bigler, Lowe, and Faulkner, the talent and the bone and sinew of the Democracy of the East, West, North and South, in the field, battling with willing hearts and hands for Pierce, King, and the Union!

On Saturday, pursuant to notice, the political friends and advocates of the election of Pierce and King assembled at the citadel of Democracy—the city of Reading—to the number of thirty thousand.

There were delegations in attendance from Philadelphia, Lancaster, Lebanon, Dauphin, Chester, Montgomery, Bucks, Schuylkill, Lehigh, and other counties. The town of Pottsville sent a strong delegation, with a fine band.

The Spring Garden delegation was very full, and had a neat white banner, with black border, having thereon the inscription—"We hail from the District of Spring Garden." They were headed by the United States brass band, in their splendid uniforms.

The delegation from the Northern Liberties looked remarkably well. They were accompanied by a band of music, and had a number of beautiful flags.

The delegation from the district of Penn made a very creditable appearance, and were preceded by a tasty banner, bearing these words—"District of Penn—Pierce and King."

The delegation from Dauphin county turned out in goodly numbers, and were preceded by an excellent brass band, and displayed several pretty star-spangled banners.

There were also present two fine German bands from Philadelphia.

The Ringgold Artillery, of Reading, commanded by Captain James McKnight, paraded in full uniform, with a fine band of music.

Most of the hotels were decorated with handsome flags, many of them bearing the inscription "Pierce and King;" and all these houses were filled to overflowing with people from all parts of this State, Virginia, and Maryland.

After several delegations and the military had paraded the several streets, they gathered in front of the grand Rostrum, which was erected in Centre Square, near the western market-house. It was tastefully decorated with banners and flags, and the United States brass band and a German band were in attendance upon it, and played some lively airs in their best style.

Precisely at 12 o'clock the meeting was called to order by Horn R. Kneass, esq., one of the members of the State Central Committee; in behalf of which body he moved that the Hon. James Buchanan officiate as President of the meeting, which was unanimously agreed to amid great applause.

On motion of H. R. Kneass, esq., it was resolved unanimously that Gov. Lowe, of Maryland, and Gov. Bigler, of Pennsylvania, take position on the right and left of the President.

Horn R. Kneass, esq., here read the following list of officers of the meeting, which was unanimously agreed to:

President—Hon. JAMES BUCHANAN.

Vice Presidents.—Hon. Joel B. Dana, of Adams county; Col. Samuel W. Black, of Allegheny county; John S. Rhey, of Armstrong county; John Cessna, of Bedford county; Hon. J. Glancy Jones, of Berks county; Hon. John Laporte, of Bradford county; Hon. Thomas Ross, of Bucks county; Thomas J. Power, of Beaver county; Hon. Alfred Gilmore, of Butler county; Hon. George R. McFarlane, of Blair county; John O'Neill, of Cambria county; Asa Packer, of Carbon county; Col. James Burnside, of Centre county; Hon. John A. Morrison, of Chester county; Wm. T. Alexander, of Clarion county; George R. Barrite, of Clearfield county; Charles R. Buckalew, of Columbia county; J. Porter Brawley, of Crawford county; George W. Brewer, of Cumberland county; Hon. Wm. Dock, of Dauphin county; Alex'r McKeever, of Delaware county; Hon. J. L. Gillis, of Elk county; Hon. John Galbraith, of Erie county; Hon. John L. Dawson, of Fayette county; Hon James X. McLanahan, of Franklin county; W. F. Schell, of Fulton county; Hon. Charles Black, of Greene county; John Dougherty, of Jefferson county; Hon. Augustus Drum, of Indiana county; Hon. Andrew Parker, of Juniata county; Lot Watson, of Lawrence county; Col. Wm. B. Fordney, of Lancaster county; John Weidman, of Lebanon county; Willoughby Fogel, of Lehigh county; Hon. Andrew Beaumont, of Luzerne county; Hon. James Gamble, of Lycoming county; Hon. Robert J. Hogue, of Mercer county; Thaddeus Banks, of Mifflin county; Solomon Barstow, of McKean county; Hon. John McNair, of Montgomery county; E. H. Baldy, of Montour county; Hon. M. M. Dimmick, of Monroe county; Gen. A. H. Reeder, of Northampton county; Hon. L. Dewart, of Northumberland county; Wm. H. Miller, of Perry county: James Magee and Robt. Ewing, of Philadelphia city; Hon. Thomas B. Florence, Hon. John Robbins, jr., Hugh Malone, John S. Hoffman, and H. G. Sickles, of Philadelphia county; Henry S. Mott, of Pike county: Chas. Lyman, of Potter county; Charles Frailey, of Schuylkill county; Isaac Hugus, of Somerset county; Hon. G. A. Grow, of Susquehanna county; Hon. John R. Jones, of Sullivan county; Hon. John W. Guernsey, of Tioga county; Wm. H. Lamberton, of Venango county; Charles Schreiner, of Union county; Hon. Nathaniel P. Eldred, of Wayne county; Gen. Wm. L. Calihan, of Washington county; Hon. Wm. D. Foster, of Westmoreland county; Hon. Charlton B. Curtis, of Warren county; S. S. Winchester, of Wyoming county; and Hon. Wm. H. Kurtz, of York county.

Secretaries.—Wm. M. Heister, of Berks county; Robert J. Niven, of Susquehanna county: John Hamilton, jr., of Philadelphia city; John Oakford, John Batzig, and Henry L. Horn, of Philadelphia county; Col. L. F. Frank, of Lehigh county; Col. James Jeffries, of Dauphin county; Wm. P. Withington, of Lancaster county; Jacob Leisenring, of Northumberland county; and James C. Van Dyke, of Philadelphia city.

On motion of David Pool, esq., of Harrisburg, Col. James Jeffries, of Dauphin, was added to the list of secretaries.

The Hon. JAMES BUCHANAN being loudly called for, came forward amid repeated cheering and addressed the meeting.

He was followed by Hon. STEPHEN A. DOUGLAS, of Illinois; Gov. BIGLER, of Pennsylvania, and Gov. LOWE, of Maryland; when the president of the day, Hon. JAMES BUCHANAN, introduced to the meeting the Hon. CHAS. JAMES FAULKNER, of Virginia, as the representative in Congress of a portion of the Tenth Legion of Virginia Democracy, which annunciation was received with immense and prolonged cheering.

Mr. FAULKNER said: I thank you, fellow-citizens of Pennsylvania, for the cordial manner in which you have received one who is a perfect stranger to you. I thank you on my own account, and I thank you on behalf of the Tenth Legion of Virginia democracy. And here pemit me to say that I am reminded of an incident which occurred during our late war with Great Britain. When Decatur was bearing down on the Macedonian, and ready to open his batteries upon her, an officer came up and said: "Sir, the men wish to cheer." "Let them first take the ship, and then cheer," was the reply. Now, whilst I have not less confidence in the result of the approaching action than that which was felt by the gallant commodore, I shall hear the cheers from the democracy with much greater pleasure after the second Tuesday in November next. Let Pennsylvania do her duty, and we *shall* hear them.

Fellow-countrymen, I have come from the South in the same spirit in which the Roman student of old made his pilgrimage to the classic groves of Athens—to drink at the pure, undefiled well of northern democracy. [Cheers.] I stand in the midst of the firm, the unconquerable, the ever-conquering democracy of Berks, [cheers,] in the heart of the Tenth Legion of Pennsylvania democracy. [Cheers.] I have come here with no idle intent. I have come here with an object, and for a purpose. I have come from Virginia to see with my own eyes and to hear with my own ears how the men of Pennsylvania respond to the true principles of our great federal compact. Virginia and Pennsylvania, united in the field of party warfare, have so far proved themselves equal to a world in arms. From the foundation of the government to the present hour, the republican party has never sustained a defeat when these two powerful States have stood shoulder to shoulder in the fight. I can, then, say to you with emphasis and power, that

Virginia is sound—sound to the core; safe beyond dispute or cavil, and with untold thousands to spare from the ballot-box. The Scott column of Virginia—following the lead of false guides and treacherous counsels—is now fairly hemmed in between the Caudine forks. Any attempt to pass its northern or its southern defile must be alike fatal to it. On the south stands a democratic host, panting for the contest and flushed with the hopes of anticipated victory. On the north yawns the fearful chasms of abolition. No free-soil triumph will ever flash its glories over that field of fight. Though Scott be a native of the Old Dominion, she knows him not in his present claim upon her sympathies. As the Spartan mother said to her recreant son, who returned from battle without his shield—" Go back and return *with* your shield, or *upon* it"—so does Virginia say to Winfield Scott: Return with the principles which I taught you before you left my soil, or return never more. So long as Scott headed our gallant army against Mexico, and fought in the true line of his profession, his march was triumphant, his career brilliant. But the Samson of war has been shorn of his strength by the modern Delilahs of abolition; and if he should ever hereafter again, under the custody of his Philistine guardians, acquire strength and power, it can only be, I fear, to pull down upon your heads and mine, and his own, the pillars of our constitution. I have told you what the prospect of the campaign is in Virginia. Is it equally safe in Pennsylvania? [Shouts from the crowd, "It is—it is."] If so, then the Union is safe, the constitution is safe, sectional agitation will be forever extinguished, and the plotters and conspirators against our peace will be driven to their obscure dens, where the light of day will never reach them.

Freemen of Pennsylvania, if I cannot find patriots here, where can I go to look for them? If you do not love the Union, and reverence that constitution under whose glorious auspices you enjoy the unnumbered blessings which seem everywhere showered upon you, where upon this continent are friends of the Union to be found? God, in his goodness, never gave to man a nobler heritage than that which you here possess; and every object that met my eye, as the merry and rattling car brought me in view of your luxuriant fields, your well-cultivated farms, your richly-stored granaries, and your comfortable homesteads, all prove that you know how to value the blessings which a kind Providence has bestowed upon you.

I come from the Valley of Virginia—from a soil not inferior to your own in natural fertility, but somewhat inferior to yours in careful and judicious cultivation. A large portion of that beautiful valley has been settled by Pennsylvanians, and the descendants from the farmers of old Berks may be now seen occupying some of the fairest portions of that productive region. Your instinct in finding out good land is as unerring as your instinct in discerning what is safe in politics. Many names that I have heard to-day are as familiar to me as household words in my own county. My people are not strangers to you in blood. There are many amongst us who are bone of your bone and flesh of your flesh. My own mother was a Pennsylvanian, and some portion of the love we bear our mother is always very naturally transferred to the soil from which she sprung. My grandfather was for many years a resident of this State; he had the command of a Pennsylvania company in the battle of Brandywine, fought not far distant from this spot, was shot down in that bloody encounter, and carried in his body to the grave the British lead which he received on that day.

In that valley resided a noble and glorious son of Pennsylvania—a man of the temper and intellect of Luther—bold, original, and reforming, and suited by his genius to grace alike the pulpit or the plume of battle. I mean General Peter Muhlenberg—a patriot of the Revolution; a man who as early as the 16th of June, 1774, announced at a public meeting in Woodstock the great principles, and foreshadowed the results, of the Declaration of Independence, and who shed, by his early career, a military halo over the fame of Virginia, and by his declining life, a civil glory over that of Pennsylvania.

I must, even at the risk of being regarded tedious, relate an incident in the life of this extraordinary man, which is not generally known. At the commencement of the revolutionary war he was a clergyman of the Lutheran church, his father having been the founder of that church in America. In December, 1775, Virginia called for six additional regiments. Peter Muhlenberg and Patrick Henry were commissioned as colonels—the only two civilians to whom regiments were assigned. Muhlenberg gave notice to his congregation of his intention to deliver his farewell sermon in Woodstock. The day came, and with it an immense concourse of his friends and admirers, for all in that valley were such. At the close of an eloquent sermon he recounted the dangers which threatened the liberties of his country, and the obligations which devolved upon every man to unsheath his sword in the cause of freedom. He told them, in the language of Holy Writ, there was a time for all things—a time to preach, and a time to pray—but that these times had now passed; and then, in a voice that reached the hearts of all who heard him, and which re-echoed through the church like a trumpet blast of war, he exclaimed, that "there was a time to *fight*, and that time had now come." Then throwing aside his clerical gown, he stood before them in the full uniform of a Virginian colonel—a girded warrior ready for battle. He ordered the drums to be beat at the church door, and there was formed, in that valley, the celebrated 8th regiment of Virginia—or, as it was more commonly called, the "German Regiment of Virginia," which continued in service until the close of the war, and became one of the most distinguished in the revolutionary army.

Muhlenberg, subsequent to the war, removed from the valley of Virginia to Pennsylvania, and represented your State in the House of Representatives and Senate of the Union, and filled other important offices. I learn to-day from his relative, a member of the committee who so politely escorted us from Philadelphia, and who, if he lives, is destined to be your representative in the next Congress—having, as I learn, been nominated by the democratic party by acclamation—that he has now in his possession the original flag of this German Regiment of Virginia. Precious relic! may it continue to inspire in your bosoms the noble patriotism which animated those who so often carried it aloft amidst the storm and carnage of battle.

Your distinguished President has referred to me as being the representative of a portion of the Tenth Legion of Virginia democracy.

In the centre of that great valley there are some three or four prosperous and densely populated counties, which were originally settled almost entirely from this State, and to a great extent from this county. Although not elected as a democrat, but as an INDEPENDENT CANDIDATE, I have the honor to represent upon the floor of the House of Representatives two of those counties. Like yourselves, your descendants in that valley are almost wholly and exclusively democratic. A whig as naturally perishes there as a sucker caught in one of your beautiful streams would perish if thrown upon its bank. Since the days of Thomas Jefferson, those counties have been called the Tenth Legion of Virginia democracy. And well have they been so called, for this has been the Tenth Legion of the mighty Julius of democracy,—the Imperial Guard of Napoleon,—the reserved corps which has never yet failed to turn back the tide of disaster and defeat, and to achieve certain and secure victory. Even in 1840, when the republic seemed to reel and totter under the maddening and intoxicating influence of political frenzy,—when democratic Pennsylvania bowed her head, Virginia stood firm; but she stood firm solely by virtue of this Tenth Legion of her democratic army. My friends, I do not know whether that term is applied to you here, but in my State the county of Berks is familiarly known as the Tenth Legion of Pennsylvania democracy. Can't you propose it to yourselves to acquire a fame as imperishable as that which attaches to your descendants in Virginia? Can't you resolve that Pennsylvania shall never again bow her head in a blind and heedless enthusiasm for mere military renown? A thousand times has the taunt been repeated by your enemies from lip to lip, "Pennsylvania is safe for Scott; Pennsylvania has never yet cast her vote against a military candidate; stick up a man in uniform, put epaulettes upon his shoulders and a plume in his cap, and dub him a general, and all Pennsylvania will follow at his heels." This is the language of taunt and sarcasm in which whigs have indulged, and which has led your Johnstons and your Stevens to propose for your acceptance for the office of President of the United States *the Commander-in-Chief of your Regular Army*. Now, that General Scott does possess real solid, substantial, distinguished military merit, is not to be questioned by me. And it is only a subject of my most profound regret, that such exalted military fame should be seized upon by unprincipled demagogues and knaves, as the means to advance their own selfish and mischievous purposes. But it is for you, my fellow-citizens, to teach these blind advocates of gunpowder availability that they have miscalculated your intelligence and firmness; that you can distinguish between military merit and civil qualifications, and give to each their appropriate rewards; and that in rejecting and repudiating the claims of Winfield Scott for the Presidency, surrounded, as he unhappily is, with the foul miasma of Abolition, you do so, not because you respect the Cæsar of war less, but because you love Rome and her institutions more.

What has given to the democratic party its present commanding power and influence in this confederacy? What must ever make it the predominant party, so long as it continues faithful to the principles upon which it was originally founded by Jefferson and Madison, of Virginia, and by the two Muhlenbergs—par nobile fratrum—Rush, Dallas, Leiper, Lieb, and others, of your State? Your enemies ascribe its power to causes not very flattering to human nature, nor very honorable to American intelligence and patriotism. But examine its history from 1798 to the present hour, and you will find that the true secret of its strength is to be found in its sacred observance of the limitations, the guarantees, the letter and spirit of our great federal compact. I do not mean to say that within that period there have not been departures—very wide departures—from the true latitude and longitude of constitutional interpretation. But I do mean to say that the democratic party have sought to make the constitution the polar star by which the vessel of State should be steered through the stormy ocean of politics; and whilst the winds of faction, and the occasional mutiny of a portion of the crew, have sometimes driven it from the true line of its direction, it has not been long before it had corrected its log, and placed the old ship, in the language of Mr. Jefferson, "on the true republican tack." We are told in the *Holy Scriptures* that the gates of hell shall not prevail against that church which is built upon the rock of living and eternal truth. And so I say. Build your party upon the rock—the solid, unchanging, and adamantine rock—of your constitution, and the storms of faction, of federalism, and of free-soilism, will dash in vain against its base.

This constitution was the work of great and illustrious men—of men of mighty intellects, of tried patriotism, of exalted public virtue. It bears upon every page of it the breathing of a divine power, moulding with consummate skill the destinies of the greatest republic on earth. It was made at a period when the heart of the nation was purified from all selfishness, and when all its pulsations responded to the true glory and happiness of the people. It took time to perfect it—it required sacrifices from all sections to mature it—and when finally adopted, confusion and chaos hid their heads, and it emerged above the horizon as a second sun in the heavens, diffusing light and heat and gladness over this continent.

Gentlemen, there are provisions in that great national covenant under which you of the North have prospered in commercial, in manufacturing, and in agricultural wealth, beyond any example in the records of the human race. And while we of the South have not prospered in commerce, or manufactures, or agriculture, as you have done, yet there are provisions in that instrument under which we of the South have expected to find quiet and repose, domestic tranquillity and peace.

It is known to you, gentlemen, that there existed at the formation of our Union, in most of the Northern and in all of the Southern States, the institution of African slavery. With you it was regarded but as a temporary interest; with us it existed in such numbers, and was so intimately interwoven with all our social habits, as to have acquired the character of a fixed and permanent institution amongst us. It is not for me here to inquire how and by whose capital and enterprise slavery was introduced amongst us. It is sufficient for you and me to know that it did exist, and that the great patriots and statesmen of that day had to consider it deeply and profoundly in arranging the terms of our national compact.

Now, two of the fundamental principles agreed upon by our fathers in arranging the basis of our Union were—

1st. That each State should remain sovereign and supreme in all matters relating to its own local concerns, and should be the sole and exclusive judge of its own domestic policy; that no power beyond the limits of that State should interfere, directly or indirectly, with its own local and peculiar institutions. This threw upon the people of each State the sole responsibility for its own domestic policy, and relieved the federal government, and the people of all other States, from any responsibility whatsoever in regard to it. And the people of Massachusetts and the people of Pennsylvania have no more right to interfere with the sort of labor which we choose to use in Virginia than we have the right to prescribe to you that you shall use mules instead of your fine Conestoga horses, or the Angora goats, in place of sheep.

But there was another principle agreed upon no less important than the first—and it was this: that inasmuch as our slaves might readily escape into the free States, a power should exist somewhere that would enable us to reclaim them. This power might have been left to the States in which the fugitive sought an asylum, and certainly every principle of good neighborhood, of fraternal sympathy, and of international courtesy, would have required and justified its exercise by the States. But it was deemed most expedient to devolve that authority upon the national government, because its jurisdiction was co-extensive with the limits of the whole Union; because it was a government in which the South could be represented, and upon which it could rely for a faithful enforcement of the stipulation, and because it thereby relieved the anti-slavery feeling of any particular State from all responsibility of action in the matter.

Now, of the vast and overshadowing importance of this provision of the federal compact to the South no reflecting man can entertain a doubt. It is not the mere money value of the slaves who escape into the free States which has aroused the united action of the South on this question. It is the fact, well known to us, that if such a provision did not exist in the constitution, and was not faithfully enforced, a spirit of insubordination would very probably be infused into our slave population that would lead to the most fearful and tragic consequences. Let no man, then, suppose that when the South assumes the position which she has done on this question, she is governed by any mere consideration of dollars and cents. She is acting upon the solemn conviction that upon the faithful execution of this plain and express guarantee of the constitution depend her domestic tranquillity and peace. And we are forced to regard all men in the free States who stimulate opposition to the fugitive slave law, and who seek to frustrate and nullify its provisions, as not merely violating an express obligation of the constitution, but as seeking to enact that "*drama of blood*" which Governor Johnston, in his earlier and better days, charged to be the purpose of those who sought to embarrass the legal rights of the slaveholder. We are compelled to regard all such persons as enemies to the South, and as enemies to the Union. [Cheers.]

We of the South do not ask you gentlemen of the free States to love the institution of slavery, or to think of it otherwise than as you think proper. We have never made any such demand upon you. We have never claimed to exercise any such constraint over your opinions. It is the false allegation—the false issue which the enemies of your peace and my peace, and the peace of the Union, make for the purpose of stimulating sectional agitation for their own vile and nefarious purposes. All that we ask of you, gentlemen, is to act upon this question as sound patriots and as honest men. We ask you to love and obey the constitution of your country. We ask you, as honest men, to accord to us those rights which our great national covenant secures to us, and which we have purchased with a price. We ask you to maintain the principles of that federal Union which was framed by your fathers and mine—by patriots who, shoulder to shoulder, had poured out their best blood in the war of our Revolution. We ask you to discharge with fidelity the great national obligations which you have assumed to discharge, and which you *cannot* refuse to discharge without heaping dishonor and infamy upon the memory of your patriotic ancestors, and committing moral treason against the constitution of your country. Is this asking more than we have a right to expect? [Cries of No! no! from the crowd—you shall have it!] I know, gentlemen, we shall get it from the northern democrats. But I fear I should look in vain for any such response from northern whigs.

Now, one of the great and distinguishing features between the whig and the democratic parties of this State—at least since my attention has been specially drawn to the inquiry—is, that whilst the whig party of your State has been seeking to gain power by pandering to anti-masonry, native-Americanism, and to all those crude and uninformed anti-slavery prejudices that may be so easily aroused in every human bosom in those States in which the institution does not exist and cannot be known, the democratic party of the North, and more particularly of your State, has manifested a fixed and determined purpose to oppose itself to this unwise and dangerous agitation, to stand by the constitution, and to preserve inviolate the rights secured by that instrument. The just, patriotic, and constitutional course of the democracy of Pennsylvania has been fully observed and gratefully acknowledged in the South.

It was for this reason, amongst others, that so large a portion of the South has of late years directed its attention to a great and distinguished statesman of your commonwealth—that gentleman who presides this day with so much dignity over your meeting. [Cheers.] The feeling of confidence which Virginia cherishes for the democracy of Pennsylvania was forcibly illustrated in the recent national convention held at Baltimore. Pennsylvania's favorite son was Virginia's unchanging choice. For thirty-three successive ballots, and until all hope of the accomplishment of her wishes failed, Virginia presented an unbroken front for your noble and glorious son, James Buchanan. [Cheers.] And richly did he earn the compliment thus bestowed upon him. His gigantic intellect, his long and distinguished public services, his uniform respect for the guarantied rights of the South, his fidelity to the constitution, his love of the Union, had designated him as one worthy of the most exalted honors of this republic. [Cheers.]

Now let me illustrate this distinctive difference between the two parties in Pennsylvania by a reference to a few facts.

We of the South are in the habit of regarding the position of parties in the North upon the fugitive slave law, as presenting an infallible test of constitutional orthodoxy. And why? Because it is a plainly-written provision of the constitution—clear, distinct, positive—admitting of no evasion or equivocation; and the man who would nullify that provision, would strike down the whole instrument whenever it suited his purpose. Again, because the Supreme Court of the United States has solemnly announced that the act of 1793 was delusive and inefficient for the objects contemplated by the constitution, and that we were entitled to a full and adequate remedy from the national government. Now, I maintain that any party that would throw itself in direct opposition to the plain requirements of the constitution of the United States, and in opposition to the solemn adjudication of the highest judicial tribunal in the land, and do so, for the purpose of waging a reckless and unprincipled warfare against our peace and happiness, cannot be expected to command much of *our* respect and confidence, and ought not to command the respect and confidence of any portion of the country.

Let us, then, for a moment look at the course of the two parties upon this great and vital question.

In the Senate of the United States not one single *northern whig senator* is found to vote for the passage of the bill.

In the House of Representatives it received the vote of *one* solitary whig member from the northern States, and two whig members from the northwestern States.

But this would lead me into too extensive a field of inquiry. My object is to examine the course of parties in this State, and to that I will for the present restrict myself.

You had two Senators in Congress—Daniel Sturgeon and James Cooper—the first, a democrat; the second, a whig; Sturgeon, the democrat, voted for the bill; Cooper, the whig, against it.

In the House of Representatives, the same state of things was exhibited. Of your twenty-four members, every whig whose vote was recorded—and ten are so recorded—was found in opposition to the bill. Every democrat whose vote stands recorded, is found in support of the bill.

There was, as usual upon exciting test-questions, some *dodging*; but that would seem to have been principally confined to whigs, as I would infer, at least, from a pretty coarse practical joke perpetrated by Thaddeus Stevens, of your State—himself a whig, and as appears on the pages of the *Congressional Globe*.

After the passage of the bill, Mr. Stevens rose and suggested to the Speaker to send a page and notify the *whig* members of the House that the Fugitive Slave Bill had been disposed of, and that they could now come back into the Hall. (Laughter.)

Look also to your own State legislation and State action. After the Compromise measures passed, the democratic party proceeded in good faith to facilitate their execution, and to bring the whole weight and power of their party to maintain and uphold them. In your State conventions and county conventions you declared:

Resolved, That the democratic party of Pennsylvania are true to the Union, the Constitution, and the laws, and will faithfully observe and execute, so far as in them lies, all the measures of compromise adopted by the late Congress for the purpose of settling the questions arising out of domestic slavery; and this, not only from a sense of duty as good citizens of the Republic, but also from the kind and fraternal feelings which they cherish towards their brethren of the slave-holding States.

Again, at a subsequent convention the following resolution was adopted:

Resolved, That the democracy of Pennsylvania will maintain with fidelity and energy the faithful execution of the Fugitive Slave Law; and that we pledge ourselves to use our best efforts to secure the speedy repeal of such portions of the "State Obstruction Law" as deny the use of our jails for the detention of fugitives from labor while awaiting their trial, or in any other manner interfere with the constitutional rights of citizens of our sister States, in relation to their property.

Most nobly have you redeemed your pledges to the constitution and to your southern brethren. Early in 1851 you did, in opposition to the unanimous vote of the whig party, pass through both houses of your General Assembly an act repealing the most obnoxious sections of the unconstitutional obstruction law of 1847. But your sound and patriotic purposes were, for the time, frustrated by the veto of Wm. F. Johnston, the whig Governor of your State. Did you pause in your patriotic exertions here? No! You nailed the flag of the constitution to your mast-head, and took an appeal to the people of Pennsylvania. You re-affirmed your declaration to maintain the constitutional rights of the South. You nominated the gallant Bigler as your standard-bearer, and you made a direct issue with your opponents on this question. What was the result? Why, that result which always follows a faithful observance of the constitution. The abolition forces were routed. The constitution was maintained, and democracy was triumphant; and the repealing law, which Johnston vetoed, was again passed by a democratic legislature against a solid whig vote, and approved by a democratic governor.

Now what was the course of the whig party during all this time? Why, the very reverse of yours. They were for overthrowing the constitution, whilst you were nobly maintaining it.

Why, gentlemen, in the whig convention which assembled in July, 1852, and which nominated Scott for the Presidency, and Johnston for Governor, the following resolution was submitted for its adoption, and voted down by an overwhelming majority:

Resolved, That the provisions of the constitution in reference to the rendition of fugitives held to service or labor demand, and *shall receive from our party*, a faithful, manly, and unequivocal support.

This was voted down in a whig convention of this State, by an overwhelming vote. Mark its language! It is not that the provisions of the *Fugitive Slave Law* passed by Congress, but that *provisions of the constitution*, shall receive their support; and this resolution was voted down by the whig party of Pennsylvania! thus exhibiting the spectacle of infernal fiends assaulting the very citadel of Heaven—the very constitution of the land itself.

Now, gentlemen, you may see the force and bearing of some remarks embraced in Mr. Fillmore's last annual message to Congress. I will read you a few lines from it, and you will see how he impales these moral traitors before the public gaze:

"Some objections have been urged against the details of the act for the return of fugitives from labor; but it is worthy of remark that the main opposition is aimed *against the constitution itself*, and proceeds from persons and classes of persons, many of whom declare their wish to see that constitution overturned. They avow their hostility to any law which shall give full and practical effect to this requirement of the constitution.

"*Cases have heretofore arisen in which individuals* have denied the binding authority *of acts of Congress*, and even States have proposed to nullify such acts, upon the ground that the constitution was the supreme law of the land, and that those acts of Congress were repugnant to that instrument; *but nullification is now aimed, not so much against particular laws as being inconsistent with the constitution as against the constitution itself*, and it is not to be disguised that a spirit exists, and has been actively at work, to rend asunder this Union, which is our cherished inheritance from our revolutionary fathers."

Is it surprising, when you look to the respective opinions entertained by the whig party of Pennsylvania, and by Millard Fillmore, that he should have received, in fifty-four ballots, but one single vote from the whig party of your State in the late National Convention? It can surprise no one.

Perhaps one of the most striking illustrations of this distinguishing characteristic between the northern whig and democratic parties is to be found in the course of William F. Johnston, late whig Governor of your State. You will thus perceive how the same man may perform the functions of a political chameleon, and reflect through his transparent skin the color and complexion of the party to which he at the time belongs.

In 1837 Governor Johnston was a democrat, and a member of the House of Delegates of Pennsylvania, from the county of Armstrong. On the 27th of January, of that year, a petition was presented to the House, praying the Legislature to grant the trial by jury to fugitive slaves. How did the democratic representative of the county of Armstrong then meet this proposition? He denounced it in the following just and appropriate remarks. I can only take a short extract from his speech:

"Suppose, sir, we would legitimately act upon this prayer of the petitioners, (giving the right of trial by jury to slaves,) would it be politic in this House to do so? By the original compact between the States, Pennsylvania has recognised the right of the southern man in the property of his slave; and she has no right to pass laws which would embarrass the recovery of his property. Can the owner of the slave be expected to undergo the delays of a jury trial, the procrastination of the law, and the expense incident thereof? *It would almost amount to a positive prevention to the recovery of his legal right*, and particularly when we take into consideration the fact, that in many of the counties of the Commonwealth a large and respectable portion of the citizens have *conscientious scruples* upon the subject of slavery, which would most effectually prevent the recovery of the slave. It appeared to him, that if such an act were passed, it would virtually amount to the emancipation of every negro who might be fortunate enough to escape the pursuit of his master and put his foot in Pennsylvania. *Such action would be the first act in that drama of blood which some men appear to be so anxious to bring upon the country*. Let these infatuated and misled philanthropists pursue their own course, but he confidently hoped this House would refuse to endorse their errors."

Now, what was the course of this same Wm. F. Johnston in 1850 and 1851, after he had abandoned the democratic party, and when he stood forward the embodiment and representative of Pennsylvania whiggery? Is it not as notorious as any fact in the history of your

State politics, that, as the whig candidate for the office of Governor, he denounced the fugitive slave act in the most unmeasured terms, from one end of the State to the other, and especially the feature denying a jury trial? It has been well said, what is to be thought of that religion which worships a monkey for its God? And I say, what is to be thought of that party in your State which now seems to breathe only through the nostrils of Wm. F. Johnston? Gov. Johnston cannot plead ignorance as an apology. His speech in 1837 shows that he had a full perception of that "drama of blood" which he was so zealously struggling to see enacted upon our southern soil, and that he was, with his eyes open, and with a clear view of the consequences of his act, perpetrating a violent outrage against the constitution of his country, and against the peace of his brethren of the South. [Immense cheering.]

How strikingly in contrast with the course of Governor Johnston was the conduct of his democratic predecessor—the lamented Gov. Shunk—and has been that of his democratic successor, Governor Bigler.

In the summer of 1847 I had several slaves stolen from me, which were carried to Pennsylvania. The slaves were very promptly returned. I made a demand through the Governor of Virginia upon Gov. Shunk, of Pennsylvania, for the surrender of the fugitive from justice, upon the sole and exclusive charge of his having committed a *felony*, under the laws of Virginia, *in stealing my slaves*. In a similar case from Virginia, I well know that Governor Seward, of New York, had declined to comply with the demand, and for reasons fatal to the peace of the country. I did not know much of Governor Shunk; and as he was then in the midst of an excited canvass for the office of Governor, I thought it quite likely that he would resort to the usual delays of temporizing politicians, and, like Governor Johnston, keep my demand in his *breeches-pocket* until after the election. But I soon found that Gov. Shunk (eternal honor to his memory) knew his constitutional duties, and had the firmness to discharge them. In other words, I soon learned that he was a democrat; and as rapidly as the mail could carry my letter to him, and his reply to me, I received a warrant from him under the seal of your State, and with his bold and manly signature appended to it, calling all the civil and judicial officers of your State to *arrest the felon*. [Cheers.] I gave myself no further concern about the fugitive, as I was sufficiently satisfied in seeing the constitution of the country so nobly vindicated by a democratic Governor of Pennsylvania, and the atrocious doctrines of Wm. H. Seward rejected and discountenanced by an authority equal in intellect and far superior in political virtue to his late excellency the Governor of New York.

Mr. Faulkner here proceeded to state his objections to the election of General Scott. He had none to his private or to his military character. He was prepared to concede to him all the qualifications of a gentleman and of a successful and distinguished military leader. His objections were wholly political. He was the candidate, and as such was forced upon the country by that portion of the northern whig party which had for years been making capital by the agitation of the subject of slavery, and by warring against the constitution and the rights of the South. Scott was emphatically a sectional candidate. His election would give a new and vigorous impulse to that Abolition feeling which presented a topic of greatest danger to the permanency of the Union. If Scott was personally sound, it would not be in accordance with human nature to suppose that he could throw off the influence of those who elevated him to the office of President of the United States. If elected, he must know he will be indebted for that honor to the anti-slavery sentiment of the North. Amongst that party he must find his confidential friends and advisers. Under him, they must acquire influence and power. His destiny and theirs are inseparably connected, and it is idle for any man to suppose that he can elect Scott without giving a commanding power to Seward, Johnston, and all that class of politicians who have lived upon the pernicious agitation which they have for years been fomenting.

The whigs of the North had dealt treacherously with the whigs of the South. Under the pretension that they were the conservative constitutional party of the Union, they have succeeded in inducing many honest and patriotic men of the South to combine with them. They had used the South to promote their selfish and mercenary schemes, so far as the powers of the federal government could be stretched to promote them. But when the first occasion occurred to manifest whether they had any real respect for the constitution, or any sympathy with their southern brethren, they proved false to the constitution and to the South. They voted in a body against recognising rights solemnly secured to us by the plain language of the compact. Scott is now before the country, the creature, the representative of the same sentiment of feeling of the North. It is manifest, from the exhibition of the last several years, that the South can alone find any security for its rights in a firm and cordial alliance with the democracy of the North.

The democracy, guided by that overruling Providence which seems to prosper all its measures, and to connect in one destiny *its* triumphs and the glory of our common country, has selected a ticket which I can support with my whole heart. Unambitious of office, and yet ready to obey his country's call, in peace or war, whenever the public good demands it, Franklin Pierce dreamt as little of the high destiny which now awaits him, as Cincinnatus whilst toiling at his plough. No nomination in the present condition of the country could have been less liable to any sectional or personal objection, and none could have been hailed with more universal favor by the country. By birth and residence a northern man, the South has unbounded confidence in him, because his whole public career indicates a statesman of the most enlarged and comprehensive American feeling. To use his own emphatic declaration, he knows "no North, no South, no East, no West, under the constitution, but a sacred maintenance of the common bond, and a true devotion to the common brotherhood."

This has been called the canvass of "falsehood and frauds," and such it truly has been. Without resorting to falsehood, what could be said against Franklin Pierce? At first he was charged with being a drunkard; but that soon sunk into the kennel of loathsome and forgotten calumnies. Then he was charged with intolerance to his Catholic fellow-citizens; but these very Catholics promptly rose *en masse*, with their reverend pastor at their head, and pronounced the statement false.

Then came the Foss fabrication, but that has now sunk to the tomb of the Capulets. The whigs have one fact left, and upon that they exhaust all the powers of their wit and eloquence. "General Pierce fainted on the battle-field of Churubusco!" Well, gentlemen, the fact is so. We can't deny it. General Pierce did faint on the battle-field of Churubusco; and yet the man who could reproach him with that fact is destitute of an American heart in his bosom, and is no better than a Mexican dog. It is the proudest incident in the military history of Franklin Pierce. Hear what General Scott and General Pillow say. [Mr. F. here read the official accounts of the action from the despatches of Scott, Pillow, &c.]

And this is the incident that is made the subject of whig jest, of whig wit, and of whig buffoonery. General Pierce is not the first brave man that ever fainted upon a battle-field. Messena—the brave Marshal Messena—he whom Napoleon called his right arm—whom history has styled the favorite child of victory—whom poetry and song have chaunted as the thunderbolt of war—fainted upon one of the bloodiest fields of his fame, and from the same causes that caused General Pierce to faint—pain and bodily exhaustion; and if the whigs will have it so, let history then designate Pierce as the fainting Messena of the Mexican war—as one whose gallant spirit led where his frail, diseased, and worn-down body could not follow; and believe me, gentlemen, if poetry or painting shall ever do justice to that historical scene, it will paint the prostrate body of the wounded and exhausted soldier stretched upon the ground, whilst his gallant spirit will be seen to hover over the smoke and carnage of battle, cheering his comrades on to victory, and sighing that it cannot mingle in the dread affray.

One word more, and I am done. As I told you in the opening of my remarks, I came here to see with my own eyes, and to hear with my own ears, how far the democracy of Pennsylvania mean to stand by the constitutional rights of the South. I know what politicians have said, and I know what conventions have said; but I wish to hear from the people themselves what they have to say. When I return to Virginia—to the bosom of my own constituents—shall I be able to tell them that fidelity to all the guarantees of the constitution is, and continues to be, a cardinal principle of democratic faith? ["You may—you may!" came from a hundred voices in the crowd.] That you will never cease to war with the whigs of your State, until every right secured to us by that sacred compact is fully recognised and enforced? [We will! the constitution must be preserved!" declared several voices from the crowd, to which the whole meeting responded.] Then, gentlemen, I go away satisfied. I have an answer, not from politicians or conventions, but from the great masses of the people themselves, and you have furnished me an armor more impenetrable than the sevenfold shield of Achilles. [Mr. Faulkner took his seat, when three cheers were given for the speaker and the Tenth Legion of Virginia democracy.]

SPEECH

OF

HON. JAMES C. JONES,

OF TENNESSEE.

DELIVERED IN THE UNITED STATES SENATE AUGUST 9, 1856.

Mr. JONES. Mr. President, I am indebted to the kindness and courtesy of the Senate for allowing me the privilege of addressing them to-day. As I announced a few days ago, it is not my purpose to attempt to enlighten the Senate upon the subject of the resolution now pending. My object is a wholly different one; and I feel that I owe to the Senate a debt of gratitude for the permission extended to me to be heard to-day.

Mr. President, in a letter addressed to my constituents in April last, I made them the following pledge:

"Left, as I am, to decide for myself what I ought to do in view of all the difficulties that lie in my way, fully impressed with the responsibility that rests upon me, I have calmly surveyed the whole ground, and my judgment is deliberately formed. I shall stand where I am, just as I am, and wait the coming of future developments. We have before us the names of the candidates of the American party and their principles. I shall wait and see who the Democratic party will present to us, and what principles they proclaim. When the candidates are all before us, I will cast my vote for that man and with that party which I think most likely to protect the constitution, preserve the Union, and drive back the horde of Northern vandals who seek to usurp our rights, and finally to possess themselves of the citadel of liberty. For the present I have but one political ambition—but one active, absorbing, political principle: ambitious to be an humble agent in preserving our rights, protecting our honors, and forever crushing out and annihilating these disturbers of the peace, invaders of our rights, and traitors to the constitution; to be one of the humblest in the accomplishment of this, is all I ask—it would be glory enough for me."

I now propose to redeem that pledge, as far as I may, trusting that the results will inure to the honor of our country, to its peace, safety, and prosperity.

Never, since the formation of this government, have we witnessed such a state of political affairs as now exists. Never was there a period in the history of this government which more imperiously demanded the exercise of a cool and dispassionate judgment, than the present. Never were our institutions surrounded with more difficulties. Never was there a crisis so full of danger, demanding the exercise of a larger or purer patriotism than the present.

Since the inauguration of this great experiment of self-government, we have been called to pass through many trying scenes—trials that filled the heart of the patriot with emotions of the deepest solicitude for the safety of the country, and the success of this greatest, and it may be, last effort for the establishment of a government predicated upon the will of the people, subject to the requirements of the Constitution and laws of their own creation. Amidst these trials the hearts of the stoutest have sometimes sunk within them, and nerves hitherto unstrung, have trembled for the safety of the country.

But, thanks to a kind, beneficent Providence—thanks to the self-sacrificing patriotism of our ancestors, we have passed these fearful trials, and *we yet live.* We are now surrounded with difficulties far greater, far more portentous, than our fathers were ever called to meet. Will that same kind Providence preside over us, to direct and preserve us? Will the same spirit of concession, patriotism, and devotion to the country, mark our present course and efforts, as illustrated those of our fathers? This is a momentous question, submitted to each and all of us, to every patriot, to every one who loves his country more than party or self. On the solution of this question hangs the last hope of freedom. All the great and happy results that ought to flow from the labor, toils, and anxieties of our fathers, are suspended on the decision we are called to make.

That the dangers that surround us are imminent cannot be disguised. In view of these dangers the question is, how shall we avert them; how shall we dissipate the gathering storm; how restore peace to a distracted country, and concord and brotherly love between members of this great family of States and individuals? This is a field that invokes the energies of the wisest and best. This is a cause invoking the efforts of the highest and purest patriotism. Although the signs are portentous of evil; although the clouds are dark and gathering swiftly; although the hope of the patriot may sink within him, all seeming dark and gloomy, and the way of escape not clearly discernible, yet I do not despair. I will "hope on, hope ever." I will hope against hope—hope to the last.

I put my trust in the same Providence—in that same patriotism that has rescued us heretofore, and hope that I shall yet see the clouds and darkness that now overshadow our political heavens dispelled, and the sun, the bright sun of peace, concord, and brotherly love, dispelling the gloom and shedding its rays of hope and confidence and love throughout the land, filling the hearts of all with gratitude and joy.

To accomplish so great a result requires the efforts of every patriot. How shall this be accomplished? This is the great question to which I would address myself to-day.

Never, since our national existence, have we witnessed so strange a condition of things as is now presented to our minds. We are on the eve of another presidential election, and each and all of us are required to take our position and play our part in the coming contest. There are three regularly nominated candidates in the field, from whom an election is to be made to fill the chief executive office of the government. Who are they? What are they? What do they propose? I propose briefly, Mr. President, to inquire into these three questions. It is known to you, sir, that I do not belong to either of these parties or political organizations; and the question propounded to himself by the great statesman of Massachusetts, on an occasion of similar difficulty, has a thousand times presented itself to my mind—"Where shall I go?"

Belonging to neither of these parties, never expecting to belong to either of them, I might, yielding to the counsel of my feelings, stand off as a silent spectator; and such would certainly be my course if there was nothing more involved in the contest than the triumph of one party or another—a mere struggle for power and place. But believing that there are questions involved of vital importance to the preservation of the constitution and perpetuity of the Union, I am constrained by considerations of duty and patriotism to waive the suggestions of my feelings, and bear my part in this contest in such manner as in my judgment will best promote the peace of the country, preserve its honor, and perpetuate our institutions. I cannot be indifferent if I would, and would not if I could. There is too much involved in the struggle—interests too holy to be disregarded or treated with indifference.

I have said that there are three candidates presented to the country; one of whom, unless there shall be a departure from the contemplations of the Constitution, must be called to preside over the destinies of the country. I have asked who they are, what are they, and what do they profess? Taking them in the order in which they stand, of seniority, I may ask, first, who is James Buchanan? It is not necessary for me to stop to inquire into the personal history and character of Mr. Buchanan. He has been identified with the history of this country for almost half a century. His public acts are known to all men. Whatever he is, whatever he has been, is matter of record. With him, as James Buchanan, therefore, I have nothing to do; but he is the candidate of the Democratic party, he has been selected by their convention as their standard-bearer, and is presumed to be the exponent of their principles. I proceed to inquire what those principles are.

The Democratic party have given to us and to the world a platform of principles. I have no great confidence in platforms. I think that, generally, they are cunningly-devised schemes of modern invention, intended to catch votes and to gull the people. They are admirably adapted for a presidential canvass—very good for the candidates to run by and swear by; but often very easily forgotten after the election. For this reason I confess that, generally, I have had but little confidence in platforms. I prefer to judge of the men who profess to stand upon them, rather than to inquire particularly into the creed they proclaim. Inasmuch, however, as the various candidates have been placed upon their platforms, it is but just to them—it is but just to the parties which have presented them, that we should presume, at least, that it is their honest purpose to stand upon them, and to observe them. I desire, very briefly, to inquire into these platforms in order that I may satisfy my constituents and my country that I have not been guided by passion or prejudice in the conclusions at which I have arrived.

The Democratic convention, which assembled at Cincinnati, presented to the country a platform of principles. They re-endorsed the platform of 1852, filled very much with truisms that nobody ever controverted, or ever will controvert; but they were intended to have their effect on the popular mind. With all that I have nothing to do. I examined that platform in other days which are passed and gone. All that it is necessary for me now to say is, that I dissent much from it; but upon the main point in that platform it had then, as it has now, my concurrence, because it was identical in fact, in essence, and in substance, with the platform of the party to which I then belonged, to which I now belong, and to which I intend to belong as long as I belong to anything—the old Whig party. Upon the great vital question of the rights of the South and the equality of the States, or, in other words, the great question of slavery, the Democratic and Whig platforms of 1852 were identical in every essential. It is not necessary, therefore, for me to consider that large portion of the Cincinnati platform which is simply a reiteration of that of 1852. Some additions, however, have been made to it. Going on with the tide of time, and the progress of the age in which we live, the Democratic party have felt it to be their duty to make additions to their old platform; and it is to these additions that I now desire to call the attention of the Senate and the country. The first to which I direct your notice is in the following words:

"*Resolved*, That the foundation of this union of States having been laid in, and its prosperity, expansion, and pre-eminent example in free government built upon, entire freedom in matters of religious concernment, and no respect of person in regard to rank or place of birth, no party can justly be deemed national, constitutional, or in accordance with American principles, which bases its exclusive organization upon religious opinions and accidental birth-place. And hence a political crusade in the nineteenth century, and in the United States of America, against Catholic and foreign-born, is neither justified by the past history or the future prospects of the country, nor in unison with the spirit of toleration and enlarged freedom which peculiarly distinguishes the American system of popular government."

This resolution asserts a principle which, in my judgment, must commend itself to the heart of every patriot. It asserts the great principle of universal freedom of conscience in matters of religion, and that there shall be no proscription predicated upon a man's birth-place or religion. I do not pretend to say that any person whatever is amenable to the charge of interfering with these sacred rights. I am not here to assail or to denounce, but to approve and condemn; and, as this resolution finds a response in my heart, I readily yield to it the suggestion which that response requires. I maintain the position here, and can maintain it elsewhere, that, whatever gentlemen may profess—whatever articles they may insert in their creed, if there be any American nationality, if there be an American Constitution broad enough to shield every American citizen wherever he may be, at home or abroad, upon the land or the sea, this resolution will stand the test of time.

I come, Mr President, to consider the next resolution in this *addenda* to the Democratic platform—this codicil to their old will and testament. It is in the following words:

"*Resolved*, That claiming fellowship with, and desiring the co-operation of, all who regard the preservation of the Union under the Constitution as the paramount issue, and repudiating all sectional parties and platforms concerning domestic slavery, which seek to embroil the States and incite to treason and armed resistance to law in the Territories, and whose avowed purposes, if consummated, must end in civil war and disunion; the American Democracy recognise and adopt the principles contained in the organic laws establishing the Territories of Kansas and Nebraska, as embodying the only sound and safe solution of the 'slavery question,' upon which the great national idea of the people of this whole country can repose in its determined conservatism of the Union—NON-INTERFERENCE BY CONGRESS WITH SLAVERY IN STATE AND TERRITORY, OR IN THE DISTRICT OF COLUMBIA."

In this resolution, in my humble judgment, is comprised the whole issue now before the country. I am called on either to affirm this resolution or to enter my protest against it. What does it propose? It asserts the great doctrine of the equality of the States. Is there an American Senator here who will assume, or pretend to maintain for a single moment, that the equality of the States is not right beyond controversy and dispute? This resolution goes further, and asserts the principles contained in the Kansas-Nebraska bill. What are those principles? It is not necessary for me to attempt to enlighten Senators on that point. They are known and read of all men; but I am not left to conjecture and to construction as to whether squatter sovereignty is in it. I come to the resolution itself, and I find there the construction given by the Democratic party to be this "non-interference by Congress with slavery in the States and Territories, or in the District of Columbia."

The attempt being made before the country to-day is to assert and maintain that Congress has jurisdiction over the question of slavery, not only in the Territories, but in the District of Columbia. I maintain that they have no such jurisdiction. Is there a Southern man here, is there a constitutional man here, is there a national man here who will maintain that Congress has the power to abolish slavery in the District of Columbia? I know there are those upon the floor of the Senate who maintain this doctrine, but I deny their nationality or their constitutionality. This, then, is an addition to the platform of the Democratic party which commends itself not only to my head but to my heart, because it goes home directly to the preservation of the rights of my constituents, and the honor of those who are dearer to me than life itself.

I come now to the next resolution presented by the Democratic party, and which is the real issue:

"*Resolved*, That we recognise the right of the people of all the Territories, including Kansas and Nebraska, acting through the legally and fairly-expressed will of a majority of actual residents, and whenever the number of their inhabitants justifies it, to form a constitution, with or without domestic slavery, and be admitted into the Union upon terms of perfect equality with the other States."

In the three resolutions which I have read, the principle is asserted, that a State has a right to admission into this Union with a constitution prohibiting or allowing slavery, as her people may choose to elect. Is there a man here who controverts that? I regret to know that there are some who do. But is there a southern man prepared to controvert it? If there is, let him stand up and present himself to the country. Is there a man who recognises the rights of the States, according to the compact under which we live, who can maintain that any other restriction shall be placed upon the State asking admission into the Union, than that which is prescribed by the constitution itself? But one single condition is prescribed by the wisdom of our fathers, and that is, that the State desiring admission shall have a constitution republican in its form. Now, we are told, that it is competent for the Congress of the United States to reject a State, not on account of this constitutional inability, or a want of conformity to republican institutions, but because the people of that State, in their wisdom, or it may be in their folly, elected that slavery shall exist there. This is one of the great issues before the country on which the Republican party, as they term themselves, have taken their stand, and upon which the Democratic party have planted themselves. Which is right, and which is wrong? Who is able to stand here and maintain that, if Kansas shall present herself with a constitution recognising the right of her people to hold slaves, she shall not, under the federal compact, be admitted to her place in the States of this Union? There are here gentlemen who controvert that point; but surely no southern man—no conservative, national man—can object to the Democratic party on that ground. They maintain it; they assert it; and I accord with them in it.

The next resolution, in the additions of the Cincinnati convention to the platform of 1852, is in these words:

"*Resolved*, That our geographical and political position, with reference to the other States of this continent, no less than the interest of our commerce and the development of our growing power, requires that we should hold as sacred the principles involved in the Monroe doctrine: their bearing and import admit of no misconstruction; they should be applied with unbending rigidity."

This is, I believe, the first time in the history of parties in this country when any party has asserted, as one of the principles of its creed—one of the planks of its platform—the so-called Monroe doctrine. My honorable friend from Kentucky, [Mr. Thompson,] for whom I cherish feelings not only of the greatest confidence and respect, but of kindness and affection, in addressing the Senate a few weeks ago, entered his protest against the Democratic party on account of this resolution affirming the Monroe doctrine. I will read for the benefit of the Senate what my honorable friend said on that occasion:

"Again: one resolution of the Cincinnati platform adopts the Monroe doctrine. I know that the Monroe doctrine, as explained by Mr. Calhoun, amounted to nothing, but was a mere temporary thing, suggested by Mr. Canning, the English Prime Minister, to Mr. Monroe, and carried out only in reference to its bearing on the then revolutions progressing in the South American States; but still, as generally interpreted, taken in its popular understanding, in the latitude in which the people construe it, it is a virtual declaration of war against the whole human family."

I think my friend from Kentucky is a little mistaken. He claims to be a Whig, as I do, and to be now standing upon the Whig platform, maintaining all the principles of the Whig party; and yet he enters his solemn protest against the Democratic party because of the assertion and maintenance of the Monroe doctrine. I propose, very briefly, to look into the Monroe doctrine and its history. I have heard a great deal of it; the Senate has been enlightened upon it time after time; and I am not so vain as to presume that I can add anything to the stock of wisdom now existing in the Senate. My friend from Kentucky maintains that, as understood by the country, this doctrine is a declaration of war against the whole world. If that be the Monroe doctrine, I am against it. I read from Mr. Monroe's message of December 2, 1823.

"We owe it, therefore, to the country, and to the amicable relations subsisting between the United States and those Powers, to declare that we should consider any attempt on their part to extend their system to any portion of this hemisphere as dangerous to our peace and safety."

How can that be tortured into a declaration of war against the world? How can it be tortured into the idea that it is but the precursor to the conquest of all the continent or which we live? To suppose so is a stretching of terms, a perversion of language, not authorized, in my judgment, by the plain words employed. Here is a simple declaration, that we should regard the extension of the European system to this continent as dangerous to our peace and our safety. It has been said, and I believe that is the sentiment of my friend from South Carolina, (Mr. BUTLER,) for whom I cherish the profoundest respect, that this Monroe doctrine is not to be construed as of general or universal application, but is to be considered in regard to each case as it presents itself. I do not care in what sense you take it; I am for it when applied to isolated individual cases; I am for it when applied to every foot of land on the American continent. I grant that it originated first in a disposition upon the part of this government to arrest the interference of the Holy Alliance with the affairs of South America; but why shall it not be of universal application? Is the principle in itself right? I maintain that it is. Why not, then, have the nerve and the manliness to say to Europe—"We plant ourselves upon this American principle, and we will maintain it against the whole combined power of Europe in regard to every acre of land in America?" Why not? You say it is to be considered, when the question arises, as applicable to individual cases. Let us look at it in that light.

Take the island of Cuba, and suppose that England should enter into negotiations to purchase Cuba, would my honorable friend from South Carolina, or any other senator upon this floor, be willing to see the island of Cuba pass into the possession and dominion of England? If there be a senator who would be willing to see England purchase Cuba, let him rise and answer. There is not one. Then the Monroe doctrine is true and just, and eminently American, when you apply it to Cuba. Suppose, next, we apply it to Mexico. Would you be willing to see Mexico pass into the possession and under the control and dominion of England? If there is a senator here who would be willing to see that, I call upon him to rise and say so. There is not one. If it is applicable to Cuba and to Mexico, why may it not be general and universal in its application? Would you be willing to-morrow to recognise the possession, by England, of Nicaragua, or any of the Central American States? If there is a senator here who would consent to that, let him answer. There is not one. Then go to South America. Name a State that you are willing that England shall possess. There is not one. Thus we have traversed the whole continent; and I maintain that the Monroe doctrine is of universal application, because there is no senator who will assume to say that there is a single spot on this continent which he will be willing to allow England to take possession of. Have we not grown large enough to assert our rights? Have we not power, and strength, and manliness enough to say what we feel? I am for saying what I feel, and always feeling what I say. I am in favor of the Monroe doctrine applied to isolated cases, or applied universally throughout the whole American continent.

My distinguished and honorable friend from Kentucky seemed to think this was eminently a democratic doctrine. I deny it. In the name of the old Whig party, that you are told is dead and buried, but which I believe will have a glorious resurrection some of these days, and in the name of its champions and leaders, I deny that the Monroe doctrine was a democratic doctrine. It was an American doctrine, and no more the doctrine of the democratic party at the time it was proclaimed than of every other party in the United States. Now, let us see. The name of Mr. Clay is invoked to sustain gentlemen in their positions. I am not here to pronounce the eulogy of Mr. Clay. That has been done. He sleeps his last sleep; and forever damned be he who will rudely disturb his ashes or tarnish his memory! But, sir, I maintain that this Monroe doctrine had the assent and approval of Mr. Adams and Mr. Clay at the time it was promulgated. When gentlemen talk to me about standing by the doctrines of Henry Clay, I ask them to stand by them. I will stand by them, live by them, and die by them. You all remember that, when Mr. Adams was President of the United States, and Mr. Clay his Secretary of State, a proposition was made to send ministers to the Panama Congress. The President of the United States was called upon by Congress to assign his reasons for proposing to send ministers to this Congress. What reason does he assign? He assigns the reason contained in Mr. Monroe's message, the establishment of the Monroe doctrine. Here is his message; and he quotes the identical language of Mr. Monroe to sustain the wisdom, the patriotism, and the Americanism of the Congress of Panama. Mr. Clay was Secretary of State at the time. Then, I call on the friends of Henry Clay to stand by the Monroe doctrine, for he was for the Monroe doctrine before there was any such organization as the present Democratic party.

But, Mr. President, we come down to later times. Have we not spent weeks and weeks in the last four years—in what? In vindicating our construction of the Clayton-Bulwer treaty. If there is a Senator on this floor who is willing to yield the American construction of that treaty, I challenge him to rise now and stand up and say so. Every man in the Senate has stood firmly, honestly, consistently, persistently, and patriotically in defence of the Clayton-Bulwer treaty as we construe it. What is that? It is nothing more nor less than the assertion of the Monroe doctrine, and its application to Central America.

Then you all stand to the Monroe doctrine—at least so far as Central America is concerned; and by your silence, your refusal to answer, you stand before the world in favor of its universal application.

The next resolution in the series of the amendments of the Democratic party is in the following words :

"*Resolved*, That, in view of so commanding an interest, the people of the United States cannot but sympathize with the efforts which are being made by the people of Central America to regenerate that portion of the continent which covers the passage across the inter-oceanic Isthmus."

I regret that my friend from Kentucky dissented from that sentiment. He declared that it was the endorsement of the government of William Walker. If it was intended to do that, I, as a Tennesseean, the land that gave birth to Walker and myself both, tender to the Democratic party the gratitude of my heart. If they meant by that resolution to endorse Walker, I owe them, as I give them, my sincerest gratitude. But, sir, frankness compels me to say that I do not so read the resolution. What does it profess? It simply professes a sympathy with the struggle going on for the establishment of free and liberal institutions in Central America. Oh, that the shade of Henry Clay might preside over us! What American citizen who ever read those burning words of patriotism and liberty which fell from the lips of Henry Clay in defence of liberty everywhere, and particularly in defence of the liberty of South America, expressing not only his sympathy for her, but urging this government to proclaim her independence,—what citizen, I ask, can claim to be a disciple or follower of Henry Clay, that will not accord his sympathy to the struggle now going on in Central America for free institutions? The Democratic party was a little too cautious for me in that. I would prefer they had gone further ; but I am to take them as they are. I say they express their sympathy, and I accord with them in that expression. I myself, being responsible to nobody, to no party, and I thank Heaven nobody being responsible for me, choose to go further than that. They not only have my sympathy, but my prayers for their success. I yet hope to see the banner of liberty and freedom streaming from the mast of every vessel there, and the name of William Walker, the savior of that country, inscribed upon it.

Sir, I have heard William Walker denounced on the floor of the Senate, and I desired then to vindicate him, but the occasion forbade. Now, I have to say, that those who chose to denounce William Walker as a plunderer, a marauder, a pirate, do that which they have no right to do. I know him. He was born and raised in my State—the son of as honest a man as ever breathed the breath of life ; his mother as honest a woman as ever Kentucky gave birth to. Tell me that a man thus born, thus reared, thus educated, is a plunderer? It is a vile, unmitigated calumny. When you were struggling for your liberty, La Fayette, Pulaski, and others, came here to aid you in your struggle. Did you announce to the world that they were plunderers and pirates? No, sir. Their names are now canonized and held dear in the heart of every true American patriot, for doing precisely what Walker is doing. Yet you glorify the one while you condemn and anathematize the other. I trust and believe the time will come when justice will be done to the motives and deeds of this man ; and when, instead of being denounced as a plunderer and murderer, he will be hailed as the savior of his country, and generations yet unborn rise up to call him blessed!

But, Mr. President, I pass from that, and come now to the consideration of the platform of the American party, being the second in the series ; and I must be permitted to say, that, like all other platforms I have ever seen or read, it is made up very much of truisms and facts and principles that no human being controverts. I believe it says the Bible is a very good school-book. Who denies that? I believe it says the constitution ought to be maintained. Who denies that? That the Union ought to be preserved? Who controverts that? So, like other platforms, it is made up of truisms to catch the votes of the people. But I come to that which is real and substantial and tangible in the platform. The first point is :

"V. A radical revision and modification of the laws regulating immigration and the settlement of immigrants ; offering to the honest immigrant who, from love of liberty, or hatred of oppression, seeks an asylum in the Uuited States, a friendly reception and protection, but unqualifiedly condemning the transmission to our shores of felons and paupers."

To that extent I am an American. I think, to every extent, I am really an American ; but in the political sense in which this thing is construed, I am an American. I will go as far as he who would go furthest to prevent the introduction of criminals and paupers here. I have so announced at all times. Why, I ask, have they not sent from the other branch of Congress a bill to that effect? The majority of that House were sent here as Americans ; and why have they not asked us to endorse it? I proclaim to the world I am for that doctrine ; but I maintain that it is a question outside of the jurisdiction of the federal government. I believe the States have the power, and are now exercising that power. In my State we have a law under that exact clause, saying that free negroes shall not come into the State. Is not that exercising jurisdiction over that subject? I do not know of a single State which is not to-day exercising that power. It was but a few months ago, I believe, that, from Boston, they sent back some paupers and criminals, or refused to permit them to land. If the power resides with the State, why put it in the creed? Why call on the federal government to interpose, if the States have jurisdiction? If the States have not jurisdiction, the federal government has; and if it be decided that the federal government has it, I will go as far as any friend of the American party. But, sir, their next resolution is:

"The essential modification of the naturalization laws."

I am for that. I believe it is the interest and duty of this government to revise and amend the naturalization laws. I do not believe that there is any largely organized party in this country that is not in favor of it. The extent of that remodeling and reorganization is a different thing. How far I might be willing to go will depend on the facts which may be elicited by investigation. If it shall be found that five years is too short—and I think it is—I will agree to extend it to eight, to ten, to twelve, to any number of years that may be found necessary to protect us, to guarantee to us, to secure us all the benefits conferred by the Constitution in that clause giving us jurisdiction over the subject of naturalization. Then there is no controversy between the American party and myself on that subject.

Another of their resolutions is in the following words:

"VIII. Resistance to the aggressive policy and corrupting tendencies of the Roman Catholic church in our country, by the advancement to all political stations, executive, legislative, judicial, or diplomatic, of those only who do not hold civil allegiance, directly or indirectly, to any foreign power, whether civil or ecclesiastical, and who are Americans by birth, education, and training, thus fulfilling the maxim, 'AMERICANS ONLY SHALL GOVERN AMERICA.'"

If I correctly construe and interpret that, I find no great objection to it. But I maintain that religion and politics have no connexion, and there should be no test made by blending religious questions with civil and political ones. But, as they circumscribe their terms here, and make them applicable to those who acknowledge allegiance to some foreign potentate and power, if there be any such, I would apply it to them, and I would go outside of Americanism itself; I would take up all such men upon one single act, for carrying out that purpose. I would try them for treason; because it is treason, and nothing else. It is moral treason, it is political treason, for a citizen of the United States to hold allegiance to any foreign potentate or power. Therefore I do not think there is any very great controversy on this point. If there is any such class, in the name of Heaven exclude them from office—exclude them from your country; I do not want them here, in any shape or form.

These constitute the political items contained in that platform, and I do not object very much to them.

Thirdly and lastly, as regards platforms, I come to the platform of—shall I call you Republicans, gentlemen? If you consider it more courteous, I will call you Republicans, for the sake of decency, and nothing else. The Republican party have presented to the country a platform, and they have placed their man upon it. Now, what is that platform? In part, just like the two I have noticed, it contains a great many things that nobody would controvert and every one believes; but it contains one, and but one, single and isolated principle—and what is it? Opposition to the Kansas-Nebraska bill and all its principles; in other words, opposition to slavery here and elsewhere, now and forever.

Well, sir, I heard a Senator, on the day before yesterday, say, on this floor, that he did not like to trust his temper to speak on this subject of Kansas. I thought it was the most Christian sentiment I ever heard from him, and I have improved upon it, and I will not trust myself to talk much upon that question to-day, because I do not know that I can talk about it quietly and dispassionately, or according to the rules of the Senate; and I have made up my mind never to violate the rules of the Senate if I can help it. If I find it necessary to violate them, I will postpone it until I get outside of these walls. As I do not mean to violate them intentionally, I had better forbear to speak what I think of this party, and particularly of its leaders.

But, Mr. President, as I have said, the real issue before the country, as I understand it and believe it to exist, is upon the Kansas-Nebraska bill. I ask the attention of the Senate to the resolution passed by the American party in their council, or convention, on this subject, in the following words:

"And regarding it the highest duty to avow their opinions upon a subject so important in distinct and unequivocal terms, it is hereby declared, as the sense of this national council, that Congress possesses no power under the Constitution to legislate upon the subject of slavery in the States where it does or may exist, or to exclude any State from admission into the Union because its constitution does, or does not, recognise the institution of slavery as a part of its social system; and expressly pretermitting any expression of opinion upon the power of Congress to establish or prohibit slavery in any Territory, it is the sense of the national council that Congress ought not to legislate upon the subject of slavery within the Territories of the United States, and that any interference by Congress with slavery as it exists in the District of Columbia would be a violation of the spirit and intention of the compact by which the State of Maryland ceded the District to the United States, and a breach of the national faith."

To that I object. Against that I enter my solemn protest before the people of Tennessee and the country. The issue is fairly made by the Republican party, that Congress has the power to prohibit slavery in the Territories. The Democratic party have come up boldly, openly, and manfully, and asserted that Congress has no such power. The American party say, we *pretermit* any expression of opinion on that subject. What do you mean by the term "pretermit?" What does it mean, according to lexicographers? It means to pass by, or omit. Then you omit to declare any opinion upon the great and vital question now before the country, as to whether Congress has power to prohibit slavery in the Territories. I maintain that Congress has no such power. The Kansas-Nebraska bill maintains that Congress has no such power. The Democratic party maintains that Congress has no such power. Why pretermit that? If you may pretermit an opinion on a vital question of that sort, what will be the result? Suppose a question arises whether Congress shall abolish slavery in the District of Columbia, may you excuse yourselves before the world by saying "we pretermit any opinion on that subject?" Mr. President, if they may pretermit an opinion on a great vital question of this sort, affecting the rights of the people of the South, they may upon every question. If you were to ask them whether Congress should abolish the slave-trade between the States, they might stand back and say, we pretermit any opinion on that subject. In my humble judgment the time has passed for the pretermission of opinion. The time is when men should stand out boldly and openly and proclaim their position. It is eminently so on this delicate question, affecting the rights of the people of the whole South.

But, Mr. President, there is something more in this term "pretermission" than seems to be implied. When Mr. Fillmore himself comes to speak, what does he say? He says, speaking of the repeal of the Missouri compromise:

"This repeal seems to have been a Pandora's box, out of which have issued all the political evils that now afflict the country, scarcely leaving a hope behind, and many, I perceive, are ready to attribute all these to our southern brethren. But is this just? [No! no!] It must be borne in mind that this measure originated with a northern senator, and was sustained and sanctioned by a northern President. I do not recollect that ever a petition from a southern State solicited this repeal; and how could southern members of Congress refuse a boon thus offered by the North to the South? It could only be done by sacrificing themselves upon the altar of their country for their country's good; and this is certainly expecting too much from political men in times like these. The blame, therefore, it appears to me, with all due deference, is chiefly chargeable to those who originated this measure; and, however we may deplore the act, it affords no just ground for controversy with our southern brethren—certainly none by which they should be deprived of their political rights."

I entertain no unkind feelings towards Mr Fillmore. I believe that if he were President of the United States he would make a conservative, a safe, and a national President; but I do protest against his pandering to northern fanaticism as he does in the extract which I have just read. He there denounces the repeal of the Missouri compromise, and charges to it all the evils now afflicting the country To that extent I join issue with Mr. Fillmore himself. I voted for it; and if those who did so are responsible for all these evils, I am willing to bear my full share of the responsibility. Why go out of the way and assail us, and charge that all the evils which now afflict the country have grown out of the repeal of the Missouri compromise? Is he not to that extent giving aid and comfort to the Republican party? Is he not to that extent striking a blow upon every man who voted for it? Take that in connexion with the resolution of pretermission, and then take another circumstance within my knowledge, and the impression is fixed upon my mind that the American party do not mean to stand firmly and fully by the Kansas-Nebraska bill.

In my own State, I see evidence, strong and conclusive, that they do not mean to justify the repeal of the Missouri compromise. My colleague and myself differ on that question. I have never sought to make an issue with him, or with any of my colleagues in the House, who differed with me on that occasion, believing them to be as honest as I knew myself to be; but I proclaim here and to the world, that, if war is to be made upon me by indirection, here or elsewhere, in consequence of my support of the Kansas-Nebraska bill, I am ready to meet it, here or elsewhere, now and forever. Mr. Fillmore had no right to say this. He was not called to bear his share in that battle. He chooses to pronounce sentence of condemnation on me, who have shed more drops of sweat for him than he ever did for himself; he charges me as one of the authors of the evils which now afflict the country. It is unjust; it is cruel; it is ungenerous. But, sir, I am held up to the Clay doctrine. I wish everybody could stand by it as firmly as I do. I maintain the doctrine of the Kansas-Nebraska bill, that Congress has no power over the subject of slavery in the Territories, or in the District of Columbia, or anywhere else. What did Mr. Clay think about it? He sleeps the long, last quiet sleep of repose, in his own beloved State; but yet his burning words live to speak for him. What does he say?

"I deny that the general government has any authority whatever from the constitution to abolish what is called the slave-trade, or, in other words, to prohibit the removal of slaves from one slave State to another slave State." * * * * * *

"No power whatever was granted to the general government in respect to domestic slavery, but that which relates to taxation and representation, and the power to restore fugitive slaves to their lawful owners."—*Mr. Clay's Speech of February* 7, 1839.

Let the voice of the sage of Ashland rise and rest upon the hearts of those who constantly invoke his name. He says the constitution gives no power over the subject of slavery except upon the three isolated points to which he alludes. Then he says Congress has no power to prohibit slavery in the Territories. Now, if you are the friends of Henry Clay, and his words have any force and meaning with you, stand by them, or else in shame forever seek not to invoke his name.

Mr. President, I have gone through with these pretermissions, and I come now to another question; and, as it is personal to myself, I regret exceedingly to trouble the Senate with it—I mean personal, so far as my own relations are concerned. The question is constantly propounded to me, why I cannot support the American party? I have given some reasons; but I would like to ask the question, why I should do so? I have often answered my friends in that way. When you ask me why I cannot support Mr. Fillmore and the American party, I ask you why I should do it? What claims have they on me as a Whig? You tell me you are still Whigs. You have abandoned that party and gone into a new organization.

There is not only no reason why I should support you, but there is an insuperable objection to my doing so, when I find that in your own declaration of principles you say—

"The American party having arisen upon the ruins and in spite of the opposition of the Whig and Democratic parties, cannot be held in any manner responsible for the obnoxious acts and violated pledges of either."

How, in the name of departed and sacred memory, can you call upon me as a Whig to stand by you, when you have already proclaimed to the world that you have risen upon the ruins of the only party that I ever knew to love? I never fought under any other banner. And, sir, next to the star-spangled banner of my country, the old Whig banner was endeared to my heart. You have torn down that banner; you have torn it from the mast-head, where it was nailed by Henry Clay and Daniel Webster; you have trodden it under foot; and then turn and say to me, "Come over and join us." No, sir; never. Let other rude hands do the deed, but may God palsy this arm before it ever tears down that flag! You have torn it down, and the Black Republicans of the North have stolen it, and run off with it; and now, in the South, men are called to bury it, and you turn to me, and ask me to join you. If you have risen on the ruins of the Whig party, stand on those ruins; but you will never get me to stand with you. If you have risen on those ruins, and despite their efforts, go on with your triumphs, if they have any joy for you. They have none for me.

But the cruelty does not end there. Was it not enough—though I suppose a large majority of you were once members of the old Whig party—to go off in peace, with the conviction that you were doing your duty, without sending an arrow in the bosoms and hearts of those who remained true to their faith? Why inflict still deeper wounds on us when we were already bleeding at every pore? Why taunt us with saying, "We have risen on your ruins, and despite your efforts?" But the cruelty is not yet refined!

"We cannot be held in any manner responsible for the obnoxious acts or violated pledges of either"—

not only standing upon our ruins, but writing the epitaph upon the stone that marks our fall, "violated pledges!" I maintain that Henry Clay never violated a pledge. I maintain that the old Whig party, in its purity and in its honesty, never violated any pledge. Yet, sir, these are your denunciations. We who stand by the integrity of that old Whig party are called upon, on the pains and by the penalties of denunciation and proscription, to go over and join the party that thus wrote our epitaph. I never can do it.

No man living feels more deeply, more acutely, more painfully than I do, the separation from friends who have stood by me in the hour of darkness, when the shafts of calumny were hurled from a thousand sources—who, when all the batteries of Democracy, with their envenomed darts, were hurled at me, were ready to throw themselves into the breach to protect me. Would that I could sacrifice myself to save them; but I cannot do violence to my own conscience by concurring in the doctrines that they preach to the American people. I would go to any length of personal sacrifice. I would give up everything but my convictions of honor and public duty to concur with them, if I could. I can never concur with them in this crisis; it is impossible that I can. I wish to God that I could! I know my own comfort, my own political safety, if I sought it—everything of ease, requires it. But, Mr. President, I have spent anxious hours, and, if one so unworthy as myself may be permitted to say so, prayerful hours, in trying to come to the point of concurrence with those old friends whom I love and mean to love and honor; but I have not been able to do it.

I am willing to believe they are honest; I know most of them are. All I ask is—and I do not expect the poor boon to be accorded to me—that I may receive the same charity which I extend to others; but I do not even hope for that. I have made up my mind calmly; I have made up my mind deliberately with my convictions of duty. I would rather maintain my own self-respect by a faithful discharge of duty in the retirement of private life, than stand in power and place. I am separating myself from most of my friends, or rather, they have separated from me. I do not know but one public man in the State of my old associates who concurs with me. I know I am separating from those who have cherished me—who have loved me—who have delighted to honor me, and I have delighted to return all their kindness. I have served them honestly and faithfully, and with all the ability I possessed; I could no more. I say to Democratic senators, and to Democrats everywhere, you owe me nothing—nothing—nothing; I ask nothing in return; I expect nothing, and want nothing. I am an old-line Whig; and, in voting with you, it is not because I love Democracy, but because I hate Black Republicanism. I love my country; and I believe the safety of the country depends on the success of the Democratic party at this time. I have made up my mind, I say, to this course. I know that it may be the end of my political existence. Be it so; the world will never be the loser; and all that I ask is, the poor privilege of gathering around me as I fall my old mantle of the Clay Whig party, and die in peace; and when they come to write an inscription on my tomb, let them say, "He lived true to his principles, and died defending them."

But, Mr. President, I have said that I intended no injustice to Mr. Fillmore. I believe he would make a safe and conservative President, and I should consider the country safe in his hands. If I believed that Mr. Fillmore could be elected—if I believed that he was a stronger man than Buchanan, with all my conviction of the injustice he has heaped upon us, I should not hesitate to vote for him; but has he any chance of success?

I submit it to the calm deliberation of the Senate, has Mr. Fillmore any chance of election? What prospect has he? The most sanguine friends of his with whom I have talked, claim the following States: New York, Delaware, Maryland, North Carolina, Kentucky, Tennessee, and Missouri. Suppose he should receive all of them, what would they amount to? Eighty-nine electoral votes; sixty minus of an election. But is there a sane man in the world who believes that Mr. Fillmore can get all of these States? I am taking the most favorable view that can be presented. In my judgment, I say honestly, there is not a certainty of his getting any one of them. Not a single one of the States which I have enumerated is sure for Mr. Fillmore. He may carry some of them; he may carry all of them; but if he should carry all of them, that does not make his election. If the signs of the times are to be credited, he stands a poor chance of carrying any of them. If he cannot be elected by the people, what will be the result then? Will he fare any better in the House of Representatives? Remember that the present House of Representatives has to make the election. How many States has Mr. Fillmore in the present Congress? Just three, and no more; Delaware, Maryland, and Kentucky. These are the only States Mr. Fillmore has in the present House of Representatives; and they are to choose a President, if the election goes before them. Now, in the name of justice and common sense, does anybody suppose these three States will be able to attract to them States enough to make an election? No man can think that. Then, I argue, that Mr. Fillmore has no reasonable chance of success.

Hence, the question is, whether Mr. Fremont or Mr. Buchanan shall be elected? That is the issue; and I have conversed with my friends in regard to it. Some of my interviews are very pleasant, and some painful; for whatever my faults may be—and Heaven knows they are numerous—I believe nobody ever charged me with a want of devotion to my friends. They meet me, and ask the question, "Is it possible that you are going to vote for Buchanan and Breckinridge?" I have said to them, it is possible. They ask me,

How is it? Can it be possible that I, who, from my earliest political existence, have been making war upon Democracy, can vote the Democratic ticket? I have ever opposed the Democratic party. I would not withdraw a single blow I ever gave them; and if the old issues are ever revived, and I am living, I shall be found maintaining them. My friends say to me, "How is it possible you are going to vote for Buchanan?" Now, Mr. President, will my friends permit me to ask one question, or, in Yankee phrase, to answer them by asking another? Inasmuch as I am in the minority, they ought to answer the question at once. Tell me how you reconcile yourselves to vote for Andrew Jackson Donelson? When you answer that, I will answer yours. You are taking to your confidence a man born, reared, and educated in the Democratic faith; raised at the feet of the political Gamaliel; taught to despise and contemn Henry Clay and every Whig in the nation. You find no difficulty whatever; but with perfect complacency, with perfect self-satisfaction, you can vote for Andrew Jackson Donelson; and when I talk about voting for Buchanan and Breckinridge you say, "In the name of Heaven, how can you do it?" I do it as a choice of evils. I do it, as I said before, not because I love them, but because I believe the interest and honor of the country now demand their election; and you, who are swallowing Andrew Jackson Donelson, cannot say one word to any man. You are taking the medicine in broken doses; but I would rather take a full dose at once. I prefer, if I have to take the medicine, to take it all at once. That is the difference. If I were talking to my friends in Tennessee, I would ask them how they took a great many men whom they took there last year? Why, sir, many of them were conceived in Democratic sin, and brought forth in political iniquity, and yet they could swallow them; and now they say to me, "In the name of Heaven, how can you vote for Buchanan?" I confess it is difficult, and I do not disguise it. My old political friends, by abandoning the Whig party, have forced the necessity on me of choosing between evils. As a freeman, I make the choice, and take all the responsibility that attaches to it.

But then they say Mr. Buchanan has antecedents which will not do. I expect he has; but where will you show me a man who has been twenty, or thirty, or forty years in the public councils of the country, or in politics, whose antecedents you can trust? You say Mr. Buchanan's antecedents will not do. I do not like some of them; I am against a great many of them; and if you get on the old track, and give me such a man as Henry Clay, I will oppose him again. But if you go into Mr. Buchanan's antecedents, how would you like to have Mr. Fillmore's examined? He has not been quite as long—not so many years—in politics; but both of them have enough sins to damn them altogether, if antecedents alone are to be relied on.

Then, that is not a safe rule to swear by. You must take the men by what they are now, what they profess now, and the amount of confidence you repose in them. There are one or two things about Mr. Buchanan which they say are rather hard to swallow. They say Mr. Buchanan once declared that, if there was a drop of Democratic blood in his veins, he would let it out. Now, that is a beautiful argument to make to me! I have been trying all my lifetime to let the last drop of Democratic blood out of the body-politic, and it is no objection with me to Mr. Buchanan that he said, if he had any Democratic blood in his veins, he would let it out. It is rather a recommendation to me, because it proves to my mind that he was once right. You had better make that argument to somebody else; make it to Democrats, to whom I have made it several times; and I have asked some Democrats, How can you vote for him, as he is not Democratic? [Laughter.] But you say if he was not Democratic, he was a Federalist.

Then I am obliged to take him either as a Federalist or Democrat. If I were forced to the issue between the two, I should be in a close place. I have no such objection to Federalism as some. I am not a Federalist myself; I do not believe in their doctrines; I think they were extreme in some things; but I do say, and am ready to say here and everywhere, that I believe the old Federal party was as honest a party as ever lived. I believe that Washington himself was called a Federalist, and I know that Hamilton was; and I should not be ashamed to be classed with such men. Hamilton was a Federalist; he at least was honest, and the government of the United States have paid a deserved compliment to Alexander Hamilton, to his patriotism, and virtues, and acknowledged ability, by publishing his works and distributing them in the country.

That is no objection to Mr. Buchanan. I do not care whether he was a Federalist or not. But then you say—and this is the point to which I wish to direct the attention of the Senate—Mr. Buchanan ought not to be voted for by me, as I profess to have been a friend of Mr. Clay during his lifetime, and to cherish his memory now that he is dead. Why not? They say that Buchanan, if not the author, was the propagator of the vile old calumny, in 1824, of bargain and intrigue.

Mr. President, pending the question as to who should be the candidate of the Democratic party, I expressed my opinions freely, and said to some gentlemen now in my presence, that I had understood (I had not investigated it) Mr. Buchanan had failed to do Mr. Clay justice, and, unless that question were cleared up, I would never vote for Mr. James

Buchanan, though he might be nominated by a thousand conventions. I repeat to-day, that if I believed Mr. Buchanan had originated, or even circulated, or given countenance to, that old vile calumny, I would not vote for him. It was on that account, not having investigated it, that I said to the friends of Mr. Buchanan, "If you nominate him, I do not think I can vote for him. I will certainly not vote for him unless I can be satisfied on that question." It was on that ground, in part, that I preferred the Senator from Illinois. I am glad he is not in his seat. I preferred that he should be nominated. Why, sir, did I prefer him? Because I had seen him here standing up, day and night, vindicating the rights of my constituents. I had seen him standing here, as Leonidas at Thermopylæ, to vindicate and maintain the interests and honor of the people of the South. I had seen the arrows in showers hurled at him, and I had seen him bare his proud bosom to the storm in vindication of our rights. I now predict that the time will come when passion and prejudice shall sleep, when the South will do honor to STEPHEN A. DOUGLAS. [Applause in the galleries.] I predict the time will come when a returning sense of justice will rally around his standard, or, if not around his standard, at least around his name and memory, to say, "There was a man who dared to die for others." Who has received so much of slander, and calumny, and detraction, as STEPHEN A. DOUGLAS? And for what? In the name of all that is grateful on the part of the South, I conjure them—hate him, despise him as you may, for other things—do him justice for the noble, manly, gallant, fearless, undying devotion, which he has manifested in defence of the rights and honor of the South. I preferred him on that account.

But, sir, to return to Mr. Buchanan and this charge of bargain and corruption. I repeat, I have examined this question faithfully, thoroughly, and honestly, and I say here that I will make the record so plain in my judgment that no fair man will ever controvert it. I repeat, that if I believed he was guilty of any participation in that calumny, I would never, never support him. I have seen it said in some newspaper that the very bones of the sage of Ashland would move in their dull cold resting-place at the idea of Whigs like me voting for Mr. Buchanan. Well, sir, if all that ever was said by Andrew Jackson Donelson was contrasted with what Mr. Buchanan said against Mr. Clay, and if the bones would move at the name of Buchanan, the spirit itself would burst its cerements and rise in judgment against those who are ready to elevate to power and place Andrew Jackson Donelson. I have the records here about that bargain, intrigue, and corruption charge.

Mr. Clay voted for Mr. Adams in 1824 for the Presidency, and thereupon Mr. George Kremer published a communication in some Pennsylvania newspaper saying that there had been a corrupt bargain between Mr. Clay and Mr. Adams. Mr. Clay was then a member of the House of Representatives. With his wonted boldness, gallantry, and integrity, he at once demanded an investigation, and a committee was appointed. Mr. Kremer was summoned to present his proofs; and Mr. Kremer retired to his dark chamber of calumny, like Judas Iscariot, and never attempted to make good his charge.

But afterwards it was renewed by General Jackson, or an intimation made, that the bargain had been proposed to him by a distinguished member of Congress, and it was said that Mr. Buchanan was that member of Congress. As soon as the charge was made, Mr. Buchanan published a letter in reply to General Jackson, in which he says: "It is not so; I never approached you to make any corrupt bargain. I never was authorized by Mr. Clay or his friends to approach you." There was the result of that publication.

I hold in my hand a book, and it is a very important book, written in 1831, a few years after these things transpired. And by whom was it written? By one of the most gifted and talented men in this nation—George D. Prentice, of the Louisville Journal. Mr. Prentice was the confidential friend of Mr. Clay, and his biographer. When the facts were fresh before the country—when they were fresh in the public mind—what did Mr. Prentice say in his biography? A thing that is to live after Mr. Clay, and Mr. Prentice, and all, all of us are consigned to the final resting-place of our fathers, as the solemn record—the history of the life and character of the most illustrious statesman that ever lived. What does he say? Let us read. Mr. Prentice says:

"Not satisfied with private hints and declarations, Mr. Clay's distinguished accuser [General Jackson] finally stated, in a public letter, that overtures of a bargain had been made to him, during the pendency of the Presidential election in the House of Representatives, by the friends of Mr. Clay. With his usual promptitude of character, Mr. Clay demanded through whom those overtures had been made. In reply, General Jackson gave up the name of Mr. James Buchanan, one of his own personal and political friends. Mr. Buchanan, however, was an honorable man, and hesitated not to say, publicly, that he had never made to General Jackson the overtures in question, or any that bore the least resemblance to them."

Now, if you were trying Mr. Buchanan before an impartial tribunal, I ask you, would you not hold that to be testimony—at least prima facie? Here is Mr. Prentice, an eminent man, a man of superior talents, the warm personal and political friend of Mr. Clay, his biographer, who a few years after the transaction says Mr. Buchanan, like an honorable man as he was, came out promptly and denied the whole thing. Yet you tell me I ought not to vote for Mr. Buchanan because of the charge of bargain.

I am not done, sir, with this charge. Allow me to read you a letter, dated Lancaster, August 27, 1827, only two years after this charge :

"MY DEAR SIR : Yours of the 9th instant came to hand last night. The one by Mr. A. I received a few days since by private hand, from the county of Harlan. With your letter of the 9th, Mr. Buchanan's response to the hero was received. This answer is well put together. As they say in Connecticut, 'there is a great deal of good reading' in Buck's reply. It is modest and genteel, yet strong and *conclusive.* I am truly delighted with the manner in which B. has acquitted himself. I really feared and believed he was placed in such a dilemma by the General, that he could not extricate himself with any sort of credit. But he has come forth victoriously. I am greatly gratified with the result, and must believe it will have a happy effect upon the presidential election. It is impossible it should turn out otherwise. Virginia, after this, will not—cannot support the General. I never had the least hope of Virginia until now.

"I presume Buck's reply supersedes the necessity of any reference to the conversation in my room. I am glad of it."

Who do you suppose wrote that letter? Robert P. Letcher, the warm personal and political friend of Mr. Clay; a man who enjoyed his confidence to an extent equal to any man in the Union. When the facts were all fresh before him, Mr. Letcher wrote that letter, in which he says Mr. Buchanan has come out, and is fully acquitted. Now, I ask you—I ask any honest man to tell me how you can resist the testimony of two such devoted personal intimate friends of Mr. Clay as Mr. Prentice and Mr. Letcher, given at the time these things were being investigated? Is that not enough to satisfy the *gourmand* appetite of calumny? But I do not rest it there. I have more than that. I want to show what Mr. Clay says; and if you will not believe him now, you would not believe him though he should rise from the dead. What does he, the only man who had a personal interest in the matter, say? Here is a letter addressed to Mr. Francis Brooke :

"WASHINGTON, *August* 14, 1827.

"MY DEAR SIR : I received your obliging favor from Waynesborough. I should be very glad if I could participate with you and Mr. Southard in the pleasure and benefit of the springs. My health is, however, not bad.

"I hope you are not mistaken in the good effect of my Lexington speech. Mr. Buchanan has presented his communication to the public; and, although he evidently labors throughout the whole of it to spare and cover General Jackson, he fails in every essential particular to sustain the General. *Indeed, I could not desire a stronger statement from Mr. Buchanan.* The tables are completely turned upon the General. Instead of any intrigues on my part and that of my friends, they were altogether on the side of General Jackson and his friends. But I will leave the statement to your own reflections. I directed a copy to be enclosed yesterday to Mr. Southard. It must confirm any good impression produced by my speech.

"Tell Mr. Southard that his children are much better, and that he need not entertain any fear about them.

"With my best wishes that you may both realize much benefit from the mineral waters."

There is a letter of Mr. Clay, in which he says he could not desire a fuller response from Mr. Buchanan than he had received. If Mr. Clay was himself satisfied—if his friends at the time were satisfied—I ask any man to tell me who shall complain now, when twenty-five or thirty years have passed by? Two years after the occurrence, and after Mr. Buchanan had spoken out publicly, Mr. Clay proclaims to his friends that it was all that he could desire or expect from him.

Mr. President, I submit whether there can be any fairness in pursuing Mr. Buchanan with that charge? I have produced this testimony, not for the purpose of vindicating Mr. Buchanan—I care nothing about that—but for the purpose of vindicating myself for the vote which I shall give in November next. Unless my mind changes between this and that time, I shall assuredly vote for him, unless I shall believe that Mr. Fillmore, or somebody else, stands a better chance to defeat the Black Republican party than he does. I mean to give this evidence as a vindication of my vote.

My friend from Kentucky said in his speech—I do not suppose that he intended it for me particularly, as there are several of us in the same category :

"Besides, let me tell them that a man who is turned down to the foot hardly ever gets to the head again. When the estate comes to be divided under the statute of distribution, as I understand, these men not being of the household will come in as foreigners, aliens, or bastards, in the family. They will be treated as having worked for a time for wages, and when the estate comes to be distributed, they will not get a distributive share. They will have to wait for the second table all the time they work too. This is a bad fix for any man to get into."

I know my friend did not mean to insinuate that those who were going for Mr. BUCHANAN, or might do so, were doing it with the hope of reward, and for the mere sake of the loaves and fishes. Never, sir. I assert now that I expect nothing from him, and I want nothing from him. But is that the sort of doctrine to proclaim in this country? Are we a set of Swiss soldiers, fighting for pay? Is there no patriotism in the land? Has it fled the country?

Mr. THOMPSON, of Kentucky. I never thought of the gentleman in that connexion, though I had a private belief that the prodigal son went back because his father had a fatted calf. [Laughter.] But it never occurred to my mind to think anything of that kind about my friend from Tennessee, for I did not think him capable of being governed by such motives.

Mr. JONES, of Tennessee. I have no idea that he thought particularly of me; but I wanted to give my friend an opportunity to put himself right before the country, because the idea here conveyed is, that if we vote for Mr. Buchanan we shall come in at the second table, and can never expect to sit at the first table. Now, my friend from Kentucky is an old-fashioned Whig, and a Clay Whig, as he announced to us; but I know he also declared his determination to vote the American ticket. He does not belong to them; he repudiates any connexion with them, except to vote for them. Will my friend tell me what table he expects to sit at?

Mr. THOMPSON, of Kentucky. The first table all the time. Whenever Kentucky decides the question, there is where I will be.

Mr. JONES, of Tennessee. If you never get to any table until you get to the first one, you will starve to death, [laughter,] because they tell you in their creed—at least they say in my part of the State of Tennessee, in their creed—you shall not eat at all unless you belong to the family, [laughter;] so you are bound to starve any way; and I can but starve if I go. [Laughter.] Now, Mr. President, I do not go for any such thing. As for the table, I do not care a copper about it. I do not ask them to invite me to their table; and it is questionable with me whether, if they were to ask me, I would accept it, only on the score of politeness or hospitality. I am as independent of the Democratic party as they are of me; and I reiterate it again, they owe me nothing, and they will owe me nothing after this contest is over. I do not care whether they invite me to their table or not. Thank God, I have a table of my own. I have the table of my country, and all can feed at that table—food enough for every generous American heart—food enough for me, food enough for all. As for your sectional party tables, if you think there is any honor in sitting at them, sit at them. I choose to sit at the great national table, and to do my duty to my country as I understand, leaving the results to Heaven and the country.

I am reminded of a story which my friend from South Carolina told me this morning, and I will tell it now for the benefit of those who are in doubt. It will do for the Senate, because this is a ministerial affair. I have been frequently taunted the last week by friends saying, "I have heard that Father Cass is going to perform the service of baptism." I think if anybody could do that, he might; but I am not going to take the water at all, and I want to illustrate my position by an anecdote which my friend told. There was a Baptist preacher in South Carolina by the name of Cartlin, an honest, good man; and a gentleman, by the name of Jack Crawford, sought admission into the church. You know the Baptist church is a real democratic concern; they take a man just as he is, big or little; and when Jack Crawford came up, they considered his right, and the old man Cartlin voted against him. He would not take Jack at all, for he was a terrible fellow; but the church overruled him, just as General Taylor's cabinet overruled him, and outvoted him; and they decided to take Jack in. Of course the duty of administering baptism devolved upon the old man Cartlin. When he went to baptize him, he said to him, "Jack, I voted against this thing, but the church has overruled me, and it is my duty to baptize you; but I will tell you what is the fact; I do not believe you are fit to be baptized, and you ought not to be baptized;" but he finally concluded that he was obliged to do it—he baptized him. "Now, you see, Jack, you are baptized, and if you can get religion, there is no sinner on earth that need fear hereafter." (Great laughter.) I think that, if I can vote for Mr. Buchanan, nobody need fear; for I believe I have been, and am still, as good a Whig as any in the world, and I think I am a better one than many of those who would chide me for the course I feel it my duty to pursue. I at least have never forsaken it. I cling to it still; and, should its banner ever again be given to the breeze, I shall be found standing beneath it.

I have another reason why I am going to vote this Democratic ticket; and it is a hard thing for me to say. I regard the present Democratic party as affording the only and last hope of security to the South. Gentlemen may say, "this is sectional." Be it so; I do not care whether you call it sectional or not. It is a fact, and I mean to establish it from the records. I say that, in my judgment, the Democratic party affords the best, if not last, hope of safety and security to the South. Why do I say so? We have had a Democratic party, and we have had a Whig party. We have had contest after contest. What has become of the Whig party of the North? The northern wing of the Whig party has gone off—where? They have become thoroughly abolitionized. And the American party, rising upon the ruins of the Whig party, did it upon the hope and assurance, as I believe, that they would be able to establish a national party. They did establish a national party; and how long did it last? It lasted until they had the first national convention, when they broke asunder—the North going to itself, and the South standing by itself, with a few exceptions in the North. I maintain there is but one party that is national, and that is maintaining the rights of the South. I do not pretend to say that the South Americans are not as conservative, national, and true to the constitutional rights of the South as any party—I know they are; but I know, at the same time, they have no such support at the North as to give them power to carry out their purposes. Then where are we to look?

I ask you to go to the record, and begin as far back as 1845, and let us see how it stands. In 1845 Florida proposed to be admitted into the Union as a slave State. How stood the vote on that question? In the House, northern Democrats voted—yeas 58, nays 4; all others from the North, nays 37. In the Senate, northern Democrats—12 yeas, nays none; all other northern men—yeas none, nays 9. Therefore Florida would not have been admitted, and never could have been admitted, but for the votes of the northern Democrats.

Again: when Texas sought to be annexed, how stood the vote? I was opposed to the acquisition of Texas, and therefore I make every allowance. I opposed it upon the grounds of opposition to all territorial aggrandizement; but when the question came here, how did the vote stand? Northern Democrats in the House—yeas 37, nays 3; all others from the North—yeas none, nays 46. Then it got not a single northern vote except Democratic ones. Now I ask southern gentlemen if that is not significant? If that does not teach something? If it does not point to something? Here is a southern State asking for admission. We are not strong enough to admit her, and we have to look to the North for her admission. Who comes to our assistance! Northern Democrats, and northern Democrats alone.

Again: when the fugitive slave law was passed, how did the vote stand? Northern Democrats—yeas 28, nays 14; all others from the North—yeas 3, nays 62. Then the fugitive slave law never could have been passed but by northern Democratic votes. It only received three northern votes outside of the Democratic party, and I believe they were Whigs, and therefore it never could have been passed but for the Democratic party.

But I come down to later times, when the Kansas-Nebraska bill was here. Gentlemen say that was not a northern and southern question. I will not pretend to argue that. All that I know is what I find on the record. How did the vote stand? Northern Democrats in the House—yeas 45, nays 38; all other representatives of the North—not one yea, nays 54. Then the Kansas-Nebraska bill, which I regard as a southern measure, did not receive a single northern Whig vote in the House of Representatives. How did it stand in the Senate? Northern Democrats—yeas 14, nays 4. How many northern Whigs voted for it? Not one.

Upon each and every one of these measures we have had to rely on the northern Democrats to carry and to sustain them, and without them they would have been lost. I will state another fact in regard to the Kansas bill. If there had not been a southern Senator in the world—if the last one of us had been ingulfed before the vote was taken, the northern Democrats would have passed it over all opposition. It received northern Democratic votes enough to pass it without the vote of a single southern Senator; and not one northern Whig would stand by us to vote for it. It may be said there is nothing in that; but is it not a strange coincidence, that in each of these measures the Democrats sustained what are supposed to be the rights and interests of the South, and all others from the North voted against them?—none except Democrats standing with us, except three, on the fugitive slave bill.

Now, sir, when you come to the election of Mr. Speaker Banks, how does the record stand? After ten weeks of toil and labor, how does it stand? In the final vote Mr. Banks received one hundred and three votes, and Mr. Aiken one hundred. How many northern votes did Mr. Aiken get, and who were they? Mr. Aiken did not receive a single northern vote which was not a Democratic vote. Where were the North Americans then, who mean to do us justice—who mean to stand by us in the preservation of our rights? Did a single one of them vote for Mr. Aiken? Not one. Every northern vote for him was a Democratic vote, and every other northern vote was cast against him. He received every southern vote, American and all, except one or two; but not one northern vote except from the Democratic party. How was it upon the Topeka convention bill in the other House a few days ago? The very same thing substantially in regard to that. Now, I ask southern men—and I wish my voice could reach to every man in the South—how do you think, with these facts before you, your rights are to be preserved? You tell me I ought not to vote for the Democratic party. Where shall I flee for safety and protection for myself, for my wife, for my children, and the graves of my ancestors? Whom shall I trust at the North? Here and there is a man whom you may trust; but what organized party there may you trust, when the rights of the South are in danger? If there were no other question in the world, and there was that isolated fact staring me in the face, I should feel bound now, as a man consulting the interests of the country, to cast the vote which I have suggested.

There is another consideration. Are we not bound by an obligation, as high, as solemn as honor itself, to stand by those who have succored us in our hours of trial? What interest have these gentlemen of the North to stand by us? If they were but consulting the prejudices, and passions, and fanaticism of their people, they would go on with the great tide, swimming, gloriously and quietly. Yet when the question comes here, they stand by the constitution; they stand by its compromises; they stand by the country. For that they receive anathemas at the North, and, be it said to our shame, too often anathemas at the South. To the South I would say in solemn condemnation, "Go on in your work of ingratitude, if you choose to peril all; treat these men with the ingratitude and injustice with which you are treating some of them; and when the dark hour comes, you know that you are in a hopeless minority, you know that that minority is becoming weaker every day; and when another storm shall come, whom will you call upon to succor you? You banish those men who have stood by you; you denounce them as enemies to the country; you have treated them with ingratitude and injustice; and when the hour of trial and danger comes, where will you find your support—where? This solemn warning comes up as an echo, and answers, Where? I appeal to this record; if you find them not there, you will find them not at all. If you find them not at all, what will you do? Men of the South, what can you do? No allies at the North; no support there; no succor there. Your venerable men are taken away from the public councils, swallowed up in fanaticism, and what will you do? You have but one last refuge, and that is your own right arm to defend yourself. Then the end has come, and then all our cherished devotion to the constitution and the Union will avail us nothing; we of the South shall be left to defend ourselves, our own firesides, our own household gods, our wives, and our daughters—we shall be left single and alone to stem the fearful tide. Fearful as this may be, we will stand by them and die by them.

Now, Mr. President, one word and I have done. I do not know that I shall ever address the Senate again on this subject. I do not care ever to do so. I think it likely that the days of my political existence are numbered. This has no terror to me. I shall die as I have lived, however deluded I may be or may have been, honest and sincere in the convictions which I entertain; and I do not know that I can better close this address than by reading a sentiment from that immortal patriot and sage who now sleeps quietly beneath the soil at Marshfield. I conclude what I have to say, as an ovation, dedicated to him as an evidence of my willingness to stand by the Union, to live by it as long as I can in honor; and when honor is to be maintained, there is no sacrifice, in my judgment, too great to be made. I conclude, therefore, with an extract from that inimitable speech of Mr. Webster, in which he said:

"While the Union lasts, we have high, exciting, gratifying prospects spread out before us, for us and our children. Beyond that I seek not to penetrate the veil. God grant, in my day, at least, that curtain may not rise! God grant that on my vision never may be opened what lies behind! When my eyes shall be turned to behold, for the last time, the sun in heaven, may I not see him shining on the broken and dishonored fragments of a once glorious Union—on States dissevered, discordant, belligerent—on a land rent with civil feuds, or drenched, it may be, in fraternal blood. Let their last feeble and lingering glance rather behold the gorgeous ensign of the Republic, now known and honored throughout the earth, still full high advanced, its arms and trophies streaming in their original lustre, not a stripe erased or polluted, nor a single star obscured, bearing for its motto no such miserable interrogatories as '*What is all this worth?*' nor those other words of delusion and folly, '*Liberty first and Union afterwards;*' but everywhere, spread all over, in characters of living light, blazing on all its ample folds as they float over the sea and over the land, and in every wind under the whole heavens, that other sentiment, dear to every American heart, LIBERTY AND UNION, NOW AND FOREVER, ONE AND INSEPARABLE!"

KANSAS AFFAIRS.

SPEECH

OF

HON. GEORGE E. PUGH, OF OHIO,

DELIVERED

IN THE SENATE OF THE UNITED STATES, JULY 2, 1856.

The Senate having under consideration the report in favor of printing twenty thousand extra copies of the bill to enable the people of the Territory of Kansas to form a constitution—

Mr. PUGH said:

Mr. PRESIDENT: I am not disposed to renew this discussion at any other time; and as it is necessary that I should correct one misrepresentation of my colleague, personal to myself, I will say a few words, also, in reference to the topics which have been debated.

I had objections, Mr. President, to the bill which passed the Senate last week, but I did not think it worth while, after a continuous session of twenty hours, when all around me were so much exhausted, to explain those objections at any length. I doubted whether Kansas had a sufficient population to warrant her admission as a State; but I never said, (as my colleague asserts,) that the lack of ninety thousand inhabitants was an insuperable objection. I did say the lack of thirty thousand was an insuperable objection; and I said, also, from the votes cast in October, 1855, the Territory could not have contained that number, by five or six thousand, at the time of the session of the Topeka convention. I confess, sir, I have no distinct evidence, to this hour, that Kansas contains thirty thousand inhabitants; and it was upon this point, chiefly, I had to overcome doubts.

Mr. WADE. I stated only from recollection what my colleague said. It occurred to me that he did say there should be ninety-three thousand, the amount required in the original bill; but it may be as he has stated. I did not profess to be accurate on the point. I quoted from memory.

Mr. PUGH. I should not have referred to the subject at all, but that, when I rose to correct my colleague's statement—supposing he had misapprehended me—he refused to allow the correction, and insisted upon the accuracy of his own words. I knew what my views were at the time, and thought I remembered my language. Since the occurrence, however, I have examined the report of my speech, and it was just as I said. My insuperable objection was to the lack of thirty thousand inhabitants, and because I believe the Constitution requires that number in the case of every new State, when it declares that the ratio for Representatives shall never be less than thirty thousand. I thought the admission of new States, with ten or twenty thousand inhabitants, would be an infringement of the Federal compact, and, considering the number of our Territories at present, of very dangerous consequence.

The Senator from Vermont, [Mr. COLLAMER,] when he submitted his views as a member of the Committee on Territories, only claimed twenty-five thousand inhabitants for Kansas, and that claim was based upon the votes given in October last. I repeat, sir, the evidence is not conclusive to my mind, that the population of Kansas has increased, even as yet, to thirty thousand. But the Senator from New York [Mr. SEWARD] declares that it is forty thousand; and one of the Senators from Massachusetts [Mr. SUMNER] has risen to nearly or quite sixty thousand. It seemed to be conceded on all sides, and affirmed by the vote of the other House, that there had been a large increase of population in Kansas during the past eight months; and so, for the sake of peace, assenting to what appeared to be the opinion of those Senators with whom I generally vote—assenting to what I supposed were the wishes of the Opposition—assenting to the course adopted by the House of Representatives—I consented to act upon the supposition that Kansas had now attained the limit of thirty thousand inhabitants. The Senator from Missouri [Mr. GEYER] appeared to have some doubt in this regard, and expressed himself to that effect; but he sacrificed all doubts, nobly, for the sake of conciliation and peace.

The Senator from Kentucky [Mr. CRITTENDEN] also expressed a doubt. What those two Senators said, just before the final vote, so fully explained my own views, that I did not wish to add a single word. So much for the inconsistency of which my colleague accused me. I said also, in my speech, that I would not be disposed to admit a State with less population, by two thirds, than the existing ratio of representation. I would only agree to that in extraordinary circumstances. I still adhere to the declaration. But, sir, these are extraordinary circumstances, and they have become so, in a great degree, since my speech was delivered. If what my colleague has said be true—if there be any foundation at all for the constant assertions of those with whom he acts—this is a case in which I am bound to surrender every consideration short of constitutional duty, in order to establish peace in the Territory; and—if it be not, alas! too late—restore peace to our almost distracted Union.

Mr. President, I care little whether the motion under debate be or be not adopted. I do not imagine that twenty thousand copies of the "pacification" bill (as it has been rightly named) will answer the public demand, or even suffice to inform the country of its provisions. I have no such idea. Nor do I believe that one hundred thousand copies would accomplish the purpose. To me, therefore, it is immaterial whether the motion be adopted or rejected. Already, in the newspapers of the Opposition, a studious attempt has been made to deceive the people as to its character. It is called "the Kansas slave State bill," not only in editorial paragraphs, but in letters and telegraphic dispatches. And even here, to our very faces, several Senators have asserted—not that the bill was calculated to make Kansas a slave State—not that such would be its tendency or effect—but that the purpose, the intention, the deliberate design of those who voted for it was to make Kansas a slave State. The Senator from Maine [Mr. FESSENDEN] has asserted this, and asserted also that it is a parliamentary charge. I say that it is not. It is unparliamentary, improper, and abusive; and if the Senator expects to employ such language in any debate with me, he might as well prepare for a retort. I maintain, sir, that the rules of the Senate do not tolerate an assertion like that. On reflection, to be sure, he has excepted the Senator from Kentucky [Mr. CRITTENDEN] out of this unprecedented denunciation; but he persists in the charge that all the rest of us, from the North as well as from the South, although upon the sanction of our oaths, before God and the country, we have professed that our sole purpose, intention, and design, was to adopt a fair measure—one which should truly ascertain the will of the actual inhabitants of Kansas, are perpetrating a deliberate falsehood. Who is this Senator, pray, that he should thus pronounce other Senators to be hypocrites and knaves? This, I suppose, is the "free speech" of which we have heard so much, and which no man must presume to question in or out of the Senate Chamber. I repeat, sir, such language is neither parliamentary nor excusable.

I agree that any Senator has a right to declare that the provisions of the bill are such, or the circumstances under which it is proposed are such, that the legitimate consequence will be to make Kansas a slave State. That is a proposition I can discuss with him; and to that even the Senator from Massachusetts [Mr. WILSON] confined himself in his last address. But when a Senator exceeds that limit, and undertakes to impute an intention to his fellow Senators, contrary to what they have professed, he violates all the decorum of debate, and the privileges of those who are compelled to hear him. And, sir, whenever it is attempted, offensively, towards me, I shall claim an equal degree of indulgence—and the right to say (what I now say of the assertion of the Senator from Maine) that, so far as I am concerned, it is entirely without foundation or excuse.

Well, Mr. President, we attempted to settle the Kansas question fairly, so far as we could settle it. I have stated the points upon which I yielded. I do not agree with the Senator from New York, that the day for compromise has passed. I agree with the Senator from Kentucky that, saving the Constitution, I will compromise to the last syllable of recorded time, if I can thereby promote the peace of the Union, and the welfare of the individual States. I have contributed my share; other Senators have made their contributions. The bill was not introduced at my suggestion, nor after any consultation with me. I found it here upon my return from the

West, and examined it as well as I could. The result was a determination to give it my support. I sympathized also in the invitation extended by the distinguished Senator from Kentucky to those who claim to be the especial friends of the free-State party in Kansas—an invitation to propose any amendment which would render the bill more acceptable to them, and yet preserve its principles. I had read, in the Globe newspaper, that the Senator from New Hampshire [Mr. HALE] declared it a bill almost unexceptionable—such, perhaps, was his very language—and I rejoiced in the hope that, from all this confusion and tumult, this bitterness in Congress and out of Congress, in Kansas and everywhere else, a path of deliverance had been discovered, and that we could all agree, at last, upon terms of fair and honorable adjustment. That Senator has not assigned an excuse satisfactory, in my judgment, for since voting against the bill.

If any reason, worthy to be called such, had been alleged for his motion to strike out the 4th of July, 1856, and insert a later period, I should have voted in favor of it. But, sir, what was the pretext alleged? Merely, that he had no confidence in the President of the United States. Did the Senator expect those of us who voted for Franklin Pierce to unite in a condemnation so broad and unqualified? The very pretext was an insult to us.

This question, then, is not to be settled; that is the notice which we have received. Its settlement is to be postponed until after the presidential election. And wherefore?

At the commencement of the session, you will recollect, the Senator from New York [Mr. SEWARD] proclaimed that Kansas stood at our door knocking for admission; and he demanded whether the Senate would drive her away from this place of refuge—would coldly drive her back to anarchy and bloodshed? That inquiry was propounded time and again. Kansas, it was said, is ready to rush into your arms; will you receive her? For if you receive her—it was also said—everything will be well. Now, Mr. President, we have agreed to receive her; we have opened the doors of the Senate Chamber; we have invited her to present us a constitution adopted by her people, and take her place in the Union as a State. But, sir, how quickly has the tune changed? These gentlemen now tell us that Kansas does not wish to be admitted as a State for twelve or eighteen months.

What other amendments were proposed by Senators of the Opposition? Two only of material consequence; and the first of these was a recognition of the Topeka constitution. Well, sir, I say of that constitution, as I said before, it never was adopted by the people of Kansas, according to its own requirements. I do not need any other answer; this alone is conclusive. The constitution required, in terms, that it should be submitted to a vote of the qualified electors, and be ratified by them. It never was so ratified; it did not receive the votes of the free-State partisans; it received no votes of any consequence.

It is not, therefore, the voice of the people; it is not even the voice of the free-State partisans; it is only the voice of a handful of men (we know not whom) assembled in various precincts—for in many precincts no votes at all were received—assembled under the sanction of no law, and with no tests, of any sort, whereby to ascertain the qualification of those who voted. We are asked to impose this constitution, thus promulgated at a time when the population did not exceed twenty-five thousand, on a people which now numbers (if the Senator from Massachusetts is to be believed) some sixty thousand. Sir, I am ready to argue the cause on that issue. Senators need not imagine there is any sentiment of fear in my bosom as to the verdict of the American people when a proposition so monstrous shall have been fairly exposed.

What else was offered in the way of amendment? Why, sir, at the last hour, with a vain hope—vain, indeed, it proved—that some further concession might satisfy Senators upon the other side, I invited them to suggest additional safeguards. It had been alleged, in the course of the discussion, that the 4th day of July, 1856, was not a fair date by which to ascertain the residence of voters, because a large number of the free-State partisans had been driven out of the Territory. This, certainly, is an exaggeration. How many actual settlers have been driven out? I do not speak of the number of men lately sent thither, who may have been prevented from entering the Territory. I ask how many actual settlers have been driven out? A thousand? Where are they? Are they in your State? Are they in Illinois? I know they are not in Ohio. Where, then, upon the face of the earth, will you find this vast concourse of sufferers? Sir, this exaggeration is too bold—too apparent. Those who have been driven out, if any, are few in number. But, to avoid even this objection, the Senator from Illinois [Mr. DOUGLAS] added a clause to the bill, under which all who have left the Territory through fear, or in consequence of any ill usage, are allowed to return, to register their names, and to vote. The commissioners will be in session, for this purpose, three or four months. What more could be asked?

But, it is said, you do not protect these persons in returning, and after they shall have returned. What protection do they desire? One Senator alleges that a line of sentinels has been stationed upon the western border of Missouri, to prevent free-State men from entering Kansas through that State. Well, sir, suppose this to be true—I do not know whether it is true or false; I am rather inclined to believe it is false, as the statement comes from a quarter whence so many falsehoods have emanated;—but suppose, I say, that it were true: what power has Congress over the State of Missouri? What can we do with any such sentinels? What relief can we afford to the citizens of San Francisco, in California, against the irresponsible, despotic, armed oligarchy which now enslaves them, and threatens to subvert even their State government?

The question is not what would be the best remedy for all the grievances alleged, but what is the best remedy within our power? There are other routes into the Territory; they are not the most eligible ones, but they are complete, and are the only routes over which Congress can exercise the least control. What protection, then, is requisite? Let these men return by the way of Iowa and Nebraska. This moment, I understand, Colonel Lane has an encampment in the State of Iowa.

What is the nature of the protection which Senators demand. Must we send military officers to search for every persecuted free-State man, and assign him a body-guard during the next four months? Is there no limit, Mr. President, to human absurdity?

We have invited these men to return, and register their names as qualified voters. They pretend to have been oppressed by certain laws, and we have stricken those laws out of existence. It is alleged that they have been prevented, by violence, from approaching the polls: we station the troops of the United States by the side of each ballot-box to protect all voters from abuse or molestation. And we have intrusted this election to five commissioners, who shall be nominated by the President and confirmed by the Senate—commissioners who, as the Senator from Michigan [Mr. CASS] was authorized to state, will represent both parties. We have furnished, therefore, every possible safeguard—more than our opponents ever suggested, or even imagined. Will it be, then, a fair election? What more can be asked? What more can we provide? I call upon the Senate and the country to take notice of the fact, that Senators upon the other side have been invited again and again to propose any additional safeguards—and have been able to propose none. At the last hour, almost, I renewed the invitation. I asked them to suggest a provision (if they could) for the more effectual protection of the inhabitants, and especially those who have been driven out.

Such, Mr. President, was my request; and how was it answered? I realized the wisdom of the Scriptures. I asked for bread, and received a stone—for a fish, and received only a serpent. The Senator from Illinois [Mr. TRUMBULL] rose to name *his* measure of pacification. We had been told that Kansas was in a miserable condition—that men were slain, women were outraged, and property was destroyed. What remedy did the Senator propose for all these terrible evils? He proposed that even the faint vestiges of law in the Territory should be expunged, and that fair domain given over to legitimized anarchy and lawlessness. This, then, is the proposition of Senators who have talked so much about peace and justice—the utter abrogation of every law, and the nullification of the power of every magistrate. All government there is to be at an end; and the thousands of people, men, women, and children, who have gone thither in the faith of our protection, are suddenly to be outlawed by the *fiat* of Congress, and exposed to the wanton outrages of any individual. Let me tell the Senator from Illinois, and all his supporters, that I am prepared for an appeal to the country upon that issue also. Indeed, sir, this is the whole question to be decided; all else is of no consequence. If it were ever so true that we had abandoned some abstract doctrine, heretofore professed, they could derive no justification from the fact. They ought rather to congratulate us upon a conversion so marvelous, and not assail us with new phrases of abuse and vituperation. It would be in better taste, even, to lift up their sanctimonious eyes, like the Pharisee of old, and thank God they are better than us publicans and sinners, who stand afar off, and humbly smite our breasts with remorse.

Sir, I will meet the question, whether we have or have not departed from the acknowledged principles of the Democratic party, but I will not debate it with the Senator. It is a question with which he has no concern. How does it become his affair whether I regard the doctrines of my party or not? If I do not regard them, here or elsewhere, I shall be called to account by the constituted authorities of the party, and tried and convicted in due form; but, with all respect, I do not consider the Senator one of those authorities. I do not care what he may have been in times past. I find by the newspapers that he attended a "Republican" convention not long since, and approved the nomination of Messrs. Frémont and Dayton.

In my judgment, however, the pacification bill violates no doctrine proposed or advocated by the Democratic party heretofore. I believe that I understand the doctrine of "popular sovereignty" quite well; and, so far as I do understand it, there is nothing to restrain or abridge its full operation in the bill which has received the sanction of the Senate.

The question presented upon this subject is, whether the actual inhabitants of a Territory shall decide the character of their local institutions, or submit to the arbitrary decision of Congress in that regard? Popular sovereignty and congressional domination stand opposed to each other. The Senator maintains that it is the right of Congress to govern the Territories in all respects, without reference to the will of their inhabitants. I deny both the righfulness and expediency of such legislation. I have held this faith ever since I had a vote, and expect to continue in the faith.

Popular sovereignty is not a new idea; nor was its application to the case of our Territories first suggested by the venerable Senator from Michigan, [Mr. CASS,] although I acknowledge that he first expressed it in a definite and consistent form. It was suggested by Jefferson at the time of the Missouri compromise; and that will appear from several of his letters, those especially which he addressed to President Monroe. Jefferson denied the power of Congress in this regard; and he prophesied of the Missouri compromise exactly what has since come to pass.

The same views were entertained by Madison, Monroe, Jackson, and Calhoun; but it was reserved for the venerable Senator from Michigan to proclaim the doctrine of popular sovereignty in that definite form in which it was accepted by the Democratic party eight years ago. He was nominated for the Presidency upon that platform.

General Taylor came into office without having announced any opinions on this subject. He was represented by his friends at the North as a staunch "Wilmot proviso" man, and at the South as exactly the opposite. All parties, therefore, felt great anxiety to learn what course he would pursue. But whatever his own opinions, or the professions of his friends, General Taylor found himself compelled to adopt the doctrine which had been professed by General CASS—the doctrine of congressional non-intervention and popular sovereignty—and during the brief period of his administration he endeavored to maintain that doctrine, so far as he could by executive influence, in reference to California, New Mexico, and Utah.

The administration of Mr. Fillmore came next, and with it the great adjustment of 1850. What was the principle of that adjustment? It was, that all our Territories, when they came to be admitted as States, should be received with slavery, or without slavery, as the people might decide, and not as Congress might decide. What is now the doctrine of our opponents? I do not presume to declare what it may be in Illinois, but I know what it is in Ohio. I need not go beyond the resolutions presented here, at this session, from the Republican majority of the Legislature. I need not give my recollection of any man's speeches, nor appeal to any obsolete platform. The resolutions are here, and have been printed by order of the Senate. They declare that no slaveholding State shall be received into the Union, henceforth, in any circumstances, or upon any pretext. If that does not contradict, directly, the compromise of 1850, I confess myself unable to understand the force of the English language.

The issue, therefore, is whether Congress or the people shall decide upon the institutions of a new State. There are some Senators belonging to the Democratic party who stop at that point. I believe the Senator from Louisiana [Mr. BENJAMIN] does; and, at all events, the Senator from Mississippi [Mr. BROWN] and the Senator from Georgia [Mr. TOOMBS] do. I do not. They hold that the Constitution of the United States restrains the people of the Territories from excluding slavery, by law, during the period of the territorial government. I do not so understand the Constitution. I agree with them, however, in this: If the Constitution has restrained the people, as alleged, let them be restrained! Whatever the Constitution provides in this particular, by that I will stand. I desire no better law than the Constitution; and God knows that I advocate no "higher law" for the government of our political relations.

This question being a mere question of construction, a question as to the powers conferred in the Federal Constitution, we have agreed that it shall be referred to the judicial authorities for determination; and, both as a Senator and a citizen, I mean to be bound by whatever the judicial authorities decide in that respect. At present, however, and until the decision, I will entertain, and, if necessary, defend my own opinion. Finding no such restraint in the Constitution as Senators have alleged, I believe that, under the terms of the Kansas-Nebraska act, each Territorial Legislature may prohibit or admit slavery at will—not as a permanent decision, to be sure, but during the territorial period, or until otherwise lawfully provided.

This question, however, is not involved in the pacification bill. We are not debating what shall be the condition of affairs in Kansas during a territorial form of government; and hence the utter inappropriateness of two amendments proposed by the Senator from Illinois, [Mr. TRUMBULL,] against which I voted. We are now looking to the admission of Kansas as a State into the Union; and upon that issue the Democratic Senators, North and South, East and West, all agree. We agree, sir, that if the actual inhabitants of Kansas do now, fairly, and in a legitimate mode, exclude slavery, or establish it, by an organic act, their exclusion or establishment—I care not which—shall be decisive and ultimate. This, in my judgment, is not a *favor* conferred on the inhabitants. They have a *right* to decide the issue; and I will maintain their right in all places, and at all times, even as against the supposed sanctity of a hundred Missouri compromises.

The pacification bill which the Senate has adopted, so far as I am able to judge of its provisions, is eminently just toward all parties. Its object is to secure a fair election. If any amendment can be suggested to perfect this design, or more certainly to prevent violence, to prevent irregularities, to prevent fraud, to assure each citizen of the Territory in the free exercise of his right of suffrage, I hope that it will be proposed by the House of Representatives; and, for one, I am ready to concur in it. Then, sir, as soon as the citizens of Kansas shall have adopted their State constitution, whether that constitution excludes slavery or establishes it, I will vote for the admission of the State without any further question. Even the Senator from Vermont [Mr. COLLAMER] and the Senator from Illinois [Mr. TRUMBULL] acknowledge that those citizens, when they come to organize a State government, have the right to establish slavery, or exclude it, without any reference to the Missouri compromise, or any other species of territorial legislation.

Having provided a fair election under this bill, with all the safeguards which occur to me, or can be suggested by others, I have done my part. The citizens of Kansas must do the rest. If they wish to be a non-slaveholding State, and so declare, I shall demand of the Senator from Missouri, [Mr. GEYER,] and all other supporters of the bill, a vote for unqualified admission. On the other hand, if the citizens of Kansas declare that they wish to become a slaveholding State—much as I shall regret, individually, their choice—I can discover no pretext founded upon the Constitution, or in any principle of good faith, which would justify me for resisting their admission into the Union.

How can it be said, therefore, with any regard to truth or justice, that there is any unfairness in the bill? Where is the "fraud" so lustily asserted? Where is the "cheat" to be found? These are hard words. They have been used frequently in the course of this session, as if certain Senators had an unlimited prerogative to accuse, insult, and revile the rest of us. It seems to be considered parliamentary, as well as courageous, in their code, to impute the worst motives, and apply the worst language, to their opponents—to make accusations here, under the shadow of senatorial privilege, which they would not dare to make elsewhere, and upon equal terms.

The Territory of Kansas is now convulsed by civil war. These Senators themselves proclaim the fact. They represent it as worse, much worse, than I have seen reason to believe. They tell us that the people—our fellow-citizens—men, women, children—are in a condition of horrible distress. What remedies are proposed? None, sir, that can be effectual, or satisfactory, except the bill to which the Senate has given its approval. Will those Senators defeat the bill? Will their partisans in the other House reject it? I adjure you to consider the consequences. Do you desire peace in Kansas? Do you wish to have a fair election? Do you intend to allow those inhabitants their undoubted rights as American citizens? Then assist in the adoption of the Senate bill. There is nothing else. If you do not assist—if you defeat that bill—if you prolong the sorrowful condition of Kansas—if you stimulate this unnatural controversy to greater lengths—then, I tell you, the curse of every crime which may henceforth be committed there—the blood of every man who may be slain—the honor of every woman who may be violated—will rise up in judgment against you. I will not now make the charge—although, as a retort, it would be justifiable—that you desire a continuance of this anarchy, public distress, and civil war, in order that you may influence the results of the presidential election. That, however, is a question for the country at large; and I shall endeavor, in my humble sphere, to make the country understand and appreciate it.

Here is the substantive proposition: That with all the safeguards suggested in either House of Congress, an election is to be held in Kansas—a State government formed—and peace happily restored. What is proposed on the other side? First, the Senator from Illinois [Mr. TRUMBULL] wishes to abolish all the laws of the Territory at once, and thus legitimate the outrages, the bloodshed, the anarchy, which he pretends to deplore. Second, he and his political associates offer to subjugate the citizens of the Territory to a constitution which they never ratified—which was formed without authority of law—and which modestly declares itself unalterable, in any particular, for nine years!

Let the people of the United States consider such an issue—ay, sir, let them *decide* it. This involves everything, connected with our Government, which is worthy of consideration. If passion, prejudice, fanaticism—aided by all the modern arts and adjuncts of falsehood—can so mislead the American people that they will not distinguish good from evil—will no longer respect the fundamental principles of their own Government—will rashly mutilate that sacred compact, THE FEDERAL CONSTITUTION, in which all the securities of our Union, our peace, our liberty, our happiness, reside,—it is of little consequence who may be the next President, and whether Congress should ever again assemble. The experiment of popular institutions will have utterly failed; for, without patriotism, intelligence, virtue, and self-command, a popular government must fall into confusion and despotism at last.

In any event, Mr. President, I can do nothing more. I have sacrificed every scruple, every minor consideration, to an ardent desire for peace. I have gone to the extremity of concession. I have agreed to whatever is honest and fair; and I am yet willing to vote for any amendment or scheme of that character which can be suggested. If the Opposition will not meet us in this spirit—if the Senate pacification bill should be rejected by the House—I must discharge myself henceforth of all responsibility as a Senator and a citizen. I shall have performed my duty to the uttermost; no blood will be upon my skirts, nor any reproach upon my conscience.

KANSAS INVESTIGATION.

MINORITY REPORT

OF THE

KANSAS INVESTIGATING COMMITTEE,

OF

THE HOUSE OF REPRESENTATIVES,

BY

HON. M. OLIVER, OF MISSOURI.

WASHINGTON:
PRINTED AT THE UNION OFFICE.
1856.

MINORITY REPORT.

JULY 11, 1856.—Ordered to be printed.

Mr. MORDECAI OLIVER, from the Select Committee, submitted the following views of the minority.

The undersigned, member of the committee of three appointed by the House of Representatives to investigate the state of affairs in Kansas, disagreeing with the views and conclusions of his two colleagues, in the written statement submitted by them touching the result of their investigations, begs leave, under the permission of the House, to present a counter-statement.

The authority under which the committee acted was an order of this House, passed the 19th of March last, directing them to "proceed to inquire into, and collect evidence in regard to, the troubles in Kansas generally, and particularly in regard to any fraud or force attempted or practiced in reference to any of the elections which have taken place in said Territory, either under the law organizing said Territory or any *pretended law* which may be alleged to have taken effect there since; and when the investigation was completed, to report the evidence so collected to the House."

Under this resolution the committee entered upon the discharge of the duties imposed on them with as much dispatch as possible. Their labors were closed at Westport, Missouri, on the 9th of June, 1856. The paper in the nature of a report, drawn up by the colleagues of the undersigned on the committee, was not read to or by him, and he knew nothing of its contents or character until it was presented to the House. It was not the expectation of the undersigned that any other report would be submitted by them than the testimony taken. A full execution of the commission of the House, he thought, was the presentation of the evidence collected. But as the majority of the committee have thought proper to comment on the character of the testimony, and to give their version of the substance of the facts, which is altogether at variance from his understanding of both, the undersigned feels it incumbent on him to follow their example, by presenting like comments on his part.

It must have been apparent to all, that the report of the majority was not only *ex parte* and one-sided, but highly partisan in its character from beginning to end. This appears all through the paper, in the manner of their statement of all things referred to by them, as facts, many of which statements of facts thus made rest upon no evidence whatever collected by the committee.

To justify this remark, the undersigned will, in the beginning of what he has to offer, barely allude to a few statements in the report of the majority, from which its whole character may be judged. It is, for instance, said by the majority that "a party under H. C. Pate, composed *chiefly of citizens of Missouri*, were taken prisoners by a party of settlers; and while your committee were at Westport, a company, chiefly of Missourians, accompanied by the sitting delegate, went to relieve Pate and his party, and a collision was prevented by the United States troops."

Now, the undersigned affirms most positively that this statement has not one particle of proof, taken before the committee, to rest upon? There is no testimony in the whole mass collected by the committee on that matter—none at all. But the undersigned affirms, that, in his opinion, and according to the best of his information and belief, the fact is contrary to the statement of the majority; at all events, so far as relates to Captain Pate. Since that report has been made, under indulgence granted by this House, testimony has been taken on that point, from which it is made very clearly to appear that this statement, made without proof in the first instance, was founded wholly in error. Captain Pate himself—a man of character and integrity—swears that, to the best of his knowledge, "not one of them were citizens of Missouri." This deposition the undersigned here refers to, without spreading it out at large, and makes it a part of his report as fully and completely as if it were given in full in this place.

Again. The statement about the "young man being seized in the town of Atchison, and, under circumstances of gross barbarity, tarred and cottoned, and in that condition sent to his family," is entirely unsustained by any proof in the mass of that taken by the committee. It is true, testimony was taken as to the alleged facts of this character; but when it was proposed to go fully into the investigation of the whole truth of such charges, and not to rest them on *ex parte* statements alone, the majority of the committee abandoned the investigation, and struck out the testimony which they had taken. But the undersigned has not time to go on with such specifications. He will here barely add, that all like statements in the report, as to the existing condition of the Territory, are wholly gratuitous and unsupported by any testimony taken by the committee. For the correctness of what he now affirms, the undersigned appeals to the testimony on file; and to counteract the impression of such statements by the majority of the committee, he begs leave to refer to the sworn depositions hereunto appended and made part of his report, as fully as if the same was set forth at large.

The undersigned affirms, most positively and distinctly, that the testimony taken by the committee contains no matter going to disprove or deny in the slightest degree these great, leading, and controlling facts in the merits of the controversy which gave rise to the organization of this committee, to wit: that an election for a Territorial legislature was held in Kansas Territory on the 30th of March, 1855, in pursuance of the proclamation of A. H. Reeder, governor of the Territory under the organic law; that, in that proclamation, the time and places of voting were set forth; that the judges of election were appointed by him, with instructions as to how their places were to be filled if they or any of them refused or failed to act; that he reserved the power to himself to judge, in the first instance, of the election returns, and that he did so act; that the returns were made to him, and he did set aside the election of but nine members of the twenty-six elected to the house of representatives, and three of the thirteen elected to the council, and gave his certificate of election to the other seventeen members of the house, and ten members of the council, being a majority of both branches of the legislature; that he ordered new elections in those districts where he had set aside the returns; that the governor convened the legislature, thus constituted, according to law, on the 1st of July, 1855, and communicated with them officially after they were organized, and recognized them as legally and a properly constituted law-making body; and never, until August, 1855, after he was removed from the office of governor, did he object to the election of a majority of the legislature, both in the council and in the house of representatives, to whom he had previously given certificates.

These great leading and essential facts, upon which the validity or invalidity of laws, or "*pretended laws*," of Kansas must rest, are not denied, or even assailed, by a particle of testimony taken by the committee; and, with these facts unassailed and unimpeached, it is beyond the comprehension of the undersigned how the majority could come to the conclusion that the laws passed by the Territorial legislature were null and void in consequence of any illegality, even if such had been proved, in the election of its members. All questions relating to that election were closed by their waiver at the proper time, and without an investigation by the proper authority. This is a well-fixed principle in all our representative institutions; upon it they all rest, and with the correctness of it Governor Reeder himself seems to be duly impressed. This the testimony clearly discloses. In a letter found in the streets of Lawrence, and proven before the committee to be in the hand-writing of Governor Reeder, and bearing his genuine signature, dated in this city on the 12th of February, 1856, and addressed to a friend of his in Kansas Territory, he says:

"As to putting a set of laws in operation in opposition to the territorial government, my opinion is confirmed instead of being shaken; my predictions have all been verified so far, and will be in the future. *We will be, so far as legality is concerned, in the wrong; and that is no trifling matter, in so critical a state of things, and in view of such bloody consequences.* * * * * * I may speak my plain and private opinion to our friends in Kansas, for it is my duty. But to the public, as you will see by my published letter, I show no divided front."

This letter, and another also found, were addressed, as it is understood, to Grosvenor P. Lowrey, his friend, and formerly his private secretary, while he was governor of Kansas; and so important a bearing had they upon the *main facts of the case*, which are the *legality of the territórial legislature and their enactments*, that the majority of the committee, after they had admitted them as evidence, as it was clearly understood by all parties, attempted to reject them. The following is their action in regard to them:

"The counsel for J. W. Whitfield having, at Leavenworth city, offered in evidence before the committee two letters written by A. H. Reeder—one dated Washington, January 20, 1856, the other dated Washington, February 12, 1856; and, before offering the said letters, their authenticity, both as to the signature and hand-writing in the body of said letters, was proved to be the proper hand-writing and signature of A. H. Reeder, and of which facts the committee were satisfied; but a majority of the committee—Messrs. Howard and Sherman—not being satisfied, at the time, of the propriety of the admission of such evidence, took the matter under consideration; and now, at this day, at the sitting of the committee at Westport, the question of the admission of said letters as evidence came up for consideration and decision, and a majority of the committee, Messrs. Howard and Sherman—Mr. Oliver dissenting—decline to receive said letters in evidence, and to be engrafted into and constitute a portion of the evidence taken by the committee in their investigations, upon the ground that they, the committee, have not the rightful possession of them; they having been found in the street, and being clearly private letters, or so declared to be by the majority of the committee. The said majority of the committee take no objection to the relevancy or competency of said letters as evidence; but place their objection solely upon the grounds above stated, not denying that said letters might be evidence against said A. H. Reeder in a criminal prosecution. The committee admit that the copies of said letters, furnished to the committee for the purpose of having them transcribed into the evidence, are true and genuine copies of the originals offered in evidence, and which said copies are hereto appended, marked (A) and (B,) and made part of this protest.

"The counsel for J. W. Whitfield, and on behalf of the law and order party in Kansas Territory, offer said letters in evidence for the double purpose of showing the opinions and admissions of A. H. Reeder, in reference to the matters and subjects connected with the elections of the 30th of March, 1855, in the Territory, and the contest now pending between Whitfield and Reeder in the House of Representatives, as well as to show the complicity of A. H. Reeder in all the troubles which have led to bloodshed and civil war in the Territory.

"To the refusal of the majority of said committee to receive said letters in evidence, Mr. Oliver enters his protest; and also, the said John W. Whitfield, by his attorneys, protests against the action of a majority of the committee in refusing the admission of said letters in evidence, as depriving him of his just rights in the investigation before the committee, and in showing to the country the true ground and source of all the difficulties in Kansas Territory.

"J. W. WHITFIELD.
By his Attorneys,
"AUSTIN A. KING,
"JOHN SCOTT.

"WESTPORT, Mo., *June* 7, 1856.

"The above protest was this day presented, and the accompanying copies of letters, marked by me 'Exhibit A, accompanying protest,' and 'Exhibit B, with protest.'

"WM. A. HOWARD,
"*Chairman K. C.*

"WESTPORT, *June* 7, 1856."

But the undersigned insists that they were not only competent, but pertinent to the main issue which the committee were sent out to investigate. He therefore incorporates copies of them in this report; he appends them to it, and makes them part of the same as fully as if here entered at large.

These remarks, touching the general character of the majority's report, and what has not been proved, are preliminary to such comments as the undersigned intends to submit on the matters which were elicited by the investigation. And another fact on the same line of preliminary observations, deserving, in his opinion, to be noticed, is, that witnesses were examined by the committee in but three places in the Territory, to wit: Lawrence, Tecumseh, and Leavenworth city; except that the testimony of Daniel Woodson, secretary of the Territory, was taken informally at Lecompton, in regard to the loss of poll-books in certain districts, and also a certain letter said to have been written by him. All the places in which witnesses were examined touching the election of the 30th of March, 1855, were in districts where the elections had been set aside by Governor Reeder himself, as before stated. All the testimony they took touching the elections at other places, was given by witnesses sent for and examined out of the vicinage; and much the larger portion of the testimony taken at the instance of the contestant was taken at Lawrence, the great rendezvous of the malcontents in the Territory. The object of the testimony of the witnesses produced by Governor Reeder was to show that the election of the legislature on the 30th of March was carried by illegal votes from Missouri, notwithstanding he had officially adjudicated that question as governor of the Territory.

And before proceeding to notice in detail the testimony, such as it is, adduced for that purpose, it may be proper here to advert to some strange inconsistencies in the report of the majority, and which are apparent upon its face. They say, for instance, "this unlawful interference has been continued in every important event in the history of the Territory. *Every election* has been controlled, not by the actual settlers, but by citizens of Missouri; and, as a consequence, every officer in the Territory, from constables to legislators, except those appointed by the President, owe their positions to non-resident voters. None have been elected by the settlers, and your committee have been unable to find that any political power whatever, however unimportant, has been exercised by the people of the Territory."

This is certainly very broad and sweeping language; and who, after having heard it read, was not surprised to hear the same gentlemen admit, in an after part of their report, in speaking of the first election for a delegate to Congress, November 29, 1854, and after giving all the facts in relation to that election, that General Whitfield was duly elected a delegate to Congress? They say, "*of the legal votes cast, General Whitfield received a plurality*," and was consequently duly elected. And if he was duly elected by *legal votes*, as they were forced to admit from the evidence, then the result could not have been affected by non-resident voters.

The undersigned does not deem it necessary for him to say more upon the subject of that election, which was the first object of their inquiry.

The majority admit that General Whitfield was duly elected by the actual settlers of the Territory, and those who were entitled to vote. This admission is a sufficient answer to their previous statement, that no person had been elected by the settlers, and that they had been unable to find that any political power whatever, however unimportant, had been exercised by the people of the Territory. Like inconsistencies appear in their statements concerning the election of members of the legislature on the 30th of March, 1855.

They say, in the first place, in relation to this election, that companies of men from Missouri "were arranged in regular parties, and sent into *every council district in the Territory*, and into *every representative* district *but one*. That numbers were so distributed as to control the elections in *each district*."

And then, under the head of "tenth district," they say, "this and the 'eighth election district' formed one representative district, and was the *only one* in which the invasion from Missouri did not extend." But under the head of "twelfth district," they say, "the election in this district was conducted fairly; no complaint was made that illegal votes were cast."

And again, under the head of "seventeenth district," they say, "the election in this district seems to have been fairly conducted, and not contested at all. In this district the pro-slavery party had a majority."

These contradictory statements, to the undersigned, seem wholly inexplicable, and he leaves them for the majority to reconcile or explain as best they may. But the undersigned affirms, that the weight of testimony shows that the majority of legal voters in fourteen out of the eighteen election districts in the Territory were in favor of the party electing a majority of the legislature, as returned and certified to by the governor. And the testimony as to the other districts, while it is contradictory on some points, is far from being conclusive that a like majority did not exist in them. This, moreover, appears from the report of the majority itself, without referring to the testimony.

The Territory was divided into ten council election districts and fourteen representative districts. The first council district embraced the city of Lawrence—the stronghold of the abolition or free State party, as it is called. In this council district, the whole entire vote cast for the free State ticket was but 255. The whole number of legal voters in that district, by the census in February before, was 446. These figures are taken from the tabular exhibit given by the majority themselves. And it is also in proof by Mr. Ladd, one of Gov. Reeder's main witnesses, that at least fifty illegal votes were given for the free State ticket in Lawrence by eastern emigrants just arrived, and not entitled to vote.

These figures and this fact show that the free State ticket did not receive a majority of the legal voters in this district; for if fifty be taken from the 255 cast for their ticket, it would leave only 205, being 61 short of a majority of the 466 legal voters in the district. That Missourians may have voted there illegally, does not, and cannot, vary this result. But the election at Lawrence was set aside by Governor Reeder for informality in the return.

The undersigned has compiled tables, comparing the votes cast for the free State ticket in the several council districts and representative districts in the Territory. This is taken from the tables exhibited by the majority. It is part of their own showing. In it will be seen the number of votes cast in each district for the free State tickets, compared with the number of voters at the time the census was taken in each respectively; and from this it will appear that the free State votes fell far short of being sufficient to elect a majority in either branch of the legislature, even if there had been no increase of voters, by *bona fide* settlers, between the time the census was taken and the election.

But the concurrent testimony of a number of witnesses establishes the fact conclusively, in the opinion of the undersigned, that the emigration of *bona fide* settlers from the southern States was greater in the month of March, after the census was taken, than in any equal time previous.

Here are the tables:

REPRESENTATIVE DISTRICTS.				COUNCIL DISTRICTS.			
No. of representative district.	No. of voters by census.	No. of votes for free State ticket.	No. of representatives.	No. of council district.	No. of voters by census.	No. of votes for free State ticket.	No. of councilmen.
1	97	19	1	1	466	255	2
2	369	253	3	2	212	12	1
3	212	12	2	3	193	44	1
4	101	4	1	4	442	156	2
5	92	49	1	5	253	....	1
6	253	35	2	6	201	140	1
7	242	152	4	7	247	....	1
8	99	120	1	8	215	60	1
9	102	26	1	9	208	....	1
10	83	....	1	10	468	66	2
11	47	54	2				
12	215	....	2				
13	203	....	2				
14	335	59	3				

This shows that the aggregate of the votes cast in the Territory for the free State ticket fell short of 800, while the census shows that there were 2,905 legal voters in the Territory in the February previous. The free State ticket, therefore, did not receive one third of the legal voters of the Territory, even if all be excluded from the account who emigrated to the Territory after the census was taken.

This fact was apparent to the majority of the committee. But they attempted to break its force in two ways: First, by comparing the names on the poll-books with those on the census returns, from which comparison they argue that only a fraction over 1,300 of the legal voters upon the census returns voted at that election. And secondly, by arguing that the abolitionists were prevented from voting by violence, threats, and intimidation.

On the first point, the undersigned deems it unnecessary to say more than that no comparison between the poll-books and the census returns was made except by districts. Between the time of taking the census and the election, settlers had changed their residence from one part of the Territory to another, and doubtless voted in a place different from that in which they were registered when the census was taken. The committee did not compare the names on the poll-books with the names on the census returns throughout the Territory, and the comparison alluded to by the majority, therefore, by no means proves what they claim for it.

On the second point the undersigned will barely state that there is no evidence that any violence was resorted to, or force employed, by which men were prevented from voting at a single election precinct in the Territory, or that there was any greater disturbance at any election precinct than frequently occurs in all our State elections in exciting times. A number of witnesses on both sides swear that men on both sides had arms, guns, pistols, bowie knives, &c., and made threats, &c. But no one of them swears that any one was prevented from voting by the use of these weapons in a single instance, to the best of the undersigned's recollection. The testimony from beginning to end does not disclose the fact of a single assault and battery at or about the polls, or on account of the side on which any one wished to vote or had voted, in the whole Territory, on the day of election.. Some quarrels and fights occurred at two or three places, but not about voting, and not as many in the whole Territory as the undersigned is informed occurred at one precinct in this city at the late municipal election.

The undersigned will now take up and proceed with the districts in their order. He now refers to the election districts. There were eighteen of these.

First Election District.

The testimony in this district shows that a great many strangers were present, some with wagons and tents; that considerable excitement prevailed. But there is no positive evidence of but a very few persons, known at that time to be citizens of Missouri, being present. All else is hearsay, vague and uncertain. While this is so, Mr. Salster, in his deposition hereunto appended and made part of this report, testifies as follows:

"I emigrated into the Territory of Kansas in June, 1854, and settled in the neighborhood of Lawrence, and have resided there ever since."

"My acquaintance was reasonably extensive in that district. I knew about 400 voters who resided in the district, but I did not know near all of the resident voters of that district. So far as I know, all the resident voters of that district were present and voted."

"At the time of the election of the 30th March, 1855, there was a majority of pro-slavery residents in the Lawrence district. I was well acquainted in the district. There were about 200 free State resident voters in that district, and there were from 300 to 400 pro-slavery voters at the polls that day, whom I knew to be residents of that district, and a great many of them voted in my presence, and the others told me they had voted."

Besides this, the testimony of other witnesses shows that a large immigration of *bona fide* settlers from Missouri came into the district after the census was taken, and before the election. (1) The parties, says one witness, were pretty nearly divided—perhaps more of the free State than pro-slavery party; but the free State party were divided, and many voted for the pro-slavery candidates. (2) There was *no intimidation or force* used to prevent any of the free State party from voting, and all could have voted who wished to vote. (3.) In the afternoon some one hundred men, who had come in with Dr. Charles Robinson from the east, marched over to the polls and voted the free State ticket. (4) They were said to have come into the Territory that very day. (5.)

From this testimony, it is difficult for the undersigned to see how the majority of the committee could come to the conclusion to which they arrived, that even in the Lawrence district there was a majority of the legal voters for the free State ticket.

Second District.

In regard to this district, the testimony is conflicting and contradictory; but the weight of the evidence, in the opinion of the undersigned, shows that there were many settlers came into this district after the census was taken, and before the March election. On the morning of election the free State judges took arms with them into the judges' room. The free State men, under the lead of Judge Wakefield, took possession of the polls, and required all the pro-slavery men to be sworn without discrimination, and did not swear any free State men. The pro-slavery residents objected to this, and declared that both parties ought to be sworn alike. After some time the free State judges resigned, and other judges were selected by the crowd. No intimidation was used to prevent the free State men from voting, but all were asked to come up and vote. The pro-slavery ticket had a majority in the district, as the free State party were not united on their ticket, (6.) In addition to the general testimony relating to this district, the

(1.) Horatio Owens, James Whitlock, A. B. Wade.
(2.) James Whitlock, A. B. Wade.
(3.) Horatio Owens, J. Whitlock, A. B. Wade.
(4.) J. Whitlock, A. B. Wade, J. M. Banks.
(5.) James Whitlock, John M. Banks.
(6.) George W. Ward.

undersigned begs to call the attention of the House especially to the testimony of Parris Ellison, one of the judges to hold said election, appointed by Governor Reeder himself, which deposition, with others in relation to the election in that district, is hereunto appended, and made part of this report. Mr. Ellison, in his deposition, among other things, says:

"The undersigned, Parris Ellison, states on oath: That I emigrated from Missouri to Kansas, and settled at Douglas, the second district, in October, 1854, and have resided there ever since. I was present at the election held at Mr. Burson's in the second district, on the 30th March, 1855. I was appointed by Governor Reeder as one of the judges, and Mr. Burson and Mr. Ramsay, I think, were the other two. We met at Mr. Burson's house in the morning before the hour to open the polls. Mr. Burson was a magistrate, appointed by Governor Reeder, and he qualified me, and qualified Ramsay. Ramsay qualified Burson. We appointed the clerks, and qualified them. George W. Taylor was one of the clerks. My son Parris was very sick at the time, and I wanted to resign. I proposed to resign if the other judges would permit me to name a man to serve in my place. Judge Wakefield, one of the candidates on the free State ticket, was in the room, and interfered, telling the judges that they had power to name the man. They refused to let me appoint a man in my place, and I determined to serve, and did serve. I remarked to the other judges that we were sworn to act impartially during the whole day. They said, yes; we are sworn to act impartially. We agreed that, inasmuch as they knew a great many voters that I did not know, and I knew a great many that they did not know, that those whom I knew should vote without swearing, and those whom they knew I would not require of them to be sworn. Under this agreement we commenced the election. After some twenty-nine or thirty votes were taken, the pro-slavery party had some two to one against the free State party. The other two judges began to grumble. Dr. Brooks came up to vote. I knew Dr. Brooks had a claim in that district, and had been on it, and had put a house on it.

"Dr. Brooks was a single man, and afterwards brought his mother there, and has resided there ever since. At the time of the election, Dr. Brooks claimed to be a citizen of the district. I knew him to be a resident, and under our agreement I wanted to take his vote without swearing, but the other two judges refused to take his vote unless he would swear; this he refused to do, because he said that he had understood that, under the agreement, if Mr. Ellison took his vote without requiring him to swear that was all that was necessary. The other two judges still refused to take his vote. The doctor stood at the window a long time, and said, that unless they would let him vote, as he was a citizen of the district, and had been for some time previous, no other man should vote there that day. I told them that if they refused his vote it would create a fuss and confusion, and that it would be violating the agreement made before the election began; but still refused. Sherman Woffal then came up to vote; but they refused to take his vote without swearing. Sherman said that he could prove by me that he was a citizen of the district, and had been a citizen of the district from the fall before. I knew that Mr. Woffal was a resident of the district, for he was living there when I went to the district to live. I bought hay of Mr. Woffal before the election, which he had made and cured the summer before. They still refused to let him vote, unless he would swear. He refused to swear because they, the judges, would not let him prove his residence. He said he would not swear. I had not, up to this time, objected to any of the persons that came up to vote which the other two judges said they knew. I had kept the agreement made between us to the word and letter. On account of this conduct on the part of the other two judges, a fuss and confusion arose in the crowd outside of the house. While the fuss was going on, I proposed to adjourn, as I told them I thought it would be over in half an hour or so. Mr. Burson, thereupon adjourned for half an hour. He proclaimed the adjournment aloud. I told each one of the judges to pick up a poll-book. I took the ballot-box which one of the judges tried to take from me. I think it was Ramsay, but am not certain. Sharp words passed between us, but I kept the ballot-box, and they took the poll books and went off. A man by the name of Jones asked me where the poll-books were? I told him that Burson and Ramsay had taken them off. He followed them and brought the poll-books back. I waited until the half hour had expired, and the other two judges did not come back. I waited ten minutes longer. I called them, but they did not come. I called them again, and they did not appear. I told the people that I would wait five or ten minutes longer, and if the other two judges did not come they would have a right to select two men to act in their places. I waited ten minutes and they did not come, and the people elected two men to act in their places, namely, Sherman Woffal and Frank Labay. They were qualified. I asked Mr. Taylor to repeat the oath to them which he did; but, by mistake, Mr. Taylor signed the oath instead of myself. Mr. Tay, lor had been sworn in as a clerk by Mr. Burson and Mr. Ramsay. Messrs. Woffal and Labay and I then opened the polls, and the election went off quietly during the remainder of the day. We kept the polls open until six o'clock in the evening. Andrew McDonald was the pro-slavery candidate for council, and Judge Wakefield was the free State candidate for council. O. H. Brown and Mr. Ward were the pro-slavery candidates for the house of representatives, and Jesse was one of the free State candidates for the house, and the other I do not remember. All the votes received after we began the second time were for the pro-slavery candidates. The ballot-box which I took possession of at the time of the adjournment I carefully preserved, and did not open it until 6 o'clock in the evening. It was then opened in presence of the other two judges, who had been selected by the people, and the clerks. The ballots were counted, and there were twenty-one votes for the pro-slavery ticket, and twelve votes for the free-State ticket. When we commenced the election the second time, we got another ballot-box.

"When I got there in the morning, there were some thirty or forty men present about the house, and when I went into the house I saw some fifteen or twenty guns standing in one corner of the house, which had been brought there by the free State men. When the adjournment took place, the guns were taken away by the free State men. These guns were all the guns that I saw on the ground. I did not see a gun in the hands of a pro-slavery man that day. There was no charge made with either guns or pistols or other weapons at the window, nor were there any threats of violence made by the pro-slavery men. There was no violence committed by the pro-slavery men there that day to the judges, nor were there any threats of violence offered, as I saw. I did not see Mr. Samuel Jones pull out his watch and say to the judges, Ramsay and Burson, that he would give them five minutes to resign, nor did I hear him afterwards say to them that he would give them one minute to resign. If this had occurred, I should have seen and heard it, for I was in the house all the time, and was at the door when these two judges came out. I did not see Samuel Jones in the house at any time while Ramsay and Burson were there. In my neighborhood I was well acquainted with the settlers there, and at the time of the election and before. The residents were almost all pro-slavery. From what I knew myself, and the information received from the census taker and others, I am satisfied that the pro-slavery party had a decided majority in the second district."

This is the district in which it is represented that Sheriff Jones figured so conspicuously. The testimony of Mr. Ellison clearly disproves all such allegations. Other depositions, herewith filed and made part of this report, fully confirm the testimony of Mr. Ellison.

Third District.

The testimony in relation to this district is, that the pro-slavery party had a majority among the actual settlers of the district. (7)

Fourth District.

The testimony in relation to this district shows that the pro-slavery party had a majority among the actual settlers. (8)

Fifth District.

In this district the testimony goes to show that there was a majority for the free State party.

Sixth District.

The testimony goes to show that the pro-slavery party had a majority of the actual settlers in this district, and also that most of the free State men voted for the pro-slavery candidates. (9)

Seventh District.

The testimony shows that the pro-slavery party had a majority among the actual settlers in this district. (10)

---

(7) George Holmes.
(8) A. S. Johnson, T. Mockbee.
(9) Wm. Barbee, Joseph C Anderson, S. A. Williams, T. B. Arnett.
(10) C. A. Linkenauger, Andrew Johnson.

Eighth District.

As to this district, no testimony was taken on either side, so far as the undersigned now remembers.

Ninth District.

The testimony shows that in this district the pro-slavery party were in the majority among the actual settlers. (11)

Tenth District.

The testimony shows that the election was conducted fairly in this district, and the result would not have been changed by the rejection of all the illegal votes on both sides.

Eleventh District.

In this district there is no evidence to impeach the correctness of the election returns as made to and sanctioned by the governor.

Twelfth District.

There is no evidence to impeach the correctness of the returns of election for this district.

Thirteenth District.

The evidence shows that there was a pro-slavery majority of the actual residents in this district, and that there was no force or intimidation used to prevent free State men from voting. (12)

Fourteenth District.

The evidence shows that the pro-slavery party was largely in the majority among the actual residents in this district; that the election was peaceable and quiet, and that no intimidation was used prevent any one from voting. (13)

Fifteenth District.

The evidence in regard to this district shows that the pro-slavery party were largely in the majority among the actual residents—probably ten to one—and that there was no force or intimidation used to prevent any man from voting. (14)

Sixteenth District.

The evidence shows that the election in this district was conducted peaceably and quietly, and no intimidation or force used to prevent any one from voting. There was a decided pro-slavery majority among the actual settlers in this district. (15)

Seventeenth District.

The evidence shows that in this district the election was conducted peaceably and quietly, and that the pro-slavery party were in the majority among the actual settlers. (16)

Eighteenth District.

The evidence shows that the election was conducted peaceably and quietly, and that there was a decided pro-slavery majority among the actual settlers in this district. (17)

(11) C. R. Mobley, Thomas Reynolds.
(12) Wm. Tebbs, O. H. Tebbs, and others.
(13) W. P. Richardson, William P. Hall, J. H. Whitehead, J. P. Blair, and others.
(14) John W. Martin, N. Williams.
(15) W. G. Matthias, L. J. Eastin, R. R. Rees, Amos Rees, A. T. Pattie, J. H. Day, A. McAuley, and others.
(16) Cyprian Chouteau, Rev. T. Johnson.
(17) R. L. Kirk, J. W. Foreman.

Upon an examination of the testimony taken before the committee, what the undersigned has affirmed in relation to these several districts will be found to be sustained by the proof. And from all the testimony collected, when compared and weighed properly, the undersigned feels confident that it will appear to every unprejudiced mind, not only that General Whitfield was duly elected, by the actual and *bona fide* residents, a delegate to Congress at the first election, in November, 1854, but that the free State party was in the minority in the Territory at the March election in 1855, for members of the legislature; and that that election was not carried either by force, violence, or non-residents, but that a majority of the legislature was duly elected as certified to by the governor, and was properly constituted as a law-making body; and, as a consequence, that the laws passed by them, as far as they are consistent with the Constitution of the United States and the organic act of the Territory, are valid; and, as a further consequence, that the sitting delegate, having been duly elected a delegate to Congress under a Territorial law thus passed, is entitled to a seat on this floor as such.

And having gone through this branch of the subject, the undersigned now begs leave to refer to other matters alluded to by the majority of the committee in their report. They speak of a certain secret political society formed in the State of Missouri, known by different names, such as "Social Band," "Friend's Society," "Blue Lodge," "Sons of the South"—the object of which was to send emigrants into Kansas for the purpose of making it a slave State.

In reply to this part of their report it is only necessary to state that the evidence shows that these organizations were formed for the purpose of counteracting similar and other organizations, first started at the east and elsewhere, for the purpose of colonizing the Territory with persons for the avowed object of making Kansas a free State, and in this way ultimately affecting injuriously the institutions of Missouri.

The first society of this kind was formed in the City of Washington, immediately after the passage of the Kansas-Nebraska bill. It was composed of members of Congress of both branches, and others.

The undersigned refers, in this connexion, to the testimony of the Hon. Daniel Mace, a member from Indiana, which is appended to this report and made part thereof. In his deposition he states that such an association was formed in Washington immediately after the passage of the Kansas-Nebraska act. It was called the Kansas Aid Society, the members of which subscribed various sums of money, he himself subscribing $50 or $100, he is not certain which amount. The object of the movement was to induce persons to go to Kansas who would make that their home, and who would at all elections vote against the institution of slavery. Mr. Goodrich, a member of the House of Representatives from Massachusetts, was the president of the society.

Soon after this society was formed, other societies were formed in the eastern States for the same object; that is, for the purpose of sending persons to Kansas to control the elections there. A society of this kind formed in Boston, Massachusetts, commenced sending emigrants to Kansas for this avowed object. To show the object of this last-named Emigrant Aid Company, the undersigned begs leave to refer to a letter written by Thomas H. Webb, corresponding secretary of the company, and which is among the testimony taken by the committee. It is as follows:

BOSTON, *August* 14, 1854.

DEAR SIR: By the pamphlet mailed you, much of the information which you desire can be obtained.

The next party will leave here on the 29th instant, at quarter past 2, p. m.; they will go *via* Buffalo, Detroit, Chicago, Alton, and St. Louis, and will disembark at Kansas City, near the mouth of Kansas river. The fare through will be about $25 for first-class accommodations, meals extra, which need not cost, on an average, more than twenty cents. Each person is allowed 100 pounds of baggage, and for all excess will be liable to pay about $3 per 100. Children under three years will be taken free; between three and twelve, pay half price. No pledges are required from those who go; but as our principles are known, we trust those who differ from us will be honest enough to take some other route.

The agent who located our pioneer party will accompany the next one, and furnish all requisite information.

Yours respectfully,

THOMAS H. WEBB,
Sec. Em. Aid Co.

A. JENNINGS, *Provincetown, Mass.*

The undersigned also refers to a pamphlet admitted in evidence before the committee, from which he submits the following extracts:

"THE PIONEER PARTY.—Charles H. Branscomb, esq., one of the company's agents, went up with the pioneer party, and located them on a beautiful tract of land previously selected by him as an advantageous position for a town site. This spot is situated six miles above the Wakarusa, a tributary of the Kansas river, and about thirty-five miles above the mouth of the latter stream, on its south side. For a brief description, the reader is referred to the paragraph commencing on page eleven, and continued on page twelve, of this pamphlet.

"Mr. B. travelled in various sections of the Territory, and says it is impossible for one who has not been in that region to conceive of its beauty and fertility; he confirms all the statements that have been made respecting it in our pamphlet.

"The second party left this city on Tuesday, the 29th of August. They reached Kansas City, September 6th, and entered the Territory under the guidance of Charles Robinson and S. L. Pomeroy, agents of the company. They were cordially received by the pioneer party, and have made a joint settlement at the beautiful site selected by Mr. Branscomb.

"The third party, under the guidance of Mr. Branscomb, (who has returned twice from Kansas since July,) left Boston, September 26th. It numbered eighty-six persons, to which accessions were made at Worcester, Rochester, and elsewhere westward. Messrs. Pomeroy and Robinson are making great exertions to accommodate the parties for the winter, and to provide the materials for the erection of houses in the spring. This pressure of business involves a large expenditure, which their experience will enable them to make with prudence and discretion. But their drafts cannot be met with the funds in the hands of the trustees, unless '*material aid*,' furnished by those who wish for success to the enterprise, shall be very much greater than it has been thus far.

"The fourth party left this city the 17th of October. It numbered 123 individuals, to which sixty were added at Worcester, a number at Springfield, Albany, Rochester, and Buffalo. At Chicago a large accession was anticipated, and ere leaving St. Louis the number will exceed 250."

This was all in the summer and fall of 1854, and prior to the first election for a delegate to Congress, in November of that year. Whatever organizations, therefore, were formed in Missouri, of the character alluded to by the majority of the committee, were formed solely and expressly for the purpose of counteracting those organizations previously formed elsewhere. This the testimony abundantly proves.

The testimony also shows that emigrants going out under those and similar organizations were supplied with arms and munitions of war. Great numbers of Sharpe's rifles aud several pieces of artillery were sent to the Territory. And if arms were taken by emigrants from Missouri, it was only for the purpose of defence against arms in the hands of emigrants from other quarters.

The testimony shows that large numbers of persons sent out by these eastern societies went into the Territory during the month of March, just before the election, declaring it to be their intention to vote; that they came there for that purpose; and in a few days after the election, great numbers of these persons were seen returning to the north and east, saying, many of them, that they had voted.* The testimony also shows that a large number of Missourians went over to the Territory on the day of election, merely to prevent illegal voting on the part of these eastern emigrants, and few of these Missourians, and only a few, are proven to have voted, and their names given, by the testimony; not as many in all as those of the eastern emigrants, who it is proven voted illegally at Lawrence.

The majority of your committee in their report say, that the only cause of the hostilities in the Territory was the known desire of the citizens of Lawrence to make Kansas a free State, and their repugnance to laws imposed upon them by non-residents.

The undersigned, however, is unable to concur with them in that allegation. On the contrary, he affirms, what he believes to be the truth of the matter, that the cause of all the difficulties in the Territory of Kansas, from its organization down to the present time, is to be found, first, as before stated, in the various organizations of members of Congress, and in the northern and eastern States, with the avowed purpose of colonizing the Territory with persons of anti-slavery sentiments, to the end of making Kansas a free State; secondly, that finding themselves defeated and thwarted in their purpose of electing a legislature in favor of making Kansas a free State, as shown in a former part of this report, being chagrined and mortified, they, the anti-slavery party in the Territory

---

* F. M. Mahan, H. M. Blossom, and others.

of Kansas, in a fit of desperation, determined to set themselves up in opposition to, and in resistance of, the laws passed by the Kansas legislature, and to resist them to a "bloody issue," if necessary to their defeat and utter subversion. Indeed, the undersigned affirms, that even before the legislature convened, there were propositions made to form an organization of a military character, to resist any and all laws which might be enacted by that legislature, by force of arms, even should such resistance result in the subversion of the government of the Territory, and to the peril of the Union itself.

In proof of this allegation, the undersigned begs leave to refer to the testimony of Dr. J. N. O. P. Wood, which is as follows:

"I came into the Territory first about the 1st of April, 1854; I located permanently in Lawrence about the 7th of October, 1854; I resided there until some time the last of March, or the 1st of April last, and then I went to Lecompton. About the time I came there, there was considerable difficulty between what was called the Lawrence Association, of which Dr. Robinson was president, and the settlers that were not members of this association. The members of the association held a meeting two or three evenings after I got there, and elected a judge, and a Mr. Grover marshal, and organized a company, which I think they called the 'shot-gun battalion,' for the purpose of preventing persons that did not belong to their association from settling about the place, and taking timber and stone from the claims of those who did live there. They said there was no law in the Territory; that the organic act was unconstitutional--made so by the repeal of the Missouri compromise; and that they intended to form an association, and make and enforce their own laws, irrespective of the laws of Congress, until there could be a change in Congress, by which the Missouri compromise could be restored, and the organic act set aside.

"There was no open opposition to the execution of the laws until Governor Reeder appointed justices of the peace, and one or two members of this association were arrested. They refused to recognize the power of the justice of the peace, and refused to attend as witnesses, and would only attend their own provisional court, as they termed it.

"When the legislature was about to be elected, they held a meeting, and brought out their candidates. After the legislature was elected, and before they met, there were several meetings held in Lawrence, and at those meetings they passed resolutions declaring they would submit to no laws passed by that legislature. This was what was called the Lawrence association, different from the town association. It was composed of men sent out under the auspices of the Emigrant Aid Society, and Dr. Robinson was at the head of the association. Many belonging to this association lived in different parts of the Territory. They were allowed to vote at the meetings of the association, which I sometimes attended, and those who were not enrolled as members of the association were not allowed to vote or debate at their meetings. Some of them lived at Ossawatomie, Topeka, Manhattan, and other places in the Territory. They resolved not to obey the laws that would be passed by the legislature, and only obey their own provisional laws until they could form a provisional government for the Territory.

"The first general meeting, while the legislature was in session, was held in Lawrence in July or August, 1855. Before that time their meetings had been of the association; but this was the first general meeting. That was the first meeting at which I recollect hearing Colonel Lane take ground in opposition to the laws that the legislature, then in session, should pass. All the public speakers that I heard there, said they did not intend to obey the laws that should be passed, but intended to form a provisional government for themselves. After the legislature adjourned, the first meeting at which I heard any declarations with regard to the resistance of the laws was held at Blanton's bridge. Col. Lane, Mr. Emery, and Mr. John Hutchinson, addressed the meeting, urging the people to resist the laws, let the consequences be what they might.

"In private conversation with those men, they always expressed their determination to resist the laws, and said the officers and posse should not enforce the laws. They said they had a new code of laws called Sharpe's Revised Statutes, and they were going to use them in preference to any others. It was a common remark, that they would use Sharpe's Revised Statutes in preference to any others.

"I think the first box of rifles came there marked Revised Statutes. I think after Mr. Dietzler came back, he said he brought the rifles with him. When they were brought to Lawrence they wanted to put them in my warehouse. They were lying at my door, and I inquired what they were, and Mr. Salter, who was keeping the warehouse for me, said they were emigrant aid guns. I objected to their being put in my warehouse, and they were taken and put in Mr. Simpson's office. I told them I would not be the first to harbor guns brought there for revolution.

"I often expostulated with Lane, Robinson, and others, both publicly and privately, as to their course, and addressed the meeting at Blanton's bridge in opposition to their course. They said they would resist the laws regardless of consequences.

"The next public meeting I recollect of was the Big Springs convention. At that convention I had but little conversation, except with Governor Reeder and Judge Johnson. Prior to the meeting several days, Governor Reeder came up to our place. I heard that he was urging the people to resist the laws, and to do so by setting a different day for the election of delegate to Congress, on which he should be voted for. I called on him at his room, and asked him if he had recommended that course, and he said that he had intended to have returned to Pennsylvania, but upon reflection he had concluded that if they would take that course at the convention, he would be a candidate for Congress, and had returned from Kansas City, where he had taken his trunks and baggage. He said he had understood since he came there that Lane, Roberts, and others, would be candidates before the convention; but if they would withdraw, and the course he had indicated was taken, he would be a candidate for Congress. He said it would give him an opportunity to bring the matter before Congress, and with the majority they had then in Congress against the Democratic party, he thought he could succeed in ousting General Whitfield, if elected.

"A meeting was held in Lawrence, and it was agreed upon that a different day should be fixed upon for the election; and the candidates who were there—Robinson, Lane, and some others—agreed to withdraw in favor of Governor Reeder. This was four or five days before the Big Springs convention.

"I rode up to that convention in company with General Pomeroy, who invited me to go up with him. At the convention I had another conversation with Governor Reeder. We had always been on the most intimate terms, and I talked with him as I would with any friend. I talked with him, and said that I thought that by taking that course, and thereby repudiating the laws, it would bring a state of anarchy upon the Territory, that he nor I would probably live to see the end of. I said it would be opening the door, and giving an invitation to outlaws outside of the Territory to come and make that the field of operations; that it would bring about a state of things that would be injurious to the country, by preventing capitalists from risking their means in such a country.

"He replied that he thought differently; that they had determined to adopt the platform of the Topeka convention, held before that time, recommending the formation of a provisional government. I think he took a pencil and draughted a resolution recommending the calling of a convention to form a State constitution. He said he would offer that resolution; they could go on and form their State constitution, appoint an executive committee to issue a proclamation calling for the election of delegates to form a free State constitution, and they would elect their members to the legislature, pass their laws; and if Congress did not admit them, they would pass their own laws, and go on independently of Congress, until such time as they could be admitted.

"I remarked, that would bring them immediately in conflict with the acts of the Territorial legislature, one or the other of which must become supreme; and I thought it would necessarily bring on a collision between the two opposing parties, and involve the country in an armed difficulty.

"He replied, that they had made up their minds to resist the laws, and by forming a free State constitution they could get the aid and sympathy of the North to help them enforce their provisional laws; that they were determined to resist the territorial laws. That was about the substance of the conversation.

"In his speech before the convention, he urged them to resist the territorial laws at all hazards. I have read the speech of Gov. Reeder as reported in the proceedings of the Big Springs convention, in a printed copy now before me. I cannot say that it contains all his speech. He spoke for an hour, or a little over an hour. I understood him distinctly to say this: that he wanted them, if they had any regard for their rights, not to appeal to the laws for redress, nor answer others if appealed to. He called them 'bogus' laws, meaning thereby the territorial laws. That, I think, is about the substance of what he said.

"I came down home, I believe, in company with Judge Johnson, who disapproved of the course adopted. I had conversations with Governor Reeder afterwards, but we held our respective positions.

"A proclamation was issued by what was called the Executive Committee, calling an election for State officers and legislature, a convention to form a State constitution having met and formed a State constitution. I talked with Lane and Robinson often about this matter. There were free State men in Lawrence who opposed this course, and oppose it yet. I myself co-operated with the free State party, until they took these revolutionary steps, and then I left them.

"I lived in Illinois twelve years before I came to this Territory."

Indeed the undersigned affirmed, upon the testimony, that either before the meeting of the legislature, or during its session, or after its adjournment, there were other organizations formed, to resist by force of arms the execution of any laws the legislature might pass, or any which they had passed, at all hazards, even to the destruction of the territorial government, and the dismemberment of the confederacy itself. In proof of this assertion the undersigned begs leave to refer to the testimony of Pat. Laughlin, and the testimony of Dr. Andrew J. Francis.

Pat. Laughlin testifies, in substance, that he came to Kansas from the State of Kentucky, in May, 1855. He settled in Doniphan and favored the freesoil sentiment. He became a freesoiler about the middle of August, 1855, and had a meeting of that party on the 25th of the same month; at which meeting S. Collins presided.

The meeting—although it was one intended for all of the fourteenth election district, as designated by Governor Reeder, in his official proclamation governing the spring election of 1855—had but about forty members in it, and that, too, in a district far more thickly populated than any other district in the Territory of Kansas.

This meeting was addressed by A. Lazelere, Dr. G. A. Cutler, C. W. Stewart, B. Harding, and others, all of whom urged very strongly on the meeting the necessity of forming a society something on the order of the "Know-nothings," by which they could unite their small party, and labor more effectually against the pro-slavery party. This idea was received with general acclamation by every member of the meeting but himself. He thought this a good sign of their "Know-nothing" origin. He therefore opposed the manœuvres they were making; told them if they went into such measures, they would find in him an unrelenting enemy. They, sooner than cause any disturbance in their yet feeble ranks, gave up all thoughts of such organizations. The meeting then went on; and, after disposing of all business before it, we had speeches from several of the leading men—S. Collins, Dr. G. A. Cutler, C. W. Stewart, John Fee, A. Lazelere, B. Harding, B. G. Cady, and others—many of whom strongly urged that the people ought to rise in arms, and with their might resist the authorities; and sooner than permit slavery in Kansas, or even to submit to the repeal of the Missouri compromise, to go with all their might for a disunion of the States; and, in order to effect their purpose, shed, if necessary, the last drop of their blood. Those speeches were received with acclamation by the poor deluded listeners. He was appointed at this meeting, together with several others, to represent the people of this (14th) district at the Big Springs convention, to be held on the 5th of September. Next day several of the delegates met, and solicited him to go before the rest several days, that he might find out what our party was doing in other parts of the Territory. He started for Lawrence on the 27th of August, and after riding as far as Ocena, in Atchison county, he stopped at the house of Mr. Crosby, and made himself known to him. He then made him acquainted with the secret military organization, which organization had been on foot from the 4th of April, 1855. (There was another society previous to this.) Mr. Crosby then gave him a letter of introduction to G. W. Brown, of the Herald of Freedom.

He went to Lawrence, and after acquainting Brown with his business, and giving him the letter of Mr. Crosby, he showed him a great number of Sharpe's rifles—he supposed about 75 or 100—and told him they were sent to them by the Emigrant Aid Society, of Boston; that the society had also sent, and would continue to send, men and means to make Kansas a free State by force, if necessary. He told him that the arms and munitions of war were sent generally as dry goods or books to the agent of the society; and were sent concealed in this manner, that they might not be detected by the United States officers. He told him that when our regiment would number thirty men, we could send a delegate to Boston; but that he must first visit Lawrence, where he would get letters of introduction to the society in Boston, who would furnish us with as many rifles as we had men to bear them in the neighborhood; and, furthermore, that he would get them gratis.

While in Lawrence, a box of goods came, directed to C. Robinson; it was taken into the room where they hold their secret meetings. A friend of his invited him to go up with him to see the kind of goods they received from the east. He went up, and, to his surprise, saw in the box a lot of blue jackets and white pants for military uniform; also a drum and drum-sticks.

The lookers-on winked with their eyes, as though they meant something. There was a large house, which answered the double purpose of a hotel and fort, and with which the public is very familiar; it was then in the course of erection by the Emigrant Aid Society of Boston; it had port-holes in it for guns. He was told by Mr. Brown, Mr. Conway, Hutchison, and Lowry, and many other leading men among the abolitionists, that this hotel was intended principally for a fortification for their town, for they expected their conduct would bring them, before long, into a collision with the authorities.

A. H. Reeder seemed very well acquainted with the secret military order. Immediately after he told his business to Mr. Brown, and let him know he was a member of the secret order, he had an introduction to A. H. Reeder. They both then got up and went into the back room, where the rifles were, about twenty-five feet from him, and stood in a position on the floor where he had a full view of them. He could see from their actions, and from part of their conversation, which he overheard, that he and the society were the principal topics of their conversation. When they finished their interview a preacher came in, and he was introduced as late of Boston. The three then began a conversation, in which the topic was, what men and means they could get by the next election, which was to come off in the fall, for delegate to Congress. They spoke of a preacher who had gone to Boston for the express purpose of getting voters and other means to insure success at the coming election.

Pursuant to public notice, the convention of the abolitionists met at Big Springs, on the 5th of September, 1855; also the executive committee. This committee claimed the sole right to govern the Territory. He was introduced to this convention by A. H. Reeder. His manner of introducing him was very strange, and he was made a member without being proposed in his hearing. Shortly after he was introduced to the committee, a man whose name, he thought, was McCullough, and whose accent and outward demeanor bespoke him to be from the eastern States, offered the following resolution:

"*Resolved*, That every reliable free State man in the Territory be furnished with a rifle, a brace of pistols, and a sabre, gratis; and that he be required to take an oath to come when called upon, and muster into service under his superior officer, and to sacrifice his life, if necessary, to rescue the person and property of any person who would be brought under the jurisdiction of the present laws of the Territory."

The above resolution was seconded, and received by loud stampings in every part of the house, except the chairman, (C. Robinson,) who remained silent a few moments, as though lost in deep thought. He at last spoke up, and asked the gentleman to withdraw his motion, and they would act upon it in a more private manner. All seemed silent and seemed to wonder at the chairman's course. Another spoke up, and said he thought the resolution interfered with provisions already made.

The chairman said he thought not; but, for reasons he cared not to give at present, he wished the gentleman to withdraw his resolution, and let them act upon it in a more private manner. It was then withdrawn. This committee, in assuming the government of the Territory, appointed two governing committees of three men each side of the Kansas river, whose duty it was to establish post offices, mail routes, and mail carriers, to carry and take care of all freesoil and abolition mails, which was confined to the Territory. These two governing committees had the power to appoint persons who would arbitrate all difficulties arising in their respective districts. Persons so appointed were subject to removal, and responsible to the governing committee for any neglect of duty or abuse of power. In like manner, the governing committees were responsible to the executive committee.

All expenses of the above named officials were to be borne by the executive committee, who would derive the necessary aid from the eastern States and the Emigrant Aid Society of Boston. The executive committee issued orders for all free State men to give into the governing committees all the statements they could which would affect anything in weakening the pro-slavery party. He being further north than any of the other two who were on the committee with him, he had all the statements to take of those north of him, and any other direction that was convenient.

There were many who gave him their statements against the legislature and private individuals. All those who gave him any statements, had it in such language as was capable of being construed into a more dangerous meaning for the pro-slavery party, than what the real definition should be. Many of them told him they were making use of language that would make the pro-slavery party appear to the world more guilty than they in reality were; and no matter how false a meaning was put on their statements, they would be easy in conscience if they could realize their object. Many told them, when called upon, they were willing to swear that thousands of Missourians came over and voted, although he saw none; but admitted to him that they saw no Missourians vote, nor did they know of any who did. He had heard A. H. Reeder urge the people to rebellion and bloodshed, while they listened to him as though he were one of the prophets and patriarchs of old. He had heard men say, who appeared to take and hold a high position among the abolitionists, openly boast that they had helped to run off negroes from the south into Canada, and hoped the day was near at hand when they would succeed in all their designs, and settle those gentlemen of color along the shores of Kansas, where they could make war on the institutions of the south—particularly of Missouri—till there would not be a slave left in it. Such are the principles of those who keep Kansas in a state of rebellion, and such are the men who are the leaders of the abolitionists—leading them on to thievery, treason, and death.

He has heard Judge Johnson, of the United States supreme court for the Territory, often instruct the people that, when called on to swear in the Territory, they might swear to what suited them, and they would not be perjured, as there was no law in the Territory. Whilst in Lawrence as delegate to the convention of the free State men to be held at Big Springs, he heard many of the people say many of their people returned after the spring election. There were a great many camps at Lawrence then. Some of those forming the camps told him that they would return to the States in the latter part of the fall. At the fall and winter election for a delegate to Congress, for a State constitution and the formation of a State government, the judges of the polls had instructions publicly, that in case of Indian or other troubles they might adjourn from day to day, and finally to any other district in the Territory, to hold their election. But the private instructions were, if pro-slavery men attempted to vote, and were likely to have a majority, they must adjourn from day to day, and finally to any freesoil district in the Territory. He heard many of the people in Lawrence curse the Emigrant Aid Society of Boston, and say if it did not pay them soon they would return to the States, for it had failed to pay them for some time. He was told by several of the emigrants in Lawrence that the Emigrant Aid Society of Boston paid the expenses of all men who would come out to Kansas to vote for it to be a free State.

The following is an extract from the deposition of Andrew J. Francis:

" Offers were made to me by various persons to introduce me to a secret political organization. The only name I ever received as a member of the lodge was 'Kansas Regulator.' The next morning I was conversing with Governor Reeder, Jas. H. Lane, G. P. Lowry, and several others, one by the name of Chapman and one by the name of Hornsby; but both these gentlemen had merely come up to us as we were standing on the corner of the street talking. I had noticed black ribbons tied in the shirt-bosoms of several gentlemen; I noticed one or two tied to Governor Reeder's shirt-bosom. I made the inquiry as to what those black ribbons meant. Colonel Lane asked me to go with him, and he would show me something that would please me better than what I had seen the night before. The night before I had attended a masonic lodge. Colonel Lane was in the lodge while I was there. I made some reply to Lane, as though awaiting to go with him, saying that I would have to see something that would please me extraordinarily well, if it pleased me better than what I had seen the night before. I went with Colonel Lane to the law-office of John Hutchinson, as I afterwards found out. Governor Reeder did not go into the room where I was initiated. Doctor Robinson was standing just before the door, with a lady, I think. Colonel Lane asked him to leave the lady and go into the office with us. Robinson rather objected at first, but finally came in with us and said he would explain the nature of the organization he was about to initiate me into. The substance of the explanation was that Kansas was a beautiful country and well adapted to freedom, and the best territory in the world for the friends of freedom to operate on, more especially for those who were engaged in the free white State cause. After proceeding in that strain for awhile, he asked me if I was willing to pledge my word and honor that I would keep secret what I saw there and who I saw there, provided he would pledge his word and honor that there was nothing that would interfere with my duties as a citizen, or that was disloyal in any respect. I replied that I was willing. He then gave me some other instructions that I do not now recollect, of about the same import as the first. Colonel Lane then took me in hand and told me that he could administer the grand obligation, which was done by my repeating after him, as follows:

"I, of my own free will and accord, in the presence of Almighty God and these witnesses, do solemnly swear that I will always hail, forever conceal, and never reveal any of the secrets of this organization to any person in the known world, except it be to a member of the order, or within the body of a just and legal council. I furthermore promise and swear, that I will not write, print, stain, or indite them on anything movable or immovable, whereby the least figure or character may become intelligible to myself or any other person. I furthermore promise and swear, that I will, at all times, and under all circumstances, hold myself in readiness to obey, even to death, the orders of my superior officers. I furthermore promise and swear, that I will at all times, and under all circumstances, use my influence to make Kansas a free white State. I furthermore promise and swear, that all things else being equal, I will employ a free State man in preference to a Missouri man, or a pro-slavery man. I furthermore promise and swear, that all business that I may transact, so far as in my power, shall be transacted with free State men. I furthermore promise and swear, that I will at all times, and under all circumstances, hold myself in readiness to take up arms in defence of free State principles, even though it should subvert the government. I furthermore promise and swear, that I will at all times, and under all circumstances, wear upon my person the regalia of my office and the insignia of the order. I furthermore swear, that I will, at all times, and under all circumstances, wear on my person a weapon of death. I furthermore promise and swear, that I will, at all times, and under all circumstances, keep in my house at least one gun, with a full supply of ammunition. I furthermore promise and swear, that I will at all times, and under all circumstances, when I see the sign of distress given, rush to the assistance of the person giving it, even when there is a greater probability of saving his life than of losing my own. I furthermore promise and swear, that I will, to the utmost of my power, oppose the laws of the so-called Kansas legislature. I furthermore promise and swear, that when I hear the words of danger given, I will repair to the place where the danger is. I furthermore promise and swear, that if any part of my obligation is at this time omitted, I will consider the same as binding when legally informed of it. I furthermore promise and swear, that, at the first convenient opportunity, I will commit this obligation to memory. To all of this I solemnly swear, without equivocation or self-evasion, binding myself under the penalty of being declared a perjuror before Heaven and a traitor to my country."

"I then remarked to Colonel Lane, that that was a very serious obligation. He replied it was; and also stated that it was necessary for me to become acquainted with the signs and pass-words. The sign of recognition is given by placing the right thumb under the chin, and the fore-finger of the right hand by the side of the nose, quietly scratching or rubbing it two or three times. The answer to it was given by placing the thumb and fore-finger of the left hand on the lower lip, as if rubbing it. The grip was given by locking the two first fingers of the right hand over each other. The words accompanying the grip are these: The one giving you the grip would ask: 'Are you in favor of Kansas becoming a free State?' The answer was: 'I am, if Missouri is willing.' The means by which persons procured admission into the council was, by going to the door the sentinel would then present himself. The person applying would then say 'Kansas,' accenting the last syllable. The person would then advance to the center of the room and salute the colonel, by placing his right hand just above his forehead. The regalia was this: The private members wore a black ribbon tied upon their shirt-bosoms; the colonel wore a red sash; the lieutenant colonel a green sash; the major a blue sash; the captains white sashes; the lieutenants yellow sashes; the orderly sergeant a very broad black ribbon upon the shirt-bosom. Colonel Lane then remarked to me that I had been made acquainted with the principles of the institution, and that it was the determination of the free State party not to submit to the laws of the legislature, or to any opposition that might come from Missouri or any other quarter. I remarked to the colonel that I was sworn to support those laws in taking my oath as a lawyer, and that I considered that that oath was administered by a higher power than he exercised, and hence I should not keep the obligation he had given to me; and under no circumstances would I do anything to subvert the institutions of the country, or place myself in opposition to the laws; and he might depend upon it, I would expose it the first convenient opportunity. I also told him I could not consistently keep both obligations that had been imposed upon me; that I was also a member and minister of a religious denomination, and that it would not be consistent with my Christian duties to keep the obligation he had imposed on me; that I should most certainly, when the subject came up, expose it. He stated then to me, that if that was my determination, and I did express myself so publicly, I would hardly get away from the city with my life. I replied to him that I would express myself so under all circumstances, both in public and private."

It now being most fully shown, as the undersigned believes, that the anti-slavery party formed secret political organizations of a military character to resist, with force of arms, the execution of the laws of the Territory, and to defend themselves against any effort which might be made by officers to enforce obedience to the laws and authorities of the Territory; after preparing the minds of the people to embark in any measures, however reckless and desperate in their nature and characters, the primary objects of these seditious, secret associations were boldly developed at a convention held by the anti-slavery party at Big Springs on the 5th and 6th days of September, 1855. But, before proceeding further in relation to this convention, the undersigned deems it proper to remark, that after the legislative election in March, 1855, Governor Reeder issued his proclamation, convening the legislature at Pawnee city, upon the express understanding that if there were not sufficient accommodations there for the members and officers of the legislature, they could, strictly in accordance with the provisions of the organic act, adjourn to any other point in the Territory, and if they did so he would co-operate with them. In proof of this, reference is made to the testimony of the Rev. Thomas Johnson, a member of the council. The legislature consequently met at Pawnee city. They remained there but a short time, as they found no accommodations for the members and officers of the legislature, the great majority of them having to camp out and cook their own provisions, there not being boarding-houses in the place sufficient to receive and accommodate them. The cholera also broke out there, and several deaths occurred in consequence. The legislature then adopted a resolution adjourning to Shawnee Mission. It is evident that Pawnee city was not a suitable place for the convening of the legislature, because of the absence of all accommodations for members, as well as being 145 miles from the Missouri river, whence they derived chiefly their supplies for subsistence. The house in which they were convened had neither doors nor windows, and but a temporary floor.

While in session, however, at Pawnee, the governor recognized them as a legally constituted legislative body, as will be more fully shown by reference to his message to that body; but, after they removed to Shawnee Mission, he vetoed all the bills they passed, of every description, upon the ground that they were sitting then at a place not authorized by law—the only ground alleged.

Meanwhile, "The governor, instead of exercising constant vigilance, and putting forth all his energies to prevent or counteract the tendencies to illegality which are prone to exist in all imperfectly organized and newly associated communities, allowed his attention to be diverted from his official obligations by other interests, and himself set the example of a violation of law in the performance of acts which [as it seems] rendered it the duty of the President of the United States, in the sequel, to remove him from the office of chief executive magistrate of the Territory."

The undersigned, in proof of the want of accommodations at Pawnee city, refers to the testimony of Rev. Thomas Johnson, member of the council, A. S. Johnson, Thomas Barbee, Wm. G. Mathias, and other members of the legislature, as taken before a justice of the peace, and properly certified, which the undersigned begs to have considered a part of this report.

After the removal of Governor Reeder, chagrined as he evidently was, he is found an active member of the Big Springs convention, held on the 5th and 6th days of September; at which convention, as it is proven by the testimony of Marcus J. Parrott, a free State man, and a member of the free State legislature, taken before your committee, the following resolutions, drawn up in the hand-writing of Governor Reeder, were adopted. They are taken by the undersigned from a certified copy of the proceedings of said convention, in evidence before your committee, and are as follows:

"*Resolved*, That we owe no allegiance or obedience to the tyrannical enactments of this spurious legislature; that their laws have no validity or binding force upon the people of Kansas, and that every freeman amongst us is at full liberty, consistently with all his obligations as a citizen and a man, to defy and resist them, if he chooses to do so.

"*Resolved*, That we will resist them, primarily, by every peaceable and legal means within our power, until we can elect our own representatives, and sweep them from the statute-book; and that, as the majority of the Supreme Court have so far forgotten their official duty, have so far cast off the honor of the lawyer and the dignity of the judge, as to enter, clothed with the judicial ermine, into a partisan contest, and by extrajudicial decision, given opinions in violation of all propriety, have prejudged our case before we could be heard, and have pledged themselves to these outlaws in advance, to decide in their favor, we will, therefore, take measures to carry the question of the validity of these laws to a higher tribunal, where judges are unpledged, and dispassionate, where the law will be administered in its purity, and where we can at least have the hearing before the decision.

"*Resolved*, That we cannot and will not quietly submit to surrender our great 'American birthright'—the elective franchise—which, first by violence, and then by chicanery, artifice, weak and wicked legislation, they have so effectually accomplished to deprive us of, and that we with scorn repudiate the 'election law,' so-called, and will not meet with them on the day they have appointed for the election, but will ourselves fix upon a day for the purpose of electing a delegate to Congress.

"*Resolved*, That we will endure and submit to these laws no longer than the best interests of the Territory require, as the least of two evils, and will resist them to a *bloody issue*, as soon as we ascertain that peaceful remedies shall fail, and forcible resistance shall furnish any reasonable prospect of success; and that, in the mean time, we recommend to our friends throughout the Territory the organization and discipline of volunteer companies, and the procurement and preparation of arms."

And, finally, as the natural result of the foregoing proceedings of the freesoil party in the Territory, the laws were violated, their execution openly resisted by them, till at length came the difficulties at Lawrence, in the fall of 1855, and after the Big Springs convention, in regard to which, as the most reliable testimony taken by your committee, the undersigned begs to refer to the evidence of Governor Wilson Shannon, which is as as follows: "That, as to the origin, progress, and conclusion of the difficulties at Lawrence last fall, (1855,) he begs leave to refer to his two dispatches to the President of the United States, with the accompanying documents—the first dated on the 28th day of November, and the second on the 11th day of December, 1855—as containing what deponent believes to be a correct history and account of those transactions."

The following are the dispatches and documents referred to by the witness:

EXECUTIVE OFFICE, SHAWNEE MISSION,
Kansas Territory, November 28, 1855.

SIR: Affairs in this Territory are daily assuming a shape of real danger to the peace and good order of society. I am well satisfied that there exists in this Territory a secret military organization which has for its object, among other things, resistance to the laws by force.

Until within a few days past I have looked upon the threats of leading men and public papers who have placed themselves in an attitude of resistance to the laws, as not intended by those who made them to be carried into execution. I am now satisfied of the existence of this secret military organization, and that those engaged in it have been secretly supplied with arms and munitions of war, and that it is the object and purpose of this organization to resist the laws by force. The strength of this organization is variously estimated at from one to two thousand, but I have no satisfactory data from which to estimate its real strength, and I do not believe they can command for any given purpose more than one thousand men. They are said to be well supplied with Sharpe's rifles and revolvers, and that they are bound by an oath to assist and aid each other in the resistance of the laws when called upon so to do. Independent of the disclosures made by those who formerly belonged to this association and the hints thrown out in some of the public journals in their interest, the most practical proof of the truth of these allegations consists in their own acts. A few days since a difficulty took place in Douglas county, some ten miles south of Lawrence, between one of these men and a man by the name of Coleman, from Virginia, in relation to a claim; in which the former was shot and died immediately. Coleman was taken into custody for trial, by the sheriff of that county, and to avoid all ground of objection as to legal authority, Judge Lecompte was written to and requested to attend at the county seat (it being in his judicial district) and sit as an examining court. In the meantime a large body of armed men, said to be from three to four hundred, collected at and near Lawrence for the avowed purpose of rescuing Coleman from the sheriff and executing him without a trial. Coleman claims that he shot the man strictly in self-defence, and is willing to abide a judicial investigation and trial. On Monday last a warrant was issued against one of this band of men for threatening the life of one of his neighbors, and placed in the hands of the sheriff of the county for execution, who, with a posse of some ten men, arrested him on Tuesday night, and as he was conveying the prisoner to Lecompton, he was met about two o'clock in the morning by a band of these men, consisting of between forty and fifty, all armed with Sharpe's rifles and revolvers, who forcibly rescued the prisoner out of his hands, and openly proclaimed that there were no officers or law in this Territory. In the settlement in which these transactions took place there were from sixteen to twenty law and order families, and about one hundred freesoil families. At the last advices three of the houses of the former had been burnt down by this armed band.

Cattle had been killed, and a considerable amount of corn and other personal property destroyed, and the whole law and order population of that neighborhood, induced by terror, had fled, except two families, whose lives were threatened. Helpless women and children have been forced by fear and threats to flee from their homes, and seek shelter and protection in the State of Missouri. Measures were being taken by the legal authorities to procure warrants against these lawless men, and have them arrested and legally tried. Under these circumstances the sheriff of the county has called on me for three thousand men to aid him in the execution of the warrants in his hands, and to protect him and his prisoner from the violence of this armed force. The force required by the sheriff is far beyond what I believe to be necessary, and indeed far beyond what could be raised in this Territory. From five to eight hundred men will be amply sufficient, I have no doubt, to protect the sheriff, and enable him to execute the legal process in his hands. With the view of giving to the sheriff the requisite aid, I have issued orders to Major General Richardson, of the northern division of militia of this Territory, a prudent and discreet man, a copy of which I send you herewith. I also send you a copy of a request I have made of General Strickler, who resides in the adjoining county to Douglas. These are the only orders I have thought it necessary to issue, by means of which I believe a sufficient force will be raised to protect the sheriff, and enable him to execute the legal process in his hands.

The time has come when this armed band of men, who are seeking to subvert and render powerless the existing government, have to be met and the laws enforced against them, or submit to their lawless dominion. If the lives and property of unoffending citizens of this Territory cannot be protected by law, there is an end to practical government, and it becomes a useless formality.

The excitement along the border of Missouri is running wild, and nothing but the enforcement of the laws against these men will allay it. Since the disclosure of the existence and purposes of this secret military organization in this Territory, there has been much excitement along the borders of Missouri, but it has been held in check, heretofore, by assurances that the laws of the Territory would be enforced, and that protection would be given to the citizens against all unlawful acts of this association. This feeling and intense excitement can still be held in subordination if the laws are faithfully executed; otherwise there is no power here that can control this border excitement, and civil war is inevitable. This military organization is looked upon as hostile to all southern men, or rather to the law and order party of the Territory, many of whom have relations and friends, and all have sympathizers, in Missouri, and the moment it is believed that the laws will not furnish adequate protection to this class of citizens against the lawless acts of this armed association, a force will be precipitated across the line to redress real and supposed wrongs inflicted on friends that cannot be controlled, or for the moment resisted. It is in vain to conceal the fact; we are standing on a volcano, the upheavings and agitations beneath we feel, and no one can tell the hour when an eruption may take place. Under existing circumstances the importance of sustaining the sheriff of Douglas county, and enabling him to execute his process, independent of other considerations connected with the peace and good order of society, will strike you at once; and to do this by the aid and assistance of the citizens of this Territory is the great object to be accomplished, to avoid the dreadful evils of civil war. I believe this can be done; in this, however, I may be mistaken. No efforts shall be wanting on my part to preserve good order in the Territory, and I will keep you constantly advised of the progress and state of things here.

I have the honor to be, your obedient servant,

WILSON SHANNON.

His Excellency FRANKLIN PIERCE.

HEADQUARTERS, SHAWNEE MISSION,
Kansas Territory, November 27, 1855.

SIR: Reliable information has reached me that an armed military force is now in Lawrence and that vicinity, in open rebellion against the laws of this Territory, and that they have determined that no process in the hands of the sheriff of that county shall be executed. I have received a letter from S. J. Jones, sheriff of Douglas county, informing me that he had arrested a man under a warrant placed in his hands, and while conveying him to Lecompton he was met by an armed force of some forty men, and that the prisoner was taken out of his custody, and open defiance bid to the law. I am also duly advised that an armed band of men have burnt a number of houses, destroyed personal property, and turned whole families out of doors in Douglas county. Warrants will be issued against those men, and placed in the hands of the sheriff of Douglas county for execution. He has written to me, demanding three thousand men to aid him in the execution of the process of the law and the preservation of peace.

You are, therefore, hereby ordered to collect together as large a force as you can in your division, and repair without delay to Lecompton, and report yourself to S. J. Jones, the sheriff of Douglas county, together with the number of your forces, and render to him all the aid and assistance in your power, if required in the execution of any legal process in his hands. The forces under your command are to be used for the sole purpose of aiding the sheriff in executing the law, and for no other purpose.

I have the honor to be, your obedient servant,

WILSON SHANNON.

Major General WILLIAM P. RICHARDSON.

HEADQUARTERS, SHAWNEE MISSION,
Kansas Territory, November 27, 1855.

SIR: I am this moment advised, by letter from S. J. Jones, sheriff of Douglas county, that while conveying a prisoner to Lecompton, whom he has arrested by virtue of a peace warrant, he was met by a band of armed men, who took said prisoner forcibly out of his possession, and bid defiance to the execution of all law in this Territory. He has demanded of me three thousand men to aid him in the execution of the legal process in his hands. As the southern division of the militia of this Territory is not organized, I can only request you to collect together as large a force as you can, and at as early a day as practicable report yourself, with the forces you may raise, to S. J. Jones, sheriff of Douglas county, and to give him every assistance in your power, in the execution of the legal process in his hands. Whatever forces you may bring to his aid are to be used for the sole purpose of aiding the said sheriff in the execution of the law, and no other. It is expected that every good citizen will aid and assist the lawful authorities in the execution of the laws of the Territory and the preservation of good order.

Your obedient servant,

WILSON SHANNON.

General H. J. STRICKLER.

EXECUTIVE OFFICE, SHAWNEE MISSION,
Kansas Territory, December 11, 1855.

SIR: In my dispatch to you of the 28th ultimo, I advised you of the threatened difficulties in relation to the execution of the laws of this Territory in Douglas county. The excitement which then existed continued to increase, owing to the aggravated reports from Lawrence and that vicinity in relation to the military preparations that were being made to attack the sheriff and resist the execution of the laws. The excitement increased and spread, not only throughout this whole Territory, but was worked up to the utmost point of intensity in the whole of the upper portion of Missouri. Armed men were seen rushing from all quarters towards Lawrence, some to defend the place, and others to demolish it. The orders I had issued to Major General Richardson and General Strickler had brought to the sheriff of Douglas county a very inadequate force for his protection, when compared with the forces in the town of Lawrence. Indeed, the militia of the Territory being wholly unorganized, no forces could be obtained except those who voluntarily tendered their aid to the sheriff, or to Generals Richardson and Strickler. The whole force in the Territory thus obtained did not amount to more than three or four hundred men, badly armed, and wholly unprepared to resist the forces in Lawrence, which amounted, at that time, to some six hundred men; all remarkably well armed with Sharpe's rifles and other weapons. These facts becoming known across the line, in the State of Missouri, large numbers of men from that State, in irregular bodies, rushed to the county of Douglas, and many of them enrolled themselves in the sheriff's posse. In this state of affairs, I saw no way of avoiding a deadly conflict but to obtain the use of the United States forces at Fort Leavenworth, and with that view I addressed you a telegraphic despatch, and received on the 5th instant your very prompt and satisfactory reply of the 4th instant, a copy of which I immediately transmitted, by special dispatch, to Colonel Sumner, with the request that he would accompany me with his command to the scene of difficulty. In reply, I was informed he would immediately do so, having no doubt that in due time proper instructions would be received from the War Department. Information, however, which I received from both parties, convinced me that my presence was necessary to avoid a conflict, and without waiting for Colonel Sumner, I repaired to the seat of threatened hostilities, at the same time advising Colonel Sumner, by special dispatch, of this movement. On my way to Lawrence, I met a dispatch from Colonel Sumner, informing me that, upon reflection, he had changed his determination, and that he would not march with his command until he had received orders from the proper department, but that he would be ready to move with his command the moment such orders came to hand. I proceeded as rapidly as possible to the camp of General Strickler, on the Wakarusa, six miles east of Lawrence, and arrived in camp about three o'clock on the morning of the sixth instant. I found that General Strickler, as well as General Richardson, had very judiciously adopted the policy of incorporating into their respective commands all the irregular forces that had arrived. This was done with the view of subjecting them to military orders and discipline, and to prevent any unlawful acts or outbreaks. The great danger to be apprehended was from an unauthorized attack on the town of Lawrence, which was being strongly fortified, and had about one thousand and fifty men, well armed, to defend it, with two pieces of artillery, while, on the other side, there was probably in all near two thousand men, many of them indifferently armed, but having a strong park of artillery. I found in the camp at Wakarusa a deep and settled feeling of hostility against the opposing forces in Lawrence, and apparently a fixed determination to attack that place and demolish it and the presses, and take possession of their arms. It seemed to be a universal opinion in the camp that there was no safety to the law and order party in the Territory while the other party were permitted to retain their Sharpe's rifles, an instrument used only for war purposes. After mingling with all the leading men in the Wakarusa camp, and urging on them the importance of avoiding a conflict of arms, that such a step would probably light the torch of civil war and endanger the very Union itself, I still found that there was a strong desire with all, and a fixed determination with many, to compel the forces in Lawrence to give up their arms. Believing that such a demand would lead to a conflict which, if once commenced, no one could tell where it would end, and seeing no way to avoid it except by the aid of the United States forces, I again wrote another communication to Colonel Sumner, and sent it to him by special dispatch about three o'clock on the morning of the 7th instant, requesting his presence; a copy of which I send you herewith, marked E. I received no reply until my return to this place, after the difficulty had been arranged. I send you a copy of this reply, marked F. Early on the morning of the 7th instant, I repaired to the camp at Lawrence, and found them busily engaged in their fortifications, and in drilling their forces, and had a full and satisfactory interview with the committee appointed by the forces in Lawrence, in relation to the impending difficulties. So far as the execution of the laws was concerned, we had no difficulty in coming to a satisfactory understanding. It was at once agreed that the laws of the Territory should have their regular course, and that those who disputed their validity should, if they desired to do so, test that question in the judicial tribunals of the country; that, in the mean time, no resistance should be made to their due execution, and the citizens of Lawrence and vicinity were, when properly called on, to aid in the arrest of any one charged with their violation, and aid and assist in the preservation of the peace and good order of society; while, on my part, I gave them every assurance in my power that they should be protected in all their rights, and defended against any unlawful aggressions. It is proper I should say, that they claimed that a large majority of them had always held and inculcated the same views. The assurances I received entirely satisfied me that no one against whom a writ had issued was then in Lawrence; that they had all fled, and that they were harboring, concealing, or defending no one against whom a writ had been issued, and that hereafter there would be no combined effort made to prevent the service of any process in the county of Douglas. This was entirely satisfactory, and all that had been desired. But to satisfy the forces that surrounded Lawrence, so that they could be induced to retire in order, was the great difficulty to be overcome. To issue an order to the sheriff to disband his *posse*, and to Generals Richardson and Strickler to disband their forces, would have been to let loose this large body of men, who would have been left without control to follow the impulse of their feelings, which evidently was to attack and disarm the people of Lawrence. Early on the morning of the 8th, through the influence of some leading men, I procured thirteen of the leading captains in the Wakarusa camp to be appointed a committee to confer with a committee from the Lawrence camp, to meet at Franklin, midway between the two hostile forces. I proceeded to the Lawrence camp, and returned to Franklin in the evening, with the committee, where the proposed interview took place. This interview, which lasted for some time, resulted in producing a better state of feeling, and the committee from the Wakarusa camp were satisfied to retire without doing anything more, and so reported to the army. This, with the active exertions of myself and others, produced a better feeling among the men, and by daylight on the morning of the 9th, I felt I could with safety order the forces to disband, and accordingly did so. They retired in order, and refrained from any act of violence, but it was evident there was a silent dissatisfaction at the course I had taken. But I felt conscious I was right, and that my course would be sanctioned alike by the dictates of humanity and sound policy. I returned to Lawrence on the 9th, and remained until the morning of the 10th, when, everything being quiet and safe, I returned to this place. Everything is quiet now; but it is my duty to say to you, frankly, that I have forebodings as to the future. The militia volunteer corps cannot be relied on to preserve the peace in these civil party contests, or where partisans are concerned. A call on the militia will generally only bring in conflict the two parties. I am satisfied that the only forces that can be used in this Territory in enforcing the laws, or preserving the peace, are those of the United States, and with this view I would suggest that the executive of this Territory be authorized to call on the forces of the United States when, in his judgment, the public peace and tranquility, or the execution of the laws, may require their assistance. Should there be an outbreak, it will most probably be sudden, and before orders can be obtained from Washington the crisis will have passed. I send you herewith the copies of various affidavits, letters, &c., which will give you some information in detail touching the subject-matter of this dispatch.

I have the honor to be, your obedient servant,

WILSON SHANNON.

His Excellency FRANKLIN PIERCE.

UNITED STATES OF AMERICA, *Territory of Kansas.* } *ss.*

Be it remembered, that on this sixth day of December, in the year A. D. 1855, personally appeared before me, J. M. Burrell, one of the associate justices of the supreme court of the said Territory of Kansas, Harrison Buckley, of lawful age, who being by me duly sworn, saith that he is a citizen of the county of Douglas, and has resided therein since 30th day of March last, and has resided during all that time at Hickory Grove; that he was informed on good authority, and which he believed to be true, that Jacob Branson had threatened his life, both before and after the difficulty between Coleman and Dow, which led to the death of the latter. I understood that Branson swore that deponent should not breathe the pure air three minutes after I returned, this deponent at this time having gone down to Westport, in Missouri; that it was these threats, made in various shapes, that made this deponent really fear his life, and which induced him to make affidavit against the said Branson, and procure a peace warrant to issue, and be placed in the hands of the sheriff of Douglas county; that this deponent was with the said sheriff (S. J. Jones) at the time the said Branson was arrested, which took place about two or three o'clock in the morning; that Branson was in bed when he was arrested by said sheriff; that no pistol or other weapon was presented at the said Branson by any one; that after the arrest, and after the company with the sheriff had proceeded about five miles in the direction of Lecompton, the county seat of Douglas county, the said sheriff and his posse were set upon by about between thirty and forty men, who came out from behind a house, all armed with Sharpe's rifles, and presented their guns cocked, and called out who they were; and said Branson replied that they had got him a prisoner; and these armed men called on him to come away. Branson then went over on their side, and sheriff Jones said they were doing something they would regret hereafter in resisting the laws; that he was sheriff of Douglas county, and, as such, had arrested Branson. These armed men replied that they had no laws, no sheriff, and no governor, and that they knew no laws but their guns. The sheriff, being overpowered, said to these men, that if they took him by force of arms he had no more to say, or something to that import, and then we rode off. This deponent further states that there have been three houses burned in the Hickory Point settlement; one was this deponent's house, another belonged to Josiah Hargis, and the third to said Coleman. All I had in the world was burned up, leaving my wife and children without clothing. This deponent's wife and four children fled to Missouri, where they still remain with their relatives. The house of deponent was burned down, as it is said, shortly before daylight in the morning. The wives and children of both Coleman and Hargis also fled to Missouri, where they still remain. There were about fifteen or sixteen law-abiding families in the settlement called the Hickory Grove, settlement about the time these difficulties sprung up; they have all been forced by terror and threats of these armed men to flee with their wives and children to the State of Missouri for protection, and still remain there. These armed men have repeatedly in my presence said that they would resist the law by force, and there was no law in this Territory. These threats have been repeatedly made by these men for the last three months. And further this deponent saith not.

H. H. BUCKLEY.

Sworn and subscribed the day and year above stated, before me.

J. M. BURRELL,

Associate Justice Supreme Court, Kansas Territory.

UNITED STATES OF AMERICA, } ss.
Territory of Kansas, }

Be it remembered, that on this 7th day of December, A. D. 1855, personally came before me, S. G. Cato, one of the associate justices of the supreme court of the Territory of Kansas, Josiah Hargis, of lawful age, who being by me duly sworn, deposeth and saith, that on or about the 26th day of November, 1855, in Douglas county, sheriff Jones called upon me, with nine others, to act as a posse to arrest one Jacob Branson, under a peace warrant issued by Hugh Cameron, a justice of the peace; that he proceeded with said sheriff to Hickory Point, in said county, and there arrested said Branson, with whom they proceeded in the direction of Lawrence. When near a house on the Wakarusa an armed mob of persons, amounting to between thirty and forty, rushed from behind said house, and by force did rescue said Branson out of the hands of said sheriff and posse, and in defiance of said sheriff's command, take said Branson and refuse to deliver him to said sheriff. That the said sheriff told the said mob that he held said Branson under a peace warrant properly issued by a legally authorized officer; and that he was sheriff of said county of Douglas, and charged with the execution of said writ. The leader of said mob replied to said officer that they knew him as Mr. Jones, but not as sheriff of Douglas county. He then told them that he would call out the militia to enforce the law. Their reply was that he could not get men to enforce said law. He told them then that he would call on the governor for assistance; to which the said mob replied that they had no laws and no officers, and to pitch in. Said mob stood with their guns cocked and presented at the time of said rescue.

This deponent further saith, one H. H. Buckley, of said county of Douglas, was with said sheriff at the time of said rescue, as one of said sheriff's posse; that during the same night on which said rescue was made, said affiant saw a light in the direction of said Buckley's house, and that he fully believes said house was at that time burned. That he believes, from circumstances within his knowledge, that said house, together with his own, was burned by persons concerned with said mob; and that he has reason to believe that some of said houses were fired by said Branson aforesaid, assisted by a German, commonly called Dutch Charley; and they were counselled and advised thereto by one Farley. This affiant further says, that at the time of the rescue of said prisoner he was at a house near Hickory Point, and that he there saw three women, who told him that there had been an armed force that day who notified them to leave, and all other pro-slavery families in the neighborhood; and since, said families had left said neighborhood and fled to the State of Missouri. Said affiant says that he believes there were at that time in said neighborhood about fifteen pro-slavery families, nearly all of whom have fled, as aforesaid, to the State of Missouri, for protection. Said armed force was represented to consist of from one hundred to one hundred and fifty armed men.

S. N. HARGIS.

Sworn and subscribed before me. S. G. CATO,
Associate Justice of Kansas Territory.

In relation to events which have transpired since the appointment of your committee, the majority of your committee use this language: "Your committee did not deem it within their power or duty to take testimony as to events which have transpired since the date of their appointment." The undersigned begs to say that a majority of your committee did, however, take testimony as to events which "transpired since the date of their appointment." They admitted to record the testimony of Pardee Butler, as to his being tarred and cottoned at Atchison, and that of others touching other events, all happening after the date of their arrival in Kansas Territory, and consequently after that of their appointment. Having admitted testimony as to some events of the kind, it was but justice to all parties that counter testimony relating to those as well as other events of the same kind, should be admitted. And thus the undersigned thought, when the counsel of General Whitfield sought to introduce evidence as to the Pottawatomie Creek murders, and other outrages. Having established a precedent, it was inconsistent for the majority of your committee to refuse to take such testimony upon the ground that they had no "power," and that it was not their "duty" to investigate occurrences that "transpired since the date of their appointment." They exercised such a "power," and in part fulfilled such a "duty," when they took testimony prejudicial to the pro-slavery party; but when testimony unfavorable to the free State party was sought to be introduced, it was then, and not till then, that the majority of your committee concluded that it was not within "their power or duty to take testimony as to events which transpired since the date of their appointment." But the majority of your committee extricated themselves from the dilemma in which they had, in this regard, placed themselves, by expunging testimony favorable to the free State party side—testimony already received in relation to alleged violence shown to Pardee Butler and others, so that they could consistently refuse to admit testimony as to outrages committed by the free State people, which in savage barbarity and demoniac cruelty have scarcely an equal in the history of civilized man. But, notwithstanding that the majority deemed it without their "power or duty" to investigate matters occurring since the time of their appointment, they have reported, and in their report dwelt with much warmth of expression upon, events which they admit "transpired since the date of their appointment"—events for which they do not claim to have a shadow of authority for their truth except vague rumor, and for which in fact there is none as yet shown; and the testimony in regard to at least one of which events they had expunged from the record, to wit, the tarring and cottoning of Pardee Butler. The undersigned is of the opinion, that if the majority of your committee are justified in reporting and dwelling upon occurrences for the truth of which they offer no proof, he is equally, if not much more strongly justified, in reporting and dwelling upon occurrences for the proof of which he has sworn testimony. The majority of your committee having presented, in their report, scarcely anything but what is favorable to the abolition party in Kansas and prejudicial to the law and order party, the undersigned deems it a duty, no less to the House than to the country and the cause of truth, to give some facts on the other side favorable to the other party in Kansas, so that in presenting both sides, the world may have a fair chance to get at the truth, and arrive at a just conclusion. The minority of your committee (the majority having alluded, in their report, to events as to which they refused to take testimony) has fortunately been furnished with sworn testimony to which he desires to refer, and which he considers important to lay before the House and the public. First in order of time are the murders committed on the night of the 24th of May, 1856, on Pottawatomie creek. In this massacre, it is known that five persons were killed in one night, viz: Allen Wilkinson, William Sherman, William P. Doyle, father, and William and Drury Doyle, sons. The undersigned begs leave to refer to various affidavits which he appends to and makes a part of his report.

Allen Wilkinson was a member of the Kansas legislature—a quiet, inoffensive man. His widow, Louisa Jane Wilkinson, testifies, that on the night of the 24th of May last, between the hours of midnight and day-break, she thinks, a party of men came to the house where they were residing and forcibly carried her husband away; that they took him in the name of the "Northern Army," and that next morning he was found about 150 yards from the house, dead. Mrs. Wilkinson was very ill at the time with measles. Here follows an extract from her affidavit: "I begged them to let Mr. Wilkinson stay with me, saying that I was sick and helpless, and could not stay by myself. My husband also asked them to let him stay with me until he could get some one to wait on me; told them that he would not run off, but would be there the next day, or whenever called for; the old man who seemed to be in command looked at me, and then around at the children, and replied, 'you have neighbors.' I said, 'so I have, but they are not here, and I cannot go for them.' The old man replied, 'it matters not,' and told him to get ready. My husband wanted to put on his boots, and get ready, so as to be protected from the damp and night air, but they would not let him. They then took my husband away. * * * After they were gone I thought I heard my husband's voice in complaint. * * Next morning Mr. Wilkinson's body was found about 150 yards from the house, in some dead brush. A lady, who saw my husband's body, said that there was a gash in his head and his side. Others said that he was cut in the throat twice." Mr. Wilkinson was a poor man, and of course his widow was left destitute; but, regardless of this fact, they took away some property, including the only horse they had. Mrs. Wilkinson was presented at Westport, Missouri, with the necessary means to go to her father's in Tennessee. She has two small children. Mrs. Wilkinson's description of the leader of the men who murdered her husband suits Captain John Brown, a well known character in the abolition party. She says that her husband was a quiet man, and was not engaged in arresting or disturbing anybody. He took no active part in the pro-slavery cause, so as to aggravate the abolitionists; but he was a pro-slavery man.

The circumstances attending William Sherman's assassination are testified to by Mr. James Harris, of Franklin county, Kansas. Mr. Sherman was staying over night at the house of Harris, when, on the night of the 24th of May, about two o'clock, Captain John Brown and party came there, and after taking some property and questioning Harris and others, Sherman was asked to walk out. Mr. Harris, in his affidavit, says: "Old man Brown asked Mr. Sherman to go out with him, and Sherman then went out with Brown. I heard nothing more for about fifteen minutes. Two of the 'Northern Army,' as they styled themselves, staid with us until we heard a cap burst, and then these two men left. Next morning, about ten o'clock, I found William Sherman dead in the creek near my house. I was looking for him; as he had not come back, I thought he had been murdered. I took Mr. William Sherman (body) out of the creek and examined it. Mrs. Whiteman was with me. Sherman's skull was split open in two places, and some of his brains were washed out by the water; a large hole was cut in his breast, and his left hand was cut off, except a little piece of skin on one side."

In relation to the assassination of James P. Doyle and sons, the affidavit of Mrs. Mahala Doyle, the widowed mother, was procured. Willlam Doyle, one of the murdered, was twenty-two years of age; Drury Doyle, the other, was twenty years of age. Mrs. Doyle was left very poor, with four children—one of them only eight years old—to support. Mrs. Doyle testifies: "That a party of armed men came to her house about 11 o'clock, she thinks, on the night of the 24th of May; they first inquired where Mr. Wilkinson lived, and then made Mr. Doyle open his door, and went into the house, saying they were from the 'Army of the North,' and asked them to surrender." Says Mrs. Doyle: "They first took my husband out of the house, then they took two of my sons—the two eldest, William and Drury—out, and then took my husband and the two boys away. My son John (sixteen years old) was spared, because I asked them, in tears, to spare him. In a short time afterwards I heard the report of pistols—two reports; after which I heard moaning, as if a person was dying; then I heard a wild whoop. * * * I went out next morning in search of them, and found my husband and William, my son, lying dead in the road, near together, about two hundred yards from the house. They were buried the next day. On the day of the burying I saw the dead body of my son Drury. Fear for myself and the remaining children induced me to leave the home which we had been living at, and I went to the State of Missouri."

The testimony of John Doyle goes to corroborate that of his mother. Here follows an extract: "I found my father and one brother (William) lying dead in the road, about two hundred yards from the house. I saw my other brother lying dead on the ground, about one hundred and fifty yards from the house, in the grass, near a ravine. His fingers were cut off; his head was cut open; there was a hole in his breast. William's head was cut open, and a hole was in his jaw, as though it was made by a knife, and a hole was also in his side. My father was shot in the forehead and stabbed in the breast. I have talked often with northern men and eastern men in the Territory, and these men talked exactly like eastern men and northern men talk—that is, their language and pronunciation were similar to those of eastern and northern men with whom I had talked. An old man commanded the party; he was of dark complexion, and his face was slim. My father and brothers were pro-slavery men, and belonged to the *law and order party*."

There seems to be little or no doubt that a certain notorious leader of the free State party (as they call themselves) in Kansas, whose name it is not here deemed proper to give, was at the head of the party engaged in this fiendish massacre. Mr. Harris testifies that one John Brown, one of the leaders of the free State party, was engaged in the killing of Sherman, and it will hardly be doubted that they who murdered Sherman also killed the rest—all being murdered on the same night and in the same neighborhood. Those who were killed, it is testified, were pro-slavery people; and the undersigned has no hesitation in saying that these ill-fated men were deprived of their lives, and their wives and children made widows and orphans, in consequence of the insurrectionary movements instigated and set on foot by the reckless leaders of the Topeka convention.

Next in order are the outrages committed on the property of Morton Bourn and that of J. M. Bernard. The affidavit of Mr. Bourn shows that, on the night of Wednesday, the 28th day of May, 1856, a party of abolitionists entered his house forcibly, threatened to take his life if he did not leave the Territory immediately; took all the money he had, which they said they wanted to carry on the war. They also took guns, saddles, and horses, and then robbed his store of various articles. Mr. Bourn, on oath, says: "I own slaves, and have a crop of corn and wheat growing. Have never taken any active part with the pro-slavery party, only voted the pro-slavery ticket, and was for sustaining the laws. * * * These men said I must leave in a day or two or they would kill me, or hinted as much—said I would not fare well or words to that effect. I left for fear of my life and the lives of my family. They said that the war was commenced, that they were going to fight it out, and drive the pro-slavery people out of the Territory, or words to that amount. The men that robbed my house, and drove me away from my property were abolitionists, or freesoilers. * * * * I believe they hated me so because I am a pro-slavery man, and in favor of the territorial laws, and because I served on the last grand jury at Lecompton."

But the most flagrant case of robbery that occurred while your committee were in Kansas was the plundering of Mr. Joab Bernard's store and premises. Mr. Bernard is quite a young man, and of highly respectable family. While prosecuting his business, he was warned that his life was in danger, and was compelled to leave his home for safety; and during his absence his store was robbed of nearly four thousand dollars' worth of goods and money, and his premises of cattle and horses of the value of at least one thousand more. The facts of this case are testified to by Messrs. John Miller and Thomas S. Hamilton. Mr. Bernard testifies himself as to his life being threatened, and the amount of goods in his store and other property on the premises. Messrs. Miller and Hamilton corroborate his testimony, and the undersigned makes their depositions a part of his report. St. Bernard, J. M. Bernard's place, is situated in Douglas county, on the California and Fort Scott road, about thirty miles from Lecompton. The robbery took place on the 27th day of May, 1856. In his affidavit, Mr. Miller says: "I was in the store with Mr. Davis. Whilst there a party of thirteen men came to the store on horseback, armed with Sharpe's rifles, revolvers, and bowie-knives. They inquired for Mr. Bernard. I told them that he had gone to Westport. One of them said to me, 'You are telling a God damned lie,' and drew up his gun at me. Some of them came into the store, and the rest remained outside. They called for such goods as they wanted, and made Mr. Davis and myself hand them out, and said if we 'didn't hurry' they would shoot us. They had their guns ready. After they had got the goods—they wanted principally blankets and clothing—they packed them upon their horses and went away. Mr. Joab Bernard is a pro-slavery man." Mr. Miller recognized one of the party as an active free State man. They on the next day came back with a wagon, and took the remainder of the goods in the store, except about one hundred and fifty dollars' worth—including flour, sugar, coffee, bacon, and all kinds of provisions, as well as two fine horses, three saddles, two bridles, and all the money there was in the store. In the conclusion of his affidavit, Mr. Miller says: "When they first came, they looked up at the sign, and said they would like to shoot at the name." The affidavits accompanying this report are full and explanatory, and the undersigned begs to make them a part of his report. They are sworn to before a justice of the peace for Jackson county, Missouri, and the seal of the Jackson county court is attached to the clerk's certificate, as to the official character of the justice of the peace. The undersigned thinks that, in reviewing these outrages, he did not inappropriately characterize the Pottawatomie creek murders as instances of "savage barbarity and demoniac cruelty," while the robberies of Bourn and Bernard are almost without parallel in the history of crime in this country. In this connexion, the undersigned deems it proper to state that the report so currently circulated throughout the country, to the effect that the lamented Wilkinson, Sherman, and the Doyles were caught in the act of hanging a free State man, and were shot by a party of freesoilers, is without the least foundation in truth—that it is entirely false.

In conclusion, the undersigned begs to report the following facts and conclusions, as he believes, established by the testimony and sanctioned by the law:

First. That at the first election held in the Territory under the organic act, for delegate to Congress, General John W. Whitfield received a plurality of the legal votes cast, and was duly elected such delegate, as stated in the majority report.

Second. That the territorial legislature was a legally constituted body, and had power to pass valid laws, and their enactments are therefore valid.

Third. That these laws, when appealed to, have been used for the protection of life, liberty and property, and for the maintenance of law and order in the Territory.

Fourth. That the election under which the sitting delegate, John W. Whitfield, was held, was in pursuance of valid law, and should be regarded as a valid election.

Fifth. That as said Whitfield, at said election, received a large number of legal votes without opposition, he was duly elected as a delegate to this body, and is entitled to a seat on this floor as such.

Sixth. That the election under which the contesting delegate, Andrew H. Reeder, claims his seat, was not held under any law, but in contemptuous disregard of all law; and that it should only be regarded as the expression of a band of malcontents and revolutionists, and consequently should be wholly disregarded by the House.

Seventh. As to whether or not Andrew H. Reeder received a greater number of votes of resident citizens on the 9th, than J. W. Whitfield did on the 1st of October, 1855, no testimony was taken by the committee, so far as the undersigned knows, nor is it material to the issue.

All of which is respectfully submitted.

M. OLIVER.

www.ingramcontent.com/pod-product-compliance
Lightning Source LLC
LaVergne TN
LVHW021229110826
845150LV00002B/276

* 9 7 8 1 4 2 5 5 6 5 4 2 8 *